NUMERICAL SIMULATION – FROM THEORY TO INDUSTRY

Edited by **Mikhaylo Andriychuk**

Numerical Simulation – From Theory to Industry
http://dx.doi.org/10.5772/2600
Edited by Mikhaylo Andriychuk

Contributors

Canan Çelik Karaaslanlı, DongBin Lee, C. Nataraj, Oscar Esquivel-Flores, Héctor Benítez-Pérez, Jorge Ortega-Arjona, Sandile Motsa, Stanford Shateyi, Magdi Shoucri, T. T. Truong, M. K. Nguyen, Sergiu Spinu, Dumitru Amarandei, Oleg A. Yurtsev, Grigory V. Ptashinsky, Mykhaylo Andriychuk, Abel García-Barrientos, Francisco R. Trejo-Macotela, Liz del Carmen Cruz-Netro, Volodymyr Grimalsky, Takuichi Hirano, Kenichi Okada, Jiro Hirokawa, Makoto Ando, Saadeddine Khemissi, Salvador Pinillos Gimenez, Marcello Bellodi, I. Lăncrănjan, R. Savastru, D. Savastru, S. Micloş, Jean-Luc Autran, Sergey Semikh, Daniela Munteanu, Sébastien Serre, Gilles Gasiot, Philippe Roche, Takaaki Uda, Masumi Serizawa, Shiho Miyahara, Julien Touboul, Christian Kharif, Mohamed Riahi, Taieb Lili, Manabendra Pathak, Dumitru Toader, Stefan Haragus, Constantin Blaj, A. Aoufi, G. Damamme, Masoud Ziabasharhagh, Arash Mohammadi, Jian-Xun Fu, Weng-Sing Hwang, Nur Syahroni, Mas Irfan Purbawanto Hidayat, Hossein Jalalifar, Naj Aziz

Published by InTech
Janeza Trdine 9, 51000 Rijeka, Croatia

Publishing Process Manager Marina Jozipovic
Technical Editor InTech Prepress, Novi Sad
Cover InTech Design team

Additional hard copies can be obtained from orders@intechopen.com

Numerical Simulation – From Theory to Industry, Edited by Mikhaylo Andriychuk
p. cm.
ISBN 978-953-51-0749-1

For EU product safety concerns:
IN TECH d.o.o., Prolaz Marije Krucifikse Kozulić 3, 51000 Rijeka, Croatia,
info@intechopen.com or visit our website at intechopen.com.

Meet the editor

Dr Mykhaylo I. Andriychuk received the M.Sc. degree in the computational mathematics from the Lviv National University, and the Ph.D. degree in the mathematical modeling from the Kyiv National University in 1976 and 1987, respectively. Currently, he is the senior scientist at the Pidstryhach Institute for Applied Problems in Mechanics and Mathematics (IAPMM), NASU, Lviv, Ukraine. In 1996, Dr. Andriychuk received the academic status "senior scientist" in the computational mathematics from the IAPMM. His professional performance includes 5 books, more than 100 papers in the scientific journals and international conference proceedings, which concern to the diffraction and antenna synthesis theory, optimization methods, nonlinear integral and matrix equations. His professional experience includes also teaching in two Lviv Universities. He is in position of the visiting professor at the Lviv Polytechnic National University now. Dr. Andriychuk is IEEE Member since 1995, and IEEE Senior Member since 2003.

Contents

Preface

Starting from the sixties of previous century, numerical simulation has become a significant, and at times, a crucial role in the progress of many areas of science. This book contains original and innovative research studies related to modeling and simulation of the physical phenomena in a very wide range of applications, including the macro- and micro-electrodynamics radiation and scattering, the fluid dynamics turbulence and emulsification, as well as the various industrial processes.

Recent numerical techniques, as well as the most accurate and advanced software are applied in order to perfectly explain the nature of the considered phenomena. The book can be useful for theoretical and applied researchers, who deal with numerical simulation in various areas of science.

The book chapters are divided into four sections according to the considered problems and corresponding areas of application. **Section 1** contains the latest advances in the bifurcation theory, network scheduling, epidemiology, physics of plasma, and mechanics.

Chapter 1, authored by Canan Çelik Karaaslanli, is aimed to study the bifurcation phenomena for the solution of ordinary differential equations and systems of such equations in conjunction with the analytical computation and numerical analysis. The governing equations of the bifurcation analysis are derived for the case of one dimension, for which the saddle-node, transcritical and pitchfork bifurcations are examined. For the two-dimensional case, the Hopf bifurcation theorem determines the condition providing the bifurcation of two types, namely, subcritical and supercritical bifurcation. It was substantiated and proved that Hopf bifurcation is possible for the systems consisting of two or more differential equations; such type of bifurcation is described in literature as Poincare-Andronov-Hopf bifurcation. The main theoretical result consists in center manifold reduction for Hopf bifurcation, this result allows to circumscribe the Hopf bifurcation for various types of the differential equation systems. The numerous exercises demonstrate initial equilibrium properties of the systems under consideration, as well as explain the difference between arising types of bifurcation.

A time-varying control approach designed for a nonlinear system is studied by Dong Bin Lee and C. Nataraj in **Chapter 2**. A cart-pole nonlinear dynamic model with the unknown system parameters is developed for the application of a proposed control algorithm and expressed in a state space form. The error signals are formulated from desired model-based reference system and applied for a trajectory tracking control. Based on the analysis of the developed time-varying error system, state transition matrix is given in a series form, and then a special form of this matrix is derived for the second-order error differential equation, which is used for obtaining the grammian matrix and the closed-loop controller. The control system is also applicable to reject disturbances via a projection-based adaptive control approach and modify laws for the parameter update. Results of numerical simulation demonstrate the validity of the proposed system. The developed approach can be extended to other nonlinear time-varying dynamic systems such as aerial, marine, or ground vehicles.

Oscar Esquivel-Flores at al. discuss in **Chapter 3** the communication network control system based on scheduling strategy and applied for the real time controller design of 2-DOF helicopter prototype. The architecture and overview of the network control system is presented and explored. The True Time simulation tool based on the Matlab/Simulink software, presenting the kernel and network blocks, is scheduled in order to take into account the global network activity. This leads to considering a real time distributed system with three sets of frequency transmission parameters: minimum, real, and maximum frequency rates. The real frequency rate is determined as a solution to respective linear algebraic system with limitation to four sensor nodes. For the implementation purpose, the mathematical model of the 2-DOF helicopter prototype is studied, and the parameters for the network control are defined. The values of pitch and yew angles, as well as the values of their derivatives are the parameters under real time control. The network control flowchart integrated into closed control loop of the 2-DOF helicopter is constructed and applied for the dynamical adjustment of the helicopter position.

In **Chapter 4**, Sandile Motsa and Stanford Shateyi apply the nonlinear system of partial differential equations for SIR model which describes the temporal dynamics of a childhood disease in the presence of a preventive vaccine. The main stage of solving the problem consists of reduction of the obtained system to non interconnected equations. In spite of the fact that this system contains two initial unknown functions, the proposed quasilinearization method allows solving the respective equations related with one function only. Rearranging the unknown functions in right and left hand sides of equations, authors received such representation of the system which allows solving it by the effective iterative procedure. The numerical results are carried out for different cases of the DFE and EE phenomena. The approach is validated with calculations by the MATLAB initial value solver ode45. It is shown that for the case of absence of the disease eradication the scheme of zero order is sufficient to describe toward process adequately.

Magdi Shoucri in **Chapter 5** discusses the rigorous analytical description of the phenomena related to charge separation and electromagnetic field properties at the cylindrical plasma edge. The problem is formulated in coupled set of equations consisting of the normalized 2D Vlasov equation for ions distribution function and normalized 2D guiding-center equation for electron properties. The effective leapfrog scheme is proposed in order to split the equations in one-time step. The proposed scheme foresees three stages, in the first of them a set of homogeneous equations for determination of the distribution function and electron density profile is solved for half-time step. The second step gives the solution to homogeneous equations with regard to missing in the first step terms. The values of electron density, calculated in the previous step, are substituted in the equations which are solved in the first step in order to receive the solution with half-time step again in the third step. The analysis of modeling results provides with understanding a series of physical phenomena, what is the considerable contribution to the neoclassical Tokamak theory and its applications.

T. T. Truong and M. K. Nguyen use theoretical study and numerical simulation for describing the recent developments in the Compton scatter tomography (CST) in **Chapter 6**. The mathematical model foresees the calculation of the reconstructed electron density for the cases of internal and external scanning. The combination of the Radon transform along the respective curves in the conjunction with Chebyshev integral transform of initial equation for the reconstructed electron density is applied for this purpose. In the process of numerical simulation, the resulting expression for the reconstructed electron density is obtained using the explicit formula for curves of integration what leads to representation of integrals by discrete sums; the recurrence relations for arising integrals, as well as, a simple linear approximation of derivatives is used. The validation of approach is realized on the Shepp-Logan medical phantom investigation. It is observed that the quality of reconstruction is improved by passing from first to third CST modality, proposed by authors and adopted from the literature. The proposed approach can be used for research and development in the field of non-invasive imaging for biology, medicine and industry.

Numerical simulations of the slip-stick elastic contact related to the contact mechanics and theory of elasticity is considered by Sergiu Spinu and Dumitru Amarandei in **Chapter 7**. The novelty of proposed approach is determined by utilization of the non-linear theory of elasticity for study of the stress-strain state of materials with various dissimilarly elastic characteristics. The mathematical model of the slip-stick elastic contact problem in terms of normal and tangential forces is discussed. It is underlined that owing to the interdependency of the normal and tangential forces' components the model is essentially non-linear. Based on the two dimensional convolution product, the mathematical description of the discretized model is given in very clear and useful manner. The algorithm for solving the received disretized problem, involving the combination of the conjugate gradient method and uncoupled determination of normal and tangential forces is described very precisely and accurate. The additional taking into account of the torsional contact is validated by consideration of problem with spherical indenter and comparison of solution with known analytical one for such problem.

Section 2 is devoted to numerical simulation in the areas of macro- and micro-electrodynamics, as well as to the numerical investigation of the electromagnetic field characteristics in semiconductor devices of micro- and nano-electronics.

In **Chapter 8**, Oleg A. Yurtsev and Grigory V. Ptashinsky apply numerical simulation for study of radiation characteristics of the dipole and loop antennas. The well approved Pocklington's integral equation is used for accurate formulation of the problem of determining the exciting current in the antenna elements. The respective linear algebraic system is derived and applied for numerical calculation of sought currents. The radiation and scattering characteristics, normalized cross section, input resistance, resonance frequency, and percentage bandwidth for the dipole antennas and Yagi-Uda antennas, dipole antennas with reduced dimensions, flat and convex dipole and Yagi arrays, linear antenna arrays with series excitation, are discussed during the numerical modeling. The high emphasis is placed onto investigation of various modifications of loop antennas. The constructions of such antennas, the interaction of array elements are studied in the terms of input resistance, voltage-standing wave ratio, gain, and matched bandwidth. The optimal parameters of antennas are determined for various geometries, and simulation results complete the existing data regarding the dipole antennas to a considerable degree.

Mykhaylo Andriychuk proposes the variational approach for solving the synthesis problems of antennas according to the given (desired) amplitude radiation pattern (RP) in **Chapter 9**. The absence of requirements to the phase RP is used as an additional possibility to improve the quality of approximation to the desired amplitude RP, but the incompleteness of initial data in the problem yields a class of essentially ill-posed problems, which are described by the nonlinear integral or matrix equations. The methods of nonlinear functional analysis which allow localization of the branching solutions are applied for investigation of solutions and determination of their number and qualitative characteristics. Depending on the restrictions which are imposed on the sought distribution of current or field in the antenna elements and type of antenna, the problems of amplitude-phase, amplitude, and phase synthesis are considered for the specific antennas. The methods of successive approximations are applied for solving the derived nonlinear integral equations; the direct optimization of the proposed functionals by the gradient methods is performed too.

The physical phenomena of amplification of the space charge waves in n-InP films are numerically studied by Abel García-Barrientos et al. in **Chapter 10.** The mathematical description of model is similar to the case of GaAs films. Since the 2D model of electron gas in the n-InP film is used, the respective Poisson's equation is reduced to the two dimensional case. The fast Fourier transform is used for solving this equation. The unknown coefficients in the series for potential and E-components are determined by satisfaction of boundary conditions what yields the respective linear algebraic system with three-diagonal matrix. A series of physical phenomena is studied in the framework of numerical simulation. The spatial increment of instability of the space charge waves, distribution of spectral components of the electric field, the spatial distribution of alternative part of electric field components, the components of electron drift velocity, and alternative part of the electron concentration are analyzed. The modeling results show a better performance of the investigated n-InP films in comparison with the GaAs ones.

The subject of **Chapter 11**, prepared by Takuichi Hirano at al., is electromagnetic simulation of the RF circuits S-parameters applied to structures on a Si CMOS substrate. The engineering features of method, the detailed description of the investigated ICs and de-embedded techniques, as well as the mathematical description of toward processes in three types of patterns are discussed. Electromagnetic modeling consists of calculation of transmission coefficients using the conventional HFSS software. The amplitude and phase of transmission coefficients are received for three types of lumped ports configuration for symmetric and asymmetric IC patterns. The comparison of accuracy between proposed variants of de-embedding techniques for the guided microstrip line is done for the attenuation and phase constant, as well as for the extracted characteristic impedance. A good agreement between the calculation and measurement results was obtained for the above characteristics. Summarizing the obtained results on the whole, one can conclude that the proposed de-embedded techniques on the base of numerical simulation and HFSS solver is effective instrument for investigation of transmission parameters of a wide class of RF circuits on chip.

Saadeddine Khemissi studies the conductive characteristics of the GaAs metal-semiconductor field effect transistors (MESFETs) within the framework of the elaboration of analytical model and numerical simulation in **Chapter 12**. Firstly, the respective Poisson's equation supplemented by proper boundary conditions is considered. The boundary conditions deciding the connections between the intrinsic gate-source, drain-source voltages, and electric field in the depletion-layer edges are specified in the second step of research. The Green's function approach and superposition technique are applied for extension of the initial model to the 2D one. The resulting depletion layer parameters are determined as a combination of initial values from 1D model and total tension function. Calculation of conductive characteristics consists of determination of the drain current for linear, pinch-off, and saturation regimes. In order to calculate the extrinsic characteristics, the effects of parasitic resistance are taken into account. Since they require the calculation of drain currents, which are also contained in the first terms of respective formulas, the iterative procedure for calculation of the drain currents is proposed.

In **Chapter 13**, the comparative study of the Diamond SOI MOSFETs and the conventional ones is performed by Salvador Pinillos Gimenez and Marcello Bellodi using the numerical simulation. The ATLAS device simulator is applied for the comprehensive three-dimensional modeling of the devices under consideration. Lombardi's vertical and horizontal electric-field-depend mobility model which takes into account the effects of low and high electric field is a theoretical background of the proposed approach. It is substantiated that the Diamond SOI nMOSFETs have more than two times larger drain current than conventional ICs, what can be used for increasing the fun-out and fun-in capability of the logic gates. The better performances regarding the transconductance (two times and more) can be used for improving the voltage gain and unit voltage gain frequency of the amplifiers used in the analog ICs. Comparative study of the electrical and physical behavior in the wide temperature range demonstrates also the advantages of the Diamond nMOSFETs. The results reported in Chapter give the important information regarding the electrical characterization of the novel Diamond SOI MOSFETs and comprehensive understanding of their electrical and physical internal behaviors.

Comparison of the output characteristics of the passively Q-switched solid state lasers obtained by the numerical simulation, based on the coupled differential equations system for photon distribution function, and the measurement data, is performed in **Chapter 14** authored by Ion Lancranjan et al. It is established that the accurate definition of photon density and population inversion constitutes a key role in the passive optical Q-switching solid state laser numerical simulation. The numerical simulation and comparison with experimental results are carried out for rod laser and slab laser oscillator/amplifier. For the first example, the good coincidence for the full width and half maximum characteristic, as well as the measured power density and predicated photon density curve is observed. In the case of slab laser oscillator/amplifier, a wide set of the output parameters was simulated and compared with experimental results for four types of prism samples. The analysis of the difference between the first passively Q-switched laser pulse and the next one, generated by a continuous and quasi-continuous wave pumped laser system, regarding the recovery condition to initial state of laser system, is reported firstly.

Jean-Luc Autran et al. in **Chapter 15** suggest a complete general purpose simulation platform for the numerical evaluation of the sensitivity of advanced semiconductor memories, such as static RAMs, subjected to natural radiation at ground level. It is substantiated that the atmospheric radiation environment and the telluric radiation sources are two major sources which cause soft error in the digital circuits. The structure of the TIARA-G4 Monte Carlo simulation code applied to the soft error rate evaluation of different SRAM CMOS built circuits of various technologies is discussed and explained from the utilization point of view. The simulation results illustrate the capabilities of the TIARA-G4 code trough studies on the simulation of 65 and 40 nm CMOS bulk SRAM circuits, subjected to different sources of atmospheric particles. The impact of thermal and low energy neutrons, the soft error rate estimation under high energy atmospheric neutrons, and effects of low-energy muons are investigated and various possible scenarios are discussed. In conclusion, it is accentuated that the novel TIARA-G4 simulation tool provides the researchers with the possibility of the comprehensive numerical evaluation of the sensitivity of advanced semiconductor memories, such as static RAMs.

The evolutionary processes caused by water wave propagation in the sea environment, the problems of instability of water waves, the fluid turbulent flows, and emulsification processes are simulated in **Section 3**.

In **Chapter 16**, the numerical model for prediction of beach changes in the various conditions of shoreline is elaborated and compared with experimental studies by Takaaki Uda et al. The proposed model is used for investigation of extension of sand spit on shallow seabed and formation of a cuspate foreland on step coast, a tidal flat facing on inland sea, and formation of slender sand bar in the case of depth seabed. The comprehensive numerical experiments regarding formation of barrier island on flat shallow seabed and formation of cuspate foreland on steep coast are carried out. The experiment foresees prescribing the initial data the adequate to the field conditions, accurate study of bathymetric phenomena, investigation of influence of change in wave field and sand transport flux. The results on change in longitudinal profiles of areas near shoreline present a specific practical importance. The numerical simulation is performed also for the case of formation of a slender sand bar in the condition of real coast. The results of Chapter are applicable to prediction of changes in shoreline and creating the marine nature-conservative objects.

Julien Touboul and Christian Kharif discuss the problem of propagation of the wave trains caused by the wind and dissipation effects in **Chapter 17**. The theoretical background of investigation is based on the potential flow theory, but new non-potential effects caused by wind and viscosity of water waves can be taken into account through modification of the boundary conditions at the surface of waves. More exact, fully nonlinear approach upcoming in the framework of two-dimensional flows and based on the high-order spectral method is used to solve numerically the governing partial differential equations. In order to investigate the long time behavior of periodic water waves characterizing by the modulation instability, a special treatment is engaged. The main computational problem due to the instability phenomenon is calculation of vertical velocity of propagating waves. Prescribing the initial conditions for the propagating wave's trains is important for receiving the stable or non-stable solution. The numerical results testify that the propagation waves under action of wind and viscosity feature can not be considered likely a stationary and periodic.

Study and clarification of the physical properties of the compressible turbulent flows under rapid distortion theory consideration is the aim of **Chapter 18**, presented by Riahi Mohamed and Lili Taieb. The mathematical model of the physical processes consists of a set of equations describing the linear compressible flows in the absence of inertial effects. The liquid flow is interpreted as a homogeneous compressive turbulent shear flow described by a set of conventional equations. Using the Fourier transform, authors reduce the initial problem to a set of equations in the respective spectral space. The initial velocity components are determined by integration of additional double correlations which are contained in the velocity components. It is substantiated that growth of initial gradient Mach number yields the different regimes of flow. The numerical results explain the physical effects arising in the process of the compressible turbulent flow propagation. Determination of dominant parameter in the turbulent kinetic energy budget is very important for better understanding the physics of flow. The limit values of Reynolds stress anisotropy tensor providing with the equilibrium state of homogeneous compressible turbulence are assessed.

The phenomenon of droplet dynamics in membrane emulsification is studied in **Chapter 19** by Manabendra Pathak in order to determine the optimal geometrical parameters and physical properties for obtaining the stable condition of process. The conservation mass equation leading to continuity equation, the momentum or unsteady Navier-Stokes equation are specified in the framework of the volume of fluid method; the respective non-slip and impermeability boundary conditions are applied in order to rigorously describe the existing physical processes. Because of a large set of initial variables, the governing equations have been reduced in the dimensionless form. Two non-dimensional numbers (Reynolds' and Weber's ones) influence the emulsification process to the considerable extent. The characteristics of the growth and detachment of the droplets, effects of dispersed phase flow rate, velocity fields during droplets growth, effects of surface tension are investigated and optimal parameters of emulsification process are determined. It is substantiated that three important factors must be considered in order to obtain a high production rate of membrane emulsification, namely, a proper combination of continuous and dispersed phases, a proper distribution of pores in ground membrane, and sufficient cross-flow velocity.

In Section 4, the numerical modeling and computational approach are used for study of some industrial problems in the energetic, metallurgy and building.

In **Chapter 20**, Dumitru Toader et al. discuss the application of the numerical modeling for study of the transients in medium voltage networks. The mathematic model of electric circuits is based on the state-variable method and consists of a system of algebraic and differential equations. The first system is a result of applying the Kirchhoff's law to the circuit's topology, and the second one represents the temporal change of the circuit currents and voltages. As a result, the state-variable equations are obtained by elimination of the algebraic equations in the initial equation system. To obtain the transient characteristics, the conventional PSPICE tool is used. Simple ground and double grounding faults are analyzed for the different values of initial phase of voltage. It is concluded that the values of the initial phase of voltage does not exert a sufficient influence in the case of single phase-to-ground faults in the overcompensated and resonance regimes, but in the case of the double phase-to-ground faults this value influences the transient characteristics too much.

A. Aoufi and G. Damamme in **Chapter 21** deal with the numerical analysis of the processes of ignition and propagation of TiC combustion, described by the interconnected set of equations. The mathematical modeling takes into account the interaction between the all essential phenomena, namely, the equations describing the heat capacity characteristics, thermal conductivity, enthalpy balance, and adiabatic temperature of reaction are applied for rigorous description of process in whole. The numerical discretization scheme requires very precise arrangement because of the complexity of the mathematical model. The questions of dependence of the combustion front propagation, contribution of furnace temperature, ratio of released/absorbed energy by the boundary conditions, contribution of the cut-off temperature to the ignition and propagation, as well as analysis of double-front propagation are studied for a large set of the initial parameters of problem. The extension to 2D and 3D models provides with data corresponding to specific TiC components. The essential peculiarity of the proposed approach is the fact that it can be successfully extended to study of other ceramic materials, such as silicium carbide (SiC), and etc.

The process of combustion in porous media is studied numerically by Arash Mohammadi and Ali Jazayeri in **Chapter 22**. The background of combustion, including stability of flame, premixed and non-premixed mixture, reciprocating flow, hydrogen production, and the materials for porous media combustion, are introduced. The numerical step-by-step modeling foresees consideration of governing equations for the one-, two-, and three-dimensional models. The last model is considered for the cases of simple turbulence and radiation models, as well as for more complicate combustion model. The latter foresees the consideration of the chemical mechanisms: continuity, gas phase momentum, and gas phase energy equations, as well as the effects of turbulence. The finite volume equation formulation is applied for discretization of problem, the algorithms of discretization are explained in details. The numerical simulations are carried out on the example of thin cylinder domain. The distribution of gas and solid fractions, gas phase temperature, and temperature of solid phase are investigated in the temporal range. Obtained numerical results are explained from the physical point of view and they confirm a series of the known chemical and physical phenomena of combustion.

In **Chapter 23**, the numerical simulation of slab broadening in a continuous casting of steel, validated by a series of experimental and factory results, is described by Jian-Xun Fu. The slab broadening in the process of casting is considered in both terms of the ratio of apparent shrinkage and the ratio of ultimate broadening. It is substantiated that the mechanical stresses, including the bending stress, straightening stress, roller-miss-alignment stress, the stress of rollers acting on the slab, and the static pressure of molten steel, determine the degree of broadening. An influence of the factory parameters, such as casting speed, width and thickness of slab, change of mold size, contraction of roll gap in the process of broadening, is carefully investigated and compared with the specific industrial data. The industrial experiments related to investigation of influence of the static pressure of molten steel on the broadening were performed and validated the proposed approach. General conclusion, that the higher casting speed, the lower intensity of secondary cooling, the thinner slab shell, the larger static pressure of molten steel, and the lower hardness of steel at high temperature increase slab broadening, summarizes the Chapter.

Syahroni Nur and Hidayat Mas in **Chapter 24** use 3D finite element simulation for study of residual stresses and distortions depending on the various welding sequences. The investigation of the thermomechanical effects of various welding sequences on the T-joint fillet weld is carried out. Theoretical background of approach foresees the study of basic mechanism of welding residual stresses, including the residual stresses due to mismatch and uneven distribution of non-elastic strains, as well as the analysis of welding distortions upon residual stresses. The existing thermal, stress and strain phenomena are examined in details and are evaluated from the engineering point of view. In the first part of procedure, welding simulation deals with determination of the temperature distributions for the different welding sequences. The temperature characteristics and peak temperature are determined. Using the above data the distribution of residual stresses and change of the welding structure are examined in the second part of investigations. The optimal welding sequences, resulting in the process with the smallest longitudinal and transverse residual stresses, as well as with the smallest angular distortion and difference, are revealed in the process of numerical simulation.

Hossein Jalalifar and Naj Aziz study the application of numerical simulation to prediction of the stressed-deformed state of composite materials in **Chapter 25**. The mathematical model foresees consideration of fully grouted rock bolt medium with bolt, grout, rock, and two interfaces under axial and lateral loading. Authors discuss the advantages of existing models from the points of adequate modeling and necessary computational resources. The mathematical modeling deals with description of finite elements for concrete, grout, and bolt; the specific finite elements are applied for the different areas in order to precisely describe the stresses and strains in each of material's component. The special attention is paid to modeling the bolts under lateral loading and bolt modeling under axial loading. The first part of investigations is devoted to obtaining the strain and stress development for the materials with various conditions and features, namely the different strength rock and pre-tension loads were examined. The conditions, at which the materials start to crush, are substantiated in the second part of research.

I would like to thank all authors for their responsibility, patience, and improvement of their chapters in the process of preparing the book. In conclusion, I express my sincere thanks to Ms. Mariana Jozipovich, who finished this project, as well as to Mr. Marijan Polic, who started as publishing manager for this book, for their professional assistance during the publishing process.

Mykhaylo I. Andriychuk
Pidstryhach Institute for Applied Problems
in Mechanics and Mathematics, NASU, Lviv,
Ukraine

Section 1

Simulation Background and Advances

Chapter 1

Bifurcation Analysis and Its Applications

Canan Çelik Karaaslanlı

Additional information is available at the end of the chapter

http://dx.doi.org/10.5772/50075

1. Introduction

Continuous dynamical systems that involve differential equations mostly contain parameters. It can happen that a slight variation in a parameter can have significant impact on the solution. The main questions of interest in this chapter are: How to continue equilibria and periodic orbits of dynamical systems with respect to a parameter? How to compute stability boundaries of equilibria and limit cycles in the parameter space? How to predict qualitative changes in system's behavior (bifurcations) occurring at these equilibrium points? This chapter will also cover the classification of bifurcations in terms of equilibria and periodic orbits. Especially it will present the specific bifurcation called "Hopf bifurcation" which refers to the development of periodic orbits from stable equilibrium point, as a bifurcation parameter crosses a critical value. Since the theory of bifurcation from equilibria based on center manifold reduction and Poincaré-Normal forms, the direction of bifurcations for the mathematical models will also be explained using this theory. Finally, by introducing several software packages and numerical methods this chapter will also cover the techniques to determine and continue in some control parameters all local bifurcations of periodic orbits of dynamical systems and relevant normal form computations combined with the center manifold theorem, including periodic normal forms for periodic orbits.

In general, in a dynamical system, a parameter is allowed to vary, then the differential system may change. An equilibrium can become unstable and a periodic solution may appear or a new stable equilibrium may appear making the previous equilibrium unstable. The value of parameter at which these changes occur is known as "bifurcation value" and the parameter that is varied is known as the "bifurcation parameter".

In this chapter, we also discuss several types of bifurcations, saddle node, transcritical, pitchfork and Hopf bifurcation. Among these types, we especially focus on Hopf bifurcation. The first three types of bifurcation occur in scalar and in systems of differential equations. The fourth type called Hopf bifurcation does not occur in scalar differential equations because this type of bifurcation involves a change to a periodic solution. Scalar autonomous differential equations can not have periodic solutions. Hopf bifurcation occurs in systems of differential equations consisting of two or more equations. This type is also referred to as a "Poincare-Andronov-Hopf bifurcation".

For a given system of differential equations first we shall consider the stability and the local Hopf bifurcation. By using the Hopf bifurcation theorem we prove the occurrence of the Hopf bifurcation. And then, based on the normal form method and the center manifold reduction introduced by Hassard et al.,[10], we derive the formulae determining the direction, stability and the period of the bifurcating periodic solution at the critical value of the bifurcation parameter. To verify the theoretical analysis, numerical simulations for bifurcation analysis are given in this chapter. For references see [1]-[22].

We also introduce the Hopf bifurcation for continuous dynamical systems and state the Hopf bifurcation theorem for these models. As it is well known, Hopf bifurcations occur when a conjugated complex pair of eigenvalues crosses the boundary of stability. In the time-continuous case, a limit cycle bifurcates. It has an angular frequency which is given by the imaginary part of the crossing pair. In the discrete case, the bifurcating orbit is generally quasi-periodic, except that the argument of the crossing pair times an integer gives just 2π. If we consider an ordinary differential equation (ODE) that depends on one or more parameters α

$$x' = f(x,\alpha), \tag{1}$$

where, for simplicity, we assume α to be the only parameter. There is the possibility that under variation of α nothing interesting happens to Equation (1). There is only a quantitatively different behavior. Let us define Equation (1) to be structurally stable in the case there are no qualitative changes occurring. However, the ODE (Ordinary Differential Equation) might change qualitatively. At that point, bifurcations will have occurred.

Many of the basic principles for one dimensional systems apply also for two-dimensional systems. Let us define a two-dimensional system

$$\begin{aligned} x' &= f(x,y,\alpha), \\ y' &= g(x,y,\alpha), \end{aligned} \tag{2}$$

where biologically we mostly interpret x as prey or resource and y as predator or consumer. Equilibria can be found by taking the equations equal to zero, i.e.,

$$\begin{aligned} f(x,y,\alpha) &= 0, \\ g(x,y,\alpha) &= 0. \end{aligned}$$

We have three possibilities for the stability of an equilibrium. Next to the stable and unstable equilibrium, there is the saddle equilibrium. A two-dimensional stable equilibrium is attracting in two directions, while a two-dimensional unstable equilibrium is repelling in two directions. A saddle point is attracting in one direction and repelling in the other direction. In the less formal literature saddles are often considered just unstable equilibria. A second remark is that also the dynamics of the system around the equilibria can differ.

The attracting or repelling can occur via straight orbits (a node) or via spiralling orbits (a spiral or focus). Note that, it is not possible to have a saddle focus in two dimensions. It is possible though in three of higher dimensional systems.

To prove the existence of Hopf bifurcation, we first obtain the Hopf bifurcation theorem hypothesis, i.e., the existence of purely imaginary eigenvalues of the corresponding characteristic equation with respect to the parameter α and also we prove the transversality condition

$$\frac{d\lambda}{d\alpha}(\alpha = \alpha_0) \neq 0 \tag{3}$$

at the critical value α_0 where Hopf bifurcation occurs. Then based on the normal form approach and the center manifold theory introduced by Hassard et. al,[10], we derive the formula for determining the properties of Hopf bifurcation of the model.

Finally in this chapter, to support these theoretical results, we illustrate them by numerical simulations. In numerical analysis, generally MATLAB solver packages are used to analyze the dynamics of nonlinear models. In these solvers, differential equation systems are simulated by difference equations. In this chapter, we also give some examples from biology (such as well known predator-prey models with time delay) with numerical simulations and by graphing the solutions in two or three dimensions, we illustrate the occurrence of periodic solutions. For some examples see references by Çelik, [4], [5] and [6].

2. Basic concepts of bifurcation analysis

As it is stated above, in dynamical systems, a bifurcation occurs when a small smooth change made to the parameter values (the bifurcation parameters) of a system causes a sudden "qualitative" or topological change in its behavior. Generally, at a bifurcation, the local stability properties of equilibria, periodic orbits or other invariant sets changes. It has two types;

Local bifurcations, which can be analyzed entirely through changes in the local stability properties of equilibria, periodic orbits or other invariant sets as parameters cross through critical thresholds; and

Global bifurcations, which often occur when larger invariant sets of the system "collide" with each other, or with equilibria of the system. They cannot be detected purely by a stability analysis of the equilibria (fixed or equilibrium points, see the next section).

2.1 Equilibrium points

In dynamical systems, only the solutions of linear systems may be found explicitly. The problem is that in general real life problems may only be modeled by nonlinear systems. The main idea is to approximate a nonlinear system by a linear one (around the equilibrium point). Of course, we do hope that the behavior of the solutions of the linear system will be the same as the nonlinear one. But this is not always true. Before the linear stability analysis, we give some basic definitions below.

Definition (Equilibrium Point): Consider a nonlinear differential equation

$$x'(t) = f(x(t), u(t)),$$

where f is a function mapping $R^n x R^3 \to R^n$. A point $\bar{x}$ is called an equilibrium point if there is a specific $\bar{u}\, \epsilon R^m$ such that

$$f(x(t), u(t)) = 0_n.$$

Suppose $\bar{x}$ is an equilibrium point (with the input $\bar{u}$). Consider the initial condition $x(0) = \bar{x}$, and applying the input $u(t) = \bar{u}$ for all $t \geq t_0$, then resulting solution $x(t)$ satisfies

$$x(t) = \bar{x},$$

for all $t \geq t_0$. That is why it is called an equilibrium point or solution.

Example: As an example, consider the logistic growth equation (the rate of population density)

$$x' = rx(1 - \frac{x}{K}),$$

where $x(t)$ denotes the population density at time t, r and K are positive constants, K is the carrying capacity. Then by setting right hand side function equal to zero,

$$f(x) = rx(1 - \frac{x}{K}) = 0,$$

we obtain two equilibrium points $x = 0$ and $x = K$.

2.2 Linear stability analysis

Linear stability of dynamical equations can be analyzed in two parts: one for scalar equations and the other for two dimensional systems;

2.2.1 Linear stability analysis for scalar equations

To analyze the ODE

$$x' = f(x)$$

locally about the equilibrium point $x = \bar{x}$, we expand the function $f(x)$ in a Taylor series about the equilibrium point $\bar{x}$. To emphasize that we are doing a local analysis, it is customary to make a change of variables from the dependent variable x to a local variable. Now let

$$x(t) = \bar{x} + \varepsilon(t),$$

where it is assumed that $\varepsilon(t) \ll 1$, so that we can justify dropping all terms of order two and higher in the expansion. Substituting $x(t) = \bar{x} + \varepsilon(t)$ into the RHS of the ODE yields;

$$\begin{aligned} f(x(t)) &= f(\bar{x} + \varepsilon(t)) \\ &= f(\bar{x}) + f'(\bar{x})\varepsilon(t) + f''(\bar{x})\frac{\varepsilon^2(t)}{2} + ... \\ &= 0 + f'(\bar{x})\varepsilon(t) + O(\varepsilon^2), \end{aligned}$$

and dropping higher order terms, we obtain

$$f(x) \approx f'(\bar{x})\varepsilon(t).$$

Note that dropping these higher order terms is valid since $\varepsilon(t) \ll 1$. Now substituting $x(t) = \bar{x} + \varepsilon(t)$ into the LHS of the ODE,

$$\varepsilon'(t) = f'(\bar{x})\varepsilon(t).$$

The goal is to determine if we have growing or decaying solutions. If the solutions grows, then the equilibrium point is unstable. If the solution decays, then the fixed point is stable.

To determine whether or not the solution is stable or unstable we simply solve the ODE and get the solution as

$$\varepsilon(t) = \varepsilon_0 \exp(f'(\bar{x})t),$$

where ε_0 is a constant. Hence, the solution is growing if $f'(\bar{x}) > 0$ and decaying if $f'(\bar{x}) < 0$. As a result, the equilibrium point is stable if $f'(\bar{x}) < 0$, unstable if $f'(\bar{x}) > 0$ as it is stated in the following theorem.

Theorem: Suppose for scalar differential equation

$$x' = f(x),$$

the derivative function f' is continuous on an open interval I where the equilibrium point $\bar{x}\epsilon I$. Then the equilibrium point $\bar{x}$ is locally stable if $f'(\bar{x}) < 0$ and it is unstable if $f'(\bar{x}) > 0$.

If the equilibrium point is stable and in addition

$$\lim_{t\to\infty} x(t) = \bar{x},$$

then it is called asymptotically stable equilibrium point.

Example: Determine the stability of the fixed points to the Logistic growth equation

$$N' = f(N) = rN(1 - \frac{N}{K}), \text{ where } r > 0.$$

We first find the equilibrium points by setting

$$f(\bar{N}) = 0, \text{ which yields two points } \bar{N} = 0, K.$$

Next we compute $f^{'}(N)$ and evaluate it at the equilibrium points.

$$\begin{aligned}
&f'(N) = r(1 - \frac{2N}{K}) \\
&\text{at } \bar{N} = 0, \; f'(0) = r > 0, \text{ so it is unstable} \\
&\text{at } \bar{N} = K, \; f'(K) = -r < 0, \text{ so it is locally stable.}
\end{aligned}$$

2.2.2 Linear stability analysis for systems

Consider the two dimensional nonlinear system

$$x' = f(x,y),$$
$$y' = g(x,y),$$

and suppose that $(\bar{x},\bar{y})$ is a steady state (equilibrium point), i.e.,

$$f(\bar{x},\bar{y}) = 0 \text{ and } g(\bar{x},\bar{y}) = 0.$$

Now let's consider a small perturbation from the steady state $(\bar{x},\bar{y})$

$$x = \bar{x} + u,$$
$$y = \bar{y} + v,$$

where u and v are understood to be small as $u \ll 1$ and $v \ll 1$. Is is natural to ask whether u and v are growing or decaying so that x and y will move away form the steady state or move towards the steady states. If it moves away, it is called unstable equilibrium point, if it moves towards the equilibrium point, then it is called stable equilibrium point.As in scalar equations, by expanding the Taylor's series for $f(x,y)$ and $g(x,y)$;

$$\begin{aligned} u' &= x' = f(x,y) \\ &= f(\bar{x}+u,\bar{y}+v) \\ &= f(\bar{x},\bar{y}) + f_x(\bar{x},\bar{y})u + f_y(\bar{x},\bar{y})v + \text{higher order terms...} \\ &= f_x(\bar{x},\bar{y})u + f_y(\bar{x},\bar{y})v + \text{higher order terms....} \end{aligned}$$

Similarly,

$$\begin{aligned} v' &= y' = g(x,y) \\ &= g(\bar{x}+u,\bar{y}+v) \\ &= g(\bar{x},\bar{y}) + g_x(\bar{x},\bar{y})u + g_y(\bar{x},\bar{y})v + \text{higher order terms...} \\ &= g_x(\bar{x},\bar{y})u + g_y(\bar{x},\bar{y})v + \text{higher order terms....} \end{aligned}$$

Since u and v are assumed to be small, the higher order terms are extremely small, we can neglect the higher order terms and obtain the following linear system of equations governing the evolution of the perturbations u and v,

$$\begin{bmatrix} u' \\ v' \end{bmatrix} = \begin{bmatrix} f_x(\bar{x},\bar{y}) & f_y(\bar{x},\bar{y}) \\ g_x(\bar{x},\bar{y}) & g_y(\bar{x},\bar{y}) \end{bmatrix} \begin{bmatrix} u \\ v \end{bmatrix},$$

where the matrix $\begin{bmatrix} f_x & f_y \\ g_x & g_y \end{bmatrix}$ is called Jacobian matrix J of the nonlinear system.The above linear system for u and v has the trivial steady state $(u,v) = (0,0)$, and the stability of this trivial steady state is determined by the eigenvalues of the Jacobian matrix, as follows:

Theorem : An equilibrium point $(\bar{x}, \bar{y})$ of the differential equation is stable if all the eigenvalues of J, the Jacobian evaluated at $(\bar{x}, \bar{y})$ have negative real parts. The equilibrium point is unstable if at least one of the eigenvalues has a positive real part.

As a summary,

Asymptotically stable : A critical point is asymptotically stable if all eigenvalues of the jacobian matrix J are negative, or have negative real parts.

Unstable: A critical point is unstable if at least one eigenvalue of the jacobian matrix J is positive, or has positive real part.

Stable (or neutrally stable) : Each trajectory move about the critical point within a finite range of distance.

Definition(Hyperbolic point): The equilibrium is said to be hyperbolic if all eigenvalues of the jacobian matrix have non-zero real parts.

Hyperbolic equilibria are robust(i.e., the system is structurally stable): Small perturbations of order do not change qualitatively the phase portrait near the equilibria. Moreover, local phase portrait of a hyperbolic equilibrium of a nonlinear system is equivalent to that of its linearization. This statement has a mathematically precise form known as the Hartman-Grobman. This theorem guarantees that the stability of the steady state $(\bar{x}, \bar{y})$ of the nonlinear system is the same as the stability of the trivial steady state $(0, 0)$ of the linearized system.

Definition(Non-Hyperbolic point): If at least one eigenvalue of the Jacobian matrix is zero or has a zero real part, then the equilibrium is said to be non-hyperbolic.

Non-hyperbolic equilibria are not robust (i.e., the system is not structurally stable). Small perturbations can result in a local bifurcation of a non-hyperbolic equilibrium, i.e., it can change stability, disappear, or split into many equilibria. Some refer to such an equilibrium by the name of the bifurcation (See the section below).

Example: Consider the following nonlinear autonomous system

$$\begin{aligned} \dot{x}(t) &= y(t)[x(t) - y(t)], \\ \dot{y}(t) &= x(t)[2 - y(t)]. \end{aligned} \tag{4}$$

The equilibria are the points $(\bar{x}, \bar{y}) = (0, 0)$ and $(\bar{x}, \bar{y}) = (1, 2)$ and the Jacobian matrix is

$$J = \begin{bmatrix} y & x-1 \\ 2-y & -x \end{bmatrix}.$$

We compute the Jacobian at the equilibrium point (0,0) where $J(0, 0) = \begin{bmatrix} 0 & -1 \\ 2 & 0 \end{bmatrix}$ which implies that the eigenvalues are purely imaginary

$$\lambda_{1.2} = \pm\sqrt{2}i,$$

by solving the characteristic equation

$$det(J - \lambda I) = 0.$$

Since the point is non-hyperbolic, the linearized system can not tell about the stability. Later on we will show that this is a center.

For the equilibrium point (1,2), the Jacobian $J(1,2) = \begin{bmatrix} 2 & 0 \\ 0 & -1 \end{bmatrix}$ thus the point is locally unstable (as

$$\lambda_1 = 1 \quad \text{and} \quad \lambda_2 = -1,$$

where one of the eigenvalues is strictly positive). Since it is a hyperbolic equilibrium point, the stability of fixed point is the same as in the linearized system. So it is also unstable.

3. Bifurcation analysis

Consider a family of ODE's that depend on one parameter λ

$$x' = f(x, \lambda), \tag{5}$$

where $f : \mathbb{R}^{n+1} \rightarrow \mathbb{R}^n$ is analytic for $\lambda \epsilon \mathbb{R}$, $x \epsilon \mathbb{R}^n$. Let $x = x_0(\lambda)$ be a family of equilibrium points of equation (5), i.e., $f(x_0(\lambda), \lambda) = 0$. Now let's set

$$z = x - x_0(\lambda).$$

Then

$$z' = A(\lambda)z + O(|z|^2),$$

where $A(\lambda) = \frac{\partial f}{\partial x}(x_0(\lambda), \lambda)$.

Let $\lambda_1, \lambda_2, ... \lambda_n(\lambda)$ be the eigenvalues of $A(\lambda)$. If, for some i, $Re\lambda_i(\lambda)$ changes sign at $\lambda = \lambda_0$, we say that λ_0 is a bifurcation point of equation (5).

3.1 Bifurcation in one dimension

We may assume that $n = 1$ so that $f : \mathbb{R}^2 \rightarrow \mathbb{R}^1$, and $x_0(\lambda)$ is a real valued analytic function of λ provided

$$\lambda_1(\lambda) = \frac{\partial f}{\partial x}(x_0(\lambda), \lambda) = A(\lambda) = 0.$$

Therefore, the equilibrium point is asymptotically stable if $\lambda_1(\lambda) < 0$, and unstable if $\lambda_1(\lambda) > 0$. This implies that λ_0 is a bifurcation point if $\lambda_1(\lambda_0) = 0$. Hence, bifurcation points $(x_0(\lambda), \lambda)$ are solutions of

$$f(x, \lambda) = 0 \quad \text{and} \quad \frac{\partial f}{\partial x}(x, \lambda) = 0.$$

The most common bifurcation types are illustrated by the following examples.

3.1.1 Saddle-node bifurcation

A saddle-node bifurcation or tangent bifurcation is a collision and disappearance of two equilibria in dynamical systems. In autonomous systems, this occurs when the critical equilibrium has one zero eigenvalue. This phenomenon is also called fold or limit point bifurcation.

Now consider the dynamical system defined by

$$x' = a - x^2, \quad \text{for} \quad a \quad \text{is real.} \tag{6}$$

An equilibrium solution (where $x' = 0$) is simply $x = \pm\sqrt{a}$. Therefore,

if $a < 0$, then we have no real solutions,

if $a > 0$, then we have two real solutions.

We now consider each of the two solutions for $a > 0$, and examine their linear stability in the usual way. First, we add a small perturbation:

$$x = \bar{x} + \varepsilon.$$

Substituting this into the equation yields

$$\frac{d\varepsilon}{dt} = (a - \bar{x}^2) - 2\bar{x}\varepsilon - \varepsilon^2,$$

and since the term in brackets on the RHS is trivially zero, therefore

$$\frac{d\varepsilon}{dt} = -2\bar{x}\varepsilon,$$

which has the solution

$$\varepsilon(t) = A\exp(-2\bar{x}t).$$

From this, we see that for $x = +\sqrt{a}$, $|x| \to 0$ as $t \to \infty$ (linear stability); for $x = -\sqrt{a}$, $|x| \to 0$ as $t \to \infty$ (linear stability).

As sketched in the "bifurcation diagram" below, therefore, the saddle node bifurcation at $a = 0$ corresponds to the creation of two new solution branches. One of these is linearly stable, the other is linearly unstable.

3.1.2 Transcritical bifurcation

In a transcritical bifurcation, two families of fixed points collide and exchange their stability properties. The family that was stable before the bifurcation is unstable after it. The other fixed point goes from being unstable to being stable.

Now consider the dynamical system

$$\frac{dx}{dt} = az - bx^2, \quad \text{for} \quad x, a, b \quad \text{real.}$$

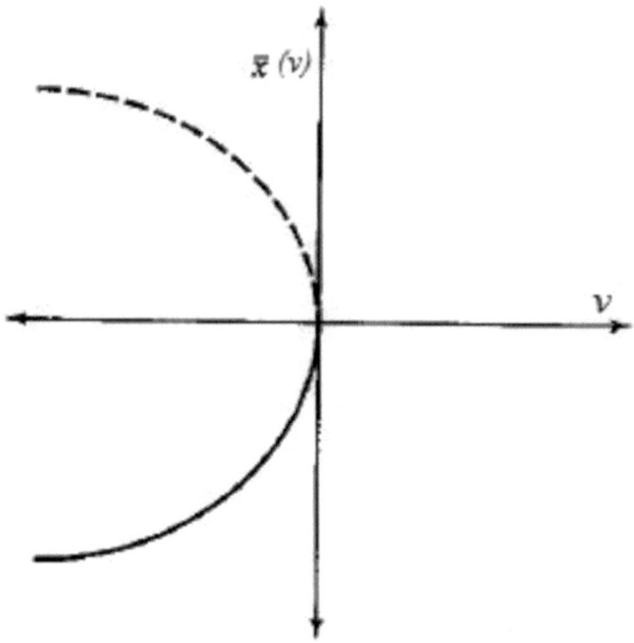

Figure 1. Bifurcation diagram corresponding to the saddle-node bifurcation

Again, a and b are control parameters. We can find two steady states $(x' = 0)$ to this system

$$x = \bar{x}_1 = 0, \forall a, b$$
$$x = \bar{x}_2 = \frac{a}{b}, \forall a, b, b \neq 0.$$

We now examine the linear stability of each of these states in turn, following the usual procedure.

For the state $\bar{x}_1$, we add a small perturbation

$$x = \bar{x}_1 + \varepsilon,$$

which yields

$$\frac{d\varepsilon}{dt} = a\varepsilon - b\varepsilon^2$$

with the linearized form

$$\frac{d\varepsilon}{dt} = a\varepsilon$$

has the solution

$$e(t) = A\exp(at).$$

Therefore, perturbations grow for a > 0 and decay for a < 0. So

the state $\bar{x}_1$ is unstable if $a > 0$,
the state $\bar{x}_1$ is stable if $a < 0$.

Now for the state $\bar{x}_2$, we add a small perturbation

$$x = \bar{x}_2 + \varepsilon,$$

which yields the linearized form

$$\frac{d\varepsilon}{dt} = -a\varepsilon$$

has the solution

$$e(t) = A\exp(-at).$$

Therefore, perturbations grow for a >0 and decay for a <0. So

$$\text{the state } \bar{x}_2 = \frac{a}{b} \text{ is linearly stable if } a > 0,$$
$$\text{the state } \bar{x}_2 = \frac{a}{b} \text{ is linearly unstable if } a < 0.$$

It can be easily seen that the bifurcation point $a = 0$ corresponds to an exchange of stabilities between the two solution branches.

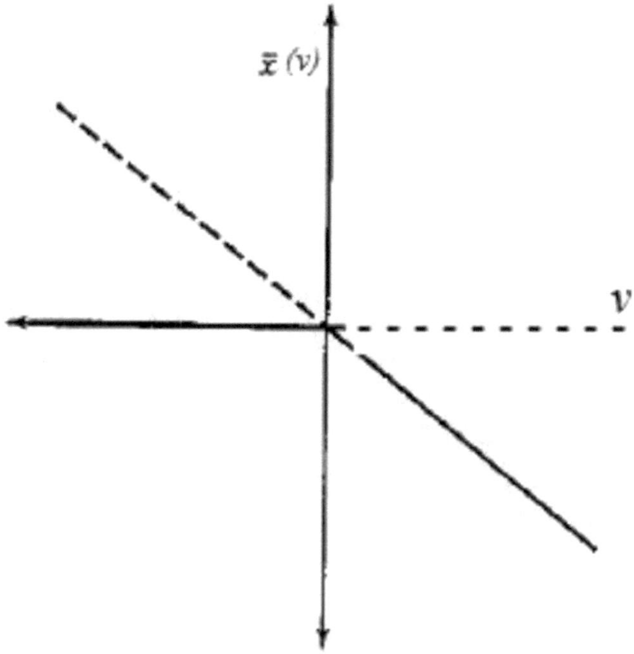

Figure 2. Bifurcation diagram corresponding to the transcritical bifurcation

3.1.3 The pitchfork bifurcation

In pitchfork bifurcation one family of fixed points transfers its stability properties to two families after or before the bifurcation point. If this occurs after the bifurcation point, then pitchfork bifurcation is called supercritical. Similarly, a pitchfork bifurcation is called subcritical if the nontrivial fixed points occur for values of the parameter lower than the bifurcation value. In other words, the cases in which the emerging nontrivial equilibria are stable are called supercritical whereas the cases in which these equilibria are called subcritical.

Consider the dynamical system

$$x' = ax - bx^3, \text{for} \quad a, b \quad \text{real.}$$

As usual, a and b are external control parameters. Steady states, for which $x' = 0$ are as follows:

$$x = \bar{x}_1 = 0, \forall a, b,$$

$$x = \bar{x}_2 = -\sqrt{a/b}, \text{ for } a/b > 0,$$

$$x = \bar{x}_3 = \sqrt{a/b}, \text{ for } a/b > 0.$$

Note that the equilibrium points $\bar{x}_2$ and $\bar{x}_3$ only exist when $a > 0$ if $b > 0$ and for $a < 0$ if $b < 0$.

As usual, we now examine the linear stability of each of these steady states in turn. (This can be done for a general b). First we write the perturbation for $\bar{x}_1 = 0$,

$$x = \bar{x}_1 + \varepsilon$$

that yields the linearized equation

$$\frac{d\varepsilon}{dt} = a\varepsilon,$$

with the solution

$$e(t) = A\exp(at).$$

So we see that

the state $\bar{x}_1 = 0$ is linearly unstable if $a > 0$,

the state $\bar{x}_2 = 0$ is linearly stable if $a < 0$.

For the states $x = \bar{x}_2$ and $x = \bar{x}_3$, setting

$$\bar{x} = \pm\sqrt{a/b} + \varepsilon,$$

$$\frac{d\varepsilon}{dt} = a\varepsilon - 3b\bar{x}^2\varepsilon,$$

with the solution

$$e(t) = A\exp(ct) \text{ where } c = -2a.$$

Thus it is obvious that

the states $\bar{x}_2$ and $\bar{x}_3$ are linearly stable if $a > 0$,
the states $\bar{x}_2$ and $\bar{x}_3$ are linearly unstable if $a < 0$,

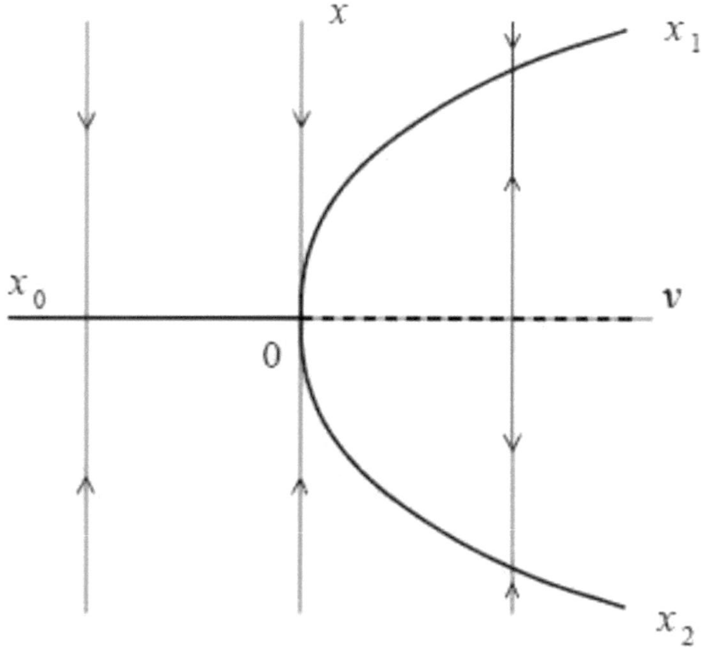

Figure 3. Bifurcation diagram corresponding to the pitchfork bifurcation

3.2 Bifurcation in two dimension

3.2.1 Hopf bifurcation

Definition : A Hopf or Poincare-Andronov-Hopf bifurcation is a local bifurcation in which a fixed point of a dynamical system loses stability as a pair of complex conjugate eigenvalues of linearization around the fixed point cross the imaginary axis of the complex plane.

3.3 Hopf bifurcation theorem

Consider the two dimensional system

$$\frac{dx}{dt} = f\left(x, y, \tau\right), \qquad (7)$$
$$\frac{dy}{dt} = g\left(x, y, \tau\right),$$

where τ is the parameter and suppose that $\left(\overline{x}\left(\tau\right), \overline{y}\left(\tau\right)\right)$ is the equilibrium point and $\alpha\left(\tau\right) \pm i\beta\left(\tau\right)$ are the eigenvalues of the Jacobian matrix which is evaluated at the equilibrium point.

In addition let's assume that the change in the stability of the equilibrium point occurs at $\tau = \tau^*$ where $\alpha\left(\tau^*\right) = 0$.

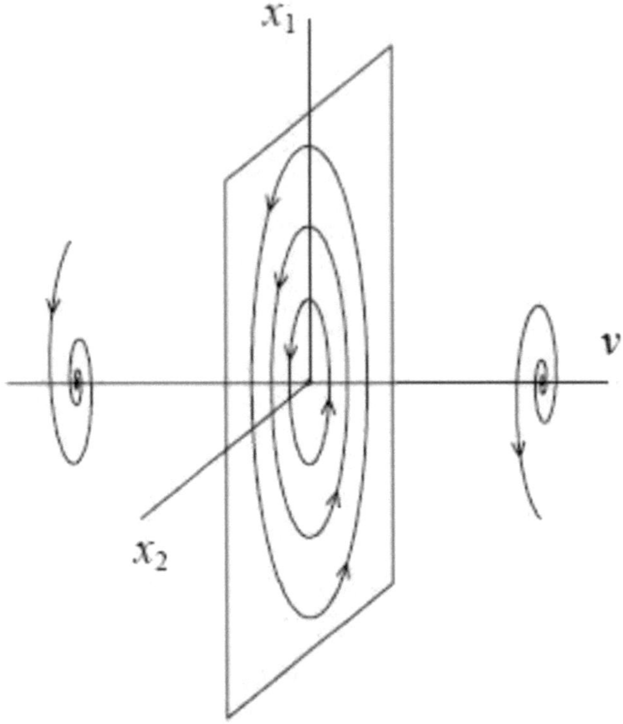

Figure 4. Hopf bifurcation diagram

First the system is transformed so that the equilibrium is at the origin and the parameter τ at $\tau^* = 0$ gives purely imaginary eigenvalues. System (7) is rewritten as follows;

$$\frac{dx}{dt} = a_{11}(\tau)x + a_{12}(\tau)y + f_1(x, y, \tau), \tag{8}$$

$$\frac{dy}{dt} = a_{21}(\tau)x + a_{22}(\tau)y + g_1(x, y, \tau).$$

The linearization of the system (7) about the origin is given by $\frac{dX}{dt} = J(\tau)X$, where $X = \begin{bmatrix} x \\ y \end{bmatrix}$ and

$$J(\tau) = \begin{bmatrix} a_{11}(\tau) & a_{12}(\tau) \\ a_{21}(\tau) & a_{22}(\tau) \end{bmatrix}$$

is the Jacobian matrix evaluated at origin.

Theorem (Hopf bifurcation theorem)

Let f_1 and g_1, in system (8) have continuous third order partial derivatives in x and y. Suppose that the origin is an equilibrium point of (8) and that the Jacobian matrix $J(\tau)$ as above, is valid for all sufficiently small $|\tau|$. Moreover, assume that the eigenvalues of matrix $J(\tau)$ are $\alpha(\tau) \pm i\beta(\tau)$ where $\alpha(0) = 0, \beta(0) \neq 0$ such that the eigenvalues cross the imaginary axis with nonzero speed, i.e.,

$$\frac{d\alpha}{d\tau}\,|_{\tau=0}\neq 0.$$

Then in any open set U containing the origin in $\mathbb{R}^2$ and for any $\tau_0 > 0$, there exists a value $\bar{\tau}, |\bar{\tau}| < \tau_0$ such that the system of differential equations (8) has a periodic solution for $\tau = \bar{\tau}$ in U. (Allen, L.J.S).

Note: The Hopf bifurcation requires at least a two dimensional differential equation system to appear.

Definition: The bifurcation stated in the Hopf bifurcation theorem is called "**supercritical**" if the equilibrium point $(0,0)$ is asymptotically stable when $\tau = 0$ (at the bifurcation point) and it is called "**subcritical"** if the equilibrium point $(0,0)$ is negatively asymptotically stable (as $t \to -\infty$) when $\tau = 0$.

In a supercritical Hopf bifurcation, the limit cycle grows out of the equilibrium point. In other words, right at the parameters of the Hopf bifurcation, the limit cycle has zero amplitude, and this amplitude grows as the parameters move further into the limit-cycle. (See the figure below)

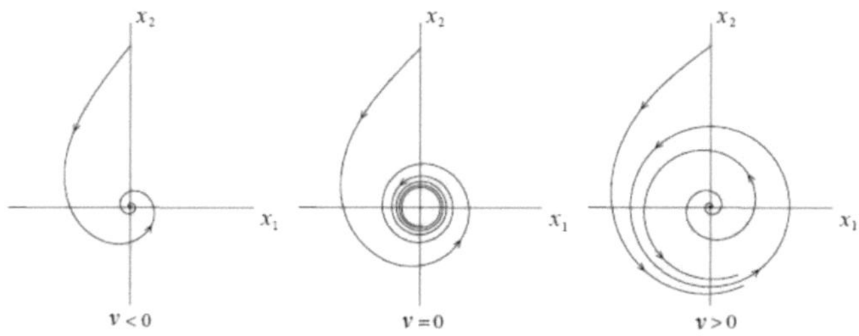

Figure 5. Bifurcation diagram corresponding to Supercritical Hopf bifurcation

However in a subcritical Hopf bifurcation, there is an unstable limit cycle surrounding the equilibrium point, and a stable limit cycle surrounding that. The unstable limit cycle shrinks down to the equilibrium point, which becomes unstable in the process. For systems started near the equilibrium point, the result is a sudden change in behavior from approach to a stable focus, to large-amplitude oscillations.(See the figure below).

Example: Consider the two dimensional system

$$\frac{dx}{dt} = x^2 - \alpha, \qquad (9)$$

$$\frac{dy}{dt} = -(x^2+1)y,$$

where α is a parameter. When we compute the equilibrium points depending on parameter α;

If $\alpha < 0$, then there is no x-nullclines, hence the system has no equilibrium points.

If $\alpha = 0$, then the system has exactly one equilibrium point at $(0,0)$.

If $\alpha > 0$, then the system has two equilibrium points $(-\sqrt{\alpha},0)$ and $(\sqrt{\alpha},0)$.

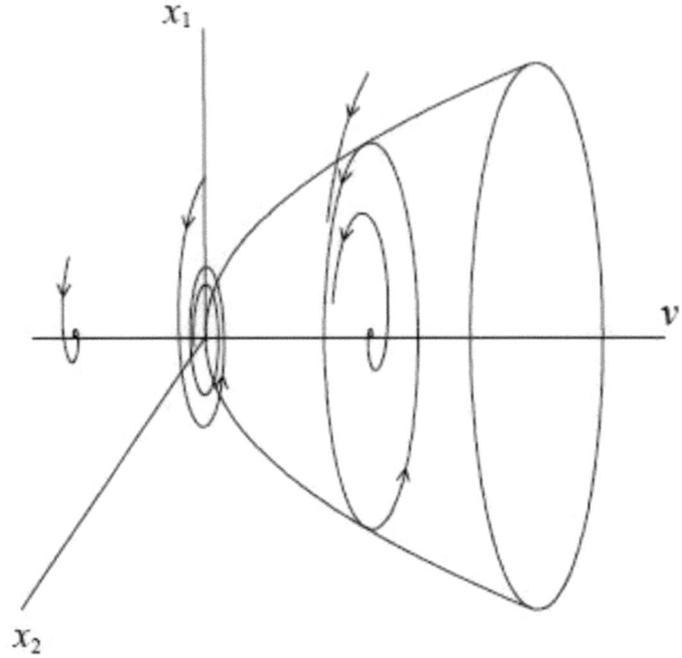

Figure 6. Supercritical Hopf bifurcation

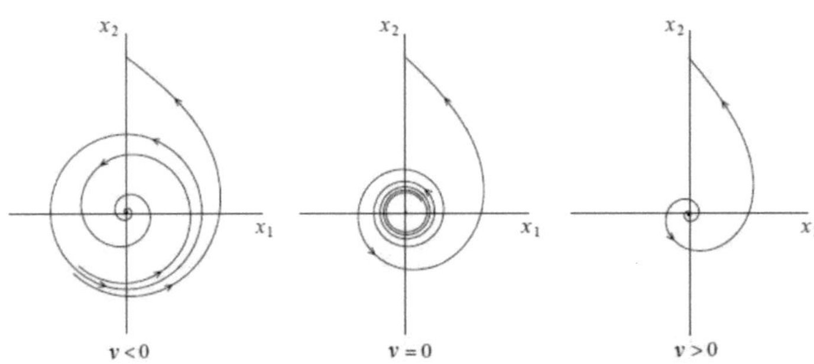

Figure 7. Diagram for Subcritical Hopf bifurcation

Then the Jacobian matrix is

$$J = \begin{bmatrix} 2x & 0 \\ -2xy & -(x^2+1) \end{bmatrix},$$

where at the equilibrium points $J(0.0) = \begin{bmatrix} 0 & 0 \\ 0 & -1 \end{bmatrix}, J(\sqrt{\alpha},0) = \begin{bmatrix} -2\sqrt{\alpha} & 0 \\ 0 & -\alpha-1 \end{bmatrix}$ and $J(\sqrt{\alpha},0) = \begin{bmatrix} 2\sqrt{\alpha} & 0 \\ 0 & -\alpha-1 \end{bmatrix}$.

For $\alpha = 0$, there will be a line equilibrium (since one of the eigenvalues is zero) and for $\alpha > 0$, the point $(-\sqrt{\alpha},0)$ is a sink and $(\sqrt{\alpha},0)$ is a saddle point so that $\alpha = 0$ is the bifurcation point for this differential equation system.

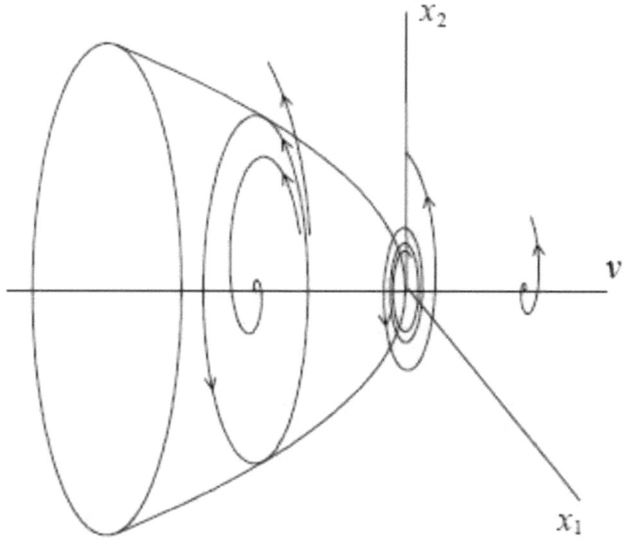

Figure 8. Subcritical Hopf bifurcation

Example: Consider the two dimensional system

$$\frac{dx}{dt} = y + \alpha x, \qquad (10)$$
$$\frac{dy}{dt} = -x + \alpha y,$$

where α is the bifurcation parameter. We can easily show that the conditions of the Hopf Bifurcation theorem hold. In this system f_1 and f_2 are zero. Then the Jacobian matrix is

$$J = \begin{bmatrix} \alpha & 1 \\ -1 & \alpha \end{bmatrix}$$

for which the eigenvalues are $\lambda_{1,2} = \alpha \pm i$ where $\text{Re}\lambda(\alpha) = \alpha$ and the imaginary part $\text{Im}\lambda(\alpha) = \pm 1$.It follows that $\text{Re}\lambda(0) = 0$ and $\text{Im}\lambda(0) \neq 0$. and also

$$\frac{dRe\lambda(\alpha)}{d\alpha} |_{\alpha=0} = 1 \neq 0.$$

Hence, we conclude that there exists a periodic solution for $\alpha = 0$ in every neighborhood of origin.

4. Center Manifold teorem

Let $f(0) = 0$, for the dynamical system

$$x' = f(x), \; x \in \mathbb{R}^n, \qquad (11)$$

and let the eigenvalues of the Jacobian matrix be $\lambda_1, \lambda_2, ..., \lambda_n$. Suppose that, the real parts of the eigenvalues are zero and if not, suppose there are n_+ numbers of eigenvalues with $\operatorname{Re}\lambda > 0$, n_0 number of eigenvalues with $\operatorname{Re}\lambda = 0$ and n_- number of eigenvalues with $\operatorname{Re}\lambda < 0$. Let T^c be the eigenspace on imaginary axis corresponding to n_0 eigenvalues. The eigenvalues on the imaginary axis ($\operatorname{Re}\lambda = 0$) are called the critical eigenvalues as on the eigenspace T^c. And suppose the function φ^t denote the flow corresponding to the equation (11).

With these assumption, we state the Center Manifold theorem as follows;

Theorem: (Center Manifold theorem)

There exists a locally invariant C^∞ center manifold $W^c_{loc}(0)$ such that

$$W^c_{loc}(0) = \{(x, y) : y = h(x); |x| < \delta, h(0) = 0; DJ(0) = 0\}$$

such that the dynamics of the system

$$x' = A^c x + r_1(x, y),$$

$$y' = A^s y + r_2(x, y),$$

(where A^c and A^s are are the blocks in the canonical form whose diagonals contain the eigenvalues with $\operatorname{Re}\lambda = 0$ and $\operatorname{Re}\lambda < 0$; respectively) restricted to the center manifold are given by

$$x' = A^c(x) + r_1(x, h(x)).$$

And the manifold W^c_{loc} is called center manifold.

Remark: Center manifolds are not unique.

4.1 Center Manifold reduction for two dimensional systems

Example: Consider the two dimensional system of differential equations

$$x' = xy, \qquad (12)$$

$$y' = -y + x^2.$$

The only equilibrium point is $(0, 0)$, we linearize around that and obtain

$$J(0,0) = \begin{bmatrix} 0 & 0 \\ 0 & -1 \end{bmatrix}.$$

Now we look for $y = h(x) = ax^2 + bx^3 + cx^4 + dx^5 + O(x^6)$. Then,

$$y' = h'(x)x' = xh'(x)h(x)$$

$$= 2a^2x^4 + 5abx^5 + O(x^6)$$

and on the other hand,

$$\begin{aligned} y' &= -h(x) - x^2 \\ &= -(a+1)x^2 - bx^3 - cx^4 - dx^5 + O(x^6). \end{aligned}$$

Comparing the two expressions, we deduce that $a = -1, b = 0, c = -2, d = 0$ and the center manifold reduction takes the form

$$y = h(x) = -x^2 - 2x^4 + O(x^7).$$

Hence for the last equation $x = 0$ is asymptotically stable and therefore $(0,0)$ is asymptotically stable for the original system.

Example: Consider the two dimensional system

$$\begin{aligned} x' &= x^2y - x^5, \\ y' &= -y + x^2. \end{aligned} \tag{13}$$

Again $(0,0)$ is an equilibrium point and the jacobian matrix for the linearized system is

$$J(0,0) = \begin{bmatrix} 0 & 0 \\ 0 & -1 \end{bmatrix}.$$

Consider the transformation $y = h(x) = ax^2 + bx^3 + cx^4 + dx^5 + O(x^6)$, which leads

$$\begin{aligned} y' &= h'(x)x' \\ &= 2a^2x^5 + [2a(b-1) + 3ab]x^6 + O(x^7), \end{aligned}$$

and

$$\begin{aligned} y' &= -h(x) + x^2 \\ &= -(a+1)x^2 - bx^3 + O(x^4) \\ &= 2a^2x^4 + 5a - bxbx^5 + O(x^6), \end{aligned}$$

from which we deduce that $a = 1$ and $b = 0$ and

$$x' = x^4 + O(x^5).$$

For this reduced equation, $x = 0$ is unstable and hence, $(0,0)$ is also unstable for the original system.

4.2 Center Manifold reduction for Hopf bifurcation

The aim of this section is to give a formal framework for the analytical bifurcation analysis of Hopf bifurcations in delay differential equations

$$x' = f(x, \tau), x \epsilon \mathbb{R}^3 \tag{14}$$

with a single fixed time delay τ to be chosen as a bifurcation parameter. Characteristic equations of the delay differential equation form (14) are often studied in order to understand changes in the local stability of equilibria of certain delay differential equations. It is therefore important to determine the values of the delay at which there are roots with zero part. We give a general formalization of these calculations and determine closed form algebraic equations where the stability and amplitude of periodic solutions close to bifurcation can be calculated.

We shall determine the direction of Hopf bifurcation and the stability of the bifurcating periodic solutions by applying the normal form theory and the center manifold theorem by Hassard et al.,[10], and throughout this section, we assume that the three dimensional system of delay differential equations (14) undergoes Hopf bifurcations at the positive equilibrium (N_0^*, P_0^*, S_0^*) at $\tau = \tau_k$, and $i\omega_1$ is the corresponding purely imaginary root of the characteristic equation at the positive equilibrium (N_0^*, P_0^*, S_0^*). For the sake of simplicity, we use the notation $i\omega$ for $i\omega_1$.

We first consider the system (14) by the transformation

$$x_1 = N - N_0^*,\ x_2 = P - P_0^*,\ x_3 = S - S_0^*,\ t = \frac{t}{\tau},\ \tau = \tau_k + \mu$$

which is equivalent to the following Functional Differential Equation(FDE) system in $C = C([-1,0], \mathbb{R}^3)$,

$$\dot{x}(t) = L_\mu(x_t) + f(\mu, x_t), \tag{15}$$

where $x(t) = (x_1(t), x_2(t), x_3(t))^T \epsilon \mathbb{R}^3$, and $L_\mu : C \to \mathbb{R}^3$, $f : \mathbb{R} \times C \to \mathbb{R}^3$ are given

respectively, by

$$L_\mu(\phi) = (\tau_k + \mu) \begin{bmatrix} a_1\ a_2\ a_3 \\ a_4\ a_5\ a_6 \\ a_7\ a_8\ a_9 \end{bmatrix} \begin{bmatrix} \phi_1(0) \\ \phi_2(0) \\ \phi_3(0) \end{bmatrix}$$

$$+(\tau_k + \mu) \begin{bmatrix} b_1\ b_2\ b_3 \\ b_4\ b_5\ b_6 \\ b_7\ b_8\ b_9 \end{bmatrix} \begin{bmatrix} \phi_1(-1) \\ \phi_2(-1) \\ \phi_3(-1) \end{bmatrix},$$

and

$$f(\mu, \phi) = (\tau_k + \mu) \begin{bmatrix} f_{11} \\ f_{12} \\ f_{13} \end{bmatrix}.$$

By Riesz representation theorem, there exists a function $\eta(\theta, \mu)$ of bounded variation for $\theta \epsilon [-1, 0]$, such that

$$L_\mu \phi = \int_{-1}^{0} d\eta(\theta, 0)\phi(\theta), \text{ for } \phi \epsilon C.$$

Indeed we may take

$$\eta(\theta, \mu) = (\tau_k + \mu) \begin{bmatrix} a_1\ a_2\ a_3 \\ a_4\ a_5\ a_6 \\ a_7\ a_8\ a_9 \end{bmatrix} \delta(\theta) - (\tau_k + \mu) \begin{bmatrix} b_1\ b_2\ b_3 \\ b_4\ b_5\ b_6 \\ b_7\ b_8\ b_9 \end{bmatrix} \delta(\theta + 1),$$

where δ is the Dirac delta function. For $\phi \epsilon C^1([-1,0],\mathbb{R}^3)$, define

$$A(\mu)\phi = \begin{cases} \frac{d\phi(\theta)}{d\theta} & \theta\epsilon[-1,0), \\ \int_{-1}^{0} d\eta(\mu,s)\phi(s) & \theta = 0 \end{cases}$$

and

$$R(\mu)\phi = \begin{cases} 0 & \theta\epsilon[-1,0), \\ f(\mu,\phi), \theta = 0. \end{cases}$$

Then the system (15) is equivalent to

$$\dot{x}_t = A(\mu)x_t + R(\mu)x_t,$$

where $x_t(\theta) = x(t+\theta)$ for $\theta\epsilon[-1,0)$. For $\psi\epsilon C^1([-1,0],(\mathbb{R}^3)^*)$, define

$$A^*\psi(s) = \begin{cases} -\frac{d\psi(s)}{ds} & s\epsilon(0,1], \\ \int_{-1}^{0} d\eta^T(t,0)\psi(-t) & s = 0 \end{cases}$$

and a bilinear inner product

$$\langle\psi(s),\phi(\theta)\rangle = \bar{\psi}(0)\phi(0) - \int_{-1}^{0}\int_{\xi=0}^{\theta} \bar{\psi}(\xi-\theta)d\eta(\theta)\phi(\xi)d\xi, \tag{16}$$

where $\eta(\theta) = \eta(\theta,0)$. Then $A(0)$ and A^* are adjoint operators. Suppose that $q(\theta)$ and $q^*(s)$ are eigenvectors of A and A^* corresponding to $i\omega\tau_k$ and $-i\omega\tau_k$, respectively. Then suppose that $q(\theta) = (1,\beta,\gamma)^T e^{i\omega\tau_k\theta}$ is the eigenvector of $A(0)$ corresponding to $i\omega\tau_k$, then $A(0)q(\theta) = i\omega\tau_k q(\theta)$. Then in the following, we use the theory by Hassard et al.,[10], to compute the coordinates describing center manifold C_0 at $\mu = 0$. Define

$$z(t) = \langle q^*, x_t\rangle, \qquad W(t,\theta) = x_t - 2Rez(t)q(\theta). \tag{17}$$

On the center manifold C_0, we have

$$W(t,\theta) = W(z(t),\bar{z}(t),\theta) = W_{20}(\theta)\frac{z^2}{2} + W_{11}(\theta)z\bar{z} + W_{02}(\theta)\frac{\bar{z}^2}{2} + ...,$$

where z and $\bar{z}$ are local coordinates for center manifold C_0 in the direction of q and $\bar{q}^*$. Note that W is real if x_t is real. We consider only real solutions. For the solution $x_t\epsilon C_0$, since $\mu = 0$ and (15), we have

$$\begin{aligned} \dot{z} &= i\omega\tau_k z + \langle q^*(\theta), F(0, W(z,\bar{z},\theta) + 2Rezq(\theta))\rangle \\ &= i\omega\tau_k z + \bar{q}^*(0)F(0, W(z,\bar{z},0) + 2Rezq(0)) \\ &\stackrel{def}{=} i\omega\tau_k z + \bar{q}^*(0)F_0(z,\bar{z}) \\ &= i\omega\tau_k z + g(z,\bar{z}), \end{aligned}$$

where

$$g(z,\bar{z}) = \bar{q}^*(0)F_0(z,\bar{z}) = g_{20}\frac{z^2}{2} + g_{11}z\bar{z} + g_{02}\frac{\bar{z}^2}{2} + g_{21}\frac{z^2\bar{z}}{2} + ... \tag{18}$$

By using (17), we have $x_t(x_{1t}(\theta), x_{2t}(\theta), x_{3t}(\theta)) = W(t,\theta) + zq(\theta) + \overline{zq}(\theta)$, $q(\theta) = (1, \beta, \gamma)^T e^{i\omega\tau_k\theta}$, and

$$\begin{aligned}
x_{1t}(0) &= z + \bar{z} + W_{20}^{(1)}(0)\frac{z^2}{2} + W_{11}^{(1)}(0)z\bar{z} + W_{02}^{(1)}(0)\frac{\bar{z}^2}{2} + O(|(z,\bar{z})|^3),\\
x_{2t}(0) &= \beta z + \bar{\beta}\bar{z} + W_{20}^{(2)}(0)\frac{z^2}{2} + W_{11}^{(2)}(0)z\bar{z} + W_{02}^{(2)}(0)\frac{\bar{z}^2}{2} + O(|(z,\bar{z})|^3),\\
x_{3t}(0) &= \gamma z + \overline{\gamma\alpha} + W_{20}^{(3)}(0)\frac{z^2}{2} + W_{11}^{(3)}(0)z\bar{z} + W_{02}^{(3)}(0)\frac{\bar{z}^2}{2} + O(|(z,\bar{z})|^3),\\
x_{1t}(-1) &= ze^{-i\omega\tau_k\theta} + \bar{z}e^{i\omega\tau_k\theta} + W_{20}^{(1)}(-1)\frac{z^2}{2} + W_{11}^{(1)}(-1)z\bar{z} + W_{02}^{(1)}(-1)\frac{\bar{z}^2}{2}\\
&\quad + O(|(z,\bar{z})|^3).
\end{aligned}$$

From the definition of $F(\mu, x_t)$, we have

$$g(z,\bar{z}) = \bar{q}^*(0)f_0(z,\bar{z}) = \bar{D}\tau_k(1, \bar{\beta}^*, \bar{\gamma}^*)\begin{bmatrix} f_{11}^0 \\ f_{12}^0 \\ f_{13}^0 \end{bmatrix}$$

and we evaluate $g(z,\bar{z})$.

To determine g_{21}, we need to compute $W_{20}(\theta)$ and $W_{11}(\theta)$. By (15) and (18), we have

$$\begin{aligned}
\dot{W} &= \dot{x}_t - \dot{z}q + \dot{\overline{zq}} \\
&= \begin{cases} AW - 2Re\{\bar{q}^*(0)f_0 q(\theta)\}, & \theta\epsilon[-1,0) \\ AW - 2Re\{\bar{q}^*(0)f_0 q(\theta)\} + f_0 & \theta = 0, \end{cases} \\
&\overset{def}{=} AW + H(z.\bar{z},\theta),
\end{aligned} \tag{19}$$

where

$$H(z.\bar{z},\theta) = H_{20}(\theta)\frac{z^2}{2} + H_{11}(\theta)z\bar{z} + H_{02}(\theta)\frac{\bar{z}^2}{2} + ... \tag{20}$$

Note that on the center manifold C_0 near to the origin,

$$\dot{W} = W_z\dot{z} + W_{\bar{z}}\bar{z}. \tag{21}$$

Thus we obtain,

$$(A - 2i\omega\tau_k)W_{20}(\theta) = -H_{20}(\theta), \qquad AW_{11}(\theta) = -H_{11}(\theta). \tag{22}$$

By using (19), for $\theta\epsilon[-1,0)$,

$$H(z.\bar{z},\theta) = \bar{q}^*(0)f_0 q(\theta) - q^*(0)f_0(0)\bar{q}(\theta) = -gq(\theta) - \bar{g}\,\bar{q}(\theta). \tag{23}$$

Comparing the coefficients with (20), we obtain the following

$$H_{20}(\theta) = -g_{20}q(\theta) - \bar{g}_{02}\bar{q}(\theta), \qquad H_{11}(\theta) = -g_{11}q(\theta) - \bar{g}_{11}\bar{q}(\theta). \tag{24}$$

From (22) and (24) and the definition of A, we get

$$\dot{W}_{20}(\theta) = 2i\omega\tau_k W_{20}(\theta) - g_{20}q(\theta) - \bar{g}_{02}\bar{q}(\theta).$$

Noticing $q(\theta) = q(0)e^{i\omega\tau_k\theta}$, we evaluate $W_{20}(\theta)$ by $E_1 = (E_1^{(1)}, E_1^{(2)}, E_1^{(3)})\epsilon\mathbb{R}^3$ is a constant vector. From the definition of A and (22), we obtain

$$\int_{-1}^{0} d\eta(\theta)W_{20}(\theta) = 2i\omega\tau_k W_{20}(0) - H_{20}(0), \tag{25}$$

and

$$\int_{-1}^{0} d\eta(\theta)W_{11}(\theta) = -H_{11}(0), \tag{26}$$

where $d\eta(\theta) = \eta(\theta, 0)$. Next we compute $W_{20}(\theta)$ and $W_{11}(\theta)$ from (25) and (26) and determine the following values to investigate the qualities of bifurcating periodic solution in the center manifold at the critical value τ_k. For this purpose, we express the direction of Hopf bifurcation in terms of $g_{ij}'s$ and eigenvalues $\lambda\tau_k$. And then we can evaluate the following values;

$$
\begin{aligned}
c_1(0) &= \frac{i}{2\omega\tau_k}(g_{20}g_{11} - 2|g_{11}|^2 - \frac{|g_{02}|^2}{3}) + \frac{g_{21}}{2},\\
\mu_2 &= -\frac{Re\{c_1(0)\}}{Re\{\lambda'(\tau_k)\}},\\
\beta_2 &= 2Re\{c_1(0)\},\\
T_2 &= -\frac{Im\{c_1(0)\} + \mu_2 Im\{\lambda'(\tau_k)\}}{\omega\tau_k}
\end{aligned}
\tag{27}
$$

and we state this as in the following theorem.

Theorem : μ_2 determines the direction of Hopf bifurcation; if $\mu_2 > 0$, then the Hopf bifurcation is supercritical and the bifurcating periodic solutions exist for $\tau > \tau_0$, if $\mu_2 < 0$, then the Hopf bifurcation is subcritical and the bifurcating periodic solutions exist for $\tau < \tau_0$. β_2 determines the stability of the bifurcating periodic solutions; bifurcating periodic solutions are stable if $\beta_2 < 0$, unstable if $\beta_2 > 0$. T_2 determines the period of the bifurcating solution; the period increases if $T_2 > 0$, it decreases if $T_2 < 0$.

In the following section, we shall give a numerical example to verify the theoretical results.

4.2.1 Numerical example of Center Manifold reduction

Consider the following system with discrete time delay τ;

$$
\begin{aligned}
\frac{dN(t)}{dt} &= r_1 N(t) - \epsilon P(t)N(t),\\
\frac{dP(t)}{dt} &= P(t)(r_2 - \theta\frac{S(t)}{N(t-\tau)}),\\
\frac{dS(t)}{dt} &= \alpha P(t) - \alpha S(t).
\end{aligned}
\tag{28}
$$

Now we present some numerical simulations by using MATLAB(7.6.0) programming (Çelik-3). We simulate the predator-prey system (28) by choosing the parameters $r_1 = 0.45$, $r_2 = 0.1$, $\theta = 0.05$, $\epsilon = 0.03$, and $\alpha = 1$, i.e., we consider the following system

$$\begin{aligned}\frac{dN(t)}{dt} &= 0.45N(t) - 0.03P(t)N(t),\\ \frac{dP(t)}{dt} &= P(t)(0.1 - 0.05\frac{S(t)}{N(t-\tau)}),\\ \frac{dS(t)}{dt} &= P(t) - S(t),\end{aligned} \qquad (29)$$

which has only one positive equilibrium $E^* = (N_0^*, P_0^*, S_0^*) = (7.5, 15, 15)$. By algorithms in the previous sections, we obtain $\tau_0 = 1.5663$, $\omega_1 = 0.0045$, $z_1 = \omega_1^2$ and $g'(z_1) = 1.1944 \times 10^{-4} > 0$ which leads to $\frac{dRe\lambda(\tau_0)}{d\tau} = 5.8982 > 0$. So by the theorem above, the equilibrium point E^* is asymptotically stable when $\tau \epsilon [0, \tau_0) = [0, 1.5663)$ and unstable when $\tau > 1.5663$ and also Hopf bifurcation occurs at $\tau = \tau_0 = 1.5663$ as it is illustrated by computer simulations.

By the theory of Hassard et al.,[10], as it is discussed in previous section, we also determine the direction of Hopf bifurcation and the other properties of bifurcating periodic solutions. From the formulae in Section 5.2 we evaluate the values of μ_2, β_2 and T_2 as

$$\mu_2 = 0.0981 > 0,\ \beta_2 = -0.5785 < 0,\ T_2 = 7.1165 > 0,$$

from which we conclude that Hopf bifurcation of system (29) occurring at $\tau_0 = 1.5663$ is supercritical and the bifurcating periodic solution exists when τ crosses τ_0 to the right, and also the bifurcating periodic solution is stable.

In computer simulations, the initial conditions are taken as $(N_0, P_0, S_0) = (50, 25, 25)$ and MATLAB DDE (Delay Differential Equations) solver is used to simulate the system (29). We first take $\tau = 1.5 < \tau_0$ and plot the density functions $N(t)$, $P(t)$ and $S(t)$ in Figs.9,10,11 respectively which shows the positive equilibrium is asymptotically stable for $\tau < \tau_{0.}$. Moreover in Fig.12, we illustrate the asymptotic stability in three dimension.

However in Figs.13,14,15 and 16 below, we take $\tau = 2 > \tau_0$ sufficiently close to τ_0 which illustrates the existence of bifurcating periodic solutions from the equilibrium point E^*.

4.3 Exercises

1. Consider the Van der Pol equation

$$\ddot{x} - (1 - x^2)\dot{x} + x = 0$$

and convert this into a system and check the stability of fixed points.

2. Let y_0 be an equilibrium point of the equation

$$\frac{dy}{dt} = f(y).$$

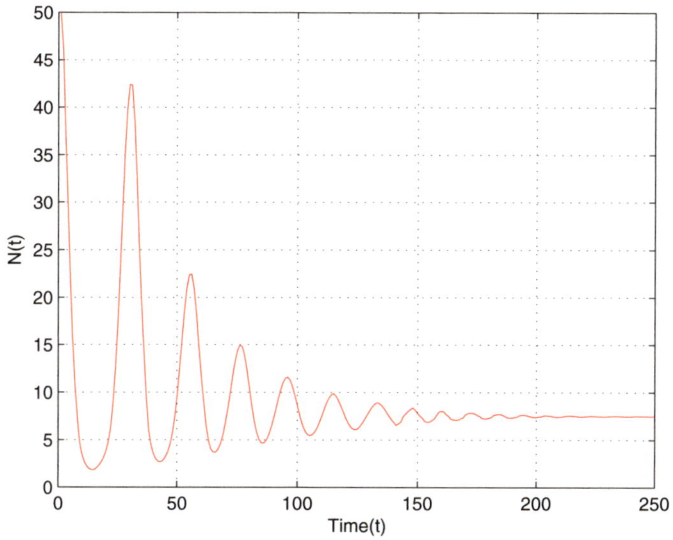

Figure 9. The trajectory of prey density versus time with the initial condition $N_0 = 50$. The graph of solutions of the model (29) when $\tau = 1.5 < \tau_0$, where the equilibrium point E^* is asymptotically stable.

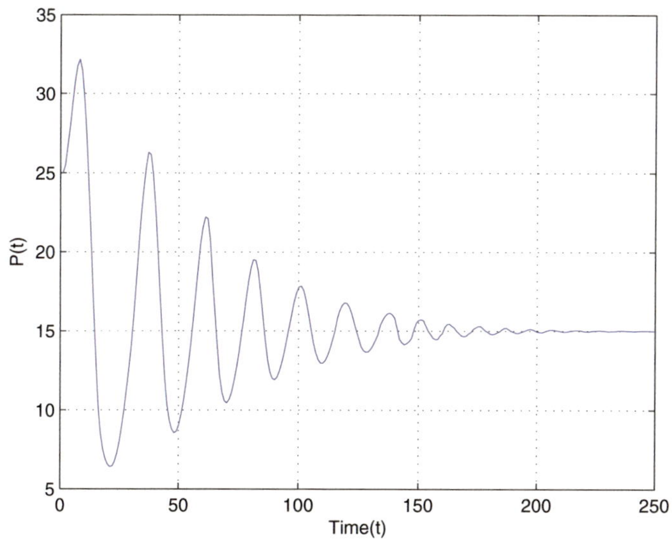

Figure 10. The trajectory of predator density versus time with the initial condition $P_0 = 25$. The graph of solutions of the model (29) when $\tau = 1.5 < \tau_0$, where the equilibrium point E^* is asymptotically stable.

Let $g(y)$ be a positive function. Deduce the stability of y_0 as an equilibrium solution of the equation

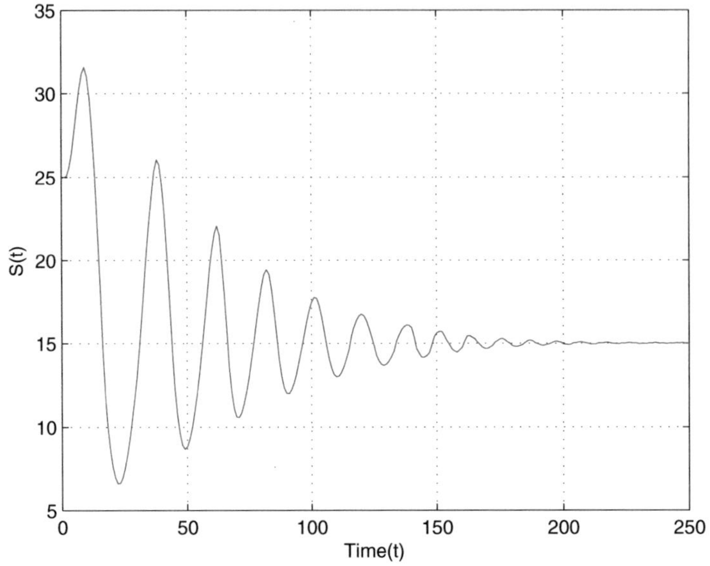

Figure 11. The trajectories of $S(t)$ versus time with the initial condition $S_0 = 25$. The graph of solutions of the model (29) when $\tau = 1.5 < \tau_0$, where the equilibrium point E^* is asymptotically stable.

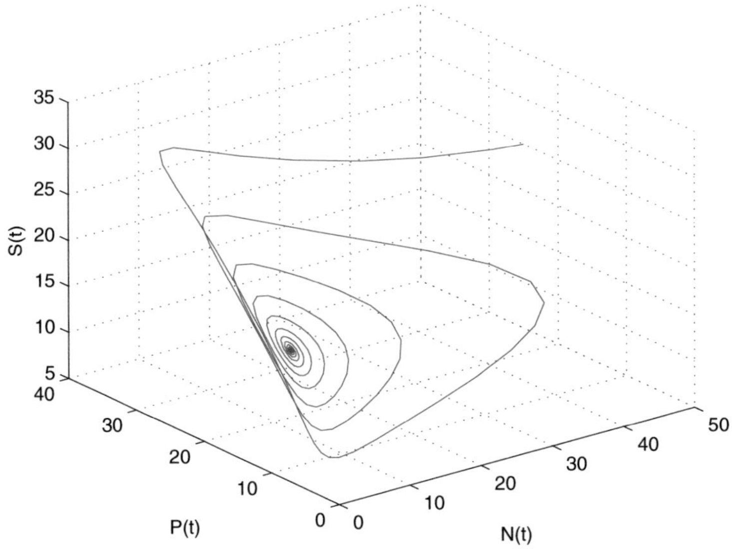

Figure 12. The trajectory of N, P, S in three dimension with the initial condition $(50, 25, 25)$ when $\tau = 1.5 < \tau_0$ for which the equilibrium point E^* is asymptotically stable.

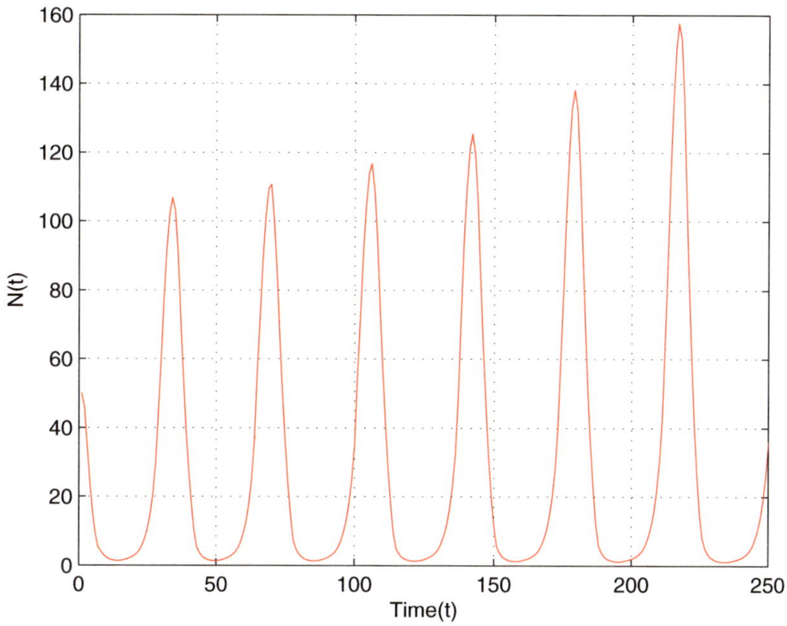

Figure 13. The trajectory of $N(t)$ when $\tau = 2 > \tau_0$.

$$\frac{dy}{dt} = f(y)g(y)$$

from its stability as an equilibrium solution of the equation $\frac{dy}{dt} = f(y)$. Repeat the same question if $g(y)$is a negative function.

3. For the following nonlinear system

$$x' = -x^3 - y,$$
$$y' = x - y^3,$$

determine the stability of fixed points.

4. For the following nonlinear system

$$x' = y - xy^2,$$
$$y' = -x + x^2 y,$$

classify the fixed points.

5. Analyze the bifurcation properties of the following problems choosing r as bifurcation parameter,

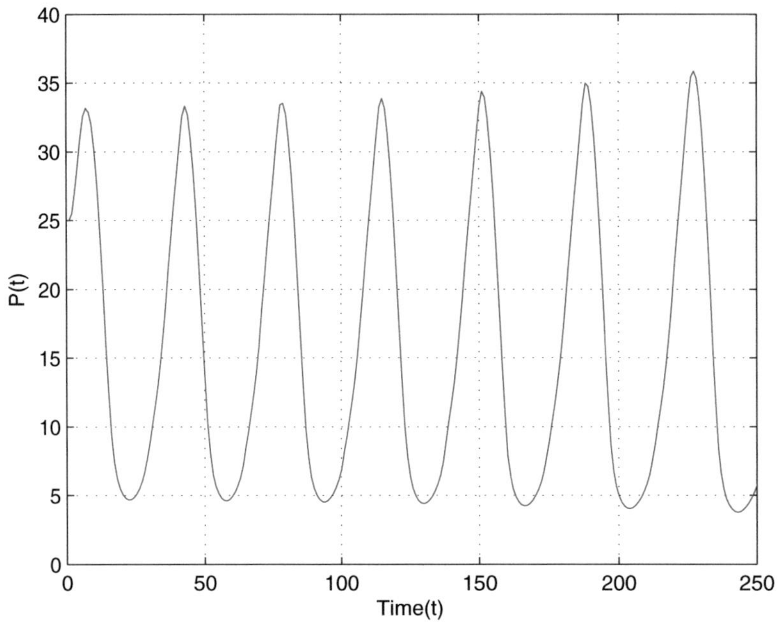

Figure 14. The trajectory of $P(t)$ when $\tau = 2 > \tau_0$.

$$a)x' = -x + \beta \tanh x,$$

$$b)x' = rx - 4x^3,$$

$$c)x' = rx - sin(x),$$

$$d)x' = rx + 4x^3,$$

$$e)x' = rx - \sin h(x),$$

$$c)x' = x + \frac{rx}{1+x^2}.$$

6. Find the equilibrium points and identify the bifurcation in the following system, and sketch the appropriate bifurcation diagram and phase portraits:

$$\frac{dx}{dt} = (1+\tau)y - x - 2x^3,$$

$$\frac{dy}{dt} = x - y - y^3.$$

Then compute the extended center manifold near the bifurcation point by choosing τ as bifurcation parameter.

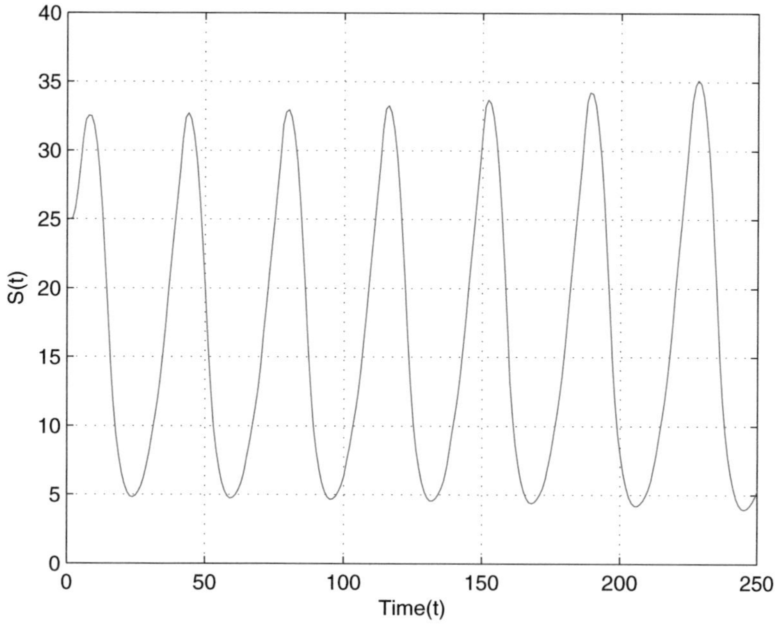

Figure 15. The trajectory of $S(t)$ when $\tau = 2 > \tau_0$.

7. Show that the following system is structurally unstable,

$$\frac{dx}{dt} = x + y - x^2 + y^2,$$

$$\frac{dy}{dt} = -2x - y + xy,$$

and the following system is structural stable. Explain our reason.

$$\frac{dx}{dt} = 2x + y - x(x^2 + y^2),$$

$$\frac{dy}{dt} = -x + 2y - y(x^2 + y^2).$$

8.

$$\frac{dx}{dt} = xy,$$
$$\frac{dy}{dt} = 1 - y^2 - x^2,$$

for the above system, classify the fixed points.

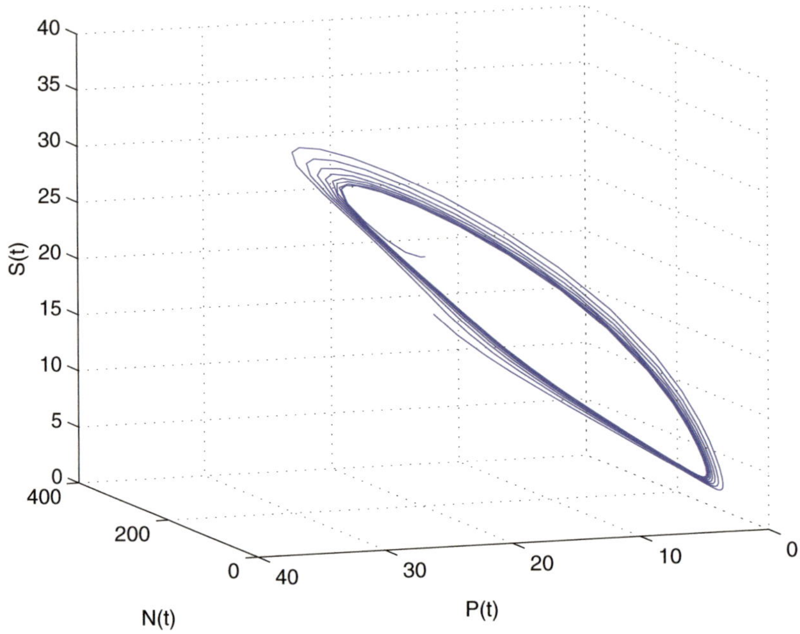

Figure 16. When $\tau = 2 > \tau_0$ a stable periodic orbit bifurcates from the equilibrium point E^*.

9. For $r \in R$, consider the differential equation

$$x' = rx - 2x^2 + x^3$$

on the real line.

(a) Show that $x^* = 0$ is a fixed point for any value of the parameter r, and determine its stability. Hence identify a bifurcation point r_1.

(b) Show that for certain values of the parameter r there are additional fixed points. For which values of r do these fixed points exist? Determine their stability and identify a further bifurcation points r_2.

(c)Using a Taylor expansion of the differential equation above, determine the normal form of the bifurcation at r_1. What type of bifurcation takes place.

(d) Similarly, determine the normal from of the bifurcation at r_2. What type bifurcation takes place?

(e) Sketch the bifurcation diagram for all values of r and x^*. (Use a full line to denote a curve of stable fixed points, and a dashed line for a curve of unstable fixed points).

10. Consider the system of differential equations

$$x' = y - xy^2,$$
$$y' = -x + yx^2,$$

in the (x, y) plane.

(a) Determine all fixed points of the system.

(b) Let $r^2 = x^2 + y^2$. Show that $r' = 0$ Considering the result of (c), what does this imply for the trajectories?

(c) Sketch the phase portrait in the (x, y) plane, including trajectories through $(1, 0)$ and $(2, 0)$. Which fixed point does the trajectory through $(2, 0)$ approach?

11. Consider the Lorenz system (the model of heat convection by Rayleigh-Benard occurring in the earth's atmosphere) in three dimension as follows;

$$\begin{aligned} x' &= \sigma(y - x), \\ y' &= rx + -xz - y, \\ z' &= xy - bz, \end{aligned}$$

where σ, r, b are constants. Perfom the stability analysis of this nonlinear system.

12. For the Holling-Tanner type Predator-Prey model

$$\begin{aligned} x' &= x(1 - x) - \frac{x}{a + x}y, \\ y' &= y(\delta - \beta\frac{y}{x}), \end{aligned}$$

where $x(0) > 0, y(0) > 0$ and a, δ, β are positive constants. Find the equilibria and classify them.

13. Consider the Delayed Predator-Prey model

$$\begin{aligned} x'(t) &= rx(t) - bx(t)x(t - \tau) - \alpha x(t)y(t), \\ y'(t) &= -cy(t) + \beta x(t)y(t), \end{aligned}$$

with time delay τ and positive constants r, b, α, c and β. By choosing τ as bifurcation parameter, check whether bifurcating periodic solutions occur around the equilibrium points or not.

Author details

Canan Çelik Karaaslanlı
Bahçeşehir University, Turkey

5. References

[1] Allen L.J.S., An Introduction to Mathematical Biology, 2007.
[2] Andronov A.A., Leontovich E.A., Gordon I.I., Maier A.G., Theory of Bifurcations of Dynamical Systems on a Plane, Israel Program Sci. Transl., 1971.
[3] Arnold V.I., Geometrical Methods in the Theory of Ordinary Differential Equation, Grundlehren Math. Wiss.,(250), Springer, 1983.

[4] Çelik C., The stability and Hopf bifurcation for a predator-prey system with time delay, Chaos, Solitons & Fractals, 2008, (37), 87–99.

[5] Çelik C., Hopf bifurcation of a ratio-dependent predator-prey system with time delay, Chaos, Solitons & Fractals, 2009, (42), 1474–1484.

[6] Çelik C., Dynamical Behavior of a Ratio Dependent Predator-Prey System with Distributed Delay, Discrete and Continuous Dynamical Systems, Series B, 2011, (16), 719-738.

[7] Guckenheimer J., Holmes P., Nonlinear Oscilllations, Dynamical Systems and Bifurcations of Vector Fields, Springer, 1983.

[8] Guckenheimer J., Myers M., Sturmfels B. Computing Hopf Bifurcations I, 1997, SIAM Journal on Numerical Analysis.

[9] Hairer E., Norsett S.P., Wanner G., Solving Ordinary Differential Equations I: Nonstiff Problems (Second ed.). New York: Springer-Verlag, 1993.

[10] B.D. Hassard B.D., Kazarinoff N. D., Wan Y-H., Theory and Applications of Hopf Bifurcation, Cambridge University Press, Cambridge, 1981.

[11] Hale J., Koçak H., Dynamics and Bifurcations. Texts in Applied Mathematics, New York: Springer-Verlag, 1991.

[12] Iooss G., Bifurcations of Maps and Applications, North-Holland, 1979.

[13] Kahoui M.E., Weber A., Deciding Hopf bifurcations by quantifier elimination in a software component architecture. Journal of Symbolic Computation, 2000, 30 (2), 161-179.

[14] Kelley A., The stable, center stable, center, center unstable and unstable manifolds, J. Diff. Eq., 1967, (3), 546-570.

[15] Kirk P., Toni T., Stumpf M.P., Parameter inference for biochemical systems that undergo a Hopf bifurcation, Biophysical Journal, 2008, 95, (2), 540-549, doi:10.1529/biophysj.107.126086. PMC 2440454. PMID 18456830.

[16] Kuang Y., Delay Differential Equations with Applications in Population Dynamics, Academic Press, 1993.

[17] Kuznetsov Y.A., Elements of Applied Bifurcation Theory, New York: Springer-Verlag, 2004.

[18] Marsden J., McCracken M., Hopf Bifurcation and Its Applications, Springer, 1976.

[19] Murray J.D., Mathematical Biology, Springer-Verlag, New York, 1993.

[20] Strogatz S.H., Nonlinear Dynamics and Chaos. Addison Wesley publishing company, 1996.

[21] Whitley D.C., Discrete dynamical systems in dimensions one and two, Bull. London Math. Soc., 1983, (15), 177-217.

[22] Wilhelm T., Heinrich R., Smallest chemical reaction system with Hopf bifurcation, Journal of Mathematical Chemistry, 1995, (17,1), 1-14. doi:10.1007/BF01165134.

Chapter 2

Model-Based Adaptive Tracking Control of Linear Time-Varying System with Uncertainties

DongBin Lee and C. Nataraj

Additional information is available at the end of the chapter

http://dx.doi.org/10.5772/51625

1. Introduction

This primary purpose of this research is concerned with adaptive tracking control of a nonlinear system [6, 9]. Particularly, time-varying control approach has been designed for tracking of the system with application to a nonlinear dynamic model [1]. Furthermore, the time-varying system is further complicated by parametric uncertainty or disturbances such as external forces, continuous or discrete noise where the parameters are unknown. Over the past several years, trajectory tracking issue as a high-level control of a nonlinear system has been received a wide attention from control community. Hence, the discussion here is principally devoted to model-based adaptive trajectory tracking control algorithm of linear time-varying (LTV) systems in the presence of uncertainty [4, 5].

A system undergoing slow time variation in comparison to its time constants can usually be considered to be linear time invariant (LTI) and thus, slow time-variation is often ignored in dealing with systems in practice. An example of this is the aging and wearing of electronic and mechanical components, which happens on a scale of years, and thus does not result in any behavior qualitatively different from that observed in a time invariant system on a day-to-day basis. There are many well developed techniques for dealing with the response of linear time invariant systems such as Laplace and Fourier transforms, but not applicable to linear time varying or nonlinear systems, nor feasible to implement for complicated real-world systems. In addition, time-varying system may be difficult to satisfy global controllability or to show whether the time-varying system is even stable or not, due to difficulties in computing or finding solution. Unlike LTI systems, linear time varying systems may behave more like nonlinear systems [1, 2, 3]. In general all systems are time-varying in principle and a large number of systems arising in practice are time-varying. Time variation is a result of system parameters changing as a function of time [5], such as aerodynamic coefficients of aircrafts, hydrodynamic terms in marine vessels, circuit parameters in electronic circuits, and mechanical parameters in machinery. Thus, we characterize systems as time-varying if the parameter variation is happening on time scales close to that of the system dynamics. Time variation also occurs as a result of linearizing a nonlinear system about a family of operating points and/or about a time-varying trajectory for developing control system. However, due to the desire to achieve better accuracy and quality in a wide range of applications [11], there have been increasing interests to include the effects of time-variation [12] while designing controllers or observers at the time analyzing and/or applying to such systems.

In this work, tracking error system is formulated based on its model-reference system which has a reference input and the nonlinear dynamic model of the inverted pendulum. We found a solution of the tracking nonlinear system after developing its linear time varying systems. For the development of subsequent control approach, the error system is linearized about given desired trajectory using a perturbation approach and produced a linear time-varying tracking error equation [3] with system matrices, $A(t)$ and/or $B(t)$. At this time the controllability of this time-varying system only shows that the system is stable in an instant time or about a trajectory which can be locally controllable or stabilized. Then, a novelty of this research is that a controllability grammian matrix is found to be a necessary and sufficient conditions of the global controllability and the inverse of the grammian matrix exists, which is nonsingular, and is used for the designing the control input of the closed-loop system. In this research, a complicated solution of state transition matrix is obtained based on Taylor series expansion, categorized into feasible forms based on the system and the shape of matrix. The control input of the tracking system is designed from the state transition matrix and the grammian matrix, which makes the system globally controllable, and the control input of the actual system is redesigned via the tracking controller while compensating for the uncertainty as disturbances, which also yields the system globally stable. This chapter consists of as follows: a time-varying system is briefly described relative to a time-invariant system and a non-homogeneous system is introduced for linear time-varying system for the development of the solution which is state transition matrix in Section II followed by Introduction. Then a cart-pole nonlinear dynamic model where the system parameters are unknown is developed for the application of a proposed control algorithm and expressed into a state space form. For the trajectory tracking control, error signals are formulated from desired model-based reference system. Based on the analysis of the developed time-varying error system, the solution of the system, state transition matrix, is derived in a series form and then a special form of the matrix is obtained for the second-order error differential equation, which is used for the grammian matrix and the closed-loop controller. The control system is also developed to reject disturbances via a projection-based adaptive control approach and update laws for the parameter update in Section III. Numerical simulation results with analyses demonstrate the validity of the proposed system. This approach can be extended to other nonlinear time-varying dynamic systems such as aerial-, marine, or ground vehicles.

2. Linear time-varying system

A linear time-invariant system (LTI) is described as

$$\dot{x} = Ax(t),\ \forall t \geq 0 \tag{1}$$

where the equilibrium point is at the origin and if det(A)≠0, the fixed point is isolated and the stability of the origin depends on the location of the eigenvalues of the matrix $A(\cdot) \in \Re^{n \times n}$ which is not a function of time. The solution of (1) with the initial state $x(t_0)$ is given by

$$x(t) = \exp(At)x(t_0) \tag{2}$$

Another LTI state equations is given by

$$\dot{x} = Ax + Bu \tag{3}$$

where A and B are time-invariant. It is known that the solution of the equation (3) using an integrating factor yields $A(\cdot) \in \Re^{n \times n}$ can be time-varying or time-invariant. The solution of (3) with the initial state $x(t_0)$ is given by

$$x(t) = \Phi(t,t_0)x(t_0) + \int_{t_0}^{t} \Phi(t,\tau)Bu(\tau)d\tau \tag{4}$$

where this is a convolution control solution and the state transition matrix $\Phi(t,t_0) = e^{A(t-t_0)}$ and $\Phi(t,\tau) = e^{A(t-\tau)}$. The solutions (2) and (4) make clear the importance of the matrix exponential $\exp(At)$ and its eigenvalues. However, these techniques are not strictly valid for time-varying systems.

2.1. Homogeneous system

A time-varying system is described as

$$\dot{x} = A(t)x(t),\ \forall t \geq 0 \tag{5}$$

where $\dot{x}(t),\ x(t) \in \Re^{n}$, and the matrix $A(\cdot) \in \Re^{n \times n}$ is not a constant as a function of time; it is nonautonomous [6, 7]. The general solution of the (5) in n-dimensional linear vector space, $\dot{x}_i(t) = A(t)x_i(t) \in \Re^{n}$, is unique for the space on $[t_0,\ t]$ in case $A(t)$ is smooth where x_{i0} $(i = 0,\ \ldots\ ,\ n)$ is a basis set of n linearly independent initial condition. According to the linearly independent solutions, a system is defined as

$$\dot{X}(t) = A(t)X(t) \tag{6}$$

where $X(t) = [x_1,\ \ldots\ ,\ x_n] \in \Re^{n \times n}$ is a matrix which has the linearly independence solutions which shows $\dot{X}(t) = [A(t)x_1,\ \ldots,\ A(t)x_n] \in \Re^{n \times n}$. The general solution of (6) is given as

$$\dot{X}(t) = X(t_0)\Phi(t,\ \tau) \tag{7}$$

where $X(t_0)$ is the matrix of the initial value of state, $\Phi(t,\ \tau) \in \Re^{n \times n}$ is called the state transition matrix as known as a fundamental solution matrix associated with $A(t)$, having a form of exponential function.

2.2. Nonhomogeneous system

A linear time-varying system (LTV) is described as

$$\dot{x} = A(t)x(t) + B(t)u(t) \tag{8}$$

where $B(t)u(t) \in \Re^n$, $B(t) \in \Re^{n \times n}$, $u(t) \in \Re^n$, $B(t)u(t) \in \Re^n$, in which $B(t) \in \Re^{n \times n}$ can be input configuration matrix and $u(t) \in \Re^n$ is the control input where n is the number of control inputs. Note that in case the control input is underactuated, then $B(t) \in \Re^{n \times m}$ and $u(t) \in \Re^m$ where n-m is the underactuation, or the number of underactuated inputs. For the controllability of time-varying systems given in (8), the state transition matrix (or known as fundamental solution matrix) is the overall solution and used to perform the function of integrating factor where the solution is derived from a linear independence on the columns of a matrix that was a function of $\Phi(\cdot)$ and $B(\cdot)$.

2.3. Solution of the state transition matrix

The system is controllable if the controllability gramian (or grammian) matrix $G_C \in \Re^{n \times n}$ below is nonsingular, *i.e.*, invertible for the necessary and sufficient condition

$$G_C = \int_{t_0}^{t} X(\tau)X^{\mathrm{T}}(\tau)d\tau \tag{9}$$

where the rows of the matrix product $X(\tau) = \Phi(t_0,\tau)B(\tau)$ are linearly independent in an interval. In order to prove the invertible exists, the control input $u(t)$ of the system can be designed based on the gramian matrix as

$$u = -KB^{\mathrm{T}}(\tau)\Phi^{\mathrm{T}}(t_0,\tau)G_C^{-1}(t_0,\tau)x(t_0) \tag{10}$$

where $K = diag\{k_1,...,k_l\} \in \Re^{n \times n}$ is a control input gain matrix and $G_C^{-1}(t_0,\tau)$ is the inverse of (9). Convolution integral solution to determine the state at the end of the interval, $x(t_1)$, yields

$$x(t_1) = \Phi(t_1,t_0)x(t_0) + \int_{t_0}^{t_1} \Phi(t_1,\tau)B(\tau)u(\tau)d\tau \tag{11}$$

where the solution of linear time-varying system $\Phi(t,\tau)$ is given by

$$x(t) = \Phi(t,t_0)x(t_0) + \int_{t_0}^{t} \Phi(t,\tau)B(\tau)u(\tau)d\tau \tag{12}$$

The expression (11) yields by factoring $\Phi(t_1,t_0)$ of the left side as

$$x(t_1) = \Phi(t_1,t_0)\left[x(t_0) - G_C G_C^{-1} x(t_0)\right] = 0 \tag{13}$$

where (9) was used and this implies the control input, $u(t)$ in (10), drives the system to reach the zero state, in which K should be the identity matrix. Now the system is controllable and shows that the controllability gramian is invertible.

3. Application to nonlinear inverted pendulum system

3.1. Dynamic model

A continuous nonlinear time-varying system is given as a combined model based on the inverted pendulum [1] expressed by the second-order differential equation by

$$\ddot{\theta} = \frac{g}{\hat{L}}\sin\theta + u \tag{14}$$

where $\theta(t)$ is the angle of the pole of the inverted pendulum which is subjected to the external force $u(t) \in \Re^1$, g is the gravitational force, and L is the combined parameter term given by

$$\hat{L} = \frac{\hat{J} + \hat{m}\hat{l}^2}{\hat{m}\hat{l}},$$

where $\hat{L}$ is an unknown lumped parameter, in which $\hat{J}$ is the inertia of the pole, $\hat{m}$ is the mass of the pole, and $\hat{l}$ is the length of the pole. The system can be expressed into a state space model in order to analyze as

$$\begin{aligned} \dot{x}_1 &= x_2 \\ \dot{x}_2 &= \frac{g}{\hat{L}}\sin x_1 + u \end{aligned} \tag{15}$$

where $u(t)$ is the actual control input of the inverted pendulum to be designed later. Let $\dot{x}_{2d}(t)$ be the desired model-based reference system as follows

$$\begin{aligned} \dot{x}_{1d} &= x_{2d} \\ \dot{x}_{2d} &= -k_1 x_{2d} + \frac{g}{\hat{L}}\sin x_{1d} + u_r \end{aligned} \tag{16}$$

where the first term $k_1 x_{2d}(t)$ in the right side of the second row equation is added because the response of the second equation can be divergent due to the positive reference input u_r, in which k_1 is a positive constant.

3.2. Error formulation

Then, the error equation can be derived from the subtraction between the desired and the actual system as

$$\dot{e}_1 \equiv x_{2d} - x_2 = e_2 \tag{17}$$

and subtracting $\dot{x}_2(t)$ from $\dot{x}_{2d}(t)$ and substituting the second equation of (16) yields

$$\dot{e}_2 \equiv \dot{x}_{2d} - \dot{x}_2 = \frac{g}{\hat{L}}(\sin x_{1d} - \sin x_1) + u_r - k_1 x_{2d} - u. \tag{18}$$

Let the error, $e_1(t)$, assumed to be small. Then, $e_1(t)$ produces

$$e_1 = x_{1d} - x_1 \equiv \varepsilon_0 x_{1d}, \tag{19}$$

which results in $x_1 = (1-\varepsilon_0)x_{1d}$ where ε_0 is positive constant. Substituting this $x_1(t)$ into the parenthesis term for $\sin x_1(t)$ in (18) and using the sum of sines yields

$$\sin x_{1d} - (\sin x_{1d}\cos\varepsilon_0 x_{1d} - \cos x_{1d}\sin\varepsilon_0 x_{1d}) = e_1\cos x_{1d}. \tag{20}$$

where $\cos\varepsilon_0 x_{1d} = 1$ and $\sin\varepsilon_0 x_{1d} = \varepsilon_0 x_{1d} = e_1$. Hence, (18) yields

$$\dot{e}_2 = \frac{g}{\hat{L}}\cos x_{1d} e_1 + u_r - k_1 x_{2d} - u \tag{21}$$

where the parameter L is unknown. Putting (17) and (21) together into a matrix yields

$$\begin{bmatrix} \dot{e}_1 \\ \dot{e}_2 \end{bmatrix} = \begin{bmatrix} 0 & 1 \\ \frac{g}{\hat{L}}\cos x_{1d} & 0 \end{bmatrix}\begin{bmatrix} e_1 \\ e_2 \end{bmatrix} + \begin{bmatrix} 0 \\ 1 \end{bmatrix}\overline{u} \tag{22}$$

where

$$\overline{u} \equiv u_r - k_1 x_{2d} - u. \tag{23}$$

3.3. Solution of the linear time-varying system

The solution of linear time-varying error system for (22) is given by

$$e(t) = \Phi(t,t_0)e(t_0) + \int_{t_0}^{t} \Phi(t,\tau)Bu(\tau)d\tau \tag{24}$$

However, it is difficult to find the state transition matrix of (22) since the system has a function of time in the $A(t)$ and coupled. However, the fact that (17) and (21) can be considered as decoupled between two equations helps to find the state transition matrix, $\Phi(t,\tau)$. The solution of the first equation in (22), i.e., (17), yields

$$e_1 = e^{t-\tau}e_{20} \tag{25}$$

where $e_2(\tau) = e_{20}$. Substituting (25) for $e_1(t)$ into the second differential equation of (22) produces

$$\dot{e}_2 = f(t)e^{t-\tau}e_{20} + \overline{u} \tag{26}$$

where $f(t) = \frac{g}{\hat{L}} \cos x_{1d}$ and the equation can be easily decoupled from the (25).

Thus, the state transition matrix, $\Phi(t,\tau)$, yields

$$\Phi(t,\tau) = \exp[\int_{\tau}^{t} f(v) e^{t-\tau} dv] \tag{27}$$

where it is identified that $A(t)$ is a scalar form, $f(t)e^{t-\tau}$. In this case the gramian matrix is defined by utilizing (27) as

$$G_C(t_0, t_1) = \int_{t0}^{t} \Phi(\tau, t_0) B B^{\mathrm{T}} \Phi^{\mathrm{T}}(\tau, t_0) d\tau, \tag{28}$$

where this gramian matrix is positive definite and nonsingular, whose inverse exists and satisfies the sufficient and necessary condition of the controllability due to the time-varying system. Applying (27) to (24) for solving (26) yields

$$e_2(t) = \exp[\int_{\tau}^{t} f(v) e^{(v-\tau)} dv] e_{20} + \int_{\tau}^{t} \exp[\int_{v}^{t} f(v') e_2^{(v'-\tau)} dv'] B \bar{u}(v) dv \tag{29}$$

where $e_2(t_0) = e_{20}$. Then the open-loop control input for the second equation of (22) using a controllability gramian term is

$$\bar{u} = -K B^{\mathrm{T}} \Phi^{\mathrm{T}}(\tau, t_0) G_C^{-1}(t_0, \tau) e_2(\tau) \tag{31}$$

where $B = 1$ and K is the control input gain constant, and $u(t)$ in (29) will be designed in the next. From the definition of $\bar{u}(t)$ in (23), the control input $u(t)$ is designed in the presence of the parametric uncertainty as

$$u = u_1 + \frac{g}{\hat{L}} \cos x_{1d} e_1 + \frac{1}{\gamma_e} \tilde{\Theta} \dot{\hat{\Theta}} \tag{32}$$

where the first term, $u_1(t)$, is designed for subsequent control development as

$$u_1 = u_r - k_1 x_2 + k_2 e_1, \tag{33}$$

the second term, $\hat{L}$, in (32) is the estimated parameter term of (14) and the following adaptation laws are used for the parameter estimator, $\hat{\Theta}(t)$, while compensating the parametric uncertainty.

3.4. Adaptation laws for parameter update

Substituting (32) for $u(t)$ into $\bar{u}(t)$ and rearranging yields

$$\dot{e}_2 = Y_d \tilde{\Theta} e_1 + \tilde{u} \tag{34}$$

where $Y_d(t) = g\cos x_{1d}$, $\tilde{\Theta} = \frac{1}{L} - \frac{1}{\hat{L}}$, and

$$\tilde{u} = -k_1 e_2 - k_2 e_1 - \frac{1}{\gamma_e}\tilde{\Theta}\dot{\hat{\Theta}}, \tag{35}$$

in which γ_e is constant gain value. Rearranging yields

$$\dot{e}_2 = \tilde{\Theta}(Y_d e_1 - \frac{1}{\gamma_e}\dot{\hat{\Theta}}) - k_1 e_2 - k_2 e_1 \tag{36}$$

Then, the adaptation law is designed as

$$\dot{\hat{\Theta}} = \gamma_e Y_d e_1 \tag{37}$$

Hence, the final error system utilized (37) results in

$$\dot{e}_2 + k_1 e_2 + k_2 e_1 = 0 \tag{38}$$

The following is assumed to define the upper and lower bounds of each unknown parameters

$$\underline{\hat{\Theta}} \le \hat{\Theta} \le \overline{\hat{\Theta}} \tag{39}$$

where $\hat{\Theta}$ is the estimated constant parameters, $\underline{\hat{\Theta}}$, $\overline{\hat{\Theta}}$ are unknown lower and upper bounds of the estimated parameters as shown in system parameters, respectively, which will be set to the amount of percentage of their true values. $\dot{\hat{\Theta}}(t)$ vector is designed to update using a projection-based algorithm as

$$\dot{\hat{\Theta}} = \mathrm{Pr}oj\left\{\gamma_e Y_d e_1, \hat{\Theta}\right\} \tag{40}$$

where $\mathrm{Pr}oj\{\cdot\}$ is the projection operator [8] and each parameter is adaptively updated using adaptation laws for online estimation of unknown parameter as follows:

$$\mathrm{Pr}oj\left\{\dot{\hat{\Theta}}\right\} = \begin{cases} \gamma_e Y_d e_1 & \text{if } \hat{\Theta} > \underline{\hat{\Theta}} \text{ and } \hat{\Theta} < \overline{\hat{\Theta}} \\ \gamma_e Y_d e_1 & \text{if } \hat{\Theta} = \overline{\hat{\Theta}} \text{ and if } \gamma W \le 0 \\ \gamma_e Y_d e_1 & \text{if } \hat{\Theta} = \underline{\hat{\Theta}} \text{ and if } \gamma W > 0 \\ 0 & \text{elsewhere} \end{cases} \tag{41}$$

It is straightforward to make a conclusion that the above adaptive control approach is applied to (36) and then the parenthesis term in (36) will be going to zero, resulting in (38) if both are perfectly canceled, which yields globally stable tracking result.

4. Numerical results

The initial condition of inverted pendulum angles is given as $x_1(0) = [0.1,\ 0.5,\ 1.0]$ (rad) $\cong$ $\cong$ [6, 17, 57] (deg) as shown in Figure 1 where each actual angle of the pendulum track the desired angle $x_{1d} = 0$, starting from its initial value. Note that the initial angular rate, $x_2(0)$, is zero. In Figure 2, the actual angular rate tracks the desired angular rate of the inverted pendulum. In Figure 3, their tracking angle errors are shown in the top plot and the error rates are shown in the bottom plot, where the errors and error rates are close to zero and thus the tracking system works well. The control inputs are in Figure 4; the control input shown in plot (a) is the designed control input in (32), which is used for the control input of the system dynamic model given in (15), the control input shown in plot (b) is the control solution given in (31) of the tracking error dynamics in (34), which enables the global stability, and finally the plot in (c) is proposed controller of this research, i.e., the closed-loop adaptive tracking control input designed in (35). Figure 5 is the estimate of the time varying parameter, $\hat{L}$ of L, in which the simulation parameters such as mass (m), length of the pole (l), and inertia of the pole (J) are combined together and the values used in simulation are as follows: $m = 0.127$ [kg], $l = 0.3$ [m], $J = 0.05$ [kgm^2], and $g = 9.81$ [m/s^2]. The percentage of the upper and lower bounds given in (39) is set to 100%. The nominal value of $1/L$ is 0.612. Thus, the upper bound is 1.232 and lower bound is zero as shown in Figure 5 and the time-varying parameter estimate is varying within the bounds. The error dynamics, $\dot{e}_2(t)$, developed in the main body of this chapter are shown in Figure 6; the plot (a) is the second equation of (22) with the control input given in (31), the plot (b) is the output of the error dynamics given in (34) with the control input (35), and the plot in (c) is the final error dynamics given in (38). In Figure 7, those velocity errors with regard to the dynamics are shown. The reference velocity, error control gain constants, gain value, and control input gain matrix are

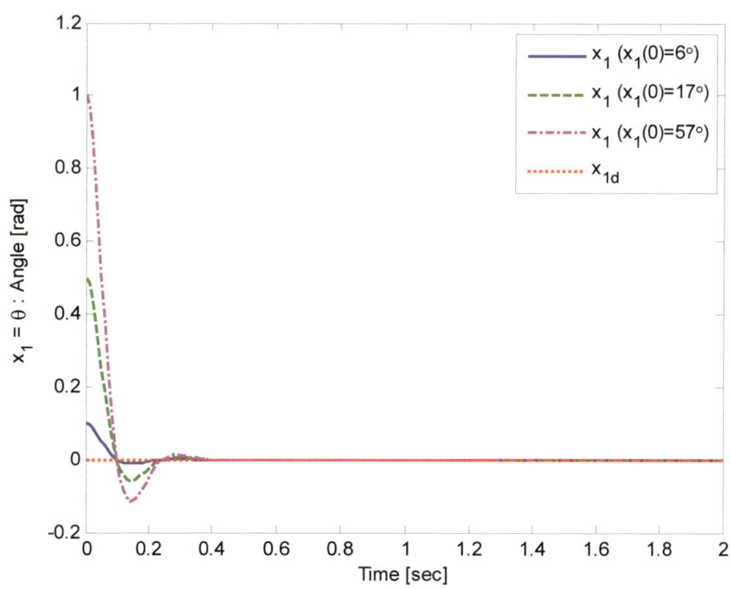

Figure 1. Tracking Angle ($x_1(t)$, $x_{1d}(t)$)

$$u_r = 0\ [m/s],\ k_1 = 30,\ k_2 = 700,\ \gamma_e = 100, \text{ and } K = I_2$$

where I_2 is 2×2 identity matrix.

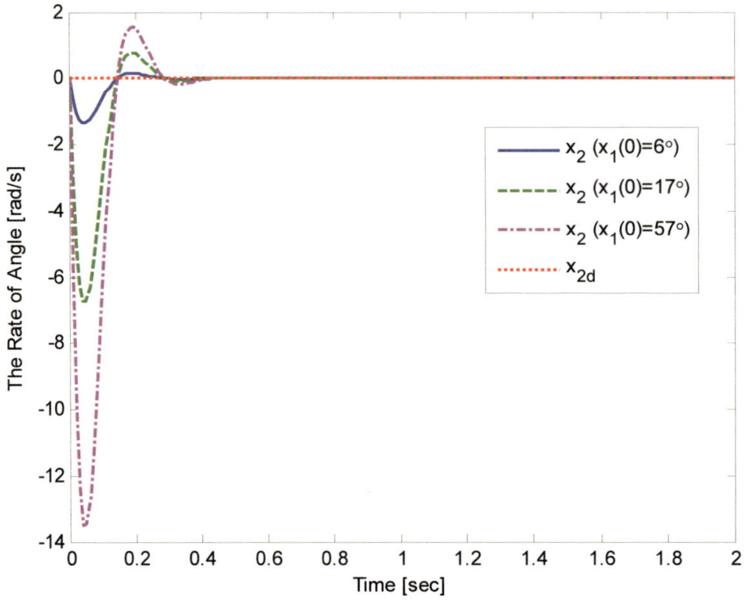

Figure 2. Tracking Angular Rate ($x_2(t)$, $x_{2d}(t)$)

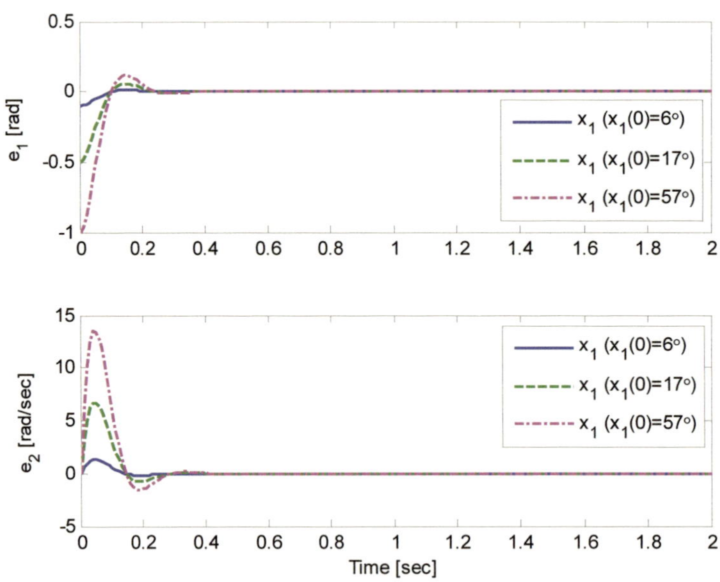

Figure 3. Angle and Angular Rate Errors : ($e_1(t)$, $e_2(t)$)

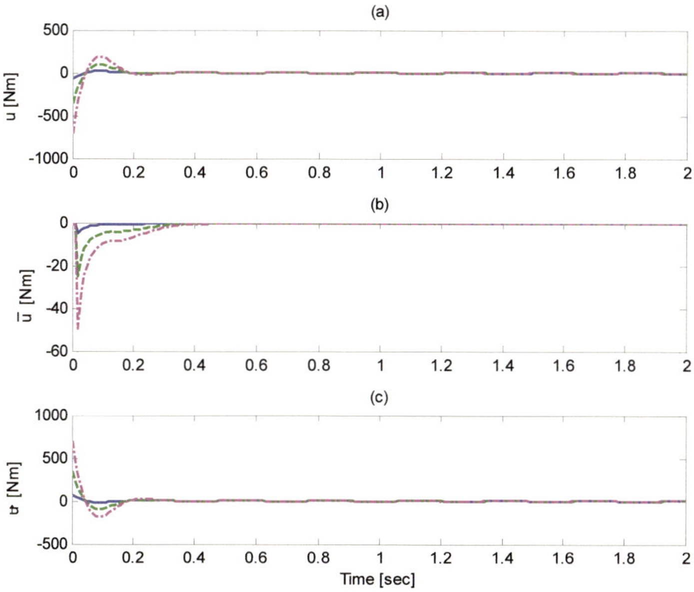

Figure 4. Control Inputs: (a) $u(t)$ in (32), (b) $\overline{u}(t)$ in (31), and (c) $\tilde{u}(t)$ in (35)

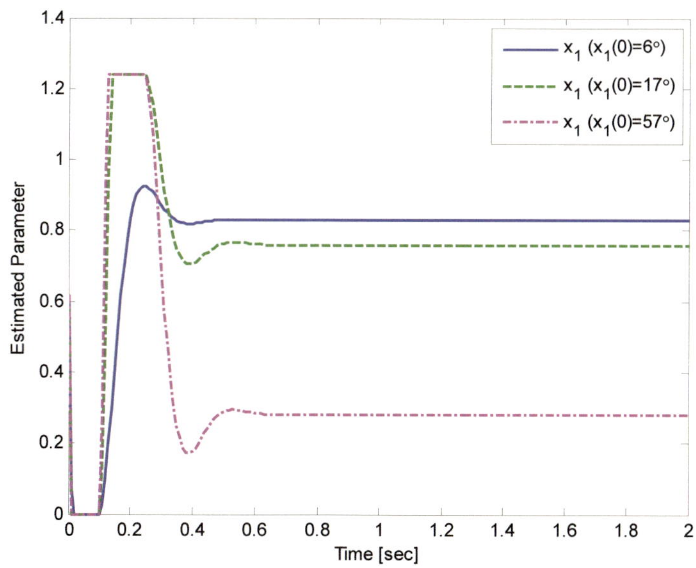

Figure 5. Parameter Estimate ($\hat{L}(t)$)

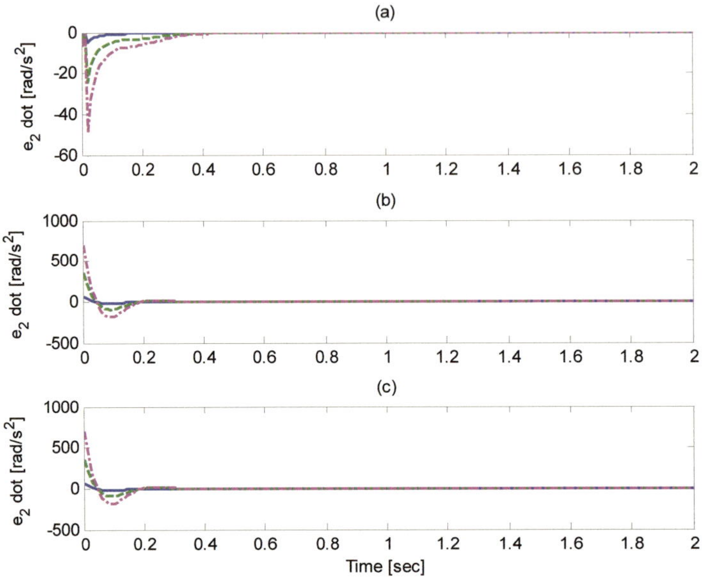

Figure 6. Error Dynamics of the Pendulum (a) $\dot{e}_2(t)$ in (22), (b) $\dot{e}_2(t)$ in (34), and (c) $\dot{e}_2(t)$ in (35)

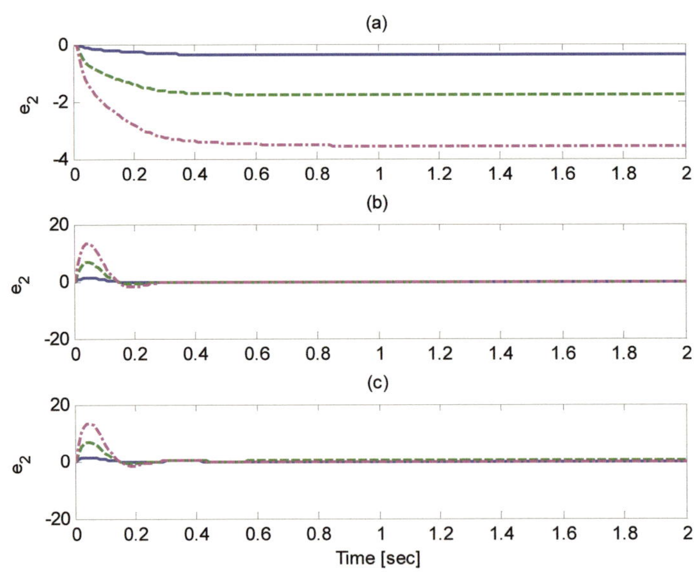

Figure 7. Velocity Errors from (a) $e_2(t)$ from (22), (b) $e_2(t)$ in (34), and (c) $e_2(t)$ in (35)

5. Conclusion

A tracking control of a model-based linear time-varying system is developed in application to the nonlinear inverted pendulum model. A novelty of this paper is that not only found a gramian matrix which is difficult to find or compute but also utilized to the linear time-varying tracking controller which satisfies the necessary and sufficient of the global stability of the system. Another is that the linear time-varying system is further complicated by parametric uncertainty where the combined parameters are unknown. The suggested adaptive control approach and update laws are applied for estimating the parameters while preserving the system to be stable and converging the tracking error close to zero. Numerical simulation results are demonstrated the validity of the proposed system.

Author details

DongBin Lee and C. Nataraj
Villanova University, PA, USA

Acknowledgement

This research is supported by Office of Naval Research (ONR, N00014-09-1-1195), which we gratefully acknowledge.

6. References

[1] P. J. Antsaklis and A. N. Michel, Linear Systems. Birkhauser, Boston, 2nd Ed., 2006.
[2] K. Tsakalis and P. Ioannou, Linear Time-Varying Systems, Engelwood Cliffs, NJ, Prentice-Hall, 1993.
[3] C. Nataraj and P. Kasliwal, "Linear time varying control of unmanned surface vehicles," *Intelligent Ships Symposium* VI, American Society of Naval Engineers, 2005
[4] M. Wu, "A note a stability of linear time-varying systems," *IEEE transactions on Automatic Control*, 19, pp. 155–162, 1974.
[5] J. Zhu and C. Morales, "On linear ordinary differential equations with functionally commutative coefficient matrices," *Linear Algebra and Its Applications*, 170, pp. 81–105, 1992.
[6] M. Vidyasagar, Nonlinear Systems Analysis, 2nd Ed., *SIAM: Society for Industrial and Applied Mathematics*, 2002.
[7] Bay, J. S., Fundamentals of Linear State Space Systems, WCB/McGraw-Hill, Inc. , 1999.
[8] J. B. Pomet and L. Praly, "Adaptive Nonlinear Regulation: Estimation from the Lyapunov Equation," *IEEE Trans. on Automatic Control*, Vol. 37, pp. 729-740, June 1992.
[9] C. Nataraj, Vibration of Mechanical Systems, Cengage Learning, India, 2011
[10] Wilson J. Rugh, Linear System Theory, 2nd Ed., Prentice-Hall, 1996.

[11] C. Nataraj and R. Thimmaraya, "Tracking Control of Unmanned Surface Vehicles with Abkowitz Steering Model," *Proc of the* ASME *Dynamic Systems and Control Conference(DSCC)*, Cambridge, MA, Sept, 2010.
[12] D. Lee and C. Nataraj, "Adaptive Tracking Control of Linear Time-varying Unmanned Surface Vehicles with Disturbances", Intelligent Ships Symposium IX (ISSIX) 2011, Intelligent Control, May 25-26, Philadelphia, PA

Chapter 3

Issues on Communication Network Control System Based Upon Scheduling Strategy Using Numerical Simulations

Oscar Esquivel-Flores, Héctor Benítez-Pérez and Jorge Ortega-Arjona

Additional information is available at the end of the chapter

http://dx.doi.org/10.5772/48578

1. Introduction

Nowadays, industry has successfully used Network Control Systems (NCS) therefore several lines of research have arisen. A NCS is a current application of a Real-Time Distributed Systems (RTDS), composed of a number of nodes capable of developing a complete control process. In these systems several nodes exchange information through a communication network to achieve specific control goals, nevertheless network traffic increases. This affects the overall system performance. Several approaches have been developed to satisfy requirements of both control and communication performance. Particularly, some methodologies focus on saving bandwidth, one of such methodologies is network scheduling. The objective of this methodology is the accurately use of the computing resources. NCS research is categorized into two main parts [5]:

1. *Control of network:* Study and research on communications and networks to make them suitable for real-time NCS, e.g. routing control, congestion reduction, efficient data communication, networking protocol.
2. *Control over network:* This area deals with control strategies and control systems design over the network trying to minimize the effect of adverse network parameters on NCS performance such as network delay.

These systems have many challenges to maintain the the Quality of Service (QoS) and Quality of Control (QoC). In the networks, QoS is the idea that transmission rates, error rates, and other characteristics can be measured and improved. The QoS can be degraded due to congestion and interference.

1.1. Architecture and overview of a NCS

There are two general NCS configurations, *Direct structure* and *Hierarchical structure* [14]. Direct structure consists of a controller and a remote system containing a physical plant, sensors and actuators. The controller and the plant are physically located at different points and are directly linked by a data network in order to perform remote closed-loop control. Fig. 1 presents a schematic diagram of a direct structure of a NCS [15].

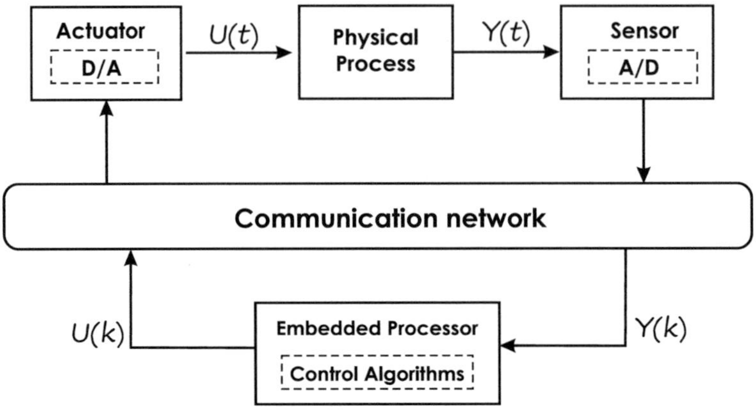

Figure 1. Schematic diagram of a direct structure of a NCS

1.2. Effect of sampling period on NCS

Network scheduling deals with to elect a sampling rate, aiming to reduce the number of data transmitted over the network . The effectiveness of the control system depends on such a sampling rate [8–10]. A region is acceptable in networked control performance terms if it is contained within two sampling rate boundaries, which can be statistically determined.

The use of a common-bus network architecture and a particular network protocol introduces different forms of time delay uncertainties between, sensors, actuators and controllers [8]. Hence, it is quite important to explore different network protocols and network scheduling strategies, before to implement the RTDS, in order to obtain a desired control performance.

For networked control, the minimum transmission frequency (f_m) is necessary to guarantee good system performance without decreasing the network performance. As the transmission frequency increases the system performance improves; however, the load on the network also increases until a maximum transmission frequency (f_h) is reached, then the system performance decreases because the network performance is overloaded.

This phenomenon represents non-linear situations with respect to sudden changes in state of the network, failure situations, or saturation in the channel or traffic, among others. However; it is possible to propose a linear model in the context of proper use of the network, thereby deferring the modeling of nonlinearity in these systems until future work.

The main objective of this work is to explore several issues on communication network scheduling of a RTDS, besides to implement a particular network scheduling strategy to evaluate its effectiveness using numerical simulations. This is presented using a simulated case study, based upon a 2-DOF helicopter simulation benchmark [13]. This simulation provides an approximation to system response, in which, for demonstration purposes, the main results are obtained for a typical fault scenario. Thus, for this simulation, a scheduling strategies is implemented using TrueTime [1, 2] performing dynamic scheduling. Several researches have focused on control over network, shared-network control systems have special interest.

2. Real-time simulation tool TrueTime

This section gives a brief overview of TrueTime simulator and exposes basic examples to initialize typical TrueTime blocks.

According to Cervin *et al.*, nowadays simple embedded control systems often contain a multi-tasking real-time kernel and support networking, besides time control algorithm and control software designs need to be considered together. Thus new computer-based tools for real time and control design are needed [1]. Networked control loops consist of sensor, actuator and control calculations residing on different nodes; within the individual nodes the controllers are implemented as one or several tasks on microprocessor with a real-time operating system, this operating system typically uses multiprogramming to execute various tasks. Communication bandwidth and CPU time can be considered as shared resources for which the task compete. Different sources of temporal nondeterminism as execution times of the tasks or communications delays affect the control performance, nevertheless this nondeterminism can be reduce by the accurate choice of implementation platforms. The constraints of the implementation platform must be considered in systems with limited computer resources [1], therefore some tools are available to analyze and simulate the effects of temporal constrains affects control performance.

TrueTime [1, 2, 6, 7, 12] is a simulator for networked and embedded control system based on Matlab/Simulink, it has been developed at Lund University since 1999 [2]. TrueTime can be used as an experimental platform for research on dynamic real-time control systems. For instance, it is possible to study compensation schemes that adjust the control algorithm based on measurements of actual timing variations [1]. TrueTime make it possible to study more general and detailed timing models of computer-controlled systems. TrueTime can be used: to investigate how timing nondeterminism affects the system behavior, to develop new outlines to adjust control parameters dynamically, to experiment new approaches as codesign of control and network scheduling and to simulate control systems based on event-driven task [1].

The simulator software consists of a Simulink block library, the kernel block simulates a Real-Time kernel executing user-defined task and interrupt handlers. To communicate kernel blocks (nodes) several network blocks may be used, thus it makes quite simple to develop networked control system simulations.

2.1. The kernel block

A computer node is simulated using TrueTime kernel block, this node has a generic real-time kernel, A/D and D/A converters, and network interfaces. An initialization scrip is used to configure the block, in this script it is possible to create several objects as task, timers, interrupt handlers, semaphores, etc., this objects establish the software executing in the computer node. The kernel continuously calls the code functions of the tasks and interrupt handlers. Either Matlab m-files code or C++ language may be used to write initialization scripts and the code functions, the main advantage to use C++ is the speed, nevertheless m-file code is very easy to use. Several scheduling policy is able to use in TreTime kernel block, these can be fixed-priority scheduling and earliest-deadline-first scheduling and custom scheduling policies [2].

The *task* is the main construction in the TrueTime environment, this object is used to simulate periodic and aperiodic activities, for example controller and I/O tasks can be periodic and communication and event-driven controller can be aperiodic tasks. A set of attributes and a code function define a task; attributes as name, release time, worst-case execution time, budget, relative and absolute deadlines, priority (if fixed priority scheduling is used), period (if the task is periodic). Release time and absolute deadline are attributes constantly updated bye the kernel during simulation, while period and priority are kept constant, although can be changed by callas to kernel primitives trough execution [1]. An example of the definition of a task is shown below:

```
function sensor_init(arg)
% Initialize TrueTime kernel
  ttInitKernel(1, 0, 'prioFP'); %Inputs,Outputs,FixedPriority
% Create sensor task
  offset = 0;
  prio = 1;
  period = 0.010;
  ttCreatePeriodicTask('sens_task', offset, period, ...
  prio, 'senscode', data);
```

The kernel primitive `ttInitKernel()` initializes a sensor node. The kernel is initialized by specifying the number of A/D and D/A channels and scheduling policy. The built-in priority function `prioFP` specifies fixed-priority scheduling. Rate monotonic `prioRM`, earliest deadline first `prioEDF`, and deadline monotonic `prioDM` scheduling are additional predefined scheduling policies [6].

Interrupts can be generated in two ways: An external interrupt is associated with one of the external interrupt channels of the computer block; when the signal of the corresponding channel changes value the interrupt triggers. The usefulness of this type of interrupt lies to simulate distributed controllers that execute when measurements arrive on the network. Internal interrupts work to construct timers, when a timer expires the interrupt is triggered. A user-defined interrupt handler is scheduled when an external or internal interrupt occurs. An interrupt, as a task, handles works but it is scheduled on a higher priority level. An interrupt handler is defined by name, a priority and a code function [1]. An example of a definition of a interrupt handler is as follows:

```
%Initialize the network
 ttCreateInterruptHandler('nw_handler1', prio, 'msgRcvSensor');
 ttInitNetwork(4, 'nw_handler1'); % node #4 in the network
```

Cervin *et al.* [1, 2] mentions that simulated execution occurs at three distinct *priority* levels: the interrupt (highest priority), kernel and task (lower priority) levels. The execution may be preemptive or non-preemptive. At interrupt level, interrupt handlers are *scheduled* according to fixed priorities. At task level, dynamic-priority scheduling may be used. At each scheduling point, the priority of task is given by user-defined priority function which is a function of the task attributes, this makes it easy to simulate different scheduling policies. Predefined priority functions exist for most of the commonly used scheduling schemes.

The *code* associated with task and interrupt handlers is scheduled and executed bye the kernel while simulation progresses. The code may be divided in segments, which can interact with other tasks and with the environment at the beginning of each code segment. The simulated execution time of each segment is returned by the code function and can be modeled as constant, random, or even data-dependent [1]. During the simulation the kernel saves the current segment and calls the code functions with proper arguments. Execution resumes in the next segment when the task has been running for the time associated with previous segment [7]. An example of a sensor code is given bellow:

```
function [exectime, data] = senscode(seg, data)
switch seg,
 case 1,
  % Receive data from analog input
  data.y = ttAnalogIn(1);
  exectime = 0.0005;
 case 2,
  % Shows the current time
  ttCurrentTime
  % Send message (80 bits) to node 3 (controller)
  ttSendMsg(3, data, 80)
  exectime = 0.0004;
 case 3,
  exectime = -1; % finished
end
```

This function implements a simple sensor node. In the first segment, the plant is sampled using a execution time of .5 ms. In the second segment, the control signal is sent to the controller node. The third segment indicates the end of execution by returning a negative execution time. The structure `data` represent the local memory and is used to store the measured variable between calls to the different segments. The kernel primitives `ttAnalogIn` and `ttAnalogOut` can be perform A/D and D/A conversion. Besides A/D and D/A conversion, a large set of kernel primitives exist which can be called from code function [12].

Monitors and events support *sincronization* between tasks. Monitors are used to guarnatee mutual exclusion when accessing comon data. Events are associated with monitors to represent condition variables [1].

Different *output graphs* are generated by truetime blocks. Each computer block will produce two graphs: A computer graph will display the execution trace of each task and interrupt handler during the simulation. If the signal is high, it means that the task is running. A medium signal indicates that the task is ready but not running, a low signal means that the task is idle. Otherwise a monitor graph shows which tasks are holding and waiting on the different monitors during simulation [1].

2.2. The network block

The TrueTime network block simulates the physical layer and the medium-access layer of several local-area networks. CSMA/CD (Ethernet), CSMA/AMP (CAN), Round Robin

(Token Bus), FDMA, TDMA (TTP), Switched Ethernet, WLAN (802.11b), and ZigBee (802.15.4) are some types of network supported [2]. The network blocks are mainly configured using blocks dialogs. Some parameters common to all types of networks are bit rate, the minimum frame size, and the network interface delay. For each type of network there are some parameters that specifie the number of nodes, data rate (bits/s), preprocessing delay, minimum frame size, maximum frame size, frame overhead, etc. The network blocks may be used having one kernel block for each node in the network. The tasks into the kernels can send and receive arbitrary Matlab structure arrays over the network using `ttSendMsg` and `ttGetMsg` kernel primitives. This way is to quite flexible but requires to program some routines to configure the system. An useful network scheduler viewer shows the network activity for all nodes involved. An overview of all Truetime's primitives can be found on [12].

3. Frequency transmission scheduling

In this section a formal definition of task model is provided and it gives an overview of the control of frequency transmission in a distributed systems and how it impacts over quality performance.

3.1. Task model

Chen *et al.* [3] gives a formal definition of system model of a typical distributed systems consisting of a set of processors and a set of tasks. A distributed system are characterized as follows. A set of processors $\Omega = \{S_1, S_2, ..., Sm\}$ where Ω is the processor set, S_i is the $i - th$ processor and m is the total number of processors. In this model, all processors are assumed to be identical to assure same execution time for each task on different processors. It is also supposed that enough processors are provided. A set of primary copy of real-time tasks $\Phi = \{\tau_1, \tau_2, ..., \tau_n\}$, where $\tau_i = \{c_i, p_i\}$, $i = \{1, 2, ..., n\}$. Here Φ is the set of tasks, τ_i is the $i - th$ task, n is the number of tasks which are periodic, independent and preemptive, c_i denotes the execution time of τ_i, p_i denotes the period of task τ_i.

3.2. Control of frequency transmission

An approach to schedule a real time distributed system based upon modifications on frequency transmission of individual components in the system is presented in [4], this shows that scheduling of a distributed system can be accomplished through modifications on transmission frequencies into a region where the system performance is not affected. A linear time invariant model in which the coefficients of the state matrix are the relations between the transmission frequencies of each agent and through a feedback controller to modify transmission frequencies bounded between maximum and minimum values of transmission. This approach drives the frequency transmission based on three parameters: minimum frequency (f_m), maximum frequency (f_h) and real frequency (f_r). Frequency transmission dynamics can be modeled as a linear time-invariant subsystem which state variables are transmission frequencies of the sensor nodes involved on the system. Note that for each primary task of a sensor S_i, $i = 1, ..., m$ frequency can be expressed as $f_i = 1/p_i$. There is a relationship between nodes' frequencies an external input frequencies which serves as coefficients of the linear system. Therefore it is possible to control the NCS through the input vector u such that the outputs y are nodes' frequencies into a region L bounded by maximum and minimum transmission frequencies, see Fig. 2.

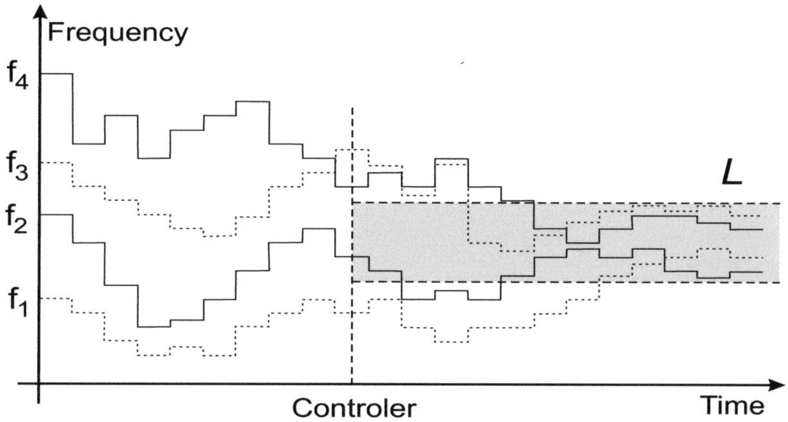

Figure 2. Transmission frequencies bounded by a schedulability region

The objective of controlling the frequency is to achieve coordination through the convergence of values. Each sensor S_i knows its minimum and maximum frequencies based upon messages sent to controller and it could be estimated its own real transmission frequency. Let a NCS with a set $\Omega = \{S_1, S_2, ..., S_l\}$ nodes that performs a set of task $\tau_i = \{c_i, p_i\}$ for $i = \{1, 2, , n\}$, a subset of Ω is sensor nodes subset $\Omega_s = \{S_1, S_2, ..., S_m\}$.

3.3. Network scheduling based on frequency transmission

An approach that modifies the frequency transmission uses f_m, f_r, f_x frequencies. RTDS dynamics, is modeled as a linear time-invariant system, whose state variables are frequencies transmission rates of the n nodes that compose the RTDS [4]. Frequency rates of a node are affected by some external input frequency rates, minimal frequencies of all nodes and particular ratios serve as coefficients of the linear system. So, it is possible to control the NCS using the input vector u, such that the output vector y contains the frequency rates of all nodes within a nonlinear region L, bounded by the maximum and minimum transmission frequency rates. Let we assume that there is a relationship amongst real frequencies $f_r^1, f_r^2, ..., f_r^m$ and external input frequencies $u_1, u_2, ..., u_m$ which serve as coefficients of the linear system:

$$\begin{aligned} x_{k+1} &= Ax_k + Bu_k, \\ y_k &= Cx_k. \end{aligned} \tag{1}$$

A, B, C are matrices with appropriate dimensions. A is the matrix of relationships between frequencies of sensor nodes, B is the scale frequencies matrix, C is the matrix with frequencies ordered, x_{k+1} is a real frequencies vector in time $t = k + 1$, y_k is the vector of output frequencies. The input u_k is a function of reference frequencies and real frequencies of the nodes in the distributed system, hence $u = K(f_m - f_r)$ where f_m, f_r are vectors. Then, the state vector in equation (1) can be written as:

$$\begin{aligned} x_{k+1} &= Ax_k + Bu_k, \\ x_{k+1} &= Af_{rk} + B\left(K(f_{mk} - f_{rk})\right). \end{aligned} \tag{2}$$

Note that K is the control gain defined as the basics of a LQR algorithm. Matrices A, B and C has the proper dimensions and matrix A include the following restriction [11]:

$$U = \sum_{i=1}^{n} c_i / p_i \leq 1,$$

as a new state of the system (1). For simplicity, frequency transition model will be described using a sensor node subset $\Omega_s = \{S_1, S_2, S_3, S_4\}$. The elements of the matrices for system 2 are defined as follows:

$$\bar{a}_{ij} = \begin{cases} \frac{\Lambda\left(f_m^1, f_m^2, f_m^3, f_m^4\right)}{f_m^i} & i = j \\ \\ \frac{f_m^j}{f_m^i} & i \neq j \end{cases},$$

$$\bar{b}_{ij} = \begin{cases} f_h^i & i = j \\ 0 & i \neq j \end{cases},$$

$$\bar{c}_{ij} = \begin{cases} 1 & i = j \\ 0 & i \neq j \end{cases}.$$

Note that $\Lambda\left(f_m^1, f_m^2, f_m^3, f_m^4\right)$ is the greatest common divisor of minimum frequencies, that is the planning cycle Γ expressed in terms of frequencies of the backup task, for shortening, it will be written only as Λ. f_m, f_h, and f_r are vectors of respective frequencies.

Considering the execution time c_i of each task executing in respective sensor nodes in Ω_s as an additional state, we can rewrite (2) as follows:

$$\begin{bmatrix} x_{k+1}^1 \\ x_{k+1}^2 \\ x_{k+1}^3 \\ x_{k+1}^4 \\ x_{k+1}^5 \end{bmatrix} = \begin{bmatrix} \frac{\Lambda}{f_m^1} & \frac{f_m^2}{f_m^1} & \frac{f_m^3}{f_m^1} & \frac{f_m^4}{f_m^1} & 0 \\ \frac{f_m^1}{f_m^2} & \frac{\Lambda}{f_m^2} & \frac{f_m^3}{f_m^2} & \frac{f_m^4}{f_m^2} & 0 \\ \frac{f_m^1}{f_m^3} & \frac{f_m^2}{f_m^3} & \frac{\Lambda}{f_m^3} & \frac{f_m^4}{f_m^3} & 0 \\ \frac{f_m^1}{f_m^4} & \frac{f_m^2}{f_m^4} & \frac{f_m^3}{f_m^4} & \frac{\Lambda}{f_m^4} & 0 \\ c_1 & c_2 & c_3 & c_4 & 1 \end{bmatrix} \begin{bmatrix} f_r^1 \\ f_r^2 \\ f_r^3 \\ f_r^n \\ x_c \end{bmatrix} + \begin{bmatrix} f_h^1 & 0 & 0 & 0 & 0 \\ 0 & f_h^2 & 0 & 0 & 0 \\ 0 & 0 & f_h^3 & 0 & 0 \\ 0 & 0 & 0 & f_h^n & 0 \\ 1 & 1 & 1 & 1 & 1 \end{bmatrix}$$

$$\cdot \left(\begin{bmatrix} K_1 & 0 & 0 & 0 & 0 \\ 0 & K_2 & 0 & 0 & 0 \\ 0 & 0 & K_3 & 0 & 0 \\ 0 & 0 & 0 & K_4 & 0 \\ 0 & 0 & 0 & 0 & K_c \end{bmatrix} \left(\begin{bmatrix} f_m^1 \\ f_m^2 \\ f_m^3 \\ f_m^4 \\ x_c^r \end{bmatrix} - \begin{bmatrix} f_r^1 \\ f_r^2 \\ f_r^3 \\ f_r^n \\ x_c \end{bmatrix} \right) \right),$$

$$\begin{bmatrix} y_k^1 \\ y_k^2 \\ y_k^3 \\ y_k^4 \\ y_k^5 \end{bmatrix} = \begin{bmatrix} 1\,0\,0\,0\,0 \\ 0\,1\,0\,0\,0 \\ 0\,0\,1\,0\,0 \\ 0\,0\,0\,1\,0 \\ 0\,0\,0\,0\,1 \end{bmatrix} \begin{bmatrix} f_r^1 \\ f_r^2 \\ f_r^3 \\ f_r^4 \\ x_c \end{bmatrix}.$$

x_c is a real execution time and x_c^r is a reference execution time.

Thus

$$\begin{bmatrix} x_{k+1}^1 \\ x_{k+1}^2 \\ x_{k+1}^3 \\ x_{k+1}^4 \\ x_{k+1}^5 \end{bmatrix} = \begin{bmatrix} \frac{\Lambda}{f_m^1} & \frac{f_m^2}{f_m^1} & \frac{f_m^3}{f_m^1} & \frac{f_m^4}{f_m^1} & 0 \\ \frac{f_m^1}{f_m^2} & \frac{\Lambda}{f_m^2} & \frac{f_m^3}{f_m^2} & \frac{f_m^4}{f_m^2} & 0 \\ \frac{f_m^1}{f_m^3} & \frac{f_m^2}{f_m^3} & \frac{\Lambda}{f_m^3} & \frac{f_m^4}{f_m^3} & 0 \\ \frac{f_m^1}{f_m^4} & \frac{f_m^2}{f_m^4} & \frac{f_m^3}{f_m^4} & \frac{\Lambda}{f_m^4} & 0 \\ c_1 & c_2 & c_3 & c_4 & 1 \end{bmatrix} \begin{bmatrix} f_r^1 \\ f_r^2 \\ f_r^3 \\ f_r^n \\ x_c \end{bmatrix} + \begin{bmatrix} K_1 f_h^1 (f_m^1 - f_r^1) \\ K_2 f_h^2 (f_m^2 - f_r^2) \\ K_3 f_h^3 (f_m^3 - f_r^3) \\ K_4 f_h^4 (f_m^4 - f_r^4) \\ K_1(f_m^1 - f_r^1) + K_2(f_m^2 - f_r^2) + \\ K_3(f_m^3 - f_r^3) + K_4(f_m^4 - f_r^4) + \\ K_c(x_c^r - x_r) \end{bmatrix},$$

$$\begin{bmatrix} y_k^1 \\ y_k^2 \\ y_k^3 \\ y_k^4 \\ y_k^5 \end{bmatrix} = \begin{bmatrix} 1\,0\,0\,0\,0 \\ 0\,1\,0\,0\,0 \\ 0\,0\,1\,0\,0 \\ 0\,0\,0\,1\,0 \\ 0\,0\,0\,0\,1 \end{bmatrix} \begin{bmatrix} f_r^1 \\ f_r^2 \\ f_r^3 \\ f_r^4 \\ x_c \end{bmatrix}.$$

4. Real-Time Distributed System

This section exposes the RTDS used for implementation purposes, it is a 2-DOF helicopter prototype [13]. The following section briefly introduces and describes this 2-DOF helicopter prototype and its controller design.

The case of study is a prototype of a helicopter system integrated to a CanBus network with two propellers that are driven by DC motors. The front propeller controls the elevation of the helicopter nose about the pitch axis (θ) and the back propeller controls the side to side motions of the helicopter about the yaw axis (ψ). The pitch and yaw angles are measured using high-resolution encoders. A brief description of the helicopter model is presented, however detailed information can be found in [13]. The dynamics of the helicopter is developed based on kinetic and potential energy, this model is used to design a position controller. The helicopter centre of mass is described in xyz cartesian coordinates with respect the pitch and yaw angles, see Fig. 3.

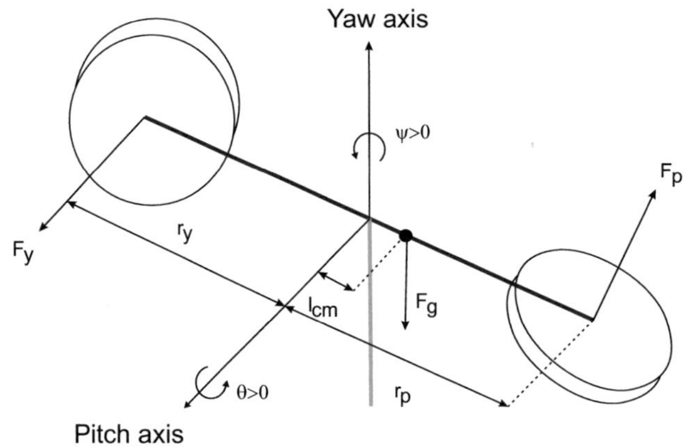

Figure 3. Dynamics of the 2DOF helicopter

The Euler-Lagrange equations are used to obtain nonlinear equations of motion for the 2 DOF Helicopter, which are used to derive the linear state model, and subsequently, to design the position controller. As the helicopter represents a non-linear system, it is required to perform a linearization around a point, this linearization point is

$$\left[\theta_0 = 0, \psi_0 = 0, \dot{\theta}_0 = 0, \dot{\psi}_0 = 0\right].$$

From this, the linearization of the motion equation is obtained as follows:

$$\left(J_{eq,p} + m_{heli} l_{cm}^2\right) \ddot{\theta} = K_{pp} V_{m,p} + K_{py} V_{m,y} - B_p \dot{\theta} - m_{heli} g l_{cm}, \tag{3}$$

$$\left(J_{eq,y} + m_{heli} l_{cm}^2\right) \ddot{\psi} = K_{pp} V_{m,y} + K_{yp} V_{m,p} - B_p \dot{\psi} - 2 m_{heli} l_{cm}^2 \theta \dot{\psi} \dot{\theta}. \tag{4}$$

Substituing $x = \left[\theta, \psi, \dot{\theta}, \dot{\psi}\right]'$ in (3) and (4) and solving for $\dot{x}$ the following linear model of state space is obtained:

$$\dot{x} = \begin{bmatrix} 0\,0 & 1 & 0 \\ 0\,0 & 0 & 1 \\ 0\,0 & -\frac{B_p}{J_{eq,p}+m_{heli}l_{cm}^2} & 0 \\ 0\,0 & 0 & -\frac{B_y}{J_{eq,y}+m_{heli}l_{cm}^2} \end{bmatrix} x + \begin{bmatrix} 0 & 0 \\ 0 & 0 \\ \frac{K_{pp}}{J_{eq,p}+m_{heli}l_{cm}^2} & \frac{K_{py}}{J_{eq,p}+m_{heli}l_{cm}^2} \\ -\frac{K_{yp}}{J_{eq,y}+m_{heli}l_{cm}^2} & -\frac{K_{yy}}{J_{eq,y}+m_{heli}l_{cm}^2} \end{bmatrix} u,$$

$$y = \begin{bmatrix} 1\,0\,0\,0 \\ 0\,1\,0\,0 \\ 0\,0\,1\,0 \\ 0\,0\,0\,1 \end{bmatrix} x.$$

where K_{pp}, K_{yy}, K_{py}, K_{yp} are the torque-constants used to obtain coupled torques acting on the pitch and yaw axes; for the state space model the input u and output y vectors are $u = \left[V_{m,p}, V_{m,y}\right]'$ and $y = \left[x_1, x_2, x_3, x_4\right]'$, V_{mp} is the input pitch motor voltage and V_{my} is the input yaw motor voltage. Notice that, since the output matrix is the identity matrix, all states are measurable.

The model makes use of several Simulink and Matlab programs to develop the helicopter basic dynamics, by running a simulation of the closed-loop response, using the position controller. Regarding control issues, two controllers are designed: a FF-LQR and a FF+LQR+I. The FF+LQR regulates the pitch axis of the helicopter, using feed-forward (FF) and proportional-velocity (PV) compensators, while the yaw axis only makes use of a PV control. The FF+LQR+I controller uses an integrator in the feedback loop to reduce the steady-state error, by a feed-forward and proportional-integral-velocity (PIV) algorithms to regulate the pitch, and only a PIV to control the yaw angle. This work focuses on the FF+LQR+I controller, as follows. The FF+LQR control converges $(\theta, \psi, \dot{\theta}, \dot{\psi}) \rightarrow (\theta_d, \psi_d, \dot{\theta}_d, \dot{\psi}_d)$ where θ_d is the desired pitch angle and ψ_d is the desired yaw angle, such that:

$$\begin{bmatrix} u_p \\ u_y \end{bmatrix} = \begin{bmatrix} K_{ff} \frac{m_{heli} g l_{cm} \cos\theta_d}{K_{pp}} \\ 0 \end{bmatrix}.$$

The addition of an integrator requires to introduce the states $\dot{x}_5 = \theta$ and $\dot{x}_6 = \psi$, so the linear state-space model is augmented as:

$$\dot{x} = \begin{bmatrix} 0\,0 & 1 & 0 & 0\,0 \\ 0\,0 & 0 & 1 & 0\,0 \\ 0\,0 & -\frac{B_p}{J_{eq,p}+m_{heli}l_{cm}^2} & 0 & 0\,0 \\ 0\,0 & 0 & -\frac{B_y}{J_{eq,y}+m_{heli}l_{cm}^2} & 0\,0 \\ 1\,0 & 0 & 0 & 0\,0 \\ 0\,1 & 0 & 0 & 0\,0 \end{bmatrix} x + \begin{bmatrix} 0 & 0 \\ 0 & 0 \\ \frac{K_{pp}}{J_{eq,p}+m_{heli}l_{cm}^2} & \frac{K_{py}}{J_{eq,p}+m_{heli}l_{cm}^2} \\ -\frac{K_{yp}}{J_{eq,y}+m_{heli}l_{cm}^2} & -\frac{K_{yy}}{J_{eq,y}+m_{heli}l_{cm}^2} \\ 0 & 0 \\ 0 & 0 \end{bmatrix} u,$$

$$y = \begin{bmatrix} 1\,0\,0\,0\,0\,0 \\ 0\,1\,0\,0\,0\,0 \\ 0\,0\,1\,0\,0\,0 \\ 0\,0\,0\,1\,0\,0 \\ 0\,0\,0\,0\,1\,0 \\ 0\,0\,0\,0\,0\,1 \end{bmatrix} x.$$

Using the adequate Q and R weighting matrices, the control gain is as follows:

$$k = \begin{bmatrix} 18.9 & 1.98 & 7.48 & 1.53 & 7.03 & 0.77 \\ -2.22 & 19.4 & -0.45 & 11.9 & -0.77 & 7.03 \end{bmatrix}.$$

Thus, the FF+LQR+I controller is:

$$\begin{bmatrix} u_p \\ u_y \end{bmatrix} = \begin{bmatrix} K_{ff} \frac{m_{heli} g l_{cm} \cos\theta_d}{K_{pp}} \\ 0 \end{bmatrix} - \begin{bmatrix} k_{11} & k_{12} & k_{13} & k_{14} \\ k_{21} & k_{22} & k_{23} & k_{24} \end{bmatrix}$$
$$\begin{bmatrix} \theta - \theta_d \\ \psi - \psi_d \\ \dot{\theta} \\ \dot{\psi} \end{bmatrix} - \begin{bmatrix} k_{15}(\theta - \theta_d) + \int k_{16}(\psi - \psi_d) \\ k_{25}(\theta - \theta_d) + \int k_{26}(\psi - \psi_d) \end{bmatrix}.$$

5. Experimental approach

In order to study the impact of network utilization on closed control loop, the 2-DOF Helicopter control model is built as a NCS. Several nodes are connected through a common communication network. The experiment focuses on network scheduling, and the main objective is to balance the amount of data sent through the network, in order to avoid latency and under sampling.

The NCS for the experiment consists of 8 processors. These real-time kernel processors and the network are simulated using TrueTime [2, 12] based on Matlab/Simulink. The network used is a CSMA/AMP(CAN) with a transmission rate of 80000 bits/second, and not data loss. The NCS model is shown in Fig. 4.

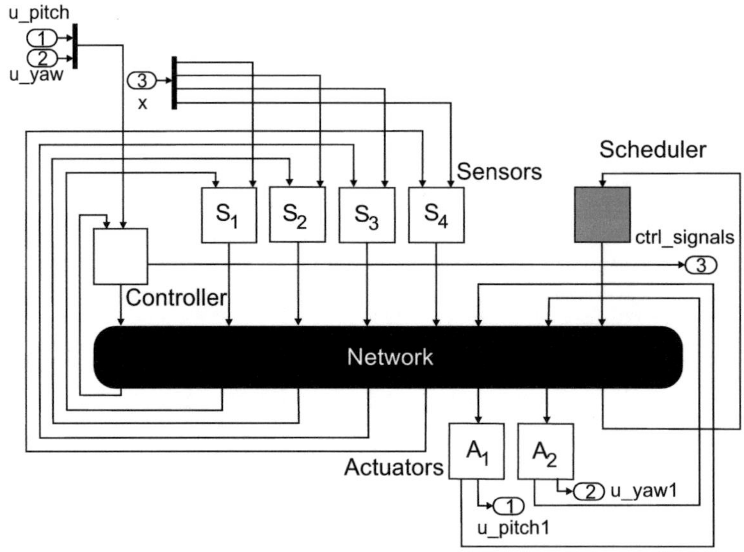

Figure 4. Networked Control System to analyze frequency transmission over the network

Four sensor nodes execute periodic tasks to sense control signals, as well as other additional periodic tasks. Each task has a period p_i and time consumption c_i (Fig. 4). The sensed control signals are $x = (\theta, \psi, \dot{\theta}, \dot{\psi})$. This model has a controller node, depicted on the left side (Fig. 4). This controller takes the control law from the FF+LQR module by means of a task, which activates by event. The time consumption of the controller task is the maximum average time it takes to compute the control law. The controller node uses the values from sensors, and sends control outputs u_p and u_y, that correspond to the pitch and yaw voltages. Two actuator nodes, located on the bottom right corner (Fig. 4), receive signals from the controller node. Finally, the scheduler node, located on the top right corner (Fig. 4), organizes the activity of the other seven nodes, and it is responsible for periodic allocation bandwidth, used by these nodes. Each node initializes, specifying the number of inputs and outputs of the respective TrueTime kernel block, defining a scheduling policy, and creating periodic tasks for the simulation. These tasks involve parameters about the periodic times and the consumption times. The task periodic times define the time interval between tasks, whereas the consumption times refer to the execution time of the task. Fig. 5 shows the 2-DOF Helicopter model, with a RTDS, where feedback control loop is closed through a communication network.

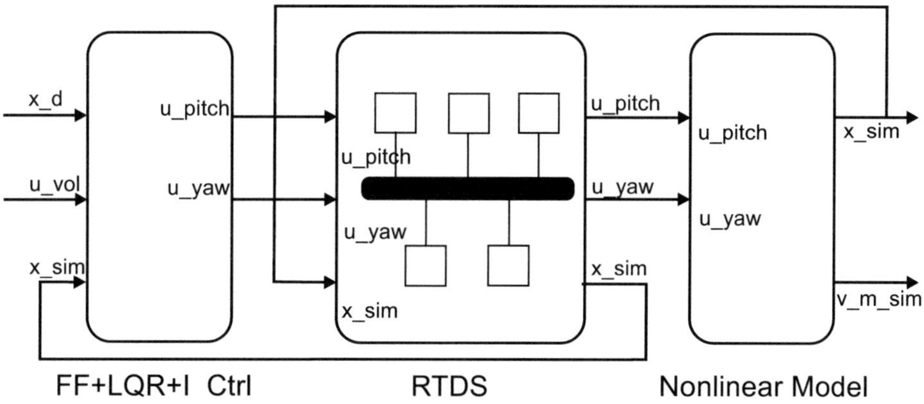

Figure 5. Networked control integrated into closed control loop of the 2DOF Helicopter

Changes on the real-time task parameters of the RTDS commonly impact on network utilization, and therefore, on the control performance [8, 9]. The problem to tackle, thus, is to find a proper way to schedule the common communication network of the RTDS, based on managing an accurate sampling period, capable of keeping both, the network load and required integrated performance.

A criteria to quantify the system's quality performance is the integral of the absolute value of the error (commonly expressed as IAE) is used:

$$IAE = \int_{t_0}^{t_f} |e(t)|\, dt \approx \sum_{k=k_0}^{k_f} |r(kh) - y(kh)| \tag{5}$$

where $r(t)$ is reference signal or setpoint, $y(t)$ is system output signal, $t_0(k_0)$ and $t_f(k_f)$ are the initial and final continuous(discrete) times of evaluation period [15].

5.1. Numerical simulations

In this section numerical simulations using the Network scheduling strategy based on Frequency Transmission are exposed. The network scheduling strategy dynamically adjusts the frequencies, considering the participation of several nodes of the NCS. These scheduling approach shows a way to manage the network resources, especially with a limited network bandwidth. These techniques avoid network delays during transmission. Numerical simulations shows that the dynamical changes of this strategy improve the RTDS response under fault scenarios.

The relationship amongst IAE and sampling periods of the primary sensing tasks is shown in Fig. (6). When the network transmits data without overloading or under sampling the output signals of pitch and yaw angles are similar to induced reference signal, so that the value of IAE is small. In contrast, when the transmission rate of sensor task set exceeds the upper bound data transmission rate the system becomes unstable, IAE increases accordingly.

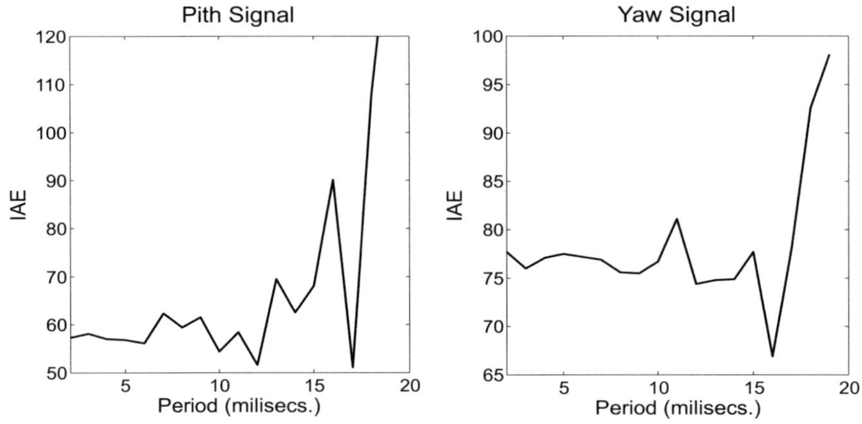

Figure 6. Values of the IAE using different sampling periods

The sensing periods was fixed in 10 miliseconds, sampling during the time simulation with this rate. In a fault-free scenario the pitch and yaw singnals track the reference signal, this behaviour is presented in Fig. 7

It is assumed that in a fault scenario the change in periods of tasks may be produced, this induces a network utilization that possibily can not be supported by the bandwidth or perhaps stops data tranmission continuity. The effect of a fault over the RTDS is shown in the Fig. 8. In this case the periods of sensor tasks produce a low sampling resulting in loss of control.

For the particular case study was made off-line analysis of the frequencies with which can be transmitted without increasing the value of the IAE for the sensing tasks. These ranges serve as parameters for the calculation of new transmission frequencies using the proposed model.

When fault occurs a signal is transmitted to the scheduler, this signal contains the *id* of sensor with fail and the parameters of the tasks on execution before the failure. The scheduler uses the frequency range and time of execution of the sensor tasks that has just entered, scheduler knows frequencies ranges of the tasks that continue without fail. This information feeds frequency transition model to compute a new frequency transmission range through a LQR

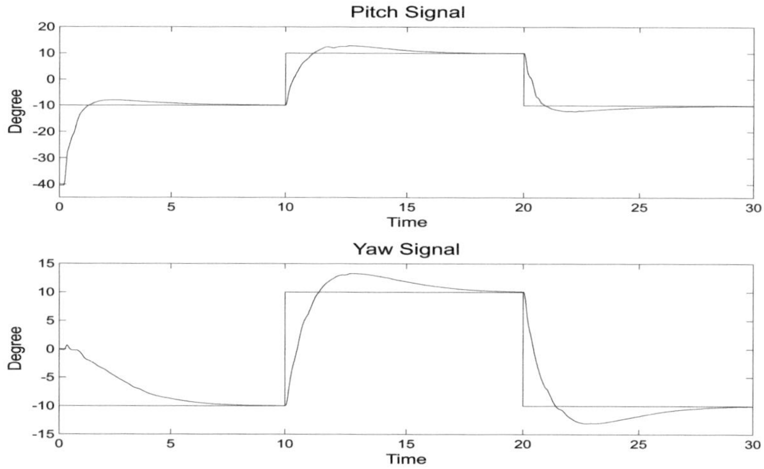

Figure 7. Pitch and yaw signals in a fault-free scenario

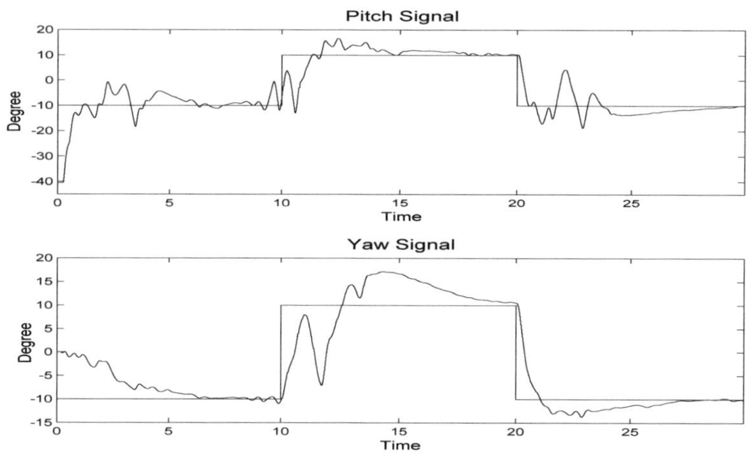

Figure 8. Pitch and yaw signals in a fault scenario

control scheme, new frequencies are assigned to the sensor nodes in which the task period is changed therefore the effect of fault scenario is minimized balancing the amount of data sent over the network.

Numerical simulations were performed using the values of the maximum, minimum, and real frequencies besides the computational time, the values used for the sensor nodes are shown in the table 1.

Figure 9 shows the frequencies controlled, this control bounds the frequency into a schedulability region where the IAE is low.

Figure 10 shows system behavior during 30 seconds using frequency transition model. Nominal frequencies start in schedulability region during 8 secs, system transmits with this

Node	Max. Freq.	Min. Freq.	Real Freq.	Consume
1	70	280	40	0.002
2	50	260	250	0.002
3	50	250	100	0.002
4	55	300	50	0.002

Table 1. Maximum, minimum, and real frequencies besides the computational time

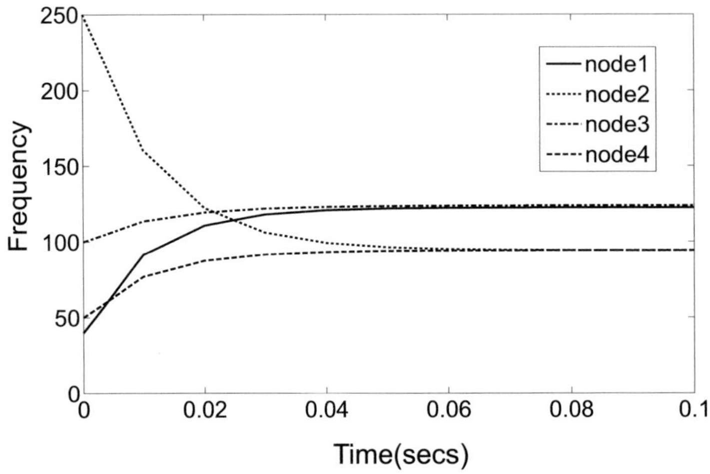

Figure 9. Frequencies bounded into a schedulability region usign a frequency transmission controller

rate. In second 9 fault appears with a change of context, system transmits with this frequency until second 18. In second 19 frequency transition model change frequencies of backup tasks.

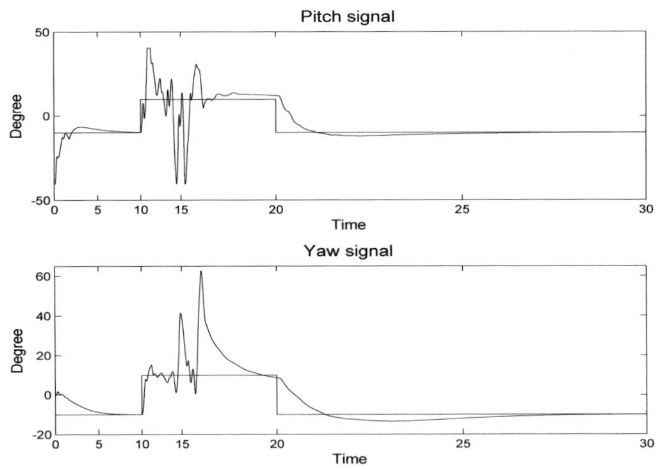

Figure 10. Pitch and yaw signals in a fault scenario using frequency transmission model

Figure 11 shows the computer network as well

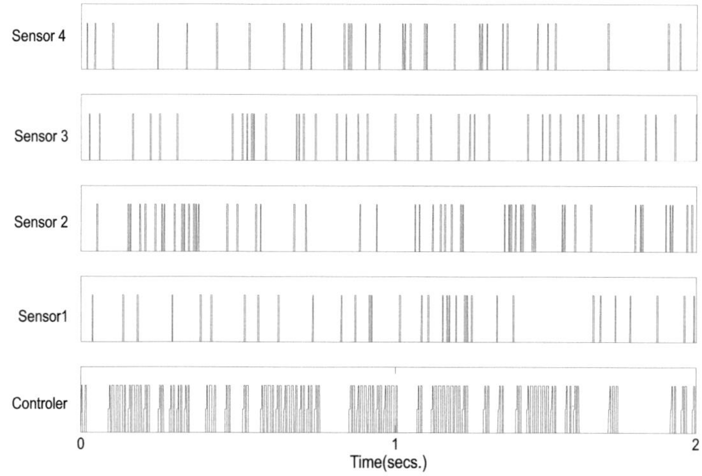

Figure 11. Sensing activiity and the related use of the computer networking using the Truetime toolbox

6. Conclusions

This work show a study of network scheduling strategy using numerical simulations. A simulation of a particular RTDS, a 2-DOF helicopter, is built using TrueTime as real-time simulation tool. A network scheduling strategy based on changes of frequency transmission rates is implemented in order to expose the advantages of using dynamic scheduling in an ad-hoc implementation for the network of a NCS. The use of numerical simulations aid to explore several considerations in design and analysis of a NCS.

Author details

Oscar Esquivel-Flores, Héctor Benítez-Pérez and Jorge Ortega-Arjona
Universidad Nacional Autónoma de México, México

7. References

[1] Cervin, A., Henriksson, D., Lincoln, B., Eker, J. & Årzen, K.-E. [2003]. How does control timing affect performance? analysis and simulation of timing using jitterbug and truetime, *Control Systems, IEEE* 23(3): 16 – 30.

[2] Cervin, A., Ohlin, M. & Henriksson, D. [2007]. Simulation of networked control systems using truetime, *Proc. 3rd International Workshop on Networked Control Systems: Tolerant to Faults*, Nancy, France.

[3] Chen, H., Luo, W., Wang, W. & Xiang, J. [2011]. A novel real-time fault-tolerant scheduling algorithm based on distributed control systems, *Computer Science and Service System (CSSS), 2011 International Conference on*, pp. 80 –83.

[4] Esquivel-Flores, O., Benítez-Pérez, H., Méndez Monroy, E. & Menéndez, A. [2010]. Efficient overloading techniques for primary-backup scheduling in real-time systems, *ICI Express Letters Part B: Applications* 1(1): 93–98.

[5] Gupta, R. & Chow, M.-Y. [2010]. Networked control system: Overview and research trends, *Industrial Electronics, IEEE Transactions on* 57(7): 2527 –2535.

[6] Henriksson, D., Cervin, A., Andersson, M. & Årzén, K.-E. [2006]. Truetime: Simulation of networked computer control systems, *Proceedings of the 2nd IFAC Conference on Analysis and Design of Hybrid Systems*, Alghero, Italy.

[7] Henriksson, D., Redell, O., El-Khoury, J., Cervin, A., Törngren, M. & Årzén, K.-E. [2006]. Tools for real-time control systems co-design, *in* H. Hansson (ed.), *ARTES – A network for Real-Time research and graduate Education in Sweden 1997–2006*, Department of Information Technology, Uppsala University, Sweden.

[8] Lian, F.-L., Moyne, J. & Tilbury, D. [2001]. Time delay modeling and sample time selection for networked control systems. *International Mechanical Engineering Congress and Exposition, Proceedings of ASME-DSC*, Vol. XX.

[9] Lian, F.-L., Moyne, J. & Tilbury, D. [2002]. Network design consideration for distributed control systems, *Control Systems Technology, IEEE Transactions on* 10(2): 297 –307.

[10] Lian, F.-L., Yook, J., Otanez, P., Tilbury, D. & Moyne, J. [2003]. Design of sampling and transmission rates for achieving control and communication performance in networked agent systems, *American Control Conference 2003, Proceedings of*, Vol. 4, pp. 3329 – 3334.

[11] Liu, C. L. & Layland, J. W. [1973]. Scheduling algorithms for multiprogramming in a hard-real-time environment, *J. ACM* 20(1): 46–61.

[12] Ohlin, M., Henriksson, D. & Cervin, A. [2007]. *TRUETIME 1.5 Reference Manual*.

[13] Quanser [2006]. *Quanser 2 DOF Helicopter. User and Control Manual*, Quanser. Innovate-Educate.

[14] Tipsuwan, Y. & Chow, M.-Y. [2003]. Control methodologies in networked control systems, *Control Engineering Practice* 11(10): 1099 – 1111.

[15] Xia, F. & Sun, Y. [2008]. *Control and Scheduling Codesign. Flexible Resource Management in Real-Time Control Systems*, Springer.

Chapter 4

On New High Order Iterative Schemes for Solving Initial Value Problems in Epidemiology

Sandile Motsa and Stanford Shateyi

Additional information is available at the end of the chapter

http://dx.doi.org/10.5772/48264

1. Introduction

Most problems arising from mathematical epidemiology are often described in terms of differential equations. However, it is often very difficult to obtain closed form solutions of such equations, especially those that are nonlinear. In most cases, attempts are made to obtain only approximate or numerical solutions. In this work, we revisit the SIR epidemic model with constant vaccination strategy that was considered in [11], where the Adomian decomposition method was used to solve the governing system of nonlinear initial value differential equations.

In this work we develop new accurate iterative schemes which are based on extending Taylor series based linearization method to obtain accurate and fast converging sequence of hybrid iteration schemes. At first order, the hybrid iteration scheme reduces to quasilinearization method (QLM) which was originally developed in [1]. More recently Mandelzweig and his co-workers [8–10] have extended the application of the QLM to a wide variety of nonlinear BVPs and established that the method converges quadratically. In this work we demonstrate that the proposed hybrid iteration schemes are more accurate and converge faster than the QLM approach.

To implement the method we consider the SIR model that describes the temporal dynamics of a childhood disease in the presence of a preventive vaccine. In SIR models the population is assumed to be divided into the standard three classes namely, the susceptibles (S), who can catch the infection but are so far uninfected, the infectives (I), those who have the disease and can transmit it to the susceptibles, and the removed (R), who have either died or who have recovered and are therefore immune.

The governing equations for the problem are described [11] by

$$\frac{dS}{dt} = (1-P)\pi N - \beta\frac{SI}{N} - \mu S, \tag{1}$$

$$\frac{dI}{dt} = \beta\frac{SI}{N} - (\kappa+\mu)I, \tag{2}$$

$$\frac{dR}{dt} = P\pi N + \kappa I - \mu R, \tag{3}$$

where $S(t)$, $I(t)$ and $R(t)$ denote the susceptibles, infectives and the removed classes respectively.

The total population is denoted by $N = S + I + R$, μ is the death rate, P is the fraction of citizens vaccinated at birth each year, β is the average contact rate, π is the constant birth rate, and κ is the rate at which an individual recovers from the disease and enters the removed group which also contains vaccinated individuals. Equations (1 - 3) are solved using the new hybrid iteration schemes and the results are compared with results from the Runge-Kutta MATLAB in-built solver `ode45`.

2. Numerical solution

To simplify the formulation of the solution, equations (1) - (3) are scaled by dividing by N. We define new variables $z_1 = S/N$, $z_2 = I/N$ and $z_3 = R/N$. This leads to $z_1 + z_2 + z_3 = 1$ and if we assume that $\pi = \mu$, the scaled new system becomes

$$z_1'(t) = (1-P)\pi - \beta z_1(t)z_2(t) - \pi z_1(t), \quad z_1(0) = s_0, \tag{4}$$
$$z_2'(t) = \beta z_1(t)z_2(t) - (\pi + \kappa)z_2(t), \qquad z_2(0) = i_0, \tag{5}$$

where s_0 and i_0 are given constants. The solution for $z_3(t)$ can be obtained from $z_3 = 1 - z_1 - z_2$.

Previous studies [4–7, 12] have shown that the long term behaviour of systems like (4) - (5) can be classified into two categories namely, endemic or eradication. From the long term behaviour of $z_1(t)$ and $z_2(t)$ it holds that the solution asymptotically approaches a disease free equilibrium (DFE) or the endemic equilibrium (EE) where

$$\lim_{t\to+\infty}(z_1(t), z_2(t)) = \text{DFE} = (1-P, 0), \tag{6}$$

$$\lim_{t\to+\infty}(z_1(t), z_2(t)) = \text{EE} = \left(\frac{1-P}{R_v}, \frac{\pi}{\beta}(R_v - 1)\right). \tag{7}$$

Here R_v, the vaccination reproduction number, is the threshold that determines the stability of the equilibria and is defined by

$$R_v = \frac{\beta(1-P)}{\gamma + \pi}. \tag{8}$$

It was shown in [11] that the DFE is locally stable if $R_v < 1$ and the EE is locally stable provided $1 < R_v \leq 4(\kappa + \pi)/\pi$. In this work, we use develop new iteration schemes to solve the system (4) - (5) using parameters that yield both the DFE and EE.

3. Method of solution

To develop the method of solution, we assume that the true solution of (4 - 5) is $z_{s,\alpha}$ $(s = 1, 2)$ and $z_{s,\gamma}$ are the initial approximations. We introduce the following coupled system,

$$L_j z_j + f_j(z_{1,\gamma}, z_{2,\gamma}) + \sum_{s=1}^{2}(z_s - z_{s,\gamma})\frac{\partial f_j}{\partial z_s}(z_{1,\gamma}, z_{2,\gamma}) + g_j(z_1, z_2) = \Psi_j, \tag{9}$$

$$g_j(z_1, z_2) = f_j(z_1, z_2) - f_j(z_{1,\gamma}, z_{2,\gamma}) - \sum_{s=1}^{2}(z_s - z_{s,\gamma})\frac{\partial f_j}{\partial z_s}(z_{1,\gamma}, z_{2,\gamma}), \tag{10}$$

where

$$L_1 z_1 = z_1' + \pi z_1, \quad L_2 z_2 = z_2' + (\pi + \kappa) z_2, \tag{11}$$

$$f_1(z_1, z_2) = \beta z_1 z_2, \quad f_2(z_1, z_2) = -\beta z_1 z_2, \quad \Psi_1 = (1 - P)\pi, \quad \Psi_2 = 0. \tag{12}$$

This idea of introducing the coupled equations of the form (9-10) have previously been used in [3] the construction of Newton-like iteration formulae for the computation of the solutions of nonlinear equations of the form $f(x) = 0$.

We write equation (9) as

$$L_j z_j + \sum_{s=1}^{2} z_s \frac{\partial f_j}{\partial z_s}(z_{1,\gamma}, z_{2,\gamma}) + g_j(z_1, z_2) = \Phi_j(z_{1,\gamma}, z_{2,\gamma}), \tag{13}$$

where

$$\Phi_j(z_{1,\gamma}, z_{2,\gamma}) = \Psi_j + \sum_{s=1}^{2} z_{s,\gamma} \frac{\partial f_j}{\partial z_s}(z_{1,\gamma}, z_{2,\gamma}) - f_j(z_{1,\gamma}, z_{2,\gamma}). \tag{14}$$

We use the quasilinearization method (QLM) of Bellman and Kalaba [1] to solve equation (13). The QLM determines the $(i+1)$th iterative approximation $z_{j,i+1}$ as the solution of the differential equation

$$L_j z_{j,i+1} + \sum_{s=1}^{2} z_{s,i+1} \frac{\partial f_j}{\partial z_s}(z_{1,\gamma}, z_{2,\gamma}) + g_j(z_{1,i}, z_{2,i}) + \sum_{s=1}^{2}(z_{s,i+1} - z_{s,i})\frac{\partial g_j}{\partial z_s}(z_{1,i}, z_{2,i}) = \Phi_j(z_{1,\gamma}, z_{2,\gamma}), \tag{15}$$

which can be written as

$$L_j z_{j,i+1} + \sum_{s=1}^{2} \left[\frac{\partial f_j}{\partial z_s}(z_{1,\gamma}, z_{2,\gamma}) + \frac{\partial g_j}{\partial z_s}(z_{1,i}, z_{2,i})\right] z_{s,i+1} = \tag{16}$$

$$\sum_{s=1}^{2} z_{s,i} \frac{\partial g_j}{\partial z_s}(z_{1,i}, z_{2,i}) - g_j(z_{1,i}, z_{2,i}) + \Phi_j(z_{1,\gamma}, z_{2,\gamma}),$$

subject to

$$z_{1,i+1} = s_0, \qquad z_{2,i+1} = i_0. \tag{17}$$

We assume that $z_{j,0}$ is obtained as a solution of the linear part of equation (13) given by

$$L_j z_{j,0} + \sum_{s=1}^{2} z_{s,0} \frac{\partial f_j}{\partial z_s}(z_{1,\gamma}, z_{2,\gamma}) = \Phi_j(z_{1,\gamma}, z_{2,\gamma}), \tag{18}$$

which yields the iteration scheme

$$L_j z_{j,r+1} + \sum_{s=1}^{2} z_{s,r+1} \frac{\partial f_j}{\partial z_s}(z_{1,r}, z_{2,r}) = \Phi_j(z_{1,r}, z_{2,r}). \tag{19}$$

We note that equation (19) is the standard QLM iteration scheme for solving (4 - 5).

When $i = 0$ in (16) we can approximate z_j as

$$z_j \approx z_{j,1}. \tag{20}$$

Thus, setting $i = 0$ in (16) we obtain

$$L_j z_{j,1} + \sum_{s=1}^{2} \left[\frac{\partial f_j}{\partial z_s}(z_{1,\gamma}, z_{2,\gamma}) + \frac{\partial g_j}{\partial z_s}(z_{1,0}, z_{2,0}) \right] z_{s,1} = \sum_{s=1}^{2} z_{s,0} \frac{\partial g_j}{\partial z_s}(z_{1,0}, z_{2,0})$$
$$-g_j(z_{1,0}, z_{2,0}) + \Phi_j(z_{1,\gamma}, z_{2,\gamma}), \tag{21}$$

which yields the iteration scheme

$$L_j z_{j,r+1} + \sum_{s=1}^{2} \left[\frac{\partial f_j}{\partial z_s}(z_{1,r}, z_{2,r}) + \frac{\partial g_j}{\partial z_s}(z^{(0)}_{1,r+1}, z^{(0)}_{2,r+1}) \right] z_{s,r+1} = \sum_{s=1}^{2} z^{(0)}_{s,r+1} \frac{\partial g_j}{\partial z_s}(z^{(0)}_{1,r+1}, z^{(0)}_{2,r+1})$$
$$-g_j(z^{(0)}_{1,r+1}, z^{(0)}_{2,r+1}) + \Phi_j(z_{1,r}, z_{2,r}), \tag{22}$$

where $z^{(0)}_{j,r+1}$ is the solution of

$$L_j z^{(0)}_{j,r+1} + \sum_{s=1}^{2} z^{(0)}_{s,r+1} \frac{\partial f_j}{\partial z_s}(z_{1,r}, z_{2,r}) = \Phi_j(z_{1,r}, z_{2,r}). \tag{23}$$

The general iteration scheme obtained by setting $i = m$ ($m \geq 2$) in equation (16), hereinafter referred to as scheme-m is

$$L_j z_{j,r+1} + \sum_{s=1}^{2} \left[\frac{\partial f_j}{\partial z_s}(z_{1,r}, z_{2,r}) + \frac{\partial g_j}{\partial z_s}(z^{(m-1)}_{1,r+1}, z^{(m-1)}_{2,r+1}) \right] z_{s,r+1} = \sum_{s=1}^{2} z^{(m-1)}_{s,r+1} \frac{\partial g_j}{\partial z_s}(z^{(m-1)}_{1,r+1}, z^{(m-1)}_{2,r+1})$$
$$-g_j(z^{(m-1)}_{1,r+1}, z^{(m-1)}_{2,r+1}) + \Phi_j(z_{1,r}, z_{2,r}), \tag{24}$$

where $z^{(m-1)}_{j,r+1}$ is obtained as the solution of

$$L_j z^{(m-1)}_{j,r+1} + \sum_{s=1}^{2} \left[\frac{\partial f_j}{\partial z_s}(z_{1,r}, z_{2,r}) + \frac{\partial g_j}{\partial z_s}(z^{(m-2)}_{1,r+1}, z^{(m-2)}_{2,r+1}) \right] z^{(m-1)}_{s,r+1} = \sum_{s=1}^{2} z^{(m-2)}_{s,r+1} \frac{\partial g_j}{\partial z_s}(z^{(m-2)}_{1,r+1}, z^{(m-2)}_{2,r+1})$$
$$-g_j(z^{(m-2)}_{1,r+1}, z^{(m-2)}_{2,r+1}) + \Phi_j(z_{1,r}, z_{2,r}). \tag{25}$$

The initial approximation for solving the iteration algorithms, scheme-m is obtained by solving the linear part of the governing equations (4 - 5). This gives

$$z_{1,0} = (1 - P)(1 - e^{-\pi t}) + s_0 e^{-\pi t}, \qquad z_{2,0} = i_0 e^{-(\pi+\kappa)t}. \tag{26}$$

The iteration schemes (19),(24 - 25) can be solved numerically using standard methods such as finite difference, finite elements, spline collocation methods,etc. In this study we use the Chebyshev spectral collocation method to solve the iteration schemes. For brevity, we omit the details of the spectral methods, and refer interested readers to ([2, 13]). Before applying the spectral method, it is convenient to transform the domain on which the governing equation is defined to the interval [-1,1] on which the spectral method can be implemented. We use the transformation $t = t_F(\tau+1)/2$ to map the interval $[0, t_F]$ to [-1,1], where t_F is a finite time. The basic idea behind the spectral collocation method is the introduction of a differentiation matrix D which is used to approximate the derivatives of the unknown variables z at the collocation points as the matrix vector product

$$\frac{dz}{dt} = \sum_{k=0}^{N} \mathbf{D}_{jk} z(\tau_k) = \mathbf{D}\mathbf{Z}, \qquad j = 0, 1, \ldots, N, \tag{27}$$

where $N+1$ is the number of collocation points (grid points), $\mathbf{D} = 2D/t_F$, and $\mathbf{Z} = [z(\tau_0), z(\tau_1), \ldots, z(\tau_N)]^T$ is the vector function at the collocation points τ_j.

Applying the Chebyshev spectral method to (19), for instance, gives

$$\left[\begin{array}{c|c} \mathbf{D} + \pi I + \mathbf{a}_{11} & \mathbf{a}_{12} \\ \hline \mathbf{a}_{21} & \mathbf{D} + (\pi+\kappa) I + \mathbf{a}_{22} \end{array}\right] \left[\begin{array}{c} z_{1,r+1}(\tau_0) \\ z_{1,r+1}(\tau_1) \\ \vdots \\ z_{1,r+1}(\tau_N) \\ \hline z_{2,r+1}(\tau_0) \\ z_{2,r+1}(\tau_1) \\ \vdots \\ z_{2,r+1}(\tau_N) \end{array}\right] = \left[\begin{array}{c} \Phi_{1,r+1}(\tau_0) \\ \Phi_{1,r+1}(\tau_1) \\ \vdots \\ \Phi_{1,r+1}(\tau_N) \\ \hline \Phi_{2,r+1}(\tau_0) \\ \Phi_{2,r+1}(\tau_1) \\ \vdots \\ \Phi_{2,r+1}(\tau_N) \end{array}\right], \tag{28}$$

where

$$\mathbf{a}_{ji} = \frac{\partial f_i}{\partial z_i} \tag{29}$$

and I is an $(N+1) \times (N+1)$ identity matrix.

4. Results and discussion

In this section we present the results of solving the governing equations (4-5) using the iteration scheme-m. For illustration purposes we present the results for $m = 0, 1, 2$ to illustrate the effect of increasing m in the accuracy and convergence of the iteration schemes. The number of collocations points in all the results presented here is $N = 40$. In order to assess the accuracy of the proposed method, the present numerical results were compared against results generated using the MATLAB initial value solver `ode45`. In the numerical simulations presented here, following [11], the governing parameters were carefully selected in order to represent the cases which give rise to both the disease free equilibrium (DFE) and endemic equilibrium (EE). We consider the following cases

1. Case 1: $s_0 = 1, \;\; i_0 = 0, \;\; \beta = 0.8, \;\; \kappa = 0.03, \;\; \pi = 0.4, \;\; P = 0.9.$
   In this case we observe that $R_v = 0.186 < 1$, hence we expect the disease to be eradicated from the population after some time.
2. Case 2: $s_0 = 0.8, \;\; i_0 = 0.2 \;\; \beta = 0.8, \;\; \kappa = 0.03, \;\; \pi = 0.4, \;\; P = 0.9.$
   In this case we observe that $R_v = 0.186 < 1$ and as expected, using these parameters, the disease should be eradicated as $t \to \infty$.

3. Case 3: $s_0 = 0.8, \;\; i_0 = 0.2 \;\; \beta = 0.8, \;\; \kappa = 0.03, \;\; \pi = 0.4, \;\; P = 0.$
   In this case$R_v = 1.86 > 1$ which leads to the endemic equilibrium (no disease eradication).
4. Case 4: $s_0 = 0.8, \;\; i_0 = 0.2 \;\; \beta = 0.8, \;\; \kappa = 0.03, \;\; \pi = 0.4, \;\; P = 0.3.$
   In this case $R_v = 1.32 > 1$ which leads to the endemic equilibrium (no disease eradication).

The results for Case 1 are shown on Figs. 1 - 2. In this case, the initial guess and the first few iterations match the numerical solution all the iterative schemes in the plots of $s(t), r(t)$. We observe that $s(t)$ decreases monotonically with time while $r(t)$ increases with time. The graph of the profile for $i(t)$ is not shown because $i(t) = 0$ in this particular case.

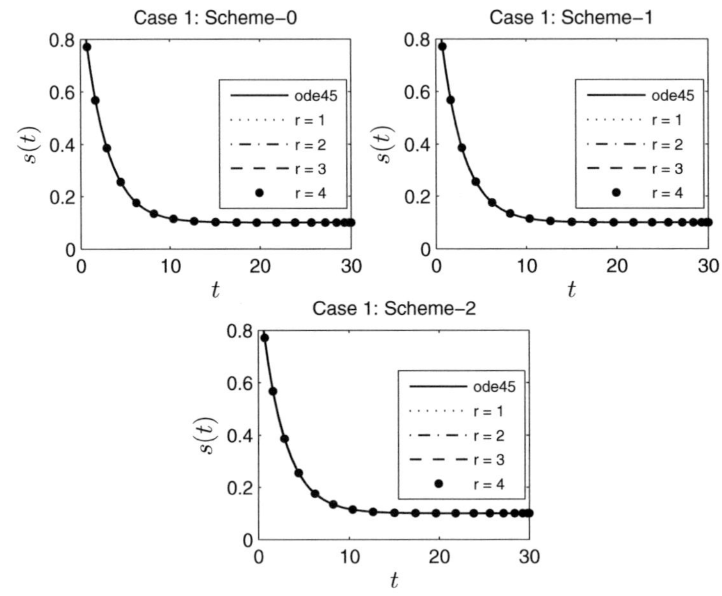

Figure 1. Case 1: Comparison of the numerical solution of the population fractions $s(t)$ against the results from the iteration schemes-0, 1 and 2

Figs. 3 - 5 show the numerical approximation of the profiles of the different classes for Case 2. Again, all the iterative schemes rapidly converge to the numerical solution. The population of the susceptibles decreases with time and that of the removed (those recovered with immunity) increases with time. The infected population initially increases and reaches a maximum, then gradually decreases to zero as $t \to \infty$.

Figs. 6 - 8 show the numerical approximation of the profiles of the different classes for Case 3. It can be noted from the graphs that the Scheme-2 converges fastest towards the numerical results. Only 10 iterations are required for full convergence in Scheme-2 compared to 14 iterations in Scheme-1 and 28 iterations in Scheme-1.

Figs. 8 - 11 shows the variation all the population groups with time for Case 4. Again, we observe that Scheme-2 converges fastest towards the numerical results. Only 5 iterations are required for full convergence in Scheme-2 compared to 6 iterations in Scheme-1 and 12 iterations in Scheme-1.

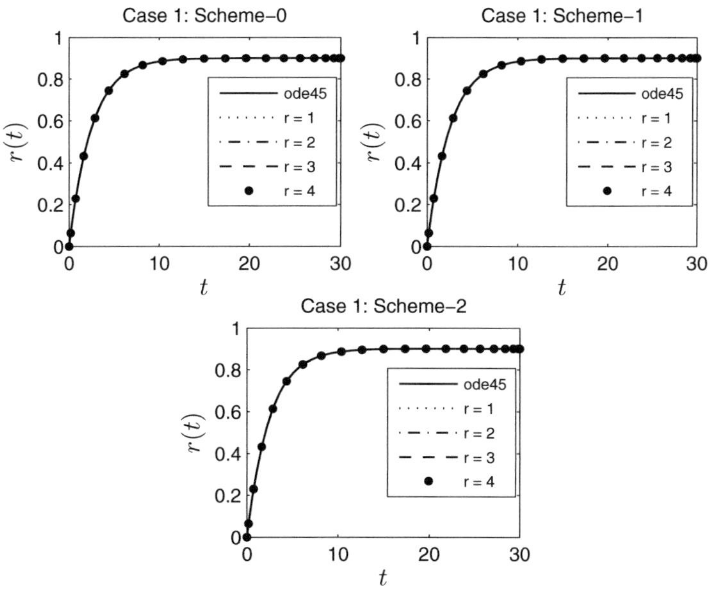

Figure 2. Case 1: Comparison of the numerical solution of the population fractions $r(t)$ against the results from the iteration schemes-0, 1 and 2

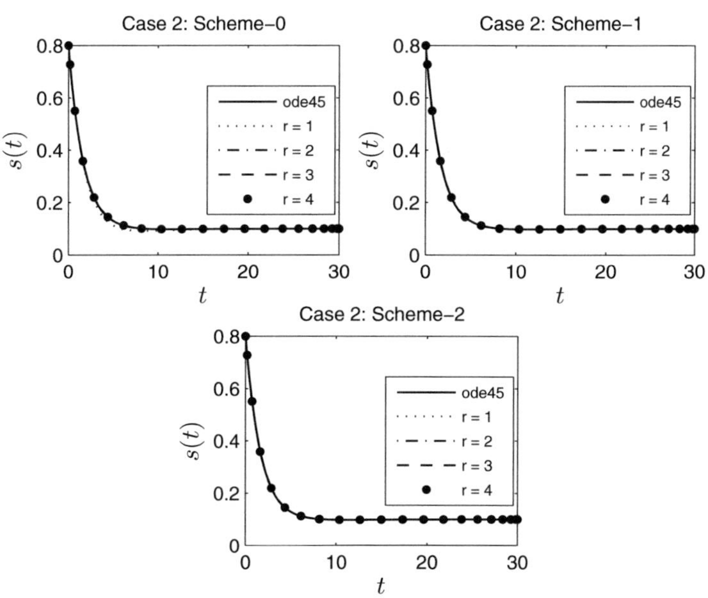

Figure 3. Case 2: Comparison of the numerical solution of the population fractions $s(t)$ against the results from the iteration schemes-0, 1 and 2

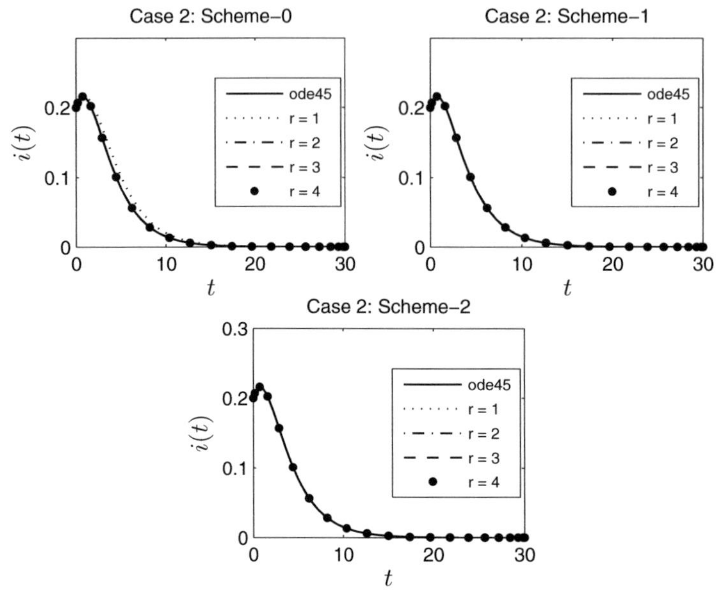

Figure 4. Case 2: Comparison of the numerical solution of the population fractions $i(t)$ against the results from the iteration schemes-0, 1 and 2

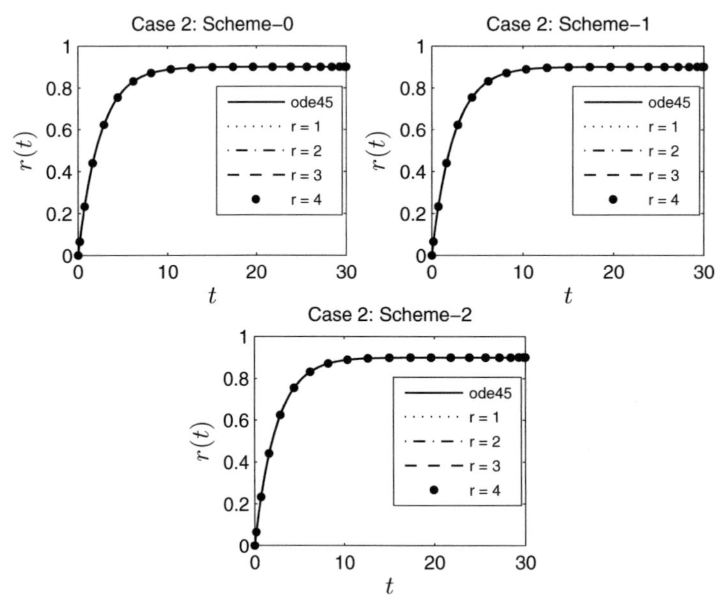

Figure 5. Case 2: Comparison of the numerical solution of the population fractions $r(t)$ against the results from the iteration schemes-0, 1 and 2

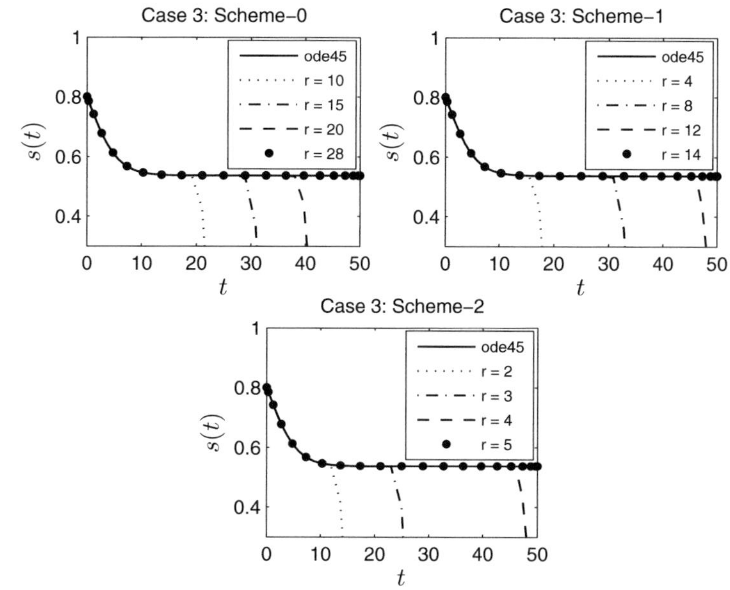

Figure 6. Case 3: Comparison of the numerical solution of the population fractions $s(t)$ against the results from the iteration schemes-0, 1 and 2

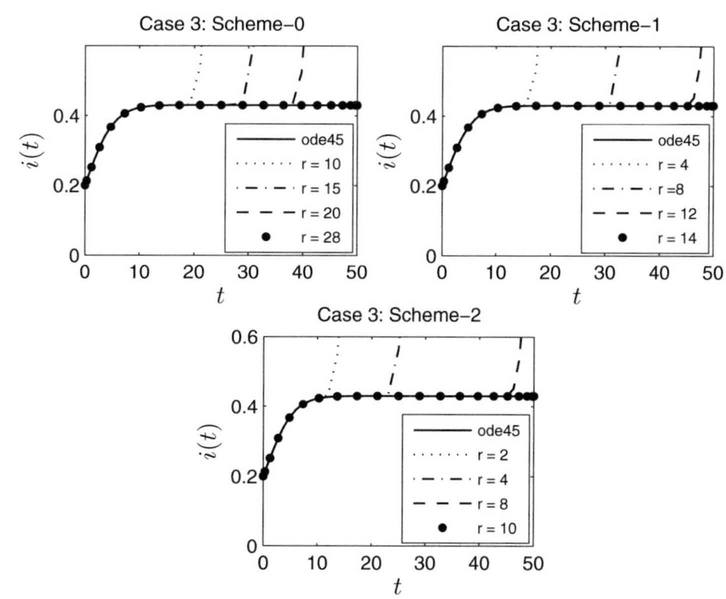

Figure 7. Case 3: Comparison of the numerical solution of the population fractions $i(t)$ against the results from the iteration schemes-0, 1 and 2

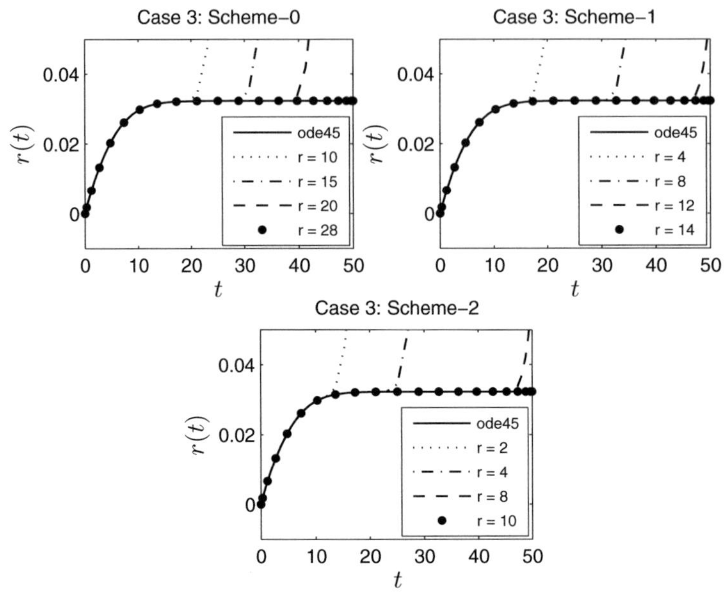

Figure 8. Case 3: Comparison of the numerical solution of the population fractions $r(t)$ against the results from the iteration schemes-0, 1 and 2

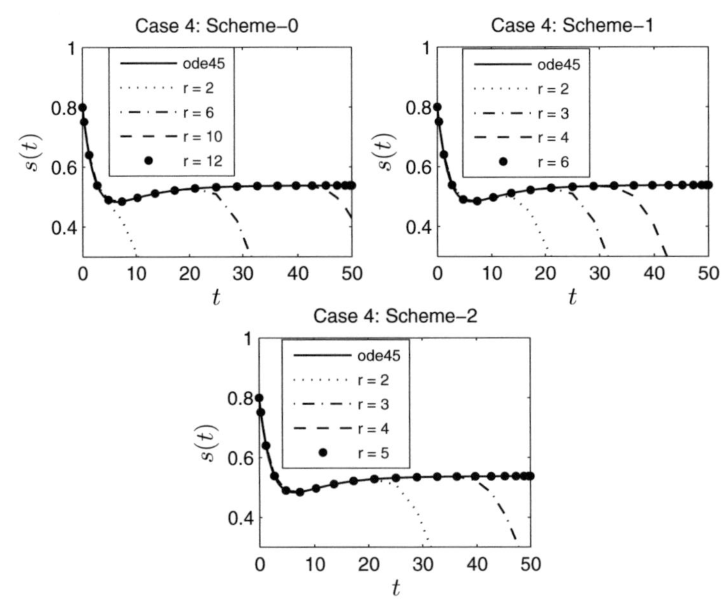

Figure 9. Case 4: Comparison of the numerical solution of the population fractions $s(t)$ against the results from the iteration schemes-0, 1 and 2

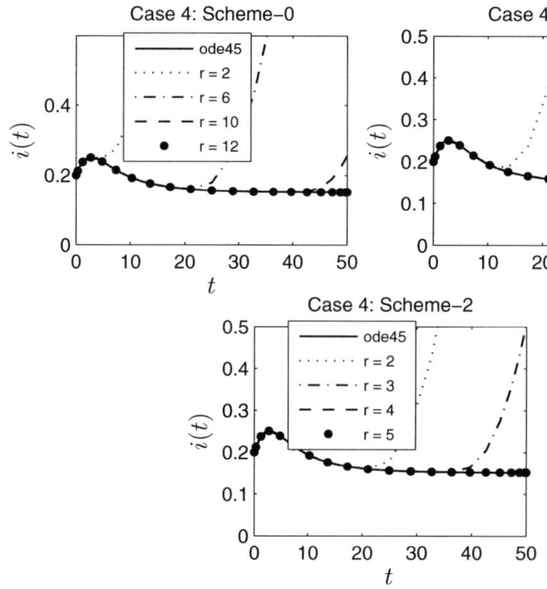

Figure 10. Case 4: Comparison of the numerical solution of the population fractions $i(t)$ against the results from the iteration schemes-0, 1 and 2

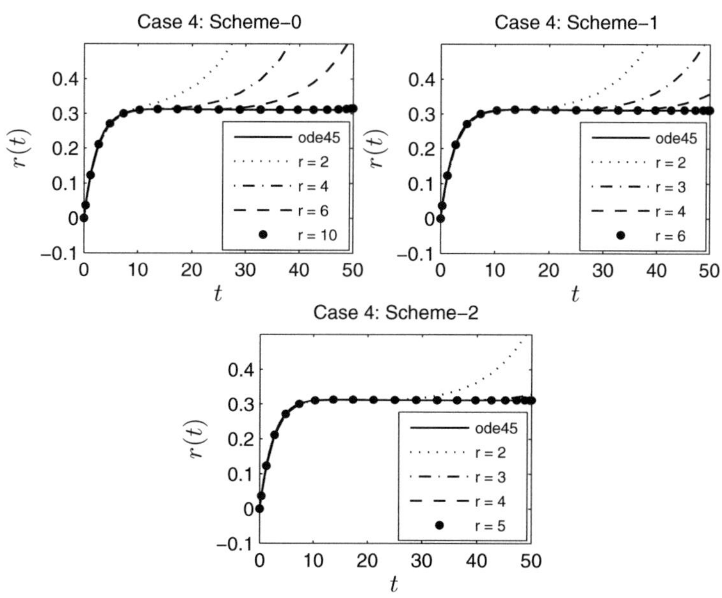

Figure 11. Case 4: Comparison of the numerical solution of the population fractions $r(t)$ against the results from the iteration schemes-0, 1 and 2

5. Conclusion

In this work, a sequence of new iteration schemes for solving nonlinear differential equations is used to solve the SIR epidemic model with constant vaccination strategy. The proposed iteration schemes are derived as an extension to the quasi-linearization method to obtain hybrid iteration schemes which converge very rapidly. The accuracy and validity of the proposed schemes is confirmed by comparing with the `ode45` MATLAB routine for solving initial value problems. It is hoped that the proposed method of solution will spawn further interest in computational analysis of differential equations in epidemiology and other areas of science.

Author details

Sandile Sydney Motsa
School of Mathematics, Computer Science and Statistics, University of KwaZulu Natal, Private Bag X01, Scottsville 3209, Pietermaritzburg, South Africa

Stanford Shateyi
University of Venda, Department of Mathematics, Private Bag X5050, Thohoyandou 0950, South Africa

6. References

[1] R.E. Bellman and R.E. Kalaba, (1965) Quasilinearization and Nonlinear Boundary-Value Problems, Elsevier, New York.
[2] C. Canuto, M.Y. Hussaini, A. Quarteroni, and T.A. Zang (1988). Spectral Methods in Fluid Dynamics, Springer-Verlag, Berlin.
[3] C. Chun, (2005) Iterative methods: Improving Newton's method by the Decomposition method, Computers and Mathematics with Applications, Vol 50, pg 1559–1568.
[4] H. Khan, R.N. Mohapatra, K.Vajravelu, and S.J. Liao, Explicit series solution of SIR and SIS epidemic models, Appl. Math.Comput, doi:10.1016/j.amc.2009.05.051(2009).
[5] W.O. Kermack and A.G. McKendrick,(1927) Contribution to the mathematical theory of epidemics, Proc. Roy. Soc, A115:700-721.
[6] H. W. Hethcote, (2000) The mathematics of infectious diseases, SIAM Review, 42(4):599–653.
[7] R. Casagrandi, L. Bolzoni, S.A. Levin. V. Andreasen, (2006) The SIRC model and influenza A, Math. BioSc. Vol 200, pg 152–169.
[8] R. Krivec, V.B. Mandelzweig, (2001) Numerical investigation of quasilinearization method in quantum mechanics, Computer Physics Communications Vol 138, pg 69–79
[9] V.B. Mandelzweig, F. Tabakin, (2001) Quasilinearization approach to nonlinear problems in physics with application to nonlinear ODEs, Computer Physics Communications, Vol 141, pg 268–281
[10] V. B. Mandelzweig, (2005) Quasilinearization Method: Nonperturbative Approach to Physical Problems, Physics of Atomic Nuclei, Vol 68(7) pg 1227–1258.
[11] O. D. Makinde, (2007) Adomian decomposition approach to a SIR epidemic model with constant vaccination strategy, Appl. Math.Comput, Vol 184, pg 842-848.
[12] Murray, J.D. Mathematical Biology, Springer-Verlag, 3rd.ed., 2001.
[13] Trefethen,L.N., (2000) Spectral Methods in MATLAB, SIAM.

Chapter 5

Charge Separation and Electric Field at a Cylindrical Plasma Edge

Magdi Shoucri

Additional information is available at the end of the chapter

http://dx.doi.org/10.5772/48353

1. Introduction

There are number of physical situations where plasmas neutrality breaks down through boundary layers called plasma sheaths, which are either free or in contact with a wall. The plasma sheaths transition problems are at the heart of an industrial revolution whose theme is the design of matter on the molecular scale.The study of the charge separation at a plasma edge requires generally the solution of the kinetic equations of plasmas which, for a collisionless plasma, usually reduce to the well-known Vlasov equation. Some examples for the solution of the Vlasov equation for sheaths transition problems have been presented in Shoucri, 2008a, 2009a. A problem of interest is the problem involving the generation of radial electric fields and poloidal flows to achieve radial force balance at a steep density gradient in the presence of an external magnetic field. This problem is of great importance in the steep density gradients pedestal of the high confinement mode (H-mode) in tokamaks, since it largely affects the edge physics of the H-mode. In the present work, we shall study the problem of the generation of a charge separation and the associated electric field at the edge of a cylindrical plasma column, in the presence of an external magnetic field directed along the cylinder axis. In previous publications on this problem (Shoucri *et al.*, 2003, 2004, 2008b, 2009b), we have considered the case where the electrons were frozen by the magnetic field lines, with a constant density profile which changes rapidly along the gradient over an ion orbit size. Along the gradient the electrons bound by the magnetic field cannot move across this field to exactly compensate the ion charge which results from the finite ions' gyroradius. This effect is especially important for large values of the ratio ρ_i / λ_{De}, where ρ_i is the ions' gyroradius and λ_{De} is the Debye length. Accurate calculation of the charge separation is important for the accurate calculation of the self-consistent electric field. This requires also an accurate calculation of the exact ion orbits using a kinetic equation. In the present work, we use an Eulerian Vlasov code to study the evolution of the ion distribution function for the problem of the charge separation at the edge of a cylindrical plasma, in the presence of an external magnetic field directed along the cylinder axis. Eulerian codes have the advantage of a very low noise level and make it possible to measure accurately a very small charge separation (Shoucri *et al.*, 2003, Shoucri *et al.*, 2004 & Shoucri, 2009a,b), and allows accurate results in the low density regions of the phase-space.

It was pointed out in the analysis of H-mode power threshold in a tokamak by Groebner *et al.*, 2001, that the changes in the electron density n_e and ∇n_e in the transition to H-mode are small, and changes in T_e are barely perceptible in the data. Electrons and ions have a density profile which varies rapidly along the gradient over an ion orbit size. In previous publications (Shoucri *et al.*, 2003, 2004, Shoucri, 2002, 2008a,b, 2009a,b) the electrons density and temperature profiles were kept constant. In the present work we will allow the electrons to move, and it will be sufficient for the purpose of our study to describe the motion of the electrons, having a small gyroradius, by a guiding center equation (Shoucri *et al.*, 1997). This allows a more accurate description of the contribution of the electrons, with respect to the approximation previously used in Shoucri *et al.*, 2003, 2004, 2009a, where the profile of the electrons was assumed constant in time. The electrons motion across the magnetic field in the gradient region is limited by the guiding center equation, and the magnetized electrons cannot move sufficiently across the magnetic field to compensate the charge separation which results from the ions motion due to the finite ion orbits. To determine this charge separation at the plasma edge along the gradient, it is important to calculate the ion orbits accurately by using an Eulerian Vlasov code. The larger the ions' gyroradius, the bigger the charge separation and the self-consistent electric field at the edge. (Hence the important role played by even small fractions of impurity ions, because of their large gyroradii, in enhancing the electric field at the plasma edge).

In full toroidal geometry, there are "neoclassical" effects which can play a role in this problem, such as the neoclassical enhancement of the classical ion polarization drift, or the neoclassical damping of poloidal flows (Stix, 1973, Hirshman 1978, Waltz *et. al.*, 1999). We focus for simplicity in the present work on a cylindrical geometry for the problem of the generation of an electric field and poloidal flow at a plasma edge due to the finite ions' gyroradius, when the external magnetic field is applied along the axis of the cylinder. The solution we present is a two-dimensional (2D) solution in a cylindrical geometry, with the external magnetic field assumed uniform along its axis. We compare the radial electric field calculated along the gradient with the macroscopic values calculated from the kinetic code for the gradient of the ion pressure in the radial direction, and we find that this quantity balances the radial electric field fairly well, a result similar to what has been presented in one-dimensional geometry (Shoucri, 2002, Shoucri *et al.* 2003, 2004). The contribution of the Lorentz force term along the gradient is negligible. For the parameters we use in the present work, the solution allows for a small value of E_θ to exist, especially on the high field side of the cylinder as it will be discussed below, which causes a small oscillation in the radial direction.

As mentioned above, the ions are described by a kinetic Vlasov equation and the electrons are described by a guiding center equation. These equations are solved numerically using a method of characteristics. There have been important advances in the last few decades in the domain of the numerical solution of hyperbolic type partial differential equations using the method of characteristics. The application of the method of characteristics for the numerical solution of the kinetic equations of plasmas and for the guiding center equations has been recently discussed in several publication (see for instance Shoucri, 2008a,c, 2009a). These methods are Eulerian methods which use a computational mesh to discretize the equations on a fixed grid, and have been successfully applied to different important problems in plasma physics involving kinetic equations, such as laser-plasma interaction (Ghizzo *et al.*, 1990, 1992, Strozzi *et al.*, 2006, Shoucri, 2008d), the calculation of an electric field at a plasma edge (Shoucri, 2002, 2008b, 2009b, Shoucri *et al.*, 2000, 2003, 2004), the applications of gyro-kinetic codes to study edge physics problems in plasmas (Manfredi *et al.*, 1996, Shoucri, 2001, Shoucri *et al.*, 2005, Pohn & Shoucri, 2008) and to collisional plasmas (Batishchev *et al.*, 1999). These methods present the great advantage of having a low noise level, and allow accurate results in the low density regions of the phase-space (Shoucri, 2008c). In the applications presented (Shoucri, 2008a,c, 2009a), the computation was usually done on a fixed grid, so no dynamical grid adjustment was necessary, and interpolation was restricted to the use of a cubic spline, which compared favourably with other methods (see, for instance, Pohn *et al.*, 2005), so altogether the method was accurate and remained relatively simple. Interpolation in several dimensions using a tensor product of cubic *B*-splines has been also successfully applied (Sonnendrücker *et al.*, 1999, Shoucri, 2008a, 2009a, 2011). The method of characteristics has been also successfully applied in fluids to problems having shock wave solution (Shoucri & Shoucri, 2007). Large Courant-Frederichs-Levy (CFL) computation parameter is possible, and therefore the time-step numerical limitation by large velocities can be removed, if the physics makes it possible. A more complete study on splines can be found in the book of Ahlberg *et al.*, 1967, and an important theoretical study on the method of characteristics can be found, for instance, in the book of Abbott, 1966. More applications to plasma physics problems can be found in the several references we have cited.

2. The relevant equations and the numerical method

We consider the cylindrical coordinate system (r,θ,z). The plasma is uniform in the z direction. The radial direction in the cylindrical plasma is normal to a vessel surface which is located at $r = r_{max}=R$. The constant magnetic field is in the z direction which represents the toroidal direction, and θ is the poloidal direction. The constant magnetic field in the z direction is given by:

$$\vec{B} = \frac{B_0 \vec{e}_z}{1+\varepsilon\cos\theta} \tag{1}$$

where B_0 is the magnetic field along the axis of the cylinder at $\theta = \pi/2$, and $\varepsilon = r / R_{maj}$ where R_{maj} is the major radius of the tokamak. We assume that at $r = r_{max}=R$ we have R / R_{maj} =0.2. In this case we can also write $\varepsilon = r / R_{maj} = 0.2r / R$. We consider a deuterium plasma,

$m_i / m_e = 2\text{x}1836$. The ions are described by the normalized 2D Vlasov equation for the ions distribution function $f_i(r,\theta,v_r,v_\theta,t)$:

$$\frac{\partial f_i}{\partial t} + v_r \frac{\partial f_i}{\partial r} + \frac{v_\theta}{r}\frac{\partial f_i}{\partial \theta} + \left(E_r + \omega_{ci} v_\theta + \frac{v_\theta^2}{r} \right) \frac{\partial f_i}{\partial v_r} + \left(E_\theta - \omega_{ci} v_r - \frac{v_r v_\theta}{r} \right) \frac{\partial f_i}{\partial v_\theta} = 0 \tag{2}$$

where from Eq.(1) the ion cyclotron frequency $\omega_{ci} = \omega_{ci0} / (1 + \varepsilon \cos\theta)$. The electrons are described by the normalized 2D guiding-center equation:

$$\frac{\partial n_e}{\partial t} + \nabla . \vec{V}_d n_e = 0 \tag{3}$$

where the drift velocity $\vec{V}_d = \vec{E} \text{x} \vec{B} / B^2$. Equation (3) can be developed in our 2D system to give the following equation:

$$\frac{\partial n_e}{\partial t} + V_{dr} \frac{\partial n_e}{\partial r} + V_{d\theta} \frac{\partial n_e}{\partial \theta} = -n_e E_\theta \frac{\partial}{\partial r} \frac{1+\varepsilon\cos\theta}{\omega_{ci0}} + n_e E_r \frac{1}{r}\frac{\partial}{\partial \theta} \frac{1+\varepsilon\cos\theta}{\omega_{ci0}} \tag{4}$$

where $V_{dr} = E_\theta \dfrac{1+\varepsilon\cos\theta}{\omega_{ci0}}$; $V_{d\theta} = -\dfrac{E_r}{r}\dfrac{1+\varepsilon\cos\theta}{\omega_{ci0}}$

This system is coupled to Poisson's equation:

$$\frac{1}{r}\frac{\partial}{\partial r}(r \frac{\partial \phi}{\partial r}) + \frac{1}{r^2}\frac{\partial^2 \phi}{\partial \theta^2} = -(n_i - n_e);\ E_r = -\frac{\partial \phi}{\partial r};\ E_\theta = -\frac{1}{r}\frac{\partial \phi}{\partial \theta} \tag{5}$$

Time is normalized to the inverse plasma frequency ω_{pi}^{-1}, velocity is normalized to the acoustic velocity $C_s = \sqrt{T_e / m_i}$, and length is normalized to the Debye length $\lambda_{De} = C_s / \omega_{pi}$. T_e is the electron temperature and m_i is the ion mass. The potential is normalized to T_e / e, and the electric field is normalized to $T_e / (e\lambda_{De})$, and the density is normalized to the peak initial central density. The ion cyclotron frequency ω_{ci} as previously defined is normalized to ω_{pi}. The system is solved over a length $r_L = 175$ Debye lengths in front of the vessel surface, with an initial ion distribution function for the deuterons over the domain $r = \{R - r_L, R\}$ given in our normalized units, by:

$$f_i(r,\theta,v_r,v_\theta) = n_i(r) \frac{e^{-\left(v_r^2+v_\theta^2\right)/2\,T_i}}{2\pi T_i}\ ; \tag{6}$$

$n_i(r)$ and $n_e(r)$ are the initial ion and electron density profiles respectively, with $n_e(r) = n_i(r)$ in the initially neutral system. R is the radius of the cylinder as we previously mentioned. We also use the following parameters:

$$\frac{T_i}{T_e} = 1 ; \quad \frac{\rho_i}{\lambda_{De}} = \sqrt{\frac{2T_i}{T_e}} \frac{1}{\omega_{ci0} / \omega_{pi}} = 20 \tag{7}$$

In the present calculations the parameter $\omega_{ci0} / \omega_{pi} = 0.1 / \sqrt{2}$. With the initial distribution function for the ions in Eq. (6), we have $T_{i\theta} = T_{ir} = T_i$ spatially constant, the factor $2T_i$ in Eq. (7) in the calculation of the gyroradius takes into account the fact that the perpendicular temperature is $\langle v_\perp^2 \rangle = \langle v_r^2 \rangle + \langle v_\theta^2 \rangle = \frac{2T_i}{m_i}$.

Equations (2) and (3) are solved by a method of fractional step (Yanenko, 1971), first applied for a Vlasov equation by Cheng & Knorr, 1976, and Gagné & Shoucri, 1977, coupled to a method of characteristics. For the general case where several dimensions are involved, the fractional step technique allows the reduction of the multi-dimensional equation to an equivalent set of reduced equations. To advance Eq. (2) and Eq.(3) for one time-step Δt, the splitting of the equations is applied as follows.

Step 1. We solve for $\Delta t/2$ the equations:

$$\frac{\partial f_i}{\partial t} + v_r \frac{\partial f_i}{\partial r} + \frac{v_\theta}{r} \frac{\partial f_i}{\partial \theta} = 0 \tag{8}$$

$$\frac{\partial n_e}{\partial t} + V_{dr} \frac{\partial n_e}{\partial r} + V_{d\theta} \frac{\partial n_e}{\partial \theta} = 0 \tag{9}$$

Equations (8) and (9) are solved by interpolation along their characteristics, to be described below. We then solve Poisson's equation in Eq.(5) to calculate the new electric field.

Step 2. We solve for Δt the equations:

$$\frac{\partial f_i}{\partial t} + \left(E_r + v_\theta \omega_{ci} + \frac{v_\theta^2}{r} \right) \frac{\partial f_i}{\partial v_r} + \left(E_\theta - \omega_{ci} v_r - \frac{v_r v_\theta}{r} \right) \frac{\partial f_i}{\partial v_\theta} = 0 \tag{10}$$

$$\frac{\partial n_e}{\partial t} = -n_e E_\theta \frac{\partial}{\partial r} \frac{1 + \varepsilon \cos\theta}{\omega_{ci0}} + n_e E_r \frac{1}{r} \frac{\partial}{\partial \theta} \frac{1 + \varepsilon \cos\theta}{\omega_{ci0}} \tag{11}$$

Again Eq.(10) is solved by a method of characteristics, to be described below.

Step 3. We repeat **Step1** for $\Delta t/2$, and then solve Eq.(5) to calculate the new electric field $E_r^{n+1}, E_\theta^{n+1}$.

This completes a one time-step cycle Δt.

2.1. The solution for Step 1

For the solution of Eq. (8), we first solve the characteristic equations:

$$\frac{dr}{dt} = v_r \ ; \qquad \frac{d\theta}{dt} = \frac{v_\theta}{r} \tag{12}$$

at a given (v_r, v_θ) in velocity space. The solution of Eqs (12) originating at (r_o, θ_o) at time *t*, and reaching the grid point (r, θ) at $t = t + \Delta t/2$ can be written as follows, for a half time-step $\Delta t/2$:

$$r_o = r - v_r \Delta t/2; \ \theta_o = \theta - \frac{v_\theta}{v_r} \ln \frac{r}{r - v_r \Delta t/2} \tag{13}$$

For $v_r \, \Delta t/2 \ll 1$, the second equation reduces to $\theta_o = \theta - \frac{v_\theta}{r} \Delta t/2$. Therefore the solution of Eq. (8) can be written, for half a time-step $\Delta t/2$, as follows:

$$f_i^*\left(r, \theta, v_r, v_\theta, t + \Delta t/2\right) = f_i\left(r - v_r \ \Delta t/2, \theta - \frac{v_\theta}{v_r} \ln \frac{r}{r - v_r \Delta t/2}, v_r, v_\theta, t\right) \tag{14}$$

The right hand side of Eq. (14) is calculated by interpolation using a tensor product of cubic *B*-splines, in which θ is periodic (Shoucri *et al.*, 2004, Shoucri, 2008a, 2009a). For each v_r and v_θ, we write for the interpolation function $s(r, \theta)$:

$$s(r, \theta) = \sum_{j=0}^{N_r} \sum_{k=0}^{N_\theta} \eta_{jk} B_j(r) B_k(\theta) \tag{15}$$

taking into account that θ is periodic. $B_j(r)$ and $B_k(\theta)$ are cubic splines.The cubic *B*-spline is defined as:

$$B_j(x) = \frac{1}{6h^3} \begin{cases} (x - x_j)^3 & x_j \le x < x_{j+1} \\ h^3 + 3h^2(x - x_{j+1}) + 3h(x - x_{j+1})^2 & \\ \qquad - 3(x - x_{j+1})^3 & x_{j+1} \le x < x_{j+2} \\ h^3 + 3h^2(x_{j+3} - x) + 3h(x_{j+3} - x)^2 & \\ \qquad - 3(x_{j+3} - x)^3 & x_{j+2} \le x < x_{j+3} \\ (x_{j+4} - x)^3 & x_{j+3} \le x < x_{j+4} \end{cases} \tag{16}$$

and $B_j(x) = 0$ otherwise. The grid size *h* (either Δr or $\Delta\theta$ in our notation), is assumed uniform. For the calculation of the coefficients η_{jk} of the cubic *B*-spline interpolation function $s(r, \theta)$ for periodic θ in Eq.(15) see details in Shoucri *et al.*, 2004 and Shoucri, 2008a, 2009a.

We then solve Eq.(9) for a half time-step $\Delta t/2$ along the characteristics:

$$\frac{dr}{dt} = V_{dr}(r, \theta) = E_\theta \frac{1 + \varepsilon \cos\theta}{\omega_{ci0}} \ ; \qquad \frac{d\theta}{dt} = V_{d\theta}(r, \theta) = -\frac{E_r}{r} \frac{1 + \varepsilon \cos\theta}{\omega_{ci0}} \tag{17}$$

Equations (17) are solved using an iterative process. We assume that at the time-step $t_{n+1/2} = t_n + \Delta t/2$, r is at the grid point j_r and θ is at the grid point j_θ. The following leapfrog scheme can be written for the solution of Eq.(17):

$$\frac{r_{j_r} - r(t_n)}{\Delta t/2} = V_{dr}(r^{n+1/4}, \theta^{n+1/4}) = V_{dr}\left(\frac{r_{j_r} + r(t_n)}{2}, \frac{\theta_{j_\theta} + \theta(t_n)}{2}\right) \tag{18}$$

$$\frac{\theta_{j_\theta} - \theta(t_n)}{\Delta t/2} = V_{d\theta}(r^{n+1/4}, \theta^{n+1/4}) = V_{d\theta}\left(\frac{r_{j_r} + r(t_n)}{2}, \frac{\theta_{j_\theta} + \theta(t_n)}{2}\right) \tag{19}$$

where $(r(t_n), \theta(t_n))$ is the point where the characteristic is originating at t_n (not necessarily a grid point). Put:

$$\Delta_r = \frac{r_{j_r} - r(t_n)}{2}; \; \Delta_\theta = \frac{\theta_{j_\theta} - \theta(t_n)}{2} \tag{20}$$

we can rewrite Eqs.(18,19) as follows:

$$\Delta_r = \frac{\Delta t}{4} V_{dr}(r_{j_r} - \Delta_r, \theta_{j_\theta} - \Delta_\theta) \tag{21}$$

$$\Delta_\theta = \frac{\Delta t}{4} V_{d\theta}(r_{j_r} - \Delta_r, \theta_{j_\theta} - \Delta_\theta) \tag{22}$$

which are implicit equations for $(\Delta_r, \Delta_\theta)$, and which are solved by iteration. Usually, two iterations are sufficient for convergence. We start with $(\Delta_r^0 = 0, \Delta_\theta^0 = 0)$. We get at the first iteration:

$$\Delta_r^1 = \frac{\Delta t}{4} V_{dr}(r_{j_r}, \theta_{j_\theta}) = \frac{\Delta t}{4} E_\theta(r_{j_r}, \theta_{j_\theta}) \frac{1 + \frac{r_{j_r}}{R}\cos\theta_{j_\theta}}{\omega_{ci0}} \tag{23}$$

$$\Delta_\theta^1 = \frac{\Delta t}{4} V_{d\theta}(r_{j_r}, \theta_{j_\theta}) = -\frac{\Delta t}{4} \frac{E_r(r_{j_r}, \theta_{j_\theta})}{r_{j_r}} \frac{1 + \frac{r_{j_r}}{R}\cos\theta_{j_\theta}}{\omega_{ci0}} \tag{24}$$

Second iteration:

$$\Delta_r^2 = \frac{\Delta t}{4} V_{dr}(r_{j_r} - \Delta_r^1, \theta_{j_\theta} - \Delta_\theta^1) = \frac{\Delta t}{4} E_\theta(r_{j_r} - \Delta_r^1, \theta_{j_\theta} - \Delta_\theta^1) \frac{1 + \frac{r_{j_r} - \Delta_r^1}{R}\cos(\theta_{j_\theta} - \Delta_\theta^1)}{\omega_{ci0}} \tag{25}$$

$$\Delta_\theta^2 = \frac{\Delta t}{4} V_{d\theta}(r_{j_r} - \Delta_r^1, \theta_{j_\theta} - \Delta_\theta^1) = -\frac{\Delta t}{4} \frac{E_r(r_{j_r} - \Delta_r^1, \theta_{j_\theta} - \Delta_\theta^1)}{r_{j_r} - \Delta_r^1} \frac{1 + \frac{r_{j_r} - \Delta_r^1}{R} \cos(\theta_{j_\theta} - \Delta_\theta^1)}{\omega_{ci0}} \tag{26}$$

The quantities $E_r(r_{j_r} - \Delta_r^1, \theta_{j_\theta} - \Delta_\theta^1)$ and $E_\theta(r_{j_r} - \Delta_r^1, \theta_{j_\theta} - \Delta_\theta^1)$ are calculated by a cubic *B*-spline interpolation, similar to what is described in Eq.(15). Finally to advance Eq.(9) by $\Delta t / 2$, we calculate:

$$n_e^*(r_{j_r}, \theta_{j_\theta}, t + \Delta t / 2) = n_e(r_{j_r} - 2\Delta_r^2, \theta_{j_\theta} - 2\Delta_\theta^2, t) \tag{27}$$

where the right hand side of Eq.(27) is calculated again using a cubic *B*-spline interpolation as indicated in Eq.(15).

2.2. The solution for Step 2

We go to **Step2** and solve for Δt Eqs.(10,11). We first solve the equation:

$$\frac{\partial f_i}{\partial t} + \left(E_r + \omega_{ci} \upsilon_\theta + \frac{\upsilon_\theta^2}{r} \right) \frac{\partial f_i}{\partial \upsilon_r} + \left(E_\theta - \omega_{ci} \upsilon_r - \frac{\upsilon_r \upsilon_\theta}{r} \right) \frac{\partial f_i}{\partial \upsilon_\theta} = 0 \tag{28}$$

The electric field E_θ remained small, since $E_\theta = -\frac{1}{r}\frac{\partial \phi}{\partial \theta}$, and $r \sim R$ =5000 towards the edge in our calculation.

$$\frac{dv_r}{dt} = E_r + v_\theta \omega_{ci} + \frac{v_\theta^2}{r}; \qquad \frac{dv_\theta}{dt} = E_\theta - \omega_{ci} v_r - \frac{v_r v_\theta}{r} \tag{29}$$

Following the same iterative steps as described for Eq.(27), to an order $O(\Delta t)^2$ the solution of Eq. (29) yields the following solution to Eq.(28):

$$f_i^{**}(r, \theta, v_r, v_\theta, t + \Delta t) = f_i^*(r, \theta, v_r - 2a, v_\theta - 2b, t) \tag{30}$$

Again the 2D interpolation in Eq. (30) is done using a tensor product of cubic *B*-spline, as explained in Eq.(15), and *a* and *b* are calculated with similar iterative steps as in Eqs.(23-26) and are given, to an order $O(\Delta t)^2$, by the expressions:

$$a = \frac{\Delta t}{2} \left\{ E_r + \omega_{ci} \left(v_\theta - b^1 \right) + \frac{(\upsilon_\theta - b^1)^2}{r} \right\} \tag{31}$$

$$b = \frac{\Delta t}{2} \left\{ E_\theta - \omega_{ci} \left(v_r - a^1 \right) - \frac{(\upsilon_\theta - b^1)(\upsilon_r - a^1)}{r} \right\} \tag{32}$$

where $a^1 = \frac{\Delta t}{2}\left\{E_r + \omega_{ci}\upsilon_\theta + \frac{\upsilon_\theta^2}{r}\right\}$; $b^1 = \frac{\Delta t}{2}\left\{E_\theta - \omega_{ci}\upsilon_r - \frac{\upsilon_\theta \upsilon_r}{r}\right\}$

The density $n_e^{**}(r,\theta,t+\Delta t)$ is calculated by integrating Eq.(11) as follows:

$$n_e^{**}(r,\theta,t+\Delta t) = n_e^{*}\exp\left(-E_\theta \frac{\partial}{\partial r}\frac{1+\frac{r}{R}\cos\theta}{\omega_{ci0}}\Delta t + E_r \frac{1}{r}\frac{\partial}{\partial \theta}\frac{1+\frac{r}{R}\cos\theta}{\omega_{ci0}}\Delta t\right) \tag{33}$$

where n_e^* is calculated in Eq.(27). To calculate f_i^{n+1} and n_e^{n+1}, we then repeat **Step 1** for the solution of Eqs. (8,9) for $\Delta t/2$ using f_i^{**} and n_e^{**} calculated from Eq.(30) and Eq.(33). The electric field is then updated to calculate $E_r^{n+1}(r,\theta)$ and $E_\theta^{n+1}(r,\theta)$ by solving Poisson equation.

2.3. The solution of Poisson's equation

Equation (5) is solved by first Fourier transforming the equation in the periodic direction θ:

$$\phi(r,\theta) = \sum_m \phi_m(r)e^{im\theta} \tag{34}$$

and the resulting equation is then discretized in the radial direction over a uniform grid following the method of Knorr *et al.*, 1980 (also rediscussed more recently in Crouseilles *et al.* 2009):

$$-A_m\phi_{m,j+1} + B_m\phi_{m,j} - C_m\phi_{m,j-1} = \frac{(\Delta r)^2}{12}(\rho_{m,j+1} + 10\rho_{m,j} + \rho_{m,j-1}) \tag{35}$$

where

$$A_{m,j} = 1 + \frac{\Delta r}{2r_j} - \frac{m^2(\Delta r)^2}{12r_j^2}; B_{m,j} = 2 + \frac{10m^2(\Delta r)^2}{12r_j^2}; C_{m,j} = 1 - \frac{\Delta r}{2r_j} - \frac{m^2(\Delta r)^2}{12r_j^2} \tag{36}$$

and $\phi_{m,j} = \phi_m(r_j)$; $\rho = n_i - n_e$; $n_i = \iint f_i(r,\theta,v_r,v_\theta)dv_r dv_\theta$

Equation (35) is solved using a tridiagonal algorithm. To get the boundary conditions, we assume in the present calculation that the deuterons and electrons currents hitting the cylindrical wall surface at $r = R$ are collected by a floating potential cylindrical vessel. Therefore we have the relations for the charge collected:

$$\left.\frac{\partial E_r(r,\theta)}{\partial t}\right|_{r=R} = -(J_{ri}|_{r=R} - J_{re}|_{r=R}) \quad \text{or} \quad E_r(r,\theta)|_{r=R} = -\int_0^t (J_{ri}|_{r=R} - J_{re}|_{r=R})dt \tag{37}$$

where

$$J_{ri}(r,\theta) = \int v_r f_i\left(r,\theta,v_r,v_\theta,t\right) dv_\theta dv_r \quad ; \qquad J_{re} = n_e V_{dr} \tag{38}$$

and V_{dr} is defined in Eq.(17). $E_r\big|_{r=R} \equiv E_r\big|_R$ from Eq.(37) is used to obtain for the potential the following boundary condition at $r = R$:

$$E_r\big|_R = -\frac{\partial \phi}{\partial r}\bigg|_R \tag{39}$$

By integrating the relation $\nabla.\vec{E} = \rho$, we get a relation between the charge collected on the cylindrical wall and the charge appearing in the initially neutral plasma:

$$R\,E_r\big|_R - (R - r_L)E_r\big|_{R-r_L} + \int_{R-r_L}^{R} \frac{\partial E_\theta}{\partial \theta} dr = \sigma;\ \text{where } \sigma = \int_{R-r_L}^{R} \rho r dr \tag{40}$$

where r_L is the width of the plasma slab, which extends from $R - r_L$ to R at the edge of the cylindrical plasma of radius R. σ is the charge appearing in the system. From Eq.(40), we get the following relation:

$$E_r\big|_{R-r_L} = -\frac{\partial \phi}{\partial r}\bigg|_{R-r_L} = (R\,E_r\big|_R - (\sigma - \int_{R-r_L}^{R} \frac{\partial E_\theta}{\partial \theta} dr)) / (R - r_L) \tag{41}$$

We assume that the plasma particles are allowed to enter or leave at the boundary at $r = R - r_L$. So the difference between the electric fields at the boundary $r = R - r_L$ and at $r = R$ must be such that Eq. (40) must be satisfied at every time-step in every direction θ. In the present simulation, $E_r\big|_{r=R}$ is calculated from Eq. (37), which defines the derivative of the potential at the right boundary to be used in the solution of Eq. (35). We fix the potential to be zero at the boundary at $r = R - r_L$ and solve Poisson equation in Eq.(35) for the potential. Then the resulting electric field at $E_r\big|_{r=R-r_L}$, calculated at $r = R - r_L$ from Eq. (5), must satisfy Eq. (41).

The initial density profiles at the neutral plasma edge are given by:

$$n_i(r) = n_e(r) = 0.5(1 + \tanh\left(\left(R - r - 2r_L / 5\right) / 4\right)) \tag{42}$$

The profiles in Eq. (42) situate the steep gradient to be centered at a distance of $2r_L / 5$ from the wall of the vessel, which put the plasma relatively close to the floating wall of the vessel. The wall of the vessel will collect the charge coming from the plasma, especially due to the large ions gyroradius. The system is solved for an edge thickness $r_L = 175$, and R=5000 for the radius of the cylinder (we expect this radius to be large in a tokamak, so in the domain $r = (R - r_L, R)$, the variation of the quantity r / R remains very close to 1.

We use N=250 grid points in space in the radial direction, and 128 grid points in the azimuthal direction. 80 grid points are used in each velocity direction. The velocity extrema for the ions velocities are $\pm 4\sqrt{T_e / T_i}$ in our normalized units, with T_e/T_i =1 in the present simulations.

3. Results

The code was executed for a sufficiently long time to reach a steady state. We noted around t=500 that the code has indeed reach a steady state. Since $\omega_{ci0} = 0.1/\sqrt{2}$ (normalized to ω_{pi}), then the gyroperiod $\tau = 2\pi / \omega_{ci0} \approx 88$. This means that the code has executed more than 5 gyroperiods. Figure(1) shows the electric field at $\theta = 0$ (full curve), $\theta = \pi/2$ (broken curve) and $\theta = \pi$ (dashed-dotted curve), at time $t = 495$ (left figure) and t=500 (right figure). At the edge and along the gradient the electric field E_r is directed towards the center to the interior of the plasma. The electric field at the floating vessel wall at $r = R$ was calculated using Eq. (37) at 128 points over the 2π circle. We see from Fig. (1) that the electric field at $\theta = 0$ is higher (in absolute value) than the one at $\theta = \pi$, and we note that the curves for $0<R-r<75$ have reached a steady state stable equilibrium, with the charge collected at $r=R$ remaining constant, while towards the center for $75<R-r<175$, the curve at $\theta = \pi$ shows a small steady state oscillation around zero. The charge collected on the floating wall of the cylindrical vessel at $\theta = 0$, $\pi/2$ and π are respectively -0.1455, -0.1389 and -0.063 at t=500. For the solution of Poisson equation, we set the value of the electric field $E_r\big|_{r=R}$ at the cylindrical vessel wall exactly equal to the charge collected on the wall according to Eq.(37). If the charge collected on the wall is equal to the charge appearing in the system, then according to Eq.(41) :

$$E_r\big|_R \approx (\sigma - \int_{R-r_L}^{R} \frac{\partial E_\theta}{\partial \theta} dr)) / R \quad ; \qquad E_r\big|_{R-r_L} \approx 0 \tag{43}$$

which is what we see for the curves at θ=0 and $\pi/2$ in Fig.(1). Indeed the code calculate for the charge appearing in the system $(\sigma - \int_{R-r_L}^{R} \frac{\partial E_\theta}{\partial \theta} dr)) / R$ the values of -0.1475 and -0.1399, very close to the values of -0.1455 and -0.1389 calculated for $E_r\big|_R$ at θ=0 and $\pi/2$ as we previously mentioned. And the quantity $E_r\big|_{R-r_L}$ was negligible by an order of magnitude ($2.\text{x}10^{-3}$ and $1.\text{x}10^{-3}$ at θ=0 and $\pi/2$ respectively).

In our code, we allow at $r = R - r_L$ for the possibility of plasma to flow across the boundary. Note that for our present set of the parameters the electric field E_θ calculated remained negligible from θ=0 to $\pi/2$ (see Fig.(6) below), and small around $\theta = \pi$.

Around $\theta = \pi$,the charge appearing in the system is not exactly equal to the charge collected at the cylindrical vessel wall, but shows a small oscillation due the fact that there is a small plasma circulation at $r = R - r_L$. In this case the electric field $E_r\big|_{r=R-r_L}$ is calculated from Eq.(41). At t=500, the value calculated for the right hand side of Eq.(41) is $-1.144\text{x}10^{-2}$, while the value calculated by the code is $-1.155\text{x}10^{-2}$ (which is the value we see in the right figure in Fig.(1) for the $\theta = \pi$ curve). The agreement is very good.

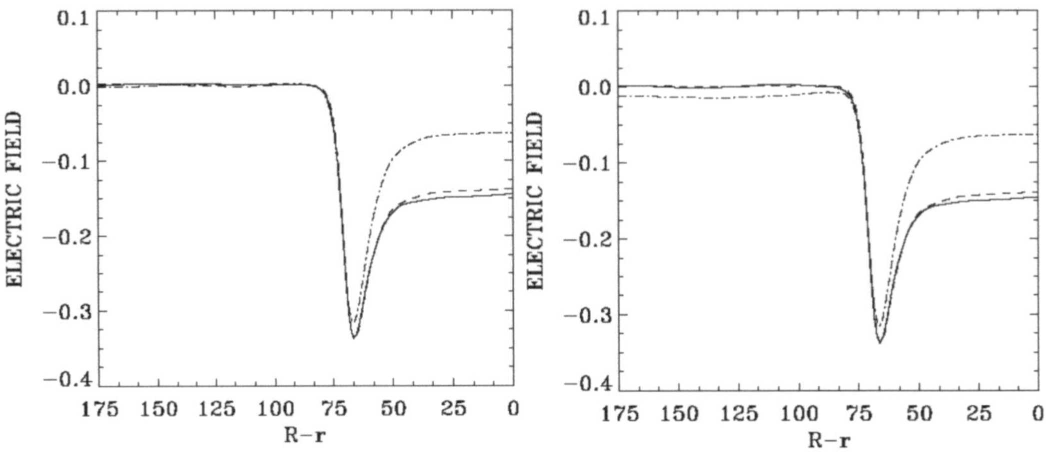

Figure 1. Electric field E_r at $\theta = 0$ (full curve), $\theta = \pi / 2$ (broken curve), and $\theta = \pi$ (dashed-dotted curve), at t=495 (left figure) and t=500 (right figure).

Figure(2) shows the potential at $\theta = 0$ (full curve), $\theta = \pi/2$ (broken line) and $\theta = \pi$ (dashed-dotted line), at time $t = 495$ (left figue) and t=500 (right figure). The curves at $\theta = 0$ and $\theta = \pi/2$ show negligible oscillation, while the curve at $\theta = \pi$ shows a small oscillation. Since as indicated in Fig.(1) the E_r profiles are essentially constant, especially for 0<R-r<75 along the gradient, then the oscillation of the curves at $\theta = \pi$ (dashed-dotted line) is taking place in such a way that the slope of the potential $\frac{\partial \phi}{\partial r} = -E_r$ remains constant for 0<R-r<75. Only for 75<R-r<175 does the small oscillation of the curve at $\theta = \pi$ in Fig.(2) (dashed-dotted line) translates into a small oscillation of the electric field E_r..

Figure(3) gives at time $t = 500$ and for $\theta = 0$ the electric field E_r (full curve). Also at $\theta = 0$ the dashed-dotted curve in Fig.(2) gives the Lorentz force, which in our normalized units is given by $-<v_\theta> \omega_{ci} / \omega_{pi} = -\frac{0.1}{\sqrt{2}} <v_\theta> /(1.+0.2\frac{r}{R}\cos\theta)$, and the broken curve gives the pressure force $\nabla P_i / n_i$, $P_i = 0.5\, n_i (T_{ir} + T_{i\theta})$, with the following definition:

$$T_{ir,\theta}(r,\theta) = \frac{1}{n_i} \int dv_r\, dv_\theta\, (v_{r,\theta} - <v_{r,\theta}>)^2\, f_i(r,\theta,v_r,v_\theta) \tag{44}$$

$$<v_{r,\theta}> = \frac{1}{n_i} \int dv_r\, dv_\theta\, v_{r,\theta}\, f_i(r,\theta,v_r,v_\theta)\ ; \qquad n_i(r,\theta) = \int dv_r\, dv_\theta\, f_i(r,\theta,v_r,v_\theta) \tag{45}$$

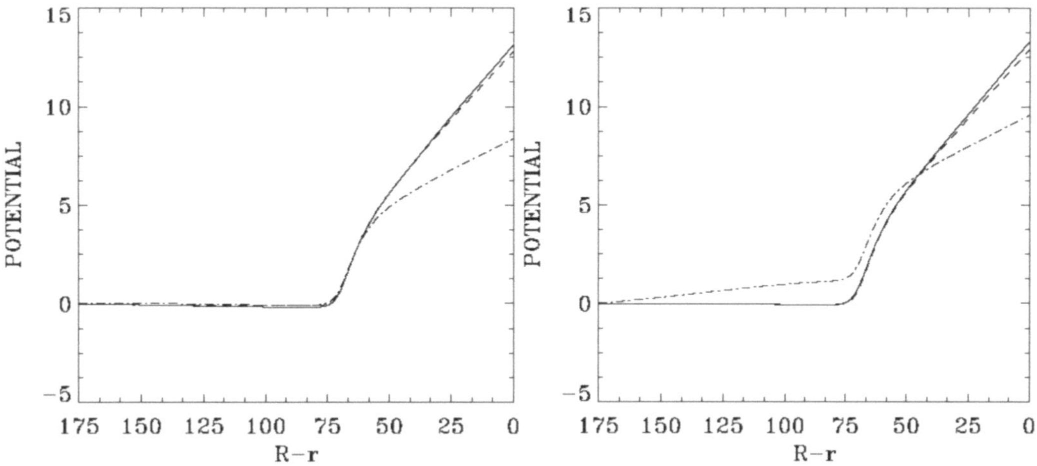

Figure 2. Potential at $\theta = 0$ (full curve), $\theta = \pi / 2$ (broken curve) and $\theta = \pi$ (dashed-dotted curve) at t=495 (left gigure) and t=500 (right figure).

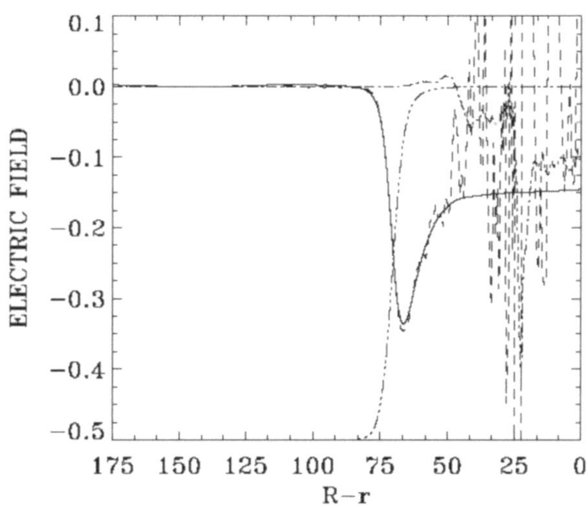

Figure 3. Plot at $\theta = 0$ of the electric field E_r (full curve), the Lorentz force $-(0.1/\sqrt{2}) < v_\theta > /(1. + 0.2(r / R)\cos\theta)$ (dashed-dotted. curve), and the pressure force $\nabla P_i / n_i$ (broken curve). The curve $-n_i/2$ is plotted for reference (dashed- 3 dotted curve). At time t =500.

The $\nabla P_i / n_i$ term (broken curve) shows a very good agreement along the gradient with the solid curve for E_r, and the Lorentz force appears negligible along the gradient. In a region of about two gyroradii from the wall (around 40 Debye lengths from the wall), we have small irregular oscillations in space (and time), the accuracy of $\nabla P_i / n_i$ being degraded by the division with a very small value of the density n_i appearing close to the vessel surface. To avoid this problem, we plot in Fig. (4) the quantities $-(0.1/\sqrt{2})n_i < v_\theta > /(1. + 0.2(r / R)\cos\theta)$, $n_i E_r, \nabla P_i$, at $\theta = 0$ (note that $J_{\theta i} = n_i < v_\theta >$). We see that there is a very nice agreement for the relation $n_i\, E_r \approx \nabla P_i$ along the gradient (the density $-n_i / 10$ is also plotted in Fig.(4) to locate the different profiles with respect to the gradient). The Lorentz force term remains negligible in the gradient region, and remains very small in the bulk at 75<*R-r*<175. The $\nabla P_i / n_i$ term is zero in the bulk since n_i and T_i are essentially flat in that region. We have seen in this case that the total charge $(\sigma - \int_{R-r_L}^{R} \frac{\partial E_\theta}{\partial \theta} dr)) / R$ appearing in the system and calculated by the code by integrating the charge as in Eq. (40) and by calculating E_θ from Poisson equation, is essentially equal to the electric field $E_r\big|_{r=R}$. We note that curves similar to Fig.(4) can be calculated at different angles θ, showing $n_i E_r$ essentially balanced by the ∇P_i.

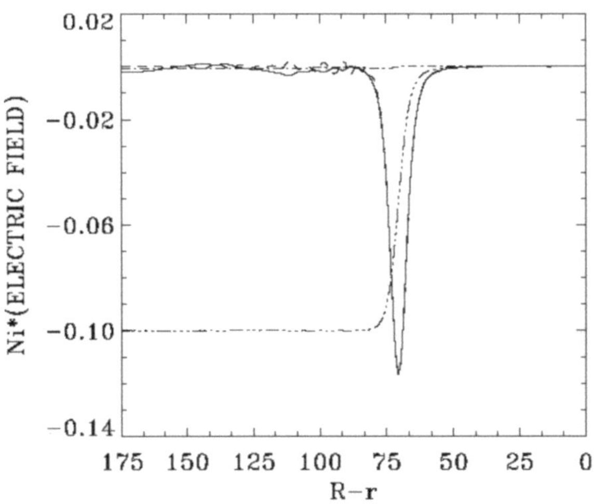

Figure 4. Plot at $\theta = 0$ of $n_i E_r$ (solid curve), $-(0.1/\sqrt{2}) n_i < v_\theta > /(1.+0.2(r/R)\cos\theta)$ (dash-dot curve), and ∇P_i (broken-curve). The curve $-n_i/10$ is plotted for reference (dashed-3 dotted curve). At time *t*=500.

The initial density profiles are given in Eq.(42), so the initial charge is zero. Fig.(5) shows the charge density $n_i - n_e$ at the time $t = 500$ and $\theta = 0$ (full curve), $\theta = \pi / 2$ (broken curve) and $\theta = \pi$ (dashed-dotted curve). It is interesting to note that the code was able to maintain the steep density gradients (see Fig.(4) for a plot of n_i). The stable in time steep density profile changes in space rapidly along the gradient over an ion orbit size ($\rho_i / \lambda_{De} = 20$), and the relaxation of the steep gradients during the simulation determines the charge density $n_i - n_e$. The charge density is important along the gradient at the plasma edge. The electrons, described by the guiding center equation given in Eq.(3) cannot compensate along the gradient the charge separation caused by the finite ion gyroradius, which results in the charge density we see in Fig.(5).

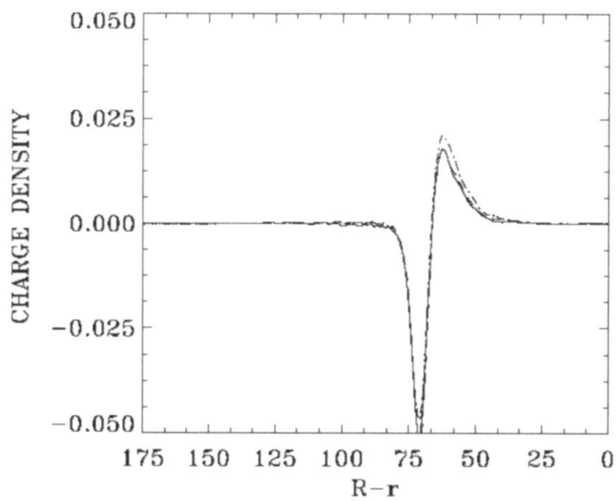

Figure 5. Charge density at $\theta = 0$ (full curve), $\theta = \pi / 2$ (broken curve) and $\theta = \pi$ (dashed-dotted curve), at *t*=500.

We have noted in Fig.(1) the constant value of the E_r profiles, especially for 0<*R*-*r*<75 along the gradient, translates the constant slope of the potential. However, the potential profile at $\theta = \pi$, although keeping essentially the same slope for 0<*R*-*r*<75, shows an oscillation in time. This results in a θ variation with an electric field $E_\theta = -\frac{1}{r}\frac{\partial \phi}{\partial \theta}$ which, as we mentioned before, is small for the parameters we are using. Figures (6) presents this electric field E_θ at *t*=485 and *t*=495. It shows no oscillation E_θ in at $\theta = 0$ (full curve, essentially equal to zero), a negligible oscillation at $\theta = \pi/2$ (broken curve), and a small oscillation for the $\theta = \pi$ (dashed-dotted curve), on the high field side of the cylinder. The curve at $\theta = \pi$ is interesting, it shows the oscillating curve for E_θ having a constant flat value in the gradient region, and a linear variation in the inner region.

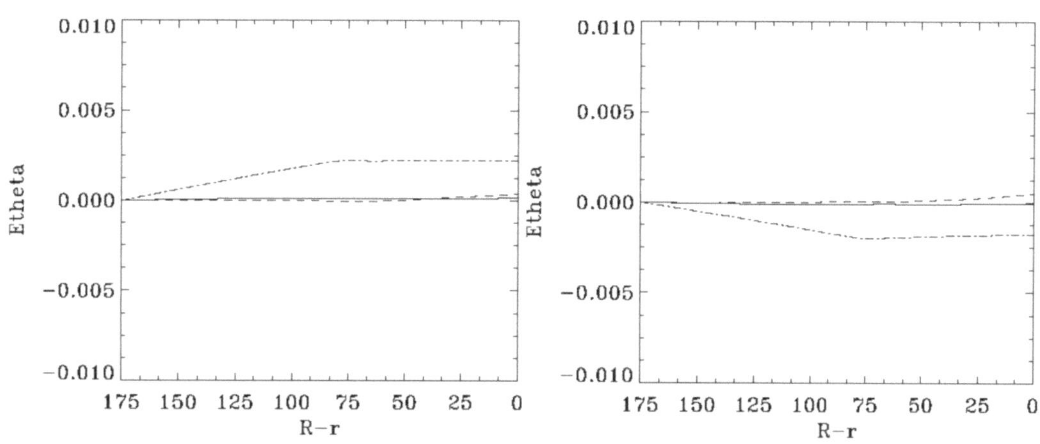

Figure 6. Electric field E_θ at $\theta = 0$ (full curve), $\theta = \pi / 2$ (broken curve), and $\theta = \pi$ (dash-dot curve), at *t*=485 (left figure) and *t*=495 (right figure).

Figure (7) gives at $t = 500$ the temperature T_{ir} as defined in Eq. (43), for $\theta = 0$ (full curve), $\theta = \pi/2$ (broken curve) and $\theta = \pi$ (dashed-dotted curve). The dashed-3 dotted curve is for $n_i T_{ir}$, which is essentially the same for all angles θ. Figure (8) presents similar results for $T_{i\theta}$ as defined in Eq.(43). Note in Fig.(7) and Fig.(8) the division by the very small density at the edge gives irregular oscillations. However the dashed-3 dotted curve in Fig.(7) and Fig.(8) is very smooth, and is for $n_i T_{ir}$ and $n_i T_{i\theta}$ respectively, which removes the problem of the division by the very small density at the edge. We present in Fig.(9) the total pressure $P_i = 0.5\, n_i \left(T_{ir} + T_{i\theta}\right)$ for $\theta = 0$ (full curve), $\theta = \pi/2$ (broken curve) and $\theta = \pi$ (dashed-dotted curve). We see that these curves are essentially identical, for the parameters we are using in the present simulation there is no variation in θ for the total pressure term.

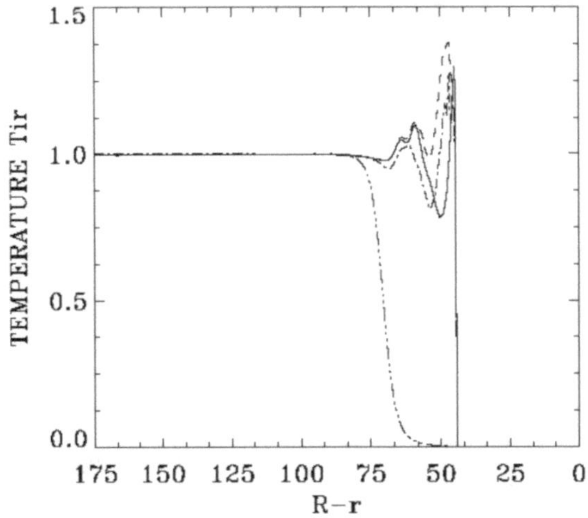

Figure 7. Temperature T_{ir} at $\theta = 0$ (full curve), $\theta = \pi/2$ (broken curve) and $\theta = \pi$ (dashed-dotted curve). The dashed -3 dotted curve is for $n_i T_{ir}$, which is essentially the same for all θ. Time t=500.

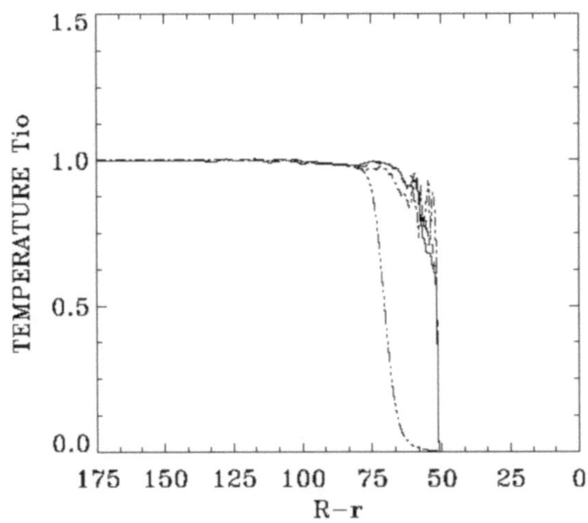

Figure 8. Temperature $T_{i\theta}$ at $\theta = 0$ (full curve), $\theta = \pi/2$ (broken curve) and $\theta = \pi$ (dash-dot curve). The dashed-3 dotted curve is for $n_i T_{i\theta}$, which is essentially the same for all θ. Time t=500.

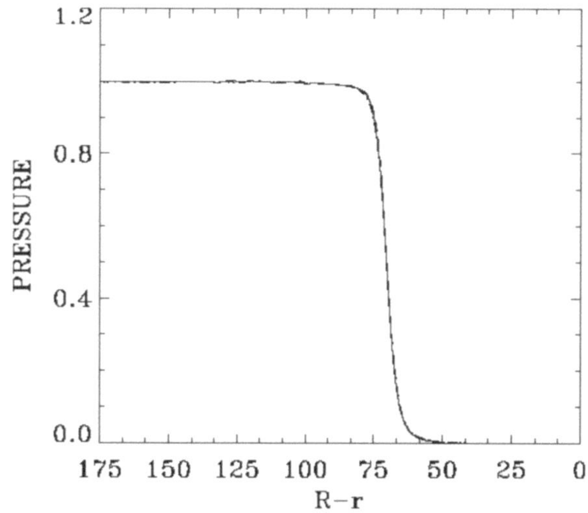

Figure 9. Pressure $P_i = 0.5\, n_i \left(T_{ir} + T_{i\theta}\right)$ at $\theta = 0$ (full curve), $\theta = \pi / 2$ (broken curve) and $\theta = \pi$ (dashed-dotted curve), at t= 500.

Figure(10) presents the plot of the θ component of the $\vec{E} \times \vec{B} / B^2$ drift, which in our normalized units is written $-E_r \,\left(1 + 0.2(r / R)\cos\theta\right)\sqrt{2} / 0.1$, at θ= 0 (full curve), θ= π/2 (broken curve) and θ= π (dashed-dotted curve). The curves for 0<R-r<75 have reached a stable equilibrium as discussed in Fig.(1) for E_r, while towards the center for 75<R-r<175 the curves at θ= π shows a small steady state oscillation around zero, as previously mentioned for E_r in the right figure in Fig.(1). Note in Fig. (10) that this azimuthal (*i.e.* poloidal) $\vec{E} \times \vec{B} / B^2$ drift is flat close to the edge, and is below the acoustic speed at θ= π at the edge, and above the acoustic speed at θ= 0 and θ= π/2 at the edge (velocities are normalized to the acoustic speed C_s). We plot in Fig. (11) the total poloidal current (in the θ direction) $n_i \left(\vec{E} \times \vec{B} / B^2 + \vec{v}_D\right)$, where the diamagnetic drift is $\vec{v}_D = \vec{B} \times \nabla n_i T_i / \left(n_i e B^2\right)$. We see that the total current is essentially zero, *i.e.* the profile is adjusting itself so that the $\vec{E} \times \vec{B} / B^2$ drift and the diamagnetic drift are essentially equal and opposite (in our units, the total poloidal current is $\left(-n_i E_r + \nabla p_i\right)\,\left(1 + 0.2(r / R)\cos\theta\right)\sqrt{2} / 0.1$, essentially equal to zero , showing a small oscillation around zero in Fig.(11), at the left boundary). So the $\vec{E} \times \vec{B} / B^2$ drift is balanced fairly well by the diamagnetic drift. This is the result we get if we calculate the poloidal current:

$$J_{\theta i}(r,\theta) = \int v_\theta f_i\left(r,\theta,v_r,v_\theta,t\right) dv_\theta dv_r \qquad (46)$$

We get indeed a negligible value for $J_{\theta i}$. (note that $J_{\theta i} = n_i < v_\theta >$).

We note that due to the small E_θ field (see Fig.6), the $\vec{E} \times \vec{B} / B^2$ drift has a small oscillating component $E_\theta\ \left(1 + 0.2(r / R)\cos\theta\right)$ in the radial direction, with a curve similar to what is presented in Fig.(6). This radial oscillation is negligible around $\theta = 0$ and $\theta = \pi / 2$, and is small on the high field side around $\theta = \pi$, as previously discussed for E_θ in Fig.(6).

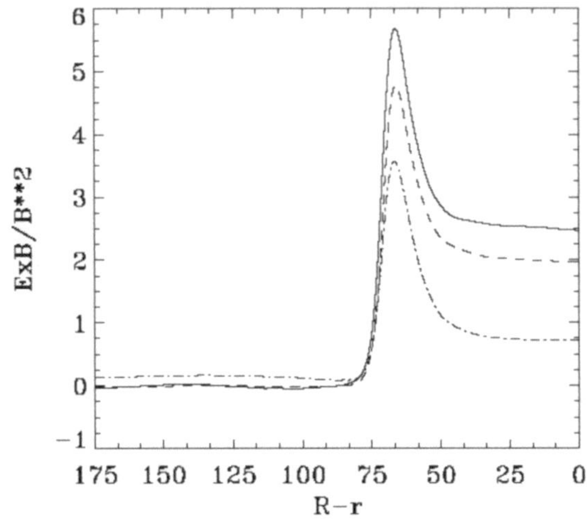

Figure 10. Plot of $-E_r \left(1+0.2(r/R)\cos\theta\right)\sqrt{2}/0.1$ for $\theta = 0$ (full curve), $\theta = \pi/2$ (broken curve) and $\theta = \pi$ (dashed-dotted curve). At time *t*=500.

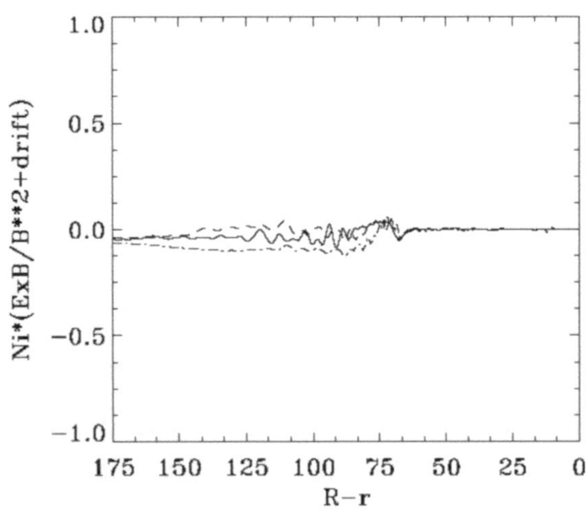

Figure 11. Plot of the total poloidal current $\left(-n_i E_r + \nabla P_i\right)\left(1+0.2\,(r/R)\cos\theta\right)\sqrt{2}/0.1$ for $\theta = 0$ (full curve), $\theta = \pi/2$ (broken curve) and $\theta = \pi$ (dashed-dotted curve). At time *t*=500.

4. Conclusion

We have presented in this work the self-consistent kinetic solution for the problem of the generation of a charge separation and an electric field at a plasma edge, under the combined effect of a large ratio of the ions' gyroradius to the Debye length ρ_i / λ_{De} (equal to 20 in the simulation we have presented) and a steep density gradient, when the electrons which are bound to the magnetic field cannot compensate along the gradient the charge separation due to the finite ions' gyroradius. In the cylindrical geometry considered, a fully kinetic equation has been used to describe the ions, and a guiding center equation has been used to describe the electrons bound to the magnetic field. These equations have been solved using the method of characteristics (Shoucri, 2008a,b,c,d, 2009a). The numerical method used for the solution in cylindrical geometry, based on an integration of the equations along the characteristics coupled to a two-dimensional interpolation (Shoucri *et al.*, 2004) applied successively in configuration space and in velocity space, is producing accurate results.

The problem of the formation of a charge separation is of great importance in the study of the H-mode physics in tokamaks. We have considered the case where the gradient in the density profiles is located in front of a floating cylindrical vessel. So the charge appearing in the system is essentially equal to the charge collected on the walls of the floating vessel. The solution shows in the radial direction that the electric field along the gradient is balanced by the radial gradient of the pressure, and the total poloidal current is essentially zero. The present results where electrons are described by a guiding center equation are close to what has been previously reported when assuming the electrons stationary and frozen by the magnetic field, and the code shows that a solution with a steep gradient, maintaining a charge separation, where the electron and ion densities vary rapidly over an ion gyroradius, is possible. Also the calculation with the present set of parameters which allow a small value of the poloidal field E_θ to exist, shows the presence of a small oscillation of E_θ on the high field side around $\theta = \pi$ (see Fig.(6)), to which is associated a small radial oscillation due to the radial component of the $\vec{E} \times \vec{B} / B^2$ drift , equal to $E_\theta \ \left(1 + 0.2\,(r / R)\cos\theta\right)\sqrt{2} / 0.1$ in our normalized units.

The present code is a step closer to a code which will include "neoclassical" effects due to toroidal geometry, which can play a role in this problem, such as the neoclassical enhancement of the classical ion polarization drift, or the neoclassical damping of poloidal flows (Stix, 1973, Hirshman 1978, Waltz *et. al.*, 1999).

Author details

Magdi Shoucri
Institut de Recherche Hydro-Québec (IREQ), Varennes, Québec, Canada

Acknowledgement

The author is grateful to Dr. Rejean Girard for his support, and to the Centre de calcul scientifique de l'IREQ (CASIR) for computer time for the simulations presented in this work.

5. References

Abbott, B.A. (1966). *An Introduction to the Method of Characteristics*; Thames and Hudson, London.

Ahlberg, J.H., Nilson, E.N. & Walsh, J.L. (1967). *The Theory of Splines and their Applications*; Academic Press, New York, N.Y.

Batishchev, O., Shoucri, M., Batishcheva, A. & Shkarofsky, I. (1999). Fully Kinetic Simulation of Coupled Plasmas and Neutral Particles in Scrape-off Layer Plasmas of Fusion Devices. *J. Plasma Physics*, Vol. 61, pp. 347- 364

Cheng, C.Z. & Knorr, G. (1976). The Integration of the Vlasov Equation in Configuration Space. *J. Comp. Phys.*, Vol. 22, pp. 330-351

Crouseilles, N., Respaud, T. & Sonnendrücker, E. (2009). A Forward Semi-Lagrangian Method for the Numerical Solution of the Vlasov Equation. *Comp. Phys. Comm.*, Vol. 180, pp.1730-1745

Gagné, R. & Shoucri, M. (1977). A Splitting Scheme for the Solution of a One-Dimensional Vlasov Equations. *J. Comp. Phys.*, Vol. 24, pp. 445-449

Ghizzo, A., Bertrand, P., Shoucri, M., Johnston, T., Feix M. & Fijalkow, E. (1990). A Vlasov Code for the Numerical Simulation of Stimulated Raman Scattering. *J. Comp. Phys.*, Vol. 90, pp. 431-457

Ghizzo, A., Bertrand, P., Shoucri, M., Johnston, T., Fijalkow, E., Feix M. & Demchenko, V.V. (1992). Study of Laser-Plasma Beat Wave Current Drive with an Eulerian Vlasov Code. *Nucl. Fusion*, Vol. 32, pp. 45-65

Groebner, R.J., Thomas, D.M. & Deranian, R.D. (2001). Evidence for Edge Gradients as Control Parameters of the Spontaneous High-Mode Transition. *Phys. Plasmas* , Vol. 8, pp. 2722-2732

Hirschman, S.P. (1978). The Ambipolarity Paradox in Toroidal Diffusion, Revisited. *Nucl. Fus.*, Vol.18, pp. 917- 927

Knorr, G., Joyce, G. & Marcus, J. (1980). Fourth-Order Poisson Solver for the Simulation of Bounded Plasmas. *J. Comput. Phys.*, Vol. 38, pp. 227-237

Manfredi, G., Shoucri, M., Dendy, R.O., Ghizzo, A. & Bertrand, P. (1996). Vlasov Gyrokinetic Simulations of Ion-Temperature-Gradient Driven Instabilities. *Phys. Plasmas* , Vol. 3, pp. 202-217

Pohn, E., Shoucri, M. & Kamelander G. (2005). Eulerian Vlasov Codes. *Comp. Phys. Comm.*, Vol. 166, pp. 81-93

Pohn, E. & Shoucri, M. (2008). Collisionless Diffusion of Particles across a Magnetic field at a Plasma Edge in the Presence of Turbulence. *Proc. Vlasovia workshop*, in *Commun. Nonlinear Sci. Numer. Simul.*, Vol. 13, pp. 183-188

Shoucri, M., Lebas, J., Knorr, G., Bertrand, Ghizzo, A., Manfredi, G. & Christopher, I. (1997). Effect of Viscous Dissipation on the Generation of Shear Flow at a Plasma Edge in the Finite Gyroradius Guiding Center Approximation. *Physica Scripta,* Vol. 55, pp. 617-628

Shoucri, M., Pohn, E., Knorr, G., Bertrand, P., Kamelander, G., Manfredi, G. & Ghizzo, A. (2000). Charge Separation at a Plasma Edge in the Presence of a Density Gradient. *Phys. Plasmas,* Vol. 7, pp. 2517-2525

Shoucri, M. (2001). Numerical Simulation of Plasma Edge Turbulence due to *ExB* Flow Velocity Shear. *Czech. J. Phys.*, Vol. 51, pp.1139-1151

Shoucri, M. (2002). Comments on 'Evidence for Edge Gradients as Control Parameters of the Spontaneous High- Mode Transition', *Phys. Plasmas,* Vol. 9, pp. 731-734

Shoucri, M., Gerhauser, H. & Finken, K.H. (2003). Numerical Simulation of the Formation of an Electric Field at a Plasma Edge in the Presence of a Density Gradient. *Proceedings of EPS 2003 30th Conference on Contr. Fusion and Plasma Phys.*, ECA Vol. 27A, P.1-170, St. Petersbourg, Russia, July 7-11

Shoucri, M., Gerhauser, H. & Finken, K.H. (2004). Study of the Generation of a Charge Separation and Electric Field at a Plasma Edge using Eulerian Vlasov Codes in Cylindrical Geometry. *Computer Physics Communications,* Vol. 164, pp. 138-149

Shoucri, M., Pohn, E.& Kamelander, G. (2005). Numerical Simulation of the Collisioless Diffusion of Particles across a Magnetic Field at a Plasma Edge. *Proceedings of EPS 2005 32nd Conference on Contr. Fusion and Plasma Phys.*, ECA Vol. 32D, P.-5.001, Tarragona, Spain, June 27-July 1

Shoucri, M. (2008a). *Numerical Solution of Hyperbolic Differential Equations,* Nova Science Publishers, ISBN 978-1-60456-459-4, New York

Shoucri, M. (2008b). Numerical Simulation For the Formation of a Charge Separation and an Electric Field at a Plasma Edge. *Proceedings of EPS 2008 35th Conference on Contr. Fusion and Plasma Phys.*, ECA Vol. 32D, P.-4.006, Hersonissos, Crete, Greece, June 9-13

Shoucri, M. (2008c). Eulerian Code for the Numerical Solution of the Vlasov Equation. *Proc. Vlasovia workshop*, in *Commun. Nonlinear Sci. Numer. Simul.*, Vol. 13, pp. 174-182

Shoucri, M. (2008d). Numerical Simulation of Wake-Field Acceleration using an Eulerian Vlasov Code. *Commun. Comp. Phys.*, Vol. 4, pp. 703-718

Shoucri, M. (2009a). The Application of the Method of Characteristics for the Numerical Solution of Hyperbolic Differential Equations, In: *Numerical Simulation Research Progress,* S.P. Colombo & C.L. Rizzo (Ed.), Nova Science Publishers, ISBN 978-1-60456-783-0, New York

Shoucri, M. (2009b). The Formation of a Charge Separation and an Electric Field at a Steep Plasma Edge. *Proceedings of EPS 2009 36th Conference on Contr. Fusion and Plasma Phys.*, ECA Vol.32D, P.- 4.105, Sofia, Bulgaria, June 29- July 3

Shoucri, M. (2011). In:*Eulerian Codes for the Numerical Solution of the Kinetic Equations of Plasmas.* M. Shoucri (Ed.), Nova Science Publishers, ISBN 978-1-61668-413-6, New York

Shoucri, R. & Shoucri, M. (2007). Applications of the Method of Characteristics for the Study of Shock Waves in Models of Blood Flow in the Aorta. *Cardiovasc. Eng.*, Vol. 7, pp.1-6

Sonnendrücker, E., Roche, J., Bertrand, P. & Ghizzo, A. (1999). The Semi-Lagrangian Method for the Numerical Resolution of the Vlasov Equation. *J. Comp. Phys.*, Vol. 149, pp. 201-220

Stix, T. (1973). Decay of Poloidal Rotation in a Tokamak Plasma. *Phys. Fluids,* Vol.16, pp.1260-1269

Strozzi, D., Shoucri, M., Bers, A., Williams, E.A. & Langdon, A.B. (2006). Vlasov Simulations of Trapping and Inhomogeneity in Raman Scattering. *J. Plasma Phys.*, Vol. 72, pp. 1299-1302

Waltz, R.E., Candy, J., Rosenbluth, M.N. & Hinton, F.L. (1999). Progress on a Full Radius Electromagnetic Gyrokinetic Code. *Proceedings of EPS 1999 26th Conference on Contr. Fusion and Plasma Phys.*, ECA Vol. 23J, pp. 1233-1236, Maastricht, Holland, June 14-18

Yanenko, N.N. (1971). *The Method of Fractional Steps*, Springer-Verlag, New York.

Chapter 6

Recent Developments on Compton Scatter Tomography: Theory and Numerical Simulations

T. T. Truong and M. K. Nguyen

Additional information is available at the end of the chapter

http://dx.doi.org/10.5772/50012

1. Introduction

Progress in nuclear physics acquired during World War II has naturally led many scientists to devote their research activities to the field of tomographic imaging techniques using ionizing radiation. This was, in the post-war booming economy, particularly of great importance for medical diagnostic as well as for industrial non destructive evaluation (NDE). As the objective is to extract information on the inner part of objects of interest, penetrating radiation was the most appropriate agent for this purpose. With the availability of high quality X-ray and gamma-ray sources (either directly originated from nuclear transitions or from pair annihilation) and the emergence of sensitive detectors, three types of imaging have been introduced and developed throughout half a century. Nowadays they have emerged as mature standard investigation methods for several domains of application.

These are: a) the X-ray transmission Computed Tomography (CT), which exploits the physical law of radiation attenuation in matter, b) the Single Photon Emission Tomography (SPECT), which uses the possibility of implanting radiation sources inside objects, c) the Positron Emission Tomography (PET), which uses the possibility of implanting positron sources in objects and exploits the properties of electron-positron pair annihilation. Milestones of their sensational evolution throughout decades are vividly recalled in recent reviews, see *e.g.* [35, 47].

It is observed that all three cited imaging methods deal exclusively with primary (or non-deviated) radiation. The physical quantity, which is non-uniformly distributed over an object and responsible for the imaging process, is respectively: the linear attenuation coefficient for CT, the γ-ray radio-activity density inside the object for SPECT, and the β^+-ray (or positron) radio-activity density for PET.

However right at the start, scientists were also attracted by the idea of using scattered radiation by Compton effect (the scattering of X- or gamma photons by an electron) to image the inner parts of an object by reconstructing its electron density map. While this last imaging technology has not yet reached the same level of maturity as the three quoted above, it has gone through revolutionary conceptual steps which have led to what is nowadays known as Compton scatter tomography (CST). Yet it has stirred continuous interest in numerous applications, see *e.g.* [2], [4], [11], [18], [5], [22], [29], [1], [23]. The aim of this chapter is to recount the past episodes of research, to give a comprehensive account of what has been accomplished in CST and to describe some new ideas which have arisen recently, see [42, 54]. The emphasis of the discussion shall be placed at the theoretical level. Negative effects on imaging such as beam attenuation and multiple scattering, which complicate enormously the analytic treatment, shall be dealt with conventional retrieval or compensation methods. The crux of the matter is to see how fertile ideas evolve in time and generate new fruitful concepts.

2. Compton scattering

To appreciate the role of scattered radiation for imaging purposes, it is useful to recall some of the key points on Compton scattering. When a thin pencil of X- or gamma radiation shines through a medium, its intensity weakens as its traverses matter. One of the cause for this attenuation process is Compton scattering: deflected rays by scattering will not reach a detector placed along the incident direction.

From the geometry and kinematics of this scattering, see *e.g.* [6], one may infer that:

• the scattered photon flux density in a given spatial direction is given by the differential Compton scattering cross-section $d\sigma_C/d\Omega = \pi r_e^2 P(\omega)$, where $r_e = 2.82 \times 10^{-15}$ m is the classical electron radius and $P(\omega)$, the Klein-Nishina scattering probability under a scattering angle ω.

• the scattered photon energy E is directly connected to the scattering angle ω by the so-called Compton relation

$$E = E(\omega) = E_0 \frac{1}{1 - \epsilon \cos \omega}, \tag{1}$$

where E_0 is the energy of incident photons and ϵ the ratio of E_0 to the electron rest energy.

Then the number of particles d^2N_{sc} scattered in a solid angle $d\Omega_{sc}$ along a direction making an angle ω with the incident direction follows from the definition of the differential scattering cross section $d\sigma_C/d\Omega$, if the following quantities are given: a) ϕ_{in}, the incident photon flux density, b) $n(\mathbf{M})$, the electron density at the scattering site $\mathbf{M}$, surrounded by volume element $d\mathbf{M}$. Thus, for a given incident energy, the angular distribution of scattered photons around the scattering site $\mathbf{M}$ is no longer isotropic. The final form of this number of scattered photons in the direction given by the angle ω is

$$d^2N_{sc} = \phi_{in}\; n(\mathbf{M})d\mathbf{M}\, \pi\, r_e^2 P(\omega)\; d\Omega_{sc}. \tag{2}$$

But this is still not realistic. For radiation emitted from a point source and incident on site $\mathbf{M}$, see Fig. 1, attenuation effects in matter before and after scattering are to be taken into account, as well as beam spreading due to straight line propagation, in the evaluation of the detected photon flux density. Equation 2 reads now for a point source emitting isotropically I_0 photons per second and per steradian

$$d^2N_{sc} = \frac{I_0}{4\pi}\, m_\sigma(SM)\, \mathcal{A}_{in}(SM)\, n(\mathbf{M})d\mathbf{M}\, \pi\, r_e^2 P(\omega)\, \mathcal{A}_{out}(MD)\, m_{\sigma'}(MD)\, d\Omega_{sc}, \tag{3}$$

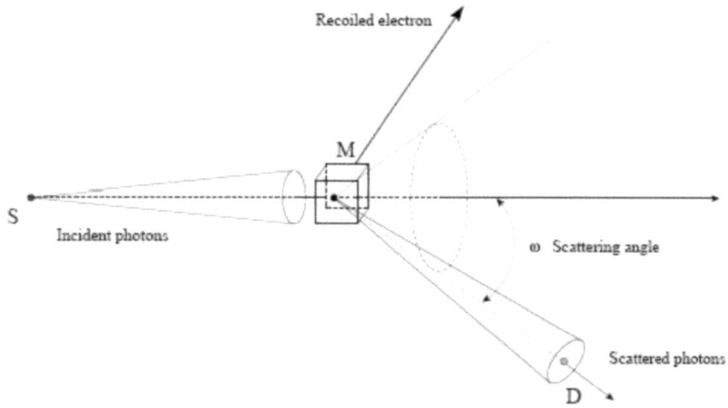

Figure 1. Compton scattering

where the attenuation factors on the traveled distances SM and MD are given by

$$\mathcal{A}_{in}(SM) = \exp\left(-\int_0^{SM} ds\, \mu(\mathbf{S}+s\mathbf{M})\right), \quad \text{and} \quad \mathcal{A}_{out}(MD) = \exp\left(-\int_0^{MD} ds\, \mu(\mathbf{M}+s\mathbf{D})\right). \tag{4}$$

In equation 4, $\mu(\mathbf{M})$ is the matter linear attenuation coefficient at site $\mathbf{M}$ and the respective beam spreading factor $m_\sigma(r)$ is of the form

$$m_\sigma(r) = \left(\frac{1}{\pi\sigma}\tan^{-1}\frac{\sigma}{2r}\right)^2, \tag{5}$$

with σ the linear size of scattering volume and r the traversed distance. Note that for $\sigma \to 0$, $m_\sigma(r) \sim 1/r^2$, a well known photometric factor, which shall be used later. Equation 3 is fundamental to the image formation by scattered radiation.

When E_0 is chosen in such a way that competing events such as photoelectric absorption and pair creation are virtually absent, then Compton scattering becomes the main phenomena to be considered for imaging, and the relevant physical quantity is $n(\mathbf{M})$, the electron density in matter at site $\mathbf{M}$, from which other quantities such as chemical composition may be deduced. As $n(\mathbf{M})$ appears also in the attenuation process, its determination becomes quite involved since it must be retrieved from a non-linear expression in $n(\mathbf{M})$. It is clear that, in CST imaging, $n(\mathbf{M})$ plays the role of the attenuation map in CT, the gamma-ray activity density in SPECT and the beta-plus-ray activity density in PET.

3. The earlier CST modalities

Equation 3 has inspired many of the earlier CST modalities which shall be described below.

3.1. Point by point scanning CST

The simplest and earliest procedure is schematically described by Fig. 2. Both point source and detector are equipped with an axial collimator (lead cylindrical tube). Their axis lie in a plane and the detector is connected to a multichannel analyzer. When the axis of a collimated point-like detector is made to intersect the incident pencil beam, the intersection site is actually a scattering site of the Compton effect. So by measuring the scattered photon flux density at a given energy, by estimating the strength of the attenuation factors, and by evaluating the beam spreading factors one can obtain $n(\mathbf{M})$. The process is then repeated for all sites in a trans-axial slice. It is interesting to note that equation 3 has been recast in the framework of an inverse problem by E. M. A. Hussein et al.[33], who have set up a discretization scheme to solve it.

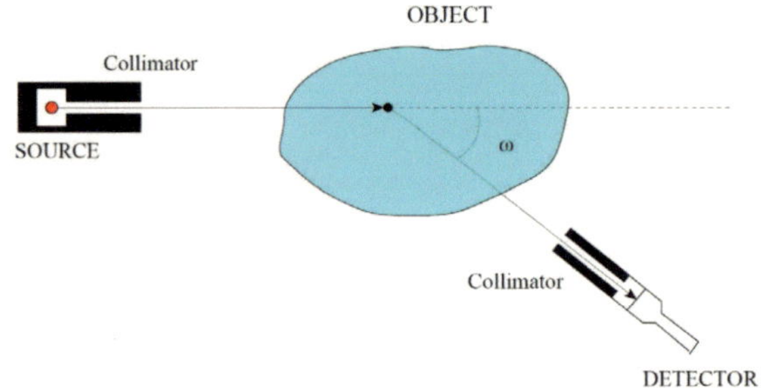

Figure 2. CST point by point scanning

At the turn of the twentieth century, the idea of using scattered gamma rays for investigating hidden structures in tissues seems to have been proposed for the first time by F. W. Spiers [52]. In 1959, P. G. Lale [40], realizing that radiographic images of organs fail to reveal their inner structure, has suggested a technique using Compton scattered radiation from a thin pencil of X-rays. Using equation 1, it is possible to move a collimated detector in space to measure the scattered radiation flux density and deduce the electron density at a precise point on the incoming pencil of X-rays. When this measurement can be performed in a planar slice of an object, it said that an image of the slice is obtained by Compton scatter tomography (CST). Of course this is clearly a point by point procedure which is quite time consuming.

An analogous problem arises in nuclear industry. There heat transfer research in circulating two-phase fluids requires knowledge and measurement of their densities without disturbing or arresting their flow. It was realized that penetrating gamma-radiation would be the most suitable for this purpose. As matter density is responsible for traversing radiation attenuation (since most of the attenuation occurs as a result of Compton scattering) measurements of radiation attenuation along linear paths crossing the section of a pipe can be easily done. D. Kershaw [36] has shown how the matter density distribution can be reconstructed from these measurements. In fact this problem is practically identical to the medical computed tomography which was developed simultaneously at that time and Kershaw has actually performed the mathematical inversion of the classical Radon transform, but most probably without being aware of the seminal works of J. Radon [49] and A. M. Cormack [15]. But it was N. N. Kondic [37], who has first suggested the use of scattered radiation for obtaining the two-phase fluid density in a pipe.

In 1973, R. L. Clarke et al. [13] used both transmitted and scattered gamma-rays to measure bone mineral content. In [14], they have introduced the term gamma-tomography for their apparatus which is made of a fixed collimated pencil source and four focussing collimated detectors positioned so as the scattering angle is about 45^0. The investigated object is placed on a moving platform which allows a raster scanning motion. The detected number of photons at each point (in fact a small "sensitive volume") is directly mapped onto the screen of an oscilloscope which yields a density image in a slice.

Later on, S. R. Gautam et al. [21] presented an imaging system called Compton Interaction Tomography, which consists of a pencil incident beam falling on a large object, the backscattered pencil is registered by a collimated detector situated on a line parallel to the large object. This is also a point by point determination of the electron density, but with the idea that the object is on one side of the line source-detector. Numerous works have been done by the NDE community in the 80's, see *e.g.* [10], [27], [30], including some reviews such as [31],[32],[8], and the use of dual sources by [28].

3.2. Line by line CST

In 1971, F. T. Farmer & M. P. Collins [19] advocated the use of a *wide angle* collimated detector limited by two plates parallel to the incident radiation pencil. Fig. 3 shows how schematically how this procedure works. The detector is coupled to a multichannel analyzer. This design allows to obtain rapidly the electron density profile along the probing incident radiation pencil. This is the reason why it is called line scanning technique. A global image of an object slice is realized when parallel lines are put together. This technique has been refined in [20].

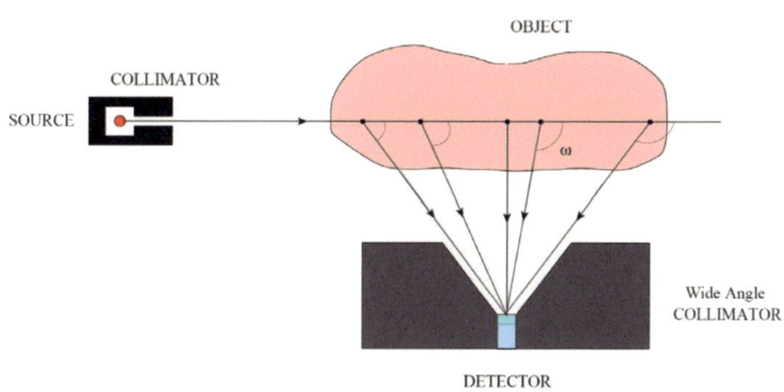

Figure 3. CST with line by line scanning

Variants of this design have been developed by the NDE community to combat the low efficiency of the single voxel technique. In [25], G. Harding described a Compton scatter imaging system for NDE with horizontal scanning and incident pencil beam perpendicular to the scanning direction. Scatter detectors are disposed on both sides of the incident beam. Fig. 4 shows a sketch of the COMSCAN (Compton Scatter Scanner), developed by the Philips Research Laboratories in Hamburg, Germany which was quite successful (see [26]).

3.3. Plane by plane CST

Then emerged several planar scatter imaging systems as extensions of linear scatter imaging systems in NDE [30], [53] as well as in medicine [24], which work at fixed scattering angle with relative success, since most of the reconstruction methods are still mathematically ill-defined and the technological problems not yet under control. Fig. 5 shows a plane by plane scanning

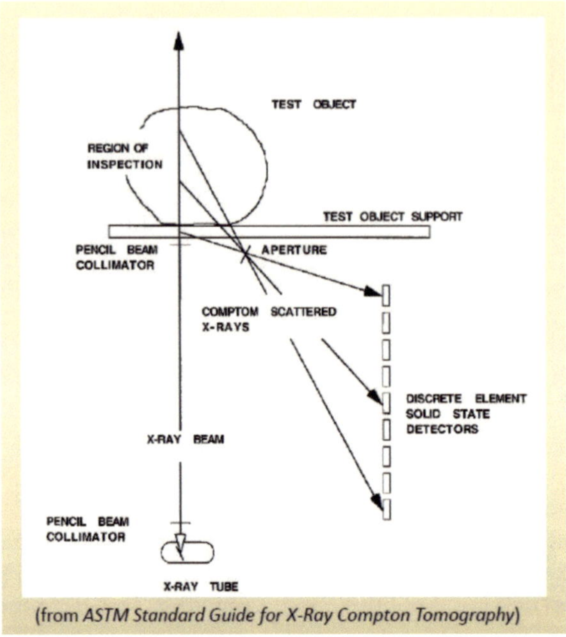

Figure 4. Philips Research Laboratory Compton Scatter Scanner (COMSCAN)

at fixed scattering angle ω using an movable collimated gamma camera. However this technique seemed to suffer from lack of sensitivity.

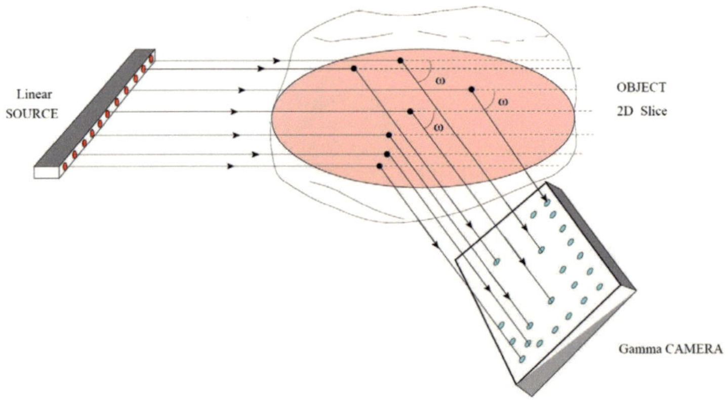

Figure 5. CST with plane by plane scanning

By now, Compton scatter tomography as set up by these workers seemed to be well established with spatial resolutions of better than 1cm and tissue density resolutions of better than 5/100 for a radiation dose of less than 1 rad. Yet two problems arose: reduction in image contrast and impaired tissue density resolution due to photon multiple scattering and attenuation artifacts. J. J. Battista et al. [7] has offered a way to cure for an improved Clarke scanner.

In the meantime the inversion problem has been formulated as a matrix inverse problem in [3] and [33], which was then solved numerically. It was realized that CST has considerable advantages over transmission CT in the low energy and low Z (atomic number) region, *i.e.* in medical range, and that CST has wide ranging NDE applications: viewing the interior of munitions, or structural material such as concrete, however with poor resolution because scanning was performed by hand moving the source-detector unit from pixel to pixel across the object. At this point, a remarkable leap forward, which provides a sound theoretical framework for CST, came into play.

4. Recent CST modalities

As early as 1978, a very original idea came from N. N. Kondic [38], who advocated the use of wide-angle collimators for *both* source and detector, instead of ray like collimators. Up to now, most proposed devices work with thin pencil-like beam source and with sharply (or widely) collimated detector coupled to a multichannel-analyzer. Kondic described a new way of irradiating a slice of an object by using a source's collimator with a wide planar angle as well as recording scattered radiation with a detector's collimator with wide angle. Thus the source takes the form of a fan beam and the wide angle collimator of the detector would delimitate an area in which an object is to be placed. In Fig. 6, we show a sketch of this proposal. Kondic made the crucial observation that when such a detector is connected to a multichannel analyzer, each measured energy channel, because of the Compton relation, is due to the sum of all scattering sites located on a circular arc starting from the source and ending at the detection site. Kondic called such an arc an *isogonic line*, wrote down the expression of the photon flux density registered at given scattering energy (including attenuation factors) and for the first time stated the electron density reconstruction problem in terms of *integral* data. Unfortunately a theoretical solution was not yet at hand. Expansion of this method and its variants were made later in [39]. Kondic cited also the advantages of using the isogonic lines. As collimation of the initial and scattered radiation in earlier modalities allows the detection of relatively few scattered photons, the counting statistics are very poor. The use of wide angle collimators would allow to work with higher counting rates which improves the data statistics and reduces the corresponding error, see [22]. Moreover Kondic did stress the need of varying the source - detector relative positions and (see item 6 on page 1146 of [39]), and proposed a rotation of the tomographic assembly in order to scan the whole field. Thus the photon flux density collected in an energy channel of a multichannel analyzer is due to the contribution not from a single scattering site but to the whole set of scattering sites corresponding to the same value of the scattering energy (or equivalently the same scattering angle ω). From elementary geometry, it can be seen that these sites lies on a circular arc passing through the source and the detection sites and subtending an inscribed angle of $(\pi - \omega)$. The measured quantity is essentially an integral of the electron density over a curve in a first approximation whereby attenuation and other effects are set aside.

In 1985, elaborating on Kondic's ideas, D. E. Bodette & A. M. Jacobs [9] were the first to realize that the scattered radiation data at constant energy may be expressed as an *integral transform* of the electron density on the isogonic line of Kondic. They pointed out the analogy with CT for which a measurement is also proportional to the integral of the linear attenuation coefficient along a straight line. They also conceded that the analytic derivation of a solution would be out of hand and offered a numerical treatment to extract a few first moments of the electron density from which several collective properties can be determined.

In 1993, starting from these ideas, T. H. Prettyman et al. [48] conceived a device which he called an *energy dispersive projective scatterometer*. Fig. 7 represents a sketch of this 1993 scatterometer device with two heavy wide angle collimators positioned at the gamma-ray source and at the detector. He then produced a numerical algorithm to deduce the electron density from the obtained measurements. He also pointed out that more complete data can be obtained by *rotating* the object, but one could have as well *rotate* the scatterometer. The coupling of the detector to a multichannel analyzer allows to collect the object projection data at constant scattering energy $E(\omega)$ as an integral on an isogonic arc of circle. More importantly, he observed that *"different projections can be obtained by rotating the sample."*, hinting that, as in the case of CT, a large number of projections, generated by a spatial rotation, would be necessary for image reconstruction. However the concept of an integral transform is still missing in the formulation of this forward problem.

In a sectional slice, the electron density $n(\mathbf{M})$ is a function of two coordinates. The necessary scatterometer data to recover $n(\mathbf{M})$ should depend also on two variables. One of them obviously would be ω the scattering angle (or alternatively the scattering energy $E(\omega)$, which can be read off on a multichannel analyzer). But there are many ways to choose the second variable. We shall discuss three of them. The situation is very reminiscent of Synthetic Aperture Radar imaging which admits two approaches, one of them makes use of integrals of the ground reflectivity function over circles on a planar ground. Hence this approach turns the reconstruction problem into a problem of integral geometry in the sense of I. M. Gelfand, which consists of reconstructing a function on a two-dimensional space by its circular arc integrals.

In the sequel, we shall discuss *three* modalities based on *three* classes of circular arcs in the plane. They are illuminating examples of mathematical contributions to imaging science. Moreover as pointed out in S. J. Norton [44], the existence of an analytic inverse formula for an integral transform could provide the basis for a computationally efficient and robust imaging algorithm, which should be also resistant to noise.

The original idea of Kondic has led Bodette and Jacobs to conclude that a true CST should to be founded on a generalized Radon transform in the same way CT, SPECT and PET imaging have as mathematical foundation the classical Radon transform. In reality, SPECT and PET imaging need a more complicated transform called the attenuated Radon transform which includes an attenuation factor in the form of the exponential of a line integral to account for a realistic functioning. But the presence of such a factor has made the inversion problem extremely complicated even if the attenuation map is known *a priori*. After decades of effort, the inversion of this transform was finally and successfully performed by R. G. Novikov [46], thanks to an ingenious *tour de force* in complex analysis. Here we are facing the formidable inversion problem of an attenuated Radon transforms on circular arcs in the plane.

If a straight line in a plane is defined by two parameters, a circle requires three parameters: the two coordinates of its center and its radius. Thus to reconstruct a function of two variables such as $n(\mathbf{M})$, a condition should be imposed in order to bring down the circle parameters to two. But there exists an infinite number of ways to define a two-parameter circle in the plane. In the CST context, the scattering angle ω, or any related function of it, appears to be a necessary parameter. The second parameter may be taken from the rotational symmetry of the problem and is simply a polar angle ϕ specifying the geometric position of the circle with respect to a reference direction. The integral transform may be then written down by

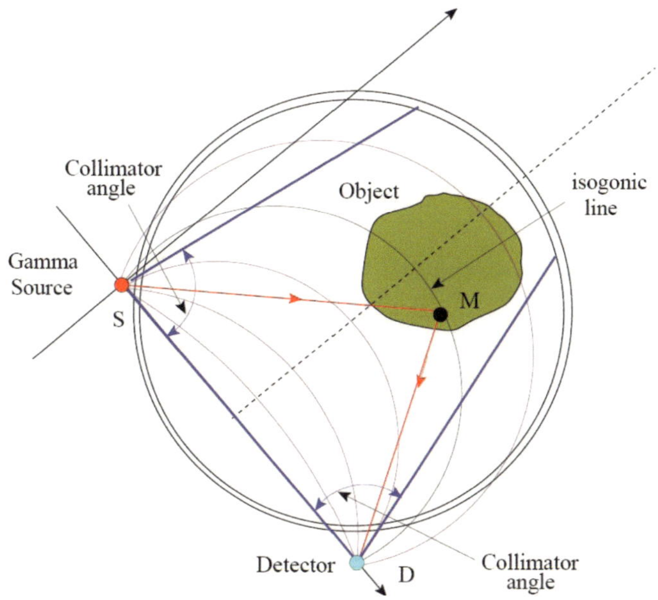

Figure 6. Sketch of Kondic's 1978 proposal

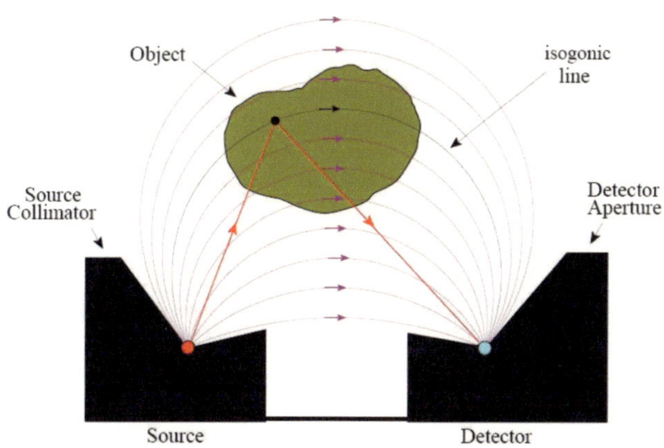

Figure 7. Sketch of Prettyman's 1993 Scatterometer

summing equation 3 over the scattering sites **M**. The result $\widehat{n}(\omega, \phi)$ is called the attenuated Radon transform of $n(\mathbf{M})$ on a circular arc. Then, for fixed **S** and **D**, we have

$$\widehat{n}(\omega, \phi) = \int_{\mathbb{R}^2} d\mathbf{M} \, \frac{I_0}{4\pi} \, m_\sigma(SM) \, \mathcal{A}_{in}(SM) \, n(\mathbf{M}) \, \pi \, r_e^2 P(\omega) \, \mathcal{A}_{out}(MD) \, m_{\sigma'}(MD) \, \delta(\text{Circ.Arc}), \tag{6}$$

where $\delta(\text{Circ.Arc})$ symbolizes the Dirac distribution concentrated on the chosen circular arc.

In the rest of the chapter, we shall discuss CST modalities, which are based on integral measurements, *i.e.* for which data are integrals of the electron density on arcs of circle linking the source point to the detection point in the plane. At present there are three of such CST modalities, corresponding to three choices of circle families in the plane. To remain on the track of the basic ideas, attenuation and beam spreading factors shall not be taken into account at first since solving such a general problem would be out of reach. Consequently we shall first concentrate on the problem of integral transform inversion. Attenuation and propagation spreading would be dealt with later. We shall see that in some cases the beam spreading effect can be included in the exact solution but attenuation must be either corrected or compensated for.

4.1. First CST modality (Norton 1994)

The first CST scanner which integrates the notion of Radon transform on Kondic isogonic arcs was proposed by S. J. Norton [44]. At that time it was known that A. M. Cormack [16] had established that the Radon transform on circles intersecting a fixed point in the plane is invertible. Norton proposed to use this result in the conception of his CST scanner, which was patented in 1995, see [45]. The Norton scanner has a gamma-ray source at fixed point **S** and a detector **D** movable on a line intersecting the source site, as sketched in Fig. 8.

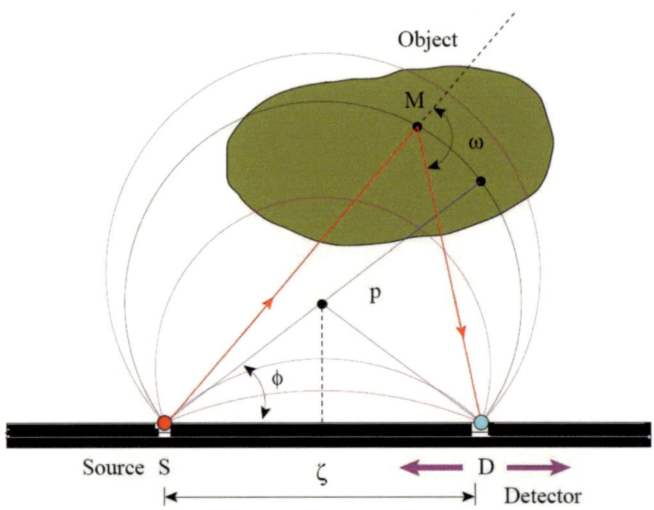

Figure 8. Fisrt CST modality

The point source **S** emits primary radiation towards an object, of which **M** is a running point. A point detector **D** moves along an Ox-axis and collects, at given energy $E(\omega)$, scattered radiation from the object. The physics of Compton scattering demands that the registered radiation flux energy $\widehat{n}(\mathbf{D})$ at site **D** is due to the contribution of all scattering sites **M** lying on an arc of circle from **S** to **D** subtending an angle $(\pi - \omega)$, where ω is the scattering angle corresponding to the outgoing energy $E(\omega)$, as given by equation 1.

Mathematically, $\widehat{n}(\mathbf{D})$ is essentially the integral of the object electron density $n(\mathbf{M})$ on such arc of circles, when radiation attenuation and beam spreading effects due to radiation propagation are neglected. If polar coordinates with **S** as origin are used, then a running point **M** on a circle of diameter p, with center at the point of polar coordinates $(p/2, \phi)$, is given by (r, θ) with $r = p\cos(\theta - \phi)$. Thus, calling $\gamma = (\theta - \phi)$ and recalling that the circle arc element is $ds = p\,d\gamma$, we have $\widehat{n}(\mathbf{D}) = \widehat{n}(p, \phi)$ with

$$\widehat{n}(p,\phi) = \int_{\text{arc}\,SD} ds\; n(r, \gamma + \phi) = p \int_{-\phi}^{\pi/2} d\gamma\; n(p\cos\gamma, \gamma + \phi), \tag{7}$$

where, for ease of notations, we have absorbed in the definition of $\widehat{n}(\mathbf{D})$ the Compton differential cross-section and the emitted flux density of the source and assumed no attenuation and beam spreading factors on the paths SM and MD. Equation 7 is not really the circular Radon transform of $n(\mathbf{M})$ in A. M. Cormack [16], since the integral goes over only the upper circular arc, which physically corresponds to the scattering angle ω and the detected energy $E(\omega)$. Note that the lower arc SD, is related to the scattering angle $(\pi - \omega)$ and the scattering energy $E(\pi - \omega)$, which is according to equation 1 not equal to $E(\omega)$. Yet Norton argued that for an object situated above the line SD, which means that the support of $n(r, \theta)$ is situated in the upper half-plane, the inversion procedure of A. M. Cormack should work. A closed form inverse formula, which mathematically well defined, has been given in [17] as

$$n(r,\theta) = \frac{1}{2\pi^2 r} \int_0^{2\pi} d\phi \int_0^{\infty} dp\, \frac{\partial \widehat{n}(p,\phi)}{\partial p}\, \frac{1}{r/p - \cos(\theta - \phi)}. \tag{8}$$

In his work of 1994 [44], Norton has also derived an alternative inversion formula *via* the radial Fourier transform of $n(r, \theta)$.

We now give some details on how equation 8 is derived. Assuming that both $n(r, \theta)$ and $\widehat{n}(p, \phi)$ can be represented by their angular Fourier series

$$n(r,\theta) = \sum_l n_l(r)\, e^{il\theta}, \quad \text{with} \quad \widehat{n}(p,\phi) = \sum_l \widehat{n}_l(p)\, e^{il\phi}, \tag{9}$$

then equation 7 takes the form of a Chebyshev [1] transform, *i.e.*

$$\widehat{n}_l(p) = 2 \int_0^p dr\, \frac{\cos l\left(\cos^{-1}(r/p)\right)}{\sqrt{1 - (r/p)^2}}\, n_l(r), \tag{10}$$

which can be inverted using the following identity, (see [16]),

$$\int_s^t \frac{dx}{x}\, \frac{\cosh\left(l \cosh^{-1}(s/x)\right)}{\sqrt{(s/x)^2 - 1}}\, \frac{\cos l(\cos^{-1}(t/x))}{\sqrt{1 - (t/x)^2}} = \frac{\pi}{2}. \tag{11}$$

The inverse formula for $n_l(r)$ is given in [17] as

$$n_l(r) = \frac{1}{\pi r} \left(\int_0^r dp\, \frac{d\widehat{n}_l(p)}{dp}\, \frac{\left((r/p) - \sqrt{(r/p)^2 - 1}\right)^l}{\sqrt{(r/p)^2 - 1}} - \int_r^{\infty} dp\, \frac{d\widehat{n}_l(p)}{dp}\, U_{l-1}(r/p) \right), \tag{12}$$

where $U_{l-1}(\cos x) = \sin lx / \sin x$. Then $n(r, \theta)$ in equation 8 is obtained by resumming the series in equation 9.

[1] This name comes from the fact that the Chebyshev polynomial of the first kind is $T_l(\cos x) = \cos lx$.

4.2. Second CST modality (Nguyen-Truong 2010)

There are two scanning modes in this modality. If the object is "small", or can be put inside a circle of radius p (a mechanical adjustable parameter), one can make an "internal" scanning inside this circle. If the object is "large" or situated far way from the observer, one can use the "external" scanning mode. The two modes shall be discussed separately.

4.2.1. Internal scanning

The second modality has originated from an proposal in [41]. At the time only numerical simulation and reconstruction using the Singular Value Decomposition method were performed on a turbine blade with encouraging results. One may conceive this modality as an evolved Prettyman's scatterometer, which can rotate around an axis perpendicular to its plane, realizing what Prettyman had foreseen long ago to generate more useful data for his numerical reconstruction method. In fact, as will be shown the rotational motion is necessary for the reconstruction the electron density in a trans-axial slice.

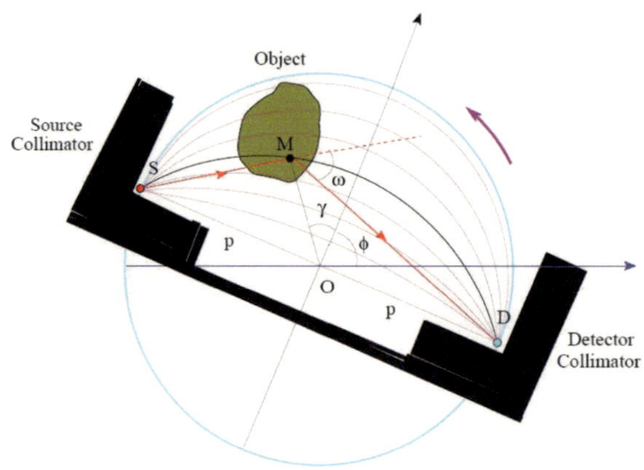

Figure 9. Second CST modality: internal scanning

The apparatus is is sketched in Fig. 9. An emitting radiation point source **S** is placed at a distance $2p$ from a point detector **D**. The segment SD joining them rotates around its middle point **O**. At site **D** is collected the single-scattered radiation flux density from the scanned object for a given angular position of the line SD and at a given scattering energy $E(\omega)$, (equivalently at scattering angle ω). Then at fixed ϕ, a multichannel analyzer records the photon counts in each energy channel. Data acquisition is performed for every angular position ϕ of SD.

Thus, thanks to the physics of the Compton effect, the detected radiation flux density is proportional to the integral of the electron density $n(\mathbf{M})$ on a class of circular arcs sharing a chord of fixed length $2p$, which rotates about its fixed middle point **O**.

With a polar coordinate system centered at **O**, the equation of a circular arc lying inside a circle of center O and radius p reads (see [42])

$$r = r(\cos(\theta - \phi)) = p\left(\sqrt{1 + \tau^2 \cos^2(\theta - \phi)} - \tau \cos(\theta - \phi)\right), \tag{13}$$

which is defined by two parameters τ and ϕ: a) ϕ is the angle made by its symmetry axis with the reference direction Ox and b) τ is related to the scattering angle ω by $\tau = \cot\omega$. Note that τ is positive for $0 < \omega < \pi/2$ and the range of θ is $(\phi - \pi/2) < \theta < (\phi + \pi/2)$.

Again to simplify the notation by assuming that attenuation and beam spreading are neglected as well as by absorbing the Compton kinematic factor into one single function, we can say that the detected photon flux density $\hat{n}(\tau,\phi)$ is the Radon transform of the electron density $n(r,\theta)$ along arcs of circle given by equation 13. Thus using the auxiliary angle $\gamma = (\theta - \phi)$ as in the previous subsection, we may express $\hat{n}(\tau,\phi)$ with ds, the integration arc element given by

$$ds = r\,d\gamma\,\sqrt{\frac{1+\tau^2}{1+\tau^2\cos^2\gamma}} = dr\,\frac{\sqrt{1+\tau^2}}{\tau\sin\gamma}. \tag{14}$$

Now introducing the angular Fourier components of $\hat{n}(\tau,\phi)$ and $n(r,\theta)$ as given by equation 9, we see that they are related by

$$\frac{\tau\,\hat{n}_l(\tau)}{\sqrt{1+\tau^2}} = 2\int_{p(\sqrt{1+\tau^2}-\tau)}^{p} \frac{dr}{\sqrt{1-\frac{1}{4\tau^2}\left(\frac{p}{r}-\frac{r}{p}\right)^2}}\,\cos\left[l\cos^{-1}\left(\frac{1}{2\tau}\left(\frac{p}{r}-\frac{r}{p}\right)\right)\right]\,n_l(r). \tag{15}$$

At first this Chebyshev transform looks a bit hopeless. However if one introduces a new variable g defined by

$$g = \frac{1}{2}\left(\frac{p}{r}-\frac{r}{p}\right), \tag{16}$$

one can put it under the form

$$\frac{\tau\,\hat{n}_l(\tau)}{\sqrt{1+\tau^2}} = 2\int_0^{\tau} dg\,\frac{\cos l\cos^{-1}\left(\frac{g}{\tau}\right)}{\sqrt{1-\frac{g^2}{\tau^2}}}\,\frac{p(\sqrt{1+g^2}-g)}{\sqrt{1+g^2}}\,n_l(p(\sqrt{1+g^2}-g)). \tag{17}$$

Then defining new functions by

$$\widehat{N}_l(\tau) = \frac{\tau\,\hat{n}_l(\tau)}{\sqrt{1+\tau^2}} \quad \text{and} \quad N_l(g) = \frac{p(\sqrt{1+g^2}-g)}{\sqrt{1+g^2}}\,n_l(p(\sqrt{1+g^2}-g)), \tag{18}$$

we obtain

$$\widehat{N}_l(\tau) = 2\int_0^{\tau} dg\,\frac{\cos l\cos^{-1}\left(\frac{g}{\tau}\right)}{\sqrt{1-\frac{g^2}{\tau^2}}}\,N_l(g), \tag{19}$$

which is precisely of the form of equation 10, obtained in the Radon problem on circles passing through a fixed point. Hence an inversion formula exists in the (τ, g) variables, *i.e.*

$$N_l(g) = \frac{1}{\pi g}\left(\int_0^{g} dp\,\frac{d\widehat{N}_l(\tau)}{d\tau}\,\frac{\left((g/\tau)-\sqrt{(g/\tau)^2-1}\right)^l}{\sqrt{(g/\tau)^2-1}} - \int_g^{\infty} d\tau\,\frac{d\widehat{N}_l(\tau)}{d\tau}\,U_{l-1}(g/\tau)\right). \tag{20}$$

A closed form of the inversion formula can be deduced from equation 8

$$N(g,\theta) = \frac{1}{2\pi^2 g} \int_0^{2\pi} d\phi \int_0^{\infty} d\tau \, \frac{\partial \widehat{N}(\tau,\phi)}{\partial \tau} \, \frac{1}{g/\tau - \cos(\theta - \phi)}. \tag{21}$$

Finally going back to the original functions $n(r,\theta)$ and $\widehat{n}(\tau,\phi)$, via equations 18, the reconstructed electron density is

$$n(r,\theta) = \frac{1}{2\pi^2} \frac{\sqrt{1 + \frac{1}{4}\left(\frac{p}{r} - \frac{r}{p}\right)^2}}{\frac{r}{2}\left(\frac{p}{r} - \frac{r}{p}\right)} \int_0^{2\pi} d\phi \int_0^{\infty} d\tau \, \frac{1}{\frac{1}{2\tau}\left(\frac{p}{r} - \frac{r}{p}\right) - \cos(\theta - \phi)} \, \frac{\partial}{\partial \tau}\left(\frac{\tau\,\widehat{n}(\tau,\phi)}{\sqrt{1+\tau^2}}\right). \tag{22}$$

4.2.2. External scanning

This scanning mode is illustrated by Fig. 10. Data acquisition is the same as for internal scanning, except for an object of compact support, the rotational motion may be replaced by a back and forth radar type sweeping motion.

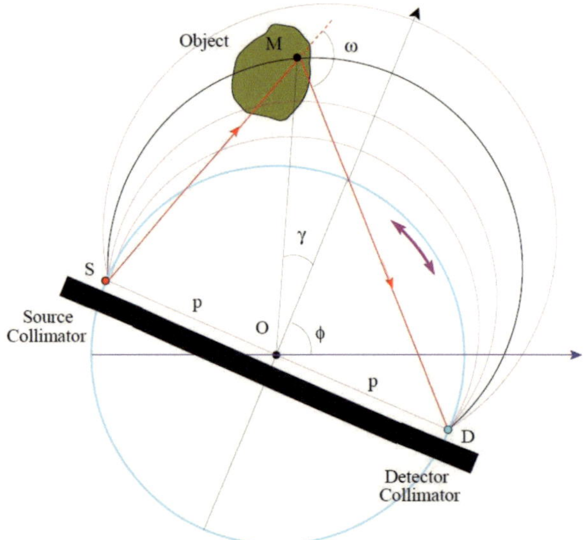

Figure 10. Second CST modality: external scanning

The working is similar to the internal scanning mode, except that one uses the scattering angle range $\pi/2 < \omega < \pi$ and the "external" arc of circle given by the equation

$$r = r(\cos(\theta - \phi)) = p\left(\sqrt{1 + \tau^2 \cos^2(\theta - \phi)} + \tau \cos(\theta - \phi)\right), \tag{23}$$

where $\tau = -\cot\omega > 0$ and $(\phi - \pi/2) < \theta < (\phi + \pi/2)$. This arc of circle Radon transform has not yet been considered in [42]. Similarly the Radon transform of the electron density on this arc of circle is now expressed by the following Chebyshev integral transform for its angular components

$$\frac{\tau\,\hat{n}_l(\tau)}{\sqrt{1+\tau^2}} = 2\int_p^{p(\sqrt{1+\tau^2}+\tau)} \frac{dr}{\sqrt{1-\frac{1}{4\tau^2}\left(\frac{r}{p}-\frac{p}{r}\right)^2}}\, n_l(r)\, \cos\left[l\cos^{-1}\left(\frac{1}{2\tau}\left(\frac{r}{p}-\frac{p}{r}\right)\right)\right]. \quad (24)$$

This equation will take the form of equation 10, as equation 19, when the intermediate variable

$$g' = \frac{1}{2}\left(\frac{r}{p}-\frac{p}{r}\right), \quad (25)$$

and the functions

$$\widehat{N}_l(\tau) = \frac{\tau\,\hat{n}_l(\tau)}{\sqrt{1+\tau^2}} \quad \text{and} \quad N_l(g') = \frac{p(\sqrt{1+g'^2}+g')}{\sqrt{1+g'^2}}\, n_l(p(\sqrt{1+g'^2}+g')), \quad (26)$$

are used. Finally, following the same steps as in the previous scanning mode, the reconstruction formula for $n(r,\theta)$ reads

$$n(r,\theta) = \frac{1}{2\pi^2}\,\frac{\sqrt{1+\frac{1}{4}\left(\frac{r}{p}-\frac{p}{r}\right)^2}}{\frac{r}{2}\left(\frac{r}{p}-\frac{p}{r}\right)} \int_0^{2\pi} d\phi \int_0^{\infty} d\tau\, \frac{1}{\frac{1}{2\tau}\left(\frac{r}{p}-\frac{p}{r}\right)-\cos(\theta-\phi)}\, \frac{\partial}{\partial\tau}\left(\frac{\tau\,\hat{n}(\tau,\phi)}{\sqrt{1+\tau^2}}\right). \quad (27)$$

4.3. Third CST modality (Truong-Nguyen 2011)

In this subsection we discuss two scanning modes of a third CST modality proposed in [54]. This modality has originated from a search for curves in the plane such that the Radon transform on these curves may be reduced to a Chebyshev integral transform of the form of equation 10, for circles passing through a fixed point. It turns out that Radon transforms on arcs of circles orthogonal to a fixed circle *do have this property*. The pair source-detector still moves on a circle of radius p (still an adjustable parameter) and centered at **O**, the origin of a polar coordinate system. But their separation distance is no longer constant as in the second CST modality: it depends on the scattering angle ω. The positions of **S** and **D** are given by an opening angle γ_0, measured from the symmetry axis of the circular arc.

4.3.1. Internal scanning

In this case, the Radon transform is defined on the following circular arc of equation

$$r = p(\tau\cos(\theta-\phi) - \sqrt{\tau^2\cos^2(\theta-\phi)-1}), \quad (28)$$

where $\tau = 1/\cos\gamma_0$ and $-\gamma_0 < (\theta-\phi) < \gamma_0$. Inspection of Fig. 11 shows that $\gamma_0 = (\pi/2-\omega)$ for $0<\omega<\pi/2$. Hence $\tau = 1/\sin\omega > 1$. So data acquisition works as follows. For fixed ϕ, the pair source - detector must be *simultaneously* displaced on the circle of radius p so that the opening angle $\widehat{SOD} = 2\gamma_0 = (\pi-2\omega)$, before registering at **D** a photon count. The number of isogonic lines is thus equal to the number of positions of the pair $(\mathbf{S},\mathbf{D})$.

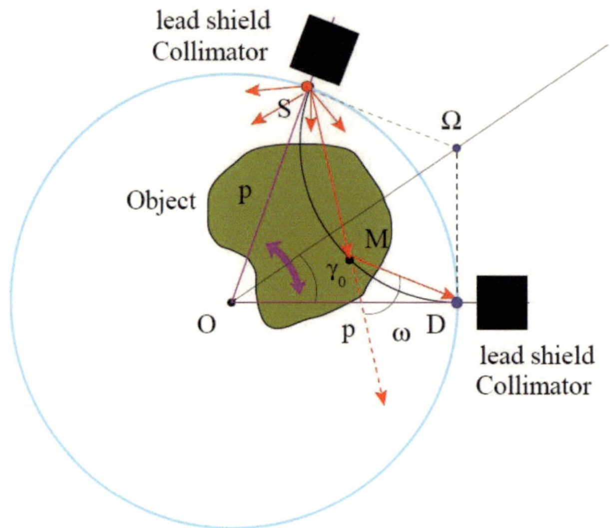

Figure 11. Third CST modality: internal scanning

The integration arc element being now

$$ds = r\,d\gamma\,\sqrt{\frac{\tau^2-1}{\tau^2\cos^2\gamma}-1} = dr\,\frac{\sqrt{\tau^2-1}}{\tau\sin\gamma}, \tag{29}$$

the Radon transform of the electron density $\widehat{n}(\tau,\phi)$ becomes, in terms of the angular components $n_l(r)$ and $\widehat{n}_l(\tau)$, a Chebyshev transform similar to equation 17, *i.e.*

$$\frac{\tau\,\widehat{n}_l(\tau)}{\sqrt{\tau^2-1}} = 2\int_{p(\tau-\sqrt{\tau^2-1})}^{p} \frac{dr}{\sqrt{1-\frac{1}{4\tau^2}\left(\frac{p}{r}+\frac{r}{p}\right)^2}}\; n_l(r)\;\cos\left[l\cos^{-1}\left(\frac{1}{2\tau}\left(\frac{p}{r}+\frac{r}{p}\right)\right)\right]. \tag{30}$$

The structural similarity with equations 15 and 24 suggests an intermediate variable g'' of the form

$$g'' = \frac{1}{2}\left(\frac{r}{p}+\frac{p}{r}\right), \tag{31}$$

which yields the following Chebyshev transform

$$\frac{\tau\,\widehat{n}_l(\tau)}{\sqrt{\tau^2-1}} = 2\int_1^{\tau} dg''\,\frac{\cos l\cos^{-1}\left(\frac{g''}{\tau}\right)}{\sqrt{1-\frac{g''^2}{\tau^2}}}\,\frac{p(g''-\sqrt{g''^2-1})}{\sqrt{g''^2-1}}\,n_l(p(g''-\sqrt{g''^2-1})). \tag{32}$$

Now redefining the functions by

$$\widehat{N}_l(\tau) = \frac{\tau\,\widehat{n}_l(\tau)}{\sqrt{\tau^2-1}} \quad \text{and} \quad N_l(g'') = \frac{p(\sqrt{g''-g''^2-1})}{\sqrt{g''^2-1}}\,n_l(p(g''-\sqrt{g''^2-1})), \tag{33}$$

we obtain the form of equation 10, nevertheless with a lower integration bound equal to $\tau = 1$ and not zero. This does not spoil the inversion procedure based on the identity 11, as shown in [54]. Consequently we recover the electron density in closed form as

$$n(r,\theta) = \frac{1}{2\pi^2} \frac{\sqrt{\frac{1}{4}\left(\frac{p}{r}+\frac{r}{p}\right)^2 - 1}}{\frac{r}{2}\left(\frac{p}{r}+\frac{r}{p}\right)} \int_0^{2\pi} d\phi \int_0^{\infty} d\tau \frac{1}{\frac{1}{2\tau}\left(\frac{p}{r}+\frac{r}{p}\right) - \cos(\theta-\phi)} \frac{\partial}{\partial\tau}\left(\frac{\tau\,\hat{n}(\tau,\phi)}{\sqrt{\tau^2-1}}\right). \tag{34}$$

4.3.2. External scanning

This scanning mode is shown in Fig. 12. It has the same data acquisition procedure as for internal scanning. It is appropriate for large objects or objects situated far away from the scanner, *e.g.* buried objects underground or undersea, with a back and forth radar type of scanning motion.

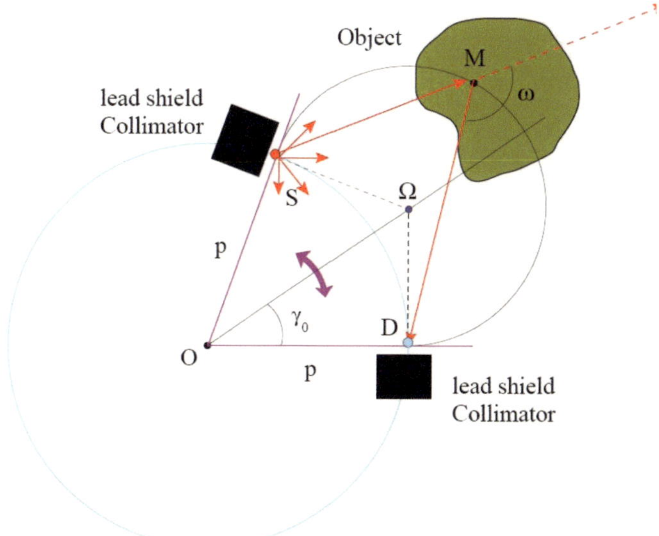

Figure 12. Third CST modality: external scanning

The Radon transform is now defined on the external circular arc with respect to the reference circle of radius p of equation

$$r = p(\tau\cos(\theta-\phi) + \sqrt{\tau^2\cos^2(\theta-\phi) - 1}). \tag{35}$$

Here $\pi/2 < \omega < \pi$ and $\gamma_0 = (\omega - \pi/2)$ [2]. As for the case of internal scanning, we have also $\tau = 1/\cos\gamma_0$ and $-\gamma_0 < (\theta-\phi) < \gamma_0$ with the same data acquisition procedure.

The integration arc element is the same as in the previous scanning mode, see equation 29. Then the Radon transform of the electron density $\hat{n}(\tau,\phi)$ becomes, in terms of function angular components, the following Chebyshev transform

$$\frac{\tau\,\hat{n}_l(\tau)}{\sqrt{\tau^2-1}} = 2\int_p^{p(\tau-\sqrt{\tau^2-1})} \frac{dr}{\sqrt{1-\frac{1}{4\tau^2}\left(\frac{p}{r}+\frac{r}{p}\right)^2}}\, n_l(r)\, \cos\left[l\cos^{-1}\left(\frac{1}{2\tau}\left(\frac{p}{r}+\frac{r}{p}\right)\right)\right]. \tag{36}$$

[2] Note that the two arcs of equations 28 and 35 belong to the same circle.

We see that the intermediate variable g'' of equation (31) can be used again so that

$$\frac{\tau \widehat{n}_l(\tau)}{\sqrt{\tau^2-1}} = 2\int_1^\tau dg'' \, \frac{\cos l \cos^{-1}\left(\frac{g''}{\tau}\right)}{\sqrt{1-\frac{g''^2}{\tau^2}}} \, \frac{p(g''+\sqrt{g''^2-1})}{\sqrt{g''^2-1}} \, n_l(p(g''+\sqrt{g''^2-1})). \tag{37}$$

Now redefining the functions by

$$\widehat{N}_l(\tau) = \frac{\tau \widehat{n}_l(\tau)}{\sqrt{\tau^2-1}} \quad \text{and} \quad N_l(g'') = \frac{p(\sqrt{g''}+g''^2-1)}{\sqrt{g''^2-1}} \, n_l(p(g''+\sqrt{g''^2-1})), \tag{38}$$

we obtain the form of equation 10, and surprisingly the same equation as for internal scanning. Consequently one end up with the same reconstruction formula (34), which is a remarkable advantage for this modality. This is due to the fact that the two arcs are on the same circle.

5. Numerical simulations

This section is devoted to showing that the analytic formulas of inversion do lead to robust computation algorithms. As we have shown, it is sufficient develop a *single* reconstruction algorithm for the Radon transform on circles passing through a fixed point, since all other cases can be reduced to that one by a change of variable and a change of functions. Since we use the formalism of angular Fourier components, we shall adapt a procedure set up long ago by C. H. Chapman & P. W. Carey [12] for the classical Radon transform.

5.1. Algorithm

The idea is to start with the result of A. M. Cormack [15] (see his equation 18b) for the reconstructed angular Fourier component of $n(r,\theta)$ given by

$$n_l(r) = \frac{1}{\pi r}\left(\int_0^r dp \, \frac{d\widehat{n}_l(p)}{dp} \, \frac{\left((r/p)-\sqrt{(r/p)^2-1}\right)^l}{\sqrt{(r/p)^2-1}} - \int_r^\infty dp \, \frac{d\widehat{n}_l(p)}{dp} \, U_{l-1}(r/p)\right). \tag{39}$$

We compute first $n_l(r)$ from a discretized version of equation 39, which shall be set up now, and get $n(r,\theta)$ back by its angular Fourier series using equation 9.

To this end, we change the form of equation 39 by making the following change of variables

$$p = \frac{r}{\cosh x} \quad \text{and} \quad p = \frac{r}{\cos x}, \tag{40}$$

respectively in the first and in the second integral of (39). Hence

$$n_l(r) = \frac{1}{\pi}\left(\int_1^\infty dx \, \frac{d\widehat{n}_l(p)}{dp} \, \frac{e^{-lx}}{\cosh^2 x} - \int_0^{\pi/2} dx \, \frac{d\widehat{n}_l(p)}{dp} \, \frac{\sin lx}{\cos^2 x}\right). \tag{41}$$

Then these integrals will be approximated by discrete sums in which we take for simplicity the same step δ for the variable r as well as for the variable p. Hence $n_l(r) \simeq n_l(j\delta)$, with

$$n_l(j\delta) = \frac{1}{\pi}\left(\sum_{k=1}^{j-1} \frac{d\widehat{n}_l(p)}{dp} \int_{x_j^k}^{x_j^{k+1}} dx \, \frac{e^{-lx}}{\cosh^2 x} - \sum_{k=j}^{K-1} \frac{d\widehat{n}_l(p)}{dp} \int_{x_j^k}^{x_j^{k+1}} dx \, \frac{\sin lx}{\cos^2 x}\right), \tag{42}$$

where K is the maximal value taken by k. Now introducing the indefinite integrals

$$I_l(x) = \int^x dz \, \frac{e^{-lz}}{\cosh^2 z} \quad \text{and} \quad J_l(x) = \int^x dz \, \frac{\sin lz}{\cos^2 z}, \tag{43}$$

we see that they obey the following recursion relations, see [50]

$$(l-2)I_l(x) = 2\,(\tan x \, \sin(l-2)x - \cos(l-2)x) - l\, I_{l-2}(x), \tag{44}$$

with $I_0(x) = 1/\cos x$ and $I_1(x) = -2\ln(\cos x)$, and

$$l\, J_{l+1}(x) = -\frac{1}{x^l(1+x^2} - (l+2)J_{l-1}(x), \tag{45}$$

with

$$J_0(x) = \frac{x}{2(1+x^2)} + \frac{1}{2}\tan^{-1} x \quad \text{and} \quad J_1(x) = \ln\left(\frac{x}{\sqrt{1+x^2}}\right) + \frac{1}{2(1+x^2)}. \tag{46}$$

The derivatives of $d\widehat{n}_l(p)/dp$ are replaced by a simple linear interpolation $\widehat{n'}_l(k)$, *i.e.*

$$\frac{d\widehat{n}_l(p)}{dp} \simeq \frac{n_l(k+1) - n_l(k)}{\delta} = \widehat{n'}_l(k). \tag{47}$$

Then the discretized value of the reconstructed angular component of $n_l(r)$, with $r \sim j\delta$, is

$$n_l(j\delta) = \frac{1}{\pi}\left(\sum_{k=1}^{j-1} \widehat{n'}_l(k)\,(I_l((k+1)\delta) - I_l(k\delta)) - \sum_{k=j}^{K-1} \widehat{n'}_l(k)\,(J_l((k+1)\delta) - J_l(k\delta))\right). \tag{48}$$

Equation 48 shall be used in numerical simulations[3].

5.2. Simulation results

In this subsection, we present numerical simulations on the first CST modality applied to the Shepp-Logan medical phantom, see [50]. The source **S** is placed below on the left of the image and the detector moves along the line SD. The relevant space is represented by 256 × 256 (length unit)^2. Let N_ϕ be the number of angular steps and let N_p be the number of radii for circles going through the origin O. Then the following sampling steps $\delta_\phi = 2\pi/N_\phi$ and $\delta = 4 \star 256/N_p$ are taken. Since there is no rotation around the object, the (ϕ, p)-space is very large in comparison to the studied image. To have a good representation of the object, we need a large maximum value of p, (*e.g.* four times the image size).

To estimate the reconstruction quality, we use the normalized mean square error ($NMSE$) and the normalized mean absolute error ($NMAE$) (expressed as a percentage), defined by

$$NMSE = \frac{100}{N^2}\frac{\sum_{(i,j)\in[1,N]^2} |\mathcal{I}_r(i,j) - \mathcal{I}_o(i,j)|^2}{\max_{(i,j)\in[1,N]^2}\{\mathcal{I}_o(i,j)\}^2} \quad \text{and} \quad NMAE = \frac{100}{N^2}\frac{\sum_{(i,j)\in[1,N]^2} |\mathcal{I}_r(i,j) - \mathcal{I}_o(i,j)|}{\max_{(i,j)\in[1,N]^2}\{\mathcal{I}_o(i,j)\}},$$

[3] For difficulties on the handling of the inversion formula of S. J. Norton, see [55]

where $\mathcal{I}_r$ is the reconstructed image and $\mathcal{I}_o$ is the original image.

In order to reduce the artifacts generated around the object by the circular harmonic decomposition approach, we can use information given by the contours of the projection data. If the projection data are vanishing, this means that the corresponding circular arc does not intersect the object. Therefore if the object of interest is bounded in space, a null set in the projection space corresponds to a null set in the original space. This approach gives a very interesting image quality in the reconstruction of the Shepp-Logan phantom. Contours and small structures are nicely recovered. A maximum value p_{max} is to be fixed in numerical computation. But a sharp cut-off of p and the ensuing loss of data generate significant artifacts. Moreover an increase of p_{max} leads to an increase of the detector length in the first CST modality.

The original Shepp-Logan phantom is given in Fig. 13.

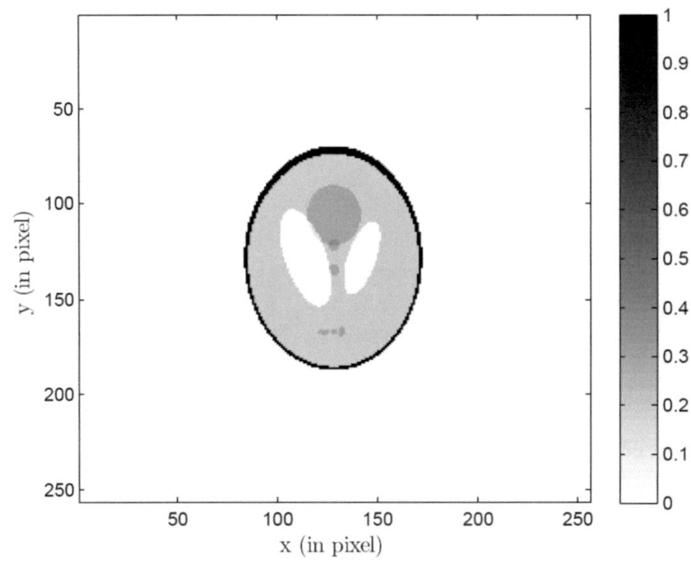

Figure 13. Shepp-Logan original phantom, reprinted from [51]

Fig. 14 illustrates the first CST modality data, obtained by application of the Radon transform on circles passing through the coordinate origin. Finally the reconstructed image by the first CST modality is given in Fig. 15.

Now using the same algorithm but in different function spaces, one can achieve the reconstruction with the two other CST modalities. With the second CST modality for small objects, collected data and image reconstruction are given in Fig. 16, see [51].

We see that generally a reasonable image quality in the reconstruction of the medical phantom is obtained. Contours and small structures are correctly recovered. The numerical error measurements are very close to those of the ordinary Radon transform and are even better for a medical phantom. Artifacts arise if the studied object occupies the whole medium since the boundary parts are not well scanned and less information are available from these parts.

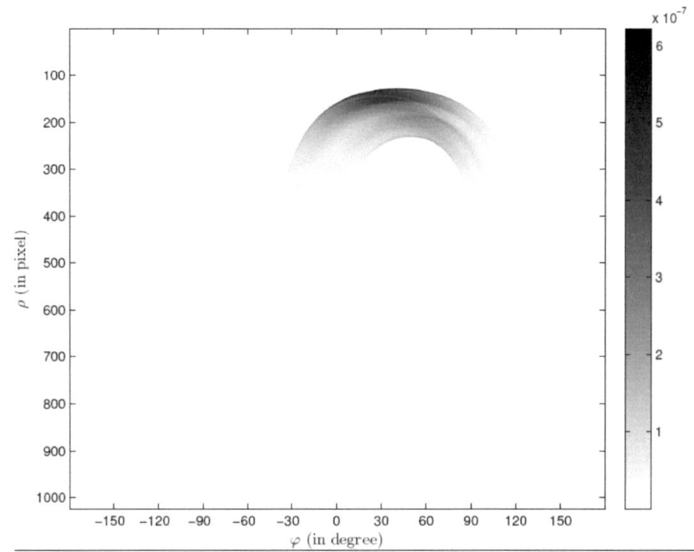

Figure 14. Data of the first CST modality (Norton 1994), reprinted from [51]

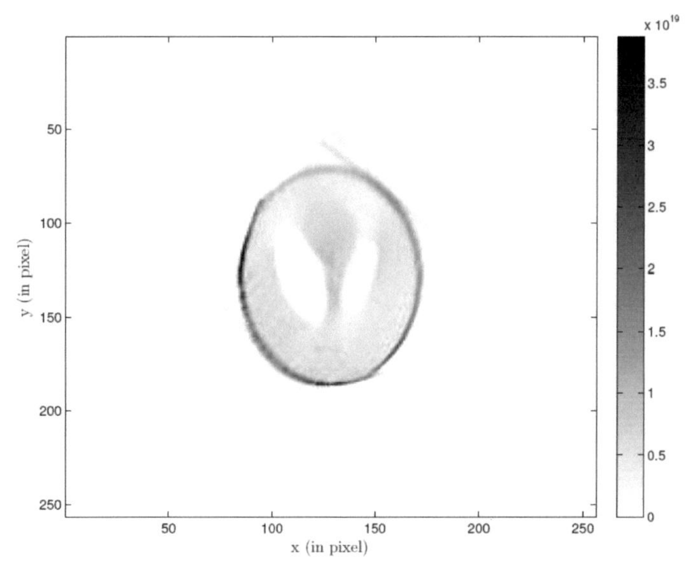

Figure 15. Shepp-Logan phantom reconstructed by the first CST modality (Norton 1994), reprinted from [51]

As the set up works with radial parameters, an object of circular symmetry fits better to this modality: this is the case of a medical phantom.

As for the CST third modality for small objects, the simulations results are displayed in Fig. 17, see [43].

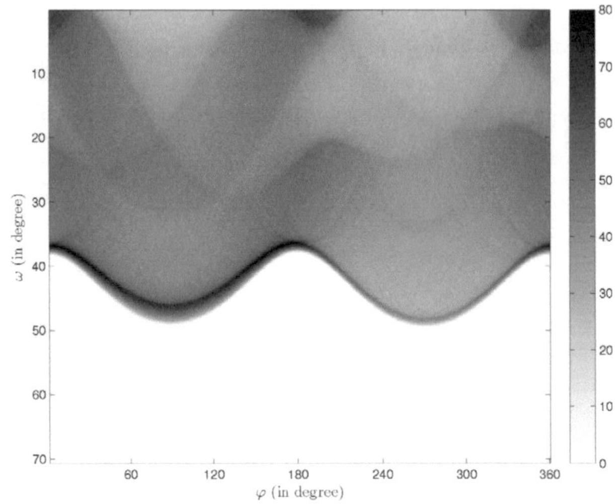

(a) Data of the second CST modality, reprinted from [50]

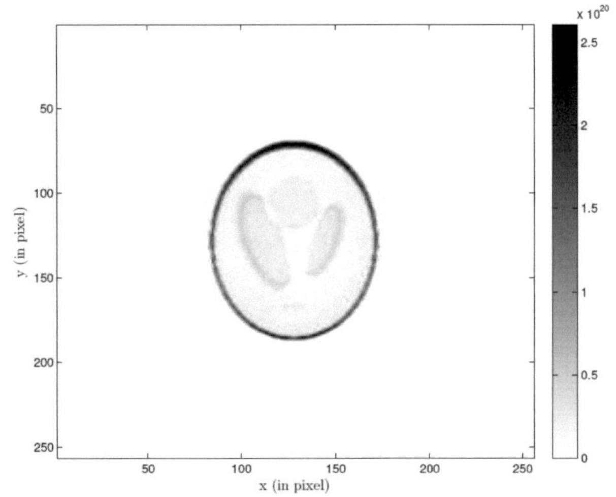

(b) Image reconstruction by the second CST modality, reprinted from [50]

Figure 16. Second CST modality simulation results illustration

The modified Chapman & Carey approach used here gives in general a reasonable image quality in the reconstruction of the medical phantom (Fig. 17) with (Normalized Mean Absolute Error =2.2% (NMAE) and Normalized Mean Square Error = 0.038 (NMSE). Contours and small structures are well recovered. The numerical error measurements obtained using the algorithm described above are of the same order of magnitude as in existing scanning devices. Nevertheless we observe some artifacts. They can be reduced by a better acquisition of the data. Indeed the (ϕ, τ)-space is very large but the (ϕ, ω)-space is bounded. Hence with a good resolution, the loss of data is less important.

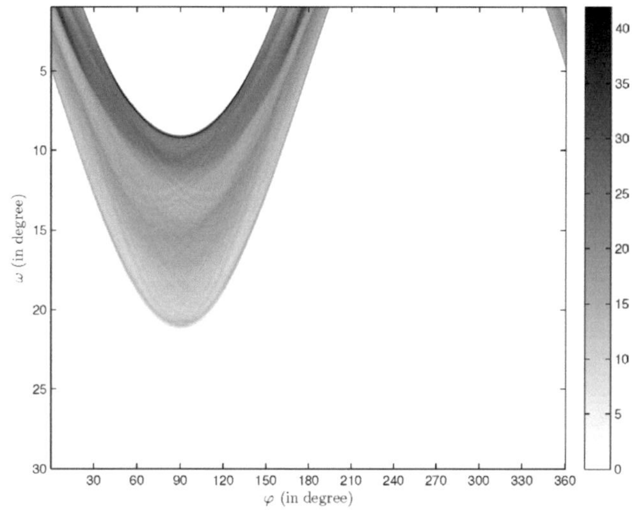

(a) Data of the third CST modality, reprinted from [43]

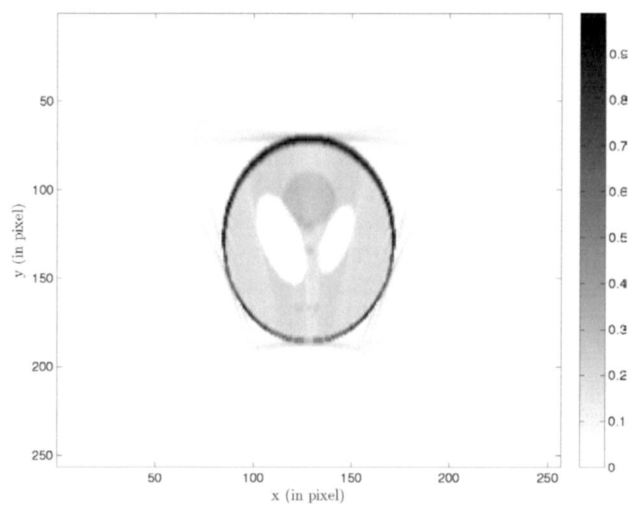

(b) Image reconstruction by the third CST modality reprinted from [43]

Figure 17. Third CST modality simulation results illustration

5.3. Open problems

Of course what is presented here does not claim neither completeness nor perfection. There are still many important problems to tackle.

1) *Attenuation.* This question, as mentioned before, has no analytic answer, even in the near future. One way to solve practically the problem is to produce an approximate iterative corrective algorithm, see *e.g.* [51].

2) *Beam spreading.* In the limit of vanishingly small detecting pixel, the inclusion of beam spreading factors proportional to the inverse distances (or inverse square distances) $SM^{-1,-2}$

(or $MD^{-1,-2}$) does not spoiled the inversion procedure. One may redefine an "effective" electron density and an "effective" Radon transform. This is due to the fact that the product $(SM \times MD)^{-1,-2}$ is of the form of a product of a function of τ and a function of r, see [42, 54].

3) *Multiple scattering.* This degrading factor is due to the use of wide angle collimator and is difficult to be removed by theoretical means. As in other gamma-ray imaging systems, such as Single Photon Emission Computed Tomography (SPECT) and Positron Emission Tomography (PET), this problem can be only approximatively fixed by corrective measures adapted to each particular scanner.

4) *Noise.* Radiation processes carry fluctuations as noise which could drastically affect numerical simulations in image reconstruction. So algorithm robustness should be tested against noise systematically. There is no universal receipt and an adapted de-noising procedure is to be set up for each scanner type. An example of such de-noising procedure is given in [51].

6. Conclusion and perspectives

Compton scatter tomography (CST) is an outstanding example of the use of Compton scattered radiation for non-invasive imaging. CST provides high resolution and high sensitivity imaging with virtually any material, including lightweight structures and organic matter, which normally pose problems in conventional x-ray computed tomography because of low contrast. However it also suffers from the usual degrading factors of radiation imaging, such as multiple scattering, attenuation, noise and fluctuations, etc., which have to be treated by appropriate (existing or to be developed) methods. Yet it has undergone a very impressive theoretical evolution. In this chapter, we have shown how the expression of the differential cross-section of the Compton effect has led to the idea of measuring the value of matter electron density point by point. The ensuing progress brought to light the successive line by line and plane by plane scanning procedures, however with limited success. A quantum leap in redefining CST was made in the 80's by N. N. Kondic, who advocated the use or wide angle collimators and pointed out the occurrence of integral measurements along circular arcs corresponding to a definite measured photon energy. Then a concept of integral transform of Radon type has emerged from this type of integral measurement in [9]. Later in the 90's, elaborating on a proposal of N. N. Kondic, T. H. Prettyman has constructed a scanner on this principle and called an energy dispersive projective scatterometer. He also realized that a relative motion between this apparatus and the object is necessary to generate the data needed for image reconstruction. This is the starting point for recent CST modalities which are now based on Radon transform on Kondic isogonic circular arcs. We have presented and discussed three existing CST modalities based on three "circular-arc" Radon transforms. Two of them are of recent origin and have arisen as new elements of integral geometry. The remarkable aspect is that they share a common inversion method based on the inversion of the Radon transform on circles intersecting a fixed point. As numerical simulations show their feasibility and viability as imaging systems, CST appears as a promising area of research and development which could bring interesting advances in the field of non-invasive imaging for medicine and industry. Work towards more efficient ways for data processing, *e.g.* setting faster back-projection types of reconstruction methods, is underway in this context.

Author details

Truong T. T.
Laboratoire de Physique Théorique et Modélisation, University of Cergy-Pontoise/CNRS UMR 8089, F-95302 Cergy-Pontoise Cedex, France

Nguyen M. K.
Laboratoire Équipes Traitement de l'Information et Systèmes, ETIS-ENSEA/University of Cergy-Pontoise/CNRS UMR 8051, F-95014 Cergy-Pontoise Cedex, France

7. References

[1] Adejumo O. O., Balogun F. A.& Egbedokun G. G. O., (2011). Developing a Compton Scattering Tomography System for Soil Studies: Theory, *Journal of Sustainable Development and Environmental Protection*, Vol. 1, No. 3, pp. 73-81. ISSN 2251-0605

[2] Anghaie S., Humphries L. L. & Diaz N. J., (1990). Material characterization and flaw detection, sizing, and location by the differential gamma scattering spectroscopy technique. Part1: Development of theoretical basis, *Nuclear Technology*, Vol. 91, pp. 361-375. ISSN 0029-5450

[3] Arendtsz N. V. & Hussein E. M. A., (1993). Electron density tomography with Compton scattered radiation, *SPIE Mathematical Methods in Medical Imaging II* , Vol. 2035, Joseph N. Wilson; David C. Wilson; Eds., pp. 230-41. ISSN 0924-9907

[4] Babot D., Le Floch C. & Peix G., (1992). Contrôle et caractérisation des matériaux composites par tomodensitométrie Compton, *Revue Pratique du Contrôle Industriel*, Vol. 173, pp. 64-67, ISSN 0766-5210

[5] Balogun F. A. & Cruvinel P. E., (2003). Compton scattering tomography in soil compaction study, *Nuclear Instruments and Methods in Physics Research A*, Vol. 505, pp. 502-507. ISSN 0167-5087, 0168-9002

[6] Barrett H. H., (1984). The Radon Transform and its Applications, in *Progress in Optics*, vol. 21, pp. 219-286, Ed. E. Wolf, North Holland. ISSN 0079-6638

[7] Battista J. J., Santon L. W. & Bronskill M. J., (1977). Compton scatter imaging of transverse sections: corrections for multiple scatter and attenuation, *Phys. Med. Biol.*, Vol. 22, No. 2, pp. 229-244. ISSN 0031-9155

[8] Berodias M. G. & Peix M. G., (1988). Nondestructive measurement of density and effective atomic number by photon scattering, *Materials Evaluation*. Vol. 46, No. 8, pp. 1209-1213. ISSN 0025-5327

[9] Bodette D. E. & Jacobs A. M., (1985). Tomographic two-phase flow distribution measurement using gamma-ray scattering, *ISA 1985*, Paper 85-0362, pp. 23-34. ISSN 0019-0578

[10] Brateman L., A. M. Jacobs & L. T. Fitzgerald, (1984). Compton scatter axial tomography with x-rays: SCAT-CAT, *Phys. Med. Biol*, Vol. 29, pp. 1353, ISSN 0031-9155

[11] Brunetti A., Cesareo R., Golosio B., Luciano P. & Ruggero A., (2002). Cork quality estimation by using Compton tomography, *Nuclear instruments and methods in Physics research B*, Vol. 196, pp. 161-168. ISSN 0168-583X

[12] Chapman C. H. & Carey P. W., (1986). The circular harmonic Radon transform, *Inverse Problems*, Vol. 2, pp. 23-49. ISSN 0266-5611

[13] Clarke R. L. & Van Dyk G., (1973). A new method for measurement of bone mineral content using both transmitted and scattered beams of gamma-rays, *Phys. Med. Biol.*, Vol. 18, No.4, pp. 532-539. ISSN 0031-9155
[14] Clarke R. L., Milne E. N., & Van Dyk G., (1976). The use of Compton scattered gamma rays for tomography, *Invest. Radiol.*, Vol.11, No.3, pp. 225-235. ISSN 0020-9996
[15] Cormack A. M., (1964). Representation of a function by its line integrals, with some radiological applications, *J. Appl. Phys*, Vol. 34, No. 9, pp. 2722-2727. ISSN 0021-8979
[16] Cormack A. M., (1981). The Radon transform on a family of curves in the plane, *Proceedings of the American Mathematical Society*, Vol. 83, No. 2, pp. 325-330. ISSN 0002-9939
[17] Cormack A. M., (1984). Radon's problem - Old and New, *SIAM - AMS Proceedings*, Vol. 14, pp. 33-39. ISSN 0080-5084
[18] Evans B. L., Martin J. B., Burggraf L. W. & Roggemann M. C., (1998). Nondestructive inspection using Compton scatter tomography, *IEEE Transactions on Nuclear Science*, Vol. 45, No. 3, pp. 950-956. ISSN 0018-9499
[19] Farmer F. T. & Collins M. P. (1971). A new approach to the determination of anatomical cross-sections of the body by Compton scattering of gamma-rays, *Phys. Med. Biol.*, Vol. 16, No. 4, pp. 577-586. ISSN 0031-9155
[20] Farmer F. T. & Collins M. P., (1974). A further appraisal of the Compton scattering method for determining anatomical cross-sections of the body, *Phys. Med. Biol.*, Vol. 19, No.6, pp. 808-818. ISSN 0031-9155
[21] Gautam S. R., Hopkins F. F., Klinksiek R. & Morgan I. L., (1983). Compton interaction tomography, *IEEE Transactions on Nuclear Science*, Vol. NS-30, No. 2, pp. 1680-1684. ISSN 0018-9499
[22] Gorshkov V. A., Kroening M., Anosov Y.V. & Dorjgochoo O., (2005). X-Ray scattering tomography, *Nondestructive Testing and Evaluation*, Vol. 20, No. 3, pp. 147-157. ISSN 1058-9759
[23] Grubsky V., Romanov V., Patton N. & Jannson T., (2011). Compton imaging tomography technique for NDE of large nonuniform structures, *Proceedings of the SPIE Conference on Penetrating Radiation Systems and Applications XII*, Vol. 8144, pp. 14-17, ISBN 9780819487544 , San Diego California USA, August 2011,
[24] Guzzardi R. & Licitra G., (1988). A critical review of Compton imaging, *CRC Critical Reviews in Biomedical Engineering*, Vol. 15, No. 3, pp. 237-268. ISSN 0278-940X
[25] Harding G., (1982). On the sensitivity and application possibilities of a novel Compton scatter imaging system, *IEEE Transactions on Nuclear Science*, Vol. NS-29, No. 3, pp. 1260-1265. ISSN 0018-9499
[26] Harding G., Strecker H. & Tischler R., (1983-1984). X-ray imaging with Compton scatter radiation, *Philips Tech. Rev.*, Vol. 41, No. 2, pp. 46-59. ISSN 0031-7926.
[27] Harding G., (1985). X-ray scatter imaging in nondestructive testing, *International Advances in Nondestructive Testing*, Vol. 11, pp. 271-295. ISSN 0140-072X
[28] Harding G. & Tischler R., (1986). Dual-energy Compton scatter tomography, *Phys. Med. Biol.* Vol. 31, No. 5, pp. 477-489. ISSN 0031-9155
[29] Harding G. & Harding E. (2010). Compton scatter imaging: a tool for historical exploitation, *Appl. Radiat. Isot.*, Vol. 68, No. 6, pp. 993-1005. ISSN 0969 8043
[30] Holt R. S., (1985). Compton imaging, *Endeavour*. Vol. 9, No. 2, pp. 97-105. ISSN 0160-9327
[31] Holt R. S. & Cooper M. J., (1987). Gamma-ray scattering NDE, *NDT International*. Vol. 20, No. 3, pp. 161-165. ISSN 0308 9126

[32] Holt R. S. & Cooper M. J., (1988). Non-destructive examination with a Compton scanner, *British Journal of Nondestructive Testing*. Vol. 30, No. 2, pp. 75-80. ISSN 0007 1137

[33] Hussein E. M. A., Meneley D. A., & Barnejee S., (1986). On the solution of the inverse problem of radiation scattering imaging, *Nuclear Science and Engineering*, Vol. 92, pp. 341-349. ISSN 0029 5639

[34] Hussein E. M. A., (1989). Radiation scattering methods for nondestructive testing and imaging, *Int. Advances in Nondestructive Testing*, Vol. 14, pp. 301-321. ISSN 0140-072X

[35] Jaszczak, R. J. (2006). The early years of single photon emission computed tomography (SPECT): an anthology of selected reminiscences, *Phys. Med. Biol.*, Vol. 51, April 2006, pp. R99-R115. ISSN 0031-9155

[36] Kershaw D., (1970). The determination of the density distribution of a gas flowing in a pipe from mean density measurements, *J. Inst. Maths Applics*, Vol. 6, pp. 111-114. ISSN 0020 2932

[37] Kondic N. N. & Hahn O. J. (1970). Theory and application of the parallel and diverging radiation beam method in two-phase systems, in *Heat Transfer 1970*,U Grigull & E. Hahne Eds., paper MT 1.5, Elsevier, Paris-Versailles France, Aug. 31 - Sept. 5, 1970.

[38] Kondic N. N., (1978). Density field determination by an external stationary radiation source using a kernel technique, in *Measurements in polyphase flows*, papers of the ASME Winter Annual Meeting, D. E. Stock Ed., pp. 37-51, ASME, ISBN 9789993764281, San Francisco California USA, December 10-15, 1978.

[39] Kondic N. N., Jacobs A. M. & Ebert D., (1983). Three-dimensional density field determination by external stationary dtectors and gamma sources using selective scattering, in *Thermal-hydraulics of nuclear reactors, Vol.2*, M. Merilo Ed., pp. 1443-1455, ANS, ISBN 089448110X, 9780894481109, Santa Barbara California USA, January 11-14, 1983.

[40] Lale P. G., (1959). The examination of internal tissues, using gamma-ray scatter with a possible extension to megavoltage radiography, *Phys. Med. Biol.*, Vol. 4, pp. 159-167. ISSN 0031-9155

[41] Nguyen M. K., Driol C., Truong T.T., Paindavoine M. & Ginhac D., (2009). Nouvelle tomographie Compton, *Proceedings of the 22nd GRETSI*, Dijon France, September 8-11 2009.

[42] Nguyen, M. K. & Truong, T. T. (2010). Inversion of a new circular-arc Radon transform for Compton tomography, *Inverse Problems*, Vol.26, No.6, pp. 065005 , ISSN 0266 5611

[43] Nguyen M. K., Faye C., Rigaud G. & Truong T. T., (2012). A novel technological imaging process using ionizing radiation properties, *Proceedings of the 9th IEEE - RVIF International Conference on Computing and Communications Technologies* (4 pages), Ho-Chi-Minh City Vietnam, Feb. 2012, ISSN 978-1-4673-030

[44] Norton S. J., (1994), Compton scattering tomography, *J. Appl. Phys*, Vol. 76, No. 4, pp. 2007-2015. ISSN 0021-8979

[45] Norton S. J., (1995). Compton scattering tomography, US Patent No 5,430,787 (July 4, 1995)

[46] Novikov R. G., (2002). An inversion formula for the attenuated x-ray transformation, *Ark. Mat.*, Vol. 40, pp. 145-167. ISSN 0004-2080

[47] Nutt R., (2002). The history of positron emission imaging, *Molecular Imaging and Biology*, Vol. 4, No 1, pp. 11-26. ISSN 1536-1632

[48] Prettyman T. H., Gardner R. P., Russ J. C. & Verghese K., (1993). A combined transmission and scattering tomographic approach to composition and density imaging, *Appl. Radiat. Isot.*, Vol. 44, No. 10/11, pp. 1327-1341. ISSN 0969-8043

[49] Radon J., (1917). Über die Bestimmung von Funktionnen durch ihre Integralwerte längs gewisser Mannigfaltikeiten, *Ber.Verh.Sächs.Akad.Wiss. Leipzig-Math.-Natur.Kl.*, Vol. 69, pp. 262-277. ISSN 0366-001X (0080-5254 old)

[50] Rigaud G., Nguyen M. K. & Louis A. K., (2012). Modeling and simulation results on a new Compton scattering tomography modality, *Simulat. Pract. Theory*, http://dx.doi.org/10.1016/j.simpat.2012.03.007, ISSN 1569 190X

[51] Rigaud G., Nguyen M. K. & Louis A. K., (2012). Novel Numerical Inversions of two Circular-Arc Radon Transforms in Compton scattering tomography, *Inverse Problems in Science and Engineering*, doi: 10.1080/174 15977.2011.653008, ISSN 1741-5977

[52] Spiers F. W. (1946). Effective atomic number of energy absorption in tissues, *British Journal of Radiology*, Vol. 19, pp. 52-63. ISSN 0007 1285

[53] Strecker H., (1982). Scattered imaging of aluminium castings using an X-ray fan beam and pinhole camera, *Materials Evaluation*, Vol. 40, pp. 1050-1056. ISSN 0025-5327

[54] Truong, T. T. & Nguyen, M. K., (2011). Radon transforms on generalized Cormack's curves and a new Compton scatter tomography modality, *Inverse Problems*, Vol.27, No.12, pp. 125001, ISSN 0266 5611

[55] Wang J. J., Chi Z. & Wang Y. M., (1999). Analytic reconstruction of Compton scattering tomography, *Journal of Applied Physics*, vol. 86, No. 3, pp. 1693-1698. ISSN 0021 8979

Chapter 7

Numerical Simulation of Slip-Stick Elastic Contact

Sergiu Spinu and Dumitru Amarandei

Additional information is available at the end of the chapter

http://dx.doi.org/10.5772/48451

1. Introduction

Fretting defines a condition in which mechanical contacts are subjected to alternating tangential displacements, small compared to dimensions of contact area, due to oscillating loading conditions. Fretting wear and fretting fatigue are between the most important factors responsible for contact failure, especially when high loads are transmitted through non-conforming contacts, leading to highly localized stress concentrators in the vicinity of the contact region. Prediction of life span of machine elements working in such conditions requires assessment of stress and strain in the contacting bodies, which is the main subject of Contact Mechanics. Although fretting is intrinsically a multidisciplinary process, involving adhesion, oxidation, abrasion and pitting, modern approach suggests that contact stresses play a chief role.

While analytic solutions in this research field lead to complex mathematical models, many without closed-form solution, numerical approach reveals itself as a useful engineering tool, capable of extending the few existing analytical results to technologically important contact scenarios. A numerical study may advance the understanding of fretting contact and provide assistance to the design of contacts with improved load-carrying capacity.

Elastic contact analysis considering interfacial friction and slip-stick behaviour originated in the works of Cattaneo (Cattaneo, 1938) and Mindlin (Mindlin, 1949). They proved independently that, even when the contacting bodies are globally sticking, a peripheral region of slip is to be assumed in order to remain in the frame of Linear Theory of Elasticity and to obey the Coulomb's law of friction. Based on these results, Johnson (Johnson, 1985) advanced the closed-form solution for the contact between similarly elastic materials undergoing a fretting loop.

In case of dissimilarly elastic materials, when the effects of normal and tangential tractions are coupled, an iterative solution has been achieved (Hills et al., 1993) only for the plane (i.e. cylindrical) contact. Many authors employ the so-called Goodman approximation

(Goodman, 1962) when dealing with this type of contact, which neglects the influence of shear tractions on pressure, but retains that of pressure on tangential tractions. As proved in (Hills et al., 1993), this approximation is satisfactory in case of plane (cylindrical) contacts if Poisson's ratio is large enough, but the inaccuracy introduced in the simulation of the three dimensional contact between dissimilarly elastic materials cannot be a priori assessed.

In order to overcome this obstacle, recent works aimed to solve the problem numerically, using a method derived from the boundary element method, also referred to as semi-analytical (SAM) in a review paper by Renauf et al. (Renauf et al., 2011). The strong point of this technique is that only a small region of the boundary of the contacting bodies, enclosing the contact area, is to be meshed, leading to a dramatic decrease in computational complexity compared to finite element method, in which discretization of the entire bulk is required.

Chen and Wang (Chen & Wang, 2008) advanced an algorithm for the non-conforming contact of dissimilarly elastic materials, and predicted the additional effect of an increasing tangential loading. Wang, Meng, Xiao, and Wang (Wang et al., 2011) investigated numerically the supplementary effect of a torsional moment, while Wang et al. (Wang et al., 2010) applied the algorithm advanced in (Chen & Wang, 2008) to contact of elastic layered half-spaces. However, the loading history was not accounted for in these studies, i.e. the full load was applied in one step.

Gallego, Nélias, and Deyber (Gallego et al., 2010) applied numerical analysis in an incremental approach to study different fretting modes, and concluded that assumptions adopted in existing analytical models lead to arguably inaccurate results. It is asserted in (Gallego et al., 2010) that, due to irreversibility of friction, which is a dissipative process, loading history should be considered although a purely elastic contact analysis is intended.

An incremental iterative algorithm for the fully coupled elastic contact with slip and stick is advanced in this work. Existing algorithms for the uncoupled normal or tangential contact problems are adapted for modeling of transient contact, and combined in an iterative approach based on the mutual adjustment between contact tractions, resulting in a three level nested loop algorithm. The use of modern numerical methods allows for a fine discretization in both spatial and temporal domain, leading to well converged numerical solutions.

2. Formulation of continuous slip-stick elastic contact problem

In contact problem formulation, it is convenient to describe the initial geometries $hi^{(i)}(x_1, x_2)$ of the two contacting bodies $i = 1,2$ in a Cartezian coordinate systems having its x_1 and x_2 axes contained in the common plane of contact (i.e. the plane passing through the first point of contact, chosen as to separate best the bounding surfaces). The direction of x_3 -axis will be referred to as the normal direction, while the other two are tangential. In the three dimensional case, forces and moments transmitted through the contact have components along all three axes, namely the normal force W, the tangential force $\mathbf{T}(T_1, T_2)$, the bending (or flexing) moments M_1, M_2 and the torsional moment M_3. Superscripts denote the contacting body, and subscripts are used for the direction of the referred quantity. Under load, the bodies deform unless assumed rigid, leading to elastic displacements $u_i^{(j)}$, and move as rigid-bodies with translations $\omega_i^{(j)}$ and rotations $\phi_i^{(j)}$, with $i=1,2,3, j=1,2$.

In Contact Mechanics, it is also assumed that contact area dimensions are small compared to extents of the contacting bodies, and therefore stresses in the contact region are independent of other boundary conditions. This assumption is well verified in case of non-conforming contacts, when stresses induced by the contact process are highly localized in the vicinity of the contact region.

Once a contact area is established, the imposed forces and moments lead to contact tractions, i.e. pressure $p^{(j)}$ in the normal direction and shear traction $\mathbf{q}^{(j)}(q_1,q_2)$ in the tangential direction. The latter appears only if interfacial friction is assumed, leading to three possible cases, in relation to the magnitude of the tangential load: full stick, partial slip (or slip-stick), or gross slip. The latter case is trivial, as shear tractions are related to pressure through Coulomb's law on all contact area. On the other hand, the works of Cattaneo (Cattaneo, 1938) and Mindlin (Mindlin, 1949) prove that the full-sticking contact cannot be solved in the Frame of Linear Theory of Elasticity, as it leads to infinite stresses at the boundary of the contact area. The study of the partial slip contact, which is found in fretting contact processes, concluding with assessment of contact tractions, is the main goal of this work.

2.1. The contact model in the normal direction

Based on the works developed in (Johnson, 1985; Polonsky & Keer, 1999), the model for the contact in the normal direction consists in the following equations and inequalities:

1. The static force equilibrium:

$$W(t) = \iint_{\Gamma_C(t)} p(x_1, x_2, t)dx_1 dx_2; \tag{1}$$

$$M_1(t) = \iint_{\Gamma_C(t)} p(x_1, x_2, t)x_2 dx_1 dx_2; \; M_2(t) = \iint_{\Gamma_C(t)} p(x_1, x_2, t)x_1 dx_1 dx_2. \tag{2}$$

2. The geometrical condition of deformation:

$$h(x_1, x_2, t) = hi(x_1, x_2) + u_3(x_1, x_2, t) - \omega_3(t) - \phi_1(t)x_2 - \phi_2(t)x_1, \quad (x_1, x_2) \in \Gamma_C(t). \tag{3}$$

3. The contact complementarity conditions:

$$\begin{cases} p(x_1, x_2, t) > 0 \wedge h(x_1, x_2, t) = 0, & (x_1, x_2) \in \Gamma_C(t); \\ p(x_1, x_2, t) = 0 \wedge h(x_1, x_2, t) > 0, & (x_1, x_2) \notin \Gamma_C(t). \end{cases} \tag{4}$$

The temporal dimension t is included in this model along the spatial dimensions x_1, x_2 to provide basis for reproduction of the loading history. Consequently, $\Gamma_C(t)$ denotes the contact area, and $h(x_1,x_2,t)$ the surface separation, both established at a specified point t on the loading curve. When $t=0$, $h(x_1,x_2,0)=hi(x_1,x_2)=hi^{(1)}(x_1,x_2)+hi^{(2)}(x_1,x_2)$. The other relative (composite) quantities, lacking the superscript indicating the contacting body, are defined in a similar way: $\omega_3(t)=\omega_3^{(1)}(t)+\omega_3^{(2)}(t)$, and $\phi_i(t)=\phi_i^{(1)}(t)+\phi_i^{(2)}(t), i=1,2$. Computation of the relative normal displacement $u_3(x_1,x_2,t)$ will be discussed in Section 3.2.

The complementarity conditions in Eq. (4) show that only compressive normal traction (i.e. pressure) is allowed on the contact area, meaning adhesion is not accounted for. While adhesion cannot be ruled out in case of rubber, the metallic materials are found to show little adhesion effects, as the actual contact area, established between the peaks of the inherent surface microtopography (i.e. roughness), is much smaller than the theoretical one. Therefore, study of adhesion effects is beyond the point of this study.

The framework leading to Eq. (3), discussed in detail in (Johnson, 1985), is depicted in Fig. 1. The tilting angles, resulting from application of flexing moments, are omitted for brevity. The dashed lines show the initial (i.e. at $t=0$, in undeformed state) profile of the contacting bodies, but in positions (relative to the initial point of contact O) corresponding to rigid-body translations $\omega_3^{(1)}(t)$ and $\omega_3^{(2)}(t)$, which have opposite signs due to the fact that the contacting bodies are compressed. In order to accommodate the interpenetration distance $\omega_3(t)$ (it should be remembered that the bodies are assumed impenetrable in the frame of Linear Theory of Elasticity), the bodies deform elastically, resulting in normal displacements $u_3^{(1)}(t)$ and $u_3^{(2)}(t)$ pointing inward the corresponding body, as both normal contact tractions are compressive. Superposition of these processes yield the profiles on the contacting bodies in deformed state (at a specified time t), depicted using continuous lines in Fig. 1.

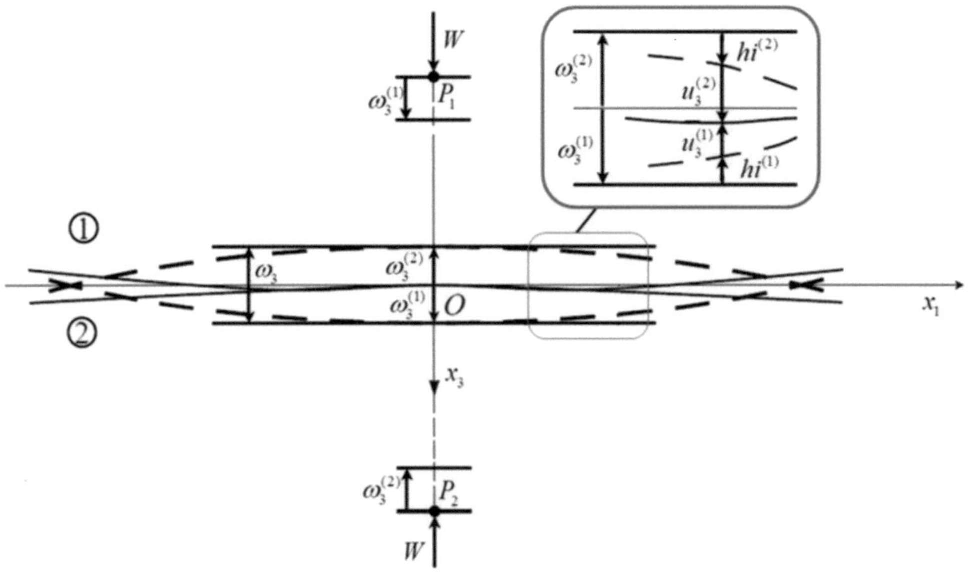

Figure 1. Geometrical condition of deformation in the normal direction

2.2. The contact model in the tangential direction

An analogous model can be established for the contact in the tangential direction, when a slip-stick regime is assumed. The model for this contact process, also developed in (Johnson, 1985; Chen & Wang, 2008), consists in the following equations and inequalities:

1. The static force equilibrium (at any time t):

$$T_i(t) = \iint_{\Gamma_C(t)} q_i(x_1,x_2,t)dx_1dx_2, \quad i=1,2; \tag{5}$$

$$M_3(t) = \iint_{\Gamma_C(t)} \left[q_2(x_1,x_2,t)x_1 - q_1(x_1,x_2,t)x_2\right]dx_1dx_2. \tag{6}$$

2. The geometrical condition of deformation in the time frame $[t_1,t_2]$, in which the tangential load is not allowed to change sign:

$$\begin{bmatrix} s_1(x_1,x_2,t_2)-s_1(x_1,x_2,t_1) \\ s_2(x_1,x_2,t_2)-s_2(x_1,x_2,t_1) \end{bmatrix} = \begin{bmatrix} u_1(x_1,x_2,t_2)-u_1(x_1,x_2,t_1) \\ u_2(x_1,x_2,t_2)-u_2(x_1,x_2,t_1) \end{bmatrix} - \dots$$
$$\begin{bmatrix} \omega_1(t_2)-\omega_1(t_1) \\ \omega_2(t_2)-\omega_2(t_1) \end{bmatrix} - \left(\phi_3(t_2)-\phi_3(t_1)\right)\begin{bmatrix} x_2 \\ x_1 \end{bmatrix}, \quad (x_1,x_2)\in\Gamma_C(t_2). \tag{7}$$

3. The contact complementarity conditions:

$$\begin{cases} \left\|\mathbf{q}(x_1,x_2,t_2)\right\| \le \mu p(x_1,x_2,t_2) \wedge \left\|\mathbf{s}(x_1,x_2,t_2)-\mathbf{s}(x_1,x_2,t_1)\right\| = 0, & (i,j)\in\Gamma_S(t_2); \\ \left\|\mathbf{q}(x_1,x_2,t_2)\right\| = \mu p(x_1,x_2,t_2) \wedge \left\|\mathbf{s}(x_1,x_2,t_2)-\mathbf{s}(x_1,x_2,t_1)\right\| > 0, & (i,j)\in\Gamma_C(t_2)-\Gamma_S(t_2). \end{cases} \tag{8}$$

Here, Γ_S is the stick area, $\Gamma_C - \Gamma_S$ the slip region, μ the frictional coefficient and $\mathbf{s}(s_1,s_2)$ the relative slip distances. The base for Eq. (7) is presented in Fig. 2, which depicts the slip-stick contact process in the direction of $\vec{x}_1$. Rigid-body motion and elastic deformation due to torsion are omitted for brevity. The time parameter is also omitted, meaning all quantities are bound to the considered time frame $[t_1,t_2]$. Let us consider two points P_1 and P_2 on the contacting bodies (1) and (2), respectively, located at t_1 on the same axis normal to the common plane of contact. The depths of these points are large enough as to assume that the corresponding tangential deformations can be neglected. The axis intersects the bounding surfaces in the points A_1 and A_2, respectively, where the bodies deform due shear tractions.

Firstly, the above mentioned axis is assumed to pass through the initial point of contact, therefore $A_1(t_1) \equiv A_2(t_1) \equiv O$. In the considered time frame, all points in the contacting bodies undergo rigid-body translations $\omega_1^{(1)}$ and $\omega_1^{(2)}$ along the direction of $\vec{x}_1$, and points A_1 and A_2 also undergo tangential displacements. If for these points the composite parameters cancel each other, i.e. $\omega_1(t_2) = u_1(t_2)$, with $\omega_1 = \omega_1^{(1)} + \omega_1^{(2)}$ and $u_1 = u_1^{(2)} - u_1^{(1)}$; therefore, $A_1(t_2) \equiv A_2(t_2) \equiv O$ and consequently a stick regime is established in O.

Secondly, the P_1P_2 axis intersects the contact area in the peripheral region, where, although $A_1(t_1) \equiv A_2(t_1)$, $A_1(t_2)$ diverge from $A_2(t_2)$ with a relative (composite) slip distance $s_1 = s_1^{(1)} + s_1^{(2)}$. This position corresponds to a region in relative slip (also referred to as micro-slip). It should be noted that any point in the current contact area is either in stick, where the norm of the shear traction is smaller than the limiting friction, or in slip, where the shear traction norm equals the limiting friction. The existence of slip is intrinsically conditioned by an increase or decrease in the level of tangential load, and therefore a purely static model is not appropriate.

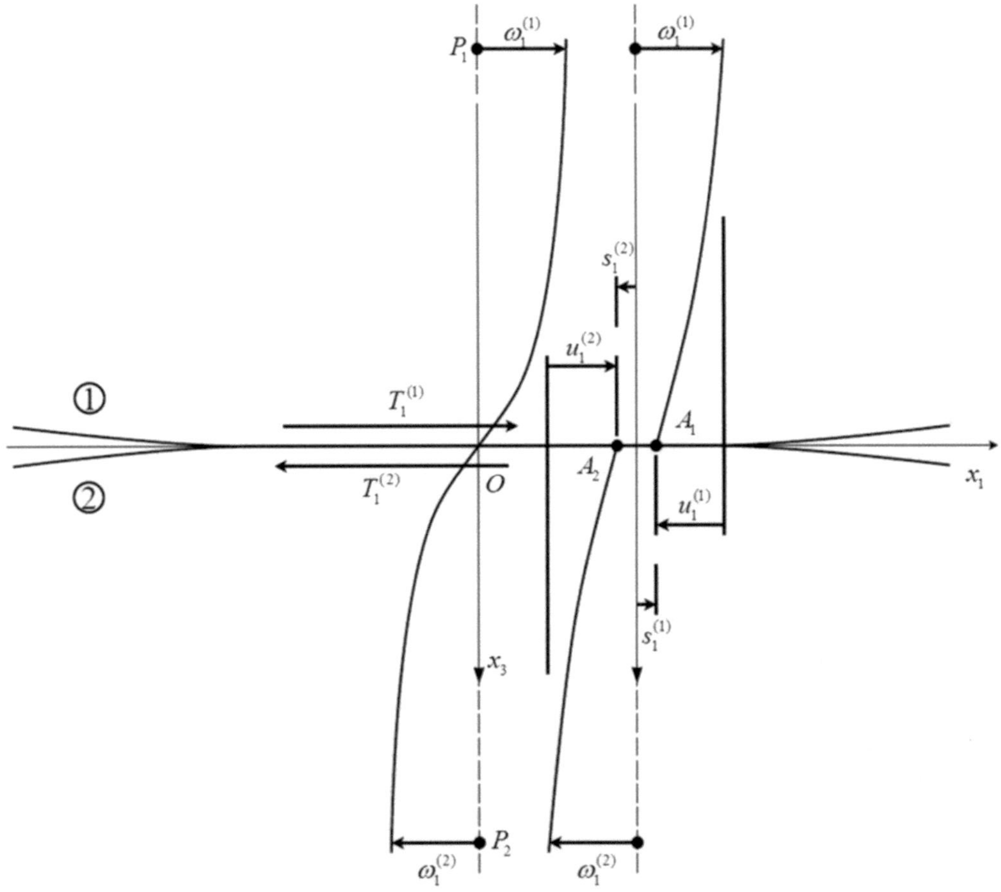

Figure 2. Geometrical condition of deformation in the tangential direction

3. Formulation of discrete slip-stick elastic contact problem

The main obstacles in solving the continuous contact problem consist in the fact that neither the contact and stick area, nor the tractions distributions are known in advance. A trial-and-error approach is therefore necessary, but this infer integration of arbitrary functions (contact tractions distributions) over irregular domains (contact or stick area) in displacements computation. As this cannot generally be performed analytically, numerical integration, although computationally intensive, is preferred. The basic principles of contact problem discretization are discussed in this section, and the advantages of this approach are outlined. Computation of displacements fields using fast numerical methods derived from the theory of Digital Signal Processing (DSP) is also discussed.

3.1. Principles of problem discretization

Numerical resolution of elastic contact problem relies on considering continuous distributions as piecewise constant on the elementary cells of a mesh established in the common plane of contact, enclosing the contact area at any point on the loading path. In case of non-conforming contacts, the Hertz contact parameters (Hertz, 1895) provide a good guess value for the estimated domain. If during application of additional loading increments the current contact area reaches the boundaries of the initial mesh, the contact simulation has to be restarted with a larger domain. However, only a small surface domain Γ_P of the contacting bodies needs to be considered, which constitutes an important advantage of SAM over other numerical techniques. In Γ_P, contact geometry should be known, or can be extrapolated from existing data. The directions of the grid sides are aligned with those of the Cartesian coordinate system in the continuous problem formulation. The elementary cell area $\Delta = \Delta_1 \Delta_2$ depends on the grid steps Δ_i in the direction of $\vec{x}_i$, $i = 1,2$. The grid control points (centroids of rectangular elementary patches) are identified by a pair of indices (i,j), with $1 \le i < N_1$, $1 \le i < N_2$. Any continuous distribution $f(x_1,x_2)$ is assumed to be constant over each patch, and equal to value computed in the control point. A simplified notation can thus be used, assuming that $f(i,j) = f(x_1^*, x_2^*)$, where x_1^*, x_2^* are the coordinates of the control point of cell (i,j).

The limiting surfaces of the contacting bodies are sampled in two height arrays corresponding to grid control points. Such data can be obtained from an optical profilometer or can be generated numerically. The sum of the two heights at node (i,j) yields the composite initial surface height $hi(i,j)$. For the half-space approximation to remain valid, the slope of the initial separation should be small everywhere over Γ_P.

To simulate the loading history, additional discretization is performed in the temporal domain, meaning the load is imposed in small steps $k = \overline{1,N_\ell}$. Consequently, $p(i,j,k)$ denotes the nodal (elementary) pressure at the intersection of the line i with the column j of the rectangular grid, achieved after application of k loading increments. When only two indexes are employed, the referred quantity does not vary with the loading level, e.g. coordinates of grid nodes; one index is used for parameters varying with the loading level only, e.g. rigid-body translations; when no index is present, the denoted quantity is a constant in the numerical program, e.g. the grid steps.

Digitization of Eqs. (1) - (4) lead to the following numerical model, which will be referred from now on as the NC:

$$W(k) = \Delta \sum_{(i,j) \in A_C(k)} p(i,j,k); \tag{9}$$

$$M_1(k) = \Delta \sum_{(i,j)\in A_C(k)} p(i,j,k)x_2(i,j); \quad M_2(k) = \Delta \sum_{(i,j)\in A_C(k)} p(i,j,k)x_1(i,j); \tag{10}$$

$$h(i,j,k) = hi(i,j) + u_3(i,j,k) - \omega_3(k) - \phi_1(k)x_2(i,j) - \phi_2(k)x_1(i,j), (i,j) \in A_P; \tag{11}$$

$$\begin{cases} p(i,j,k) > 0 \wedge h(i,j,k) = 0, & (i,j) \in A_C(k); \\ p(i,j,k) = 0 \wedge h(i,j,k) > 0, & (i,j) \in A_P - A_C(k). \end{cases} \tag{12}$$

In a similar way, the continuous model consisting in Eqs. (5) - (8) has its discrete counterpart, referred to as the TC:

$$T_n(k) = \Delta \sum_{(i,j)\in A_C(k)} q_n(i,j,k), n = 1,2; \tag{13}$$

$$M_3(k) = \Delta \sum_{(i,j)\in A_C(k)} \left[q_2(i,j,k)x_1(i,j) - q_1(i,j,k)x_2(i,j) \right]; \tag{14}$$

$$\begin{bmatrix} s_1(i,j,k) - s_1(i,j,k-1) \\ s_2(i,j,k) - s_2(i,j,k-1) \end{bmatrix} = \begin{bmatrix} u_1(i,j,k) - u_1(i,j,k-1) \\ u_2(i,j,k) - u_2(i,j,k-1) \end{bmatrix} - \begin{bmatrix} \omega_1(k) - \omega_1(k-1) \\ \omega_2(k) - \omega_2(k-1) \end{bmatrix} - \dots$$
$$\left(\phi_3(k) - \phi_3(k-1) \right) \begin{bmatrix} x_2(i,j) \\ x_1(i,j) \end{bmatrix}, \quad (i,j) \in A_C(k); \tag{15}$$

$$\begin{cases} \left\| \mathbf{q}(i,j,k) \right\| \le \mu p(i,j,k) \wedge \left\| \mathbf{s}(i,j,k) - \mathbf{s}(i,j,k-1) \right\| = 0, (i,j) \in A_S(k); \\ \left\| \mathbf{q}(i,j,k) \right\| = \mu p(i,j,k) \wedge \left\| \mathbf{s}(i,j,k) - \mathbf{s}(i,j,k-1) \right\| > 0, (i,j) \in A_C(k) - A_S(k). \end{cases} \tag{16}$$

In these equations, A_P, A_C and A_S are the discrete counterparts of Γ_P, Γ_C and Γ_S, respectively, consisting in sets of elementary patches. Consequently, in the numerical formulation, the contact or the stick area can only vary in equal increments Δ. A fine mesh is thus required for accurate estimation of contact domains.

3.2. Numerical computation of displacement fields

In Contact Mechanics, it is common practice to assimilate the contacting bodies with elastic half-spaces. This assumption holds if the dimensions of contact area are small compared to significant dimensions of contacting bodies, and allows expressing displacements according to superposition principle applied to Green functions for the elastic half-space:

$$u_{ij}^{(k)}(x_1,x_2) = \iint_{\Gamma_C} p_j^{(k)}(x_1',x_2') \cdot G_{ij}^{(k)}\left(x_1 - x_1',\ x_2 - x_2'\right) dx_1' \, dx_2'; i,j = 1,2,3; k = 1,2, \tag{17}$$

where $G_{ij}^{(k)}\left(x_1,x_2\right)$ denotes displacement of a point in body (k), in the direction of $\vec{x}_i$, induced by a unit point force applied in origin along direction of $\vec{x}_j$. The functions G for the elastic half-space, also referred to as fundamental solutions or Green functions, were derived by Boussinesq, (Boussinesq, 1969) and Cerruti (Cerruti, 1882). Integral in Eq. (17)

cannot be performed analytically except for a few cases; however, its discrete counterpart can be computed numerically for any contact area and any distribution of tractions:

$$u_{\zeta\xi}^{(n)}(i,j)=\sum_{(k,\ell)\in A_C} K_{\zeta\xi}^{(n)}(i-k,j-\ell)\cdot p_{\xi}^{(n)}(k,\ell), \tag{18}$$

where $K_{\zeta\xi}^{(n)}(i-k,j-\ell)$ is the influence coefficient, expressing the displacement in the direction of $\vec{x}_{\zeta}$, induced in the cell (i,j) of the body (n) by a unit contact traction, uniformly distributed in the cell (k,ℓ), acting along direction of $\vec{x}_{\xi}$. The influence coefficients yield from integration of Green functions over rectangular elementary patches:

$$K_{\zeta\xi}^{(n)}(i-k,j-\ell)=\int_{x_2(\ell)-\Delta_2/2}^{x_2(\ell)+\Delta_2/2}\int_{x_1(k)-\Delta_1/2}^{x_1(k)+\Delta_1/2} G_{\zeta\xi}^{(n)}\left(x_1(i)-x_1',x_2(j)-x_2'\right)dx_1'dx_2'. \tag{19}$$

Eq. (18) is in fact a two-dimensional convolution product, and can be written in an equivalent manner using the symbol "$\otimes$" to denote discrete cyclic convolution:

$$u_{\zeta\xi}^{(n)}=K_{\zeta\xi}^{(n)}\otimes p_{\xi}^{(n)}. \tag{20}$$

The assembly of contributions of all contact tractions to displacements can be expressed as:

$$\begin{bmatrix}u_1\\u_2\\u_3\end{bmatrix}=\begin{bmatrix}u_1^{(2)}-u_1^{(1)}\\u_2^{(2)}-u_2^{(1)}\\u_3^{(2)}+u_3^{(1)}\end{bmatrix}=\begin{bmatrix}K_{11}^{(2)}&K_{12}^{(2)}&K_{13}^{(2)}\\K_{21}^{(2)}&K_{22}^{(2)}&K_{23}^{(2)}\\K_{31}^{(2)}&K_{32}^{(2)}&K_{33}^{(2)}\end{bmatrix}\otimes\begin{bmatrix}q_1^{(2)}\\q_2^{(2)}\\p^{(2)}\end{bmatrix}-\begin{bmatrix}K_{11}^{(1)}&K_{12}^{(1)}&K_{13}^{(1)}\\K_{21}^{(1)}&K_{22}^{(1)}&K_{23}^{(1)}\\-K_{31}^{(1)}&-K_{32}^{(1)}&-K_{33}^{(1)}\end{bmatrix}\otimes\begin{bmatrix}q_1^{(1)}\\q_2^{(1)}\\p^{(1)}\end{bmatrix}=$$
$$=\begin{bmatrix}K_{11}^{(2)}+K_{11}^{(1)}&K_{12}^{(2)}+K_{12}^{(1)}&K_{13}^{(2)}-K_{13}^{(1)}\\K_{21}^{(2)}+K_{21}^{(1)}&K_{22}^{(2)}+K_{22}^{(1)}&K_{23}^{(2)}-K_{23}^{(1)}\\K_{31}^{(2)}-K_{31}^{(1)}&K_{32}^{(2)}-K_{32}^{(1)}&K_{33}^{(2)}+K_{33}^{(1)}\end{bmatrix}\otimes\begin{bmatrix}q_1\\q_2\\p\end{bmatrix}. \tag{21}$$

When the second subscript is omitted, the referred displacement is the sum of all contributions. The positive sign in computation of u_3 is related to the fact that normal displacements are computed in coordinate systems linked to each body, having the x_3 axes pointing inward. It should also be noted that from pressure definition $p^{(2)}=p^{(1)}=p$, but $q_i^{(2)}=-q_i^{(1)}=q_i, i=1,2$, as the mutual actions of two bodies upon each other are equal, but directed to contrary parts. The influence coefficients $K_{\ell m}^{(n)}$ can be computed using the following relations:

$$K_{\ell m}^{(n)}(\nu^{(n)},E^{(n)},i,j)=$$
$$k_{\ell m}^{(n)}(\nu^{(n)},E^{(n)},x_1(i,j)+\frac{\Delta_1}{2},x_2(i,j)+\frac{\Delta_2}{2})+k_{\ell m}^{(n)}(\nu^{(n)},E^{(n)},x_1(i,j)-\frac{\Delta_1}{2},x_2(i,j)-\frac{\Delta_2}{2})-\ldots \tag{22}$$
$$k_{\ell m}^{(n)}(\nu^{(n)},E^{(n)},x_1(i,j)+\frac{\Delta_1}{2},x_2(i,j)-\frac{\Delta_2}{2})-k_{\ell m}^{(n)}(\nu^{(n)},E^{(n)},x_1(i,j)-\frac{\Delta_1}{2},x_2(i,j)+\frac{\Delta_2}{2});$$

$$k_{33}^{(n)}\left(\nu^{(n)},E^{(n)},x_1,x_2\right)=\frac{1-\left(\nu^{(n)}\right)^2}{\pi E^{(n)}}\left[x_1\ln\left(x_2+\sqrt{x_1^2+x_2^2}\right)+x_2\ln\left(x_1+\sqrt{x_1^2+x_2^2}\right)\right]; \tag{23}$$

$$k_{13}^{(n)}\left(\nu^{(n)},E^{(n)},x_1,x_2\right)=\frac{(1+\nu^{(n)})(1-2\nu^{(n)})}{2\pi E^{(n)}}\left[2x_1\tan^{-1}\left(\frac{\sqrt{x_1^2+x_2^2}-x_2}{x_1}\right)-x_2\ln\left(\sqrt{x_1^2+x_2^2}\right)\right]; \quad (24)$$

$$k_{11}^{(n)}\left(\nu^{(n)},E^{(n)},x_1,x_2\right)=\frac{1+\nu^{(n)}}{\pi E^{(n)}}\left[x_2\ln\left(x_1+\sqrt{x_1^2+x_2^2}\right)-x_2+(1-\nu^{(n)})x_1\ln\left(x_2+\sqrt{x_1^2+x_2^2}\right)\right]; \quad (25)$$

$$k_{21}^{(n)}\left(\nu^{(n)},E^{(n)},x_1,x_2\right)=-\frac{\nu^{(n)}(1+\nu^{(n)})}{\pi E^{(n)}}\sqrt{x_1^2+x_2^2}; \quad (26)$$

$$k_{23}^{(n)}\left(\nu^{(n)},E^{(n)},x_1,x_2\right)=k_{13}^{(n)}\left(\nu^{(n)},E^{(n)},x_2,x_1\right); \quad (27)$$

$$k_{31}^{(n)}\left(\nu^{(n)},E^{(n)},x_1,x_2\right)=-k_{13}^{(n)}\left(\nu^{(n)},E^{(n)},x_1,x_2\right); \quad (28)$$

$$k_{12}^{(n)}\left(\nu^{(n)},E^{(n)},x_1,x_2\right)=k_{21}^{(n)}\left(\nu^{(n)},E^{(n)},x_1,x_2\right); \quad (29)$$

$$k_{22}^{(n)}\left(\nu^{(n)},E^{(n)},x_1,x_2\right)=k_{11}^{(n)}\left(\nu^{(n)},E^{(n)},x_2,x_1\right); \quad (30)$$

$$k_{32}^{(n)}\left(\nu^{(n)},E^{(n)},x_1,x_2\right)=-k_{23}^{(n)}\left(\nu^{(n)},E^{(n)},x_2,x_1\right), \quad (31)$$

where $E^{(n)}$ and $\nu^{(n)}$ are the elastic constants (Young modulus and Poisson's ratio, respectively) of materials of the two contacting bodies. If $E^{(1)}=E^{(2)}=E$ and $\nu^{(1)}=\nu^{(2)}=\nu$, then $K_{ij}^{(1)}=K_{ij}^{(2)}=K_{ij}, i,j=1,2,3,$ and Eq. (21) takes a simplified form:

$$\begin{bmatrix}u_1\\u_2\\u_3\end{bmatrix}=2\begin{bmatrix}K_{11}&K_{12}&0\\K_{21}&K_{22}&0\\0&0&K_{33}\end{bmatrix}\otimes\begin{bmatrix}q_1\\q_2\\p\end{bmatrix}. \quad (32)$$

The most efficient way to compute the two-dimensional convolution products in Eqs. (21) or (32) is by using spectral methods. According to convolution theorem, the convolution of two signals, each having N samples, requires $O(N^2)$ operations in time/space domain, but only $O(N\log N)$ operations in the frequency domain, where it reduces to element-wise product.

However, when transferring to frequency domain via fast Fourier transform (FFT), presumption of signal periodicity is automatically assumed, which leads to contamination of convolution result due to spurious neighbouring periods. Liu & al. (Liu & al., 2000) advanced a fast and robust algorithm to circumvent the periodicity error, which is also applied here. This algorithm is able to assess linear convolution by computing the discrete cyclic convolution of the two terms on an extended domain, with a special, "warp-around" arrangement of influence coefficients. The base for this approach is discussed in detail in (Press et al., 1992).

4. Algorithm description

Considering the similarity between NC and TC, the same type of algorithm could be used to solve either model considered independently. Indeed, in both cases, a linear system arising from Eqs. (11) and (15) respectively, is to be solved, having as unknowns the normal or the tangential tractions. The main difficulties consist in the fact that the systems are essentially non-linear, due to presence of terms containing rigid-body motions, and their size, related to the number of cells in A_C and A_S respectively, is not known in advance. Moreover, resolution of a linear system with N unknowns has an order of computation of $O(N^3)$ when direct methods like Gaussian elimination are used. In contact problems, grids with $N = 10^3$ nodes on the contact area are usually considered for nominal contact surfaces, in order to get an accurate estimation of contact area extents and to minimize the discretization error (i.e. the error introduced by digitization of problem parameters). When deterministic rough surfaces are studied, a minimum of $N = 10^6$ points is required to reproduce the detailed features of rough contact behaviour. Consequently, only fast numerical methods, based on iterative approaches, are suitable for this type of problem. According to a review paper by Allwood (Allwood, 2005), the Conjugate Gradient Method (CGM) has the fastest convergence. Implementation of CGM to this type of problem is authorised by the fact that the influence coefficients matrix is symmetrical and positive definite, therefore convergence is assured.

The algorithm used in this study is based on the modified CGM advanced by Polonsky and Keer (Polonsky & Keer, 1999) for the study of frictionless rough contact problems under normal loading. Existence and uniqueness of the solution is discussed by Kalker and van Randen (Kalker & van Randen, 1972). This algorithm was later enhanced by Spinu and Diaconescu (Spinu & Diaconescu, 2008) to allow for a bending moment on the contact area, and it was recently applied by Spinu and Frunza (Spinu & Frunza, 2011a) to solve numerically the Cattaneo-Mindlin problem.

4.1. Numerical solution of uncoupled contact problems

Eq. (21) suggests that, in case of dissimilarly elastic materials (i.e. $E^{(1)} \neq E^{(2)}$ and / or $\nu^{(1)} \neq \nu^{(2)}$), computation of displacements in either direction require the knowledge of contact tractions on every direction. From this yields the coupling between the NC and the TC. However, in case of similarly elastic materials, Eq. (32) proves that normal displacements are independent of shear tractions, and tangential displacements are independent of pressure. In the latter case, solution of NC is decoupled from that of TC; however, pressure distribution is still needed in the TC for assessment of shear tractions in the slip zone, according to Coulomb's law. In the framework developed herein, we refer to the solution of uncoupled NC or TC as being the solution of NC when shear tractions are known, but otherwise arbitrarily distributed, as well as the solution of TC when pressure is known, but otherwise arbitrarily distributed.

It should be noted that in some cases, matching names will be used for variables having the same role in the algorithm structure, although their content might be different in the NC from that in the TC. Let us assume that a new loading increment k is applied. In both NC and TC, all parameters are specific to the achieved loading level; therefore, the third formal parameter, related to the loading history, will be omitted for brevity. An additional symbol

"δ" is used to denote the increment of the referred quantity after application of the k-th loading increment, i.e. $\delta u_1(i,j) = u_1(i,j,k) - u_1(i,j,k-1)$.

The contact tractions corresponding to the new loading level $p(k)$ or $\mathbf{q}(k)$ can be assessed using the same type of algorithm, consisting in the sequences described in the following paragraphs.

1. Initialize auxiliary variables:

$$\begin{aligned} NC: &\quad \theta = 0; R_{old} = 1; d_3(i,j) = 0, p_{old}(i,j) = 0, (i,j) \in A_P; \\ TC: &\quad \theta = 0; R_{old} = 1; d_1(i,j) = 0, d_2(i,j) = 0, \mathbf{q}_{old}(i,j) = \mathbf{0}, (i,j) \in A_P. \end{aligned} \tag{33}$$

Here, $d_i, i = 1,2,3$ is the initial descend direction in the CGM. The role of the other variables will be discussed later.

2. Adopt the initial guess for contact tractions, using the static force equilibrium. In a first approximation, it will be considered in the NC that all cells are in contact, i.e. $A_C = A_P$, and in the TC that all cells in the contact area are in stick, i.e. $A_S = A_C$. The contact tractions are sought in the following form:

$$\begin{aligned} NC: &\quad p(i,j) = a_3 + a_1 x_2(i,j) + a_2 x_1(i,j), \quad (i,j) \in A_P; \\ TC: &\quad \begin{cases} q_1(i,j) = a_3 x_2(i,j) + a_1; \\ q_2(i,j) = a_3 x_1(i,j) + a_2; \end{cases} \quad (i,j) \in A_C, \end{aligned} \tag{34}$$

where the unknown coefficients $a_i(k), i = 1,2,3$ are computed by plugging Eq. (34) into Eqs. (9), (10) and (13), (14), respectively, yielding:

$$\begin{aligned} NC: &\quad \begin{bmatrix} a_3 & a_1 & a_2 \end{bmatrix}^T = \mathbf{M}^{-1} \cdot \begin{bmatrix} W & M_1 & M_2 \end{bmatrix}^T / \Delta; \\ TC: &\quad \begin{bmatrix} a_1 & a_2 & a_3 \end{bmatrix}^T = \mathbf{M}^{-1} \cdot \begin{bmatrix} T_1 & T_2 & M_3 \end{bmatrix}^T / \Delta; \end{aligned} \tag{35}$$

$$\begin{aligned} NC: \quad \mathbf{M} &= \begin{bmatrix} \sum\limits_{(i,j)\in A_C} 1 & \sum\limits_{(i,j)\in A_C} x_2(i,j) & \sum\limits_{(i,j)\in A_C} x_1(i,j) \\ \sum\limits_{(i,j)\in A_C} x_2(i,j) & \sum\limits_{(i,j)\in A_C} x_2^2(i,j) & \sum\limits_{(i,j)\in A_C} x_2(i,j)x_1(i,j) \\ \sum\limits_{(i,j)\in A_C} x_1(i,j) & \sum\limits_{(i,j)\in A_C} x_1(i,j)x_2(i,j) & \sum\limits_{(i,j)\in A_C} x_1^2(i,j) \end{bmatrix}; \\ TC: \quad \mathbf{M} &= \begin{bmatrix} \sum\limits_{(i,j)\in A_S} 1 & \sum\limits_{(i,j)\in A_S} 0 & \sum\limits_{(i,j)\in A_S} x_2(i,j) \\ \sum\limits_{(i,j)\in A_S} 0 & \sum\limits_{(i,j)\in A_S} 1 & \sum\limits_{(i,j)\in A_S} x_1(i,j) \\ \sum\limits_{(i,j)\in A_S} x_2(i,j) & \sum\limits_{(i,j)\in A_S} x_1(i,j) & \sum\limits_{(i,j)\in A_S} \left[x_1^2(i,j) + x_2^2(i,j) \right] \end{bmatrix}. \end{aligned} \tag{36}$$

3. Compute the relative displacement field over the grid domain using Eq. (21). It should be remembered that in the NC, pressure was adopted in step 2 and shear tractions are assumed as known, but arbitrarily distributed, while in the TC, shear tractions were adopted in step 2, and pressure is assumed known but arbitrarily distributed. It should also be noted that in case of TC, the increment of displacement field, $\delta u_1(i,j), \delta u_2(i,j)$, is needed.
4. Estimate the rigid-body motions in order to linearize Eqs. (11) and (15). According to complementarity conditions in Eqs. (12) and (16), the following relations hold:

$$\begin{aligned} &NC: \quad hi(i,j) + u_3(i,j) - \omega_3 - \phi_1 x_2(i,j) - \phi_2 x_1(i,j) = 0, \, (i,j) \in A_C; \\ &TC: \quad \begin{bmatrix} \delta u_1(i,j) \\ \delta u_2(i,j) \end{bmatrix} - \begin{bmatrix} \delta\omega_1 \\ \delta\omega_2 \end{bmatrix} + \delta\phi_3 \begin{bmatrix} x_2(i,j) \\ x_1(i,j) \end{bmatrix} = \begin{bmatrix} 0 \\ 0 \end{bmatrix}, \, (i,j) \in A_S, \end{aligned} \tag{37}$$

resulting in linear systems having a number of equations equal the number of cells in the contact and in the stick area, respectively. When convergence is reached, the equations in every of these two systems are not all independent; however, during iterations, they appear to be independent. To get the best possible estimates of rigid-body motions, the systems are treated as over-determined and the best fit is sought using least square minimization. The functional $\aleph$ is defined as the square sum of the residuals:

$$\begin{aligned} &NC: \aleph(\omega_3, \phi_1, \phi_2) = \sum_{(i,j)\in A_C} \left(hi(i,j) + u_3(i,j) - \omega_3 - \phi_1 x_2(i,j) - \phi_2 x_1(i,j) \right)^2; \\ &TC: \aleph(\delta\omega_1, \delta\omega_2, \delta\phi_3) = \sum_{(i,j)\in A_S} \left(\left(\delta u_1(i,j) - \delta\omega_1 - \delta\phi_3 x_2(i,j) \right)^2 + \left(\delta u_2(i,j) - \delta\omega_2 - \delta\phi_3 x_1(i,j) \right)^2 \right). \end{aligned} \tag{38}$$

The rigid-body motions that minimize the goal function in Eq. (38) are found by setting the partial derivatives of $\aleph$ to zero, leading to the following solution:

$$\begin{aligned} &NC: \begin{bmatrix} \omega_3 \\ \phi_1 \\ \phi_2 \end{bmatrix} = \mathbf{M}^{-1} \cdot \begin{bmatrix} \sum_{(i,j)\in A_C} \left[u_3(i,j) + hi(i,j) \right] \\ \sum_{(i,j)\in A_C} \left[\left(u_3(i,j) + hi(i,j) \right) x_2(i,j) \right] \\ \sum_{(i,j)\in A_C} \left[\left(u_3(i,j) + hi(i,j) \right) x_1(i,j) \right] \end{bmatrix}; \\ &TC: \begin{bmatrix} \delta\omega_1 \\ \delta\omega_2 \\ \delta\phi_3 \end{bmatrix} = \mathbf{M}^{-1} \cdot \begin{bmatrix} \sum_{(i,j)\in A_S} \delta u_1(i,j) \\ \sum_{(i,j)\in A_S} \delta u_2(i,j) \\ \sum_{(i,j)\in A_S} \left[\delta u_1(i,j) x_2(i,j) + \delta u_2(i,j) x_1(i,j) \right] \end{bmatrix}. \end{aligned} \tag{39}$$

With this approximation, Eqs. (11) and (15) finally reduce to linear systems having the nodal contact tractions as unknowns. The systems sizes are given by the extents of the contact and of the stick area, respectively, both a priori unknown. A trial-and-error approach is used, in which the systems are solved on successive contact and stick areas, until static equilibrium equations and complementarity conditions are fully satisfied for every cell in the grid.

5. Start the conjugate gradient loop by computing the residuals $r_\ell(i,j), \ell=1,2,3$:

$$\begin{aligned} NC: &\ r_3(i,j) = hi(i,j) + u_3(i,j) - \omega_3 - \phi_1 x_2(i,j) - \phi_2 x_1(i,j),\ (i,j)\in A_P; \\ TC: &\ \begin{bmatrix} r_1(i,j) \\ r_2(i,j) \end{bmatrix} = \begin{bmatrix} \delta u_1(i,j) \\ \delta u_2(i,j) \end{bmatrix} - \begin{bmatrix} \delta\omega_1 \\ \delta\omega_2 \end{bmatrix} + \delta\phi_3 \begin{bmatrix} x_2(i,j) \\ x_1(i,j) \end{bmatrix},\ (i,j)\in A_S, \end{aligned} \tag{40}$$

and the square sum of the residuals on the indicated domains:

$$\begin{aligned} NC: &\ R = \sum_{(i,j)\in A_C} \left(r_3(i,j)\right)^2; \\ TC: &\ R = \sum_{(i,j)\in A_S} \left[\left(r_1(i,j)\right)^2 + \left(r_2(i,j)\right)^2\right]. \end{aligned} \tag{41}$$

6. Compute the descend direction $d_i, i=1,2,3$ in the CGM algorithm. In the multidimensional space of contact tractions, every new descend direction is constructed from the residual to be $\mathbf{K}$ - orthogonal (Shewchuk, 1994) to all previous residuals and search directions:

$$\begin{aligned} NC: &\ d_3(i,j) \leftarrow \begin{cases} r_3(i,j) - \left(R\theta/R_{old}\right) d_3(i,j), & (i,j)\in A_C; \\ 0, \ (i,j)\in A_P - A_C; \end{cases} \\ TC: &\ \begin{bmatrix} d_1(i,j) \\ d_2(i,j) \end{bmatrix} \leftarrow \begin{cases} \begin{bmatrix} r_1(i,j) \\ r_2(i,j) \end{bmatrix} + \dfrac{R\theta}{R_{old}} \begin{bmatrix} d_1(i,j) \\ d_2(i,j) \end{bmatrix}, (i,j)\in A_S; \\ \begin{bmatrix} 0 & 0 \end{bmatrix}^T, (i,j)\in A_C - A_S, \end{cases} \end{aligned} \tag{42}$$

and overwrite the content of R_{old} : $R_{old} \leftarrow R$.

7. Assess the length of the step to be made in the computed descend direction:

$$\begin{aligned} NC: &\ \alpha = \sum_{(i,j)\in A_C} r_3(i,j) d_3(i,j) \Big/ \sum_{(i,j)\in A_C} c_3(i,j) d_3(i,j); \\ TC: &\ \alpha = \frac{\sum_{(i,j)\in A_S} r_1(i,j) d_1(i,j) + \sum_{(i,j)\in A_S} r_2(i,j) d_2(i,j)}{\sum_{(i,j)\in A_S} c_1(i,j) d_1(i,j) + \sum_{(i,j)\in A_S} c_2(i,j) d_2(i,j)}, \end{aligned} \tag{43}$$

where $c_i, i=1,2,3$ denotes the convolution of the influence coefficients matrix with the descend direction:

$$\begin{aligned} NC: &\quad c_3 = \left[K_{33}^{(2)} + K_{33}^{(1)} \right] \otimes d_3; \\ TC: &\quad \begin{bmatrix} c_1 \\ c_2 \end{bmatrix} = \begin{bmatrix} K_{11}^{(2)} + K_{11}^{(1)} & K_{12}^{(2)} + K_{12}^{(1)} \\ K_{21}^{(2)} + K_{21}^{(1)} & K_{22}^{(2)} + K_{22}^{(1)} \end{bmatrix} \otimes \begin{bmatrix} d_1 \\ d_2 \end{bmatrix}. \end{aligned} \tag{44}$$

8. Memorize the current contact tractions in a new variable for subsequent error computation: $p_{old} \leftarrow p$, $\mathbf{q}_{old} \leftarrow \mathbf{q}$.
9. Update the system solution by making a step of length α , computed using Eq. (43), along direction $d_i, i = 1,2,3$, derived in Eq. (42):

$$\begin{aligned} NC: &\quad p(i,j) \leftarrow p(i,j) - \alpha d_3(i,j), (i,j) \in A_C; \\ TC: &\quad \begin{bmatrix} q_1(i,j) \\ q_2(i,j) \end{bmatrix} \leftarrow \begin{bmatrix} q_1(i,j) \\ q_2(i,j) \end{bmatrix} - \alpha \begin{bmatrix} d_1(i,j) \\ d_2(i,j) \end{bmatrix}, (i,j) \in A_S. \end{aligned} \tag{45}$$

10. Impose complementarity conditions to adjust the size of the system. In the NC, the contact or non-contact status of every cell in the contact domain is to be determined, while in the TC, the stick or slip regime of every cell in the contact area must be assessed.

In the NC, cells having negative pressure are removed from the current contact area, and the corresponding nodal pressures are set to zero. It should be remembered that the current model cannot incorporate adhesion; therefore, normal contact tractions can only be compressive, not tensile. This assumption leads to specific cells passing from the contact zone to the non-contact area, in order to obey the non-adhesion hypothesis.

On the other hand, as bodies are considered impenetrable in the frame of Linear Theory of Elasticity, specific cells having vanishing pressure but negative gap $h(i,j)$ (which equals the residual), are reinstated in the current contact area. To this end, the corresponding nodal pressures are adjusted with a quantity proven (Polonsky & Keer, 1999) to be positive at all times, i.e. $-\alpha r(i,j)$.

$$\begin{cases} A_C \leftarrow A_C - \{(i,j)\}, p(i,j) = 0, (i,j) \in \{(i,j) : p(i,j) < 0\}; \\ A_C \leftarrow A_C \cup \{(i,j)\}, p(i,j) \leftarrow p(i,j) - \alpha h(i,j), (i,j) \in \{(i,j) : p(i,j) = 0 \wedge h(i,j) < 0\}. \end{cases} \tag{46}$$

In the TC, cells for which Coulomb's friction law is not verified are removed from the stick region, and the corresponding shear tractions are set to the value of limiting friction. Also, cells having micro-slip $\mathbf{s}(i,j)$ not opposite to shear tractions $\mathbf{q}(i,j)$ pass from the slip to the stick region, yielding an adjusted stick area:

$$\begin{cases} A_S \leftarrow A_S - \{(i,j)\}, \mathbf{q}(i,j) \leftarrow \mu p(i,j) \dfrac{\mathbf{q}(i,j)}{\|\mathbf{q}(i,j)\|}, (i,j) \in \{(i,j) : \|\mathbf{q}(i,j)\| > \mu p(i,j)\}; \\ A_S \leftarrow A_S \cup \{(i,j) : \mathbf{q}(i,j) \cdot \mathbf{s}(i,j) > 0\}. \end{cases} \tag{47}$$

In either the NC or the TC, if any cell is removed from or re-enters the contact or the stick area, auxiliary variable θ is set to zero, otherwise it is set to unity. This variable allows resetting the conjugate directions d_i once new cells enter or leave the system. Indeed, these new cells have no precedent in the minimization process and therefore a new search for the optimal path in the CGM algorithm must be conducted.

11. Adjust contact tractions (i.e. system solution) according to the static equilibrium equations. The correction is sought in the same form as in step 1 of the algorithm:

$$\begin{aligned} &NC: \ p(i,j) \leftarrow p(i,j) + a_3 + a_1 x_2(i,j) + a_2 x_1(i,j), \quad (i,j) \in A_P; \\ &TC: \ \begin{bmatrix} q_1(i,j) \\ q_2(i,j) \end{bmatrix} \leftarrow \begin{bmatrix} q_1(i,j) \\ q_2(i,j) \end{bmatrix} + \begin{bmatrix} a_3 x_2(i,j) + a_1 \\ a_3 x_1(i,j) + a_2 \end{bmatrix}; \quad (i,j) \in A_S, \end{aligned} \tag{48}$$

yielding the following correcting parameters:

$$\begin{aligned} &NC: \ \begin{bmatrix} a_3 \\ a_1 \\ a_2 \end{bmatrix} = \mathbf{M}^{-1} \cdot \begin{bmatrix} W/\Delta - \sum\limits_{(i,j)\in A_C} p(i,j) \\ M_1/\Delta - \sum\limits_{(i,j)\in A_C} p(i,j) x_2(i,j) \\ M_2/\Delta - \sum\limits_{(i,j)\in A_C} p(i,j) x_1(i,j) \end{bmatrix}; \\ &TC: \ \begin{bmatrix} a_1 \\ a_2 \\ a_3 \end{bmatrix} = \mathbf{M}^{-1} \cdot \begin{bmatrix} T_1/\Delta - \sum\limits_{(i,j)\in A_C} q_1(i,j) \\ T_2/\Delta - \sum\limits_{(i,j)\in A_C} q_2(i,j) \\ M_3/\Delta - \sum\limits_{(i,j)\in A_C} \left[q_2(i,j) x_1(i,j) + q_1(i,j) x_2(i,j) \right] \end{bmatrix}. \end{aligned} \tag{49}$$

12. Verify convergence to the imposed precision ε :

$$\begin{aligned} &NC: \ \sum_{(i,j)\in A_C} \left| p(i,j) - p_{old}(i,j) \right| \Big/ \sum_{(i,j)\in A_C} p_{old}(i,j) \le \varepsilon; \\ &TC: \ \sum_{(i,j)\in A_C} \left\| \mathbf{q}(i,j) - \mathbf{q}_{old}(i,j) \right\| \Big/ \sum_{(i,j)\in A_C} p(i,j) \le \varepsilon, \end{aligned} \tag{50}$$

and return to step 2 if the precision goals are not met. The algorithm can be summarized in the flow-chart depicted in Fig. 3.

4.2. Numerical solution of coupled contact problems

In the general case, the NC and the TC cannot be solved independently, as the two problems are coupled, i.e. solution of each one requires resolution of the other. While the NC can be decoupled from the TC by neglecting the normal displacements induced by tangential tractions, as in case of Goodman approximation, solution of NC is always required to solve the TC, as shear tractions are linked to pressure in the slip area through Coulomb's law. The solution of the partial slip-stick elastic contact problem, involving the coupled NC and TC, can be obtained in an iterative manner, using the algorithm consisting in the following steps.

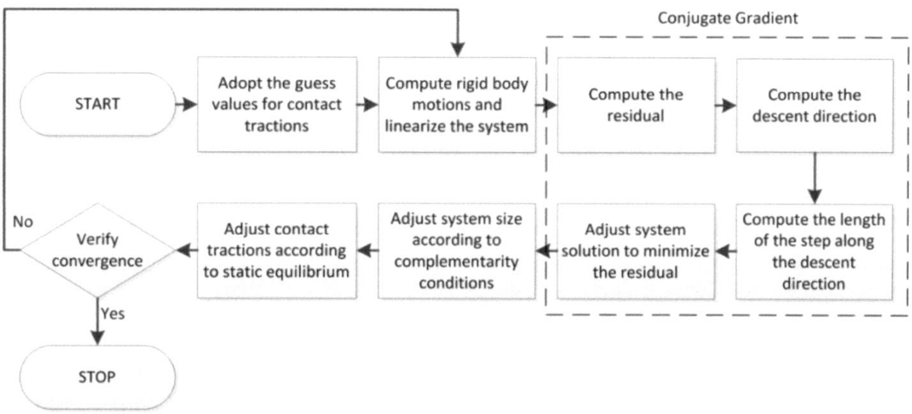

Figure 3. Flow-chart for the uncoupled NC or TC

1. Acquire the state after $k-1$ loading increments and establish the new increment.
2. Adopt vanishing guess value for the increment of shear tractions $\delta\mathbf{q}(i,j)$, i.e. $\mathbf{q}(i,j,k)=\mathbf{q}(i,j,k-1), (i,j)\in A_C(k-1)$.
3. Solve the uncoupled NC using the algorithm described in the previous section, and obtain pressure $p(i,j,k),(i,j)\in A_C(k)$.
4. Memorize the obtained pressure for subsequent error computation: $p_{old}(i,j,k)\leftarrow p(i,j,k)$.
5. Solve the uncoupled TC having as input the previously computed pressure, and obtain the shear tractions $\mathbf{q}(i,j,k),(i,j)\in A_C(k)$. The latter constitutes a better approximation to coupled problem solution compared to shear tractions adopted in step 2.
6. Solve the uncoupled NC again, using as input the shear tractions computed in step 5. The resulting pressure distribution $p(i,j,k)$ is in its turn a better approximation to coupled problem solution than the one obtained in step 3.
7. Verify if pressure distributions resulted in two subsequent computations, $p(i,j,k)$ and $p_{old}(i,j,k)$, vary within an imposed precision goal. If convergence is not met, return to step 4.

This algorithm can be used to simulate any loading history in the fully coupled three dimensional elastic contact with slip and stick. Essentially, three levels of iterations are employed. The inner level is responsible for solving either the normal (NC), or the tangential (TC) unconnected contact problem. The intermediate level mutually adjusts these solutions, based on the contribution of tractions in each direction to displacement fields. The outer level is employed to reproduce the loading history, and is related to friction being a dissipative process. Spinu and Frunza (Spinu & Frunza, 2011b) recently proved that results obtained by simulating the loading history are a closer match to existing analytical solutions than when the full load is applied in one step.

5. Results and discussions

The newly advanced algorithm is validated in this section by comparison with existing closed-form solutions for the contact of similarly elastic materials. The results are then extended by simulating the three-dimensional contact between dissimilarly elastic materials, proving the capacity of the program to solve a large variety of problems incorporating the slip-stick processes in elastic mechanical contacts.

5.1. Simulation of a fretting loop

The newly proposed algorithm is first validated by comparison with the closed-form solution advanced in (Johnson, 1985) for the spherical contact undergoing a fretting loop. A steel ball of radius $R = 18\ mm$ is pressed against an elastic half-space having the same elastic properties, with a normal force $W = 1\ kN$. In this case, the NC is uncoupled from the TC, as shown by Eq. (32). A tangential force T_1 oscillating between two limiting values $T_{\lim}$ and $-T_{\lim}$, where $T_{\lim} = 0.9\mu W$, is subsequently applied. During a fretting contact process, it is expected that friction vary on the contact area, as well as with accumulation of debris particles resulted from additional wear. However, for validation purposes, a frictional coefficient uniform over all contact area and constant during load application is assumed in this study. The numerical approach can equally handle mapped distributions of μ , if such information is available. The loading history for fretting processes is depicted in Fig. 4, in which the load is applied incrementally in $N_\ell = 700$ equal steps.

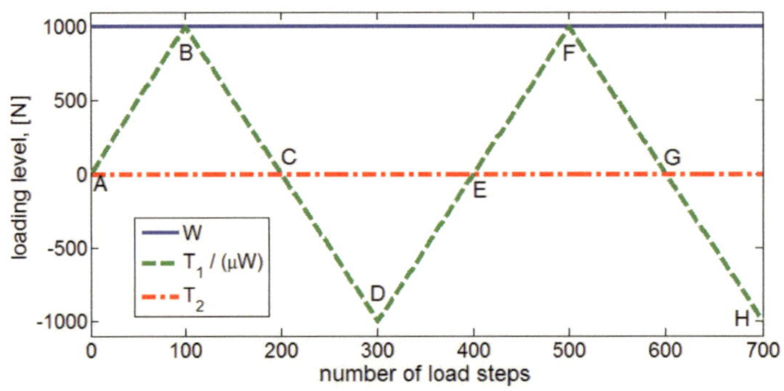

Figure 4. The loading history in simulation of a fretting loop; all moments are assumed to vanish

N_ℓ is chosen differently in the following simulations. When studying the contact between similarly elastic materials, accurate (i.e. concurring with the existing closed-form solution) results can be obtained with even a small number of increments ($N_\ell = 42$ increments in simulations depicted in Figs. 5 and 6). Moreover, it is found that every different state on the loading path can be obtained by simulating only the states when the tangential load changes its sign of, e.g. every state M on the trajectory DF require computation of three states: the ones corresponding to points B and D, as well as the current one (corresponding to point M). This is not the case when simulating the contact between dissimilarly elastic materials. It is found that a large number of increments is required to obtain the detailed contact behaviour, due to non-overlapping stick regions from one loading step to the next. This feature was also observed by Gallego et al. (Gallego et al., 2010), who pointed out that a waved shear tractions profile is predicted numerically when the number of increments is small. Although some perturbations still appear, the large number of increments used in the current simulations $N_\ell = 700$ led to well converged numerical solutions.

The Hertz frictionless theory for the similarly elastic contact scenario predicts a central pressure $p_H = 1.996\,GPa$ and a contact radius $a_H = 0.489\,mm$, which are used as normalizers. Shear tractions profiles corresponding to equal loading levels but laying on different trajectories are depicted in Fig. 5, proving that the current state depends not only on the present load level, but also on its past evolution, thus showing a hysteretic behaviour or memory effect. Only profiles corresponding to states on AD are shown in Fig. 5. States on the DF trajectory can be obtained from those on AD by symmetry with respect to the x_1-axis, and states on FH overlap those on BD corresponding to the same loading level.

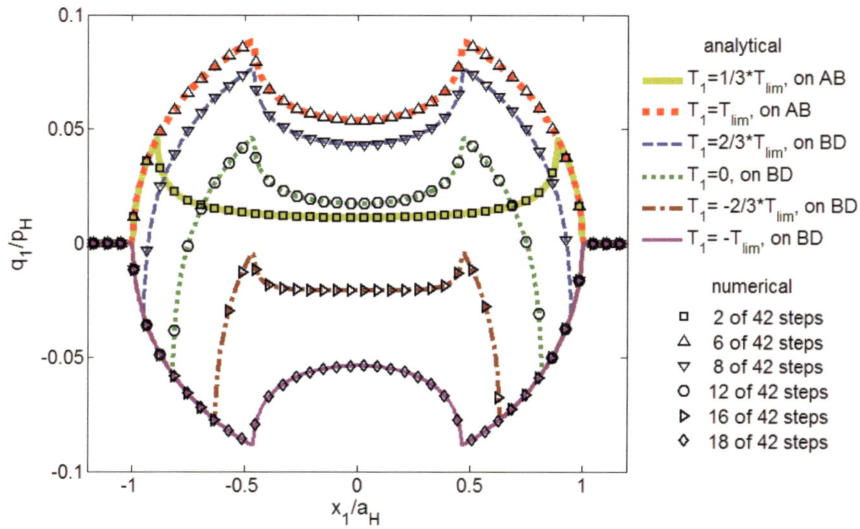

Figure 5. Profiles of shear tractions in the plane $x_2 = 0$ corresponding to different points on the loading curve, $\mu = 0.1$

As depicted in Fig. 6, the force-displacement curve forms a hysteretic loop, also referred to as a fretting loop. The rigid-body tangential displacement is normalized by its value $\omega_{\lim}$ corresponding to $T_{\lim}$. The analytical model predicts that the states corresponding to points B and F on the loading curve should overlap, which is also obtained through numerical simulation, within an imposed precision.

From a mechanical point of view, regions undergoing the most severe stresses are of interest, leading to prediction of yield inception or crack nucleation in the contacting bodies. An algorithm to assess stresses due to known, but otherwise arbitrarily distributed contact tractions is readily available (Liu & Wang, 2002). A typical distribution of von Mises equivalent stress σ_{VM}/p_H in the plane $x_2 = 0$, corresponding to point B on the loading path, is depicted in Fig. 7. Evolution of magnitude and of depth of von Mises maximum stress in a fretting loop is depicted in Figs. 8-9, for various frictional coefficients.

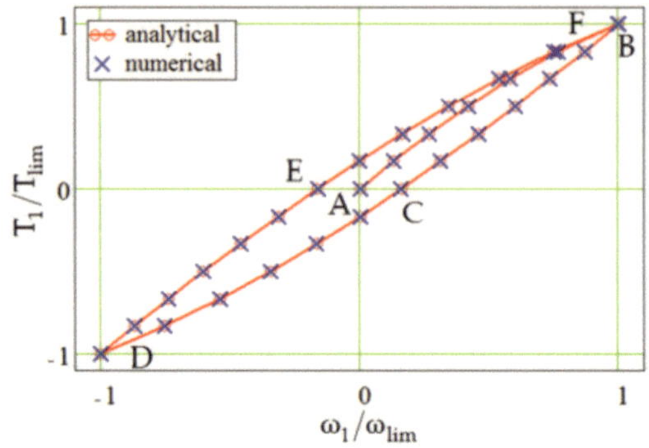

Figure 6. The force-displacement curve in the fretting contact between similarly elastic materials

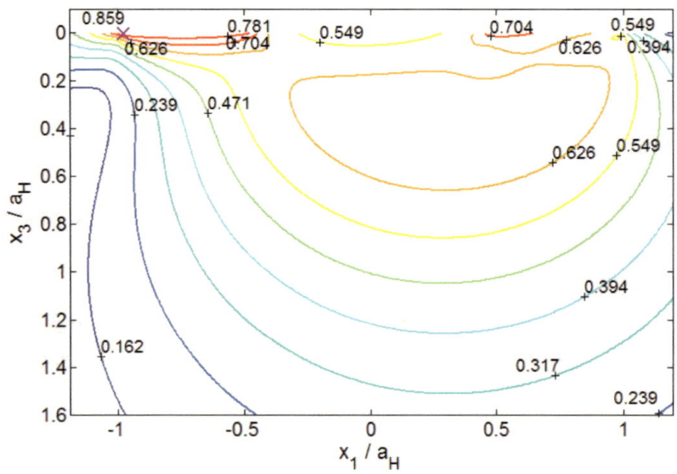

Figure 7. Contour lines of von Mises equivalent stress σ_{VM}/p_H in the plane $x_2 = 0$, corresponding to point B on the loading path; position of maximum is denoted by the symbol "x"

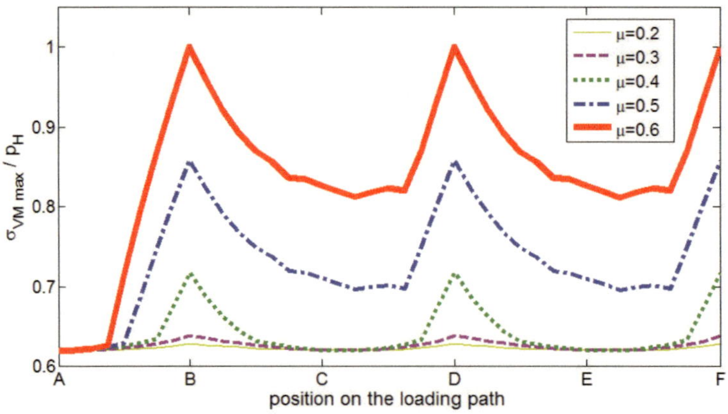

Figure 8. Magnitude of maximum von Mises equivalent stress versus loading level (indicated by the corresponding point on the loading curve)

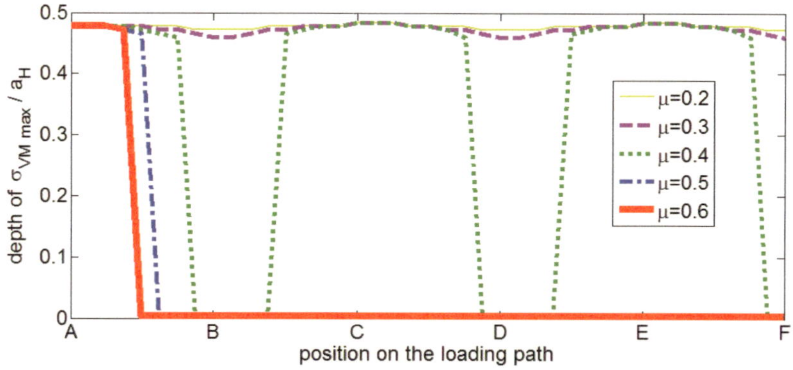

Figure 9. Dimensionless depth of maximum von Mises equivalent stress versus loading level (indicated by the corresponding point on the loading curve)

It is found through numerical simulation that shear tractions have a weak impact on the maximum von Mises stress when $\mu < 0.2$. However, larger friction processes lead to a competition between the in-depth maximum, which fluctuates around its position in the frictionless contact (corresponding to point A in Fig. 9), and a second extremum developing on the surface, at the trailing edge of the contact. The latter can seriously diminish the load-carrying capacity of the contact, especially in case of surfaces with poorly controlled surface quality, due to superimposition of microtopography-induced stress perturbations.

5.2. Simulation of torsional contact

Program validation is subsequently performed in case of a spherical contact undergoing torsion applied simultaneously to a normal constant force. Based on the results of this author, (Mindlin, 1949), Johnson (Johnson, 1985) presents the closed-form solution for this contact scenario when a partial slip regime is established on the contact area (i.e. when the torsional moment M_3 is smaller than a limiting value $M_{3\,\lim} = 3\pi\mu W a_H / 16$). The solution is later reviewed and enhanced for the case of viscoelastic materials by Dintwa et al. (Dintwa et al., 2005).

A spherical indenter of radius $R = 18\,mm$ is pressed with a normal force $W = 1\,kN$ against an elastic half-space, having the same elastic parameters, and subsequently an increasing torsional moment $M_3 \le M_{3\,\lim}$ is applied, leading to shear tractions q_1 and q_2 depicted in Figs. 10a and b, respectively. The norm of these tractions $\|\mathbf{q}(i,j)\| = \sqrt{q_1(i,j) + q_1(i,j)}$ is compared in Fig. 11 with analytical results, using cylindrical coordinates.

Figure 12 depicts the dimensionless stick radius when the torsional moment M_3 is varied in the domain corresponding to partial slip. In all investigated cases, a good agreement between analytical results and numerical predictions is found, giving further confidence in the newly advanced computer program.

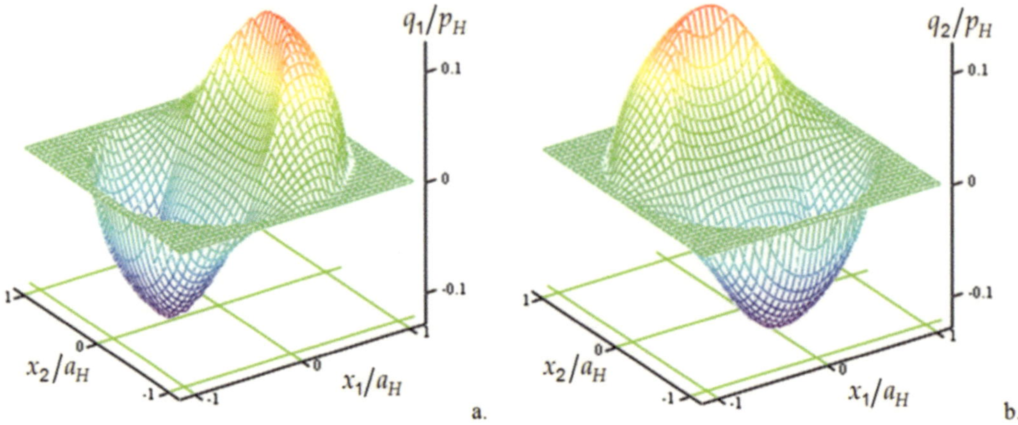

Figure 10. Distribution of shear tractions in torsional contact, $\mu = 0.1$, $M_3 = 0.9M_{3\,\mathrm{lim}}$

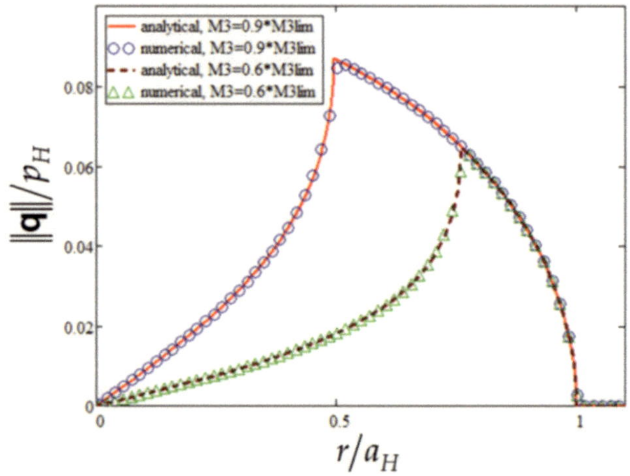

Figure 11. Profiles of radial shear tractions, $\mu = 0.1$

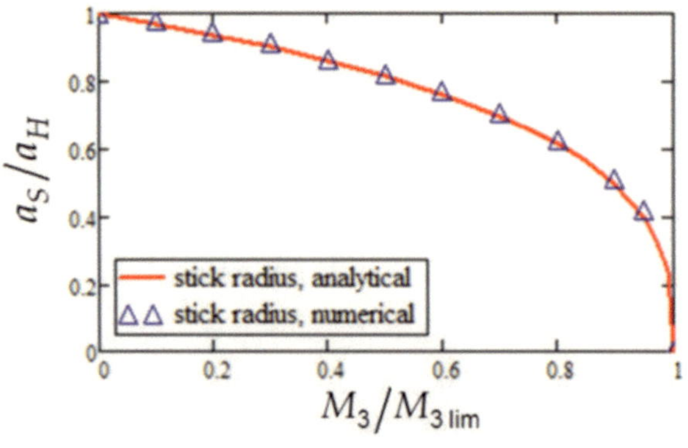

Figure 12. Dimensionless stick radius versus torsional moment

5.3. Extension of results

The numerical program advanced in this study is subsequently used to simulate the fretting contact between dissimilarly elastic materials. To our best knowledge, an analytical solution to this contact process has not been advanced yet. The ball in the previous example is considered rigid, and the loading history is simulated using $N_{\ell} = 700$ equal increments.

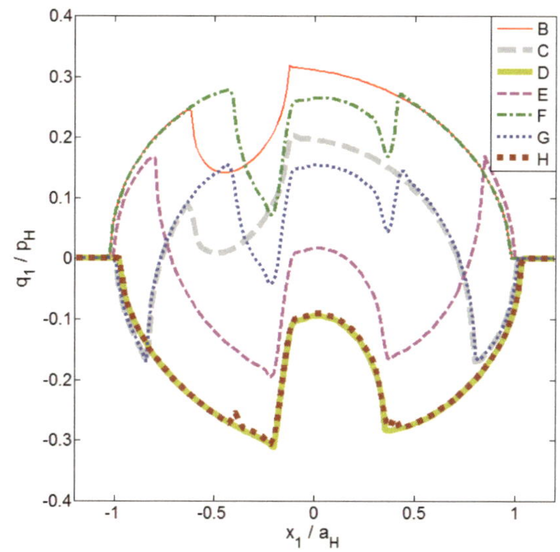

Figure 13. Shear tractions profiles in the fretting contact between dissimilarly elastic materials, corresponding to different points on the loading path, $\mu = 0.3$

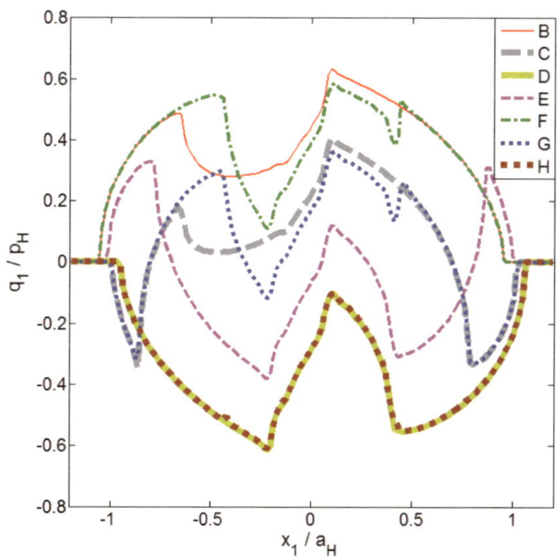

Figure 14. Shear tractions profiles in the fretting contact between dissimilarly elastic materials, corresponding to different points on the loading path, $\mu = 0.6$

Numerical simulations predict that the investigated fretting contact exhibits a unique behaviour in the first two loading cycles, after which it stabilizes to a fixed path. Figures 13 and 14 suggest that the shear tractions profiles corresponding to the BD and FH trajectories no longer match, as in case of similarly elastic materials. However, states D and H overlap, beside a few perturbations induced by the former boundaries of the stick area. Presumably, these perturbations are related to the discretization error, and the D and H states can be considered as concurring. Subsequent oscillating loading is expected to lead to states following the same fixed path, as in case of similarly elastic materials. An analogous behaviour was observed by Wang et al. (Wang et al., 2010) when studying numerically the partial slip contact of elastic layered half-spaces.

6. Conclusions

The work reported herein advances a numerical model for the fretting contact between dissimilarly elastic materials. A numerical approach is required to simulate this type of contact process, as analytical models can incorporate neither the loading history, which must be reproduced when friction is accounted for, nor the coupling of normal and tangential effects.

The implemented algorithm is based on three levels of iterations, fully incorporating the interconnectivity between normal and tangential tractions. The innermost level solves, in a conjugate gradient type loop, either the normal, or the tangential uncoupled contact problem, while the intermediate loop iterates between these solutions, until pressure convergence is reached. The outer level reproduces the loading history, and is based on the assumption that irreversibility of friction requires simulation of all previous states in an incremental load process.

The strong points of this algorithm consist in reduced computational complexity, compared to finite element analysis, as well as in its ability to handle arbitrarily shaped contact geometries or imposed frictional coefficient maps. Comparison with existing closed-form solutions for the spherical contact undergoing a fretting loop or torsion, when a uniform frictional coefficient is assumed, gives confidence in the newly advanced model.

Evolution of stress state during a fretting loop in the spherical contact between similarly elastic materials is assessed. It is found that for specific combinations of loading levels and frictional coefficients, the most severely stressed region can be found on the bounding surfaces, at the trailing edge of the contact.

Numerical simulations suggest that the fretting contact between dissimilarly elastic materials exhibits a unique path in the first two loading cycles, which stabilizes with subsequent oscillating loading to a fixed trajectory, as in case of similarly elastic materials.

The newly advanced algorithm is expected to solve a large variety of contact problems involving interfacial friction, leading to a better understanding of complex multidisciplinary phenomena like fretting wear and fretting fatigue, in which transient contact tractions and induced subsurface stresses play an important role, as well as to a more accurate prediction of contact failure through yield inception or crack nucleation. Study of partial slip elastic-plastic contact is anticipated for future contributions, by addition of the residual term, related to development of plastic strains.

Author details

Sergiu Spinu and Dumitru Amarandei
Department of Mechanics and Technologies, "Stefan cel Mare" University of Suceava, Romania

Acknowledgement

This paper was supported by the project "Progress and development through post-doctoral research and innovation in engineering and applied sciences – PRiDE - Contract no. POSDRU/89/1.5/S/57083", project co-funded from European Social Fund through Sectorial Operational Program Human Resources 2007-2013.

7. References

Allwood, J. M. (2005). Survey and Performance Assessment of Solution Methods for Elastic Rough Contact Problems. *ASME Journal of Tribology*, Vol. 127, No. 1, pp. 10-23, ISSN: 0742-4787.

Boussinesq, J. (1969). *Application des potentiels á l'etude de l'equilibre et du mouvement des solides élastiques*, Reed. A. Blanchard, ISBN: 978-2853670715, Paris.

Cattaneo, C. (1938). Sul contatto di due corpi elastici: distribuzione locale degli sforzi, *Accademia Nazionale Lincei, Rendiconti, Ser. 6*, Vol. 27, pp. 342–348, 434–436, 474–478, ISSN: 0392-7881.

Cerruti, V. (1882). Ricerche intorno all'equilibrio de'corpi elastici isotropi. *Reale Accademia dei Lincei, Ser. 3*, Vol. 13, pp. 81–122, Roma.

Chen, W. W. & Wang Q. J. (2008). A Numerical Model for the Point Contact of Dissimilar Materials Considering Tangential Tractions. *Mechanics of Materials*, Vol. 40, No. 11, pp. 936-948, ISSN: 0167-6636.

Dintwa, E., Zeebroeck, M. V., Tijskens, E., & Ramon, H. (2005). Torsion of Viscoelastic Spheres in Contact. *Granular Matter*, Vol. 7, No. 2, pp. 169–179, ISSN: 1434-5021.

Gallego, L., Nélias, D., & Deyber, S. (2010). A Fast and Efficient Contact Algorithm for Fretting Problems Applied to Fretting Modes I, II and III, *Wear*, Vol. 258, No. 1-2, pp. 208-222, ISSN: 0043-1648.

Goodman, L. E. (1962). Contact Stress Analysis of Normally Loaded Rough Spheres. *ASME Journal of Applied Mechanics*, Vol. 29, No. 3, pp. 515-522, ISSN: 0021-8936.

Hertz, H., (1895). Uber die Beruhrung fester elasticher Korper. *Gesammelte Werke*, Bd. 1, Leipzig, pp. 155-173.

Hills, D. A. Nowell, D., & Sackfield, A. (1993). *Mechanics of Elastic Contacts*, Butterworth Heinemann Ltd., ISBN: 978-0750605403, Oxford, United Kingdom.

Johnson, K. L. (1985). *Contact Mechanics*, Cambridge University Press, ISBN: 978-0521347969, Cambridge, United Kingdom.

Kalker, J. J., & van Randen, Y. A. (1972). A Minimum Principle for Frictionless Elastic Contact with Application to Non-Hertzian Half-Space Contact Problems. *Journal of Engineering Mathematics*, Vol. 6, No. 2, pp. 193-206, ISSN: 0022-0833.

Liu, S. B., & Wang, Q. (2002). Studying Contact Stress Fields Caused by Surface Tractions With a Discrete Convolution and Fast Fourier Transform Algorithm. *ASME Journal of Tribology*, Vol. 124, No. 1, pp. 36–45, ISSN: 0742-4787.

Liu, S. B., Wang, Q., & Liu, G. (2000). A Versatile Method of Discrete Convolution and FFT (DC-FFT) for Contact Analyses. *Wear*, Vol. 243, No. 1-2, pp. 101–111, ISSN: 0043-1648.

Mindlin, R. D. (1949). Compliance of Elastic Bodies in Contact. *ASME Journal of Applied Mechanics*, Vol. 16, No. 3, pp. 259–268, ISSN: 0021-8936.

Polonsky, I. A., & Keer, L. M. (1999). A Numerical Method for Solving Rough Contact Problems Based on the Multi-Level Multi-Summation and Conjugate Gradient Techniques. *Wear*, Vol. 231, No. 2, pp. 206–219, ISSN: 0043-1648.

Press, W. H., Teukolsky, S. A., Vetterling, W. T., & Flannery, B. P. (1992). *Numerical Recipes in C – The Art of Scientific Computing – Second Edition*, Cambridge University Press, ISBN: 0-521-43108-5, Cambridge, United Kingdom.

Renouf, M., Massi, F., Fillot, N., & Saulot, A. (2011). Numerical Tribology of a Dry Contact. *Tribology International*, Vol. 44, No. 7-8, pp. 834-844, ISSN: 0301-679X.

Shewchuk, J. R., (1994). *An Introduction to the Conjugate Gradient Method without the Agonizing Pain*, School of Computer Science, Carnegie Mellon University, Retrieved from http://www.cs.cmu.edu/~quake-papers/painless-conjugate-gradient.pdf.

Spinu, S., & Diaconescu, E., (2008). Numerical Simulation of Elastic Conforming Contacts under Eccentric Loading. *Proceedings of the STLE/ASME International Joint Tribology Conference IJTC2008*, ISBN: 978-0-7918-3837-2, October 20-22, Miami, Florida, USA, pp. 649-651.

Spinu, S., & Frunza, G. (2011). A Numerical Approach to the Cattaneo-Mindlin Problem. *Proceedings of VI International Conference Balttrib'2011*, Kaunas, Lithuania, November 17-19, 2011, pp. 105-110, ISSN: 1822-8801.

Spinu, S., & Frunza, G. (2011). Numerical Analysis of Elastic Contact Considering Tangential Friction. *Proceedings of VI International Conference Balttrib'2011*, Kaunas, Lithuania, November 17-19, 2011, pp. 111-116, ISSN: 1822-8801.

Wang, Z. J., Meng, F. M., Xiao, J. X., & Wang, W. Z. (2011). Numerical Analysis of Partial Slip Contact under a Tangential Force and a Twisting Moment. *Proceedings of the Institution of Mechanical Engineers, Part J: Journal of Engineering Tribology*, Vol. 225, No. 2, pp. 72-83, ISSN: 1350-6501.

Wang, Z. J., Wang, W. Z., Wang, H., Zhu, H., & Hu, Y. Z. (2010). Partial Slip Contact Analysis on Three-Dimensional Elastic Layered Half Space. *ASME Journal of Tribology*, Vol. 132, No. 2, pp. 021403-1-12, ISSN: 0742-4787.

Section 2

Electromagnetics and Microelectronics

Chapter 8

Numerical Simulations of Radiation and Scattering Characteristics of Dipole and LOOP Antennas

Oleg A. Yurtsev and Grigory V. Ptashinsky

Additional information is available at the end of the chapter

http://dx.doi.org/10.5772/47760

1. Introduction

Dipole and loop antennas are used in communication lines, in radar and navigation systems, TV and other fields of radio-engineering. Structures of antennas depend on their bandwidth. In VHF, UHF, L and S ranges, these antennas are made, as a rule, of conductors with a radius $A_0 << \lambda$ (λ – wavelength in the air). Further, we will study wire dipole and loop antennas. Dipole and monopole antennas [Balanis, 1997; Markov, 1960], a Yagi-Uda antenna [Volakis, 2007; Aisenberg, Jampolsky and Terjoshin, 1977), bicone and discone antennas [Drabkin and Zuzenko, 1961], loop antennas consisting of one or two loops located in one plane [Rothammels, 1995] are well known. The length of a loop perimeter is $L \approx \lambda$. This ensures tuning of the antenna in resonance (a reactive part of input resistance is $X_r \approx 0$). To reduce sizes of dipole antennas, conductor with surface reactive resistance is used. Such a conductor can be implemented, for example, in the form of a cylindrical helix with a radius $A << \lambda$ [Yurtsev, Runov and Kazarin, 1974]. To tune antennas in resonance, reactive resistances are used. Linear arrays of dipole antennas with series excitation are described briefly [Rothammels, 1995].

In communication nodes and antenna arrays, dipole and loop antennas function in the conditions of strong coupling. Therefore, one of the problems of numerical simulation is the research into the influence of interaction on the electrical characteristics of antennas.

Scattering characteristics of antennas are a strong factor that facilitates radar reconnaissance. These characteristics of loop and dipole antennas have hardly been studied in the literature.

In the literature, there is no enough information or there is no information at all about a number of questions related to research into and the versions of construction of dipole and loop antenna. The following is related to these problems:

- optimization of dipole and loop antennas of complex shape according to various criteria (input resistance, directional pattern, bandness); Yagi-Uda multielement antennas, discone and bicone antennas, loop antennas with a quasi-isotropic directional pattern in the E-plane, a combination of loop and dipole antennas, all these antennas are attributed to complex antennas;
- arrays of dipole and loop antennas with series excitation;
- interaction of dipole and loop antennas in the near-field region;
- scattering characteristics of dipole and loop antennas.

The above specified questions are the contents of the present chapter.

2. Method of analysis and mathematical model of wire antenna

2.1. Integral and matrix equations to determine current in arbitrary thin conductor

Wire antennas are simulated numerically by the method of integral equations. In the present chapter, we have used Pockington's integral equation [Mittra, 1973]. The integral equation is solved by Galerkin method (method of the moments) [Harrington, 1968; Mittra, 1973; Fletcher, 1984]. To integrate the integral equation to a system of linear algebraic equations, impulse functions have been used further as basis and weight functions. In this case, the basic part of each matrix coefficient of this system is defined by an exact analytical expression. That ensures the enhancement of accuracy of solution of the integral equation and reduces this problem time.

According to [Mittra, 1973], Pockington's integral equation looks like:

$$Z_s(l_p)\cdot I(l_p)+Z_l(l_p)\cdot I(l_p)+\int\limits_0^L \mathrm{I}(\mathrm{l_q})Z(l_p,l_q)dl_q=U(l_p)\,, \tag{1}$$

where

$I(l_q)$ is the sought current that flows in a conductor under the influence of an extraneous field, which excites the conductor;
$Z_s(l_p)=R_s+iX_s$ is the surface resistance of a conductor;
$Z_l(l_p)$ is the lumped complex impedance connected to the rupture of an antenna conductor – a load;
L is the conductor length.

The kernel of the integral equation $Z(\mathrm{l_p},l_q)$ is defined by the expression:

$$Z(\mathrm{l_p},l_q)=-i30k\left[G(l_p,l_q)\cdot(\vec{l}_0,\vec{S}_0)-\frac{1}{\mathrm{k}^2}\frac{d^2G(l_p,l_q)}{dl_p dl_q}\right]. \tag{2}$$

The right side depends on distribution of the extraneous field that excites the conductor:

$$U(l_p) = -(\vec{E}_{os}(l_p), \vec{l}_o),\qquad (3)$$

where $i = \sqrt{-1}$; $k = \frac{2\pi}{\lambda}$ is the wave number of free space, λ is the wavelength of the field that excites the conductor;
$\vec{E}_{os}$ is the vector of the extraneous electric field that excites the conductor.

Green's function is defined by the expression:

$$G(l_p, l_q) = \frac{e^{ikR}}{R}.\qquad (4)$$

The remaining quantities included in (1) – (4) are shown in fig. 1.

When solving an integral equation by the method of moments, a conductor of arbitrary shape is divided into M rectilinear segments of length $\Delta L << \lambda$. Coordinates of the beginning ($X1_m, Y1_m, Z1_m$) and the end ($X2_m, Y2_m, Z2_m$) of each segment are calculated (m is the segment number, $1 \le m \le M$).

The use of impulse basis and weight functions leads to the following system of linear algebraic equations:

$$Z_{sn} + Z_{lk} + \sum_{m=1}^{M} I_m K_{mn} = U_n,\qquad (5)$$

where

M is the number of segments, into which the whole conductor of length L is divided;
m is the number of a segment, in which point Q (source point) is located (fig. 1), $1 \le m \le M$;
n is the number of a segment, in which point P (point of observation) is located (fig. 1), $1 \le n \le M$;
Z_{sn} is the surface resistance in a segment with number n;
Z_{lk} is the series load resistance of a conductor, k is the number of a segment, to which the resistance is connected;
I_m is the sought current in a segment with number m.

The matrix coefficients are determined by the expression:

$$K_{mn} = \int_{\Delta L_n} \int_{\Delta L_m} \left[Z(l_p, l_q)(\vec{l}_{on}, \vec{S}_{om}) \right] dl_q dl_p = A_{mn} + B_{mn},\qquad (6)$$

where

$\Delta L_n, \Delta L_m$ are the lengths of segments with numbers n and m;
$\vec{l}_{on}, \vec{S}_{om}$ are unit vectors, tangent to a conductor in the centre of segments with numbers n and m;

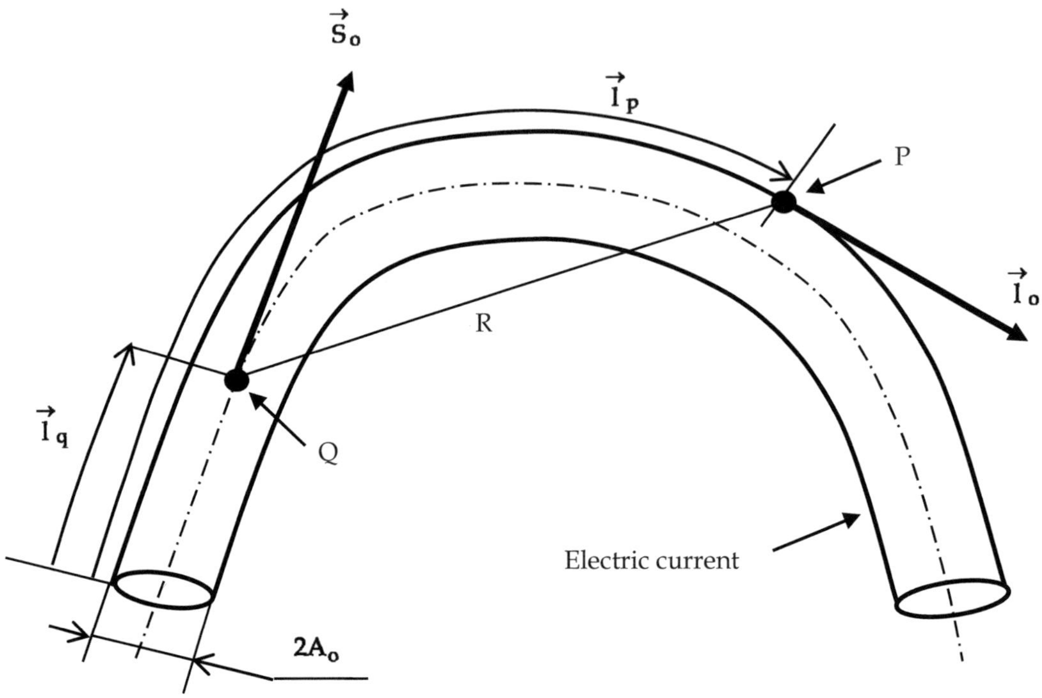

Figure 1. Conductor model

$$A_{mn} = -i30k \int_{Z_{n1}}^{Z_{n2}} \int_{Z_{m1}}^{Z_{m2}} G(z_p, z_q) dz_q dz_p; \tag{7}$$

$$B_{mn} = i\frac{30}{k}[G_{22} - G_{12} - G_{21} + G_{11}]; \tag{8}$$

$$G_{22} = \frac{e^{ikR_{22}}}{R_{22}}; \quad G_{12} = \frac{e^{ikR_{12}}}{R_{12}}; \tag{9}$$

$$G_{21} = \frac{e^{ikR_{21}}}{R_{21}}; \quad G_{11} = \frac{e^{ikR_{11}}}{R_{11}}; \tag{10}$$

$$R_{22} = \sqrt{(X_{n2} - X_{m2})^2 + (Y_{n2} - Y_{m2})^2 + (Z_{n2} - Z_{m2})^2 + a_o^2}; \tag{11}$$

$$R_{12} = \sqrt{(X_{n1} - X_{m2})^2 + (Y_{n1} - Y_{m2})^2 + (Z_{n1} - Z_{m2})^2 + a_o^2}; \tag{12}$$

$$R_{21} = \sqrt{(X_{n2} - X_{m1})^2 + (Y_{n2} - Y_{m1})^2 + (Z_{n2} - Z_{m1})^2 + a_o^2}; \tag{13}$$

$$R_{11} = \sqrt{(X_{n1} - X_{m1})^2 + (Y_{n1} - Y_{m1})^2 + (Z_{n1} - Z_{m1})^2 + a_o^2} \ . \qquad (14)$$

The right side of the system of equations (5) according to (3) turns out to be equal to:

$$\mathrm{U_n} = -\int_{\Delta L_n} (\vec{E}_{os}, \vec{1}_{on}) f_n(l_p) dl_p \ . \qquad (15)$$

The weight function is distinct from zero and is equal to unity only within a segment with number n. Therefore, it follows from (15) that:

$$\mathrm{U_n} = -\int_{\Delta L_n} E_{\tau n}(l_p) dl_p = |U_n| \exp(\Psi_n), \qquad (16)$$

where

$E_{\tau n}$ is the component of an extraneous field, tangent to a conductor in a segment with number n;
$|U_n|$, Ψ_n are the amplitude and the phase of an exciting voltage in a segment with number n.

The further transformation into (16) is different for radiation and scattering problems.

2.2. Radiation problem

When solving a radiation problem, the extraneous field is considered to be distinct from zero only in the space of excitation and constant as for its amplitude and phase within the space. In this case, it follows from (16) that:

$$\mathrm{U_n} = -U, \qquad (17)$$

where

U is the excitation voltage;

$U_n \neq 0$ only in those segments, which are within the space of excitation. It means that, in the system of equations (5), the right side is given in accordance with (17) in the equations, the numbers of which correspond to the numbers of segments within the space of excitation.

As a result of numerical solution of the system of linear algebraic equations (5), the current in each segment I_m is found. The amplitude and the initial phase of the current within each segment is considered to be constant. According to the current distribution in a conductor and the given voltage U, the input resistance $\mathrm{Z_{inp}} = \mathrm{R_{inp}} + i\mathrm{X_{inp}}$ is determined,

where

$$\mathrm{Z_{inp}} = \frac{\mathrm{U}_{inp}}{\mathrm{I_{inp}}}, \qquad (18)$$

U_{inp}, I_{inp} are the input voltage and the input current. The input voltage is the given voltage U in the space of excitation. The input current is the current at the ends of the segment (segments) that fills (fill) the space of excitation in a conductor model. The situation is explicated by fig. 2 that shows a part of a conductor of an antenna and some segments.

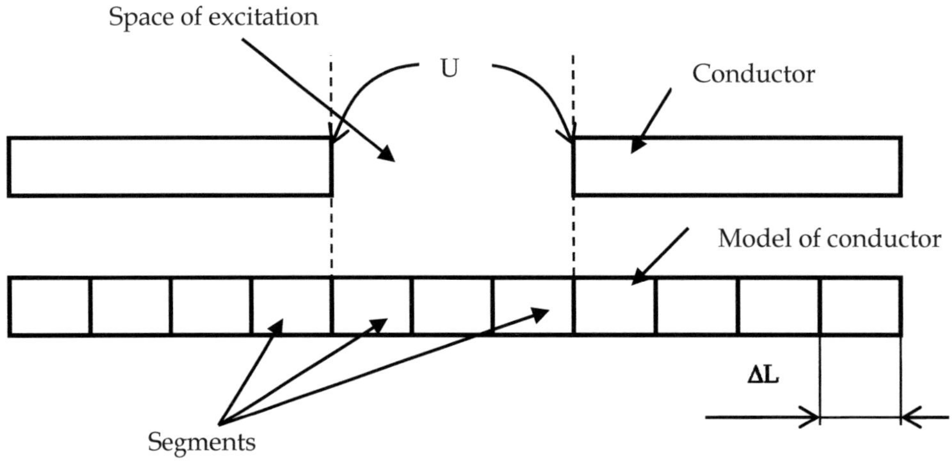

Figure 2. Conductor and its model

If there is one segment in the space of excitation, $I_{inp} = I_{n_o}$ is the current in a segment of excitation, n_o is the number of a segment of excitation. The current in each segment is the complex quantity $I_{inp} = \mathrm{Re}(I_{inp}) + i\,\mathrm{Im}(I_{inp})$. Therefore, $Z_{inp} = R_{inp} + iX_{inp}$, where R_{inp} and X_{inp} are the active and reactive parts of input resistance of the antenna:

$$R_{inp} = U\frac{\mathrm{Re}(I_{inp})}{\left|I_{inp}\right|^2}; \quad X_{inp} = -U\frac{\mathrm{Im}(I_{inp})}{\left|I_{inp}\right|^2} \tag{19}$$

According to the found current distribution in the conductor, the geometry of the conductor, it is easy to determine numerically the conductor field in space in any zone, and further, the basic characteristics and parametres of a wire antenna: its directional pattern, phase diagram, polarization pattern, directivity factor. These questions compose the contents of an exterior problem of the theory, it will be studied in more detail below.

2.3. Scattering problem

The mathematical model of a wire antenna in the scattering mode includes the above relationships that determine current in scattering conductors, and the expression that defines the right side of the matrix equation (3). We will study (3) for the case of excitation of a conductor by a plane wave falling from the given direction. The problem is explicated by fig. 3.

The figure shows a scattering conductor in the X, Y, Z coordinate system, vectors $\vec{E}_i$ $\vec{H}_i$ of a field of an incident wave, vector $\vec{\Pi}_i$ of power flux density of an incident wave. The direction of the incident wave propagation is set by an angle θ_i that is the angle between the Z axis and vector $\vec{\Pi}_i$. The wave field $\vec{E}_i$, $\vec{H}_i$ is extraneous, and $\vec{E}_{os} = \vec{E}_i$. In general, the vector $\vec{E}_i$ and the unit vector $\vec{l}_o$ in the expression (3) have three orthogonal components:

$$\vec{E}_i = E_{ix} \cdot \vec{x}_o + E_{iy} \cdot \vec{y}_o + E_{iz} \cdot \vec{z}_o, \tag{20}$$

where E_{ix}, E_{iy}, E_{iz} are the complex amplitudes of the vector $\vec{E}_i$ components;

$$\vec{l}_o = \vec{x}_o \cos\alpha_x + \vec{y}_o \cos\alpha_y + \vec{z}_o \cos\alpha_z, \tag{21}$$

where $\cos\alpha_x$ $\cos\alpha_y$ $\cos\alpha_z$ are the direction cosines of the vector $\vec{l}_o$ in relation to the X, Y, Z coordinate axes;

$\vec{x}_o$, $\vec{y}_o$, $\vec{z}_o$ are the unit vectors of the coordinate system of X, Y, Z.

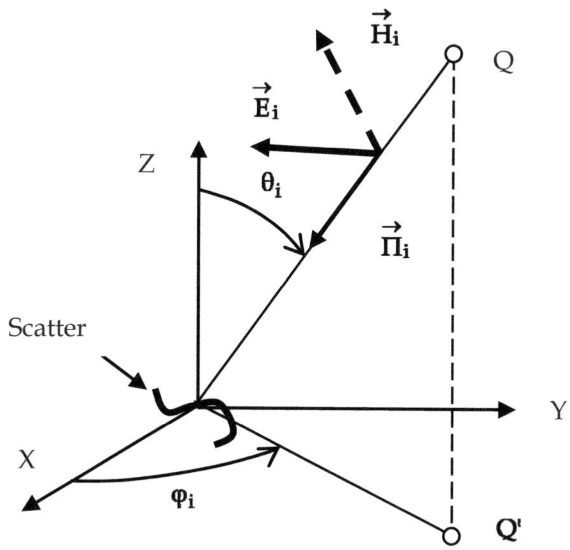

Figure 3. Scatterer conductor in space

It follows from (3), (20), (21) that:

$$U(l_p) = E_{ix}(l_p) \cdot \cos\alpha_x + E_{iy}(l_p) \cdot \cos\alpha_y + E_{iz}(l_p) \cdot \cos\alpha_z . \tag{22}$$

If the antenna is irradiated by a plane electromagnetic wave, the amplitude of the electric field is the same at all the points of the antenna and equal to E_{io}. In this case, in the expression (20):

$$\left|E_{ix}(l_p)\right| = E_{io}\cos\theta_i \sin\varphi_i; \left|E_{iy}(l_p)\right| = E_{io}\cos\theta_i \cos\varphi_i; \left|E_{iz}(l_p)\right| = E_{io}\sin\theta_i, \tag{23}$$

where θ_i φ_i are the angular coordinates of a transmitter of an irradiating electromagnetic wave located at point Q (see fig. 3, angle φ_i is calculated from the X axis to the Y axis).

The phase $U(l_p)$ in a segment with number m depends on the segment position in space, and is determined by the expression:

$$\Psi_m = -k(X_m \cos\theta_i \cos\varphi_i + Y_m \sin\theta_i \sin\varphi_i + Z_m \cos\theta_i), \tag{24}$$

where X_m, Y_m, Z_m are the coordinates of the centre of the segment with number m.

2.4. Radiation (scattered) field of thin conductor

The field at an arbitrary point of space P is determined according to the found current distribution $I(l_q)$ in a conductor. The positon of the point P is set by spherical coordinates R, θ, φ - fig. 4. To calculate the electric field at the point P, the vector-potential method has been used [Stratton, 1941; Volakis, 2007]:

$$\vec{E} \approx -i\frac{60\pi}{\lambda}\int_L I(l_q)\cdot \vec{S}_o \frac{e^{-kR_{pq}}}{R_{pq}} dl_q, \tag{25}$$

where R_{pq} is the distance from point of observation P to point Q on the antenna (see fig. 1).

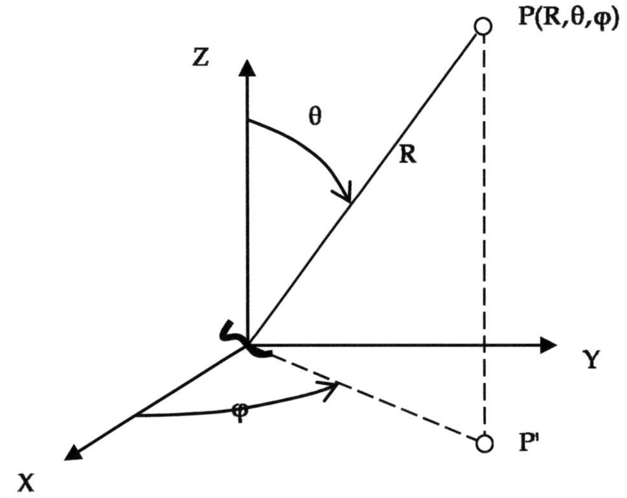

Figure 4. Point of observation in space

When calculating the current $I(l_q)$, all the antenna conductors are divided into rectilinear segments of length $\Delta L << \lambda$. The current amplitude $|I_m|$ and the current phase Ψ_m are considered to be constant within each segment with number m. Therefore, the integral (25) is transformed into the sum of fields of M segments:

$$\vec{E} \approx E_o \sum_{m=1}^{M} I_m \vec{S}_{om} \frac{e^{-kR_m}}{R_m}. \tag{26}$$

where $E_o = -i60\pi \cdot \Delta L / \lambda$; R_m is the distance from a segment with number m to point P:

$$R_m = \sqrt{(X_m - X_p)^2 + (Y_m - Y_p)^2 + (Z_m - Z_p)^2}, \tag{27}$$

$\vec{S}_{om}$ is the unit vector, tangent to a conductor in a segment with number m.

Vectors $\vec{S}_{om}$ and $\vec{E}$ are represented in the form of the sum of projections on the X, Y, Z axes:

$$\vec{S}_{om} = \frac{X_{m2} - X_{m1}}{\Delta L} \vec{x}_o + \frac{Y_{m2} - Y_{m1}}{\Delta L} \vec{y}_o + \frac{Z_{m2} - Z_{m1}}{\Delta L} \vec{z}_o, \tag{28}$$

$$\vec{E} = E_x \vec{x}_o + E_y \vec{y}_o + E_z \vec{z}_o. \tag{29}$$

The cross components E_θ and E_φ can be expressed by the projections E_x, E_y, E_z:

$$\begin{aligned} E_\theta(\theta,\varphi) &= -E_z \sin\theta + (E_x \cos\varphi + E_y \sin\varphi)\cos\theta, \\ E_\varphi(\theta,\varphi) &= -E_x \sin\varphi + E_y \cos\varphi. \end{aligned} \tag{30}$$

2.5. Directional pattern, directivity factor and gain

The directional pattern $F(\theta,\varphi)$ is determined by a field of the antenna in the radiation mode, the scattering pattern $F_s(\theta,\varphi)$ is determined by the field in the scattering mode. The fields in the radiation and scattering modes are described by the same expressions (30). Therefore, the directional pattern and the scattering pattern of the antenna are determined by the same expression:

$$F(\theta,\varphi) = E(\theta,\varphi) / E_{\max} = F_s(\theta,\varphi), \tag{31}$$

where $E_{\max}$ is the maximum value of a field on a sphere $R = const$.

The shape of $F(\theta,\varphi)$ and $F_s(\theta,\varphi)$ is different, as the current distribution is different in antenna conductors in the radiation and scattering modes.

The directivity factor (D) is determined by a directional pattern [Balanis; Aisenberg, Jampolsky and Terjoshin, 1977]:

$$G = \frac{4\pi}{\int\limits_{\varphi=0}^{2\pi} \left[\int\limits_{\theta=0}^{\pi} F^2(\theta,\varphi) \sin\theta \cdot d\theta \right] d\varphi}. \tag{32}$$

The antenna gain (G) characterises the antenna directional properties and power heat loss in antenna elements [Mittra, 1973]:

$$G = R^2 \frac{E_{\max}^2}{30U_{inp} \cdot I_{inp}}. \tag{33}$$

2.6. Radar Cross Section

The radar cross section (RCS) of antennas can exceed considerably the effective area of an object, on which the antennas are installed. That is why it is necessary to take into consideration the scattering properties of the antenna, when developping countermeasures to radar reconnaissance. In accordance with [Crispin and Maffett, 1965; Scolnic, 1970;]

$$S = 4\pi R^2 \left| \frac{E}{E_i} \right|^2, \tag{34}$$

where

S is the radar cross section;
R is the distance from an antenna to a point of observation in space;
E is the amplitude of a scattered field in the point of observation;
E_i is the amplitude of the electric field of an irradiating wave in the place of antenna location.

The scattering pattern and RCS depend on the antenna structure, frequency, polarization, and direction of falling of an electromagnetic wave on the antenna. RCS is described in general by the polarization scattering matrix:

$$S = \begin{vmatrix} S_{\theta\theta} & S_{\theta\varphi} \\ S_{\varphi\theta} & S_{\varphi\varphi} \end{vmatrix}, \tag{35}$$

where

$S_{\theta\theta}$ is the RCS calculated according to a scattered field component E_θ, when the object is irradiated by a field $E_{i\theta}$;
$S_{\theta\varphi}$ is the RCS calculated according to a scattered field component E_θ, when the object is irradiated by a field $E_{i\varphi}$;
$S_{\varphi\theta}$ is the RCS calculated according to a scattered field component E_φ, when the object is irradiated by a field $E_{i\theta}$;
$S_{\varphi\varphi}$ is the RCS calculated according to a scattered field component E_φ, when the object is irradiated by a field $E_{i\varphi}$.

The scattered field and RCS of the antenna can be represented as the sum of two components: antenna component S_a and structural component S_s [Sazonov and

Shkolnikov, 1974]. The irradiating wave creates conduction currents in the antenna conductors. These currents radiate the field that is a structural component of the scattered field. The RCS corresponding to this field is S_s. At the same time, the antenna currents excite the transmission line connected to the antenna. The wave in the transmission line is reflected from a load and is radiated by the antenna. This scattered field is the antenna component. The RCS corresponding to this field is S_a. If the load is matched to the transmission line, S_a=0. The antenna components and the structural components of the scattered field differ from each other not only by their scattering pattern, but by their phase diagram as well. Therefore, after having determined separately the components S_a, S_s and the scattered fields corresponding to these components, it is impossible to found the total RCS as their arithmetical sum [Crispin and Maffett, 1965]. The antenna component of the RCS is related to an antenna gain and a VSWR in the transmission line. When calculating the RCS by the formula (34), it is necessary to connect the matched load to the antenna port. Such an oppotunity is provided in the integral equation (1). The number of the segment k, to which the load Z_{lk} is connected, shall coincide with the number of a segment of excitation.

The scattering pattern differs from the directional pattern (DP) of an antenna in the transmission (reception) mode. It is related to the fact that a structural component predominates over an antenna component in a scattered field. The structural component of the scattered field is the result of radiation of the currents created by an incident EMW in the antenna. Distribution of these currents can differ essentially from current distribution in the antenna in the transmission mode.

2.7. Interaction of antennas located in near-field region

An integral equation and the subsequent part of a mathematical model of a wire antenna allow modelling wire antennas with an arbitrary geometry, located in the near-field region. If several antennas are located in the near-field region, the length L is the total length of conductors of all the antennas. If, in the radiation mode, only one antenna from group functions (an active antenna), and entries of all the remaining antennas are loaded with matched loads (passive antennas), it is possible to determine an isolation ratio between the active antenna and every other passive antenna. The isolation ratio of a field is calculated as the ratio of complex amplitudes of currents at the entry of the active antenna $(I_{inp})_a$ and a passive antenna $(I_{inp})_p$. The power isolation ratio K_p is equal to:

$$K_p = \left| \frac{(I_{inp})_a}{(I_{inp})_p} \right|^2 . \qquad (36)$$

The described mathematical model has been used in the program, with the help of which the results below have been obtained.

3. Modelling of radiation and scattering characteristics of dipole antennas

3.1. Dipole antennas and Yagi-Uda antenna

Fig.5 shows a Yagi-Uda antenna. Antenna elements: 1 is a linea reflector; 2 is a dipole; 3 are directors. Plane and corner reflectors are used too(see fig. 6). The polarization of the antenna is linear. Plane XZ is E-plane; plane YZ is H-plane. According to fig. 4, in XZ-plane $\varphi=0$, in YZ-plane $\varphi=90°$.

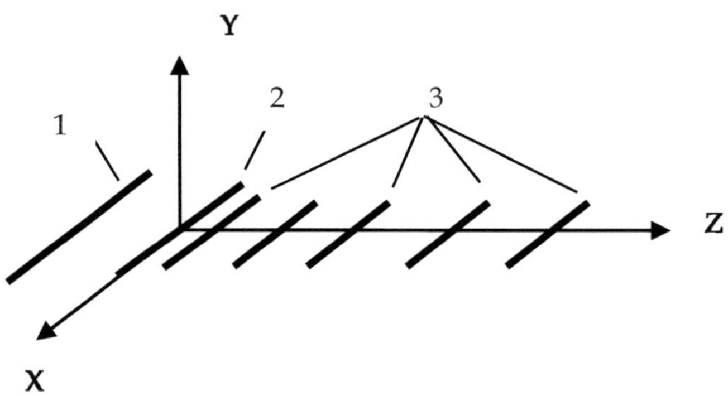

Figure 5. Yagi-Uda antenna

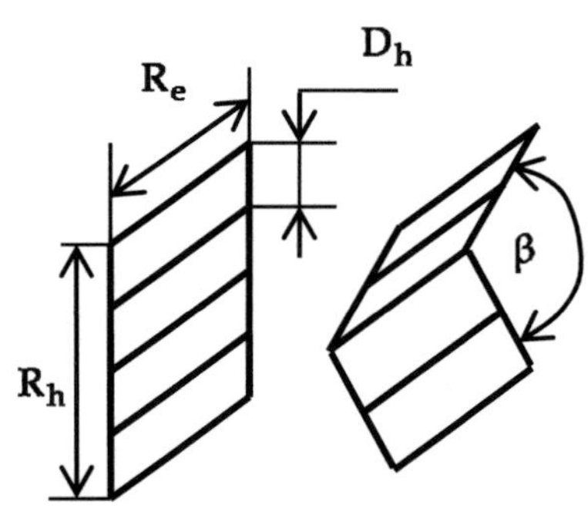

Figure 6. Versions of reflectors

The antenna is optimised as for its input resistance, gain, backscattered radiation level («Front to back» parameter: F/B). Its directional pattern, input resistance, directivity factor, gain depend on the antenna geometrical parametres, frequency, the surface resistance of conductors and the connected lumped resistances. Further, all the regularities are illustrated by the example of antennas intended for a medium frequency f=300 MHz. Size values of the antenna elements are not shown because of the lack of space.

3.1.1. Radiation characteristics

Fig. 7 shows the dependence of a directivity factor (D) of the relations F/B on the number of directors (N). The antenna reflector is linear. For each N value, sizes of the antenna elements are selected so that the input resistance was equal to $R_{inp} \approx 50$ Ohm, $X_{inp} \approx 0$. The results have been obtained for the case Z_s=0. Fig. 8 shows (as an example) a directional pattern in the E-plane at N=10. Fig. 9 shows the dependences of gain and «Front to Bback» ratio (F/B) on the reflector sizes in the H-plane at a different distance between conductors of the reflector: D_h=0,05 λ = 50 mm and D_h=0,1 λ = 100 mm; fig. 10 shows the dependence of G and F/B on the reflector size in the E-plane.

It follows from the cited and other results of simulation that the antenna gain and input resistance depend little on reflector sizes. If R_e changes in the interval (0,2 … 1)λ, the active input resistance varies in the interval (48,5 … 50) Ohm, and the reactive input resistance varies in the interval (0 …-1,7) Ohm. If the distance between the conductors of the reflector is D_h<0,1 λ, the antenna parametres hardly depend on Dh. The maximum of the F/B parametre corresponds to $R_e \approx R_h \approx$ (0,6 … 0,7) λ.

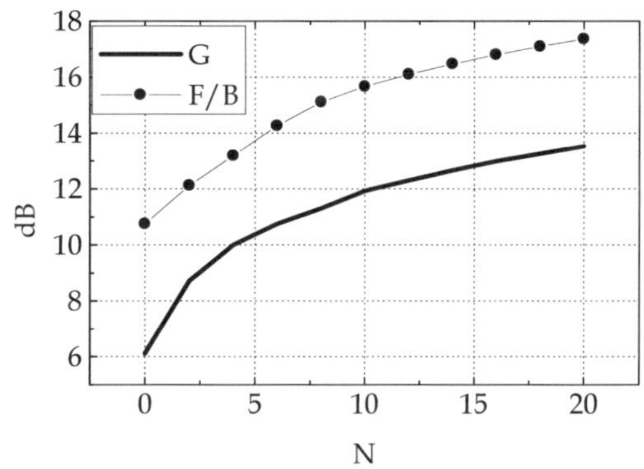

Figure 7. Gain and Front to Back ratio

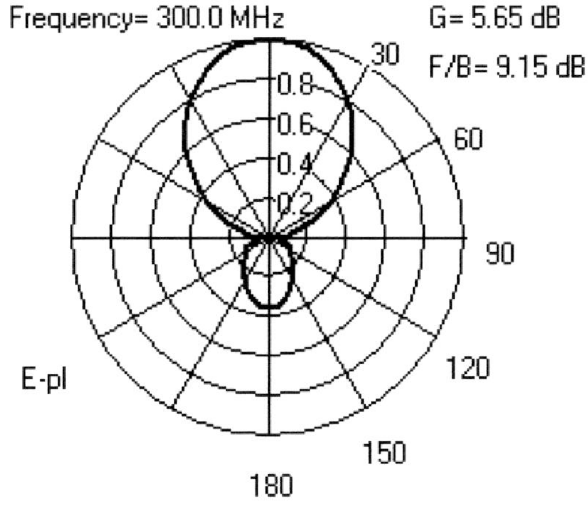

Figure 8. Radiation pattern

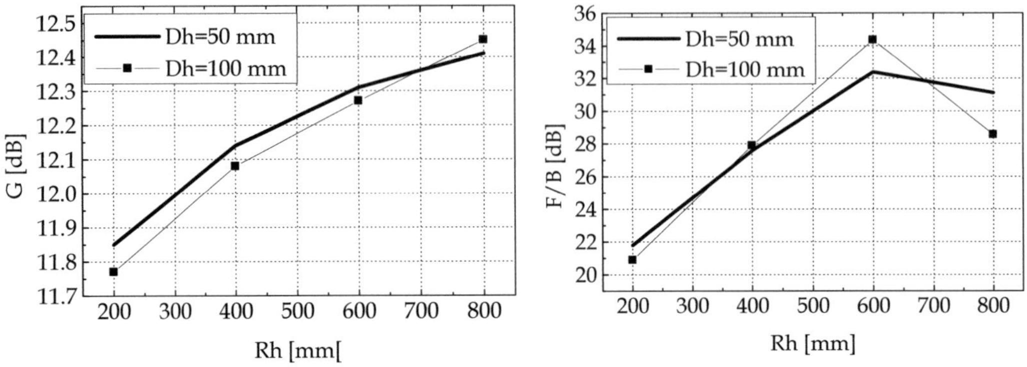

(a) Gain

(b)Front to Back ratio

Figure 9. Dependence of Gain (G) and Front to Back ratio (F/B) on reflector size in H-plane

The graph in fig. 11 illustrates the influence of shape of a reflector on the antenna parametres. The dependences of G and F/B on an angle β are shown for the reflector sizes $R_e = R_h$ = 0,6 λ = 600 mm, D_h=0,1 λ and N=10. It follows from fig. 11 that when an angle β decreases, the F/B parametre worsens, and that the gain hardly depend on β. When β increases, the input resistance increases.

3.1.2. Scattering characteristics

By the example of a dipole, it is convenient to show the dependence of current distribution in the scattering mode on the direction of radiation. Fig. 12 shows current distribution in a dipole with nonresonant length L=1,25λ. The dipole is irradiated from the direction that is perpendicular to the dipole axis (along the Z axis, see fig. 5), and at an angle of 45° to the axis. Fig. 13 shows the corresponding scattering patterns in the E-plane. The figures give the values of $RCSN = RCS / \lambda^2$ in the direction of a maximum of the scattering pattern.

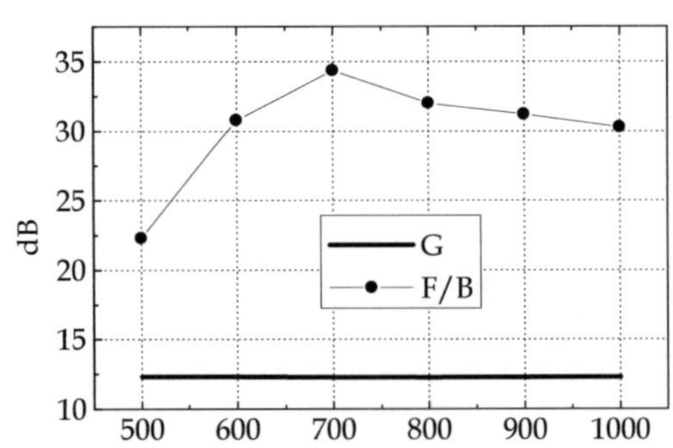

Figure 10. Dependence of G and F/B on reflector size in E-plane

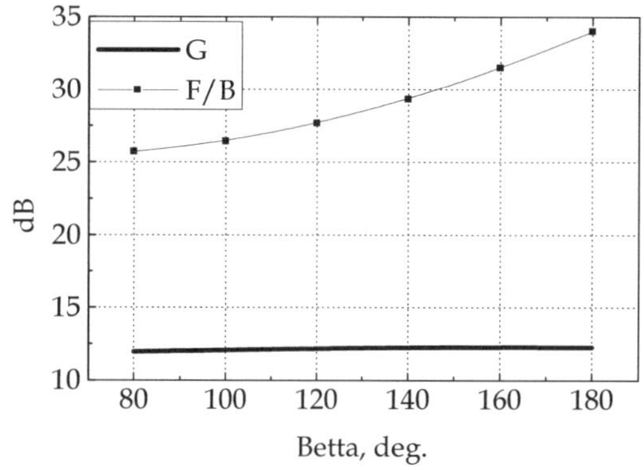

Figure 11. Dependence of G and F/B on angle β

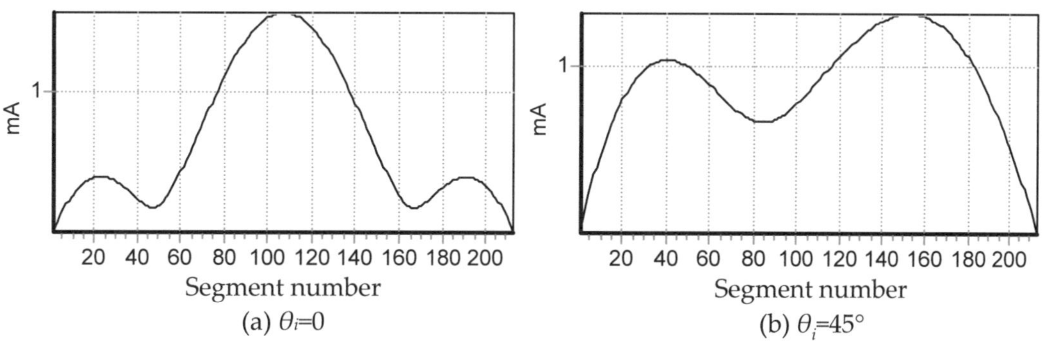

Figure 12. Current distribution

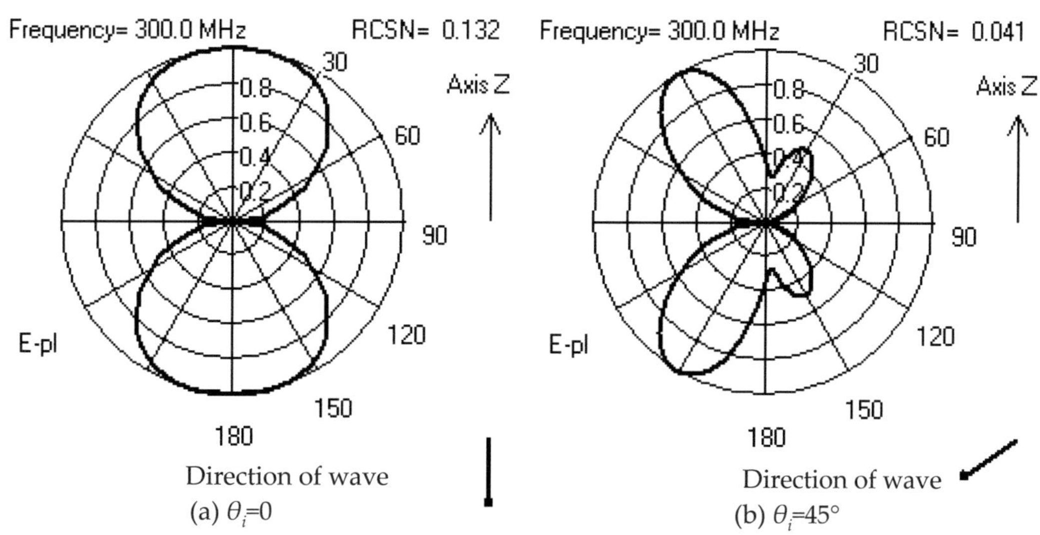

Figure 13. Scattering pattern of dipole

Fig. 14 illustrates the difference of a directional pattern and a scattering pattern and the dependence of the scattering pattern on the direction of propagation of an irradiating wave in relation to the antenna axis (Z axis). The calculations have been made for a Yagi-Uda antenna with a linear reflector, frequency f=300 MHz, N=10.

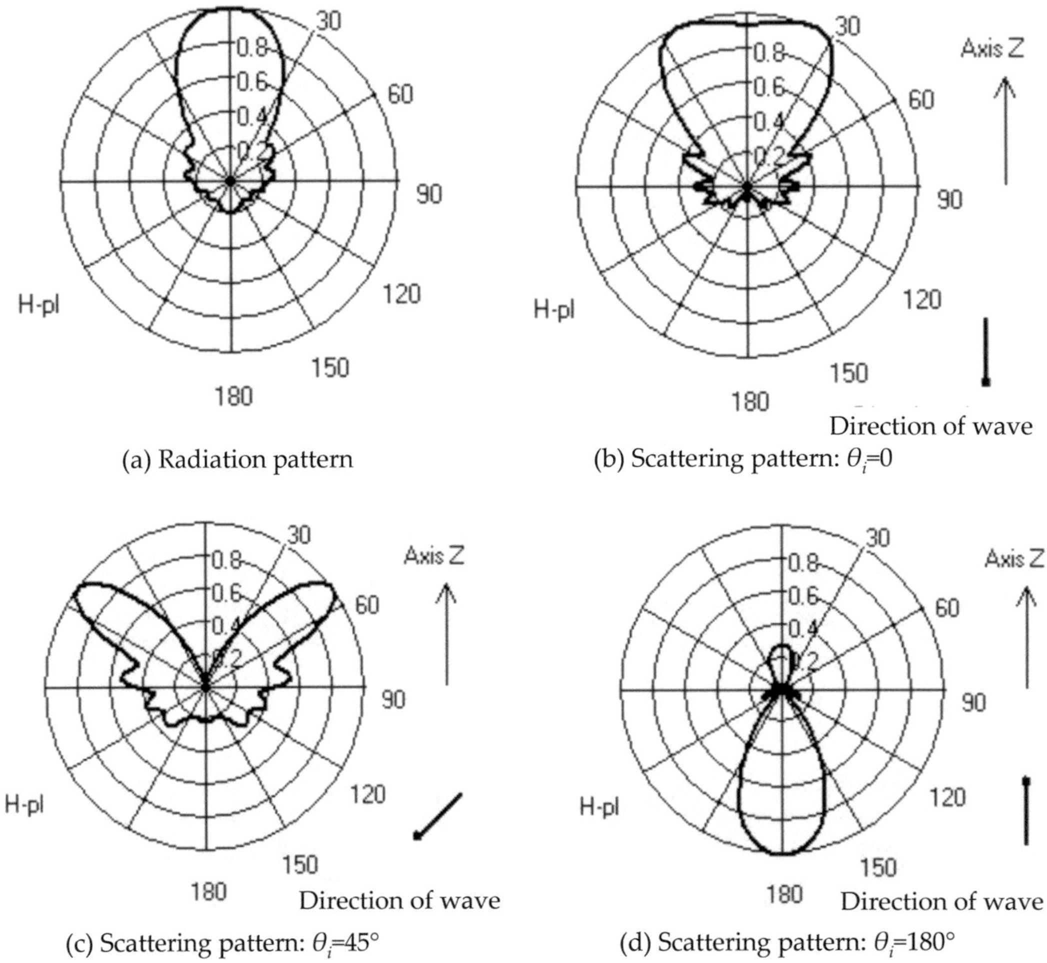

(a) Radiation pattern

(b) Scattering pattern: θ_i=0

(c) Scattering pattern: θ_i=45°

(d) Scattering pattern: θ_i=180°

Figure 14. Radiation pattern (a) and scattering pattern (b, c, d)

Fig. 15 shows the dependence of RCSN in the direction of a maximum of the scattering pattern on the number of directors N. The calculation has been made for the matched load of the antenna $Z_l = Z_{inp}^*$ and for the short-circuit load ($Z_l = 0$). It follows from fig. 15 that a structural component of RCS is much more bigger, than its antenna component.

3.1.3. Dipole antennas with reduced dimensions

In case of increase of a surface inductive reactance X_s, resonance frequency fo of an antenna decreases. The most practical version of implementation of the surface resistance is the application of, instead of a smooth conductor, a conductor rolled into a helix with a radius A_o, fig. 16. The surface resistance is the ratio of the tangential components of vectors $\vec{E}$ and $\vec{H}$ of the helix field on a cylinder of the radius A_o, namely $Z_s = R_s + iX_s = E_t / H_t$.

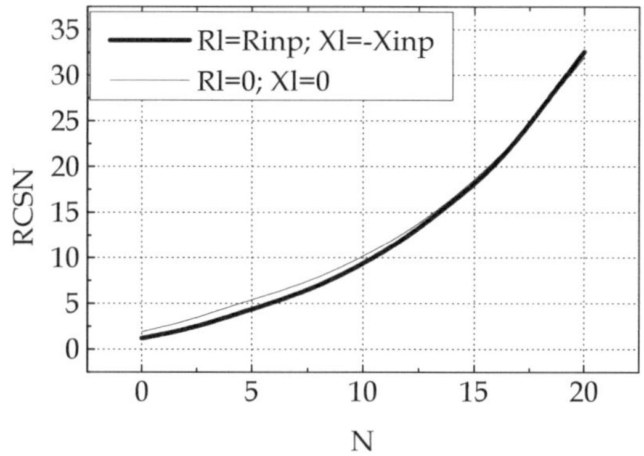

Figure 15. Dependence of RCSN on number of directors

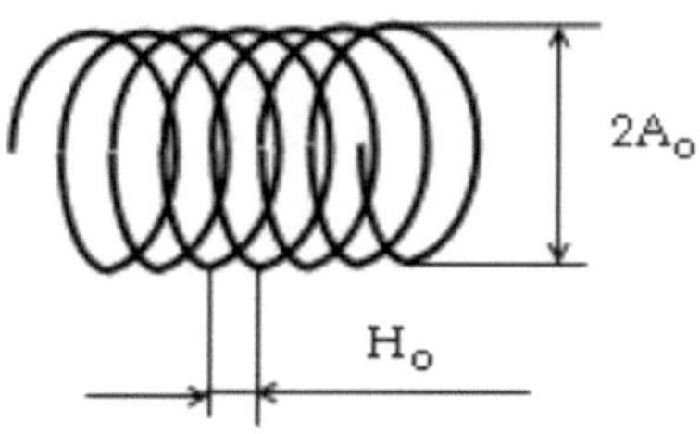

Figure 16. Helix

For the case $A_o << \lambda$, the reactance X_s turns out to be equal to [Yurtsev, Runov, Kazarin 1974]:

$$X_s \approx 480\pi^4 \left(\frac{A_o}{\lambda}\right)\left(\frac{A_o}{H_o}\right)^2 \left[\text{Ohm}\right]. \quad (37)$$

The more the ratio A_o / H_o, the more X_s and the less the antenna resonance frequency. Fig. 17 shows the dependence R_{inp} and X_{inp} on frequency at two values of A_o for a dipole tuned in resonance at a frequency of 300 MHz at X_s=0.

In case of decrease of Ho and $Ao = const$, the resonance frequency and a frequency band according to a matching criterion decreases. Fig. 18 shows the dependence of a resonance frequency f_o for a Yagi-Uda antenna with a linear reflector and one director, depending on Ho at $A_o = 0{,}003\lambda = 3$ mm. The antenna of a smooth conductor with a radius A_o=3 mm was tuned to a frequency of 300 MHz. In case of decrease of Ho, the resonance frequency f_o decreases, the band properties worsen, the F/B parametre decreases, the antenna gain G decreases. Fig. 19 shows the dependence of the percentage bandwidth df / f_o, in which

VSWR <2 (the antenna input resistance at a medium frequency f_o is equal to R_{inp}=50 Ohm, X_{inp}=0, the wave resistance of a feeder is ρ=50 Ohm).

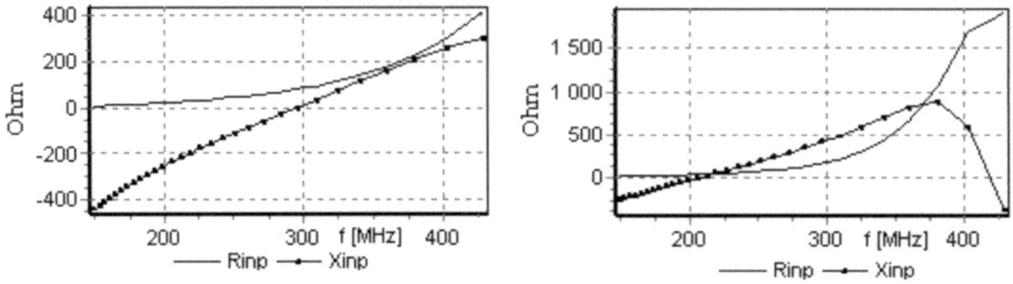

(a) Ao=0

(b) Ao=0 ,01λ

Figure 17. Dependence of input resistance on frequency at $H_o = 0{,}01\lambda$

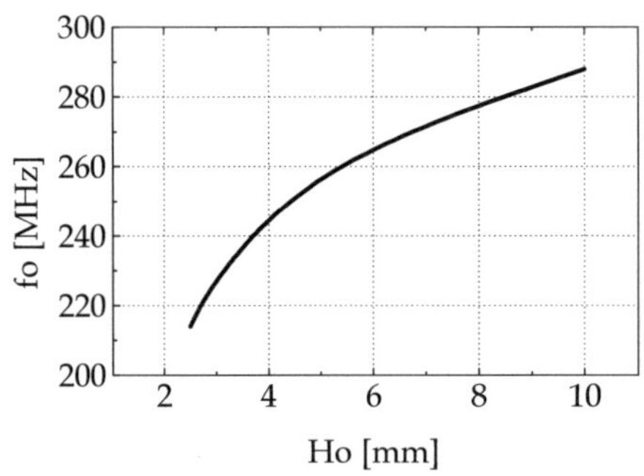

Figure 18. Resonance frequency

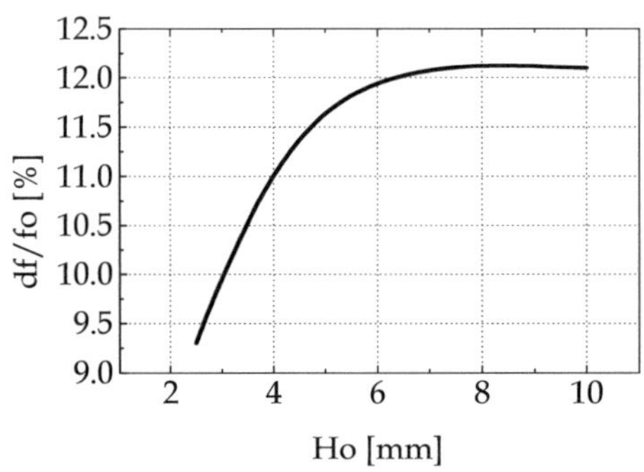

Figure 19. Percentage bandwidth

In case of change of H_0 from 10 mm to 2.5 mm, G decreases from 7 dB to 5 dB, F/B decreases from 20 dB to 14 dB.

3.2. Flat and convex dipole and Yagi arrays

One of the main questions of the numerical analysis of antenna arrays and antennas as a part of a group in the near-field region is the question of interaction of antennas. The coupling effect of antennas, located in a near-field region, results in changes of all the characteristics of the antennas. Further, the differences in interaction between emitters in plane and convex arrays have been studied by the example of comparison of linear and arc arrays. The interaction of two Yagi-Uda antennas has also been studied, depending on a distance between them and their cross orientation. It is important for the organisation of communication nodes.

The received regularities are illustrated by the example of a Yagi-Uda antenna with the number of directors N=1. The antenna is tuned so that the input resistance is equal to 50 Ohm at a medium frequency of 300 MHz.

Fig. 20 shows directional patterns of the antenna located at the centre of a fragment of a plane array with the number of emitters N_x on the X axis, and N_y on the Y axis. The distances between the emitters on the X, Y axes are equal to 0,55 λ. It ensures the absence of diffraction maximums in the directional pattern at the phase scanning in a sector of $\pm 40°$. All the emitters of the fragment, except for the central one, are loaded with matched loads. The numerical simulation shows that, with the increase of the number of the emitters in the fragment, the shape of the directional pattern in some angular sector tends to become right-angled. The degree of interaction of two emitters between themselves can be evaluated by the isolation ratio $S12 = (I_1 / I_2)^2$, where I_1 is the amplitude of an input current of an emitter in the radiation mode, I_2 is the amplitude of an input current of a passive emitter loaded with a matched load. Fig. 22 shows the dependence $S12$ on $R' = R / \lambda$, where R is the distance between emitters. The calculations have been made for a Yagi-Uda antenna at the number of directors N=1 and N=5 with the location of antennas in the E-plane and the H-plane. It follows from the simulation results that $S12$ depends little on the number of directors. If the antennas are located in the H-plane, the interaction is stronger. If the distance is $R > \lambda$, the interaction of the antennas is negligible. It means that it is sufficient to take into consideration the interaction of a Yagi-Uda antenna as a part of a plane array only with an environment of two rings.

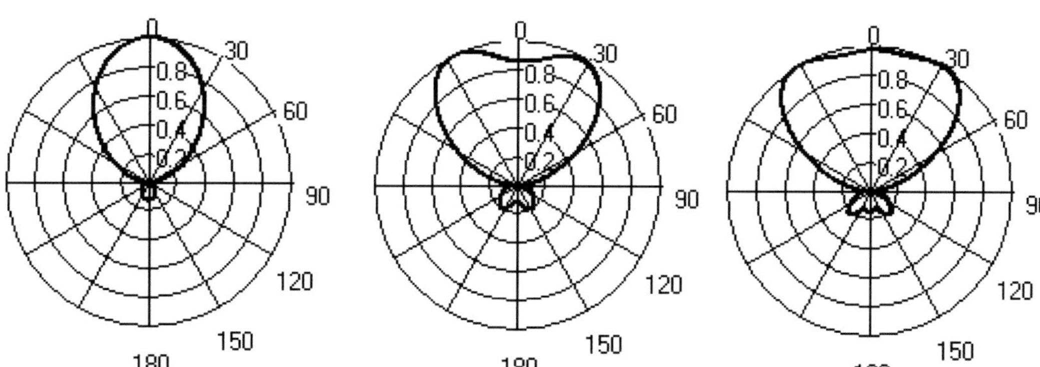

(a) $N_x = N_y = 1$ (b) N_x=3, N_y=1 (c) N_x=5, N_y=1

Figure 20. Radiation pattern in E-plane

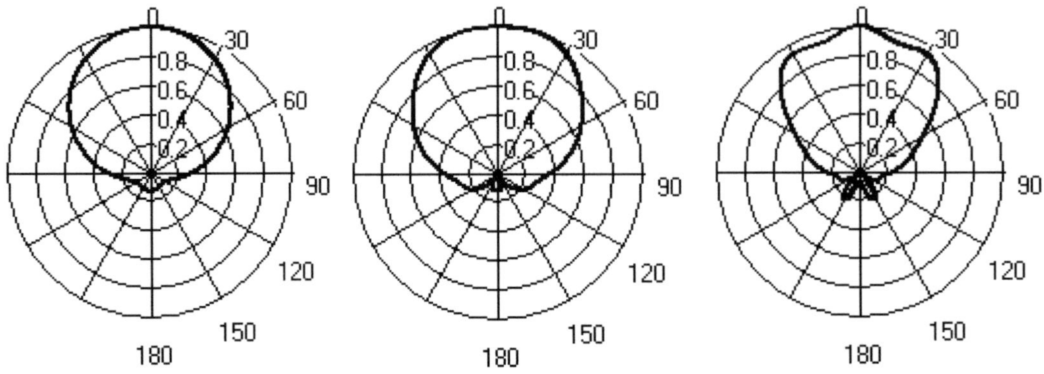

(a) N_x=N_y=1 (b) N_x=1, N_y=3 (c) N_x=1, N_y=5

Figure 21. Radiation pattern in H-plane

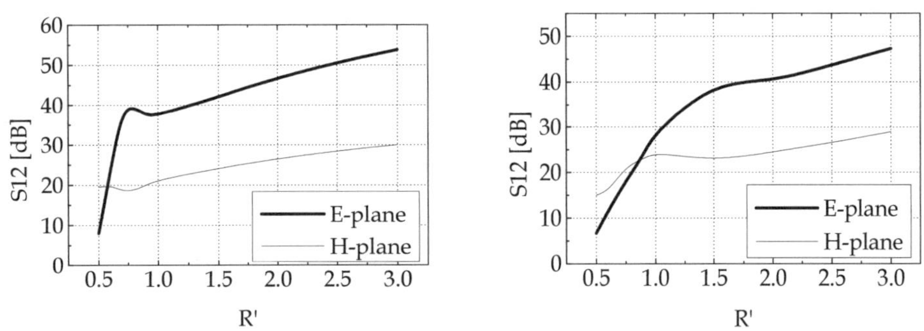

(a) N=1 (b) N=5

Figure 22. Isolation ratio between two antennas

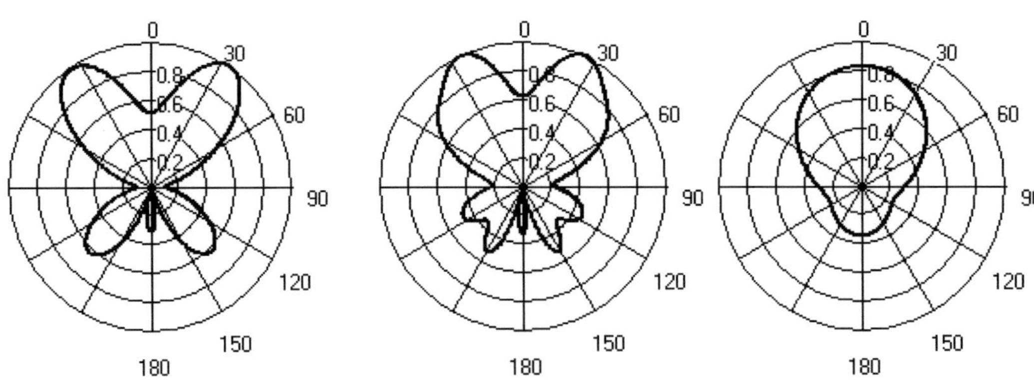

E-plane H-plane

(a) N=3 (b) N=5

Figure 23. Directional pattern of director antenna as part of arc array

The influence of interaction on the directional pattern of a Yagi-Uda antenna is different in plane and convex arrays. Fig. 23 shows the directional patterns in the E-plane of a director antenna with N=1 in the arc array for the number of emitters M=3 and M=5 at a distance between emitters D=0,55 λ. The angle between the axes of the neighboring antennas is equal to β =22°. In both cases, the middle antenna is excited, the remaining ones are loaded with matched loads.

It follows from the comparison of fig. 20b, c and fig. 23b, c that, at the same linear distance between the neighboring emitters (D), the interaction between director antennas as a part of an arc array results in more considerable changes, than if they are a part of a linear array. The dependence of an isolation ratio between two director antennas on an angle between their axes of antennas (β) is shown in fig. 24 for two distances between the antennas entries D' =D/ λ = 0,5 and D' =D/ λ = 0,7 and two values of the number of directors N=1 and N=5.

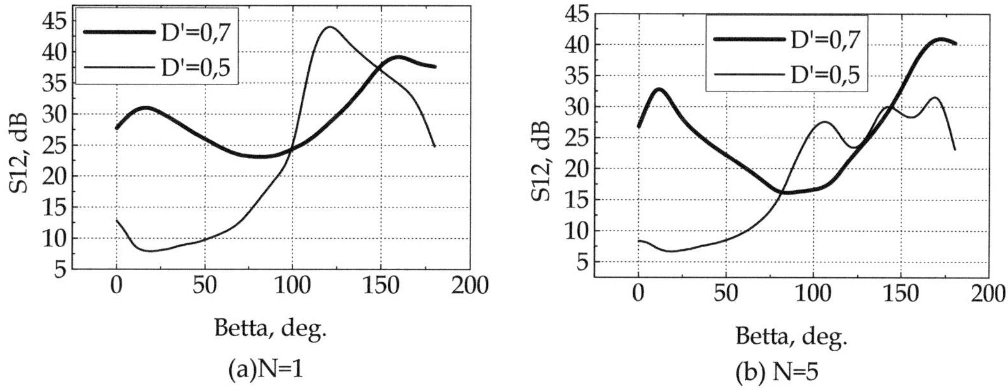

Figure 24. Dependence of isolation ratio on angle between axes of antennas

It follows from the results of numerical simulation that

1. If $D < (0{,}5 - 0{,}6)\lambda$, when an angle β increases, the isolation ratio decreases at first, then it increases and reaches a maximum at β =110°-120°.
2. If $D > (0{,}65 - 0{,}7)\lambda$, when an angle β increases, the isolation ratio increases at first, then it decreases and reaches a minimum at $\beta \approx 90°$.

3.3. Linear Antenna Array with Series Excitation

The dipole arrays of half-wave dipoles with series excitation are decribed briefly in the book [Rothammels, 1995] with the reference to the works [Brown, Liwis and Epstein, 1937; Bruckmann, 1938). Such antennas are gone by the name of Franklin antennas (Franckin C.S. – British patent № 242342, 1924). Versions of such antennas are shown in fig. 25. The drawing symbols are the following: A is half-wave dipoles: B is closed quarter-wave stubs; C is double-wire line exciting line; D is stub bonding; L is dipole length; H is stub length; d is stub width; P is point of observation in space; P_1 is projection of point P on XY plane; R, θ, ϕ are the spherical coordinates of point P.

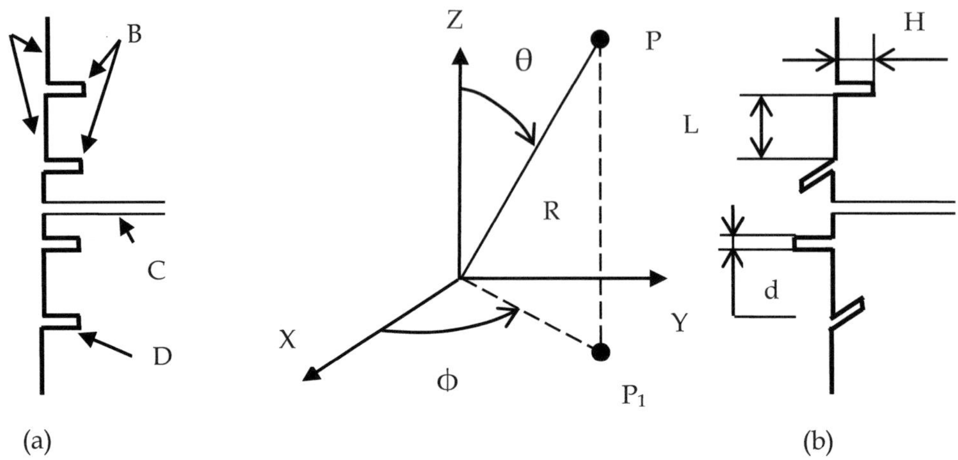

Figure 25. Fig. 25. Franklin antennas

The polarization of an antenna radiation field is linear: the E-plane is the plane ϕ=const, the H-plane is the plane XY. In the H-plane, the directional pattern is quasi-isotropic.

Antenna characteristics depend on geometrical sizes of L, H, d, the number of dipoles in the antenna, an angle between the neighbouring stubs, frequency f. In the literature, these regularities are not studied, and they are the subject of the numerical simulation in the present chapter. Besides, in the chapter, we study the modifications of a Franklin antenna that are more wideband as for the matching criterion and have a sector-shaped directional pattern in the E-plane.

The version shown in fig. 25a at a resonance frequency, which corresponds to the equality to zero of a reactive part of an input resistance (X=0), has a high active input resistance (R). For illustration, in fig. 26, the dependences R(f) X(f) are shown for an antenna with geometrical sizes: L=0,5 λ_0 ; H=0,25 λ_0 ; d=0,1 λ_0 , where λ_0 is the medium wavelength of the given bandwidth. The calculations have been made for λ_0 =300 mm (medium frequency f_0 =1000 MHz) and two cases with the number of dipoles N=3 and N=5. It is evident that at N=3, there is a frequency, at which X=0. At N$\geq$5, there is no such a frequency (X <0). It complicates the antenna matching with a transmission line.

The more convenient version for matching is the one, in which the exciting voltage is introduced into a bonding rupture. Such a version is shown conditionally in fig. 27. The place of the antenna excitation is marked by a big point. The dependences R(f) and X(f) are shown in fig. 28 a. In such an antenna, the choice of values L, H, d can be X=0, and R=50 Ohm or 75 Ohm. The graphs of fig. 28 correspond to the antenna tuning to a frequency of 1000 MHz in order to obtain R=50 Ohm, X=0 (L=142 mm; H=71,5 mm; d=8 mm). The symbols of R and X are the same as in fig. 26.

The numerical simulation shows that with increase of the number of dipoles in the antenna (N), the antenna band properties worsen. The VSWR minimum does not match to the most acceptable directional pattern in the E-plane. Fig. 29 shows the directional patterns at three frequencies of the band, in which VSWR<2. The frequency values, gain (G), R, X, VSWR are also given. The graphs of directional patterns in the H-plane give the values of nonuniformity of the directional pattern (Nu). The nonuniformity Nu decreases, if to direct the neighbouring stubs in the contrary directions (fig. 25b).

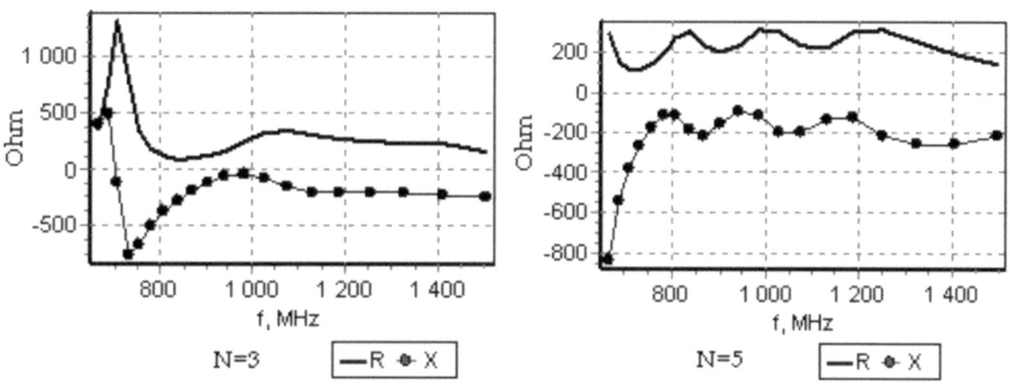

Figure 26. Dependences of input resistance on frequency

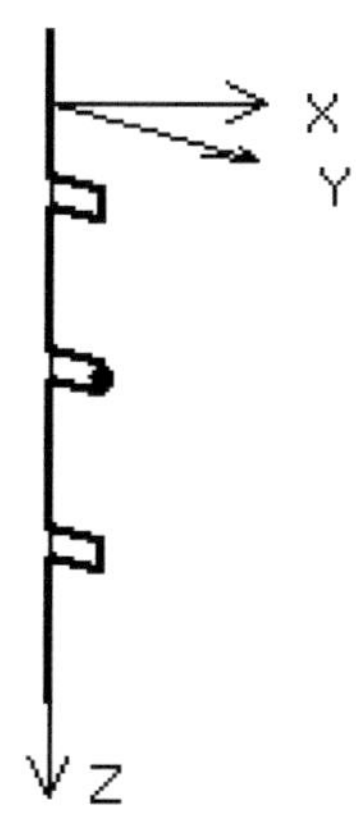

Figure 27. Antenna

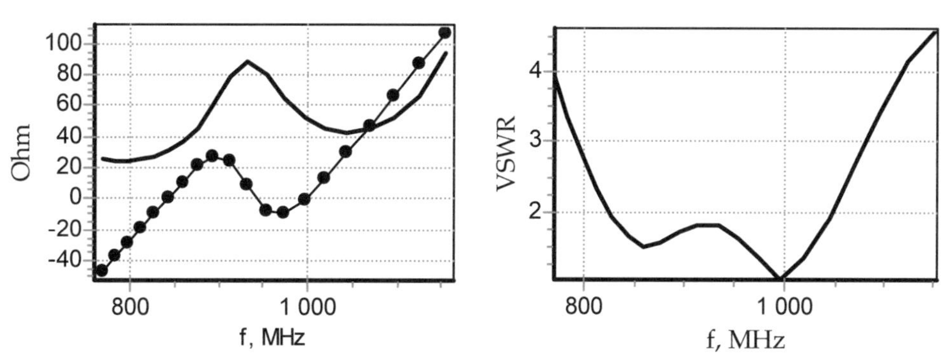

Figure 28. Input resistance and VSWR in bandwidth

Antenna characteristics depend on a number of an excited stub. In fig. 27, the central stub is excited. If to displace an excitation point from the central stub, the maximum of a directional pattern in the E-plane declines from a normal to the Z axis. Fig. 29 illustrates these properties by the example of the antenna with N=6. When the frequency increases, the angle of deflection of the maximum of a directional pattern decreases. Fig. 30 shows the DP of the antenna with N=13 within a bandwidth, in which VSWR<2. The lower stub is excited, as in fig. 29. The band of matching frequencies depends little on the number of dipoles in the antenna, if the extreme stub is excited. For illustration, fig. 31 shows the dependence of VSVR(f) at different values of the number of dipoles.

When the number of dipoles increases, the misphasing between the stub that is excited and the extreme stubs increases. Therefore, when the number of dipoles increases, the antenna gain at first increases promptly, then slowly. The dependence of gain (G) on the number of dipoles is shown in fig. 32. At N=1, the antenna represents a half-wave dipole that has G=2 dB. The lower stub is excited in the antenna. It follows from fig. 32 that there is no sense to make the number of dipoles N> 5.

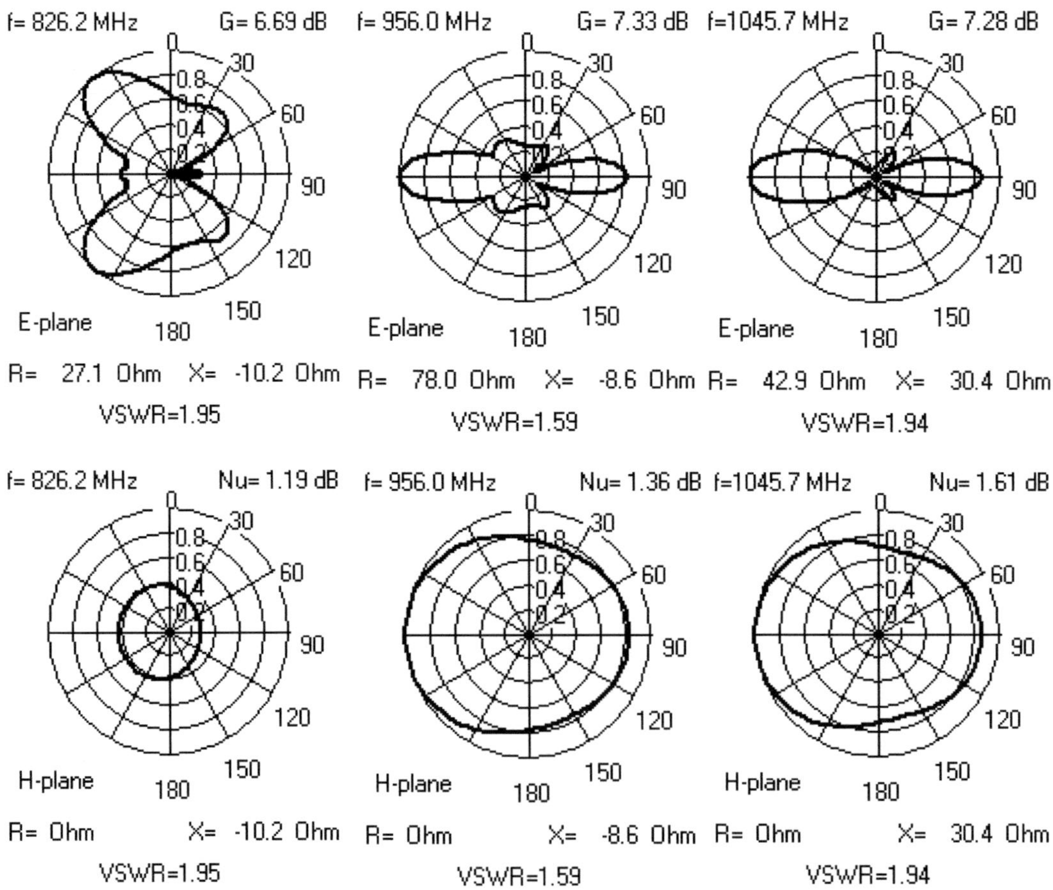

Figure 29. Directional patterns in E and H-planes

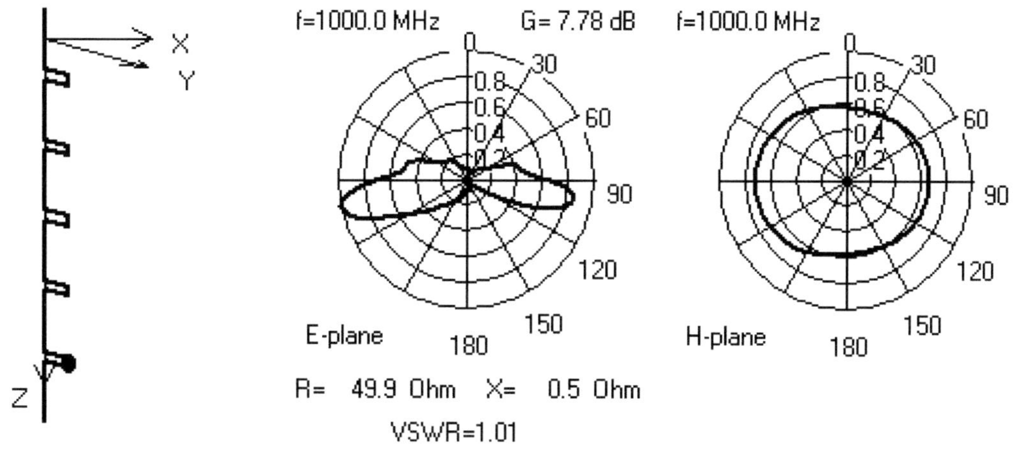

Figure 30. Nonsymmetric excitation of antenna

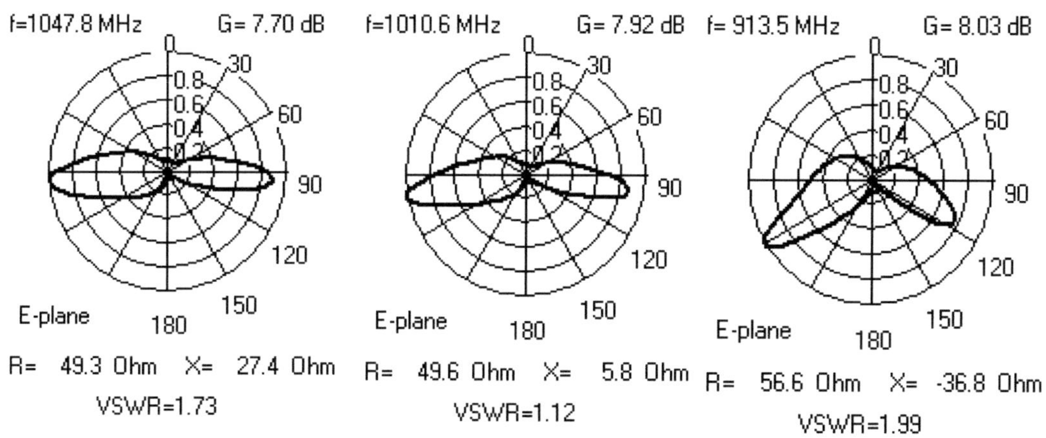

Figure 31. Directional patterns within bandwidth: N=13, the lower stub is excited.

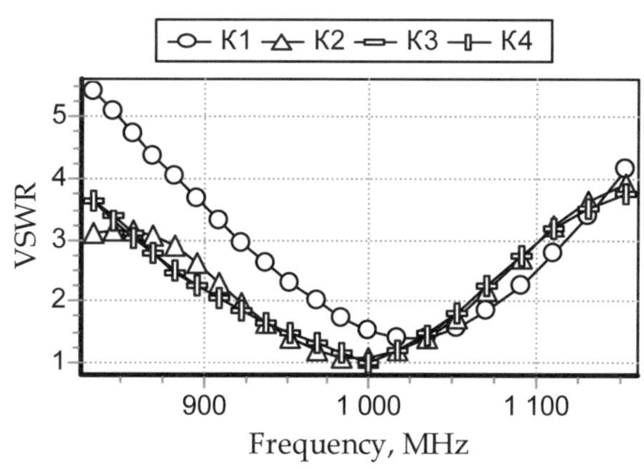

Figure 32. Dependence of VSWR on frequency
K1 – N=2; K2 – N=4; K3 – N=7; K4 – N=13

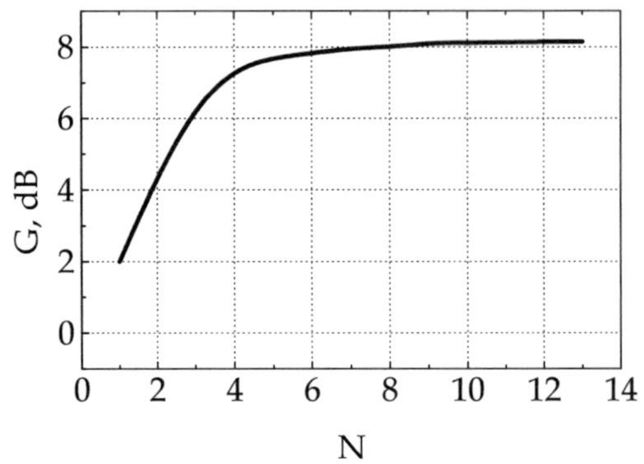

Figure 33. Dependence of Gain on number of dipoles

K1 - N=2; K2 - N=4; K3 - N=7; K4 - N=13

If to apply a system of reflectors or (and) directors to an antenna, it is possible to make a directional pattern sector-shaped in the H-plane. Fig. 33 shows such an antenna and its directional pattern.

A Franklin antenna and its modifications can be used as transmitting antennas in radio links.

4. Modelling of radiation and scattering characteristics of frame antennas

4.1. Loop antenna of closed and open arrays

Various types of loop antennas are used in radio communication, radiolocation, TV. Further in this chapter, two types of loop antennas are studied: on the basis of closed arrays with a lateral length $L \approx 0{,}25\lambda$ (fig.34a) and on the basis of open arrays with a lateral length $L \approx 0{,}5\lambda$ (fig.34b). Double loop antennas and arrays of such antennas are studied. The double loop antennas are used with a reflector (fig.34c) and without a reflector. The distance between the plane of the array and the reflector is H.

The polarization of the antenna is linear. The E-plane is the XY plane, the H-plane is the plane ϕ=const. The antenna characteristics depend on geometrical sizes of L, β, d, Le, Lh, Dh, H. The antenna is excited by voltage between points 1 and 2. In version (a), the resistance between points (input resistance of the antenna) can be made equal to 50 Ohm, in version (b) – an active part of the input resistance – 200-300 Ohm. Gain in the version (b) of the antenna is 3 dB bigger, than in the version (a) of the antenna. In versions (a) and (b), directors can be used to increase the gain, fig. 35.

In the literature, the methods of antenna excitation were studied, their key properties were studied briefly [Rothammels K, 1995], but there is no information about the main regularities. Further, these regularities are examined for version 34a only, because this version is generally used.

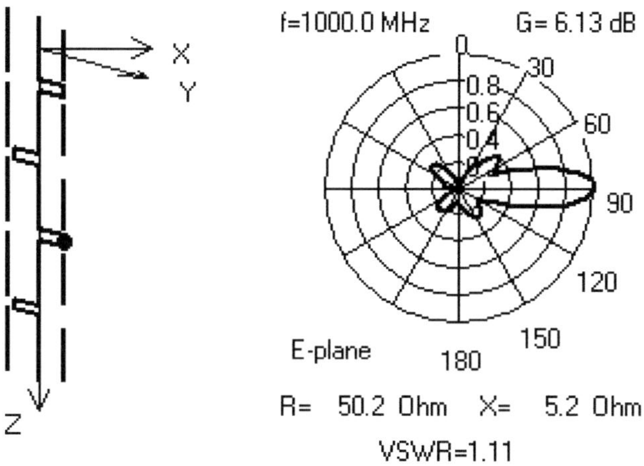

Figure 34. Franklin antenna with linear reflectors and directors

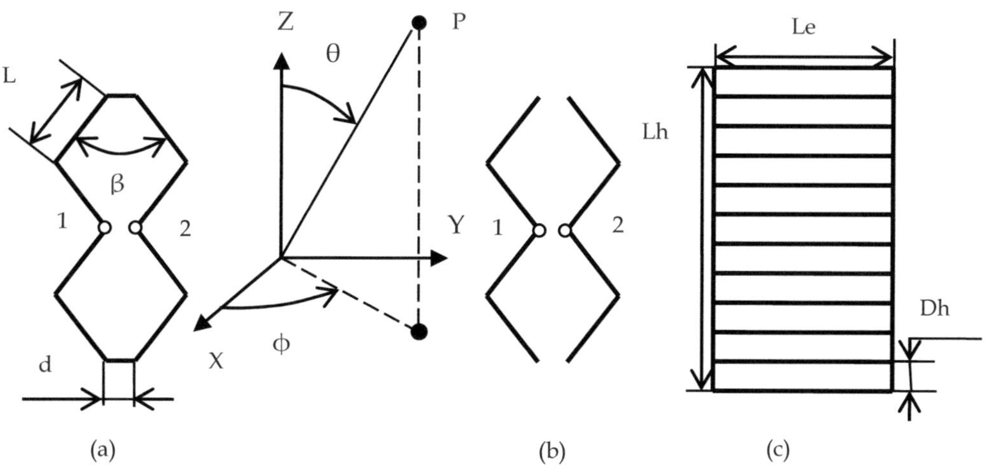

Figure 35. Loop antennas

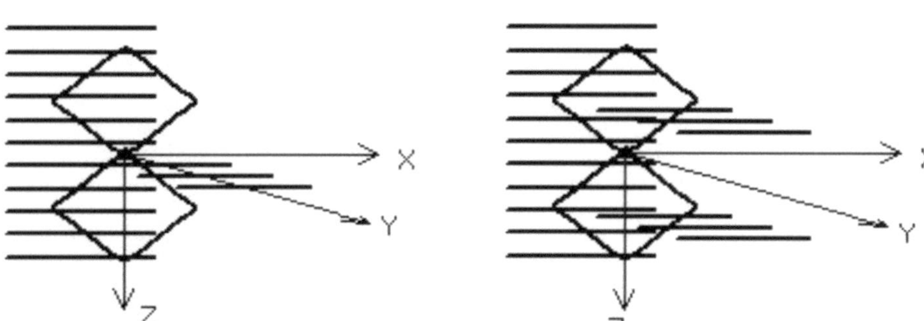

Figure 36. Loop antennas with directors

Fig. 36a shows the dependence of an active part of an input resistance (R) on an angle β, if a reactive part of the input resistance is equal to zero ($X \approx 0$). The condition $X \approx 0$ is met by changing a lateral length of an array (L) for each preset value of $H' = H / \lambda$. Fig. 36b shows the dependence of $L' = L / \lambda$ on an angle β (values of L' meet the condition $X \approx 0$). The calculations have been made for the antenna with a wire diameter of Do=0,006 λ, d=0,006 λ.

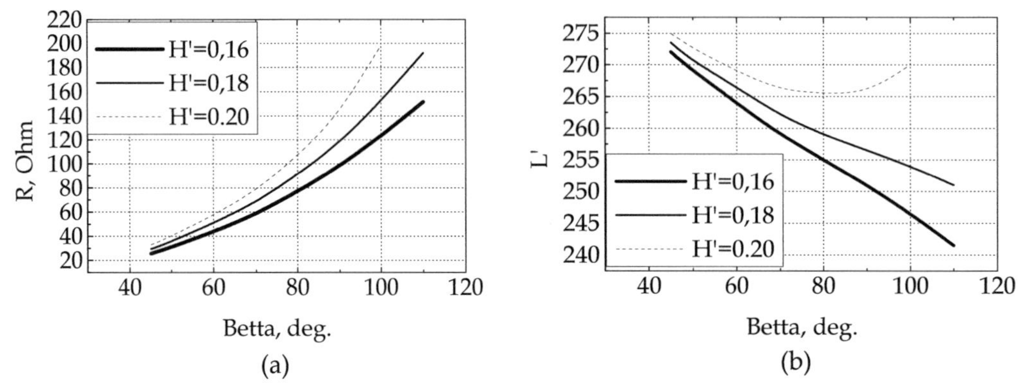

Figure 37. Dependence of input resistance (a) and array lateral length (b) on angle β

It follows from fig. 36a that, by selecting the values of L and β at preset H, it is possible to make input resistance R preset and to meet the condition $X \approx 0$.

The antenna band properties are illustrated by fig. 37, 38. The calculation has been made for the antennas calculated so that at a frequency of 300 MHz the input resistance was equal to $R \approx 50$ Ohm, $X \approx 0$, see fig. 37a, and $R \approx 75$ Ohm, $X \approx 0$, see fig. 37b. Fig. 38a shows the dependence of VSWR on frequency. For antenna 1 with the input resistance of 50 Ohm at a frequency of MHz, VSWR has been calculated in a line with the characteristic resistance of 50 Ohm (graph 1), for antenna 2 with the input resistance of 75 Ohm, VSWR has been calculated in a line with the characteristic resistance of 75 Ohm (graph 2). It is evident that the antenna with a higher input resistance is matched to a bigger bandwidth. Fig. 38b shows the dependences of gain and F/B parametre for the second antenna.

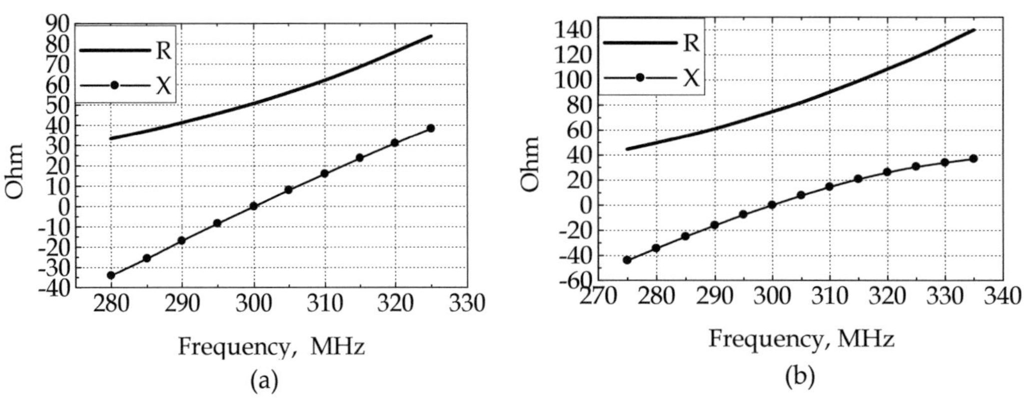

Figure 38. Dependence of input resistance on frequency

It follows from the results of the numerical simulation, that at a level of VSWR<2, the percentage bandwidth is $\delta f = (f_{max} - f_{min}) / f_o \cdot 100 \approx$ (10-20)%. The values of Gain and F/B in the said bandwidth vary little. The matched bandwidth increases, if R increases at a medium frequency. To widen the matched bandwidth, additional elements are used in the loop antenna.

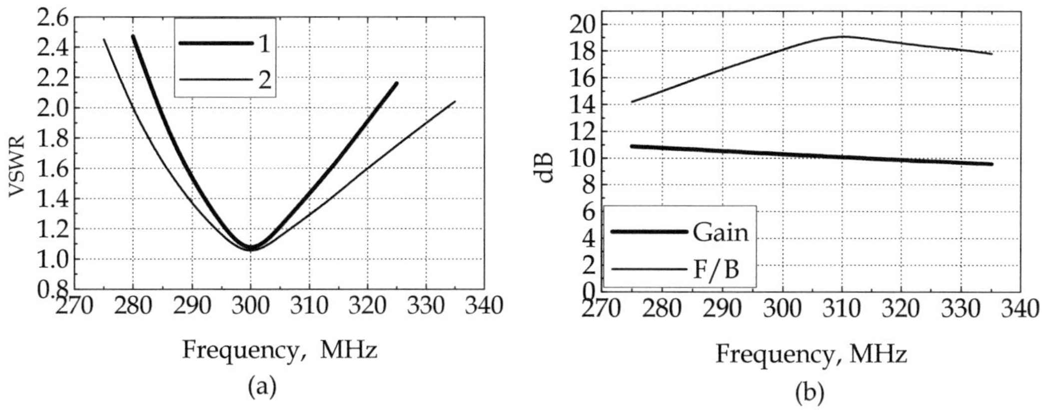

Figure 39. Dependence of VSWR, Gain and F/B parametre on frequency

4.2. Interaction of loop antennas as part of antenna array

Interaction of loop of antennas as a part of an array results in changing of their characteristics. It shall be taken into consideration, when designing antenna arrays. Fig. 39 shows directional patterns in the E and H-planes of a loop antenna with an input resistance of 50 Ohm: isolated one (a); when taking into account its interaction with two neighbouring emitters – one on the left and one on the right (b); and taking into account its interaction with four neighbouring emitters – two on the left and two on the right. The values of input resistance, gain and parametre F/B are also shown in the figures. The calculations have been made for a linear array, in which emitters are located in the E-plane, at a frequency of 300 MHz (as an example). The distance between the neighbouring emitters is equal to 0,65λ. It follows from the results of simulation that the interaction influences an input resistance and F/B parametre insignificantly. The directional pattern and gain influence the interaction greatly, but differences in influence of various number of interacting loop antennas are insignificant (fig.39b and 39c). It means that when simulating multiple-unit arrays of loop antennas, it is possible to take into consideration interaction of each emitter only with its nearest emitters, and further to use the theorem of multiplication of directional patterns.

Fig. 40 illustrates difference in influence of interaction in a linear array and in an annular array. The figure shows directional patterns of a loop antenna with the same geometrical sizes without taking interaction into consideration (a), when taking interaction into consideration with two neighbouring emitters (b), and with four neighbouring emitters (c). The linear distance between the neighbouring emitters is equal to 0.65λ, the angle between axes of antennas is equal to 12°.

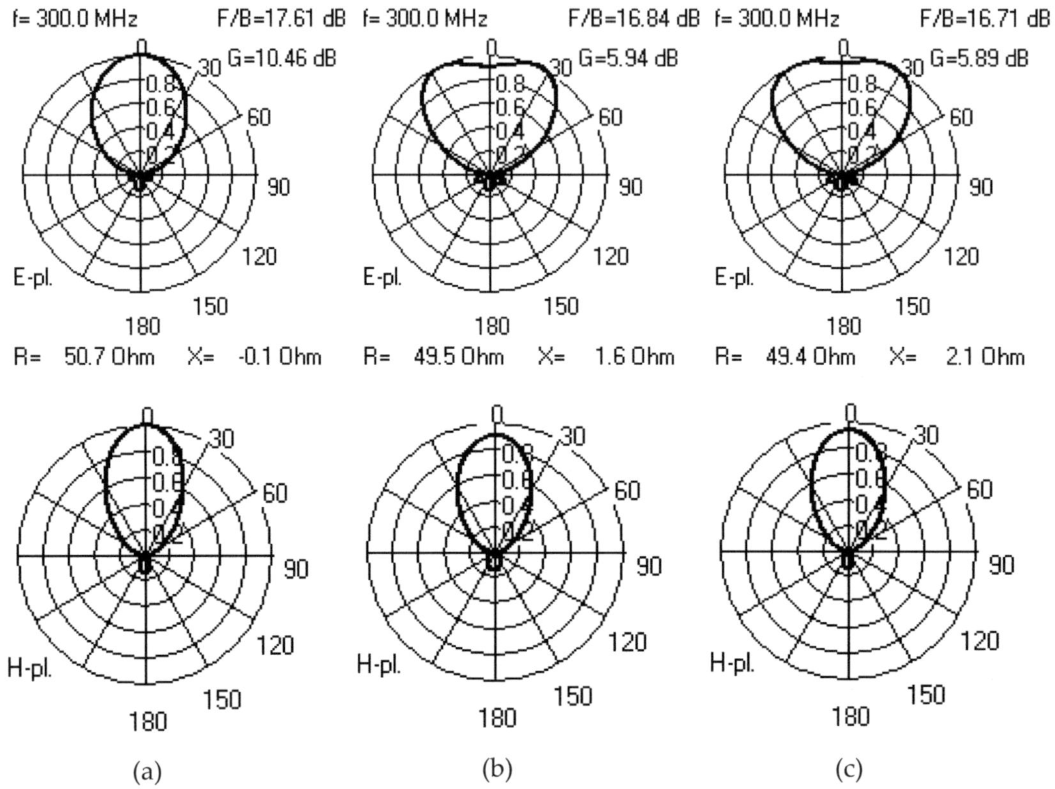

Figure 40. Loop antenna directional patterns (a) and when taking into consideration its interactions as a part of a linear array (b), (c).

It follows from the comparison of fig. 39 and fig. 40 that interaction between loop antennas in an annular array is less than interaction in a linear array.

4.3. Linear antenna arrays with coherent excitation

To increase gain, it is possible to use linear arrays of loop antennas with series excitation. Fig. 41 shows the schema of connections of arrays among themselves at a lateral length of the array $L \approx 0{,}25\lambda$ (a) and at a lateral length of the array $L \approx 0{,}5\lambda$ (b) by the example of the antennas with Mp=4. The gain increases, if the number of the arrays increases due to narrowing of the main lobe in the H-plane. Fig. 42 shows the dependence of the gain on the number of Mp arrays at $L \approx 0,25\lambda$. Fig. 42b illustrates the dependence of the input resistance on the number of arrays. The sizes of elements of the arrays are chosen so that the input resistance was equal to 50 Ohm at Mp=2.

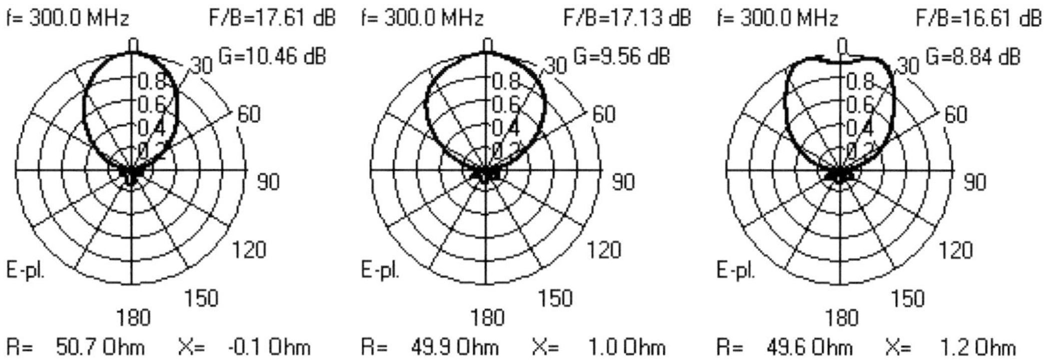

(a) (b) (c)

Figure 41. Directional patterns of a loop antenna, when taking into consideration its interaction as a part of an annular array

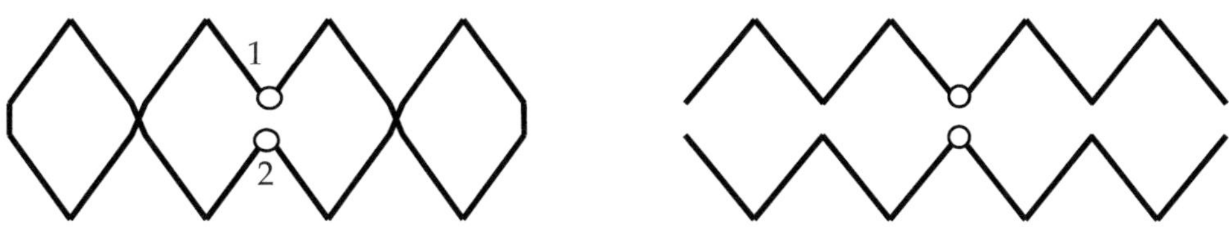

(a) (b)

Figure 42. Connecting pattern of arrays in linear array

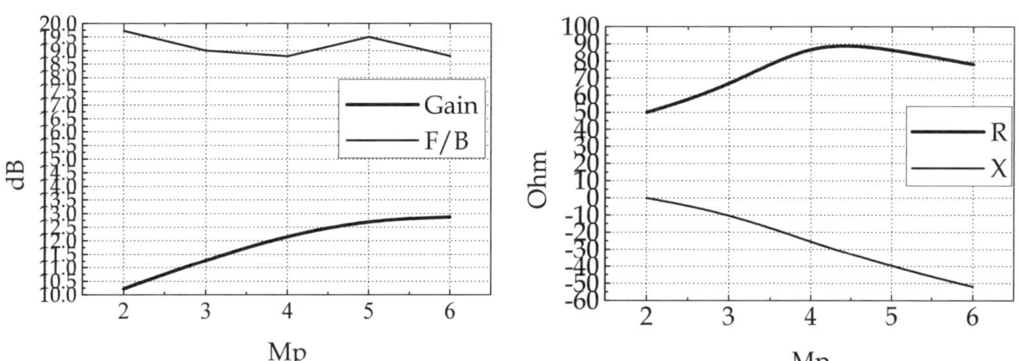

Figure 43. Dependence of parametres of a loop antenna on the number of arrays at $L \approx 0,25\lambda$

It follows from the results of simulation that it is not reasonable to make Mp>4 in the antenna. For each M value, it is necessary to optimise the sizes of elements of arrays in order to obtain the preset input resistance.

In a linear array consisting of arrays with a lateral length $L \approx 0,5\lambda$, the gain is 3 dB more approximately.

Fig. 43a shows the version of a linear array with a quasi-isotropic directional pattern in the E-plane. Such a pattern can be obtained, if to bend all the arrays along the Z axis at an angle α =35-40°. It is possible to ensure the preset input resistance by choosing the sizes of elements. Fig. 43b,c shows the directional patterns and the values of the parameters of G (Gain), NR (nonuniformity of a directional pattern in the E-plane), R, X, values of VSWR in a line with a wave resistance of 50 Ohm.

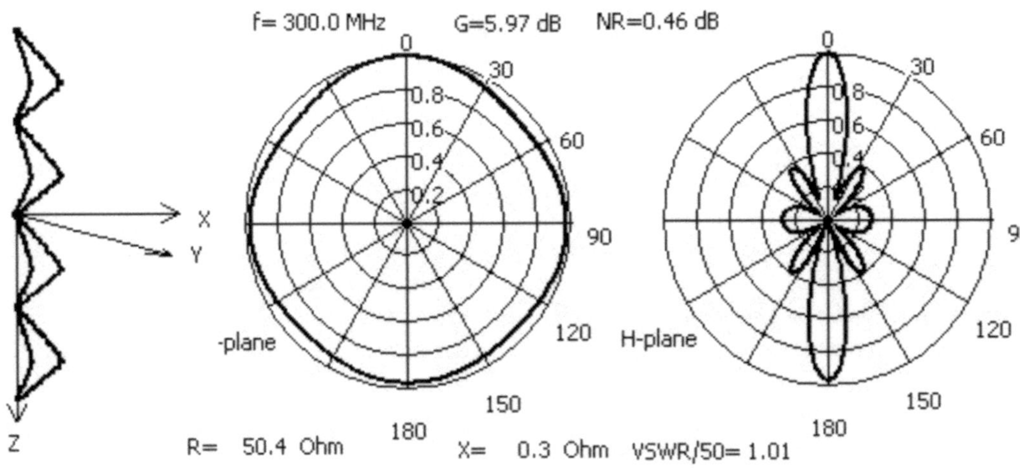

(a) (b) (c)

Figure 44. Loop antenna with quasi-isotropic directional pattern in E-plane

5. Conclusion

The simulation results, given in this chapter, complete the information about dipole and loop antennas that is available in the literature, and can be used to choice a type of an antenna according to specified requirements and after estimating its main characteristics. Numerical simulation of an antenna can be done with the use of the formulas given in the description of a mathematical model. When using a program developed on the basis of these formulas, it is necessary to carry out research into the convergence of the results of calculation. The most sensitive parametre of the antenna in relation to the number of segments of division of conductors (M) is the input resistance. When using impulse functions as the basis and weight ones, it is possible to be oriented towards the following recommendations: the ratio of a segment length to a conductor diameter $\Delta L / 2Ao \approx 0{,}8\text{-}1{,}2$; the number of segments at a wavelength: 80-200.

In some cases, the results given in the graphs can be used directly with the use of electrodynamic scaling.

We express aur gratitude to D.Moskalev and V.Kizimenko for the useful discussion of the results described in this chapter.

Author details

Oleg A. Yurtsev and Grigory V. Ptashinsky
Belarusian State University of Informatics and Radioelectronics, Belarus

6. References

Antenna Theory. (1997). Analysis and design. Second Edition Balanis, C.A. John Wiley&Sons. Inc.

Aisenberg, G.Z, Jampolsky, V.G. and Terjoshin, O.N. (1977). *Antennas UHF.* M.Svjaz. Russia.

Brown, G.H., Epstein, J and Liwis, R.F. (1937). Groud System as a Factor in Antenna Efficiency.//Proc. IRE, June 1937, pp.753-787.

Bruckmann, H. (1938).*Uber die Theorie der Erdvarluste von Antennen*.//TFT 27, H.2 pp.29-38.

Crispin, J.W., Maffett A.L.(1965). *Radar Cross-Section Estimation for Complex Shapes*.//Proceeding of the IEEE. –Vol. 53. – № 8. – 1965. pp.1115-1125.

Computer Techniques for Electromagnetics. Edition by Mittra, R. (1973). Pergamon Press. New York.

Drabkin, A.L. and Zuzenko, V.L. (1961). *Antenna-feeder devices*. M. Sovetskoe radio. Russia.

Franckin, C.S. (1924). British patent № 242342.

Fletcher, C.A.J. (1984). *Computational Galerkin method*. Springer-Verlag, New York.

Fradin, A.Z. (1977). *Antenna-feeder devices*. M.Sviaz. Russia.

Harrington, R.F. (1968). *Field Computating by Moment Methods.* Macmillan, New York.

Markov, G.T. (1960). *Antennas.* M.-L. Gosenergoizdat. Russia.

Radar Handbook.(1970). M.I.Skolnik. EDITOR - IN - Chief. Mc Graw-Hill Company, 1970.

Rothammels, K. (1995). *Antennenbuch.* Franckh-Kosmos. Verlags-GmbH&Co., Stuttgart.

Sazonov, D.M and Shkolnikov, A.M. (1974).*The scattering of electromagnetic waves by a loaded antenna array*//Radiotechnology and Electronics. –1974. – № 4. pp.689-686.

Stratton, J.A. (1941). *Electromagnetic Theory*. McGraw-Hill.

Volakis, J.L. (2007). *Antenna Engineering Handbook*. Mc Graw-Hiil Companies.

Kazarin, A.N. , Runov, A.V. and Yurtsev, O.A. (1974). *Helix Antennas*. M. Sovetskoe radio. Russia.

Chapter 9

Synthesis of Antenna Systems According to the Desired Amplitude Radiation Characteristics

Mykhaylo Andriychuk

Additional information is available at the end of the chapter

http://dx.doi.org/10.5772/46164

1. Introduction

The problems of antenna synthesis, which use the amplitude RP as input information, are often used in the process of antenna design for many practical applications [4, 16, 27, 31]. In spite of the fact that the respective mathematical problems are ill-posed [32] and they have the branching solutions [29], the antenna synthesis according to the desired amplitude characteristics is very useful and perspective.

As a rule, the branching of solutions depends on the properties of prescribed amplitude RP, geometrical and physical parameters of the considered antenna. The methods of nonlinear functional analysis [23] allowing to localize the branching solutions are applied for investigation of solutions and determination of their number and qualitative characteristics. Such approach too much simplifies determination of the optimal solutions by the numerical methods. The iterative processes for the numerical solving of the corresponding non-linear equations were elaborated in [3, 8, 11].

The Chapter is organized as follows.

In Section 2 we derive the main formulas for RP of antennas and introduce the objective functionals for the synthesis problem. Also in Section 2 we consider the variational statement of problems and derive the fundamental nonlinear equations of the synthesis.

Section 3 contains the application of the proposed approach to several types of antennas. Depending on the restrictions which are imposed on the sought distribution of current or field in the antenna elements and type of antenna, the problems of amplitude-phase, amplitude, and phase synthesis are considered for the specific antennas. The methods of successive approximations are applied for solving the derived non-linear integral equations; the convergence of the elaborated methods is discussed. The direct optimization of the proposed functionals by the gradient methods is performed and successfully applied to solving the amplitude and phase synthesis problems.

In Section 4 conclusions are formulated.

2. The theoretical background of the synthesis problems

In this Section, we present the necessary information about the properties of the electromagnetic (EM) field in far zone, introduce the variational approach to the antenna synthesis problems, as well as discuss the arising nonlinear integral and matrix equations.

2.1. RP of electromagnetic field

The EM field in the non-limited homogeneous medium satisfies the Maxwell equations [25]

$$\text{rot}H = ik\varepsilon E + \frac{4\pi}{c}I, \tag{1}$$

$$\text{rot}E = -ik\mu H, \tag{2}$$

$$\text{div}E = \rho/\varepsilon, \tag{3}$$

$$\text{div}H = 0, \tag{4}$$

where E is a component of electric field, H is a component of magnetic field, I is the extrinsic current density, ρ is the volume density of electric charge.

The scalar and vector potentials are used for solving the equations (1)-(4). Introducing the vector potential A^e as [34]

$$H = \text{rot}A^e, \tag{5}$$

we satisfy the equation (4). Substituting (5) into (2), we receive the equation

$$\text{rot}(E + i\omega\mu A^e) = 0, \tag{6}$$

which testifies that the vector field in the parenthesis of (6) is potential. This yields the equation

$$E = -i\omega\mu A^e - grad\varphi^e, \tag{7}$$

where φ^e is the scalar potential. Substituting (5) and (7) into (1), we receive the following equation for I:

$$\nabla^2 A^e + \omega^2\varepsilon\mu A^e - \text{grad}(\text{div}A^e + i\omega\varphi^e) = -I. \tag{8}$$

Using Lorentz lemma [15]

$$\text{div}A^e + i\omega\varepsilon\varphi^e = 0, \tag{9}$$

we receive the inhomogeneous Helmholtz equation for the vector potential

$$\nabla^2 A^e + k^2 A^e = -I, \tag{10}$$

where $k = \omega\sqrt{\varepsilon\mu}$ is a propagation coefficient. For a free space, the values ε and μ are real and related with the light velocity as $c = 1/\sqrt{\varepsilon\mu}$, and coefficient $k = \omega/c = 2\pi/\lambda$ is the wavenumber, λ is the length of wave.

The vector potential A^e in the arbitrary observation point $Q(x,y,z)$ is determined by formula [26]

$$A^e(x,y,z) = \frac{1}{4\pi}\int\limits_V I(x',y',z')\frac{-e^{ikR_{PQ}}}{R_{PQ}}dV, \tag{11}$$

where $R_{PQ} = \sqrt{(x-x')^2 + (y-y')^2 + (z-z')^2}$ is the distance between the observation point $Q(x,y,z)$ and integration point $P(x',y',z')$, $I(x',y'z')$ is the density of current in the domain V.

Using formulas (5), (7), and (11), we receive the solution to system (1)-(4) in the term of electric vector potential

$$E = -i\omega\mu A^e - \frac{1}{\omega\varepsilon}\text{graddiv}A^e, \tag{12}$$

$$H = \text{rot}A^e. \tag{13}$$

In the process of solving the synthesis problem, the representation of field in far zone is of interest. Using the approximate representation of distance R_{PQ} in far zone, we receive the formula for vector potential in this region

$$A^e_\infty(Q) = \frac{-e^{ikr}}{4\pi r}\int_V I(x',y',z')e^{ikr'\cos\alpha}dV + O(\frac{1}{r^2}), \tag{14}$$

where α is the angle between the vectors, directed into observation and integration point, r' and r are the radius-vector of the points P and Q, respectively.

Substituting (14) into (13) and neglecting by terms of $O(\frac{1}{r^2})$ order, we receive the formulas for components of magnetic field H in term of vector potential A^e_∞. These formulas in the spherical coordinates have form

$$H_r = 0, \quad H_\theta = ikA^e_{\infty\varphi}, \quad H_\varphi = -ikA^e_{\infty\theta}. \tag{15}$$

Consequently, the formulas for E are the following

$$E_r = 0, \quad E_\theta = -i\omega\mu A^e_{\infty\theta}, \quad E_\varphi = -i\omega\mu A^e_{\infty\varphi}. \tag{16}$$

Using formulas (15), (16) and relation

$$E = -\frac{1}{\omega\varepsilon}\text{rot}H, \tag{17}$$

we receive the formulas for non-zero E components of EM field

$$E_\theta(r,\theta,\varphi) = -i\omega\mu\frac{e^{-ikr}}{4\pi r}f_\theta(\theta,\varphi), \tag{18}$$

$$E_\varphi(r,\theta,\varphi) = -i\omega\mu\frac{e^{-ikr}}{4\pi r}f_\varphi(\theta,\varphi). \tag{19}$$

Function $\frac{e^{-ikr}}{4\pi r}$ is a spherical wave and it depends on r only. The second terms in (18) and (19) are the functions of angular coordinates of the observation point and are determined by the current $I(x',y',z')$

$$\begin{gathered} f_\theta(\theta,\varphi) = \int_V [I_x(x',y',z')\cos\theta\cos\varphi + I_y(x',y',z')\cos\theta\sin\varphi - \\ I_z(x',y',z')\sin\theta]e^{ik(x'\sin\theta\cos\varphi + y'\sin\theta\sin\varphi + z'\cos\theta)}dV, \end{gathered} \tag{20}$$

$$\begin{gathered} f_\varphi(\theta,\varphi) = \int_V [I_y(x',y',z')\cos\varphi - I_x(x',y',z')\sin\varphi]\times \\ e^{ik(x'\sin\theta\cos\varphi + y'\sin\theta\sin\varphi + z'\cos\theta)}dV. \end{gathered} \tag{21}$$

The functions (20) and (21) characterize the angular distribution of E components in far zone.

In such a way, the vectors E and H in far zone are expressed by formulas [4]

$$E(r,\theta,\varphi) = -i\omega\mu\frac{e^{-ikr}}{4\pi r}\{0, f_\theta(\theta,\varphi), f_\varphi(\theta,\varphi)\}, \tag{22}$$

$$H(r,\theta,\varphi) = ik\frac{e^{-ikr}}{4\pi r}\{0, f_\varphi(\theta,\varphi), -f_\theta(\theta,\varphi)\}. \tag{23}$$

The functions $f_\theta(\theta,\varphi)$ and $f_\varphi(\theta,\varphi)$ are defined as the RPs. Function

$$N(\theta,\varphi) = |f_\theta(\theta,\varphi)|^2 + |f_\theta(\theta,\varphi)|^2 \tag{24}$$

is the power RP and it characterizes the angular distribution of power intensity radiation. The functions $f_\theta(\theta,\varphi)$, $f_\varphi(\theta,\varphi)$, and $N(\theta,\varphi)$ are used in the process of formulating and solving the synthesis problems for various antennas.

2.2. Variational statement of the synthesis problems

Abstracting of the specific type of antenna, we present the functions f_θ and f_φ in the formulas (22)-(24) by the linear operator $\mathbf{A} = \{A_\theta, A_\varphi\}$:

$$\mathbf{f} = \mathbf{A}I, \quad (f_\nu = A_\nu I, \quad \nu = \theta, \varphi), \tag{25}$$

acting from some complex Hilbertian space H_I, to which the distribution functions of current or field belong, into the complex space $C_f^2 = C[\Omega] \oplus C[\Omega]$ of vector-valued continuous functions on the compact $\bar{\Omega} \in R^2$ (or $\bar{\Omega} \in R^1$) [29]. The form and properties of the operators A_ν depend on a type and geometry of antenna. In many practical applications, one can reduce the synthesis problem to separate consideration of the f_θ and f_φ components. This allows to reduce the synthesis problem to the scalar one. In that way, we will use more simple formula

$$f = AI \tag{26}$$

for operator expression of the RP f.

The specific form of the operator A depends on the antenna type. This operator is integral for the continuous antennas. As an example, for a cylindrical antenna with curvilinear generatrix and with current polarized along the cylinder axis, the RP in the transversal plane has form [21]

$$f = AI := \int_S I(S)e^{ikr(\varphi')\cos(\varphi-\varphi')}dS_{\varphi'}, \tag{27}$$

where $f$and I are nonzero components f_θ and I_z respectively; φ is the angular coordinate of the point in far zone, φ' is the angular coordinate of the point in antenna, $r = r(\varphi')$ describes the generatrix in polar coordinates, $dS_{\varphi'} = \sqrt{r^2 + (dr/d\varphi')^2}$ is an element of arc. In the case of array, the operator A is described by a finite sum.

In the previous subsection, we consider the direct external problem of electrodynamics consisting of determination of the asymptotic (RP) of EM field in far zone. The inverse problem, namely determination of such a current I that create EM field with the desired RP f, is of specific interest in the antenna design. The characteristic parameters of antenna can be fixed or be subject to determination in process of solving this problem. In such interpretation, the inverse problem is defined as the synthesis problem, namely the problem of determination of the current according to the desired RP.

The RPs are due to satisfy a series of requirements for the main lobe and sidelobes. In one case, the RP with narrow main beam is required, another time, this beam should have the specific wide (for example, cosecant) form; the sidelobes be as low as possible.

The angular distribution of the radiation power is characterized by the amplitude of RP, but not the whole RP. Therefore, only amplitude $|f|$ of function f is interesting in the process of statement and solving the synthesis problem. In this case, the freedom of choice of the phase $\arg f$ of function f is used for better approximation to the amplitude RP. In the synthesis theory, function $|f|$ is amplitude RP, and function $\arg f$ is phase RP.

In this way, in the process of synthesis we prescribe not the whole complex function f, but only its amplitude. We denote this function as F, the created (synthesized) by antenna amplitude RP is denoted by $|f|$. The both functions are real and positive. Of course, these functions can not coincide in any real-world situation. This fact yields to use the variational statement of the synthesis problem. In such statement, one requires not the whole coincidence of the functions $|f|$ and F, but the better approximation of function $|f|$ to F in a certain sense only. The mean-square deviation of both RPs is used as the criterion of optimization.

Let us introduce the Hilbertian spaces of radiation patterns H_f and currents H_I. Let $(\cdot,\cdot)_f$ be an inner product in H_f, and norm of f is defined as [4]

$$||f||^2 = (f,f)_f. \tag{28}$$

The functional

$$\sigma = (F - s|f|, F - s|f|)_f \tag{29}$$

is used in most cases as optimization criterion. Dependence of σ on the sought distribution of the current I in antenna is determined by formula (26). The additional multiplier s in (29) can be either prescribed (for example, $s = 1$) or determined from the condition $\partial\sigma/\partial s = 0$. In the latter case

$$s = (F,|f|)_f/(f,f)_f. \tag{30}$$

Let us introduce the normalization $(F,F)_f = 1$, then (29) can be written as

$$\sigma = 1 - Q\kappa^2, \tag{31}$$

where

$$Q = ||I||^2/||f||^2, \tag{32}$$

$$\kappa = (F,|f|)_f/||I||, \tag{33}$$

and $||I||$ is the norm of current, determined by inner product $(\cdot,\cdot)_I$ in the Hilbertian space H_I of currents: $||I||^2 = (I,I)_I$. The factor Q characterizes the goodness (reactivity) of antenna, and κ determines its power efficiency, namely the part of power radiated by the RP.

The generalized functional, allowing to diminish the mean-square deviation of RPs and relative norm of current, has the form

$$\sigma_t = (F - |f|, F - |f|)_f + t||I||^2. \tag{34}$$

Choosing the weight multiplier t, one can regularize the value of mean-square deviation of the RPs and norm of current. Similar functional appears when the method of Lagrange multipliers [16] is used to solving the conditional extremum problems. Simultaneously, one can use some weight function $p \geq 0$ in the definition (28) and to improve the approximation to prescribed amplitude RP F in the appointed angular range.

2.3. The fundamental equations of synthesis

Let us demonstrate how one can receive the respective Lagrange-Euler's equation [17] in the process of minimization of functional σ. Let $s = 1$. It is known [30] that the equality to zero of functional's gradient is requirement of its extremum. This yields determination of the maximum of the following value

$$\frac{\partial\sigma}{\partial z} = \frac{1}{||z||}\lim_{\varepsilon\to 0}\frac{\sigma(I+\varepsilon z)-\sigma(I)}{\varepsilon}. \tag{35}$$

In order to determine the derivative $\frac{\partial\sigma}{\partial z}$, one requires to factorize $\sigma(I+\varepsilon z)$ in series relatively to ε

$$\sigma(I+\varepsilon z) = \sigma(I) + \varepsilon\delta\sigma(I,z) + O(\varepsilon^2) \tag{36}$$

and to extract the linear term $\delta\sigma$. Evidently, $\frac{\partial\sigma}{\partial z} = \frac{\delta\sigma}{||z||}$. The increment of amplitude RP $|f|$ should be known in order to calculate $\delta\sigma$. This increment has the form [4]

$$|A(I+\varepsilon z)| = |f| + \varepsilon\mathrm{Re}[A(z)e^{-i\arg f}] + O(\varepsilon^2). \tag{37}$$

Substituting this expression into (35), we receive

$$\frac{\partial\sigma}{\partial z} = -2(F,\mathrm{Re}[A(z)e^{-i\arg f}])_f + 2\mathrm{Re}(f,Az)_f, \tag{38}$$

or

$$\frac{\partial\sigma}{\partial z} = -2\mathrm{Re}[(A^*(f - Fe^{-i\arg f}),z)_I], \tag{39}$$

where A^* is an operator adjoint to A in the following sense:

$$(AI_1,f_2)_f = (I_1,A^*f_2)_I. \tag{40}$$

If A is an integral operator then A^* is the same with the complex conjugate kernel and integration with respect to the second argument.

Using the Cauchy-Bunyakovsky-Schwarz inequality [10] and maximizing $\frac{\partial\sigma}{\partial z}$, we receive the expression for gradient of σ:

$$z = A^*(f - Fe^{-i\arg f}), \tag{41}$$

which is used usually for the numerical minimization of σ. In order to receive the Lagrange-Euler's equation one should equate to zero the function z (condition of σ minimum)

$$A^*(f - Fe^{-i\arg f}) = 0. \tag{42}$$

The equation (42) contains f as an unknown function. One can turn out that its solutions represent the unreliazable patterns [20]. In order to avoid such solutions, it is necessary to substitute formula (26) into (42) instead of f. In this way, we receive the integral equation for the optimal current distribution

$$A^*AI = A^*A(Fe^{-i\arg AI}). \tag{43}$$

If operator A is integral (consequently, A^* is also integral) then (43) is the nonlinear Hammerstein equation [38].

One can receive the similar expression for z in the process of κ maximization:

$$z = A^*(Fe^{-i\arg f}) - I. \tag{44}$$

Equating the right part of (44) to zero, we receive the explicit expression for I:

$$I = A^*(Fe^{-i\arg f}). \tag{45}$$

Equations (26) and (45) yield the system of nonlinear integral equations for the optimal current I and RP f created by it.

System of nonlinear equations (26), (45) can be reduced to one nonlinear equation

$$f = AA^*(Fe^{-i\arg f}). \tag{46}$$

Since right hand side of (46) is a result of acting by the operator A on some function, any solution to this equation represents the realizable RP. Once this equation is solved, the optimal distribution of current is determined by formula (45). The equation (46) is more simple than system (26), (45) because determination of its solution does not require additional operation of A and A^*.

Taking into account the above considerations, we receive the following nonlinear Hammerstein equation of the second kind for the RP f

$$tf + AA^*f = AA^*(Fe^{-i\arg f}) \tag{47}$$

in the case of functional σ_t minimization. As in the case of (46), the solution to this equation (at $t \neq 0$) represents the realizable RP. Having the solution to (47), we determine the optimal current distribution by formula

$$I = -1/tA^*(f - Fe^{-i\arg f}). \tag{48}$$

The integral equations (43), (46), and (47) are the fundamental equations for the synthesis problems according to the prescribed amplitude RP F.

2.4. The numerical solution of the integral equations

The equations (43), (46), and (47) are solved numerically by the method of successive approximations. The new approximation is determined by explicit formula

$$f_{n+1} = AA^*(Fe^{-i\arg f_n}) \tag{49}$$

in the process of κ maximization. The equation

$$A^*AI_{n+1} = A^*A(Fe^{-i\arg AI_n}) \tag{50}$$

is solved when the synthesis problem is formulated in the term of functional σ minimization. If functional σ_t is minimized then the respective iterative procedure has form

$$tf_{n+1} + AA^* f_{n+1} = AA^*(Fe^{-i \arg f_n}). \tag{51}$$

In the last case, one can use the iterative process

$$f_{n+1} = -1/tAA^*(f_n - Fe^{-i \arg f_n}), \tag{52}$$

but the convergence domain of this process is limited.

In accordance with the procedure used in Subsection 2.3, the solutions to the nonlinear equations (43), (46), and (47) are the stationary points of the respective functionals. Since the used functionals are nonconvex, the several solutions can appear, what corresponds to existence of several local minima or saddle points. The number of solutions can vary depending on the physical parameters of the problem what requires the special careful analysis of the obtained solutions [11].

3. Application to specific antennas

3.1. Amplitude-phase synthesis of cylindrical antenna

In this Subsection, we consider the application of variational approach to the synthesis problem of cylindrical curvilinear antenna. Functional (34) is used as criterion of optimization, complex function I is optimizing function. Since both the amplitude and phase of complex function I are optimizing parameters, the considered problem is the amplitude-phase synthesis problem.

3.1.1. The integral equation approach

Let the generatrix of the antenna has the length $2l$ and be parallel to Oz axis, and form of cross-section be determined by close curve S which be described by formula $r = r(\varphi')$, where φ' is the angular coordinate on S.

In many practical applications, the antennas with currents linearly polarized along Oz axis are of interest. For such case, the RP has only the component $f_\theta(\theta, \varphi)$, denote it as $f(\theta, \varphi)$. On account of formula (18):

$$f(\theta, \varphi) = \int\limits_S \int\limits_{-l}^{l} I(r(\varphi'), z) \sin\theta e^{ik[r(\varphi')\sin\theta\cos(\varphi-\varphi')+z\cos\theta]} dS_{\varphi'} dz. \tag{53}$$

Let the current distribution in antenna surface be determined as

$$I(r, z) = I_1(r(\varphi')) \cdot I_2(z), \tag{54}$$

then the spatial RP is completely determined by the RP $f_1(\theta, \varphi)$, created by the distribution of current $I_1(r(\varphi'))$ in S, and RP $f_2(\theta)$ in the longitudinal plane, created by the current distribution in the generatrix of cylinder

$$f(\theta, \varphi) = f_1(\theta, \varphi) \cdot f_2(\theta). \tag{55}$$

Function $f_2(\theta)$ is the RP of a linear antenna with length $2l$. Function

$$f_1(\theta, \varphi) = \int\limits_S I_1 r(\varphi'), z) \sin\theta e^{ik[r(\varphi')\sin\theta\cos(\varphi-\varphi')]} dS_{\varphi'} \tag{56}$$

is the RP of a plane curvilinear antenna with form S. Consequently, one can reduce the synthesis problem of cylindrical antenna to two independent problems for synthesis of linear and plane curvilinear antennas.

There is a many literature sources on the synthesis problem of linear antennas (see, e.g. [9] and references there). Therefore we consider here the synthesis problem for plane curvilinear antenna.

It is easily seen from formula (53) that the angle θ determines effective electrical scale of antenna. Therefore one can suppose $\theta = \pi/2$. Omitting the indices "1"' in the distribution of current and RP, we represent the RP (56) in form

$$f(\varphi) = AI := \int\limits_0^{2\pi} I(\varphi') e^{ik[r(\varphi')\cos(\varphi-\varphi')]} \sqrt{r^2 + (dr/d\varphi')^2} d\varphi', \tag{57}$$

that is, RP is determined due to action of linear bounded operator A.

The amplitude-phase synthesis problem for closed plane curvilinear antenna according to desired amplitude RP F consists of determination of such distribution of the current $I(\varphi')$, that the amplitude RP $|f(\varphi)|$ created (synthesized) by it, is the most close to $F(\varphi)$. The functional (34) is used as the criterion of optimization. The inner products in the spaces of the RPs and currents are defined as

$$(f_1, f_2)_f = \int\limits_0^{2\pi} p(\varphi) f_1(\varphi) f_2^*(\varphi) d\varphi, \tag{58}$$

$$(I_1, I_2)_I = \int\limits_0^{2\pi} I_1(\varphi') I_2^*(\varphi') \sqrt{r^2 + (dr/d\varphi')^2} d\varphi'. \tag{59}$$

Using (47), (57), and definitions (58) and (59), we receive the nonlinear equation with respect to RP f

$$tf(\varphi) + \int\limits_0^{2\pi} p(\varphi_1) K(\varphi, \varphi_1) f(\varphi_1) d\varphi_1 = Bf, \tag{60}$$

where $K(\varphi, \varphi_1)$ is the kernel of operator AA^*

$$K(\varphi, \varphi_1) = \int\limits_0^{2\pi} e^{ikr(\varphi')[\cos(\varphi-\varphi')-\cos(\varphi_1-\varphi')]} \sqrt{r^2 + (dr/d\varphi')^2} d\varphi', \tag{61}$$

and nonlinear operator B is determined as

$$Bf = \int\limits_0^{2\pi} p(\varphi_1) K(\varphi, \varphi_1) F(\varphi_1) e^{i \arg f(\varphi_1)} d\varphi_1. \tag{62}$$

The methods of successive approximations are applied for solving the nonlinear equation (60). The simplest of them

$$f_{n+1} = 1/t(B - AA^*)f_n \tag{63}$$

has the limited region of convergence determined by formula

$$t > 2\sqrt{2\pi}l(\int_0^{2\pi} p^2(\varphi)d\varphi)^{1/2}, \tag{64}$$

where l is the length of contour S. Once the function f is found, the optimal current I is determined by formula (48).

The iterative process (51) is more preferable, it yields the converging sequence of functional σ_t which satisfies the condition

$$\sigma_t(f_{n+1}) < \sigma_t(f_n) \tag{65}$$

for arbitrary t.

3.1.2. The gradient methods of optimization

Above we mentioned the methods of successive approximations for solving the arising nonlinear equations. The direct optimization of σ_t functional by the gradient methods can be also applied for solving the synthesis problem. The simplest gradient method is defined by the formula

$$I_{n+1} = I_n + \delta_n z_n, \tag{66}$$

where δ_n is an optimizing multiplier, z_n is a gradient of functional σ_t (34) on the function I_n:

$$z_n = A^*(f_n - Fe^{i\arg f_n}) + tI_n, \tag{67}$$

and

$$\delta_n = ||z_n||/a_n, \tag{68}$$

where a_n is a number determined by known values in the $n+1$-th iteration [4].

The disadvantage of method (66) is that only the information about optimizing function from previous iteration is used, in addition it has the slow convergence at the end of iterative process. The method of conjugate gradients [28]

$$I_{n+1} = I_n + \delta_n h_n, \tag{69}$$

and proposed in [3] generalized gradient method

$$I_{n+1} = \sum_{m=1}^{M} \delta_n^{(m)} r_n^{(m)}, \tag{70}$$

do not have such disadvantage. Here h_n is a combination of z_n from previous iterations, and $r_n^{(1)} = I_n, r_n^{(2)} = z_n, r_n^{(3)} ..., r_n^{(M)}$ is a set of some orthogonal functions, δ_n and $\delta_n^{(m)}$ are the coefficients subject to determination.

For method (70), the problem of minimization of σ_t is reduced to the solution of nonlinear algebraic system

$$\sum_{m=1}^{M} [t(r_n^{(m)}, r_n^{(j)})_I + (Ar_n^{(m)}, Ar_n^{(j)})_f]\delta_n^{(m)} = (Fe^{i \arg f_{n+1}}, Ar_n^{(j)})_f, (j = 1, ..., M) \qquad (71)$$

with unknown $\delta_n^{(m)}$. This system is solved effectively by the method of successive approximations substituting in its right hand side the function $\arg f_n$ from previous iteration. Such iterative process is converging and similarly to iterative process (51) yields the converging sequence of σ_{tn} which satisfies the condition (65).

3.1.3. The numerical results

The numerical results are shown for the prescribed amplitude RPs $F(\varphi) = \sin^2(\varphi/2)$ and $F(\varphi) = \sin^{128}(\varphi/2)$ (Fig. 1a and Fig. 1b respectively). The influence of the parameter t in the functional (34) on the quality of synthesis is investigated. One can see that decrease of t improves the proximity of given F and synthesized $|f|$ RPs. But the norm $||I||$ of currents grows if t decreases. In the case of narrow F it is necessary to diminish t in order to decrease the mean-square deviation of the RPs. The detailed information about the synthesis quality is shown in Table 1.

	$F(\varphi) = \sin^2(\varphi/2)$			$F(\varphi) = \sin^{128}(\varphi/2)$	
t	σ	κ	t	σ	κ
0.1	0.0024	0.3419	0.01	0.0411	0.3450
1.0	0.1437	0.4367	0.10	0.0612	0.3581
10.0	1.2744	1.1065	1.0	0.0977	0.4272

Table 1. The values of σ and κ for two desired RPs $F(\varphi)$

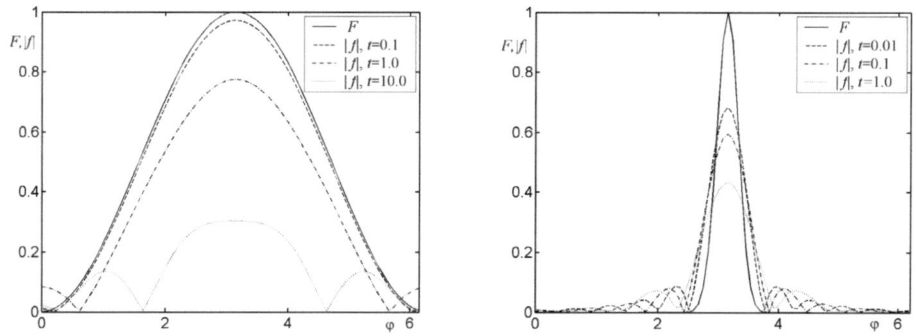

(a) $F(\varphi) = \sin^2(\varphi/2)$ (b) $F(\varphi) = \sin^{128}(\varphi/2)$

Figure 1. Dependence of synthesis quality on the parameter t in the functional σ_t

3.2. The problem of amplitude synthesis for resonant antennas

Resonant antennas are a new type of antennas [24], which allow to form the radiation characteristics satisfying a wide spectrum of practical requirements. Such antennas are formed by several surfaces, one of which is semitransparent. Antennas with one semitransparent and other metal boundary are considered here.

The synthesis problem consists of determination of such parameters of antenna (the geometry of inner boundary and transparency of the outer boundary), which form the amplitude RP or front-to-rear factor (FRF) the most close to the prescribed ones.

3.2.1. *Generalization of variational statement*

The generalized method of eigen oscillations [1] is the mathematical basis for solving the analysis (direct) problem of resonant antennas. The two-dimensional model of antennas (the case of E- polarization) is considered.

The main constructive parameter of resonant antennas is the cophased field in the outer surface. This field can be considered quite real (i.e., only its amplitude can be considered) since the constant phase shift of field does not change the amplitude RP. In this connection, the synthesis problem for resonant antennas is formulated as the amplitude synthesis problem.

The direct problem consists of determination of the RP $f(\varphi)$ by the known field $v(S)$ in the outer boundary S of the given form. The RP created by this field can be presented similarly to (26). The operator A in the case of circular external boundary has form [37]

$$Av = \int_0^{2\pi} K(\varphi, \varphi')v(\varphi')d\varphi', \tag{72}$$

where kernel

$$K(\varphi, \varphi') = \sum_{n=0}^{\infty} \frac{i^n \cos n(\varphi - \varphi')}{(1 + \delta_{0n})H_n^2(ka)}, \tag{73}$$

δ_{0n} is the Kronecker delta, function $H_n^2(ka)$ is the Hankel function of second kind, a is the circle radius.

In the case of resonant antenna with arbitrary outer boundary, the method of auxiliary sources [2, 12, 18] is used for determination of the RP f by the field v. In this method, the field $u(r, \varphi)$ outside of antenna is represented approximately by the finite sum

$$u(r, \varphi) = \sum_{n=1}^{N} a_n H_0^2(kR_n), \tag{74}$$

where $R_n = \sqrt{r^2 + r_n^2 - 2rr_n \cos(\varphi - \varphi_n)}$ is the distance between an observation point and n-th auxiliary source; r, φ and r_n, φ_n are the polar coordinates of a point of observation and n-th source, respectively; a_n are the unknown coefficients subject to determination in the process of solving the synthesis problem.

The RP is given by

$$f(\varphi) = \sqrt{\frac{2}{\pi}} e^{i\pi/4} \sum_{n=1}^{N} a_n e^{ikr_n \cos(\varphi - \varphi_n)}. \tag{75}$$

Solving the synthesis problem, we determine the field in outer boundary S of the antenna and transparency of this boundary. The form of inner boundary S_0 is determined as a curve of constant phase of the field $u(r,\varphi)$ [37].

Additionally, the restrictions on a field in some areas of a near zone can be prescribed. The functional

$$\sigma_t = \int_0^{2\pi} p(\varphi)[F(\varphi) - |f(\varphi)|]^2 d\varphi + \sum_{i=1}^{M} \int_{S_i} p_i(S_i)[U_i(S_i) - |u_i(S_i)|]^2 dS_i + t\int_0^{2\pi} v^2(\varphi)d\varphi, \quad (76)$$

which is generalization of (34), allows to take into account these requirements. Here $U_i(S_i)$ are prescribed values of the field's amplitude in the areas of restriction, $u_i(S_i)$ are the obtained values of the field. Functions $p(\varphi)$, $p_i(S_i)$ are the weight functions, allowing to adjust a degree of proximity of the given and received values of RP and field, t is the parameter limiting norm of the field v.

In the first step of solving the synthesis problem, the field v on the outer boundary S is determined from a condition of minimum of the functional (76). Minimization of functional can be carried out by the gradient methods, or by solving the respective Lagrange-Euler's equation. In the first case, the generalized gradient method [3]

$$v_{n+1} = \delta_n^{(1)} v_n + \delta_n^{(2)} z_n + \delta_n^{(3)} h_n \quad (77)$$

is used. The gradient z of the functional (76) (by virtue of the requirement of real field) has form

$$z = tv - \mathrm{Re}A^*[F\exp(i\arg f) - f] - \sum_{i=1}^{M} \mathrm{Re}B_i^*[U_i\exp(i\arg u_i) - u_i], \quad (78)$$

where A^* and B_i^* are the operators adjoined to A and B_i, respectively [4]. Each step of iterative process (77) reduces σ_t. Since σ_t is limited from below ($\sigma_t \geq 0$), the process (77) is converging.

In the second step, the transparency ρ of the outer boundary S and the form of inner metal boundary S_0 are determined.

For the antenna with circular outer boundary, the transparency distribution can be presented in the explicit form

$$\rho(\varphi) = \pi k v(\varphi)/(2\sum_{n=0}^{N} \frac{a_n \cos n\varphi}{J_n^2(ka) + N_n^2(ka)}), \quad (79)$$

where J_n and N_n are the Bessel and Neumann functions, respectively.

In the case of antenna with arbitrary outer boundary, similarly to [37], the distribution of transparency is determined by the formula

$$\rho(\varphi) = 1/[\frac{\partial\psi(S(\varphi))}{\partial N}]. \quad (80)$$

3.2.2. The numerical results

The numerical calculations are carried out for the resonant antenna with a given outer elliptic boundary. The prescribed amplitude RP is: $F(\varphi) = \sin^8(\varphi/2)$. In Fig. 2, the results are presented for the antenna with parameters $kb = 15$ and different ka: $ka = 12.75, ka = 14.25,$

where b and a are the big and small semiaxes of ellipse. For such antenna the level of side lobes in the synthesized amplitude RP $|f|$ is smaller than –20 dB, and distribution of transparency is smoother in the area of main radiation (the continuous lines in Figs. 2a, 2b correspond to $ka = 12.75$, and the dashed ones correspond to $ka = 14.25$). The outer elliptic boundaries (dashed lines), the found form of inner metallic boundaries (continuous lines), and the inner contour S_a of placement of the auxiliary sources (dash-and-dot lines) are shown in Figs. 3a, 3b. The auxiliary sources are distributed uniformly on the S_a.

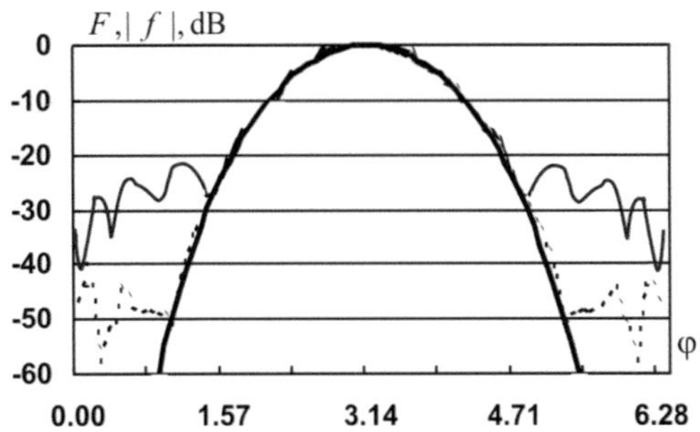

(a) the prescribed F (thick line) and synthesized RPs $|f|$

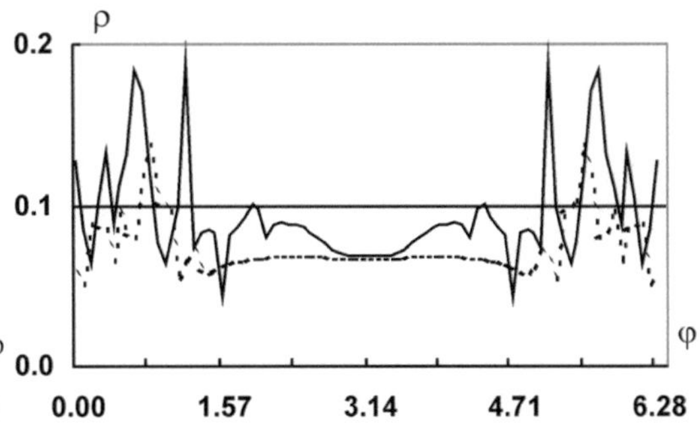

(b) the transparency ρ of outer boundary S

Figure 2. Synthesis of resonant antenna with elliptic outer boundary

The distribution of transparency ρ in the area opposite to direction of main radiation has a spasmodic character. Such distribution cannot be realized by the physical reason. Therefore the values of ρ are averaged in this range in order to receive the smooth distribution of ρ. This leads to some change of field v on S, but the numerical calculations show small change of the synthesized amplitude RP $|f|$. The more smooth distribution of ρ in the area mentioned above can be achieved by increasing the number of auxiliary sources here.

The numerical results for solution of the synthesis problem with restrictions on the field in a near zone are given for the antenna with circular outer boundary. The prescribed amplitude RP is: $F(\varphi) = \sin^8(\varphi/2)$; $ka = 15$. Minimization of a field was carried out in two points $\varphi = \pi/2, 3\pi/2$ on the additional circle with radius $kb = 20$. These points were allocated in the second summand of the functional (76) using the weight function $p_1(\varphi) = \delta(\pi/2, 3\pi/2)$; $p(\varphi) \equiv 1, t = 0.01$. In Fig. 4a, the prescribed RP F (thick continuous line) and synthesized $|f|$ (thin continuous line) amplitude RP are shown. The amplitude $|u_1|$ of obtained field on the circle of restrictions is marked by dashed line.

It can be seen that the field at restriction points is reduced up to level -37 dB. The synthesized field v (continuous line) and transparency ρ (dashed line) are presented in Fig. 4b. The form of the inner synthesized metallic boundary is more complicate than in the previous example.

3.3. Waveguide resonant antenna

Synthesis of resonant antenna with waveguide excitation is carried out according to the FRF. The optimizing functional enables to take into account a various requirements to the FRF of antenna in the operating frequency range, as well as outside this range.

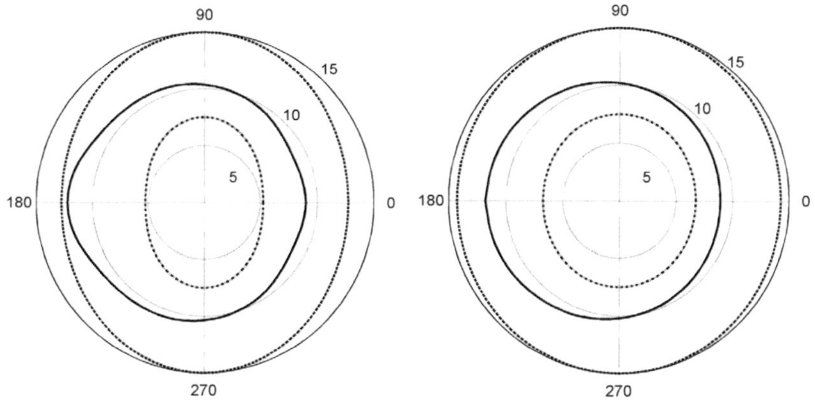

(a) $ka = 12.75$ (b) $ka = 14.25$

Figure 3. Form of antenna boundaries S and S_0

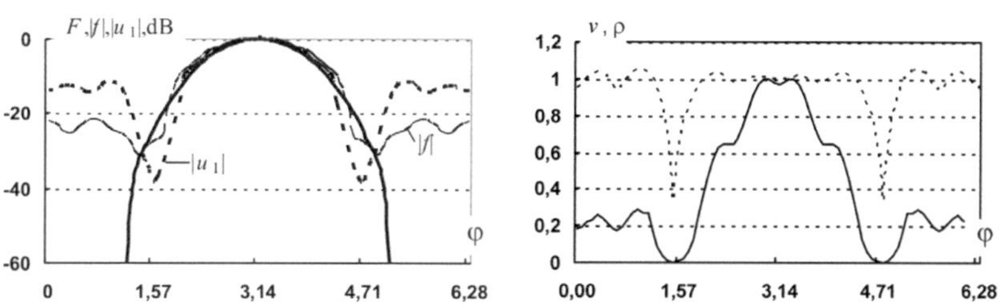

(a) the RPs and field in area of restriction (b) the field v and transparency ρ in outer boundary

Figure 4. Synthesis of resonant antenna with restriction on the field

3.3.1. The physical description of problem

The geometrical parameters of resonant antenna with waveguide excitation are shown in Fig. 5. In order to create RP enough narrow, the width L of antenna should be much larger than the wavelength λ. The height d is of the order of $\lambda/2$. Excitation is carried out by a metal single-mode waveguide with semitransparent grid at its end; the width l of waveguide is of the order $\lambda/2$, and both its length and the length D of the antenna along the Ox axis are of the order of L.

The RP of antenna has form

$$f(\theta, \varphi) = \iint\limits_{S} u(x, y) \exp[ik(x \sin\theta \cos\varphi + y \sin\theta \sin\varphi)] dxdy. \tag{81}$$

The direct (analysis) problem on determination of the electromagnetic field components in the semitransparent aperture is reduced to two separate problems in the planes xOz and yOz respectively. We consider here the case of E-polarization. The unknown function u is the E_y

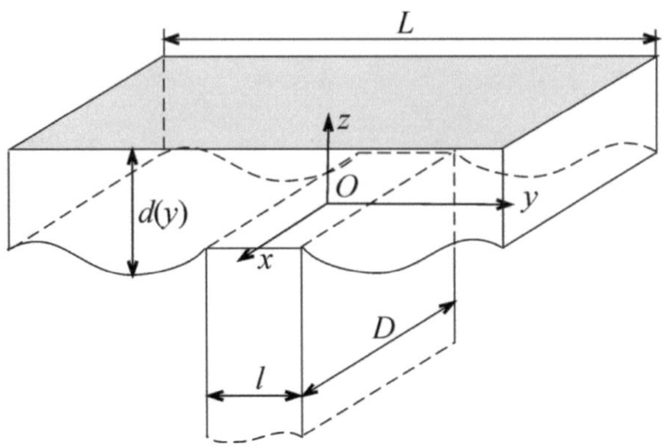

Figure 5. Geometry of the resonant antenna

component of electromagnetic field. In the region over the antenna this component satisfies the Helmholtz equation and the boundary conditions

$$u = 0 \tag{82}$$

on the all metallic walls;

$$u^+ = u^-, \quad \frac{\partial u^-}{\partial x} - \frac{\partial u^+}{\partial x} = \frac{u}{\rho(S)} \tag{83}$$

on the semitransparent upper boundary, the same conditions in the aperture of the exciting waveguide; the condition of radiation on the infinity

$$u\Big|_{\substack{r \to \infty \\ x > 0}} = \frac{\exp(-ikr)}{\sqrt{kr}} f(\varphi), \tag{84}$$

and asymptotical condition in the exciting waveguide

$$u\Big|_{\substack{x \to -\infty \\ y+ < a}} = \cos\frac{\pi y}{2a}(\exp(-i\beta_1 x) + R_1 \exp(i\beta_1 x)). \tag{85}$$

The problem of determination of the field $u(x, y)$ in the semitransparent boundary S is solved in three steps [37]. In the first step, the field in the irregular region of antenna is determined using the cross-section method [19]. In the second step, the field over the exciting waveguide is sought for, and the matching of field in the regular and irregular regions of antenna is fulfilled. The reflection coefficient R_1 is determined by the fulfillment of the adjoint boundary conditions (85) in the third step.

Under condition of the linear polarization of field in the aperture of exciting waveguide, the RP (81) can be represented as product of two functions, namely the RP of plane antenna with variable height $d(y)$ of the upper wall and transparency $\rho(y)$ of the lower wall, and RP of the linear antenna in the xOz plane.

In such a way, the RP in the yOz plane can be written down in the form [37]

$$f(\theta,\varphi) = k\sin\theta \int_{-L/2}^{L/2} u(y,0)\exp(iky\sin\varphi)dy. \tag{86}$$

Numerical calculations can be essentially simplified, if one assumes that the field above the antenna is represented approximately in the form [37]

$$u\Big|_{\substack{|y|<L/2 \\ z\to+0}} \cong u(y,0)\exp(-ikz). \tag{87}$$

3.3.2. The objective functionals

In the process of statement of the synthesis problem one requires to provide the best approximation to the prescribed FRF in the operating frequency range $[k_1,k_2]$ and the minimal values of the FRF outside this range, that is for $k \in [k_0,k_1)$ and $k \in (k_2,k_3]$.

The variational approach for solving this problem was developed in [37]. Modification of variational statement of the synthesis problem is proposed. The problem consists of determination of functions $d(y)$ and $\rho(y)$, which maximize FRF η_1 in the operating range $[k_1,k_2]$. In this case, the least value of FRF in this range is specified as a criterion of optimization, and this value is maximized by a choice of functions d and ρ. That is, the functional is maximized

$$\eta_1 = \max \min_{k_1\le k\le k_2} \eta(k). \tag{88}$$

The additional parameter of optimization $1-|R_1(k)|^2$, where $R_1(k)$ is the reflection factor of the main wave in exciting waveguide, with some weight multiplier can be included into functional (88). In this case, the transparency of waveguide aperture can be also used as an additional parameter of optimization.

Minimization of FRF outside the operating frequency range is one of requirements of electromagnetic compatibility for radiating systems [36]. Thus, the value of FRF should remain the largest in the main frequency range. Under these requirements, the following generalization of the variational statement of problem is considered: to find functions d and ρ, maximizing the functional η_1, and, at the same time, minimizing additionally the following functional [6]

$$\eta_2 = \min \max_{k_0\le k<k_1,k_2<k\le k_3} \eta(k), \tag{89}$$

that is, minimization of the maximal FRF value outside the $[k_1,k_2]$ range is required. Of course, it is necessary to take into account the restrictions on the functions $d(x)$ and $\rho(x)$ owing the physical reason:

$$d_0 < d(y) < d_m, \quad \rho_0 < \rho(y) < \rho_m. \tag{90}$$

For example, d_0, d_m are the boundary values of height, which provide the single-mode conditions in antenna, and ρ_0, ρ_m are the boundary values of transparency, which provide a good quality of antenna in the required ranges. Moreover, the received functions should satisfy the additional conditions of smoothness, which can be formulated as restriction on the second derivatives

$$|d''(y)| \leq M_1, \quad |\rho''(y)| \leq M_2. \tag{91}$$

3.3.3. The modeling results

The numerical results are shown in Fig. 6. Calculations were carried out for the problem of η maximization in range $\pm 5.0\%$ in neighborhood of the central frequency ($k_c = 6.0$). It is necessary to minimize the FRF outside of this range for $5.2 < k < 5.6$ and $6.4 < k \leq 6.8$. Parameters of antenna are the following: the length of antenna $L = 6.0$, half-width of excited waveguide $l/2 = 0.3L$, number of considered reflected waves in waveguide $N_1 = 5$, number of waves in a background $N_2 = 20$.

The optimized values of FRF are marked by solid line in the basic and additional ranges; the dashed line corresponds to not optimized values of η in the main and additional ranges.

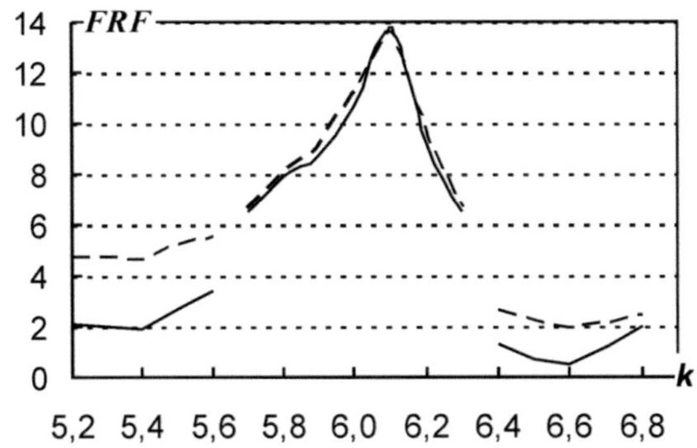

Figure 6. Optimized values of FRF in the basic and additional ranges versus the frequency (k)

Process of additional optimization is carried out on the simplified procedure, that is the control of decrease of the FRF in the basic range is omitted [6]. Therefore, the values of FRF in the basic range are slightly decreased in comparison with the FRF values for initial problem.

The optimal form $d(y)$ of the lower boundary of antenna and transparency $\rho(y)$ of the upper boundary are slightly different for the both cases of optimization.

In Fig. 7, the change of the FRF values at three points of main and additional ranges of frequency (two extreme points and middle one) is shown. The width of main range is equal to 8.33% , and width of additional range is equal to 10.0% . In Fig. 7a, curve 1 corresponds to the central value of frequency $k = 12.0$, and curves 2 and 3 correspond to the extreme points $k = 11.0$ and $k = 13.0$ respectively. In Fig. 7b, curve 1 corresponds to the central frequency $k = 14.0$, and curves 2 and 3 correspond to the frequency values $k = 13.01$ and $k = 15.0$. One can see that the main optimization takes place in the first iterations; there is the improvement only in low-order digit in the next steps. Therefore, it is enough to make 3-5 steps for the main range and 9-11 steps for the additional range, in iterative procedure to receive the practically interesting results.

The total number of iterations also depends on the width of the considered frequency ranges.

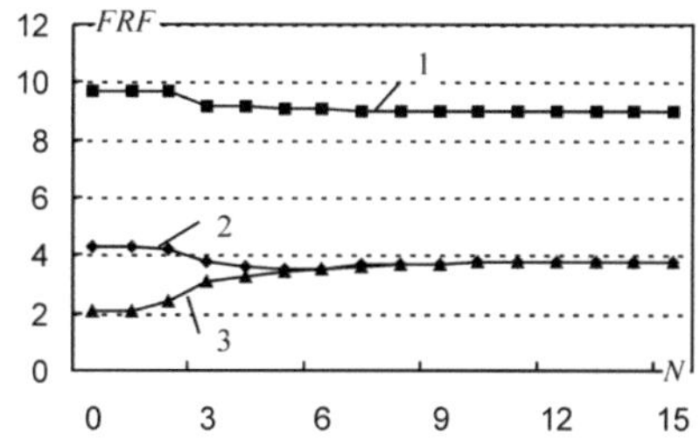

(a) the main range

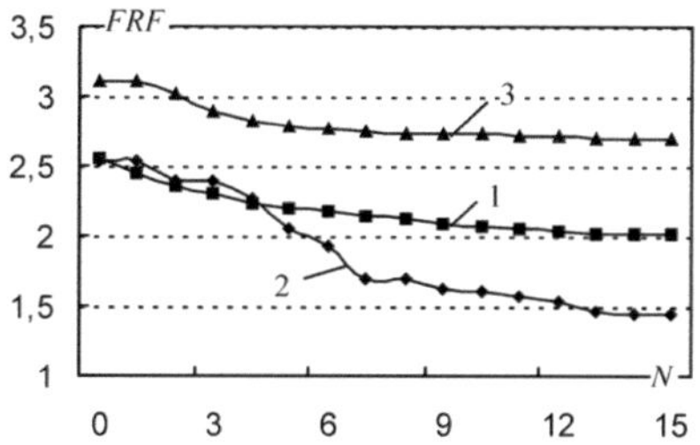

(b) the additional range

Figure 7. The FRF values versus the iteration number N

3.4. Phase synthesis problem for cylindrical array

The phase distributions of excitation currents in the array's elements are the optimizing parameters in the problem of phase synthesis. The optimization of considered functionals is reduced to the solution of the corresponding system of nonlinear equations. The gradient methods for direct optimization of functionals are used in practical applications.

3.4.1. The RP of array

A series of simplifications in process of synthesis of the cylindrical array is used in order to reduce the computing time [9, 22]. Separation of variables onto the vertical and horizontal components for the distributions of currents in the array elements, as well as for the RPs, is one of the simplifications.

Thus, the expressions for current $I_{nm}(x, y)$ in radiators and RP $f(\theta, \varphi)$ have the form [4]

$$I_{nm}(x, y) = I^1_{nm}(x) \cdot I^2_{nm}(y), \tag{92}$$

$$f(\theta, \varphi) = f_1(\theta) \cdot f_2(\varphi). \tag{93}$$

It is assumed that the radiating elements are flat apertures, for example, end of open waveguide. The RP depends on the angular coordinates θ and φ. From the practical point of view, the consideration of such models of the arrays is justified by the fact that they allow to receive the values of required radiation characteristics with the accuracy of 2% - 5%, while the time of solution for the respective problems of analysis (determination of the RP of array), considerably decreases. Such approach to the solution of direct electrodynamic problems is effective especially for the arrays with constant coordinate surfaces, e.g., for the plane, cylindrical and conical arrays. Proceeding from the above assumptions, we separate the synthesis problem of such arrays into two synthesis problems for the linear and circular arrays.

The spatial RP of cylindrical array [9] is:

$$f(\theta, \varphi) = \sum_{m=1}^{M} \sum_{n=1}^{N} I_{nm} f_{nm}(\theta, \varphi) \exp(ik(z_m \cos\theta + a \sin\theta \cos(\varphi - \varphi_n))), \tag{94}$$

where N is the number of radiators in circular subarray (identical for all subarrays), M is the number of circular subarrays, a is radius of cylinder. The currents I_{nm} are complex numbers, by means of which choice the approximation to the given amplitude RP $F(\vartheta, \varphi)$ is carried out.

The functions $f_{nm}(\vartheta, \varphi)$ are the RPs of separate radiators, (z_m, a, φ_n) are the coordinates of radiators. The RP of separate radiators is identical and can be presented in the following form

$$f_{nm}(\theta, \varphi) = f_n(\varphi - \varphi_n) f_m(\theta). \tag{95}$$

Following the above assumptions, the RP (94) can be written as

$$f(\theta, \varphi) = f_l(\theta) f_c(\varphi), \tag{96}$$

where

$$f_l(\vartheta) = A_1 I := \sum_{m=1}^{M} I_m f_m(\vartheta) \exp(ikz_m \cos\vartheta) \tag{97}$$

is the RP of linear array, and

$$f_c(\theta, \varphi) = A_2 I \equiv \sum_{n=1}^{N} I_n f_n(\varphi - \varphi_n) \exp(ika \sin\theta \cos(\varphi - \varphi_n)) \tag{98}$$

is the RP of circular array for each θ. Below we consider the synthesis problem for the circular array.

3.4.2. *Optimization criteria*

The complex currents in the array elements are determined by their amplitudes and phases. We denote these values $|I_n|$ and ψ_n, respectively. The amplitudes $|I_n|$ of currents are prescribed together with the amplitude RP F in the problem of phase synthesis. The phases ψ_n are the optimizing parameters. We use the functionals (29) and (33) for optimization.

The equalities

$$\chi = \arg A(|I|e^{i\psi}), \tag{99}$$

$$\psi = \arg A^*(Fe^{i\chi}). \tag{100}$$

should be satisfied at the points of functional (33) maximum. This set yields the system of transcendental equations for the phases ψ of current and phase RP χ.

Using normalization of the current I values: $||I|| = 1$, we write down the functional (33) in two equivalent forms

$$\kappa = (Fe^{i\chi}, A(|I|e^{i\psi}))_f = (A^*(Fe^{i\chi}), |I|e^{i\psi})_I, \tag{101}$$

where $\chi = \arg f$ is the phase RP. The operator A^* is adjoint to A and determined similarly to [4].

At first, we consider the problem of κ maximization. Substituting (99) into (100), we receive the system of nonlinear algebraic equations for optimal phase distribution of currents

$$\psi_n = \arg A^*(F \exp(i \arg A(|I|e^{i\psi}))), n = 1, 2, ..., N. \tag{102}$$

In practice, the system (99), (100) is more convenient for the numerical solution. For this reason, we use the following iterative process

$$\arg f^{(k)} = \arg A(|I| \exp(i\psi^{(k)})), \tag{103}$$

$$\psi^{(k+1)} = \arg A^*(F \exp(i \arg f^{(k)}) \qquad (104)$$

to find the phases $\psi^{(k+1)}$.

The gradient methods are more convenient to solve the minimization problem for the functional σ. The method of conjugated gradients [28] is the most suitable for this purpose. In this method the next approximation of phase vector $\psi = \{\psi_n, n = 1, ...N\}$ is calculated by the formula

$$\psi^{(k+1)} = \psi^{(k)} + \delta^{(k)} h^{(k)}. \qquad (105)$$

Here

$$h^{(k)} = z^{(k)} + \gamma^{(k)} h^{(k-1)}, \qquad (106)$$

$z^{(k)}$ is the gradient of σ with respect to the phases of currents in the "point" $\psi^{(k)}$. The components of vector $z^{(k)}$ are the following

$$z_n^{(k)} = -\text{Im}\{(A^*((F - s|f^{(k)}|) \exp(i \arg f^{(k)})))_n \cdot I_n^{(k)}\}, n = 1, 2, ..., N. \qquad (107)$$

Parameter $\delta^{(k)}$ is determined from minimum of σ being a function of this parameter.

In practice, it is necessary to solve the problem of discrete phase synthesis [9, 22], because the arbitrary phase distributions cannot be realized in the array radiators. These distributions are prescribed as a set of discrete values, which are multiple to the given phase discrete value Δ, that is $\psi_n = \lambda_n \Delta$, the integers λ_n are unknown in this case [5, 7].

The algorithm consisting of two enclosed iterative processes is used for the solution of this problem. The value of phase ψ_n is improved in the n-th step of the internal iterative process, the phases in other radiators remain fixed. At the same time, the mean-square deviation of the synthesized RP and function $F \exp(i \arg f^{(k)})$, where $\arg f^{(k)}$ is the phase RP, which is received in the previous step of external iterative process, is minimized. The phase RP $\arg f$ is improved in the external iterations.

The internal cycle consists of the successive improvement of phases in the separate radiators changing their number from 1 up to N. The value of σ decreases in each step of internal cycle.

The new phase RP $\arg f^{(k+1)}$ is calculated by the found values of $\{\psi\}$ in external cycle. The values of σ corresponding to new phase RP also decrease, what provides the convergence of the whole algorithm. In view of the step-type behavior of ψ_n values, this convergence exists not only for a sequence of σ, but also for the phase distributions. The iterative process is considered completed, if there is no change of ψ_n in the internal cycle.

The problem of discrete phase synthesis is solved in two steps. In the first step, the synthesis (with small accuracy) without the account of phase discrete values is carried out. After that, the found phases are approximated up to the nearest discrete values. In the second step, the described above algorithm of discrete synthesis is used. As a rule, one is enough to make several external cycles in the latter algorithm.

3.4.3. The results of numerical modeling

The numerical results are given for the sector array. The RPs of separate radiators have a cosine form, and mutual coupling of separate radiators is not taken into account [35]. The number of radiators $N = 32$, the radiators are placed in active sector $\beta = 90^o$.

The synthesis results are shown in Fig. 8 for the bi-directional RP

$$F(\varphi) = \begin{cases} |\sin 18\varphi, |\varphi| < 5.0^0, \\ 0, |\varphi| \geq 5.0^0. \end{cases} \quad (108)$$

The thick line corresponds to the prescribed amplitude RP F, and thin line corresponds to the synthesized RP $|f|$. The prescribed F and synthesized $|f|$ RPs coincide in the main lobe up to level –20 dB, the level of side lobes does not exceed -20 dB (see Fig. 8a).

In the practical applications, the problem of phase scanning [35] is considered for arrays. The array alongside with creating the amplitude RP which is more close to the desired one should provide the moving this RP along the angular coordinate in the scanning process. This moving is carried out by the change of the phase distribution $\{\psi_n\}$ only; the amplitudes $\{|I_n|\}$ of current remain constant. In fact, the problem of phase synthesis is solved for each scanning angle φ_s separately.

The difference between the results of continuous and discrete synthesis depends on the value of phase discrete Δ. The smaller the difference, the smaller this value. In Fig. 8b the values of σ for two types of synthesis are shown for the process of scanning, φ_s is changed in range from 1^0 up to 9^0. Solid line corresponds to the case of continuous synthesis, and dashed line correspond to the case of discrete synthesis, the value of $\Delta = 22.5^0$. This value of Δ gives not big difference for two types of synthesis. So, the difference between F and $|f|$ in main lobe of RPs does not exceed 1dB, and this difference does not exceed 10dB in the side lobes. Such difference is satisfactory for the engineering practice. Of course, the above mentioned difference grows if the scanning angle φ_s approaches to the left or right border of the active sector β.

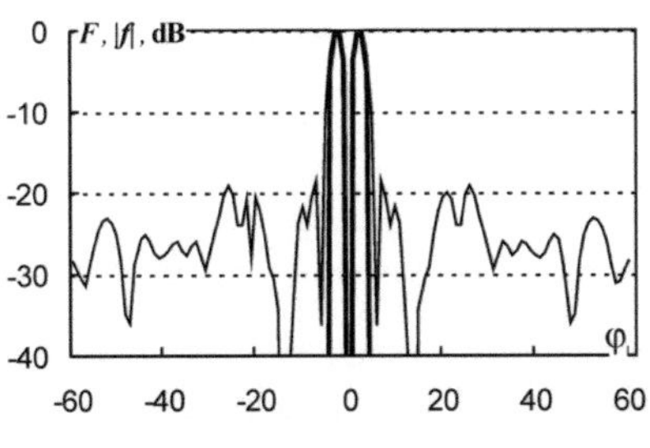

(a) the prescribed and synthesized RPs for the angle of scanning $\varphi_s = 0^0$

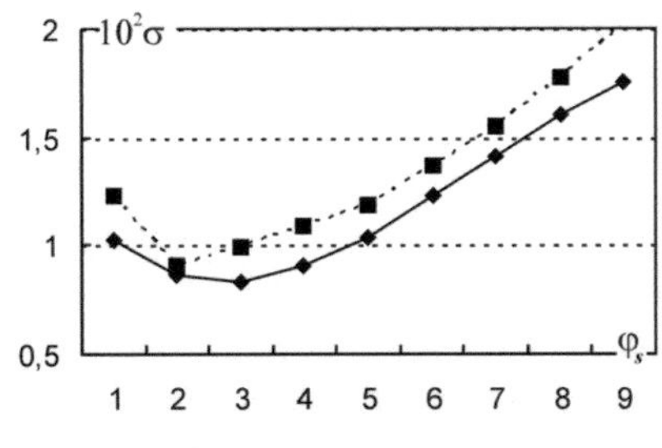

(b) the normalized values of σ for the continuous and discrete phase synthesis

Figure 8. Synthesis of bi-directional RP F

3.5. Investigation of branching solution

The problem of the non-uniqueness of solutions for phase synthesis problem is investigated on the example of linear array.

The various modifications of the Newton method have been developed for solving the nonlinear equations in [13], and have been detailed for the synthesis problems in [11]. We consider here the above approach for determination of the number of solutions and investigation of its properties by the example of the nonlinear equation (46), corresponding to functional κ (33).

Let the operator A describe the RP (array factor) of linear array [4].

$$f(\xi) = Av := \sqrt{\frac{c}{2\pi}} \sum_{n=-M}^{M} v_n \exp(icn\xi), \tag{109}$$

where $c = ka \sin\alpha$, a is the radius of array, α is the angle in which the RP F is non-zero, $N = 2M + 1$ is a total number of array elements, ξ is the generalized angular coordinate. The operator A^*acts in the following way

$$A^* f = \sqrt{\frac{c}{2\pi}} \int_{-\pi/c}^{\pi/c} f(\xi) \exp(-icn\xi) d\xi, \tag{110}$$

In this case, the functional (33) can be presented as

$$\kappa(\psi) = \int_{-\pi/c}^{\pi/c} |f(\xi)| F(\xi) d\xi. \tag{111}$$

3.5.1. The numerical results

The numerical calculations are carried out for the prescribed amplitude radiation pattern $F(\xi) = \cos(\pi\xi/2)$ and are shown in Figs. 9 and 10. In Fig. 9a, the values of κ and σ are shown for various types of initial approximation of the current's phase $\psi^{(0)}(x)$. For this case, the maximization problem of κ is equivalent in some sense to minimization problem of σ [4].

The solid lines correspond to values of κ, and the dashed lines correspond to values of σ. The number of array elements $N = 11$, parameter c changes from $c = 0$ up to $c = 2$. For the values of Nc which do not exceed $Nc = 5$ all types of solutions give the same values of κ and σ. At $Nc \approx 2\pi$ the branching of solutions appears, and optimal value for κ and σ functionals gives the solution with even phase ψ. The prescribed amplitude radiation pattern F and synthesized $|f|$ are shown in Fig. 9b. The amplitudes $|f|$ in the considerable extent differ from the amplitude F because of small value of c parameter ($c = 1.6$).

The optimal values of sought phase distributions ψ are shown in Fig. 10a, the given current amplitude distribution is $|I| \equiv 1$. The optimal phase distributions ψ keep the parity properties of corresponding initial approximations ψ_0. The optimal values of κ and σ provide the solution with phase distribution $\psi_0(x) = \cos(x)$ (see Fig. 9).

The quality of approximation to prescribed amplitude pattern F too much depends on the parameter c (see Fig. 10b). At $c = 3.14$ the κ and σ values are noticeably smaller than for $c = 1.6$, although the value of N is larger in case of Fig. 9.

3.6. Synthesis of waveguide array

The mutual coupling of the separate elements of array is taken into account in the process of solution of a direct problem (analysis problem) [7, 14].

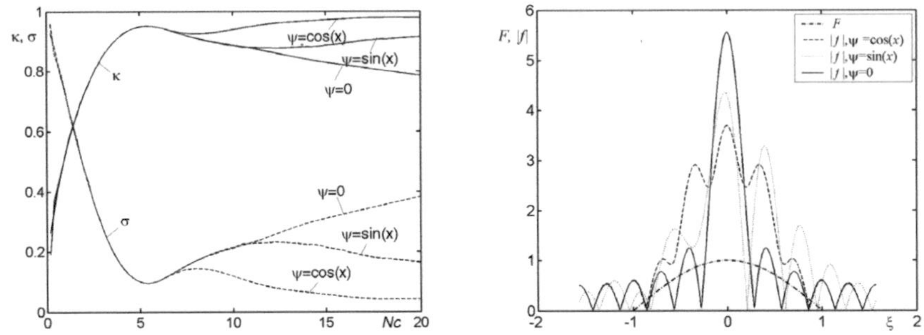

(a) the κ and σ values versus the array electrical size Nc

(b) the synthesized amplitude radiation patterns for various types of current phase, $c = 1.6$

Figure 9. The values of optimizing functionals and synthesized RPs for various type of solutions

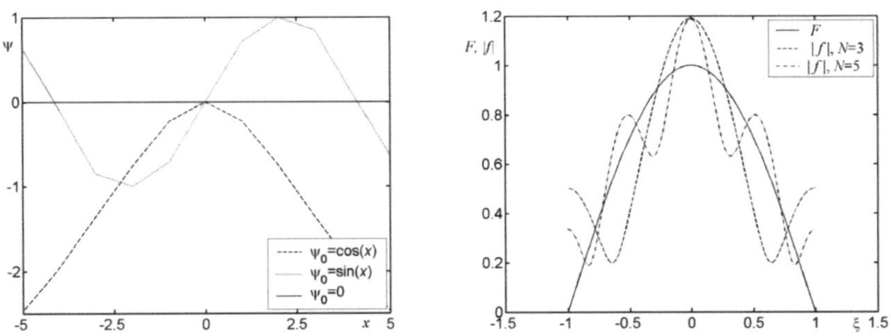

(a) the optimal phase distributions

(b) the desired F and synthesized $|f|$ RPs

Figure 10. The optimal phase distributions at $N = 11$ (a), and synthesis results at $c = 3.14$ (b)

3.6.1. Statement of synthesis problem

The objective functional is formulated as [4]

$$\sigma = \iint\limits_{\Omega} (F(\theta,\varphi) - |f(\theta,\varphi)|)^2 d\theta d\varphi + t\sum_{n=1}^{N} \int\limits_{S_n} |I_n(x_n, y_n)|^2 dx_n dy_n, \tag{112}$$

where $N = 2M + 1$ is a number of exciting waveguides, $F(\theta, \varphi)$ is the prescribed amplitude RP, $|f(\theta, \varphi)|$ is the amplitude of synthesized RP, $I_n(x_n, y_n)$ are the currents in the waveguide apertures. Geometry of waveguide array is shown in Fig. 11.

The determination of the currents $I_n(x_n, y_n)$ in the waveguide apertures (the solution of analysis problem) results in solution of the integral equation system [14].

The RP (array factor) [9] of array is:

$$f(\theta,\varphi) = \sum_{n=1}^{N} a_n \exp[ik(x_{n_0} \sin\theta\cos\varphi + y_{n_0} \sin\theta\sin\varphi)], \tag{113}$$

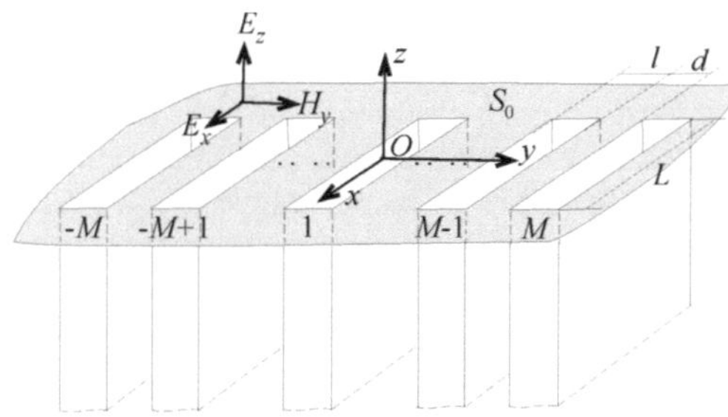

Figure 11. Geometry of plane periodical waveguide array

where x_{n_0} and y_{n_0} are the coordinates of central points of apertures, a_n is the complex excitation coefficient for n-th waveguide.

Introducing the generalized angular coordinates ξ_1 and ξ_2, we receive the expression for the RP

$$f(\xi_1,\xi_2) = \sum_{n=1}^{N} a_n \exp[ik(x_{n_0}\xi_1 + y_{n_0}\xi_2)], \tag{114}$$

where

$$\xi_1 = \sin\theta\cos\varphi, \quad \xi_2 = \sin\theta\sin\varphi, \tag{115}$$

and finally

$$f(\xi_1,\xi_2) = A\vec{a} := \sum_{n=1}^{N} a_n f_n(\xi_1,\xi_2), \tag{116}$$

where $\vec{a} = \{a_1, a_2, ...a_N\}$, $f_n(\xi_1,\xi_2)$ are the RPs of separate waveguides.

The expression (116) indicates that the calculation of array factor $f(\xi_1,\xi_2)$ using the excitation coefficients a_n is realized by the linear operator A. The coefficients a_n will be the optimization parameters in the synthesis problem. Solving the synthesis problem, we minimize the functional σ_t (34).

3.6.2. *The modeling results*

The results of numerical calculations are presented for the waveguide arrays consisting of 15 and 31 radiators; $kl = 1.2$, $kL = 18.75$, k is wavenumber, l and L are width and length of waveguide aperture respectively. The prescribed amplitude RP is: $F(\theta,\varphi) = F_1(\theta)F_2(\varphi)$, where

$$F_1(\theta) = \begin{cases} 1, |\theta| \le \pi/20 \\ 0, |\theta| > \pi/20 \end{cases}, F_2(\varphi) = (\cos\varphi)^{64}. \tag{117}$$

In Fig. 12, the dependence of the synthesis results on the value N of waveguides is shown. It is easy to see, that the synthesized amplitude RP has narrower main lobe if N increases. The level of the first sidelobe is -30.26dB and -30.71dB respectively. The low level of sidelobes and velocity of its decrease is very important characteristic of the synthesized amplitude RPs. As rule, one requires the level of first sidelobe not greater than -20dB and not very slow decreasing the next sidelobes. The above mentioned characteristic for the synthesized amplitude RP in the plane $\xi_2 Oz$ are shown in Table 2. The amplitude RP $|f|$ at $N = 31$ has lower first sidelobe -30.71dB and faster decrease of the far sidelobes.

Sidelobe:	1st	2nd	3rd	4th	5th
$N = 15$	−30.26	−40.43	−46.25	−50.63	−53.27
$N = 31$	−30.71	−40.83	−47.52	−52.45	−56.33

Table 2. The level of sidelobes (in dB) corresponding to array with various N

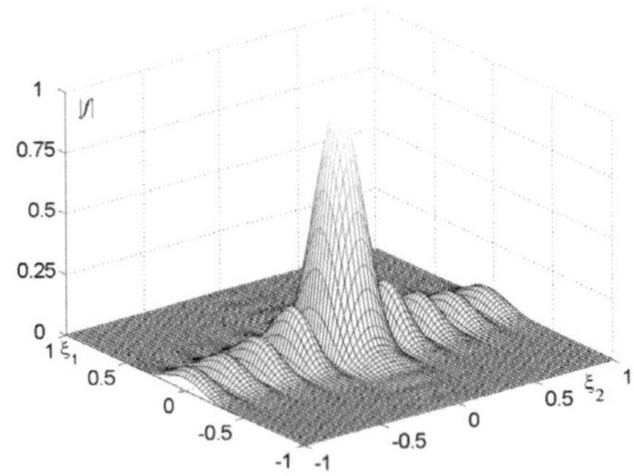

(a) $N = 15$

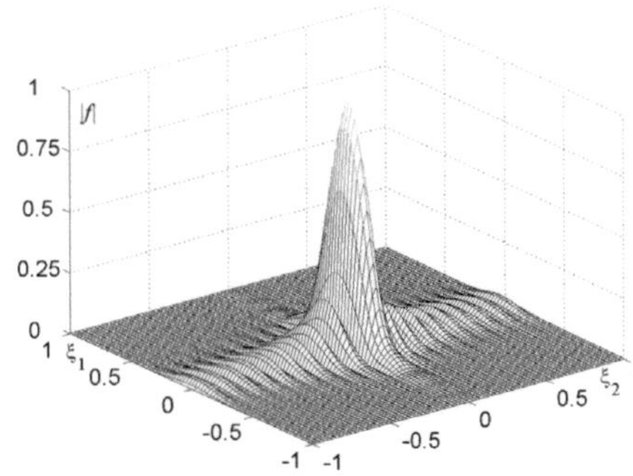

(b) $N = 31$

Figure 12. The synthesized amplitude RPs for various N

4. Conclusions

In the process of solving the amplitude-phase synthesis problem, the influence of weight multiplier t on the synthesis results was investigated. It turned out that the mean-square deviation of the prescribed F and synthesized $|f|$ amplitude RPs diminishes if t decreases. At the same time the norm $||I||$ of current grows. This testify that one should take into account the above fact in order to receive the solution with smaller mean-square deviation of the RPs or with small norm of current. The elaborated iterative procedures guarantee convergence of the successive approximation methods for numerical solving the arising non-linear equations.

The proposed approach for solving the synthesis problems of resonant antennas is universal, and it provides the possibility to synthesize antennas with the arbitrary form of external boundary. The calculation time of the RP of antenna is small enough what it is very important in the process of solution of the synthesis problem. The used variational statement of the synthesis problem also allows to take into account restrictions on the field at the given points (areas) of a near zone.

The synthesis of the resonant antenna with waveguide excitation gives the possibility to take into account the various requirements to the FRF in the operating frequency range. The developed algorithms enable to optimize the values of FRF in the single range, as well as in the several frequency ranges. The values of the objective parameters d and ρ, which are received in the process of numerical calculations, are constructive characteristics of resonant antenna and they can be directly used in the antenna design.

The variational approach for solving the phase synthesis problem can be applied effectively for the plane, cylindrical and conical arrays. It allows to decrease the computational time, at the same time the accuracy of determination of the array characteristics is sufficient for practice. The branching solutions are investigated for the case of linear array. It is shown that one can receive the solutions with various properties starting the iterative process with different initial approximations.

The considered optimization problems of waveguide array give the possibility to take into account the requirements to the amplitude RP and amplitude-phase distribution of field in the aperture of exciting waveguides. The developed algorithms enable to achieve the minimal mean-square deviation σ of the prescribed and synthesized amplitude RPs, and to optimize simultaneously the restrictions on the phase or amplitude characteristics of the excited fields.

Author details

Mykhaylo Andriychuk
Pidstryhach Institute for Applied Problems in Mechanics and Mathematics, NASU, Ukraine

5. References

[1] Agranovich, M. S., Katsenelenbaum, B. Z., Sivov, A. N., Voitovich, N. N. (1999). *Generalized Method of Eigenoscillations in Diffraction Theory*. Berlin, Wiley-VCH.

[2] Alexidze, M. A. (1978). *Solution of Boundary Problems by Decomposition on Non-orthogonal Functions*, (in Russian). Moscow, Nauka.

[3] Andriychuk, M. I., Voitovich, N. N. (1985). Synthesis of a Closed Planar Antenna with Given Amplitude Pattern. *Radio Eng. and Electron. Phys.*, Vol. 30, No 5, pp. 35-40.

[4] Andriychuk, M. I., Voitovich, N. N., Savenko, P. A., Tkachuk, V. P. (1993). *The Antenna Synthesis According to Amplitude Radiation Pattern: Numerical Methods and Algorithms*, (in Russian). Kiev, Nauk. Dumka.

[5] Andriychuk, M. I. (1998). The Analytical-numerical Solution Method of the Nonlinear Problems of the Antenna Phase Synthesis. *Proc. of IIIrd Intern. Seminar/Workshop on Direct and Inverse Problems of Electromagnetic and Acoustic Wave Theory (DIPED-98), Tbilisi, Georgia*, pp. 86-89.

[6] Andriychuk, M. I., Zamorska, O. F. (2004). The Antenna Systems Synthesis According to the Amplitude Characteristics under Condition of Electromagnetic Compatibility. *2004 Second Intern. Workshop on Ultrawideband and Ultrashort Impulse Signals, Sevastopol, Ukraine. Sept. 2004*, pp. 135-137.

[7] Andriychuk, M. I., Klakovych, L. M., Savenko, P. O., Tkach, M. D. (2005). Numerical Solution of Nonlinear Synthesis Problems of Antenna Arrays with Regard for Coupling of Radiators. *Proc. of Vth International Conference on Antenna Theory and Techniques, 24-27 May 2005, Kyiv, Ukraine*, pp. 213-216.

[8] Andriychuk, M., Zamorska, O. (2006). Waveguide Antenna Synthesis According to the Amplitude Radiation Characteristics in the Frequency Band. *Proc. of Ist European Conference on Antennas and Propagation. 6-10 November 2006. Nice, France*, 6 p.

[9] Balanis, C. A. (2005). *Antenna Theory: Analysis and Design*. 3rd Edition. Hoboken, NJ, Wiley.

[10] Bityutskov, V. I. (2001). Bunyakovskii Inequality, in M. Hazewinkel, *Encyclopedia of Mathematics*. Springer.

[11] Bulatsyk, O. O., Katsenelenbaum, B. Z., Topolyuk, Y. P., and Voitovich, N. N. (2010). *Phase Optimization Problems. Application in Wave Field Theory*. Weinheim, Wiley-VCH.

[12] Cupradze, V. D. (1967). About Approximate Solution of Mathematical Physics Problem, (in Russian). *Uspekhi Mat. Nauk*, vol. 22, No 2, pp. 59-107.

[13] Deuflhard, P. (2004). *Newton Methods for Nonlinear Problems. Affine Invariance and Adaptive Algorithms.* Series Computational Mathematics, **35**, Springer.
[14] Dmitriev, V. I., Berezina, N. I. (1986). *Numerical Methods of Solution of the Synthesis Problems for the Radiating Systems*, (In Russian). Moscow, MGU.
[15] Feld, Ya. N. (1992). On the Quadratic Lemma in Electrodynamics. *Sov. Phys. - Dokl.*, 37, pp. 235-236.
[16] Fourikis, N. (2000). *Advanced Array Systems. Applications and RF Technologies. Phased Array Systems*. Ascot park, Academic Press.
[17] Gelfand, I. M., Fomin, S. V. (2000). *Calculus of Variations*. Dover Publ.
[18] Kaklamani, D. I., Anastassiu, H. T. (2002). Aspects of the Method of Auxiliary Sources (MAS) in Computational Electromagnetics. *IEEE Antennas & Propagation Magazine*, vol. 44, No 6, pp. 48-64.
[19] Katsenelenbaum, B., Marcader del Rio, L., Pereyaslavets, M., at al. (1998). *Theory of Nonuniform Waveguides*, London, IEE Series.
[20] Katsenelenbaum, B. Z. (2003). *Electromagnetic Fields – Restriction and Approximation*. Weinheim, Wiley-VCH.
[21] Katsenelenbaum, B. Z. (2006). *High-Frequency Electrodynamics*. Weinheim, Wiley-VCH.
[22] Khzmalyan, A. D., Kondratyev, A. S. (2003). The Phase-Only Shaping and Adaptive Nulling of an Amplitude Pattern. *IEEE Trans. Antennas and Propag.*, vol. AP-51,No 2, pp. 264-272.
[23] Krasnoselsky, M. A., Zabreiko, P. P. (1975). *Geometric Methods of Nonlinear Analysis*, (in Russian). Moscow, Nauka.
[24] Kumar, A., Hristov, H. D. (1989). *Microwave Cavity Antennas*. Boston– London, Artech House.
[25] Landau, L., Lifshitz, E. (1984). *Electrodynamics of continuous media*. London, Pergamon Press.
[26] Markov, G. T., Petrov, B. M., Grudinskaya, G. P. (1979). *Electrodynamics and Propagation of Waves*, (in Russian). Moscow, Sov. Radio.
[27] Milligan, T. A. (2005). *Modern Antenna Design*. Hoboken, NJ, John Wiley & Sons.
[28] Polak, E. (1971). *Computational Methods in Application. A Unified Approach*. New York, Academic Press.
[29] Savenko, P. O. (2002). *Nonlinear Synthesis Problems of Radiating Systems*. Lviv, Ukraine, IAPMM.
[30] Smirnov, V. I. (1958). *Higher Mathematics*, (in Russian). Vol. 4, Moscow, GIFML.
[31] Styeskal, H. l, Herd, J. S. (1990). Mutual Coupling Compensation in Small Array Antennas. *IEEE Trans. on AP*, Vol. 38, No. 12, pp. 1971-1975.
[32] Tikhonov, A. N., Arsenin, V. Y. (1977). *Solutions of Ill-Posed Problems*. New York, Wiley.
[33] Vapnyarskii, I. B. (2001). Lagrange Multipliers, in M. Hazewinkel, *Encyclopedia of Mathematics*, Springer.
[34] Veinstein, L. A. (1998). *The Electromagnetic Waves*, (in Russian). Moscow, Radio i Svyaz.
[35] Vendik, O. G., Parnes, M. D. (2002). *Antennas with Electrical Scanning*, (in Russian). Saint Petersburg, Science Press.
[36] Vladimirov et al. (1985). *Electromagnetic Compatibility of Radioelectronic Devices and Systems*, (in Russian). Moscow, Radio i Svyaz.
[37] Voitovich, N. N., Katsenelenbaum, B. Z. Korshunova, E. N. , at al. (1989). *Electrodynamics of Antennas with Semitransparent Surfaces*, (in Russian). Moscow, Nauka.
[38] Weinberg, M. M., Trenogin, V. A. (1969). *Theory of the Branching of Solutions of Nonlinear Equations*, (in Russian). Moscow, Nauka.

Chapter 10

A Numerical Study of Amplification of Space Charge Waves in n-InP Films

Abel García-Barrientos, Francisco R. Trejo-Macotela,
Liz del Carmen Cruz-Netro and Volodymyr Grimalsky

Additional information is available at the end of the chapter

http://dx.doi.org/10.5772/47764

1. Introduction

The millimeter and sub-millimeter microwave ranges are very important for applications in communications, radar, meteorology and spectroscopy. However, the structure of semiconductor devices (transistors, diodes, etc.), required for such a short wavelength, becomes very complex, which makes its fabrication difficult and expensive. One potential alternative to explore the use of such a part of the electromagnetic spectrum resides in the use of non-linear wave interaction in active media. For example, the space charge waves in thin semiconductor films, possessing negative differential conductivity (InP, GaAs, GaN at 300K and strained Si/SiGe heterostructures at 77K), propagate at frequencies that are higher than the frequencies of acoustic and spin waves in solids. This means, for example, that an elastic wave resonator operating at a given frequency is typically 100000 times smaller than an electromagnetic wave resonator at the same frequency. Thus attractively small elastic wave transmission components such as resonators, filters, and delay lines can be fabricated.

The scope of space charge waves' applications is very large, because it can be useful to implement monolithic phase shifters, delay lines, and analog circuits for microwave signals. Space charge waves have been researched since a long time ago, which can be traced back to the 1950s [Benk]. The early experimental work on the amplification of space charge waves with a perturbation field started in the 1970s [Dean] and continues today [Kumabe *et al.* & Barybin *et al.*]. The first monolithic device using space charge waves was a two-port amplifier developed in the beginning of 1970s in the United States. This device contained an *n*-GaAs film on a dielectric substrate, and a couple of source and drain ohmic contacts. A microwave signal applied to the input electrode modulates the electron density under this electrode. These modulations are drifted to the drain and amplified due to the negative resistance effect. The amplified signal is taken from the output electrode placed near the drain, see Fig. 1a. Obviously, the output signal is maximal when all the waves reach the output electrodes with the same phase [Wang *et al.*]. The majority of devices based on space charge waves are fabricated on GaAs films, although InP is recognized to have superior characteristics compared to GaAs for power generation in the millimeter wave range [Wandinger & Dragoman *et al.*]. The threshold electric field is 3.2 kV/cm for gallium arsenide and 10 kV/cm for indium phosphide. The peak electron drift velocity is about 2.2 x 10^7 cm/s for gallium arsenide and 2.5 x 10^7 cm/s for indium phosphide. The maximum negative differential mobility is about -2400 cm^2/V-s for GaAs and -2000 cm^2/V-s for indium phosphide [Sze]. An electric field in excess of 10 kV/cm applied to an *n*-InP sample causes the differential electron mobility to become negative. To analyze wave phenomena in GaAs films semiconductors, a set of equations to describe the charge transport is commonly used [Kazutaka]. In the case of InP, the same set of equations can be used, because the band structure of InP is very similar to the one of GaAs. In this theory, with small initial perturbations, continuity, momentum and energy equations, and Poisson's equation are solved. The solutions show that the modulations of electron density travel along the beam in the form of waves called space charge waves; these results, for n-GaAs thin films, are in [Grimalsky, *et al.*]. In this paper, the non-linear interaction of space charge waves including the amplification in microwave and millimeter wave range in *n*-InP films, possessing the negative differential conductance phenomenon, is investigated theoretically; also the spatial increment of space charge waves in InP films is compared with the results in GaAs. The results suggest that the increment observed in the gain is due to the larger dynamic range in n-InP than in n-GaAs films, where the optical scattering mechanisms play a drastic role rather than acoustic and ionized impurity scattering.

The study of microwave frequency conversion under negative differential conductivity will be one of the most relevant topics in microelectronics and communications in the coming years, due to the potential it represents in terms of amplification of micro- and millimeter-waves. However, in order to understand the behavior of non-stationary effects, a special attention must be paid to the transverse inhomogeneity, carrier-density fluctuations, in the plane of the film, because it may affect, in a negative way, the non-linear wave interaction. Thus, a creation of effective algorithms and computer programs for simulations of non-linear interaction of space charge waves in semiconductor films, where the effects of non-locality and transverse inhomogeneity should be taken into account, becomes of high importance.

2. The equations for space charge waves

Consider n-InP film placed onto substrate without an acoustic contact. It is assumed that the electron gas is localized in the center of film. The thickness of the n-InP film is $2h < 1$ μm, see Fig. 1a. The coordinate system is chosen as follows: X-axis is directed perpendicularly to the film, the electric field E_0 is applied along Z-axis, exciting and receiving antennas are parallel to Y-axis. 2D model of electron gas in the *n*-InP film is used. Thus, 2D electron concentration is presented only in the plane $x = 0$. The space charge waves possessing phase velocity equal to drift velocity of the electrons $v_0 = v(E_0)$, $E_0 = U_0/L_z$, are considered, where U_0 is bias voltage, L_z is the length of the film. Generally, a non-local dependence of drift velocity v_d of electrons on the electric field takes place.

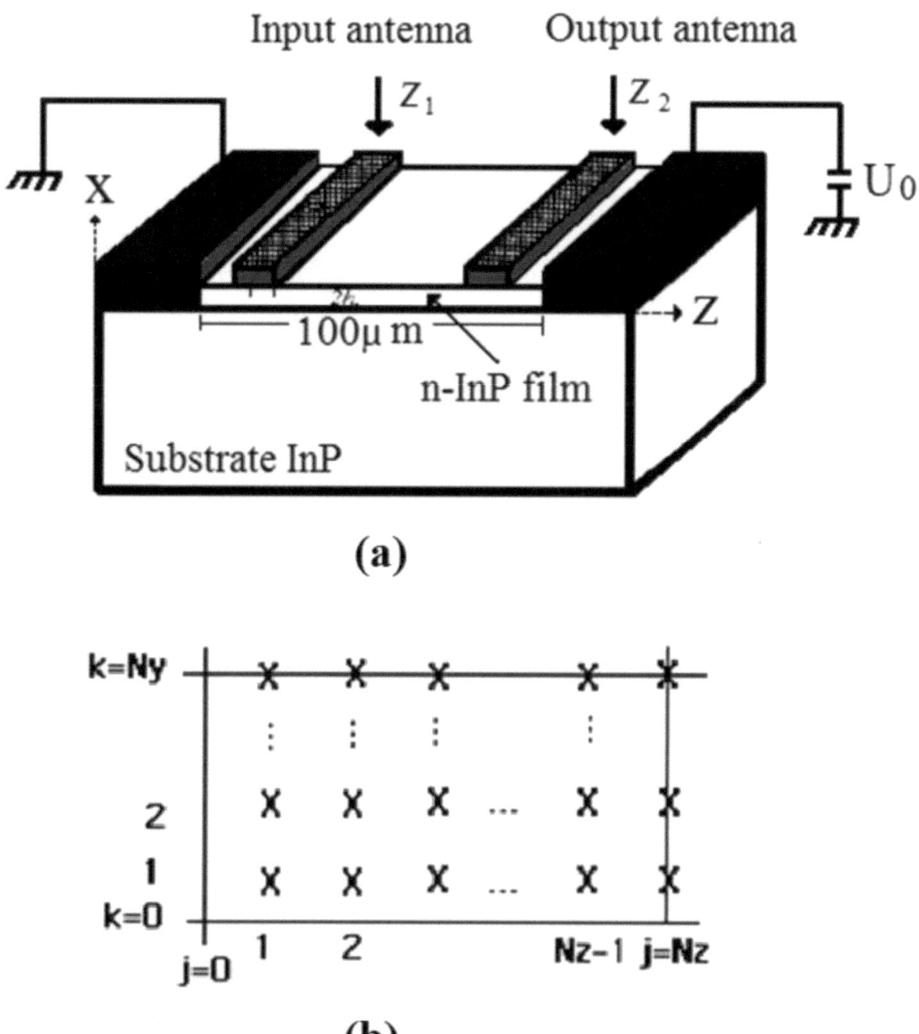

Figure 1. The structure of the *n*-InP traveling-wave amplifier fabricated with an epitaxial layer (a), scheme in device surface for calculating nodes *j* and *k* (b).

In simulations, an approximation of two-dimensional electron gas is used. The set of balance equations for concentration, drift velocity, and the averaged energy to describe the dynamics of space charge waves within the *n*-InP film takes a form, like in GaAs film [Carnez, *et al.*]:

$$\begin{aligned}
&\frac{d\left(m(w)\vec{v}_d\right)}{dt} = -q\left(\vec{E} - \frac{\vec{v}_d E_s}{v_s}\right) \\
&\frac{dw}{dt} = -q\left(\vec{E}\vec{v}_d - E_s v_s\right) \\
&\frac{\partial n}{\partial t} + div\left(n\vec{v}_d - D\tilde{N}n\right) = 0 \\
&D(w) = \frac{2}{3}\frac{\tau_p(w)}{m(w)}\left(w - \frac{1}{2}mv^2\right) \\
&\vec{E} = \vec{e}_z E_0 - \tilde{N}\varphi + \vec{e}_z \tilde{E}_{ext} \\
&\Delta\varphi = \frac{q}{\varepsilon_0 \varepsilon}\left(n - n_0\right)\delta(x)
\end{aligned} \tag{1}$$

where v_d is drift velocity, ϕ is the potential, $n = n_0 + \tilde{n}$ where n_0 is constant electron concentration, $\tilde{n}$ is the varying part, w is the electron energy, **D** is the diffusion coefficient, and ε_0 is the lattice dielectric permittivity of *n*-InP, *m*(w) is averaged effective mass, *q* is the electron charge, $\tau_{p,w}$(w) are relaxation times, and E_0 is the bias electric field. It should be noticed that the delta function in equation Poisson implicitly defines the density which is important to correctly interpret the equation in actual physical quantities. It is assumed that a condition of occurring negative differential conductivity is realized. Because the signal frequencies are in microwave or millimeter wave range, it is possible to separate diffusion and drift motions. For a sake of simplicity, instead of relaxation times, the parameter E_s is introduced [Carnez *et al.*]:

$$\begin{aligned}
&\frac{m(w)}{\tau_p(w)} = \frac{E_s}{v_s(E_s)} \\
&\frac{w - w_0}{\tau_w(w)} = qE_s v_s(E_s)
\end{aligned} \tag{2}$$

In such a representation, the mean energy and effective mass of electron are denoted by w and *m(*w*)*, the equilibrium value of w is w_0; A direct correspondence between local field dependence and non-local effects is well seen. Because a dependence $E_s = E_s(w)$ is unique, it is possible to express the parameters w and v_s through the value of E_s. The dependencies of drift velocity, averaged electron energy and averaged electron mass on electric field in InP films are taken from our Monte Carlo simulation results (see Fig. 2), which are in good agreement with measured data and the set of parameters used in the simulations are very similar from literature [Fischetti].The maximum value of drift velocity in InP is when the electric field is 10 kV/cm, under these high-field conditions some of the electrons can acquire enough energy from the electric field to transfer via inter-valley scattering to the upper valley. Since the mobility of electrons in the upper valley is smaller than in lower valley, the conductivity decreases with increasing field, leading to a negative differential resistance (see Fig. 2a). A comparison of the results for GaAs and InP films reveals that for the field strength considered most of the electrons in GaAs are in higher valley while in InP less than are transferred. This is due to the difference in the separation of the valleys (0.3 eV in GaAs and 0.6 eV in InP) in spite of the higher field applied in InP [Deb, *et al.*]. A large negative differential conductance appears when increasing electric field more than the threshold fielded; the electrons have not enough energy to make the inter-valley scattering. Beyond this value, the optical scattering mechanisms play a drastic role rather than acoustic and ionized impurity scattering. Since this process is inelastic, the electron energy curves have sensitive variation in its slope; in fact it does not increase as fast as increasing in initial fields (see Fig. 2b).

A small microwave electric signal E_{ext} is applied to the input antenna. When this signal is applied, the excitation of space charge waves in 2D electron gas takes place. These waves are subject to amplification, due to negative differential conductivity. The set of equations (1) form a set of non-linear coupled time dependent partial differential equations. These differential equations are discretized, using a finite-difference scheme and is solved numerically. Calculations are performed for two dimensional grid (see Fig. 1b):

$j = 0,1,2,3,\ldots, N_z$, along the Z axis.

$k = 0,1,2,3,\ldots N_y$, along the Y axis.

For potential calculations, we use two dimensional Poisson's equation

$$\frac{\partial^2\varphi}{\partial y^2}+\frac{\partial^2\varphi}{\partial z^2}=-\chi\tilde{n}\delta(x) \tag{3}$$

We use the Fast Fourier Transform, the sine transform along the Z axis and cosine transform along the Y axis with boundary conditions:

$$\varphi(x,y,z)=\sum_{j=1}^{N_z}\sum_{k=0}^{N_y}\phi_{jk}(x)\,SinK_{zj}z*CosK_{zj}y \tag{4}$$

$$\varphi|_{z=0}=\varphi|_{z=l_z}=0;\ \frac{\partial\varphi}{\partial y}\bigg|_{y=0}=\frac{\partial\varphi}{\partial y}\bigg|_{y=l_z}=0;K_{zj}=\frac{\pi k}{l_z};K_{yk}=\frac{\pi k}{l_y} \tag{5}$$

$$E_y\big|_{y=0}=E_y\big|_{y=l_y}=0;\ v_y\big|_{y=0}=v_y\big|_{y=l_y}=0 \tag{6}$$

by replacing the equation (4) in (3) we obtain

$$\frac{d^2\phi_{jk}(x)}{dx^2}-\left(K_{zj}{}^2+K_{yk}{}^2\right)\phi_{jk}(x)=\frac{d^2\phi_{jk}(x)}{dx^2}-\Theta_{jk}{}^2\phi_{jk}(x)=-\chi\tilde{N}_{jk}\delta(x) \tag{7}$$

now

$$\tilde{n}(y,z)=\sum_{j=1}^{N_z}\sum_{k=0}^{N_y}\tilde{N}_{jk}\,SinK_{zj}z*CosK_{zj}y \tag{8}$$

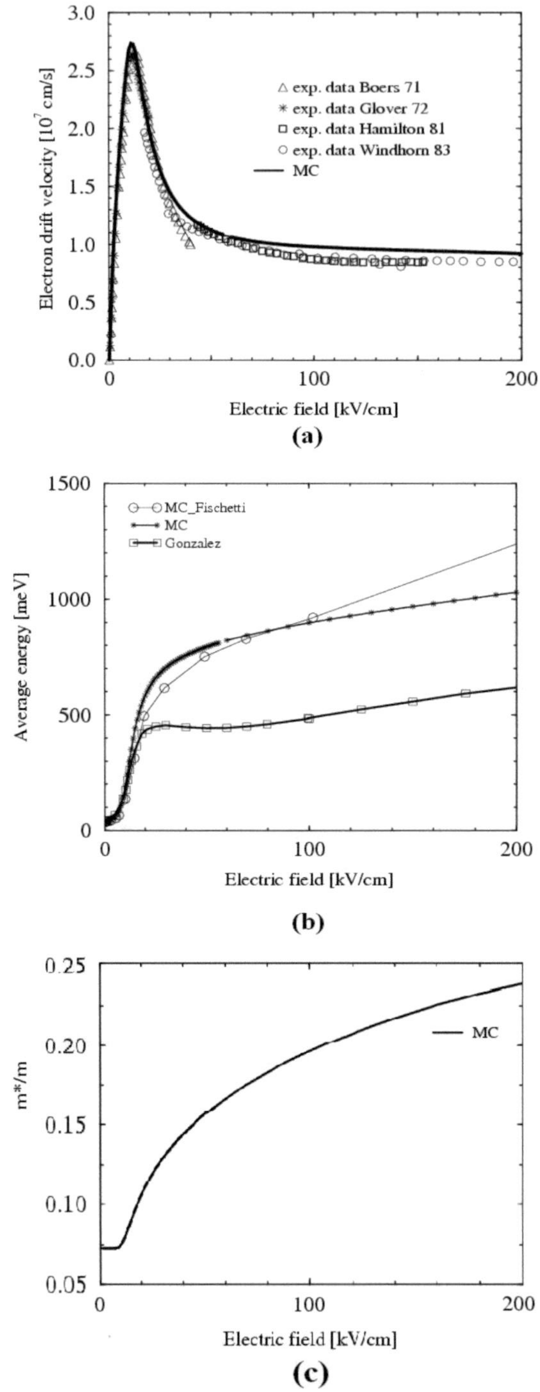

Figure 2. Electron drift velocity (a), average electron energy (b), averaged mass (c) versus electric field used in simulations; (-) MC data, (○) Fischetti, and (□) Gonzalez and experimental data: (Δ) Boers, (*) Glover, (□) Hamilton, and (○) Windhorn.

the solution of equation (7) is in the follow form:

$$\phi_{jk}(x) = \frac{\chi}{2\Theta_{jk}} \tilde{N}_{jk} e^{-\Theta_{jk}|x|} \tag{9}$$

For calculations v_z, v_y, E_y and E_z is necessary to calculate first values $y = 0$ y $y = N_y$ ($k = 0$ y $k = N_y$), then we made the same along the Z axis (increasing j) one by one, as shown in Fig. 1b, for each value of j (j = 1.2 3, ..., N_z) is needed to solve a problem with a tridiagonal matrix. In this case, values $v_z|_{z=0} = v_z|_{z=lz} = 0$; $E_z|_{z=0} = E_z|_{z=lz} = 0$ are already known. We can obtain from potential $\tilde{E}_z$ and $\tilde{E}_y$.

$$\varphi(x, y, z) = \frac{\chi}{2} \sum_{j=1}^{N_z} \sum_{k=0}^{N_y} \frac{\tilde{N}_{jk}}{\Theta_{jk}} e^{-\Theta_{jk}|x|} Sin K_{zj} z * Cos K_{zj} y \tag{10}$$

$$\tilde{E}_z\Big|_{x=0} = -\frac{\partial \varphi}{\partial z}\Big|_{x=0} = -\frac{\chi}{2} \sum_{j=1}^{N_z} \sum_{k=0}^{N_y} \frac{\tilde{N}_{jk}}{\Theta_{jk}} K_{zj} Cos K_{zj} z * Cos K_{yk} y \tag{11}$$

$$\tilde{E}_y\Big|_{x=0} = -\frac{\partial \varphi}{\partial y}\Big|_{x=0} = \frac{\chi}{2} \sum_{j=1}^{N_z} \sum_{k=0}^{N_y} \frac{\tilde{N}_{jk}}{\Theta_{jk}} K_{yk} Sin K_{zj} z * Sin K_{yk} y \tag{12}$$

For $\tilde{E}_z$ we have cosine transform along the Z direction and also for Y axis, and for $\tilde{E}_y$ we have the sine transform in the Z direction and also for Y direction, therefore the program was conducted, the Fourier transform of the sine in the Z direction and in the Y direction cosine transform for $\tilde{n}(y,z)$, and for calculations φ_{jk} (x=0) we use the Inverse Fast Fourier Transform (IFFT). We use the IFFT (Sine-Cosine) for calculations φ(x=0), and for $\tilde{E}_z$ we used the IFFT (Cosine - Cosine) and for $\tilde{E}_y$ we used the IFFT (Sine - Sine).

For calculations v_z we use equation (1), replacing the partial derivatives by their equations in difference

$$\frac{(mv_z)_{j,k}^{p+1} - (mv_z)_{j,k}^{p}}{\tau} + (v_z)_{j,k}^{p+1} \frac{(mv_z)_{j,k}^{p+1} - (mv_z)_{j-1,k}^{p+1}}{h_z} + (v_z)_{j,k}^{p+1} \frac{(mv_z)_{j,k+1}^{p+1} - (mv_z)_{j,k-1}^{p+1}}{2h_y} = \gamma_2 \left[(E_z)_{j,k}^{p+1} - \left(\frac{E_s}{v_s}\right)_{j,k}^{p+1} (v_z)_{j,k}^{p+1} \right] \tag{13}$$

ordering the terms to get a system from equation (13)

$$\alpha_{-1}(v_z)_{j,k-1}^{p+1} + \alpha_0(v_z)_{j,k}^{p+1} + \alpha_{+1}(v_z)_{j,k+1}^{p+1} = f_k \tag{14}$$

This difference equation is only for j = 1,2,3,…,N_z and for k = 1,2,3,…,N_y – 1 forming a tridiagonal matrix system, because for $y = 0$ or $y = l_y$ ($k = 0$ o $k = N_y$) $v_y = 0$. Furthermore, if we substitute for $y = 0$, equation (13) is like in the case of one dimension so we can obtain:

$$(v_z)_{j,0}^{p+1} = \frac{(mv_z)_{j,0}^{p} + \gamma_2 \tau (E_z)_{j,0}^{p+1}}{m_{j,0}^{p+1} + \frac{\tau}{h_z}\left((mv_z)_{j,0}^{p+1} - (mv_z)_{j-1,0}^{p+1}\right) + \gamma_2 \tau \left(\frac{E_s}{v_s}\right)_{j,0}^{p+1}} \tag{15}$$

And the same form for $(v_z)_{j=0,Ny}^{p+1}$, we take into account $(v_z)_{j=0,k}^{p+1} = v_s(E_0)$ from boundary conditions. And for calculations v_y, in the same form like v_z

$$\frac{(mv_y)_{j,k}^{p+1} - (mv_y)_{j,k}^{p}}{\tau} + (v_y)_{j,k}^{p+1} \frac{(mv_z)_{j,k}^{p+1} - (mv_z)_{j-1,k}^{p+1}}{h_z} + (v_y)_{j,k}^{p+1} \frac{(mv_y)_{j,k+1}^{p+1} - (mv_y)_{j,k-1}^{p+1}}{2h_y} = \gamma_2 \left[(E_y)_{j,k}^{p+1} - \left(\frac{E_s}{v_s}\right)_{j,k}^{p+1} (v_y)_{j,k}^{p+1}\right] \tag{16}$$

$$-\frac{\tau}{2h_y} m_{j,k-1}^{p+1} (v_y)_{j,k}^{p+1} (v_y)_{j,k-1}^{p+1} + \left[m_{j,k}^{p+1}\left(1 + \frac{\tau}{h_z}(v_z)_{j,k}^{p+1} + \gamma_2 \tau \left(\frac{E_s}{v_s}\right)_{j,k}^{p+1}\right)\right] (v_y)_{j,k}^{p+1} + \frac{\tau}{2h_y} m_{j,k+1}^{p+1} (v_y)_{j,k}^{p+1} (v_y)_{j,k+1}^{p+1} = (mv_y)_{j,k}^{p} + \frac{\tau}{h_z} (v_z)_{j,k}^{p+1} (mv_y)_{j-1,k}^{p+1} + \gamma_2 \tau (E_y)_{j,k}^{p+1} \tag{17}$$

also $(v_y)_{j,0}^{p+1} = (v_y)_{j,N_y}^{p+1} = 0.$

for calculations n, we use the continuity equation in two dimensions, with their respective boundary conditions, also to make it easier the calculations we use operators

$$\frac{\partial n}{\partial t} + \frac{\partial}{\partial z}\left(v_z n - D(w)\frac{\partial n}{\partial z}\right) + \frac{\partial}{\partial y}\left(v_y n - D(w)\frac{\partial n}{\partial y}\right) = \frac{\partial n}{\partial t} + \hat{A}_z n + \hat{A}_y n = 0 \tag{18}$$

$$n|_{z=0} = n|_{z=l_z} = n_0 \text{ and } \left.\frac{\partial n}{\partial y}\right|_{y=0} = \left.\frac{\partial n}{\partial y}\right|_{y=l_y} = 0 \tag{19}$$

where $\hat{A}_z$ y $\hat{A}_y$ are operators and dependent from v_z, v_y and D, and they are defined as:

$$\hat{A}_z n = \frac{\partial}{\partial z}\left(v_z n - D(w)\frac{\partial n}{\partial z}\right) \text{ and } \hat{A}_y n = \frac{\partial}{\partial y}\left(v_y n - D(w)\frac{\partial n}{\partial y}\right) \tag{20}$$

we use the approximation

$$\frac{\frac{3}{2}n^{p+1} - 2n^{p} + \frac{1}{2}n^{p-1}}{\tau} + \hat{A}_z n + \hat{A}_y n = 0 \tag{21}$$

A transverse inhomogeneity of the structure in the plane of the film along Y axis is taken into account. The following parameters are chosen: 2D concentration of electrons in the film is $n_0 = 5\text{x}10^{14}$ cm^{-2}, the initial uniform drift velocity of electrons is $v_0 = 2\text{x}10^7$cm/s, the length of the film is $l_z = 0.1$ mm, the thickness of the film is $2h = 0.1 - 1$ μm.

3. Spatial increment of space charge waves

In this section, a description of propagation of longitudinal space charge waves in a negative differential conductance medium, using the drift - diffusion equations to find the dispersion relation, is presented; the equation of continuity (22) and Poisson's equation (23) for electrons are

$$\frac{\partial n}{\partial t}+\frac{\partial}{\partial z}\left[v(E_z|_{x=0})n-D\frac{\partial n}{\partial z}\right]=0 \tag{22}$$

$$\Delta\varphi=-\frac{q}{\varepsilon_0\varepsilon}(n-n_0)\delta(x) \tag{23}$$

where n is the surface concentration, n_0 is the equilibrium density, D is the diffusion constant and $E_z=-\frac{\partial\varphi}{\partial z}$. Let us introduce $n=n_0+\tilde{n}$, $\varphi=\varphi_0+\tilde{\varphi}$ and $E=E_0+\tilde{E}_s$, with E_0 equal to the *dc* (direct current) applied field, and $\tilde{E}_s$ is the *rf* (radio frequency) field, with some approximations and mathematical tools the equations (22) and (23) can be written as

$$\frac{\partial \tilde{n}}{\partial t}+\frac{\partial}{\partial z}\left[v_0\tilde{n}+\frac{dv}{dE}n_0\tilde{E}_s-D\frac{\partial \tilde{n}}{\partial z}\right]=0 \tag{24}$$

$$\Delta\tilde{\varphi}=-\frac{q}{\varepsilon_0\varepsilon}(\tilde{n})\delta(x) \tag{25}$$

If one assumes that $\tilde{n}=\tilde{N}exp(-i\omega t+ikz)$ and $\tilde{\varphi}=\phi(x)exp(-i\omega t+ikz)$, then

$$\tilde{N}\left(-i\omega+ikv_0+Dk^2+ik\frac{dv}{dE}n_0\tilde{E}\Big|_{x=0}\right)=0 \tag{26}$$

$$\frac{d^2\phi}{dx^2}-k^2\phi=-\frac{q}{\varepsilon_0\varepsilon}\tilde{N}\delta(x) \tag{27}$$

The equation (27) is equivalent to:

$$\frac{d^2\phi}{dx^2}-k^2\phi=0 \text{ for } x\neq 0 \tag{28}$$

$$\frac{d\phi}{dx}\Big|_{x=+0}-\frac{d\phi}{dx}\Big|_{x=-0}=-\frac{q}{\varepsilon_0\varepsilon}\tilde{N} \tag{29}$$

ϕ is continuous at $x=0$. A proposed solution is

$$\phi=\begin{cases}Aexp(-kx), x>0\\ Bexp(kx), x<0\end{cases} \tag{30}$$

If $\phi|_{x=+0}=\phi|_{x=-0}$ then A=B and

$$\tilde{\varphi}=\frac{q}{\varepsilon_0\varepsilon}\frac{\tilde{n}}{2k}exp(-k|x|) \tag{31}$$

then

$$\tilde{E}_z\big|_{x=0} = -ik\tilde{\varphi}|_{x=0} = -i\frac{q\tilde{n}}{2\varepsilon_0\varepsilon} \tag{32}$$

If one substitutes the equation (32) into the equation (26) one obtains

$$\tilde{N}(-i\omega + ikv_0 + Dk^2) + ik\frac{dv}{dE}n_0\frac{(-i)q\tilde{N}}{2\varepsilon_0\varepsilon} = 0 \tag{33}$$

or

$$\omega = v_0k - iDk^2 - i\frac{qn_0}{2\varepsilon_0\varepsilon}\frac{dv}{dE}k \tag{34}$$

Using the Drift-Diffusion equation, a study about of how a small, periodic disturbance may propagate in this InP film has been introduced by means the dispersion equation $D(\omega,k) = 0$, because it determines the modes of propagation, their phase velocities and group velocities and also show if any instability can exists. For our present purpose, which is when the negative differential conductivity shows up, $dv/dE < 0$, space charge waves will get amplified instead of being damped. In general, we consider the cases where $\omega = 2\pi f$ is real and $k = k' + ik''$ has real and imaginary part. The case $k'' > 0$ corresponds to spatial increment (amplification), whereas the case $k'' < 0$ corresponds to the decrement (damping). In Fig. 3, the spatial increment of space charge waves in an *n*-InP film is shown in the curve 2, where the electron concentration is n_0 = 0.8 x 10^{14} cm^{-2}, the bias electric field is E_0 = 20 kV/cm. In curve 3, the electron concentration is n_0 = 5 x 10^{14} cm^{-2} with the same bias electric field, E_0 = 20 kV/cm. Curve 1 is the result for *n*-GaAs films where the electron concentration is n_0 = 5 x 10^{14} cm^{-2} and the bias electric field is E_0 = 4.5 kV/cm. The stationary values of E_0 have been chosen in the regime of negative differential conductivity ($dv/dE < 0$) for all cases. One can see that an amplification of space charge waves in InP films occurs in a wide frequency range, and the maximal spatial increment is k'' = 3x10^5 m^{-1} at the frequency f = 35 GHz. When compared

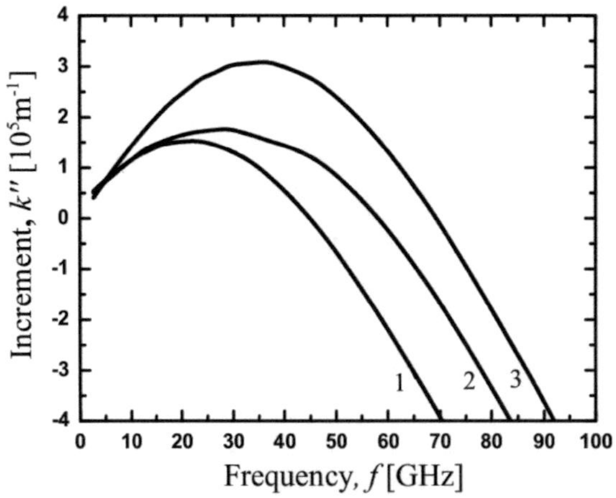

Figure 3. Spatial increments of instability $k''(f)$ of space charge waves. Curve 1 shows results for an *n*-GaAs film [Garcia-B. *et al.*]. Curve 2 is for InP films with E_0 = 20 kV/cm, n_0 = 0.8x10^{14} cm^{-2} and film thickness $2h$ = 0.05 μm and curve 3 is for the electron concentration is n_0 = 5 x 10^{14} cm^{-2} with the same bias electric field, E_0 = 20 kV/cm.

with a case of the GaAs film, it is possible to observe an amplification of space charge waves in InP films at essentially higher frequencies $f > 44$ GHz. To obtain an amplification of 25 dB, it is necessary to use a distance between the input and output antennas of about 0.09 mm.

4. Results and simulation

The propagation and amplification of space charge waves in *n*-GaAs thin films with negative difference conductance have been studied in the last decade [Mikhailov *et al.*], however *n*-InP films have not been addressed yet, and are subject of this work. We address the device presented in Fig. 1 by means of numerical simulations. An *n*-InP epitaxial film of thickness 0.1 - 1 μm is put on an InP semi-insulating substrate. The two-dimensional electron density in the film is chosen to be $n_0 = 5 \times 10^{14}$ cm^{-2}. On the film surface are the cathode and anode ohmic contacts (OCs), together with the input and output coupling elements (CEs). Designed as a Schottky-barrier strip contacts, the CEs connect the sample structure to microwave sources. A dc bias voltage (above the Gunn threshold, 20 kV/cm) was applied between the cathode and anode OCs, causing negative differential conductivity in the film. The CEs perform the conversion between electromagnetic waves and space charge waves, where the excitation of space charge waves in the 2D electron gas takes place. In the simulations an approximation of two-dimensional electron gas is used.

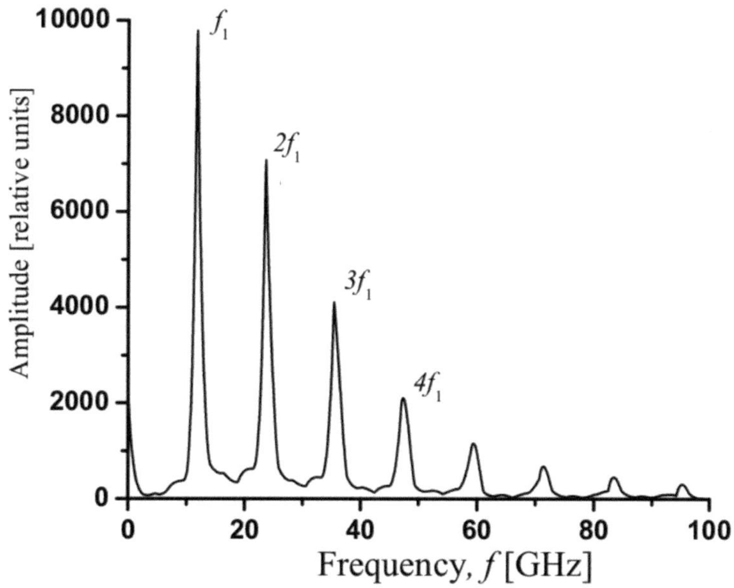

Figure 4. Spectral components of the electric field of space charge waves. The effective excitation of harmonics is presented. The input carrier frequency is $f = 12$ GHz.

A small microwave electric signal $E_{ext} = E_m \cdot \sin(\omega t) \cdot \exp(-((z-z_1)/z_0)^2-((y-y_1)/y_0)^2)$ is applied to the input antenna. Here z_1 is the position of the input antenna, z_0 is its half-width. Therefore, the parameter $2t_0$ determines the duration of the input electric pulse. In our simulations, this parameter is $2t_0 = 2.5$ ns. The carrier frequency f is in the microwave range: $f = 1$ GHz – 100

GHz. When a small microwave signal is applied to the input antenna, the excitation of space charge waves in the 2D electron gas takes place. The space charge waves are subject to amplification, due to the negative differential conductivity. The stable implicit difference scheme is used. The following parameters have been chosen: 2D electron concentration in the film is n_0 = 5x10^{14} cm^{-2}, the initial uniform drift velocity of electrons is $v_0 \approx$ 2x10^7 cm/s (E_0 =15 – 20 kV/cm), the length of the film is L_z = 0.1 mm, the thickness of the film is $2h$ = 0.1 - 1 μm. The typical output spectrum of the electromagnetic signal is given in Fig. 4. The input carrier frequency is f = 12 GHz. The amplitude of the input electric microwave signal is E_m = 25V/cm. Although the growth rate decreases as the *rf* frequency increases, for our case an amplification of 25 dB is obtained. The maximum of the input pulse occurs at t_1 = 2.5 ns. One can see both the amplified signal at the first harmonic of the input signal and the harmonics generations of the input signal, which is generated due to the non-linearity of space charge waves.

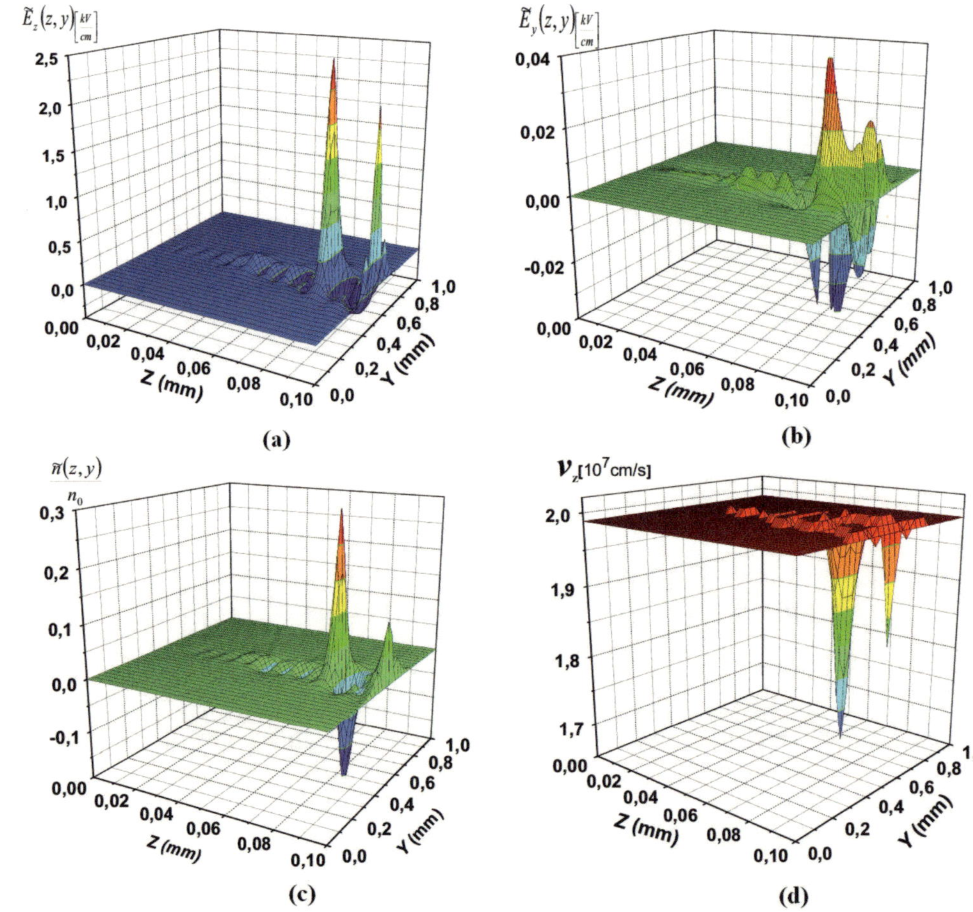

Figure 5. The spatial distributions of the alternative part of the electric field component $E^{\sim}_z$ of space charge wave (a); the component of electric field $E^{\sim}_y$ (b); alternative part of the electron concentration $n^{\sim}$ (c); and the component of the electron drift velocity v_z (d). The length of the film is 0.1 mm. The transverse width of the film along Y axis is 1 mm.

The spatial distributions of the alternate component of the electric field $E^{\sim}_z$, $E^{\sim}_y$, the alternate part of the electron concentration $\tilde{n}$, and the drift velocity v_z are given in Fig. 5, at the time moment t = 4 ns. One can see the maximum variations are in the output antenna and the spatial distribution in direction $E^{\sim}_z$ is bigger than in $E^{\sim}_y$, it is because the propagation of space charge wave. The length of the film is 0.1 mm. The transverse width of the film along Y axis is 1 mm. The duration of the input electric pulse is 2.5 ns. The spatial distributions are presented for the time moment 1.5 ns after the maximal value of the input signal. Direct numerical simulations have confirmed pointed below results on linear increments of space charge waves amplification. Also a possibility of non-linear frequency doubling and mixing is demonstrated. To get the effective frequency doubling in the millimeter wave range, it is better to use the films with uniform doping.

5. Conclusions

A theoretical study of two-dimensional amplification and propagation of space charge waves in n-InP films is presented. A microwave frequency conversion using the negative differential conductivity phenomenon is carried out when the harmonics of the input signal are generated. A comparison of the calculated spatial increment of instability of space charge waves in n-GaAs and n-InP films is performed. An increment in the amplification is observed in InP films at essentially higher frequencies $f > 44$ GHz than in GaAs films, which is due to its larger dynamic range. The maxi mum amplification (gain of 25 dB) is obtained at $f = 35$ GHz, using a distance between the input and output antennas of about 0.09 mm.

Author details

Abel García-Barrientos and Francisco R. Trejo-Macotela
Polytechnic University of Pachuca, Hidalgo, Mexico

Liz del Carmen Cruz-Netro
Polytechnic University of Altamira, Tamaulipas, Mexico

Volodymyr Grimalsky
Autonomous University of Morelos, Cuernavaca, Morelos, Mexico

Acknowledgement

This project has been partially funded by the CONACyT- Mexico grant CB-169062 and by the ECEST-SEP (Espacio Común de Educación Superior Tecnológica) Program under the mobility program for professors.

6. References

Barybin A.A., Mikhailov A.I., Parametric interaction of space-charge waves in asymmetric thin-film n-GaAs structures, Tech. Phys.,vol. 48, no. 6, pp. 761 – 767, 2003.

Beck A.H.W, Space-charge waves and slow electromagnetic waves, Pergamon, New York, 1958.

Boers P.M., Measurements on the velocity/field characteristics of indium phosphide, Electron.Lett., vol. 7, no.20, pp. 625-626, 1971.

Carnez B., Cappy A., Kaszynskii A., Constant E. and Salmer G., Modeling of submicrometer gate FET including effect of nonstationary dynamics, J. Appl. Phys., vol. 5, no. 1, pp. 784-790, 1980.

Dean R.H, Travelling-wave amplifier using epitaxial GaAs layer, Electron. Lett., vol. 6, no. 24, pp.775, 1970.

Deb Roy M. and Nag B. R., Velocity auto-correlation and hot-electron diffusion constant in GaAs and InP, Appl. Phys. A, vol. 28, 1982.

Dragoman M., Block M., Kremer R., Buchali F., Tegude F. J., and Jager D., Coplanar microwave phase shifter for InP-based MMICs, Microelectronics Engineering, vol. 19, pp. 421-424, 1992.

Fischetti M.V., Monte Carlo simulation of transport intechnologically significant semiconductors of thediamond and zinc-blende structures-Part I:homogeneous transport, IEEE Transactions on Electron Devices, vol. 38, no. 3, 1991.

Garcia-B. A., Grimalsky V., Gutierrez-D. E. A. and Palankovski V., Non-stationary effects of space charge in semiconductor films, J. Appl.Phys., vol. 105, no. 7, pp. 1-6, 2009.

Glover G.H., Microwave measurement of the velocity-field characteristic of n- type InP, Appl. Phys. Lett., vol. 20, pp. 224-225, 1972.

Gonzalez Sanchez, T., Velazquez Perez J. E., Gutierrez Conde P. M., and Pardo D., Electron transport in InP under high electric field conditions, Semicond. Sci. Technol.vol. 7, no. 1, 1992.

Grimalsky V., Gutierrez-D. E., Garcia-B A.. and Koshevaya S., "Resonant excitation of microwave acoustic modes in n-GaAs film, Microelectronics Journal, vol. 37, pp. 395-403 (2006).

Hamilton D.K., Measurements of dipole domains in indium phosphide using a new point-contact probe, Proc. IEE Solid-State and Electron Devices, vol. 128, no. 2, pp. 6167, 1981.

Kazutaka T., Numerical Simulation of Submicron Semiconductor Devices, London, Artech House, pp. 171-189, 1993.

Kumabe K. and Kanbe H., GaAs travelling-wave amplifier, Int. J. Electronics, vol. 58, no. 4, pp. 587-611, 1985.

Mikhailov A.I., Experimental study of the parametric interaction between space-charge waves in thin-film GaAs-based semiconductor structures, Tech. Phys. Lett.,vol. 26, no. 3, pp. 217 – 219, 2000.

Sze S. M., High Speed Semiconductor Devices, Wiley, New York, 1992.

Wandinger L., mm-Wave InP Gunn devices: Status and trends, Microwave J., vol. 24, no. 3, pp. 71 - 78, 1981.

Wang Y. and Jahandoots H., Solid-stated traveling-wave amplifiers based on multistream instability, Int. J. Electronics, vol. 58, no. 4, pp. 571-585, 1985.

Windhorn T.H., Cook L.W., Haase M.A., and Stillman G.E., Electron transport in InP at high electric fields, Appl. Phys. Lett., vol. 42, no. 8, pp. 725-727, 1983.

Chapter 11

Accuracy Investigation of De-Embedding Techniques Based on Electromagnetic Simulation for On-Wafer RF Measurements

Takuichi Hirano, Kenichi Okada, Jiro Hirokawa and Makoto Ando

Additional information is available at the end of the chapter

http://dx.doi.org/10.5772/48431

1. Introduction

Millimeter-wave CMOS RF circuits have received substantial attention in recent years, motivated by advances in CMOS processing. Figure 1 shows on-wafer measurement using probes, which is commonly used in research and development of RF front-end circuits. De-embedding is necessary to remove the effect of pads in on-wafer measurements of RF circuits. Thru-Reflect-Line (TRL) calibration technique [1][2][3] and the de-embedding technique using open and short patterns [4] have been used conventionally. The authors applied the Thru-Line (TL) de-embedding technique [5] to remove the effect of pads from the measured S-parameters of RF circuits on a Si CMOS substrate. The TL de-embedding technique requires two patterns (Thru and Line) while the TRL de-embedding requires three patterns (Thru, Reflect and Line). The TL de-embedding technique can characterize left and right pads under the assumption that left and right pads have the same characteristics while TRL de-embedding cannot characterize pads, without knowing characteristic impedance of the line used for example. Other de-embedding methods, such as double delay [6], through-only [7], and multi line (or L-2L) de-embedding [8][9], have been proposed. However, these all use approximation of pads, or parasitic component, by an equivalent circuit model while the TL de-embedding method treats pads rigorously with S-parameters. The effectiveness of TL de-embedding has been investigated in [10].

It is very difficult to keep repeatability of measurement in such high frequencies over millimeter-wave band. Hence, the electromagnetic (EM) simulation technology becomes important. This paper explains EM simulation modeling for on-wafer measurement using a GSG probe. By utilizing the result of EM simulation, the accuracy of de-embedding techniques (open-short, TRL, and TL) are compared and discussed.

The chapter is organized as follows. Section 2 describes structure of pads and transmission line considered in the chapter. Section 3 presents open-short, TRL and TL de-embedding techniques. Section 4 presents EM simulation modeling for on-wafer measurement using a GSG probe. The gap between ground (G) and signal (S) pads is excited by a lumped source. Section 5 discusses the accuracy of de-embedding techniques (open-short, TRL, and TL). The accuracy degradation of open-short de-embedding technique is quantitatively investigated via numerical simulation, which is verified in section 4.

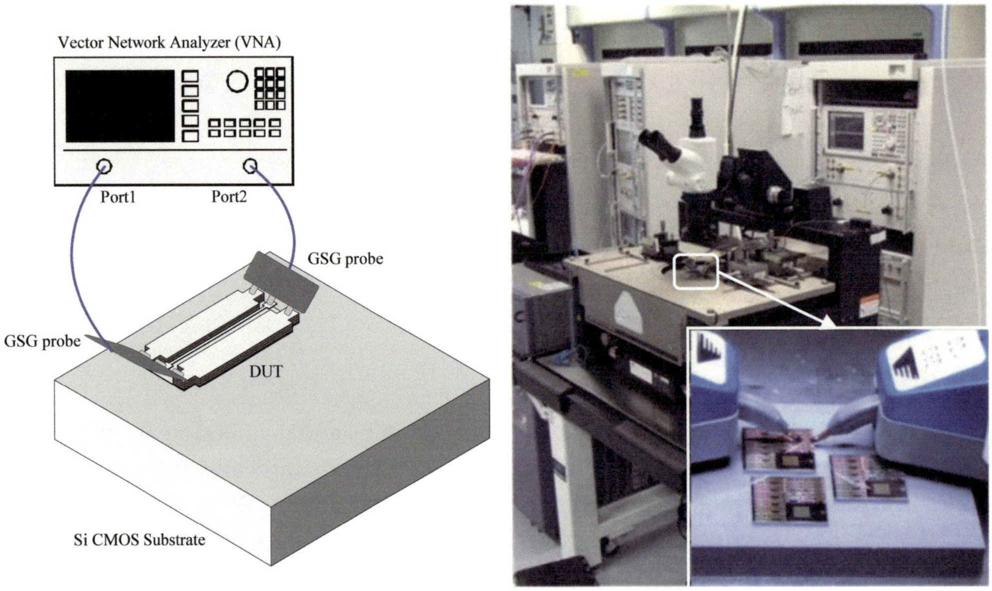

(a) Conceptual block diagram (b) Photograph of equipments

Figure 1. On-wafer measurement using probes.

2. Structure of pads and transmission line

The structure of pads and transmission lines are shown in Figure 2. The GSG pad is used for touching with the GSG probe. A guided microstrip line (G-MSL) on a Si CMOS substrate [11], which has metal walls on both sides of the signal line, is used as the transmission line between the GSG pads as shown in Figure 2. The G-MSL with dummy metal fills is shown in Figure 3. The transmission line consists of several metal (Aluminum) layers and vias which connect them. SiO_2 is used as an insulator between the metal layers. The ground plane and signal line are realized by the bottom and top metal layers, respectively. The width and thickness of the signal line are 10 μm and 1 μm, respectively. The characteristic impedance is designed to be about 50 Ohm. There are metal walls, or guides, on both sides of the signal line which consists of the metal layers and vias [11]. The role of the guide is to increase the metal density to satisfy design rules and to suppress unwanted leakage at corners. The distance from the guide walls to the edges of the signal line is 20 μm to ensure that the guide does not affect transmission characteristic of the microstrip mode.

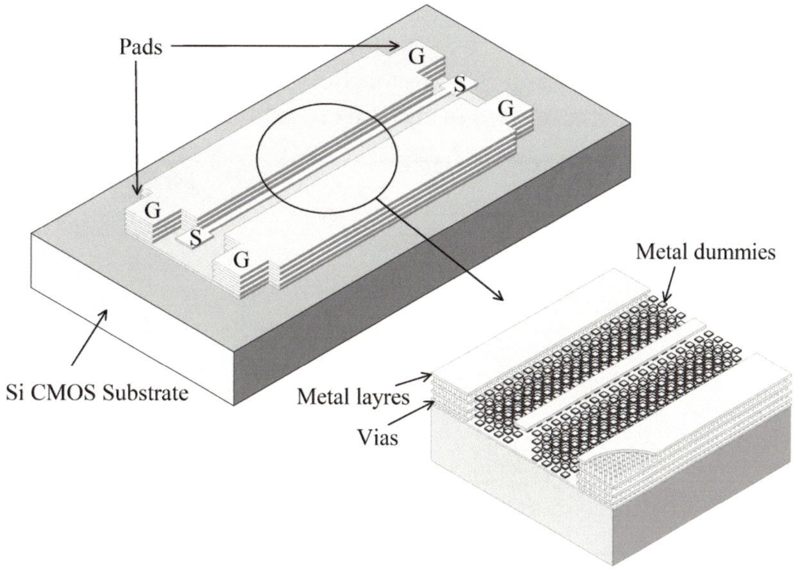

Figure 2. Structures of pads and guided microstrip line (G-MSL).

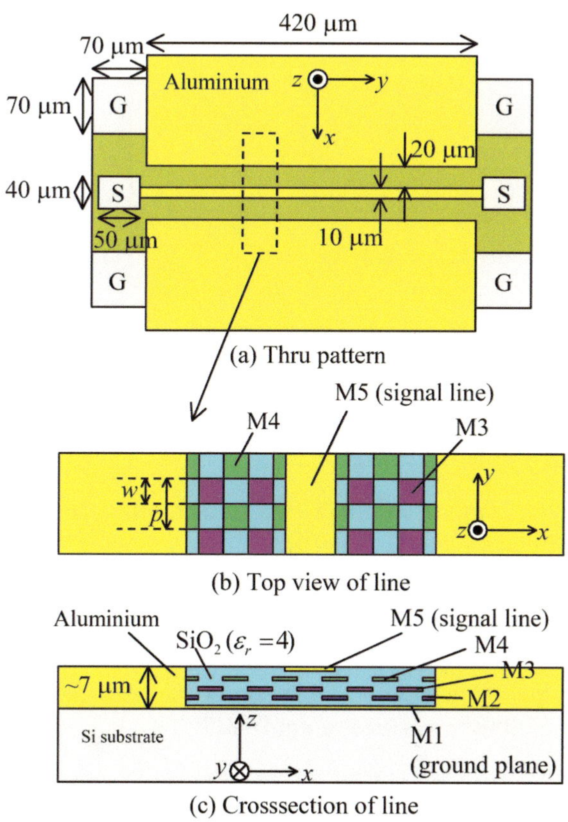

Figure 3. Thru pattern and structure of a guided microstrip line.

3. De-embedding techniques

Algorithms of open-short, TRL and TL de-embedding techniques are introduced in this section. Table 1 shows the patterns used in each de-embedding method.

Pattern		Method		
		TRL	TL	Open/Short
Thru	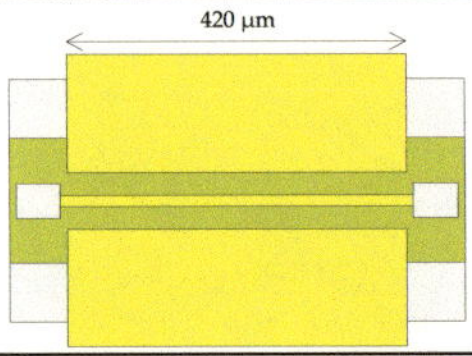	✓	✓	
Reflect (~Open)	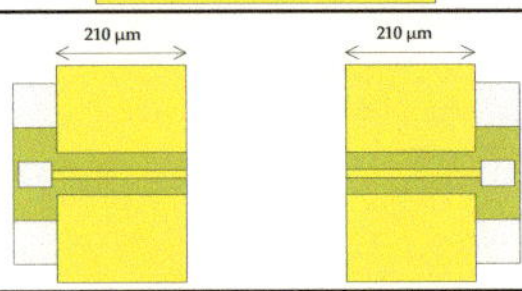	✓		✓
Line	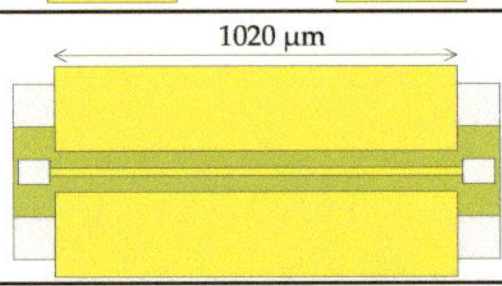	✓	✓	
Short	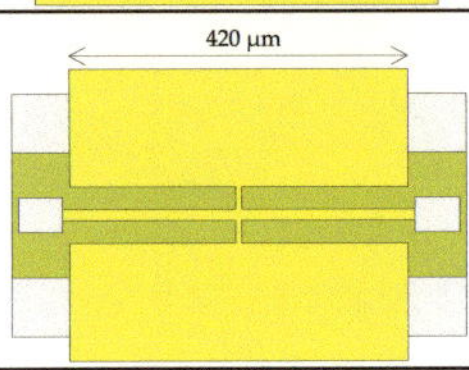			✓

Table 1. Pattern used in de-embedding methods

3.1. De-embedding techniques using open-short patterns

The open-short de-embedding technique [4] is reviewed and outlined here. In the open-short de-embedding technique, the parasitic component of pads is approximated by the equivalent circuit topology shown in Figure 4.

i) Three measurements are made to obtain the transmission line characteristics shown in Figure 4(i). The first measurement is done for the open-pattern, resulting in the open two-port Y-parameters $Y^{(\mathrm{open})}$. The second measurement is done for the short-pattern, resulting in the short two-port Y-parameters $Y^{(\mathrm{short})}$. The third measurement is done for a thru-pattern, which includes the GSG pads at both ends of a short line, described by the two-port Y-parameters $Y^{(\mathrm{SUT})}$. The thru-pattern can be replaced by an arbitrary structure with the GSG pads, which is named the structure under test (SUT).

(ii) The thru-pattern is approximated by the equivalent circuit topology shown in Figure 4(ii). Parasitic elements Y_{p1}, Y_{p2} and Y_{p3} can be determined from $Y^{(\mathrm{open})}$ by comparing with π -circuit parameters.

$$Y^{(\text{open})} = \begin{bmatrix} Y_{11}^{(open)} & Y_{12}^{(open)} \\ Y_{21}^{(open)} & Y_{22}^{(open)} \end{bmatrix} = \begin{bmatrix} Y_{p1} + Y_{p3} & -Y_{p3} \\ -Y_{p3} & Y_{p2} + Y_{p3} \end{bmatrix} \tag{1}$$

By comparing matrix elements, Y_{p1}, Y_{p2} and Y_{p3} can be determined.

$$\begin{cases} Y_{p1} = Y_{11}^{(open)} + Y_{12}^{(open)} \\ Y_{p2} = Y_{22}^{(open)} + Y_{12}^{(open)} \\ Y_{p3} = -Y_{12}^{(open)} \end{cases} \tag{2}$$

(iii) Parasitic elements Y_{p1}, Y_{p2} and Y_{p3} can be removed from $Y^{(\text{short})}$; $Y^T = Y^{(\text{short})} - Y^{(\text{open})}$. Parasitic elements Z_{s1}, Z_{s2} and Z_{s3} can be determined by comparing with T-circuit parameters after transforming Y^T into Z-parameters Z^T.

$$Z^T = \begin{bmatrix} Z_{11}^T & Z_{12}^T \\ Z_{21}^T & Z_{22}^T \end{bmatrix} = \begin{bmatrix} Z_{s1} + Z_{s3} & Z_{s3} \\ Z_{s3} & Z_{s2} + Z_{s3} \end{bmatrix} \tag{3}$$

By comparing matrix elements, Z_{s1}, Z_{s2} and Z_{s3} can be determined.

$$\begin{cases} Z_{s1} = Z_{11}^T - Z_{12}^T \\ Z_{s2} = Z_{22}^T - Z_{12}^T \\ Z_{s3} = Z_{12}^T \end{cases} \tag{4}$$

(iv) The Y-parameters for thru, only transmission line characteristic, $Y^{(\text{DUT})}$ can be obtained by removing Y_{p1}, Y_{p2}, Y_{p3}, Z_{s1}, Z_{s2} and Z_{s3}. Parasitic elements Y_{p1}, Y_{p2} and Y_{p3} can be removed by subtracting $Y^{(\text{open})}$ from $Y^{(\text{SUT})}$. Parasitic elements Z_{s1}, Z_{s2} can be removed with the fundamental matrix (F-matrix). Finally, Z_{s3} can be removed with the Z-matrix.

It is noted that a lumped element can be the DUT although the transmission line is assumed as the DUT in this paper. De-embedding technique using electromagnetic (EM) simulator [12], with higher accuracy than the open/short de-embedding technique, is also proposed when the DUT is a lumped element.

3.2. De-embedding techniques using Thru-Reflect-Line patterns

The Thru-Reflect-Line (TRL) calibration technique [1][2][3], which is widely used for network analyzer calibration, can be used for deembedding of pads directly.

3.3. De-embedding techniques using Thru-Line patterns

The Thru-Line (TL) de-embedding technique [5] uses Thru (T) and Line (L) patterns, which have different lengths as shown in Figure 5. The line pattern is longer (by ΔL) than the Thru

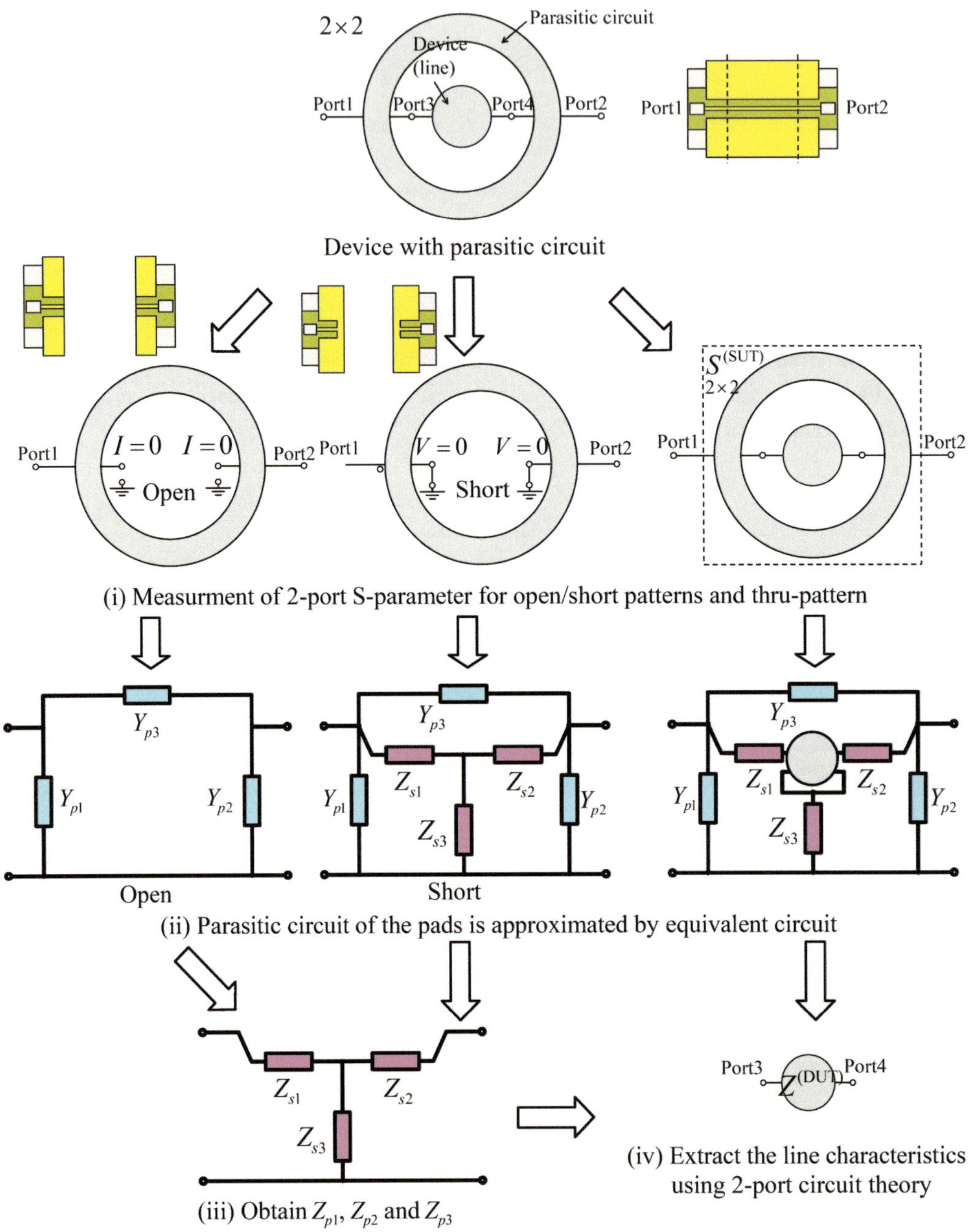

Figure 4. De-embedding technique using open and short patterns.

pattern. The overall characteristics of the Line pattern can be decomposed as a cascade connection of pads and line parts as shown in Figure 6. The assumption that two pads have completely same characteristics is necessary in TL de-embedding. From Figure 6, the total characteristics of Thru and Line patterns are

$$\begin{cases} \rho_t = S_{11} + \dfrac{S_{12}{}^2 S_{22}}{1 - S_{22}{}^2} \\ \tau_t = \dfrac{S_{12}{}^2}{1 - S_{22}{}^2} \end{cases} \qquad \begin{cases} \rho_l = S_{11} + \dfrac{S_{12}{}^2 S_{22} \Gamma^2}{1 - S_{22}{}^2 \Gamma^2} \\ \tau_l = \dfrac{S_{12}{}^2 \Gamma}{1 - S_{22}{}^2 \Gamma^2} \end{cases} \tag{5}$$

where ρ_t and τ_t are the reflection and transmission coefficients of the Thru pattern; ρ_l and τ_l are the reflection and transmission coefficients of the Line pattern; and S_{11}, $S_{12}(=S_{21})$, and S_{22} are the S-parameters of the pads. Here, ρ_t, τ_t, ρ_l, and τ_l can be measured while $S_{11}, S_{22}, S_{12}{}^2$, and $\Gamma(=e^{-\gamma \Delta L})$ are unknowns. With the four equations in (5), these unknowns can be found by solving the non-linear equations, for example by using Mathematica [13].

$$\begin{cases} S_{11} = \dfrac{\rho_l{}^2 - \rho_t{}^2 - \tau_l{}^2 + \tau_t{}^2 \pm A}{2(\rho_l - \rho_t)} \\ S_{22} = \dfrac{\rho_l{}^2 - 2\rho_l \rho_t + \rho_t{}^2 - \tau_l{}^2 + \tau_t{}^2 \pm A}{2(-\rho_l + \rho_t)\tau_t} \\ S_{12}{}^2 = -\dfrac{1}{2\tau_t}\{(\rho_l - \rho_t)^2 - 2\tau_t{}^2 \pm B \\ \qquad -\dfrac{1}{(\rho_l - \rho_t)^2}(2\rho_l{}^2\tau_l{}^2 - 4\rho_l\rho_t\tau_l{}^2 + 2\rho_t{}^2\tau_l{}^2 \\ \qquad + (\tau_l - \tau_t)(\tau_l + \tau_t)(-(\tau_l{}^2 - \tau_t{}^2) \pm B))\} \\ \Gamma = \dfrac{-\rho_l{}^2 + 2\rho_l\rho_t - \rho_t{}^2 + \tau_l{}^2 + \tau_t{}^2 \pm A}{2\tau_l\tau_t} \end{cases} \tag{6}$$

where

$$\begin{aligned} A &= \sqrt{-4(\rho_l - \rho_t)^2\tau_t{}^2 + \left\{(\rho_l - \rho_t)^2 - \tau_l{}^2 + \tau_t{}^2\right\}^2} \\ B &= \sqrt{(\rho_l - \rho_t - \tau_l - \tau_t)(\rho_l - \rho_t + \tau_l - \tau_t)(\rho_l - \rho_t - \tau_l + \tau_t)(\rho_l - \rho_t + \tau_l + \tau_t)} \end{aligned} \tag{7}$$

It must be noted that there are two sets of solutions to (6) indicated by the double sign. The propagation constant can be calculated from Γ.

$$\gamma = -\frac{\ln \Gamma}{\Delta L} \tag{8}$$

Selecting the correct solution from the two sets of solutions in (6) and (7) is uncomplicated. If the transmission line is a right-handed waveguide, the phase constant is positive, and a set of solutions which gives a positive phase constant $\beta = \mathrm{Im}[\gamma]$ is chosen at the lowest considered frequency near direct current (DC). At the next higher frequency point, in frequency sweeping, a set of solutions is chosen so that the phase constant is near the previous lower frequency point.

The effect of the pads can be de-embedded from a structure under test (SUT) by the following procedure:

(i) Measure the S-matrix of the SUT $S^{(\mathrm{SUT})}$.

(ii) Transform $S^{(\mathrm{SUT})}$ into a cascade matrix (T-matrix) $T^{(\mathrm{SUT})}$. Now $T^{(\mathrm{SUT})}$ is implied to be $T^{(\mathrm{SUT})} = T^{(\mathrm{PAD\text{-}L})}T^{(DUT)}T^{(\mathrm{PAD\text{-}R})}$, where $T^{(\mathrm{PAD\text{-}L})}$, $T^{(\mathrm{PAD\text{-}R})}$ and $T^{(DUT)}$ are the T-matrixes of the left pad, right pad, and device under test (DUT) embedded in the pads, respectively. The $T^{(\mathrm{PAD\text{-}L})}$ and $T^{(\mathrm{PAD\text{-}R})}$ values can be calculated from $S^{(\mathrm{PAD\text{-}L})}$ and $S^{(\mathrm{PAD\text{-}R})}$, with the elements obtained in (6) (See also Figure 6).

(iii) $T^{(DUT)}$ can be obtained by matrix operations: $T^{(DUT)} = \left(T^{(\mathrm{PAD\text{-}L})}\right)^{-1} T^{(\mathrm{SUT})} \left(T^{(\mathrm{PAD\text{-}R})}\right)^{-1}$. Finally, $S^{(\mathrm{DUT})}$ is obtained by transformation from $T^{(DUT)}$, and de-embedding of the pads can be performed.

A sample Mathematica source code is given in Appendix.

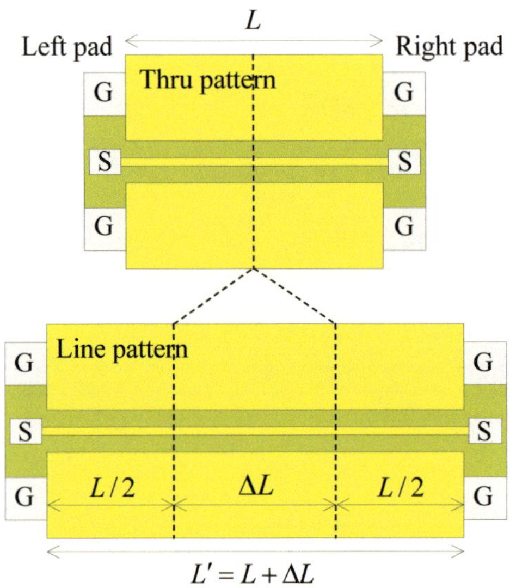

$$S_t = \begin{bmatrix} \rho_t & \tau_t \\ \tau_t & \rho_t \end{bmatrix}$$

$$S_l = \begin{bmatrix} \rho_l & \tau_l \\ \tau_l & \rho_l \end{bmatrix}$$

Figure 5. Thru and line patterns.

4. Electromagnetic modeling

This section verifies the modeling and accuracy of the electromagnetic (EM) simulator. The FEM-based EM simulator, Ansoft HFSS Ver.11 [14], was used for EM analysis in the chapter.

4.1. Symmetric pattern

Figure 7 shows the model for the analysis of the thru-pattern in HFSS. Due to the symmetry of the structure and excitation, the model for the analysis of the Figure 3 thru-pattern can be reduced to half of the whole structure, as suggested in Figure 7. A magnetic wall, or perfect magnetic conductor (PMC), is assumed at the center of symmetry. The absorbing boundary, or radiation boundary in HFSS, conditions are applied to the other outer boundary walls. The gap between ground (G) and signal (S) pads is excited by a lumped source. Lumped ports with 100 Ohm intrinsic impedances, which is double of probe impedance because of image theory, were used for the excitations.

To verify the accuracy of the EM simulation, the calculated value is compared with the measured one. A micrograph of a fabricated chip is shown in Figure 8. The chip is 2.5 mm square and an 0.18 μm CMOS process is used. In the measurements, 100 μm-pitch GSG probes were used, and the system was calibrated using the impedance standard substrate (ISS). Smith charts of the S-parameters for the thru, line, and reflect patterns are shown in Figures 9, 10, and 11, respectively. The calculated and measured results agreed very well for all three patterns.

Then, sensitivity of lumped port position and size is investigated. Figure 12 shows position and size of lumped port in the GSG pad. Reflection coefficient S_{11} and transmission coefficient S_{12} (=S_{21}) are shown in Figure 13 and Figure 14, respectively, with various sets of width (w), left pad offset (d_l) and right pad offset (d_r) (both offsets are prescribed in a similar manner). w is varied from 10 μm to 30 μm. d_l and d_r are varied from -15 μm to 15 μm. It is found that there are no significant differences in results. These results suggest that the probe positioning error is not serious in measurement. Results indicated by "edge1" and "edge2" are obtained with the excitation model in which lumped port is arranged at the edge of the GSG pad as shown in Figure 15. w_a in Figure 15 is 20 μm for "edge1" while it is 50 μm for "edge2". The phase of S_{11} begins to show different value in high frequency region. The result indicated by "vertical" is obtained with the excitation model in Figure 16. The phase of S_{12} begins to show different value in high frequency region. However, the results of these excitation models show good agreement.

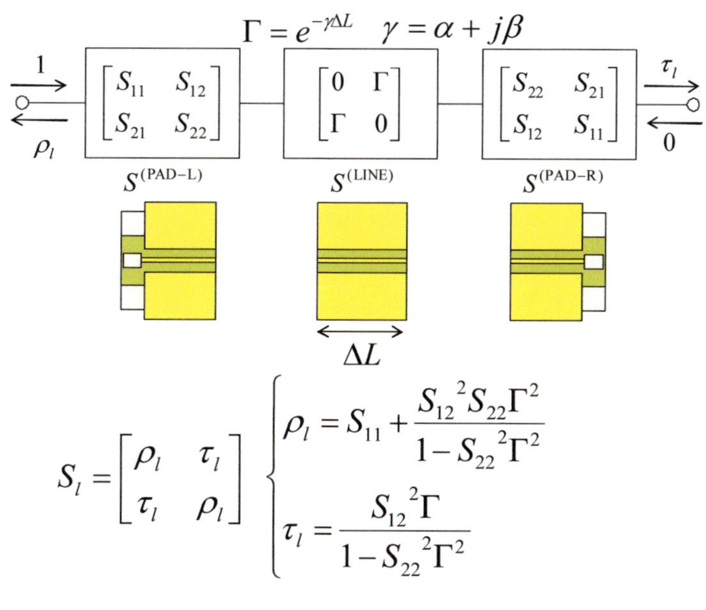

Figure 6. Cascading expression of the line pattern.

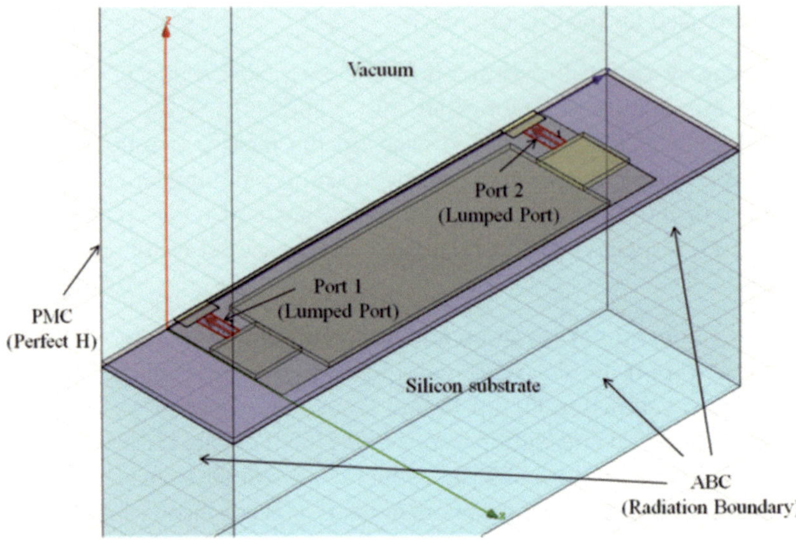

(a) Bird's eye view

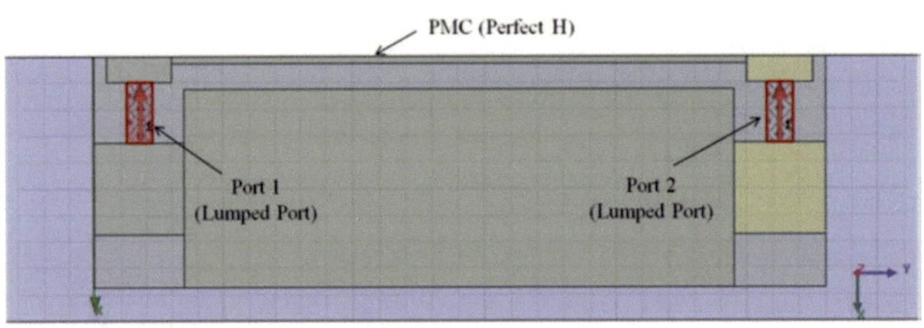

(b) Top view

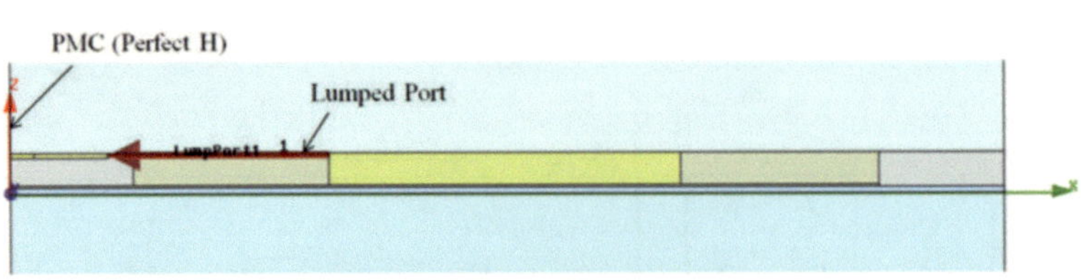

(c) Cross-sectional view

Figure 7. Analysis model of thru-pattern in HFSS.

Figure 8. Chip photo (process: CMOS 0.18μm, chip size: 2.5 mm x 2.5 mm)

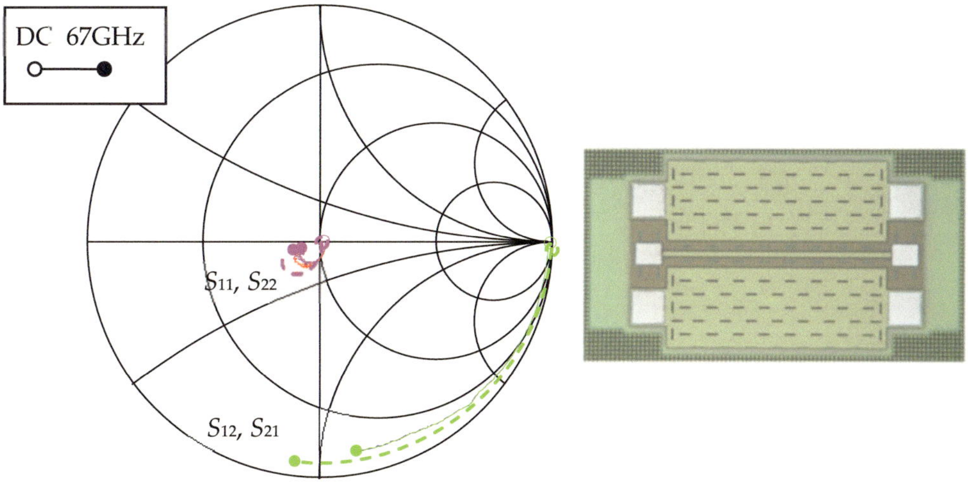

Figure 9. Smith chart of thru-pattern. (Solid line: measurements, broken line: simulation)

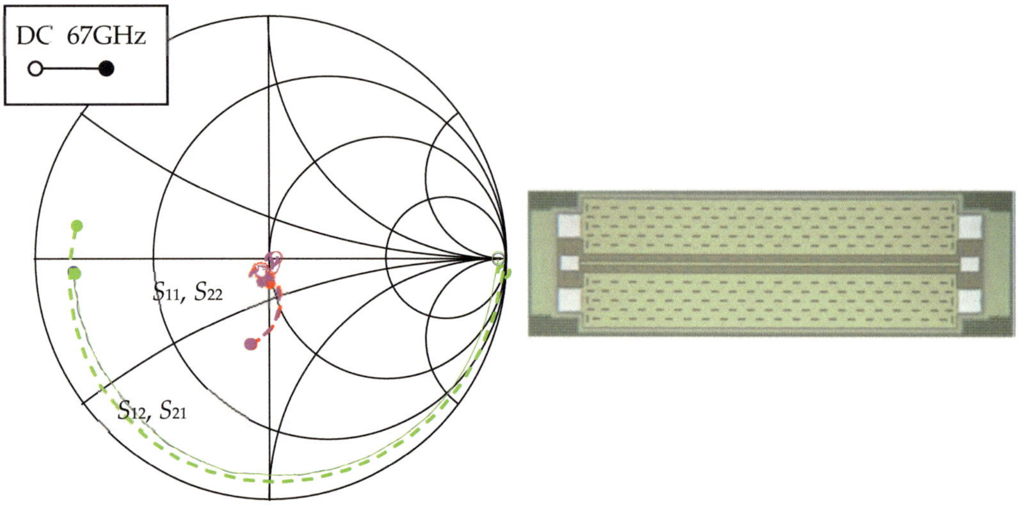

Figure 10. Smith chart of line-pattern in HFSS.

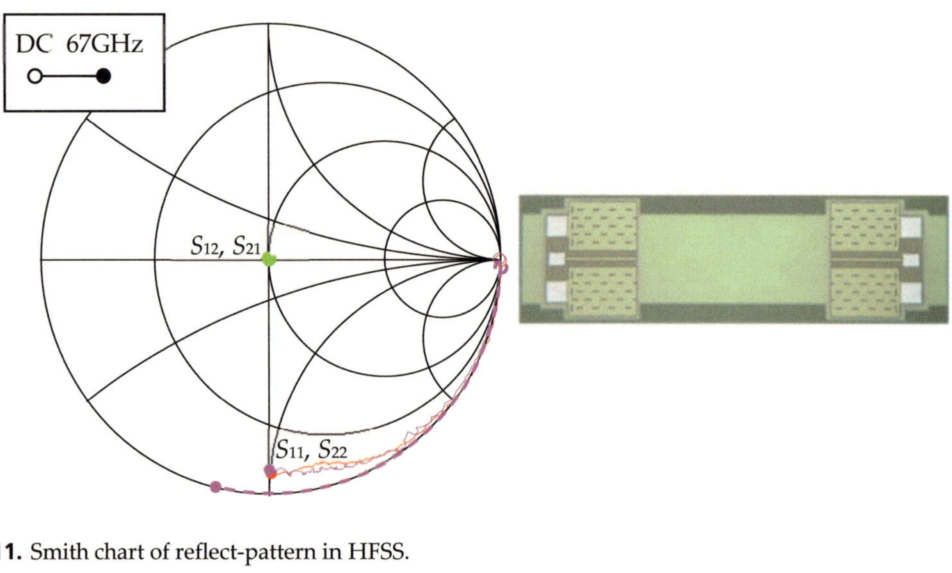

Figure 11. Smith chart of reflect-pattern in HFSS.

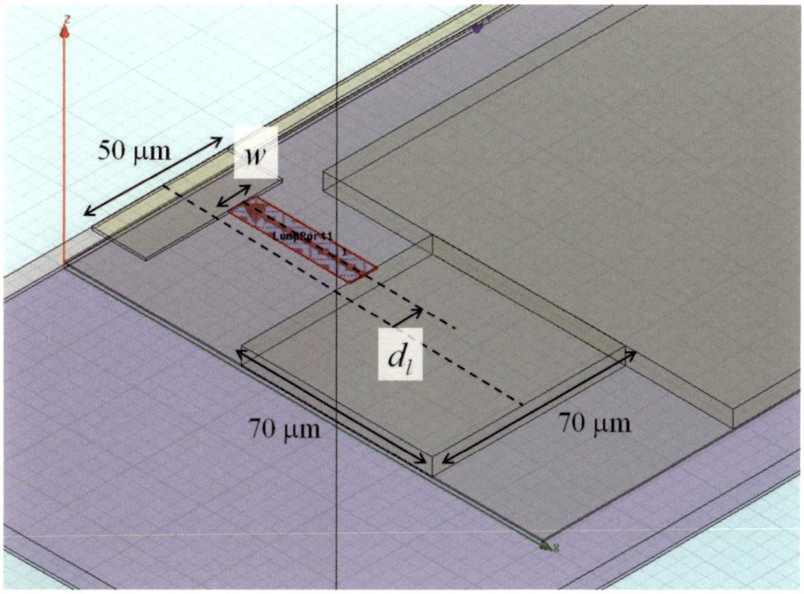

Figure 12. Position and size of lumped port in the GSG pad.

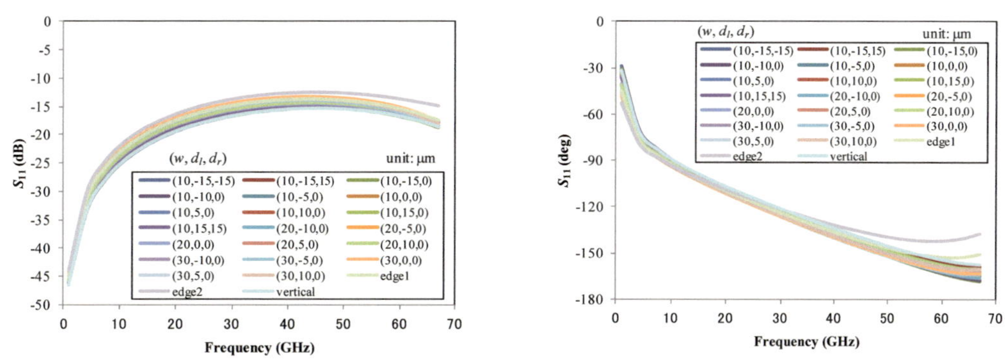

(a) Amplitude (b) Phase

Figure 13. Position sensitivity of lumped port for S_{11} of thru-pattern.

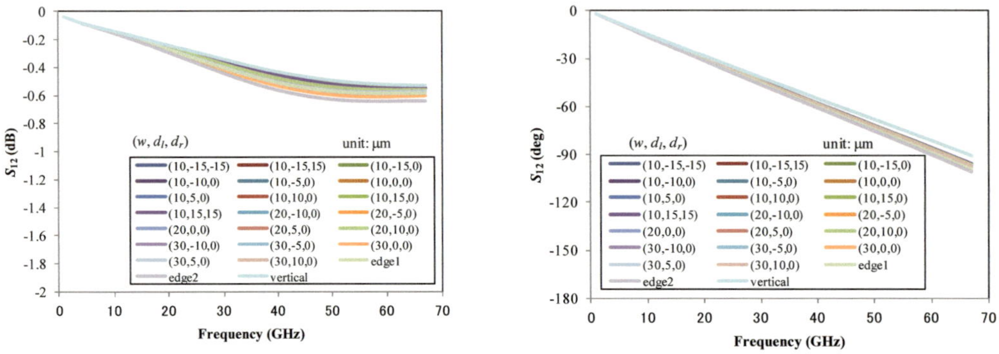

(a) Amplitude (b) Phase

Figure 14. Position sensitivity of lumped port for S_{12} of thru-pattern.

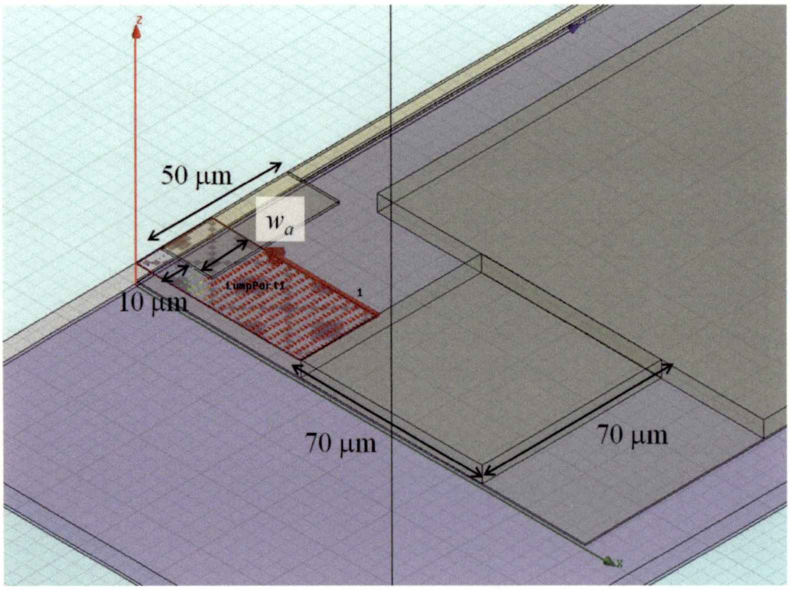

Figure 15. Lumped port arranged at the edge of the GSG pad.

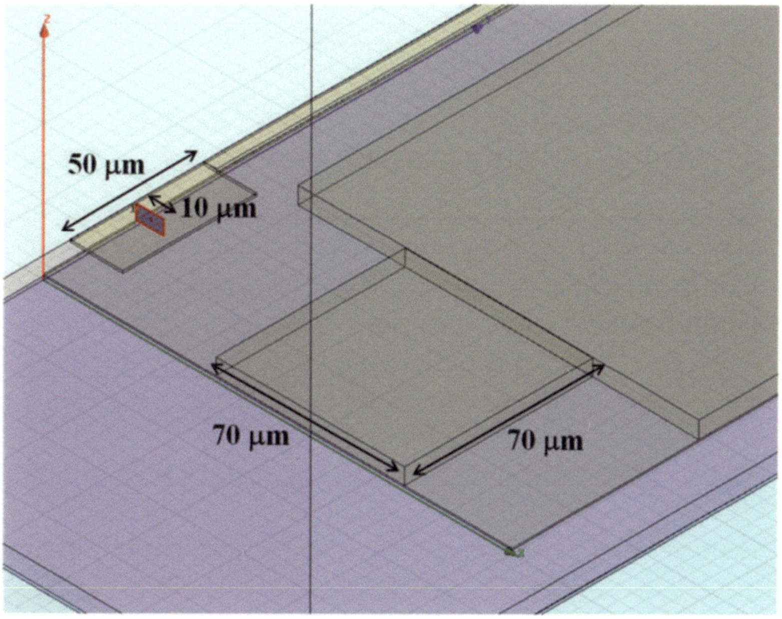

Figure 16. Lumped port arranged vertically in the GSG pad.

4.2. Asymmetric pattern

In this section, excitation modeling is extended in order to treat more general problem. Figure 17 shows EM excitation-modeling for GSG pad include asymmetric pattern while symmetric pattern is considered in the previous section. Port 1, 2, 3 and 4 have 100 Ohm intrinsic impedance when the impedance of the GSG probe is 50 Ohm. The objective of the following discussion is to convert 4×4 S-matrix obtained by simulation into 2×2 S-matrix to compare with VNA measurement. S-matrix for the Figure 17 is written as

$$\begin{bmatrix} b_1 \\ b_2 \\ \hline b_3 \\ b_4 \end{bmatrix} = \left[\begin{array}{cc|cc} S_{11} & S_{12} & S_{13} & S_{14} \\ S_{21} & S_{22} & S_{23} & S_{24} \\ \hline S_{31} & S_{32} & S_{33} & S_{34} \\ S_{41} & S_{42} & S_{43} & S_{44} \end{array}\right] \begin{bmatrix} a_1 \\ a_2 \\ \hline a_3 \\ a_4 \end{bmatrix}. \tag{9}$$

Port 1 and Port 2 are identically excited ($a_1 = a_2 = a_1'$), and Port 3 and Port 4 are also identically excited ($a_3 = a_4 = a_2'$). The GSG pad is symmetric and coming waves to Port 1 and Port 2 are identical ($b_1 = b_2 = b_1'$) because they are guided by the G-MSL. This is same for Port 3 and Port 4 ($b_3 = b_4 = b_2'$).

$$\begin{bmatrix} b_1' \\ b_1' \\ \hline b_2' \\ b_2' \end{bmatrix} = \left[\begin{array}{cc|cc} S_{11} & S_{12} & S_{13} & S_{14} \\ S_{21} & S_{22} & S_{23} & S_{24} \\ \hline S_{31} & S_{32} & S_{33} & S_{34} \\ S_{41} & S_{42} & S_{43} & S_{44} \end{array}\right] \begin{bmatrix} a_1' \\ a_1' \\ \hline a_2' \\ a_2' \end{bmatrix} \tag{10}$$

$$\begin{cases} b_1' = (S_{11} + S_{12})a_1' + (S_{13} + S_{14})a_2' \\ b_1' = (S_{21} + S_{22})a_1' + (S_{23} + S_{24})a_2' \\ b_2' = (S_{31} + S_{32})a_1' + (S_{33} + S_{34})a_2' \\ b_2' = (S_{41} + S_{42})a_1' + (S_{43} + S_{44})a_2' \end{cases} \tag{11}$$

Because of the symmetry of the GSG pad, $S_{11} = S_{22}$, $S_{12} = S_{21}$, $S_{13} = S_{14} = S_{23} = S_{24}$, $S_{31} = S_{32} = S_{41} = S_{42}$, $S_{33} = S_{44}$, $S_{34} = S_{43}$ holds. The first and second equations in (11) are identical. Also, the third and fourth equations in (11) are identical. As a result, the following 2×2 S-matrix is obtained.

$$\begin{bmatrix} S_{11}' & S_{12}' \\ S_{21}' & S_{22}' \end{bmatrix} = \begin{bmatrix} S_{11} + S_{12} & S_{13} + S_{14} \\ S_{31} + S_{32} & S_{33} + S_{34} \end{bmatrix} \tag{12}$$

If only one GSG probe is used to measure reflection, the reflection coefficient can be obtained by

$$\Gamma = \frac{b}{a} = S_{11} + S_{12} = S_{21} + S_{22}. \tag{13}$$

To verify the formulation of (12), the EM excitation-modeling for thru-pattern shown in Figure 18 is compared with the modeling shown in Figure 7. Figure 19 shows the frequency characteristic of reflection and transmission coefficient for the thru-pattern. The result indicated by "Cal" is obtained by the model in Figure 7, and the result indicated by "Cal (4-ports to 2-ports)" is obtained by the model in Figure 18. They agreed very well each other. Figure 19 shows two short-circuited lines, which have asymmetric structure as an example. Figure 20 shows the frequency characteristic of S-parameters for the structure shown in Figure 19. Calculated results agreed very well with measured results, and (12) is validated.

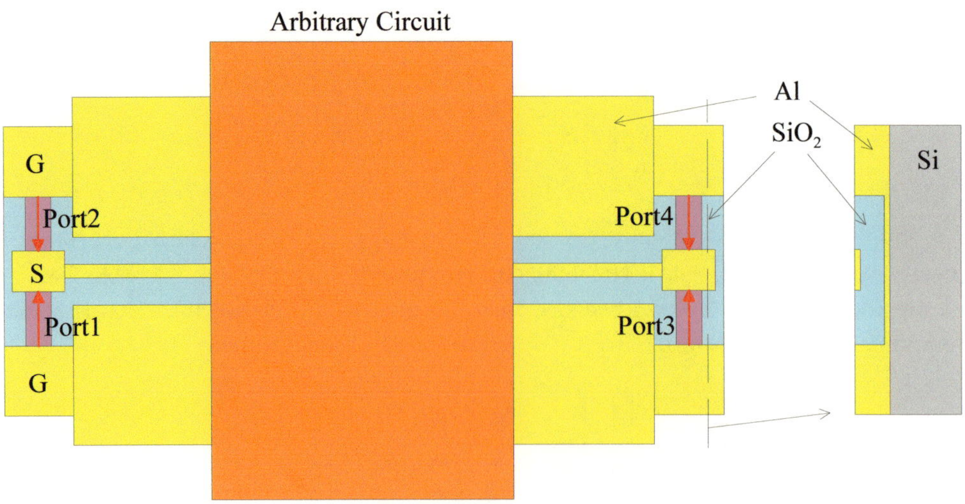

Figure 17. EM excitation-modeling for GSG pad include asymmetric pattern.

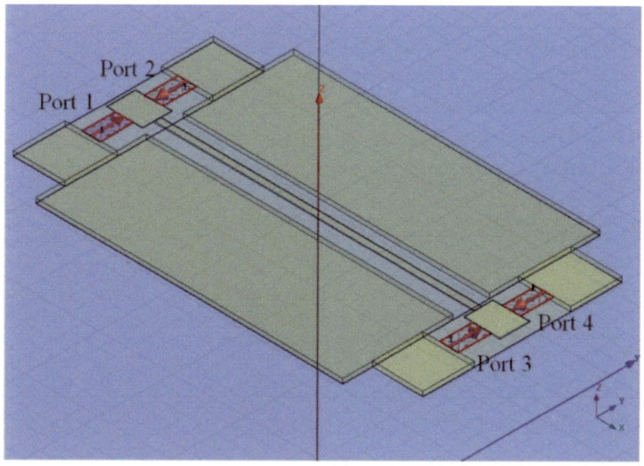

Figure 18. Four port excitation model for thru-pattern.

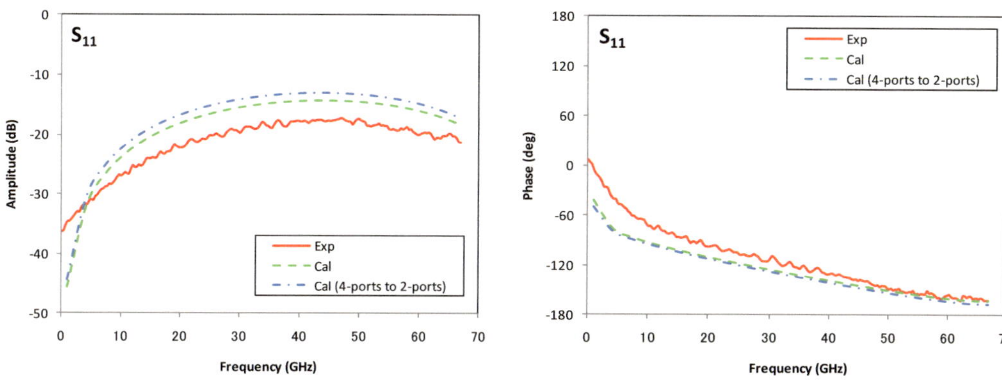

(a) Reflection coefficient S_{11}

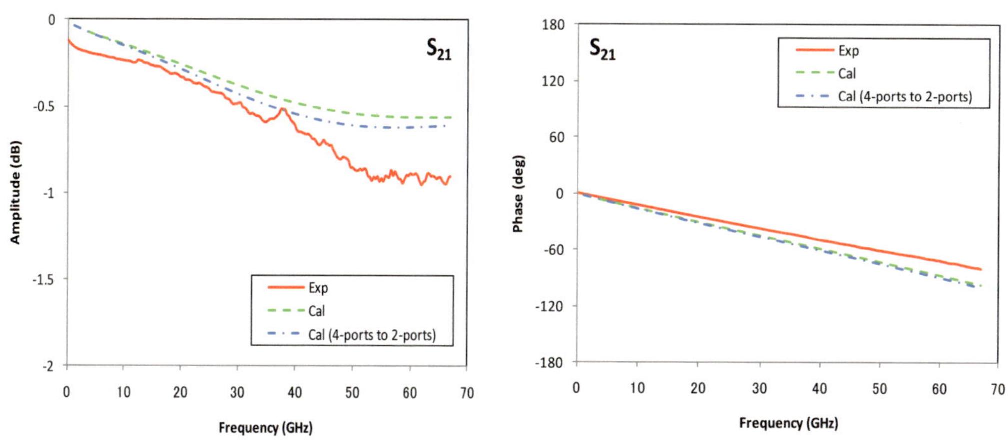

(b) Transmission coefficient S_{21}

Figure 19. Comparison between two-port and four-port excitation model for thru-pattern.

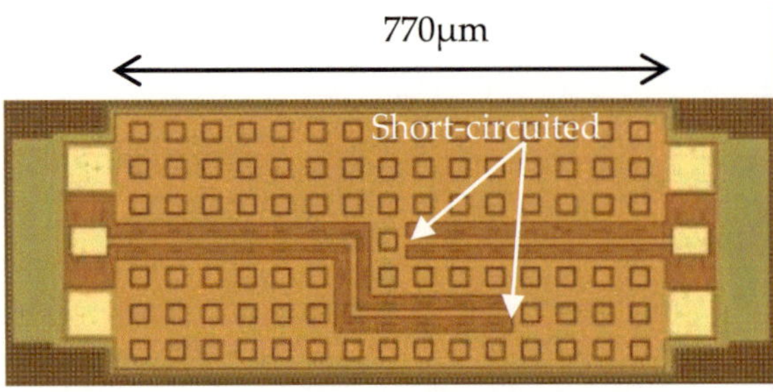

(a) Micrograph

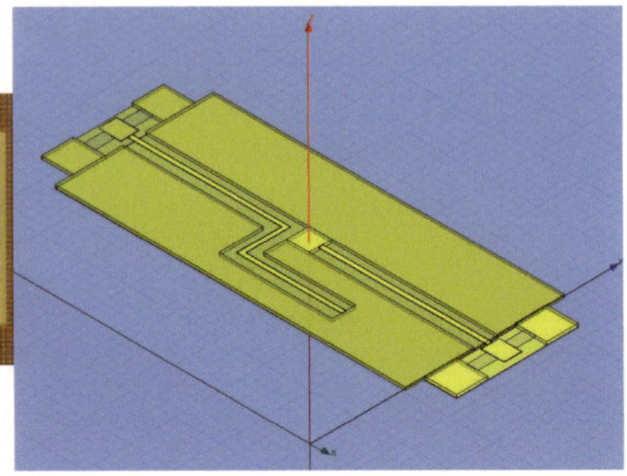

(b) Analysis model in HFSS

Figure 20. Two short-circuited lines.

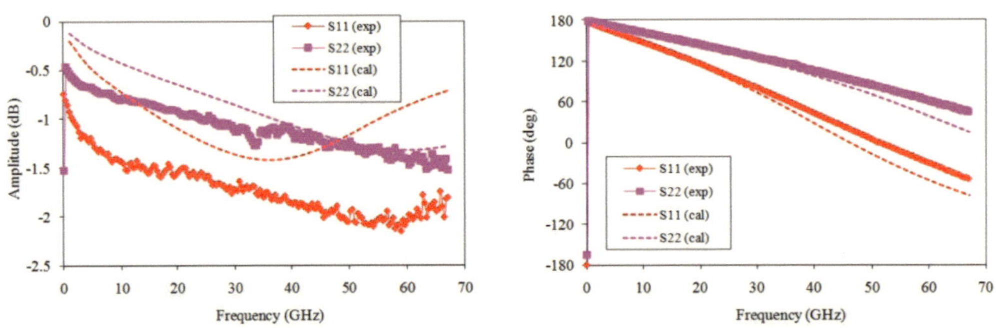

(a) Reflection coefficient S_{11} and S_{22}

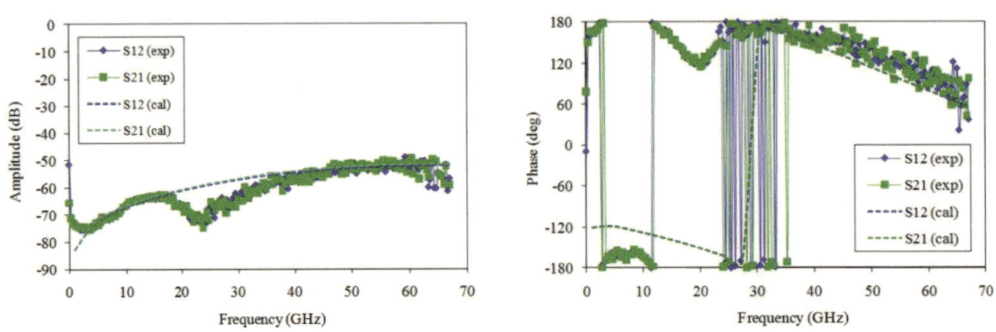

(b) Transmission coefficient S_{12}, S_{21}

Figure 21. Frequency characteristic of S-parameters for two short-circuited lines shown in Figure 20.

5. Results

5.1. Comparison of accuracy between de-embedding techniques

The frequency characteristic of the propagation constant for the G-MSL is extracted by de-embedding techniques, and shown in Figure 22. The solid and broken lines represent results without and with dummy metal fills (5 m square; w=5 m and p=10 m in Figure 3) in the G-MSL, respectively. The loss of the G-MSL with dummy metal fills is slightly larger than that without dummy metal fills. The phase constant of the G-MSL with dummy metal fills is slightly larger than that without dummy metal fills because the dummy metal fills result in an effect like an artificial dielectric compound. The line with "Cal." is the calculated result with the method in [15]. The measured results agreed well with the calculations. Figure 22 shows that the accuracy of TL de-embedding technique is as good as that of the TRL de-embedding technique.

Figure 23 shows the characteristic impedance of the transmission lines. The characteristic impedance was obtained from the ratio of the voltage V to the current I. The voltage V is calculated by the tangential line integral of the electric field from the ground plane to the signal line. One half of the current $I/2$ is calculated by the tangential line integral of the magnetic field around the signal line. The characteristic impedance is obtained using the de-embedding technique [16] together with a characterization of the pads using the TL de-embedding technique. Very good agreement between the calculated and measured results was obtained. As the frequency increases, the real part of the characteristic impedance approaches 50 Ohm and the imaginary part of the characteristic impedance approaches 0 Ohm.

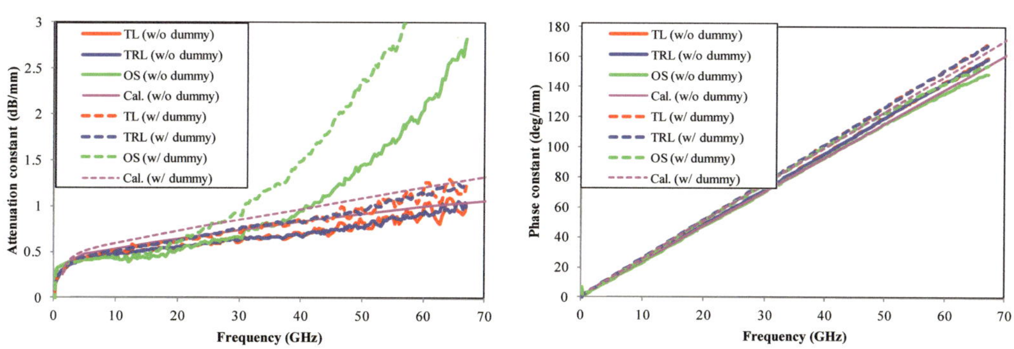

(a) Attenuation constant (b) Phase constant

Figure 22. Extracted propagation constant of the G-MSL.

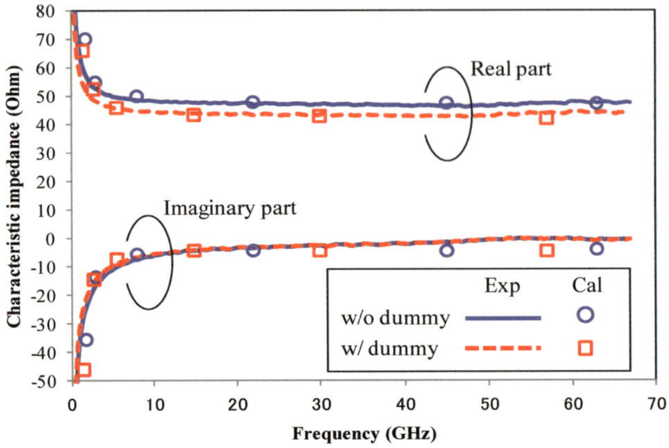

Figure 23. Extracted Characteristic impedance of the G-MSL.

5.2. Accuracy investigation of open/short de-embedding technique

The accuracy of de-embedding methods using thru-line patterns, thru-reflect-line patterns and open/short patterns will be discussed numerically in this section. Open and short patterns used in the simulation are shown Figure 24. The lengths from left and right pads to the open or short ends are $l/2$. Figure 25 shows the transmission coefficient S_{21} for the G-MSL with the length of 600 μm extracted by each method. The line with "3-D FEM (HFSS)" is the result directly obtained by the S_{21} of the 3-D FEM analysis using wave port excitation in HFSS. The line with "2-D FEM (HFSS)" is the result obtained using the propagation constant analyzed by the port solution by the 2-D FEM analysis in HFSS. These must be identical, and the differences are negligible. The results with "TRL", "TL", and "OS" are obtained after de-embedding the influence of the pads and using the TRL, TL, and open/short de-embedding techniques, respectively. Except for the "OS" they agreed very well with the results of the "3-D FEM (HFSS)," and the effectiveness of the TL and TRL de-embedding methods is verified. The accuracy of the open/short de-embedding method becomes poorer as the frequency increases. This is because the pads cannot be approximated well by an equivalent circuit in the high frequency band [12]. The accuracy of the "OS" can be improved if patterns with shorter lengths are used [17]. The accuracy of the TL de-embedding method is as good as that of TRL de-embedding method, allowing the conclusion that the accuracy of the TL de-embedding method is validated.

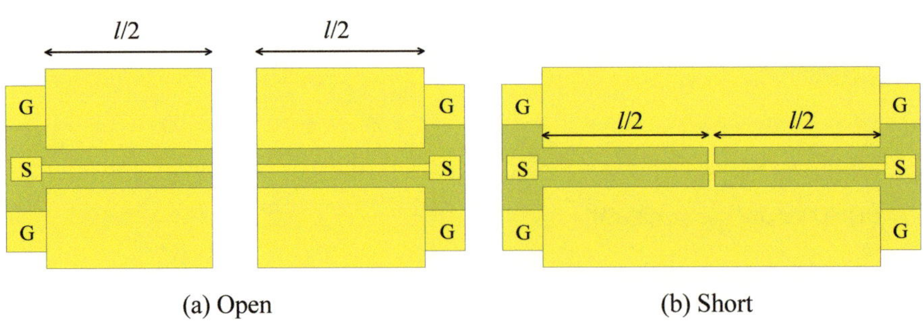

Figure 24. Extracted Characteristic impedance of the G-MSL.

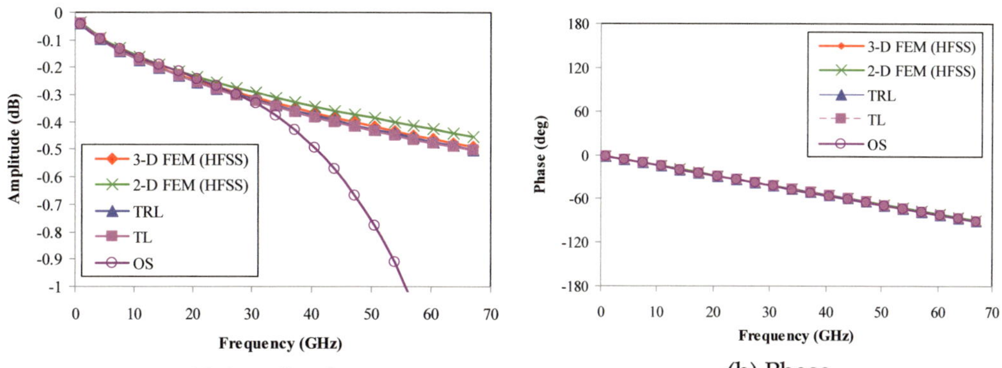

(a) Amplitude (b) Phase

Figure 25. Extracted transmission coefficient S_{21} of the 600 μm-length G-MSL (l=420 μm in Figure 24).

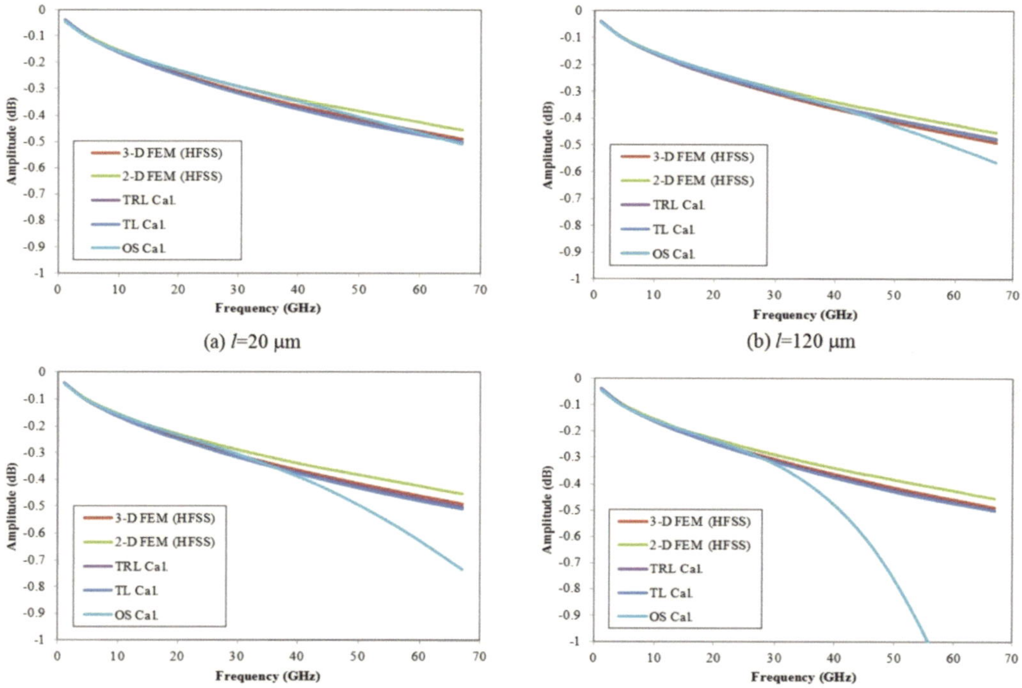

(a) l=20 μm (b) l=120 μm

(c) l=220 μm (d) l=420 μm

Figure 26. Extracted transmission coefficient S_{21} of the 600 μm-length G-MSL for several length of open/short patterns.

To investigate the accuracy of the open-short de-embedding technique, numerical simulation was performed to extract S_{21} of a G-MSL with 600 μm-length. Figure 26 shows extracted S_{21} for the 600 μm-length G-MSL using calibration patterns with l=20 μm, 120 μm, 220 μm, 420 μm, respectively. A line of "3-D FEM (HFSS)" is the result obtained by S_{21} of the 3-D FEM analysis for the 600 μm-length G-MSL. The result indicated by "2-D FEM (HFSS)" is port analysis solution. Results indicated by "TRL", "TL" and "OS" are obtained after applying TRL, TL, and open-short de-embedding techniques, respectively. Results are obtained by simulation using HFSS. The accuracy of the TRL and TL de-embedding techniques is very good while that of open-short de-embedding technique differs in high frequency. The accuracy becomes higher as the length l of the open and short patterns becomes shorter. Figure 27 shows the error of the extracted S_{21} defined by

$$error \equiv \left| \frac{S_{21}^{\text{true}} - S_{21}^{\text{extracted}}}{S_{21}^{\text{true}}} \right|. \tag{14}$$

The result indicated by "3-D FEM (HFSS)" is used for S_{21}^{true}. The error becomes larger when the length of the open and short pattern becomes longer.

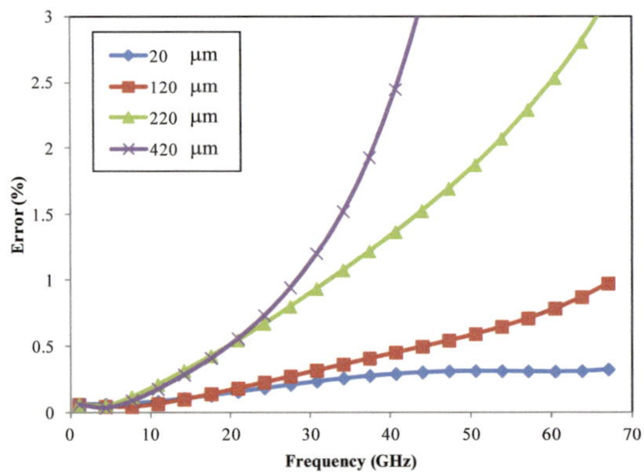

Figure 27. Error of the extracted transmission coefficient S_{21} of the 600 μm-length G-MSL with open-short de-embedding technique.

6. Conclusion

In this paper, EM simulation modeling for on-wafer measurement using a GSG probe was presented. The gap between ground (G) and signal (S) pads is excited by a lumped source. Transformation formula from 4-port to 2-port S-matrix expression was derived. The accuracy of EM simulation was verified by comparing with measurements. Results of EM simulation by changing excitation model suggest that the probe positioning error is not serious in measurement.

TL de-embedding technique was applied for on-wafer measurement using a GSG probe. The accuracy of de-embedding techniques (open-short, TRL, and TL) were compared and discussed. It was found that the accuracy of TRL and TL de-embedding technique is approximately the same. Degradation of accuracy in open-short de-embedding technique was quantitatively investigated via numerical simulation. In the open-short de-embedding technique, the accuracy becomes higher as the lengths of the open and short patterns become shorter.

Author details

Takuichi Hirano, Kenichi Okada, Jiro Hirokawa and Makoto Ando
Tokyo Institute of Technology, Japan

Acknowledgement

This work was supported in part by Semiconductor Technology Academic Research Center (STARC). The chip in this study has been fabricated in the chip fabrication program of the VLSI Design and Education Center (VDEC), the University of Tokyo in collaboration with Rohm Corporation and Toppan Printing Corporation. The authors would like to express their deepest gratitude to Toshihiko Mori of FUJITSU, Osamu Kobayashi of STARC, Naoko Ono of TOSHIBA, Toshiakira Ando of STARC/PANASONIC, and Ryuichi Fujimoto of STARC /TOSHIBA for their fruitful discussion.

Appendix

Example Mathematica [13] code is shown here.

```
In[1]:= sol = Solve[{ρl == s11 + (s12sq*s22*Γ^2)/(1 - s22^2*Γ^2), τl == (s12sq*Γ)/(1 - s22^2*Γ^2), ρt == s11 + (s12sq*s22)/(1 - s22^2), τt == s12sq/(1 - s22^2)},
        {s11, s12sq, s22, Γ}] // Simplify;
   s11A[ρl_, τl_, ρt_, τt_] = s11 /. sol[[1]];
   s12sqA[ρl_, τl_, ρt_, τt_] = s12sq /. sol[[1]];
   s22A[ρl_, τl_, ρt_, τt_] = s22 /. sol[[1]];
   ΓA[ρl_, τl_, ρt_, τt_] = Γ /. sol[[1]];

   s11B[ρl_, τl_, ρt_, τt_] = s11 /. sol[[2]];
   s12sqB[ρl_, τl_, ρs_, τs_] = s12sq /. sol[[2]];
   s22B[ρl_, τl_, ρt_, τt_] = s22 /. sol[[2]];
   ΓB[ρl_, τl_, ρt_, τt_] = Γ /. sol[[2]];

   (* Choose one of two solution sets *)
   s11[ρl_, τl_, ρt_, τt_] := s11A[ρl, τl, ρt, τt];
   s12sq[ρl_, τl_, ρt_, τt_] := s12sqA[ρl, τl, ρt, τt];
   s22[ρl_, τl_, ρt_, τt_] := s22A[ρl, τl, ρt, τt];
   Γ[ρl_, τl_, ρt_, τt_] := ΓA[ρl, τl, ρt, τt];

In[14]:= (* Formulas *)
   TransStoT[s_] := 1/s[[2, 1]] * ( -Det[s]      s[[1, 1]]
                                    -s[[2, 2]]   1         );
   TransTtoS[t_] := 1/t[[2, 2]] * ( t[[1, 2]]    Det[t]
                                    1            -t[[2, 1]] );
```

```
In[16]:= (* Thru-Line (TL) De-embedding *)
l1 = 420.0 * 10^-6; l2 = 1020.0 * 10^-6; dl = l2 - l1; dlScale = 0. * 10^-6;

(* Thru *)
smt = ( 1. * 10^-16    1.
        1.             1. * 10^-16 ); (* Read measured data *)
tmt = TransStoT[smt];
(* Line *)
sml = ( 2. * 10^-16    Exp[I * 1]
        Exp[-I * 1]    2. * 10^-16 ); (* Read measured data *)
tml = TransStoT[sml];
(* Device to be extracted *)
smd = ( 1.  2.
        3.  4. ); (* Read measured data *)
tmd = TransStoT[smd];

(* Thru *)
ρt = smt[[1, 1]];
τt = smt[[1, 2]];
(* Line *)
ρl = sml[[1, 1]];
τl = sml[[1, 2]];

In[27]:= sal = ( 1.0 * 10^-16              Γ[ρl, τl, ρt, τt]
                 Γ[ρl, τl, ρt, τt]          1.0 * 10^-16 );

spadL = ( s11[ρl, τl, ρt, τt]             √s12sq[ρl, τl, ρt, τt]
          √s12sq[ρl, τl, ρt, τt]          s22[ρl, τl, ρt, τt] );
tpadL = TransStoT[spadL];
spadR = ( s22[ρl, τl, ρt, τt]             √s12sq[ρl, τl, ρt, τt]
          √s12sq[ρl, τl, ρt, τt]          s11[ρl, τl, ρt, τt] );
tpadR = TransStoT[spadR];

γ = -Log[Γ[ρl, τl, ρt, τt]] / dl;
sdlScale = ( 1. * 10^-16                 Exp[-γ * dlScale]
             Exp[-γ * dlScale]           1. * 10^-16 );
tdlScale = TransStoT[sdlScale];
tpadL = tpadL.tdlScale;
tpadR = tdlScale.tpadR;

tal = Inverse[tpadL].tml.Inverse[tpadR];
sal = TransTtoS[tal];

tad = Inverse[tpadL].tmd.Inverse[tpadR];
sad = TransTtoS[tad];
```

Check (identical to smd?)

```
In[41]:= TransTtoS[tpadL.tad.tpadR] // Chop

Out[41]= {{1., 2.}, {3., 4.}}
```

7. References

[1] G.F. Engen and C.A. Hoer, "'Thru-Reflect-Line': an improved technique for calibrating the dual six-port automatic network analyzer," IEEE Trans. Microwave Theory Tech., vol.MTT-27, No.12, Dec. 1979.

[2] P. Colestock and M. Foley, "A generalized TRL Algorithm for S-parameter de-embedding," Fermi National Accelerator Laboratory Technical Memo, TM-1781, April 1993.

[3] D. Rytting, IEEE MTT/ED seminar on Calibration and Error Correction Techniques for Network Analysis, OGI Center for Professional Development, September, 2004.

[4] M.C.A.M. Koolen, J.A.M. Geelen, and M.P.J.G. Versleijen, "An improved de-embedding technique for on-wafer high-frequency characterization," Proc. IEEE, Bipolar/BiCMOS Circuits and Tech. Meeting, pp.188-191, Sept. 1991.

[5] S. Georgakopoulos and S. Ogurtsov, "An S-parameter extraction technique for broad-band characterization of microstrip-to-SIW transitions," IEEE AP-S Dig., 428.4, June 2009.

[6] J.C. Rautio, "A de-embedding algorithm for electromagnetics," Int. J. Microwave Millimeter-Wave Computer-Aided Eng., vol.1, no.3, pp.282-287, 1991.

[7] H. Ito and K. Masu, "A simple through-only de-embedding method for on-wafer S-parameter measurements up to 110GHz," IEEE MTT-S International Microwave Symposium (IMS), pp. 383-386, June 2008.

[8] N. Li, K. Matsushita, N. Takayama, S. Ito, K. Okada, and A. Matsuzawa, "Evaluation of a multi-line de-embedding technique up to 110 GHz for millimeter-wave CMOS circuit design," IEICE Trans. Fundamentals, vol.E93-A, No.2, pp. 431-439, Feb. 2010.

[9] Q.-H. Bu, N. Li, K. Bunsen, H. Asada, K. Matsushita, K. Okada, and A. Matsuzawa, "Evaluation of a multi-line de-embedding technique for millimeter-wave CMOS circuit design," Asia-Pacific Microwave Conference (APMC), Yokohama, Japan, Dec. 2010.

[10] T. Hirano, K. Okada, J. Hirokawa, and M. Ando, "Thru-Line (TL) calibration technique for on-wafer measurement," Proceedings of International Symposium on Antennas and Propagation (ISAP), Paper ID: 104, Macao, November 23-26, 2010.

[11] M.A.T. Sanduleanu and J.R. Long, "CMOS integrated transceivers for 60GHz UWB communication," IEEE International Conference on Ultra-Wideband (ICUWB), pp.508-513, Singapore, September 2007.

[12] T. Hirano, H. Nakano, Y. Hirachi, J. Hirokawa, and M. Ando, "De-embedding method using an electromagnetic simulator for characterization of transistors in the millimeter-wave band," IEEE Transactions on Microwave Theory and Techniques, Vol.58, No.10, pp.2663-2672, October 2010.

[13] Mathematica, Wolfram Research, Champaign, IL [Online]. Available: http://www.wolfram.com/
[14] Ansoft HFSS. ver. 11, Ansoft, Pittsburgh, PA, 2009. [Online]. Available: http://www.ansoft.com/products/hf/hfss/
[15] Y. Ono, T. Hirano, K. Okada, J. Hirokawa, and M. Ando, "Eigenmode Analysis of Propagation Constant for a Microstrip Line with Dummy Fills on a Si CMOS Substrate," IEICE Trans. Electron., Vol.E94-C No.6, pp.1008-1015, June 2011.
[16] A.M. Mangan, S.P. Voinigescu, M.-T. Yang, and M. Tazlauanu, "De-embedding transmission line measurements for accurate modeling of IC designs," IEEE Trans. Electron Devices, vol.53, No.2, pp.235-241, Feb. 2006.
[17] T. Hirano, K. Okada, J. Hirokawa, and M. Ando, "Accuracy investigation of the de-embedding technique using open and short patterns for on-wafer RF characterization," Asia-Pacific Microwave Conference (APMC), TH3G-44, poster, pp.1436-1439, Yokohama, Japan, Dec. 2010.

Chapter 12

Analytical Model and Numerical Simulation for the Transconductance and Drain Conductance of GaAs MESFETs

Saadeddine Khemissi

Additional information is available at the end of the chapter

http://dx.doi.org/10.5772/47741

1. Introduction

The analytical model and simulation numerical of semiconductor devices is one of the important steps for Integrate Circuit fabrication, verification and characterization. Each semiconductor device has models that satisfies the requirements to the device under different operating conditions. GaAs MESFET is a promising semiconductor device used in many applications in the microwave domain. The elements which compose the MESFET transistors can be gathered in two distinct categories. There are extrinsic and intrinsic elements; the first category represents the different structures of access like the side resistances *Rs* and *Rd*. The intrinsic elements like the transconductance g_m and drain conductance g_d translate by their nature and their behavior localized of the device physical structure. Our main aim in these sheets related on the one hand to the optimization of a two dimensional (2D) analytical model for the static characteristics of short gate-length GaAs MESFET's, this model takes into account the different physical specific phenomena of the device, and on the other hand to calculate the variation of some intrinsic elements (transconductance and drain conductance) as a function of the biasing voltages. The model suggested has enables to us to calculate and trace the different series from curves. The results obtained are well represented and interpreted.

2. General characteristics of the model

The major features of this study are:

To solve the system of the two dimensional partial differential equations, we based for the works of Chin and Wu (1992, 1993), the Green's function technique is used in these references to solved the two dimensional Poisson's equation, this technique gives an acceptable distribution of the space charge and a form of the depletion area in agreement with the physical phenomena specific to this device.

To determine the depletion-layer width, we have considered first the one-dimensional approximation (Sze and Ng, 2007), then we add the corrective which results from the two-dimensional analysis.

To determine the electron mobility law in the semiconductor, we have considered that described by Chang and Day (1989).

To calculate the drain current expression as a function of the drain-source and gate-source voltages, we divided the channel under the gate in regions (linear, non-linear and saturated) according to the electric field.

In order to simplify the mathematical study and consequently the numerical simulation, we used some assumptions and approximations.

To determine the *I-V* extrinsic characteristics in different operations regimes, we used the iterative method.

To determine the transconductance and drain conductance as a function of the drain-source and gate-source voltages in different operations regimes, we based also for the numerical simulation methods.

2. Analytical model

2.1. Determination of the potential under the gate

The potential distribution in the active layer under the gate is modeled by solving the Poisson's equation with proper boundary conditions, in two-dimensions this equation is given by:

$$\Delta\psi(x,y) = \frac{\partial^2\psi(x,y)}{\partial x^2} + \frac{\partial^2\psi(x,y)}{\partial y^2} = -\frac{\rho(x,y)}{\varepsilon} \tag{1}$$

where $\psi(x, y)$ is the potential in the active-layer.
$\rho\ (x, y)$ is the density of the majority carriers in the channel.
ε is the dielectric permittivity of semiconductor.

If the channel doping is homogeneous, the activity area density is written

$$\rho(x,y) = \rho(y) = eN_d(y) \tag{2}$$

where $N_d(y)$ is the doping profile in semiconductor.

To simplify the study, one considers that this equation is a superposition of two simple equations. In this connection, one can write:

$$\psi(x,y) = U(y) + \varphi(x,y) \tag{3}$$

where

$$U(y) = \iint \frac{-eN_d(y)}{\varepsilon} dy^2 \tag{4}$$

and

$$\frac{\partial^2 \varphi(x,y)}{\partial x^2} + \frac{\partial^2 \varphi(x,y)}{\partial y^2} = 0 \tag{5}$$

In such a way, according to formula (3 – 5) the process of solving the initial Poisson's equation consists of looking-for of solution to one-dimensional equation (Eq. 4) and solving the two-dimensional equation (Eq. 5).

2.2. Boundary conditions

The above solution of the Poisson's equation has to verify the equations and boundary conditions expressed as:

$$\psi(x,0) = 0 \tag{6}$$

$$\psi(0,y) = Vb - Vg \tag{7}$$

$$\psi(L,y) = Vd + Vb - Vg \tag{8}$$

where Vg is the intrinsic gate-source voltage, Vd is the intrinsic drain-source voltage and Vb is the built-in voltage of the Schottky barrier.

If the drain voltage is equal to zero, the symmetry between the two gate-sides leads to the following condition:

$$\psi(0,y)\big|_{Vd=0} = \psi(L,y)\big|_{Vd=0} \tag{9}$$

At the first point of the pinch-off, the electron velocity attains its maximum and the electric field with drain side's corresponds to the saturation field E_S.

$$\left.\frac{\partial \psi(x,y)}{\partial x}\right|_{(L,a)} = E_S \tag{10}$$

The electric field must vanish in the depletion-layer edges at both gate-sides; this field may cause a large current flow. Therefore, it may be written:

$$E_{\vec{n}}\big|_S = 0 \tag{11}$$

and

$$E_{\vec{n}}\Big|_D = 0 \tag{12}$$

where $\vec{n}$ is the outward unit vector at the depletion-layer edge.

2.3. 1D approximation

By integrating the equation (4) from *0* to *h (x)*, we determine the term *U (y)*, and one obtains:

$$U(h) = \frac{eN_d}{2\varepsilon} h(x)^2 \tag{13}$$

The one-dimensional depletion layer width *hx* at any *x* coordinate is given by the one-sided abrupt junction depletion approximation (Sze and Ng, 2007).

$$h_X = \sqrt{\frac{2\varepsilon\left(V(x) + Vb - Vg\right)}{eN_d}} \tag{14}$$

where *V(x)* is the potential of the neutral channel with *V(0) = 0* at the source-end and *V(L) = Vd* at the drain-end. So that the one-dimensional depletion widths at the source and drain ends given respectively by:

$$h_S = \sqrt{\frac{2\varepsilon\left(Vb - Vg\right)}{eN_d}} \tag{15}$$

$$h_D = \sqrt{\frac{2\varepsilon\left(Vd + Vb - Vg\right)}{eN_d}} \tag{16}$$

2.4. 2D analytical model

To determine the second term, we based for the works Chin and Wu (1992, 1993), Jit et al. (2003, 2011) and Morarka and Mishra. (2005), these studies are used the Green's functions and superposition techniques. In the homogeneous medium, the solution suggested is written in the following form:

$$\varphi(x,y) = \left[A_1^S \frac{\sinh\left(k_1(L-x)\right)}{\sinh\left(k_1 L\right)} + A_1^D \frac{\sinh\left(k_1 x\right)}{\sinh\left(k_1 L\right)} \right] \sin\left(k_1 y\right) \tag{17}$$

where

$$k_1 = \frac{\pi}{2a} \tag{18}$$

$$A_1^S = Vp\left[a_1 + b_1\left(\frac{Vb - Vg}{Vp} - c_1 \right)^{1/2} \right] \tag{19}$$

and

$$A_1^D = Vp\left[a_1 + b_1\left(\frac{Vd + Vb - Vg}{Vp} - c_1\right)^{1/2}\right] \tag{20}$$

$A^S{}_1$ and $A^D{}_1$ are the first term of Fourier coefficient for the excess sidewall potential at the source and drain sides of the gate respectively.

a_1, b_1 and c_1 are constants related to the device structure.

From (13) and (17), one obtains the expression of total tension $\psi\ (x, y)$:

$$\psi(x,y) = \frac{eN_d}{2\varepsilon}h^2(x)\left[A_1^S\frac{\sinh(k_1(L-x))}{\sinh(k_1L)} + A_1^D\frac{\sinh(k_1x)}{\sinh(k_1L)}\right]\sin(k_1y) \tag{21}$$

2.5. Depletion-layer width

To calculate the two dimensional width of the depletion layer formed by the Schottky barrier W_X at any x coordinate, we have considered firstly the one-dimensional approximation h_X then we have added the corrective which results with the two-dimensional analysis. So the Eqs. (14 ~ 16) becomes respectively as follows:

$$W_X = \sqrt{\frac{2\varepsilon\left(V(x) + Vb - Vg - \varphi(x,h_X)\right)}{eN_d}} \tag{22}$$

$$W_S = \sqrt{\frac{2\varepsilon\left(Vb - Vg - \varphi(0,h_S)\right)}{eN_d}} \tag{23}$$

$$W_D = \sqrt{\frac{2\varepsilon\left(Vd + Vb - Vg - \varphi(L,h_D)\right)}{eN_d}} \tag{24}$$

where the correctives are determinate by:

$$\varphi\left(x,h(x)\right) = \left[A_1^S\frac{\sinh\left(k_1\left(L-x\right)\right)}{\sinh(k_1L)} + A_1^D\frac{\sinh\left(k_1.x\right)}{\sinh(k_1L)}\right]\sin\left(\frac{\pi}{2}\sqrt{\frac{Vb - Vg + V(x)}{Vp}}\right) \tag{25}$$

$$\varphi\left(0,h_S\right) = A_1^S\sin\left(\frac{\pi}{2}\sqrt{\frac{Vb - Vg}{Vp}}\right) \tag{26}$$

$$\varphi\left(L,h_D\right) = A_1^D\sin\left(\frac{\pi}{2}\sqrt{\frac{Vd + Vb - Vg}{Vp}}\right) \tag{27}$$

and the pinch-off voltage:

$$Vp = \frac{eN_d}{2\varepsilon} a^2 \tag{28}$$

2.6. The electron mobility law

For gallium arsenide GaAs, the analytical expression of the electron mobility dependence of the electric field which used in this study is a simplified mathematical relation (Chang and Day, 1989; Shin and Klemer 1992) given as follows:

For the feeble electric fields where $E < E_0$, the electrons are in thermodynamic balance with their mobility, the later is constant and independent of the electric field, in this connection:

$$\mu(E) = \mu_0 \tag{29}$$

As the electric field becomes more growth where $E \geq E_0$ the interactions of the carriers with the vibrations of the network involve a reduction in the mobility of the electrons. The law of this mobility in this case is given by:

$$\mu(E) = \frac{\mu_0}{\left[1 + \left(\frac{E - E_0}{E_C}\right)^2\right]^{\frac{1}{2}}} \tag{30}$$

where

$$E_C = \frac{v_S}{\mu_0} \tag{31}$$

$$E_0 = \frac{1}{2}\left[E_S + \left(E_S^2 - 4E_C^2\right)^{\frac{1}{2}}\right] \tag{32}$$

$$\left.\frac{dv(E)}{dE}\right|_{E=E_S} = 0 \tag{33}$$

2.7. I-V caractéristics

In general, it is possible that the channel current is expressed as a function of the intrinsic grille-source and drain-source voltages in terms of physical dimensions. The basic equation used to derive the *I-V* relationship (Sze and Ng, 2007) is given by:

$$Id = \frac{Zq^2N_d^2\mu(E)}{\varepsilon L}\int_{W_S}^{W_D}\left(a - W\right)WdW \tag{34}$$

By simple integration, *Id* becomes as:

$$Id = Ip\left[\left(u_D^2 - u_S^2\right) - \frac{2}{3}\left(u_D^3 - u_S^3\right)\right] \tag{35}$$

where

$$Ip = \frac{Zq^2N_d^2\mu(E)a^3}{2\varepsilon L} \tag{36}$$

$$u_D = \frac{W_D}{a} \tag{37}$$

$$u_S = \frac{W_S}{a} \tag{38}$$

u_D and u_S are the normalized dimensionless units.

The mobility law makes it possible to obtain the different expressions of the drain-current in the different operation regimes (linear, non-linear and saturated). Fig. 1 shows the structure of a MESFET with the channel under the gate. It can be divided in general into three regions (L_A, L_B and L_C) depending upon the magnitude of the electric field (Shin and Klemer, 1992; Khemissi et al. 2004, 2006). In the region L_A the electric field is below E_0, and the electron mobility is given by equation (29), region L_B correspond the electric field is between E_0 and E_S and the electron mobility is given by equation (30), the last L_C is the high field region in which the electric field exceeds E_S and the mobility is given by equation (30).

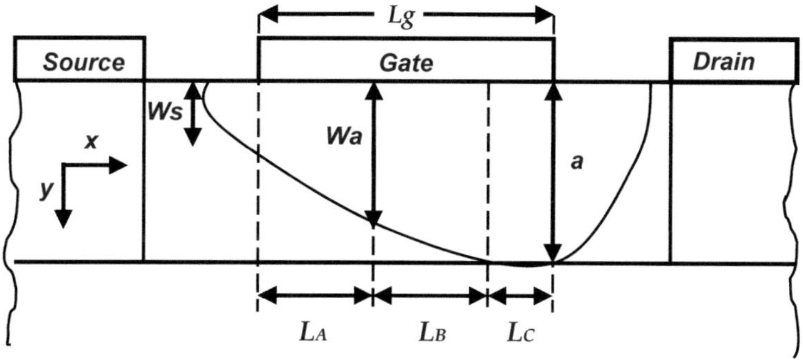

Figure 1. A cross-sectional view of a biased MESFET channel

2.8. Linear regime

This regime exists when the applied drain-source voltage is sufficiently low such that the electrical field under the gate is both smaller than E_0, the mobility is equal to μ_0 and the channel is described by L_A. The expression of the drain current in this regime is given by:

$$Id = Ip_0\left[\left(u_D^2 - u_S^2\right) - \frac{2}{3}\left(u_D^3 - u_S^3\right)\right] \quad (39)$$

where

$$Ip_0 = \frac{Zq^2 N_d^2 \mu_0 a^3}{2\varepsilon L} \quad (40)$$

2.9. Pinch-off regime

As the drain-source voltage increases, the electric field in the channel is not entirely below E_0. For this case, the channel under the gate consists of two regions: One of the lengths L_A with the field is below E_0 and the mobility is equal to μ_0. The other region of the length L_B with E is between E_0 and E_S and the mobility is given by equation (30). The expression of the current in this regime can be obtained by:

$$Id = Ip_0\left[\left(u_A^2 - u_S^2\right) - \frac{2}{3}\left(u_A^3 - u_S^3\right)\right] + Ipn\left[\left(u_D^2 - u_A^2\right) - \frac{2}{3}\left(u_D^3 - u_A^3\right)\right] \quad (41)$$

where

$$Ipn = \frac{Zq^2 N_d^2 \mu_0 a^3}{2\varepsilon L\left[1 + \left(\frac{E - E_0}{E_C}\right)^2\right]^{1/2}} \quad (42)$$

and u_A is the normalized dimensionless unit which corresponds to the drain bias equal to $(E_0.L)$.

2.10. Saturation regime

As the electric field at the drain side becomes larger than E_S, the channel is divided into three regions: The first of the length L_A, the second of the length L_B and the last of the length L_C in which the depletion-layer reaches the interface between the activate area and the semi-insulator substrate. The expression of the current in this regime can be obtained by

$$Id = Ip_0\left[\left(u_A^2 - u_S^2\right) - \frac{2}{3}\left(u_A^3 - u_S^3\right)\right] + Ips\left[\frac{1}{3} - \left(u_A^2 - \frac{2}{3}u_A^3\right)\right] \quad (43)$$

where

$$Ips = \frac{Zq^2 N_d^2 \mu_0 a^3}{2\varepsilon L\left[1 + \left(\frac{E_S - E_0}{E_C}\right)^2\right]^{1/2}} \quad (44)$$

2.11. Effect of parasitic resistances

The characteristics which we have calculated are those of the intrinsic values (*Vg, Vd* and *Id*). To obtain the extrinsic characteristics (*Vgs, Vds,* and *Ids,*) of the device it is necessary to take into account the effect of parasitic resistances (*Rs, Rd* and *Rp*) and substitute the intrinsic terms by the extrinsic terms in all the previous expressions. In this case *Vgs, Vds* and *Ids* can be respectively expressed as

$$Vgs = Vg + RsId \tag{45}$$

$$Vds = Vd + RdId \tag{46}$$

$$Ids = Id + \frac{Vds}{Rp} \tag{47}$$

where *Rs* is the resistance of the region from the source contact to the source side of the gate, *Rd* is the resistance of the drain region outside the gate and *Rp* is the parallel resistance associated with the buffer layer.

It is obviously necessary to implement an iterative technique to obtain the extrinsic drain current *Ids* for given values of the gate-source and drain-source voltages *Vgs* and *Vds* respectively.

2.12. Transconductance and drain conductance

The expression of the intrinsic drain current "*Id*" makes it possible to determine the mathematical expressions of the transconductance and the drain conductance. When the transistor is polarized at a point of operation given by the biasing, the expression of the current "*Id*" can be written as follows:

$$dId = \frac{\partial Id}{\partial Vg}dVg + \frac{\partial Id}{\partial Vd}dVd \tag{48}$$

$$dId = g_m dVg + g_d dVd \tag{49}$$

The expression of the transconductance is defined by the equation:

$$g_m = \left.\frac{\partial Id}{\partial Vg}\right|_{Vd=cst} \tag{50}$$

And the expression of the drain conductance is given by the equation:

$$g_d = \left.\frac{\partial Id}{\partial Vd}\right|_{Vg=cst} \tag{51}$$

After simple derivations of the current drain expressions in the different operation regimes, one obtains the expressions of the transconductance and the drain conductance.

3. Numerical methods

3.1. Calculation of the drain current

To calculate the extrinsic characteristics *Ids (Vds, Vgs)*, one needs to put in consideration the effect of parasitic resistances, this effect which is not negligible, is very significant for the exactitude of the analytical model, but the problem of this type of models (model analytical) is that, the effect of parasitic resistances in the hand is requires to calculate the expressions of the drain current and on the other hand the mathematical relations which express this effect are determined also by the drain current. To solve this problem, are thus needed used a sophistical numerical methods. In this study, we used the iterative method represented by the following relations:

At the beginning, the initial extrinsic drain current *Ids* is considered equal to intrinsic current *Id*.

$$Ids^{(0)} = Id \tag{52}$$

Consequently,
$$Ids^{(1)} = Ids^{(0)} + \Delta Ids^{(1)} \tag{53}$$

where: $\Delta\ Ids^{(1)}$ is on a side the difference between $Ids^{(1)}$ and $Ids^{(0)}$ and on the other side it results on the effect of parasitic resistances for $Ids = Ids^{(0)}$.

$$\begin{aligned} Ids^{(2)} &= Ids^{(1)} + \Delta Ids^{(2)} \\ &\vdots \\ Ids^{(n)} &= Ids^{(n-1)} + \Delta Ids^{(n)} \end{aligned} \tag{54}$$

The operation is stopped when:
$$\Delta Ids^{(n)} = 10^{-3}\, Ids^{(n-1)} \tag{55}$$

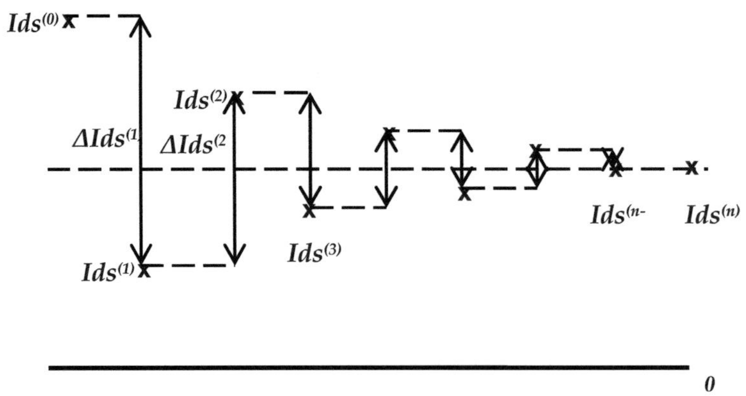

Figure 2. Diagram representative of the method

3.2. Calculation of transconductance and the drain conductance

The expressions of the transconductance and the conductance of drain are simple derivations of the drain current as a function as the drain and gate intrinsic voltages (Eqs. 50, 51), to obtain the values of these significant parameters, we based on numerical calculation as follows:

For the transconductance:

After the fixing of the drain voltage to the given value, the transconductance is obtained from the following relation:

$$g_m^{(k)} = \left.\frac{\Delta Ids^{(k)}}{\Delta Vg^{(k)}}\right|_{Vd=cst} = \left.\frac{Ids^{(k+1)} - Ids^{(k)}}{Vg^{(k+1)} - Vg^{(k)}}\right|_{Vd=cst} \tag{56}$$

where:

$$Vg^{(k+1)} - Vg^{(k)} = 0{,}01 \tag{57}$$

Same manner as the transconductance, the drain conductance is obtained after fixing of the gate voltage and after the following relation:

$$g_d^{(k)} = \left.\frac{\Delta Ids^{(k)}}{\Delta Vd^{(k)}}\right|_{Vg=cst} = \left.\frac{Ids^{(k+1)} - Ids^{(k)}}{Vd^{(k+1)} - Vd^{(k)}}\right|_{Vg=cst} \tag{58}$$

where:

$$Vd^{(k+1)} - Vd^{(k)} = 0{,}01 \tag{59}$$

4. Simulation results

In order to illustrate the exposed model, we elaborated simulation software based on different formulas and mathematical equations previously obtained and by using the numerical methods. The study carried out on a submicron gate length GaAs MESFET transistors which parameters shown in the table 1. The results obtained are exposed and interpreted in this section.

L (μm)	a (μm)	Z (μm)	Nd (At / cm^3)	μ_0 (cm^2/ Vs)	E_0 / Em
0,3	0,145	100	1,2. 10^{17}	3400	0,25
Rs (Ω)	Rd (Ω)	Rp (Ω)	a_1	b_1	c_1
6	6	600	- 0,06	0,12	0,10

Table 1. Summary of device dimensions

In the fig. 3, we have presented the network of the static characteristics in the case of the preceding device. These characteristics illustrate the relation between the extrinsic drain current *Ids* and the bias voltages *Vds* and *Vgs*. We notice the presence of three regions which correspond to the three operation regimes (linear, non-linear and saturated).

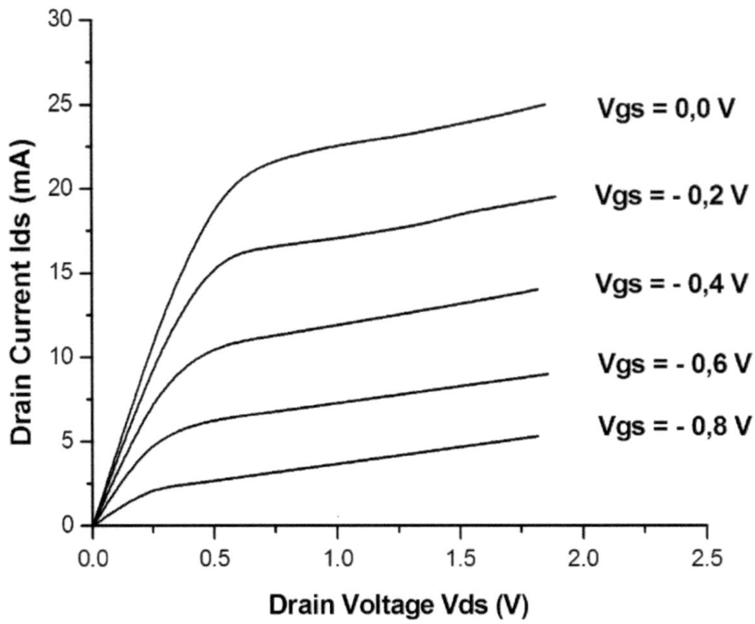

Figure 3. Drain current versus drain-source voltage at a different gate-source voltages for GaAs MESFET with parameters and device dimensions are listed in Table 1.

To demonstrate the validity of the developed model and to compare its performance with the experimental data reported in the literature (Chin and We, 1993) a submicron GaAs MESFET having the parameters and device dimensions selected in Table 2. Fig. 4 represented a comparison between the proposed model and the experimental *I-V* characteristics for this device. It is clearly seen that good agreement between the model and the experimental data are obtained, this is quite interesting to argue the validity of the mathematical analysis and the proposed numerical methods for practical short gate-length GaAs MESFET devices.

L (μm)	a (μm)	Z (μm)	Nd (At / cm^3)	μ_0 (cm^2/ Vs)	E_0 / Em
0,5	0,143	100	1,31. 10^{17}	3600	0,25
Rs (Ω)	Rd (Ω)	Rp (Ω)	a_1	b_1	c_1
6	6	1000	- 0,06	0,12	0,10

Table 2.

Fig. 5 and Fig. 6 represent the transconductance as a function of the intrinsic drain voltage *Vd* for a series of intrinsic gate voltage *Vg*. In these figures, we noticed that the transconductance increases on the one hand as the absolute value of the voltage gate decreases, and on the other hand with the increase in the drain voltage until the saturation regime where the transconductance is saturated. This is explained because, more the gate voltage increases in absolute value, more the width of space charge area increases. The extension of this area ends when this one occupies all the width of the channel. No passage of the current is then theoretically possible.

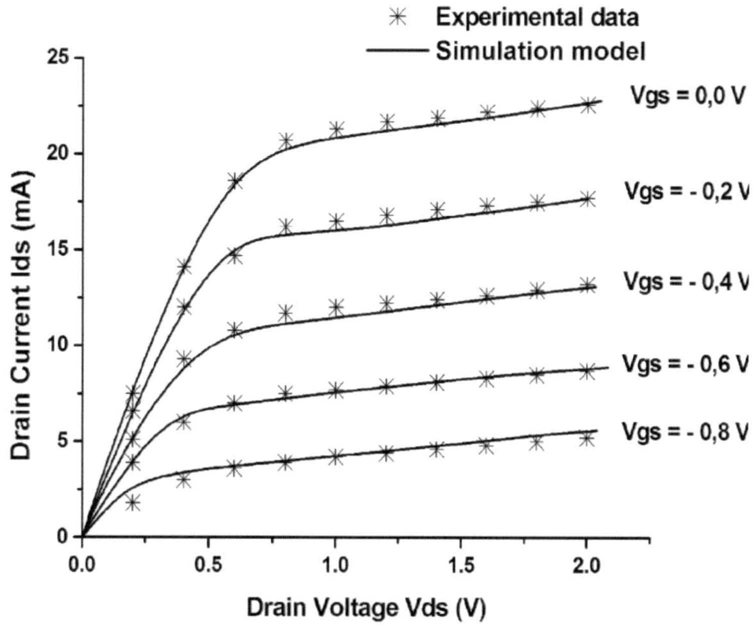

Figure 4. Comparisons of the *I-V* characteristics between the proposed model (solid line) and the experimental data (asterisks) (Chin and Wu, 1993) for the device with dimensions are listed in Table 2.

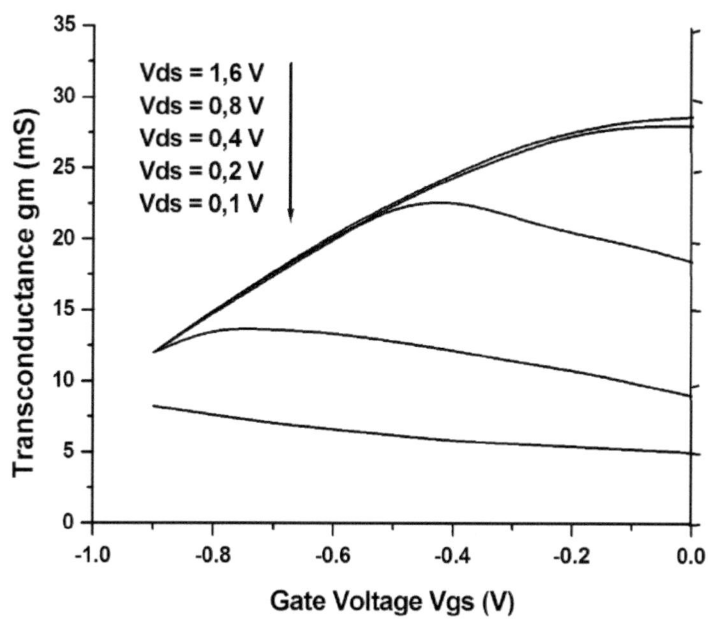

Figure 5. Variation in transconductance as a function of gate-source voltage at different drain-source voltages for a device with parameters and dimensions are listed in Table 1.

Fig. 7 represents the drain conductance as a function of the drain voltage for a series of gate voltage. We notice that the drain conductance is decreases on the one hand as the drain

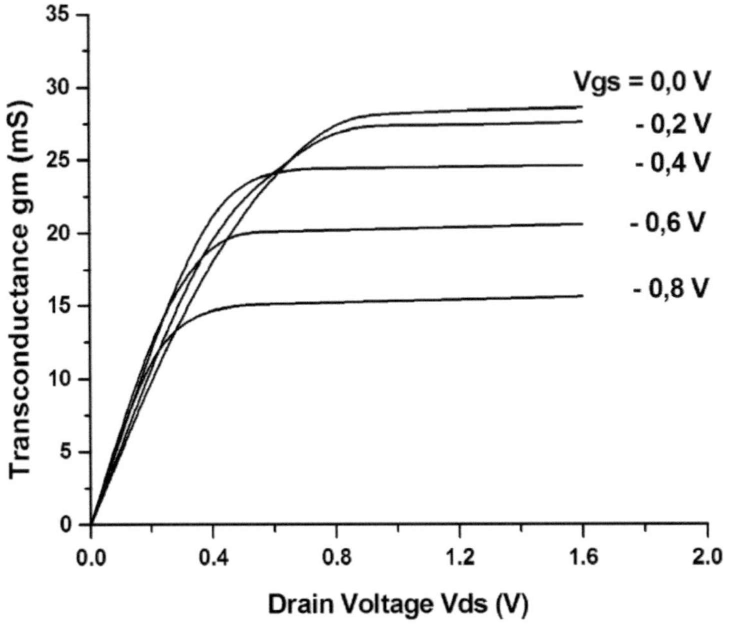

Figure 6. Variation in transconductance as a function of drain-source voltage at different gate-source voltages for a device with parameters and dimensions are listed in Table 1.

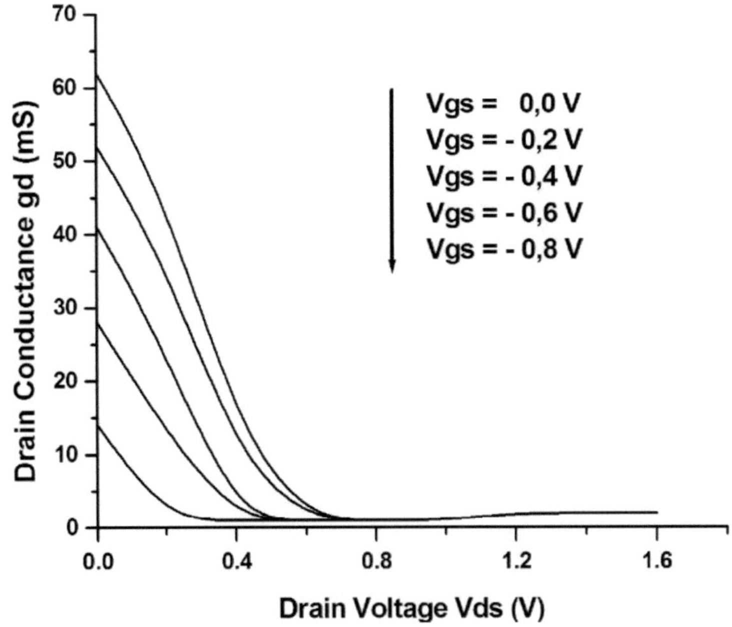

Figure 7. Variation in drain conductance as a function of drain-source voltage at different gate-source voltages for a device with parameters and dimensions are listed in Table 1.

voltage increases and on the other hand when the absolute value of the gate voltage increases. It takes its maximum value in linear regime, and is cancelled in regime of saturation. This explains why, in linear mode, the electrons available for conduction and present in the channel do not reach their speed limit. Also the drain current *Ids* varies in an important and quasi linear way with the drain voltage. On the contrary, for the strong values of *Vd* in the saturated regime, the electrons reached their speed limits and the current *Ids* progresses slightly with *Vd*.

5. Conclusion

During this work, a comprehensive new model is developed to simulate the static characteristics of short gate-length GaAs MESFET. The validity of the model is established by simulating *Ids*, *gm* and *Gd* characteristics. The performance of the model is compared with experimental results existing in the literature by calculating the I-V characteristics of a device with the gate length is equal to 0,5 μm. It has been demonstrated that the proposed model is a comprehensive one capable of simulating DC characteristics of short gate-length GaAs MESFETs. The transconductance and drain conductance curves obtained by the model have the same behavior with those of the theory, so that it has been shown that proposed model could be a useful tool for device simulators involving short channel MESFETs.

Author details

Saadeddine Khemissi
Abbes Laghrour University, Khenchela, Algeria

6. References

Chang and Day, USA(1989) "Analytical theory for current- voltage characteristics and field distribution of GaAs mesfet's", *IEEE Trans Elec Dev*, Vol 36, No 2 , pp 269-280.

Chin and Wu, Taiwen(1992). "A new two dimensional model for the potential distribution of short gate lenght MESFET's and its applications", *IEEE Tran. Elec Dev*, Vol 39, No 8, pp 1928-1937.

Chin and Wu, Taiwen(1993). "A new I-V model for short gate lenght MESFET's", *IEEE Tran. Elec Dev*, Vol 40, No 4, pp 712- 720.

Jit, Pandey and Pal, India(2003). "A New Two-Dimensional Model for the Drain-Induced Barrier Lowering of Fully Depleted Short-Channel SOI-MESFET's," *Journal of Semiconductor Technology and Science*, Vol 3, pp. 217-222.

Khemissi, Merabtine, Zaabat, Azizi and Saidi, Algeria(2006). " Influence of physical and geometrical parameters on electrical properties of short gate GaAs MESFET's", *Semiconductor Physics Quantum Electronics and Optoelectronics*, Vol 9 No 2 pp 34-39.

Merabtine, Khemissi, Zaabat and Azizi, Algeria(2004). "Accurate numerical modeling of GaAs MESFET current-voltage characteristics", *Semiconductor Physics Quantum Electronics and Optoelectronics*, Vol 7 No 4 pp 389- 394.

Morarka and Mishra, India(2005). "A 2-D model for the potential distribution and threshold voltage of fully depleted short-channel ion-implanted silicon MESFET's", *journal of semiconductor technology and science*, Vol 5, No 3, pp 173-181.

Shin, Klemer and Lion, USA(1992) "Current voltage characteristics of submicrometre GaAs MESFET's with nonuniform channel doping profils", *Solid State Electronics*, Vol 35, No 11, pp 1639- 1644.

Sze and Ng, USA(2007). "Pysics of semiconductor devices". 3rd d. New York, John Wiley, pp 374.

Tripathi and Jit, India(2011). "A Two-Dimensional (2D) Analytical Model for the Potential Distribution and Threshold Voltage of Short-Channel Ion-Implanted GaAs MESFETs under Dark and Illuminated Conditions", *Journal of semiconductor technology and science*, Vol.11, No.1, pp. 40-50.

Chapter 13

Using Numerical Simulations to Study and Design Semiconductors Devices in Micro and Nanoelectronics

Salvador Pinillos Gimenez and Marcello Bellodi

Additional information is available at the end of the chapter

http://dx.doi.org/10.5772/48334

1. Introduction

The survival of the integrated circuits(ICs) industries is directly linked to its ability to innovate in terms of the developing new semiconductor devices (planar and three-dimensional) and new manufacturing process technologies (Silicon-On-Insulator, etc), in theircapability to reduce the dimensions of semiconductor devices focusing on the increasing of integration capability of the devices into a single integrated circuit (IC) and in their efficiency to develop new digital and analog ICs applications to attend the market in different forms of consumption. In this context, the numerical simulators represent a very important role for the ICs industries and very high investments have been done in this area of the process and device simulation tools (Technology Computer-Aided Design, TCAD) in order to use the computer simulations to develop and optimize semiconductor processing technologies and devices [1-2].

Significant costs reductions can be achieved through the use of numerical simulators for developing new semiconductor manufacturing technologies and devices that are associated with ICs industries. Thinking on developing new devices, the numerical simulations are able to supply a lot of information about the devices in terms of theirs electrical characteristics curves (drain current as a function of gate voltage for the MOSFETs, etc) and mainly in terms of the internal electrical and physical behaviors of the semiconductor devices (current density, electric field density, potential distribution along of the device structure, mobile carriers density along of the channel width and length of a MOSFET, etc) previously to the physical implementation, which is impossible to be obtained, visualized and understood with only the electrical characterization of the physical devices [1-2]. The involved costs with numerical simulations are associated mainly with human resources and infra-structure (hardware and software) while that, if new devices developing were associated only with the manufacturing process use, would involve very high production costs, very high lead time and many uncertainties about the efficiency of the proposed devices [1-2].

Currently there is two-pronged research in the world focusing on developing new semiconductor devices [3]. The first one is based on designing of the new tridimensional (3D) devices, such as the multi-gates MOSFETs (FinFETs, Three-gates, Four-gates, Surrounding-gate) that involve high cost and investments related to the new techniques of ICs manufacturing process andnew materials. The other tries to explore the many real improvement opportunities of the current planar ICs manufacture technology. One of them, it is to use the "drain/source and channel region interface engineering" (D/SCRIE) approach [4-6], where it can implement new and innovative layout styles with non-conventional geometries, focusing on enhancing the device performance and consequently the performance of analog and digital ICs applications [4-7]. An example is very promising of this layout approach is the "Diamond MOSFET" that it was carefully and specially designed to improve the longitudinal (parallel) electric field ($\vec{\varepsilon}_{//}$) in order to increase the mobile carriers drift velocity in the channel region ($\vec{\nu}_{//}$) and consequently the drain current (I_{DS}), transconductance (g_m) and to reduce the on-state drain/source series resistance (R_{DS_on}) by a simple changing of the gate geometry from the conventional (rectangular) to hexagonal, as illustrated in Figure 1, showing an example of a SOI nMOSFET3D structure [4-7].

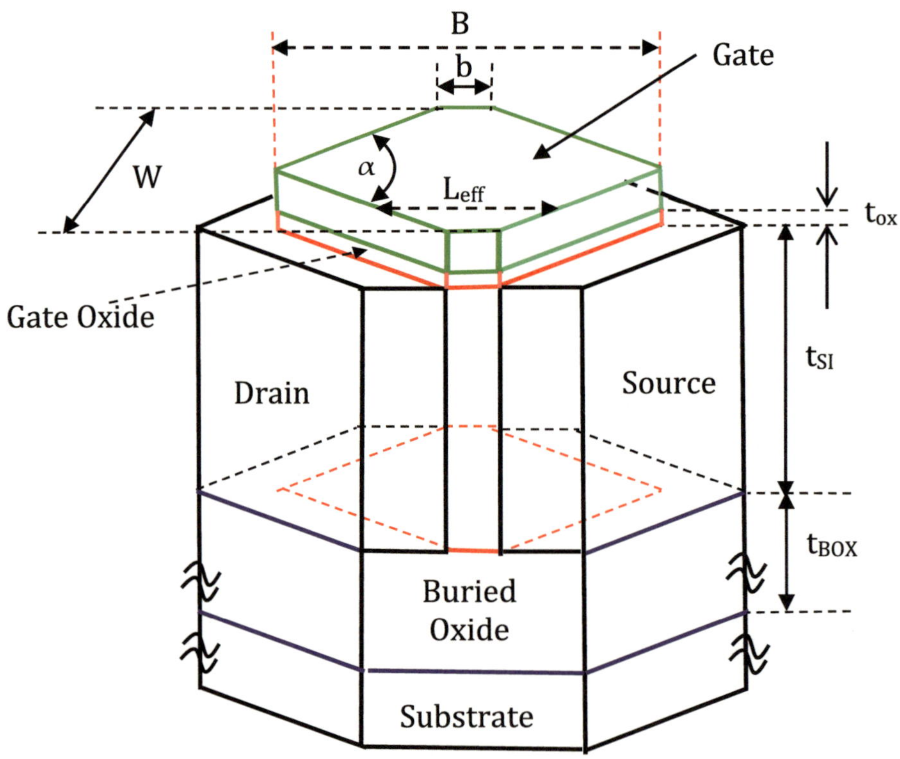

Figure 1. Example of a SOI nMOSFET 3D structure.

In Figure 1, the shorter and longer channel dimensions are represented by b and B, respectively, W is the channel width and L_{eff} is the effective channel length, α angle is the angle of the drain/channel and the channel/source interfaces due to hexagonal gate geometry, t_{ox}, t_{SI} and $t_{BOX}$are gate oxide, silicon film and buried oxide thickness, respectively.

Figure 2 presents the Diamond SOI nMOSFET layout style, where the longitudinal corner effect (LCE) acting in the point P in the channel is shown and the resultant longitudinal electric field ($\vec{\varepsilon}_{//}$) is given by the vector sum of the longitudinal electric field components ($\vec{\varepsilon}_{//1}$ and $\vec{\varepsilon}_{//2}$). Last is higher than the one observed in the conventional SOI nMOSFET counterpart. These longitudinal electric field components ($\vec{\varepsilon}_{//1}$ and $\vec{\varepsilon}_{//2}$) are generated by the drain bias (V_{DS}) and are perpendiculars to the metallurgical junctions of the drain/silicon film (channel region) [4-7].

The effective channel length (L_{eff}) of the Diamond SOI nMOSFET is given by the equation (1).

$$L_{eff} = \frac{B+b}{2} \tag{1}$$

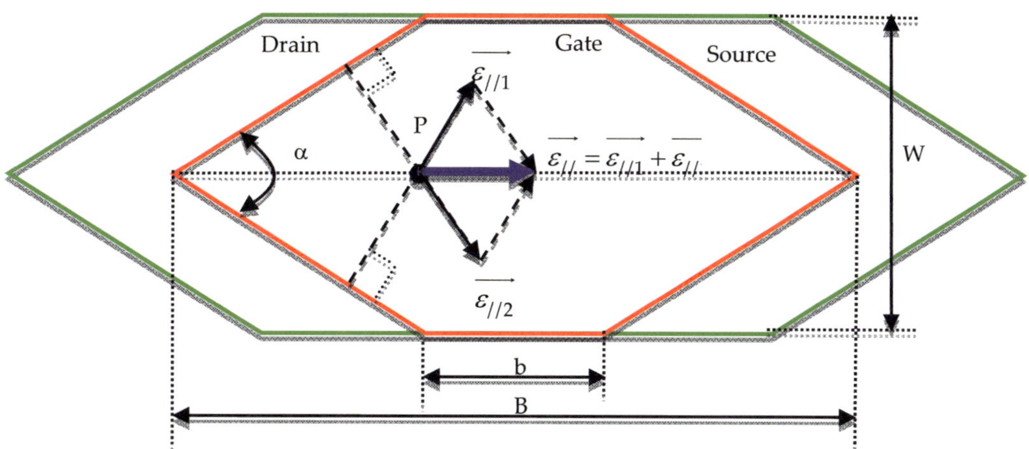

Figure 2. Example of a SOI nMOSFET 3D layout showing the LCE acting in the point P.

In this structure, the resultant longitudinal electric field ($\vec{\varepsilon}_{//}$) in the center of the gate region is higher than the one observed in the edges of the gate region, due to the higher interaction between the longitudinal electric field components ($\vec{\varepsilon}_{//1}$ and $\vec{\varepsilon}_{//2}$) in the center of the device (LCE) [4-7] than the one found in the edges of the gate region, and therefore the drain current tends to flow more in the center of the gate region than in the edges of the gate region. Besides that, the Diamond structure can be electrically represented by the parallel association of the N transistors, where the channel width of each transistor of this parallel association is given by W/N and the channel length of these transistors varies from b to B. As a consequence of this last feature, the drain current tends to flow more by the edges than by the center of the gate region. This effect is defined here by "Variable Channel Lengths of Transistors Associated in Parallel Effect" (VACLETAPE). So, in the Diamond structure occurs two effects at the same time, i.e., the LCE and the VACLETAPE generating a Diamond drain current higher than the one observed in the conventional (rectangular) SOI nMOSFET counterpart, regarding the same gate area (A_G) and bias conditions.

2. Devices used to perform the study

So, in order to qualify and quantify the benefits of Diamond layout style to improve the transistor performance, it were implemented three pairs of SOI nMOSFETs, being three Diamond transistors with different α angles and other three conventional SOI nMOSFETs counterparts, regarding the same gate area (A_G). Table I presents the devices dimensions used to implement these devices in the DevEdidt3D from (TCAD/Silvaco Inc) [8]. A similar TCAD to implement devices is the Sentaurus Structure Editor of the Synopsys, Inc [9].

Conventional SOI nMOSFET				Diamond SOI nMOSFET			
#	W (μm)	L (μm)	W/L	#	b (μm)	B (μm)	α (°)
CSM1	6.0	7.0	0.86	DSM1	1.0	13.0	53.1
CSM2	6.0	4.0	1.50	DSM2	1.0	7.0	90.0
CSM3	6.0	2.5	2.40	DSM3	1.0	4.0	126.9

Table 1. Devices Dimensions used to the study.

The constructive characteristics of these devices are: gate-oxide (t_{ox}), silicon-film (t_{SI}) and buried-oxide (t_{BOX}) thickness are 2 nm, 100 nm and 400 nm, respectively, and drain/source and channel doping concentrations are $5.5\text{x}10^{17}$ cm^{-3} and $1\text{x}10^{20}$ cm^{-3}, respectively.

3. Three-dimensional simulations results

The ATLAS (Device Simulation Software) [9] was used to perform the 3D numerical simulations of the Diamond and Conventional SOI nMOSFETs. The curves of I_{DS} versus gate voltage (V_{GS}) and I_{DS} versus drain voltage (V_{DS}) were obtained. Based on these curves, the main parameters of these devices were extracted and compared in order to verify the advantages and disadvantages of the Diamond layout style in relation to the conventional one counterpart.

Basically, the ATLAS device simulator uses two files inputs: the first one is the text file that contains commands for the ATLAS. Usually, these commands are to include a file that define the devices structure (usually built by using DevEdit3D [8]), to define the dimensions, the terminals and the meshof the structure of the device. The second one is responsible to define the physic phenomenon models (mobility, band width, impact ionizations, etc), the solution methods and the bias commands of the terminals that must be taking in account in the simulation of the device [1].

Besides that, ATLAS generates three types of output files. The first one is the "run-time output file" that provides all the error and warning messages. The second one is the "log files", which store allterminal voltages and currents of the device [direct current (DC), small signal alternate current (AC) and transient] generated the command SOLVE. This last file can be seen with the TonyPlot (visualization tool) to visualize the electrical behavior of the device. The last one is the "solution files", and it is responsible to stores the two-dimensional and three-dimensionaldata of the solution variables within the device for a single bias point (electric field, potential, etc.). This last file can be visualized by the use of TonyPlot too [1].

The following models are used to perform the 3D numerical simulations of the devices: I. Lombardi's vertical and horizontal electric-field-dependent mobility model, which includes effects of low (surface acoustic phonon scattering, optical inter-valley scattering and surface roughness) and high (Thonber's drift velocity model to calculate the velocity saturation) electric field; II. The Aurora model takes into account mobility degradation due to the lattice temperature; III. The Fowler-Nordheim Tunneling (electron and holes) model considersthe tunneling of electrons from the semiconductor Fermi level into the insulator conduction band, when high electric field across the gate is applied; IV. The Lucky-Electron Hot Carrier Injection model, considers the electrons emissions into the oxide by first gaining enough energy from the electric field in the channel to surmount the insulator/semiconductor barrier [1].

Figure 3 presents the three-dimensional numerical (3D) simulations results of the DSMs and CSMs I_{DS} as a function of V_{GS},for V_{DS} equal to 10 mV (Triode Region).

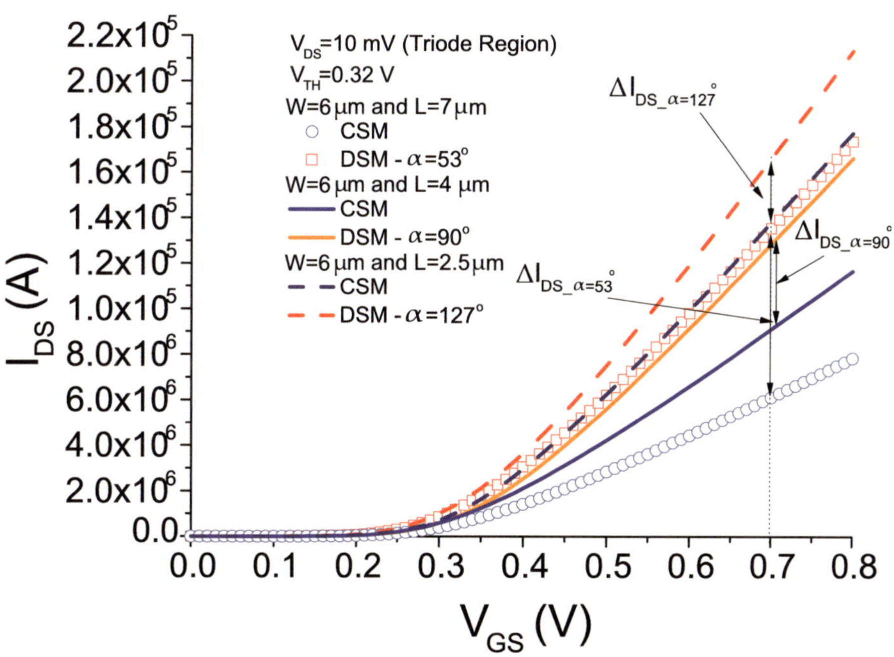

Figure 3. Curves of three-dimensional numerical simulations of the I_{DS} as a function of V_{GS} for V_{DS}=10mV.

In Figure 3, $\Delta I_{DS\_\alpha=127^o}$, $\Delta I_{DS\_\alpha=90^o}$ and $\Delta I_{DS\_\alpha=53^o}$ are respectively the differences between the I_{DS} of the DSMs with different α angles (127º, 90º and 53º) and the respective CSMs counterparts.

By analyzing the Figure 3, considering the same A_G and bias conditions in the Triode Region, it can be observe that DSMs I_{DS} with α angles equals to 127º, 90º and 53º are respectively 20.3 %, 37.2 % and 126.5 % (2.26 times) higher than those observed in the CSMs counterparts and these differences decreaseswhile the DSM α angle increases, due the two effects existents in the Diamond SOI nMOSFET (LCE and VACLETAPE). So, this innovative layout style can be used to increase the fun-out and fun-in capability of the logic gates.

Figure 4 presents the three-dimensional numerical (3D) simulations results of the DSMs and CSMs g_m as a function of gate voltage (V_{GS}),for drain voltage (V_{DS}) equal to 10 mV.

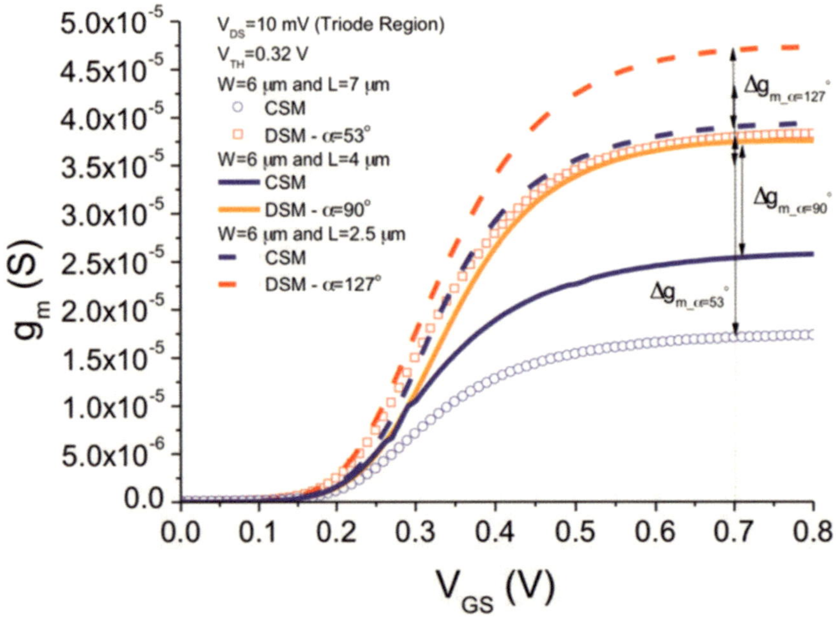

Figure 4. Curves of three-dimensional numerical simulations of the g_m as a function of V_{GS} for V_{DS}=10 mV (Triode Region).

In Figure 4, $\Delta g_{m\_\alpha=127^o}$, $\Delta g_{m\_\alpha=90^o}$ and $\Delta g_{m\_\alpha=53^o}$ are respectively the differences between the g_m of DSMs with different α angles (127º, 90º and 53º) and the respective CSMs counterparts.

Basing on Figure 4, we can see that, DSMs g_m with α angles equals to 127º, 90º and 53º are respectively 20.5 %, 47.6 % and 122.9 % (around 2.23 times) higher than those verified in the CSM counterparts and these differences also decreaseswhile DSM α angle increases, due the LCE and VACLETAPE,considering the same A_G and bias conditions.So, this Diamond structures can be used to improve significantly the voltage gain (A_V) and unit voltage gain frequency (f_T) of the amplifiers used in analog ICs.

Figure 5 presents the three-dimensional numerical (3D) simulations results of DSM (α=53°) and CSM counterpart Log(I_{DS}) as a function of gate voltage (V_{GS}),for drain voltage (V_{DS}) equal to 10 mV.

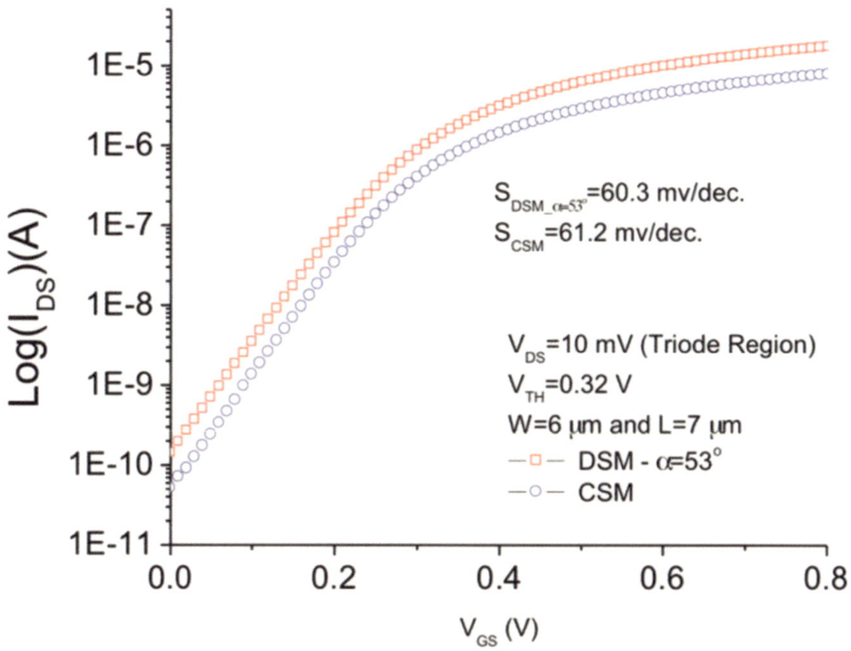

Figure 5. Curves of three-dimensional numerical simulations of DSM (α=53°) and CSM Log(I_{DS}) as a function of V_{GS} for V_{DS}=10 mV.

Analyzing Figure 5, we can see that the subthreshold slopes (S) from of the both devices are practically similar around 60 mV/decade. Similar results are found to the others devices studied.

Figure 6 presents I_{DS} as a function of V_{DS} with V_{GS} equal to 0.4 V in the saturation region to DSM with α angles equals to 127° (Figure 6.a), 90° (Figure 6.b) and 53° (Figure 6.c) respectively.

Analyzing Figure 6, it is possible toobserve that always the I_{DS} in saturation region (I_{DSsat}) of all DSMs with different α angles are higher than those found in the CSMs counterpart, considering the same A_G, geometric factor and bias conditions. Besides that, I_{DS} of DSMs with α angles equals to 127°, 90° and 53° is higher 27%, 52% and 284% (1.84 times) than those observed in CSMs counterparts. This can be justified because of LCE and VACLETAPE effects present in the Diamond structure. Additionally, itcan see that DSMs Early voltages (V_{EA}) are strongly degraded in relation to CSMs counterparts, due to the high resultant longitudinal electric field in the drain region of the Diamond structures, as for example, DSM (α=53°) V_{EA} is approximately equal to 5V while CSM counterpart V_{EA} is approximately equal to 36V (around seven times smaller) and therefore can limit the use of this device to the output stages of analog ICs.

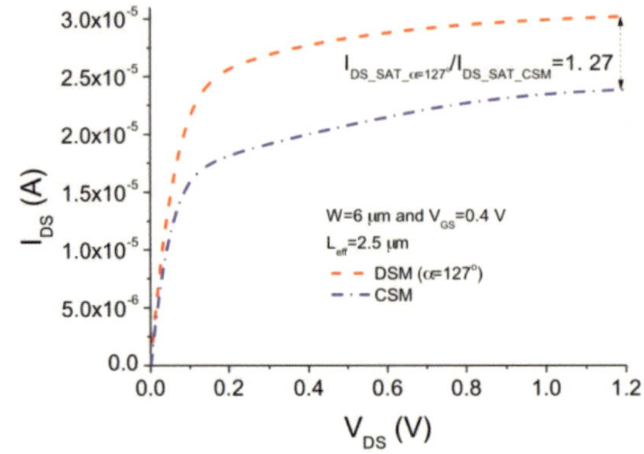

(a)

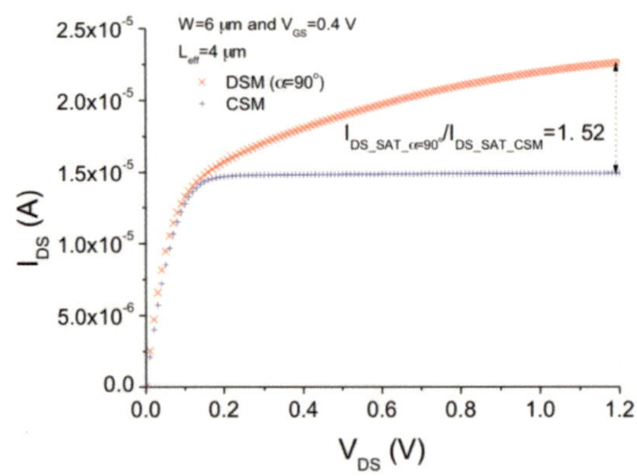

(b)

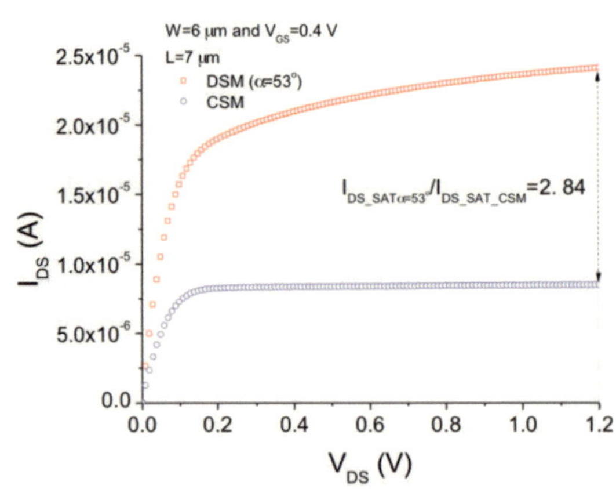

(c)

Figure 6. Curves of three-dimensional numerical simulations of I_{DS} as a function of V_{DS} for V_{GS}=0.4 V (saturation region) for DSMs with different α angles [127° (Figure 6.a), 90° (Figure 6.b) and 53° (Figure 6.c)and CSMs counterparts.

The on-state series resistance (R_{DS_on}) can be extracted from the Figure 6 in the linear region of the triode region. So, notice that, DSMs with different α angles R_{DS_on} are always higher than those observed in CSMs counterparts, as for example, DSM (α=53°) R_{DS_on} is around 82% (6 KΩ) smaller than the one found in CSM counterpart (110 KΩ) and therefore, by using DSM counterpart instead CSM, we can improve significantly the processing clock velocity of digital ICs.

4. Electrical and physical analysis

In order to understand the electrical and physical behavior of the Diamond structure in relation the to conventional one counterpart, the longitudinal electrical field vectors picture was extracted of DSM (α =90°) and CSM counterpart structures, regarding V_{GS} and V_{DS} equals to 0.4 V and 1.2 V, respectively, in saturation region, as illustrated in Figure 7.

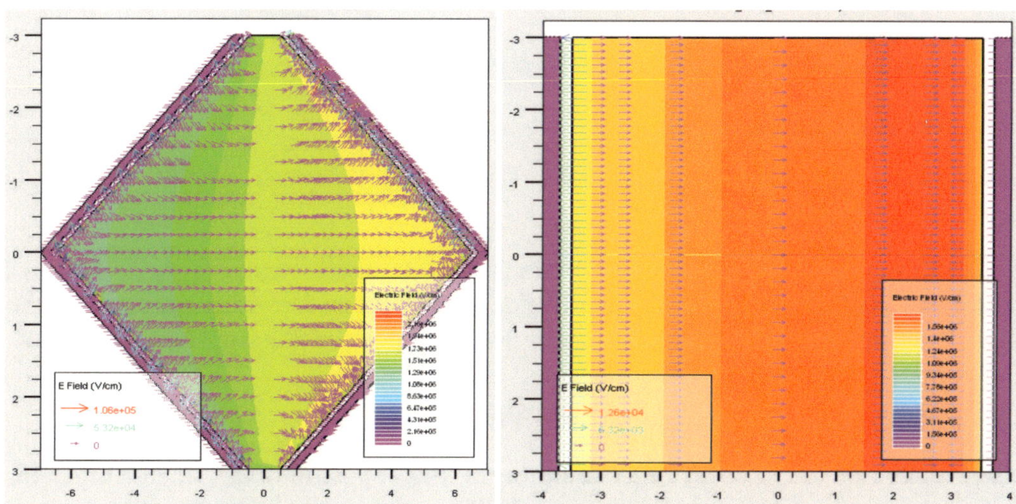

(a) (b)

Figure 7. Vectors of the resultant longitudinal electric field of the DSM (α=90°) (Figure 7.a) and CSM counterpart (Figure 7.b) channel regions for V_{GS} and V_{DS} equal to 0.4 V and 1.2 V, respectively (saturation region).

With the use of TonyPlot3D (Silvaco Inc.) [1] and analyzing Figure 7, it is possible to see how is the behavior of DSM (α =90°) resultant longitudinal electric field ($\vec{\varepsilon}_{//}$) along of the channel length. Notice that, DSM (α =90°) resultant longitudinal electrical field ($\vec{\varepsilon}_{//}$) in the channel region edges (1.5x10^6 V/cm) is smaller than the one found in the center of the channel from of the middle of the channel length (2.0x10^6 V/cm), due to the smaller interaction between the longitudinal electric field components ($\vec{\varepsilon}_{//1}$ and $\vec{\varepsilon}_{//2}$) next to DSM edges regions. Besides that, it can beverify that DSM (α =90°) average resultant longitudinal electric field (1.9x10^6 V/cm) is higher than the one observed in CSM counterpart (1.2.10^4 V/cm), due to the presence of LCE and VACLETAPE in the Diamond structure.

Additionally, it is plotted a picture of the DSM (α =53°) total drain current density, considering V_{GS} and V_{DS} equals to 0.4 V and 1.2 V, respectively, in saturation region, as illustrated in Figure 8.

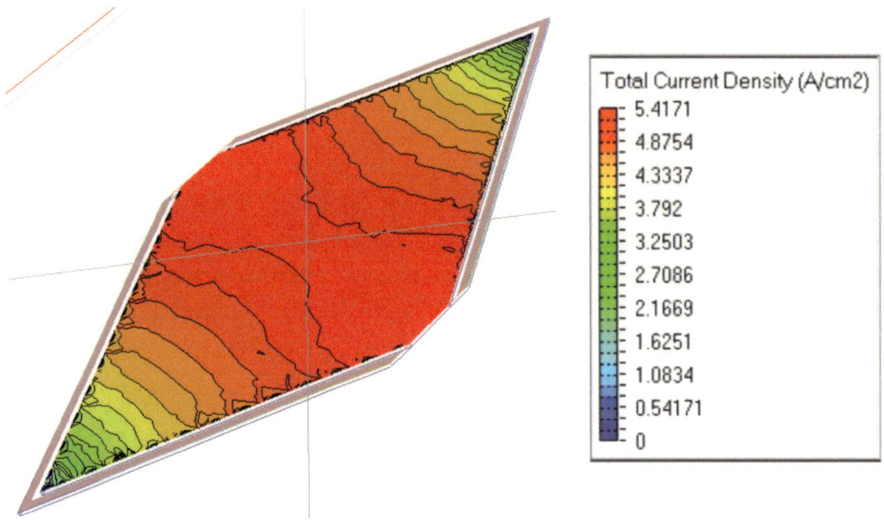

Figure 8. Curves of the total drain current density of DSM (α=53°) (Figure 8.a) and CSM counterpart (Figure 8.b) channel regions for V_{GS} and V_{DS} equal to 0.4 V and 1.2 V, respectively (saturation region).

Figure 8 shows that DSM (α =90°) total drain current density is higher in the center of the channel region than in the vertices (source/drain and channel regions interfaces) of the device, indicating that this layout style can be evolved to the octagonal gate geometric [10].

5. SOI MOSFEts investigationat high temperatures

Today, there are much electronic equipments that operate under high-temperature environment (from room temperature up to 300°C) such as avionics, automotive, aircrafts, spacecrafts, ships, train, among other [11-13], where conventional (bulk) CMOS integrated circuits can operate satisfactorily at moderate temperatures (up to 150°C), but when the temperature increases beyond this, the devices present failures arising the threshold voltage reduction and excessive drain leakage current increases [14-18].

Fortunately, thanks to the advantages of SOI CMOS technology, especially at high temperatures, their applications at high temperatures can be extended up to 300°C, where its electrical performance is less impaired than the one found in the conventional MOSFETs [18-20].

In this context, the drain leakage current (I_{DLeak}) of the Diamond SOI nMOSFET (DSM) is analyzed from room temperature up to 300°C by the three-dimensional numerical simulator ATLAS [1]. The DSM I_{DLeak}results are then compared tothe one found in the SOI MOSFETs (CSM) counterpart, taking into account the same die area, geometric factor and bias and temperature conditions.

6. Three-dimensional numerical simulations results at high temperatures

To analyze DSM operating at high temperatures, from room temperature up to 300°C, CSM and DSM with different α angles are implemented by using DevEdit3D [8].

In order to investigate I_{DLeak} behavior, it is necessary to extract the I_{DS} as a function of V_{GS} curves, at high temperatures. Once I_{DLeak} is obtained in the subthreshold region. In this study, I_{DLeak} is extracted considering V_{GS} equal to -0.5V, as it can be seen in Figure 9, for different temperatures (27°C, 100°C, 200°C and 300°C) and for all devices under evaluation in this work.

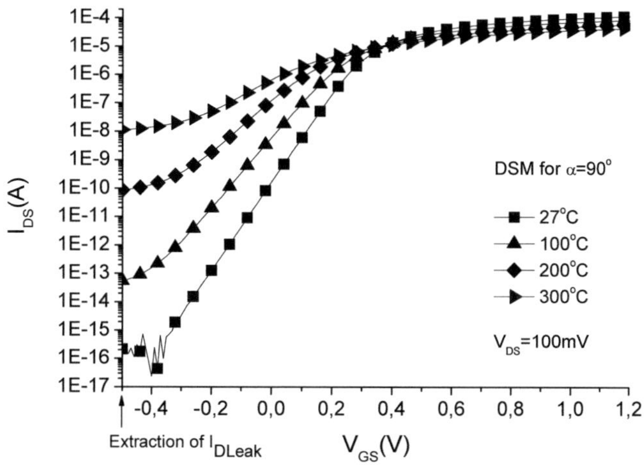

Figure 9. DSM (α=90°) Log(I_{DS}) as a function of V_{GS} with V_{DS} equal to 100 mV, considering different temperatures.

Figure 10 shows some results concerning I_{DLeak}as a function of the temperature, considering DSM with different α angles and the CSMs counterparts, operating at same bias and temperature conditions.

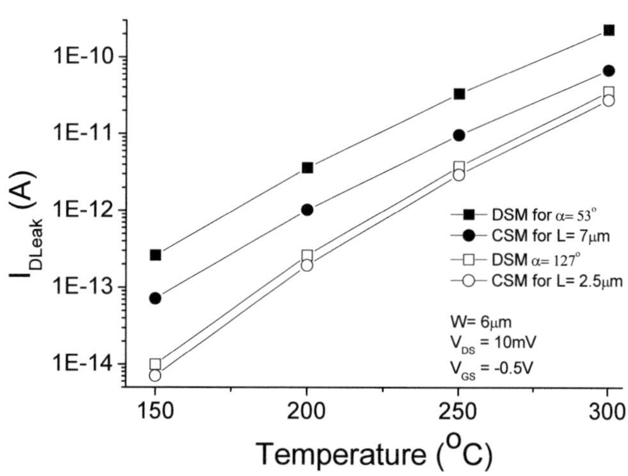

Figure 10. DSM and CSM counterpart I_{DLeak} as a function of the temperature.

From Figure 10, it is possible to observe that, as the temperature increases, I_{DLeak} also increases, as expected [11]. Besides that, I_{DLeak} is higher in DSM when compared to CSM devices, independently of the αangle and the temperature. It happens since the longitudinal electric field is higher in DSM when compared to CSMs and consequently, its drain leakage current (I_{DLeak}) is also larger. On the other hand, it worthwhile to describe that as α reduces, I_{DLeak} difference observed between both devices becomes higher. As for example, when $\alpha$is equal to 127°, DSM I_{DLeak} is 20% higher than the one observed in the CSM counterpart (L= 2.5μm) for V_{GS}=-0.5 V, but providing an I_{DS} also 20% more than rectangular gate transistor, for V_{GS}=1.2V. These increasing proportions between I_{DLeak} and drain currents are maintained for all equivalent devices, i.e., for α = 53° and 127°.

Figure 11 shows DSM I_{DLeak} behavior as a function of the angle α. It is important to comment that this comparison is possible once I_{DLeak} is normalized with the geometric factor (W/L), thus providing a more realistic comparison of I_{DLeak} as α changes. Then, analyzing the results it is possible to observe that, for the same temperature, as α increase, I_{DLeak} becomes smaller. Otherwise, for the same α, I_{DLeak} also increases according to the temperature rises.

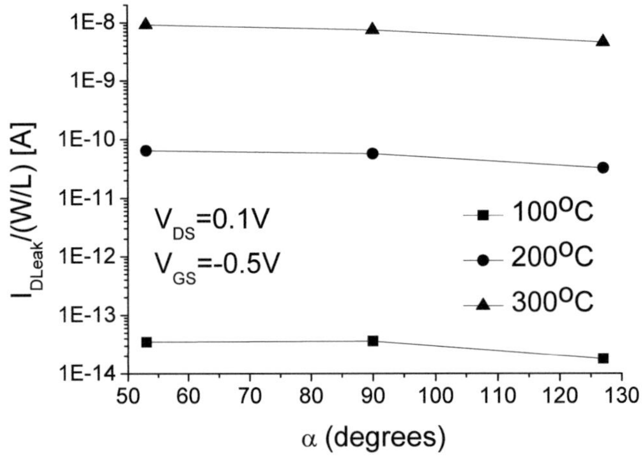

Figure 11. Diamond SOI nMOSFET I_{DLeak} behavior as a function of α, at high temperatures.

Anyway, for both CSM and DSM, I_{DLeak} increases when the temperature increases in the same proportion,mainly due to the thermal generation process [15], but in DSM I_{DLeak} is higher because the longitudinal electric field along the DSM channel length is higher than the one present in its CSM counterpart.

7. Conclusions

Comparative studies between Diamond SOI MOSFETs and Conventional ones counterparts by numerical simulations demonstrate that Diamond layout style can improve current drive, transconductance, on-state series resistance, frequency response (voltage gain and unit voltage gain frequency) when it is compared to the Conventional counterpart, considering the same gate area, geometry factor (aspect ratio) and bias conditions.

By using Diamond layout style, instead rectangular gate geometry, the die area of analog integrated circuits can be significantly reduced since the drain current of the Diamond structure is higher than the one observed in the Conventional counterpart, considering the same gate area, geometry factor (aspect ratio) and bias conditions.

Therefore, the Diamond layout style becomes an important device alternative to improve the performance of the transistors and consequently the performance of the analog and digital ICs.

This temperature studyin the Diamond layout structure shows the drain leakage current behavior in the Diamond SOI MOSFETs, in comparison to the conventional one counterpart, regarding these devices operating since room temperature (27°C) up to 300°C. From this investigation it is observed that I_{DLeak} in Diamond SOI MOSFETs is higher than the one observed in Conventional devices operating at same bias and temperatures conditions, because the longitudinal electric field along the Diamond channel length is higher than the one found in the conventional counterpart. On the other hand, the DSM drain current is increased in the same proportion of I_{DLeak}, regarding to the same die area, geometric factor and bias and temperature conditions. So, these results show that also it is possible to analyze and investigate the behavior of devices at high temperatures, through three-dimensional numerical simulations, in order to predict its performance in harsh environments before submit them in such real operation conditions, and thus, even get additional information to improve the design/performance of the ICs in harsh temperature conditions. Therefore, Diamond layout style I_{DLeak} (35 pA and 228 pA for α equals to 127° and 53°, respectively) presents practically the same magnitude order than the one observed in the CSM counterpart (67 pA and 28 pA for α equals to 127° and 53°, respectively) at 300 °C and therefore when it is used DSM instead of the conventional one, Diamond structure does not degrade the performance the battery time life of the portable electronics equipment operating in harsh (high temperature) environments.

Author details

Salvador Pinillos Gimenez and Marcello Bellodi
Department of Electrical Engineering, Centro Universitário da FEI (FEI),
São Bernardo do Campo, São Paulo, Brazil

Acknowledgement

The author would really acknowledge CNPq and FAPESP for the financial support.

8. References

[1] Atlas User's Manual (2011) Device Simulation Software, Silvaco Inc.
[2] Sentaurus Device User Guide (2009) Synopsys Inc., v. C-2009.06.
[3] Colinge J-P (2008) FinFETs and Other MOSFET Multi-Gate Transistors, Springer.

[4] Gimenez S P, Bellodi M (2010) Diamond SOI MOSFET. PI0802745-5 A2, Publication Date: 03/23/2010, (RPI 2046).

[5] Gimenez S P, Bellodi M (2009) Diamond SOI MOSFET: A New Drain and Source/Channel Interface Layout to Improve Drain Current. Int. EUROSOI2009, Goteborg, Sweden.1: 87-88.

[6] Gimenez S P (2010) Diamond MOSFET: An innovative layout to improve performance of ICs. Int. solid-state electron. j. 54: 1690-1699.

[7] Bellodi M, Gimenez S P (2009) Drain Leakage Current Evaluation in the Diamond SOI nMOSFET at High Temperatures. Int. ecstransactions. 25: 243-253.

[8] DeviEdit User's Manual (2011) Silvaco Inc.

[9] Sentaurus Structure Editor User Guide (2008) Synopsys, Inc.

[10] Gimenez S P (2009) OCTO layout style. PI0903005-0 A2, Publication Date: 10/05/2011 (RPI: 2105).

[11] McDonnald J A (1996) Int. hte rep., III-Vs Review. 9: 57-59.

[12] Grabinski W, Stricker A, Fichtner W (1998) A Versatile Setup for Semiconductor Testing up to 550ºC". Int. HITEC 1998. 1: 143.

[13] Osman M A (1998) Investigation of high temperature effects on MOSFET transconductance (g_m). Int. HITEC 1998. 1: 301.

[14] Emam M, Tinoco J C, Vanhoennacker-Janvier D, Raskin J P (2008) High-temperature DC and RF behaviors of partially-depleted SOI MOSFET transistors. Int. solid-state Electron. j. 52: 1924-1932.

[15] Colinge J-P (2004) Silicon-on-Insulator Technology: Materials to VLSI. 3rd ed., Kluwer Acad. Pub., Massachusetts.

[16] Flandre D, Francis P, Gentinne B, and Colinge J P (1993) Demonstration of the potential of accumulation-mode MOS transistors on SOI substrates for high-temperature operation (150-300C). In. ieee trans. electon. dev. 14: 10-14.

[17] Francis P, Terao A, Gentinne B, Flandre D, Colinge J-P (1992) SO1 Tecnology for high-temperature applications. Int. iedm techn. Dig. 1:353-356.

[18] Jeon Deok-Su, Burk D E (1991) A temperature-dependent SOI MOSFET model for high-temperature Application (27ºC-300ºC). Int. ieee transact. on elect. dev., j. 38: 2101-2111.

[19] Kaamouch E, Delatte P, Moussa M Si, Raskin J-P, Vanhoenacker-Janvier D (2008) Temperature Behavior of Spiral Inductors on high resistive substrate in SOI CMOS technology. Int. solid-state Electron. J. 52: 1915-1923.

[20] Eggermont J-P, Ceuster D De, Flandre D, Gentinne B, Jespers G A, Colinge J-P (1996) Design of SOI CMOS Operational Amplifiers for Applications up to 300ºC. Int. ieee journal of solid-state circ. j., 31,179-186.

Chapter 14

Numerical Simulation of Passively Q-Switched Solid State Lasers

I. Lăncrănjan, R. Savastru, D. Savastru and S. Micloş

Additional information is available at the end of the chapter

http://dx.doi.org/10.5772/47812

1. Introduction

Short laser light pulses have a large number of applications in many civilian and military applications [1-10]. To a large percentage these short laser pulses are generated by solid state lasers using various active media types (crystals, glasses or ceramic) operated in Q-switching and/or mode-locking techniques [1-10]. Among the short light pulses laser generators, those operated in Q-switching regime and emitting pulses of nanosecond FWHM duration occupy a large part of civilian (material processing - for example: nano-materials formation by using ablation technique [3,7]) and military (projectile guidance over long distances and range finding) applications. Basically, Q-switching operation relies on a fast switching of laser resonator quality factor Q from a low value (corresponding to large optical losses) to a high one (representing low radiation losses). Depending on the proposed application, two main Q-switching techniques are used: active, based on electrical (in some cases operation with high voltages up to about 1 kV being necessary) or mechanical (spinning speeds up to about 1 kHz being used) actions on an optical component at least, coming from the outside of the laser resonator, and passive relying entirely on internal to the laser resonator induced variation of one optical component transmittance.

2. Theory

Figure 1 displays a general schematic of electronic energy levels of laser active centers embedded in an active medium and of saturable absorption centers embedded into solid state passive optical Q-switch cell laser oscillator operated in passive optical Q-switching regime [11-18,26]. As laser active centers, rare earth (RE) triple ions included by substitution into crystalline or poly micro-crystalline structure of the solid state active medium are used to a large extent. The four electronic energy levels of a laser active center can be observed together with the transitions between them, transitions which constitute the laser emission cycle of the active medium. The pumping transition, sometimes denoted as pumping absorption, from level "am0" to level "am1" together with the laser emission transition from level "am2" to level "am3" are presented. The pumping transition which assures attaining the population inversion between levels "am2" and "am3" can be technologically realized, considering basically the longitudinal or transverse/perpendicular versus laser beam propagation direction, by absorption of pumping radiation using one of two possibilities: longitudinal, along the active medium axis or transverse, through its side surfaces. Usually longitudinal pumping means a distribution of population inversion density which has an important consequence upon the laser dynamics. The transitions "am1" → "am2" and "am3" → "am0" are fast non-radiative transitions [26]. The laser emission transition "am2" → "am3" has a characteristic fluorescence lifetime τ_g in the range from μs to ms. The three-levels structure of electronic energy laser active medium is possible with the main characteristic difference that the level "am3" is identical with the level "am0" [5,6,7].

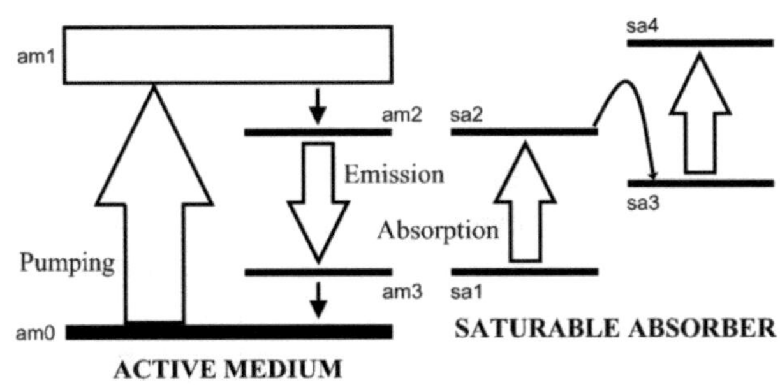

Figure 1. The schematic of a solid state laser active medium and passive optical Q-switch cell electronic energy levels. Active medium - levels: am0 - ground level; am1 - pumping level; am2 - upper laser level; am3 - lower laser level; Saturable absorber - sa1 - ground level; sa2 - upper saturable absorber level; sa3 - saturable absorber lower excited level; sa4 - saturable absorber upper excited level [26].

As can be seen in the schematic describing the functional cycle of the saturable absorber material, the absorption transition from electronic energy level "sa1" to electronic energy level "sa2" is the most important for passive optical Q-switching process, relying on its nonlinear characteristic absorption coefficient, $\alpha(I)$. The $\alpha(I)$ coefficient varies with the intensity I of the light beam incident on the saturable absorber according to an equation as [5,7]:

$$\alpha(I) = \frac{\alpha_0}{1 + \frac{I}{I_{sat}}} \tag{1}$$

I_{sat} represents the saturation value of the light beam intensity, the value for which the absorption coefficient is reduced with 50%. The function as a passive optical Q-switch cell is obtained by absorptive transition "sa1" → "sa2" which is characterized by a fluorescence lifetime of the upper level long enough to store the saturable absorption centres on the upper level and to depopulate the lower level at a fast rate. In this situation, the passive optical Q-switch cell appears as transparent (bleached) at the laser wavelength, allowing the laser radiation to circulate inside resonator. It has to be understood that simultaneously with the bleaching process, in the active medium the population inversion is accumulated, the laser active centres being stored into upper laser level. Practically, the assemble of the pumped active medium and passive optical Q-switch cell placed inside a resonator formed by two mirrors represent a laser oscillator with poor optical quality and high threshold condition. When the high energy threshold condition is attained for this low quality oscillator, a large population inversion is stored in the active medium and enhanced fluorescence emission intensity at laser wavelength is obtained. Because of the passive optical Q-switch cell bleaching effect, which is fast enough with in comparison to the upper laser level fluorescence lifetime, the optical quality of the resonator is fast growing to high values allowing laser emission [11,12,19-23]. As a consequence, the population inversion accumulated in the active medium is converted into emission of short laser pulses. The laser oscillator behaves as in free running regime in a very short early period quality and after that as in Q-switching regime characterised by emission of a short laser pulse burst.

As can be noticed, the possible situation of a non-saturable parasitic absorption of the passive optical Q-switch cell is presented. This parasitic absorption can take place between levels "sa3" and "sa4", levels "sa3" being populated by excitation transfer process from level "sa2" [20,21,27]. The non-saturable parasitic absorption can represent an embarrassment for Q-switching process in the case of a good spectral match between laser emission wavelength and "sa3" → "sa4" absorption because imposing a lower quality of the laser resonator after the bleaching of the passive optical Q-switch cell [13-16].

2.1. Laser rate equations

The parameters characteristic for a passively optical Q-switched operated solid state laser system and appearing in the equations describing its functionality, as schematically presented in Figure 2 and in Figure 5, are the following:

- Φ -the laser photon density;
- Φ_P -the laser pumping photon density;
- N_g - the population inversion density;
- N_a -the instantaneous population density of the SA ground absorbing state;
- N_{a0} -the total population density of the SA;
- l_g -the length of the gain medium;
- l_a -the length of the SA;
- c - the speed of light;
- R_p -the pumping rate of the active medium;
- K_a -the pumping radiation absorption coefficient of the active medium;
- R_1 -the reflectivity of the rear (high reflectance) laser mirror;
- R_2 -the reflectivity of the output coupler;
- L -the round trip non-saturable dissipative optical loss;
- σ_g -the stimulated emission cross section area of the gain medium;

- σ_a -the ground electronic state absorption cross section of the SA;
- σ_{ae} -the excited electronic state absorption cross section of the SA;
- τ_r -the light round trip transit time in the laser resonator;
- τ_g - the lifetime of the upper laser level of the gain medium;
- τ_a - the lifetime of the SA excited state;
- S_a -the beam cross-section area in the passive optical Q-switch cell;
- S_g -the beam cross-section area in the active medium;
- S -the pumped active medium contribution to priming spontaneous emission at the laser wavelength.

Without losing the generality degree of the mathematical approach, the photons of the laser beam are supposed to follow a Gaussian distribution in planes transverse to the laser beam optic axis, being defined as [24-26,31]:

$$\Phi(r,t) = \Phi(0,t)\exp\left(-\frac{2r^2}{w_L^2}\right) \tag{2}$$

Also without losing the generality degree of the mathematical approach, the photons of the pumping beam are supposed to follow a Gaussian distribution in planes transverse to the laser beam optic axis, being defined as [24-26,31]:

$$\Phi_P(r,t) = \Phi_P(0,t)\exp\left(-\frac{2r^2}{w_P^2}\right) \tag{3}$$

In the laser rate equation approach, Φ, N_g and N_a as functions of time are obtained by numerically solving a system of coupled differential equation. Whatever which is the used integration method, the accuracy of the solution is improved by considering physics details as intimate as possible, which means to take into account the overall purpose of the numerical performed investigation and the limits imposed by the electronic machine. In other words, an improved efficiency of the numerical simulation is a desirable purpose. Among the intimate physics details to be considered, the spatial distributions of Φ, N_g and N_a are important. By considering a cylindrical coordinate system r, Φ and z, properly suited to usual laser resonator geometry and its cylindrical symmetry, Φ, N_g and N_a are defined as functions of r and t. The Φ, N_g and N_a variations with z, the laser resonator axis coordinate are not directly considered, the implicitly ones being possible. Equations (4), (5) and (6) form a system of differential rate equations defining Φ, N_g and N_a. The system of equations (4), (5) and (6) can be numerically solved using different methods, mostly Runge-Kutta-Fehlberg [11-22,26]. It is important to underline a fact which will be demonstrated by experimentally results in the followings: the output parameters of a passively Q-switched solid state laser have large variations over very short periods before and/or after long time duration characterized by slow or zero such variations. Connected to this observation, it is worth to underline the necessity of accurate definition of the role of each term which appears in these equations. Equation (4) defines the time variation of laser photon density inside laser resonator as a sum of contributions due to amplification (gain) along the active medium, saturable losses ("sa1" → "sa2" transition in Figure 1) and parasitic losses ("sa3" → "sa4" transition in Figure 1) of the passive optical Q-switch cell, parasitic and output (R_1, R_2) laser resonator losses (L) and fluorescence emission at laser wavelength. In Equation (4), the integration over radial coordinate r is to be noticed.

$$\int_0^{\infty} \frac{\partial \Phi(r,t)}{\partial t} \cdot 2\pi r \cdot dr = \int_0^{\infty} \frac{\Phi(r,t)}{\tau_r} \left[2\sigma_g l_g N_g(r,t) - 2\sigma_a l_a N_a(r,t) - L_{par}(r,t) + \ln(R_1 R_2) - L + S(r,t) \right] \cdot 2\pi r \cdot dr . \tag{4}$$

Equation (5) defines the variation speed of the population inversion density as a sum of contributions due to the processes occurring in the active medium, namely stimulated emission, depopulation of upper laser level "am2" caused by fluorescence emission of an intensity proportional to $1/\tau_g$ and a positive term representing the pumping rate [31]:

$$\frac{dN_g(r,t)}{dt} = -c\sigma_g l_g \Phi(r,t) N_g(r,t) - \frac{N_g(r,t)}{\tau_g} + R_p(r,t) \tag{5}$$

Equation (6) defines the variation speed of the saturable absorber centres situated in the ground level "sa1" population inversion density as a sum of contributions due to the processes occurring in the passive optical Q-switch cell, namely absorption at laser wavelength (transition "sa1" → "sa2"), depopulation of first excited level "sa2" caused by fluorescence emission and/or non-radiative transitions of an intensity proportional to $1/\tau_a$:

$$\frac{dN_a(r,t)}{dt} = -\frac{S_g}{S_a} \gamma c \sigma_a l_a \Phi(r,t) N_a(r,t) + \frac{N_{ao} - N_a(r,t)}{\tau_a} \tag{6}$$

In Equation (4), the role of non-saturable losses of the passive optical Q-switch cell due to "sa3" → "sa4" absorption is considered by introducing the term L_{par} which is defined using σ_{ae} as [18,30,31]:

$$L_{par}(r,t) = 2\sigma_{ae} \left[N_{ao} - N_a(r,t) \right] \tag{7}$$

In Equation (5), the rate term $R_p(r,t)$ represents absorption of pumping radiation into active medium and is defined as:

$$R_P(r,t) = K_{abs} \int_0^{\infty} \Phi_P(0,t) 2\pi r dr \tag{8}$$

The coupled differential equations system (4), (5) and (6) is an Initial Value Problem (IVP). Accurate definitions of photon density, population inversion and saturable absorption centres population density initial values represent a key point of passive optical Q-switched solid state laser numerical simulation. The initial value of the laser photon density can be considered as proportional to the active medium fluorescence emission intensity. When the differential equation system (4), (5) and (6) is solved numerically, for practical reasons, photon density initial value is defined as a much smaller percentage of its maximum value [6,26,31]:

$$S(r,0) \approx k\Phi_m(r,t) \tag{9}$$

The initial value of the population inversion density in the active medium is defined as

$$N_g(r,0) = N_g(0,0)\exp\left(-\frac{2r^2}{w_P^2}\right) \tag{10}$$

In Equation (10) the factor $N_g(0,0)$, a factor which represents the laser oscillation threshold condition on the laser resonator axis ($r = 0$), being possible denoted as an "axial" threshold condition is defined as:

$$N_g(0,0) = \frac{\ln\left(\frac{1}{R_1R_2}\right) + \left(\frac{\sigma_{ae}}{\sigma_a}\right)\ln\left(\frac{1}{T_0^2}\right) + L}{2\sigma_g l_g}\left(1 + \frac{w_L^2}{w_P^2}\right) \tag{11}$$

The initial value of saturable absorption centres population density is most easily to define because, as a simplification corresponding to most encountered experimental configurations, these centres are uniformly distributed inside the passive optical Q-switch cell. The initial value of saturable absorption centres population density is defined as:

$$N_a(r,0) = N_{ao} \tag{12}$$

A possible development of mathematical apparatus used for numerical simulation passive optical Q-switched solid state laser can be obtained by substituting equations (2), (10) and (12) into (5) and (6) which are modified into:

$$N_g(r,t) = N_g(0,0)\exp\left(-\frac{2r^2}{w_P^2}\right)\exp\left[-\gamma c\sigma_g \exp\left(-\frac{2r^2}{w_L^2}\right) l_g \int_0^t \Phi(0,t)dt\right], \tag{13}$$

$$N_a(r,t) = N_{ao}\exp\left[-\frac{S_g}{S_a}\sigma_a c \exp\left(-\frac{2r^2}{w_L^2}\right)\int_0^t \Phi(0,t)dt\right] \tag{14}$$

In the next step, by substituting equations (2), (13) and (14) into (4), an equation describing photon density speed of variation can be obtained:

$$\frac{d\Phi(0,t)}{dt} = \frac{4\sigma_g N_g(0,0) l_g \Phi(0,t)}{w_L^2 \tau_r} K_1(t) - \frac{4(\sigma_a - \sigma_{ae}) N_{a0} l_a \Phi(0,t)}{w_L^2 \tau_r} K_2(t) - \frac{\Phi(0,t)}{\tau_r} K_3 \tag{15}$$

In Equation (15) the factors $K_1(t)$, $K_2(t)$ and K_3 are introduced for ease of numerical integration, of numerical solving procedures. These factors are defined as:

$$K_1(t)=\int_0^{\infty}\exp\left[-\gamma\sigma_g c\exp\left(-\frac{2r^2}{w_L^2}\right)\int_0^t\Phi(0,t)dt\right]\exp\left[-2\frac{r^2\left(w_L^2+w_P^2\right)}{w_L^2 w_P^2}\right]2rdr\,, \tag{16}$$

$$K_1(t)=\int_0^{\infty}\exp\left[-\frac{S_g}{S_a}\sigma_a c\exp\left(-\frac{2r^2}{w_L^2}\right)\int_0^t\Phi(0,t)dt\right]\exp\left[-\frac{2r^2}{w_L^2}\right]2rdr\,, \tag{17}$$

$$K_3=\ln\left(\frac{1}{R_1R_2}\right)+\left(\frac{\sigma_{ae}}{\sigma_a}\right)\ln\left(\frac{1}{T_0^2}\right)+L \tag{18}$$

In defining K_3, the initial small-signal transmission of the passive optical Q-switch cell is used being defined as:

$$T_0=\exp\left(-\sigma_a l_a N_{a0}\right) \tag{19}$$

For practical reasons, for comparison of experimental results with the ones obtained by numerically solving the rate coupled differential equations, a simplification was considered, namely that of a transverse to the active medium uniform pumping. Regarding the above developed mathematical apparatus, this hypothesis is equivalent to considering that pumping radiation has a distribution with $w_P \rightarrow \infty$. A direct consequence of this simplification is that while the photon density and saturable absorption centres population density initial values are kept the same, population inversion density initial value is modified as:

$$N_g(0,0)=\frac{\ln\left(\frac{1}{R_1R_2}\right)+\ln\left(\frac{1}{T_0^2}\right)+L}{2\sigma_g l_g} \tag{20}$$

The coupled differential equations system (4), (5) and (6) is simplified to:

$$\frac{d\Phi(t)}{dt}=\frac{\Phi(t)}{\tau_r}\left[2\sigma_g l_g N_g(t)-2\sigma_a l_a N_a(t)+\ln(R_1\cdot R_2)-L\right]+S\,, \tag{21}$$

$$\frac{dN_g}{dt}=-c\sigma_g l_g \varphi N_g-\frac{N_g}{\tau_g}+R_p\,, \tag{22}$$

$$\frac{dN_a}{dt}=-c\sigma_a l_a \varphi N_a+\frac{N_{ao}-N_a}{\tau_a}\,. \tag{23}$$

2.2. Iteration technique

The main idea of passive optical Q-switched solid state laser using an iteration technique consists in considering a Gaussian distribution of photon density inside laser resonator; launching it inside laser resonator at an initial, reference plane transverse to the laser beam axis; calculating its modification during round trip propagation between the laser mirrors using the ABCD matrix M_{LR} characteristic for the investigated laser resonator [36-38]. The integral equation representing the imposed condition of photon density distribution reproducibility in phase and amplitude, with the exception of a proportionality coefficient, is defined at the chosen reference plane by numeric integration corresponding to round trip propagation [9,28-30]. The numeric integration corresponding to round trip propagation is iteratively calculated for verifying that photon density distribution reproducibility is attained.

Such approach can conduct to determination of the fundamental mode parameters of the laser cavity under real pumping conditions, assuming a Gaussian distribution of pumping radiation intensity [37]. The radially variable gain profiles [32-34] as well as heat-source densities [35] which occur as a result of focusing of the pump beam in the majority of diode-pumped lasers can be considered. In analyzing this type of laser in the framework of the space-dependent rate-equation model [32-37], we assume that laser mode parameters are known a priori. The thermal guiding effect responsible for mode structure in lasers operating near threshold can be analyzed establishing its importance. Thus the developed complementary models that account for gain guiding [32,35], the Kerr effect [34], and gain-related effects [32-37] can be developed.

Mathematically, the above mentioned considerations can be expressed by differential equation defining the propagation of photon density distribution along the laser resonator axis, z being the axial coordinate:

$$\frac{1}{I_r(z)}\frac{dI_r(z)}{dz}=\frac{g(z)}{1+I_r(z)} \tag{24}$$

In Equation (24), $g(z)$ is the small-signal logarithmic gain coefficient and $I_r(z)$ is relative laser beam density defined as:

$$I_r(z)=\frac{I(z)}{I_{sat}} \tag{25}$$

I_{sat} represents the saturation intensity of the investigated laser active medium and resonator.

As mentioned previously, at the starting point the cavity matrix M_{LR} including the effective thermal lensing power of a gain medium is calculated in order to determine the incident Gaussian beam profile at the considered point of entrance (reference plane). It is considered a small value of the incident intensity magnitude compared with the saturation one. In each step of the iterative procedure the output intensity profile after passage through the gain medium is calculated according to Equations (24) and (25) as:

$$I_{r,1}\exp\left(I_{r,1}\right)=I_{r,0}\exp\left(gl_rI_{r,0}\right) \tag{26}$$

where $I_{r,1}$ is the output laser beam intensity at the reference plane and $I_{r,0}$ is the input counterpart incident on the reference plane. Equation (26) can be transformed into a Lambert W function [38]:

$$I_{r,1}=W\left[I_{r,0}\exp\left(I_{r,0}\right)G\left(l_r\right)\right] \tag{27}$$

Equation (27) can be solved using by Lambert W function tables. The general integral of this type of first-order ordinary differential equation is known as the Lambert W function.

The cavity matrix M_{LR} is defined as the product of active medium effective gain matrix M_{SG}, bare cavity M_{BC} which includes the rest of laser resonator components. The laser beam is passed through the cavity, applying the product of both matrices M_{SG} and M_{BC}. At each step we introduce the logarithmic passive losses of cavity δ_{pas}, multiplying the intensity profile at the output mirror by the factor $\exp(-\delta_{pas})$. Because of the saturated gain profile and passive losses, the peak intensity converges with the number of round-trips to finite value, for which the procedure stops. It is worth to notice that in the developed model including spatially variable gain saturation it is assumed that the fundamental laser mode is not changed. The main concept consists in application of the analytical solution of a saturable gain (or absorption) equation for a homogeneously broadened medium.

3. Comparison with experimental results

As previously mentioned, the numerical simulation methods are validated by comparison with experimental results. Special care has to be taken when applying the system coupled differential equations defining laser output parameters. In the followings, such comparison of numerical simulation results obtained using the above developed mathematical apparatus performed for two experimental passively Q-switched Nd:YAG lasers are presented: the first based on a rod active medium and the second based on a slab laser active medium.

3.1. Rod laser example

The experimental setup developed in the case of a rod laser active medium numerical simulation results for verifying the simple theory previously presented is designed for measuring the laser output parameters, mainly the FWHM laser pulse time width, at three different lengths of the resonator, keeping unchanged the components of the resonator, including the pumping chamber. As the passive Q-switch cell, a cylindrical LiF:F_2^- crystal is used. The LiF:F_2^- crystal is mounted approximately at one third of the laser resonator. The LiF:F_2^- has no dielectric AR coatings on the optical plane parallel (less than 30″ error) end faces. As observed in Figure 2 the rod laser oscillator setup consists into using a step variable length plane-plane resonator with a high reflectivity mirror (HR in Figure 2) of 99 % reflectivity and an output coupler (OC in Figure 2) manufactured of a quartz plate of about

8 % reflectivity. Into the laser resonator, in order to improve the stability laser output stability, a polarizer made of two 1 mm thick quartz plates placed at Brewster angle versus optical axis is inserted. The pumping system consists of a QUANTRON 104 B reflector made of a cylindrical Quartz block with external and the two internal holes for flash lamp and active medium optical quality polished surfaces. QUANTRON 104 B reflector is made of a colloidal silver layer chemically deposited on the external surface Quartz block surface and protected from oxidation by an electrochemically deposited Ni-Cu layer. An INP 5/60 AI flash lamp mounted on a power source which injected discharge current of about 200 μs duration is used. The adjustable repetition frequency of flash lamp pumping pulses is set at 1 Hz. The active medium is a Ø6×80 mm Nd:YAG laser rod with both ends having AR coatings. The active medium is pumped on 60 mm of its length. The QUANTRON 104 B reflector, flash lamp and laser rod are cooled with flowing de-ionized water.

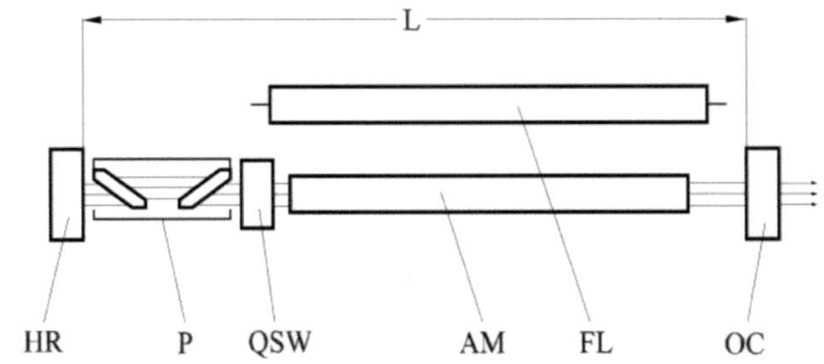

Figure 2. Schematic representation of the rod laser setup. HR - high reflectivity back mirror; P - polarizer; QSW – LiF:F_2^- passive optical Q-switch cell; AM – active medium; FL – flash lamp; OC – output coupler; L – optical resonator length

The laser output is measured with a system composed of:

- laser energy measurement - a thermoelectric GENTEC ED2S energy meter used as the "calibration unit" and a silicon photodiode ROL 021 operated in an inverse polarization mode as a service laser energy monitor;
- laser pulse time shape measurement - an ITT F4014 vacuum photodiode (about 10 ps response time) coupled to a Tektronix 519 oscilloscope (1GHz bandwidth). The response time of this measuring system was estimated to be about 1 ns.

Regarding the LiF:F_2^- crystal used as passive optical Q-switch cell, denoted as Sample C105, it can be mention the fact that it was obtained from a basic crystal with 9 mm diameter and 30 mm length grown in controlled nitrogen atmosphere by Czochralski method. In Table 1, the impurity content concentration of LiF:F_2^- passive optical Q-switch C105 sample, measured by neutron activation method is presented.

Impurity [ppm]										
Type	Na	Cl	K	Ca	Fe	Co	Sc	Zn	La	Pb
II.2	250	1.5	1.7	2.7	185	5.5	2.9	2.5	1.6	2.5

Table 1. The impurity content concentration of investigated LiF:F_2^- passive optical Q-switch C105 sample.

The saturable absorber F_2^- color centers are obtained by "high energy electrons" (about 7 MeV), denoted as "HEE", irradiation at about 1 MRad/h dose and ten Co^{60} γ additional irradiation stages operated at about 1 MRad/h dose. The irradiation procedures applied to Sample C105 are summarized in Table 2 [21].

Sample	Stage 1 [MRad]	Stage 2 [MRad]	Additional [MRad]
C105	250	200	48

Table 2. The irradiation procedures for F_2^- color center formation used for investigated LiF:F_2^- passive optical Q-switch C105 sample.

The end facets of the investigated LiF crystals were optically polished. Optical transmittance measurements were performed on the investigated LiF samples before F_2^- color centers formation by irradiation procedures using a Perkin Elmer Lambda 1050 spectrophotometer. The optical transmittance of clean LiF samples was measured to be of between 0.90 and 0.92. In Table 3, the results of the spectroscopic measurements are summarized.

Sample	Type	T_{Lin}	T_{Lfin}	T_{QswSA}
C105	II.2	0.035	0.899	0.901

Table 3. The spectroscopic characteristics of investigated LiF:F_2^- passive optical Q-switch samples.

The results of numerical simulation for photon density and population inversion density are shown in Figure 3. Experiments proved a good concordance with the simulation. Figure 4 is a plot of measured power density, which fits pretty well with the photon density curve predicted in Figure 3.

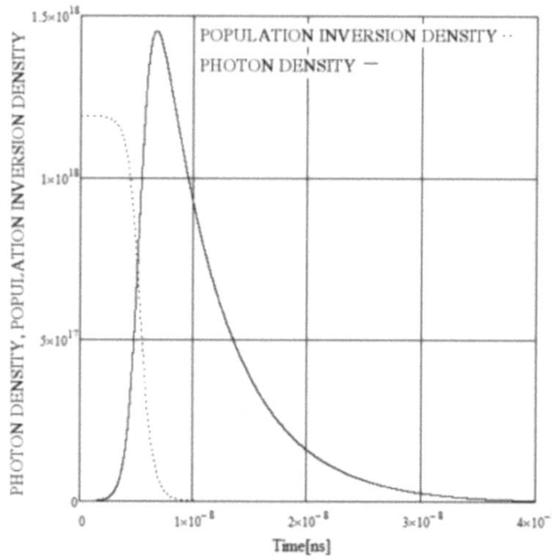

Figure 3. The numerical simulation results for photon density (continuous line) and population inversion density (dotted line).

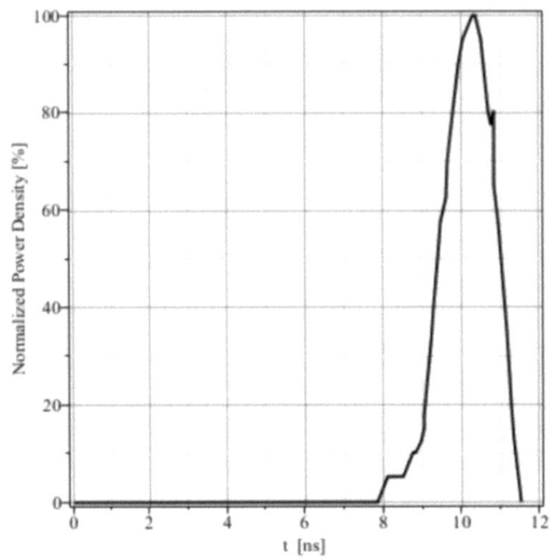

Figure 4. Laser pulse time-shape observed in Q-switching regime for the rod laser oscillator in the case of laser resonator length L = 43.5 cm. Horizontal time division is 2 ns.

3.2. Slab laser oscillator/amplifier example

The use of a slab laser oscillator/amplifier instead of a linear laser resonator offers some remarkable advantages, such as an increased power in smaller volume. Our simulation took into account the schematic presented bellow.

A schematic detail - a cross-section of the pumping chamber - of the investigated Nd:YAG slab oscillator/amplifier laser system setup is shown in Figure 5. The active medium of the investigated laser oscillator/amplifier system is a Nd:YAG crystal slab with sizes of 7 mm × 27 mm ×163 mm with a quite large clear cross-section aperture of 7 mm × 25 mm. The end facets of the active medium are cut and polished at Brewster angle to impose a polarization degree of the laser beam propagating through the laser oscillator/amplifier system. The polarization of the laser light in the case of a passively Q-switched Nd:YAG laser oscillator is useful for the stability of the output parameters, as it is experimentally observed [4]. The slab laser system used a pumping chamber consisting of four krypton flash lamps, 7 mm diameter and 4 inches (101.6 mm) length, mounted into two pairs along the large side surfaces (27 mm ×163 mm) of the Nd:YAG slab active medium. The slab active medium and the flash lamps are cooled using flowing demineralized water. As mentioned in [4], two 2 mm – thick UV cut-off filters (WG360, 360 nm cut-off wavelength) are inserted between the krypton flash lamps and the Nd:YAG crystal slab to prevent UV irradiation of active medium that causes active medium damage by forming color centers and other intrusions. The side un-pumped surfaces of the Nd:YAG crystal slab are thermally insulated by glass plates mounted in direct contact, which serve to dissipate the heat. Accordingly, regarding flash lamp pumping efficiency and considering the spectral match between the Nd:YAG slab active medium absorption bands and the flash lamp light emission, the pumping power transfer coefficient, q_g, is approximated to 2.5%. It is worth to be emphasized that the active medium of the investigated laser system can be considered as uniformly pumped and, therefore, the pumping rate can be approximated as constant in the cross-sectional area of the active medium, actually in the volume of active medium, within an error of less than 1%.

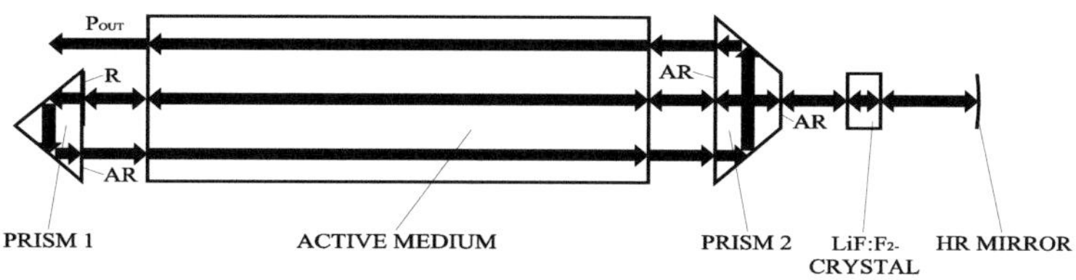

Figure 5. Schematic representation of the slab laser setup. PRISM 1, PRISM 2 – prisms; R – 53 % reflective coating as output coupler; AR – anti-reflective coating; LiF:F_2^- CRYSTAL - passive optical Q-switch cell; ACTIVE MEDIUM – Nd:YAG slab; HR MIRROR – high reflectivity mirror; P_{OUT} – outgoing laser beam.

Concerning the approximations considered in defining the system of three coupled differential equations (20) – (22), the experimentally determined time shape of the pump light emitted by the four flash lamps proved the validity of the assumption that the pumping is quasi-continuous. The rise-time and the fall-time of the pump light pulse are short compared to the overall pulse width. This justifies the approximation of using a constant value of R_p during Q-switching process. It is important to mention that the pumping light duration can be varied up to 4 ms, extremely long compared to Nd:YAG fluorescence lifetime (τ_g ~ 250 μs) and to the expected characteristic duration of the investigated Q-switching process (10^{-8} - 10^{-7} s).

The beam aperture in the laser oscillator is one third of the slab width (an area of about 81 mm^2), this value being imposed by the on axis mounted PRISM 2, more exactly, being imposed by the small facet of this prism [4]. The active facets of PRISM 2 are AR-coated to reduce the laser beam parasitic losses. It can be noticed that one third of the Nd:YAG slab active medium is used for the laser oscillator and the rest for the two amplifier stages. The off axis mounted PRISM 1 has a 14 mm hypotenuse, two thirds of the slab active medium width. The upper half of the PRISM 1 hypotenuse has a thin layer of 53% reflectivity. The upper part of the PRISM 1 acts as output mirror (output coupler) for the slab Nd:YAG oscillator. The other optically active facets of the PRISM 1 are AR-coated for the laser wavelength to reduce losses due to laser beam manipulation through the two amplifier stages. The Prism 1 is placed at a distance of about 85 cm from the rear high reflectivity mirror (5 m radius of curvature), denoted as HR MIRROR in Figure 5. Theoretically, the dimensions of the laser resonator output coupler in the transverse plane have to be extremely large compared to the characteristic laser beam transverse dimension, which is mainly imposed by the active medium. Obviously, it is practically impossible to meet this requirement, because a large prism would obstruct the output beam. In our experiment the prism is 7 mm wide, exactly equal to the slab active medium width. This implies increased scattering losses on the output coupler edges. Therefore the round trip non-saturable dissipative optical loss L will be larger, marking higher losses. In order to effectively use the entire slab active medium volume, the ratio of the width, the hypotenuse of the PRISM 1 and the aperture of PRISM 2 has to be roughly 3:2:1, this being an "on the edge" value [4].

Denoted as samples C326, C327, C328 and C329, four lithium fluoride crystals grown by Czochralski method, were cut and optically polished at dimensions of 10 mm × 10 mm × 40 mm. Each of the developed LiF:F_2^- passive optical Q-switches can be operated in two possible ways: with 10 mm or 40 mm optical length. As indicated in Figure 5, the LiF:F2- passive optical Q-switch uses the 10 mm optical length. They were irradiated by a 1.16 MeV Co60 γ–source at a dose rate of 1 MRad/hour to create the F_2^- color centers, which are the saturable absorber centers of interest to be used in the laser resonator - the final LiF:F_2^- passive optical Q-switch. The impurity content concentration in the raw LiF crystals used for creating LiF:F_2^- passive optical Q-switches are the same as in Table 1. An important feature of the developed LiF:F_2^- passive optical Q-switch is that each of them has four optical active plane facets (two pairs of plane parallel facets).

In Table 4 the parameters determined for the four samples (C326, C327, C328 and C329) of LiF:F_2^- passive Q-switches by spectral measurements are summarized [4]. Here D represents the time integrated Co^{60} γ irradiation dose, T_{in} is the initial (small signal) transmittance, T_{PL} represents the parasitic losses and T_{fin} is the final (saturated) transmittance. The fluorescence lifetime of the saturable absorption centers is τ_a = 75 ns [23]. The ground state absorption cross section of the SA is estimated to be τ_a = $1.67 \cdot 10^{-17}$ cm^{-2} [4]. Using these spectral measurements, the F_2^- color centers concentration [F_2^-] can be calculated [4].

Sample	D [MRad]	T_{in}	T_{PL}	T_{fin}	[F_2^-] [cm^{-3}]
C326	150	0.82	0.88	0.87	$4.02 \cdot 10^{15}$
C327	175	0.80	0.91	0.89	$4.19 \cdot 10^{15}$
C328	200	0.75	0.90	0.88	$4.45 \cdot 10^{15}$
C329	225	0.72	0.90	0.88	$4.61 \cdot 10^{15}$

Table 4. The parameters of the tested LiF:F_2^- passive Q-switches.

The transmittance of the lithium fluoride crystals at 1.06 μm (laser wavelength) was measured before and after the F_2^- color centers formation by Co^{60} γ irradiation to accurately determine the LiF:F_2^- passive Q-switches laser functional parameters, as described in [4]. The transmittance spectrogram of a sample of the set of investigated LiF:F_2^- passive optical Q-switches was obtained using a Perkin Elmer Lambda 1050 on a 40 mm optical length LiF:F_2^- sample. The measured transmittance at 1600 nm was considered to be T_{fin} because at this wavelength there is not reported in literature any absorption due to color centers [4]. Here the LiF:F_2^- should to be transparent, as it is recorded in the spectrogram. The measured T_{fin} indicate a low heavy metals impurity concentration. This indicates also a small concentration of colloids formed as by-product of color centers irradiation processing.

The passively Q-switched Nd:YAG slab oscillator/amplifier is basically made up of an oscillator and two amplifier stages, all operating inside the same active medium. It is assumed that the amplification factor of the laser pulses by propagation through the two amplifier stages rise up to about 3.5 - 4.0, increasing with pumping energy up to 1600 J [4]. This is an important issue in performing the numerical simulation of the slab Nd:YAG laser oscillator/amplifier system in the sense that the numeric solution of the coupled rate equations (20) – (22) can provide information about the oscillator stage and the obtained results should be multiplied by the amplification factor (3.5 – 4.0).

The application of the previously presented numerical analysis method consists in performing several successive steps. First of all, the evaluation of the pumping rate, N_{cw}. For both samples considered in this application, the pumping rate of the active medium is evaluated for a 4 ms pumping pulse width and 1040 J pumping pulse energy resulting $R_p = 4.242 \cdot 10^{19}$ cm^{-3}. The population inversion density for the investigated laser system if continuously pumped and operated in free-running regime is defined for the same pumping conditions as $N_{cw} = 1.061 \cdot 10^{16}$ cm^{-3}. The estimated value of N_{cw} is obtained considering σ_g about 230 μs [7]. The Nd:YAG emission cross-section is $\sigma_g = 6.5 \cdot 10^{-19}$ cm^2 [7]. In Table 5, the results of the simulation for laser output parameters, using the mathematical apparatus presented in Section 2, are compared to the experimental data. It can be noticed the fact that the simulated values of E_{out}, σ_{out}, P_{out} and f_{rep} are comparable with the experimental data. σ_p can be considered as fulfilling the necessary condition for multiple laser pulses emission. Considering the value of σ_p (4 ms), the laser emission is therefore quasi continuous. The next step is the simulation of laser pulses repetition frequency, first laser pulse time shape, FWHM pulse width and output energy.

For sample C326 the simulated value of laser pulse repetition frequency is $f_{rep} = 75.54$ kHz, less than the measured value of 80 kHz, while for sample C329 (see Figure 6) the simulated value of laser pulse repetition frequency is $f_{rep} = 25.54$ kHz, larger than the measured value of 20 kHz (Figure 7).

Parameter	Unit	Sample C326		Sample C329	
		Simulated	Experimental	Simulated	Experimental
E_{total}	J		26.7		25.0
N_{pulses}	-		334		82
E_{out}	mJ	26	25	105	98.5
σ_{out}	ns	70.77	68.43	28.42	30.90
P_{out}	MW	0.36	0.38	3.75	3.17
f_{rep}	kHz	75.54	80.00	25.14	20.00

Table 5. Summary of laser output parameters experimentally measured and numerically estimated for C326 and C329 samples.

For the sample C326 the simulated FWHM is ~ 72 ns, while the measured value is ~ 68 ns. Figure 8 illustrates the simulated single laser pulse time shape obtained for the sample C329. The simulated FWHM is ~ 31 ns, while the measured value is ~28 ns (see Figure 9).

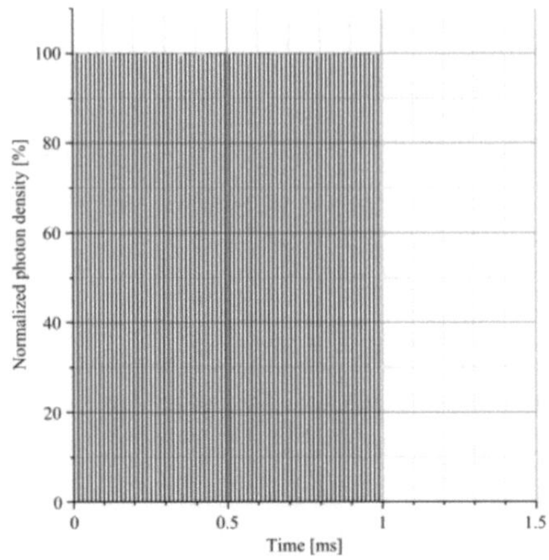

Figure 6. Simulated laser pulses train time-shape.

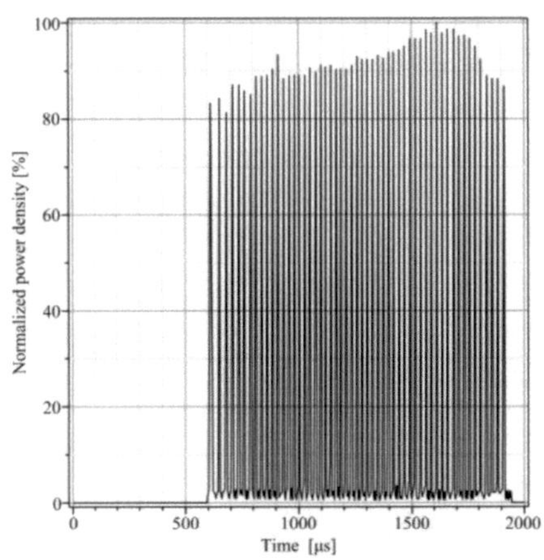

Figure 7. Measured laser pulses train time shape at a pumping pulse width of about 2 ms.

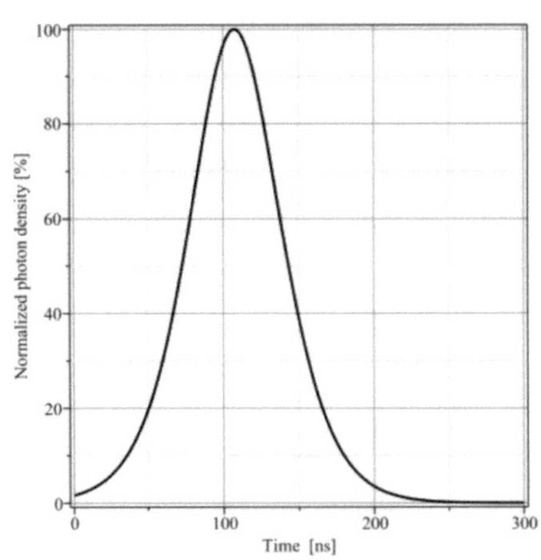

Figure 8. Simulated single laser pulse time shape.

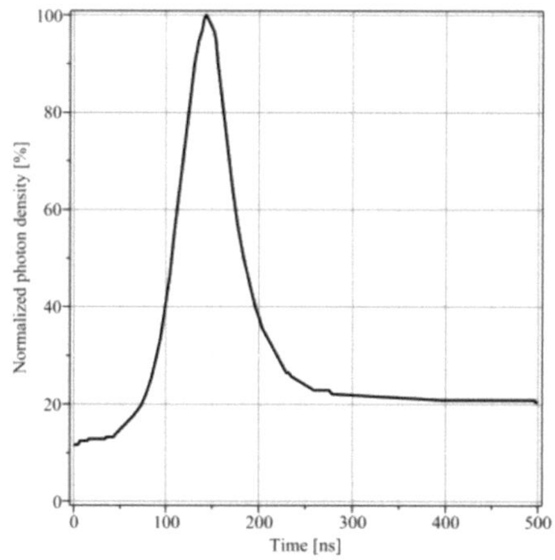

Figure 9. Measured first laser pulse time-shape.

It is worth noticing that several previously defined parameters describing the Nd:YAG slab oscillator/amplifier laser system play an important role in acquiring a certain accuracy of the developed numerical simulation method. As a rule of thumb, the coefficients used for defining the system of coupled rate differential equations (20) – (22) are measured experimentally whenever it is possible. This rule of thumb is valid, directly or through intermediate estimations, for the majority of these coefficients with several exceptions such as R_p, S and L. It is difficult to estimate an accurate value of R_p, in the case of the investigated laser system, because q_g depends on the spectral match between the pumping light emission spectrum of the flash lamps and the absorption lines of the Nd:YAG active medium. This spectral match depends on the neutral glass UV filters used for preventing destruction of the Nd:YAG active medium by the intense UV radiation. In the numerically solving the differential equations (20) – (22) q_g was set to be in the range 0.5% - 1.5%. S is extremely difficult to be accurately estimated because, in principle, it represents a certain percentage of the inverted, pumped Nd:YAG active medium fluorescence emission. S can be evaluated as a coefficient times the initial N_g value, the coefficient being the ratio between the areas subtended by the end apertures, as seen from a middle point of the active medium, on a sphere with the center in this middle point and the radius half of the active medium length. This coefficient has to be "weighted" as considering diffraction effects produced in the laser resonator. In the performed numerical simulations, S is considered as 10^{-6} of N_g initial value. The L coefficient is composed of two parts: the first one due to the non-saturable linear parasitic linear losses of the laser resonator itself and the second one, much smaller, due to the same type of losses of the passive optical Q-switch cell (denoted as T_{PL} in Table 4). For the numerical simulation of the two investigated cases, the samples C326 and C329, the contribution of the laser resonator linear losses was considered as $L = 0.1 - 0.3\ \text{cm}^{-1}$.

The simulation results presented in Table 5 are obtained by considering the best fit with experimental data set of q_g, S and L parameters. The q_g, S and L parameters were varied in the previously defined ranges and the developed simulation software was run with these coefficients until the values came close to the measured data. Afterwards, the developed simulation software was run several times in order to check the obtained results. This procedure suggests a design method for the investigated Nd:YAG laser oscillator/amplifier type, a method relying on the developed simulation procedure. The suggested design method is based on using components, mainly active medium and passive optical Q-switch cells with the parameters previously defined, but with possible different geometrical dimensions, an optimum being found for the best fit of desired output parameters with the set of q_g, S and L parameters.

4. Conclusion

This chapter presents the results obtained in the numerical simulation of a passively Q-switched solid state laser system generating high power, high output energy singular laser pulses or laser pulses trains in pulsed CW or quasi-CW pumping. An important feature of the developed simulation method consists of an analysis of the differences between the first passively Q-switched laser pulse and the next, generated by a CW or a quasi-CW pumped laser system, regarding the recovery condition to the initial state of the passive optical Q-switch cell, which is analyzed in detail for the first time. As far as we know, concerning the passive optical Q-switching, this difference is not reported in literature so far as exhaustively studied. By observing this difference, a method for estimation of laser output pulse parameters is developed. The numerical simulation results are compared to the experimental data and a fairly good agreement between them is observed.

Author details

I. Lăncrănjan
Advanced Study Center–National Institute of Aerospace Research "Elie Carafoli", Bucharest, Romania

R. Savastru, D. Savastru and S. Micloş
National Institute of R&D for Optoelectronics INOE 2000, Magurele, Ilfov, Romania

5. References

[1] Ready JF, Davis J, Berkmanns J, Kugler TR. Lasers for Materials Processing. In: Ready JF. (ed.) LIA Handbook of Laser Materials Processing. Oakland: Magnolia Press; 2001. p27-43.
[2] Steen WM. Laser Material Processing. Berlin, Heidelberg, New York: Springer; 1991.
[3] Misawa H., Juodkazis S. 3D Laser Microfabrication, Weinheim: Wiley-VCH; 2006.
[4] Dong S, Lü Q, Lancranjan I. 220 W Average Output Power From a Q-Switching Nd: YAG Slab Laser with a LiF: F_2^- Crystal. Optics and Laser Technology 1993; 25(3) 175-178.
[5] Siegman AE. Lasers, Sausalito: University Science Books; 1986.
[6] Mercer CJ, Tsang YH, Binks DJ. A Model of a QCW Diode Pumped Passively Q-Switched Solid State Laser. Journal of Modern Optics 2007; 54 (12) 1685-1694.

[7] Koechner W. Solid State Laser Engineering, Berlin: Springer; 2006.

[8] Fan TY, Byer RL. Diode Laser-Pumped Solid State Lasers. IEEE Journal of Quantum Electronics 1988; 24 (6) 895-912.

[9] Laporta P, Brussard M. Design Criteria for Mode Size Optimization in Diode-Pumped Solid-State Lasers. IEEE Journal of Quantum Electronics 1991; 27(10) 2319-2326.

[10] Siegman AE. New Developments in Laser Resonators. In: Holmes DA (ed.) Optical Resonators, 1990, Proceedings of SPIE vol. 1224; 2-14.

[11] Degnan JJ. Optimization of Passively Q-Switched Lasers. IEEE Journal of Quantum Electronics 1995; 31(11) 1890-1901.

[12] Degnan JJ. Theory of the Optimally Coupled Q- Switched Laser. IEEE Journal of Quantum Electronics 1989; 25(2) 214-220.

[13] Kuo YK, Birnbaum M, Chen W. Ho:YLiF4 Saturable Absorber Q-Switch for the 2-◎m Tm, Cr:Y3Al5O12 Laser. Applied Physics Letters 1994; 65(24) 3060-3062.

[14] Kuo YK, Huang MF, Birnbaum M. Tunable Cr^{4+}:YSO Q-Switched Cr:LiCAF Laser. IEEE Journal of Quantum Electronics 1995; 31(4) 657-663.

[15] Kuo YK, Birnbaum M. Passive Q-Switching of the Alexandrite Laser with a $Cr^{4+}:Y_2SiO_5$ Solid-State Saturable Absorber. Applied Physics Letters 1995; 67(2) 173-175.

[16] Kuo YK, Birnbaum M. Ho:YVO4 Solid-State Saturable Absorber Q Switch for 2-◎m Tm,$Cr:Y_3Al_5O_{12}$ Laser. Applied Optics 1996; 35(6) 881-884.

[17] Kuo YK, Chen W, Stultz RD, Birnbaum M. $Dy^{2+}:CaF_2$ Saturable-Absorber Q Switch for the Ruby Laser. Applied Optics 1994; 33(27) 6348-6351.

[18] Kuo YK, Birnbaum M, Unlu F, Huang MF. $Ho:CaF_2$ Solid-State Saturable Absorber Q-Switch for the 2-◎m Tm,$Cr:Y_3Al_5O_{12}$ Laser. Applied Optics 1996, 35(15) 2576-2579.

[19] Kuo YK, Lee S, Unlu F, Huang MF, Birnbaum M, Fuqua PD, Dunn B. Solid State Polymer Dye Q-Switch for Cr:LiCAF, Alexandrite, and Ruby Lasers. Electronics Letters 1996; 32(23) 2146-2148.

[20] Kuo YK, Chen HM. Cr:YSO Saturable Absorber for the Three-Level $Cr:BeAl_2O_4$ Laser at 680.4 nm, Japanese Journal of Applied Physics 2000; 39(12A) 6574-6575.

[21] Y. K. Kuo, H. M. Chen, J. Y. Chang, Numerical study of the Cr:YSO Q switched ruby laser, Opt. Eng., 9 (2001) 2031-2035.

[22] Kuo YK, Chen HM, Chang Y. Numerical Study of Passive Q switching of a Tunable Alexandrite Laser with a Cr:Y2SiO5 Solid-State Saturable Absorber. Applied Optics 2001; 40(9) 1362-1368.

[23] Zayhowski JJ, Kelley PL. Optimization of Q-Switched Lasers, IEEE Journal of Quantum Electronics 1991, 27(9) 2220-2225.

[24] Lancranjan I, Miclos S, Savastru D, Popescu A. Numerical Simulation of a DFB-Fiber Laser Sensor (II) - Theoretical Analysis of an Acoustic Sensor. Journal of Optoelectronics and Advanced Materials 2010; 12 (12) 2456-2461.

[25] Lancranjan I, Miclos S, Savastru D, Popescu A. Numerical Simulation of a DFB-Fiber Laser Sensor (I). Journal of Optoelectronics and Advanced Materials 2010; 12 (8) 1636-1645.

[26] Lancranjan I, Miclos S, Savastru D. Numerical Simulation of a Passive Optical Q – Switched Solid State Laser - High Brightness Nd:YAG Laser Case. Journal of Optoelectronics and Advanced Materials 2011; 13 (5-6) 477-484.

[27] Basiev TT, Mirov SB, Osiko VV. Room-Temperature Color Center Lasers. IEEE Journal of Quantum Electronics 1988; 24 (6) 1052-1069.

[28] Kapoor R, Mukhopadhyay PK, George J. A New Approach to Compute Overlap Efficiency in Axially Pumped Solid State Lasers. Optical Express 1999; 5(6) 125-133.

[29] Zayhowski JJ. Thermal Guiding in Microchips. In: Dube G, Jensen HP.(eds.) OSA Proceedings on Advanced Solid State Lasers 1990; 9-13.

[30] Innocenzi ME, Yura HT, Fincher CL, Fields RA. Thermal Modeling of Continuous-Wave-Endpumped Solid-State Lasers. Applied Physics Letters 1990; 56(19) 1831-1833.

[31] Zhang X, Zhao S, Wang Q, Ozygus B, Weber H. Modeling of Passively Q-Switched Lasers. Journal of Optical Society of America B 2000; 17 (7) 1166-1175.

[32] Salin F, Squier J. Gain Guiding in Solid State Lasers. Optics Letters 1992; 17(19) 1352-1354.

[33] Magni V, Cerullo G, De Silvestri S. Closed Form Gaussian Beam Analysis of Resonators Containing a Kerr Medium for Femtosecond Lasers. Optics Communications 1993; 101(5-6) 365-370.

[34] Kemp AJ, Conroy RS, Friel GJ, Sinclair B. Guiding Effects in Nd:YVO_4 Microchip Lasers Operating Well Above Threshold. IEEE Journal of Quantum Electronics 1999; 35(4) 675-681.

[35] Serrat C, van Exter MP, van Druten NJ, Woerdman JP. Transverse Mode Formation in Microlasers by Combined Gain- and Index-Guiding. IEEE Journal of Quantum Electronics 1999; 35(9) 1314-1321.

[36] Denchev O, Kurtev S, Petrov P. Modes of Unstable Resonators with a Saturable Gain Guide. Applied Optics 2001; 40(6) 921-929.

[37] Grace EJ, New GH, French PMW. Simple ABCD Matrix Treatment for Transversely Varying Saturable Gain. Optics Letters 2001; 26(22) 1776-1778.

[38] Barry DA, Parlange JY, Li L, Prommer H, Cunningham CJ, Stagnitti F. Analytical Approximations for Real Values of the Lambert W-Function. Mathematics and Computers in Simulation 2000; 53(1-2) 95-103.

Chapter 15

Soft-Error Rate of Advanced SRAM Memories: Modeling and Monte Carlo Simulation

Jean-Luc Autran, Sergey Semikh, Daniela Munteanu, Sébastien Serre, Gilles Gasiot and Philippe Roche

Additional information is available at the end of the chapter

http://dx.doi.org/10.5772/50111

1. Introduction

Single-event-effects (SEE) are the result of the interaction of highly energetic particles, such as protons, neutrons, alpha particles, or heavy ions, with sensitive regions of a microelectronic device or circuit [1-2]. They may perturb the device/circuit operation (e.g., reverse or flip the data state of a memory cell, latch, flip-flop, etc.) or definitively damage the circuit (e.g. gate oxide rupture, destructive latch-up events).

With the constant downscaling of microelectronic devices, the sensitivity of integrated circuits to natural radiation coming from the space or present in the terrestrial environment has been found to seriously increase [3-5]. In particular, ultra-scaled memory integrated circuits are more sensitive to single-event-upset (SEU) and digital devices are more subjected to digital single-event transient (DSETs). The problem has been well-known for space applications over many years (more than forty years) and production mechanisms of single-event effects (SEE) in semiconductor devices by protons or heavy ions well apprehended, characterized and modeled [6]. In a similar way for avionic applications, the interaction of atmospheric neutrons with electronics has been identified as the major source of SEE [7]. For the most recent deca-nanometers technologies, the impact of other atmospheric particles produced in nuclear cascade showers on circuits has been clearly demonstrated (protons [8-9]) or is still under exploration for some exotic particles (pions and charged muons [10-14]).

With respect to such high-altitude atmospheric environments, the situation at ground level is slightly different. Of course, atmospheric neutrons are always the primary particles but, with a flux approximately divided by a factor ~300 at sea-level with respect to the flux at avionics altitudes, the Soft-Error Rate (SER) of circuits can be now affected by an additional source of radiation, usually neglected because completely screened by neutrons in avionics: the alpha particles generated from traces of radioactive contaminants in CMOS process or packaging materials [1,15]. As a consequence of these multiple sources of radiation, the accurate modeling and simulation of the SER of circuits at ground level is rather a complex task because one can clearly separate the contribution to SER of atmospheric particles (the external constraint) from the one due to natural alpha-particle emitters present as contaminants in circuit materials (the internal constraint).

Modeling and simulating the effects of ionizing radiation has long been used for better understanding the radiation effects on the operation of devices and circuits [16-19]. In the last two decades, due to substantial progress in simulation codes and computer performances which reduce computation times, simulation reached an increased interest. Due to its predictive capability, simulation offers the possibility to reduce radiation experiments and to test hypothetical devices or conditions, which are not feasible (or not easily measurable) by experiments. Physically-based numerical simulation at device-level presently becomes an indispensable tool for the analysis of new phenomena specific to short-channel devices and for the study of radiation effects in new device architectures for which experimental investigation is still limited [19]. In these cases, numerical simulation is an ideal investigation tool for providing physical insights and predicting the operation of future devices expected for the end of the microelectronic roadmap. Last but not least, the understanding of the soft error mechanisms in such devices and the prediction of their occurrence under a given radiation environment are of fundamental importance for certain applications requiring a very high level of reliability and dependability [1].

In this framework, this chapter describes in details a complete general purpose simulation platform we have developed these last years for the numerical evaluation of the sensitivity of advanced semiconductor memories (static RAMs) subjected to natural radiation at ground level. The physical modeling approach we developed as well as the object-oriented programming implementation are very general and can be used to simulate both external or internal radiation constraints, i.e. the bombardment of the memory circuit by heavy-ions, neutrons, protons, muons, etc. or the generation of alpha-particles inside the circuit materials due to the presence of traces of radioactive contaminants.

The chapter is organized as follows. After introducing the natural radiation environment at ground level and the different types of radiation constraints in section 2 and the basic mechanisms of single-event effects on microelectronic devices in section 3, section 4 will present in details the different modules of our multi-scale and multi-physics numerical simulation chain, including some important precisions related to the modeling of the circuit architecture, the generation of particles mimicked a given radiation environment and the physical-based modeling of the circuit/cell electrical response. Finally, in section 5, we will illustrate various capabilities of our code to estimate the soft-error rate of different SRAM circuits representative of advanced technological nodes.

2. Natural radiation at ground level

As briefly stated in the introduction, natural radiation that causes soft error in digital circuits may come from various sources. At ground level, one can distinguish two major sources of radiation described in the following: i) the atmospheric radiation environment and ii) the telluric radiation sources,.

2.1. Atmospheric radiation environment

The cascades of elementary particles and electromagnetic radiation are produced in the Earth's atmosphere when a primary cosmic ray (of extraterrestrial origin) enters the atmosphere [20]. The term cascade means that the incident particle (generally a proton, a nucleus, an electron or a photon) strikes a molecule in the air so as to produce many high energy secondary particles (photons, electrons, hadrons, nuclei) which in turn create more particles, and so on.

Among all these produced secondary particles, neutrons represent the most important part of the natural radiation constraint at ground level susceptible to impact electronics. Because neutrons are not charged, they are very invasive and can penetrate deeply in circuit materials. They can interact via nuclear reactions with the atoms of the target materials and create (via elastic or inelastic processes) secondary ionizing particles. This mechanism is called "indirect ionization" and is potentially an important source of errors induced in electronic components. One generally distinguishes thermal neutrons (interacting with ^{10}B isotopes potentially present in circuit materials, but progressively removed from technological processes [5]) and high-energy atmospheric neutrons (up to the GeV scale). Figure 1 (top) shows the typical energy distribution of atmospheric neutrons, ranging from thermal energies to 1 GeV, as measured by Goldhagen et al. [21] using a Bonner multi-sphere spectrometer at the reference location (New-York City, NYC). The integration of this spectrum, also shown in Figure 1 (bottom), gives the total neutron flux expressed in neutrons per square centimeter and per hour: this flux is equal to 7.6 n/cm^2/h for the lower part (thermal and epithermal neutrons below 1 eV), 16 n/cm^2/h for the intermediate part (between 1 eV and 1 MeV) and 20 n/cm^2/h for the upper part (high energy neutrons above 1 MeV).

Atmospheric muons also represent an important part of the natural radiation constraint at ground level [20]. Muons belong to the meson or "hard" component in the atmospheric cosmic ray cascades and are the products of the decay of charged pions (instable particles with a short lifetime of 26 ns) via the weak interaction. They are easily able to penetrate the atmosphere down to sea level and they constitute the only secondary cosmic radiation able to penetrate significant depths underground. In spite of a lifetime of about 2.2 μs, most of them survive to sea level and constitute the most preponderant charged particles at sea level. But despite this abundance, muons interact extremely few with matter, excepted at low energies by direct ionization (see subsection 5.3).

In contrast and while strongly interacting with matter, pions are not enough abundant at ground level to induce significant effects in components. Furthermore, for modern technologies, the small amount of electrons and gamma-rays having very low energy are not able to disrupt electronics.

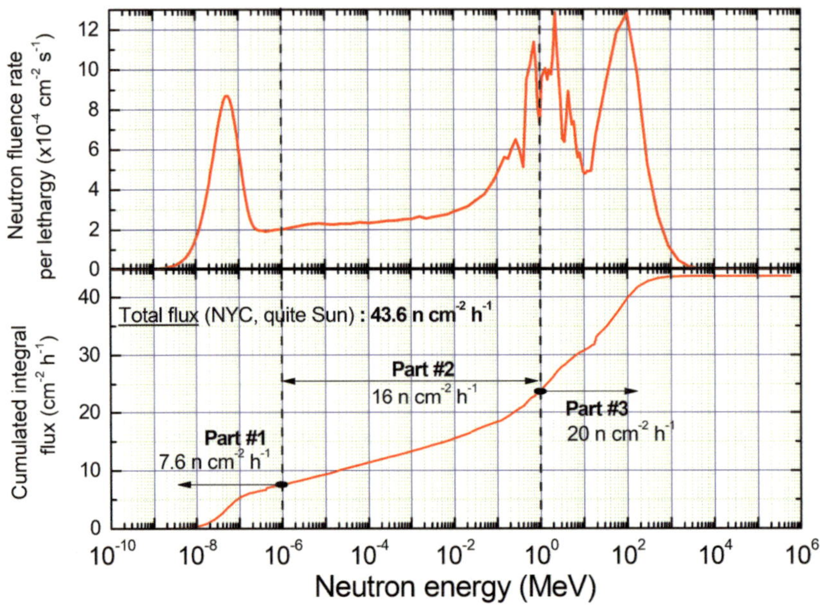

Figure 1. Top: Reference atmospheric neutron spectrum measured on the roof of the IBM Watson Research Center main building [21]. Numerical data courtesy from Paul Goldhagen (U.S. Department of Homeland Security). Bottom: Cumulated integral flux corresponding to the above spectrum. The total neutron flux is 43.6 neutrons per cm² and per hour.

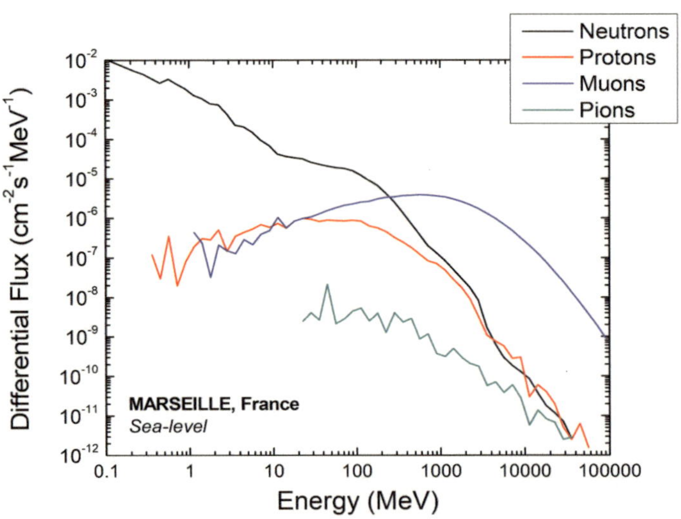

Figure 2. High energy (> 0.1 MeV) differential flux for atmospheric neutrons, protons, muons and pions at ground level. Data computed using the Qinetic Atmospheric Radiation Model [22-23] for Marseille, France (Latitude 43.18' N, Longitude 5.22' E, sea-level).

Finally, protons, although they interact with silicon as neutrons above a few tens of MeV, are one hundred times less numerous than the latter at ground level. Their low abundance allows us to consider their impact as negligible compared with that of neutrons, except at low energies (< 1 MeV) for which certain advanced technologies show an exacerbated sensitivity due to charge deposition by direct ionization.

Figure 2 shows a typical energy distribution of the differential flux for atmospheric neutrons, protons, muons and pions at ground level. Such a collection of spectra, characteristic of a given location (latitude, longitude and elevation), constitute a set of input data of primary importance for any simulation code dedicated to the evaluation of the soft error rate induced by the atmospheric radiation environment (see section 4).

2.2. Telluric radiation sources

Natural radioisotopes contained in the Earth's crust are the principal natural sources of α, β and γ radioactivity but only the alpha-particle emitters present a reliability concern in microelectronics. Beta and gamma processes are indeed not able to deposit a high enough amount of energy susceptible to significantly impact the microelectronic circuit operation. The presence of alpha-particle emitters in electronic devices can be classified as materials that are naturally radioactive (they contain a fraction of radioactive nuclei) or materials that contain residual trace of radioactive impurities [24]. Currently, several types of alpha-particle emitters have been identified at wafer, packaging and interconnection levels, including lead in solder bumps, uranium and thorium in silicon wafers and in molding compounds, more recently hafnium in new high-κ gate and platinum in silicide materials.

Considering the activity of radioisotopes in the calculation of the soft error rate of a circuit thus requires to accurately modeling the alpha-particle source mimicking the presence of these alpha-particle emitters in the circuit materials. For example, considering traces of uranium in a given material (silicon for example) requires to take into account the complete uranium disintegration chain composed of 14 daughter nuclei with 8 alpha-particle emitters. Energies of the alpha-particle are ranging from 4.20 to 7.68 MeV; their corresponding ranges

	$T_{1/2}$ (s)	Alpha Energy (MeV)	Range in Si (μm)	Corresponding initial LET (MeV/(mg/cm²))
^{238}U	$1.40\times10^{+17}$	4.19	18.95	0.677
^{234}U	$7.76\times10^{+12}$	4.68	22.17	0.634
^{230}Th	$2.38\times10^{+12}$	4.58	21.49	0.642
^{226}Ra	$5.05\times10^{+10}$	4.77	22.78	0.627
^{222}Rn	$3.30\times10^{+05}$	5.49	27.94	0.575
^{218}Po	$1.86\times10^{+02}$	6.00	31.86	0.545
^{214}Po	1.64×10^{-04}	7.68	46.22	0.468
^{210}Po	$1.20\times10^{+07}$	5.31	26.61	0.588

Table 1. Main characteristics (half-life, mean energy, range in silicon and initial linear energy transfer of the emitted alpha-particle) of the eight alpha-emitters of the disintegration chain of ^{238}U [25].

in silicon vary from 19 to 46 μm and their initial Linear Energy Transfer (LET) from 0.47 to 0.68 MeV/(mg/cm²), as summarized in Table 1.

3. Basic mechanisms of single-event effects on microelectronic devices

In this section, we briefly summarize the physical mechanisms related to the production of SEE in microelectronic devices by a charged particle. This general scheme can be applied to all particles able to directly deposit an electrical charge along their track (heavy ions, alpha-particles, low energy protons and low energy muons). As we already mentioned for neutrons, the ionization is indirect since neutron is a neutral particle but it can induce charged particles (recoil atoms or secondary particle) by nuclear reaction with the atoms of the target material. The following scenario can thus be applied separately to all secondary charged particles produced by the neutron.

Considering a single charged particle, the passage of this particle through a portion of a microelectronic circuit consists in three main successive steps: (1) the charge deposition by the energetic particle striking the sensitive region, (2) the transport of the released charge into the device and (3) the charge collection in the sensitive region of the device. Figure 3 schematically shows these successive steps in the case of the passage of the energetic charged particle through a reverse-biased n^+/p junction. In the following we succinctly describe these different mechanisms, for a detailed presentation we invite the reader to consult references [5][16-19].

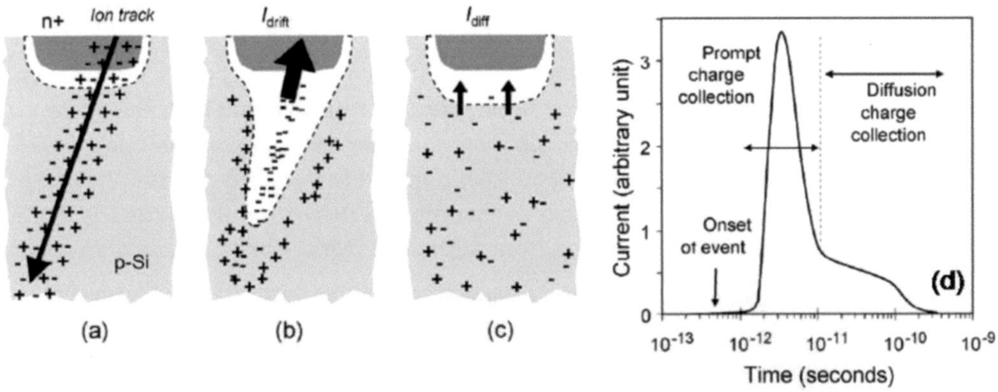

Figure 3. Charge generation, transport and collections phases in a reverse-biased junction and the resultant current pulse caused by the passage of an energetic charged particle. After Baumann [5]. © 2005 Institute of Electrical and Electronics Engineers Inc., reproduced with permission.

Charge deposition (or generation): When the particle strikes the device, an electrical charge along the particle track can be deposited by direct ionization of the target material. This direct ionization is mainly produced by inelastic interactions and transmits a large amount of energy to the electrons of the struck atoms. These electrons produce a cascade of secondary electrons which thermalize and create electron-hole pairs along the particle path [Figure 3(a)]. In a semiconductor or insulator, a large amount of the deposited energy is thus converted into electron-hole pairs, the remaining energy being converted into heat and a very small quantity in atoms displacement. It was experimentally shown that the energy necessary for the creation of an electron-hole pair depends on the material bandgap. In a Silicon substrate, one electron-hole pair is produced for every 3.6 eV of energy lost by the particle.

As already mentioned, neutrons of the terrestrial environment do not interact directly with target material since they do not ionize the matter on their passage. However, the products resulting from a nuclear reaction can deposit energy along their traces, in the same manner as that of direct ionization. Since the creation of the column of electron-hole pairs of these secondary particles is similar to that of ions, the same models and concepts can be used.

Charge transport: When a charge column is created in the semiconductor by an ionizing particle, the released carriers are quickly transported and collected by elementary structures (e.g. p-n junctions). The transport of charge relies on two main mechanisms [Figures 3(b) and 3(c)]: the charge drift in regions with an electric field and the charge diffusion in neutral zones. The deposited charges can also recombine with other mobile carriers existing in the lattice.

Charge collection: The charges transported in the device induce a parasitic current transient [Figure 3(d)], which could induce disturbances in the device and associated circuits. The devices most sensitive to ionizing particle strikes are generally devices containing reversely-biased p-n junctions, because the strong electric field existing in the depletion region of the p-n junction allows a very efficient collection of the deposited charge. The effects of ionizing radiation are different according to the intensity of the current transient, as well as the number of impacted circuit nodes. If the current is sufficiently important, it can induce a permanent damage on gate insulators (gate rupture, SEGR) or the latch-up (SEL) of the device. In usual low power circuits, the transient current may generally induce only an eventual change of the logical state (cell upset).

4. The TIARA-G4 Monte Carlo simulation code

This section describes in details the TIARA-G4 code developed these last years conjointly at Aix-Marseille University (IM2NP laboratory) and at STMicroelectronics (Central R&D, Crolles). TIARA-G4 is a general-purpose Monte Carlo simulation code written in C++ and fully based on the Geant4 toolkit for modeling the interaction of Geant4 particles (including neutrons, protons, muons, alpha-particles and heavy ions) with various architectures of electronic circuits. TIARA stands for Tool Suite for Radiation Reliability Assessment. The primary ambition of TIARA is to embed in a unique simulation platform the state-of-the-art knowledge and methodology of SER evaluation.

The initial version of TIARA [26-27] was a standalone C++ native code dynamically linked with IC CAD flow through the coupling with a SPICE solver. The code has been developed such that the addition of new radiation environments, physical models or new circuit architecture should be quite simple. On one hand, this first version was able to treat the transport and energy deposition of charged particles (heavy ions and alpha particles) without the need for a nuclear code as Geant4 [28]; only SRIM [29] tables were used as input files to compute the transport of the particles in silicon and in a simplified Back-End-Of-Line (BEOL) structure reduced to a single layer. On the other hand, for neutrons, it used separate databases compiled using a specific Geant4 application to generate nuclear events in the simulation flow resulting from the interactions of incident neutrons with the circuit.

The new version of TIARA, described here, is called TIARA-G4, in reference to the fact that it is totally rewritten in C++ using Geant4 classes and libraries and compiled as a full Geant4 application [28]. The main improvement of TIARA-G4 with respect to the first version of the code comes precisely from this transformation of the code in a Geant4 application, allowing the use of Geant4 classes for the description of the circuit geometry and materials (now including the true BEOL structure) and the integration of the particle transport and tracking directly in the simulation flow, without the need of external databases or additional files. Figure 4 shows a schematics of the TIARA-G4 simulation flow structured in several independent modules. In the following, we present the content of the main modules of the code and illustrate (also in Section 5) their capabilities for the soft error rate evaluation of different SRAM CMOS bulk circuits (65 nm and 40 nm technologies) subjected to natural radiation at ground level.

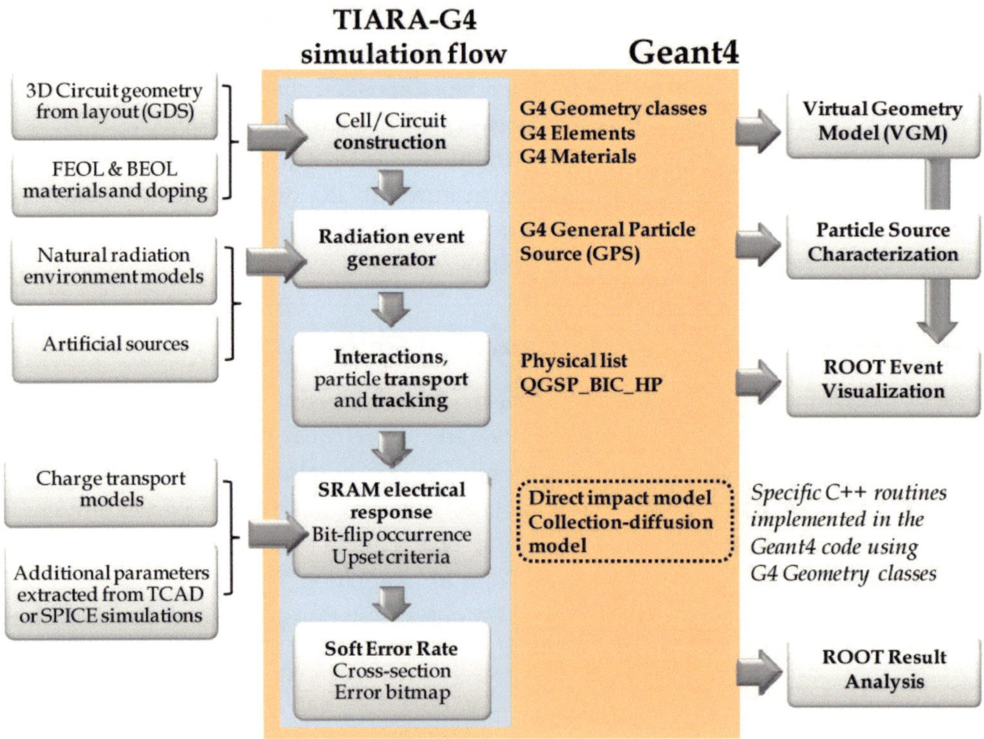

Figure 4. Schematics of the TIARA-G4 simulation flow showing the different code inputs and outputs and the links with Geant4 classes, libraries, models or external modules and visualization tools.

4.1. Circuit architecture construction module

The first step of the TIARA-G4 simulation is to construct a model of the simulated circuit from Geant4 geometry classes and libraries of elements and materials. In the framework of Geant4, the circuit under simulation is considered as the "particle detector". The structure creation in TIARA is based on 3D circuit geometry information extracted from GDS formatted data classically used in the Computer-Aided Design (CAD) flow of semiconductor circuit manufacturing. To perform such an extraction from the GDS layout description, a separate tool has been developed [30]. It parses the GDS file, obtains coordinate points of CAD layers and using geometrical computations tracks the positions and dimensions of the transistor active areas, cell dimensions, p-type and n-type and Back-End-Of-Line (BEOL) stack geometry. Based on this information and additional data concerning the depth of the wells, junctions, STI regions (obtained from TCAD or SIMS measurements) and BEOL layer composition, TIARA creates a 3D structure of the elementary memory cell and, by repetition, of the complete portion of the simulated circuit. The real 3D geometry is simplified since it is essentially based on the juxtaposition of boxes of different dimensions, each box being associated to a given material (silicon, insulator, metal, etc.) or doped semiconductor (p-type, n-type).

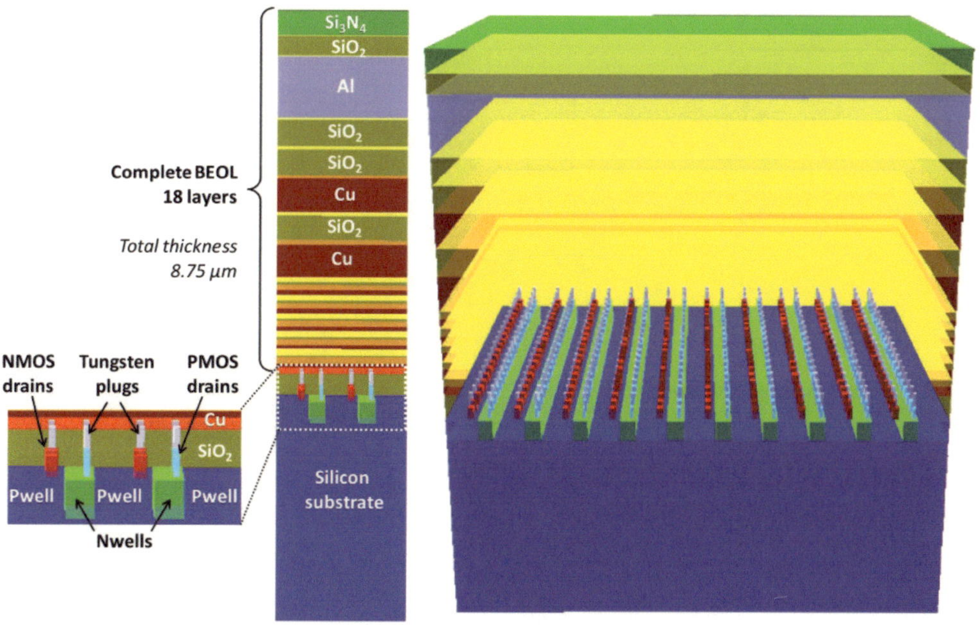

Figure 5. Left and Center: ROOT screenshots illustrating the geometry of the complete 65 nm SRAM architecture considered in TIARA-G4 simulation. Right: 3D perspective view of a 10×20 SRAM cell array covered with the BEOL.

Figure 5 (left) illustrates the geometry of a complete 65 nm SRAM architecture considered in TIARA-G4 simulation. Sensitive Pmos and Nmos drains regions are connected to the first metal layer (Cu) of the BEOL stack with tungsten plugs. The BEOL structure is composed of 18 uniform stacked layers with exact compositions and thicknesses. The 3D perspective view of a 10×20 SRAM cell array covered with the BEOL is shown in Figure 5 (right). For better visibility, BEOL layers have been rendered semi-transparent in this illustration.

4.2. Radiation event generator

To numerically generate the particles with the spectral, spatial and angular distributions mimicking all the characteristics of the natural background, as introduced and defined in section 2, we use the G4 General Particle Source (GPS) [31] which is part of the Geant4 distribution. The module allows the user to define all the source parameters, in particular the energy of the emitted particles from a given energy distribution defined in a separate input file.

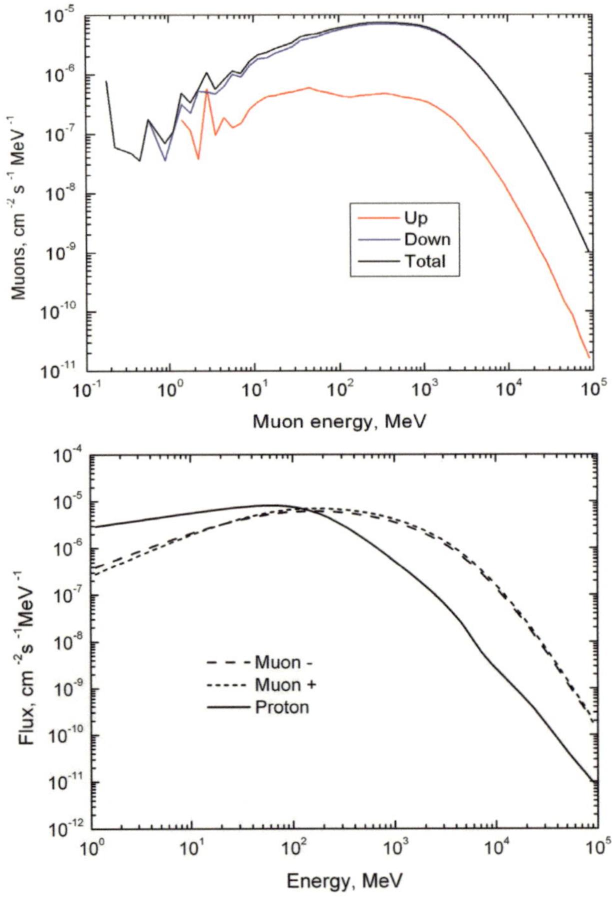

Figure 6. Differential fluxes of atmospheric muons given by the QARM (top) [22-23] and PARMA (bottom) [33-34] models at the location of the Altitude SEE Test European Platform (ASTEP, latitude North 44° 38′ 02″, longitude East 5° 54′ 26″, altitude 2555 m, see www.astep.eu). The atmospheric proton spectrum calculated with the PARMA model is also plotted (bottom).

For atmospheric particles, the energy distributions of neutrons, protons, pions and muons reaching the ground level are available in the literature or on the web as functions of latitude, longitude and altitude. They are obtained from direct measurements and/or from Monte Carlo simulations. For the neutron flux, we use the experimental atmospheric spectrum presented in Figure 1, which is actually the reference curve (for high-energy neutrons above 1 MeV) for the JEDEC Standard JESD89A [32]. For the other atmospheric particles (mainly muons and protons), we adopted the QinetiQ Atmospheric Radiation Model (QARM) [22-23] and the PARMA model [33-34], which are specifically developed for prediction of the radiation in the atmosphere for a given location and date. Figure 6 shows the differential fluxes of atmospheric muons (resp. protons) given by these two models (resp. by PARMA).

Another important issue in Monte-Carlo simulation is the strong zenith angular dependence of atmospheric showers. To make our Geant4 GPS primary particle sources more realistic, we introduce in simulations the angular dependence of the primary flux intensity in the form $I(\theta) \sim \cos^n(\theta)$ where θ is the zenith angle and n a parameter fixed to n=3.5 for neutrons [35], and for muons n=2 [36].

For the simulation of alpha-particle emitters present in the IC materials, we directly generate in the code the random positions and emission directions with uniform probability densities for each daughter element of the considered decay chain (uranium or thorium).

4.3. Interaction, transport and tracking module

Once an incident particle has been numerically generated with the radiation event generator, the Geant4 simulation flow computes the interactions of this particle with the target (the simulated circuit) and transports step-by-step the particle and all the secondary particles eventually produced inside the world volume (the largest volume containing, with some margins, all other volumes contained in the circuit geometry). The transport of each particle occurs until the particle loses its kinetic energy to zero, disappears by an interaction or comes to the end of the world volume.

The G4ProcessManager class contains the list of processes that a particle can undertake. A physical process describes how particles interact with materials. The list of physical processes employed in our simulations is based on the physics lists QGSP_BIC_HP [37], one of the standard Geant4 list covering the energy range of particles interacting in low- to medium-energy ranges. This list uses binary cascade, precompound and various de-excitation models for hadrons standard EM, with high precision neutron model used for neutrons below 20 MeV. This list is generally used for simulations in the fields of radiation protection, shielding and medical applications.

Geant4 provides a way for the user to access the transportation process and to obtain the simulation results at the beginning and end of transportation, at the end of each stepping in transportation and at the time when the particle is going into a given sensitive volume of the circuit. Tables 2 and 3 shows two intermediate output results of TIARA-G4 respectively describing a particle interaction event (Table 2, nuclear inelastic event with a silicon atom of the p-type silicon substrate of the circuit, see Figure 5) and the tracking of two secondary particles impact different sensitive volumes of the circuit (Table 3). All these output data are saved as text files during the simulation and can be used later for event visualization or post-processing. Finally, Figure 7 illustrates the visualization of an interaction event (here a negative muon capture by a silicon atom) using ROOT [38]. Such a 3D perspective view is computed using a dedicated ROOT script which directly imports geometry and event data from a collection of files saved on the machine hard disk during simulation.

```
Event #2359425
Incident particle: neutron
Energy (MeV): 5.664161e+01
Physical process: NeutronInelastic
Volume name: P-substrate
Reaction vextex positions (x,y,z): -5.656377e+00 -1.377065e+00 -5.347320e+00
-----------------------------------------------------------------------------
Number of secondary particles produced: 5
Particle       Energy (MeV)     Px                Py                Pz
Alpha          3.197153e+01     6.097439e-01      -5.070998e-01     6.091488e-01
Neutron        1.697277e+00     -9.311596e-01     3.551987e-01      8.231417e-02
Gamma          9.051714e+00     3.281911e-01      -6.857286e-02     9.421191e-01
Gamma          1.377447e+00     2.331650e-01      8.485282e-01      4.750095e-01
Mg24[0.0]      2.554443e+00     -7.370831e-01     6.733902e-01      5.704476e-02
```

Table 2. Table 2. Example of a TIARA-G4 output in case of particle interaction with the target (circuit). The present example describes a neutron inelastic process (energy of the incident neutron of 56.64 MeV) with a silicon atom of the p-type substrate of the circuit described in Figure 4. This nuclear reaction produces 5 secondary particles at the reaction vertex position; for each produced particle, the particle energy and the three components of the normalized particle momentum (Px, Py, Pz) are indicated.

Figure 7. TIARA-G4 screenshot under ROOT visualization tool showing a part of the memory circuit (65 nm SRAM) subjected to a negative muon irradiation. The resulting interaction shown here is a muon capture by a silicon atom in the active circuit region (Pwell) produced a shower of ten secondary particles.

```
Event #5477703
EventStepData.size: 5
---------------------------------------------------
StepData object #0    ParticleName: Al28[0.0]
VolumeName: Psub #0
initPoint/um: (-2.234447e+00,-1.624657e+00,-8.960758e-01)
postPoint/um: (-2.239293e+00,-1.703238e+00,-8.400000e-01)
EnergyDep/MeV: 7.491555e-02
---------------------------------------------------
StepData object #1    ParticleName: Al28[0.0]
VolumeName: Pwell #8
initPoint/um: (-2.239293e+00,-1.703238e+00,-8.400000e-01)
postPoint/um: (-2.233404e+00,-2.258219e+00,-3.596903e-01)
EnergyDep/MeV: 4.304428e-01
---------------------------------------------------
StepData object #2    ParticleName: proton
VolumeName: Psub #0
initPoint/um: (-2.234447e+00,-1.624657e+00,-8.960758e-01)
postPoint/um: (-2.230874e+00,-1.572415e+00,-8.400000e-01)
EnergyDep/MeV: 2.421962e-04
---------------------------------------------------
StepData object #3    ParticleName: proton
VolumeName: Pwell #8
initPoint/um: (-2.230874e+00,-1.572415e+00,-8.400000e-01)
postPoint/um: (-2.196440e+00,-1.069293e+00,-3.000000e-01)
EnergyDep/MeV: 2.737365e-03
---------------------------------------------------
StepData object #4ParticleName: proton
VolumeName: Nmos #168
initPoint/um: (-2.181468e+00,-8.495000e-01,-6.405073e-02)
postPoint/um: (-2.177411e+00,-7.898294e-01,0.000000e+00)
EnergyDep/MeV: 2.871799e-04
```

Table 3. Example of the tracking of two secondary particles (^{28}Al and proton) impacting different sensitive volumes (Psub, Pwell and Nmos) of the SRAM circuit. For each particle and each impacted sensitive volume, the (x, y, z) coordinates of the entry and exit points of the particle in this volume are indicated and also the energy deposited by the particle in this same volume.

4.4. SRAM electrical response module

We detail in this section the model used to calculate the electrical response of the SRAM circuit subjected to the irradiation. Starting a simulation sequence when a primary particle emitted by the particle source enters in the world volume, we already mentioned that Geant4 computes the interactions of this particle with the circuit and transports step-by-step the particle and all the secondary particles (eventually produced) until all these particles loss their kinetic energy to zero, disappear by interaction or come to the end of the world volume.

At the end of the sequence,TIARA-G4 examines the tracks of all the charged particles involved in this simulation step (including eventually the track of the incident primary particle if it is charged) and determine the complete list of the different silicon volumes (drains, Pwells, Nwells, substrates, etc.) traversed by these particles. Two very general cases can be distinguished from this pure geometrical analysis, as schematically shown in Figure 8:

1. A single or several charged particles directly pass through a sensitive drain volume. In this case, TIARA-G4 directly evaluates from Geant4 data the total energy deposited by these particles in the drain (ΔE), converts this value into a number of generated electron-hole pairs (Q_{dep} = ΔE/3.6 eV for bulk silicon) and finally compares this value with the critical charge value ($Q_{crit,P}$ for Pmos, $Q_{crit,N}$ for Nmos) of the simulated technology. If $Q_{dep} > Q_{crit}$, the memory cell is considered to be upset, in the contrary case, the electrical state of the cell is not changed [19].
2. A single or several charged particles impact one or several Nwell, Pwell and/or the silicon substrate. In this case, TIARA-G4 evaluates for each sensitive drain located in the impacted Nwell(s) (for Pmos) or Pwell(s) and substrate (for Nmos) the transient current I(t) resulting from the diffusion of carriers in excess in these regions and the collection of the charge by the sensitive nodes (see also Figure 9). Such calculations are performed using the "diffusion-collection model" detailed in the following. Until the I(t) characteristic is computed for all the considered sensitive drains, TIARA-G4 applies the "I_{max}-t_{max}" criterion, also described below, to determine if the corresponding memory cell is upset or not.

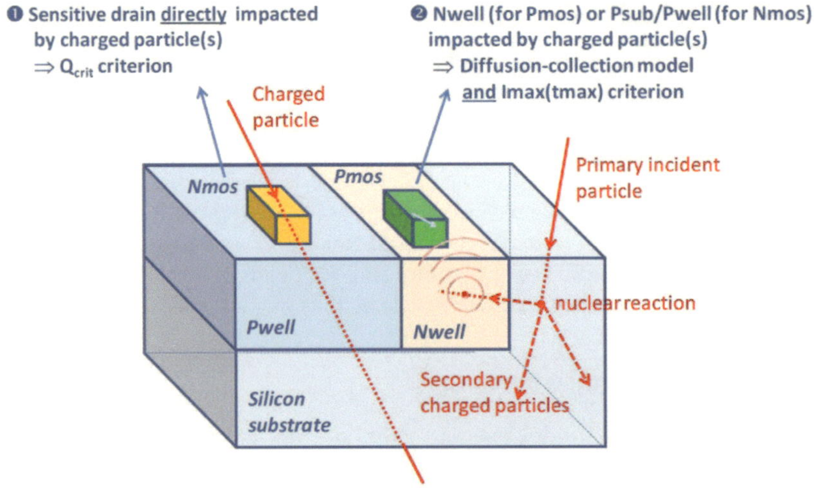

Figure 8. Schematics of the different cases envisaged in TIARA-G4 for the evaluation of cell upset in the simulated SRAM circuit.

In the diffusion-collection model [39-40], the energy lost by a charged particle in silicon along its track is converted in a succession of elementary carrier densities δQ. The model then assumes that the behavior of these quasi-point charges is governed by a pure 3D spherical diffusion law:

$$\frac{\partial n}{\partial t} = D \cdot \Delta n \tag{1}$$

where n is the carrier density in excess generated in the silicon and D is an ambipolar diffusion coefficient.

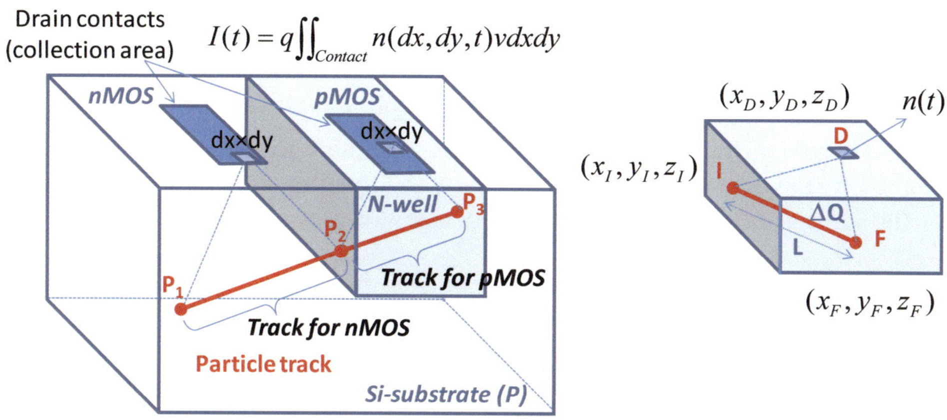

Figure 9. Left: Schematics of the "diffusion-collection model" used to compute the transient current I(t) resulting from the 3D spherical diffusion and then from the collection by a given reverse-biased drain of the charge in excess generated along a charged particle track. Right: Definition of the different points in Cartesian coordinates used to numerically evaluate n(t).

The temporal and spatial concentration n(r,t) resulting from the diffusion of a quasi-ponctual charge δQ in the silicon at the distance r from this charge is thus described by the following equation:

$$n(r,t) = \frac{\delta Q}{\sqrt[3]{4\pi Dt}} \times \exp\left(-\frac{r^2}{4Dt} - \frac{t}{\tau}\right) \tag{2}$$

where τ is the carrier lifetime, r is the distance from the element δQ, and t is the time.

In the present implementation of the diffusion-collection model, δQ is directly evaluated from Geant4 data, considering the energy lost by the particle in a given geometry volume. Figure 9 (right) illustrates the general case of a given volume impacted by a particle. The particle enters the volume in point I and exits in point F. Because drain and well volumes have reduced dimensions (typically expressed in tenths of a micron), the electrical charge δQ deposited per elementary length dl can be approximated by $Q_{dep} \times dl / L$ where L is the length of the segment IF. Considering the Cartesian coordinates of the geometrical points I, F and D defined on Figure 8, the total collected charge at point D due to the contribution of the complete segment IF can be analytically evaluated from the following expression:

$$n(t) = \frac{\delta Q / q}{8\pi DtL} \times \exp\left(-\frac{l_0^2}{4Dt} - \frac{t}{\tau}\right) \times \exp\left(-\frac{K^2}{L^2 4Dt}\right) \times \left\{ erf\left[\frac{1}{2\sqrt{Dt}}\left(L + \frac{K}{L}\right)\right] - erf\left[\frac{K}{2L\sqrt{Dt}}\right]\right\} \tag{3}$$

where quantities L, l_0 and K are defined from the Cartesian coordinates of points I, F and D:

$$\begin{cases} L=\sqrt{(x_F-x_I)^2+(y_F-y_I)^2+(z_F-z_I)^2} \\ l_0^2=(x_D-x_I)^2+(y_D-y_I)^2+(z_D-z_I)^2 \\ K=(x_I-x_D)(x_F-x_I)+(y_I-y_D)(y_F-y_I)+(z_I-z_D)(z_F-z_I) \end{cases} \quad (4)$$

The total electrical charge from the particle track collected at the level of a sensitive drain electrode is obtained by integrating Eq. (3) on the total drain surface, as illustrated in Figure 9. Then, the charge is converted into a current by multiplying n(t) by the elementary charge and by the average collection velocity via space charge region of the reverse-biased drain:

$$I(t)=q\iint_{Contact} n(t)\cdot v\cdot dxdy \quad (5)$$

Once the I(t) characteristic has been computed for all drains of the sensitive transistors in the SRAM cell matrix, TIARA-G4 applies the I_{max}-t_{max} criterion [26] to determine the cell upsets. This criterion is separately obtained from TIARA-G4 simulation and requires the combination of TCAD and PSICE analysis. The calculated $I_{max}(t_{max})$ characteristic delimitates two current-time domains, as illustrated in Figure 10. If the transient current peak is located above this curve, an upset occurs; in the contrary case the extracted transient current from the sensitive node is not able to sufficiently disturb the electrical state of the bi-stable flip-flop and consequently to upset the memory point.

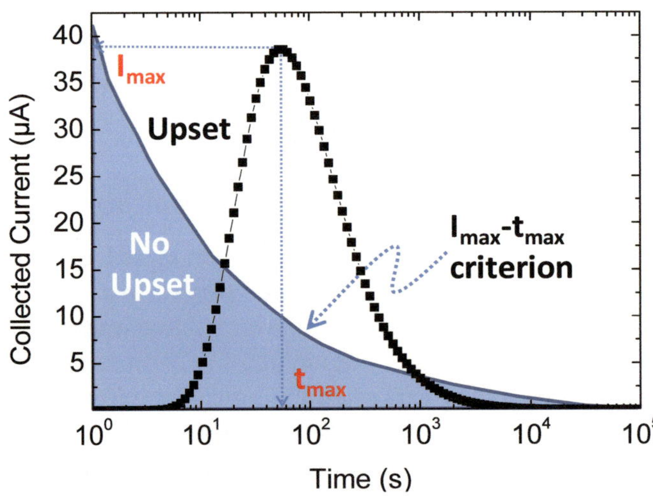

Figure 10. Example of a transient current characteristic superimposed to the I_{max}-t_{max} upset criterion. The transient current has been calculated from the "diffusion-collection model" for a ^{24}Mg particle (10 MeV) which perpendicularly impacts a Pwell at the distance of 0.25 μm from the Nmos drain contact.

4.5. Soft error rate calculation module

At the end of the simulation flow, the last module of the TIARA-G4 code evaluates the Soft Error Rate (SER) of the SRAM circuit from the following expression [32]:

$$SER[\text{FIT/Mbit}] = \frac{1024 \times 1024}{CellNum} \times \frac{IntFlux[cm^{-2}]}{NumPart} \times L_X[\text{cm}] \times L_Y[\text{cm}] \times 10^9 \times TotalUpsetNum \quad (6)$$

where TotalUpsetNum is the total number of cell upsets obtained during the simulation, CellNum is the number of memory cells of the simulated circuit, L_X and L_Y are the circuit dimensions (in cm), NumPart is the total number of primary particles incident on the simulated circuit and IntFlux is the integral flux (cm^{-2}) of the particle source used to generate the incident particles. For example, considering the atmospheric neutron spectrum of Figure 1, IntFLux = 7.6 n/cm^2 for Part #1, 16 n/cm^2 for Part #2 and 20 n/cm^2 for Part #3 of the spectrum.

5. Simulation results

In this last section, the capabilities of the TIARA-G4 code are illustrated though a few dedicated studies on the simulation of 65 nm or 40 nm CMOS bulk SRAM circuits subjected to different sources of atmospheric particles. These three examples are independent and respectively concern: i) the impact of thermal and low energy neutrons on a 40 nm SRAM circuit; ii) the SER estimation of a 65 nm SRAM under high energy atmospheric neutrons and iii) the effects of low-energy muons on the same 65 nm circuit.

5.1. Impact of thermal and low energy neutrons on a 40 nm SRAM circuit

Since the 80's, the interaction of cosmic ray induced thermal neutrons with the ^{10}B isotope of the boron has been identified as a major source of soft errors in electronic circuits [41]. ^{10}B only represents 19.9% abundance of natural boron but the very large cross section of the $^{10}B(n,\alpha)7Li$ reaction at thermal energies combined with the highly ionizing character and the range in silicon of the two nuclei produced by this fission reaction (one lithium nucleus and one alpha particle) can easily explain the danger of ^{10}B when it is present in elevated concentration in close proximity to the sensitive regions of integrated devices [41]. Modern semiconductor processes have thus completely eliminated the presence of ^{10}B in Borophosphosilicate glasses (BPSG) used in the back-end-of-line (or outright the use of the BPSG itself), considered as the principal reservoir of ^{10}B and the dominant source of boron fission in circuits. However, ^{10}B remains present at silicon level, since bulk substrate doping and source/drain implantation are not selective in isotope and continue to use natural boron [41-42]. The issue of thermal neutron sensitivity to current technologies is still relevant and remains open, in particular for ultra-scaled technologies in the natural terrestrial environment at ground level. Recent work demonstrated a substantial SER sensitivity with neutron energies for many SRAM circuits in the 0.25 μm-45 nm technology range [43-44].

Using the new TIARA-G4 code, we propose here to explore the question of thermal and low energy neutron-induced soft errors in state-of-the-art 40 nm SRAMs. Such a study can be only conducted with a code taking into account the real geometry at silicon level, including the silicon doping with natural boron in p-type regions containing 19.9% of ^{10}B. We thus constructed a 40 nm SRAM matrix with exact doping levels at the level of Pwells ([B] = 10^{16} cm^{-3}) and Pmos drains ([B] = 3×10^{20} cm^{-3}).

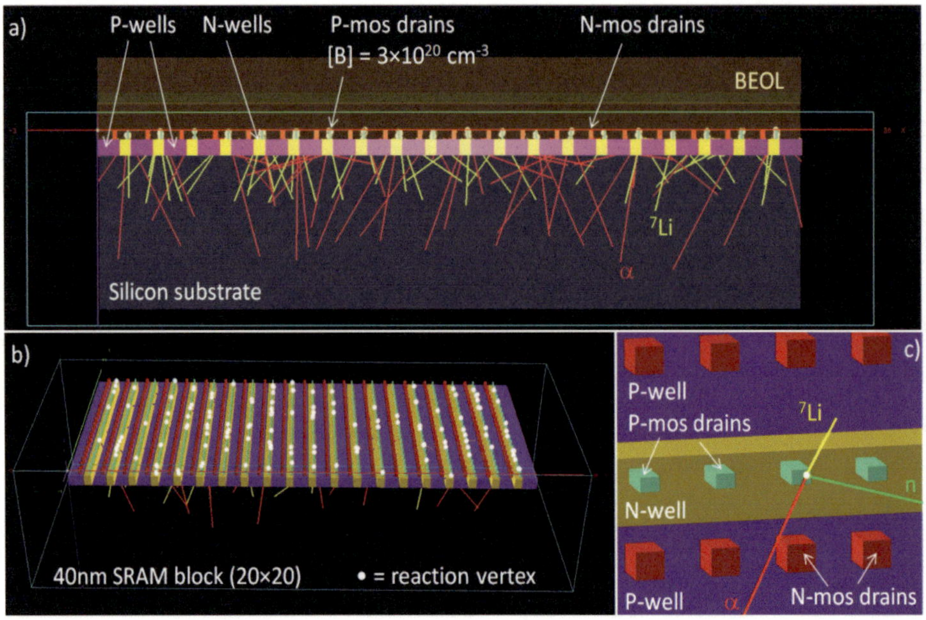

Figure 11. TIARA-G4 screenshots under ROOT illustrating the results of $2{\times}10^9$ thermal neutrons incident on the 40 nm single-port SRAM (20×20 memory cell block). White points correspond to the reaction vertex (only localized in the Pmos drain volumes); colored segments to the trajectories of the secondary ions produced (red for alpha, yellow for ^{7}Li). For clarity, BEOL and substrate have been removed from the perspective view in b). c) Detail a ^{10}B fission reaction occurring in the volume of a Pmos drain (note that the alpha-particle and the lithium nucleus are emitted in opposite directions to conserve momentum).

Figure 11 illustrates the simulation results obtained on a 20×20 SRAM matrix. This circuit was irradiated with thermal and low energy neutrons generated by the Geant4 GPS source considering Part #1 of the reference atmospheric spectrum shown in Figure 1. In order to obtain a sufficient event statistic (interaction events are relatively rare), we pushed the number of incident particles up to $2{\times}10^9$ thermal neutrons. A total 116 single bit upsets (SBU) and 24 multiple celle upsets (MCU) have been detected: they are exclusively the result of ^{10}B fission events localized in the drain volumes of the Pmos transistors (see Figure 11(b), the vertex of the reactions are indicated by the white dots).

Figure 12 shows that both the SER value and the event multiplicity distributions are in excellent agreement with experimental data performed at the LLB facility, located at CEA Saclay, France [45]. The experiment was conducted on the G3-2 beam line under a thermal neutron flux reduced to $7.88{\times}10^8$ n/cm^2/s (beam surface area of 25×50 mm2, neutron energies in the range 1.8-10 meV). For the purposes of the study, we considered a 7 Mbit 40 nm SRAM array with a layout cell area of 0.374 μm^2). We obtained an experimental thermal neutron-induced SER of 4 FIT/Mbit for the SRAM, with 75% of SBU, 17% of MCU with a multiplicity of 2 and 8% of events with multiplicities ranging from 3 to 5. All these MCU events correspond to physical adjacent bit cells in the memory plan. For comparison, results obtained with TIARA-G4 give a SER equal to 4.5 FIT/Mbit with 83% of SBU, 14% of MCU with a multiplicity of 2 and 4% of events with multiplicities ranging from 3 to 5.

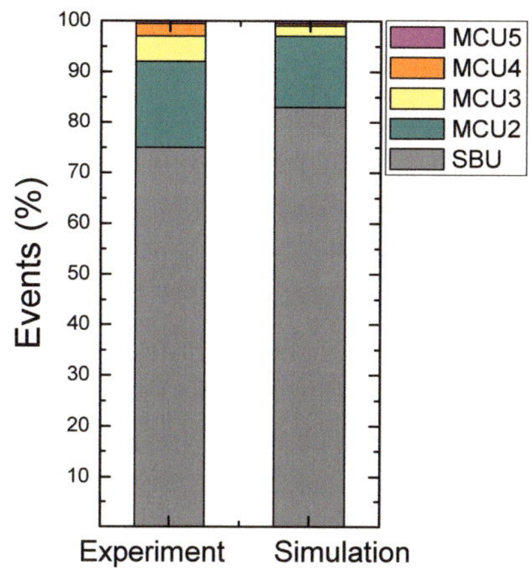

Figure 12. Event multiplicity distributions obtained for the 40 nm SRAM subjected to thermal neutrons and deduced from both experiment and numerical simulation, respectively conducted at LLB facility and obtained with the new release of the TIARA/Geant4 code.

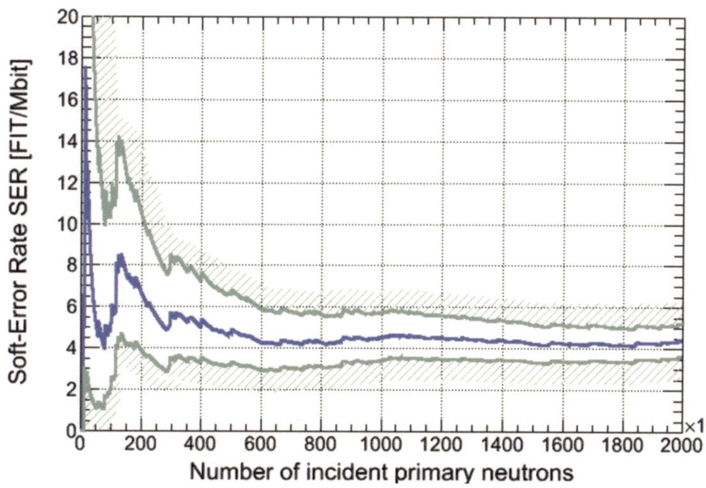

Figure 13. Convergence of the soft-error rate as a function of the number of incident primary neutrons obtained from TIARA-G4 simulation. The upper and lower limits of the SER confidence interval for 90% based on the χ^2 distribution are also plotted.

Figure 13 illustrates the convergence of the soft-error rate during the TIARA-G4 simulation as a function of the number of incident primary neutrons. The code asymptotically converges towards a unique SER value, demonstrating the invariance of the extracted SER when the statistics become satisfactory, typically above 1.5×10^9 primary neutrons in this case.

Finally, Figure 14 shows a synthesis of both experimental and simulation results obtained for the soft-error rate (expressed in bit flips) of the 40 nm single-port SRAM. "Simul. Part #1", "Simul. Part #2" and "Simul. Part #3" correspond respectively to the SER extracted from

TIARA-G4 simulations considering the parts labeled #1, #2 and #3 of the reference atmospheric spectrum (Figure 1) as the primary sources of particles. Note that the contributions of parts #1 and #2 of the neutron spectrum in the SRAM SER are very small with respect to the high energy part #3 and only represent 3% of the total SER value. "Simul. 1+2+3" is equal to the sum of these three SER simulated values and corresponds to the SER estimation for the full atmospheric spectrum, estimated around 500 FIT/MBit. The "Exp. real-time ASTEP" value (682 FIT/Mbit) corresponds to the neutron-SER extracted from a real-time experiment (conducted on the ASTEP platform at the altitude of 2252m, see www.astep.eu) and corrected from the contribution of internal chip radioactivity (alpha-particle emission). The comparison of these results evidences a ~30% discrepancy between simulation and experimental results. Such an underestimation of the total SER by simulation in such ultra-scaled technology can be easily explained by the fact that the bipolar amplification mechanism has not been yet included in the SRAM electrical response module of the simulation code. In the next validation example (see subsection 5.2) considering a less integrated technology (65 nm), the impact of bipolar amplification will be significantly reduced and its impact on SER value quasi negligible.

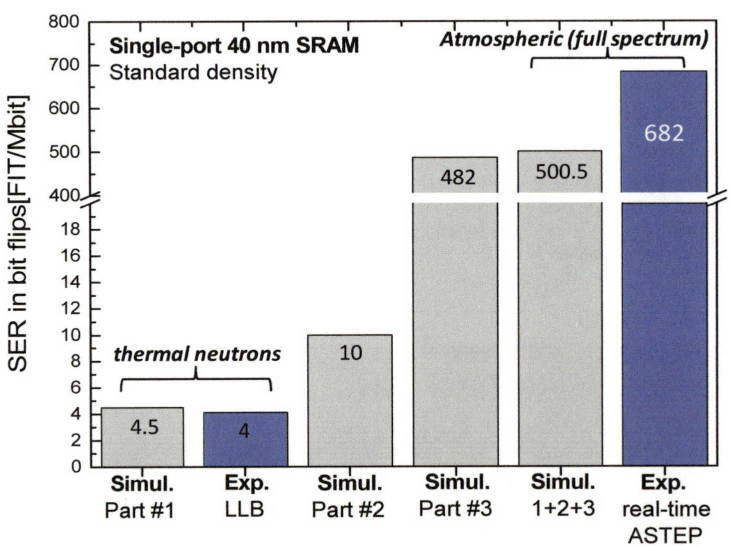

Figure 14. Synthesis of both experimental and simulation results obtained for the soft-error rate (expressed in bit flips) of the 40 nm single-port SRAM subjected to atmospheric neutrons.

5.2. SER estimation of a 65 nm SRAM under high energy atmospheric neutrons

In this second example, we simulated the complete 65 nm SRAM architecture previously defined in Figure 5. The objective was to compare neutron-induced SER results obtained by TIARA-G4 with simulation data previously obtained from the initial code TIARA [26,30] (see the introduction of section 4). Another objective was to perform simulation with and without taking into account the complete BEOL stack in order to evidence the impact of this BEOL on the neutron SER.

Figure 15 shows the comparison of the neutron-induced SER computed with the different versions of TIARA for a 20×20 65 nm SRAM array. The atmospheric neutron source considered for these simulations corresponds to the Part #3 of the reference neutron spectrum of Figure 1 (high energy neutrons below 1 MeV). Very close values are obtained with TIARA and TIARA-G4 without taking into account the complete BEOL structure (a single SiO_2 layer is used as a simplified BEOL stack in this case): respectively 266 and 251 FIT/MBit, evidencing the equivalence of the two approaches in terms of global SER values. For memory, the initial version of TIARA computes neutron-silicon interactions from pre-calculated databases using Geant4 while TIARA-G4 is a full Geant4 application. Taking into account the complete BEOL structure (defined in Figure 5) in the new code TIARA-G4 results in a significant increase of the SER (337 FIT/Mbit). This +30% variation of the SER can be attributed to additional secondary particles produced by the interactions of incoming neutrons with the different BEOL materials (mainly SiO_2, Cu and Al), these secondary particles being able to deposit electrical charges in the active silicon regions.

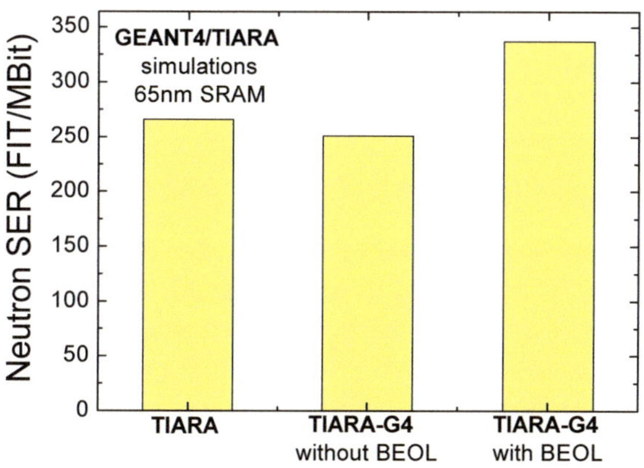

Figure 15. Comparison of simulation results obtained with the initial (TIARA) and new (TIARA-G4) versions of the code for the evaluation of the neutron-induced SER in the 65 nm SRAM architecture. Data are also plotted for TIARA-G4 with and without taking into account the real BEOL structure.

A more detailed analysis, reported in Figure 16, evidences slight differences in the distributions of the events as a function of the event size or event multiplicity (which corresponds to the number of simultaneous cell flips induced by a single primary particle interaction with the circuit). TIARA-G4 is found to generate more single bit upsets and, inversely, less multiple cell upsets than the initial TIARA code. The presence of the complete BEOL structure above silicon is also found to induce more single bit upsets and high multiplicity events than the simplified BEOL structure. This can be attributed to the production of new nuclei and recoil nuclei up to the atomic number $Z = 74$ corresponding to the tungsten, precisely present in the BEOL at the level of the plugs for the interconnection of drains with the first metal layer. The detailed analysis of this new produced nuclei shows that the majority of those inducing an upset are the result of neutron-cupper interactions in the first metal layers close to the active silicon.

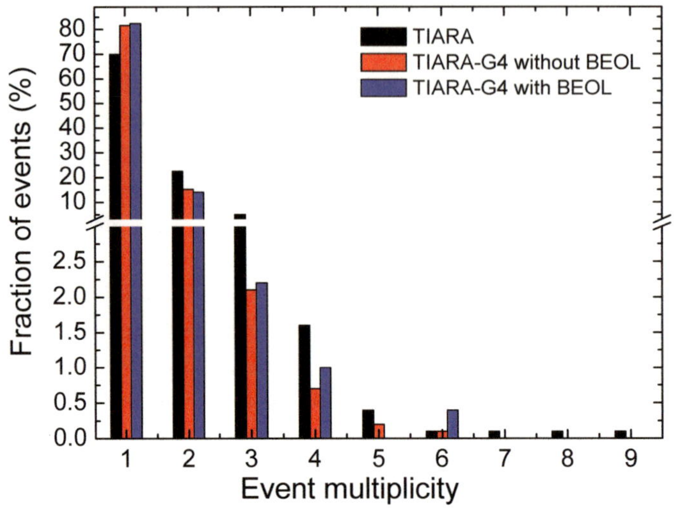

Figure 16. Event multiplicity distributions obtained with the initial (TIARA) and new (TIARA-G4) versions of the code for the evaluation of the neutron-induced SER in the 65 nm SRAM architecture. Data are also plotted for TIARA-G4 with and without taking into account the real BEOL structure.

5.3. Effects of low-energy muons on a 65 nm SRAM circuit

This last example concerns a preliminary study of the effects of low-energy muons on SRAM memories. As already introduced in subsection 2.1, atmospheric muons represent an important part of the natural radiation environment at ground level [1,20]. The muon is an elementary particle similar to the electron, with a unitary negative electric charge and a mass about 200 times the mass of an electron. The muon, denoted by μ^- and also called "negative muon", has a corresponding antiparticle of opposite charge and equal mass: the antimuon, often called "positive muon" (μ^+). Because they are charged, both negative and positive muons can loss their kinetic energy by ionization process when they travel through matter. But this interaction with matter is tenuous and muons can travel large distances in matter, thus deeply penetrating into material circuits.

Another particularity of muons is that they are unstable particles with a mean lifetime of 2.2 μs. They spontaneously decay into three particles:

$$\mu^- \rightarrow e^- + \bar{\upsilon}_e + \upsilon_\mu \qquad \mu^+ \rightarrow e^+ + \upsilon_e + \bar{\upsilon}_\mu. \tag{7}$$

Finally, when negative muons (and only negative muons) stop in silicon, about 35% decay following the previous reaction scheme and the remaining 65% are captured. If an intermediate state is assumed, the capture reaction can be written as:

$$\mu^- + Si^{28} \rightarrow Al^{28} + \nu + 100.5\,MeV \tag{8}$$

The excited ^{28}Al nucleus can decay from the following modes, thus producing secondary heavy nuclei that can deposit important charge in silicon:

$$\begin{aligned} Al^{28} &\rightarrow Al^{27} + n\,(12.4\,MeV) \\ &\rightarrow Al^{27} + n\,(14.2\,MeV) \\ &\rightarrow Na^{24} + \alpha\,(15.5\,MeV) \\ &\rightarrow Mg^{26} + d\,(18.4\,MeV) \end{aligned} \tag{9}$$

In contrast to the first version of TIARA, TIARA-G4 is now capable of simulating the impact of muons on SRAM circuits. For this first study, we considered low energy (< 1 MeV) negative and positive muons susceptible to directly deposit charge by ionization or to be captured (negative muons) after they stop in silicon. The Geant4 general particle source was then used to generate mono-energetic muons incident on the well-known 65 nm SRAM architecture (with complete BEOL) previously defined in Figure 5. Figure 17 illustrates different possible scenarios of negative and positive muon interactions with the structure. Figure 17(a) shows a negative muon decay in the top layers of the BEOL structure, this cannot lead to an upset since the muon disintegrates in light particles not able to deposit any significant charge in silicon. Figure 17(b) shows a similar event but occurring in the silicon substrate. In this case, the incoming positive muon traverses the complete BEOL structure and, statistically, can cross a sensitive drain. If the charge deposited in the impacted drain is higher than the critical charge for this transistor type and for this technology, the corresponding memory cell is upset. Figures 17 (c) and (d) show two negative muon capture events occurring in the BEOL and in silicon, respectively. These events produce large secondary particle showers, containing one or more charged particles susceptible to reach the active silicon region and to induce an upset or even a multiple cell upset. Of course, the probability to induce an upset is maximum when the muon capture-induce shower is produced in the immediate vicinity of the sensitive drain layer, as illustrated in Figure 17(d). This case corresponds to a reduced energy interval for the incoming muons in so far as the penetration depth of the muons in the structure and then the capture location primarily depends on the muon kinetic energy.

In order to illustrate this effect, we plotted in Figure 18 the distribution inside the SRAM structure of the vertex positions related to the negative muon capture reactions for three different values of the incident muon kinetic energy: 0.1, 0.3 MeV and 0.5 MeV. We clearly evidence in this figure such a dependency of the capture position (depth) with the muon kinetic energy. As a result, the soft error rate induced by negative muon irradiation presents a maximum when precisely muon captures occurs at the depth of the layer containing sensitive drains. This behavior is illustrated in Figure 19 which also plot the percentage of cell upsets induced by muon capture reactions or directly by muon impacts on sensitive drain (i.e. direct charge deposition in drain volumes). When increasing the kinetic energy of primary particles, the fraction of upsets induced by muon capture rapidly decrease as soon captures occur deeper in silicon, below the active layer. In this case, upsets become mainly induced by direct charge deposition from incident muons.

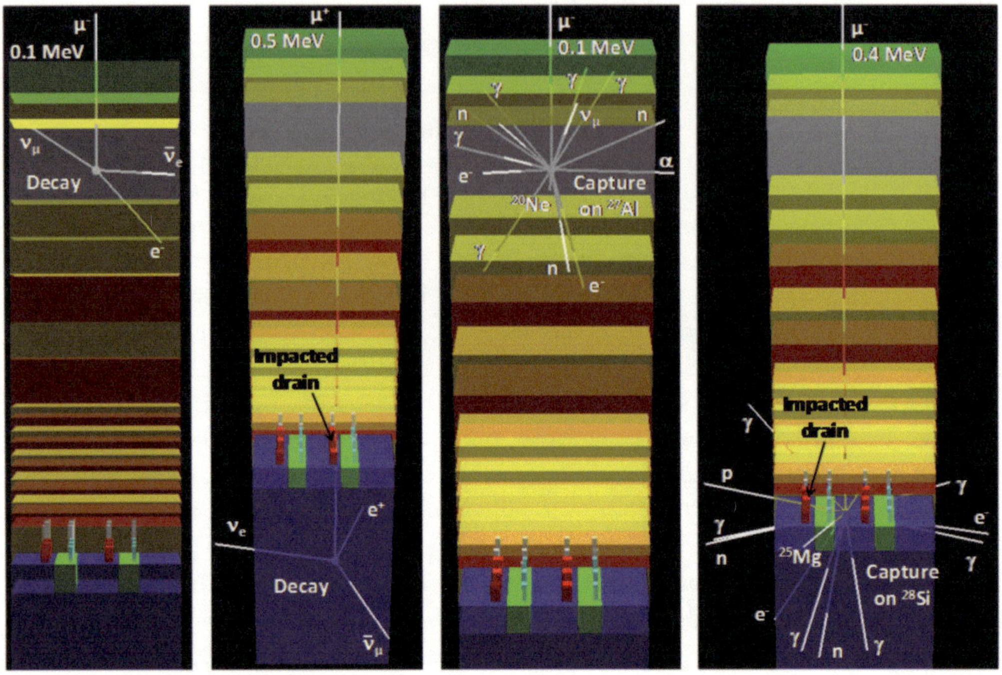

Figure 17. TIARA-G4 screenshots under ROOT of four events illustrating the interactions of low energy negative and positive muons with the complete 65 nm SRAM structure. From left to right: μ- decay in the BEOL (Al layer), μ+ upsetting a drain by direct charge deposition though the structure followed by the muon decay in the substrate, μ- capture on an aluminum atom in the BEOL, μ- capture on a silicon atom in the active circuit region (Pwell) leading to a drain upset via a direct impact by a secondary particle (proton in this case).

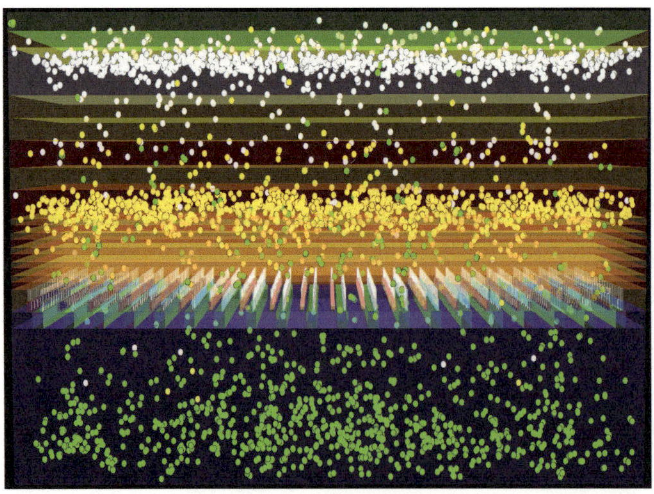

Figure 18. 3D distribution inside the SRAM circuit of the vertex positions related to the negative muon capture reactions for three different values of the incident muon kinetic energy: 0.1 MeV (white dots), 0.3 MeV (yellow dots) and 0.5 MeV (green dots).

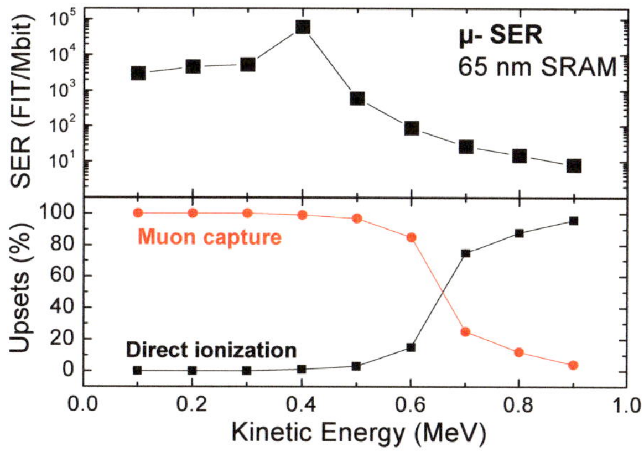

Figure 19. Estimated negative muon-induced soft error rate versus muon kinetic energy for the 65 nm SRAM. The percentage of cell upsets induced by the secondary particles produced by muon capture reactions or directly by muon impacts on sensitive drain (i.e. direct charge deposition in drain volumes) are also plotted.

6. Conclusion

In conclusion, we described in this chapter a new simulation platform, named TIARA-G4, we have developed these last years for the numerical evaluation of the sensitivity of advanced semiconductor memories (static RAMs) subjected to natural radiation at ground level. Based on the Geant4 toolkit, the application is sufficiently general and modular to simulate a user-defined circuit architecture subjected to the external irradiation by heavy-ions, neutrons, protons, muons or directly by alpha-particles generated inside the circuit materials. After defining the natural radiation environment at ground level and the different types of radiation constraints, we presented in details the different modules of our code, including the methods and approximations adopted to model the circuit architecture, to generate particles mimicking a given radiation environment and to model the circuit/cell electrical response. Finally, we illustrated the capabilities of our code to estimate the soft-error rate in deca-nanometer SRAM circuits subjected to atmospheric thermal and high energy neutrons and to mono-energetic positive and negative muons, investigating and illustrating for the first time, some unconventional physical effects, such as the ^{10}B thermal neutron capture at the level of the Pmos drains or the negative muon capture and its consequences on the SER in the SRAM circuit structure. TIARA-G4 should be used in the future to more deeply investigate the radiation response of ultimate MOS circuits and alternate nanoelectronic devices in the natural (terrestrial) environment.

Author details

Jean-Luc Autran, Sergey Semikh , Daniela Munteanu and Sébastien Serre
Aix-Marseille University & CNRS, Marseille, France

Gilles Gasiot and Philippe Roche
STMicroelectronics, Crolles, France

7. References

[1] J.F. Ziegler, H. Puchner, SER – History, Trends and Challenges, Cypress Semiconductor, 2004. See also references therein.

[2] M. Nicolaidis (Editor), Soft Errors in Modern Electronic Systems, Springer (2010).

[3] J.L. Leray, "Effects of atmospheric neutrons on devices, at sea level and in avionics embedded systems", Microelectronics Reliability, Volume 47, Issues 9-11, pp. 1827-1835, 2007.

[4] S. Mitra, P. Sanda, and N. Seifert, "Soft Errors: Technology Trends, System Effects and Protection Techniques," IEEE VLSI Test Symposium, 2008.

[5] R.C. Baumann, "Radiation-Induced Soft Errors in Advanced Semiconductor Technologies", IEEE Transactions on Device and Material Reliability, Vol. 5, pp. 305-316 (2005).

[6] R. D. Schrimpf, D. M. Fleetwood (Editors), Radiation Effects And Soft Errors In Integrated Circuits And Electronic Devices, World Scientific Publishing (2004).

[7] E. Normand, "Single Event Upset at Ground Level", IEEE Trans. Nucl. Sci., Volume NS-43, N°6, pp. 2742-2750, 1996. See also references therein.

[8] D.F. Heidel, P.W. Marshall, K.A. LaBel, J.R. Schwank, K.P. Rodbell, M.C. Hakey, M.D. Berg, P.E. Dodd, M.R. Friendlich, A.D. Phan, C.M. Seidleck, M.R. Shaneyfelt, M.A. Xapsos, "Low Energy Proton Single-Event-Upset Test Results on 65 nm SOI SRAM", IEEE Trans. Nucl. Sci., vol 55, Issue 6, pp. 3394-3400, 2008.

[9] E. H. Cannon, M. Cabanas-Holmen, J. Wert, T. Amort, R. Brees, J. Koehn, B. Meaker, and E. Normand, "Heavy Ion, High-Energy, and Low-Energy Proton SEE Sensitivity of 90-nm RHBD SRAMs", IEEE Trans. Nucl. Sci., vol 56, Issue 7, pp. 3493-3499, 2010.

[10] J. F. Dicello, C. W. McCabe, J. D. Doss, and M. Paciotti, "The relative efficiency of soft-error induction in 4K static RAMs by muons and pions", IEEE Trans. Nucl. Sci., vol 30, Issue 6, pp. 4613-4616, 1983.

[11] C. J. Gelderloos1i, R. J. Peterson, M. E. Nelson, and J. F. Ziegler, "Pion-Induced Soft Upsets in 16 Mbit DRAM Chips", IEEE Trans. Nucl. Sci., vol 44, Issue 6, pp. 2237-2242, 1997.

[12] S. Duzellier, D. Falguère, M. Tverskoy, E. Ivanov, R. Dufayel, and M.C. Calvet, "SEU Induced by Pions in Memories From Different Generations", IEEE Trans. Nucl. Sci., vol 48, Issue 6, p. 1960-1965, 2001.

[13] Brian D. Sierawski, Marcus H. Mendenhall, Robert A. Reed, Michael A. Clemens, Robert A. Weller, Ronald D. Schrimpf, Ewart W. Blackmore, Michael Trinczek, Bassam Hitti, Jonathan A. Pellish, Robert C. Baumann, Shi-Jie Wen, Rick Wong, and Nelson Tam, "Muon-Induced Single Event Upsets in Deep-Submicron Technology", IEEE Trans. Nucl. Sci., vol. 57, issue 6, pp. 3273-3278, 2011.

[14] Sierawski, B.D.; Reed, R.A.; Mendenhall, M.H.; Weller, R.A.; Schrimpf, R.D.; Wen, S.; Wong, R.; Tam, N.; Baumann, R.C, "Effects of scaling on muon-induced soft errors", International Reliability Physics Symposium (IRPS 2011), pp. 3C3.1-6.

[15] J.L. Autran, D. Munteanu, P. Roche, G. Gasiot, S. Martinie, S. Uznanski, S. Sauze, S. Semikh, E. Yakushev, S. Rozov, P. Loaiza, G. Warot, M. Zampaolo, "Soft-errors induced

by terrestrial neutrons and natural alpha-particle emitters in advanced memory circuits at ground level", Microelectronics Reliability, Vol. 50, pp. 1822-1831 (2010).

[16] P. E. Dodd, "Device Simulation of Charge Collection and Single-Event Upset", IEEE Trans. Nucl. Sci., vol. 43, no. 2, pp. 561-575, April 1996.

[17] P.E. Dodd and L.W. Massengill, "Basic mechanisms and modeling of single-event upset in digital microelectronics", IEEE Trans. Nucl. Sci., vol. 50, no. 3, pp. 583–602, Jun. 2003.

[18] P. E. Dodd, "Physics-Based Simulation of Single-Event Effects", IEEE Trans. Device Mater. Reliab., vol. 5, no. 3, pp. 343-357, Sept. 2005.

[19] D. Munteanu, J.L. Autran, "Modeling of digital devices and ICs submitted to transient irradiations", IEEE Trans. Nucl. Sci., 2008, Vol. 55, no. 4, pp. 1854-1878.

[20] L.I. Dorman, Cosmic Rays in the Earth's Atmosphere and Underground, Kluwer Academic Publishers, 2004.

[21] M.S. Gordon, P. Goldhagen, K.P. Rodbell, T.H. Zabel, H.H.K. Tang, J.M. Clem, P. Bailey, " Measurement of the Flux and Energy Spectrum of Cosmic-Ray Induced Neutrons on the Ground", IEEE Trans. Nucl. Sci., Vol. 1, 2004, pp. 3427-3434.

[22]] F. Lei, S. Clucas, C. Dyer, P. Truscott, "An atmospheric radiation model based on response matrices generated by detailed Monte Carlo Simulations of cosmic ray interactions", IEEE Trans. Nucl. Sci., 2004, Vol. 51, pp. 3442-3451.

[23] F. Lei, A. Hands, S. Clucas, C. Dyer, P. Truscott, "Improvement to and Validations of the QinetiQ Atmospheric Radiation Model (QARM)", IEEE Trans. Nucl. Sci., 2006, Vol. 53, pp. 1851-1858. See also http://qarm.space.qinetiq.com/

[24] F. Wrobel, J. Gasiot, F. Saigné, A. D. Touboul, "Effects of atmospheric neutrons and natural contamination on advanced microelectronic memories", Appl. Phys. Lett., Vol. 93, 064105, 2008.

[25] G. Adamiec and M. Aitken, "Dose-rate conversion factors: update", Ancient TL, Vol. 16, N°2, pp. 37-50, 1998.

[26] S. Uznanski, G. Gasiot, P. Roche, C. Tavernier, J-L. Autran, "Single Event Upset and Multiple Cell Upset Modeling in Commercial Bulk 65 nm CMOS SRAMs and Flip-Flops," IEEE Trans. Nucl. Sci., vol. 57, issue 4, pp. 1876-1883, Aug 2010.

[27] S. Uznanski, G. Gasiot, P. Roche, J. L. Autran, "Combining GEANT4 and TIARA for Neutron Soft Error Rate Prediction of 65 nm Flip-Flops," IEEE Trans. Nucl. Sci., vol. 58, issue 6, pp. 2599-2606, Dec 2011.

[28] S. Agostinelli et al., "Geant4—a simulation toolkit", Nuclear Instruments and Methods in Physics Research Section A: Accelerators, Spectrometers, Detectors and Associated Equipment, Vol. 506, pp.250-303, 2003.

[29] SRIM software, available online: http://www.srim.org/

[30] S. Uznanski, "Monte-Carlo simulation and contribution to understanding of Single Event Upset (SEU) mechanisms in CMOS technologies downto 20nm technological node.", Ph.D. Thesis, Aix-Marseille University, Sept. 2011.

[31] Geant4 General Particle Source, http://reat.space.qinetiq.com/gps/

[32] JEDEC Standard Measurement and Reporting of Alpha Particles and Terrestrial Cosmic Ray-Induced Soft Errors in Semiconductor Devices, JESD89 Arlington, VA: JEDEC Solid State Technology Association.

[33] T. Sato, H. Yasuda, K. Niita, A. Endo and L. Sihver "Development of PARMA: PHITS-based Analytical Radiation Model in the Atmosphere", Radiation Research, 2008, Vol. 170, pp. 244-259.

[34] EXcel-based Program for calculating Atmospheric Cosmic-ray Spectrum, available online at http://phits.jaea.go.jp/expacs/index.html

[35] U. Bravar, E.O. Flückiger, K. Godin, Z.C. Hansen, J.R. Macri, M.L. McConnell, R.S. Miller, M. R. Moser, J.M. Ryan, "Atmospheric Neutron Measurements with the SONTRAC Science Model", IEEE Nuclear Science Symposium Conference Record, 2005, N14-126.

[36] J. Kempa and I.M. Brancus, "Zenith angle distributions of cosmic ray muons", Nuclear Physics B - Proceedings Supplements, 2003, Vol. 122, pp. 279-281.

[37] http://Geant4.web.cern.ch/Geant4/support/proc_mod_catalog/physics_lists/referencePL.shtml

[38] ROOT, an object oriented framework for large scale data analysis, available online: http://root.cern.ch

[39] J.M. Palau, G. Hubert, K. Coulie, B. Sagnes, M.C. Calvet, S. Fourtine, "Device Simulation Study of the SEU Sensitivity of SRAMs to Internal Ion Tracks Generated by Nuclear Reactions", IEEE Trans. Nucl. Sci., Vol. 48, N°2, pp. 225-231, 2001.

[40] G. Hubert, A. Bougerol, F. Miller, N. Buard, L. Anghel, T. Carriere, F. Wrobel, R. Gaillard, "Prediction of Transient induced by Neutron/Proton in CMOS combinational Logic Cells", Proceedings of the 12th IEEE International On-Line Testing Symposium (IOLTS'06).

[41] R. Baumann, T. Hossain, S. Murata, H. Kitagawa, "Boron Compounds as a Dominant Source of Alpha Particles in Semiconductor Devices," IEEE International Reliability Physics Physics Symposium, 1995, pp. 297-302.

[42] R. Baumann and E. Smith, "Neutron-Induced 10B Fission as a Major Source of Soft Errors in High Density SRAMs", Microelectronics Reliability, Vol. 41, 2001, pp. 211-218.

[43] M. Olmos, R. Gaillard, A. Van Overberghe, J. Beaucour, S.Wen, S. Chung, "Investigation of thermal neutron induced soft error rates in commercial SRAMs with 0.35 μm to 80 nm technologies", IEEE International Reliability Physics Physics Symposium, 2006, pp. 212-216.

[44] S. Wen, R. Wong, M. Romain, N. Tam, "Thermal neutron soft error rate for SRAM in the 90-45 nm technology range", IEEE International Reliability Physics Physics Symposium, 2010, pp. 1036-1039.

[45] Laboratoire CEA-CNRS Léon Brillouin (LLB), http://www-llb.cea.fr/

Section 3

Fluid Dynamics

Chapter 16

BG Model Based on Bagnold's Concept and Its Application to Analysis of Elongation of Sand Spit and Shore – Normal Sand Bar

Takaaki Uda, Masumi Serizawa and Shiho Miyahara

Additional information is available at the end of the chapter

http://dx.doi.org/10.5772/48547

1. Introduction

The accurate prediction of three-dimensional (3D) beach changes on a coast with a large shoreline curvature, such as a coast with a sand spit, and a wave field that significantly changes in response to topographic changes, has been difficult to achieve in previous studies. As a result, regarding the beach changes around a sand spit, most previous studies have focused on the shoreline changes. Ashton et al. (2001) showed that when the incident angle of deep-water waves to the mean shoreline exceeds 45°, shoreline instability occurs, resulting in the development of sand spits from a small perturbation of the shoreline. They successfully predicted the planar changes in a shoreline containing sand spits using infinitesimal meshes divided in the x- and y-directions. However in Ashton et al.'s model, only the longshore sand transport equation is employed as the sand transport equation instead of a two-dimensional (2D) sand transport equation in which both cross-shore and longshore sand transport are considered. Furthermore, in evaluating the wave field, wave conditions at the breaking point are transformed into deep-water values assuming a bathymetry with straight parallel contours and using Snell's law. Since the sand transport equation is expressed using these deep-water parameters, the effect of large 3D changes in topography on the wave field cannot be accurately evaluated. Furthermore, the finite-difference scheme used to evaluate the breaker angle and the method of calculating the wave field around the wave-shelter zone are altered depending on the calculation conditions, resulting in a complicated calculation method that requires special calculation techniques. Watanabe et al. (2004) developed a model for predicting the shoreline changes of a sand spit under the conditions that the sand spit significantly changes its configuration with changes in the wave field. They selected orthogonal curvilinear coordinates parallel and normal to the shoreline of the sand spit, and the seabed topography after various numbers of time steps was inversely determined from the time-dependent shoreline configuration given by the seabed slope. They also predicted the shoreline changes due to the spatial changes in longshore sand transport. Their model is also not a definitive model for predicting the 3D topographic changes of a sand spit.

A sand spit is often formed by wave action at a location where the direction of the coastline abruptly changes. Uda & Yamamoto (1992) carried out a movable-bed experiment using a plane-wave basin to investigate the development of a sand spit. Two experiments were carried out: sand was deposited (1) on a shallow flat seabed and (2) on a coast with a steep slope. Their results showed that a slender sand spit extends along the marginal line between the shallow sea and offshore steep slope in Case 1, whereas a cuspate foreland is formed owing to the deposition of sand on the steep slope in Case 2, suggesting the importance of the effect caused by the difference in the depth of water where sand is deposited. We have developed a model for predicting beach changes based on Bagnold's concept (Serizawa et al., 2006) by applying the concept of the equilibrium slope introduced by Inman& Bagnold (1963) and the energetics approach of Bagnold (1963). Here, the BG model is used to simulate the extension of a sand spit on a shallow seabed and the formation of a cuspate foreland on a steep coast (Serizawa & Uda, 2011).

As another type of beach change due to waves on a coast with a shallow flat seabed, a tidal flat facing an inland sea is considered. On such a tidal flat subject to the action of waves with significant energy, a sandy beach may develop along the marginal line between the tidal flat and the land, and the sandy beach with a steep slope is clearly separated from the tidal flat along a line with a discontinuous change in the slope. On such beaches developing along the marginal line between the tidal flat and the land, longshore sand transport due to the oblique wave incidence to the shoreline and cross-shore sand transport during storm surges often occur. However, in addition to these sand transport phenomena, as part of the interaction between the tidal flat and the sandy beach, shoreward transport and the landward deposition of sand originally supplied from the offshore zone of the tidal flat, forming a slender sand bar, are often observed. Although this landward sand movement due to waves on the shallow tidal flat is considered to be part of the process by which sand transported offshore by river currents during floods returns to the shore, its mechanism has not yet been studied. These phenomena were observed on the Kutsuo coast, which has a very wide tidal flat and faces the Suo-nada Sea, part of the Seto Inland Sea, Japan. Here, the BG model was also used to predict the extension of a slender shore-normal sand bar observed on this coast (Serizawa et al., 2011). The observed phenomena were successfully explained by the results of the numerical simulation.

2. Numerical model (BG model)

With the elongation of a sand spit or a sand bar, the shape of the wave-shelter zone behind the spit or the sand bar changes, and therefore, the repeated calculation of the wave field and topographic changes is required. We use Cartesian coordinates (x, y) and consider the elevation at a point Z (x, y, t) as a variable to be solved, where t is time. The beach changes are assumed to take place between the depth of closure h_c and the berm height h_R. A modified version of the BG model proposed by Serizawa et al. (2009a) was used to predict the formation of a sand spit. An additional term given by Ozasa & Brampton (1980) was also incorporated into the fundamental equation of the BG model to accurately evaluate the longshore sand transport due to the effect of the longshore gradient of the wave height. The fundamental equation is given by

$$\vec{q} = C_0 \frac{P}{\tan\beta_c} \left\{ \begin{array}{l} K_n \left(\tan\beta_c \vec{e_w} - |\cos\alpha| \, \overrightarrow{\nabla Z} \right) \\ + \left\{ (K_s - K_n) \sin\alpha - \dfrac{K_2}{\tan\overline{\beta}} \dfrac{\partial H}{\partial s} \right\} \tan\beta \vec{e_s} \end{array} \right\} \tag{1}$$

$$(-h_c \le Z \le h_R)$$

$$P = \rho\, u_m^3 \tag{2}$$

$$u_m = \frac{H}{2}\sqrt{\frac{g}{h}} \tag{3}$$

Here, $\vec{q} = (q_x, q_y)$ is the net sand transport flux, Z (x, y, t) is the elevation, n and s are the local coordinates taken along the directions normal (shoreward) and parallel to the contour lines, respectively, $\overrightarrow{\nabla Z} = (\partial Z/\partial x,\ \partial Z/\partial y)$ is the slope vector, $\vec{e_w}$ is a unit vector in the wave direction, $\vec{e_s}$ is a unit vector parallel to the contour lines, α is the angle between the wave direction and the direction normal to the contour lines, $\tan\beta = |\overrightarrow{\nabla Z}|$ is the seabed slope, $\tan\beta_c$ is the equilibrium slope, $\tan\beta\ \vec{e_s} = (-\partial Z/\partial y,\ \partial Z/\partial x)$, K_s and K_n are the coefficients of longshore sand transport and cross-shore sand transport, respectively, K_2 is the coefficient of the term given by Ozasa & Brampton (1980), $\partial H/\partial s = \vec{e_s} \cdot \overrightarrow{\nabla H}$ is the longshore gradient of the wave height H measured parallel to the contour lines and $\tan\overline{\beta}$ is the characteristic slope of the breaker zone. In addition, C_0 is the coefficient transforming the immersed-weight expression into a volumetric expression ($C_0 = 1/\{(\rho_s - \rho) g (1-p)\}$, where ρ is the density of seawater, ρ_s is the specific gravity of sand particles, p is the porosity of sand and g is the acceleration due to gravity), u_m is the amplitude of the seabed velocity due to the orbital motion of waves given by Eq. (3), h_c is the depth of closure, and h_R is the berm height.

The intensity of sand transport P in Eq. (1) is assumed to be proportional to the wave energy dissipation rate ϕ based on the energetics approach of Bagnold (1963). In the model of Serizawa et al. (2006), P was formulated using the wave energy at the breaking point, but in this study, it is combined with the wave characteristics at a local point. Bailard & Inman (1981) used the relationship $\phi_t = \tau u_t = \rho C_f u_t^3$ for the instantaneous wave energy dissipation rate ϕ_t to derive their sand transport equation, where τ is the bottom shear stress, u_t is the instantaneous velocity and C_f is the drag coefficient. We basically follow their study but assume that ϕ is proportional to the third power of the amplitude of the bottom oscillatory velocity u_m due to waves instead of the third power of the instantaneous velocity. The intensity of sand transport P is then given by Eq. (2), and its coefficient is assumed to be included in the coefficients of longshore and cross-shore sand transport, K_s and K_n, respectively. u_m can be calculated by small-amplitude wave theory in shallow water using the wave height H at a local point (Eq. (3)), which can be obtained by the numerical calculation of the plane-wave field. The depth of closure h_c is assumed to be proportional to the wave height H at a local point and is given by Eq. (4), referring to the relationship given by Uda & Kawano (1996).

$$h_c = KH \qquad (K=2.5) \tag{4}$$

In the numerical simulation of beach changes, the sand transport equation and the continuity equation are solved on the x-y plane by the explicit finite-difference methodemploying staggered mesh scheme. In the estimation of sand transport near the berm top and the depth of closure, sand transport was linearly reduced to 0 near the berm height or the depth of closure to prevent sand from depositing in the area higher than the berm height and beach erosion in the zone deeper than the depth of closure.

The wave field was calculated using the energy balance equation given by Mase (2001), in which the directional spectrum D $(f,\ \theta)$ of the irregular waves varies with the energy dissipation term due to wave breaking (Dally et al., 1984). Here, f and θ are the frequency and wave direction, respectively. In this method, wave refraction, wave breaking and wave diffraction in the wave-shelter zone can be calculated with a small calculation load. The energy dissipation term due to wave breaking ϕ (Dally et al., 1984), which is incorporated into the energy balance equation (Eq. (5)), is given by

$$\frac{\partial}{\partial x}\left(DV_x\right)+\frac{\partial}{\partial y}\left(DV_y\right)+\frac{\partial}{\partial \theta}\left(DV_\theta\right)=F-\phi \tag{5}$$

$$\phi=\left(K/h\right)DC_g\left[1-\left(\Gamma/\gamma\right)^2\right] \qquad \left(\phi \geq 0\right) \tag{6}$$

Here, D is the directional spectrum, (V_x, V_y, V_θ) is the energy transport velocity in the (x, y, θ) space, F is the wave diffraction term given by Mase (2001), K is the coefficient of the wave-breaking intensity, h is the water depth, C_g is the wave group velocity ($C_g \approx \sqrt{gh}$ in the approximation in shallow-water wave theory), Γ is the ratio of the critical breaker height to the water depth on the horizontal bed and γ is the ratio of the wave height to water depth. To prevent the location where the berm develops from being excessively seaward compared with that observed in the experiment or the field, a lower limit was considered for h in Eq. (6). As a result of this procedure, wave decay near the berm top was reduced, resulting in a higher landward sand transport rate. In the calculation of the wave field on land, the imaginary depth h' between the minimum depth h_0 and berm height h_R was considered, as given by Eq. (7), similarly to in the ordinary 3D model (Shimizu et al., 1996).

$$h'=\left(\frac{h_R-Z}{h_R+h_0}\right)^r h_0 \qquad (r=1) \qquad \left(-h_0 \leq Z \leq h_R\right) \tag{7}$$

In addition, at locations whose elevation is higher than the berm height, the wave energy was set to 0. The calculation of the wave field was carried out every 10 steps in the calculation of topographic changes.

Equation (1) shows that the sand transport flux can be expressed as the sum of the component along the wave direction and the components due to the effect of gravity normal to the contours and the effect of longshore currents parallel to the contours. To investigate the physical meaning of Eq. (1), $\vec{q}$ in Eq. (1) is separately expressed as Eq. (8) when neglecting the additional term given by Ozasa & Brampton (1980), and when the inner products of $\vec{e_n}$ and $\vec{q}$ and of $\vec{e_s}$ and $\vec{q}$ are taken, Eqs. (9) and (10) are derived for the cross-shore and longshore components of sand transport, q_n and q_s, respectively. Furthermore, under the condition that the seabed slope is equal to the equilibrium slope, Eq. (10) reduces to Eq. (11).

$$\vec{q} = q_n \vec{e_n} + q_s \vec{e_s} \tag{8}$$

$$q_n = \vec{e_n} \cdot \vec{q} = C_0 K_n P |\cos\alpha| \left(\frac{\cos\alpha}{|\cos\alpha|} - \frac{\tan\beta}{\tan\beta_c} \right) \tag{9}$$

$$q_s = \vec{e_s} \cdot \vec{q} = C_0 K_s P \sin\alpha \left\{ \frac{\tan\beta}{\tan\beta_c} + \frac{K_n}{K_s} \left(1 - \frac{\tan\beta}{\tan\beta_c} \right) \right\} \tag{10}$$

$$q_s \approx C_0 K_s P \sin\alpha \qquad (\because \tan\beta \approx \tan\beta_c) \tag{11}$$

In Eq. (9), the cross-shore sand transport q_n becomes 0 when the local seabed slope is equal to the equilibrium slope, and the longshore sand transport q_s becomes 0 when the wave direction coincides with the normal to the contour lines, as shown in Eqs. (10) and (11). When a discrepancy from these conditions arises, sand transport is generated by the same stabilization mechanism as in the contour-line-change model (Uda & Serizawa, 2010).

Taking the above into account, the first term in the parentheses in Eq. (1) gives the sand transport in the case that the rates of longshore and cross-shore sand transport are equal ($K_s = K_n$), and the second term is the additional longshore sand transport in the case that the rates are different ($K_s > K_n$). The physical meaning of the second term is that longshore sand transport is generated by the small angular shift that occurs when the wave direction is incompletely reversed in the oscillatory movement due to waves, and the second term also models the additional longshore sand transport due to the effect of longshore currents, the effect of which is only partially included in the first term.

Although the applicability of the contour-line-change model to the prediction of beach changes is limited when the shape of coastal structures is complicated because it tracks the movement of lines with specific characteristics, the BG model can be applied to the prediction of topographic changes under all structural conditions, because the depth changes in the x-y plane are calculated, similarly to in the ordinary model for predicting 3D beach changes, and therefore the calculation can be carried out systematically. This is an advantage of the BG model.

3. Movable-bed experiment on elongation of a sand spit

A movable-bed experiment was carried out using a plane-wave tank of 16 m width and 21 m length (Uda & Yamamoto, 1992). A model beach was made of sand with d_{50} = 0.28 mm. A sandy beach was established as the source of sand in the right half of the plane basin and conditions were set up such that leftward longshore sand transport developed. In Case 1, a shallow seabed with a water depth of 5 cm was formed in the left half of the wave basin and an offshore bed was formed with a steep slope of 1/5. In Case 2, a steep slope of 1/5 was produced instead of a shallow sea where the sand spit was formed. The angle between the direction normal to initial shoreline and the wave direction was 20° in order for sufficient longshore sand transport to occur. The elevation of the flat surface on the land was assumed to be 10 cm above mean sea level. Regular waves with H_0' = 4.6 cm and T = 1.27 s incident to the model beach were generated for 8 hr. When a shallow sea exists, incident waves break immediately offshore of the shallow seabed, resulting in the rapid decay of waves on the shallow seabed. Because of this effect, sand is deposited near the marginal line between the shallow flat seabed and the steep offshore slope, resulting in the rapid elongation of a sand spit.

Figures 1(a)-1(c) show the initial bathymetry and the beach topography after wave generation for 1 and 8 hr in Case 1, respectively. Here, the arrows in Figs. 1(a) and 1(d) show the breaking point (the tip of the arrows), the breaker height (the length of the arrows), and the wave directionat the breaking point (the direction of the arrows) measured immediately after the start of wave generation. Because the shoreline had a discontinuity due to a sudden change in the shoreline direction between the sand supply zone and the shallow seabedwhere sand was deposited, a straight sand spit extended from the boundary, and a slender sand spit extended along the marginal line between the shallow seabed and the steepoffshore slope over time. After 8 hr, the sand spit had reached the left boundary while forming a barrier island, and the width of the barrier island expanded upcoast from the left boundary because of the continuous sand supply.

Figures 1(d) and 1(e) show the initial bathymetry and the beach topography after wave generation for 8 hr in Case 2 with a steep offshore slope. The water depth in the zone where sand was deposited was large; thus, sand was deposited while forming a steep slope.

Because this steep slope reaches a great depth, a cuspate foreland was formed without the development of a sand spit. These experimental results were used for validating the improved BG model.

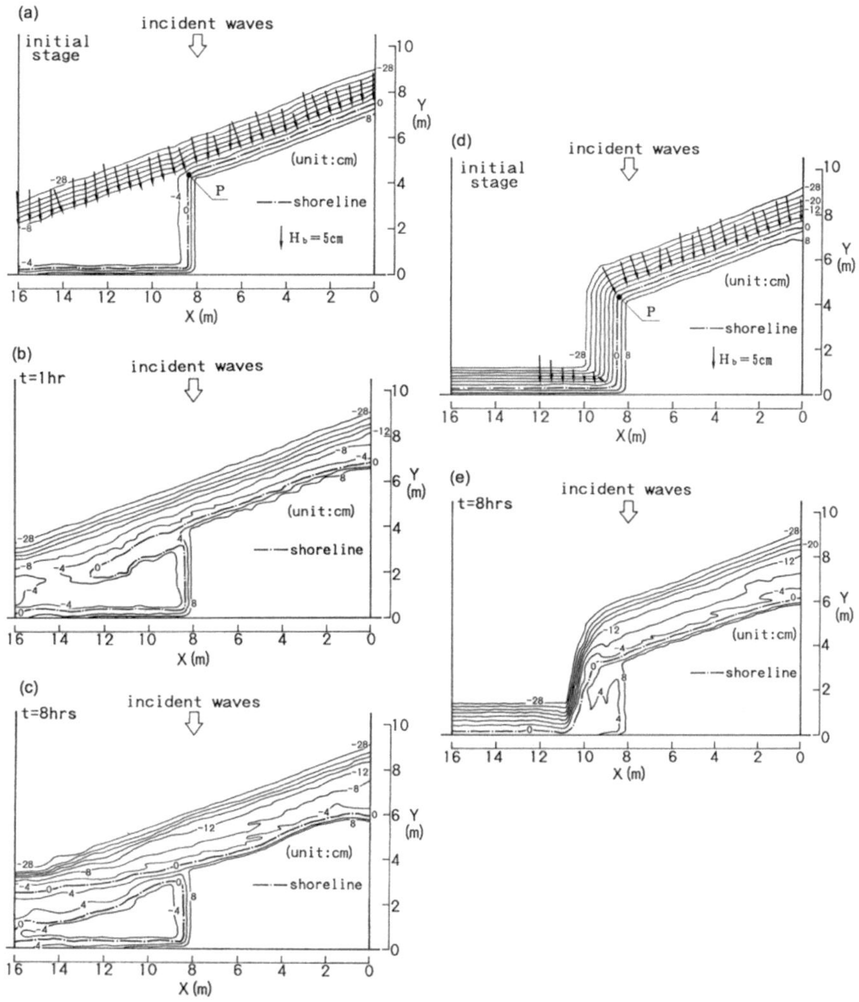

Figure 1. Experimental results for development of sand spit on a coast with abrupt change in coastline orientation (Uda & Yamamoto, 1992).

4. Field observation of formation of slender shore-normal sand bar

4.1. General conditions

The study area is the Kutsuo coast facing the Suo-nada Sea, part of the Seto Inland Sea, as shown in Fig. 2. Figure 3 shows an aerial photograph of the study area taken in 1999. The Harai River flows into the coast, which has a very wide tidal flat of approximately 1.5 km width offshore of the river. Although a river mouth bar extends on the north side of the Harai River, another slender sand bar has developed along the north side of the channel extending between the river mouth and the offshore tidal mud flat, and it intersects the river mouth bar perpendicular to the shoreline. The sand source for this slender sand bar is assumed to be the Harai River; sand transported offshore by flood currents is deposited along both sides of the channel, and is then transported shoreward owing to the wave action.In this area, the slender sand bar as shown in Fig. 3 has been continuously developing. Figure 4 shows the bathymetry around the slender sand bar relative to the reference level (0.1m below mean sealevel) in 2008. Although the slender sand bar has moved slightly north compared with its position in Fig. 3, it extends in the cross-shore direction at X = 120 m in the central part of the river mouth bar, and the shoreline slightly protrudes near the connection point. The foreshore has been developing in the zone with elevation between 1.0 and 3.0 m. This foreshore is composed of coarse and medium-size sand, and its slope is as steep as 1/10. A tidal flat extends in the offshore zone, the elevation of which is lower than 1.0 m. In addition, there is a difference in the elevation of the tidal flat on both sides of the slender sand bar extending in the cross-shore direction with the ground elevation on the south side slightly higher than that on the north side.

Figure 2. Location of Kutsuo coast facing Suo-nada Sea, part of Seto Inland Sea.

Figure 3. Aerial photograph of Kutsuo coast.

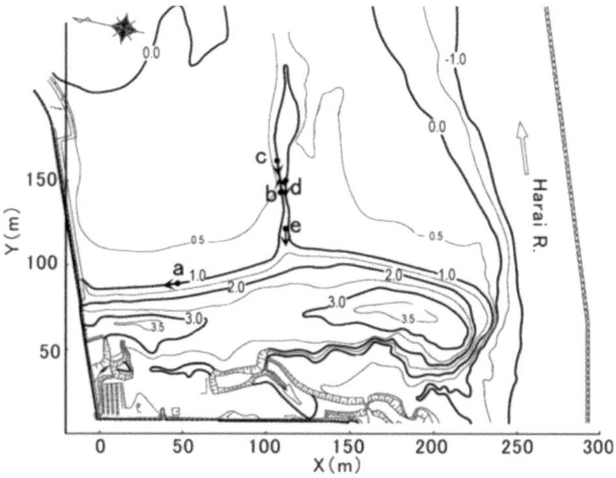

Figure 4. Bathymetry around slender sand bar on tidal flat offshore of Kutsuo coast.

4.2. Field observation

During low tide on December 27, 2009, a field observation of the tidal flat offshore of the coast was carried out. The north end of the coast is separated by a vertical seawall protecting a park, as shown in Fig. 5. A sandy beach abruptly begins with a steep slope from the mud flat covered by cohesive materials, and the mud flat and sandy beach are clearly separated along a line where the slope changes abruptly. The tidal flat is composed of cohesive materials, whereas the sandy beach is composed of coarse sand and is well compacted.

Figure 6 shows a view of the entire slender sand bar. Although the sand bar is submerged during high tide, it is completely exposed during low tide, as shown in Fig. 6. The sand bar extends in the direction normal to the mean coastline. Comparing the elevations of the mud flat on both sides of the sand bar, the elevation on the right (south) side, which is next to theoffshore channel, is higher than that on the left (north) side. On the south side of the slender sand bar, the Harai River flows into the sea, and sand supplied to the tidal flat from the river mouth is considered to be transported and deposited on the surface of the tidal flat owing to the shoreward sand transport due to waves. In this case, sand supply to the area north of the slender sand bar is obstructed by the sand bar itself, and this is assumed to be the cause of the difference in ground elevation on both sides of the sand bar.

Figure 7 shows the tip of a branch separated from the offshore part of the main slender sand bar, as shown in Fig. 3. On this sand bar, decomposed granite, which was considered to be transported offshore by flood currents of the river, has been deposited. The elevation of the sand bar gradually increases shoreward, then at the landward end suddenly drops to the tidal flat with a steep slope approximately equal to the angle of repose of the sand, implying the occurrence of shoreward sand transport.

Figure 8 shows the coastal conditions, looking landward from the tip of the slender sand bar. Although sand was deposited with a foreshore slope of 1/10 along the north side of the slender sand bar, the foreshore and flat tidal flat were clearly separated along the abrupt

Figure 5. Beach separated by vertical seawall (December 27, 2009).

Figure 6. View of entire slender sand bar (December 27, 2009).

change in the slope passing through point B. By a sieve analysis of the beach material sampled at point A, the median diameter of the beach material was determined to be d_{50} = 1.50 mm at point A. Figure 9 shows the narrow neck of the slender sand bar connected to the land. Several lines showing high tide marks extend in the cross-shore direction on the surface of the sand bar, implying that the sand bar stably exists during tidal changes. Figure 10 shows the beach condition near the point connecting the land and the slender sand bar. The triangular high tide lines show that the contour lines are parallel to these high tide lines. Therefore, if waves are incident from the direction normal to the coastline, large shoreward sand transport may occur along these contour lines because of the large incident wave angle. However, the slender sand bar is stable without rapid beach changes. Taking into account the continuity condition of sand and the fact that the slender sand bar is stable, the materials forming the sand bar are considered to have been carried from the Harai River during floods. The observation results indicate that the sand transported offshore by flood currents returns to the beach owing to shoreward sand transport due to waves. On an exposed beach, the formation of a stable sand bar extending normal to the coastline, as observed on this coast, is difficult, and such a sand bar rapidly deforms under wave action. Taking this into account, the formation of a slender sand bar observed in this study is considered to be due to the typical sand movement observed on only a very shallow tidal flat.

Figure 7. Tip of branch separated from offshore part of main slender sand bar (December 27, 2009).

Figure 8. Coastal condition, while looking landward from tip of slender sand bar (December 27, 2009).

Figure 9. Narrow neck of slender sand bar connected to land (December 27, 2009).

Figure 10. Beach condition near point connecting land and slender sand bar (December 27, 2009).

5. Application to movable-bed experiment

At locations with elevations higher than the berm height, the wave energy was set to 0. For convenience, the space scale in the calculation was set to 100-fold that in the experiment, and then the calculated results were reduced 100-fold. Although the movable-bed experiment was carried out under regular wave conditions, the wave field was calculated using the energy balance equation for irregular waves while regarding regular waves in the experiment as irregular waves, because repeated calculations were necessary owing to the bathymetric changes in this calculation.

5.1. Formation of barrier island on flat shallow seabed

Given the same initial topography and wave conditions as those in the experiment (regular waves with $H_0' = 4.6$ cm and $T = 1.27$ s obliquely incident to the model beach with an angle of 20°), the beach changes after 8 hr were predicted. The depth of closure was given by $h_c = 2.5H$ (H: wave height at a local point). The berm height was assumed to be 5 cm, and the angles of the equilibrium slope and repose slope were set as 1/5 and 1/2, respectively, on the basis of the experimental results. The calculation domain was divided by $\Delta x = \Delta y = 20$ cm intervals in the cross-shore and longshore directions, respectively, and the calculation for up to 8 hr (8×10^4 steps) was carried out using time intervals of $\Delta t = 1\times10^{-3}$ hr. Table 1 shows the calculation conditions.

5.1.1. Bathymetric changes

Figures 11(a)-11(f) show the results for the predicted development of a sand spit on a shallow flat seabed given the same conditions as those in the experiment. A slender sand spit with a length of approximately 2 m was formed until 0.5 hr because of the deposition of sand supplied from upcoast along the marginal line between the flat shallow seabed and the steep offshore bottom, as shown in Fig. 11(b). Rapid shoreward sand transport also occurred owing to the restoration effect of the beach slope corresponding to the deviation from the

Wave conditions	Incident waves: H_I= 4.6 m (4.6 cm), T = 12.7 s (1.27 s), wave direction θ_I=20°relative to normal to initial shoreline
Berm height	h_R= 5 m (5 cm)
Depth of closure	h_c = 2.5H (H: wave height)
Equilibrium slope	tanβ_c=1/5
Angle of repose slope	tanβ_g=1/2
Coefficients of sand transport	Coefficient of longshore sand transport K_s=0.045 Coefficient of Ozasa & Brampton (1980) term K_2= 1.62K_s Coefficient of cross-shore sand transport K_n= 0.1K_s
Mesh size	$\Delta x = \Delta y$ = 20 m
Time intervals	Δt = 0.001 hr (0.01 hr)
Duration of calculation	80 hr (8×10^4 steps) (8 hr)
Boundary conditions	Shoreward and landward ends: q_x = 0, left and right boundaries: q_y = 0
Calculation of wave field	Energy balance equation (Mase, 2001) •Term of wave dissipation due to wave breaking: Dally et al. (1984) model •Wave spectrum of incident waves: directional wave spectrum density obtained by Goda (1985) •Total number of frequency components N_F = 1 and number of directional subdivisions N_θ= 8 •Directional spreading parameter S_{max} = 75 •Coefficient of wave breaking K = 0.17 and Γ= 0.3 •Imaginary depth between minimum depth h_0 and berm height h_R : h_0= 2 m (2 cm) •Wave energy = 0 where $Z \geq h_R$ •Lower limit of h in terms of wave decay due to breaking: 0.7 m (0.7 cm)
Remarks	Numbers in parentheses show experimental values. Space and time scales in the calculation are 100- and 10-fold those in the experiment, respectively.

Table 1. Calculation conditions (numbers in parentheses: experimental conditions).

equilibrium slope, because the seabed had an abrupt change in the slope along this marginal line along which sand was deposited, whereas the intervals between the contours became large in the offshore zone shallower than h_c. The sand spit further extended along the marginal line with increasing time, and the length of the spit reached 3.5 m after 1 hr, as shown in Fig. 11(c). After 2 hr, the tip of the spit was connected to the left boundary and a barrier island had formed, enclosing a lagoon behind the barrier island (Fig. 11(d)). Although a slender, straight sand spit extended along the marginal line until 2 hr after the start of wave generation, sand started to be deposited upcoast of the left boundary after 4 hr because of the blockage of longshore sand transport by the left boundary. Offshore sand transport in the deep zone also occurred, as shown in Fig. 11(e). During this process, the shoreline advanced and the width of the barrier island formed by the extension of the sand spit gradually increased from the left boundary. After 8 hr, the effect of the blockage of longshore sand transport by the left boundary had reached the upcoast and the width of the barrier island had also increased at $X = 9$ m, where the sand spit first developed, as shown in Fig. 11(f).

We compared the experimental results after 1 hr with the calculated results, as shown in Figs. 1(b) and 11(c), respectively. Both sets of results indicated that a sand spit extended from the location with a sudden change in the coastline orientation along the marginal line on the flat shallow seabed and were in good agreement. However, there was some discrepancy in the location of the tip of the sand spit. Similarly, both experimental and calculated results after 8 hr, shown in Figs. 1(c) and 11(f), respectively, are in good agreement in that the width of the barrier island was increased by the blockage of longshore sand transport by the left boundary and that a gentle slope was formed at a depth of approximately 8 cm owing to erosion along with the formation of a scarp near the right boundary. With regard to the experimental results for the extension of the sand spit reported by Uda & Yamamoto (1992), Watanabe et al. (2004) successfully predicted the shoreline changes related to the extension of the sand spit using a one-line model with a curvilinear coordinate system. However, in the present study, we were able to predict the development of a barrier island after the extension of the sand spit.

Figures 12(a)-12(f) show bird's-eye view of the extension of the barrier island in Case 1, looking upcoast from above the downcoast. Although a simple sand spit extended from the boundary between the sand supply and accretion zones on the flat shallow seabed, sand had already been transported shoreward, forming a subsurface sand bar along the marginal line between the steep offshore slope and flat shallow seabed, until 0.5 hr before the extension of the sand spit, implying the generation of rapid shoreward sand transport at the abrupt change in the slope. Furthermore, sand was deposited over the steep offshore slope between 4 and 8 hr after the start of wave generation and an extremely steep slope was formed near the downcoast boundary. In contrast, a wave-cut gentle slope was formed offshore of the erosion zone located upcoast.

5.1.2. Changes in wave field

Significant changes in the wave field occurred on the shallow flat seabed with the extension of the barrier island, as shown in Fig. 13. Initially, the wave height was reduced by up to approximately 1.5 cm because of wave breaking along the marginal line of the shallow flat seabed. However, the extension of the sand spit owing to the shoreward sand transport was very rapid, and the wave height was markedly reduced on the shallow flat seabed after wave generation for 1 hr. After 8 hr, a calm wave zone extended in the entire area behind the barrier because of the rapid development of the barrier, and the wave height had a uniform distribution.

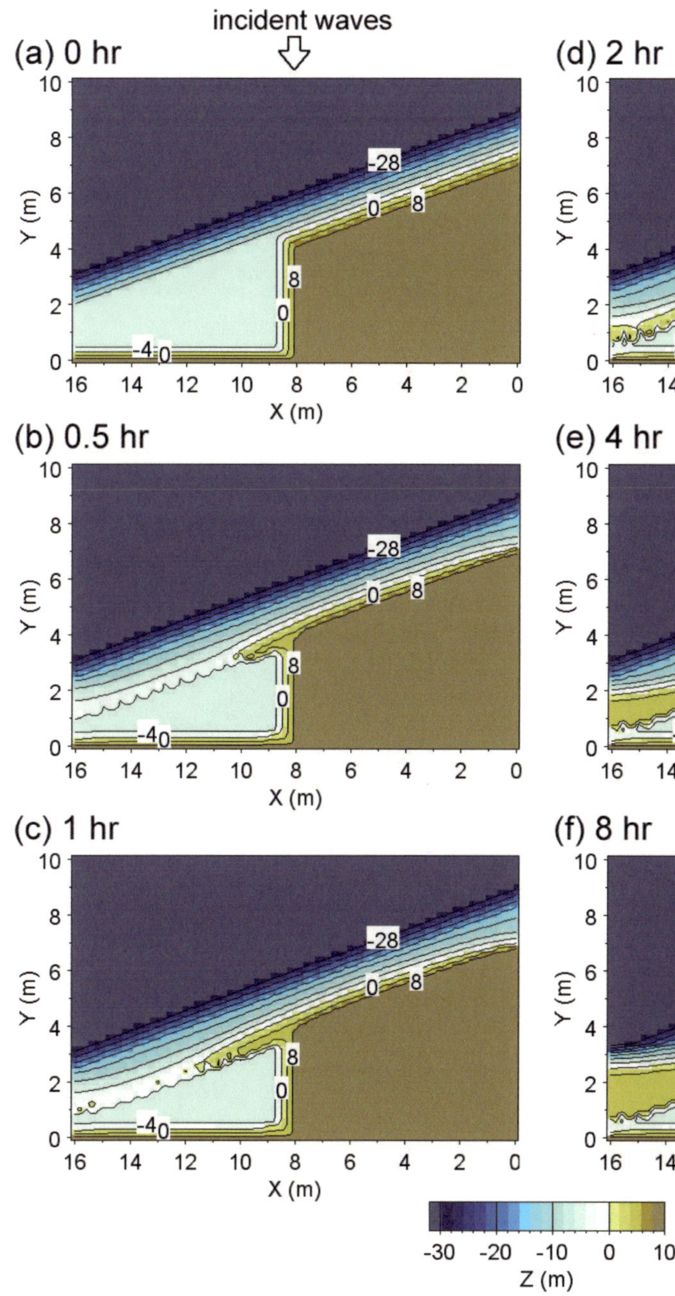

Figure 11. Results for predicted development of sand spit on a coast with abrupt change in coastline orientation (Case 1: flat shallow seabed).

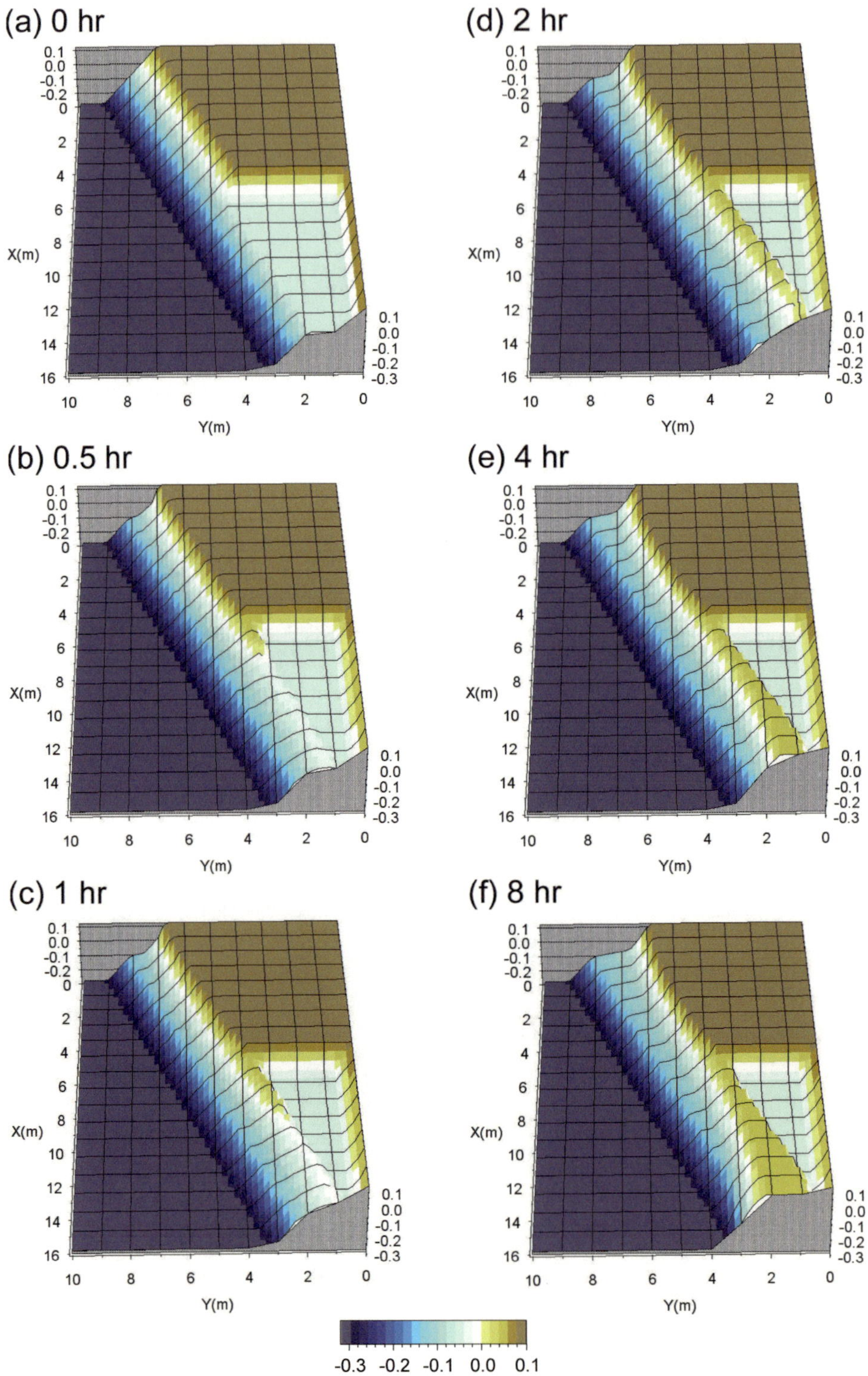

Figure 12. Bird's-eye view of topographic changes (Case 1: flat shallow seabed).

5.1.3. Sand transport flux

Figure 14 shows the sand transport flux 0, 1 and 8 hr after the start of wave generation. Although the initial sand transport flux was large in the area to the right of $X = 8$ m, where the sand source was located, the area with a large sand transport flux had moved left with the extension of the sand spit after 1 hr. In contrast, the sand transport flux decreased in magnitude near the right boundary, because the angle between the direction normal to the contour lines and the direction of incident waves was reduced. After 8 hr, the sand spit had reached the left boundary and the sand transport flux had significantly decreased, and the area with a large sand transport flux had become small.

5.1.4. Changes in longitudinal profiles

Figures 15(a)-15(d) show the experimental and predicted changes in longitudinal profiles along transect $X = 0$ m located at the right boundary, and transects $X = 9$, 12 and 14 m crossing the flat shallow seabed, respectively. Along transect $X = 0$ m, although the experimental and predicted results, which indicated that the depth of closure was -12 cm, are in agreement, as shown in Fig. 15(a), the eroded volume in the calculation was overestimated in the nearshore zone, where there was less scarp erosion. However, the sand budget in the cross section was approximately maintained and the parallel recession of the cross section while maintaining a constant slope was accurately predicted in the calculation. Along transect $X = 9$ m, the development of a berm of 5 cm height after 1 hr, as shown in Fig. 15(b), was observed in both the experiment and simulation, but the location of the berm was slightly seaward in the simulation. After 8 hr, however, the berm location had moved landward and a stable barrier island had formed. These experimental and calculated changes are in good agreement. Furthermore, no beach changes occurred on the flat shallow seabed because the elongation of the sand spit was too rapid to permit wave intrusion into the flat seabed. Along transect $X = 12$ m, the elongation of the sand spit was limited until 1 hr, as shown in Fig. 15(c), and there was little development of the berm. However, a substantial berm had developed after 8 hr. The experimental and calculated results are in good agreement regarding these points. Along transect $X = 14$ m near the left boundary, although a sand bar did not develop until 1 hr, a large amount of sand had been deposited after 8 hr, forming a barrier island with a 1.2 m width, as shown in Fig. 15(d). In this case, the seabed slope gradually steepened because of the continuous deposition of sand along the offshore steep slope, resulting in the deposition of sand up to a depth of -23 cm, which is approximately two fold larger than the depth of closure of -12 cm.

5.2. Formation of cuspate foreland on steep coast

5.2.1. Bathymetric changes

Figures 16(a)-16(f) show the results for the calculation of the development of a cuspate foreland on a steep coast $t = 0$, 0.5, 1, 2, 4, and 8 hr after the start of wave generation given the same conditions as those in the experiment. The contour lines that extended parallel to

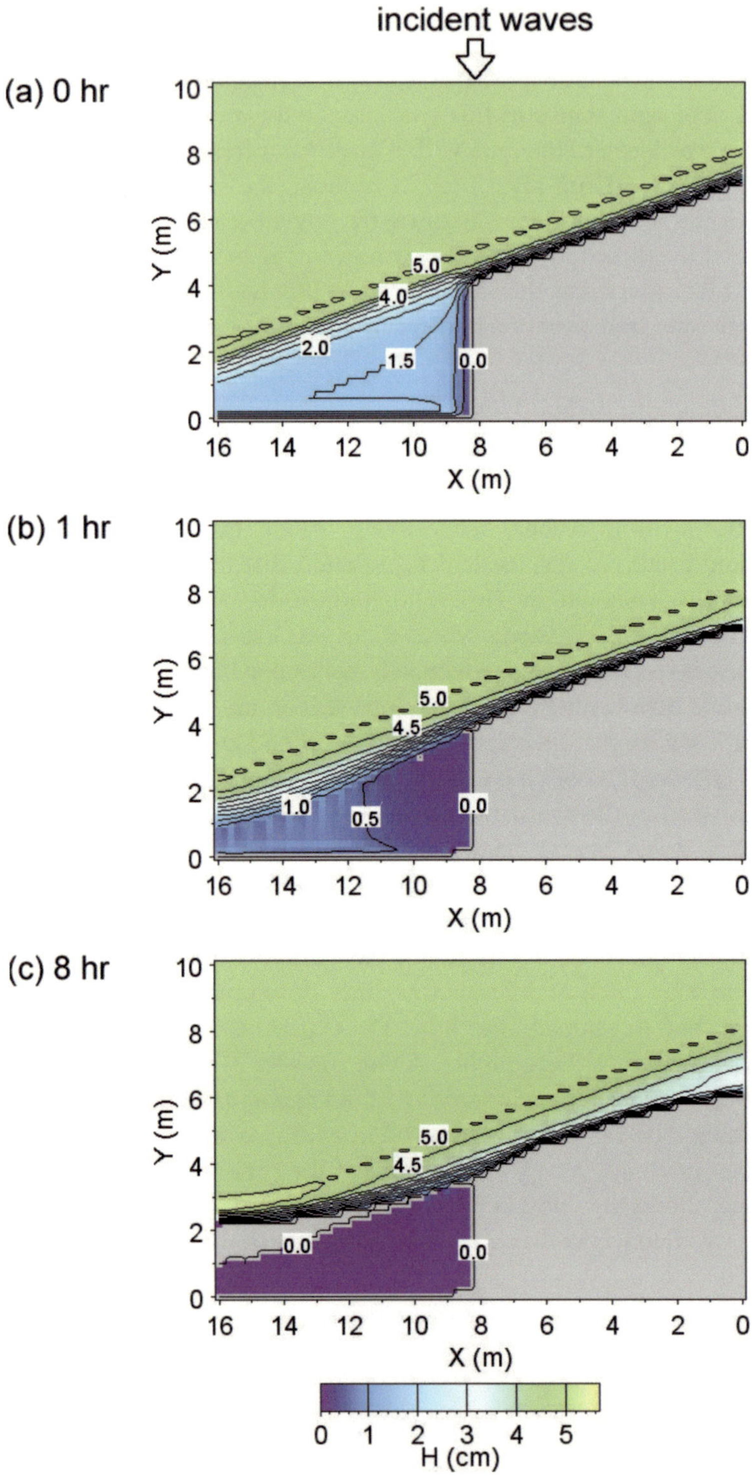

Figure 13. Changes in wave height (Case 1: flat shallow seabed).

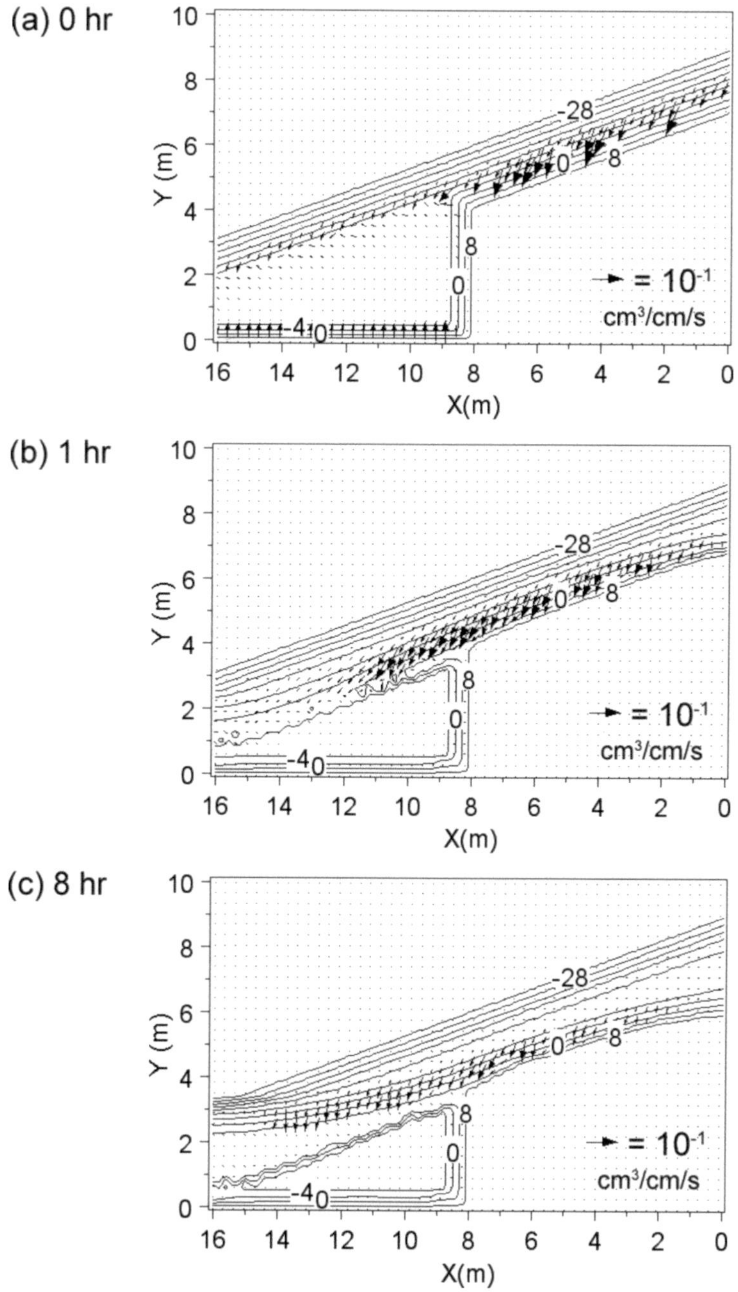

Figure 14. Sand transport flux (Case 1: flat shallow seabed).

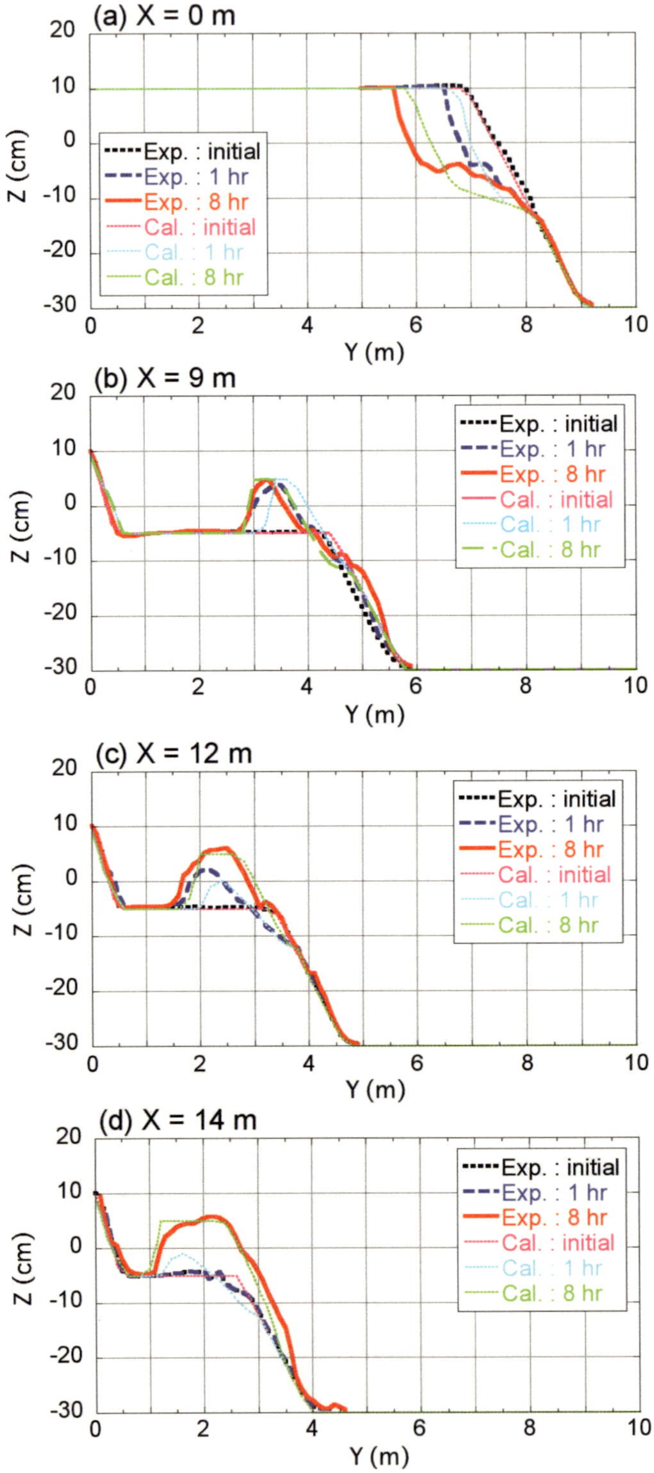

Figure 15. Changes in longitudinal profiles (Case 1: flat shallow seabed).

each other at the initial stage around the location with an abrupt change in the coastline orientation rapidly changed over time, causing sand deposition in the deep zone and the formation of a cuspate foreland after 0.5 hr. After 1 hr, the shoreline protruded further and a neck in the contour had formed downcoast of the sand deposition zone of the cuspate foreland. The size of this neck increased with time, and a sand spit that enclosed a shallow sea inside the neck had formed after 2 hr. This morphology is very similar to that of Miho Peninsula, formed by the extension of a sand spit, and Miho Bay in Shizuoka Prefecture (Uda & Yamamoto, 1994). Because of the continuous sand supply from upcoast, the sand spit elongated and the tip became connected to the downcoast shoreline. As a result, the shallow sea located inside the neck had formed a pond after 4 hr. After 8 hr, a steep slope had formed along the shoreline of the cuspate foreland owing to the continuous sand deposition in the deeper zone, whereas a wave base with a gentle slope had formed on the coast from which sand was supplied.

Figures 17(a)-17(f) show bird's-eye view of the development of a cuspate foreland on a steep coast. Although sand transported from upcoast was deposited on the steep seabed, the deposition of sand started near the location with an abrupt change in the coastline orientation, forming a neck in the contours, as shown in Figs. 17(a) and 17(b). This neck moved landward with time, and finally a sandy beach with a flat surface and a steep slope offshore of the shoreline had formed after 8 hr.

5.2.2. *Changes in wave field*

Figures 18(a)-18(c) show the distributions of the calculated wave height after wave generation for 0, 1 and 8 hr. At the initial stage, the longshore change in the wave height is large near the location with an abrupt change in the coastline orientation. Although a semicircular cuspate foreland developed until 1 hr, a marked decay in the wave height occurred over the short distance along the protruding shoreline, because the wave height was extremely low behind the protruded shoreline. The change in longshore sand transport due to this decay in wave height was successfully taken into account by the additional term given by Ozasa & Brampton (1980). The spatial change in longshore sand transport is large in this area because of the abrupt decrease in wave height, meaning that sand was rapidly deposited. However, after 8 hr, the area where the wave height abruptly decreased had disappeared and the wave height was smoothly distributed alongshore.

5.2.3. *Sand transport flux*

Figure 19 shows the sand transport flux after wave generation for 0, 1 and 8 hr. Although the sand transport flux was initially large to the right of $X = 8$ m, which is the sand supply area, as in Case 1, after 1 hr the area with a large sand transport flux had moved leftward with the elongation of the sand spit. Moreover, the sand transport flux was reduced because the angle between the direction normal to the contour lines and the direction of incident waves decreased near the right boundary. After 8 hr, the sand spit had reached the left boundary, and the absolute value of sand transport flux decreased because the angle between the direction normal to the contour lines and the wave incidence direction had been reduced near both boundaries.

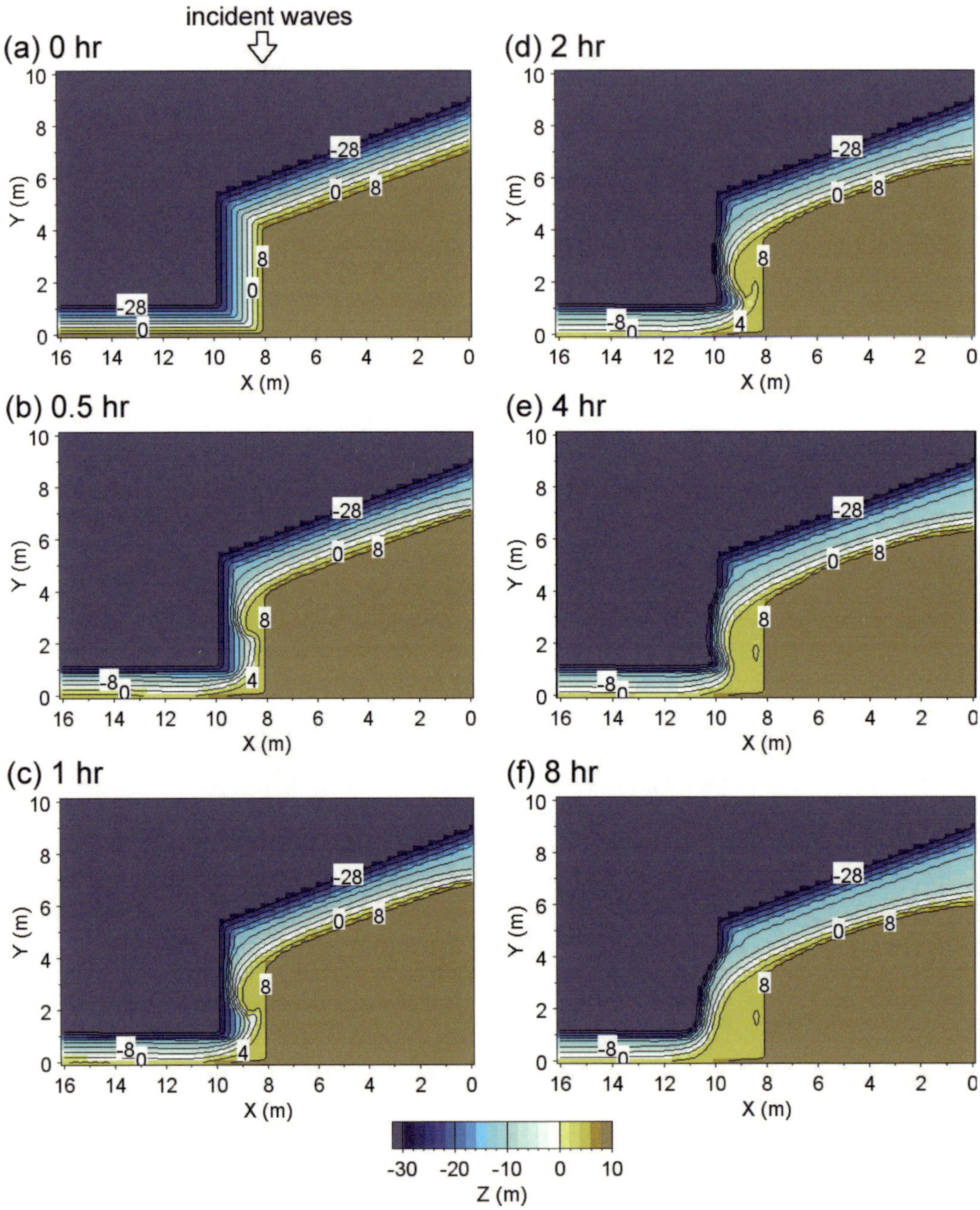

Figure 16. Predicted results for development of cuspate foreland on a coast with abrupt change in coastline orientation (Case 2: steep slope and deep seabed).

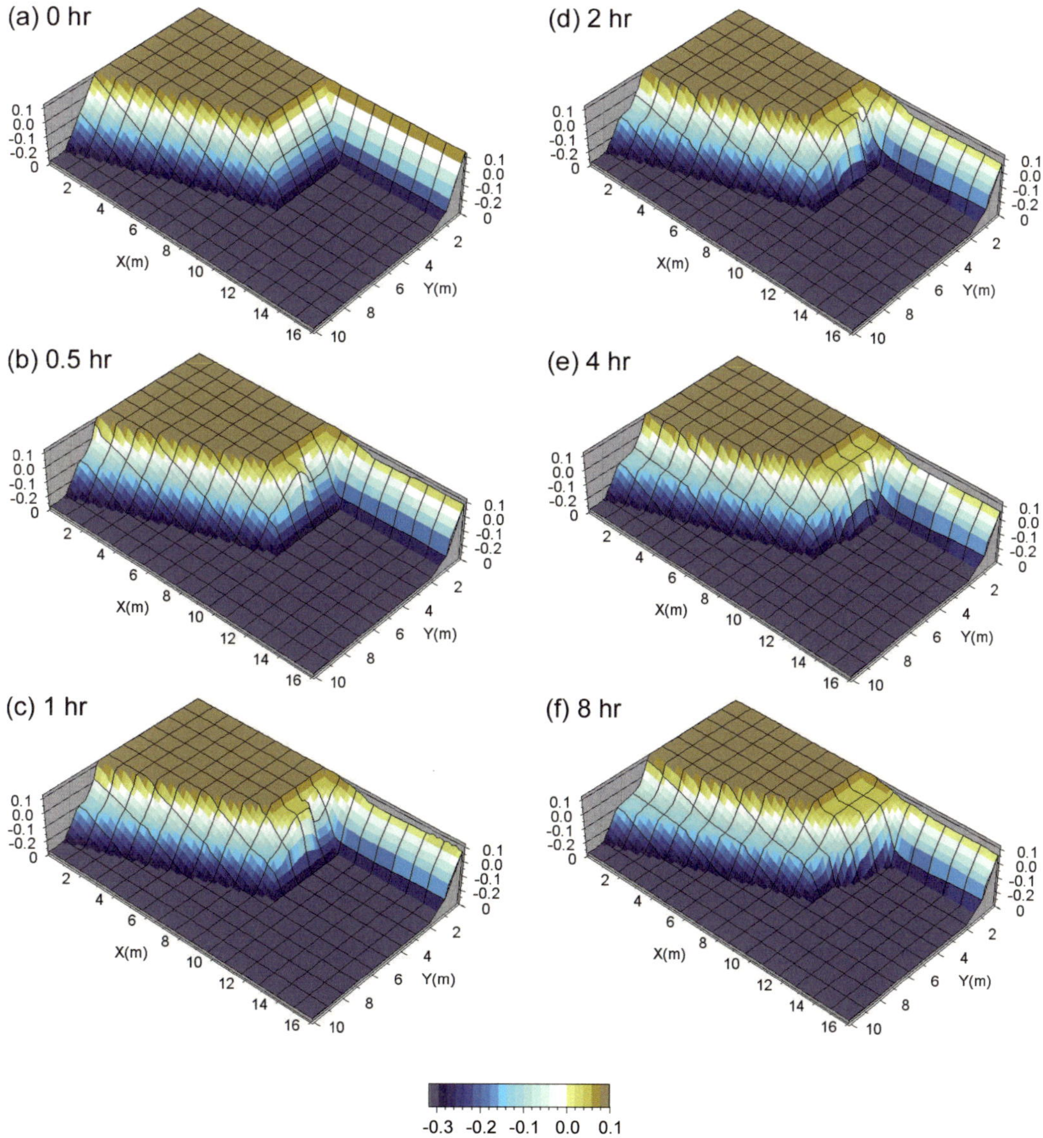

Figure 17. Bird's-eye view of topographic changes (Case 2: steep slope and deep seabed).

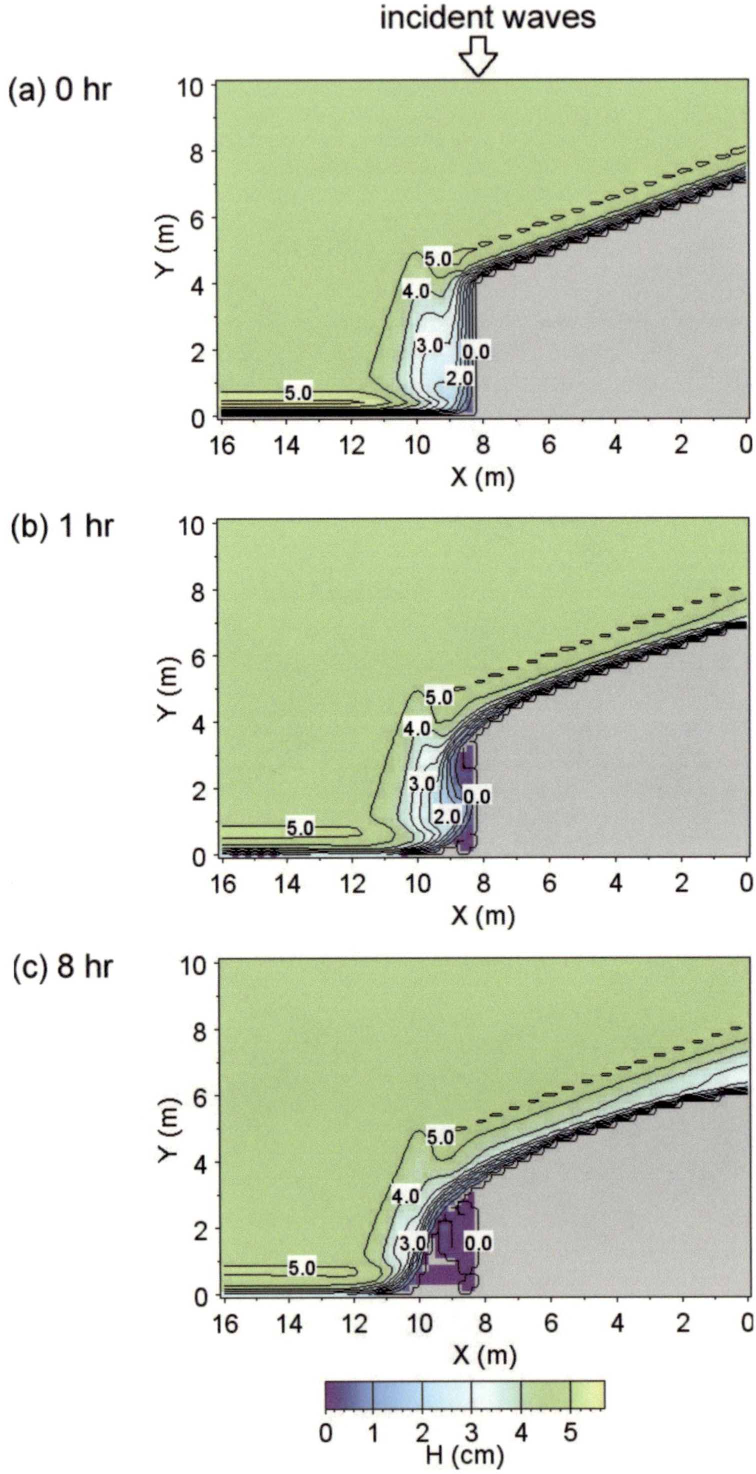

Figure 18. Changes in wave height (Case 2: steep slope and deep seabed).

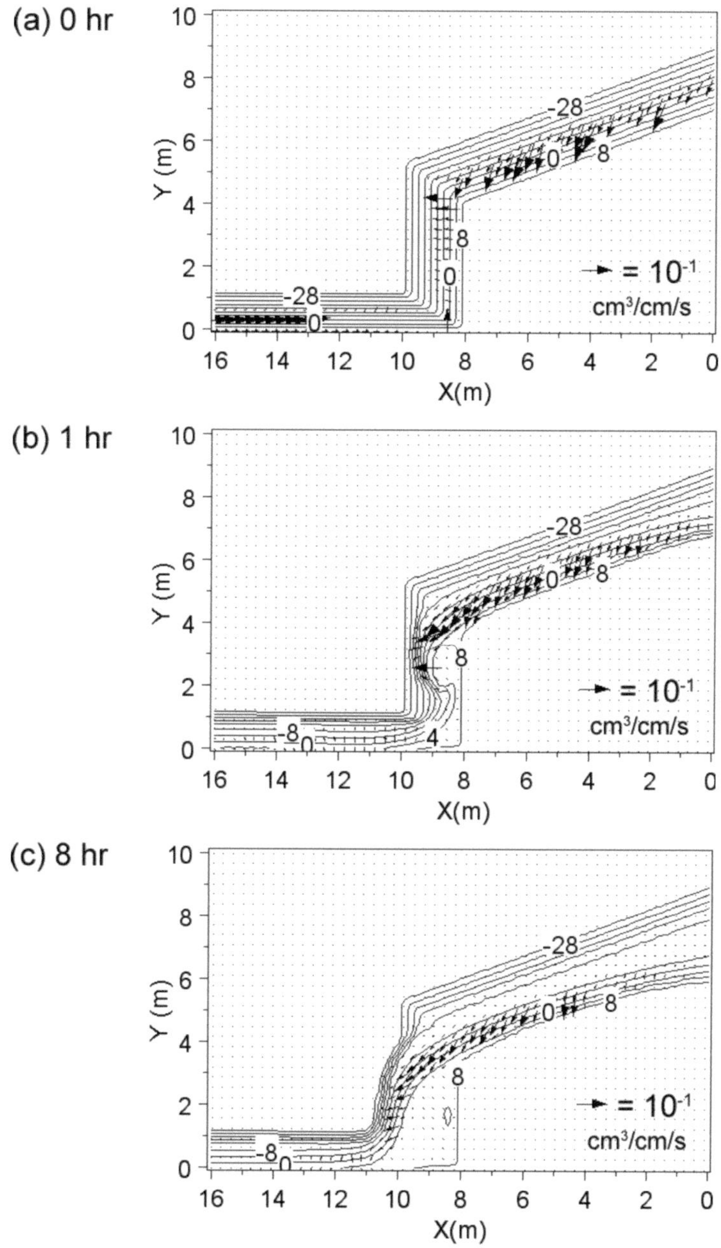

Figure 19. Sand transport flux (Case 2: steep slope and deep seabed).

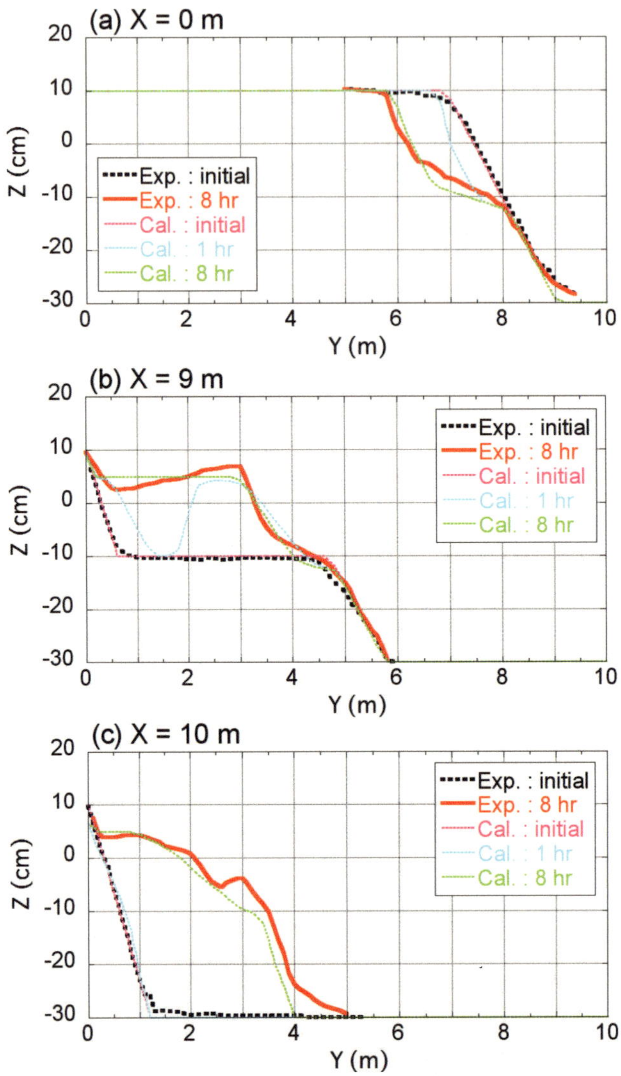

Figure 20. Changes in longitudinal profiles (Case 2: steep slope and deep seabed).

5.2.4. *Changes in longitudinal profiles*

Figures 20(a)-20(c) show the experimental and predicted changes in longitudinal profiles along transect X = 0 m located at the right boundary, transect X = 9 m near the location where the coastline orientation abruptly changes, and transect X = 10 m, respectively. Along transect X = 0 m, the parallel recession of the cross section is accurately reproduced in the calculation, as shown in Fig. 20(a). Along transect X = 9 m, a slope that slightly inclined landward had formed in the experiment after 8 hr, whereas a flat surface was predicted in the calculation. With the exception of these points, the experimental and predicted results are in good agreement, as shown in Fig. 20(b). The experimental and calculated results are also in good agreement along transect X = 10 m, as shown in Fig. 20(c).

6. Simulation of formation of slender sand bar on Kutsuo coast

To model the accumulation of sand on the tidal flat due to wave action and the formation of a slender sand bar, a point source in a single mesh (5 m×5 m) was assumed. The intensity of the point source was determined by trial and error, and it was set to 3.75×10^4 m^3/yr at the point (x, y) = (200 m, 0 m). In addition, an upper limit of 0.5 m was assumed as the elevation of the sandy island. When the elevation of the island reached this height during the calculation, the wave energy was set to 0.

Given the simplified initial topography and the conditions of the annual energy-mean waves of the Kutsuo coast (significant wave height H_i of 0.4 m and wave period T of 4 s), and assuming wave incidence from the direction normal to the coastline, the beach changes were predicted. The depth of closure was given by h_c = 2.5H (H: wave height at a local point). The water depth of the initial bottom of the tidal flat was assumed to be 2 m. This initial flat bottom was assumed to be a solid bed, and a sandy beach with a slope of 1/10 was set at the landward end of the flat bottom. The berm height was assumed to be 0.5 m, and angles of the equilibrium slope and repose slope were set as 1/10 and 1/2, respectively. The calculation domain was divided by $\Delta x = \Delta y$ = 5 m intervals in the cross-shore and longshore directions, respectively, and a calculation for up to 5000 hr (5×10^4 steps) was carried out using time intervals of Δt = 0.1 hr. Table 2 shows the calculation conditions.

6.1. Bathymetric changes

Figure 21 shows the calculation results obtained after every 10^4 steps. Initially, only a flat bottom extended offshore of the sandy beach with a straight shoreline. The solid circle in Fig. 21(a) shows the location of the sand source, and a sandy beach with a slope of 1/10 extended along the marginal line between the tidal flat and the land, as observed on the Kutsuo coast. Owing to the wave action under these conditions, a slender submerged sand bar started to form after 10^4 steps, as shown in Fig. 21(b), as a result of the deposition of sand supplied from the sand source. The landward end of the slender sand bar was sharp and similar to a comet tail formed on the lee of an island. On the other side of the slender sand bar, longshore sand transport toward the lee of the slender sand bar was induced from the nearby coast, resulting in the formation of a cuspate foreland because of the wave-sheltering effect of the sand bar. After 2×10^4 steps, the submerged sand bar had become a sandy island because of its continuous development (Fig. 21(c)). After 2×10^4 steps, the cuspate foreland behind the sandy island was more developed than that after 10^4 steps. The beach width in the zone between x = 50 and 100 m was very small and a neck was formed. After 3×10^4 steps, the widths of the sandy island and the neck behind the island had increased, and sand that had originally been supplied from the offshore point source had reached the beach, resulting in the connection of the sandy island to the beach (Fig. 21(d)). Finally, the island developed a spoonlike shape with the shoreline of a tombolo connected to the slender island.

The development of the sandy island continued up to 5×10^4 steps, and the widths of the sandy island and the neck between the island and the tombolo continued to increase (Figs. 21(e) and 21(f)). The numerical results for the development of a slender sand bar and the resultant sandy island successfully explain the results observed on the Kutsuo coast, as shown in Fig. 3, and the fact that the slender sand bar has a neck near the landward end, as shown in Figs. 8-10.

Figures 22(a)-22(f) show bird's-eye view of the development of a slender sand bar developed on a flat seabed. Sand supplied from a sand source at (x, y) = (200 m, 0 m) was deposited to form an island with the gradual shoreward movement of sand. After 2×10^4 steps, a slender island connected to the land extended with the formation of a tombolo because of the wave-sheltering effect of the island itself. Because of the continuous supply of sand, the width of the island increased and the scale of the tombolo increased with increasing number of steps. The final configuration of the slender bar was very similar to that observed on the Kutsuo coast, as shown in Fig. 9.

Wave conditions	Incident waves: $H_I = 0.4$ m, $T = 3$ s, wave direction $\theta_I = 0°$, normal to initial shoreline
Tide condition	H.W.L. = +2.0 m
Berm height	$h_R = 0.5$ m
Depth of closure	$h_c = 2.5H$ (H: wave height)
Equilibrium slope	$\tan\beta_c = 1/10$
Angle of repose slope	$\tan\beta_g = 1/2$
Coefficients of sand transport	Coefficient of longshore sand transport $K_s = 0.05$ Coefficient of Ozasa & Brampton (1980) term $K_2 = 1.62\ K_s$ Coefficient of cross-shore sand transport $K_n = 0.2\ K_s$
Mesh size	$\Delta x = \Delta y = 5$ m
Time intervals	$\Delta t = 0.1$ hr
Duration of calculation	5000 hr (5×10^4 steps)
Boundary conditions	Shoreward and landward ends: $q_x = 0$, left and right boundaries: $q_y = 0$
Calculation of wave field	Energy balance equation (Mase, 2001) •Term of wave dissipation due to wave breaking: Dally et al. (1984) model •Wave spectrum of incident waves: directional wave spectrum density obtained by Goda (1985) •Total number of frequency components $N_F = 1$ and number of directional subdivisions $N_\theta = 8$ •Directional spreading parameter $S_{max} = 10$ •Coefficient of wave breaking $K = 0.17$ and $\Gamma = 0.3$ •Imaginary depth between minimum depth h_0 and berm height h_R: $h_0 = 0.5$ m •Wave energy = 0 where $Z \geq h_R$ •Lower limit of h in term of wave decay due to breaking: 0.2 m
Remark	Point source in single mesh (3.75×10^4 m^3/yr)

Table 2. Calculation conditions.

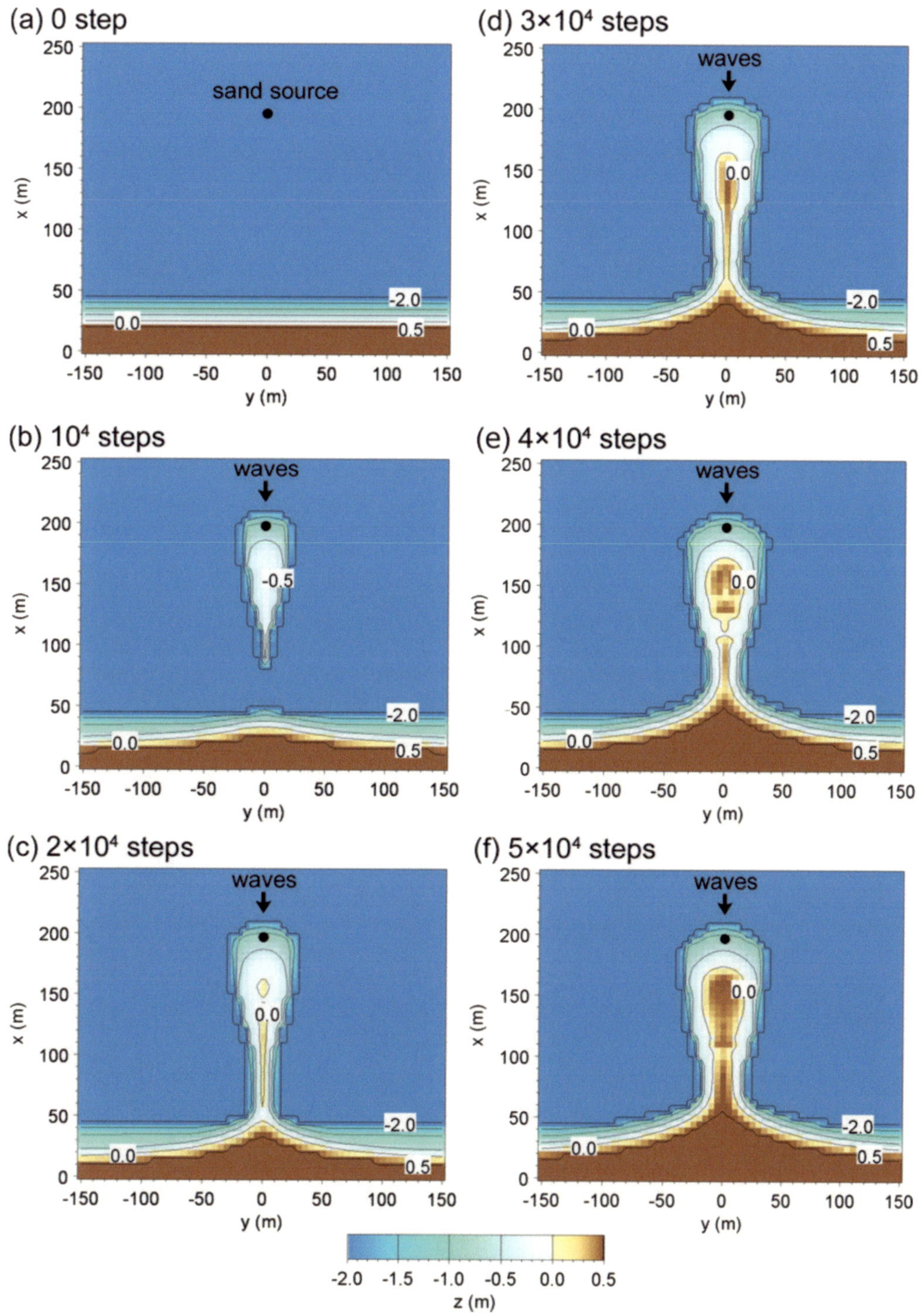

Figure 21. Calculation results observed after every 10^4 steps.

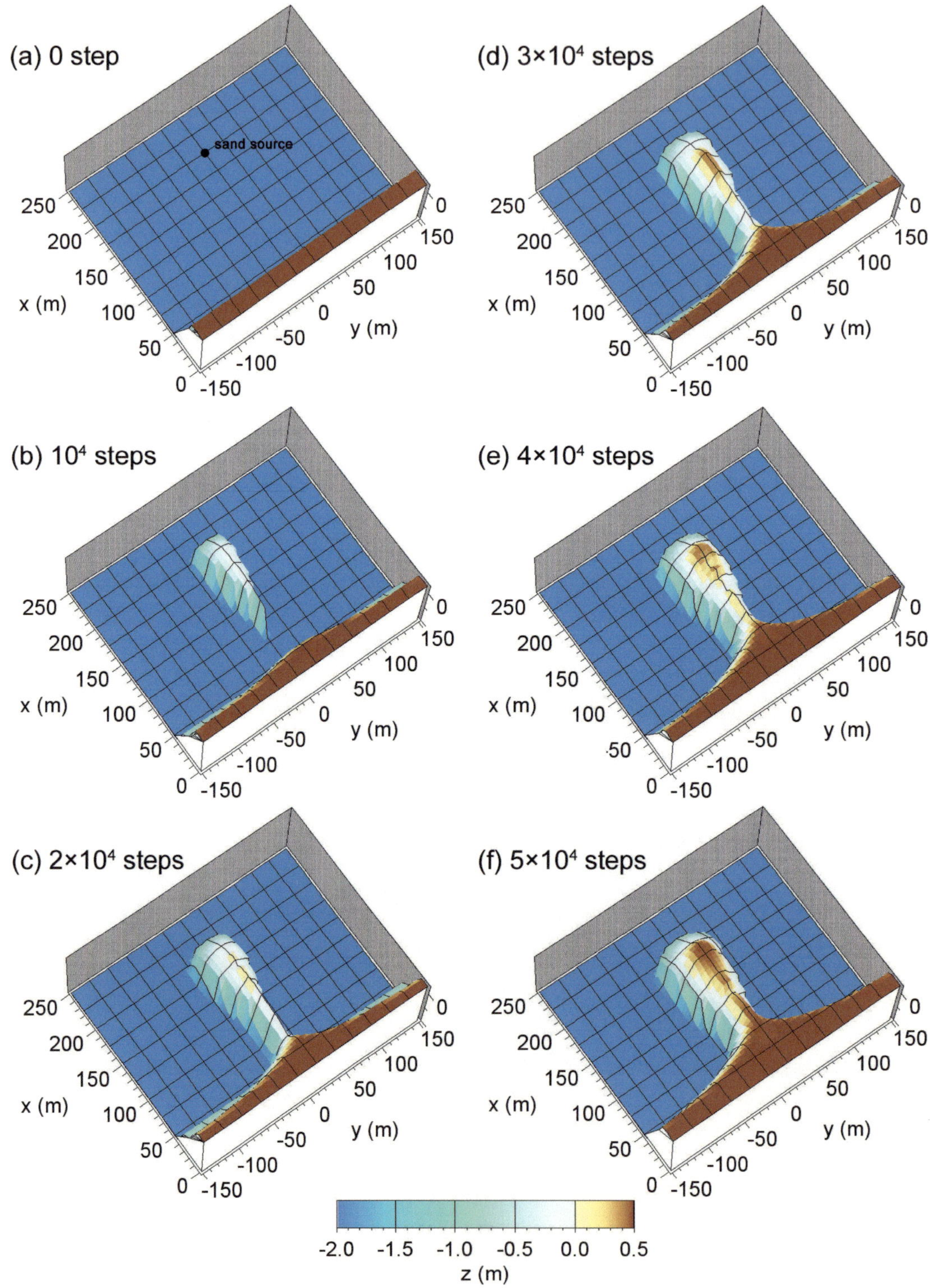

Figure 22. Bird's-eye view of topographic changes.

6.2. Changes in longitudinal and transverse profiles

Figure 23 shows the changes in the longitudinal profile along transect y = 0 m, which passes through the center of the slender sandy island, as shown in Fig. 21(f). Because the development of the sandy island along this transect was very rapid, the results obtained after not only 1 $\times 10^4$ steps but also 5×10^3 and 1.5×10^4 steps are also shown. Although the sand bar gradually extended landward, the wave height along the side slopes of the sand bar (or the resultant sandy island) was reduced owing to the wave-sheltering effect induced by the sand bar itself, resulting in a decrease in the depth of closure along the side slope. For example, a steep slope with an angle of repose of 1/2 had formed in the zone deeper than Z = -0.3 m after 1×10^4 steps. The elevation of the beach connecting the land and the sandy island increased to reach the berm height of h_R = 0.5 m.

Figure 24 shows the changes in the cross section along transect x = 100 m, which passes through the neck of the slender sandy island, and transect x = 50 m near the boundary between the sandy beach and the tidal flat under the initial conditions, as shown in Fig. 21(f). After 10^4 steps, an island with a sharp top and a side slope with a steep angle of repose on both sides of the island had formed along transect x = 100 m. The increase in the width of the sandy beach over time was slow. In contrast, because of the increase in the wave-sheltering effect owing to the development of the sandy island, the cuspate foreland was more developed along transect x = 50 m than along transect x = 100 m, and its width increased over time.

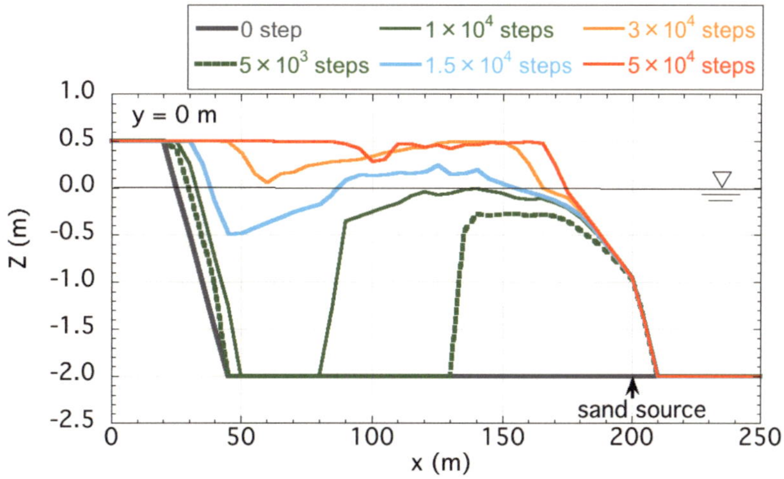

Figure 23. Changes in longitudinal profile along transect y = 0 m passing through center of slender sandy island.

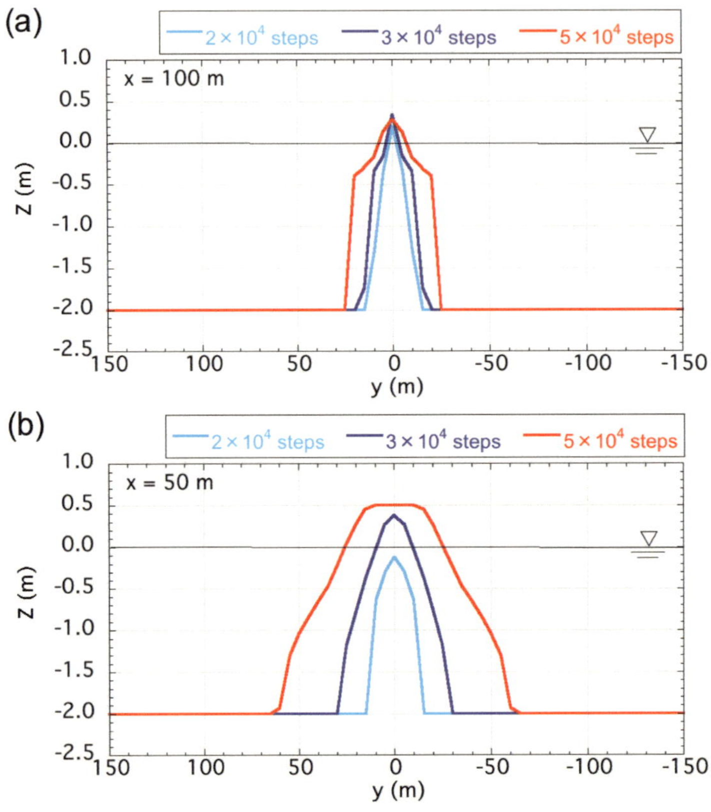

Figure 24. Changes in cross section along transect $x = 100$ m passing through neck of slender sandy island and transect $x = 50$ m near boundary between sandy beach and tidal flat.

6.3. Wave height and direction

The wave fields corresponding to the beach changes are shown in Fig. 25. The wave height on the tidal flat was initially uniform (0 step) and uniform wave decay due to wave breaking occurred on the sandy beach extending between the land and the tidal flat. After 1×10^4 steps, a submerged sand bar had been formed by the accumulation of sand supplied from a point source. This sand bar induced a change in the wave field; the wave height was reduced along the side slope of the slender sand bar, and oblique wave incidence occurred on both sides of the sand bar owing to wave diffraction by the sand bar itself. This oblique

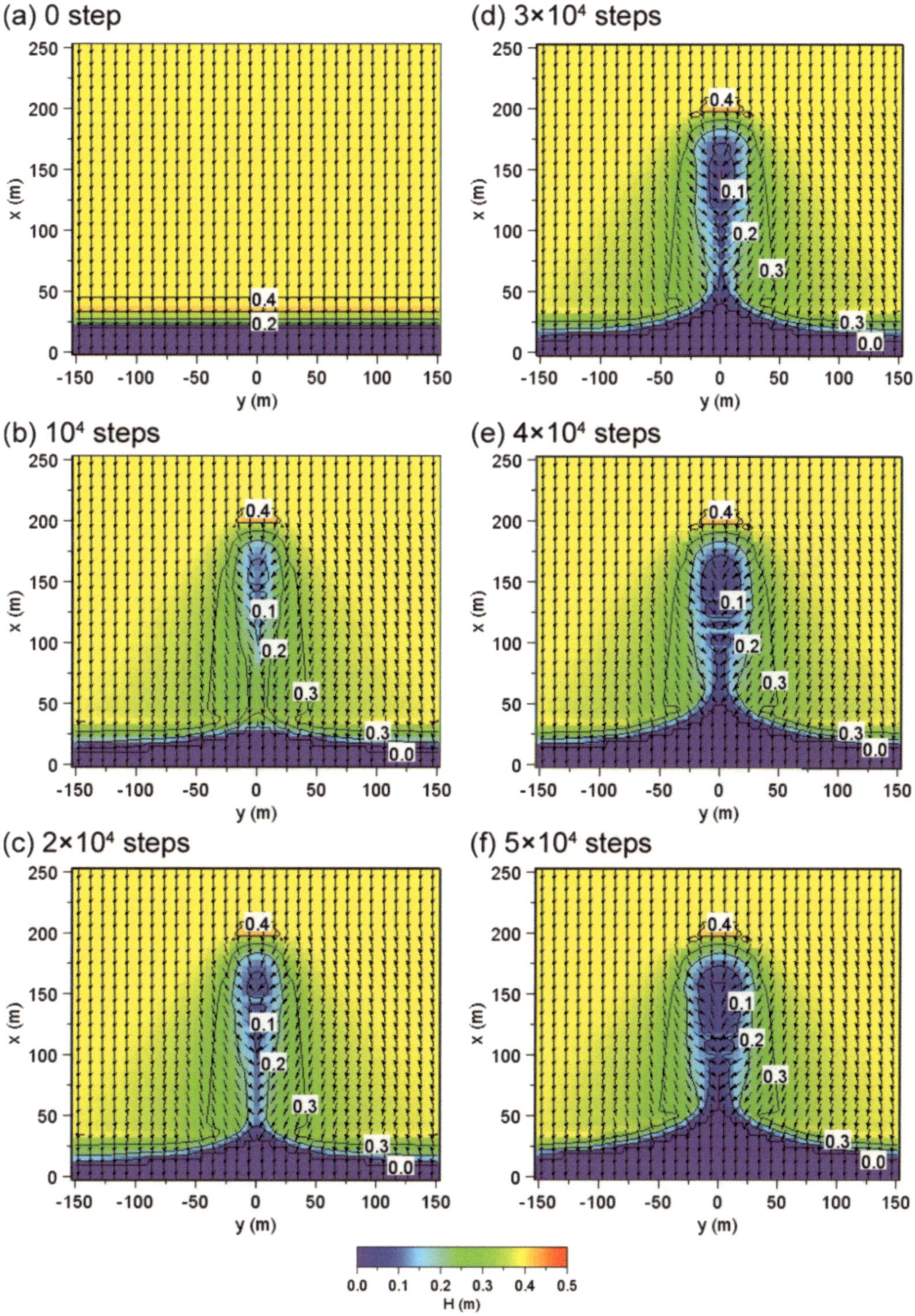

Figure 25. Wave fields corresponding to beach changes.

wave incidence caused shoreward sand transport flux along the contours of the sand bar. On the other hand, on the lee of the submerged sand bar, the wave height was reduced, similarly to in the case of a detached breakwater, inducing longshore sand transport toward the lee of the sand bar from outside the wave-shelter zone. After 2×10^4 steps, as a result of the landward extension of the slender sand bar and the decrease in water depth, wave breaking occurred there, causing a marked reduction in wave height. At the same time, the oblique wave incidence continued in this area and landward sand transport from the island to the land continuously occurred. After 4×10^4 and 5×10^4 steps, the same beach changes as those until 2×10^4 steps continued.

7. Conclusions

The BG model was applied to predict the development of a sand spit on a flat shallow seabed and the formation of a cuspate foreland on coasts with an abrupt change in the shoreline orientation. The results of the model were validated by comparison with the experimental results obtained by Uda & Yamamoto (1992). The predicted and measured results were in good agreement. As another type of beach change due to waves on a coast with a shallow flat seabed, the shoreward transport of sand originally supplied from the offshore zone of a tidal flat, forming a slender sand bar, and the landward deposition of such sand were observed on the Kutsuo coast, which has a very wide tidal flat and faces the Suo-nada Sea, part of the Seto Inland Sea. We investigated these phenomena by field observations and then performed a numerical simulation using the BG model. The observed results were successfully explained by the results of the numerical simulation. Although the BG model has been used to predict the development of river mouth bars, a single sand spit and a bay barrier (Serizawa et al., 2009b, 2009a; Uda & Serizawa, 2011), another application was demonstrated in the present study.

Author details

Takaaki Uda
Public Works Research Center, Taito, Tokyo

Masumi Serizawa and Shiho Miyahara
Coastal Engineering Laboratory Co., Ltd., Shinjuku, Tokyo

8. References

Ashton, A.; Murray, A. B. & Arnault, O. (2001). Formation of coastline features by large-scale instabilities induced by high angle waves, *Nature*, Vol. 14, No. 6861, (November 2001), pp. 296-300, ISSN 0028-0836

Bagnold, R. A. (1963). Mechanics of Marine Sedimentation, In: *The Sea*, Hill, M. N. (editor), Vol. 3, pp. 507-528, Wiley, ISBN 978-0674017306, New York

Bailard, J. A. & Inman, D. L. (1981). An energetics bedload model for a plane sloping beach: Local transport, *J. Geophys. Res.*, Vol. 86, C3, pp. 2035-2043

Dally, W. R.; Dean, R. G. & Dalrymple, R. A. (1984). A model for breaker decay on beaches, *Proc. 19th ICCE*, pp. 82-97,Houston, Texas, USA, September 1984

Goda, Y. (1985). *Random Seas and Design of Maritime Structures*, University of Tokyo Press, ISBN 978-9810232566, Tokyo

Inman, D. L. & Bagnold, R. A. (1963). Littoral Processes, In: *The Sea*, M. N. Hill (editor), Vol. 3, pp. 529-533, Wiley, ISBN 978-0674017306, New York

Mase, H. (2001). Multidirectional random wave transformation model based on energy balance equation, *Coastal Eng. J.*, JSCE, Vol. 43, No. 4, (December 2001),pp. 317-337.

Ozasa, H. & Brampton, A. H. (1980). Model for predicting the shoreline evolution of beaches backed by seawalls, *Coastal Eng.*, Vol. 4, pp. 47-64

Serizawa, M.; Uda, T.; San-nami, T. & Furuike, K. (2006). Three-dimensional model for predicting beach changes based on Bagnold's concept, *Proc. 30th ICCE*, pp. 3155-3167, ISBN 978-981-270-636-2, San Diego, California, USA, September 2006

Serizawa, M.; Uda, T.; San-nami, T.; Furuike, K. & Ishikawa, T. (2009a). Prediction of topographic changes of sand spit using BG model, *J. Coastal Res.*, SI 56, pp. 1060-1064

Serizawa, M.; Uda, T.; San-nami, T.; Furuike, K. & Ishikawa, T. (2009b). Model for predicting recovery of a river mouth bar after flood using BG model, *Asian and Pacific Coasts 2009, Proc. 5th International Conf.*, Vol. 3, pp. 96-102, Singapore, October 2009

Serizawa, M. & Uda, T. (2011). Prediction of formation of sand spit on coast with sudden change in coastline using improved BG model, *Coastal Sediments '11*, pp. 1907-1919, Miami, Florida, USA, May 2011

Serizawa, M.; Uda, T. & Miyahara, S. (2011). Model for predicting formation of slender sand bar due to shoreward sand transport on shallow tidal flat, *Asian and Pacific Coasts 2011, Proc. 6th International Conf.*, pp. 1477-1484, ISBN 978-981-4366-48-9, Hong Kong, December 2011

Uda, T. & Kawano, S. (1996). Development of a predictive model of contour line change due to waves, *Proc. JSCE*, No. 539/ II -35, pp. 121-139. (in Japanese)

Shimizu, T.; Kumagai, T. & Watanabe, A. (1996). Improved 3-D beach evolution model coupled with the shoreline model (3D-SHORE), *Proc. 25th ICCE*, pp. 2843-2856, Orlando, Florida, USA, September 1996

Uda, T. & Yamamoto, K. (1992). On relationship between seabed topography and formation of spit, *Trans. Jpn. Geomor. Union*, Vol. 13, pp. 141-157 (in Japanese)

Uda, T. & Yamamoto, K. (1994). Beach erosion around a sand spit-an example of Mihono-Matsubara sand spit-, *Proc. 24th ICCE*, pp. 2726-2740, Kobe, Japan, October 1994

Uda, T. & Serizawa, M. (2010). Model for predicting topographic changes on coast composed of sand of mixed grain size and its applications (Chap. 16), In: *Numerical simulations-examples and applications in computational fluid dynamics*,Angermann, L. (Ed.), pp. 327-358, INTECH,http://www.intechopen.com/articles/show/title/model-for-predicting-opographic-changes-on-coast-composed-of-sand-of-mixed-grain-size-and-its-appli

Uda, T. & Serizawa, M. (2011). Model for predicting formation of bay barrier in flat shallow sea, *Coastal Sediments '11*, pp. 1176-1189, Miami, Florida, USA, May 2011

Watanabe, S.; Serizawa, M. & Uda, T. (2004). Predictive model of formation of a sand spit, *Proc. 29th ICCE*, pp. 2061-2073, ISBN 981-256-298-2, Lisbon, Portugal, September 2004

Chapter 17

Numerical Simulations of Water Waves' Modulational Instability Under the Action of Wind and Dissipation

Julien Touboul and Christian Kharif

Additional information is available at the end of the chapter

http://dx.doi.org/10.5772/48595

1. Introduction

The seek of uniform, propagative wave train solutions of the fully nonlinear potential equations has been a major topic for centuries. [5] was the first to propose an expression of such waves, the so called Stokes' waves. However, pioneer works of [6] emphasized that such waves might be unstable, providing a geometric condition for this stability problem. Later on, [1] showed analytically that Stokes' waves of moderate amplitude are unstable to long wave perturbations of small amplitude travelling in the same direction. This instability is named the Benjamin-Feir instability (or modulational instability). This result was derived independently by [7] in an averaged Lagrangian approach, and by [8] who used an Hamiltonian formulation of the water wave problem. Using this approach, the latter author derived the nonlinear Schrödinger equation (NLS), and confirmed the previous stability results.

Within the last fifty years, the study of this instability became central for fundamental and applied research. The modulation instability is one of the most important mechanisms for the formation of rogue waves [9]. A complete review on the various phenomena yielding to rogue waves can be found in the book of [10]. In the absence of forcing and damping, Stokes' waves of specific initial steepness are submitted to this instability, when they encounter perturbations of specific wave numbers [11, 12]. In this case, they encounter a nonlinear quasi-recursive evolution, the so called Fermi-Pasta-Ulam recurrence phenomenon ([13]). This phenomenon corresponds to a series of modulation - demodulation cycles, during which initially uniform wave trains become modulated, leading possibly to the formation of a huge wave. Modulation is due to an energy transfer from the wave carrier to the unstable sidebands. In the wave number space, these unstable sidebands are located in a finite narrow band centered around the carrier wave number. During the demodulation, the energy returns to the fundamental component of the original wave train. Using the Zakharov equation, [14] questions the relevance of the Benjamin-Feir index to indicate the intensity of modulational instability. Indeed, this index is often used to quantify the intensity of interactions between a carrier wave and the finite amplitude sidebands. However, [14] emphasized that nonlinear interactions occur also for sidebands located beyond the Benjamin-Feir instability domain.

A damped nonlinear Schrödinger equation (dNLS) was derived by [15] who revisited the Benjamin-Feir instability in the presence of dissipation. They studied numerically the evolution of narrow bandwidth waves of moderate amplitude. More recently [2] investigated theoretically the modulational instability within the framework of the dNLS equation and demonstrated that any amount of dissipation stabilizes the modulational instability in the sense of Lyapunov. Namely, they showed that the zone of unstable region, in the wavenumber space, shrinks as time increases. As a result, any initially unstable mode of perturbation will finally become stable. [2] have confirmed their theoretical predictions by laboratory experiments for waves of small to moderate amplitude. Later, [3] developed fully nonlinear numerical simulations which agreed with the theory and experiments of [2].

From the latter study we could conclude that dissipation may prevent the development of the Benjamin-Feir instability. This effect questions the occurrence of modulational instability of water wave trains in the field. [16] speculated about the effect of dissipation on the early development of rogue waves and raised the question whether or not the Benjamin-Feir instability was able to spawn a rogue wave.

Nevertheless, these authors did not take the effect of wind into account. When considering the occurrence of modulational instability in the field, the role of wind upon this instability in the presence of dissipation needs to be addressed. Based on this assumption, [4] derived a forced and damped nonlinear Schrödinger equation (fdNLS), and extended the analysis of [2] when wind input is introduced. The influence of wind was introduced through a pressure term acting at the interface, in phase with the wave slope, accordingly to Miles' theory [17]. This quasi-laminar theory of wind wave amplification is based on the Miles' shear flow instability. This mechanism of wave amplification is a resonant interaction between water waves and a plane shear flow in air which occurs at the critical height where the wind velocity matches the phase velocity of the surface waves. Stokes waves propagating in the presence of such a forcing, when not submitted to modulational instability, encounter an exponential growth. They demonstrated, within the framework of fdNLS equation, that Stokes' waves were unstable to modulational instability as soon as the friction velocity is larger than a threshold value. Conversely, for a given friction velocity it was found that only carrier waves presenting frequencies (or wavenumbers) lower than a threshold value are subject to Benjamin-Feir instability. Otherwise, due to dissipation, modulational instability restabilizes in the sense of Lyapunov.

As it was mentioned, this physical result is based on the solution of an approached model, the fdNLS equation. Thus, a proper verification is required. However, the phenomenon at hand is based on the long-time behavior of the modulated wave train when propagating in the presence of wind and dissipation. This remark explains the difficulty to provide an experimental verification of the theory. This physical problem is then especially well adapted for a numerical verification. This verification was performed in a first time by [18], who investigated the development of the modulational instability under wind action and viscous dissipation within the framework of fully nonlinear potential equations. This work is an extension of that of [3] when wind input is considered. Later on, [19] emphasized that the equations empirically introduced by [3] were not completely representative of the dispersion relation in the presence of damping, and corrected the equations to overcome this problem, in accordance with the demonstration of [20] and [21].

This work aims to emphasize how numerical simulations can provide useful information to validate long term results based on weakly nonlinear theory. Furthermore, the numerical approach presented here constitutes an extension of the results of [4] to higher orders of nonlinearity and larger band spectra, too. The long time evolution of modulated wave trains can be investigated in a way not allowed by fdNLS equation. The numerical simulations enable to produce results concerning the long time behavior of the modulated wave train. Especially, the phenomenon of permanent frequency downshift will be investigated.

In section 2, the governing equations of the problem are presented. Section 3 presents the weakly nonlinear model obtained by [4], and summarizes their results. The numerical model used to investigate the long time behavior of the modulated wave train is developed in section 4. The initial conditions used to support the numerical strategy for validating the theory introduced by [4] is presented in section 5. Finally, the results obtained are described in section 6.

2. Governing equations of the problem

The approach used in this study is based on the potential flow theory. The fluid is assumed to be incompressible, inviscid, and animated by an irrotational motion. Thus, the fluid velocity derives from a potential ϕ. However, non-potential effects due to wind and viscosity can be taken into account through a modification of the boundary conditions at the surface.

The wind has already been introduced in the dynamic boundary condition through a pressure term acting at the free surface in several numerical potential models. Among them, one may cite [22], [23] and [24] who introduced and discussed this approach for BIEM methods and [25], [26], and [27] who extended it to HOS methods. The pressure term used here is based on the Miles' theory [17], accordingly to the approach of [4]. The viscosity was introduced heuristically by [3] who used the HOS method to address the question raised in [2] on the restabilisation of the Benjamin-Feir instability of a Stokes wave train in the presence of dissipation. The introduction was made through the addition of a damping term in the dynamic boundary condition. However, a proper derivation of the kinematic and dynamic boundary condition in the presence of viscosity was made by [20], and later on by [21]. A modification of both kinematic and dynamic condition was found, resulting in a slight difference in the dispersion relation, as it was discussed by [19]. Finally, the system of equations corresponding to the potential theory, in the presence of wind and viscous damping reads

$$\phi_{xx} + \phi_{zz} = 0 \quad \text{for} \quad -\infty < z < \eta(x,t) \tag{1}$$

$$\nabla\phi \to 0 \quad \text{for} \quad z \to -\infty \tag{2}$$

$$\eta_t + \phi_x \eta_x - \phi_z - 2\nu\eta_{xx} = 0 \quad \text{for} \quad z = \eta(x,t) \tag{3}$$

$$\phi_t + \frac{1}{2}\left[(\phi_x)^2 + (\phi_z)^2\right] + g\eta = -\frac{P_a}{\rho} - 2\nu\phi_{zz} \quad \text{for} \quad z = \eta(x,t), \tag{4}$$

where $\phi(x,z,t)$ refers to the velocity potential, $\eta(x,t)$ is the free surface elevation, $P_a(x,t)$ is the atmospheric pressure due to the wind action, applied at the free surface, and where g, ρ, and ν are respectively the gravity, the water density and the water kinematic viscosity. In this system of equations, the influence of wind has to be specified. In the absence of wind, the term P_a/ρ is equal to zero. Otherwise, the wind action is modeled through the term initially introduced by [17], which reads

$$P_a(x,t) = \frac{\rho_{air}\beta u_*^2}{\kappa^2}\frac{\partial\eta}{\partial x}(x,t), \tag{5}$$

where ρ_{air} is the air density, u_* the friction velocity, κ is the von Karman constant, and β a parameter depending on the friction velocity u_* and the wave carrier velocity c_0.

3. Weakly nonlinear approach: The nonlinear Schrödinger equation

The Nonlinear Schrödinger equation can be obtained from the fully nonlinear potential theory by using the multi-scale method. The equations are expanded in Taylor series, around a small parameter, ε, the wave steepness. In the presence of forcing and dissipation, this work was performed initially by [15], who obtained a forced and damped version of this equation. The equation obtained is an approximation of the system of equations (1 - 4), correct to the third order in ε. Recently, [4] used the forced and damped nonlinear Schrödinger equation (fdNLS),

$$i(\psi_t + c_g\psi_x) - \frac{\omega_0}{8k_0^2}\psi_{xx} - 2\omega_0 k_0^2|\psi|^2\psi = i\frac{\mathcal{W}\omega_0 k_0}{2g\rho}\psi - 2i\nu k_0^2\psi \tag{6}$$

to investigate both damping and amplification effects on the Benjamin-Feir instability. Herein, $\mathcal{W} = \rho_{air}\beta u_*^2/\kappa^2$ represents the wind effect, $c_g = \omega_0/2k_0$ is the group velocity of the carrier wave, and where all the parameters ν, ρ, ρ_{air}, g, u_*, and κ are the parameters defined in previous section. Equation (6) describes the spatial and temporal evolution of the envelope of the surface elevation, ψ, for weakly nonlinear and dispersive gravity waves on deep water when dissipation, due to viscosity, and amplification, due to wind, are considered. If considering the right hand side of this equation, it can be rewritten as

$$i\left(\frac{\mathcal{W}\omega_0 k_0}{2g\rho} - 2\nu k_0^2\right)\psi = i\mathcal{K}\psi. \tag{7}$$

[4] found that the stability of the envelope depends on the sign of the constant $\mathcal{K}$. For values of $\mathcal{K} < 0$, solutions are found to be stable, while for values of $\mathcal{K} \geq 0$, solutions are unstable. Physically, they interpreted this result in terms of frequency of the carrier wave ω_0 and friction velocity u_* of the wind over the waves. They plotted the critical curve separating stable envelopes from unstable envelopes. Namely, they showed that for a given friction velocity u_*, only carrier wave of frequency ω_0 which satisfies the following condition are unstable to

modulational perturbations

$$\frac{4\nu\kappa^2\omega_0}{\beta(\kappa c_0/u_*)su_*^2} < 1 \tag{8}$$

This condition can be rewritten as follows

$$\frac{\mathcal{A}^2\Omega}{\beta(\mathcal{A})} < 1 \tag{9}$$

where $\mathcal{A} = \kappa c_0/u_*$ is associated to wind whereas $\Omega = \omega_0/(sg^2/4\nu)^{1/3}$ is associated to dissipation. Note that $\mathcal{A}^2\Omega/\beta(\mathcal{A})$ is equal to the ratio between the rate of damping and the rate of amplification and illustrates the competition between dissipative effects and wind input. The non dimensional numbers $\mathcal{A}$ and Ω correspond to the wave age and non dimensional carrier wave frequency. The modulational instability was found to be sustained as soon as the friction velocity is larger than a threshold value. Conversely, for a given friction velocity, it was found that only carrier waves presenting frequencies (or wavenumbers) lower than a threshold value are subject to Benjamin-Feir instability. Otherwise, due to dissipation, modulational instability restabilizes in the sense of Lyapunov.

4. Fully nonlinear approach: The High Order Spectral method

Within the framework of two-dimensional flows, a High-Order Spectral Method is used to solve numerically the basic partial differential equations corresponding to equations (1 - 4). The lateral conditions correspond here to space-periodic conditions. The horizontal bottom condition corresponds to infinite depth. The velocity potential is expanded in a series of eigenfunctions fulfilling both these lateral and bottom conditions. A spectral treatment is well adapted to investigate numerically the long time behavior of periodic water waves encountering the modulational instability.

4.1. Mathematical formulation

We first introduce the following dimensionless variables into equations (1), (2), (3) and (4):

$$\tilde{x} = k_0 x,\ \tilde{z} = k_0 z,\ \tilde{\eta} = k_0\eta,\ \tilde{t} = \sqrt{gk_0}t,\ \tilde{\phi} = \phi/\sqrt{g/k_0^3} \text{ and } \tilde{p} = p/\left(\rho g/k_0\right), \tag{10}$$

where x, z, η, t, ϕ and p are dimensional variables, and where k_0 is a reference wave number. Hence, the kinematic and dynamic boundary conditions become

$$\frac{\partial\tilde{\eta}}{\partial\tilde{t}} + \frac{\partial\tilde{\phi}}{\partial\tilde{x}}\frac{\partial\tilde{\eta}}{\partial\tilde{x}} - \frac{\partial\tilde{\phi}}{\partial\tilde{z}} - 2\frac{\nu k_0}{c_0}\frac{\partial^2\tilde{\eta}}{\partial\tilde{x}^2} = 0 \quad \text{on} \quad \tilde{z} = \tilde{\eta}(\tilde{x},\tilde{t}), \tag{11}$$

$$\frac{\partial\tilde{\phi}}{\partial\tilde{t}} + \frac{\nabla\tilde{\phi}^2}{2} + \tilde{\eta} + \tilde{P}_a + 2\frac{\nu k_0}{c_0}\frac{\partial^2\tilde{\phi}}{\partial\tilde{z}^2} = 0 \quad \text{on} \quad \tilde{z} = \tilde{\eta}(\tilde{x},\tilde{t}). \tag{12}$$

Following [8], we introduce the velocity potential at the free surface $\tilde{\phi}_s(\tilde{x},\tilde{t}) = \tilde{\phi}(\tilde{x},\tilde{z} = \tilde{\eta}(\tilde{x},\tilde{t}),\tilde{t})$ into these equations, and it comes, after dropping the tilde for sake of readability,

$$\frac{\partial \eta}{\partial t} = -\phi_{s_x}\eta_x + w\left(1+\eta_x^2\right) + 2\frac{\nu k_0}{c_0}\eta_{xx} \text{ on } z = \eta(x,t) \tag{13}$$

$$\frac{\partial \phi^s}{\partial t} = -\eta - \frac{1}{2}\phi_{s_x}^2 + \frac{1}{2}w^2\left(1+\eta_x^2\right) + 2\frac{\nu k_0}{c_0}\frac{\phi_{s_{xx}} - w\eta_{xx}}{1+\eta_x^2} - P_a \text{ on } z = \eta(x,t) \tag{14}$$

with

$$w = \frac{\partial \phi}{\partial z}(x, z = \eta(x,t), t) \tag{15}$$

The main difficulty in this approach is the computation of the vertical velocity at the free surface, w. Following [28], the potential $\phi(x,z,t)$ is written in a finite perturbation series up to a given order M,

$$\phi(x,z,t) = \sum_{m=1}^{M} \phi^{(m)}(x,z,t). \tag{16}$$

The term $\phi^{(m)}$ is of order $\mathcal{O}(\varepsilon^m)$, where ε, a small parameter, is a measure of the wave steepness. Then expanding each $\phi^{(m)}$ evaluated on $z = \eta$ in a Taylor series about $z = 0$, we obtain

$$\phi_s(x,t) = \sum_{m=1}^{M}\sum_{l=0}^{M-m} \frac{\eta^l}{l!}\frac{\partial^{(l)}}{\partial z^l}\left(\phi^{(m)}(x, z=0, t)\right). \tag{17}$$

At a given instant of time, ϕ_s and η are known, and we can estimate $\phi^{(m)}$ at each order ε^m:

$$\phi^{(1)}(x, z=0, t) = \phi_s(x,t), \quad m = 1, \tag{18}$$

$$\vdots$$

$$\phi^{(m)}(x, z=0, t) = -\sum_{l=1}^{m-1} \frac{\eta^l}{l!}\frac{\partial^l}{\partial z^l}\phi^{(m-l)}(x, z=0, t), \quad m \geq 2. \tag{19}$$

The boundary conditions, together with the Laplace equations $\nabla^2\phi^{(m)} = 0$ define a series of Dirichlet problems for $\phi^{(m)}$. For $2\pi-$periodic conditions in x, say, $\phi^{(m)}$ can be written as follows in deep water

$$\phi^{(m)}(x,z,t) = \sum_{j=1}^{\infty} \phi_j^{(m)} e^{-jz} e^{ijx}. \tag{20}$$

Note that $\phi^{(m)}(x,z,t)$ satisfies automatically the Laplace equation and the boundary condition $\nabla\phi^{(m)} \to 0$ when $z \to -\infty$.

4.2. Computation of the vertical velocity

Substitution of equation (20) into the set of equations (18 - 19) provides an expression of the modes $\phi_j^{(m)}$. The vertical velocity at the free surface is then

$$w(x,t) = \sum_{m=1}^{M}\sum_{l=0}^{M-m} \frac{\eta^l}{l!}\frac{\partial^{l+1}}{\partial z^{l+1}}\phi^{(m)}(x, z=0, t) \tag{21}$$

This expression might be substituted into the kinematic and dynamic boundary conditions (13) and (14), yielding to the evolution equations for ϕ_s and η. Another version of HOSM developed by [29] can be used. The difference between both methods lies in the way of computing w from ϕ_s. [29] assume a power series for w as

$$w(x,t) = \sum_{m=1}^{M} w^{(m)}, \tag{22}$$

where

$$w^{(m)} = \sum_{l=0}^{m-1} \frac{\eta^l}{l!} \frac{\partial^{l+1}}{\partial z^{l+1}} \phi^{(m-l)}(x, z=0, t). \tag{23}$$

In fact, the version of [29] differs from the version of [28] not only in the expression of the approximated vertical velocity at the surface, but also in its subsequent treatment in the free surface equations. According to [29], the surface equations must be truncated at consistent nonlinear order if they are to simulate a conservative Hamiltonian system. This requires to treat carefully all nonlinear terms containing w in the prognostic equations. In contrast to the series used by [28], those used by [29] are naturally ordered with respect to the nonlinear parameter . The [28] formulation is not consistent, after truncation, with the underlying Hamiltonian structure of the canonical pair of free-surface equations. Thus, the formulation of [29] preserves the Hamiltonian structure of the prognostic equations.

5. Initial conditions for the numerical simulations

From a numerical point of view, one part of the initial condition is obtained by considering a Stokes wavetrain $(\bar{\eta}, \bar{\phi})$ which is computed using the approach first introduced by [30]. A very high-order Stokes wave of amplitude a_0 and wavenumber k_0 is calculated iteratively. In the absence of wind and dissipation, the infinitesimal perturbation components (η', ϕ') calculated through a perturbative approach developed by [31] correspond to a Benjamin-Feir instability of wavenumber δk. The perturbed Stokes wave is obtained by adding the infinitesimal perturbations at the sidebands $k_0 \pm \delta k$ of the fundamental and its harmonics. For fixed values of $(\mathcal{A}, \Omega)$ two kinds of initial conditions are used when wind and dissipation are considered. The first kind (unseeded case) corresponds to the unperturbed Stokes' wave $(\eta, \phi) = (\bar{\eta}, \bar{\phi})$, whereas the second kind (seeded case) corresponds to the perturbed Stokes' wave $(\eta, \phi) = (\bar{\eta}, \bar{\phi}) + \varepsilon(\eta', \phi' + \bar{\phi}_z \eta')$, with $\varepsilon = 10^{-3}$. In both cases, we consider a Stokes wavetrain such as $a_0 k_0 = 0.11$ and $k_0 = 5$. The wavenumber of the modulational instability is $\delta k = 1$. This choice of the perturbation wave number corresponds to the closest approximation of the most unstable wave number that can be fitted in the computational domain. The order of nonlinearity was taken equal to $M = 6$. In other words, nonlinear terms have been retained up to sixth-order. The highest wavenumber taken into account in the simulations is $k_{max} = 50$, corresponding to the ninth harmonic of the fundamental wavenumber. The number of mesh points was taken equal to $N = 750$, satisfying the stability criterion $N > (M+1) \times k_{max}$. In the absence of wind and damping, the unperturbed initial condition leads to the steady evolution of the Stokes' wavetrain, whereas the perturbed initial condition leads to the well known Fermi-Pasta-Ulam recurrence. We propagate these initial wavetrains under various conditions of wind and dissipation, to analyze the behavior of the modulational instability of the Stokes wavetrain.

6. Results and comparisons

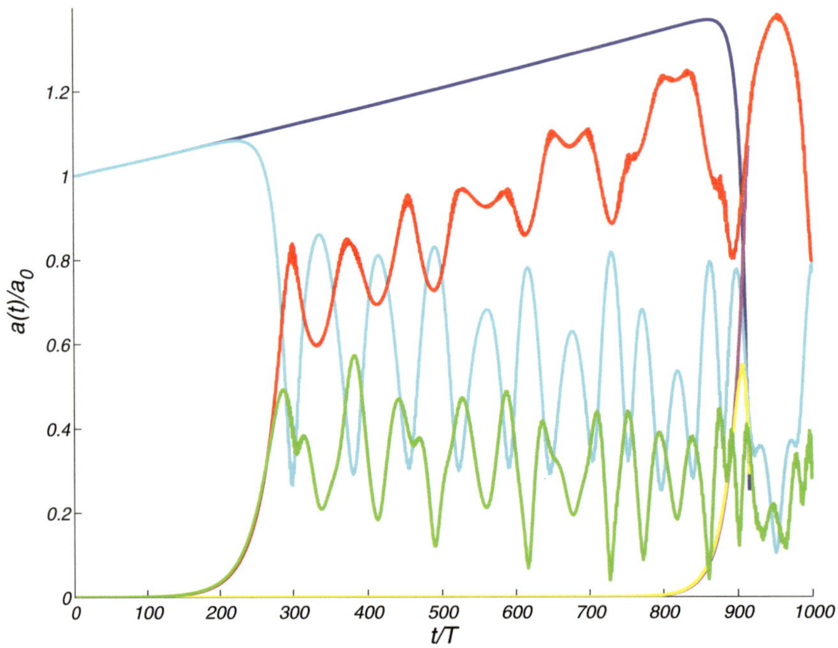

Figure 1. Time evolution of the normalized amplitudes of the fundamental mode ($k = 5$), subharmonic mode ($k = 4$) and superharmonic mode ($k = 6$) for $(\mathcal{A}, \Omega) = (4, 0.59)$. Fundamental mode amplitude (—), subharmonic mode amplitude (—) and superharmonic mode amplitude (—) for an initially unperturbed Stokes' wave (unseeded case). Fundamental mode amplitude (—), subharmonic mode amplitude (—) and superharmonic mode amplitude (—) for an initially perturbed Stokes' wave (seeded case). T is the fundamental wave period.

One of the difficulties involved in this study is to define clearly the stability. Indeed, since Stokes' waves are propagating under the action of wind and viscosity, this flow cannot be considered stationary nor periodic. Discussing of the combined influence of wind forcing and damping on the modulational instability, however, implies to define a reference flow. In order to do so, we first consider the evolution of the unperturbed Stokes' waves in the presence of forcing and dissipation (unseeded case). It is checked that the instability does not develop spontaneously in the laps of time considered. Afterwards, we consider the evolution of the initially perturbed Stokes' wave train under the same conditions of wind forcing and damping (seeded case). The nonlinear evolution of the Stokes' wavetrain perturbed by the modulational instability in the presence of wind and dissipation is then compared to that of the reference flow. In that way, the deviation from the reference flow can be interpreted in terms of modulational instability, and the influence of wind forcing and dissipation can be analyzed. Following our previous works [18, 19], the evolution of the energy of the perturbation is thus obtained.

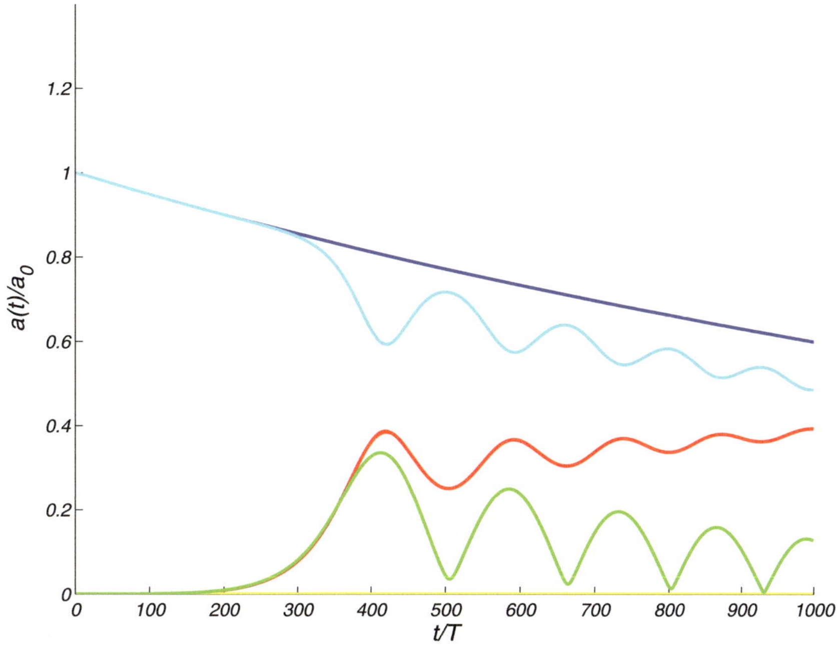

Figure 2. Time evolution of the normalized amplitudes of the fundamental mode ($k = 5$), subharmonic mode ($k = 4$) and superharmonic mode ($k = 6$) for $(\mathcal{A}, \Omega) = (4, 0.61)$. Fundamental mode amplitude (—), subharmonic mode amplitude (—) and superharmonic mode amplitude (—) for an initially unperturbed Stokes' wave (unseeded case). Fundamental mode amplitude (—), subharmonic mode amplitude (—) and superharmonic mode amplitude (—) for an initially perturbed Stokes' wave (seeded case). T is the fundamental wave period.

Figures 1 and 2 present the time evolution of the amplitudes of three components of the water waves' spectrum. The mode $k = 5$ is the fundamental mode, while modes $k = 4$ and $k = 6$ are sidebands, respectively the subharmonic and the superharmonic. Each of these figures present to two kinds of initial conditions, namely the unseeded and the seeded cases. The two figures correspond to two different conditions of wind forcing and damping.

Figure 1 shows the time evolution of the normalized amplitudes $a(t)/a_0$ of the fundamental mode $k = 5$, subharmonic mode $k = 4$ and superharmonic mode $k = 6$ with and without perturbations for the modulational instability. For both cases, the simulations correspond to a wind parameter $\mathcal{A} = 4$ and to a viscosity parameter $\Omega = 0.59$. Within the framework of the NLS equation, [4] showed that the wave train is unstable to modulational instability for these values of $\mathcal{A}$ and Ω. From this figure, it appears that both wavetrains (unseeded and seeded cases) present a similar evolution during the first hundred periods of propagation, T being the fundamental wave period. Then, the behavior of the wavetrain is strongly affected by the development of the modulational instability. For the unperturbed case (unseeded case), the fundamental component increases, since no occurrence of the modulational instability is expected. However, due to the accumulation of numerical errors, the spontaneous occurrence of the modulational instability cannot be avoided, but not before $t = 900T$. On figure 3 one can observe the persistence of the modulational instability through the evolution of the free surface. Indeed, it is observed that the wave packet is alternatively modulated, leading to the formation of a large wave, and demodulated, corresponding to a state which is closer from the origin. This is an expression of the Fermi-Pasta-Ulam quasi-recurrence.

Figure 2 corresponds to $(\mathcal{A},\Omega)$=$(4,0.61)$. Wind condition is similar to the previous numerical simulation, but the dissipative effect considered is stronger. This case correspond to a linearly stable case of the modulational instability, as obtained by [4] in the framework of the NLS equation. From this figure, one can see that wind energy goes to the subharmonic mode whereas dissipation reduces the fundamental and superharmonic components, as previously observed. However, modulation of modes decrease, and they present a monotonic behavior. For unseeded case, as expected, we observe an exponential decay of the fundamental mode. Note that there is no natural occurrence of the subharmonic mode of the modulational instability as it was found in figure 1. For seeded case, the first maximum of modulation that occurs at $t = 410T$ is followed by partial damped modulation/demodulation cycles. Figure 4 illustrates the disappearance of the modulational instability through the evolution of the free surface. In this case dissipation prevails over amplification due to wind and [2] have obtained linear and nonlinear stability of modulational perturbations within the framework of the dissipative NLS equation. More specifically they showed that dissipation reduces the set of unstable wavenumbers as time increases. Consequently every mode becomes stable. The result of this numerical simulation agrees with that of [2] and [3] who considered only dissipation. In their approach, a solution is said to be stable if every solution that starts close to this solution at $t = 0$ remains close to it for all $t > 0$, otherwise the solution is unstable. To include nonlinear stability analysis they introduced a norm and considered stability in the sense of Lyapunov.

In our previous work [18], we assumed that the dominant mode describes the main behavior of a wave train, and we introduced a norm measuring the distance between the fundamental modes of the unperturbed and perturbed Stokes wave corresponding to unseeded case and seeded case respectively. However, it is more consistent to consider the energy of the perturbation, as it was stated in [19]. Thus, another norm can be introduced as

$$E_N(t) = \frac{\int_{-\infty}^{\infty}(a_{k_S}(t) - a_{k_{US}}(t))^2 dk}{\int_{-\infty}^{\infty} a_{k_{US}}^2(0)dk}, \tag{24}$$

where $a_{k_{US}}(t)$ is the amplitude of the component of water elevation η of wave number k, for the initially unperturbed wave train (unseeded case), and $a_{k_S}(t)$ is the amplitude of the component of water elevation η of wave number k, for the initially perturbed wave train (seeded case). This norm corresponds to the potential energy of the perturbation. Its value characterizes the deviation of the perturbed solution from the unperturbed solution. Figure 5 shows the time evolution of this norm for two sets of parameters $(\mathcal{A},\Omega) = (4,0.59)$ and $(\mathcal{A},\Omega) = (4,0.61)$. For the two cases we can observe two regimes. The first regime corresponds to the development of the modulational instability and shows that it is the nonlinear interaction between the fundamental mode and its sidebands which dominates with a weak effect of the wind forcing and the dissipation. The second regime corresponding to the oscillatory evolution of the norm is dominated by the competition between wind forcing and dissipation. The nonlinear interaction between the fundamental mode and the sidebands is

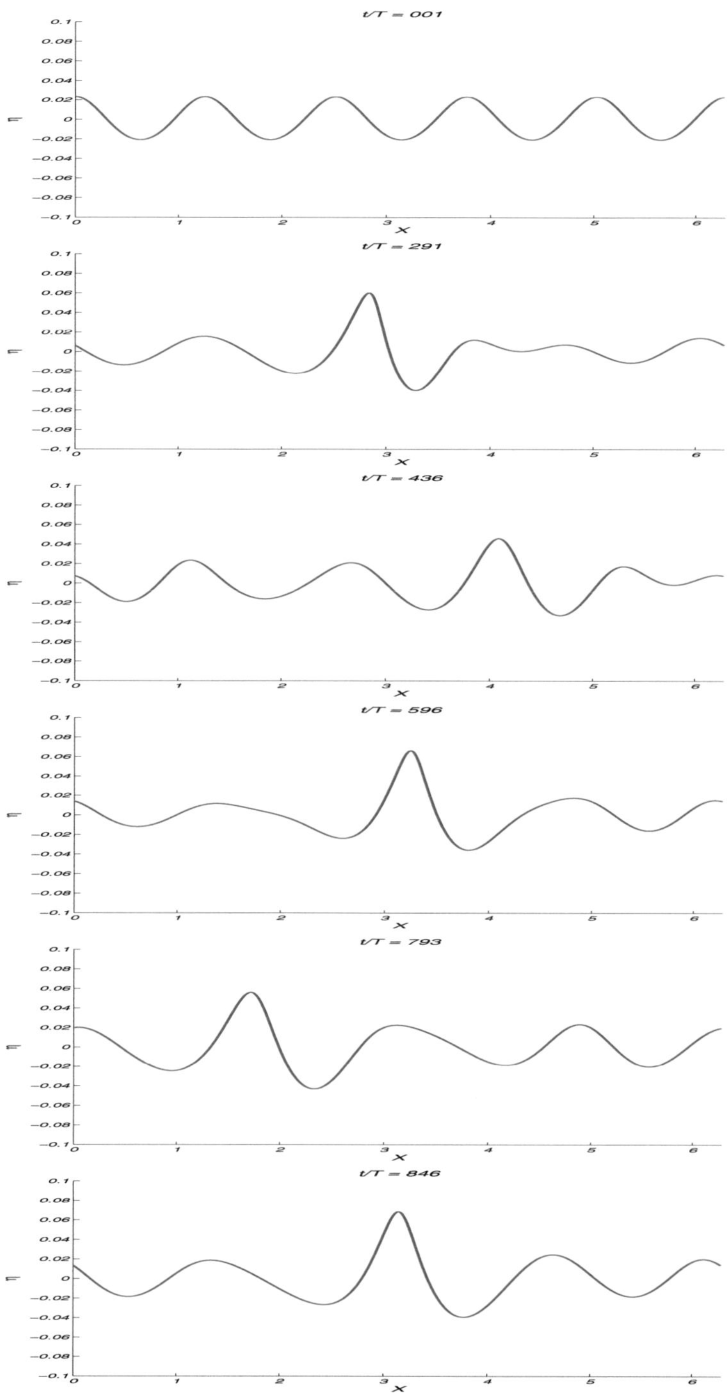

Figure 3. Surface wave profiles at different times, obtained while propagating initial condition corresponding to seeded case with $(\mathcal{A}, \Omega) = (4, 0.59)$. From top to bottom $t/T = 1$, 291, 436, 596, 793, 846.

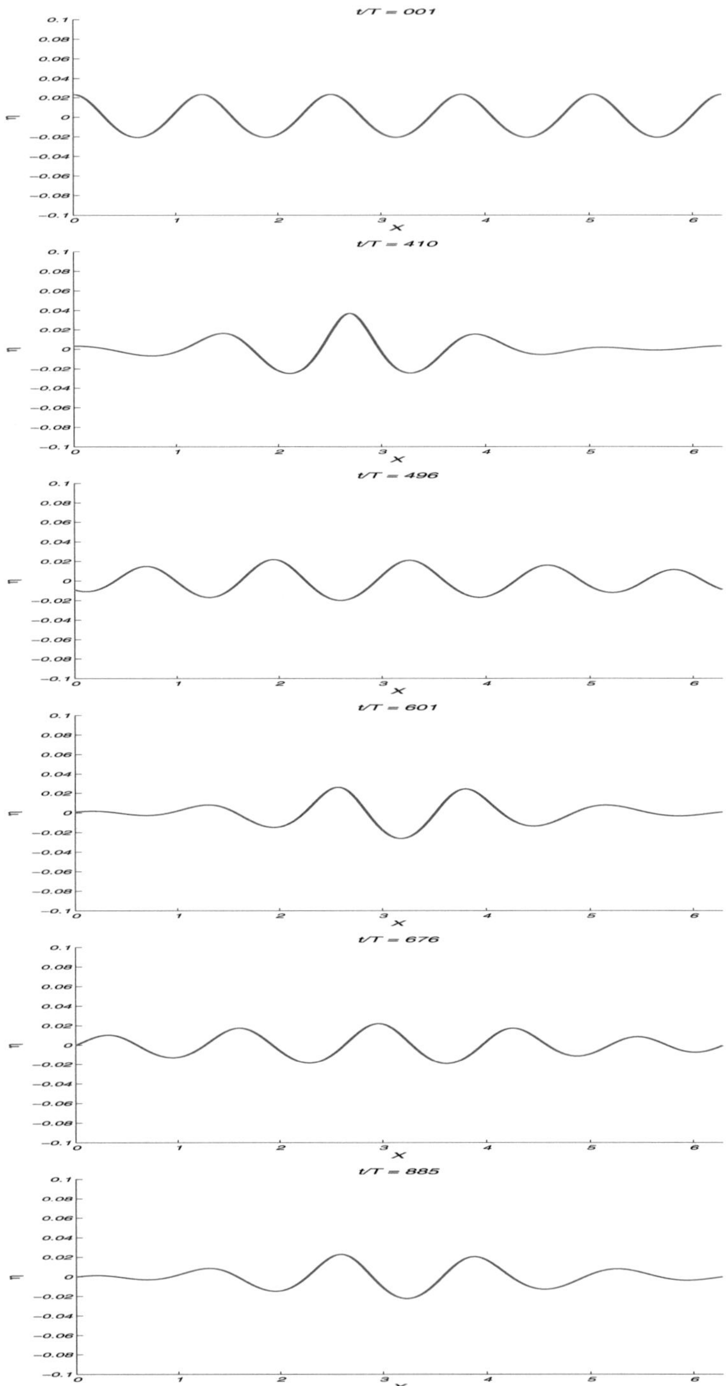

Figure 4. Surface wave profiles at different times, obtained while propagating initial condition corresponding to seeded case with $(\mathcal{A}, \Omega) = (4, 0.61)$. From top to bottom $t/T = 1$, 410, 496, 601, 676, 885.

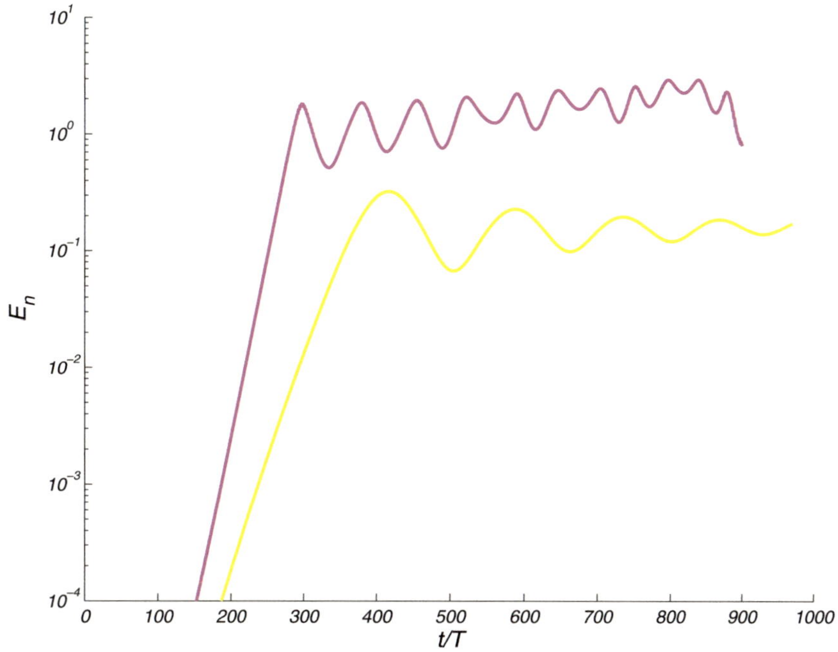

Figure 5. Time evolution of the norm E_n for $(\mathcal{A}, \Omega) = (4, 0.59)$ (—) and $(\mathcal{A}, \Omega) = (4, 0.61)$ (—).

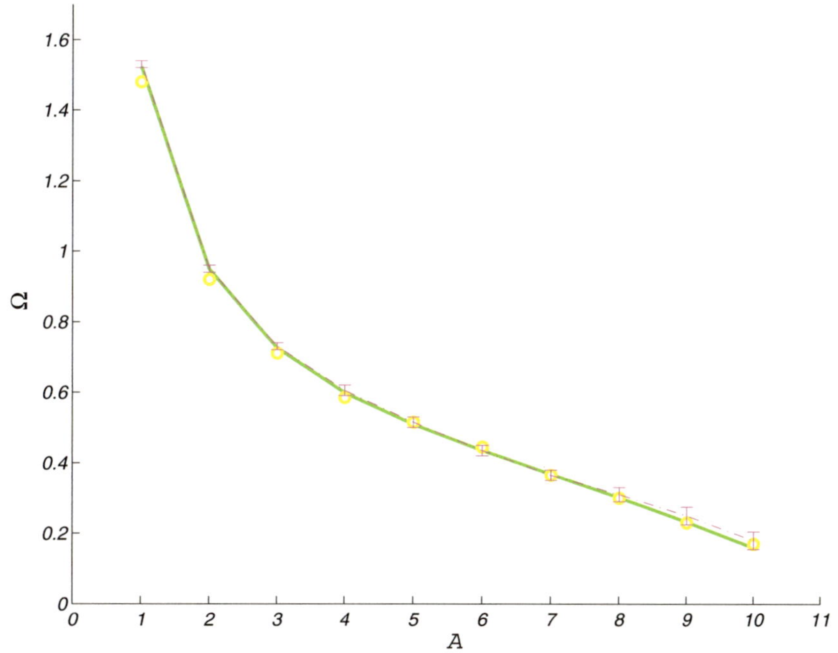

Figure 6. Theoretical (—) and numerical (– · –) marginal stability contour lines. (○) correspond to numerical results obtained in the framework of the equations suggested by [3]. The theoretical curve corresponds to the figure 1 of [4].

not the dominant mechanism. The magenta curve exhibits oscillations around an averaged value growing exponentially, whereas the yellow curve exhibits the same oscillations around a constant value. We can claim that the norm, E_N, presents globally exponential growth or asymptotical saturation corresponding to instability and stability respectively. Herein, the stability can be interpreted in terms of asymptotic stability. The first case is said to be unstable whereas the second case corresponds to a stable solution. In the latter case we expect that the solution will remain close to the unperturbed solution. In other words, nonlinear interactions are affected by the non conservative effects that are wind and dissipation, leading to a long time disappearance of these interactions.

Many numerical simulations have been run for various values of the parameters $\mathcal{A}$ and Ω. Figure 6 shows a stability diagram which presents comparison between the present numerical results and those of [4] obtained theoretically. The marginal curve corresponding to the fully nonlinear equations is very close to the theoretical marginal curve obtained within the framework the NLS equation. The region above the critical curve corresponds to stable cases, whereas the region beneath corresponds to unstable cases. Bars in figure 6 correspond to uncertainty on stability or instability. Numerical results obtained in our previous work [18] within the framework of equations suggested by [3] are plotted for the sake of reference ( ). The way of introducing damping effect into the kinematic boundary condition has little influence on the results, especially for young waves. The present numerical simulations demonstrate that the results derived by [4] within the framework of the NLS equation are correct in the context of the fully nonlinear equations.

This result provides a validation of the weakly nonlinear theory obtained in the framework of nonlinear Schrödinger equation. However, the numerical approach allows to investigate the long time evolution of the wave train, taking into account the strongly nonlinear behavior of water waves. One phenomenon especially illustrates this nonlinear behavior: the permanent frequency downshift. This phenomenon was discussed by [32] and [33] within the framework of gravity waves. These authors considered that dissipation due to breaking wave was responsible for this permanent downshift. [34] modeled the phenomenon in the presence of wind and eddy viscosity, and latter on [35] in the presence of only molecular viscosity. All these works are based on equations valid up to fourth order in nonlinearity, or higher. Indeed, it is well known that the frequency downshift cannot be observed in the framework of nonlinear Schrödinger equation, which preserves the symmetry between subharmonic and superharmonic components. In fact, [36] concluded that in the absence of wind and dissipation, it was not possible to observe the phenomenon even with higher order equations.

If going back to figure 1, for the initially perturbed case (seeded case), the development of the modulational instability is responsible for the frequency downshift observed at around $t = 500T$. Indeed, one can see that the subharmonic component increases continuously whereas the fundamental and superharmonic component decrease. The superharmonic component decreases faster than the fundamental component. Hence, wind energy goes to the subharmonic mode whereas dissipation reduces the fundamental and superharmonic components. During the modulation process, a broadening of the spectrum is observed, even if not presented here for the sake of clarity. Beyond $t = 500T$, the subharmonic mode $k = 4$ is dominant in the spectrum. To investigate the effect of wind and damping, another series of simulations is performed. Namely, the values of $\mathcal{A}$ and Ω where chosen to fulfill the condition

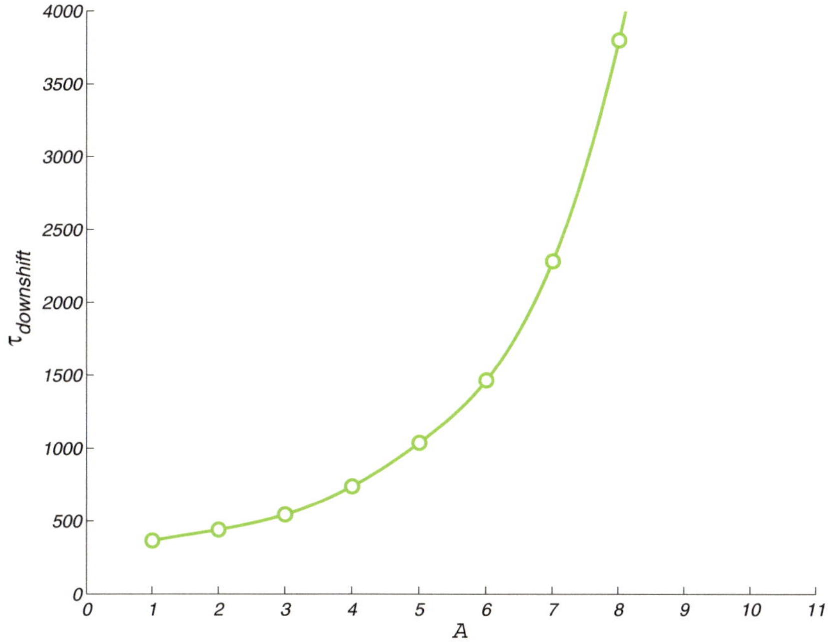

Figure 7. Nondimensional time $\tau_{downshift} = t/T$ for which the permanent frequency downshift is observed, plotted as a function of the wave age parameter $\mathcal{A}$. Ω is chosen here to be on the marginal stability curve presented on figure 6.

$\mathcal{K} = 0$ (see equation (7) for the definition of $\mathcal{K}$). This might be interpreted in terms of balance between wind forcing and damping, corresponding to an equilibrium state. Furthermore, in these conditions, the forced and damped nonlinear Schrödinger equation reduces to the canonical NLS equation. It becomes obvious that the weakly nonlinear theory does not predict any variation in behavior, since the NLS equation remains unchanged for each values of $\mathcal{A}$ and Ω. However, the results of the numerical simulations are different. Indeed, figure 7 presents the nondimensional time $\tau_{downshift}$ after which the permanent frequency downshift is observed, as a function of $\mathcal{A}$. From this figure, it seems obvious that this time is strongly dependant on the wind speed. The youngest the waves are, the fastest is the downshift.

7. Conclusion

In this work, it was evidence how numerical simulations can provide a good demonstration of a weakly nonlinear theory that cannot be achieved by means of experimental demonstration. In this study, an extension of the work of [4] to the fully nonlinear case was suggested. Within the framework of the NLS equation the latter authors considered the modulational instability of Stokes wave trains suffering both effects of wind and dissipation. The results they obtained show that the modulational instability depends on both frequency of the carrier wave and strength of the wind velocity. They plotted the curve corresponding to marginal stability in the $(\mathcal{A}, \Omega)$-plane. Here, a numerical verification is performed, by means of a fully nonlinear approach. The long term behavior of a wave group propagating under both actions of wind and dissipation was obtained thanks to this method. To distinguish stable solutions from unstable solutions, a norm based on the potential energy of the perturbations was introduced. A nonlinear stability diagram resulting from the numerical simulations of the fully nonlinear equation has been given in the $(\mathcal{A}, \Omega)$-plane which coincides with the linear stability analysis of [4]. In the presence of wind, dissipation and modulational instability it is found that wind energy goes to the subharmonic sideband whereas dissipation lowers the amplitude of the fundamental mode of the wave train yielding to a permanent frequency-downshifting. This permanent frequency downshift is strongly influenced by the wind and dissipation parameter. If the wave group is at equilibrium in energy input and dissipation, the fdNLS equation reduces to the classical NLS equation, and predict no influence of the wind. However, by considering the asymmetry between wave components, induced by strong nonlinearity (higher than fourth order), a strong influence of the wind and dissipation is observed.

Author details

Julien Touboul
Mediterranean Institute of Oceanography (MIO), Aix-Marseille Univ., Université du Sud Toulon-Var, CNRS/INSU, UMR 7294, IRD, UMR235, France

Christian Kharif
Institut de Recherche sur les phénomènes hors équilibre (IRPHE), Aix-Marseille Univ., Ecole Centrale Marseille, CNRS/INSIS UMR 7342, France

8. References

[1] T. B. Benjamin and J. E. Feir. The disintegration of wave trains on deep water. *J. Fluid Mech.*, 27:417–430, 1967.
[2] H. Segur, D. Henderson, J. Carter, J. Hammack, C. M. Li, D. Pheiff, and K. Socha. Stabilizing the benfamin-feir instability. *J. Fluid Mech.*, 539:229–271, 2005.
[3] G. Wu, Y. Liu, and D. K. P. Yue. A note on stabilizing the benjamin-feir instability. *J. Fluid Mech.*, 556:45–54, 2006.
[4] C. Kharif, R. Kraenkel, M. Manna, and R. Thomas. The modulational instability in deep water under the action of wind and dissipation. *J. Fluid Mech.*, 664:417–430, 2010.
[5] G. G. Stokes. On the theory of oscillatory waves. *Trans. Camb. Phil. Soc.*, 8:441–455, 1847.
[6] M. J. Lighthill. Contributions to the theory of waves in non-linear dispersive systems. *J. Inst. Math. Appl.*, 1:269–306, 1965.
[7] G. B. Whitham. Linear and nonlinear waves. Wiley-Interscience (New-York), 1974.
[8] V. E. Zakharov. Satbility of periodic waves of finite amplitude on the surface of a deep fluid. *J. Appl. Tech. Phys.*, 9:190–194, 1968.
[9] C. Kharif and E. Pelinovsky. Physical mechanisms of the rogue wave phenomenon. *Eur. J. Mech. B Fluids*, 22 (6):603–633, 2003.
[10] C. Kharif, E. Pelinovsky, and A. Slunyaev. Rogue waves in the ocean. In *Mathematical Aspects of Vortex Dynamics*. Springer (ISBN: 978-3-540-88418-7), 2009.
[11] J. W. Dold and D. H. Peregrine. Water-wave modulation. In *Proc. 20th Intl. Conf. Coastal Eng. (Taipei)*, volume 1, pages 163–175. 1986.
[12] M. L. Banner and X. Tian. On the determination of the onset of breaking for modulating surface gravity water waves. *J. Fluid Mech.*, 367:107–137, 1998.

[13] E. Fermi, J. Pasta, and S. Ulam. Studies of non linear problems. *Amer. Math. Month.*, 74 (1), 1967.
[14] L. Shemer. On benjamin feir instability and evolution of a nonlinear wave with finite amplitude sidebands. *Nat. Hazards Earth Syst. Sci.*, 10:1–7, 2010.
[15] S. W. Joo, A. F. Messiter, and W. W. Schultz. Evolution of weakly nonlinear water waves in the presence of viscosity and surfactant. *J. Fluid Mech.*, 229:135–158, 1991.
[16] H. Segur, D. Henderson, and J. Hammack. Can the benjamin-feir instability instability spawn a rogue wave? In *Proc. 14th 'Aha Huliko' a Hawaiian winter worshop*, pages 43–57. 2005.
[17] J. W. Miles. On the generation of surface waves by shear flow. *J. Fluid Mech.*, 3:185–204, 1957.
[18] C. Kharif and J. Touboul. Under which conditions the benjamin-feir instabilty may spawn a rogue wave: a fully nonlinear approach. *Eur. Phys. J. Special Topics*, 185:159–168, 2010.
[19] J. Touboul and C. Kharif. Nonlinear evolution of the modulational instability under weak forcing and damping. *Nat. Hazards Earth Syst. Sci.*, 10 (12):2589–2597, 2010.
[20] T. S. Lundgren. A free surface vortex method with weak viscous effects. In R. E. Calfish, editor, *Mathematical Aspects of Vortex Dynamics*, pages 68–79. SIAM Proceedings, 1989.
[21] F. Dias, A. I. Dyachenko, and V. E. Zakharov. Theory of weakly damped free-surface flows: A new formulation based on potential flow solutions. *Phys. Lett. A*, 372:1297–1302, 2008.
[22] M.I. Banner and J. Song. On determining the onset and strength of breaking for deep water waves. part ii: Influence of wind forcing and surface shear. *J. Phys. Oceanogr.*, 32 (9):2559–2570, 2002.
[23] J. Touboul, J.-P. Giovanangeli, C. Kharif, and E. Pelinbovsky. Freak waves under the action of wind: Experiments and simulations. *Eur. J. Mech. B. Fluid.*, 25:662–676, 2006.
[24] J. Touboul, C. Kharif, E. Pelinbovsky, and J.-P. Giovanangeli. On the interaction of wind and steep gravity wave groups using miles' and jeffreys' mechanisms. *Nonlin. Processes Geophys.*, 15:1023–1031, 2008.
[25] J. Touboul and C. Kharif. On the interaction of wind and extreme gravity waves due to modulational instability. *Phys. Fluids*, 18(108103), 2006.
[26] J. Touboul. On the influence of wind on extreme wave events. *Nat. Hazards Earth Syst. Sci.*, 7:123–128, 2007.
[27] C. Kharif, J.-P. Giovanangeli, J. Touboul, L. Grare, and E. Pelinovsky. Influence of wind on extreme wave events: experimental and numerical approaches. *J. Fluid Mech.*, 594:209–247, 2008.
[28] D. G. Dommermuth and D. K. P. Yue. A high-order spectral method for the study of nonlinear gravity waves. *J. Fluid Mech.*, 184:267–288, 1987.
[29] B. J. West, K. A. Brueckner, R. S. Janda, M. Milder, and R. L. Milton. A new numerical method for surface hydrodynamics. *J. Geophys Res.*, 92:11803–11824, 1987.
[30] M. S. Longuet-Higgins. Bifurcation in gravity waves. *J. Fluid Mech.*, 151:457–475, 1985.
[31] C. Kharif and A. Ramamonjiarisoa. Deep water gravity wave instabilities at large steepness. *Phys. Fluids*, 31:1286–1288, 1988.
[32] K. Trulsen and K. B. Dysthe. Frequency down-shift through self modulation. In A. Torum and O. T. Gud-Mestad, editors, *Proc. Water Wave Kinematics*, volume 178, pages 561–572. Kluwer Academic Publishers, 1990.

[33] K. Trulsen and K. B. Dysthe. Action of windstress and breaking on the evolution of a wavetrain. In M. L. Banner and R. H. J. Grimshaw, editors, *Breaking Waves*, pages 243–249. Springer Verlag, 1992.

[34] T. Hara and C. C. Mei. Frequency downshift in narrowbanded surface waves under the influence of wind. *J. Fluid Mech.*, 230:429–477, 1991.

[35] C. Skandrani, C. Kharif, and J. Poitevin. On benjamin feir instability and evolution of a nonlinear wave with finite amplitude sidebands. *Cont. Math.*, 200:157–171, 1996.

[36] E. Lo and C. C. Mei. A numerical study of water wave modulation based on a higher order nonlinear schrödinger equation. *J. Fluid Mech.*, 150:395–416, 1985.

Chapter 18

Spectral Modeling and Numerical Simulation of Compressible Homogeneous Sheared Turbulence

Mohamed Riahi and Taieb Lili

Additional information is available at the end of the chapter

http://dx.doi.org/10.5772/48617

1. Introduction

This chapter is mainly in the area of the use of Rapid Distortion Theory (RDT) to clarify and to well better increase our understanding of the physics of the compressible turbulent flows. This theory is a computationally viable option for examining linear compressible flow physics in the absence of inertial effects. In this linear limit, the statistical evolution of incompressible homogeneous turbulence can be described completely in terms of closed spectral covariance equations (see Refs. (Hunt, 1990 & Savill, 1987) and references therein). Many papers in literature deal with homogeneous compressible turbulence and RDT solution (Cambon et al., 1993; Coleman & Mansour, 1991; Blaisdell et al., 1993, 1996; Durbin & Zeman, 1992; Jacquin et al., 1993; Livescu & Madnia, 2004; Riahi et al., 2007; Riahi, 2008; Riahi & Lili, 2011; Sarkar, 1995; Simone, 1995; Simone et al., 1997). These studies have yielded very valuable physical insight and closure model suggestions. In all the above works, the fluctuation equations are solved directly to infer turbulence physics. For the case of viscous compressible homogeneous shear flow in the RDT limit no analytical solutions are known. Simone et al. (1997) performed RDT simulations of homogeneous shear flow and showed that the role of the distortion Mach number, M_d, on the time variation of the turbulent kinetic energy is consistent with that found in the direct numerical simulation (DNS) results. In this chapter, numerical solutions to the RDT equations for the special case of mean shear is described completely by finding numerical solutions obtained by solving linear double point correlations equations. Numerical integration of these equations is carried out using a second-order simple and accurate scheme (Riahi & Lili, 2011). Indeed, this numerical method is proved more stable and faster than the previous one which use linear transfer matrix (Riahi et al., 2007 & Riahi, 2008) and allows in particular to obtain accurately the asymptotic behavior of the turbulence parameters (for large values of the non-dimensional times St) characteristic of equilibrium states. To perform this work, RDT code solving linearized equations for compressible homogeneous shear flows is validated by comparing RDT results to those of direct numerical simulation (DNS) of Simone et al. (1997) and Sarkar (1995) for various values of initial gradient Mach number M_{g0} (Riahi & Lili, 2011).

A study of compressibility effects on structure and evolution of a sheared homogeneous turbulent flow is carried out using this theory (RDT). An analysis of the behavior of different terms appearing in the turbulent kinetic energy and the Reynolds stress equations permit to well identify compressibility effects which allow us to analyze performance of the compressible model of Fujiwara and Arakawa concerning the pressure-dilatation correlation (Riahi et al., 2007). The evaluation of this model stays in the field of RDT validity (Riahi & Lili, 2011).

Equilibrium states of homogeneous compressible turbulence subjected to rapid shear can be studied using rapid distortion theory (RDT) for large values of St ($St > 10$) in particular for large values of the initial gradient Mach number M_{g0} describing various regimes of flow. In fact, the study of the behavior of the non-dimensional turbulent kinetic energy $q^2(t)/q^2(0)$ (with $q^2 = \overline{u_i u_i}$) allows to check relevance of an incompressible regime for low values of initial gradient Mach number, of an intermediate regime for moderate values of M_{g0} and of a compressible regime for high values of M_{g0} (Riahi et al., 2007). The pressure-released regime is related to infinite values of M_{g0} (Riahi & Lili, 2011). The gradient Mach number M_g appears naturally when scaling the (linearized) RDT equations for homogeneous compressible turbulence (see equations (A.10), (A.11), (A.12) and (A.13) in appendix (Riahi et al., 2007)). This parameter can be viewed as the ratio of an acoustic time $\tau_a = \frac{l}{a}$ for a large eddy to the mean flow time scale $\tau_d = \frac{1}{S}$: $M_g = \frac{\tau_a}{\tau_d} = \frac{Sl}{a}$, where l is an integral lengthscale and a is the mean sound speed. The lengthscale of energetic structure is expressed by $l = \frac{q^3}{\varepsilon}$, where ε is the rate of turbulent kinetic energy dissipation. Sarkar (1995) also used $\frac{Sl}{a}$ (which he referred to as 'gradient Mach number' M_g), to quantify compressibility effects for homogeneous shear flow. In the case of shear flow, l is chosen to be the integral lengthscale of the streamwise fluctuating velocity in the shearing direction x_2. Another Mach number relevant to homogeneous shear flow and that characterize the effects of compressibility on turbulence is the turbulent Mach number $M_t = u/a$ based on a characteristic fluctuation velocity u and mean sound speed a.

2. RDT equations for compressible homogeneous turbulence

The flow to be considered is a homogeneous, compressible turbulent shear flow where we retain the same RDT equations adopted by Simone (1995), Simone et al. (1997), Riahi et al. (2007) and Riahi (2008). The linearized equations of continuity, momentum and entropy controlling the fluctuating of velocity u_i and pressure p lead to general RDT equations:

$$\left(\frac{\dot{p}}{\gamma \overline{P}}\right) = -u_{i,i}, \tag{1}$$

$$\dot{u}_i + u_j \frac{\partial \overline{U_i}}{\partial x_j} = -\frac{1}{\overline{\rho}}\frac{\partial p}{\partial x_i} + \frac{\nu}{3}\frac{\partial^2 u_j}{\partial x_i \partial x_j} + \frac{\nu}{3}\frac{\partial^2 u_i}{\partial x_j^2}, \tag{2}$$

where γ is the ratio of specific heats, $\overline{\rho}$ is the mean density and ν is the kinematic viscosity.

The dot superscript denotes a substantial derivative along the mean flow trajectories related to mean field velocity $\overline{U_i}$.

Equation (1) is derived from continuity equation

$$\left(\frac{\dot{\rho}}{\overline{\rho}}\right) = -u_{i,i} \tag{3}$$

associated to isentropic fluctuations hypothesis $\dot{s} = 0$ which is translated by

$$\left(\frac{\dot{p}}{\overline{P}}\right) = \gamma \left(\frac{\dot{\rho}}{\overline{\rho}}\right) \tag{4}$$

and leads to equation (1). So, the isentropic hypothesis $\dot{s} = 0$ simplifies governing equations by keeping the variables u_i and p and eliminating ρ. We can obviously discard the hypothesis $\dot{s} = 0$ by writing the (exact) energy equation. The linearized derived equation within the framework of RDT can be written as pressure fluctuation equation which contains some viscous terms (Livescu et al., 2004; see equation (8)). Such an equation is compatible with equation (2) which contains also viscous terms and represents the linearized equation of momentum. Concerning now the validity of isentropic hypothesis $\dot{s} = 0$, Blaisdell et al. (1993) introduced a polytropic coefficient n defined by, $\frac{p}{\overline{P}} = n\frac{\rho}{\overline{\rho}}$ $n = \gamma$ corresponding obviously to isentropic fluctuations. These authors performed direct numerical simulations (DNS) related to homogeneous compressible sheared turbulence with various initial conditions. They calculated temporal variation of an average polytropic coefficient $n = \left(\frac{\overline{p^2} / \overline{P}^2}{\overline{\rho^2} / \overline{\rho}^2}\right)^{\frac{1}{2}}$. During the period of the turbulence establishment (for early times), the evolution of n with St depends on initial conditions (and in particular of initial entropy fluctuations). However, for all of their simulations and for large values of St, n tends toward an equilibrium value independent of initial conditions and slightly less than $\gamma = 1.4$. Blaisdell et al. (1993) concluded that thermodynamic variables "follow a nearly isentropic process" for large values of *St* and for compressible sheared turbulence. As a conclusion, we retain that with isentropic fluctuations hypothesis, we can obtained a good prediction of equilibrium states $(St \to \infty)$ for compressible homogeneous sheared turbulence.

After these remarks, we consider the Fourier transform (denoted here by the symbol " ^ ") of various terms in equations (1) and (2) which leads to the following equations expressed in the spectral space and in the case of turbulent shear flow:

$$\frac{\dot{\hat{p}}}{\gamma \overline{P}} = -\hat{u}_{i,i}, \tag{5}$$

$$\dot{\hat{u}}_i + \lambda_{ij}\,\hat{u}_j + \frac{\nu}{3} k_i\, k_j\, \hat{u}_j + \frac{\nu}{3} k^2\, \hat{u}_i = -Ik_i \frac{\hat{p}}{\overline{\rho}}, \tag{6}$$

where λ_{ij} is the mean velocity gradient defined by:

$$\lambda_{ij} = S\delta_{i1}\delta_{j2} \tag{7}$$

and $I^2 = -1$.

In the Fourier space, velocity field is decomposed on solenoidal and dilatational contributions by adopting a local reference mark of Craya (Cambon et al., 1993):

$$\hat{u}_i(\vec{k},t) = \hat{\varphi}^1(\vec{k},t)\, e_i^1(\vec{k}) + \hat{\varphi}^2(\vec{k},t)\, e_i^2(\vec{k}) + \hat{\varphi}^3(\vec{k},t)\, e_i^3(\vec{k}), \tag{8}$$

where $\hat{\varphi}^1(\vec{k},t)$ and $\hat{\varphi}^2(\vec{k},t)$ are the solenoidal contributions and $\hat{\varphi}^3(\vec{k},t)$ is the dilatational contribution.

By separating solenoidal and dilatational contributions, we introduce the spectrums of doubles correlations:

$$\Phi_{ij}(\vec{k},t) = \frac{1}{2}\left[\hat{\varphi}^{i*}(\vec{k},t)\hat{\varphi}^{j}(\vec{k},t) + \hat{\varphi}^{i}(\vec{k},t)\hat{\varphi}^{j*}(\vec{k},t)\right] \quad i,j = 1..4, \tag{9}$$

where $\hat{\varphi}^4(\vec{k},t)$ is related to the pressure and takes the following form:

$$\hat{\varphi}^4(\vec{k},t) = I\frac{\hat{p}}{\overline{\rho}a} \tag{10}$$

We then write evolution equations of these doubles correlations:

$$\frac{d\Phi_{11}}{dt} = -2\nu k^2 \Phi_{11} - 2\frac{Sk_3}{k}\Phi_{12} + 2\frac{Sk_2k_3}{kk'}\Phi_{13}, \tag{11}$$

$$\frac{d\Phi_{12}}{dt} = (-2\nu k^2 + \frac{Sk_1k_2}{k^2})\Phi_{12} - \frac{Sk_1}{k'}\Phi_{13} - \frac{Sk_3}{k}\Phi_{22} + \frac{Sk_2k_3}{kk'}\Phi_{23}, \tag{12}$$

$$\frac{d\Phi_{13}}{dt} = 2\frac{Sk_1k'}{k^2}\Phi_{12} - (\frac{7}{3}\nu k^2 + \frac{Sk_1k_2}{k^2})\Phi_{13} - ak\Phi_{14} - \frac{Sk_3}{k}\Phi_{23} + \frac{Sk_2k_3}{kk'}\Phi_{33}, \tag{13}$$

$$\frac{d\Phi_{14}}{dt} = ak\Phi_{13} - \nu k^2\Phi_{14} - \frac{Sk_3}{k}\Phi_{24} + \frac{Sk_2k_3}{kk'}\Phi_{34}, \tag{14}$$

$$\frac{d\Phi_{22}}{dt} = (-2\nu k^2 + 2\frac{Sk_1k_2}{k^2})\Phi_{22} - 2\frac{Sk_1}{k'}\Phi_{23}, \tag{15}$$

$$\frac{d\Phi_{23}}{dt} = 2\frac{Sk_1k'}{k^2}\Phi_{22} - \frac{7}{3}\nu k^2\Phi_{23} - ak\Phi_{24} - \frac{Sk_1}{k'}\Phi_{33}, \tag{16}$$

$$\frac{d\Phi_{24}}{dt} = ak\Phi_{23} + (-\nu k^2 + \frac{Sk_1k_2}{k^2})\Phi_{24} - \frac{Sk_1}{k'}\Phi_{34}, \tag{17}$$

$$\frac{d\Phi_{33}}{dt} = 4\frac{Sk_1k'}{k^2}\Phi_{23} - 2(\frac{4}{3}\nu k^2 + \frac{Sk_1k_2}{k^2})\Phi_{33} - 2ak\Phi_{34}, \tag{18}$$

$$\frac{d\Phi_{34}}{dt} = 2\frac{Sk_1k'}{k^2}\Phi_{24} + ak\Phi_{33} - (\frac{4}{3}\nu k^2 + \frac{Sk_1k_2}{k^2})\Phi_{34} - ak\Phi_{44}, \tag{19}$$

$$\frac{d\Phi_{44}}{dt} = 2ak\Phi_{34}, \tag{20}$$

where $k' = \sqrt{k_1^2 + k_3^2}$ and k_1, k_2, k_3 are the components of the wave vector $\vec{k}$.

Numerical integration of these equations ((11)-(20)) is carried out using a simple second-order accurate scheme:

$$f(t + \Delta t) = f(t) + \Delta t\, f'(t) + \Delta t^2 f''(t)/2, \tag{21}$$

where the derivatives $f'(t)$ and $f''(t)$ are expressed exactly from evolution equations (11)-(20) and Δt is the time-step size.

3. RDTcode validation

3.1. Introduction

In this section, results are presented and used to verify the validity of the RDT code. For this, tests of this code have been performed by comparing RDT results with those of direct numerical simulation (DNS) of Simone et al. (1997) for various values of initial gradient Mach number M_{g0} which describe different regimes of the flow (see below). Comparisons concern the turbulent kinetic energy $q^2(t)/q^2(0)$ [Figs. 1, 2], the non-dimensional production term $\frac{2P}{Sq^2} = -2b_{12}$ [Figs. 3, 4] and the turbulent kinetic energy growth rate $\Lambda = \frac{1}{Sq^2}\frac{dq^2}{dt}$ [Figs. 5, 6]. In the same way, comparisons deal with the solenoidal and the dilatational b_{12} anisotropy tensor components [Figs. 7, 8] (Riahi & Lili, 2011). We note that $b_{12} = \frac{\overline{u_1 u_2}}{q^2}$ is the relevant component of the Reynolds stress anisotropy tensor. Tavoularis & Corrsin (1981) have shown that in the incompressible homogeneous shear flow b_{12} tends toward an equilibrium value which is independent of initial conditions.

Concerning the existence of the evolution zones where shocks develop, we neither observe any anomaly in physic parameters (no problem of realisability), nor any instability in the calculation course. In addition, it is important to specify that our code was not conceived to take explicitly into account the existence of shocks. However, we think that in the applications presented, the flow is not probably contaminated by the appearance of shocks.

3.2. Initial parameters

Intrinsic parameters that characterize the flow include the initial turbulent Mach number $M_{t0} = \frac{q_0}{a}$ (recall that $\frac{1}{2}q_0^2$ is the initial turbulent kinetic energy and a is the mean speed of sound), the initial gradient Mach number $M_{g0} = M_{t0}\, S\frac{q_0^2}{\varepsilon_0}$ (S is the constant mean shear and ε_0 the initial total rate of turbulent kinetic energy dissipation) and the initial turbulent Reynolds number $R_{et0} = \frac{q_0^4}{\nu\varepsilon_0}$. The ratio of the gradient Mach number to the turbulent Mach number $r = S\frac{q_0^2}{\varepsilon_0}$ characterizes the rapidity of the shear.

Table 1 lists ten simulations cases labelled A_1, A_2 … A_{10} corresponding to different values of the initial gradient Mach number M_{g0}. In these simulations, M_{g0} increases respectively in cases A_1 ($M_{g0} = 2.7$) to A_{10} ($M_{g0} = 66.7$) by keeping the same initial value of the turbulent Mach number M_{t0} and the turbulent Reynolds number R_{et0}.

In these cases, the initial turbulent kinetic energy spectrum is similar to that used by Simone (1995),

$$E(K,t_0) = K^4 \exp(-2\frac{K^2}{\kappa_{pic}^2}),$$

where κ_{pic} denotes the wave number corresponding to the peak of the power spectrum and K is the initial wave number.

Case	M_{t0}	M_{g0}	r_0	R_{et0}
A_1	0.25	2.7	10.7	296
A_2	0.25	4	16	296
A_3	0.25	8.3	33.1	296
A_4	0.25	12	48	296
A_5	0.25	16.5	66.2	296
A_6	0.25	24	96.1	296
A_7	0.25	32	128.1	296
A_8	0.25	42.7	170.8	296
A_9	0.25	53.4	213.5	296
A_{10}	0.25	66.7	266.9	296

Table 1. Initial parameters.

3.3. Results and discussion

All Figures 1-8 validate RDT approach and numerical code for low values of the non-dimensional times *St* (until 3.5). Indeed, comparisons carried out between our RDT results (Riahi & Lili, 2011) and DNS results of Simone et al. (1997) show that the linear analysis predicted correctly – as well qualitatively as quantitatively – the behavior of turbulence in particular for small values of *St*.

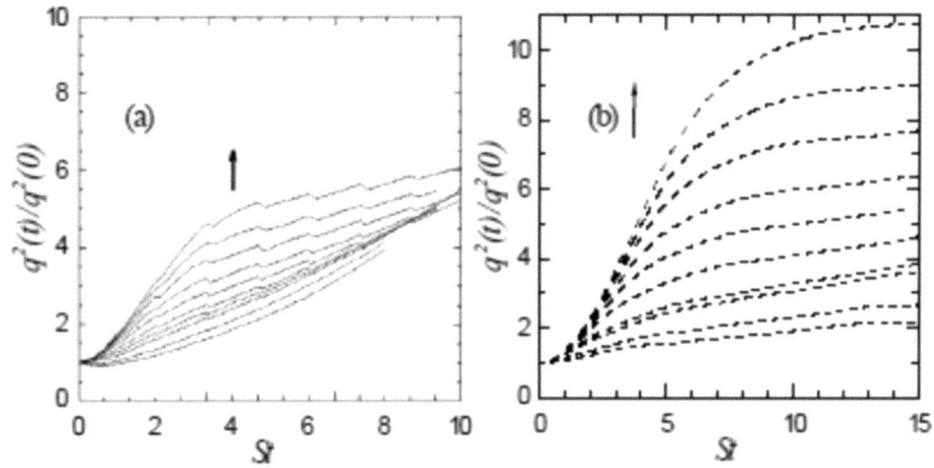

Figure 1. Histories of the turbulent kinetic energy for pure-shear flow: (a) DNS results of Simone et al. (1997) and (b) our RDT results. Initial gradient Mach number M_{g0} ranges from 2.7 to 67 for both DNS and RDT; arrows show trend with increasing M_{g0}.

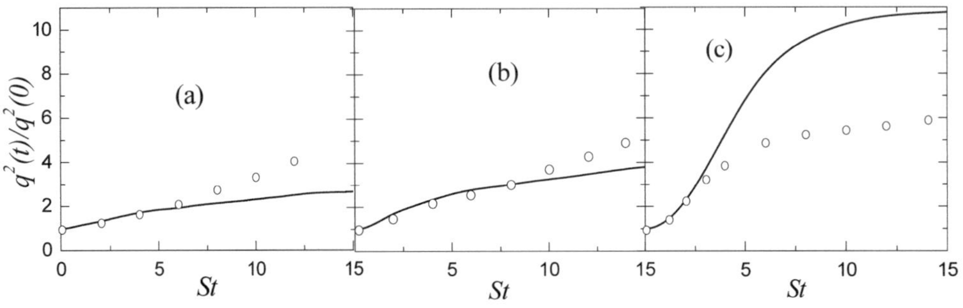

Figure 2. Evolution of the turbulent kinetic energy (a) case A_2 ($M_{g0} = 4$), (b) case A_4 ($M_{g0} = 12$) and (c) case A_{10} ($M_{g0} = 66.7$). —— : RDT results, o : DNS results of Simone et al. (1997).

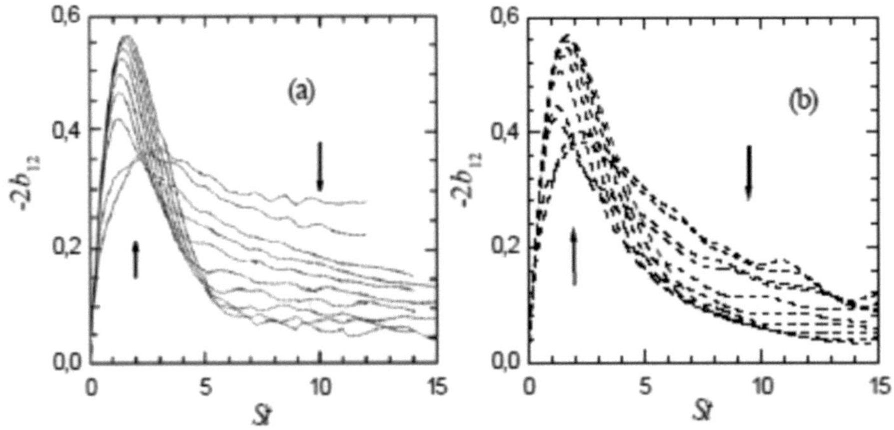

Figure 3. Histories of the non-dimensional production term $-2b_{12}$ for pure-shear flow: (a) DNS results of Simone et al. (1997) and (b) our RDT results. Initial gradient Mach number M_{g0} ranges from 2.7 to 67 for both DNS and RDT; arrows show trend with increasing M_{g0}.

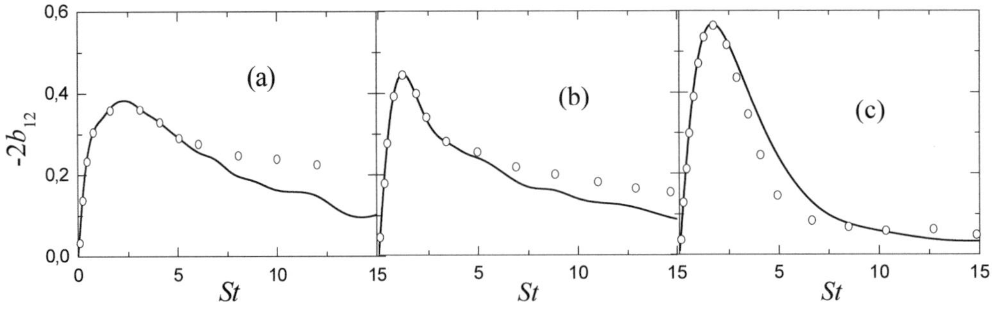

Figure 4. Evolution of the non-dimensional production term (a) case A_2 ($M_{g0} = 4$), (b) case A_4 ($M_{g0} = 12$) and (c) case A_{10} ($M_{g0} = 66.7$). —— : RDT results, o : DNS results of Simone et al. (1997).

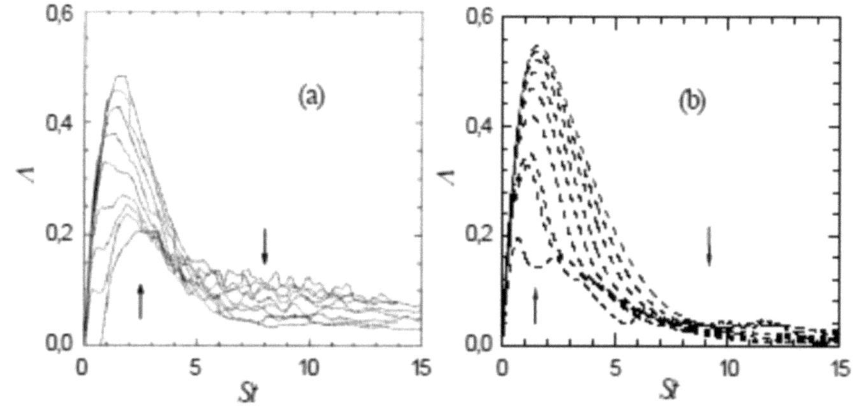

Figure 5. Histories of the temporal energy growth rate for pure-shear flow: (a) DNS results of Simone et al. (1997) and (b) our RDT results. Initial gradient Mach number M_{g0} ranges from 2.7 to 67 for both DNS and RDT; arrows show trend with increasing M_{g0}.

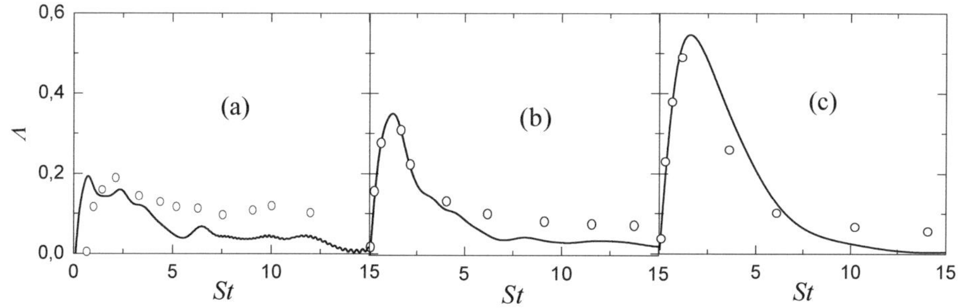

Figure 6. Evolution of the turbulent kinetic energy growth rate (a) case A_2 (M_{g0} = 4), (b) case A_4 (M_{g0} = 12) and (c) case A_{10} (M_{g0} = 66.7). ——— : RDT results, o : DNS results of Simone et al. (1997).

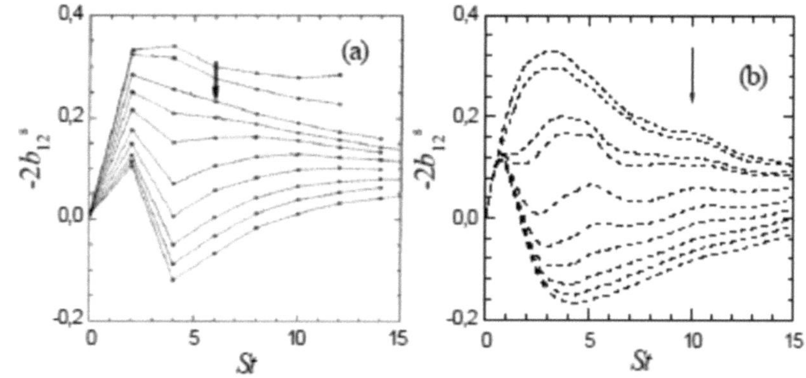

Figure 7. Histories of the solenoidal b_{12} component anisotropy tensor for pure-shear: (a) DNS results of Simone et al. (1997) and (b) our RDT results. Initial gradient Mach number M_{g0} ranges from 2.7 to 67 for both DNS and RDT; arrows show trend with increasing M_{g0}.

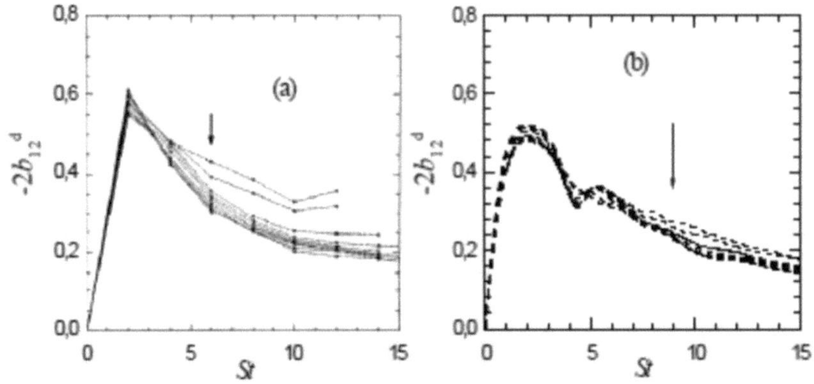

Figure 8. Histories of the dilatational b_{12} component anisotropy tensor for pure-shear flow: (a) DNS results of Simone et al. (1997) and (b) our RDT results. Initial gradient Mach number M_{g0} ranges from 2.7 to 67 for both DNS and RDT; arrows show trend with increasing M_{g0}.

In the compressible regime (M_{t0} = 0.25 and M_{g0} = 66.7), RDT and DNS equilibrium values of the non-dimensional production -2b_{12} of Simone et al. (1997) are very close [Fig. 4(c)]. As one can remark from this figure that for large values of St (St > 10), there is a small difference between RDT and DNS results of Simone et al. (1997). Thus, in this compressible regime, RDT predicts correctly equilibrium behavior of the turbulence (asymptotic behavior $(St \to \infty)$) relatively to the non-dimensional production -2b_{12} (strongly compressible regime M_{g0} = 66.7 >> 1 and r_0 >> 1) which is a rapid distortion regime compatible with the framework of RDT. The intermediate regime (case A4, M_{g0} = 12) and especially the incompressible regime, for which non-linear effects are preponderant, are poorly estimated by RDT for large values of St. Moreover, Simone et al. (1997) indicate, as general conclusion that compressibility effects on homogeneous sheared turbulence, concerning particularly b_{12} and the non-dimensional production, which are generally associated with non linear phenomena, can be explained in terms of RDT. So, non linear and dissipative effects (through the non linear cascade) are not significant for predicting equilibrium states for strongly compressible regime (Simone et al., 1997). Consequently, we can justify the resort to RDT in order to determine equilibrium states in the compressible regime.

In Figures 9-11, we present evolutions of b_{12} (which is linked to production), b_{11} and b_{22} components anisotropy tensor in the incompressible (M_{g0} = 2.2) and intermediate regimes (M_{g0} = 13.2). In the incompressible regime, as illustrated in Figures 9(a), 10(a), 11(a), we confirm that RDT validity is limited for small values of St; considerable differences appear between RDT and DNS results of Sarkar (1995) beyond. With RDT, it is not possible to predict evolution of sheared turbulence for large values of St. Consequently, we can't predict, by means of RDT, equilibrium states of sheared turbulence in the incompressible regime. We note that in the intermediate regime [Figs. 9(b), 10(b), 11(b)], the behavior of DNS results of Sarkar (1995) concerning b_{12}, b_{11} and b_{22} seems to be compatible with RDT results for large values of St. In the intermediate zone of St (between small and large values of St) differences are appreciable.

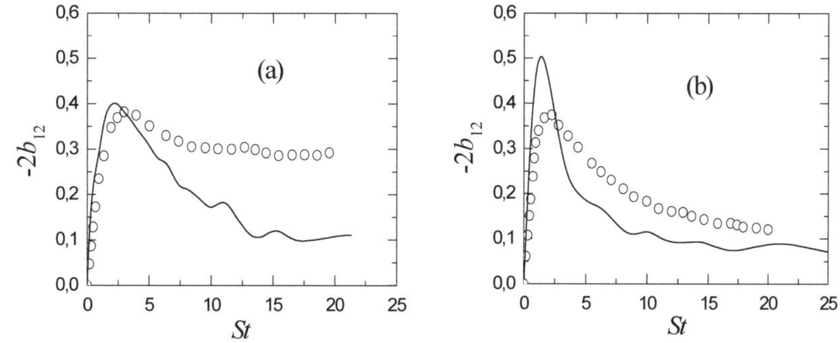

Figure 9. Evolution of the non-dimensional production term with (a): $M_{g0} = 2.2$ and (b): $M_{g0} = 13.2$. ——— : RDT results, o : DNS results of Sarkar (1995).

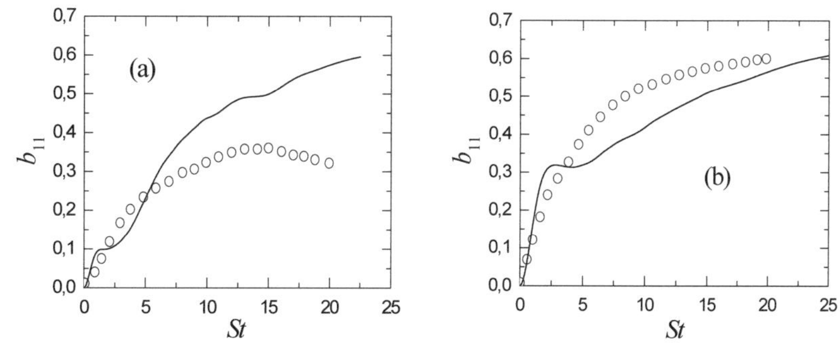

Figure 10. Evolution of b_{11} component anisotropy tensor with (a): $M_{g0} = 2.2$ and (b): $M_{g0} = 13.2$. ——— : RDT results, o : DNS results of Sarkar (1995).

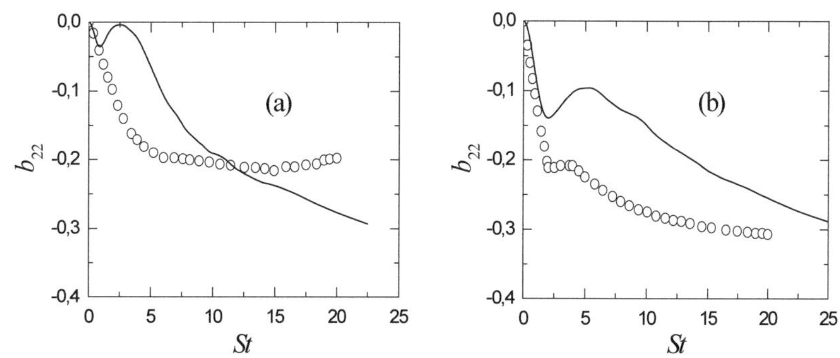

Figure 11. Evolution of b_{22} component anisotropy tensor with (a): $M_{g0} = 2.2$ and (b): $M_{g0} = 13.2$. ——— : RDT results, o : DNS results of Sarkar (1995).

In conclusion, RDT is valid for small values of the non-dimensional times St ($St < 3.5$). RDT is also valid for large values of St ($St > 10$) in particular for large values of M_{g0}. This essential feature justifies the resort to RDT in order to critically study equilibrium states in the compressible regime.

4. Various regimes of flow

The various curves of Figure 1(b) permit to determine different regimes of the flow (Riahi & Lili, 2011). This figure shows that there is an increase in the turbulent kinetic energy when M_{g0} increases for various cases considered $A_1,\ldots,A_{10}$. In addition, when initial gradient Mach number increases, we observe a break of slope which is accentuated when the value of M_{g0} becomes more significant. It appears from this figure that the turbulent kinetic energy varies quasi-linearly in cases A_1 and A_2, where M_{g0} takes respectively values 2.7 and 4. These two values of M_{g0} correspond to the incompressible regime. A weak amplification of the turbulent kinetic energy shows that cases A_4 ($M_{g0} = 12$) and A_{10} ($M_{g0} = 66.7$) correspond to the intermediate regime. From $M_{g0} = 16.5$, the regime becomes compressible. Indeed, cases $A_5,\ldots,$ A_{10} show a significant amplification of the total kinetic energy more and more marked when the initial gradient Mach number M_{g0} increases.

These different regimes permit to better understanding compressibility effects on structure of homogeneous sheared turbulence and to analyze the causes of turbulence structure modification generated by compressibility.

Several explanations were proposed these last years to analyze causes of the stabilising effect of compressibility which are still not cleared up.

5. Compressibility effects on structure of homogeneous sheared turbulence

5.1. Introduction

The study of compressibility effects on the turbulent homogeneous shear flow behavior made these last years the objective of several researches as mentioned in the works of Blaisdell et al. (1993 & 1996) and Sarkar et al. (1991 & 1992). DNS developed by Sarkar (1995) show that the temporal growth rate of the turbulent kinetic energy is extensively influenced by compressibility. Simone et al. (1997) identified the new coupling term in the quasi-isentropic RDT equations, which was responsible for long-term stabilization, comparing incompressible and compressible RDT. They concluded that the modification of the compressible turbulence structure is due to linear processes.

The prediction of compressible turbulent flows by rapid distortion theory provides useful results which can be used to clarify the physics of the compressible turbulent flows and to study compressibility effects on structure of homogeneous sheared turbulence. This study is important for the analysis of various physical mechanisms which characteristic the turbulence. Thus, physical comprehension of compressibility effects on turbulence leads it possible to better predict compressible turbulent flows and to improve existing turbulence models. The Helmoltz decomposition of the velocity field in solenoidal and dilatational parts reveals two additional terms in the turbulent kinetic energy budget. Several studies of the behavior of the different terms present in this budget and the Reynolds stress equations show the role of the explicit compressible terms. From Simone et al. (1997) and Sarkar (1995), for the case in which the rate of shear is much larger than the rate of non-linear interactions of the turbulence, amplification of turbulent kinetic energy by the mean shear caused by compressibility is due to the implicit pressure-strain correlations effects and to the anisotropy of the Reynolds stress tensor. These authors also recommend to take into account correctly the explicit dilatational terms such as the pressure-dilatation correlation and the dilatational dissipation. In contrast, the role of explicit terms was over-estimated by Zeman (1990) and Sarkar et al. (1991). These last authors show that both those terms have a dissipative contribution in shear flow, leading to the reduced growth of the turbulent kinetic energy.

The study of the budget behaviors of the turbulent kinetic energy and the Reynolds stress anisotropy by RDT enables to better understand and explain compressibility effects on structure and evolution of a sheared homogeneous turbulence.

5.2. The turbulent kinetic energy equation

In the case of homogeneous turbulence, the turbulent kinetic energy is written (Simone, 1995) as:

$$\frac{d}{dt}\left(\frac{q^2}{2}\right) = P - \varepsilon_s - \varepsilon_d + \Pi_d, \qquad (22)$$

in which $P = -S\overline{u_1 u_2}$ is the rate of production by the mean flow and $\Pi_d = \overline{p u_{i,i}}$ the pressure-dilatation correlation. $\varepsilon_s = \nu\,\overline{\omega_i \omega_i}$ and $\varepsilon_d = \frac{4}{3}\nu\,\overline{u_{i,i} u_{i,i}}$ are respectively the solenoidal and the dilatational parts of the turbulent dissipation rate given that ω_i is the fluctuating vorticity and $u_{i,i}$ denotes the fluctuating divergence of velocity. ε_s represents the turbulent dissipation arising from the traditional energy cascade which is solenoidal, ε_d represents the turbulent dissipation arising from dilatational regimes. Note that the last two terms on the right-hand side in equation (22) do not appear when the flow is incompressible. The explicit/energetic approach is embodied in the modeling of ε_d and Π_d done by Zeman (1990), Sarkar et al. (1991) and others.

5.3. Results

Figures 12(a), (b), (c) show the budget of the turbulent kinetic energy for three values of initial gradient Mach number (respectively 1, 12 and 66.7) which describe the various regimes of the flow (Riahi & Lili, 2011). It will be shown from Figures 12(b), (c) that the production P and the pressure-dilatation Π_d intervene significantly in this budget. In the compressible regime [Fig. 12(c)], the production is dominating and the pressure-dilatation Π_d remains with relatively low values (practically null until $St = 1$). Figure 12(a) shows the results for $M_{g0} = 1$ and $M_{t0} = 0.1$ (case A_0). In this case, it is still the production which is dominating. The explicitly compressible terms which are the dilatational dissipation rate ε_d and the pressure-dilatation Π_d are not negligible in spite of the small value of the initial gradient Mach number M_{g0}. Consequently, we can affirm that "the incompressible behavior" cannot be obtained in the borderline case of low values of M_{g0}; that's why we preferred to give the results for $M_{g0} = 1$ and not for $M_{g0} = 2.7$ and 4 with an aim of better approaching the "incompressible limit".

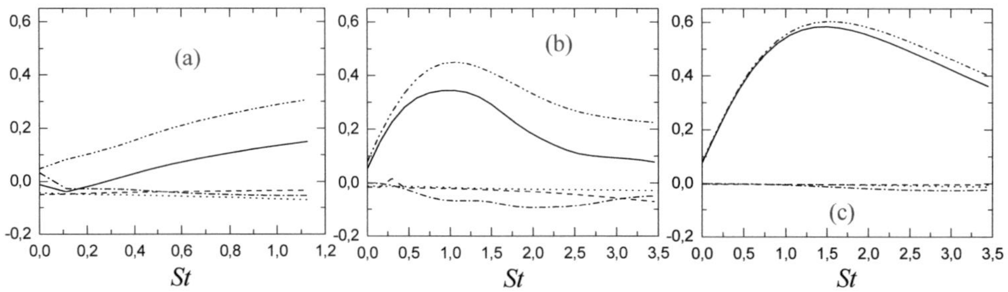

Figure 12. The turbulent kinetic energy budget (a) case A_0 ($M_{g0} = 1$), (b) case A_4 ($M_{g0} = 12$) and (c) case A_{10} ($M_{g0} = 66.7$). —— : $\frac{d}{dt}(\frac{q^2}{2}) = P - \varepsilon_s - \varepsilon_d + \Pi_d$, -···- : rate of the turbulent production (P), ···: rate of the solenoidal dissipation $(-\varepsilon_s)$, --- : rate of the dilatational dissipation $(-\varepsilon_d)$, -··- : pressure-dilatation correlation term (Π_d).

In conclusion, compressibility affects more the turbulent production term which represents the dominating parameter in the turbulent kinetic energy budget. In the compressible regime, the production becomes preponderant. This property is already observed in the analysis of the budget of the Reynolds stress equations related to $\overline{u_1^2}$ and $\overline{u_1 u_2}$ (Riahi et al., 2007).

In Figures 13(a), (b), (c), (d) are represented the different components of the anisotropy tensor b_{ij}. These figures show obviously a remarkable property concerning the anisotropy. In fact, it appears clearly that the anisotropy increases with M_{g0} i.e. with compressibility and that it is responsible of the behavior of $\overline{u_1^2}$ which becomes dominating compared to $\overline{u_2^2}$ and $\overline{u_3^2}$ in the compressible case ($M_{g0} = 66.7$). As an indication, $\frac{\overline{u_1^2}}{\overline{u_2^2}} = 12.62$ and $\frac{\overline{u_1^2}}{\overline{u_3^2}} = 13.11$ for $St = 3.5$.

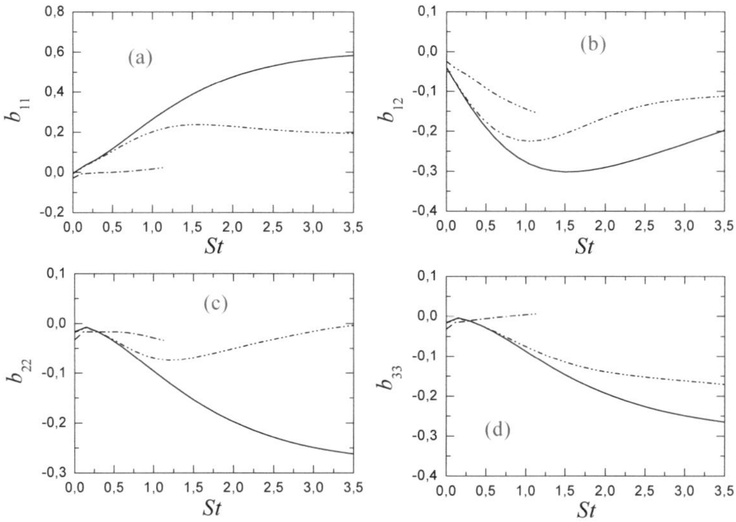

Figure 13. Components evolution of the anisotropy tensor (a) b_{11}, (b) b_{12}, (c) b_{22} and (d) b_{33}. – · – : case A_0 (M_{g0} = 1), — · · : case A_4 (M_{g0} = 12), ——— : case A_{10} (M_{g0} = 66.7).

6. Equilibrium states of homogeneous compressible turbulence

RDT is also used to determine equilibrium states in the compressible regime (Riahi & Lili, 2011) in particular for large values of *St* (*St* > 10) and M_{g0}. Evolution of the relevant component of Reynolds stress anisotropy tensor b_{12} is presented in Figure 14 for different values of the initial gradient Mach number M_{g0} (66.7, 200, 500 and 1000). Numerical results show that, for large values of *St*, b_{12} is independent of the initial turbulent Mach number M_{t0} as shown in Figure 14(a) (M_{t0} = 0.25) and in Figure 14(b) (M_{t0} = 0.6). As one can remark also from these results that b_{12} reaches its stationary value all the more quickly as M_{g0} is large (M_{g0} = 1000). At this stage, we study equilibrium states corresponding to M_{g0} = 1000, value which we assimilate to M_{g0} arbitrarily large (M_{g0} infinity). We present now some properties relative to these equilibrium states corresponding to pressure-released regime. The case corresponding to pressure-released limit has been discussed by Cambon et al. (1993), Simone et al. (1997) and Livescu et al. (2004). We begin by presenting equilibrium values of Reynolds stress anisotropy components: $\left(b_{11}\right)_\infty$ = 0.66, $\left(b_{22}\right)_\infty = \left(b_{33}\right)_\infty$ = - 0.33 and $\left(b_{12}\right)_\infty$ = 0. These values confirm the independence of the anisotropy tensor with M_{t0} in the pressure-released regime; calculation gives effectively these values for M_{t0} = 0.25, 0.4, 0.5 and 0.6. Pressure-released state corresponds thus to a particular state of one-component turbulence in the direction of the shear (x_1 direction): $\left(\overline{u_1^2}\right)_\infty = q^2$, $\left(\overline{u_2^2}\right)_\infty = 0$ and $\left(\overline{u_3^2}\right)_\infty = 0$.

Another interesting property of the pressure-released regime is the quadratic increase of $\overline{u_1^2}$ as shown in Figure 15 related to $M_{g0} = 10^6$ and M_{t0} = 0.25 (Riahi & Lili, 2011). This property has been established by Livescu et al. (2004) as analytical RDT solution in the pressure-released limit.

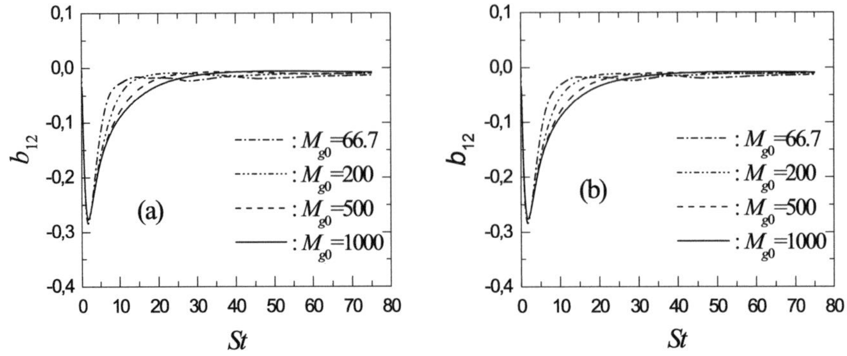

Figure 14. Evolution of the relevant component of the Reynolds stress anisotropy tensor b_{12} for various values of initial gradient Mach number M_{g0} with (a): $M_{t0} = 0.25$ and (b): $M_{t0} = 0.6$.

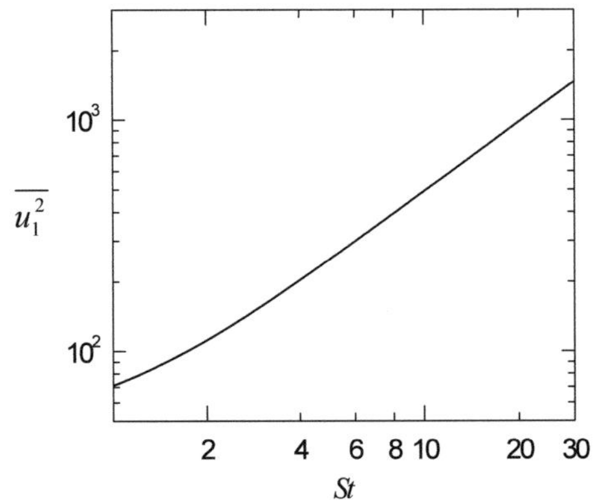

Figure 15. Quadratic evolution of $\overline{u_1^2}$.

Table 2 lists equilibrium values of the normalized dissipation rate due to dilatation $\left(\frac{\varepsilon_d}{\varepsilon_s + \varepsilon_d}\right)_\infty$, the normalized pressure-dilatation correlation $\left(\frac{\overline{pd}}{Sq^2}\right)_\infty$ and the normalized pressure variance $\left(\frac{\overline{p^2}}{\overline{\rho}^2 q^4}\right)_\infty$ for various values of initial turbulent Mach number M_{t0} (Riahi & Lili, 2011). From this table, we deduce the dependence of all these parameters with M_{t0}.

Figure 16 shows variation of the equilibrium normalized pressure variance $\left(\frac{\overline{p^2}}{\overline{\rho}^2 q^4}\right)_\infty$ with various initial turbulent Mach number ($M_{t0} = 0.25$, 0.4, 0.5 and 0.6 ($M_{t0} = 0.6$ is relatively high initial turbulent Mach number)) (Riahi & Lili, 2011). From this figure, it can be seen that this parameter can be written as $\left(\frac{\overline{p^2}}{\overline{\rho}^2 q^4}\right)_\infty = (M_{t0})^\alpha$ where $\alpha = 5.8$.

Equilibrium parameters \ M_{t0}	0.25	0.4	0.5	0.6
$\left(\frac{\varepsilon_d}{\varepsilon_s+\varepsilon_d}\right)_\infty$	0.0410	0.0277	0.0230	0.0197
$\left(\frac{\overline{pd}}{Sq^2}\right)_\infty$	0.000387	0.000311	0.000280	0.000257
$\left(\frac{\overline{p^2}}{\bar{\rho}^2 q^4}\right)_\infty$	0.00937	0.00278	0.00156	0.000973

Table 2. Equilibrium values of the normalized dissipation rate due to dilatation, the normalized pressure-dilatation and the normalized pressure variance for various initial turbulent Mach number M_{t0}.

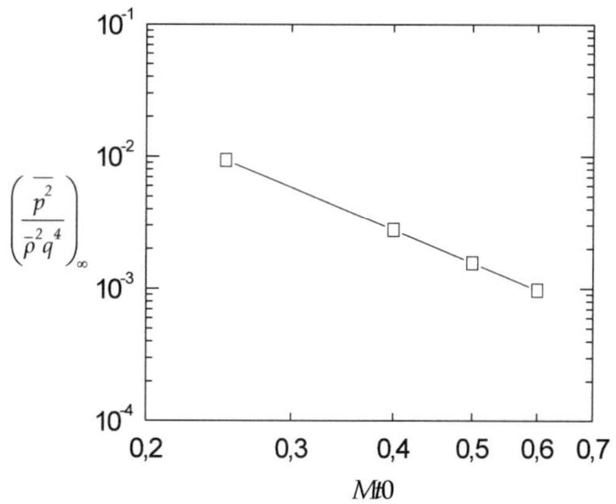

Figure 16. Variation of the equilibrium normalized pressure variance with various initial turbulent Mach number (M_{t0} = 0.25, 0.4, 0.5 and 0.6).

7. Turbulence model to be tested

7.1. Introduction

RDT is an efficient and accurate method for testing linear turbulence models. The Fujiwara and Arakawa model (1995) has been proposed in literature for pressure-dilatation correlation studying compressible turbulence. In order to verify its capacity to describe the homogeneous compressible flow, since it was established to this objective, three cases of the initial gradient Mach number (M_{g0} = 1, 12 and 66.7) are considered. The evaluation of this model, in the different regimes of flow, stays in the field of RDT validity (Riahi & Lili, 2011). Its detailed linear form is provided below.

7.2. Fujiwara and Arakawa model

The model suggested by Fujiwara and Arakawa (1995) for the pressure-dilatation correlation takes into account the compressible part (dilatational) of the kinetic energy (q_d^2). Linear part of this model has the following form:

$$\Pi_d = C_1 \bar{\rho} q^2 b_{ij} \sqrt{\frac{q_d^2}{q^2}} \frac{\partial U_i}{\partial x_j},$$

where $C_1 = 0.3$ and ε is the turbulent dissipation rate. b_{ij} is the Reynolds anisotropy tensor.

7.3. Results

Comparison between RDT and Fujiwara and Arakawa (1995) model results concerning the pressure-dilatation correlation term Π_d are represented in Figures 17(a), (b), (c). As one can remark from these results, that the contribution of Π_d obtained by this model is negligible. Except in the case of the intermediate regime (M_{g0} = 12), the Fujiwara and Arakawa model does not represent an appreciable discrepancies with the RDT results.

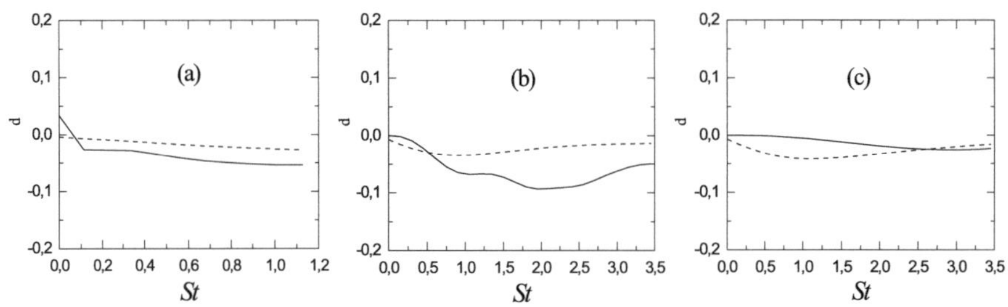

Figure 17. Evolution of the pressure dilatation correlation term Π_d (a) case A0 (M_{g0} = 1), (b) case A4 (M_{g0} = 12) and (c) case A10 (M_{g0} = 66.7). ——— : RDT results, - - - : Fujiwara and Arakawa model.

8. Conclusion

Rapid distortion theory (RDT) is a computationally viable option for examining linear compressible flow physics in the absence of inertial effects. Evolution of compressible homogeneous turbulence has been described completely by finding numerical solutions obtained by solving linear double correlations spectra evolution. Numerical integration of these equations has been carried out using a second-order simple and accurate scheme. This numerical method has proved more stable and faster and allows in particular to obtain accurately the asymptotic behavior of the turbulence parameters (for large values of *St*) characteristic of equilibrium states. In this chapter, RDT code developed by authors solves linearized equations for compressible homogeneous shear flows (Riahi & Lili, 2011). It has been validated by comparing RDT results with direct numerical simulation (DNS) of Simone et al. (1997) and Sarkar (1995) for various values of initial gradient Mach number M_{g0} which is the key parameter controlling the level of compressibility. The study of the behavior of the non-dimensional turbulent kinetic energy $q^2(t)/q^2(0)$ permit to determine various regimes of flow. This study allows to check relevance of an incompressible regime for low values of initial gradient Mach number M_{g0}, of an intermediate regime for moderate values of M_{g0} and of a compressible regime for high values of M_{g0}. Agreement between RDT and DNS of Simone et al. (1997) and Sarkar (1995) is obtained for small values of the non-dimensional times St ($St < 3.5$). This agreement gives new insight into compressibility effects and reveals the extent to which linear processes are responsible for modifying the structure of compressible turbulence. The behavior analysis of the various terms presented in the turbulent kinetic energy budget shows that compressibility affects more the turbulent production which becomes preponderant in the compressible regime. This property is already observed in the analysis of the budget of the Reynolds stress equations related to $\overline{u_1^2}$ and $\overline{u_1 u_2}$. Another important property reveals that anisotropy increases with compressibility.

Agreement of RDT with DNS (Simone et al., 1997) found for large values of St ($St > 10$) in particular for large values of M_{g0} which allows to determine equilibrium states in the compressible regime. Evolution of the relevant component of the Reynolds stress anisotropy tensor b_{12}, for different values of initial gradient Mach number M_{g0} (66.7, 200, 500 and 1000) and for large values of St, shows that b_{12} is independent of the initial turbulent Mach number M_{t0} (which is a parameter characterizing the effects of compressibility). In addition, b_{12} becomes stationary all the more quickly as M_{g0} is large (M_{g0} = 1000). Considering equilibrium states associated to this value of M_{g0} as representative of equilibrium states related to infinite M_{g0} (pressure-released regime), equilibrium values of the Reynolds stress anisotropy components $(b_{11})_\infty$ and $(b_{22})_\infty$ are independent of the initial turbulent Mach number M_{t0}. In contrast, equilibrium values of the normalized dissipation rate due to dilatation, the normalized pressure-dilatation correlation and the normalized pressure variance are dependent of M_{t0}. Variation of the equilibrium normalized pressure variance with various initial turbulent Mach number (M_{t0} = 0.25, 0.4, 0.5 and 0.6) can be written as $\left(\frac{\overline{p^2}}{\overline{\rho}^2 q^4}\right)_\infty = (M_{t0})^{\alpha}$ where $\alpha = 5.8$.

In conclusion, after a critical analysis, we were able to justify that RDT permits to well identify compressibility effects in order to develop models taking them into account satisfactorily. The analysis of rapid distortion theory showed that it is possible to better understand the compressible turbulent flows. In addition, RDT is valid to predict asymptotic equilibrium states for compressible homogeneous sheared turbulence for large values of initial gradient Mach number (pressure-released regime). RDT is an efficient method for testing linear contribution of turbulence models.

Author details

Mohamed Riahi and Taieb Lili
Faculté des Sciences de Tunis, Département de Physique, Laboratoire de Mécanique des Fluides, Campus Universitaire, Manar II, Tunis, Tunisia

Abbreviations

RDT Rapid Distortion Theory
DNS Direct Numerical Simulation

Nomenclature

M_g, M_{g0}	gradient Mach number, initial gradient Mach number
M_t, M_{t0}	turbulent Mach number, initial turbulent Mach number
S	magnitude of the mean velocity gradient
u_i	velocity fluctuation
p	pressure fluctuation
$\bar{\rho}$	mean density
ν	kinematic viscosity
λ_{ij}	mean velocity gradient
a	mean sound speed
Δt	time-step size
$q^2/2$	turbulent kinetic energy
$b_{ij} = \frac{\overline{u_i u_j}}{q^2} - \frac{\delta_{ij}}{3}$	anisotropy tensor
ε_0	initial total (solenoidal and dilatational) dissipation rate of turbulent kinetic energy
R_{et0}	initial turbulent Reynolds number
r_0	initial rapidity of the shear
γ	ratio of specific heats

9. References

Blaisdell, G.A.; Mansour, N.N. & Reynolds, W.C. (1993). Compressibility effects on the growth and structure of homogeneous turbulent shear flow. *Journal of Fluid Mechanics*, vol. 256, pp. 443-485.

Blaisdell, G. A.; Coleman, G. N. & Mansour, N. N. (1996). Rapid distortion theory for compressible homogenous turbulence under isotropic mean strain. *Physics of Fluids*, vol. 8, pp. 2692-2705.

Coleman, G. N. & Mansour, N. N. (1991). Modeling the rapid spherical compression of isotropic turbulence, *Physics of Fluids*, vol. A 3, pp. 2255-2259.

Cambon, C.; Coleman, G.N. & Mansour, N.N. (1993). Rapid distortion analysis and direct simulation of compressible homogeneous turbulence at finite Mach number. *Journal of Fluid Mechanics*, vol. 257, pp. 641-665.

Durbin, P.A. & Zeman, O. (1992). Rapid distortion theory for homogeneous compressed turbulence with application to modelling. *Journal of Fluid Mechanics*, vol. 242, pp. 349-370.

Fujiwara, H. & Arakawa, C. (1995). Modeling the pressure-dilatation correlation in isotropic and homogeneous sheared turbulence. *Proc. 10th Symposium on Turbulent Shear Flows*, vol. 26, pp. 1-6.

Hunt, J. C. R. & Carruthers, D. J. (1990). Rapid distortion theory and the problems of turbulence. *Journal of Fluid Mechanics*, vol. 212, pp. 497-532.

Jacquin, L.; Cambon, C. & Blin, E. (1993). Turbulence amplification by a shock wave and rapid distortion theory. *Physics of Fluids*, vol. A 5, pp. 2539-2550.

Livescu D. & Madnia, C. K. (2004). Small Scale Structure of Homogeneous Turbulent Shear Flow. *Physics of Fluids*, vol. 16, pp. 2864-2876.

Riahi, M.; Chouchane, L. & Lili, T. (2007). A study of compressibility effects on structure of homogeneous sheared turbulence. *The European Physical Journal Applied Physics*, vol. 39, Issue: 1, pp. 67-75.

Riahi, M. (2008). Modélisation et simulation d'une turbulence homogène compressible. *Thèse de Doctorat, Faculté des Sciences Mathématiques Physiques et Naturelles de Tunis*, Tunisie.

Riahi, M.; & Lili, T. (2011). Equilibrium states of homogeneous sheared compressible turbulence, *AIP Advances*, vol. 1, Issue: 2, pp. 022117-022117-11, ISSN 2158-3226.

Savill, A. M. (1987). Recent Developments in Rapid-Distortion Theory. *Annual Review of Fluid Mechanics*, vol. 19 pp. 531-573.

Sarkar, S.; Erlebacher, G.; Hussaini, M. & Kreiss, H.O. (1991). The analysis and modelling of dilatational terms in compressible turbulence. *Journal of Fluid Mechanics*, vol. 227, pp. 473-493.

Sarkar, S. (1992). The pressure-dilatation correlation in compressible flows, *Physics of Fluids*, vol. A 4, pp. 2674-2682.

Sarkar, S. (1995). The stabilizing effect of compressibility in turbulent shear flow. *Journal of Fluid Mechanics*, vol. 282, pp. 163-186.

Simone, A.; Coleman, G.N. & Cambon, C. (1997). The effect of compressibility on turbulent shear flow: a rapid-distortion-theory and direct-numerical-simulation study. *Journal of Fluid Mechanics*, vol. 330, (July 1996), pp. 307-338.

Simone, A. (1995). Etude théorique et simulation numérique de la turbulence compressible en présence de cisaillement ou de variation de volume à grande échelle. *Thèse de Doctorat, Ecole Centrale de Lyon*, France.

Tavoularis, S. & Corrsin, S. (1981). Experiments in nearly homogeneous turbulent shear flow with a uniform mean gradient temperature. *Part I. Journal of Fluid Mechanics*, vol. 104, pp. 311-347.

Zeman, O. (1990). Dilatation dissipation: The concept and application in modeling compressible mixing layers. *Physics of Fluids*, vol. 2, pp. 178-188, ISSN 0899-8213.

Chapter 19

Numerical Simulation of Droplet Dynamics in Membrane Emulsification Systems

Manabendra Pathak

Additional information is available at the end of the chapter

http://dx.doi.org/10.5772/50180

1. Introduction

An emulsion is a two-phase liquid system of two immiscible liquids, where the liquid with lower mass fraction is dispersed in form of small droplets in other surrounding liquid of higher mass fraction. Emulsions are widely used to produce sol–gel, drugs, synthetic materials, and food products. Based on the size of droplet, emulsions can be classified as micro and macro emulsion. Karbstein and Schubert, (1995) have made a limiting droplet size of 0.1 μm, below which the emulsion is termed as micro emulsion and above that size the emulsion is termed as macro emulsion. Size and size distribution of droplets play important roles in the stability of emulsion. There are also other factors such as sedimentation, skimming, droplet aggregation and coalescence, which may affect the stability of the droplets. Thus for making a stable emulsion it is necessary to convert the dispersed phase into tiny droplets and stabilize them against coalescence. Some amount of energy is required in the process to break the dispersed phase into droplets. The amount of energy put in the dispersing phase also controls the resulting droplet size. The stability of newly formed droplets depends on how fast the used emulsifiers are able to occupy the newly created interfaces and how well they stabilize them. The common devices used to produce emulsions are rotor-stator-systems, stirrers and high-pressure homogenizers. During last two decades, new technologies of making emulsion have been developed. Compared to conventional method of emulsification such as rotor-stator method, these new techniques of emulsification have several advantages such as low energy consumption, controllable droplet size with proper distribution and easy scalability. These new methods are based on the microdroplet formation in micrometer sized channels. Three such new methods are T-junction emulsification, flow focusing emulsification, and membrane emulsification. In all these methods, controllable droplet formations are achieved by properly maintaining the combination of continuous and dispersed phase flow rate.

In membrane emulsification process, micro or macro porous membranes are used to generate droplets by pressing the dispersed phase through the porous matrix of the membrane towards the continuous phase. At the interface, the dispersed phase forms droplets near the region of pores openings and detached by the cross-flowing continuous phase. Sometimes surfactants are used to stabilize the droplets. Compared to the conventional method, membrane emulsification process requires a lower energy input (10^5 – 10^6 J/m^3) to generate micro-sized droplets (Schubert and Behrend, 2003). Since small droplets are directly formed at the micro-pores of a membrane, rather than by disruption in zones of high energy density, smaller amount of stress is required in the process compared to the conventional method. The main disadvantage of the process is the requirement of longer production time compared to the conventional processes because of the slow rate at which the dispersed phase flows through the membrane (Joscelyne and Trägårdh, 1991, 2000). The longer production time can be reduced by increasing the flow rate of dispersed phase fluid. With the increase in dispersed phase flow rate, the droplet diameter increases first than decreases and the process shifts towards jetting phenomenon (Pathak, 2011). Thus there should be an optimum dispersed phase flux for optimum production time and droplet size in a membrane emulsification system.

The schematic diagram of a cross-flow membrane emulsification has been shown in Fig. 1. Some commonly used membranes are tubular micro-porous glass (MPG) and shirasu porous glass (SPG) membrane. Some metallic oxides such as ceramic α-Al_2O_3 or α-Al_2O_3 coated with titainia oxide or zirconia oxide are also used as membrane. These membranes contain cylindrical, interconnected, uniform micro-pores having pore sizes, typically ranging about 0.05–14 μm. In membrane emulsification system, the time of droplets formation, size and stability of droplets are three important parameters which control the emulsification system. Thus understanding the droplet dynamics in detail may enable to explore the possibilities and limits of membrane emulsification for various applications.

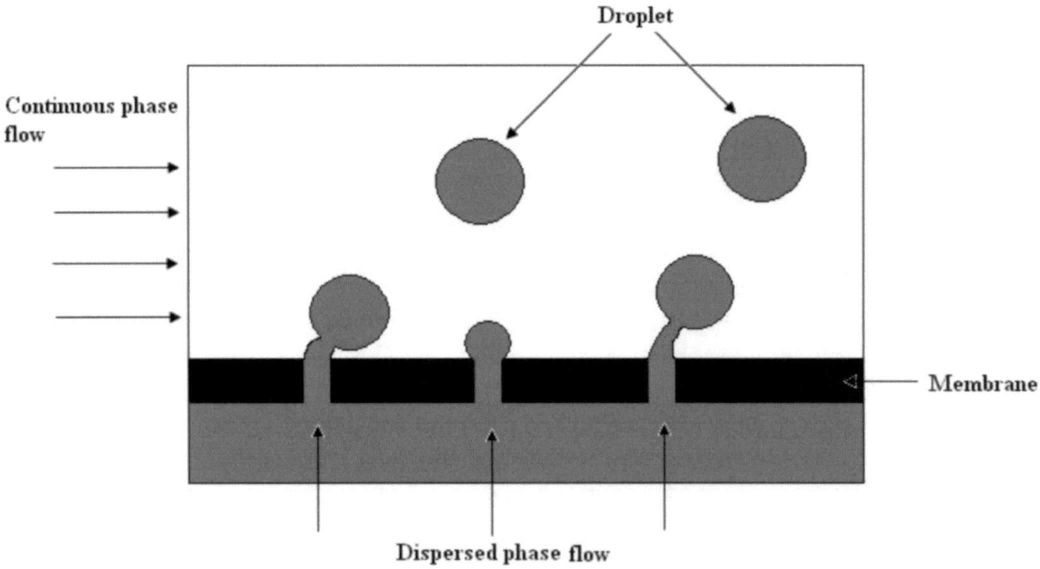

Figure 1. Schematic diagram of a cross-flow membrane emulsification process

In membrane emulsification process, the size distribution of pores and their relative spatial distribution in the membrane surface control the production of mono-disperse emulsions. The growth and detachment of the droplet i.e. droplet dynamics in membrane emulsification depends on several parameters. Luca et al., (2004) has classified them into three broad categories.

i. **Operating parameters:** cross-flow velocity, transmembrane pressure and disperse phase flux;
ii. **Membrane parameters:** pore size, active pores, distance between the pores, membrane hydrophobicity/hydrophilicity;
iii. **Phase parameters:** interfacial tension, viscosity and density of the processed phases.

Based on these parameters, the size of the droplet in membrane emulsification system depends upon the pore diameter and the dependence of the droplet diameter on pore diameter can be expressed as:

$$D_P = x\, D_0 \tag{1}$$

where D_P is the droplet diameter and D_0 is the pore diameter. Katoh et al., (1996) experimentally observed the value of x in the range of 2 to 12. The major factors affecting the value of x are: (i) the shear rates of continuous cross-flow fluid (ii) the dynamic interfacial tension, γ; and (iii) the disperse phase flux (J_d). Other parameters those implicitly control the value of x are: the average velocity of the continuous phase flow $\langle u_c \rangle$, the viscosities of the disperse phase and the continuous phases (μ_d and μ_c) the density of the continuous phase (ρ_c) the thermodynamic temperature, (T), the transmembrane pressure (P_m). The viscosity and dynamic surface tension depend upon temperature and that way temperature can influence the emulsification process.

Cross-flow velocity of continuous phase imparts drag force on the growing droplet for which the droplet detaches at the pore. With the increase in cross-flow velocity, the droplet diameter decreases. The dispersed phase flow rate or velocity influences the droplet dynamics via the inertial force competing with other forces such as drag and surface tension force. The difference between the pressure of dispersed phase in the dispersed phase channel and the average pressure of the continuous phase in the main channel is termed as transmembrane pressure.

$$\Delta p_m = p_d - \overline{p_c} \tag{2}$$

The average pressure of the continuous phase is defined as:

$$\overline{p_c} = (p_{c,in} + p_{c,out})/2 \tag{3}$$

where $p_{c,in}$ and $p_{c,out}$ are the pressure of continuous phase at the inlet and outlet of the main channel. Total transmembrane pressure consists of two parts: one is the capillary pressure (p_γ) and other is the effective transmembrane pressure (p_{eff}) or drag pressure inside the pore. Due to curvature of the droplet and dynamic interfacial tension, a small amount of pressure is required to inflate the droplet. This pressure is the capillary pressure. The capillary pressure is maximum at the starting of formation of the droplet at the pore and it decrease as the droplet grows. The capillary pressure becomes the minimum at the detachment time of the droplet. The effective or drag pressure part is responsible for the flow rate of dispersed phase. The effective pressure determines the throughput and thus the productivity of the membrane emulsification system. The transmembrane pressure controls the size of the droplet formed in membrane emulsification process. With the increase in transmembrane pressure, several researchers (Katoh et al, 1996; Peng and Williams, 1998; Schröder and Schubert, 1999) have observed the increase in droplet diameter while others (Abrahamse et al., 2002; Vladisavljevic and Schubert, 2003; Vladisavljevic et al., 2004) have observed the decrease in droplet diameter. The variation in droplet diameter with transmembrane pressure results the wide range of droplet size distribution (Abrahamse et al., 2002; Vladisavljevic et al., 2004). The wide range of droplet size also is affected by the steric hindrance between droplets or by the membrane being wetted by the dispersed phase, causing coalescence on the membrane.

The design and pore distribution of the membrane are important factors controlling the droplet dynamics in membrane emulsification. Due to presence of multi-pore and multi-droplet formation, there is a change in hydrodynamic effects caused by neighboring droplet and interactions between the droplets. The separation distance between the pores controls those hydrodynamic effects. If the separation distance of pores in the flow direction is small, the continuous phase velocity decreases and the boundary layer thickness increases as the flow approaches consecutive rows after crossing the first row. These would lead to an increase in the size of the droplets. With the increase in droplet size, there would be a caution of stability loss and coalescence of the droplets. For high efficiency of the emulsification process, narrow droplet size distribution and higher dispersed phase velocity is required. However, with the increase in dispersed phase flow rate, the droplet formation phenomenon shifts towards jetting (Pathak, 2011) and this requires a greater distance between the pores in the direction of the cross-flowing continuous phase in order to prevent drops from colliding and coalescing. In several experimental studies (Sugiura et al., 2002; Kobayashi et al, 2003, 2006) the droplet size distribution has been observed narrow up to a specific velocity of the dispersed phase, above which the diameter of the droplet distribution has been increased. Timgren et al. (2009) have investigated the effects of pore size distribution on hydrodynamic effects of droplet size and distribution. They observed that for small pore separation distance and with a low dispersed phase velocity the drop formation process was uniform, resulting an emulsion with a narrow drop size distribution. For shortest pore separation distance, with the increase in dispersed phase velocity, they observed the formation of poly dispersed emulsion, whereas pore separations of 15 and 20 times the pore diameter gave nearly mono dispersed emulsions.

The wetting behavior of membrane surface also controls the droplet growth. The wetting behavior of a membrane is represented by the static contact angle between the two liquid phases and the solid boundary. The static contact angle between the two phases and walls controls the evolution of the dispersed phase inside the micro-pore and in the continuous phase flow channel. If the angle is less than 90° the wall is said to be wetting and if it is greater than 90°, the wall is called the non-wetting.

Among different properties of the phase, surface tension controls the droplet dynamics in a greater way than any other properties. Surface tension force holds the droplet and offers the resistance against any deformation. The viscosities of both the phases have also effect on the droplet deformation. The drag force imparted by the continuous phase on the droplet depends upon the viscosity ratio of dispersed phase and continuous phase. For fixed flow rate of continuous phase the drag force increases with the increase in viscosity ratio up to some extent. After that value, the drag force becomes independent of the viscosity ratio. The densities of both phases enter into the droplet dynamics through the buoyancy or gravity force. In micro- or nano-fluidics flow the value of gravity force is very small and it can be neglected without loss of much accuracy.

1.1. Different forces acting in membrane emulsification.

All the parameters discussed in above control the droplet dynamics in membrane emulsification process with different magnitudes and output of the process can be analyzed on the basis of these operating parameters. Besides the individual effects, many of these parameters exhibit coupling effects. Different types of hydrodynamic forces act in the emulsification process. The droplet growth and deformation in membrane emulsification can be explained from the action of these and the final droplet size is a result of the interaction of these forces.

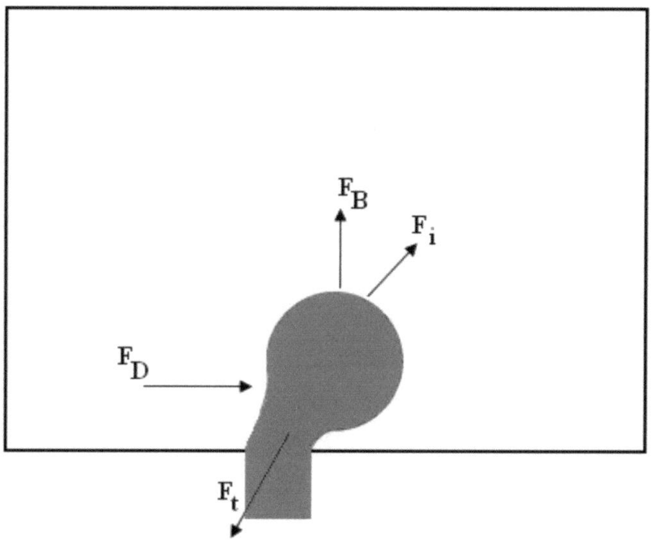

Figure 2. Different forces acting on the emulsification system

The major forces that act in the process are: drag force imparted by the flowing continuous phase, the interfacial tension force, the inertial force of the dispersed phase and the buoyancy or gravitational force. Different forces acting in the droplet formation process are shown in Fig. 2. Among these forces, interfacial tension force is the attaching force and other are detaching force. The droplet is detached from the pore when the detaching forces overcome the attaching force.

These four forces can be approximated as follows:

Drag force:

$$F_D = \frac{1}{2} C_d \rho_{cp} (v^* - v_{dp})^2 (\pi D_P^2 / 4) \tag{4}$$

Surface tension force:

$$F_t = \pi \sigma D_p \tag{5}$$

Inertial force of dispersed phase:

$$F_i = \frac{\pi \rho_{dp} D_0^2 v_{dp}^2}{4} \tag{6}$$

Buoyancy force:

$$F_B = \rho_c g V_{dr} - p_c A_n \tag{7}$$

In above v_{dp} is the velocity of dispersed phase ($v_{dp} = v_o$), v^* is the local continuous phase velocity at the centre of the drop, D_p is the diameter of the drop, D_0 is the pore diameter and V_{dr} is the droplet volume. The local continuous phase velocity is given by:

$$v^* = 2u_{cp} \left[1 - \left(\frac{D_h - D_p}{D_h} \right)^2 \right] \tag{8}$$

where u_{cp} is the average velocity of the continuous phase in the channel. D_h is the hydraulic diameter given by:

$$D_h = 2bh / (b + h) \tag{9}$$

where b and h are the width and height of the continuous phase channel respectively. The drag coefficient C_d depends upon the Reynolds number of the droplet (Re_p) and the viscosity ratio $\lambda (\mu_{dp} / \mu_{cp})$. The drop Reynolds number is defined as

$$Re_p = \frac{\rho_{dp} \left| v^* - v_{dp} \right| D_p}{\mu_{dp}} \tag{10}$$

Out of these forces, the only attaching force is the surface tension force and remaining forces, drag and inertial and buoyancy force are detaching forces. Neglecting the buoyancy or gravity force, the balance of forces at the moment of droplet detachment can be written as

$$\frac{1}{2} C_d \rho_{cp} (v^* - v_{dp})^2 (\pi D_P^2 / 4) + \frac{\pi \rho_{dp} D_0^2 v_{dp}^2}{4} = \pi \sigma D_p \tag{11}$$

For low value of *We* number, the value of inertial force (F_i) is very low. In that situation the diameter of the drop can be approximated as

$$D_p \propto \frac{\sigma}{(C_d \rho_{cp})(v^* - v_{dp})^2} \tag{12}$$

Thus analytically, droplet diameter increases with the increase in surface tension value.

1.2. Numerical simulation of droplet dynamics

Droplet formation and deformation have been studied for a long time due to complexity with the problem and practical utilities of the phenomenon. Droplet formation in a two-phase flow system possesses a rich dynamics with the involvement of several parameters such as average velocity of the liquids, their viscosities, densities, surface tension, surface chemistry and the flow geometry. Droplets formation results the creation of new surfaces which enhance the heat and mass transfer between the phases. Due to enhanced heat and mass transfer, the process has been used for wide ranges of phase-contact applications. Particularly the droplet formation in micro or nano size has received significant attention during last several years. Due to miniature size, the fabrication of experimental facility is expensive and reliable experimentation of microfluidic is very intricate. Hence the viable alternate is the numerical tools for investigating the problems. With the development of high speed computer and advanced algorithm, numerical modeling and simulation have become an essential part in the design and development of numerous engineering systems. Numerical simulations of droplet dynamics i.e. the investigations of two-phase flow in micro scale have been extensively undertaken during last several years. Various types of numerical techniques have been developed to solve the governing equations of the two-phase flow.

1.3. Different numerical methods

In numerical simulation of droplet dynamics or as a whole in the simulation of two-phase flow, there are several challenges which need to be carefully tackled to obtain reliable results. The main challenge is capturing the moving interface of the two phases accurately, which is not known priory. The accurate tracking of the interface and investigation of two-phase flow topology should be the essentiality of a good numerical method. There are several numerical methods based on interface kinematics to track the interface in free surface flows. Among them are: volume of fluid methods, front tracking methods, level set methods, phase field formulations, continuum advection schemes, boundary integral methods, particle-based methods, and moving mesh methods.

Volume of fluid method (VOF), earlier known as the volume tracking method, were originally developed by Nichols and Hirt (1975), Noh and Woodward (1976) and further extended by Hirt and Nichols (1981). Since then, the method has been extensively used and significantly improved over the years (Rudman,1997; Rider and Kothe,1998). The VOF method is based on the conservation of the volume fraction function F with respect to time and space, expressed as

$$\frac{\partial F}{\partial t} + (v.\nabla)F = 0 \qquad (13)$$

In VOF method, the computational grid is kept fixed and the interface between the two fluids is tracked within each cell through which it passes. In a computational grid cell, the interface can be effectively represented by line of the slope. To reconstruct the interface, the piecewise linear interpolation calculation (PLIC) method developed by Youngs (1982) is used in the computation. The interfacial surface forces are incorporated as body forces per unit volume in the Navier-Stokes equations; hence no extra boundary condition is required across the interface.

The basic working principle of front tracking method is based on the marker and cell (MAC) formulation (Harlow and Welch, 1966; Daly, 1967). The interface is represented discretely by Lagrangian markers connected to form a front which lies within and moves through a stationary Eulerian mesh. As the front moves and deforms, interface points are added, deleted, and reconnected as necessary. Further details of the method may be found in (Glimm et al., 1985; Churn et al., 1986; Tryggvason et al., 1998).

Level set methods have been developed by Osher and Sethian (1988). This method can compute the geometrical properties of highly complicated interface without explicitly tracking the interface. The basic principle of the level set method is to embed the propagating interface Γ(t) as the zero level set of a higher dimensional function ϕ , defined as ϕ $(x, t = 0) = \pm d$, where d is the distance from x to Γ $(t = 0)$. The function is chosen to be positive (negative) if x is outside (inside) the initial position of the interface Γ $(t = 0) = \phi$ $(x, t = 0) = 0$. Afterwards a dynamical equation for ϕ $(x, t = 0)$ that contains the embedded motion for $\Gamma(t)$ as the level set $\phi = 0$ can be derived similarly as in the volume of fluid conservation equation (13)

In phase field method, interfacial forces are modeled as continuum forces by smoothing interface discontinuities and forces over thin but numerically resolvable layers. This smoothing allows conventional numerical approximations of interface kinematics on fixed grids. The method has been used for investigating the problems governed by Navier-Stokes equations (Antanovskii, 1995; Jacqumin, 1996).

Boundary integral methods are designed to track the interface explicitly, as in front tracking methods, although the flow solution in the entire domain is deduced solely from information possessed by discrete points along the interface. The advantage of these methods is the reduction of the flow problem by one dimension involving quantities of the interface only.

Particle-based methods use discrete "particles" to represent macroscopic fluid parcels. Here, Lagrangian coordinates are used to solve the Navier-Stokes equations on "particles" having properties such as mass, momentum, and energy. The nonlinear convection term is modeled simply as particle motion and by knowing the identity and position of each particle, material interfaces are automatically tracked. By using particle motion to approximate the convection terms, numerical diffusion across interfaces (where particles change identity) is virtually zero; hence interface widths are well defined.

In moving mesh methods, the position history of discrete point's x_i lying on the interface is tracked for all time by integrating the evolution equation, forward in time.

$$\frac{dx_i}{dt} = v_i \tag{14}$$

A moving mesh is Lagrangian if every point is moved, and mixed (Lagrangian-Eulerian) if grid points in a subset of the domain are moved. Mixed methods are used for mold filling simulations, where the mold computational domain can be held stationary and the molten liquid is followed with a Lagrangian mesh.

Besides these individual methods, there are some combined method such as coupled level set and volume of fluid method. This method has been developed to tackle the inefficiency of VOF method in calculating complex geometrical properties and problem of mass imbalance of level set method. In the coupled method, the LS function is used only to compute the geometric properties (normal and curvature) at the interface while the void fraction is calculated using the VOF approach. Ohta et al. (2007) and Sussman et al. (2007) developed a novel coupled LS-VOF method to determine the sharp interface for incompressible, immiscible two-phase flows for large value of density ratio.

1.4. Issues of numerical simulation

Numerical investigation of active droplet formation is reasonably complex as it is potentially a multi-physics problem governed by a large number of partial differential equations (PDEs). Numerical simulation of droplet dynamics in membrane emulsion process requires accurate capturing of the evolving liquid–liquid interfaces. This gives sufficient challenge since the boundary between the two phases is not known priori and it is a part of the solution. In addition, the solution technique has to deal with different properties of both the phases such as density, viscosity, and velocity ratios. Numerical investigation of membrane emulsification process requires two main issues to be dealt with: one is permeation of the disperse phase through the membrane pores; the other is the mechanism of droplet detachment. Several earlier investigations have treated these issues separately; however both of them simultaneously contribute to droplet evolution and should be considered in the same framework. Both these issues have been considered in the present work. In the present work, numerical simulation of droplet dynamics in a membrane emulsification has been carried out considering multipore membrane. The hydrodynamic effects due to multipores and the effect of different operating parameters on the droplet dynamics have been investigated.

2. Problem description

The flow configuration of membrane emulsification considered in the present work has been shown in Fig. 3. Here the membrane emulsification process with two pores has been considered. A uniform pore arrangement in the membrane surface has been considered and the simulation has been mode for a row of pores consisting of two pores. The dispersed phase liquid has been injected through cylindrical pores of 10 μm diameter and a length of 100 μm. The distance between the pores in cross-flow direction has been considered as 100 μm. The height of the rectangular channel through which the continuous phase flows has been considered as 150 μm (y-direction). The width of the computational domain has been considered as 150 μm (z-direction) and a length of 500 μm (x-direction) has been considered. Since the present computational domain is a small element of whole membrane emulsification process, symmetrical boundary conditions have been considered in both the sides of computational domain in z-direction. The fluid properties used in the present simulation are within the range of properties of o/w emulsion system. Simulations have been made for different values of the non-dimensional numbers and other flow properties as shown in Table 1.

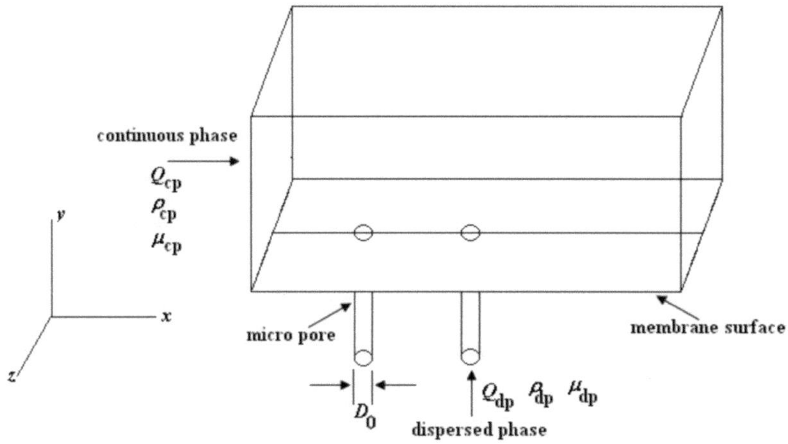

Figure 3. Schematic of computational domain

2.1. Governing equations

In the simulation of membrane emulsification system, both the phases have been considered incompressible, isothermal and laminar flow. The phase properties and the surface tension have been assumed to be constant throughout the flow domain. The conservation of mass on the whole domain (both the fluid phases and interface) leading to continuity equation is written as:

$$\frac{\partial \rho}{\partial t} + \nabla.(\rho V) = 0 \tag{15}$$

The momentum equation or unsteady Navier-Stokes equation is written as:

$$\rho\left(\frac{\partial V}{\partial t} + V.\nabla V\right) = -\nabla p + \rho g + \nabla.\left[\mu(\nabla V + \nabla V^T)\right] + f_S \tag{16}$$

In above f_S is the surface force, which includes surface tension force of the interface of the two fluids.

Parameters	Ranges
Diameter of pore	10 μm
Flow rate of continuous phase	0.27 and 0.54 liter/h
Flow rate of dispersed phase	0.0014 to 0.007 liter/h
Viscosity of continuous phase	0.001 Pa.s
Viscosity of dispersed phase	0.0036 to 0.014 Pa.s
Density of continuous phase	1000 kg/m^3
Density of dispersed phase	827 kg/m^3
Surface tension	0.0008 to 0.0024 N/m
Weber no (*We*)	0.0021 to 0.215
Capillary no (*Ca*)	0.0208 to 0.0625
Froude no (*Fr*)	6.37 to 637

Table 1. Values of physical properties used in the simulation

2.2. Interface tracking

Volume of fluid method (VOF) has been used for tracking the interface. In this method, the distribution of volume fraction is solved from its transport equation.

$$\frac{\partial F}{\partial t} + V.\nabla F = 0 \tag{17}$$

With the inclusion of volume fraction in the calculation, the volume averaged density and viscosity (ρ and μ) are defined as:

$$\rho = \rho_1 + F(\rho_2 - \rho_1) \tag{18}$$

$$\mu = \mu_1 + F(\mu_2 - \mu_1), \tag{19}$$

where subscript 1 and 2 denote the continuous and dispersed phase respectively. The surface force f_S appearing in momentum equation has been calculated using continuous surface force (CSF) model proposed by Brackbill et al. (1992) . It is defined as:

$$f_S = -\sigma\kappa\nabla F, \tag{20}$$

where σ and κ are the surface tension and surface curvature respectively. Surface curvature is calculated from:

$$\kappa = \nabla.\frac{\nabla F}{|\nabla F|}. \tag{21}$$

2.3. Boundary and initial conditions

Various types of boundary conditions have been used in the simulation of the membrane emulsification. A fully developed laminar duct flow has been considered at the inlet to the continuous phase channel and the flow has been assumed to be dominant along the stream direction thus: $u = u_{cp}$, $v = 0$, $w = 0$. At the inlet of continuous phase, the value of volume fraction has been set to zero ($F = 0$). At the inlets to the micro-pores, a velocity inlet type boundary condition has been used: $v = v_0$. The other components of the velocity have been put as $u = 0$, $w = 0$ and the value of volume fraction has been set to $F = 1$. Outflow boundary condition has been put at the outlet of the flow channel. Symmetry boundary conditions have been put at both sides of the computational domain. The top of the channel has been treated as walls where no-slip and impermeability boundary conditions have been set. At the starting of the computation, the whole flow domain has been assumed to be filled up with the continuous phase fluid. The static contact angle between the two phases and the wall influences the droplet growth in the dispersed and continuous phase channel. It has been observed that the effect of contact angle in the droplet formation is negligible when its value is greater than 165° (Sang et al., 2009). The value of static angle used in the present simulation has been set to 170°.

To reduce the number of dependable variables, the governing equations have been expressed in dimensionless form. The diameter of the pore (D_0) has been used as length scale and the average velocity (v_0) of the dispersed phase has been used as velocity scale for making non-dimensional form of the equation. The non-dimensional equations are:

$$\frac{\partial \rho^*}{\partial t^*} + \nabla.(\rho^* V^*) = 0 \tag{22}$$

$$\left(\frac{\partial V^*}{\partial t^*} + V^*.\nabla V^*\right) = -\nabla p^* + \frac{\rho^*}{Fr} + \frac{1}{\mathrm{Re}} \nabla.\left[(\nabla V^* + \nabla V^{*T})\right] + \frac{1}{We}.\ \nabla.\frac{\nabla F}{|\nabla F|} \tag{23}$$

In above starred quantities are non-dimensional parameters. The three non-dimensional numbers appeared in the problem are: Reynolds number (*Re*) , Weber number (*We*) and Froude number (*Fr*). They are defined as:

$$Re = \frac{\rho_{dp} v_0 D_0}{\mu_{dp}};\ We = \frac{\rho_{dp} v_0^2 D_0}{\sigma};\ Fr = \frac{v_0^2}{g D_0};$$

The Reynolds numbers (*Re*) is defined as the ratio of viscous force to the inertia force, Weber number (*We*) is defined as the ratio of inertia force relative to the surface tension force and Froude number (*Fr*) is defined as the ratio of inertia to gravity force. In the present work to incorporate the effect of the continuous phase fluid, the Capillary number has been introduced and is defined as:

$$Ca = \frac{\mu_{cp} u_{cp}}{\sigma} = \frac{RWe}{\lambda \mathrm{Re}}$$

where λ is the viscosity ratio ($\lambda = \mu_{dp} / \mu_{cp}$) and R is the velocity ratio ($R = u_{cp} / v_0$).

2.4. Numerical method

Commercial code Ansys Fluent (V12) based on finite volume method has been used in the simulation. The momentum and volume fraction transport equation have been discretized with 2nd order upwind scheme. The PISO (pressure implicit with splitting of operators) algorithm has been used for pressure correction. The VOF/CSF techniques have been used to track the fluid interface between the two immiscible fluids. A geometry reconstruction scheme has been used in the simulation to avoid the diffusion at the interface. The interface was reconstructed by the piecewise-linear interface calculation (PLIC) technique (Youngs, 1982). The unsteady term was treated with first-order implicit time stepping. Simulations were made with very small time steps (~10^{-7} s). The solutions have been assumed to be converged and therefore iterations have been terminated when the normalized sum of residual mass was less than 10^{-4} and variation of other variables in successive iteration was less than 10^{-2}. A non-uniform grid was used in the simulation where grids were clustered near the walls and the injection portion of the dispersed phase. The channel was decomposed into 12×10^5 numbers of control volumes and the pore with 12×10^3 after a grid independent study.

3. Results and discussions

In the present work, the dynamics of droplet formation in two pores of membrane emulsification has been investigated for different flow rates (velocities) of dispersed phase, continuous phase, surface tension and viscosity of the two phases. It is to be noted that In case of membrane emulsification process, the dispersed phase fluid gets more space to interact with the continuous phase fluid compared to the confined geometries in case of T-junction emulsification. Due to this the evolution of dispersed phase becomes different than the case of T-junction emulsion and the dependence of the process on different properties of both the phases also changes.

3.1. Growth and detachment of the droplets

In membrane emulsification system, the flow rate of dispersed phase controls the droplet dynamics via its inertial force competing with the drag force imparted by the continuous phase and interfacial tension force. In order to investigate the effect of dispersed phase flow rate, simulations have been made for different values of *We* number by changing the dispersed phase velocity i.e. inertial force and keeping the surface tension force fixed. Before discussing the effects of *We*, the growth and detachment of the droplet for a constant values of *We* (0.0086) and *Ca* (0.028) at different time levels have been shown in Fig. 4. It has been observed that both the droplet grow at their respective micro-pore and detached by the continuous phase at the same location. As the first droplet is being detached and carried away by continuous phase fluid, the second droplet starts to grow at the pore and the repetition of droplets detachment takes place periodically with constant volume of droplet. Simulation has also revealed that the growth rate of the droplet at the downstream micro pore is different than the upstream micro pore and the droplet at that pore requires more detachment time. The presence of upstream droplet changes the hydrodynamic effects and reduces the viscous drag force of continuous phase on the downstream droplet. Due to reduction in drag force, the surface tension force can hold the droplet for longer time and detachment takes place lately. Due to this the droplet size is greater than the droplet formed at the upstream pore. Moreover due to low drag force of the continuous phase, the inertia force of dispersed phase has some effect in forming the necking of the droplet in the downstream pore. The diameter of the droplet after detachment has been found as 41.3 μm, which is about 4.13 times the pore diameter. This ratio is within the range of 1-12 observed by Katoh et al. (1996).

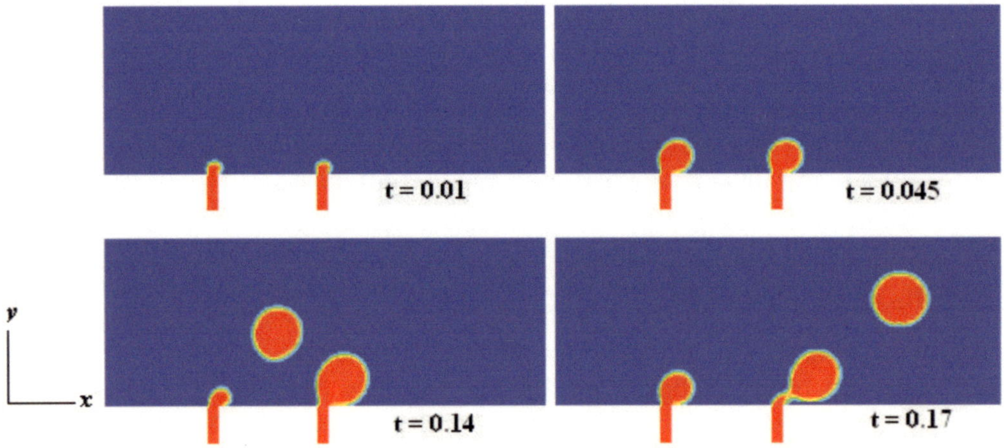

Figure 4. Growth and detachment of droplet at different time level, $We = 0.0086$, $Ca = 0.0208$

Thus the distance between the two pores should be at least five times the pore diameter for simultaneous growing of two spherical droplets without any hindrance from the neighboring pore. On the other hand the droplet deforms in the direction of flow of the continuous phase as shown in Fig. 4. Considering the deformation and growth of the droplet, it can be concluded that a distance of almost 10 times the pore diameter between the two pores in x-direction i.e. in cross-flow direction is needed to avoid contact, and thus avoid coalescence at two neighboring pores for this particular flow rate of dispersed phase and surface tension.

The investigation of droplet growth in transverse direction i.e. z-direction is important to design the pore distance in transverse direction. The growth of the droplet in a horizontal plane (x-z) at at y/D_0 = 25 μm has been shown in Fig. 5 at different time levels for We = 0.0086 and Ca = 0.0208. As the time progresses, the droplet at the first pore grows and deforms along the cross-flow fluid direction. Thus the distance between the two forming droplets decreases. It has been observed that in the transverse (z-) direction the droplet remains almost spherical throughout the formation process; therefore, the distance between the pores in that direction can be fixed at seven times the pore diameter.

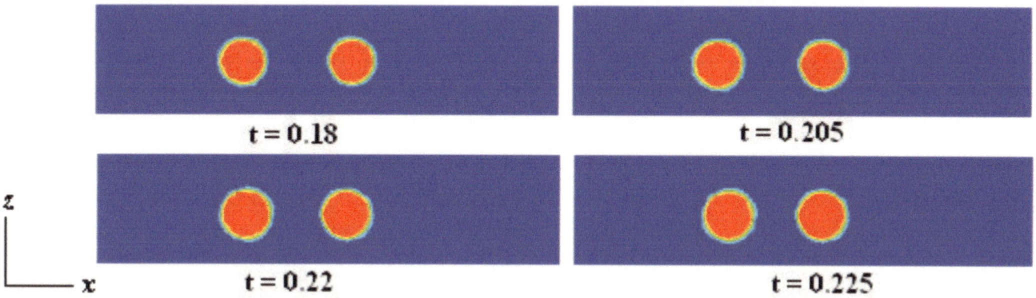

Figure 5. Growth of droplets at horizontal x-z plane at different time level, *We* = 0.0086, *Ca* = 0.0208

With the fixed distance along cross-flow and transverse direction, the maximum porosity of the membrane can be calculated. The porosity is defined as the ratio of the total pore cross-sectional area and the total membrane surface area.

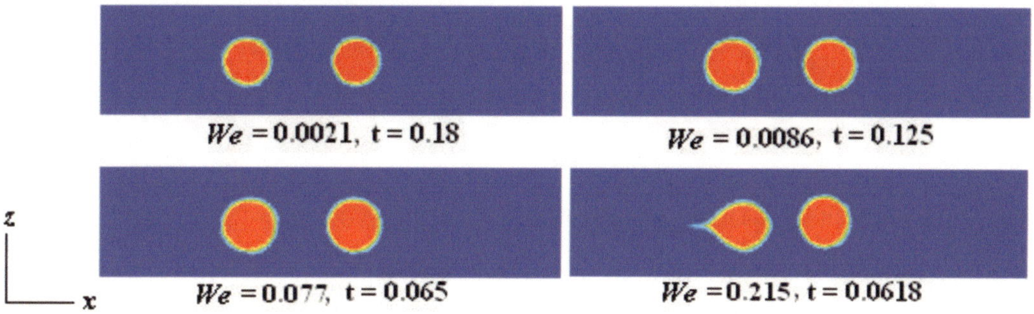

Figure 6. Growth of droplets at horizontal *x-z* plane for different values of *We*, *Ca* = 0.0208

To check the effect of *We* on the droplet growth along transverse direction, the simulated results of droplet growth at horizontal plane for different values of *We* and at different time levels have been shown in Fig 6. With the increase in *We* the droplet size increases and the distance between the two droplets decreases along the continuous phase fluid flow direction. At high value of *We* the necking phenomenon has been observed which makes the insufficient distance between the pore for avoiding coalescence. On the other hand at high value of *We* the growth of the droplet in transverse direction is same as the case in lower value of *We*. Thus the spacing of pores in transverse direction can be fixed based on droplet diameter and irrespective of the dripping or jetting mode.

3.2. Effect of dispersed phase flow rate

In order to show the effect of dispersed phase flow rate in droplet dynamics, the droplet growth before the detachment has been shown in Fig.7 for different values of *We* (0.0021 to 0.215) number. The qualitative difference in droplet growth for different values of *We* can be seen in the figure. Some key phenomena such as dripping at low *We* number, necking and jetting at higher *We* number have been observed. During the droplet formation in membrane emulsification process, the inertial force of the dispersed flow acts as detaching force, and acts against the attaching force of surface tension. When inertia force of the dispersed is less than the drag force or interfacial tension force, it cannot influence the droplet dynamics and the droplet growth and detachment are controlled by the drag force competing with the surface tension force. At the low value of *We* (*We* =0.0021) number, the droplet forms and breakups at the micro-pore which is termed as the dripping mode.

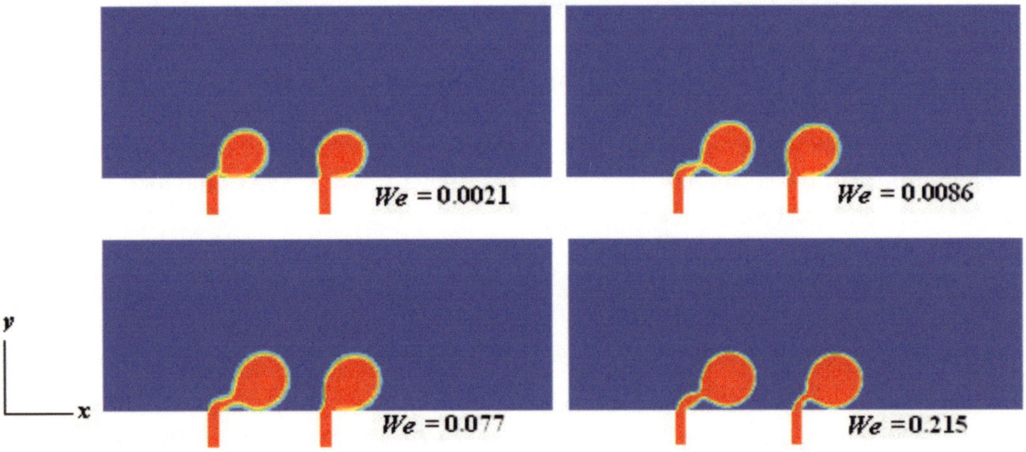

Figure 7. Growth of the droplets for different values of *We*, *Ca* = 0.0208

At intermediate values of Weber number (0.0086 and 0.077), the point of droplet detachment has been moved away from the micro-pore, and formation of dispersed phase thread and necking have been observed. With the increase in inertial force of the dispersed phase, the effective pressure overcomes the capillary pressure inside the liquid thread leading to a stretched filament and also distends the droplet neck noticeably. With the increasing in dispersed phase flow rate further (0.215), two nodes form in the liquid filament and extension of the droplet neck occurs. The detachment point of the droplets moves further downstream from the pore. Thus jetting occurs and the droplet forms at the tip of the droplet. A decrease in the resultant droplet size can be observed. Thus at higher value of *We* number, due to formation of the jetting and the droplet formation from the tip, the distance of 10 pore diameter between the pores is not sufficient to avoid the contact and coalescence of two neighboring droplets.

3.3. Velocity field during droplet growth

The droplet dynamics in membrane emulsification process is controlled by the evolving velocity field outside and inside the dispersed phase since the drag force is correlated to velocity. The velocity fields for *We* = 0.0086 in the central vertical plane (*x*-*y*) at the time level *t* = 0.125 have been shown in Fig. 8. Recirculating flows have been observed inside the both droplets and the center of recirculation is different in both the droplets.

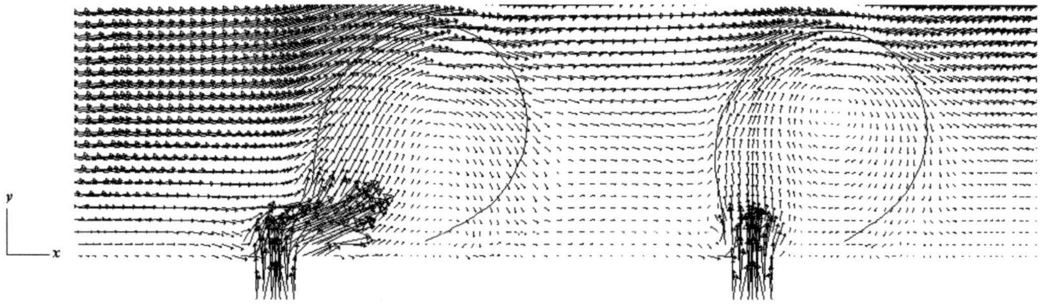

Figure 8. Velocity vector at the central plane, *We* = 0.0086, *Ca* = 0.0208

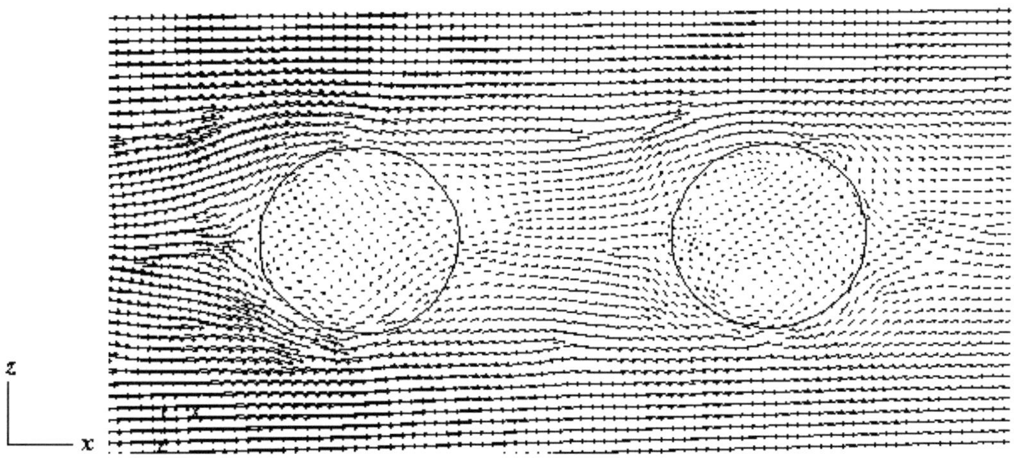

Figure 9. Velocity vector at the horizontal plane, *We* = 0.0086, *Ca* = 0.0208

As the continuous liquid phase interacts the dispersed phase, it imparts a viscous drag force on the evolving interface between the two phases. The viscous drag force produces shear stress along the interface that faces the continuous phase fluid. This initiates the recirculation inside the both droplets. The acceleration of the dispersed phase out of the pore also affects the motion inside the forming drop, especially at an early stage of drop formation. The centre point of the rotational flow inside the drop is at the top of the drop, which is controlled by the above two factors. The dispersed phase inside the interface front finally flows along the continuous liquid phase and is accelerated by the viscous drag. From the velocity diagram it can be seen that the upstream droplet has disturbed the approaching velocity field for the downstream growing droplet. Thus the droplet that grows in the "shade" of another droplet experiences a different velocity profile.

The velocity field inside and outside the dispersed phase in horizontal plane (*x*-*z*) at the time level (0.125) for *We* = 0.0086 has been shown in Fig. 9. The wake formed by the first droplet is visible from the velocity field, where velocity field is weak.

3.4. Effect of continuous phase velocity

To show the effect of continuous phase velocity, the simulation has been made for same range of Weber number (0.00 to 0.215) but with higher continuous phase flow rate (Q_{cp} = 0.54 l/h). The comparison of droplet diameter for two values of continuous phase velocities i.e. flow rates has been shown in Fig. 10. It has been observed that for the higher continuous phase flow rate, the diameter of the droplets is smaller compared to lower continuous phase flow rate. At a particular value of continuous phase flow rate, the droplet diameter increases with the increase in droplet diameter, than decreases with the increase in droplet diameter due to jetting phenomenon. It can be seen that with the increase in continuous phase velocity, the droplet diameter decreases. Due to increase in velocity, the continuous phase fluid imparts higher drag force and droplet detaches within short interval. It has been also observed that the reduction of droplet diameter during transition from dripping to jetting is less in case of higher value of continuous phase velocity compared to its lower value.

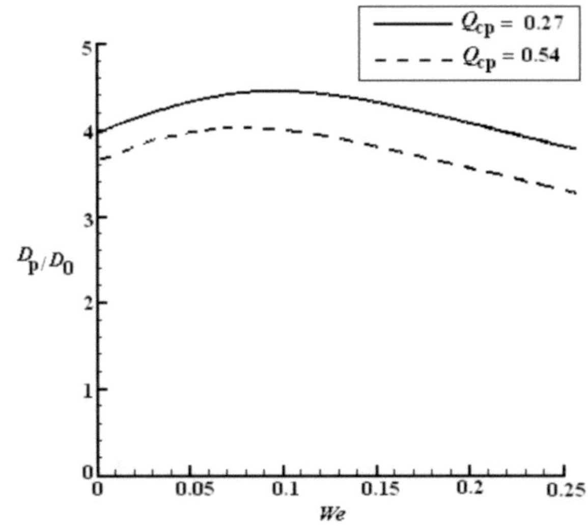

Figure 10. Effect of continuous phase velocity on droplet diameter

The detachment time of droplets for two values of flow rates of continuous phase have been shown in Fig. 11. With lower value of continuous phase flow rate, the detachment time decreases exponentially with the increase in *We* number up to some value of *We* number, after that the decrease rate reduces. At a particular *We* number, the detachment time has been observed less for higher continuous phase flow rate compared to lower continuous phase flow rate. For lower flow rate of continuous phase, the detachment time decreases with the increase of *We* number, but it does not follow the same trend as for the lower flow rate.

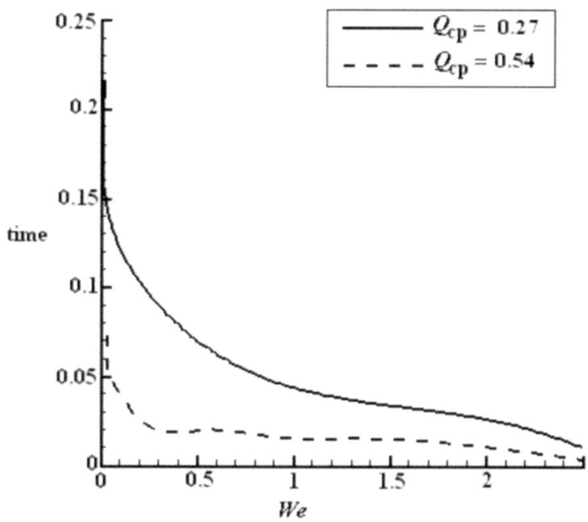

Figure 11. Detachment time of the droplet for different *We* number

3.5. Effect of surface tension

To show the effect of surface tension on the droplet formation, the simulation has been made for different values of surface tension (Ca = 0.0208 to 0.0625) at constant value of inertial force. The droplet diameters for different values of Ca and two values of continuous phase flow rate have been shown in Fig. 12. With the decrease in surface tension force i.e. increase of Ca, the droplet diameter decreases. At low value of surface tension, the attaching surface tension force cannot hold the droplet for longer time against the other detaching forces leading to formation of droplet with smaller size. At very low value of surface tension (0.0008 N/m) even at low value of We (0.0021) the phenomenon shows the jetting behavior as shown in Fig. 13. Due to jetting phenomenon, the spacing between the micro-pore is not sufficient to avoid the coalescence of the droplets at two neighbor pores.

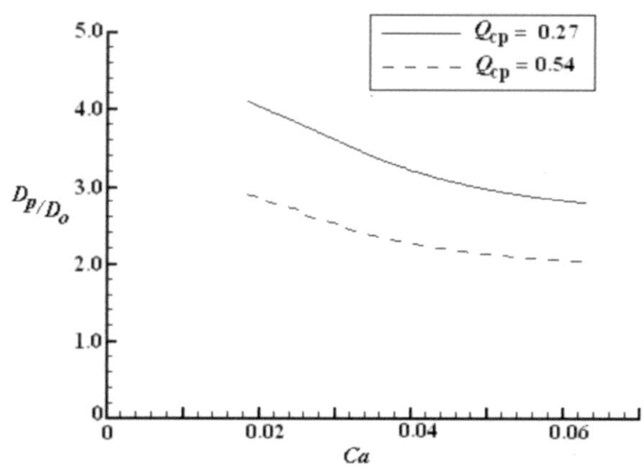

Figure 12. Effect of surface tension on droplet diameter

From the present investigation, it can be seen that dripping to jetting transition can be possible in two ways: one at constant surface tension while varying the inertial force (varying the dispersed phase flow rate) and another at constant inertial force while varying the surface tension force. A qualitative difference in flow pattern in both the transitions has been observed. During dispersed phase controlled transition, the diameter of the drop increases first then decreases rapidly while in surface tension controlled transition, the size of the droplet continuously decreases (Fig. 10 and Fig. 12).

Surface tension force is dominant over the inertial force in dripping mode, hence the droplet size increases and in jetting mode inertial force overcomes the surface tension force for which drop size decreases. In surface controlled breakup, the drag force and interfacial force take part in the droplet formation.

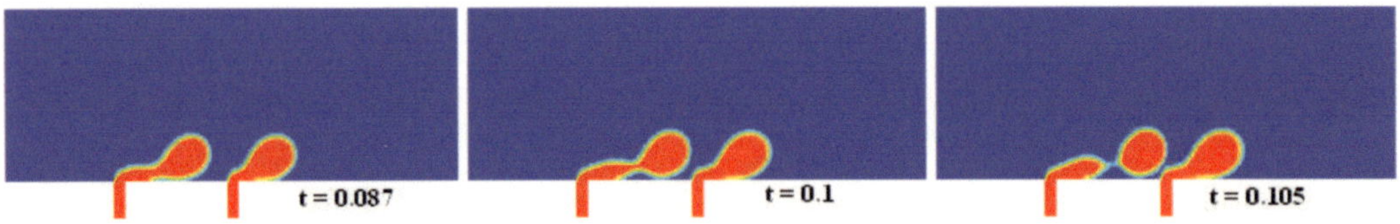

Figure 13. Jetting behavior at low surface tension value

3.6. Effect of viscosities

The viscosities of both the phases also effect the droplet growth and deformation as discussed in introduction section. The drag force which detaches the droplet depends upon the viscosity ratio of dispersed phase and continuous phase. At a constant value of continuous phase flow rate, the drag force increases with the increase in viscosity ratio up to some extent. After that, the drag force becomes independent of the viscosity ratio. Pathak (2011) has observed negligible effect of dispersed phase viscosity in the membrane emulsification system. Moreover it has been also observed that the effect viscosity on droplet dynamics is not very significant if the ratio of dispersed phase and continuous phase viscosity is high (van Dijke et al., 2010). Since the viscosity ratio of dispersed phase and continuous phase fluid is above 3, the effects of viscosities have not been investigated in the present work.

4. Conclusions

Droplet formation in a two-pore membrane emulsification has been numerically investigated in this chapter. The dynamics of droplet formation has been investigated by solving the two-phase governing equations using VOF method. The effects of various parameters, viz., dispersed and continuous phase flow rate, surface tension and viscosities on the droplet dynamics have been investigated. The dynamics of evolution of dispersed phase and droplets formation show the dripping and jetting behavior depending upon the operating conditions and properties of two-phase liquids in the emulsification system. At constant continuous phase flow rate, the dripping phenomenon occurs at low dispersed phase velocity i.e. at low *We* number and transits towards jetting with the increase in dispersed phase flow rate. At constant continuous phase flow rate, with the increase in dispersed phase flow rate, the droplet size increases initially but decreases as the system transits towards jetting. At constant dispersed phase flow rate, with the increase in continuous phase flow rate, the droplet size decreases and also detachment time. Two ways of dripping to jetting transition have been observed, one with the increasing dispersed phase flow rate at constant continuous phase flow rate and other way is reducing the surface tension at constant dispersed phase flow rate. Both the transitions show different physical structures. The effect of inertia force has been observed the negligible for high value of surface tension and significant for lower surface tension value. The distance between the pore in continuous flow direction depends upon the operating parameters leading to dripping to jetting mode but the pore distance in transverse direction is not affected by the dripping or jetting behavior. Thus at higher value of *We* number, due to formation of the jetting and the droplet formation from the tip, the distance of 10 pore diameter between the pores is not sufficient to avoid the contact and coalescence of two neighboring droplets. The droplet size in the process scales with four main forces: drag forces imparted by the continuous phase, inertia force imparted by dispersed phase, surface tension force and the gravity force. In dripping mode inertial force of dispersed phase has negligible effect as the surface tension and drag force are dominant whereas in jetting mode inertial force of dispersed phase and surface tension force take part in the droplet formation. The evolving vortices are observed in the initial stage of dripping mode but it disappears in later stage. Three important factors must be considered in order to obtain a high production rate in membrane emulsification. (i) A proper combination of continuous phase, dispersed phase flow rate and surface tension so that droplet formation is made just before the starting of surface instability in jetting region. (ii) A proper distribution of pores so that coalescence of droplets does not occur during the droplet growth. (iii) The crossflow velocity must be high enough to provide a sufficient wall shear stress at the membrane surface to transport the drops away from the pore opening and, thus avoid the static hindrance and drop coalescence.

Author details

Manabendra Pathak
Department of Mechanical Engineering, Indian Institute of Technology Patna, India

Nomenclature

A_n	Area of the droplet neck ($(\mu m)^2$)
b	Width of the continuous phase channel (μm)
C_a	Capillary number

C_d	Drag coefficient
D_h	Hydraulic diameter of the continuous phase channel (μm)
D_0	Diameter of micro-pore (μm)
D_p	Diameter of the droplet (μm)
f_s	Surface force (N)
F	Volume fraction of dispersed phase fluid
g	Acceleration due to gravity (m/s^2)
h	Height of the continuous phase channel (μm)
k_1	Constant
k_2	Constant
p	Pressure of the flow (Pa)
p_c	Pressure of the continuous phase fluid flow (Pa)
p_d	Pressure of the dispersed phase fluid flow (Pa)
p_γ	Capillary pressure (Pa)
Q_{cp}	Flow rate of continuous phase fluid (m^3/s)
Q_{dp}	Flow rate of dispersed phase fluid (m^3/s)
R	Viscosity ratio of continuous phase to dispersed phase fluid
Re	Reynolds number of the flow
R_p	Reynolds number of the drop
u	Velocity in x- direction (m/s)
u_{cp}	Velocity of continuous phase at the inlet to the channel (m/s)
v	Velocity in y- direction (m/s)
v^*	Local velocity of continuous phase fluid in the channel (m/s)
v_0	Velocity of dispersed phase at the inlet to the micro-pore (m/s)
V	Velocity vector
V_{dr}	Droplet volume((μm)^2)
w	Velocity in z- direction (m/s)
We	Webber number

Greek letters

r	Position vector of interface of the two phase
ϕ	Level set function
κ	Surface curvature (m^{-1})
λ	Viscosity ratio of dispersed phase to continuous phase fluid
μ_{cn}	Viscosity of continuous phase fluid (m^2/s)
μ_{dn}	Viscosity of dispersed phase fluid (m^2/s)
ρ_{cn}	Density of continuous phase fluid (kg/ m^3)
ρ_{dn}	Density of dispersed phase fluid (kg/ m^3)
σ	Surface tension coefficient (N/m)

5. References

Abrahamse, A. J., van der Padt, A. & Boom, R. M. (2002). Analysis of droplet formation and interactions during cross-flow membrane emulsification, J. Membr. Sci. 204: 125-137.

Antanovskii, L. K. (1995) A Phase Field Model of Capillarity. Phys. Fluids 1: 747-753.

Brackbill, J. U., Kith, D. B. & Zemach, C. (1992). A Continuum method for modeling surface tension. J Comp. Phys 100: 335–354.

Churn, I. L., Glimm, J., McBtyan, O., Plohr, B. & Yanic, S. (1986). Front tracking for gas dynamics. J. Comp. Phys. 62: 83-110.

Daly, B. J. (1967). Numerical study of two fluid Rayleigh-Taylor instabilities. Phys. Fluids 10:297-307.

Glimm, J. & McBryan, O. A. (1985). A computational model for interfaces. Adv. Appl. Math. 6: 422-435.

Harlow, F. H. & Welch, J. E. (1966). Numerical study of large-amplitude free-surface motion. Phys. Fluids 9: 842-851.

Hirt, C. W. & Nichols, B. D. (1981). Volume of fluid (VOF) method for the dynamics of free boundaries. J. Comp. Phys. 39: 201-225.

Jacqumin, D. (1996). An energy approach to the continuum surface method. AIAA paper, 96-0858.

Joscelyne, S. M. & Trägårdh, G. (1991). Food emulsions using membrane emulsification: conditions for producing small droplets. J. Food Eng., 39: 59-64.

Joscelyne, S. M. & Trägårdh, G. (2000). Membrane emulsification – a literature review. J. Membr. Sci.169: 107-117.

Karbstein, H., & Schubert, H. (1995). Developments in the continuous mechanical production of oil-in-water macro-emulsions. Chem. Engg. Process. 34: 205-211.

Katoh, R., Asano, Y., Furuya, A., Sotoyama, K. & Tomita, M. (1996). Preparation of food emulsions using membrane emulsification system. J. Membr. Sci. 113: 131-135.

Kobayashi, I., Nakajima, M. & Mukataka, S. (2003). Preparation characteristics of oil-in-water emulsions using differently charged surfactants in straight-through microchannel emulsification. Colloids Surf. A 229: 33–41.

Kobayashi, I., Uemura, K. & Nakajima, M. (2006). CFD study of the effect of a fluid flow in a channel on generation of oil-in-water emulsion droplets in straight-through microchannel emulsification. J. Chem. Eng. Jpn. 39: 855–863.

Luca, G. D., Sindona, A., Giorno, L. & Drioli, E. (2004). Quantitative analysis of coupling effects in cross-flow membrane emulsification. J. Membr. Sci. 229: 199-209.

Nichols, B. D. & Hirt, C. W. (1975). Methods for calculating multi-dimensional, transient free surface flows past bodies. Technical Report LA-UR-75-1932, Los Alamos National Laboratory. NM.

Noh, W. F. & Woodward, P. R. (1976). SLIC (simple line interface methods). In: Voore A I V, P. J. Zandbergen P J, editors. Lecture Notes in Physics 59: 330-340.

Ohta, M., Kikuchi, D., Yoshida, Y. & Sussman, M. (2007). Direct numerical simulation of the slow formation process of single bubbles in a viscous liquid. J. Chem. Eng. Jpn. 40: 939-943.

Osher, S. & Sethian, J. A. (1988). Fronts propagating with curvature-dependent speed: algorithms based on Hamilton-Jacobi formulation. J. Comp. Phys. 79:12-49.

Pathak, M. (2011). Numerical simulation of membrane emulsification: effect of flow properties in the transition from dripping to jetting. J. Membr. Sci. 382: 166-176.

Peng, S., J. & Williams, R. A. (1998). Controlled production of emulsions using a crossflow membrane, Part I: droplet formation from a single pore. Chem. Eng. Res. Des., 76: 894-901.

Rider, W. J. & Kothe, D. B. (1998). Reconstructing volume tracking. J. Comp. Phys 141:112-52.

Rudman, M. (1997). Volume tracking methods for interfacial flow calculations. Int. J. Num. Meth. Fluids. 24: 671-691.

Sang, L., Hong, Y. & Wang, F. (2009). Investigation of viscosity effect on droplet formation in T-shaped microchannels by numerical and analytical methods. Microfluid Nanofluid 6: 621–635.

Schröder, V. & Schubert, H. (1999). Production of emulsions using microporous, ceramic membranes. Colloids Surf A 152: 103-109.

Schubert, H., Ax K, & Behrend, O. (2003). Product engineering of dispersed systems. Trends Food Sci & Technol. 14: 9-16.

Sugiura, S., Nakajima, M., Kumazawa, N., Iwamoto, S. & Seki, M. (2002). Characterization of spontaneous transformation-based droplet formation during microchannel emulsification. J. Phys. Chem. B 106: 9405–9409.

Sussman, M., Smith, K. M., Hussaini, M. Y., Ohta, M. & Zhi-Wei, R. (2007). A sharp interface method for incompressible two-phase flows. J. Comp. Phys. 221: 469-505.

Timgren, A., Trägårdh, G. & Trägårdh. C. (2009). Effects of pore spacing on drop size during cross-flow membrane emulsification—A numerical study. J. Membr. Sci. 337: 232-239.

Tryggvason, G., Bunner, B., Ebrat, O. & Tauber, W. (1998). Computations of multi-phase flow by a finite difference/front tracking method. I. Multi-fluid flows. In Lecture Notes for the 29th Computational Fluid Dynamics Lecture Series, Karman Institute for Fluid Mechanics, Belgium.

van Dijke, K., Kobayashi, I., Schroe¨n, K., Uemura, K., Nakajima, M. & Boom. R. (2010). Effect of viscosities of dispersed and continuous phases in microchannel oil-in-water emulsification, Microfluid Nanofluid. 9: 77–85.

Vladisavljevic, G. T. & Schubert, H. (2003). Preparation of emulsions with a narrow particle size distribution using microporous α-alumina membranes. J. Disp. Sci. Technol. 24: 811-819.

Vladisavljevic, G. T., Lambrich, U., Kakajima, M. & Schubert, H. (2004). Production of o/w emulsion using SPG membranes, ceramic α-aluminium oxide membranes, microfluidizer anda silicon microchannel plate - a comparative study. Colloids Surf. A 232: 199-207.

Youngs, D. L. (1982). Time-dependent multi-material flow with large fluid distortion. In: Morton K W, Baines M J, editors, Numerical Methods for Fluid Dynamics, Academic Press 1982.

Section 4

Industrial Applications

Chapter 20

Numerical Methods for Analyzing the Transients in Medium Voltage Networks

Dumitru Toader, Stefan Haragus and Constantin Blaj

Additional information is available at the end of the chapter

http://dx.doi.org/10.5772/49953

1. Introduction

The analysis of transient regimes in electric networks is a complex problem due to great number of elements, some nonlinear, as well as, due to the nonsinusoidal variation of currents and voltages. Numerical simulation can solve properly such a problem

There are available a lot of simulation programs for transients. One of the first of them, dedicated to electro energetic systems, was initiated by H.W.Dommel. Electromagnetic Transient Program (EMTP) was bought by Bonneville Power Administration (USA) (Dommel, 1995). Later on, from this initial program were developed several versions, such as MicroTrans, EMTP-RV, ATP (Alternative Transients Program), PSCAD (Chuco, 2005; DeCarlo & Lin, 2001).

Comparing some of the main simulation programs is not very conclusive, because each one of them are used in some versions trying to solve a large group of problems (Iordache & Mandache, 2004; Istrate et al., 2009).

Interface becomes more and more friendly, the library becomes larger and the facilities for creating own models are simpler to use. The speed of calculations and the storage capacity do no more represent a problem. It is possible now to implement some complicated algorithms able to solve problems with high speed in the variation of variables, able to solve all kinds of nonlinearities or to handle eigenvalues highly distanced one from another (large stiffness ratio dynamical systems).

An important criterion for the selection is represented by the integration of complex dynamical systems like rotating electric machines, relays, power electronic devices, FACTS, controllers etc. in the simulation. Some of the programs, depending on the way that were conceived, allow a better integration of these subsystems.

Choosing one or other of the simulation programs depends on the previous experience of the user, as well as, on the manner the program responds to the specific demands (Chuco, 2005; Danyek et al., 2002; Foltin et al., 2006; Karlsson, 2005; Rashid & Rashid, 2006).

No mater what program is used, the numerical analysis of transients eventually must be able to solve a set of differential – algebraic equations that models the physical system. By accounting the stage the numerical integration takes place at, there are two main classes of simulation programms.

One class consists of those programs that make the integration at element level, meaning that for each step of time discretization the differential equations associated to dynamic elements are transformed in finite difference relations. Several ways of approximation can be used, more frequently the trapeze rule being used. All these algebraic relations are then assembled and as a result an algebraic system of equations is obtained and consequently solved using specific algorithms. This procedure is repeated at each iteration step, the parameters involved in the equations being modified by the results obtained at the previous step. Usually the integration step is fixed, but if this is required by a lack of convergence, the integration step can be split in half and the computation process is resumed. This method is known under the name of the implicit integration method and is used in programs such as SPICE and EMTP (Blume, 1986).

A second class of programs uses a two step procedure. In the first step the mathematic model is expressed as a system of first order differential equations, known as the system's state equations. During the next step this system of equations is integrated using algorithms with fixed step or with variable steps, depending on the systems particularities. The advantage of this method, called the state variables method, is to treat in the same way, in a unitary manner, electric networks, electric machines, drives, control devices or any other device that allows state equations. A representative of this method is SimPowerSystems™ which is an extension of Simulink® with tools for modeling and simulating of electrical power systems. It provides models of many components used in these systems, including three-phase machines, electric drives, and libraries of application-specific models such as Flexible AC Transmission Systems (FACTS) and wind-power generation. Harmonic analysis, calculation of Total Harmonic Distortion (THD), load flow, and other key power system analyses are automated (Mathworks®).

The precision of the results obtained by integration of the equations describing the simulated system is quite remarkably high. It is obvious that none of the simulation programs, no mater which of the methods is using, cannot be more precise than the mathematic models used for the simulated components. The accuracy of the values of the parameters of these models is of high importance.

2. The state-variable method for electrical circuits

Medium voltage electric networks are in fact complex circuits mainly made of power sources, resistors, inductors, capacitors and, sometimes, other electric components.

Analyzing transient regimes in such networks is the same as the analysis of any other complex electric circuit (Dessaint, et al. 1999; Mandache & Topan, 2009; SIMULINK, 1997).

Generally, an electric circuit, no mater how complex it is, is described by an algebraic linear system of equations, obtained by applying the Kirchhoff's laws. This system of equations reflects the circuit's topology. To complete the model, the voltage-current equation at the terminals of each element of circuit (called also constitutive relations) must be added.

The inductors and the capacitors are described by constitutive relations in which are involved the derivatives of currents, respectively voltages. As a result, the mathematic model of an electric circuit consists of a system of algebraic and differential equations (DAE).

In the electric circuit theory it is demonstrated that each current or voltage can be expressed as function of inductors currents and capacitors voltages. By other words if the inductors currents and the capacitors voltages are known, all remaining currents and voltages are uniquely determined and because of this they are called state-variables.

The state-variable equations are obtained by elimination of the algebraic equations in the initial DAE.

The modelization of an electric circuit made using state-equations has several important advantages.

First of all, electric circuits can be integrated with other dynamic systems, of completely different physical nature, as long as the last ones are described also by state-equations.

By the other hand, the procedures for integrating state-equations have a well-established theoretic support, being the domain of interest for quite a long period of time for famous mathematicians.

Finally, but not last, the method can be applied to linear circuits, as well as, to nonlinear circuits.

Of course there is a price to be paid for all these advantages: a certain difficulty in the elimination of the algebraic equations from the system.

In order to give an example for the basics of the state-variable method, we will analyze the simple RLC series connection circuit supplied by an ideal voltage source $u(t)$. The Kirchhoff equations and the constitutive relations for such a circuit are, respectivelly:

$$\begin{gathered} i_R(t) = i_L(t) = i_C(t), \\ u(t) = u_R(t) + u_L(t) + u_C(t), \\ u_R(t) = Ri(t), \\ u_L(t) = L\frac{di_L(t)}{dt}, \\ i_C(t) = C\frac{du_C(t)}{dt}. \end{gathered} \tag{1}$$

It is customary to write the last two equation in the form

$$\begin{aligned}\frac{di_L(t)}{dt} &= \frac{1}{L}u_L(t),\\ \frac{du_C(t)}{dt} &= \frac{1}{C}i_C(t).\end{aligned} \tag{2}$$

With the remaining equations $u_L(t)$ and $i_C(t)$ are obtained as functions of $i_L(t)$, $u_C(t)$:

$$\begin{aligned}u_L(t) &= u(t) - Ri_L(t) - u_C(t),\\ i_C(t) &= i_L(t).\end{aligned}, \tag{3}$$

By the substitution in (2) it follows

$$\begin{aligned}\frac{di_L(t)}{dt} &= \frac{1}{L}u(t) - \frac{R}{L}i_L(t) - \frac{1}{L}u_C(t),\\ \frac{du_C(t)}{dt} &= \frac{1}{C}i_L(t),\end{aligned} \tag{4}$$

or, in matrix form,

$$\frac{d}{dt}\begin{bmatrix} i_L(t) \\ u_C(t)\end{bmatrix} = \begin{bmatrix} -\frac{R}{L} & -\frac{1}{L} \\ \frac{1}{C} & 0 \end{bmatrix}\begin{bmatrix} i_L(t) \\ u_C(t)\end{bmatrix} + \begin{bmatrix} -\frac{1}{L} & 0 \end{bmatrix}\begin{bmatrix} u(t) \\ 0 \end{bmatrix}. \tag{5}$$

This is a first order differential equations system, with the variables $i_L(t)$ and $u_C(t)$.

If the initial conditions $i_L(0)$ and $u_C(0)$ are known, then, according to the uniqueness theorem for the solution of a first order differential equation, the solution $i_L(t)$ and $u_C(t)$, $t \geq 0$, exists and is unique.

Once the solutions for the variables $i_L(t)$ and $u_C(t)$ are available, immediately all the other unknowns are solved. Therefore, $i_L(t)$ and $u_C(t)$ are the state-variables of the circuit, and (5) is the matrix state equation of the circuit.

Generally, for a linear electric circuit, the matrix state equation is of the type (6):

$$\frac{d\mathbf{x}(t)}{dt} = \mathbf{A}\,\mathbf{x}(t) + \mathbf{B}\,\mathbf{u}(t), \tag{6}$$

where $x(t)$ is the column matrix of the inductor currents and of the capacitor voltages (state-vector),

$u(t)$ is the column matrix of independent supply sources (sources vector), and, A and B are matrix depending on the circuits topology and of its parameters.

The total number of the state variables is equal with the sum of the number of the inductors and capacitors from the circuit, representing the order of the circuit.

All the other unknown variables are represented by the column matrix *y*(*t*) (also called output vector) represented by a linear combination of the state-vector and the sources vector):

$$\mathbf{y}(t) = \mathbf{C}\mathbf{x}(t) + \mathbf{D}\mathbf{u}(t), \tag{7}$$

C and *D* being matrix of the same origin as *A* and *B*.

The equation given by (6) describes the model, in state-space, of a linear electric circuit.

It is possible, as the result of using ideal elements in the modelization, to occur capacitive loops or inductive sections.

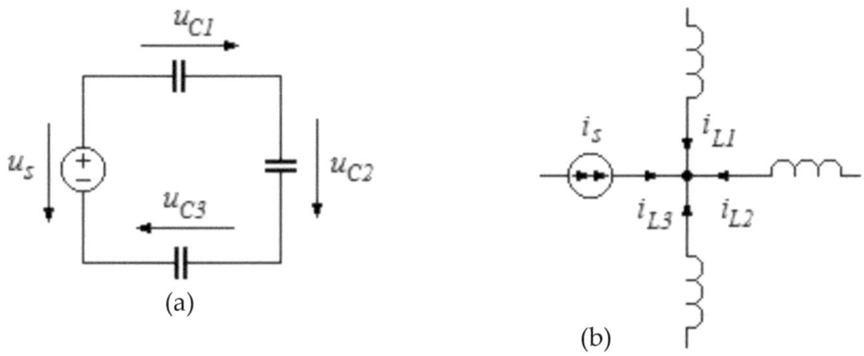

Figure 1. Capacitive loop and, respectively, inductive section

A capacitive loop (see Fig. 1a) is a loop consisting only from capacitors and, possibly, independent voltage sources.

In this case the voltages at the terminals of capacitors from the loop are no more linearly independent variables, because the second Kirchhoff's law gives:

$$-u_S + u_{C1} + u_{C2} + u_{C3} = 0\,. \tag{8}$$

One, arbitrarily selected, of the capacitor voltages can be expressed as a linear combination of the other voltages.

Such a situation is present also for inductive sections.

An inductive section is represented in Fig.1b, being composed by the convergence in a node of ideal inductors and, possibly, independent current sources. In this case the first Kirchhoff's law states that

$$-i_S + i_{L1} + i_{L_2} + i_{L_3} = 0\,. \tag{9}$$

Again anyone of the state variables can be expressed as a function of the others.

The order of an RLC circuit , meaning the number of linearly independent variables (and by consequence the number of state-equations) is equal to $n_{LC} - n_{bC} - n_{sL}$:

n_{LC} is the total number (sum) of inductors and capacitors

n_{bC} is the number of the capacitive loops

n_{sL} is the number of inductive sections.

The programs performing the analysis make the detection of capacitive loops and of the inductive sections presents in the electric circuit. Usually, it is recommended to introduce a very small value resistor in series connection with one of the elements of the capacitive loop, or to connect a high value resistor in parallel to one of the elements of the inductive section. By this the circuits differs from the original, but the difference in currents values and voltages values are insignificant

The method of state variables can be naturally extended for nonlinear circuits. In this case the circuit equations are of the form

$$\begin{aligned} f_R\left(u_R, i_R\right) &= 0, \\ u_C = \frac{dq}{dt}; \; f_C(u_C, q) &= 0, \\ i_L = \frac{d\Phi}{dt}; \; f_L(i_L, \Phi) &= 0, \end{aligned} \tag{10}$$

with f_R, f_C, f_L being the characteristics of nonlinear elements and, q and Φ, the electric charge of the capacitor, respectively the magnetic flux trough the inductor.

The procedure for obtaining the state equations is similar as for linear circuits, with the difference that the state variables are q and Φ. These variables are present in the dynamic constitutive equations.

The variables u_C and i_L are obtained as functions of q and Φ and afterwards :

$$\frac{d\boldsymbol{x}}{dt} = \boldsymbol{F}\left(\boldsymbol{x}, t\right), \tag{11}$$

In (11) x is the column matrix of state variables (state vector), and F is a matrix depending on the circuits topology and on the nonlinear characteristics.

If for linear circuits, the circuits equations can be always reduced to state equations, for certain nonlinear circuits it is not possible to allow state equations (Hasler & Neirynck, 1985).

Anyhow, for a modelization not excessively idealized and a reasonable choice of state variable it is possible to obtain always state equations. For nonlinear state equations even the problem of existing or not of a solution might occur.

State equations for linear circuits have exact analytically determined solution, available in any book of college mathematics. If the order of the circuit is higher than three, analytic solution implies calculations so complicated that this method becomes inefficient. For this kind of situations a large offer of numeric integrations methods is available embedded in the commercial programs of numeric simulation.

3. Simulation of electric circuits using PSPICE

The levels of the analysis of electric circuits performed by PSPICE are, mainly, the following (Radoi, 1994; Vladimirescu, 1999):

a. Solving a linear electric circuit, invariable with time,
b. Solving a nonlinear electric circuit,
c. Solving a time variable electric circuit.

For solving the electric circuit problems PSPICE uses the branch current method. Each element of the circuit is considered being placed between two nodes. The nodes are numbered from "0", the reference node, to N and the position of an element is given by the numbers of its terminals. A very simple circuit example is given in Fig. 2.

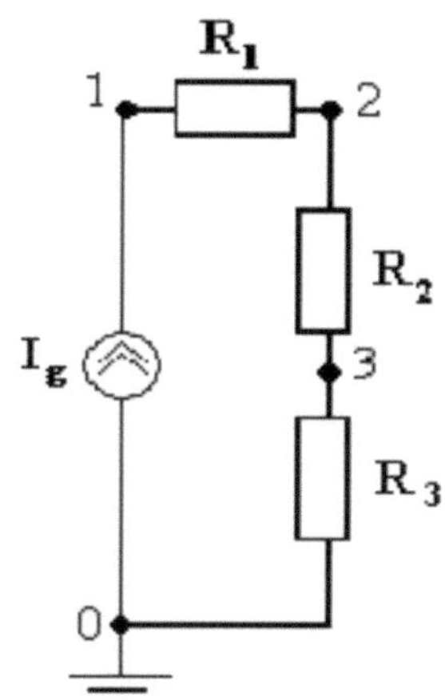

Figure 2. Simple circuit for SPICE application

$$\begin{cases} \dfrac{V_0 - V_3}{R_3} = -I_g & \textit{for node } 0, \\ \dfrac{V_1 - V_2}{R_1} = I_g & \textit{for node } 1, \\ \dfrac{V_1 - V_2}{R_1} = \dfrac{V_2 - V_3}{R_2} & \textit{for node } 2, \\ \dfrac{V_2 - V_3}{R_2} = \dfrac{V_3 - V_0}{R} & \textit{for node } 3. \end{cases} \tag{12}$$

These equations can be written in matrix form also as (13), where [I] is the column matrix of the sources for all the nodes, in the same order as the unknown nodes potentials in matrix [V]. [G] is the square conductance matrix.

The potential of the reference node, "0", is taken with "zero" value so all the other N-1 nodes potentials remain as unknown values in the equation system.

With $V_0 = 0$, system (13) is transformed into a system (14) with N-1 equations.

In this very simple example remain only 3 unknown values of nodes potentials (14).

$$\begin{bmatrix} -I_g \\ +I_g \\ 0 \\ 0 \end{bmatrix} = \begin{bmatrix} \frac{1}{R_3} & 0 & 0 & -\frac{1}{R_3} \\ 0 & \frac{1}{R_1} & -\frac{1}{R_1} & 0 \\ 0 & -\frac{1}{R_1} & \frac{1}{R_1}+\frac{1}{R_2} & -\frac{1}{R_2} \\ -\frac{1}{R_3} & 0 & -\frac{1}{R_2} & \frac{1}{R_2}+\frac{1}{R_3} \end{bmatrix} \cdot \begin{bmatrix} V_0 \\ V_1 \\ V_2 \\ V_3 \end{bmatrix} \text{ or, } [I]=[G]\cdot[V] \quad (13)$$

$$\begin{bmatrix} +I_g \\ 0 \\ 0 \end{bmatrix} = \begin{bmatrix} \frac{1}{R_1} & -\frac{1}{R_1} & 0 \\ -\frac{1}{R_1} & \frac{1}{R_1}+\frac{1}{R_2} & -\frac{1}{R_2} \\ 0 & -\frac{1}{R_2} & \frac{1}{R_2}+\frac{1}{R_3} \end{bmatrix} \cdot \begin{bmatrix} V_1 \\ V_2 \\ V_3 \end{bmatrix} . \quad (14)$$

The system (14) can be solved using the Gaussian elimination method (Ross, 2004).

An equivalent method that can be used for solving the system is the LU factorization, by decomposing the [G] matrix.

Matrix [G]=[L]·[U], with [L] being a matrix with "1" on the principal diagonal, and [U] is a matrix having only "0" below the principal diagonal. This method is more advantageous than the "classic" Gauss elimination method, mainly when the equation [I] = [G]·[V] has to be solved several times: several sources [I] for the same conductance matrix. This is the situation for solving our problem using PSPICE, so that the LU factorization method shall be used.

In the analysis of dynamical circuits either the sources, voltage or current sources, have time variation, either the topology of the circuit is changing. If the passive elements are resistors, linear or nonlinear, using a time step Δt for the discretization of the time variation (sinusoidal, exponential, linear) of the sources. For each time moment a set of values [V(t)] is calculated and memorized. These values can be used in further graph representations or printed.

The presence of inductors and/or capacitors implies replacing them with equivalent elements.

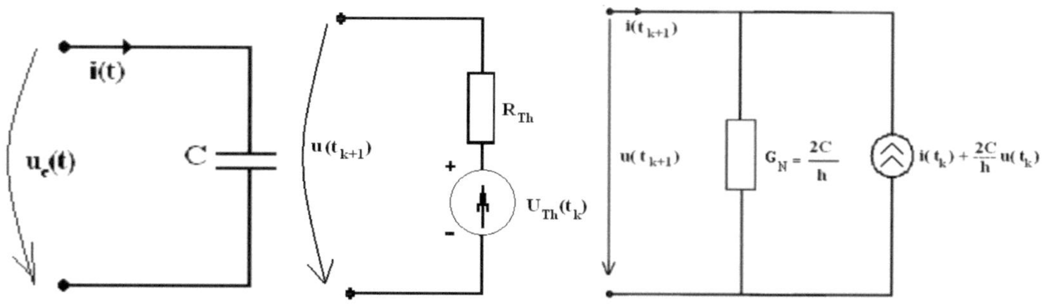

Figure 3. Thevenin and Norton generators for a capacitor , when trapeze method is used

For an iterative calculation process the capacitor can be replaced by a Thevenin or a Norton generator. The Norton generator presented in the Fig. 3 has the parameters calculated according to the trapeze method of integration. The method using the Euler's regressive algorithm and the Gear's second order algorithm can be used also, but the equivalences (parameters of the Norton or Thevenin generators) are different from those presented in Fig. 3.

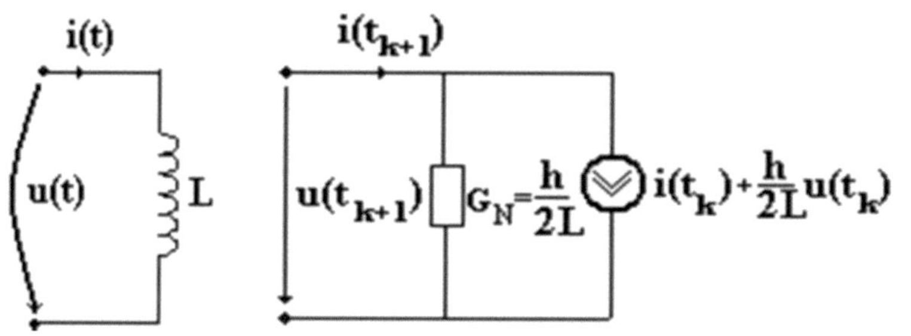

Figure 4. Norton equivalent generator representation of a inductor, when trapeze method is used

In a similar manner for an inductor can be used a Norton equivalent generator or a Thevenin equivalent generator, with parameters depending on the method used for solving the problem. Taking the nodes potentials as unknown values it is more suitable to use the Norton generator equivalent to the inductor in a dynamic circuit.

The transient regime analysis is the most important analysis that can be performed using PSPICE.

When the transient regime begins with non zero initial conditions this fact can be introduced in the program by the option UIC (use initial conditions).

The situation of the modelization of a complex network is shown in the Fig. 5.

The transient regime is triggered by closing the switch, meaning that phase one is grounded, as if a fault phase to ground is produced.

Resistor R_{17} has a value that is corresponding to the conditions of the fault.

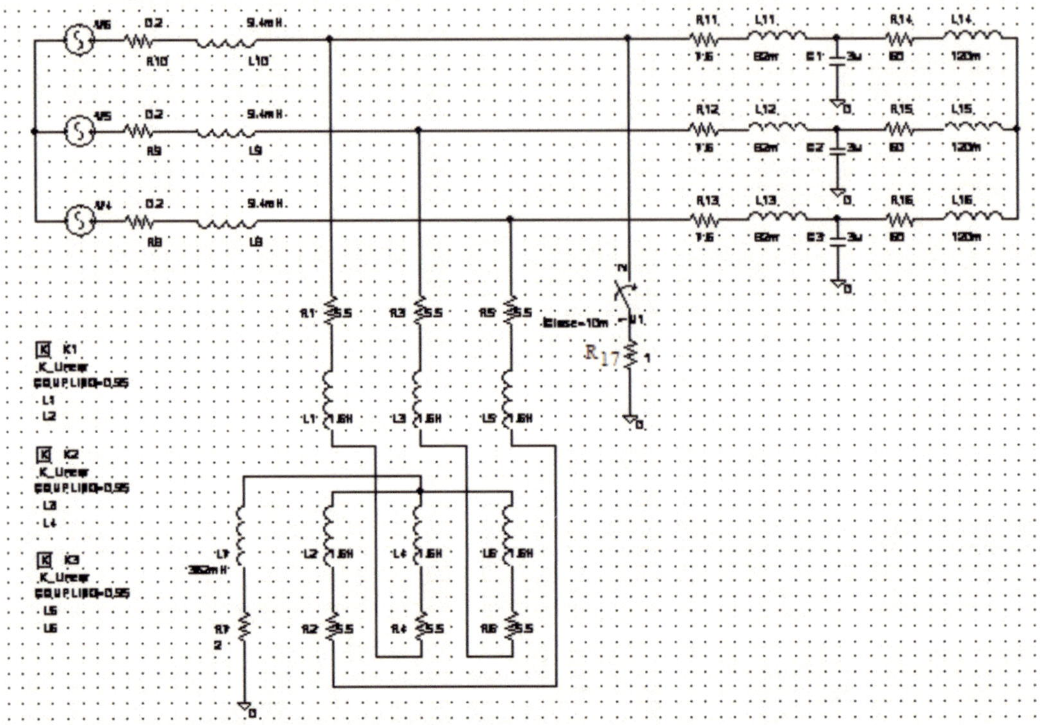

Figure 5. MVN represented as a complex circuit in SPICE drawing

Currents and voltages can be represented, as on a "soft" oscilloscope, after solving the transient regime, using the elements of the V[t] matrix, calculated for each time step, and the resulting, calculated, currents values.

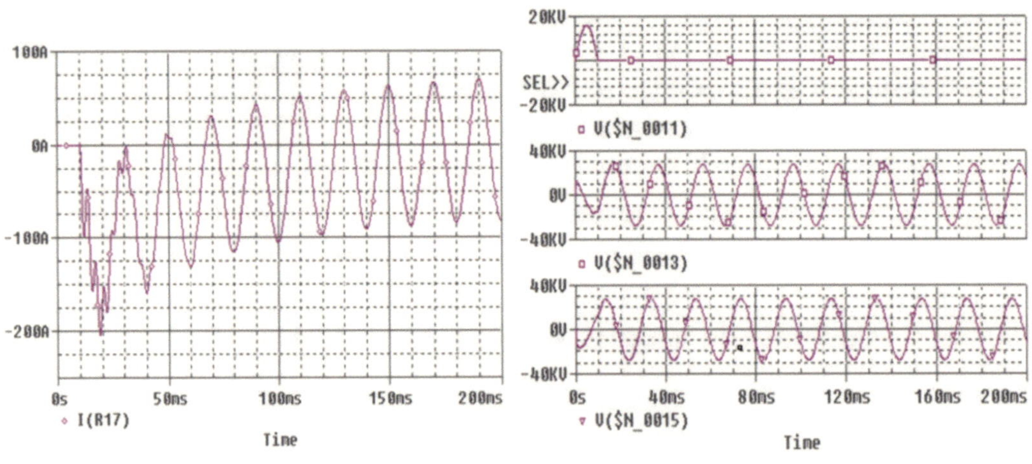

Figure 6. Current and voltages representation as SPICE output oscillogrames

4. Numeric simulation of transients triggered by faults in medium voltage networks

Faults in medium voltage networks (MVN) generate transient regimes with duration depending on the networks parameters, on the contact type at the fault place and on the default type itself. The numeric simulation performed in this chapter is based on PSPICE and the transient regimes are caused by simple and double grounding faults, as well as, by the fault produced by a broken conductor, grounded towards the consumer. A fault of the type broken conductor grounded towards the source can be treated similar as the simple grounding fault, with an insignificant error, so shall be no more analyzed in the followings (Sybille et al., 2000).

The elements that are important in the analysis are:

- the initial phase α of the faulty phase,
- the electric resistance at the fault, grounding point,
- the method used for grounding the neutral of the network,
- the functioning regime of the MVN.

4.1. The structure of MVN

The single line diagram of the MVN whose behavior is studied in case of transient caused by faults is presented in Fig. 7.

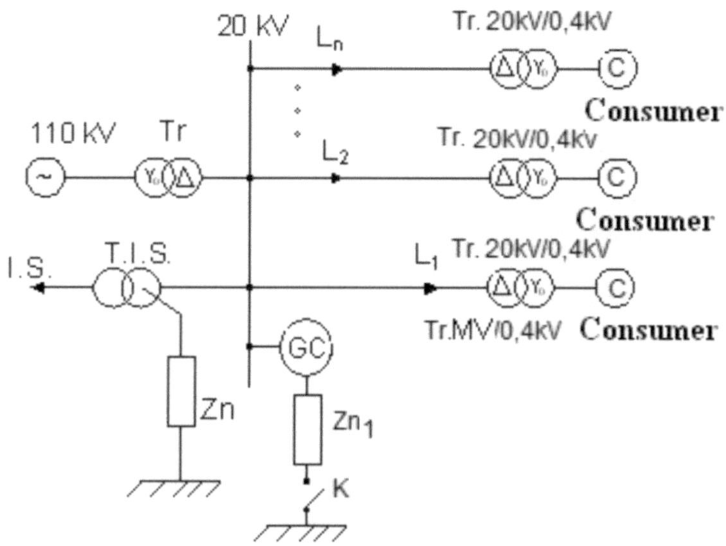

Figure 7. Single Line Diagram of the MVN

The MVN in Fig. 7 contains the following elements:

- The source, the 110kV line supplying the transformer 110kV/20kV, considered as being of infinite power supply and internal impedance zero,

- The transformer (Tr) 110kV/20kV star connection with neutral point on 110kV side and delta connection on the 20kV side,
- The lines of 20kV (L_1 ... L_n),
- The transformers TR.20kV/0.4kV supplying low voltage consumers, transformers having star or delta connection on the 20kV side and star with null or zigzag with null on the low voltage side,
- Low voltage consumers (C),
- The transformer for internal services (TIS) ; this transformer is used also for creating the artificial null of the 20kV network (has zigzag connection with null on the 20kV side and star with null on the low voltage side),
- The grounding inductor (GC) , having zigzag with null and creates the artificial null of the 20kV network,
- The impedance for treatment of the null (Z_n), impedance that might be a compensation inductor, a resistor or might be missing in the case of isolated null,
- The resistor for the null's treatment (Z_{n1}),
- The switch for the connection to the ground of the resistor Z_{n1}.

The model is designed with the possibility of changing the values of parameters.

4.2. Numerical simulation of some fault types

The numeric simulator of the three phased circuit corresponding to a MVN is shown in Fig.8. The PSPICE program is used to perform the modelization. Several types of faults are simulated using the model:

- simple grounding fault,
- double grounding fault,
- broken conductor and grounded on the consumer side.

The MVN where the faults are modelized has the following characteristics:

- nominal line voltage 20kV,
- S = 25MVA, the apparent power of the transformer 110kv/MV,
- the capacitive current of the MVN is 100A,
- the current of the two faulty lines , 8A each,
- the apparent power of the consumers is 80% of the nominal one and is uniformly distributed on the MV lines.

The simulator contains three lines, denoted with "a", "b" and "c" , so that to each index of parameter such as resistance or inductance is added a, b or c. The line "c" is considered as the healthy line and is the equivalent of all the 20kV lines without fault (Bucatariu et al., 2009; Drapela, 2009)

The line "a" is provided with the possibility of the simulation of a simple grounding fault, by connecting V_{Sa}. The same line "a" might simulate a fault of the type broken conductor (by opening the switch VSGOL). Even more, by opening the switch VSGOL and closing, in the same time, the switch VS_a it is possible to simulate a fault of the type broken conductor and grounded on the consumer's side.

The line "b" can simulate a simple grounding fault by closing the switch VS_b.

The fault of the type double grounding is simulated by closing the switch VS_a connected to the line "a" and closing the switch VS_b connected to the line "b", as well.

If a fault of the type double grounding on the same line is wanted to be simulated, the switch VS_b should be moved from line "b" to line "a".

The parameters of the Earth (resistance, inductance) are encompassed in the parameters of the electric line.

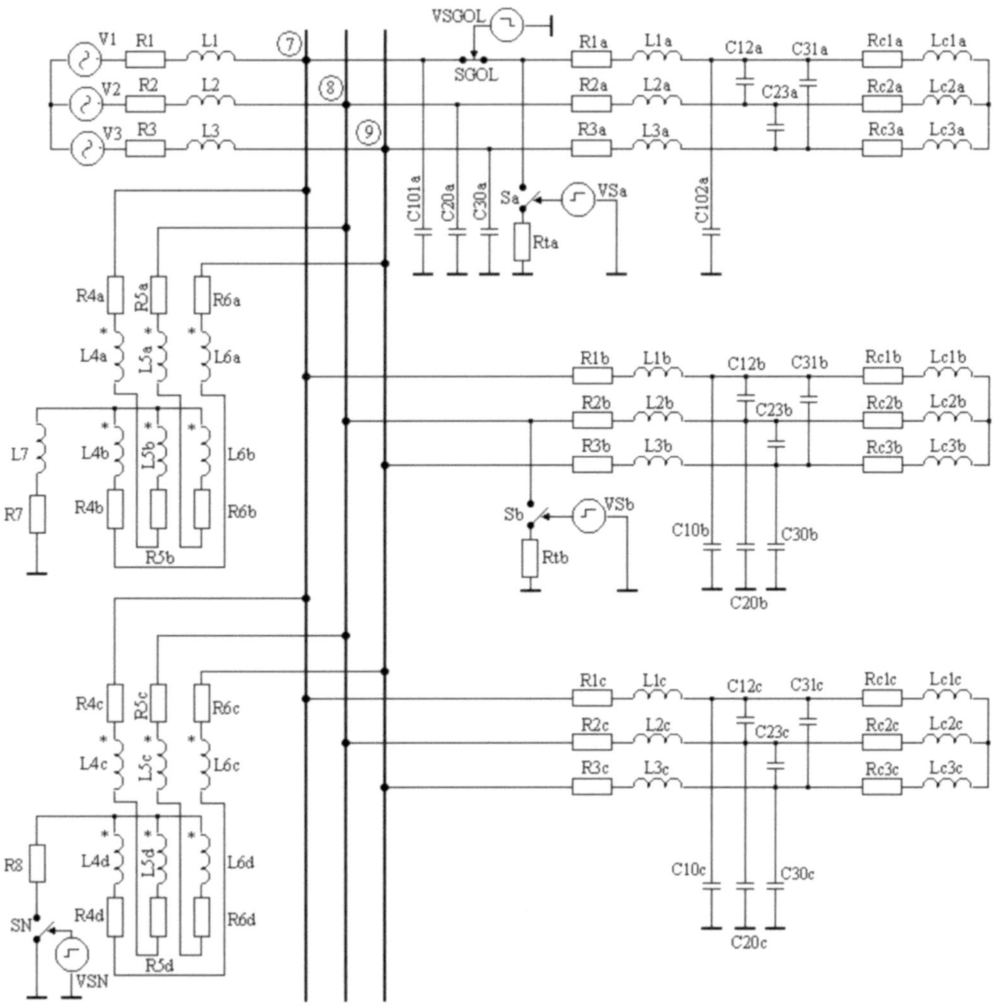

Figure 8. Three phased circuit simulating a MVN

4.2.1. The single phase-to-ground fault

Using the numerical simulator a multitude of situation could be analyzed.

One of those situations is the one when the MVN has the null grounded trough compensation inductor and the MVN functions under resonance conditions, respectively overcompensated 10%.

In these circumstances the evolution of voltages and currents during the transient is analyzed according to:

- the initial phase of the faulty phase (α) in the very moment when the fault is produced
- the electric resistance at the fault place (R_t)
- the way the null is treated
- the functioning regime (resonance, under or over compensated)

The first oscillogram, left side, is corresponding to the currents and the second corresponding to the voltages.

In these oscillograms I(S) represents the time variation of the current at the fault place, the zero sequence current of the faulty line is denoted as (I(R1a)+I(R2a)+I(R3a))/3, the zero sequence current is (I(R1b)+I(R2b)+I(R3b))/3 on the healty line, and the current trough the element for grounding the neutral point is I(L7).

In the oscillograms of the voltages , V(7), V(8) and V(9) represent, respectively, the voltages of the three phases and the zero sequence voltage of the MVN bars is represented by (V(7) + V(8) + V(9))/3.

In figures 9….20 the results correspond to the 10% overcompensated MVN with the neutral point grounded with compensation inductor. Only two values, 0 and 90°, of the initial phase of the voltage of the faulty line are taken into account. An intermediate value of 45° for this angle does not modify significantly the transient of the simple grounding fault.

From the oscillograms it can be observed that the initial phase of the faulty phase has great importance in the evolution of voltages and currents during the transient regime caused by the simple gounding fault.

Knowing, as accurate as possible, the evolution in time of the voltages gives the possibility of a good design for the MVN, strong enough to resist to the maximal applied voltage.

The maximal values of the currents are important for the correct evaluation of the mechanical forces acting on lines conductors, on the insulators and on the bars of MVN from the transformer station 110kV/MV.

The way that the electric contact is established, R_t , at the fault place, is very important in the transient evolution of the voltages and currents. If the resistance is over 100Ω the transient vanishes rapidly, in less than 5ms, and the maximal values of voltages and currents are not significant. This conclusion results by comparing oscillograms from Fig. 9 to Fig. 19, and, respectively, from Fig. 10 to Fig. 20.

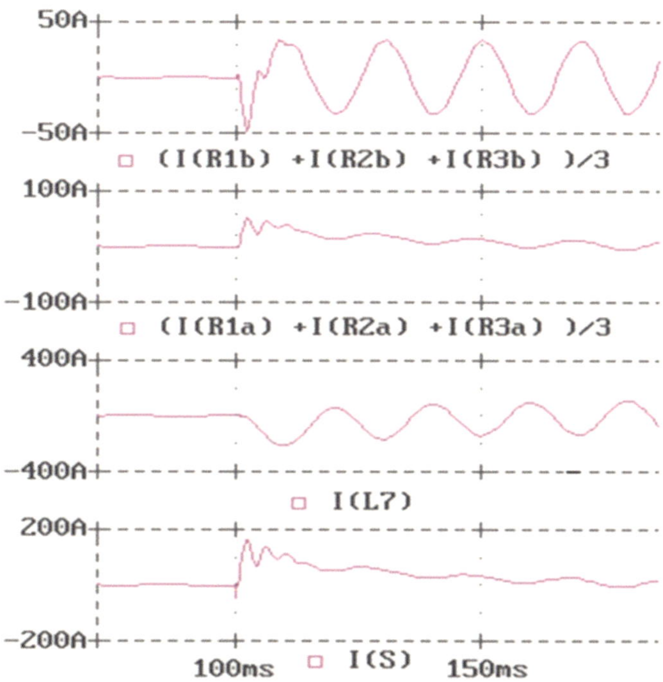

Figure 9. Time variation of the currents when MVN is 10% overcompensated and $R_t = 1\Omega$, $\alpha = 0°$

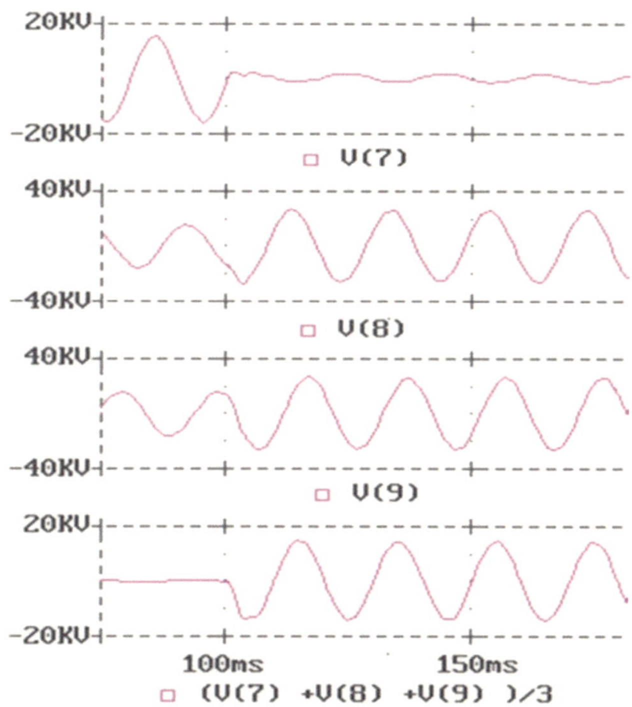

Figure 10. Time variation of the voltages when MVN is 10% overcompensated and $R_t = 1\Omega$, $\alpha = 0°$

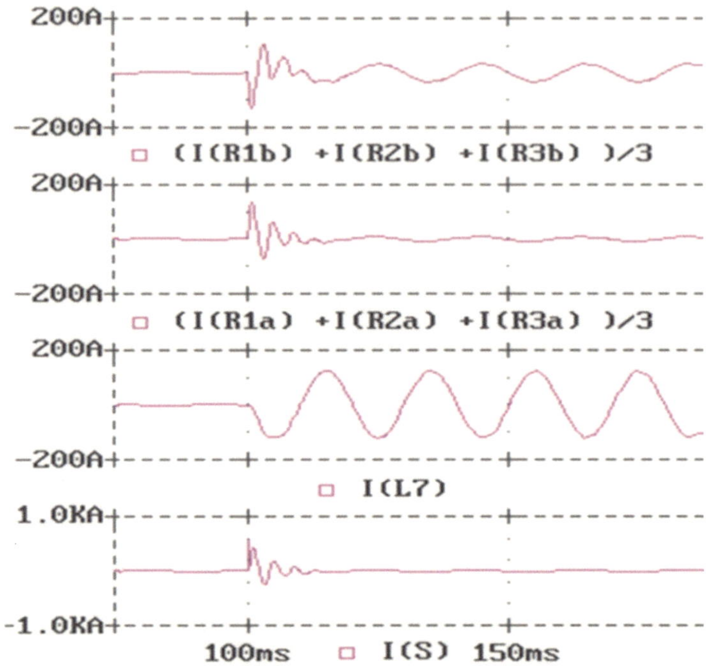

Figure 11. Time variation of the currents when MVN is 10% overcompensated and $R_t = 1\Omega$, $\alpha = 90°$

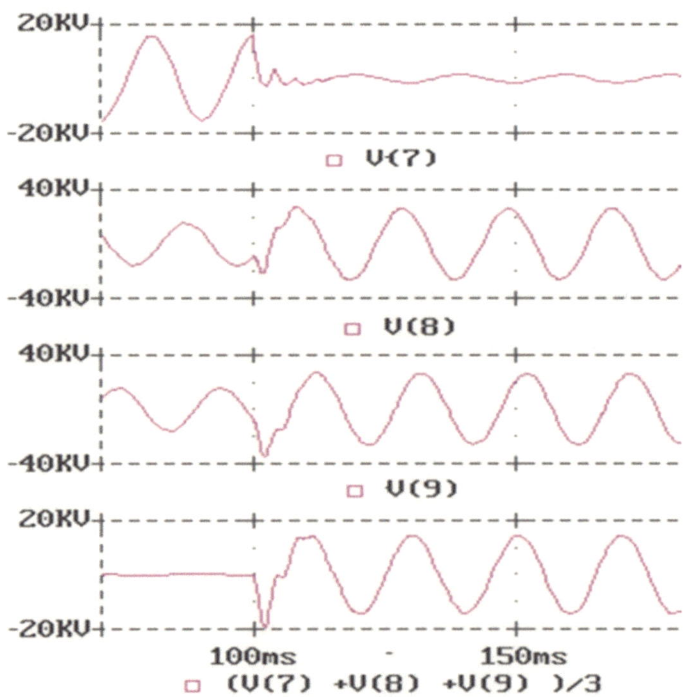

Figure 12. Time variation of the voltages when MVN is 10% overcompensated and $R_t = 1\Omega$, $\alpha = 90°$

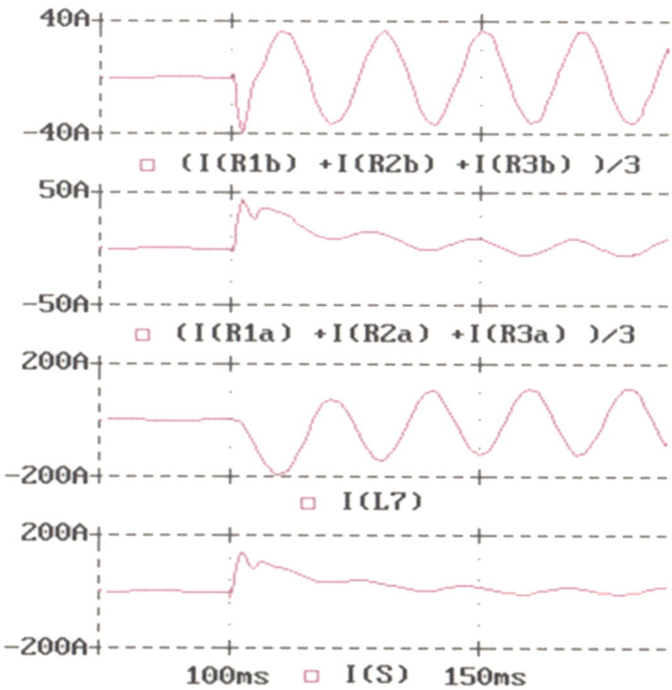

Figure 13. Time variation of the currents when MVN is 10% overcompensated $R_t = 10\Omega$, $\alpha = 0°$

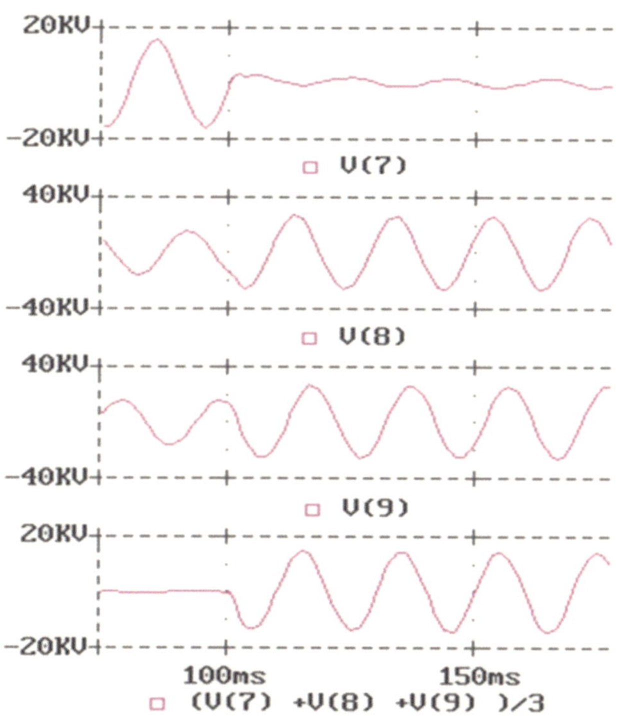

Figure 14. Time variation of the voltages when MVN is 10% overcompensated and $R_t = 10\Omega$, $\alpha = 0°$

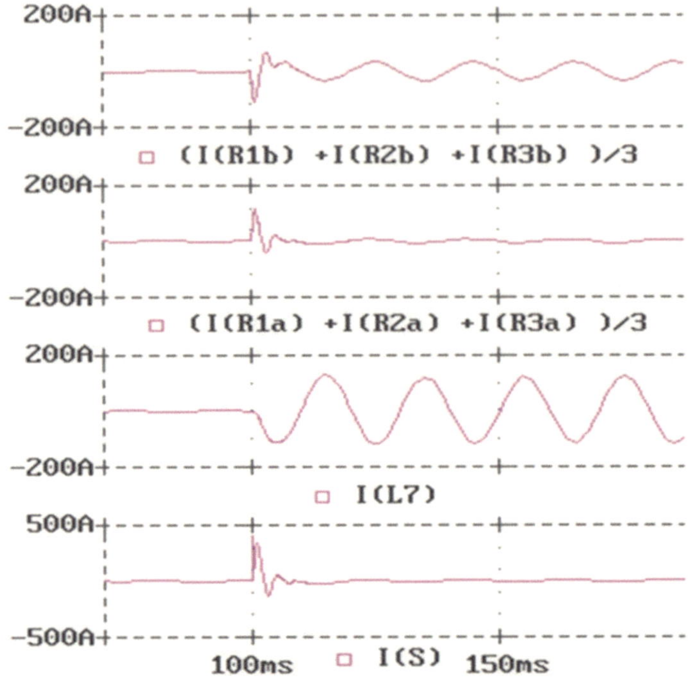

Figure 15. Time variation of the currents when MVN is 10% overcompensated $R_t = 10\Omega$, $\alpha = 90°$

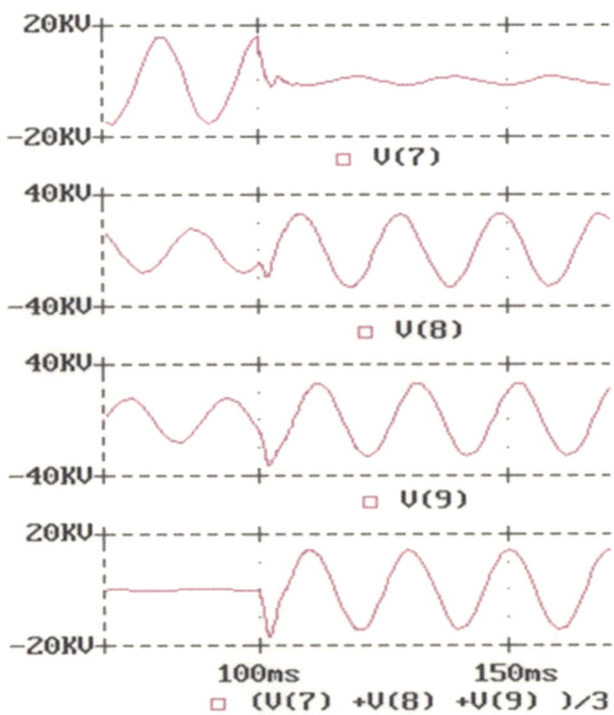

Figure 16. Time variation of the voltages when MVN is 10% overcompensated and $R_t = 10\Omega$, $\alpha = 90°$

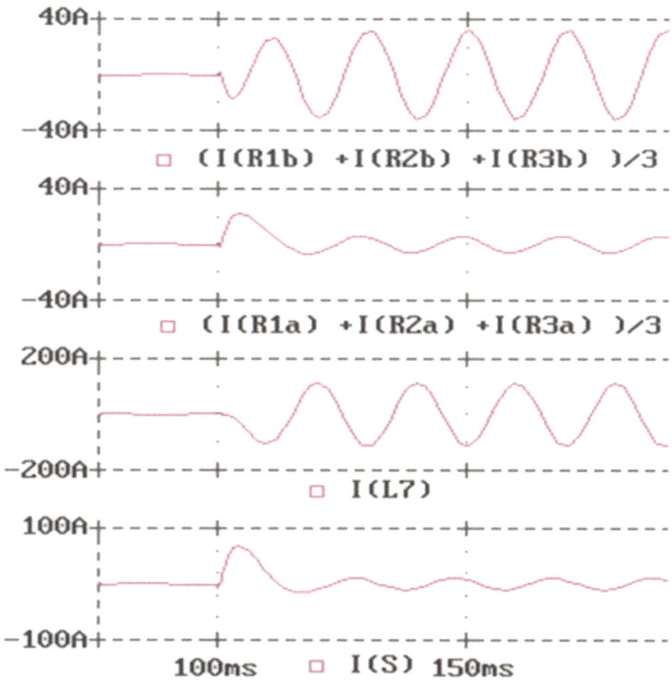

Figure 17. Time variation of the currents when MVN is 10% overcompensated $R_t = 100\Omega$, $\alpha = 0°$

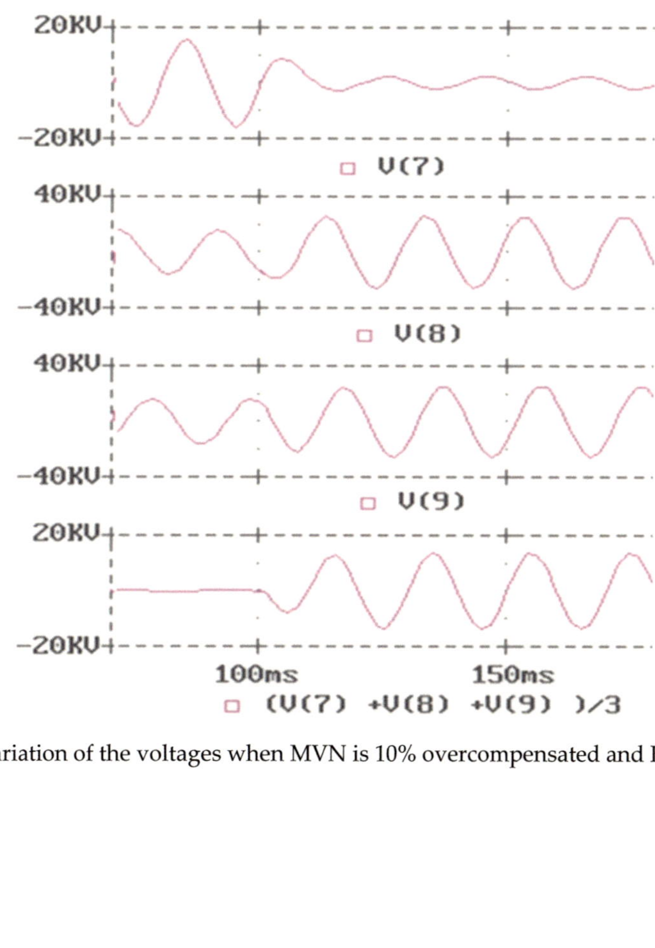

Figure 18. Time variation of the voltages when MVN is 10% overcompensated and $R_t = 100\Omega$, $\alpha = 0°$

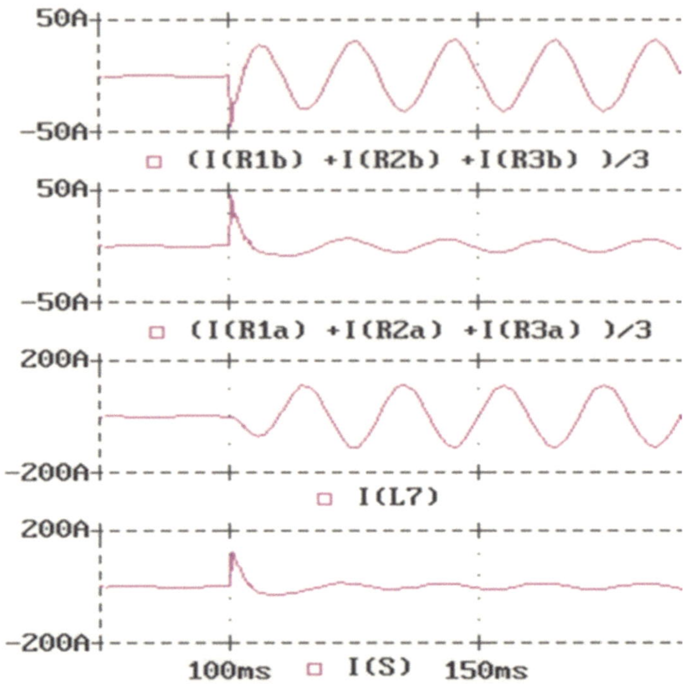

Figure 19. Time variation of the currents when MVN is 10% overcompensated $R_t = 100\Omega$, $\alpha = 90°$

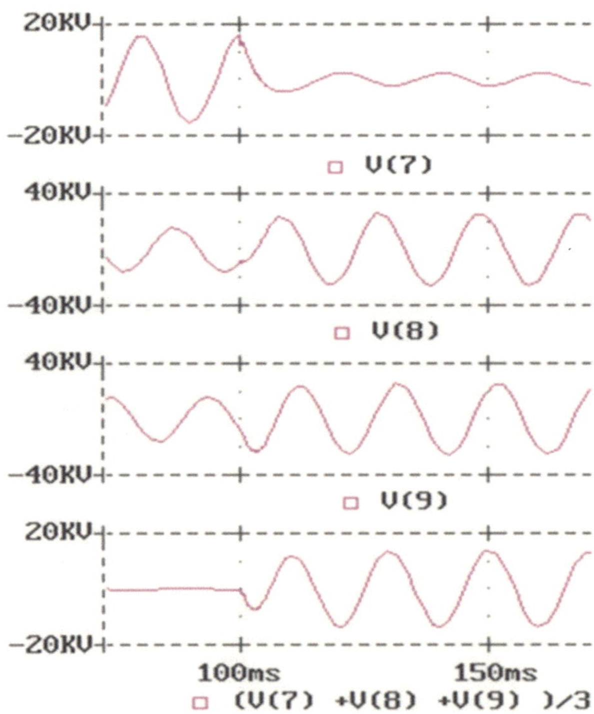

Figure 20. Time variation of the voltages when MVN is 10% overcompensated and $R_t = 100\Omega$, $\alpha = 90°$

If the MVN is functioning at resonance, the same simulation results are presented and, in addition, also the 45° value for the initial phase of the faulty phase voltage is presented.

The oscillograms show that the differences between the 10% overcompensated regime and the resonant regime are not significant.

If the functioning regime is far from being at resonance the transient regim produced by simple grounding fault is very short and the variation of voltages and currents is less important.

The maximal value of the current at fault place is obtained for 90° (comparing α values 0°, 45°, respectively 90°).

For $R_t = 1\Omega$ at $\alpha = 45°$ the current is twice its value at 0° and at 90° the current at the fault place is four times greater than the same current if $\alpha = 0°$.

If R_t becomes 10Ω the conclusions regarding the dependence of the current at the fault place on the phase α remain the same (higher α, higher value of the current) but with a decrease of about 25% of the maximal value of the current for a 10 times increase of the resistance at the fault place.

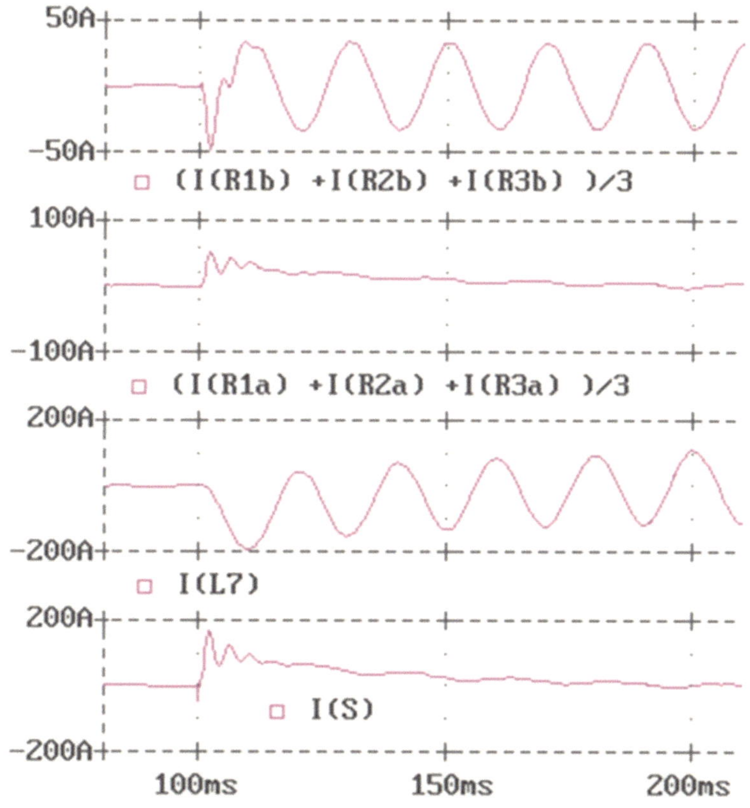

Figure 21. Time variation of the currents when MVN is at resonance , $R_t = 1\Omega$, $\alpha = 0°$

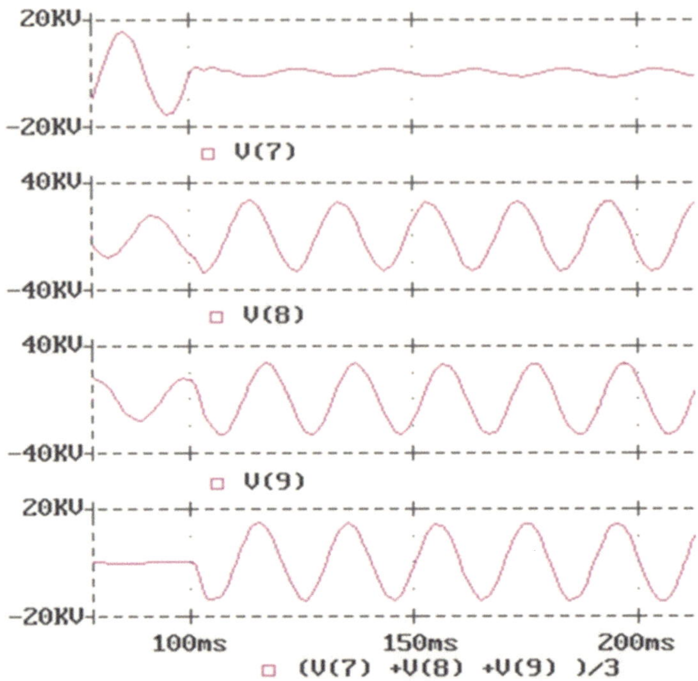

Figure 22. Time variation of the voltages when MVN is at resonance, $R_t = 1\Omega$, $\alpha = 0°$

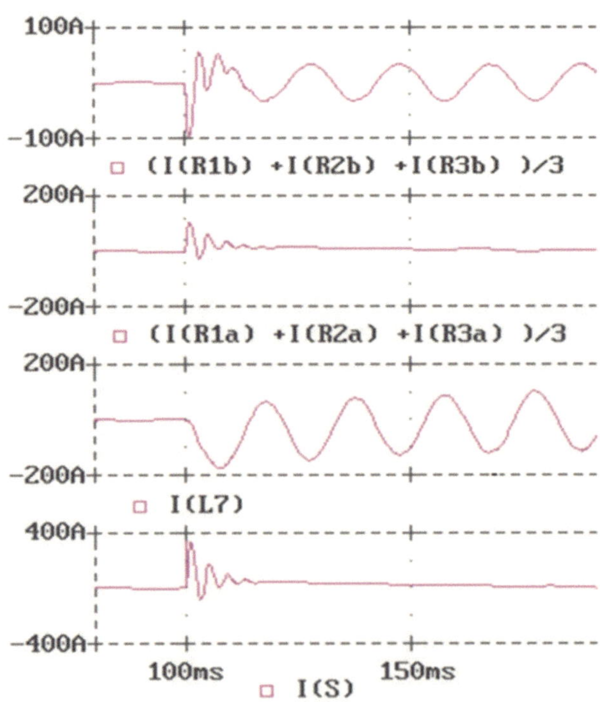

Figure 23. Time variation of the currents when MVN is at resonance , $R_t = 1\Omega$, $\alpha = 45°$

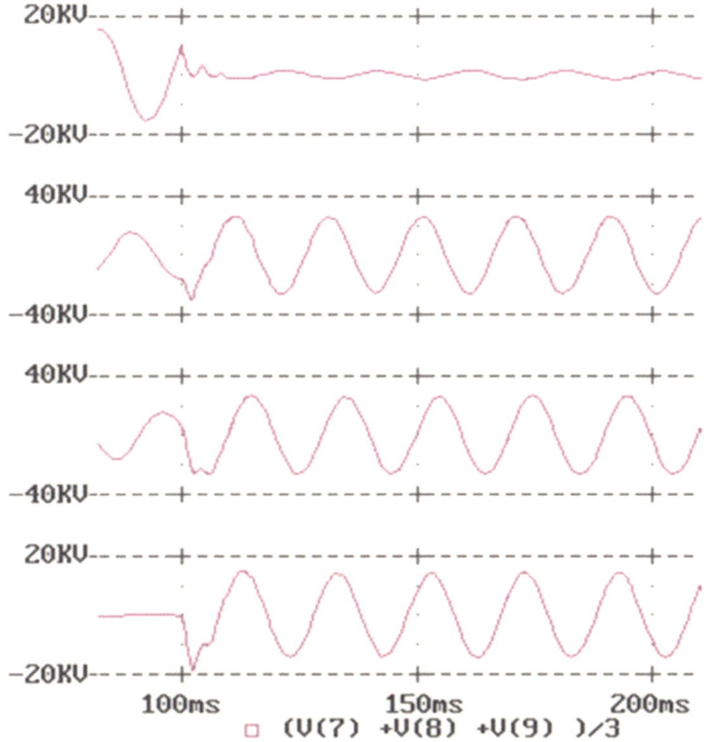

Figure 24. Time variation of the voltages when MVN is at resonance, $R_t = 1\Omega$, $\alpha = 45°$

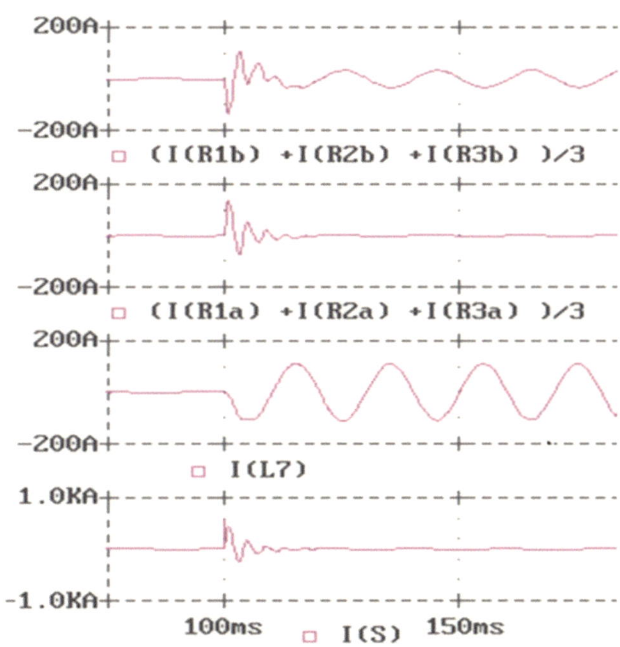

Figure 25. Time variation of the currents when MVN is at resonance , $R_t = 1\Omega$, $\alpha = 90°$

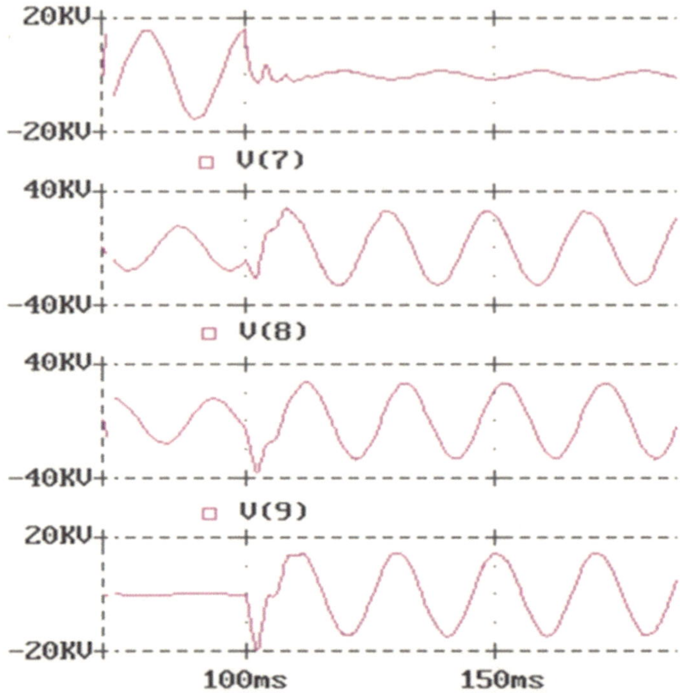

Figure 26. Time variation of the voltages when MVN is at resonance, $R_t = 1\Omega$, $\alpha = 90°$

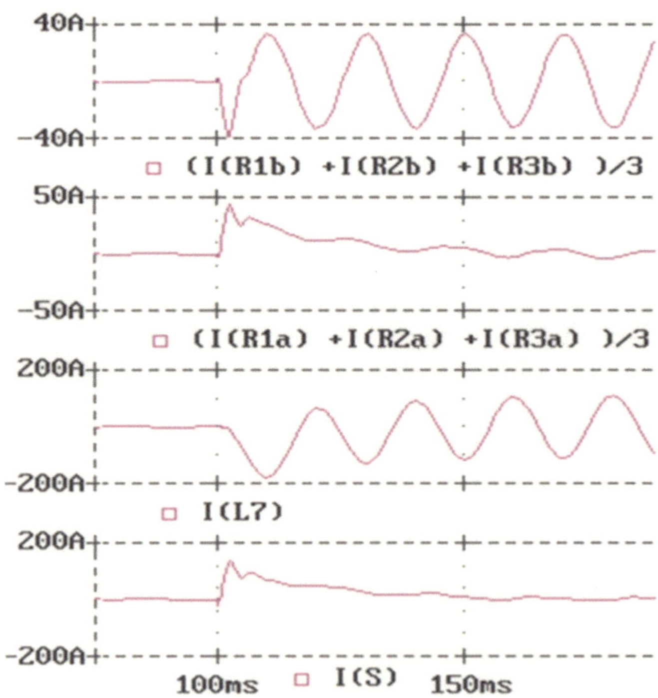

Figure 27. Time variation of the currents when MVN is at resonance , $R_t = 10\Omega$, $\alpha = 0°$

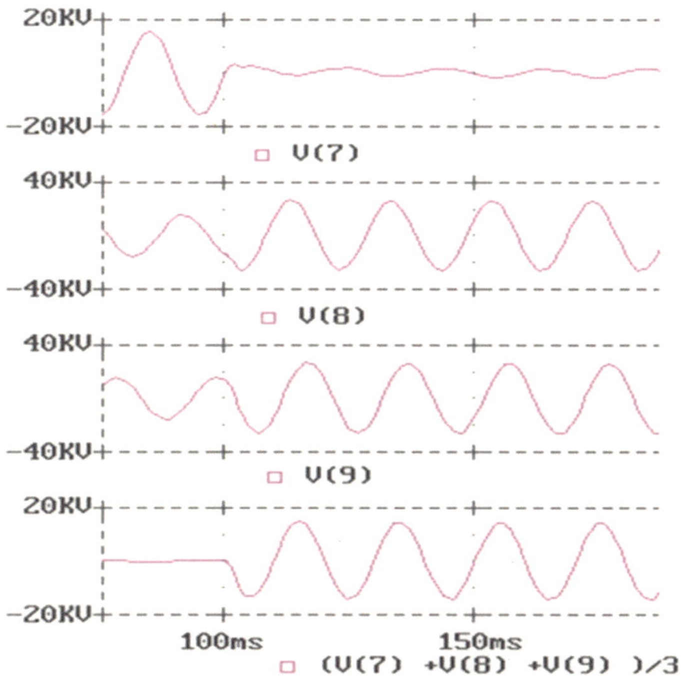

Figure 28. Time variation of the voltages when MVN is at resonance, $R_t = 10\Omega$, $\alpha = 0°$

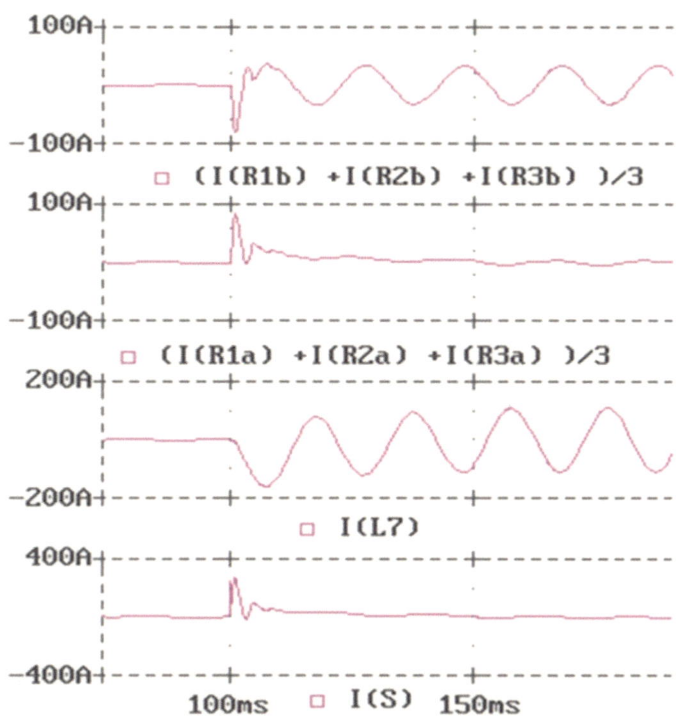

Figure 29. Time variation of the currents when MVN is at resonance , $R_t = 10\Omega$, $\alpha = 45°$

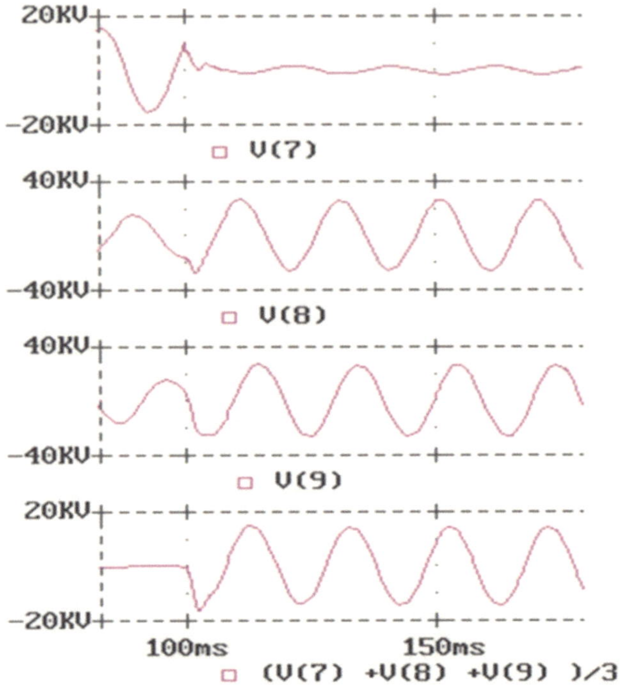

Figure 30. Time variation of the voltages when MVN is at resonance, $R_t = 10\Omega$, $\alpha = 45°$

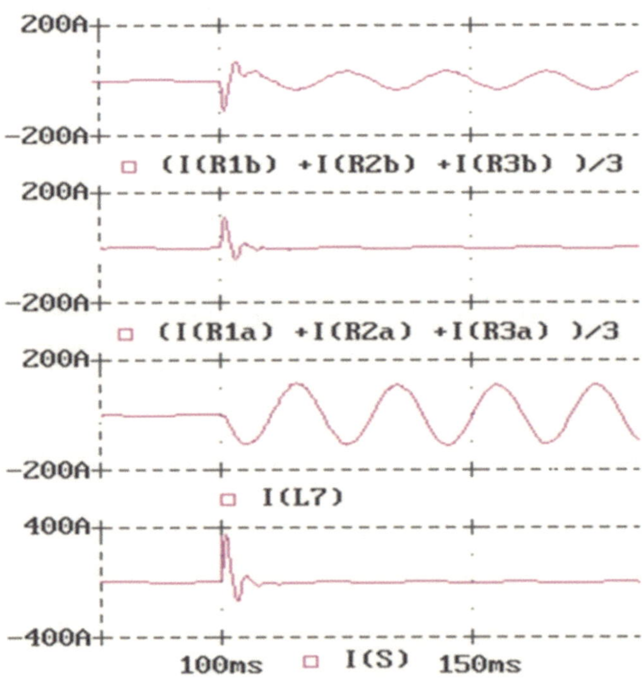

Figure 31. Time variation of the currents when MVN is at resonance , $R_t = 10\Omega$, $\alpha = 90°$

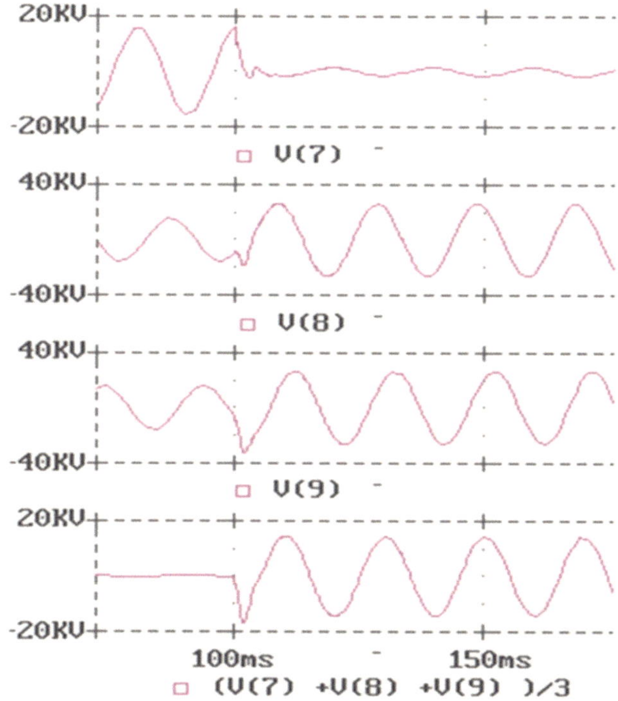

Figure 32. Time variation of the voltages when MVN is at resonance, $R_t = 10\Omega$, $\alpha = 90°$

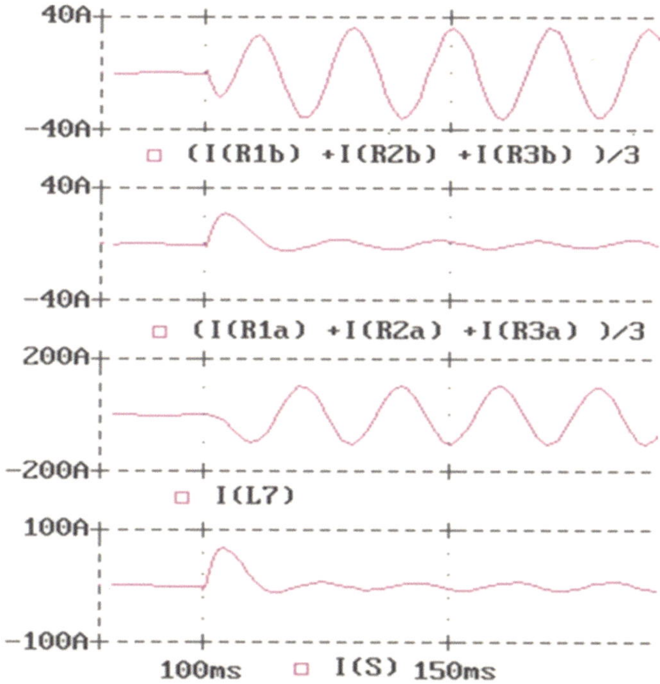

Figure 33. Time variation of the currents when MVN is at resonance , $R_t = 100\Omega$, $\alpha = 0°$

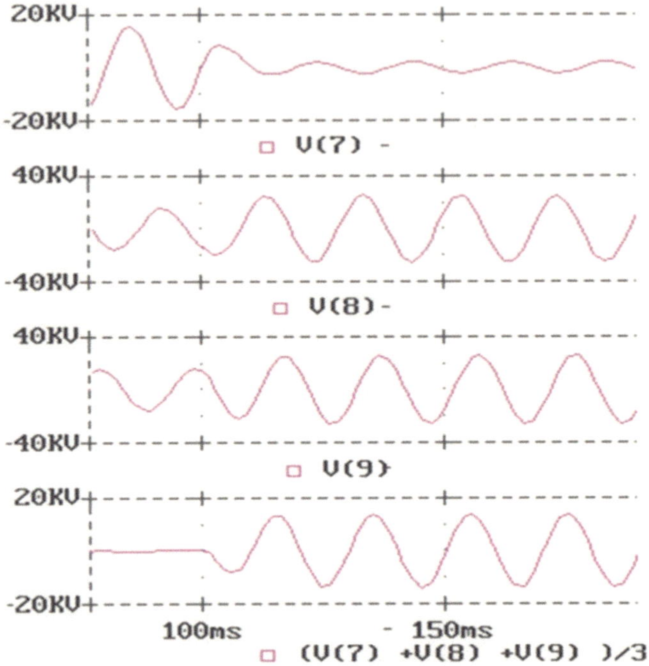

Figure 34. Time variation of the voltages when MVN is at resonance, $R_t = 100\Omega$, $\alpha = 0°$

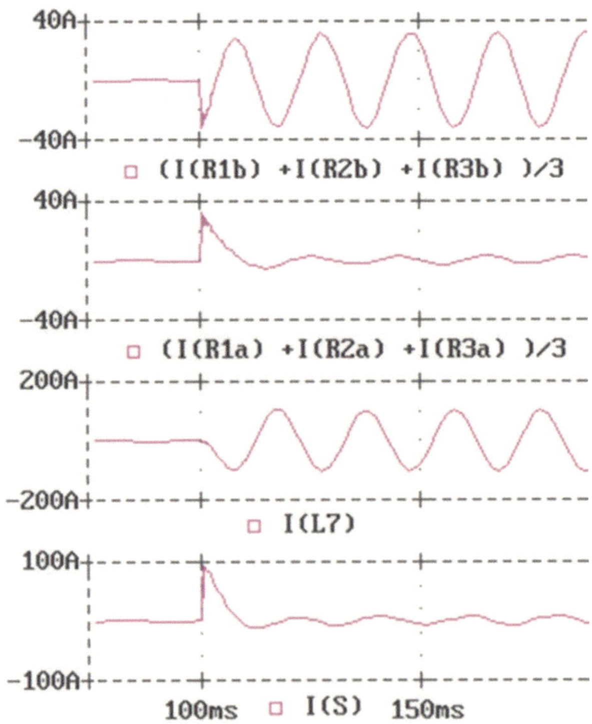

Figure 35. Time variation of the currents when MVN is at resonance , $R_t = 100\Omega$, $\alpha = 45°$

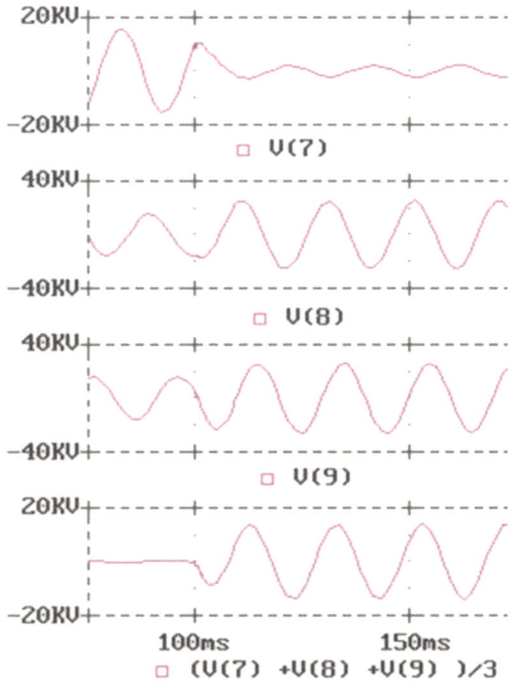

Figure 36. Time variation of the voltages when MVN is at resonance, $R_t = 100\Omega$, $\alpha = 45°$

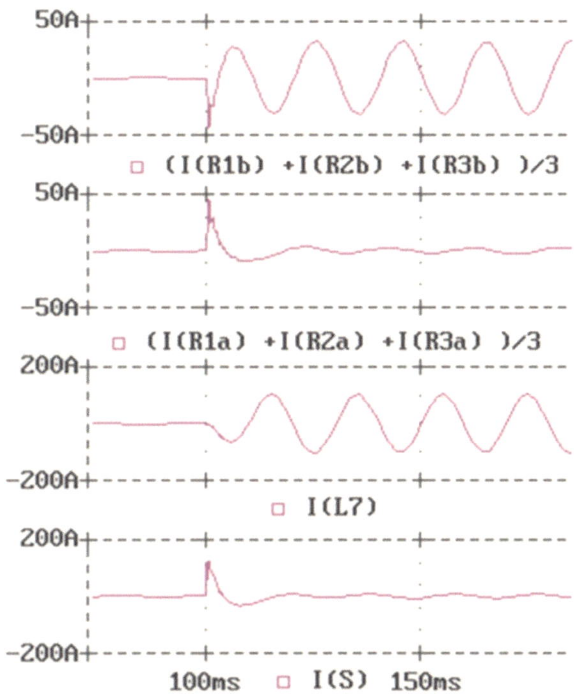

Figure 37. Time variation of the currents when MVN is at resonance , $R_t = 100\Omega$, $\alpha = 90°$

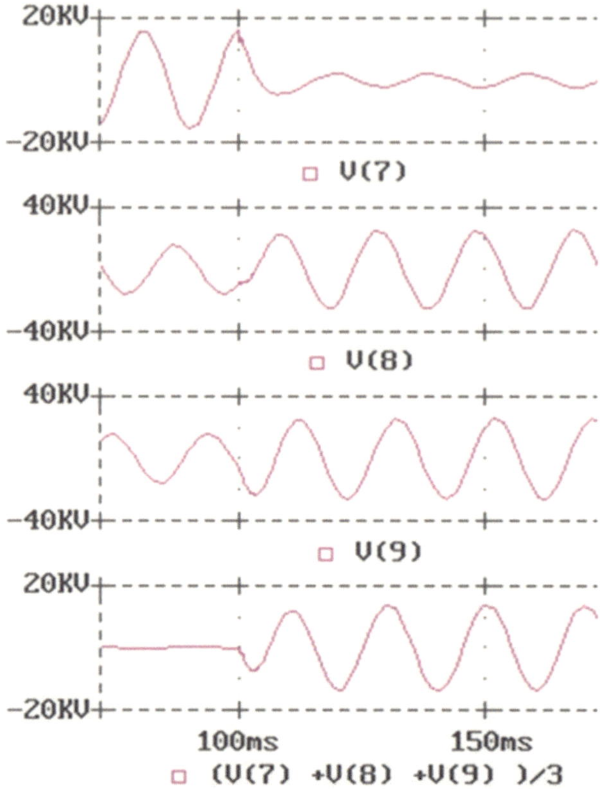

Figure 38. Time variation of the voltages when MVN is at resonance, $R_t = 100\Omega$, $\alpha = 90°$

4.2.2. The double phase-to-ground fault

The same simulation model from Fig. 8 is used with the switch VSa closed, and after 20ms the switch VSb is connected also. VSGOL remains in „closed" position.

The double phase to ground fault was simulated for neutral point grounded by compensation inductor and, respectively, by resistor.

In both cases R_t was considered consecutively with 1Ω, 100Ω, 1000Ω trough VSa switch and with 1Ω trough VSb .

In both cases $\alpha = 90°$ was considered, but also $\alpha = 0°$ was imposed for the situation with compensation inductor.

Also the situation with isolated neutral point was simulated, with same R_t values , but only with $\alpha = 90°$. (Curcanu et al., 2006).

The same symbols are used in oscillograms for the currents, just in addition the index "a" is used for the first faulty line (simulated by switch VSa) and the index "b" for the second faulty line (VSb). For the voltages the symbols are quite the same as those used previously.

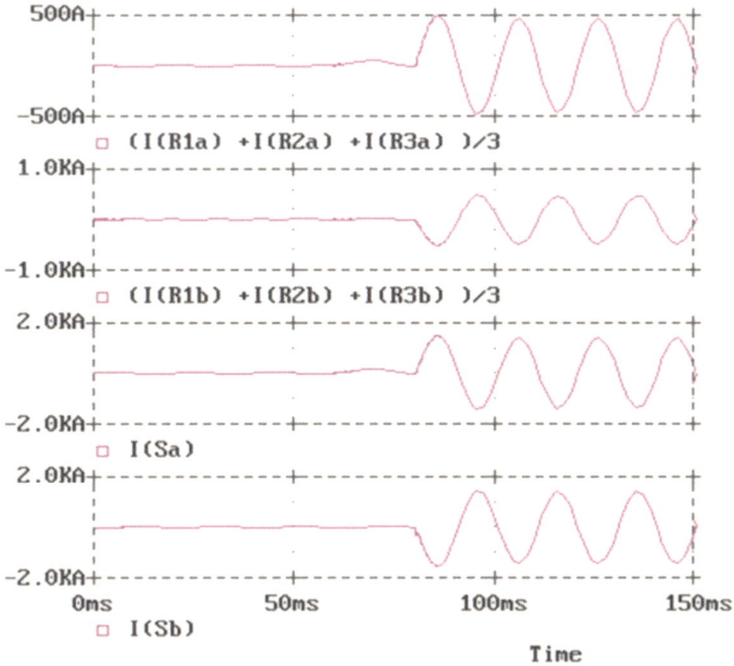

Figure 39. Time variation of the currents when MVN is at resonance , $R_t = 1\Omega$, $\alpha = 0°$

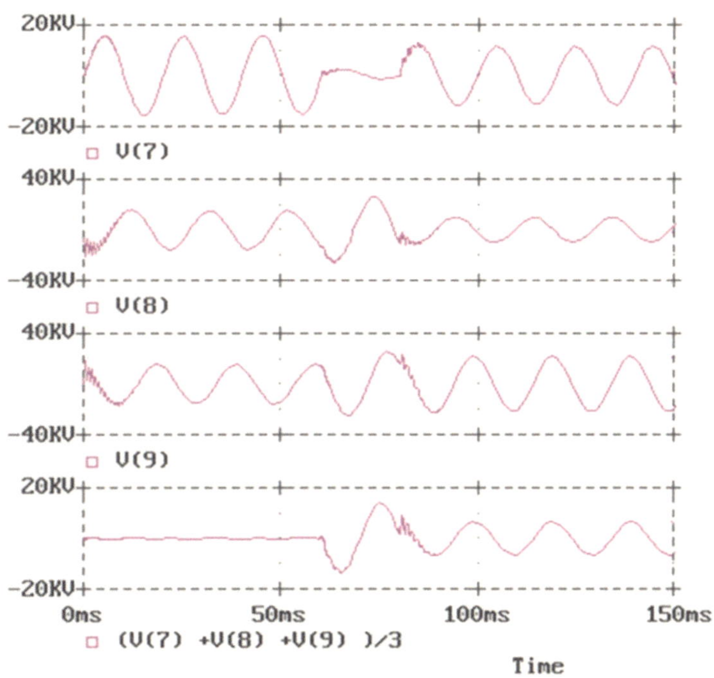

Figure 40. Time variation of the voltages when MVN is at resonance, $R_t = 1\Omega$, $\alpha = 0°$

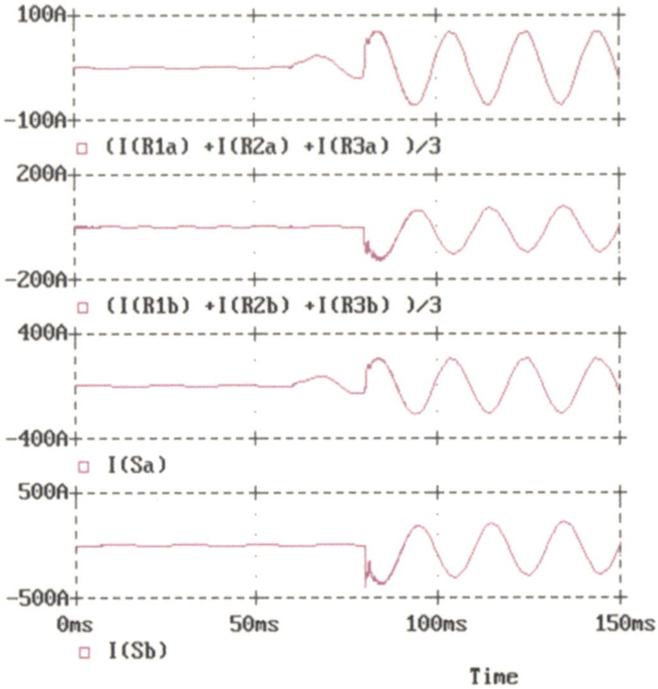

Figure 41. Time variation of the currents when MVN is at resonance , $R_t = 100\Omega$, $\alpha = 0°$

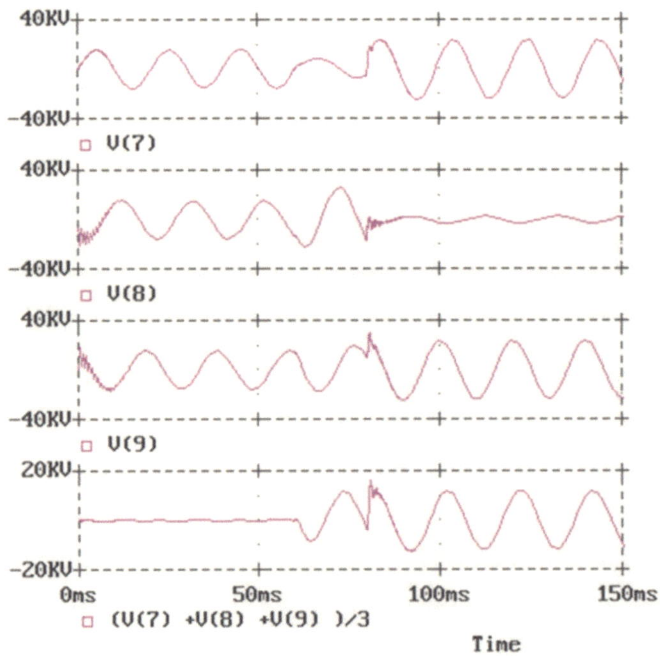

Figure 42. Time variation of the voltages when MVN is at resonance, $R_t = 100\Omega$, $\alpha = 0°$

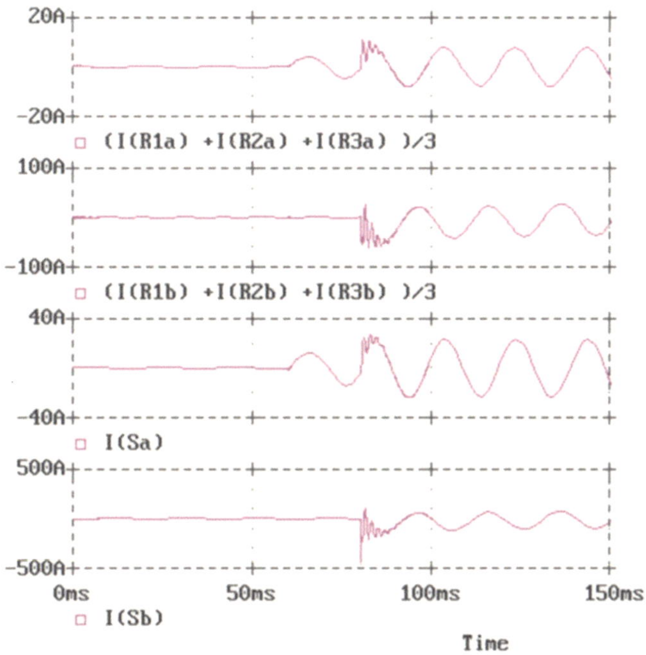

Figure 43. Time variation of the currents when MVN is at resonance , $R_t = 1000\Omega$, $\alpha = 0°$

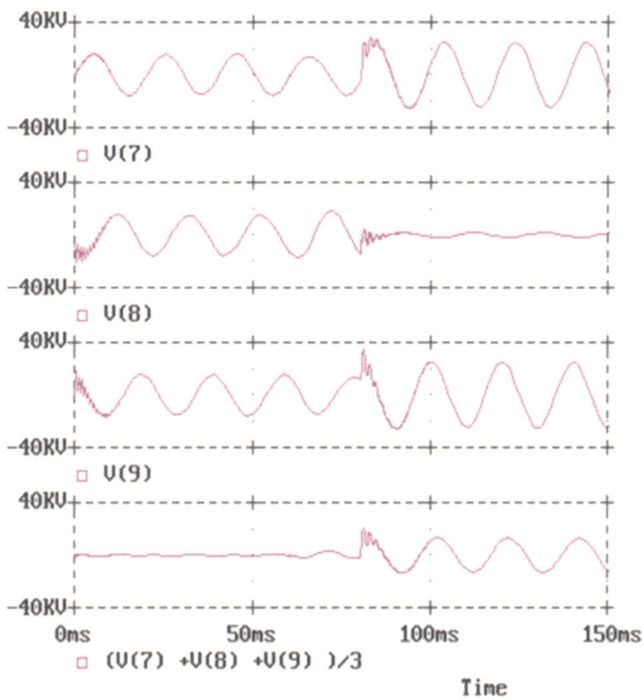

Figure 44. Time variation of the voltages when MVN is at resonance, $R_t = 1000\Omega$, $\alpha = 0°$

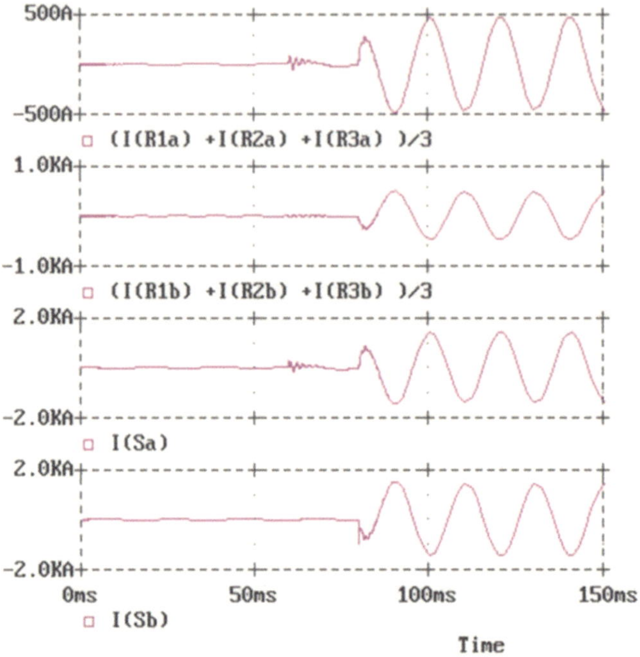

Figure 45. . Time variation of the currents when MVN is at resonance , $R_t = 1\Omega$, $\alpha = 90°$

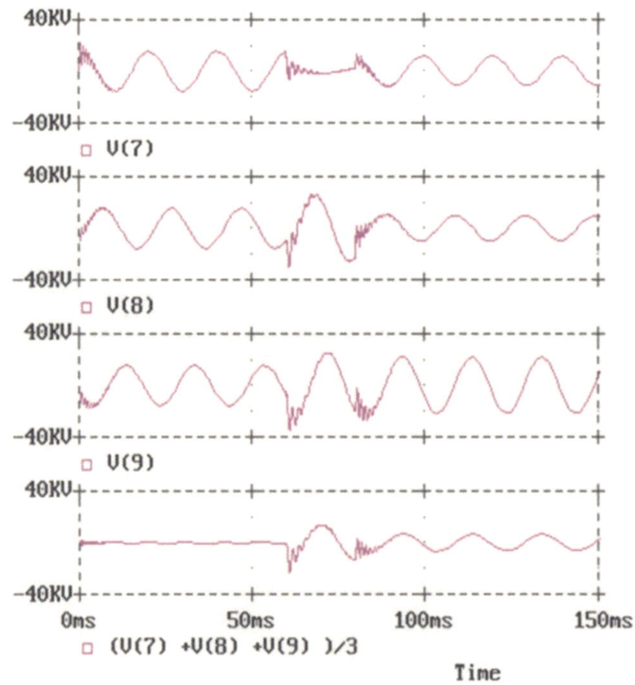

Figure 46. Time variation of the voltages when MVN is at resonance, $R_t = 1\Omega$, $\alpha = 90°$

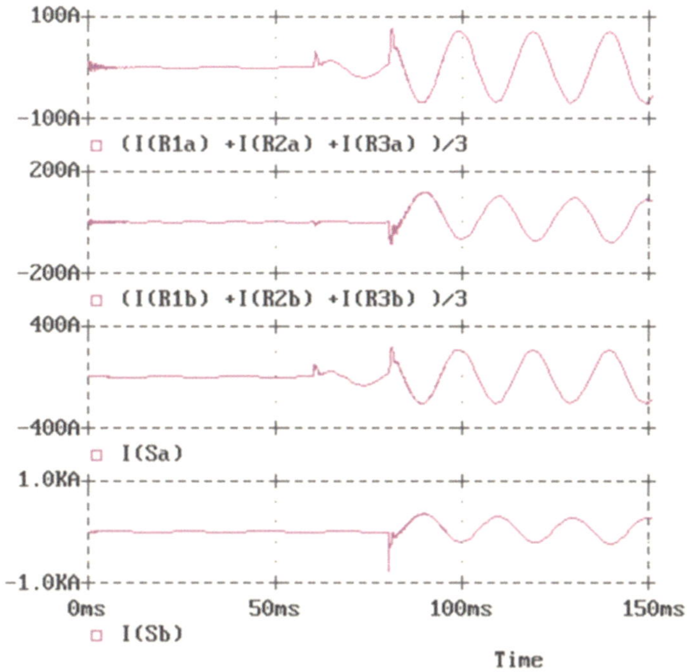

Figure 47. Time variation of the currents when MVN is at resonance , $R_t = 100\Omega$, $\alpha = 90°$

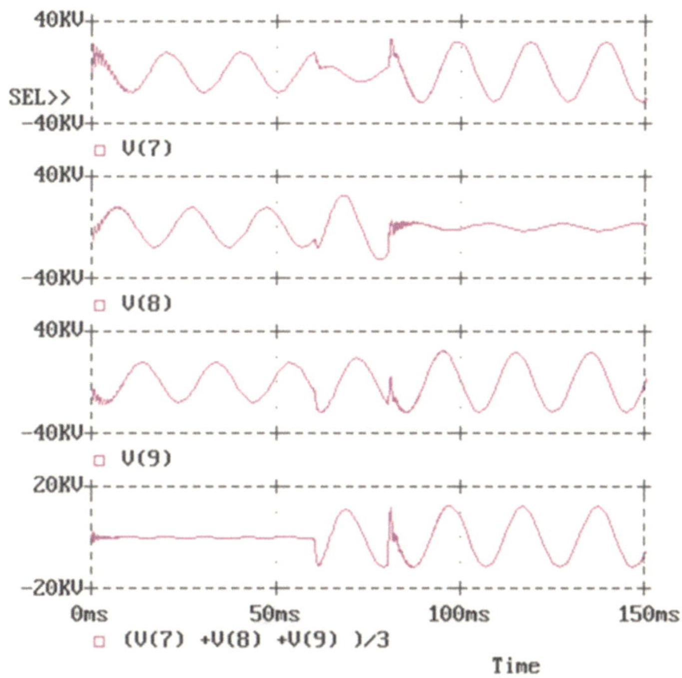

Figure 48. Time variation of the voltages when MVN is at resonance, $R_t = 100\Omega$, $\alpha = 90°$

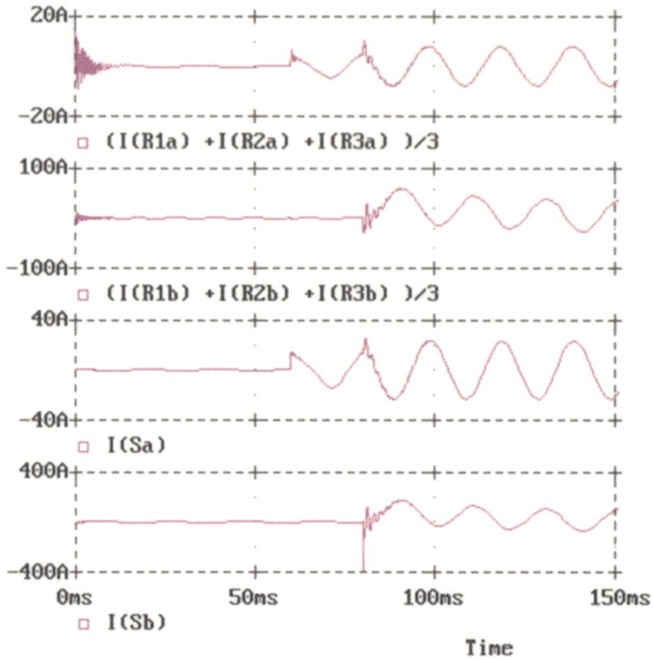

Figure 49. Time variation of the currents when MVN is at resonance , $R_t = 1000\Omega$, $\alpha = 90°$

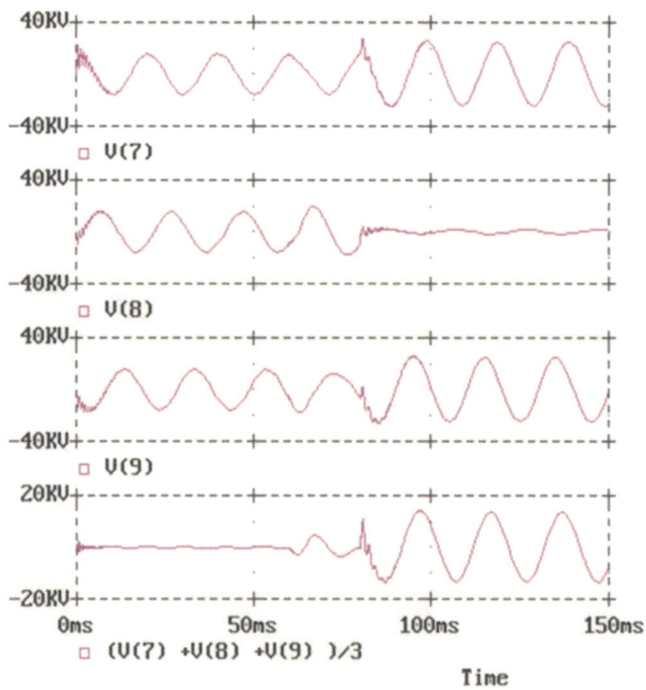

Figure 50. Time variation of the voltages when MVN is at resonance, $R_t = 1000\Omega$, $\alpha = 90°$

The double phase to ground fault has less important transient effects than the single phase to ground fault.

When the simple phase to ground fault occurs than the value of initial phase α is importans, but its variation is totaly insignifiant in the double phase to ground fault. The value of the resistance at the fault place is important in both fault types, the maximal value of the fault currents and the zero sequence currents depending strongly on the electric resistance at the fault place.

The oscillograms for the MVN grounded trough resistor are presented in Fig. 51 ... Fig. 54. The fault is simulated with the switch VSa and for $\alpha = 90°$ the transient is most important.

The current flowing trough the grounding resistor is calculated also and this is important because the value of this current is taken into account for the protection.

The resistance at the fault place is simulated with the switch VSa.

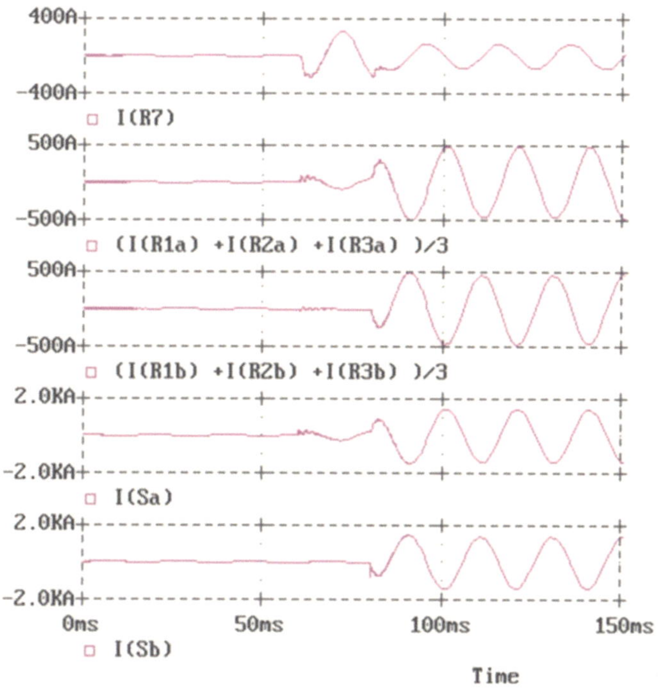

Figure 51. Time variation of the currents when MVN is grounded trough resistor, $R_t = 1\Omega$, $\alpha = 90°$

If the resistance at the fault place is increasing from 1Ω to 100Ω the current at the fault place is strongly decreasing from 1.8kA to 500A.

Oscillograms from Fig. 55 ...Fig. 60 , for isolated neutral point of the MVN, show that the double phase to ground fault gives a heavier transient for voltages than for currents.

There is not an important difference between the transient produced by the double phase to ground fault in MVN with isolated neutral point compared with the MVN grounded trough compensation inductor, but both cases are much heavier than the transient for MVN grounded trough resistor.

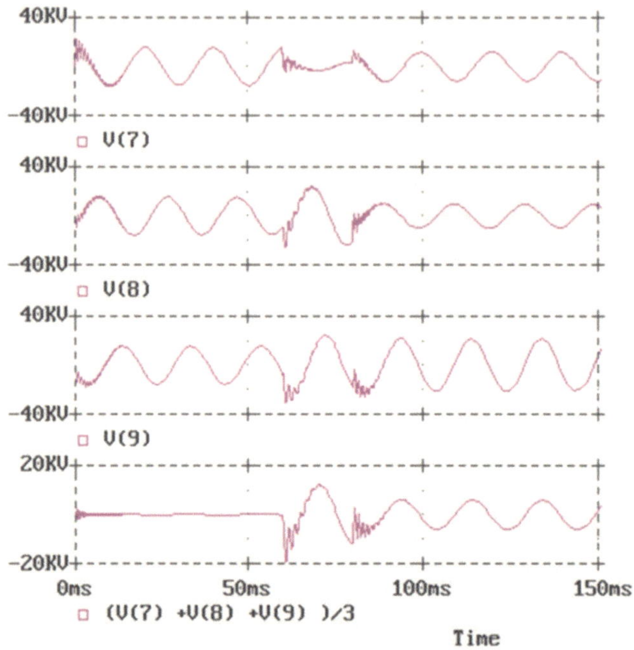

Figure 52. Time variation of the voltages when MVN is grounded trough resistor $R_t = 1\Omega$, $\alpha = 90°$

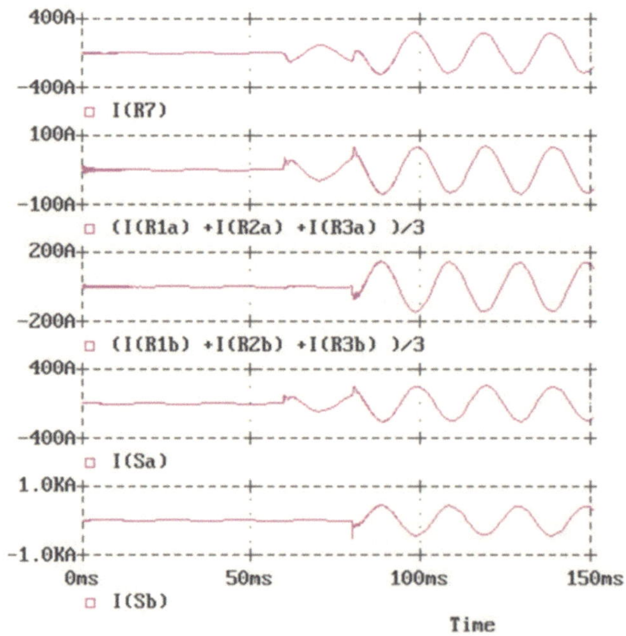

Figure 53. Time variation of the currents when MVN is grounded trough resistor, $R_t = 100\Omega$, $\alpha = 90°$

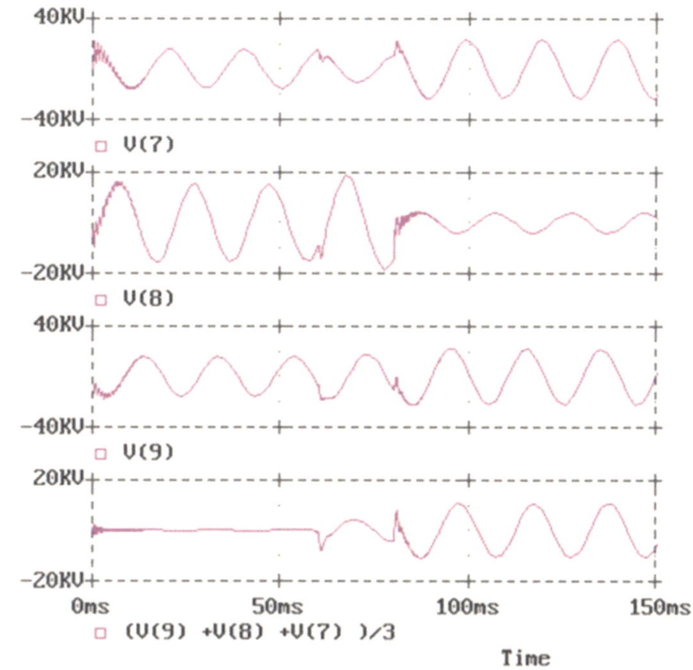

Figure 54. Time variation of the voltages when MVN is grounded trough resistor $R_t = 100\Omega$, $\alpha = 90°$

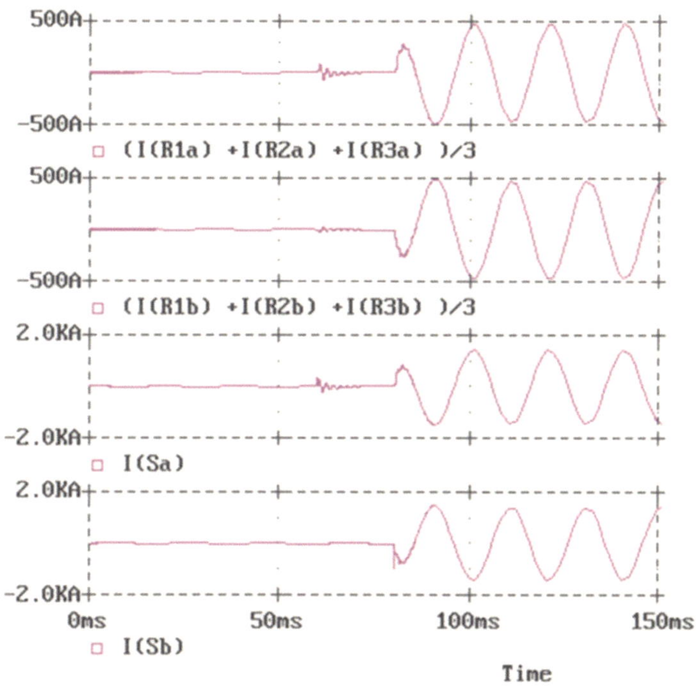

Figure 55. Time variation of the currents when the neutral point of MVN is isolated, $R_t = 1\Omega$, $\alpha = 90°$

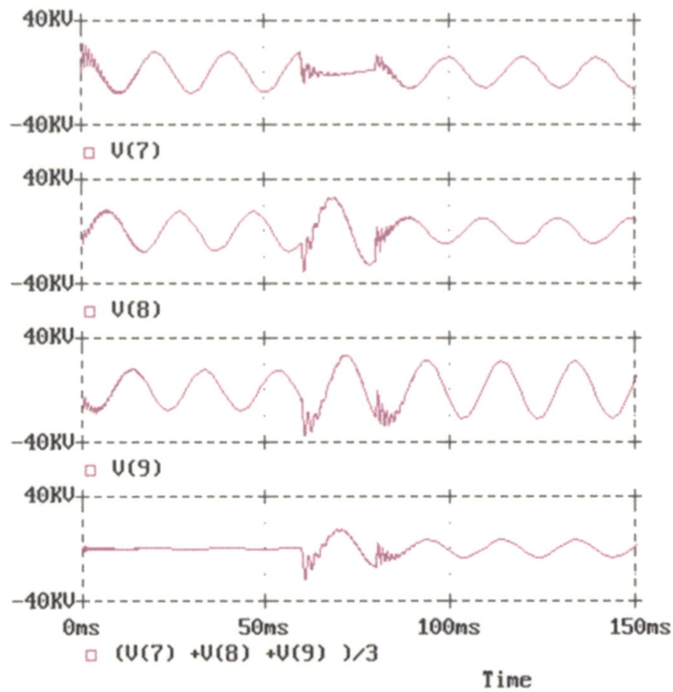

Figure 56. Time variation of the voltages when the neutral point of MVN is isolated, $R_t = 1\Omega$, $\alpha = 90°$

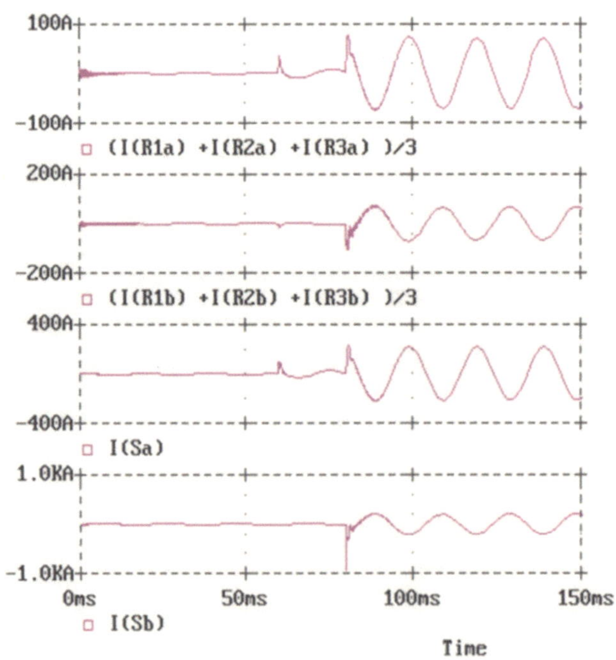

Figure 57. Time variation of the currents when the neutral point of MVN is isolated, $R_t = 100\Omega$, $\alpha = 90°$

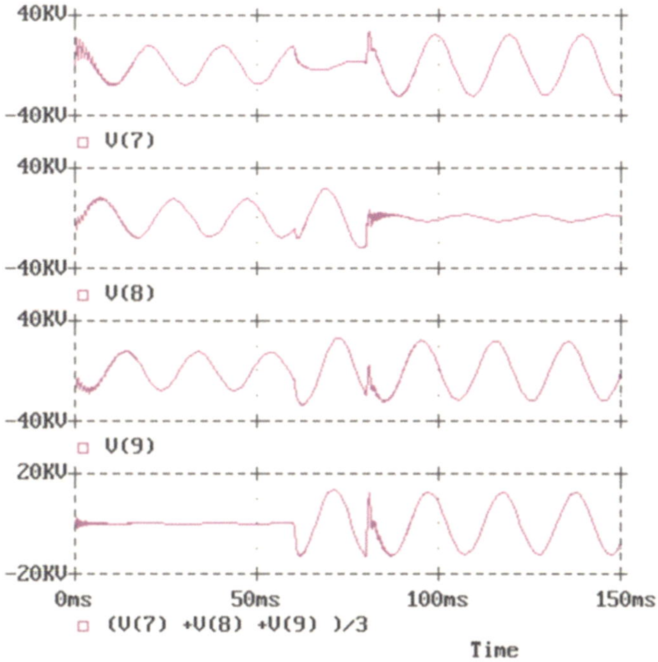

Figure 58. Time variation of the voltages when the neutral point of MVN is isolated, $R_t = 100\Omega$, $\alpha = 90°$

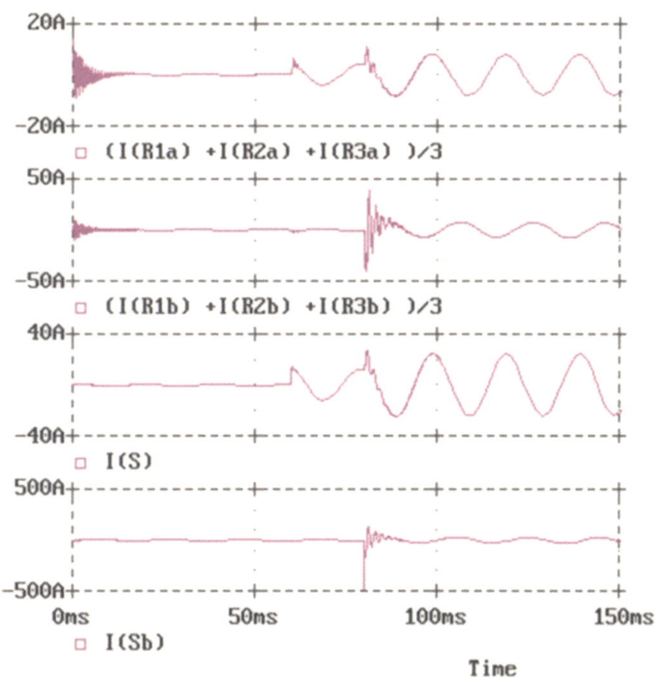

Figure 59. Time variation of the currents when the neutral point of MVN is isolated, $R_t = 1000\Omega$, $\alpha = 90°$

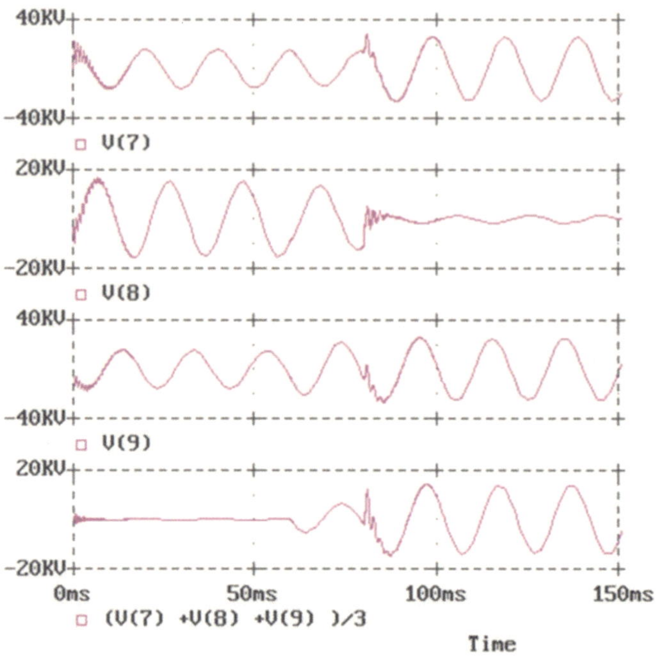

Figure 60. Time variation of the voltages when the neutral point of MVN is isolated, $R_t = 1000\Omega$, $\alpha = 90°$

The greater values of the currents at the two fault places, when the double phase to ground fault is produced, give high thermic solicitation to the instalation, as well as, higher values of the step voltages. This situatiom is dangerous for human being and animals, especially if this events are situated near the earth plate.

The time variation at the two fault places is far from being the same, no matter what grounding methos is used for the neutral point of the MVN.

4.2.3. The interrupted conductor with ground contact towards the customer fault

For this simulation VSGOL is opened , as if the phase conductor would be interrupted, and with a 20ms delay VSa is connected (simulating the ground contact of the broken conductor). The switch VSb remains opened.

The MVN functioning at resonance, with compensation inductor, was simulated with three values of R_t, namely 1Ω, 10Ω, 100Ω. Two values for α were taken into account, 0°, respectively 90°.

The equivalent capacitance of the phase conductor from the fault to the consumers is simulated by:

- C_{101a} is simulating the capacitance of phase 1 from the fault place to the bars of the MV transformer station
- C_{102a} represents the model for the capacitance of the phase conductor from the fault place to the consumers supplied by the faulty line.

Two possible situations are considered: $C_{101a} = C_{102a}$, and $C_{102a} = 0{,}1C_{101a}$.

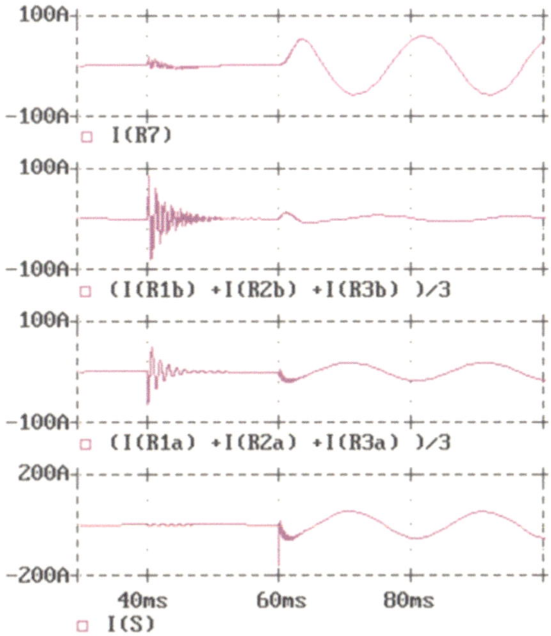

Figure 61. Time variation of the currents, neutral point of MVN is grounded by resistor and $R_t = 1\Omega$, $\alpha = 90°$, $C_{101a} = 9C_{102a}$

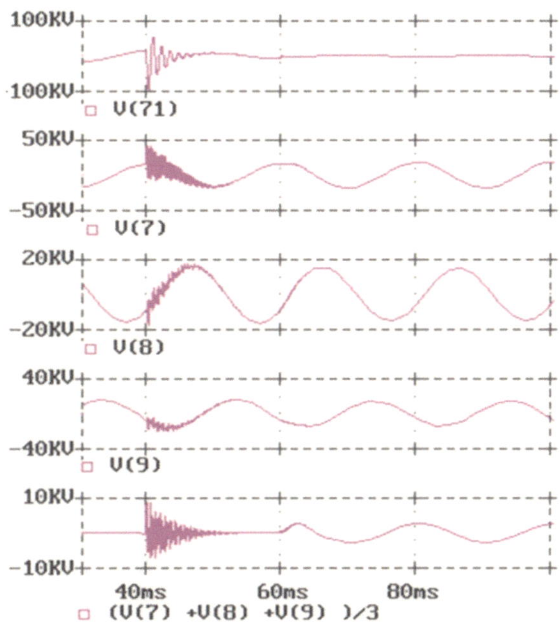

Figure 62. Time variation of the voltages, neutral point of MVN is grounded by resistor and $R_t = 1\Omega$, $\alpha = 90°$, $C_{101a} = 9C_{102a}$

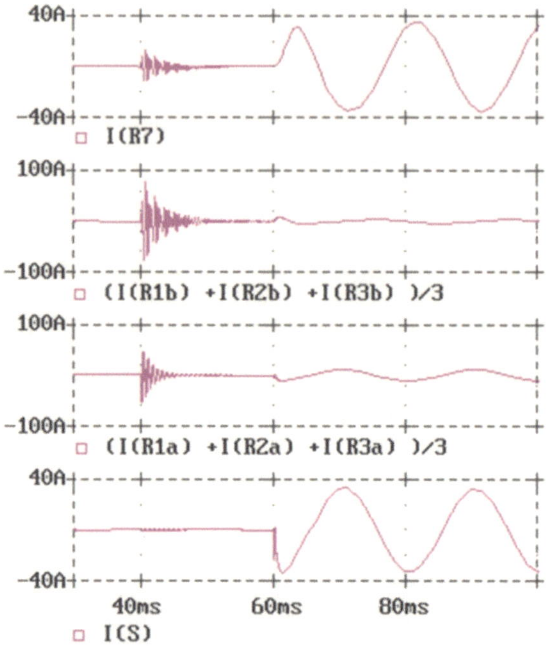

Figure 63. Time variation of the currents, neutral point of MVN is grounded by resistor and $R_t = 100\Omega$, $\alpha = 90°$, $C_{101a} = 9C_{102a}$

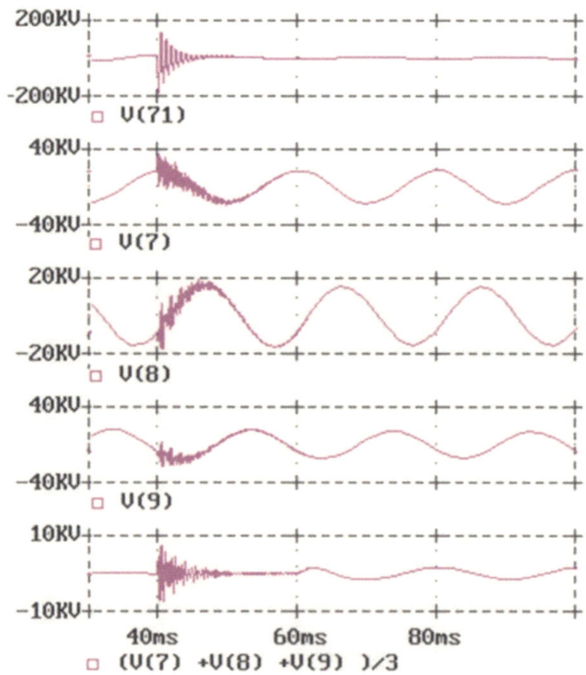

Figure 64. Time variation of the voltages, neutral point of MVN is grounded by resistor and $R_t = 100\Omega$, $\alpha = 90°$, $C_{101a} = 9C_{102a}$

In the oscillograms of the currents I(S) is the current to ground at the place of the fault, I(R_7) is the current flowing trough the grounding resistor and the zero sequence current of the faulty line is (I(R_{1a}) + I(R_{2a}) + I(R_{3a}))/3. In the oscillogramms (I(R_{1b} + I(R_{2b}) + I(R_{3b}))/3 is the zero sequence current of the healty "b" line.

The phase voltages are V(7), V(8), V(9), the zero sequence voltage on the bars of the MV transform station is (V(7) + V(8) + V(9))/3 and V(71) is the voltage of the broken conductor behind the fault place.

In each situation, either the grounding resistance is 1Ω, or 100Ω, the transient regime is stronger in the very moment of broking the phase conductor (t = 40 ms) than in the moment when the broken conductor contacts the ground (t = 60 ms). The voltage on the broken conductor might reach very high, dangerous values, jeopardizing the insulation of the line as well as the insulation of the consumer.

In Figs. 65 to 78 the oscillograms correspond to the MVN at resonance, with compensation inductor for grounding the neutral point. In this cases the current trough the compensation inductor is not represented because the protections used in MVN do not survey this current.

By the point of view of the overvoltages that might appear when the conductor is broken are more dangerous than the overvoltages in the case when the broken conductor is in contact with the ground.

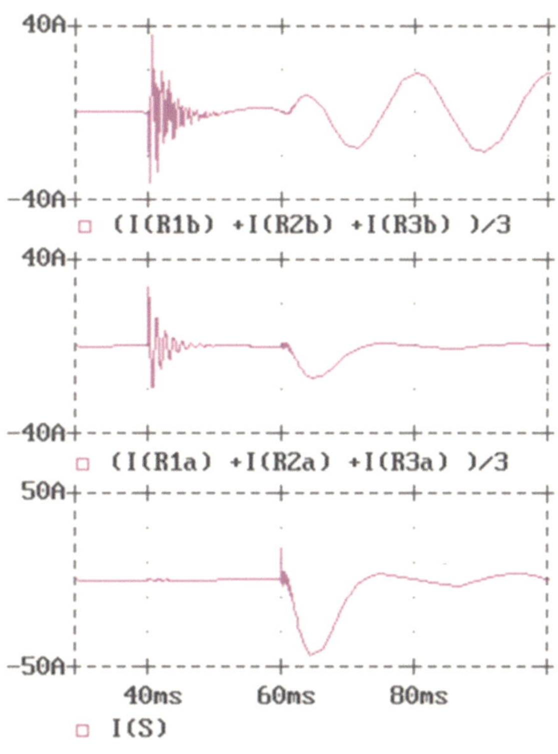

Figure 65. Time variation of the currents when MVN is at resonance, $R_t = 1\Omega$, $\alpha = 0°$, $C_{101a} = C_{102a}$

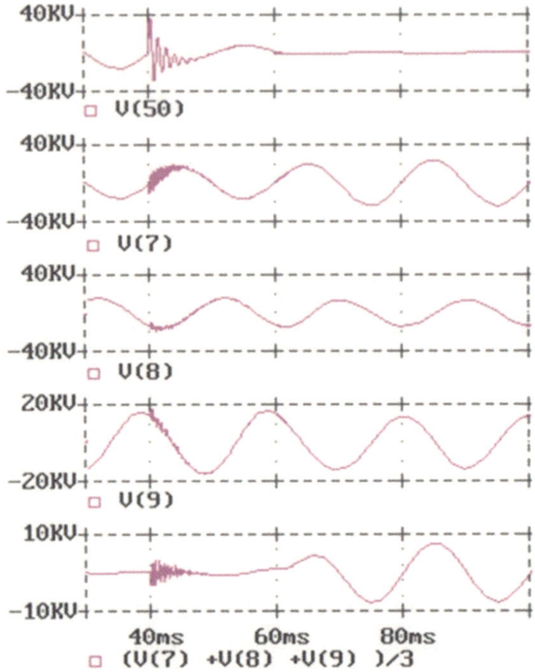

Figure 66. Time variation of the voltages, when MVN is at resonance, $R_t = 1\Omega$, $\alpha = 0°$, $C_{101a} = C_{102a}$

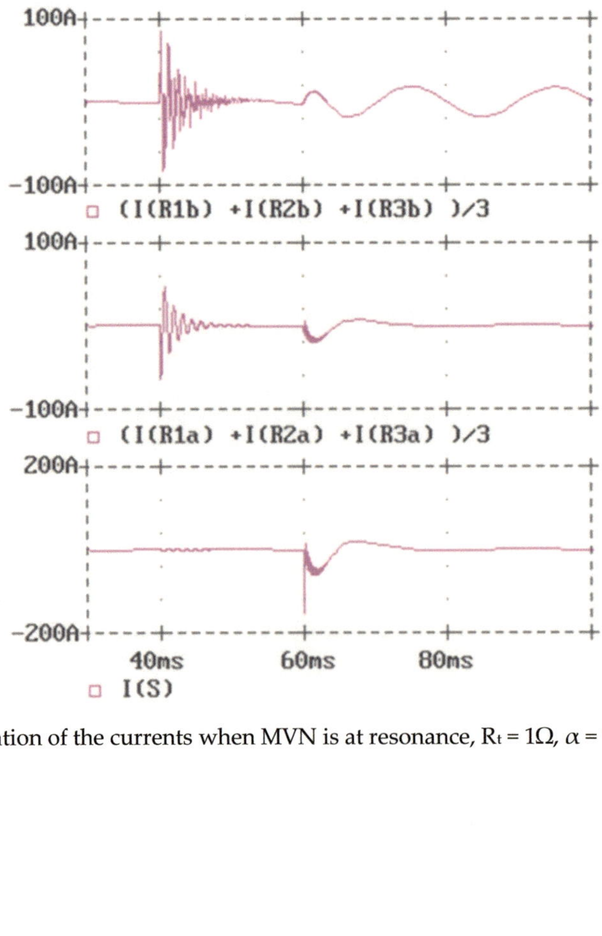

Figure 67. Time variation of the currents when MVN is at resonance, $R_t = 1\Omega$, $\alpha = 90°$, $C_{101a} = C_{102a}$

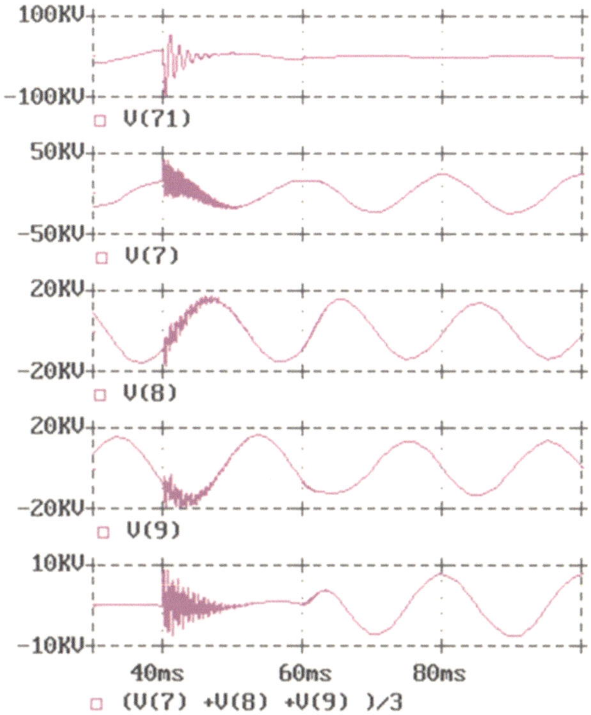

Figure 68. Time variation of the voltages, when MVN is at resonance, $R_t = 1\Omega$, $\alpha = 90°$, $C_{101a} = C_{102a}$

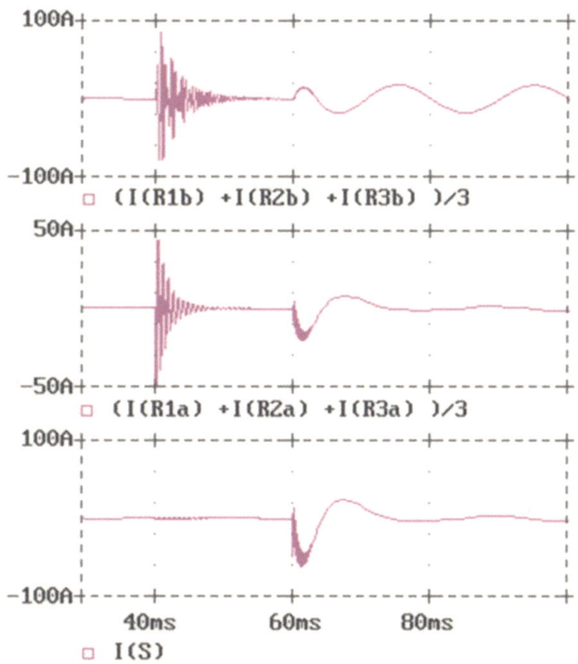

Figure 69. Time variation of the currents when MVN is at resonance, $R_t = 1\Omega$, $\alpha = 90°$, $C_{101a} = 9C_{102a}$

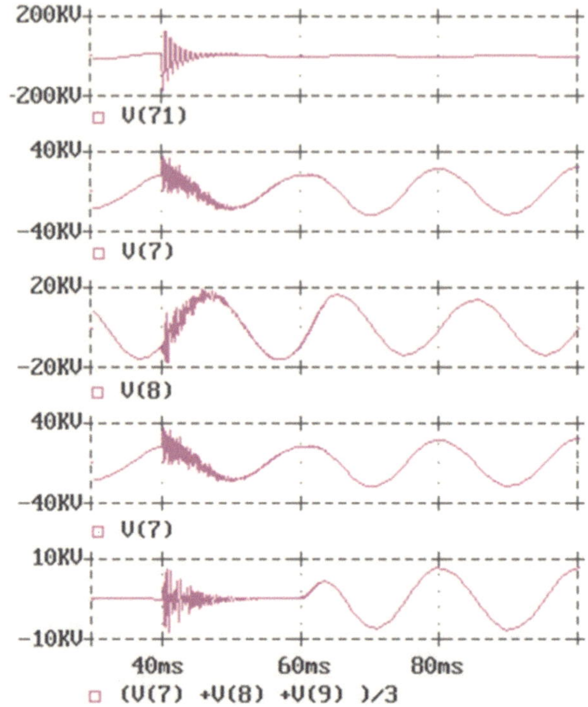

Figure 70. Time variation of the voltages, when MVN is at resonance, $R_t = 1\Omega$, $\alpha = 90°$, $C_{101a} = 9C_{102a}$

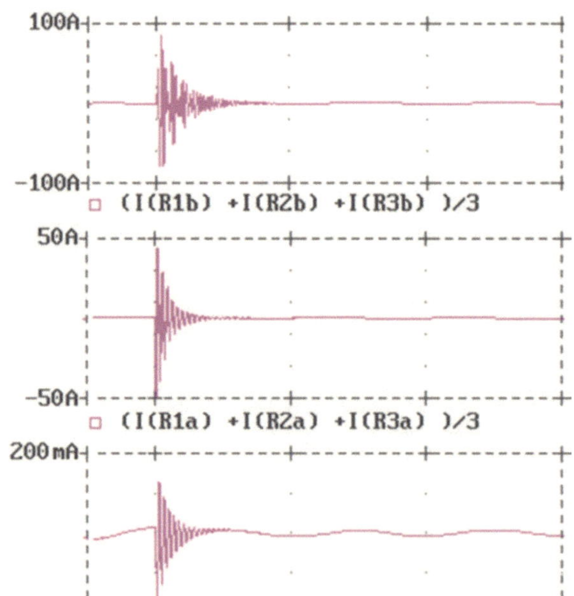

Figure 71. Time variation of the currents when MVN is at resonance, $R_t = 1M\Omega$, $\alpha = 90°$, $C_{101a} = 9C_{102a}$

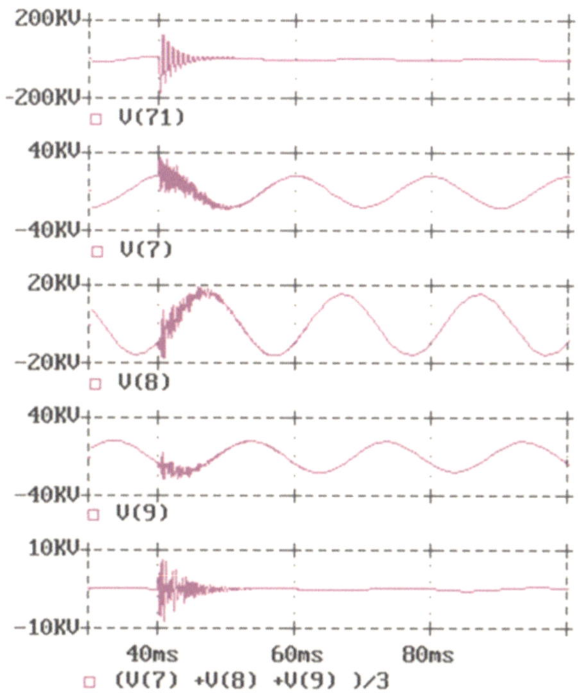

Figure 72. Time variation of the voltages. when MVN is at resonance, $R_t = 1M\Omega$, $\alpha = 90°$, $C_{101a} = 9C_{102a}$

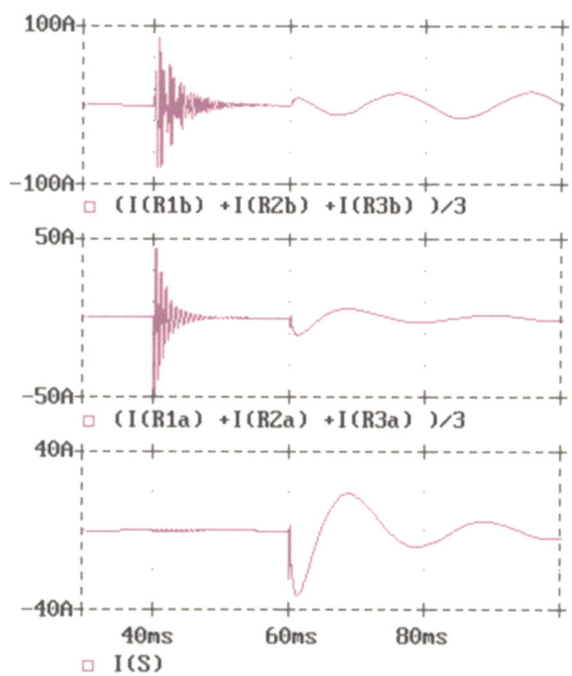

Figure 73. Time variation of the currents when MVN is at resonance, $R_t = 100\Omega$, $\alpha = 90°$, $C_{101a} = 9C_{102a}$

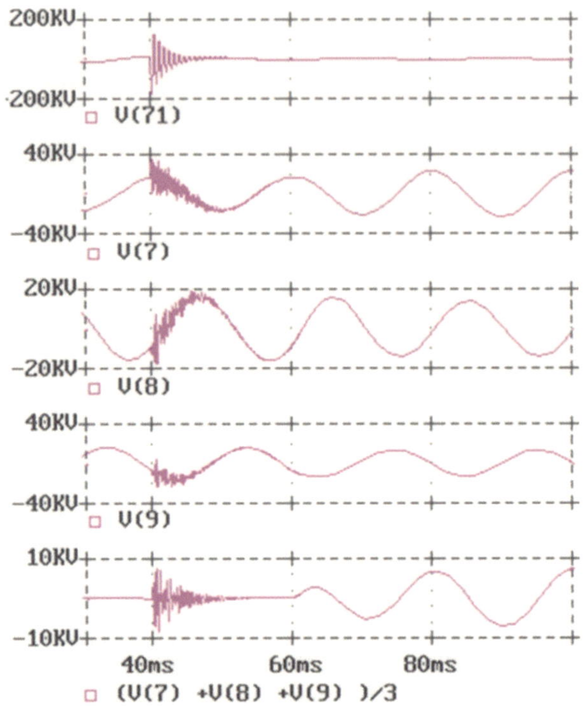

Figure 74. Time variation of the voltages, when MVN is at resonance, $R_t = 100\Omega$, $\alpha = 90°$, $C_{101a} = 9C_{102a}$

When $R_t = 1M\Omega$ the fault becomes of the type broken conductor and at t=60ms does not occur a transient regime.

When the fault is of the type interrupted conductor with ground contact towards the customer the heavyest situation is shown to be when the phase is near 90°.

For higher values of R_t the transient regime is less dangerous.

5. Measurement on real MVN

The results obtained during the measurements in the experiment area, while faults were produced on purpose, are shown in the followings.

The fault produced was of type single phase grounding.

The experimental aria contains 7 electric lines of 6kV, with total value of the capacitive current of 27A From the 7 electric linea 6 are connected at first system of bars and at the second bar system was connected the line on which the faults were produced. The capacitive current of this line is 2.7A.

The transformer station contains a transversal switch in connected position.

For recording the currents and the voltages during the experiment was used a CDR oscilloperturbograph.

Figures 75 to 83 show the following:

- the zero sequence current of the faulty line $I^0_{PT\ Turn}$,
- the current trough the compensation inductor I_B,
- the star voltages, V_a, V_b, V_c; - the zerosequence voltage of MV bars from the transformer station U^0.

The experiment was made in order to verify the concordance with the numeric simulation and to validate the accuracy of the simulator.

The experiment consisted on producing on purpose faults of the type single-phase grounding, namely:

- metallic grounding of a phase $R_t = 0$,
- grounding through the passing resistance $R_t = 250\ \Omega$,
- grounding through the passing resistance $R_t = 500\ \Omega$.

The functioning regimes of the MV network were:

- MV network functioning at resonance; -MV network functions at 10% overcompensation,
- MV network functions at 10% undercompensation.

The three recordings, corresponding to the three functioning regimes for metallic grounding are shown in Figs. 75, 76 and 77.

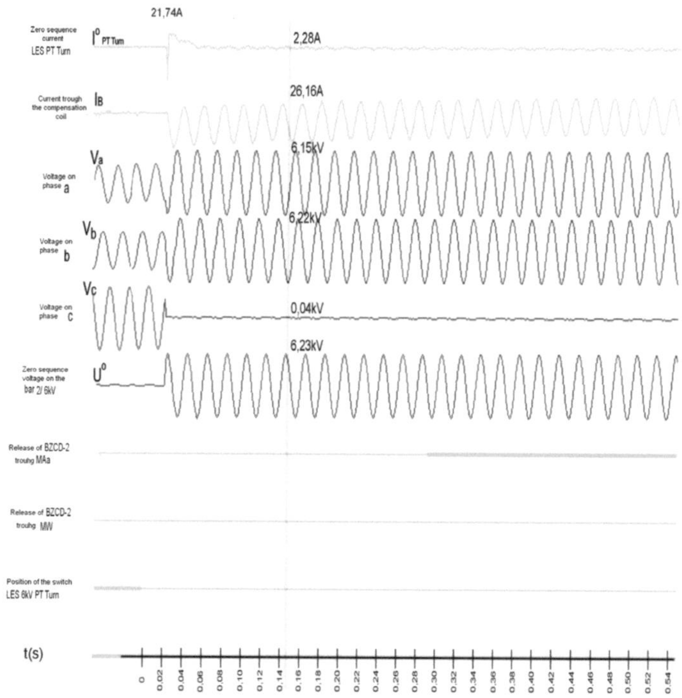

Figure 75. Single phase metallic grounding, $R_t = 5\ \Omega$, network at resonance

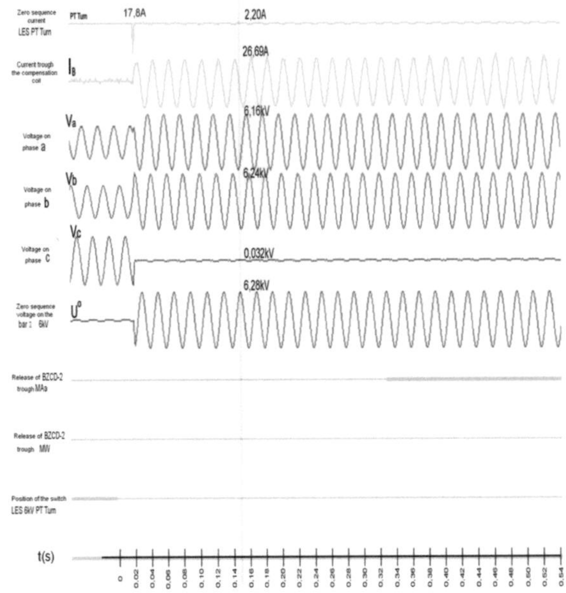

Figure 76. Single phase metallic grounding, R_t= 5 Ω, network at 10% over-compensation network

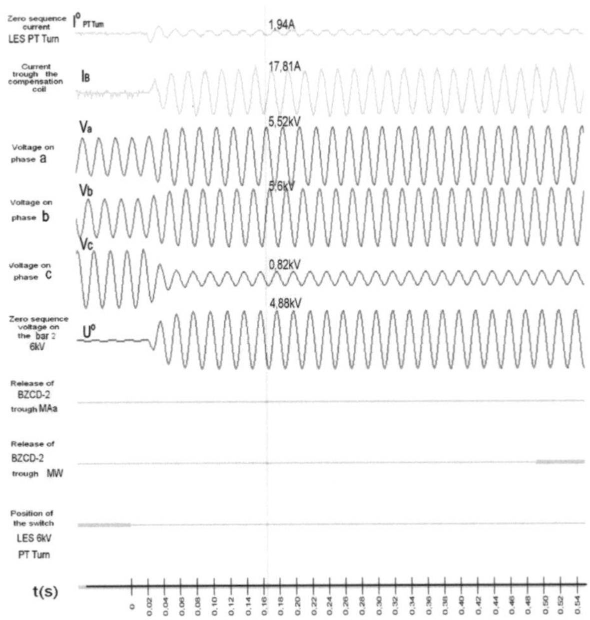

Figure 77. Single phase grounding with R_t=5 Ω, 10% under-compensated network

By comparing the shape of the current of the faulty line during the transient regime (the zero sequence current of the faulty line) obtained by numeric simulation with the one obtained by recording the same current during experiment it can be observed that the simulated current has an oscillating component greater than in recorded experiment.

This difference is due to a greater equivalent resistance of the experimental equivalent circuit than the simulated one.

In the same maner, as for the metallic grounding, but with a 250Ω grounding resistance for the three functioning regimes of the network the, results are presented in Figs. 78, 79 and 80.

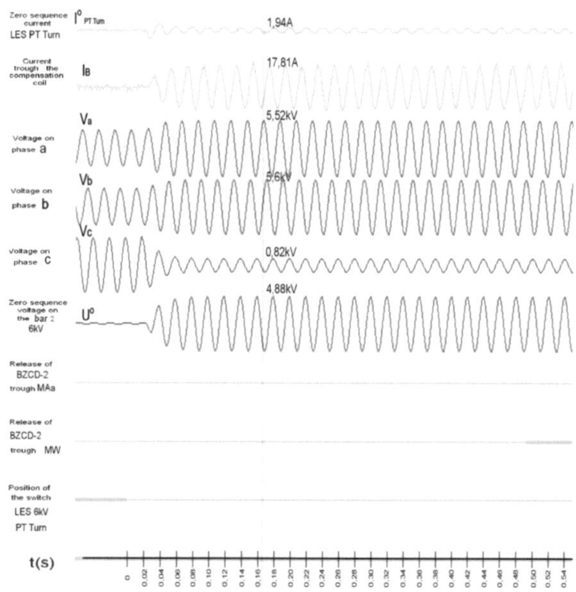

Figure 78. Single phase grounding with R_t=250 Ω, network at resonance

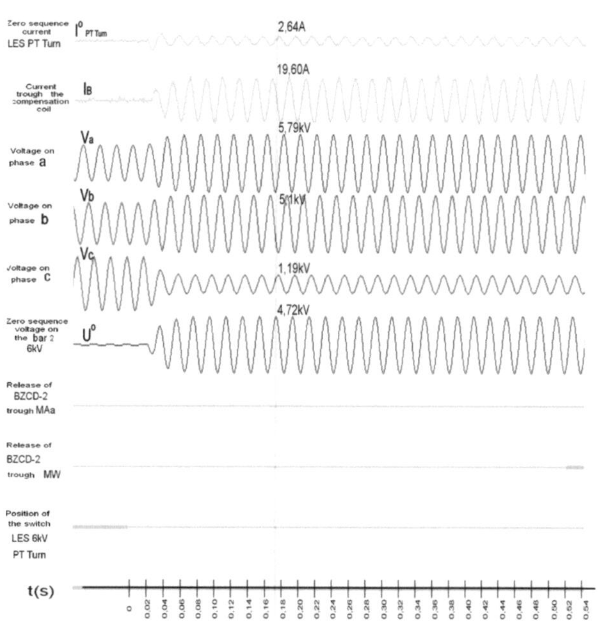

Figure 79. Single phase grounding with R_t=250 Ω, 10% over-compensated network

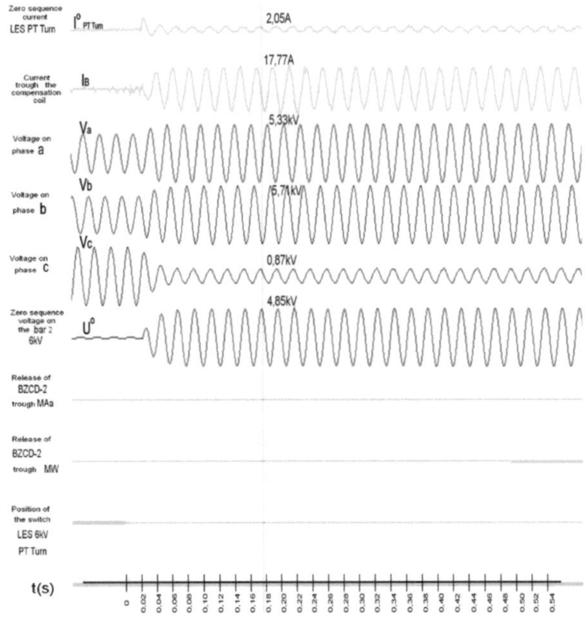

Figure 80. Single phase grounding with R_t=250 Ω, 10% under-compensated network

The third value for the grounding resistance used in the experiment is 500Ω and the results for the resonant regime, for 10% overcompensated and for 10% undercompensated are presented, respectively, in the figures 81, 82 and 83.

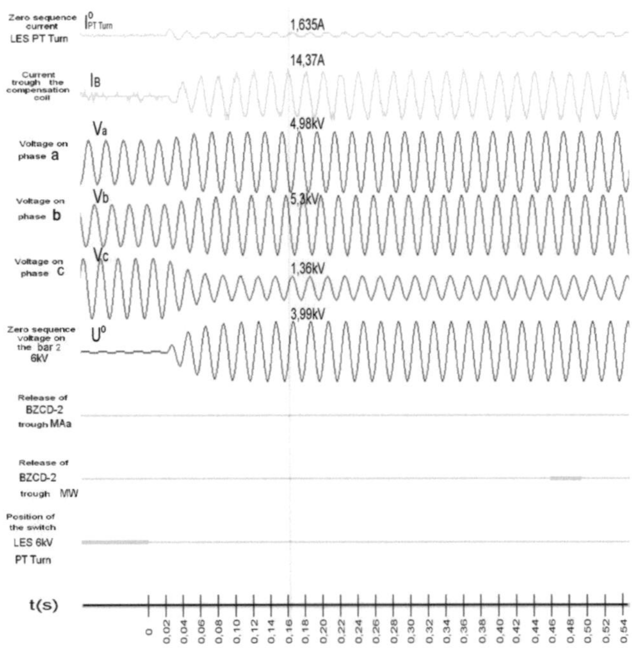

Figure 81. Single phase grounding resistance, R_t= 500 Ω, network at resonance

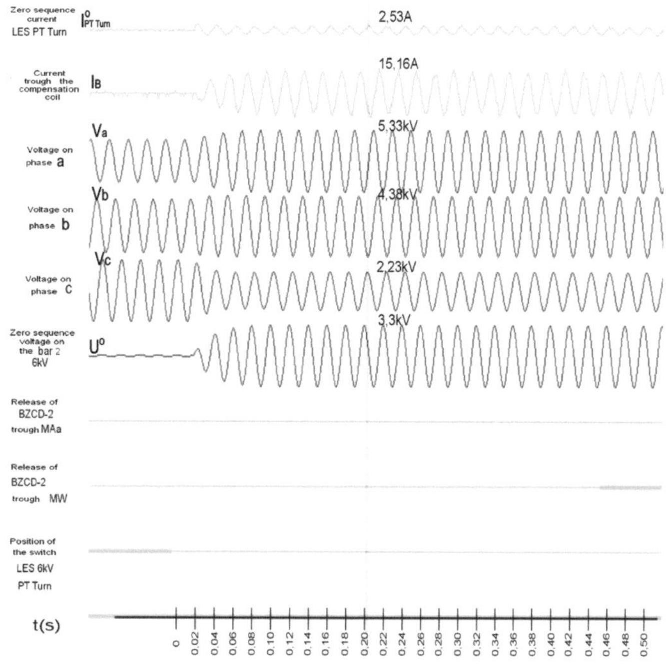

Figure 82. Single phase grounding resistance R_t= 500 Ω, network at 10% overcompensation

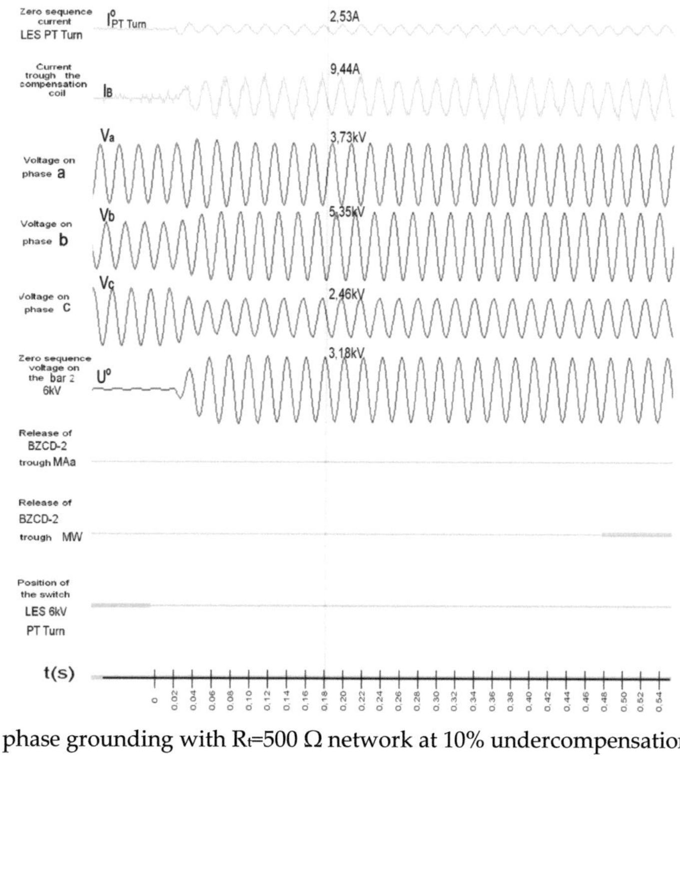

Figure 83. Single phase grounding with R_t=500 Ω network at 10% undercompensation

Table 1, campare some of the values measured during the experiment with the corresponding values obtained by numeric simulation.

The significance of the symbols from the table is as follows:

- I^0_{max} – maximal value of the zero sequence current on the faulty line,
- I_B – current trough the compensation inductor,
- I^0_{stab} – the zero sequence current of the faulty line, after the dumping of the dead-beat component,
- t_{am} – dumping time of the dead-beat component,
- U^0 – the zero sequence voltage at the MV bars of the transform station,
- U_f – voltage of the healty lines.

From Table 1. results that the differences between the values obtained by the numerical simulation and the values measured during the experiment are reasonably small.

Regime of the network	Symbol of quantities	$R_t[\Omega]$								
		5			250			500		
		Values obtained by		Error [%]	Values obtained by		Error [%]	Values obtained by		Error [%]
		Experiment	Simulation		Experiment	Simulation		Experiment	Simulation	
Resonance	I^0_{max}[A]	21,7	24,6	13,4	4,8	4,5	6,3	2,8	2,6	7,1
	I_B [A]	26,16	24,3	7,1	17,81	16,2	9,1	14,37	12,84	10,6
	I^0_{stab}[A]	2,28	2,42	6,1	1,94	1,75	9,8	1,64	1,49	9,1
	t_{am} [ms]	126	130	3,2	38	34	10,5	57	54	5,3
	U^0 [kV]	3,6	3,55	1,4	2,62	2,43	7,3	2,31	2,17	6,1
	U_f [kV]	6,22	6,03	3,1	5,6	5,46	2,5	5,3	4,78	9,8
10% Over-compensated	I^0_{max}[A]	17,8	58	226	4,2	4,5	7,1	3,2	2,9	9,4
	I_B [A]	26,69	24,82	7,0	19,6	18,3	6,6	15,16	13,86	8,6
	I^0_{stab}[A]	2,2	2,06	6,4	2,64	2,42	8,3	2,53	2,27	10,3
	t_{am} ms]	80	86	7,5	35	32	8,6	41	37	9,8
	U^0 [kV]	3,63	3,55	2,2	2,73	2,47	9,5	1,91	1,7	9,9
	U_f [kV]	6,24	5,96	4,5	5,69	5,21	8,4	4,38	4,76	8,7

Regime of the network	Symbol of quantities	$R_t[\Omega]$								
		5			250			500		
		Values obtained by		Error [%]	Values obtained by		Error [%]	Values obtained by		Error [%]
		Experi-ment	Simu-lation		Experi-ment	Simu-lation		Experi-ment	Simu-lation	
10% Under - compensated	I^0_{max}[A]	20,99	43	105	4,3	4,5	4,7	3,1	2,8	9,7
	I_B [A]	22,82	21,28	6,7	17,77	16,5	7,1	9,44	9,22	2,3
	I^0_{stab}[A]	2,5	2,32	7,2	2,05	1,91	6,8	2,53	2,31	8,7
	t_{am} ms]	198	210	6,1	31	28	8,6	23	21	8,7
	U^0 [kV]	3,59	3,56	0,84	2,8	2,53	9,6	1,84	1,67	9,1
	U_f [kV]	6,2	5,97	3,7	5,71	5,39	5,6	5,35	4,81	10,1

Table 1. Comparison of measured and simulated values

6. Conclusions

The numerical simulator designed by us allows the analysis of transients caused by diferent types of faults, such as simple groundings, double groundings, or broken conductor grounded towards the consumer.

We have compared results obtained by simulation with measured values only for simple grounding faults.

In this type of fault the simulator is validated by the measurements, no matter how the neutral point of the medium voltage network is grounded and whatever are the functioning conditions of the electrical network.

The results from Table 1. show that the simplificatory conditions, taken into account for developing the simulator, are correct.

The numerical simulation of the transient regimes caused by simple grounding faults produced in medium voltage networks shows to be an efficient method for analyzing such faults.

The most dangerous transient regimes occur when the initial phase of the voltage of the faulty line is near 90°.

The initial phase of the voltage, that happen to be in the very moment of producing the fault, was taken with the same value in simulation. The differences between the maximal values of zero sequence component, obtained by the two methods, are quite acceptable from a technical point of view and this concordance validates the model.

The resistance of the broken conductor to ground is extremely important, small values of R_t implying long damping periods. If this undesirable condition happens the currents might have high values, as well as important values of the over voltages leading to important supplementary mechanical stress and damages of the insulating devices and, eventually a simple fault can turn to a multiple fault situation.

For small values of the grounding resistance at the fault location ($R_t < 10\Omega$) difference between measured and simulated values is a litle higher than in the case of greater values ($R_t > 100\Omega$).

The model is very useful by giving the values of the voltages on the healthy lines (over voltages that might jeopardize the insulation) and zero sequence currents of the faulty lines (fixing the condition of the fault detection by protection devices).

Using the conclusions of the simulation of a MVN for the values of the currents and voltages during different types of faults it is possible to adjust the prescribed values of the protection.

Simulation of the broken conductor fault, either connected to the ground or not, shows that resonance might occur, over voltages due to this resonances being dangerous to the equipments.

When double phase to ground fault was simulated the values of the voltages showed dangerous voltages for step or touch voltage.

The numerical simulator has the advantage of analyzing rapidly several variants as models of different possible situations.

The simulator is flexible and all kinds of faults can be simulated for different MVN, just by making the proper modification in the parameters of the simulator. These modifications are slightly easier to be performed when PSPICE simulating model is used.

Either using PSPICE or Mathlab-Simulink the accuracy of the analysis is similarly good.

The precision of the results obtained by simulation depends essentially on the accuracy of the MVN parameters.

Author details

Dumitru Toader, Stefan Haragus and Constantin Blaj
"Politehnica" University of Timisoara, Romania

7. References

Blume, W. (1986). *Computer Circuit Simulation*, BYTE, July 1986

Bucatariu, I. & Surianu, F. (2009). Optimal Placement of Fixed Series Capacitor in Distribution Networks, *Proceedings of the 9thWSEA/IASMES International Conference on*

Electric Power Systems High Voltages, Electric Machines Control & Signal Processing, Genova, Italy, October 17-19, 2009, pp.65-70

Chuco, B. (2005). Electrical Software Tools Overview *in* SINATEC-IEEE

Curcanu, G., Toader, D. & Pandia, T. (2006). Determination of overvoltages in high voltage networks at single phase faults by numarical simulation and experiments, *Proceedings 12th International IGTE Symposium,* Gratz

DeCarlo, R & Lin, P. (2001). *Linear Circuit Analysis,* Oxford University Press

Danyek, M., Handl, P.& Raisz, D. (2002). Comparison of Simulation Tools ATP-EMTP and MATLAB-Simulink for Time Domain Power System Transient Studies, *Proceedings of the European EMTP-ATP Conference,* Sopron, Hungary

Dessaint, L.-A., Al-Haddad, K., Le-Huy, H., Sybille, G. & Brunelle, P. (1999). *A power system simulation tool based on Simulink,* IEEE Trans. on Ind. Electronics, vol. 46, no. 6, pp. 1252-1254, Dec. 1999

Dommel, H.W. (1995). *ElectroMagnetic Transient Program. Theory Book,* Bonneville Power Administration, Portland

Drapela, J. (2009). Performance of a Voltage Peak Detection-Based Flichermeter, *Proceedings of the 8thWSEAS International Conference on Circuits, Systems, Electronics, Control & Signal Processing,* Teneriffe, Spain, December 14-16, 2009, pp.296-301

Foltin, M., Ernek, M. & Hnat, J. (2006). SimPowerSystems in Education, *Mezinarodni Konference Technical Computing,* Prague

Hasler, M. & Neirynck, J. (1985). *Circuits non lineares,* Presses Polytechniques Romandes, Lausannes.

Iordache, M. & Mandache, A. (2004). *Computer Aided Analyse of Nonlinear Circuits (in Romanian)* , Politehnica Press Bucharest

Istrate, M., Gavrilas, M., Istrate, C. & Ursuleanu, R. (2009). Algorithms in Transmission Grids Using ATP Simulations, *Proceedings of the 9thWSEA/IASMES International Conference on Electric Power Systems High Voltages, Electric Machines Control & Signal Processing,* Genova, Italy, October 17-19, 2009, pp.109-114

Karlsson, A. (2005). *Evaluation of Simulink/SimPowerSystems and other Commercial Simulation Tools for the Simulation of Machine System Transient*, Swedish Royal Institute of Technology, Stockholm

Mandache, L. & Topan, D. (2009). *Algorithms for Electric Circuit Simulation,* Universitaria Press Craiova

Radoi , C. (1994). *SPICE Simulation and Analysis of Electronic Circuits,* Ameo Press Bucureşti.

Rashid, M.H. & Rashid, H.M. (2006) *SPICE for Power Electronics and Electric Power,* Taylor & Francis Group, Boca Raton

Ross, C.C. (2004). *Differential Equations,* Springer Science, pp.51-56

Sybille, G., Brunelle, P., Hoang Le-Huy, Dessaint, L.A. & Al-Haddad, K., (2000). *Theory and applications of power system blockset, a MATLAB/Simulink-based simulation tool for power systems*, Power Engineering Society Winter Meeting 2000, IEEE, Vol.1, pp.774-779

Vladimirescu, A. (1999). *SPICE*, Ed.Tehnica, Bucuresti

Vladimirescu, A. (1997) SIMULINK ; *Dynamic System Simulation for MATLAB, User's Guide, version 2.1*, MathWorks Inc.

Chapter 21

Multidimensional Numerical Simulation of Ignition and Propagation of TiC Combustion Synthesis

A. Aoufi and G. Damamme

Additional information is available at the end of the chapter

http://dx.doi.org/10.5772/48441

1. Introduction

The purpose of this book chapter is to analyze from a numerical point of view a reaction diffusion mathematical modelling of titanium carbide combustion synthesis from a mixture of titanium and carbide reactive powders thanks to self-propagating high temperature synthesis process. This modelling results in the coupling between a nonlinear parabolic equation expressing the enthalpy balance of the system with radiative boundary conditions and a nonlinear differential equation describing the exothermic chemical reaction in the system. An another multiphysics coupling was analyzed in [3]. This Self-propagating High temperature Synthesis (SHS) process was discovered in 1965 by Merzhanov [7], [8] and uses the energy released by the exothermic reaction itself to ensure its self-propagation inside the material after a localized heat supply has been performed for several seconds on the surface of the solid mixture. The stoichiometric solid mixture is made of several kinds of reactive powders. We analyze in this book chapter, the influence of radiative boundary conditions *related to the heat supply* over the ignition and eventual propagation of a combustion front inside the material.

Four sections are used to present our numerical simulation work. Section two presents the governing equations of the modelling. Section three outline the main aspects of the numerical scheme. Section four analyzes and discusses the main numerical simulation results of the combustion synthesis process. A conclusion summarizes the results that were obtained.

2. Mathematical modelling

This section describes the main features of the modelling which expresses the coupling between a reaction-diffusion written for the enthalpy balance and a differential equation written for the exothermic chemical kinetics. SHS (Self-propagation High-temperature Synthesis) process is a condensed phase process which converts a mixture of powders into an end product. In this paper we consider the synthesis of titanium carbide in solid phase

((s) subscript) thanks to the exothermic reaction $Ti_{(s)} + C_{(s)} \rightarrow TiC_{(s)}$. We assume that we have a stoichiometric and isotropic mixture of compacted powders of titanium and carbide. Let us denote by $T = T(M,t)$ (*resp.* $\xi = \xi(M,t)$) the temperature (*resp. conversion rate*) at point $M \in \Omega$ at time t. The system is composed of the fraction ξ of titanium carbide **TiC** end product and the fraction $(1-\xi)$ of remaining powders of titanium and carbide.

2.1. Exothermic kinetics modelling

A first order exothermic kinetics is used to describe the synthesis of titanium carbide, hence a single variable, the conversion rate $\xi \in [0,1]$ of the reaction is defined. When $\xi = 0$ (*resp.* $\xi = 1$) the reaction has not started (*resp. is ended*). The velocity of the reaction may have or not a cutoff temperature $T_s = 1166$K, which corresponds to the first allotropic phase transition of titanium α, Ti_α to titanium β, Ti_β. An Arrhenius type equation is used

$$\frac{d\xi}{dt} = k_d(T)\ (1-\xi), \qquad (1)$$
$$\xi(.,0) = 0.$$

The velocity constant $k_d(T)$ follows an Arrhenius law in temperature such that

$$k_d(T) = k_d^* \, T^d \exp\left(-\frac{E^*}{R.T}\right). \qquad (2)$$

In both cases, (with or without cut-off temperature), k_d^* is a frequency factor in s^{-1}, E^* is the activation energy of the reaction in J/mol, $R = 8.314J/(mol.K)$ is the perfect gas constant and $d \in [0,2]$ is the degree, which is not necessarily an integer. Such an expression is commonly used in literature. It is worth mentioning that the activation temperature $T^* = E^*/R = 4000\ K$ is high and gives an idea of the stiffness of the reaction-diffusion/kinetics coupling.

2.2. Heat transfer modelling

This subsection presents successively the expressions used for the heat capacity and the thermal conductivity. It then analyzes the enthalpy balance that expresses the coupling between the heat transfer by thermal diffusion with the exothermic kinetics and provides the boundary conditions to close the mathematical modelling of the system. We also define and compute the adiabatic temperature of the exothermic kinetics. Due to the high temperatures involved in the process , up to 3000K, two phase changes occur

- at $T = T_{\alpha,\beta} = 1166$K, the allotropic phase transition of Ti_α to Ti_β, characterized by its mass latent heat $L_{\alpha,\beta}$,[17], and $f_{\alpha\beta} \in [0,1]$ is the fraction of β phase,
- at $T = T_{sl} = 1943$K, titanium melting is characterized by its mass latent heat L_{sl},[17], and $f_{sl} \in [0,1]$ is the fraction of liquid phase.

2.2.1. *Equation used for the heat capacity*

The mass heat capacity at constant pressure is a function of temperature, conversion rate and porosity. Assuming that the mass of the system remains constant during the process, we can therefore apply a linear mixing law between the heat capacity of reactants $C_{p_{Ti}}(T), C_{p_C}(T)$

and the heat capacity of the product $C_{p_{\mathrm{TiC}}}(T)$ weighted by the conversion rate of the reaction ξ to obtain

$$C_p(T,\xi) = \xi . C_{p_{\mathrm{TiC}}}(T) + (1-\xi) . \frac{M_{\mathrm{Ti}}.C_{p_{\mathrm{Ti}}}(T) + M_{\mathrm{C}}.C_{p_{\mathrm{C}}}(T)}{M_{\mathrm{TiC}}}, \tag{3}$$

where M_{Ti},M_{C} et M_{TiC} denote respectively the molar mass of titanium, carbide and titanium-carbide. The expression given by Eq.(3) is also used in [5],[6].

2.2.2. *Equation used for the thermal conductivity* $\lambda(T,\xi,f_{sl})$

Thermal conductivity $\lambda(T,\xi,f_{sl})$ in $J.m^{-1}.K^{-1}.s^{-1}$ is a key parameter governing the propagation of the combustion front. Following [14] we define the effective thermal conductivity $\lambda(T,\xi,f_{sl})$ by

$$\lambda(T,\xi,f_{sl}) = \lambda_{cond}(T,\xi,f_{sl}) + \lambda_{fus}(f_{sl}) + \lambda_{rad}(T) + \lambda_{conv}(T), \tag{4}$$

where

- $\lambda_{cond}(T,\xi)$ is the thermal conductivity of the system which is a non-linear weighting between the thermal conductivity of the reactants $\lambda_{\mathrm{Ti+C}}$ and the product $\lambda_{TiC}(T_a)$ according to [17]. It is given by

$$\lambda_{cond}(T,\xi) = \left\{\lambda_{\mathrm{Ti+C}}(T) + (\lambda_{\mathrm{TiC}}(T) - \lambda_{\mathrm{Ti+C}}(T)) . \sqrt{\xi}\right\} . f(T), \tag{5}$$

  while the expression of function $f(T)$ is given in [17]. Expression used for $\lambda_{\mathrm{TiC}}(T), \lambda_{\mathrm{Ti+C}}(T)$ are given in [13].
- $\lambda_{fus}(f_{sl}) = f_{sl}(1-\xi)$ accounts for the appearance of a liquid phase when temperature $T = T_{sl} = 1943$K, i.e. the temperature for the fusion of titanium. In this case, the fraction f_{sl} will increase from 0 to 1. Moreover this temperature is reached thanks to the exothermic kinetics while a fraction $(1-\xi)$ of titanium has already been consumed during the kinetics. This expression represents the fraction of fused titanium that has not yet reacted.
- $\lambda_{rad}(T)$ expresses the contribution of the radiative heat transfer between the grains and depends on the diameter d_p of the titanium/carbide particules, their emissivity ϵ, their porosity p. The expression used is taken from [18]. It was reported in [15] that this term contributes significantly to the velocity of the combustion wave.

$$\lambda_{rad}(T) = 4\,\varepsilon\,\sigma\,T^3\,d_p\,p^{-3}. \tag{6}$$

- $\lambda_{conv}(T)$ expresses the contribution of gaz that are present in the porous system. $\lambda_{air}(T)$ is taken from [13].

$$\lambda_{conv}(T) = \lambda_{air}(T)\;p^{-3}. \tag{7}$$

2.2.3. *Enthalpy balance*

The enthalpy balance expressing the local conservation of internal energy can be written as

$$\rho\,\frac{dh}{dt} = \nabla.(\lambda\,\nabla T), \tag{8}$$

where ρ in $kg.m^{-3}$ is the density of the system, h the mass enthalpy and λ the thermal conductivity. Temperature T and conversion rate ξ are two thermodynamical variables of the problem. Moreover two scalar variables $f_{\alpha\beta}$ and f_{sl}, representing the fraction of solid and liquid phases are also used for the description of the mass enthalpy of the system. We have therefore a set of four independent variables $T, \xi, f_{\alpha\beta}, f_{sl}$ that describe the evolution of the system. The mass enthalpy is defined by

$$h\left(T,\xi,f_{\alpha\beta},f_{sl}\right) = \xi\,(\Delta_r H)_{T_a} + \int_{T_a}^{T} C_p\,(\theta,\xi)\;d\theta + f_{\alpha\beta}\,L_{\alpha\beta} + f_{sl}\,L_{sl}. \tag{9}$$

The computation of the partial derivatives $\frac{\partial h}{\partial T}, \frac{\partial h}{\partial \xi}, \frac{\partial h}{\partial f_{\alpha\beta}}$ and $\frac{\partial h}{\partial f_{sl}}$ leads to

$$\begin{aligned} \frac{\partial h}{\partial T} &= C_p\,(T,\xi)\,, \quad \frac{\partial h}{\partial f_{\alpha\beta}} = L_{\alpha\beta}, \quad \frac{\partial h}{\partial f_{sl}} = L_{sl}, \\ \frac{\partial h}{\partial \xi} &= (\Delta_r H)_{T_a} + \int_{T_a}^{T} \frac{\partial}{\partial \xi}\left[C_p\,(\theta,\xi)\,\right]\;d\theta. \end{aligned} \tag{10}$$

Thanks to the definition of $C_p\,(T,\xi)$ given by Eq.(3), we obtain

$$\frac{\partial h}{\partial \xi} = (\Delta_r H)_{T_a} + \int_{T_a}^{T}\left[C_{p_{\mathrm{TiC}}}\,(\theta) - \frac{M_{\mathrm{Ti}}.C_{p_{\mathrm{Ti}}}\,(\theta) + M_{\mathrm{C}}.C_{p_{\mathrm{C}}}\,(\theta)}{M_{\mathrm{TiC}}}\right]\;d\theta, \tag{11}$$

where the integral $I(T)$ is computed with the trapezoidal rule.

$$I\,(T) = \int_{T_a}^{T}\left[C_{p_{\mathrm{TiC}}}\,(\theta) - \frac{M_{\mathrm{TiC}}\;C_{p_{\mathrm{Ti}}}\,(\theta) + M_{\mathrm{C}}\;C_{p_{\mathrm{C}}}\,(\theta)}{M_{\mathrm{TiC}}}\right]\;d\theta. \tag{12}$$

Fig.1 represents the evolution of $\frac{I(T)}{\Delta_r H}$ for $T \in [300, 3500]$. It is observed that $\max_{300 \le T \le 3500}\left|\frac{I\,(T)}{(\Delta_r H)_{T_a}}\right| \le 2.5\;10^{-5}$. The contribution of $\int_{T_a}^{T}\frac{\partial}{\partial \xi}\left[C_p\,(\theta,\xi)\right]\,d\theta$ to $\frac{\partial h}{\partial \xi}$ is therefore neglected.

Finally the enthalpy balance for the system is written by

$$\rho.\frac{\partial h_s\,(T,\xi)}{\partial t} = \nabla.\,(\lambda\,\nabla T) + \rho.\,(-\Delta_r H)_{T_a}\,.\frac{\partial \xi}{\partial t} - \rho.L_{\alpha\beta}.\frac{\partial f_{\alpha\beta}}{\partial t} - \rho.L_{sl}.\frac{\partial f_{sl}}{\partial t}, \tag{13}$$

where

$$h_s\,(T,\xi) = \int_{T_a}^{T} C_p\,(\theta,\xi)\;d\theta. \tag{14}$$

Radiative boundary conditions are defined over $\partial\Omega$ for the system and take the form

$$-\,\lambda\,\frac{\partial T}{\partial n} = \varepsilon.\sigma.\left(T^4 - T^4_{\infty\partial\Omega}\right), \tag{15}$$

where $\epsilon = 0.7$ is the emissivity of the material while σ is the Stefan-Boltzman constant. The value of $T_{\infty\partial\Omega}$ depends on the boundary $\partial\Omega$.

The initial condition given on Ω states that the sample is at room temperature.

$$T\,(M,0) = T_a. \tag{16}$$

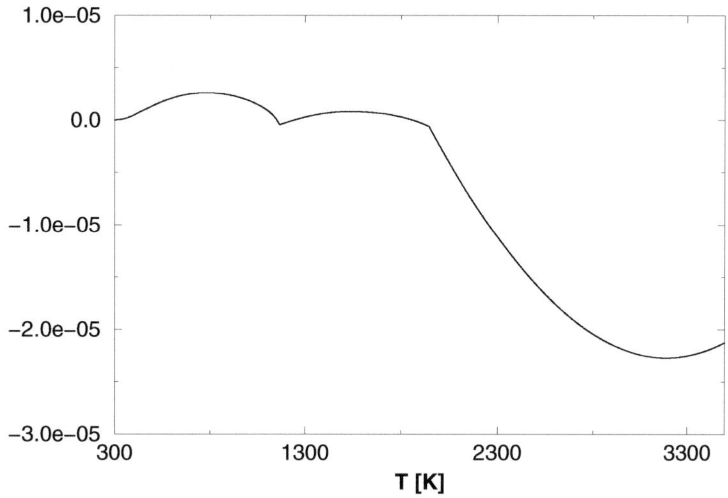

Figure 1. Evolution of $\frac{I(T)}{\Delta_r H}$ for $T \in [300, 3500]$ K.

2.2.4. Adiabatic temperature of the reaction T_{ad}

The adiabatic temperature T_{ad} of the reaction, or flame temperature, is the maximum temperature when the system is adiabatic. Titanium-carbide is obtained from titanium and carbide elements at temperature T_a. The enthalpy of the reaction corresponds to the heat of formation of TiC at temperature T_a, hence $(\Delta_r H)_{T_a} = \Delta_f H^0\,(\mathrm{TiC})_{T_a}$. Considering a thermodynamical path composed of the two steps:

(i) Titanium and carbide reactants are transformed into titanium-carbide, -TiC- at T_a,

(ii) End product TiC is heated up from T_a to T_{ad}.

One obtains that

$$\Delta_f H^0\,(TiC)_{T_a} + \int_{T_a}^{T_{ad}} C_p\,(\mathrm{TiC})\;dT = 0. \tag{17}$$

We use Janaf tables [11] for the expression of the heat capacity as a function of temperature. When $T_a = 298K$ (room temperature value), we solve numerically the integral equation Eq.(17), and obtain that the value of the adiabatic temperature is $T_{ad} = 2900K$. According to [17], we express $-\Delta_r H = \frac{\Delta H_f}{M_{TiC}}$.

2.3. Mathematical modelling of SHS process

The purpose of the numerical simulation is to determine at each point $M \in \Omega$, and at each time t, temperature field $T(M,t)$, conversion rate $\xi(M,t)$, solid fraction $f_{\alpha\beta}(M,t)$ and liquid fraction $f_{sl}(M,t)$ that will permit to determine spatial and temporal location of the reaction ignition. The mathematical modelling given by Eq.(1),Eq.(2) and Eq.(13),Eq.(14),Eq.(15) is well posed and will be solved numerically by the methods described in the next section.

3. Numerical discretization scheme

In this section we present the main features of the fully implicit finite-volume discretization scheme such as discrete maximum principle for both the reaction-diffusion and the differential equation discretization [1]. Error estimates are given in [2]. The iterative solution of penta-diagonal sparse matrix for 2D computations and hepta-diagonal sparse matrix for 3D computations is done thanks to SSOR and SIP methods. A fixed point technique is used to solve the coupled nonlinear system. A first order linearization of the exponential Arrhenius term is used which enhances the diagonal dominance of the matrix and accelerates the iterative SSOR/SIP solvers. We have used the enthalpy method to compute the phase change for which a detailed description can be found in [10]. This will be omitted from now, since we will mainly focuss our attention on the construction of the numerical scheme for the reaction-diffusion equation on a non uniform structured mesh and discard formally the specifics of the enthalpy method.

3.1. One-dimensional finite-volume discretization

We present the set of discrete equations that arise from the implicit finite-volume discretization of the enthalpy balance (reaction-diffusion equation) and the exothermic chemical reaction (differential equation).

3.1.1. *Numerical discretization of the enthalpy balance*

We integrate the enthalpy balance over a space-time finite volume $\Omega_i \times [t_n, t_{n+1}]$, where $\Omega_i = [r_i, r_{i+1}]$ is a control volume. A cell-centered approximation is used. The unknown T_i^n denotes the mean value of $T(x,t)$ at time t_n over Ω_i. $m_i = \int_{r_i}^{r_{i+1}} r^g \, dr$ is the discrete "mass" of control volume Ω_i.

$$\int_{t_n}^{t_{n+1}} \int_{\Omega_i} \rho . \frac{\partial h_s(T,\xi)}{\partial t} \, d\Omega \, dt = \int_{t_n}^{t_{n+1}} \int_{\Omega_i} \left(\nabla \left(\lambda \left(T, \xi, f_{sl} \right) \nabla \, T \right) + \frac{\rho . \Delta H_f}{M_{TiC}} k\left(T\right) \left(1 - \xi\right) \right) \, d\Omega \, dt. \tag{18}$$

Backward Euler implicit scheme is used for the temporal discretization since it is unconditionally stable, robust and well adapted for the discretization of such problems. Δt is the time-step.

We give only for internal control volumes, the finite-volume discretization of the enthalpy balance in a one-dimensional cartesian ($g = 0$), cylindrical ($g = 1$) and spherical ($g = 2$) coordinate system

$$m_i \rho \frac{h_s\left(T_i^{n+1}, \xi_i^{n+1}\right) - h_s\left(T_i^n, \xi_i^n\right)}{\Delta t} = \lambda_{i+\frac{1}{2}}^{n+1} r_{i+1}^g \frac{T_{i+1}^{n+1} - T_i^{n+1}}{d_{i+\frac{1}{2}}} - \lambda_{i-\frac{1}{2}}^{n+1} r_i^g \frac{T_i^{n+1} - T_{i-1}^{n+1}}{d_{i-\frac{1}{2}}}$$
$$+ m_i \frac{\rho \Delta H_f}{M_{TiC}} k_d(T^{n+1}) \left(1 - \xi_i^{n+1}\right). \tag{19}$$

Here $d_{i+\frac{1}{2}}$ is the distance between the center of two adjacent control volumes, and denoting by $h_i = r_{i+1} - r_i$ the length of control volume Ω_i, then $d_{i+\frac{1}{2}} = (h_{i+1} + h_i)/2$.

As pointed out by [9], in order to ensure the conservativity of the heat flux at the interface between two adjacents control volumes, $\lambda_{i+\frac{1}{2}}^{n+1}$ is computed thanks to the following harmonic mean formula:

$$\lambda_{i+\frac{1}{2}}^{n+1} = \frac{h_i + h_{i+1}}{\frac{h_{i+1}}{\lambda_{i+1}^{n+1}} + \frac{h_i}{\lambda_i^{n+1}}}, \tag{20}$$

where $\lambda_i^{n+1} = \lambda\left(T_i^{n+1}, \xi_i^{n+1}, {f_{sl}}_i^{n+1}\right)$. A decoupled iterative solution of the nonlinear system is achieved thanks to the fixed point method. A first-order linearization of both the stiff Arrhenius term, and the enthalpy term is done. This reinforces the strictly dominant three-diagonal matrix that is inverted at each step of the non-linear solver thanks to the direct (α, β) Gauss algorithm, i.e. the TDMA algorithm [9]. The numerical solution cost of the three-diagonal linear system by this method increases linearly with the number of unknowns.

3.1.2. Numerical discretization of the exothermic kinetics

We integrate the differential equation over a space-time finite volume $\Omega_i \times [t_n, t_{n+1}]$. A cell-centered approximation is used.

$$\int_{t_n}^{t_{n+1}} \int_{\Omega_i} \frac{d\xi}{dt} = \int_{t_n}^{t_{n+1}} \int_{\Omega_i} k_d(T)\ (1-\xi)\,. \tag{21}$$

The backward Euler scheme, first order accurate fully implicit scheme is used. Denoting by ξ_i^n the mean value at time t_n over Ω_i of $\xi(x,t)$, we obtain the following discrete equation

$$\xi_i^{n+1} = \frac{\xi_i^n + \Delta t\, k_d(T_i^{n+1})}{1 + \Delta t\, k_d(T_i^{n+1})}. \tag{22}$$

It was proved in [1] that the numerical scheme is L^∞ stable, moreover for each time index n and for all control volume index $i = 1, \ldots, I\ :\ \xi_i^n \in [0,1]$. For a given control volume index i, the time sequence $(\xi_i^n)_n$ is increasing, hence the discrete finite-volume approximation mimics the behavior of the continuous solution [2].

3.2. Two-dimensional finite-volume discretization

We will not detail the set of discrete equations for the chemical kinetics, since it is a straightforward extension from the 1D case. We now give the discrete equations related to the finite-volume approximation of the enthalpy balance over a space-time finite volume $\Omega_{i,j} \times [t_n, t_{n+1}]$. Each rectangular structured non uniform control volume $\Omega_{i,j} = [r_i, r_{i+1}] \times [z_j, z_{j+1}]$, has surface $m_{i,j}$ defined by :

$$m_{i,j} = \int_{\Omega_{i,j}} d\Omega = \int_{z_j}^{z_{j+1}} \left(\int_{r_i}^{r_{i+1}} r^g\, dr\right)\, dz\ = \frac{(r_{i+1})^{g+1} - (r_i)^{g+1}}{g+1} \cdot \left(z_{j+1} - z_j\right). \tag{23}$$

The enthalpy balance is written for 2D cartesian geometry $(g = 0)$ or 2D cylindrical geometry $(g = 1)$.

$$\frac{m_{i,j}}{\Delta t}.\rho.\left(h_s\left(T^{n+1}_{i,j},\xi^{n+1}_{i,j}\right)-h_s\left(T^{n}_{i,j},\xi^{n}_{i,j}\right)\right)=\lambda^{n+1}_{i+\frac{1}{2},j}r^{g}_{i+1}\frac{T^{n+1}_{i+1,j}-T^{n+1}_{i,j}}{d^{r}_{i+\frac{1}{2}}}-\lambda^{n+1}_{i-\frac{1}{2},j}r^{g}_{i}\frac{T^{n+1}_{i,j}-T^{n+1}_{i-1,j}}{d^{r}_{i-\frac{1}{2}}}$$
$$+\lambda^{n+1}_{i,j+\frac{1}{2}}\frac{T^{n+1}_{i,j+1}-T^{n+1}_{i,j}}{d^{z}_{j+\frac{1}{2}}}-\lambda^{n+1}_{i,j-\frac{1}{2}}\frac{T^{n+1}_{i,j}-T^{n+1}_{i,j-1}}{d^{z}_{j-\frac{1}{2}}}+m_{i,j}.\frac{\rho.\Delta H_f}{M_{TiC}}k\left(T^{n+1}_{i,j}\right)\left(1-\xi^{n+1}_{i,j}\right).$$

The expression used for $\lambda^{n+1}_{i+\frac{1}{2},j}$, $\lambda^{n+1}_{i-\frac{1}{2},j}$, $\lambda^{n+1}_{i,j+\frac{1}{2}}$, $\lambda^{n+1}_{i,j-\frac{1}{2}}$ is a straightforward adaptation of Eq.(20). We use the same decoupled iterative solution of the nonlinear system as in the one-dimensional case. A first-order linearization of both the stiff Arrhenius term, and the enthalpy term is done. This reinforces the strictly dominant sparse penta-diagonal matrix that is inverted at each step of the non-linear solver. It is known that the more strictly dominant a matrix is, the faster iterative solver such as the SSOR, (successive over relaxation method) converges.

3.3. Three-dimensional finite-volume discretization

We now give the discrete equations related to the finite-volume approximation of the enthalpy balance over a space-time finite volume $\Omega_{i,j,k}\times[t_n,t_{n+1}]$. Each parallelepipedic structured non uniform control volume $\Omega_{i,j,k}=[x_i,x_{i+1}]\times[x_j,y_{j+1}]\times[z_k,z_{k+1}]$, has volume $m_{i,j,k}=\int_{\Omega_{i,j,k}}d\Omega$.

$$\frac{m_{i,j,k}}{\Delta t}.\rho.\left(h_s\left(T^{n+1}_{i,j,k},\xi^{n+1}_{i,j,k}\right)-h_s\left(T^{n}_{i,j,k},\xi^{n}_{i,j,k}\right)\right) \tag{24}$$
$$=\lambda^{n+1}_{i+\frac{1}{2},j,k}\frac{T^{n+1}_{i+1,j,k}-T^{n+1}_{i,j,k}}{d^{x}_{i+\frac{1}{2}}}-\lambda^{n+1}_{i-\frac{1}{2},j,k}\frac{T^{n+1}_{i,j,k}-T^{n+1}_{i-1,j,k}}{d^{x}_{i-\frac{1}{2}}}$$
$$+\lambda^{n+1}_{i,j+\frac{1}{2},k}\frac{T^{n+1}_{i,j+1,k}-T^{n+1}_{i,j,k}}{d^{y}_{j+\frac{1}{2}}}-\lambda^{n+1}_{i,j-\frac{1}{2},k}\frac{T^{n+1}_{i,j,k}-T^{n+1}_{i,j-1,k}}{d^{y}_{j-\frac{1}{2}}}$$
$$+\lambda^{n+1}_{i,j,k+\frac{1}{2}}\frac{T^{n+1}_{i,j,k+1}-T^{n+1}_{i,j,k}}{d^{z}_{k+\frac{1}{2}}}-\lambda^{n+1}_{i,j,k-\frac{1}{2}}\frac{T^{n+1}_{i,j,k}-T^{n+1}_{i,j,k-1}}{d^{z}_{k-\frac{1}{2}}}+m_{i,j,k}.\frac{\rho.\Delta H_f}{M_{TiC}}k\left(T^{n+1}_{i,j,k}\right)\left(1-\xi^{n+1}_{i,j,k}\right).$$

The expression used for $\lambda^{n+1}_{i+\frac{1}{2},j,k}$, $\lambda^{n+1}_{i-\frac{1}{2},j,k}$, $\lambda^{n+1}_{i,j+\frac{1}{2},k}$, $\lambda^{n+1}_{i,j-\frac{1}{2},k}$, $\lambda^{n+1}_{i,j,k+\frac{1}{2}}$, $\lambda^{n+1}_{i,j,k-\frac{1}{2}}$ is a straightforward adaptation of Eq.(20). We use the same numerical procedure as the one used for the two-dimensional case. It is worth mentioning that a sparse strictly dominant hepta-diagonal matrix is inverted at each step of the non-linear solver.

3.4. Numerical implementation

Due to space constraints, we only describe key aspects of our numerical software entitled Hephaïstos; a toolbox library for multidimensional numerical computation of combustion synthesis problems written in C/C++. Detailed documented results related to the implementation on various single core, multi-core and many-core architectures are given in [4]. Auto-parallelization and openmp based speedup results on core i7 quad-core using gnu gcc, sun studio and open64 compilers are reported. A similar study is done on cuda-core using nvidia nvcc compiler [4]. Efforts were done to achieve the highest possible performance on processors that use memory cache hierarchy such as MIPS R1X00 processors and INTEL Core i7 processors. As an example, all loops invariant quantities are pre-computed and stored into one-dimensional arrays. Dynamically allocated multidimensional arrays are not used, because of pointer aliasing problems. We prefer to convert such arrays into one-dimensional arrays. A storage similar to CRS(Compact Row Storage) is used that takes into account the penta (hepta)-diagonal sparsity of the matrices that are iteratively inverted by SSOR and SIP methods. The postprocessing of the software's results saved to vtk format is done thanks to mayavi software for temporal snapshot and Paraview for interactive analysis and movie production.

4. 1D/2D/3D numerical study

In this section we analyze the ignition and propagation of the combustion front during titanium carbide-TiC- combustion synthesis. It is worth mentioning that the propagation of the combustion wave is either stable i.e. at constant velocity or oscillatory and can be determined according to [16] by the computation of the Zeldovich number Ze defined by $Ze = \dfrac{(T_{ad} - T_a)\ E^*}{R\ T_{ad}^2}$. $T_{ad}[K]$ is the adiabatic temperature of the reaction, $T_a[K]$ is the ambiant temperature and $\left(k_d^*[s^{-1}], E^*[kJ/mol]\right)$ characterizes the first order exothermic kinetics. R is the gaz constant. Experimental observations were reported in [8] to sustain this theoretical analysis. Moreover in the constant velocity case resp.(*oscillatory case i.e. periodic oscillation of the velocity of the solid flame propagation around a mean velocity*), the synthesised titanium-carbide product has uniform resp.(*non-uniform*) physical properties. For $(k_0, E^*) = (3800\,s^{-1}, 30.0\,kcal.mol^{-1})$, the Zeldovich number $Ze = 4.52 < Ze_c = 2\left(2 + \sqrt{5}\right)$, therefore the solid flame propagation is stable.

4.1. 1D numerical study

This subsection presents unpublished results related to the induction time τ_{ind} in planar/cylindrical/spherical geometry such as one depicted in Fig.(21).

The boundary conditions used to analyze the combustion front propagation in the reactive mixture of length R_e are

$$\begin{aligned} -\lambda \frac{\partial T}{\partial n}(0,t) &= \epsilon\,\sigma\left(T(0,t)^4 - \left(T_{f_{x=0}}\right)^4\right), \\ -\lambda \frac{\partial T}{\partial n}(R_e,t) &= \epsilon\,\sigma\left(T(R_e,t)^4 - \left(T_{f_{x=R_e}}\right)^4\right). \end{aligned} \tag{25}$$

4.1.1. *Tools used to analyse the numerical simulation results*

We define the induction time, starting point and ending time, three notions that will be heavily used in this section.

- The induction time τ_{ind} is the required time for the build-up of a steady-state propagation regime of the chemical reaction inside the material. It is defined as the first instant for which there exists $x \in \Omega$ such that $\xi(x, \tau_{ind}) > 0$. It depends on various parameters such as ignition temperature, heat capacity, thermal conductivity, pre-heating time, mass density.

- Starting of the reaction is $x_{ind} > 0$ such that $\xi(x_{ind}, \tau_{ind}) = 0.5$,
- Ending time of the reaction is time $\tau_{end} > 0$ such that $\forall x \in \Omega, \xi(x, \tau_{end}) = 1$,
- Thickness of reaction zone. Assuming that the reaction starts at τ_{ind}, then we can follow the evolution of the combustion front propagation in the material thanks to the computation of spatial and temporal evolution of points $x_M^{0.01}(t)$, $x_M^{0.50}(t)$ et $x_M^{0.99}(t)$ such that $\xi(x_M^{0.01}(t), t) = 0.01$, $\xi(x_M^{0.50}(t), t) = 0.50$ et $\xi(x_M^{0.99}(t), t) = 0.99$,
- A each instant t, $x_{max}(t)$ denotes the location which has the maximum temperature in domain Ω,
- The synthesis temperature characterizes the thermal history of the material from the point of view of the kinetics and is defined for $x \in \Omega$ by

$$T_{syn}(x) = \int_0^{+\infty} T(x,t) \frac{d\xi}{dt}(x,t)\, dx. \tag{26}$$

It was defined and used in [2].

A meaningful numerical simulation is presented in Fig.(2) and in Fig.(3). We observe that the "thickness" of the reaction-zone defined by $x_M^{0.99}(t) - x_M^{0.01}(t)$ is nearly constant. Moreover, the slope of the three curves is nearly the same in the steady state regime. This confirms that a stable propagation anticipated thanks to the computation of the Zeldovich number is effectively obtained. Nevertheless, the temporal evolution of $x_{max}(t)$ gives an information about the thermal history. Fig.(2) and Fig.(3) represent the temporal evolution of $x_{max}(t)$, $x(\xi = 0.01, t)$ $x(\xi = 0.50, t)$ and $x(\xi = 0.99, t)$ for wall temperature $T_{f_{r=0}} = 1600$ K. Phase changes are taken (*resp. not taken*) into account in Fig.(3) (*resp in Fig.(2)*). One observes on both Fig.(2) and Fig.(3) that $x_{max}(t)$ is equal to zero during preheating time, moreover taking into account phase changes as seen on Fig.(3) modifies the velocity of $x_{max}(t)$. When the reaction starts, the front propagates, and $x_{max}(t)$ evolves differently than $x_M^{0.01}(t), x_M^{0.99}(t)$. Moreover when the front reaches the extremity of the sample, then $x_{max}(t)$ increases rapidly and soon after decreases because the synthesis is finished and the radiative heat losses contribute significantly to the decreasing of the temperature field inside the material.

4.1.2. Combustion front propagation

Fig.(4) shows that the propagation of the stiff combustion front is stable, since each profile in the steady state propagation regime are equally distant from each other.

Fig.(5) shows that the energy released by the exothermic kinetics is nearly constant during the propagation of the combustion wave inside the material.

4.1.3. Contribution of furnace temperature

A sample of length $R_e = 1$cm is placed inside a furnace maintained at temperature $T_f \in [800, 2400]$K. Fig.(6) shows that both induction time τ_{ind} and ending time τ_{end} increase exponentially when T_f decreases, whenever phase change is taken into account or not.

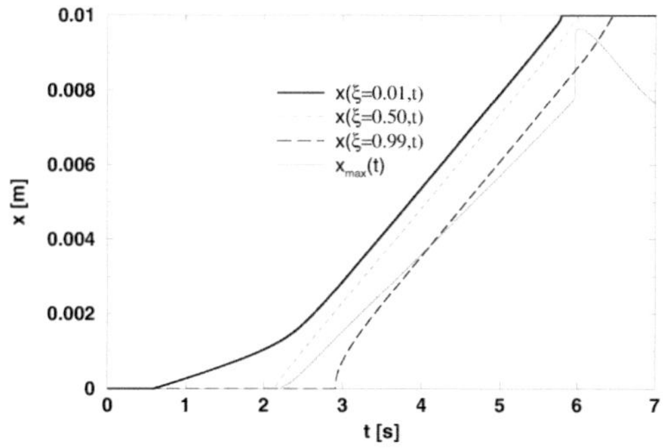

Figure 2. Temporal evolution of $x_{max}(t)$ and $x(\xi = 0.01, t)$ $x(\xi = 0.50, t)$ $x(\xi = 0.99, t)$ for wall temperature $T_{f_{r=0}} = 1600$ K. Phase changes are not taken into account.

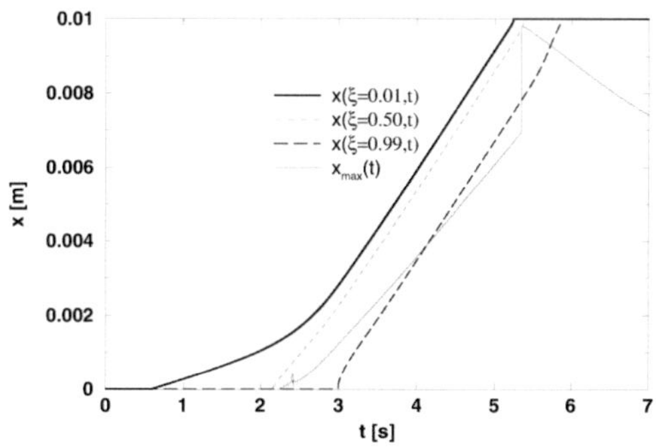

Figure 3. Temporal evolution of $x_{max}(t)$ and $x(\xi = 0.01, t)$ $x(\xi = 0.50, t)$ $x(\xi = 0.99, t)$ for wall temperature $T_{f_{r=0}} = 1600$ K. Phase changes are taken into account.

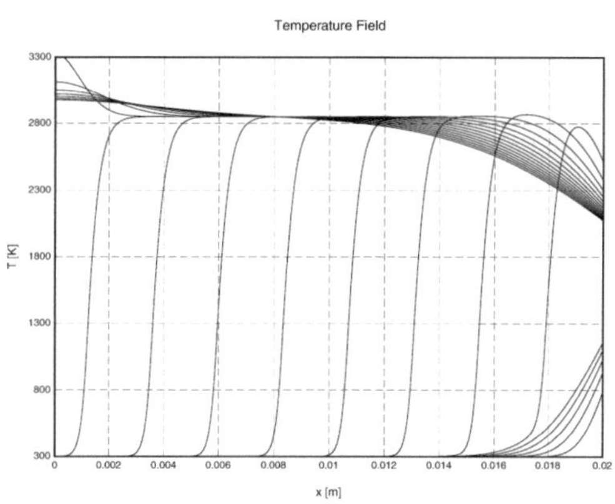

Figure 4. Temporal evolution of $T(x, t)$ at equally spaced instants. Phase change is not taken into account.

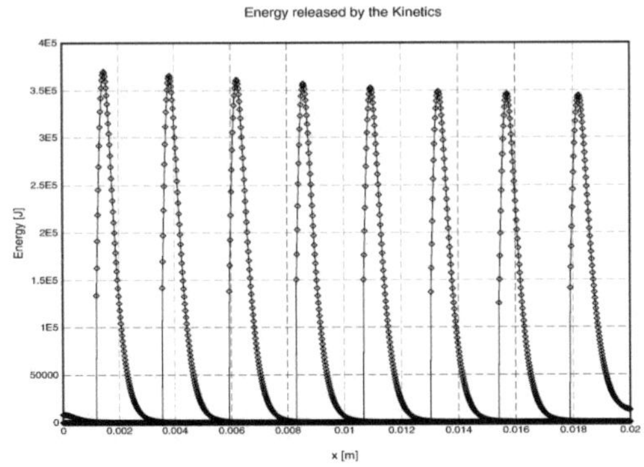

Figure 5. Temporal evolution of $\frac{\rho \Delta H_f}{M_{TiC}} k_d(T)\,(1-\xi_i)$ at equally spaced instants. Phase change is not taken into account.

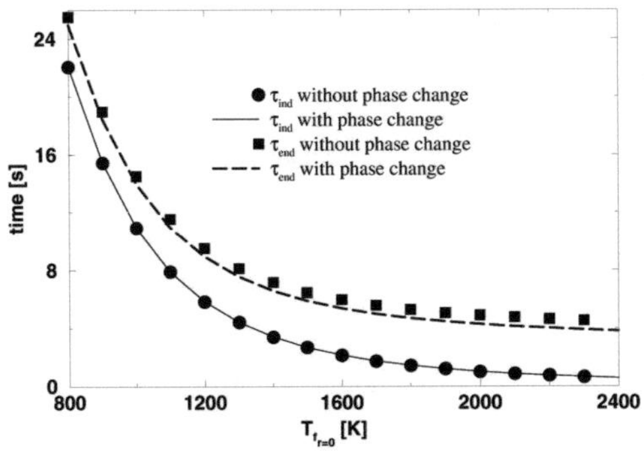

Figure 6. Evolution of τ_{ind} et τ_{end} as a function of temperature furnace $T_{f_{r=0}}$.

Fig.(7) shows that the evolution of $x_{ind}(t)$ is nearly similar whatever the furnace temperature T_f is. In fact, each curve can be translated from each other, so the behaviour is nearly independent from T_f, except from small values for which a slight curvature effect is observed. A similar conclusion can be drawn upon analyzing Fig.(8) which represents the time evolution of $T_{max}(t)$. It is also worth mentioning that a sharp peak is observed on each curve. An explanation comes from the fact that when the combustion front, at high temperature ends its propagation, it reaches the cold extremity, so an intense heat transfer occurs.

Fig.(9) shows the same behaviour for $x_{max(t)}$ whatever T_f is. The following analysis is proposed.

- A pre-heating stage, for which thanks to the heat supply at $x = 0$ (radiative boundary condition), there is a gradual increase in temperature. But $x_{max}(t) = 0$, so the temperature is below the ignition temperature.
- A combustion front propagation step $x_{max}(t)$ increases linearly with respect to time, so a constant velocity propagation of TiC synthesis is observed.
- An acceleration of the propagation which comes from the influence of the radaitive boundary condition at $x = R_e$. During a small time interval, the hot spot reaches the ending extremity of the sample.

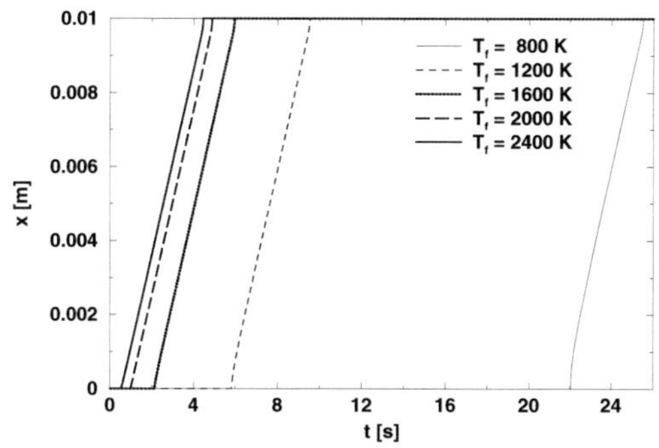

Figure 7. Temporal evolution of $x_{ind}(t)$ position , for various values of the furnace temperature $T_{f_{r=0}} \in [800, 1200, 1600, 2000, 2400]$ K.

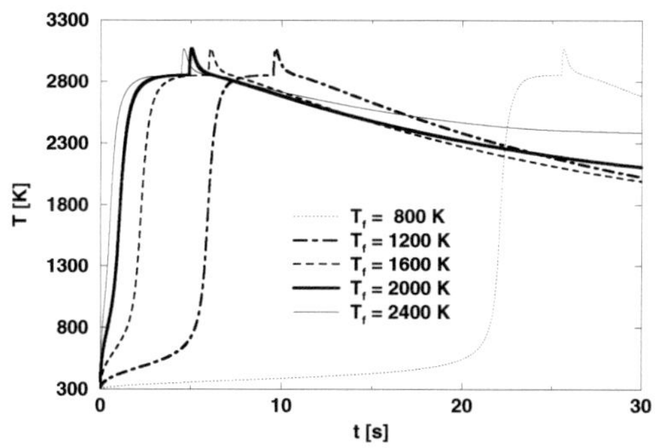

Figure 8. Time evolution of $T_{max}(t)$ for several values of temperature furnace $T_{f_{r=0}} \in [800, 1200, 1600, 2000, 2400]$.

- A cooling stage by thermal conduction, since the combustion synthesis is finished. The hot spot moves rapidly towards the center of the material thanks to the cooling. It is also observed that the velocity of the hot spot is a function of T_f.

Finally in the steady state propagation regime, each curve $x_{max}(t)$ can be translated from each other. The local heat supply induced by the boundary condition at $x = 0$ doesn't modify the characteristics of the combustion front propagation such as it's velocity. The time evolution of $T_{max(t)}$ depicted in Fig.(8) can be analyzed similarly.

Spatial distribution for different values of $T_{f_{r=0}}$ for temperature (*resp. conversion rate*) at $t = 1$s, is represented on Fig.(10). Using a suitable scaling, it is observed that their shape and stiffness is similar.

4.1.4. Energy released/absorbed by the boundary conditions

We analyze the time evolution of flux $\Phi_0(t)$, exchanged at $r = 0$ between the exterior and the material, defined by $\Phi_0(t) = -\left(\lambda \frac{\partial T}{\partial n}\right)(0,t) = \varepsilon\,\sigma\,\left(T(0,t)^4 - T_f^4\right)$. Three consecutive steps can be observed thanks to the analysis of $\Phi_0(t)$ represented by Fig.(12) and correlated to the time-evolution of $T(0,t)$

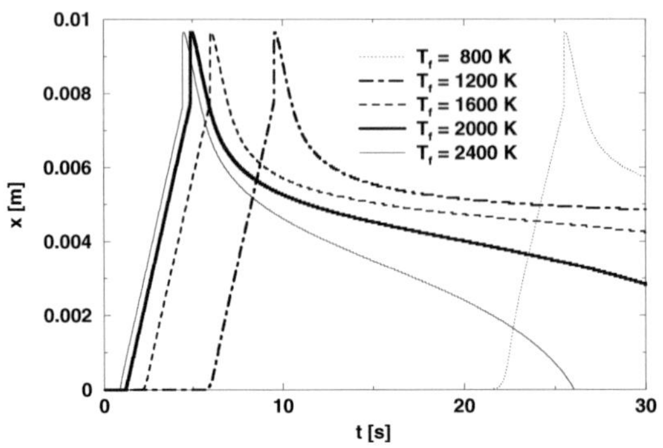

Figure 9. Time evolution of $x_{max}(t)$ for different values of furnace temperature $T_{f_{r=0}}$.

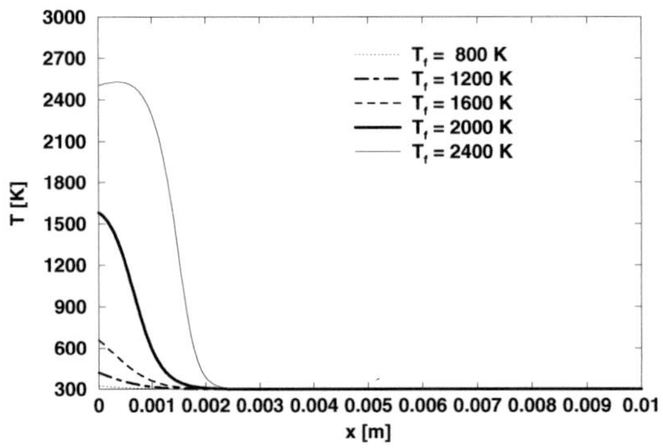

Figure 10. Spatial distribution of temperature profile at $t = 1$s, for each wall temperature $T_f \in \{800, 1200, 1600, 2000, 2400\}$ K.

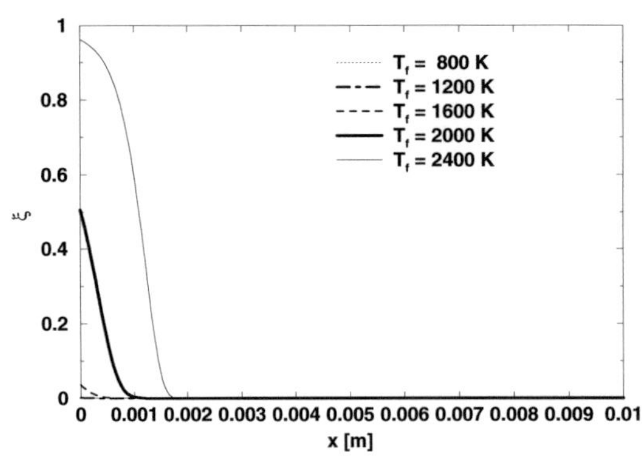

Figure 11. Spatial distribution of conversion rate profile at $t = 1$s, for each wall temperature $T_f \in \{800, 1200, 1600, 2000, 2400\}$ K.

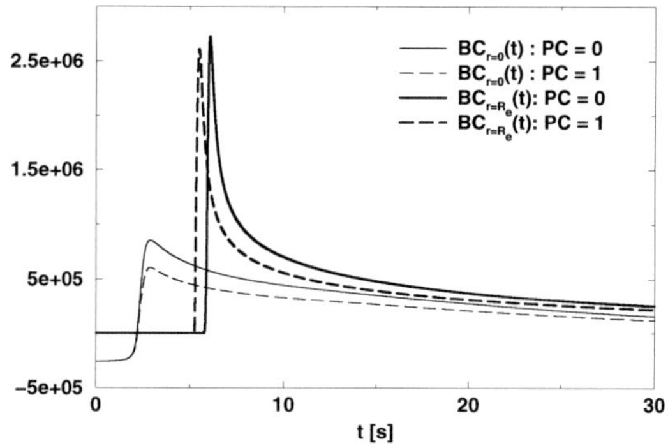

Figure 12. Time evolution of the energy released/removed by the radiative boundary conditions when phase change is taken into account or not.

(i) $T(0,t)$ increases from T_a to T_f thanks to the heat supplied by radiative heat transfer. $\Phi_0(t)$ is negative and its absolute value decreases down to zero,

(ii) $T(0,t)$ is above T_f and reaches T_{ad} ($T_f < T_{ad}$), thanks to the exothermic reaction of titanium-carbide synthesis. The sign of $\Phi_0(t)$ changes and its value increases to reach a maximum,

(iii) $T(0,t)$ decreases to T_f when the kinetics is ended. $\Phi_0(t)$ decreases asymptotically to zero.

A similar analysis can be done for $\Phi_{R_e}(t) = -\left(\lambda \frac{\partial T}{\partial n}\right)(R_e,t) = \varepsilon\,\sigma\,\left(T(R_e,t)^4 - T_f^4\right)$. It is worth mentioning that due to the thermal shock observed when the "hot" solid combustion front reaches the "cold" boundary, the amplitude $\Phi_{R_e}(t)$ is an order of magnitude higher than $\Phi_0(t)$. Taking into account phase change doesn't modify the observation done thanks to Fig.(12).

4.1.5. *Contribution of the cut-off temperature to the ignition and propagation*

We assume that the chemical kinetics has a cut-off temperature T_s equal to the first phase transition $Ti_\alpha \rightarrow Ti_\beta$ temperature, $T_{\alpha\beta} = 1166$K. We observe on Fig.(13), that the discrepancy $\tau_{ign}^{T_s=0} - \tau_{ign}^{T_s=T_{\alpha\beta}}$ increases significantly when T_f decreases whenever the phase change is taken into account or not. In practice, $\left(\tau_{ign}^{T_s=0}\right)_{T_f=900\,K} = \left(\tau_{ign}^{T_s=T_{\alpha\beta}}\right)_{T_f=1600\,K}$. A similar conclusion is drawn on Fig.(14) for the difference $\tau_{end}^{T_s=0} - \tau_{end}^{T_s=T_{\alpha\beta}}$.

Below the cut-off temperature, the kinetics is not active, therefore the modelling reduces to a non-linear diffusion equation. The main phenomena is the pre-heating of the material. When the temperature reaches locally the ignition temperature for a certain amount of time, the chemical reaction starts.

We analyze the contribution of the cut-off temperature to the spatial stiffness of the combustion front through the temperature profile on Fig.(15) and conversion rate profile on Fig.(16). In both cases, the spatial resolution of the numerical discretisation scheme is satisfactory, and we observe that temperature and conversion rate profiles are stiffer when a cut-off temperature is taken into account.

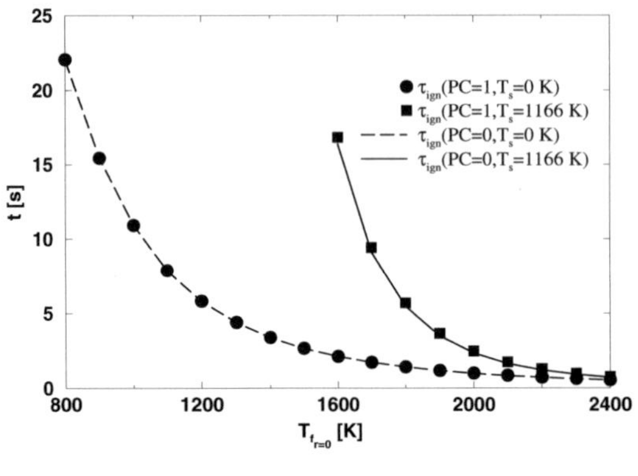

Figure 13. Evolution of τ_{ind} as a function of $t_{f_{r=0}}$ for a kinetics with/without a cut-off temperature. Phase change taken into account ($PC = 1$), or not ($PC = 0$).

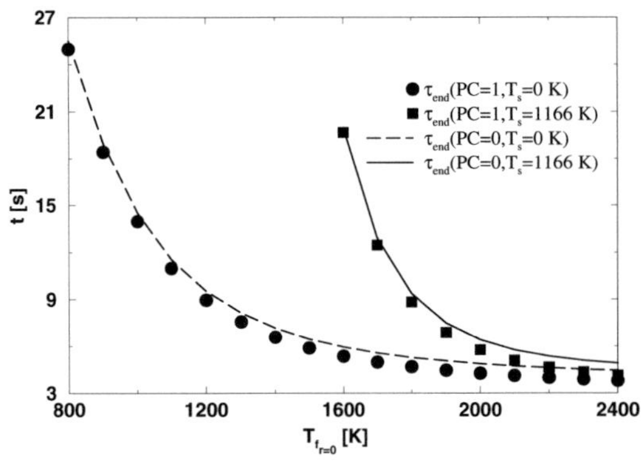

Figure 14. Evolution of τ_{ind} as a function of $t_{f_{r=0}}$ for a kinetics with/without a cut-off temperature. Phase change taken into account ($PC = 1$), or not ($PC = 0$).

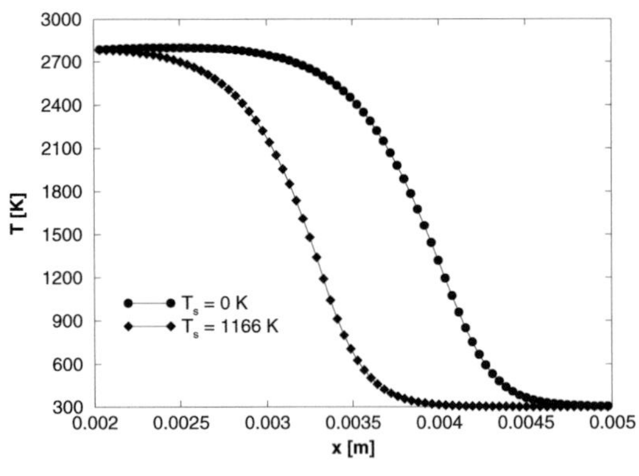

Figure 15. Spatial temperature profile at $t = 2$s, for chemical kinetic without cutoff temperature $T_s = 0$, and with cutoff temperature $T_s = T_{\alpha\beta}$.

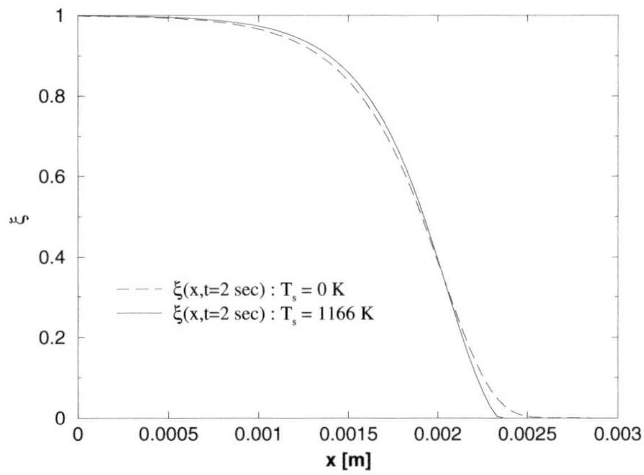

Figure 16. Spatial conversion rate profile at $t = 2$s, for chemical kinetic without cutoff temperature $T_s = 0$, and with cutoff temperature $T_s = T_{\alpha\beta}$.

4.1.6. *Analysis of a double front propagation*

We consider the situation when we heat identically both extremities of the cylinder with $T_{f_{r=0}} = T_{f_{r=R_e}} = T_f = 2400$ K. Obviously spatial profiles are similar and symmetrical with respect to $x = R_e/2$ as can be seen on Fig.(17)-(18).

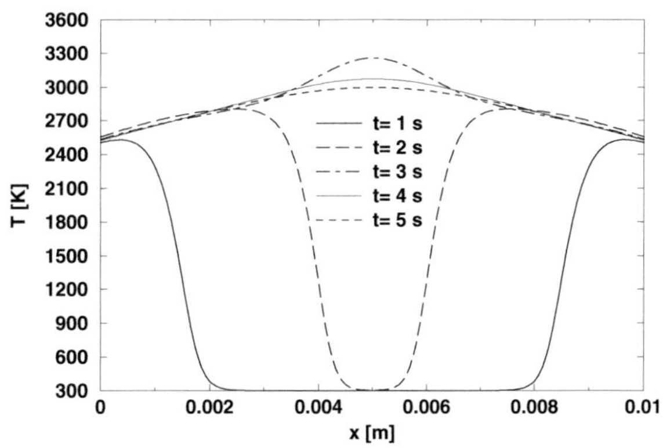

Figure 17. Spatial temperature profiles at several consecutive instants.

Moreover, when the two fronts meet each other at $x = R_e/2$, a liquid phase may appear. Temperature at the center of the material is significantly greater than the adiabatic temperature of the reaction represented in Fig.(19). The stiffness of the conversion rate in the double front case versus the single front case is also noticed in Fig.(20).

4.1.7. *Contribution of the geometry to the induction time*

Fig.(21) shows the evolution of $\log(\tau_{ind})(T_f)$ for slab, cylindrical and spherical geometry. The three profiles are similar, nevertheless it is observed that $\tau_{ind}^{\text{slab}} > \tau_{ind}^{\text{cyl}} > \tau_{ind}^{\text{sph}}$, for each value of T_f. Curvature effects may explain this result.

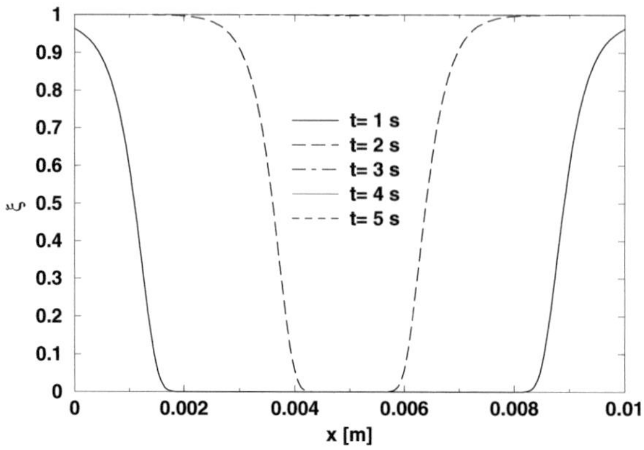

Figure 18. Spatial conversion rate profiles at several consecutive instants.

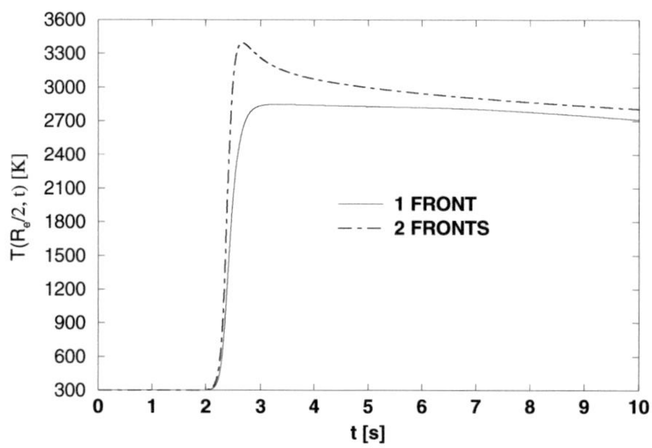

Figure 19. Temporal evolution of $T(R_e, t)$ for single and double fronts propagation.

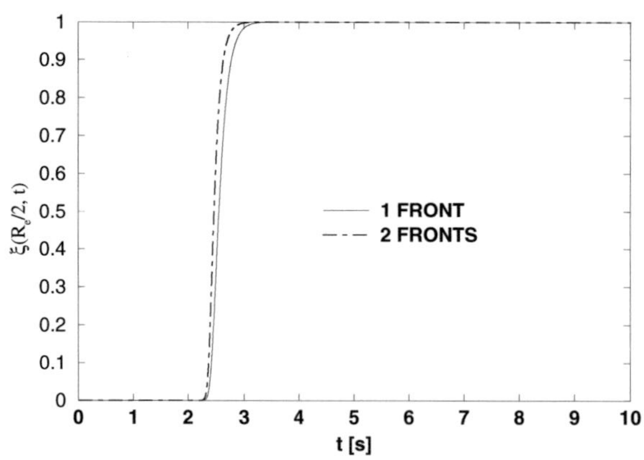

Figure 20. Temporal evolution of $\xi(R_e, t)$ for single and double fronts propagation.

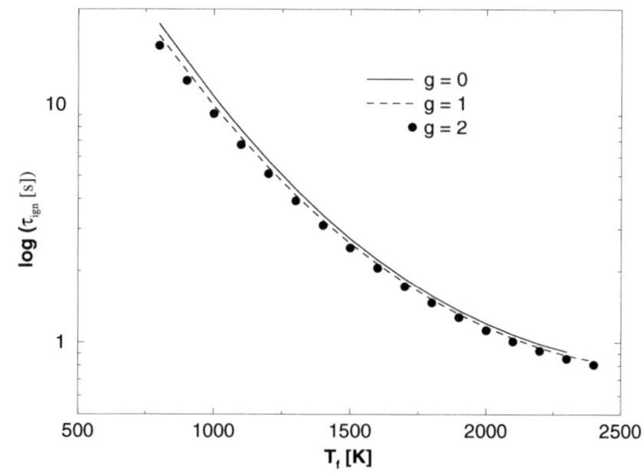

Figure 21. Evolution of the $\log(\tau_{ind})(T_f)$ for slab geometry $g = 0$, cylindrical geometry $g = 1$ and spherical geometry $g = 2$.

4.1.8. Contribution of the kinetics to the induction time

We analyze the contribution of the exponent d defined in Eq.(2) to the induction time τ_{ind} and the ending time τ_{end}. In order to obtain a better precision for $\tau_{ind}(d)$, we use fractional exponents $d \in [0, 2]$. Moreover to be able to compare the results obtained for various values of $k_d(T)$, we perform a normalization of the pre-exponential factor such that its value remain the same when $T = T_{ad}$ (the adiabatic temperature). We write therefore the equality between factors $k_0(T) = k_0^* \, exp\left(-\frac{E^*}{RT}\right)$ and $k_d(T) = k_d^* \, T^d \, exp\left(-\frac{E^*}{RT}\right)$ at $T = T_{ad}$

$$k_0^* = k_d^* . T_{ad}^d . \tag{27}$$

Fig.(22) represents the temperature dependance of $k_d(T)$. Ten numerical simulations are done for five equally-spaced values of $d \in [0, 2]$. For each value of d we take into account or not the phase change and use $T_{f_{r=0}} = 1600$K.

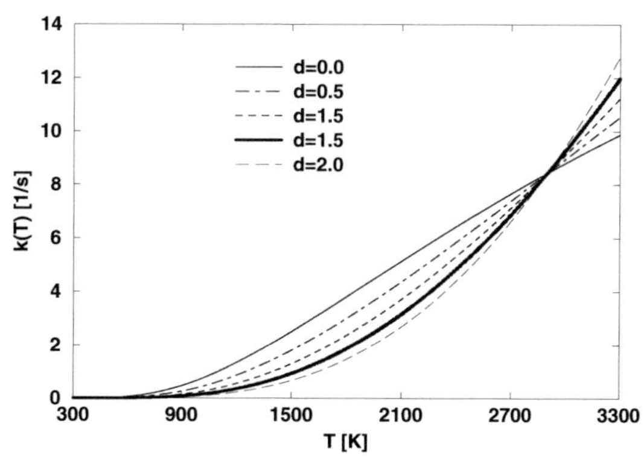

Figure 22. Temperature dependance of $k_d(T)$ for various values of exponent $d \in [0, 2]$.

We point out that

- Each curve $k_d(T)$ is an increasing function of temperature T and has the same concavity,
- When $T \leq T_{ad}$, then $k_d(T)_{d>0}$ is below $k_0(T)$,

- When $T > T_{ad}$, then $k_d(T) >> k_0(T)$. This imply that the heat released by the exothermic kinetics is significantly increasing when d increases. Temperature "overshoot" of $T_{max}(t)$ can be observed on Fig.(30).
- We conclude that the velocity of the combustion flame is higher when $d = 0$ than when $d > 0$, and the temperature obtained is super-adiabatic as seen on Fig.(30).

Fig.(23) shows that the increasing rate of the induction time τ_{ind} is super-linear, while it is linear for the ending time τ_{end} when degree d increases. It appears independent from the eventual phase change contribution. It is worth mentioning that all spatial temperature

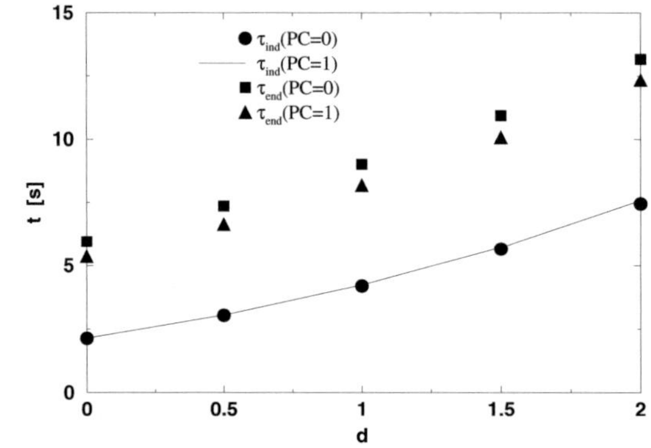

Figure 23. Comparison of induction time τ_{ind} and ending time τ_{end}, when phase change is taken into account (PC=1) or not (PC=0), for several values of exponent $d \in [0, 2]$, with $T_{f_{r=0}} = 1600$ K and $T_{f_{r=R_e}} = 300$ K.

profiles represented on Fig.(24) have a discontinuity of the time-derivative when $T = T_{sl}$. This is explained by the contribution $\lambda_{fus}(f_{sl})$ of the titanium melting to the thermal conductivity given by Eq.(4).

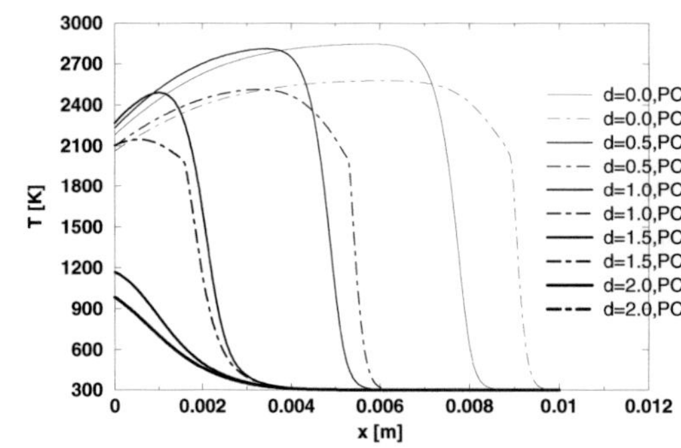

Figure 24. Spatial distribution of temperature field $T(x, t = 5\,s)$ for different values of exponent d, when phase change is taken into account (PC=1) or not (PC=0) with $T_{f_{r=0}} = 1600$ K and $T_{f_{r=R_e}} = 300$ K.

Conversion rate profiles represented on Fig.(25) are sharper when phase change is taken into account.

The spatial distribution of the synthesis temperature $T_{syn}(x, t = 30\,s)$ always increases when d increases, whether phase change is taken into account or not as seen on Fig.(26).

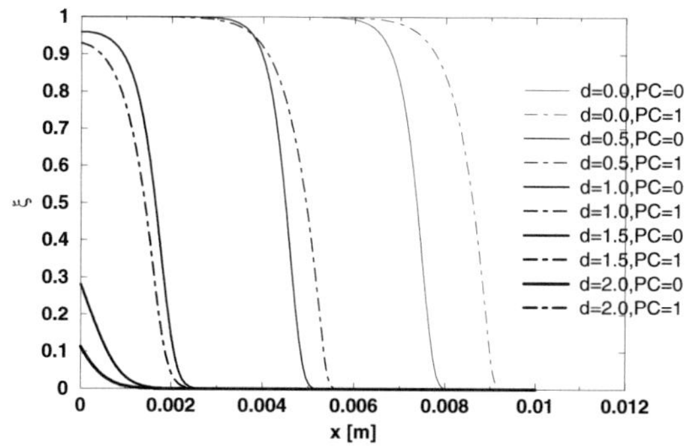

Figure 25. Spatial distribution of conversion rate field $\xi(x, t = 5\,s)$ for different values of exponent d, when phase change is taken into account (PC=1) or not (PC=0) with $T_{f_{r=0}} = 1600$ K and $T_{f_{r=R_e}} = 300$ K.

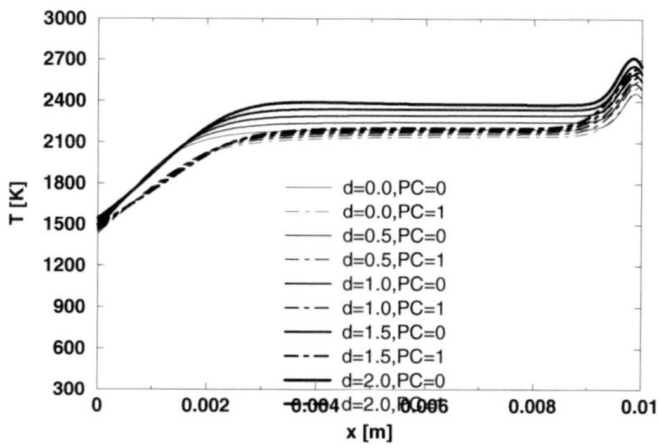

Figure 26. Spatial distribution of synthesis temperature $T_{syn}(x, t = 30\,s)$ for different values of exponent d, when phase change is taken into account (PC=1) or not (PC=0) with $T_{f_{r=0}} = 1600$ K and $T_{f_{r=R_e}} = 300$ K.

Fig.(27) shows that the time evolution of $x_{max}(t)$ has a similar shape for each value of d phase change is taken into account or not. Considering high values of d imply a significant delay for τ_{ind}. Moreover the spatial distribution of the heat released by the kinetics, as seen on Fig.(28) for $t = 5$s presents a maximum for $d = 0$, and a minimum for $d = 2$. This is correlated to the high values of induction time τ_{ind} when high values of d are used. Phase change contributes significantly to the time evolution of the front's position $x_{\xi=1/2}(t)$ as observed on Fig.(29). Without phase change, the evolution is nearly independent from the value of d since the slope of $x_{\xi=1/2}(t)$ is nearly the same. Time evolution of the front's maximum temperature $T_{max}(t)$ for different values of exponent d as seen on Fig.(30) is in fact nearly independent from d when a suitable time-translation is performed whenever phase change is taken into account or not.

4.2. 2D numerical study

This subsection computes the propagation of a dual radial/longitudinal front and a single longitudinal front for various values of the temperature furnace in which the cylindrical sample is placed. The main interest of this modelling with respect to the 1D case is to analyze the contribution of the lateral heat losses over the ignition and propagation of the

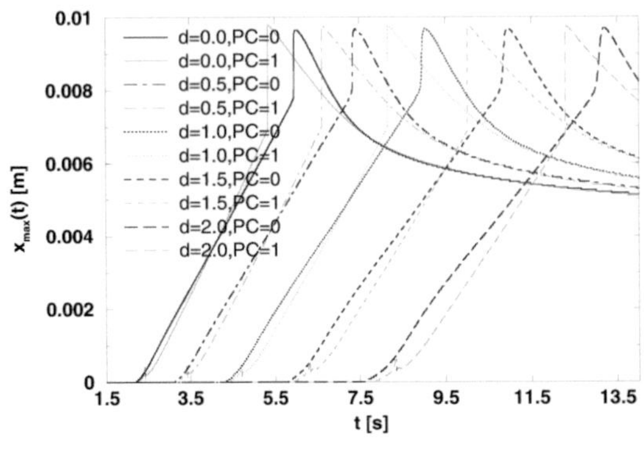

Figure 27. Time evolution of $x_{max}(t)$ for different values of exponent d when phase change is taken into account (PC=1) or not (PC=0) with $T_{f_{r=0}} = 1600$ K and $T_{f_{r=R_e}} = 300$ K.

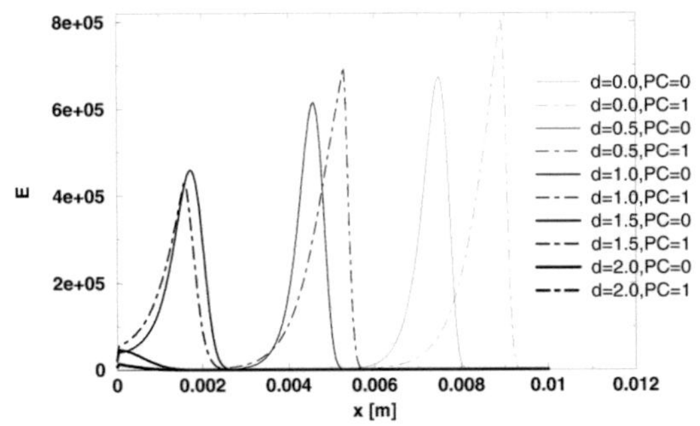

Figure 28. Spatial distribution of energy $E(x,t)$ released by the exothermic kinetics for different values of exponent d when phase change is taken into account (PC=1) or not (PC=0) with $T_{f_{r=0}} = 1600$ K and $T_{f_{r=R_e}} = 300$ K.

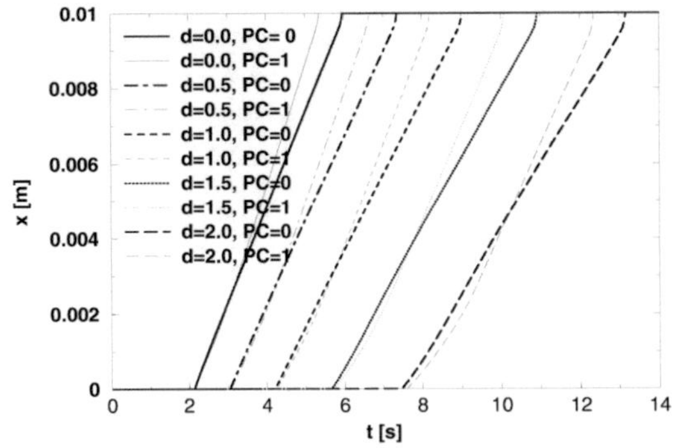

Figure 29. Time evolution of the front's position $x_{\xi=1/2}(t)$ for different values of exponent d when phase change is taken into account (PC=1) or not (PC=0) with $T_{f_{r=0}} = 1600$ K and $T_{f_{r=R_e}} = 300$ K.

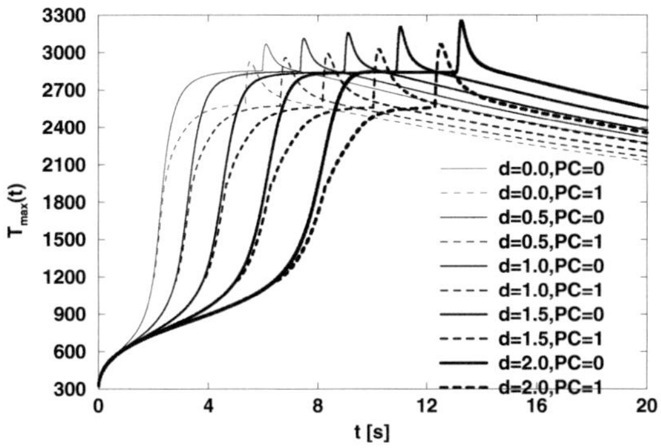

Figure 30. Time evolution of the front's maximum temperature $T_{max}(t)$ for different values of exponent d when phase change is taken into account (PC=1) or not (PC=0) with $T_{f_{r=0}} = 1600$ K and $T_{f_{r=R_e}} = 300$ K.

combustion front inside the cylindrical sample. The boundary conditions are defined over $\partial\Omega = \Gamma_{r=0} \cup \Gamma_{r=R_e} \cup \Gamma_{z=0} \cup \Gamma_{z=H_e}$ by

$$\begin{cases} \forall (r,z) \in \Gamma_{r=0} : \left(-\lambda \dfrac{\partial T(0,z,t)}{\partial n^e_{r=0}} \right) = 0, \\ \forall (r,z) \in \Gamma_{r=R_e} : \left(-\lambda \dfrac{\partial T(R_e,z,t)}{\partial n^e_{r=R_e}} \right) = \varepsilon.\sigma. \left(T(R_e,z,t)^4 - \left(T_{f_{z,r=R_e}}(t) \right)^4 \right), \\ \forall (r,z) \in \Gamma_{z=0} : \left(-\lambda \dfrac{\partial T(r,0,t)}{\partial n^e_{z=0}} \right) = \varepsilon.\sigma. \left(T(r,0,t)^4 - \left(T_{f_{r,z=0}}(t) \right)^4 \right), \\ \forall (r,z) \in \Gamma_{z=H_e} : \left(-\lambda \dfrac{\partial T(r,H_e,t)}{\partial n^e_{z=H_e}} \right) = \varepsilon.\sigma. \left(T(r,H_e,t)^4 - \left(T_{f_{r,z=H_e}}(t) \right)^4 \right). \end{cases} \tag{28}$$

The choice of the temperature triple $\left(T_{f_{z,r=R_e}}(t), T_{f_{r,z=0}}(t), T_{f_{r,z=H_e}}(t)\right)$ characterizes the way the heat supplied on the exterior surface of the cylinder (radius R_e = 2cm, height H_e = 2cm) will induce the propagation of the combustion front inside the cylinder, initially at room temperature $T = T_a = 300\,K$. Each computation will analyze the phenomena during $t = 10\,s$. The computational grid is uniform along z-axis and iso-volume along r-axis.

4.2.1. *Reaction-diffusion vs thermal diffusion*

We choose $\left(T_{f_{z,r=R_e}}(t), T_{f_{r,z=0}}(t), T_{f_{r,z=H_e}}(t)\right) = (300\,K, 1600\,K, 300\,K)$ for both simulations. The thermal diffusion case means that the kinetics is not active, i.e. $k_d = 0$, so the initial mixture of reactive powders is not transformed. At each point (r,z) of the sample and at each instant $t > 0$, we observe on Fig.(31) that $T_a \leq T(r,z,t) \leq T_f$, when the exothermic kinetics is not taken into account, moreover the numerical solution fulfills a discrete maximum principle. A similar principle is observed when the kinetics is taken into account, but the time evolution is significantly different because of the sharp rise in temperature when the synthesis starts.

Moreover $T(R_e,0,t) < T(0,0,t)$ because of the radiative heat losses at $r = R_e$.

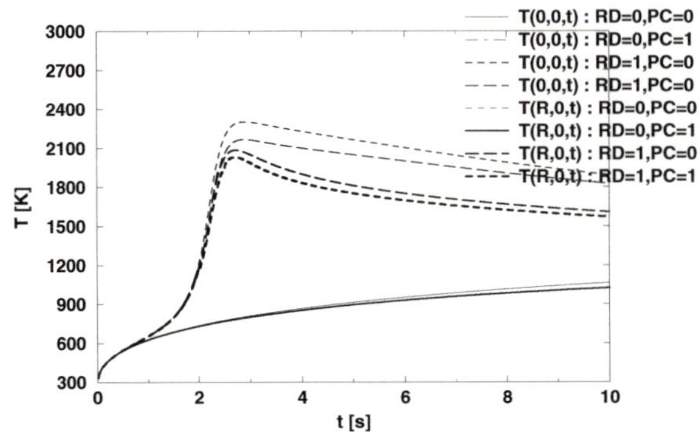

Figure 31. Time evolution of $T(0,0,t)$ et $T(R_e,0,t)$.

4.2.2. Single, dual longitudinal, dual longitudinal/single radial front

These three cases were considered and analyzed in detail in [2].

4.2.3. Dual radial-longitudinal front

We consider the case where $\left(T_{f_{z,r=R_e}}(t),\ T_{f_{r,z=0}}(t),\ T_{f_{r,z=H_e}}(t)\right) = (2400\,K, 2400\,K, 300\,K)$. At the same time a longitudinal front is moving from bottom to top, while a radial front moves from the exterior surface of the cylinder to the center, as seen on the temperature distribution at time $t = 3$s represented by Fig.(32). The conversion rate $\xi(r,z,3)$ has a similar shape. The energy released by the exothermic process is nearly uniformly distributed on Ω as seen on Fig.(33). A similar conclusion can be drawn upon the shape of the synthesis temperature $T_{syn}(r,z,5)$ represented on Fig.(34), except along the line where the two fronts are joining themselves.

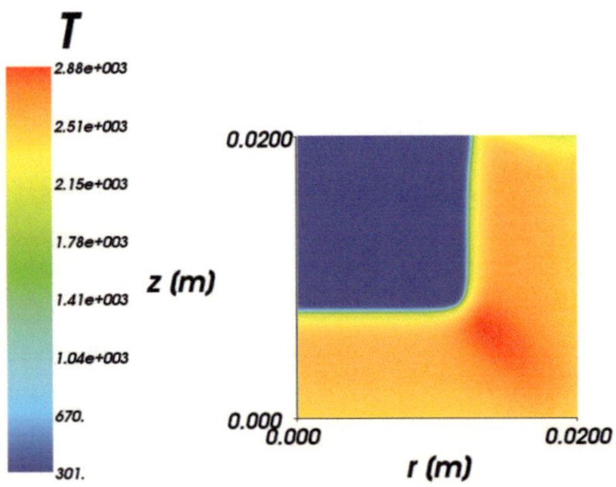

Figure 32. Temperature distribution $T(r,z,3)$ for $(r,z) \in \Omega$.

According to [2], in order to analyze the kind of propagation, we assume given a temperature $\Theta \in [300, 3000]$ and a simulation time $t_f > 0$. We define for each point $x \in \Omega$, the thermal history time $t_\Theta(x)$ which corresponds to the total time for which a given point $x \in \Omega$ remains

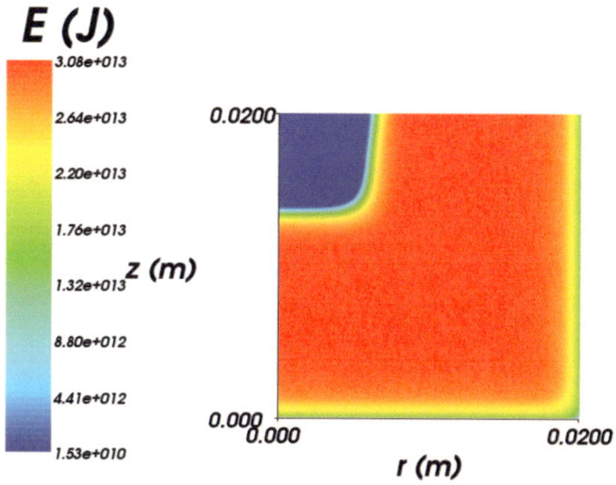

Figure 33. Integral of the energy released by the kinetics during the process at each $(r,z) \in \Omega$.

at a temperature greater or equal to Θ and gives an indication of the thermal history of the material as a function of the coupling between the exothermic reaction and the thermal diffusion. More precisely, $t_\Theta(x)$ determines if the energy involved in the reaction-diffusion process is uniformly distributed or not in Ω and what is the average temperature of the process. Fig.(35) represents such time distribution at $t = 5$s for $\Theta = 1800$K. Fig.(36) represents such time distribution at $t = 5$s for $\Theta = 2400$K. As in the previous figures, it is influenced by the propagation of the combustion wave. It is worth mentioning that on these two figures the time distribution is nearly equal, from up to 4.16s (resp. 4.70) for 1800K (resp. 2400K), and that they can be superposed.

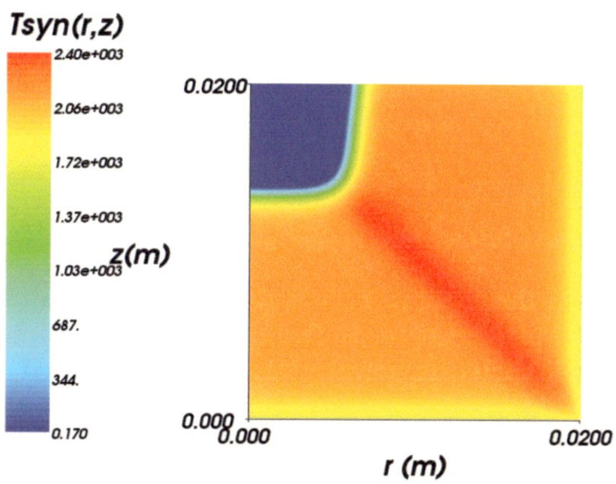

Figure 34. Synthesis temperature distribution $T_{syn}(r,z,5)$ for $(r,z) \in \Omega$.

4.3. 3D numerical study

This subsection accounts for the heterogeneity of the radiative boundary conditions to analyze the ignition and propagation of the combustion front in a cubic sample. We assume that

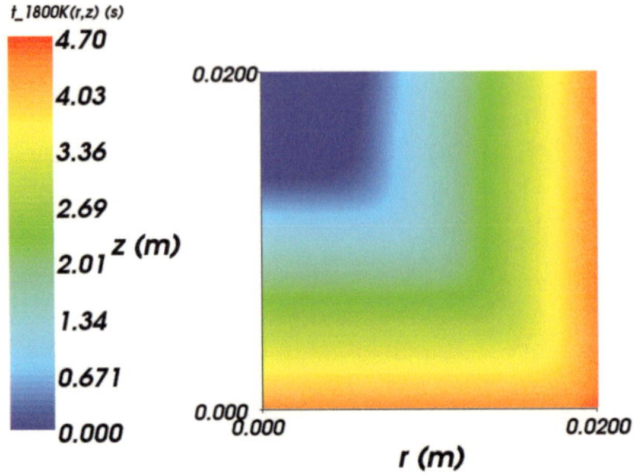

Figure 35. Time distribution of the thermal history time $T_{1800K}(r,z,5)$ for $(r,z) \in \Omega$.

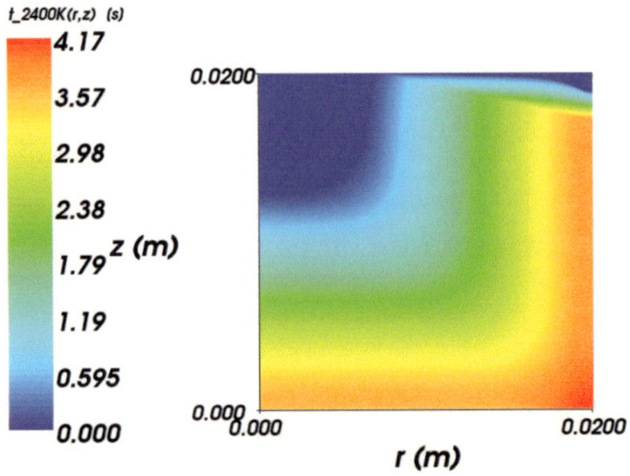

Figure 36. Time distribution of the thermal history time $T_{2400K}(r,z,5)$ for $(r,z) \in \Omega$.

the heat supplied to the six faces of the cubic sample is different, in the sense that the wall temperature that contributes to the preheating of each face of the cubic sample is different. This will induce a specific transient spatial pattern of the combustion front. A meaningful snapshot of the transient temperature profile is depicted in Fig.(37). It is clearly observed that the shape of the front's propagation inside the cube is influenced by the boundary conditions. If a regular propagation is required, providing heat supply over one single face of the cube is enough to obtain quickly titanium-carbide. So combining a different heat supply system for each face of the cube appears complicated from an experimental point of view. Numerical simulation show that the pattern of the propagation in this case is more complicated than in the single heat supply case and requires more computational power to get finely resolved. An analysis, not presented here due space constraints, and using the same methodology as in the previous 2D case show that the same conclusions can be drawn for $T_{2400K}(x,y,z,.)$, $T_{syn}(x,y,z,.)$.

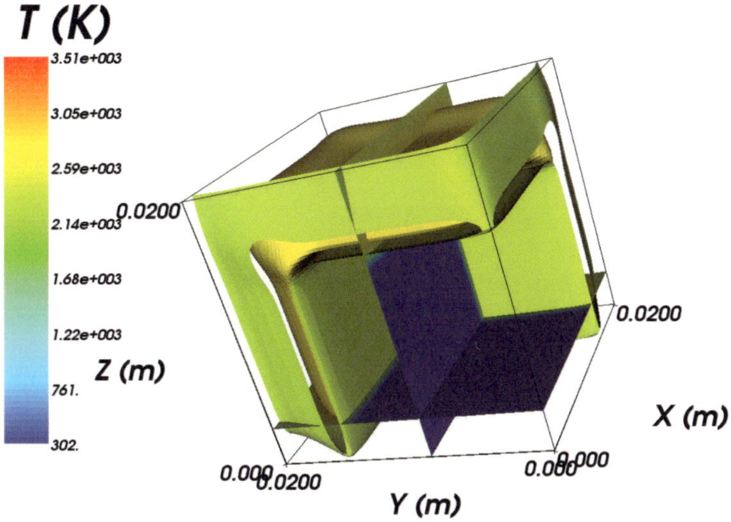

Figure 37. Temperature distribution $T(x,y,z,3)$ for $(x,y,z) \in \Omega$.

5. Conclusions and perspectives

In this book chapter, we have presented a multidimensional modelling for the numerical computation of ignition and propagation of combustion fronts during combustion synthesis of ceramic materials such as titanium-carbide. A detailed computational study was done in 1D slab/cylindrical/spherical geometry, 2D cylindrical/cartesian and 3D cartesian geometry to analyze the influence of the radiative boundary conditions over the induction time. The radiation contribution to the thermal conductivity was taken into account and the sensitivity of the induction time to several parameters such as the kinetics, wall temperature, phase change was carefully analyzed. Our numerical software Hephaïstos was presented. It implements an implicit finite-volume scheme for which error estimates, discrete maximum principles were reported and used to ensure the consistency of the numerical results. This modelling study was done for titanium carbide TiC. It can be applied to other ceramic materials such as silicium carbide-SiC-. Moreover in order to analyze the combustion front propagation for high Zeldovich number cases, an adaptive finite-volume scheme is required. A new monotonicity preserving refinement/derefinement conservative algorithm has been designed for multidimensional computations in various coordinate systems. This algorithm maintains the structured topology of the mesh. It is currently under implementation.

Author details

A. Aoufi
SMS/RMT, LCG, UMR CNRS 5146, Ecole des Mines de Saint-Etienne, 158 cours Fauriel, 42023 Saint-Etienne Cedex, France

G. Damamme
CEA, Centre DAM-Île de France, Bruyères le Châtel, 91297 Arpajon cedex, France

6. References

[1] A. Aoufi, "A finite volume scheme for a nonlinear reaction-Diffusion PDE arising in combustion", in: C. Constanda, M. Ahues, A. Largillier (Eds.), Integral Methods in Science and Engineering, Birkhauser, Basel, 2004, pp. 1-6.

[2] A.Aoufi, G.Dammame, "An implicit finite-volume discretization for the multidimensional numerical simulation of TiC combustion synthesis", Applied Mathematics and Computation, 176, 99-116 (2006).

[3] A.Aoufi, G.Dammame, "Two-Fluxes and Reaction-Diffusion Computation of Initial and Transient Secondary Electron Emission Yield by a Finite Volume Method", 89-108, in Numerical Simulations -Applications, Examples and Theory, Edited by Prof. Lutz Angermann, January 2011, InTech.

[4] A.Aoufi, "Numerical computation of multidimensional TiC combustion synthesis problems using openmp and cuda", To be submitted in (2012).

[5] Lakshmikantha M., Bhattacharya A., Sekhar J. A., "Numerical Modeling of Solidification Combustion Synthesis", Metallurgical Transactions A, 23A, 23-34, (1992).

[6] H.P.Li, J.A. Serkhar, "Dimensional Changes during micropyrectic synthesis", Material Science and Engineering, Vol A 1690 (1993), pp. 221-227.

[7] A.G. Merzhanov, The theory of stable homogeneous combustion of condensed systems, Combustion and Flame 13 (1969) 143-156.

[8] A.G. Merzhanov, Solid flames: discoveries, concept, and horizons of cognition, Combustion Science and Technology 98 (1994) 307-336.

[9] S.V. Patankar, "Numerical Heat Transfer and Fluid Flow", McGRAW-HILL BOOK COMPANY, 1980.

[10] Wei Shyy, H.S. Udaykumar, MadhuKar, M. Rao, Richar W. Smith, "Computational Fluid Dynamics with Moving Boundaries", Taylor and Francis, (1996).

[11] D.R. Stull, H. Prophet et al., "Janaf Thermochemical Tables Second Edition", NSRDS-NBS 37, Editor, US Department of Commerce, National Bureau of Standards, (1971).

[12] C.L. Tien, "Thermal Radiation in Packed Beds and Fluidized Beds", Transactions of the ASME, Vol. 110, November 1988, pp. 1230-1242.

[13] Y.S. Touloukian, D.P. Dewitt, "Thermal Radiative Properties, Nonmetallic Solids", The TPRC Data Series, Vol. 8, IFI Plenum, New-York, 1972.

[14] E. Tsotsas, H. Martin, "Thermal Conductivity of Packed Beds: A Review", Chem. Eng. Process. 22 (1987), pp. 19-37.

[15] Viljoen H.J. and Hlavacek V., "Effect of Radiation on the Combustion Rate in a Condensed Phase", AIChE J., 37, 10, 1595-1597, (1991).

[16] Transactions of mathematical monographs Volume 140 Travelling wave solutions of parabolic systems American Mathematical Society Providence Rhode Island Aizik I. Volpert, Vitaly A. Volpert, Vladimir A. Volpert 2000.

[17] D. Vrel, J.-M. Lihrmann and P. Tobaly, "Contribution of Solid-State Diffusion to the Formation of Titanium Carbide by Combustion Synthesis, Journal of Materials Synthesis and Processing, Vol. 2, No. 3, 1994, pp 179-187.

[18] N. Wakao, K. Kato, "Effective Thermal Conductivity of Packed Beds", Journal of Chemical Engineering of Japan, Vol. 2, No 1, 1969, pp. 24-32.

Chapter 22

Numerical Simulation of Combustion in Porous Media

Masoud Ziabasharhagh and Arash Mohammadi

Additional information is available at the end of the chapter

http://dx.doi.org/10.5772/50386

1. Introduction

The demand of fossil fuel resources and air pollution are the major problems that caused by using of fuels. In recent years, many researchers have developed new methods for efficient combustion of fuels. Porous media combustion, also known as filtration combustion in a packed bed, due to the interaction between two different phases, solid and gas or liquid. The theory of filtration combustion involves a new type of flame with exothermic chemical reactions during fluid flow in a porous medium. The term 'filtration combustion' was introduced by Russian scientists for combustion of gas flow through porous media. This term does not correspond to western scientific terminology, still it can be found in special literature as a synonym to combustion within porous media (PM). This process facilitates a combustion process with stability in a wide range of reactant fluid velocities, air-fuel ratios, and power density. PM combustion has some unique characteristics. It gives rise to high radiant output, low NO_x (Oxides of Nitrogen) and CO (Carbon Monoxide) emissions, high flame speed and higher power density. A porous material means a material with connected voids that flow can easily penetrate through its structure. This technology is different from conventional combustion, with free flame, thin reaction zone and high temperature gradients. Compared to conventional combustion devices, the combustion efficiency of PM burner is reasonably high and better heat transfer from burned gases to unburned mixture, takes place. On the other hand, in PM combustion three modes of heat transfer conduction, convection, and radiation are significant. In addition, there is a better homogenization of temperature across the PM and the significant amount of radiation helps to preheat the incoming air-fuel mixture at upstream. The technique of premixed combustion within PM has been studied and applied to steady combustion with great success. The porous media combustion has proved to be one of the applicable options to solve the problems to a remarkable extent in both technical and economic perspectives. This technique has been used for both gaseous and liquid fuels in steady or unsteady combustion. Flame stability in

PM with lean and rich mixtures, significant reduction in pollutants and increasing combustion efficiency, was proven.

In recent years many researchers investigated the PM combustion technology both experimentally and theoretically. The most of researches are in field of steady combustion in PM and few of them are about transient flame propagation, both approaches are employed in PM combustion. Steady combustion is widely used in radiant burners and surface combustor-heaters due to its high radiant emissivity of the solid. The combustion zone is stabilized by its solid. The other, transient leads to an unsteady reaction zone freely propagate as a filtration combustion wave in the downstream direction. Combustion in PM differs considerably from the homogeneous flames flame front. Considerable features of PM for application of combustion technology are: large specific surface area, excellent heat transfer properties, heat capacity, transparency for fluid flow, thermal resistance, mechanical resistance, recuperation of energy and electrical properties.

2. Background of combustion in porous media

2.1. Stability of flame

The flame stabilization and propagation in a PM are governed by the modified Peclet number:

$$Pe = \frac{(S_L \ d_m \ C_p \ \rho)}{k}, \tag{1}$$

where S_L is the laminar flame speed, d_m is the equivalent diameter of the average hollow space of the porous material, C_p is the specific heat of the gas mixture, ρ is the density of the gas mixture and k is the thermal conductivity of the gas mixture. For flame propagation through a porous material, the critical Peclet number of 65 has been found. Thus, $Pe < 65$ for quenching, and $Pe > 65$ for flame propagation.

2.2. Premixed and non-premixed mixture

PM may work with a premixed flow or with a non-premixed fuel flow. Premixed porous burners consist of two zones: the premixed fuel–air mixture first enters a hot solid matrix, where it is heated until it enters to the second hot solid matrix. Depending on its application, a third section, a compact heat exchanger may be added to the burner. The schematic of a two-layer premixed combustor is shown in Fig. 1.

A premixed mixture of methane-air and hydrogen-air were used in different burners with two section PM. Measurements show considerable reduction in the concentrations of NO_x, CO in the fluid gases. Also the effects of hydrogen addition to methane, were investigated. For the porous burners hydrogen was found to lower the NO_x emissions slightly, while for the other burners an increase, or no obvious effect, was found. The enhancement of the radiation flux from PM burners operating with non-premixed flames by using a vane-rotary burner, in which the swirling fuel flow was confined by an air duct, is necessary. They also studied emission characteristics of ceramic foam burners operating with non-premixed flame.

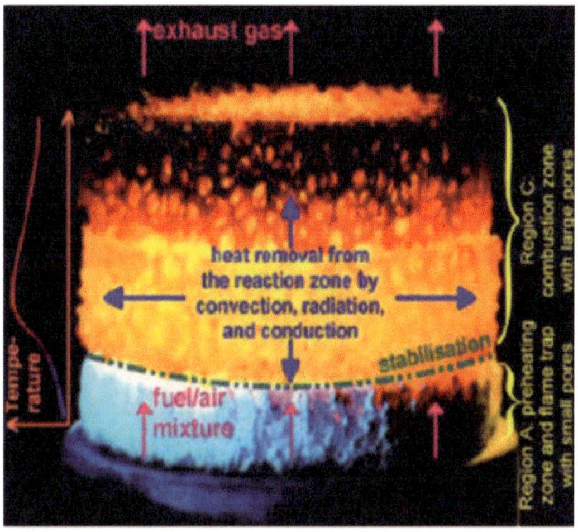

Figure 1. Schematic of a premixed combustor (M. A. Mujeebu et al. , 2009)

2.3. Reciprocating flow

For the excess enthalpy combustion, a combustion system using reciprocating flow in PM was introduced. By the reciprocating flow, the combustion gas enthalpy is regenerated into increase in enthalpy of the combustible gas through the PM, which store heat. For this technique a new arrangement of the PM that stabilized flame for a wide operating condition, was used. The mixture first flow in, and the gas and solid temperatures reaches to a maximum at the exit side. Then the flow direction is reversed by means of valves. On the reverse flow half-cycle, the fresh mixture encounters much higher solid temperatures at the entering side. Therefore, the amount of heat recycled becomes larger than that with the single flow direction. Hence in the reciprocating flow system, the heat transfer from the combustion gases raises the solid temperatures from both directions.

2.4. Hydrogen production

Production of hydrogen from gases such as methane and hydrogen-sulphide is another potential application of PM combustion. These reactants convert into products such as hydrogen, syngas (H_2 and CO), and sulfur. For both methane and hydrogen-sulphide combustion, upstream propagation corresponded to the range of equivalence ratios from stoichiometry to 1.7, and downstream wave propagation was observed for ultra-rich (1.7- 4) mixtures.

2.5. Materials for porous media combustion

Aluminum oxide (Al_2O_3), silicon carbide (SiC), and zirconium dioxide (ZrO_2) proposed as suitable materials for application. Al_2O_3 and ZrO_2 were recognized as high temperature resistant materials. SiC shows good thermal shock resistance, mechanical strength, and conductive heat transport. SiC also has high melting point (3260 K), against cyclic thermal stress and strength retention at the peak regenerator temperature (1673 K), and excellent oxidation resistance. Metallic materials were found less suitable for PM because of their inadequate thermal stability and high thermal inertia. Fe–Cr–Al-alloys and nickel-base alloys were found suitable for some applications but they were said to be comparatively less heat resistant. Structures of ceramic foams with different base materials were observed to possess high porosity, good conduction heat transport, low thermal inertia, low radiation heat transport properties and relatively high pressure drop. The effective thermal conductivity of anisotropic porous composite medium could vary largely with the component fractions.

3. Numerical modeling

The thermophysical properties of the air such as density, thermal conductivity and specific heat are assumed to be functions of the temperature. Usually, the pressure drop through the porous burner is not that high (with high porosity of PM) and its effect on the thermophysical properties can be neglected. In general, the properties of the solid phase may be assumed to be constant and assumed that there is thermal non-equilibrium between the gas and solid phases. Therefore, there are two energy equations to model the energy transport in the system. The porous material can be assumed as a scattering, emitting and absorbing medium. Gaseous radiation is assumed to be negligible compared to the solid radiation.

3.1. One-dimensional modeling

Many researchers studied the combustion and heat transfer in porous radiant burners. The PM was assumed to emit, absorb, and scatter radiant energy. Non-local thermal equilibrium between the solid and the gas is assumed for and combustion was described by a one-step, multi-steps or kinetic reactions. The effect of the optical depth, scattering albedo, solid thermal conductivity, upstream environment reflectivity, and interphase heat transfer coupling on the burner performance can be considered. Also, low solid thermal conductivity, low scattering albedo, and high inlet environment reflectivity produced a high radiant efficiency. The system consisted of a packed bed or foams in which a natural gas–air mixture combusts inside it. Radiative heat transfer in the packed bed or foams was modeled as a diffusion process, and the flow and temperature distribution in the packed bed or foams can be determined. The numerically results usually were compared with available experimental data for a similar system. Subsequently, the one-dimensional predictions of methane/air combustion in inert PM can include full mechanism (49 species and 227 elemental reactions), skeletal mechanism (26 species and 77 elemental reactions), 4-step reduced mechanism (9 species and 1-step global mechanism). The effects of these models on temperature, species, burning speeds and pollutant emissions were examined by researchers. Experimental and numerical investigations found that the flammability limits of the gaseous mixture in PM were more sensitive to their geometric properties than the physical properties.

3.1.1. One-dimensional governing equations

The following assumptions are made to simplify the problem:

1. Gas radiation is neglected, gas flow and heat transfer are one-dimensional.
2. PM is considered to be non-catalytic, homogeneous and optically thick.
3. The radiation of solid phase is treated using Rosseland approximation.
4. The PM consists of solid dispersed homogeneously, and the porosity variation near the tube wall is neglected. Under the above assumptions, a set of differential equations can be obtained in the following form.

Continuity equation:

$$\frac{\partial}{\partial t}\left(\rho_g \varepsilon\right)+\frac{\partial}{\partial x}\left(\rho_g u \varepsilon\right)=0. \tag{2}$$

Gas phase energy equation:

$$\rho_g c_g \varepsilon \frac{\partial T_g}{\partial t}+\rho_g c_g \varepsilon u \frac{\partial T_g}{\partial x}+\sum_i \rho_g \varepsilon Y_i V_i c_{gi} \frac{\partial T_g}{\partial x}+\varepsilon \sum_i \dot{\omega}_i h_i W_i=\varepsilon \frac{\partial}{\partial x}\left((k_g+\rho_g c_g D_{||}{}^D) \frac{\partial T_g}{\partial x}\right)-h_v(T_g-T_s). \tag{3}$$

Solid phase energy equation:

$$\rho_S c_S(1-\varepsilon) \frac{\partial T_s}{\partial t}=k_s(1-\varepsilon) \frac{\partial^2 T_s}{\partial x^2}+h_v(T_g-T_s)-\frac{d q_r}{d x}=0. \tag{4}$$

Species transport equation:

$$\rho_g \varepsilon \frac{\partial Y_i}{\partial t}+\rho_g \varepsilon u \frac{\partial Y_i}{\partial x}+\frac{\partial}{\partial x}\left(\rho_g \varepsilon Y_i V_i\right)-\varepsilon \dot{\omega}_i W_i=0. \tag{5}$$

$$V_i=-\left(D+D_{im}^d\right) \frac{1}{X_i} \frac{\partial X_i}{\partial x}. \tag{6}$$

density:

$$\rho=\text{constant density}. \tag{7}$$

Radiation:

$$q_r(x)=-\frac{16}{3} \frac{\sigma T_s{}^3}{\beta} \frac{d T_s}{d x}. \tag{8}$$

3.1.2 Boundary conditions for one-dimensional model

The following boundary conditions are considered in the computations:

Inlet	$T_g = T_{f,inlet}$	$\frac{\partial T_s}{\partial x} = 0$	$\frac{\partial T_s}{\partial x} = 0$
Outlet	$\frac{\partial T_g}{\partial x} = 0$	$\frac{\partial T_s}{\partial x} = 0$	$\frac{\partial Y_i}{\partial x} = 0$

3.1.3. Solution procedure

The time integration is performed using combination of implicit finite difference and finite volume method on a uniform- adaptive or non uniform mesh. The convective terms are upwinded and the diffusive terms are discretized using a second-order technique. The initial condition was also given to the system of discretized equations. For more information interested reader can see (Henneke et al , 1999)

3.2. Two-dimensional modeling

In the two dimensional model a comparison is made between the local thermal equilibrium and thermal non-equilibrium approaches by different researchers. The volume-averaged treatments unable to predict the pore-level, local high temperature region in the gas phase and the pore-level variation in the flame speed with respect to the flame location in the pore. The gas and the solid phases consider in non-local thermal equilibrium, and separate energy equations use for the two phases. The solid phase can be assumed absorbing, emitting and scattering, while the gas phase was considered transparent to radiation. The alternating direction implicit (ADI) scheme can be used to solve the transient two dimensional energy equations. Methane–air combustion with one-step, multi step and detailed chemical kinetics are used to model the combustion, like one dimensional combustion modeling. The radiative part of the energy equation can be modeled using simple Rosseland method until complex discrete ordinate method. In the flat plate burner, air flows axially through a constant area duct filled with a porous layer of thickness *L*. In the cylindrical and spherical burners, the air flows radially through an annular porous matrix.

3.2.1. Two dimensional governing equations

The energy equation for the gas phase is as follows:

$$\frac{\partial}{\partial t}(\varphi\rho_g C_{pg} T_g) + \frac{1}{r^n}\frac{\partial}{\partial r}(\varphi\rho_g C_{pg} r^n v T_g) = \frac{1}{r^n}\frac{\partial}{\partial r}\left(\varphi k_g r^n \frac{\partial T_g}{\partial r}\right) - (1-\varphi)h_v(T_g - T_s) + \varphi\Delta H_c S_{fg} \quad (9)$$

Where φ, ρ_g, r, C_{pg}, T_g, v, k_g, h_v, H_c and S_{fg} are the porosity, density, radial position, specific heat, temperature, velocity, thermal conductivity, volumetric heat transfer coefficient, enthalpy of combustion and rate of fuel consumption per unit volume, respectively. Subscripts g and s refer to gaseous and solid phases, respectively.

The energy equation for the solid phase is:

$$\frac{\partial}{\partial t}(\rho_s C_s T_s) + \frac{1}{r^n}\frac{\partial}{\partial r}\left(r^n k_s \frac{\partial T_s}{\partial r}\right) - h_v(T_s - T_g) - \nabla.F. \quad (10)$$

The term F represents the radiative transport equation and is given by:

$$\nabla . F = -(1-\omega)(G-4E_b), \tag{11}$$

where ω is the single scattering albedo and the irradiance G is governed by

$$\nabla^2 G = \eta^2 (G-4E_b),$$

$$\eta^2 = 3\beta^2(1-\omega)(1-g\omega), \tag{12}$$

where E_b is the Planck black body emitted flux and G is the radiative flux.

The conservation equation for the mass fraction of the fuel is given as follows:

$$\frac{\partial}{\partial t}(\rho_g m_f) + \frac{1}{r^n}\frac{\partial}{\partial r}(\rho_g r^n v m_f) = \frac{1}{r^n}\frac{\partial}{\partial r}\left(r^n D_{AB}\rho_g \frac{\partial m_f}{\partial r}\right) - S_{fg}\, , \tag{13}$$

where m_f is the fuel mass fraction and D_{AB} is the diffusion coefficient. The n value is set to 0, 1 and 2 for spherical, radial and axial flow burners, respectively.

A single-step Arrhenius type chemical kinetic equation as given below is normally adopted in modeling the combustion:

$$S_{fg} = f\rho_g^2 m_f m_{o_2} \exp\left(-\frac{E}{RT_g}\right), \tag{14}$$

where f, m_{O2} , E and R refer to pre-exponential factor, oxygen mass fraction, activation energy and gas constant, respectively.

3.2.2. *Boundary conditions for two-dimensional model*

The following boundary conditions are adopted for the gas, solid and species:

Gas:

$$T_{g|r=r_{in}} = 0 \quad \text{at} \quad r = r_{in}\,.$$

$$\left.\frac{\partial T_g}{\partial r}\right|_{r=r_{out}} = T_{in} \quad \text{at} \quad r = r_{out}. \tag{15}$$

Solid:

$$h_{in}\left[(T_{g,in} - T_{s|r=r_{in}})\right] + \sigma\epsilon_{in}\left[(T^4_{in,amb} - T_s^4|_{s|r=r_{in}})\right] = -k_s \left.\frac{\partial T_s}{\partial r}\right|_{r=r_{in}} \quad \text{at} \quad r = r_{in}.$$

$$h_{out}\left[(T_{out,in} - T_{s|r=r_{out}})\right] + \sigma\epsilon_{out}\left[(T^4_{out,amb} - T_s^4|_{s|r=out})\right] = -k_s \left.\frac{\partial T_s}{\partial r}\right|_{r=r_{out}} \quad \text{at} \quad r = r_{out}. \tag{16}$$

Species:

$$m_f = m_{f,in} \quad \text{at} \quad r = r_{in}.$$

$$\frac{\partial m_f}{\partial r} = 0 \quad \text{at} \quad r = r_{out}. \tag{17}$$

The control volume approach, or the finite-difference method, can be used to solve the governing equations. The solution is advanced in time by using a fully implicit technique and this was necessary due to the stiffness of the governing matrix of the problem. Also, it is necessary to use an adaptive grid, or a very fine grid, to insure the accuracy of the solution.

3.2.3. Solution procedure

The based code can be solved using alternative direction implicit (ADI) finite volume formulation. The pressure field is solved using the SIMPLE method in steady state and PISO in transient state. The gridding system should prove to be sufficient by testing several grids sizes. For more information interested reader can see (Mohammadi, 2010, Hackert et al, 1998).

4. Three-dimensional modeling

Although there exist many simulation of one-dimensional and two dimensional model in literature but only several papers discussed three-dimensional simulation in PM. Three-dimensional simulations of combustion inside the PM burner, are complex and time consuming. A finite-volume calculation for three-dimensional reacting flow in a porous burner can be used. The Navier–Stokes equations, energy for both phase of PM and species transport equations were solved, and radiative heat transfer under local thermal non equilibrium between the solid and gas phases was considered.

4.1. Three-dimensional governing equations

Following assumptions were used in modeling and simulation of the PM in modified KIVA-3V code:

1. There is thermal non-equilibrium between gas and solid phases.
2. Solid is homogeneous, isotropic, variable property with temperature and has no catalyst effects.
3. Only radiation heat transfer from the solid phase is considered and the gas phase is transparent.

Based on the above assumptions, the general governing equations are simplified as follows: Continuity equation for species *i:*

$$\frac{\partial(\varphi\rho_i)}{\partial t} + \nabla.(\varphi\rho_i\, u) = \nabla.\left[\rho\,\varphi\, D_{im}\nabla\left(\frac{\rho_i}{\rho}\right)\right] + \varphi\,\dot{\rho}_i^c + \dot{\rho}^s\,\delta_i\,, \tag{18}$$

where diffusion coefficient modified according to kinetic theory of gases. ρ is mixture density, ϕ is porosity (void fraction) of PM, ρ_i is density of species *i*, D_{im} is diffusion coefficient of species *i* in the mixture and *u* is the velocity vector.

Gas phase momentum equation:

$$\frac{\partial(\rho\, u)}{\partial t} + \nabla.(\rho\, u\, u) = -\frac{1}{a^2}\nabla P - \nabla\left(\frac{2}{3}\,\rho\, k\right) + \nabla.\sigma + F^s - \left(\frac{\Delta P}{\Delta L}\right). \tag{19}$$

The last term on the right-hand side of Eq. (19) is due to pressure drop caused by PM according to Ergan equation and σ is stress tensor. The dimensionless quantity a is used in conjunction with the Pressure Gradient Scaling (PGS) method. This is a method for enhancing computational efficiency in low Mach number flows, where the pressure is nearly uniform.

$$\left(\frac{\Delta P}{\Delta L}\right) = \left(\frac{\mu}{\alpha}\, u + c_2\, \frac{1}{2}\, \rho\, |u|\, u\right). \tag{20}$$

where α is the permeability and c_2 is the inertial resistance factor of PM, which are determined according to Eq. 21.

$$\alpha = \frac{d^2}{150}\frac{\epsilon^3}{(1-\epsilon)^2}\ ,\quad C_2 = \frac{3.5}{d}\frac{(1-\epsilon)}{\epsilon^3}. \tag{21}$$

Gas phase energy equation:

$$\frac{\partial}{\partial t}\left(\varphi\rho c_p T_g\right) + \nabla.\left(\varphi\rho c_p T_g u\right) + \varphi\sum_i \dot{\omega}_i\, H_i W_i = -\varphi P\,\nabla.u + \varphi A_0\rho\epsilon + (1-A_0)\sigma{:}\nabla u$$

$$\varphi\,\nabla.\left((k_g + \rho_g c_g D_{\parallel}^{d})\nabla T_g\right) - h_v\left(T_g - T_s\right) + \dot{Q}^s\,. \tag{22}$$

where the fourth term on the right hand side is the conduction heat transfer due to thermal conductivity of fluid and dispersion term due to existence of PM and the fifth term represent the convective heat transfer between gas and solid phase of PM which are determined according to Eqs. (23 – 25):

$$D_{\parallel}^{d} = 0.5\,\alpha_g Pe \tag{23}$$

$$Nu_v = 2 + 1.1\, Re^{0.6}\, Pr^{0.33}, \tag{24}$$

$$h_v = \frac{6\varphi}{d^2}\, k_g Nu_v \tag{25}$$

c_p is specific heat of the mixture, T_g is gas temperature, Y_i is mass fraction species i, is rate of reaction i, H_i is enthalpy of species i, W_i is molecular weight of species i, k_g is thermal conductivity of the fluid, is thermal dispersion coefficient along the length of the porous medium, h_v is volumetric heat transfer coefficient between solid and gas phase of PM. Correlation (23 - 25) was estimated from experimental data by Wakao and Kaguei for heat transfer between packed beds and fluid.

Solid phase energy equation:

$$\frac{\partial}{\partial t}\left((1-\varphi)\,\rho_s\, c_s\, T_s\right) = \nabla\cdot\left[k_s\,(1-\varphi)\nabla T_s\right] + h_v\left(T_g - T_s\right) - \nabla.q_r. \tag{26}$$

T_s is solid temperature, ρ_s is solid density, c_s is specific heat of solid phase, k_s is thermal conductivity of solid phase, q_r is the radiation heat transfer in solid in r direction.

Chemical species continuity equation:

$$\frac{\partial}{\partial t}(\varphi\rho Y_i) + \nabla.(\varphi\rho Y_i\, u) + \nabla.(\varphi\rho Y_i\, v_i) - \varphi\,\dot{\omega}_i\, W_i = 0, \tag{27}$$

$$v_i = -\left(D + D_{m\|}^{d}\right)\frac{1}{X_i}\,\nabla X_i, \tag{28}$$

$$Pe = \frac{\rho\, c_{p\,|u|\,d}}{k_g}, \tag{29}$$

$$D_{m\|}^{d} = 0.5\, D_{im} Pe, \tag{30}$$

X_i is molar fraction of species *i*, *Pe* is Peclet number, *d* is diameter of sphere in packed bed, is species dispersion coefficient, Y_i is mass fraction of species *i* and v_i is diffusion velocity of species *i* in the mixture.

Turbulence model

Since there is no model presented for simulation of turbulent compressible-flow in PM by any researcher. Hence the basic κ- ε equations were used without any modification.

The transport equation for κ turbulent kinetic energy:

$$\frac{\partial(\rho k)}{\partial t} + \nabla.(\rho u\, k) = -\frac{2}{3}\,\rho\,\kappa\,\nabla.u + \sigma : \nabla u + \nabla.\left[\left(\frac{\mu}{Pr_k}\right)\nabla k\right] - \rho\varepsilon + \dot{W}^{s}, \tag{31}$$

where σ is stress tensor. With a similar consideration dissipation rate, ε:

$$\frac{\partial(\rho\varepsilon)}{\partial t} + \nabla.(\rho u\varepsilon) - \left(\frac{2}{3}C\in_1 - C\in_3\right)\rho\varepsilon\nabla.u + \nabla.\left[\left(\frac{\mu}{\mathrm{Pr}_\varepsilon}\right)\nabla\in\right] + \frac{\in}{k}\left[C\in_1\sigma:\nabla u - C\in_2\rho\varepsilon + c_s\dot{W}^{s}\right], \tag{32}$$

The parameters, ,, and are constant whose values are determined from experiments and some theoretical considerations and is viscous stress tensor.

Equation of state:

$$P = \rho R\, T_g \,/\, \bar{W}, \tag{33}$$

R is universal gas constant, average molecular weight of mixture, *P* is pressure inside the combustion chamber and the PM.

Radiation model

Due to extreme temperature of combustion zone and solid phase, radiation heat transfer is very important. Gas phase radiation in comparison with solid phase radiation that has a high absorption coefficient, is negligible. Several relations for modeling of radiation heat transfer and derived radiation intensity are presented. The heat source term, due to radiation in solid phase that appears in Eq. 26, can be calculated from Rosseland model.

$$q_r = -\frac{16}{3}\frac{\sigma\, T_s^{\,3}}{\beta}\,\nabla T_s, \tag{34}$$

where σ is Boltzmann constant and β is extinction coefficient.

Combustion model

Chemical mechanism for oxidation of methane fuel is considered chemical production rate:

$$\omega_i = \sum_{i=1}^{NR} (v''_{k,i} - v'_{k,i}) R_{i,} \tag{35}$$

and are stoichiometric coefficients. Combustion process includes ten equations and twelve species. These equations are presented in Table .1, which includes one-step reaction for methane fuel and equations 2-4, are Zeldovich mechanism for NO formation. Rate of reactions are computed with Arrhenius method. But for six other equations that reaction rate is very quick relative to last four equations hence, equilibrium reactions are considered. In order to consider effects of turbulence on combustion the common Eddy-Dissipation model can be used.

Number	Equation
1	$CH_4 + 2\,O_2 \rightarrow CO_2 + 2\,H_2O$
2	$O_2 + 2\,N_2 \rightarrow 2\,N + 2\,NO$
3	$2\,O_2 + N_2 \rightarrow 2\,O + 2\,NO$
4	$N_2 + 2\,OH \rightarrow 2\,H + 2\,NO$
5	$H_2 \leftrightarrows 2\,H$
6	$O_2 \leftrightarrows 2\,O$
7	$N_2 \leftrightarrows 2N$
8	$O + H \leftrightarrows O\,H$
9	$O_2 + 2\,H_2O \leftrightarrows 4\,OH$
10	$O_2 + 2\,CO \leftrightarrows 2\,CO_2$

Table 1. Kinetic and equilibrium reactions

Spalding suggested that combustion processes are best described by focusing attention on coherent bodies of gas, which squeezed and stretched during their travel through the flame. This model relates the local and instantaneous turbulent combustion rate to the fuel mass fraction and the characteristic time scale of turbulence. The application of this model requires adjustment of a specific coefficient and ignition time to match the experimental combustion rate with the computational combustion rate. In combustion chamber of engine, high turbulence intensity exists and hence combustion for such device lies in the flamelets-in-eddies regime. The intrinsic idea behind the model is that the rate of combustion is determined by the rate at which parcel of unburned gas are broken down into the smaller ones, such that there is sufficient interfacial area between the unburned mixture and hot gases to permit reaction and also the turbulence length scale which is quite important can determine the turbulent burning rates. In this case, the coefficients of model were determined from experimental analysis of conventional engine.

5. Foundation of reaction

5.1. Chemical equilibrium

A general chemical equilibrium reaction with $v'_{i,s}$ and $v''_{i,s}$ representing the stoichiometric coefficient of reaction and products for the chemical species M_i

$$\sum_{i=1}^{N} v'_{i,s}\ M_i \rightleftarrows \sum_{i=1}^{N} v''_{i,s}\ M_i\,. \tag{36}$$

State of equilibrium can be interpreted as a situation, in which both the forward as well as reverse reactions progresses with identical speed.

$$K_p(T) = \prod_i \left(\frac{pi}{p0}\right)^{(v''i,s\,-\,v'i,s)}. \tag{37}$$

The equilibrium constant K_p now contains the information about the equilibrium material composition in term of partial pressure p_i of the various species i . For more information interested reader can see (Mohammadi 2010).

5.2 Reaction kinetics

A one step chemical reaction of arbitrary complexity can be represented by the following stoichiometric equation:

$$\sum_{i=1}^{N} v'_i\ M_i \rightarrow \sum_{i=1}^{N} v''_i\ M_i, \tag{38}$$

where v'_s are the stoichiometric coefficient of reactions and v''_i representing the stoichiometric coefficient of products, M_i the specification of molecule of ith chemical species, and N total number of component involved. Usually, they are represented with an Arrhenious formulation form:

$$K = AT^b \exp\left(-\frac{E_A}{RT}\right). \tag{39}$$

The constant A and the exponent b as well as the so-called activation energy E_A are summarized for many chemical reactions in extensive table.

6. The finite volume method

Customarily, CFD codes work with the finite volume method. This approach guaranties the numerical preservation of conservative quantities for the incompressible flows. The finite volume (FV) method uses the integral form of the conservation of equations. The solution domain is subdivided into a finite number of control volumes, and the conservation equations are applied to each control volume. As result, an algebraic equation for each CV is obtained. The FV method accommodates any type of grid, so it is suitable for complex geometries. However, the computational mesh ideally, be built hexahedratically. The conservation law for transport of a scalar in an unsteady flow has the general form:

$$\frac{\partial}{\partial t}(\rho\,\Phi) + \nabla.(\rho u \Phi) = \nabla.(\Gamma \nabla \Phi) + S_\Phi\,, \tag{40}$$

$(\rho u \Phi)$ designates convection, $(\Gamma \nabla \Phi)$ diffusion flows of and S_Φ the corresponding local source. For more information interested reader can see (Mohammadi 2010).

6.1. The finite volume equations formulation

Finite volume equations are derived by the integration of above differential equations over finite control volumes that taken together fully cover the entire domain of interest (Fig. 2). These control volumes are called "cells" P, for which the fluid-property value, are regarded as representative of the whole cell. It is surrounded by neighboring nodes which we shall denote by N, S, E, W, B and T. Cells and nodes for velocity components are "staggered" relative to those for all other variables.

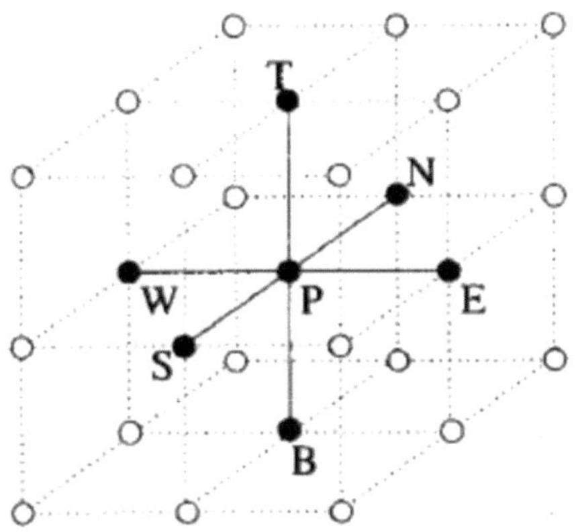

Figure 2. Computational molecule in 3D domain (Patankar, 2002)

For more information interested reader can see (Mohammadi, 2010).

6.2. Discretisation and numerical solution of the momentum equation

Finally, the momentum equation for the calculation of velocity and pressure by use of continuity equation should be considered. For numerical reasons, it is recommendable to resort to so called staggered grid, i.e. pressure and velocity are calculated on computational grids shifted to each other, the pressure for example in the cells and the velocity on the nodes. The calculations of velocity commonly take place iteratively, for which several algorithms are known (e.g. SIMPLE, PISO, SIMPLER…). In final analysis, all have the fact in common that is first step the momentum equation is solved for the velocities of momentums kept constant. In the second step, pressure corrections are then calculated with the help of a Poisson equation. For pressure with these pressure corrections, new velocities are then calculated again, and that again, until a pre-given break off threshold for the convergence is reached.

6.2.1. Discretisation of transient convection diffusion equation

Transient three dimensional convection diffusion of a general property Φ in a velocity field that govern by equation (40). The fully implicit discretisation equation is:

$$a_P \Phi_P = a_W \Phi_W + a_E \Phi_E + a_S \Phi_S + a_N \Phi_N + a_B \Phi_B + a_T \Phi_T + a^{\circ}_P \Phi^{\circ}_P + S_u \,, \qquad (41)$$

where:

$$a_P = a_W + a_E + a_S + a_N + a_B + a_T + a_P^{\circ} + \Delta F - S_P \quad (42)$$

with $a_p^{\circ} = \frac{\rho_p^{\circ} \Delta V}{\Delta}$ and $\overline{S}\Delta V = S_u + S_p\Phi_p$

For more information interested reader can see (Mohammadi, 2010).

7. Simple algorithm

As discussed in the preceding section, the governing equation for the flow may be solved in terms of derived variables, or in term of primitive variables consisting of the velocity components and the pressure.

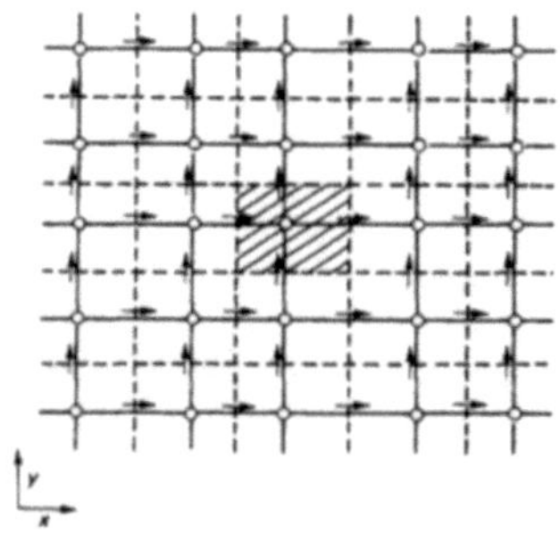

Figure 3. Staggered location for the velocity components in a two dimensional flow (Patankar, 1980)

However, in the advent of Simple (Semi Implicit Method for Pressure Linked Equations) algorithm, along with its revised version Simpler and the enhancement such as Simplec, the solution of the equations using primitive variable approach has become very attractive. In fact, Simple and Simple like algorithms are extremely popular for the solution of problems involving convective flow and transport. The basic approach involves the control volume formulation, with the staggered grid, as outlined in the proceeding section. This avoids the appearance of physically unrealistic wavy velocity fields in the solution to equations. The pressure at a chosen point is taken at arbitrary value and the pressures at other points are calculated as differences from the chosen pressure value.

Following (Patankar, 1980), if a guessed pressure field p^* is taken, the corresponding velocity field can be calculated from the discretised equations for the control volume shown in Fig. 4 These equations are of the form:

$$a_e u_e = \sum a_{nb} u_{nb}^* + b + (p_P^* - p_E^*) A_e, \quad (43)$$

where the asterisk on the velocity indicates the erroneous velocity field based on guessed pressure field. Here, a_{nb} is a coefficient that accounts for the combined convection-diffusion at the faces of the control volume, with *nb* referring to the neighbors e to the control volume, b includes the source terms except the pressure gradient, and A_e is the area on which pressure acts, being $\Delta y^*\Delta z$ for 3D. The numbers of neighbor terms are 6 for three dimensional ones. Similar equations can be written for v_n^* and w_t^*, where t lies on the z-direction grid line between grid points P and T. if p is the correct pressure and p is the correct pressure and p' the pressure correction, we may write:

$$p = p^* + p', \; u = u^* + u', \; v = v^* + v', \; w = w^* + w', \tag{44}$$

where the prime indicate corrections needed to reach the correct values that satisfy the continuity equation. Omitting the correction terms due to the neighbors, an iterative solution may be developed to solve for the pressure and the velocity field. Then, the velocity correction formula becomes:

$$u_e = u_e^* + \frac{A_e}{a_e}(p_P' - p_E').$$

$$v_n = v_e^* + \frac{A_n}{a_e}(p_P' - p_N'), \tag{45}$$

And similarly for w_t. From the time dependent continuity equation, the pressure correction equation in then developed as:

$$a_P p'_P = a_E p'_e + a_w p'_w + a_N p'_N + a_s p'_s + a_T p'_T + a_B p'_B + b, \tag{46}$$

where b is a mass source which must be eliminated through pressure correction so that continuity is satisfied. Here, T and B are neighboring grid points on the z direction grid line.

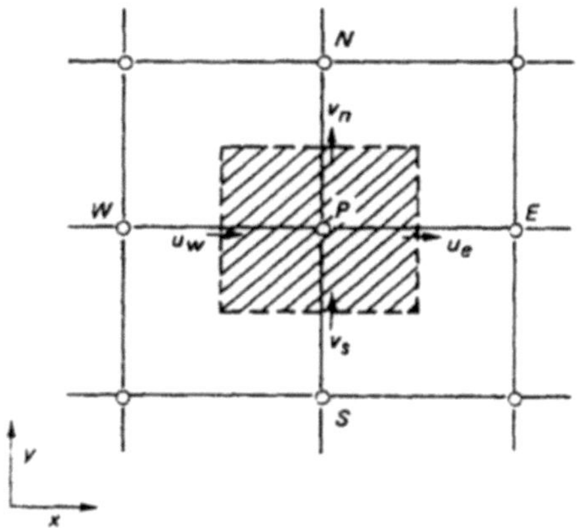

Figure 4. Control volume for driving the pressure correction equation (Patankar, 1980)

The simple algorithm has the following main steps:

1. Guess the pressure field p^*.
2. Solve the momentum equation to obtain u^*,v^*, and w^*.
3. Solve the pressure correction equation to obtain p'.
4. Add p' to p^* to obtain the corrected pressure p.
5. Calculate u, v and w from u^*, v^* and w^* using velocity correction equations.
6. Treat the corrected pressure p as the new guess p^* and iterate the preceding procedure to convergence.

The revised version Simpler is quite similar to preceding algorithm and was developed mainly to improve the rate of convergence. In this case, the mail steps are:

1. Guess the velocity field
2. Solve the pressure equation, which is similar to pressure correction equation, Eq. 46, to obtain the pressure distribution. In this equation p' is replaced by p and a different expression arise for b.
3. Treating the pressure field as p^*, solve the momentum equations to obtain u^*, v^* and w^*.
4. Solve the pressure correction equation to obtain p'.
5. Correct the velocity field but not the pressure.
6. Use the velocity field as the guessed distribution and iterate the preceding procedure to convergence.

The pressure at any arbitrary point in the computational domain is specified and pressure differentials from this value are computed. The boundary condition may be a given pressure, which makes $p' = 0$, or a given normal velocity which makes the velocity a known quantity at the boundary and not a quality to be corrected so that p' at the boundary is not needed. For further details, (Patankar, 1980) may be consulted.

8. Multi-step reaction models

Models for premixed PM combustion are complicated by the highly nonlinear radiative exchange terms in the energy equation for the solid matrix in addition to the stiffness of the set of gas phase equations. Therefore researchers have simulated the gas phase reactions using single-step chemistry. However, few researchers had taken up this issue and presented multi-step reaction models. It was concluded that use multi-step kinetics is essential for accurate predictions of the temperature distributions, energy release rates, and emissions. Single-step kinetics was shown to be adequate for predicting all the flame characteristics except the emissions for the very lean conditions under which equilibrium favors the more complete combustion process dictated by global chemistry. full mechanism (49 species and 227 elemental reactions), skeletal mechanism (26 species and 77 elemental reactions), 4-step reduced mechanism 9 species and 1-step global mechanism.

In the open literature, there are few articles concerning the interaction between a fuel spray and a PM. The PM under study was of high porosity with uniformly distributed spheres and with uniform distribution of cavities with equal mean pore size in the porous medium. The interaction between droplets during evaporation was neglected. Physical properties of fuel such as latent heat of evaporation and healing value were constant. The temperature distribution inside of the fuel droplet was uniform, but time-varying. Laminar isobaric flow consits of air, fuel droplets, gaseous combustible mixture and hot products of combustion. After evaporation the fuel mixes immediately with air to form a homogeneous combustible mixture. Mass fraction of the liquid was negligible, and the gas was optically transparent. Also, radiative heat transfer between the skeleton surfaces of the porous medium can be considered.

9. Examples

9.1. Mesh preparation

Prior to CFD simulation, computational mesh of cylinder was generated with Kiva-Prep (preprocessor for mesh generation for KIVA-3V main code). The geometry of a mesh is composed of one block. Fig. 5 shows the grid configuration of porous tube, About 300000 grids were generated for computational studies.

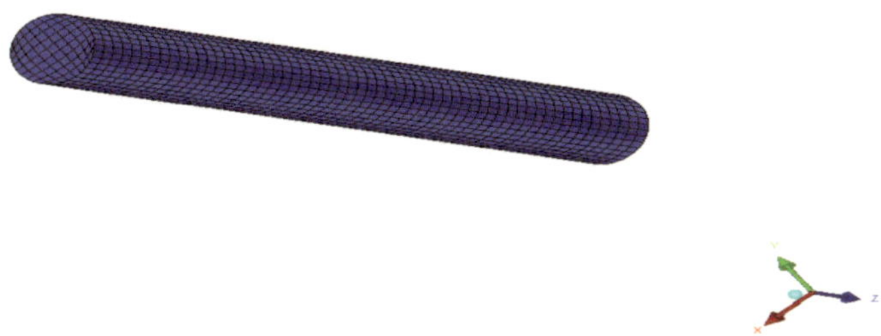

Figure 5. Computational mesh for the CFD calculation

9.2. Initial and boundary conditions

The test section was a vertical quartz glass-tube with 1.3 m in length and 0.076 m in diameter, that was isolated from the environment. The test section was filled with a packed bed of 0.0056 m solid alumina spheres. For simulation a cylinder with 0.076 m in diameter and 0.60 m in length that filled with PM, was considered (Fig. 5). The boundary condition applied to the momentum and energy equation with the assumption of zero gradients for temperature of both phase of PM and for species transport through the downstream boundary. At the upstream boundary, the gas temperature is 300K, composition is premixed methane-air with equivalence ratio 0.15, and velocity is 0.43 m/s of the premixed reactants and zero gradient for solid phase, were specified. For initial temperature for both phase of PM experimental measured data was used. Fuel is methane, porosity of PM is 0.4. The laminar flow considered for simulation. For validation of numerical simulation, modified KIVA code was used for simulation of unsteady combustion is a cylindrical tube with the experiments of Zhdanok et al. Fig. 6 plots a comparison of computation results to the experimental results of Zhdanok at the time of 147 s, which shows that the computed speed of combustion wave agrees well with the same condition of the experimental results. It is seen that methane is completely consumed in flame front that has maximum temperature.

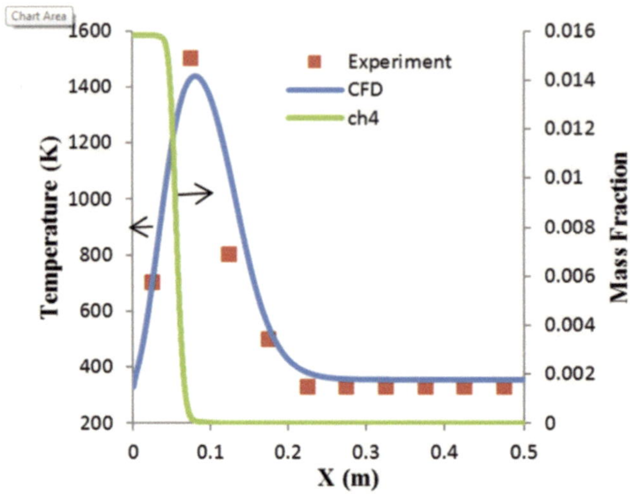

Figure 6. Comparison of combustion wave propagation between CFD and experiment in time 147 s

9.3. Discussion

In Figs. 7-10, contours of methane, carbon dioxide, temperature in gas and solid phases of PM, in cross section of tube for several times (10, 50, and 100 second) are shown. In Fig. 7 mass fraction of methane is shown. With entering of methane-air to porous tube that has high initial temperature, approximately 1800 K, in a narrow zone near inlet location, the temperature of gas increases until it reaches to self-ignition temperature. Methane consumes in a narrow region that is thicker relative to conventional flame front. In Figs. 8a, b, c, it is seen that after 10, 50 and 100 second combustion is started in respectively at x = 0.8, 2, 6 cm from entrance of mixture. The value of mass fraction of methane in PM tube is between 0.002 and this Fig indicates that the flame front has arc-shape.

Fig. 8 shows mass fraction of carbon dioxide in different time after start of simulation. Mixture flows through the porous tube that has initially heated and combustion in narrow zone of high temperature takes place. It is seen that reactions occur around the flame front in PM and its thickness is about 0.4 cm, which is very thick in compare with flame front in normal combustion. Carbon-dioxide disperses in pre heat region of entering mixture by diffusion of CO_2 and disperses in post flame by flow motion. In Fig. 9 temperature distribution in gas phase of PM in different time is shown. Flame front is recognizable from its high temperature region. Maximum fluid temperature is about 1600 K. Also, because effect of solid phase of PM, part of heat release of combustion is absorbed by it and prevents from high temperature gradient in fluid. Energy is re-circulated to the unburned gas mixture through the heat combustion and radiation of the solid. Fig. 10 shows temperature distribution in solid phase. At initial condition, mixture temperature is 300 K. The inlet temperature of solid phase is higher than gas temperature and heat is transferred from solid to gas, so allow it to reach the ignition temperature. Maximum temperature in solid phase is about 1600 K. Then the gas delivers its energy to the solid. Also, due to high heat capacity of solid phase of PM, low-temperature gradient occurs in it.

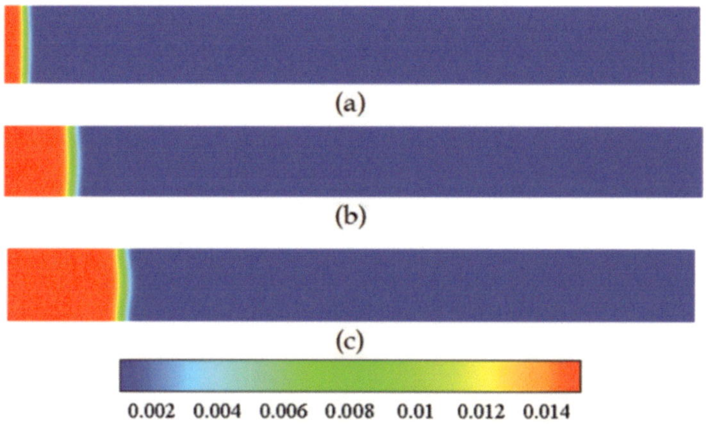

Figure 7. Mass fraction of methane in cross section x = 0 after a) t = 10 s b) t = 50 s c) t = 100 s

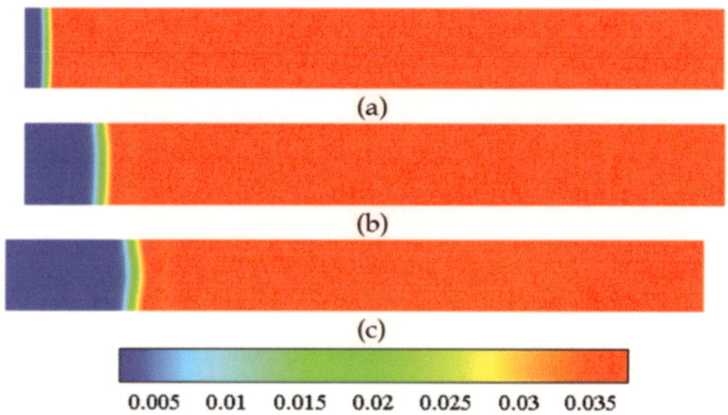

Figure 8. Mass fraction of Carbon-dioxide in cross section x = 0 after a) t = 10 s b) t = 50 s c) t = 100 s

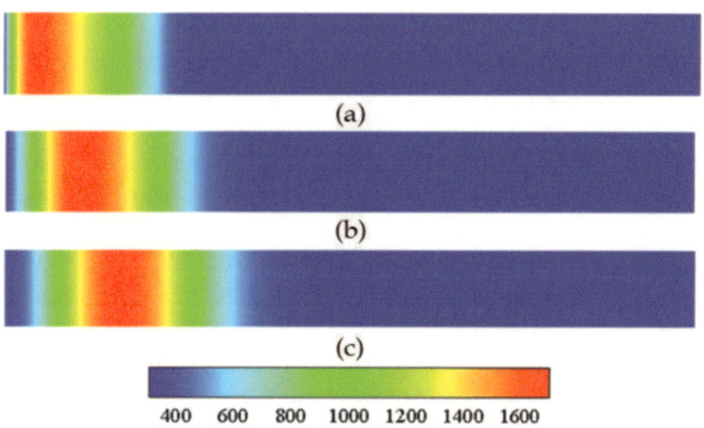

Figure 9. Gas phase temperature in cross section x = 0 after a) t = 10 s b) t = 50 s c) t = 100 s

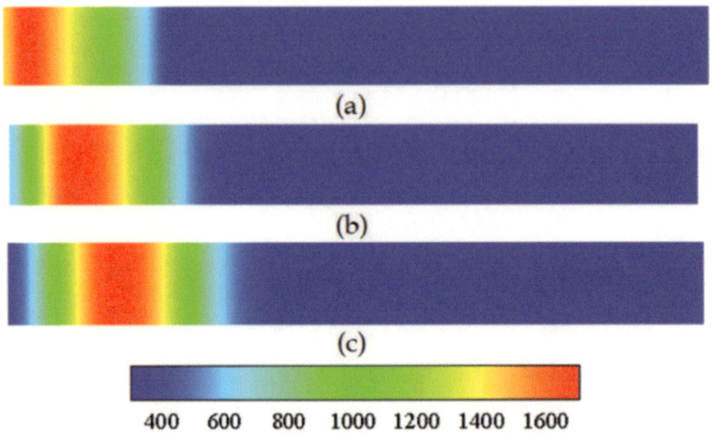

Figure 10. Temperature of solid phase in cross section x = 0 after a) t = 10 s b) t = 50s c) t= 100 s

Figs. 11, 12 show results for distribution of temperature in center line of PM tube in both phase of PM (solid and fluid) for different times versus axial direction. Heat transport is related to thermal properties of the solid material and fluid property. Flame core transports heat to incoming methane-air mixture with conduction and radiation, that its temperature is 300 K. At time t = 10 s maximum temperature in gas phase is about 1700 K. After 10 s flame moves to right with constant speed and maximum temperature of about 1600 K. After this time equilibrium between conduction, convection and radiation, causes to no change in maximum value of combustion. At the end of the tube temperature in all cases is about 325 K. In solid phase due to preheating of inlet mixture, at t = 10 s in inlet solid phase temperature is about 1450 K, in t = 50 s and t = 100 s, upstream temperature is about 850 K and 580 K, respectively and this temperature finally reach to 300 K approximately. Fig. 13 shows distribution of methane mass fraction from 10 to 100 s. Inlet mass fraction of methane is 0.016. Decrease in mass fraction of methane shows location of flame front. Flame location after 10 s is in location 3.8 cm and its thickness is thickness of 4 cm, after 50 s, is about 1.6 cm with the thickness 4.3 cm, and after 100 s is about 3.3 cm with the thickness 2.4 cm. From this Fig. inferred in 50 s and 100 s after simulation variation in flame thickness is very low value and the CH_4 is almost completely consumed in this zone. Fig. 14 shows mass fraction of CO_2 value in axial direction. Carbon dioxide is produced during combustion and its mass fraction reaches to highest value in x = 2.4, 5.5, 7.1 cm respectively to 0.036, 0.035, 0.024 mass fraction after 10, 50 and 100 s from simulation. Fig. 15 shows mass fraction of CO value in axial direction. Carbon monoxide is produced during combustion with entering of mixture and as an intermediate species produced and consumes gradually in axial direction. CO concentration reaches its highest value near the flame front at x = 1.8, 4.1, 6 cm respectively after 10, 50 and 100 s and gradually decreases at x = 4.8, 7.2 and 9.1 cm to approximately zero. With completeness of combustion and it oxidizes slowly and converted to CO_2, because of enough accessible oxygen for converting CO to CO_2. Fig. 16 shows mass fraction of CH_3 value in axial direction. Methyl concentration reaches its highest value in x = 1.4, 3.6, 9.2 cm respectively 10, 50 and 100 s after simulation. But after 100s due to fluid flow, it disperses in porous tube and oscillation occurs in value of it.

10. Two applications of PM technology

10.1. Internal combustion engines

The major target for further development of the current IC engines is to reduce their harmful emissions to environment. The most important difficulty with existing IC engines that currently exists is non-homogeneity of mixture formation within the combustion chamber which is the cause heterogeneous heat release and high temperature gradient in combustion chamber which is the main source of excess emissions such as NO_x, unburned hydrocarbons (HC), carbon monoxide (CO), soot and suspended particles. At present, the IC engine exhaust gas emission could be reduced by catalyst, but these are costly, sensitive to fuel and with low efficiency. Another strategy has been initiated to avoid the temperature gradient in IC engines that is using homogeneous charge compression ignition (HCCI)

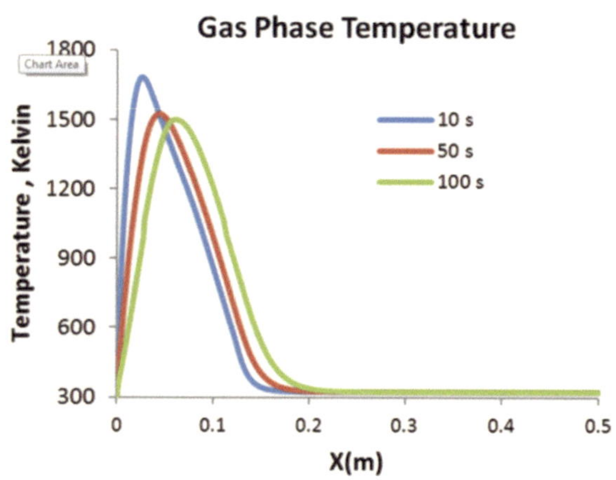

Figure 11. Mean temperature distribution in gas phase of PM versus axial direction

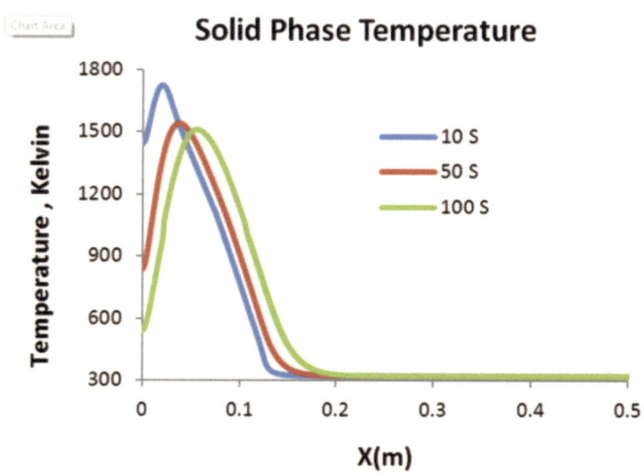

Figure 12. Mean mass fraction of methane versus axial direction

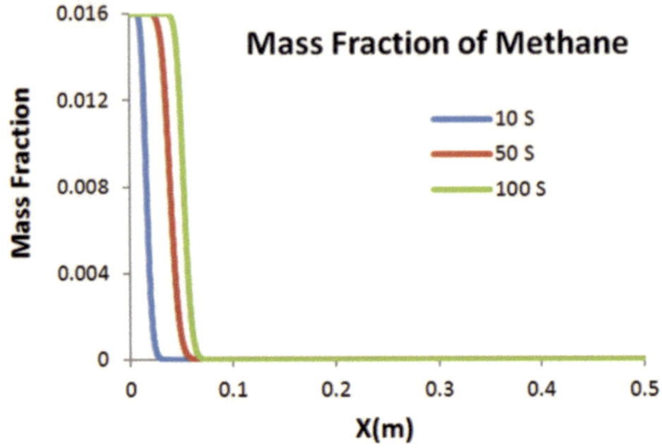

Figure 13. Mass fraction of methane versus axial direction

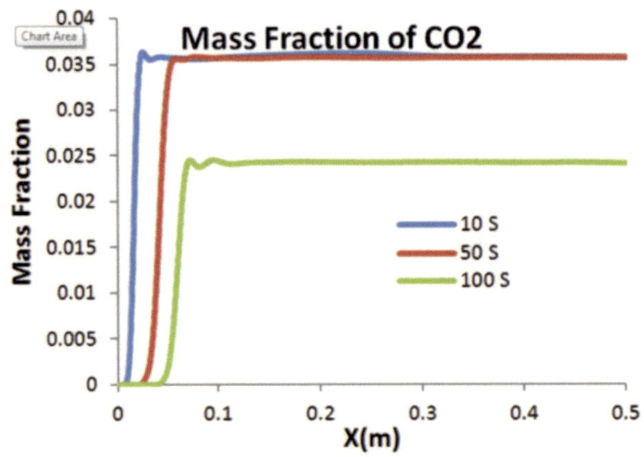

Figure 14. Mass fraction of Carbone dioxide versus axial direction

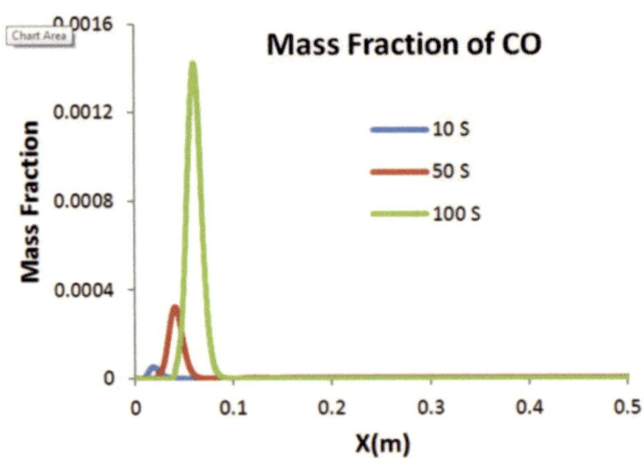

Figure 15. Mass fraction of CO versus axial direction

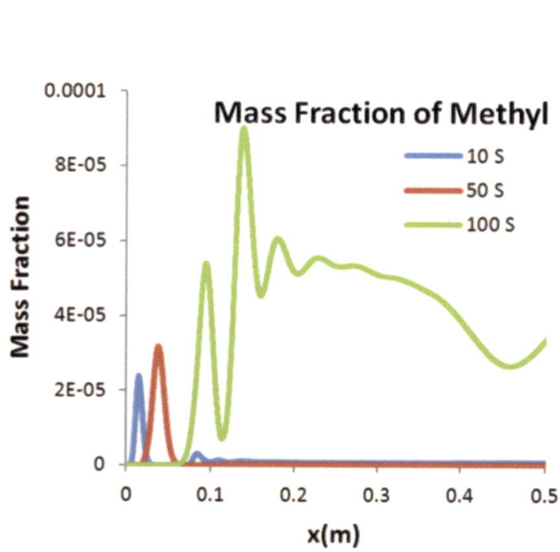

Figure 16. Mass fraction of CH_3 value versus axial direction

engines but there still exist some challenges including, higher HC and CO emissions and control of ignition time and rate of heat release under variable engine operating condition. In such engines, lean mixture with high amount of exhaust gas recycled (EGR), could be used that increases amount of CO and soot. Also by increasing the load of HCCI engine, NO_x formation and fuel consumption increases. It means that low compression ratio should be used for these engines, while in reality, the compression ratio must be high enough that temperature near the end of compression process, lead to self-ignition of mixture with reasonable time delay. Therefore, these engines are suitable for low and medium loads and it better for high loads the engine can change mode of operation to compression ignition. Also direct fuel injection engines generally have some unresolved problems due to lack of homogeneity of mixture formation and combustion. Several other technologies have been used to reduce emissions in engines, such as electronically controlled high pressure fuel injection systems, variable valve timing, EGR but still in these methods still could not solve the problem completely under all engine operating conditions. Could there be any other homogeneous combustion in IC engines to meet all operational conditions (various load and speed)? The demand target may be possible with homogeneous mixture formation and a 3D-ignition of a homogeneous charge to prevent formation of flame front that lead to temperature gradient in the entire combustion chamber which is ensuring a homogeneous temperature field. In conventional direct injection engines mechanisms also there is a lack of homogenization of combustion process. PM-engine is defined as an engine with homogeneous combustion process. The following distinct process of PM-engine is realized in PM volume: energy recirculation in cycle, fuel injection in PM, fuel vaporization for liquid fuels, perfect mixing with air, homogeneity of charge, 3D-thermal self-ignition, and homogeneous combustion. PM-engine may be classified as heat recuperation timing in an engine as: Engine with periodic contact between PM and cylinder is called closed PM-chamber and Engine with permanent contact between PM and cylinder which is called open

PM-chamber. In this paper an open PM-chamber is studied. Permanent contact between working gas and PM-volume is shown schematically in Fig. 17. The PM is placed in cylinder head. During the intake stroke there is a not much influence from PM-heat capacitor with in-cylinder air thermodynamic conditions. Also during early stages of compression stroke only a small amount of air is in contact with hot porous medium. The heat transfer process (non-isentropic compression) increases during compression, and at TDC the air penetration is cut to the PM volume. At final stages of compression stroke the fuel is injected into PM volume and with liquid fuels rapid fuel vaporization and mixing with air occurs in 3D-structure of PM-volume. A 3D-thermal self-ignition in PM-volume together with a volumetric combustion is characterized by a homogeneous temperature distribution. Therefore, all essential conditions exist for having homogeneous combustion in the PM engine. The initial idea to use PM in IC engines was proposed by Weclas. Their investigation was performed in a single-cylinder air-cooled PM Diesel engine without any catalyst. A Silicon Carbide (SiC) PM was mounted in the cylinder head between the intake and exhaust valves and fuel was injected through the PM volume. The implementation has improved engine thermal efficiency, reduced emissions and noise in comparison to the base engine. The mean cylinder temperature was about 2200 K for base engine without having any PM. The temperature reduces to about 1500 K when PM is used which is significantly even lower during combustion.

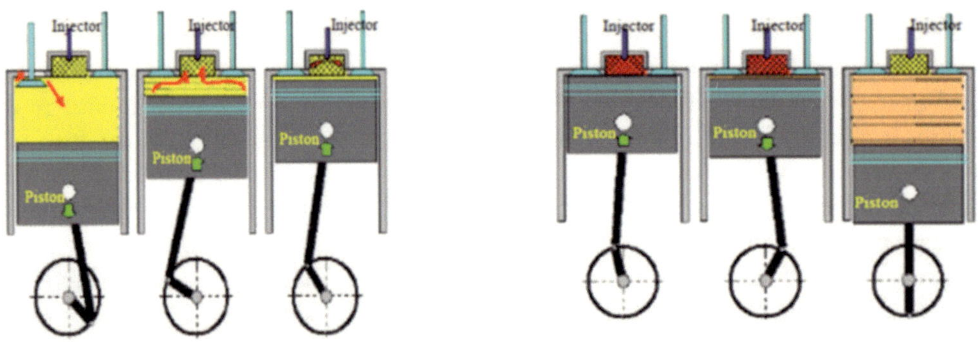

Figure 17. A permanent contact PM-engine in operation (Weclas, 2001)

The effect of SiC PM as a regenerator was simulated by Park and Kaviany. In their study a PM disk like shape was connected to a rod and was moving near piston within the cylinder of diesel engine. A two-zone thermodynamic model with single-step reaction for methane-air combustion is carried out. It is shown that the maximum cylinder pressure during combustion increases and more work is done during a full cycle, also engine efficiency increases, but due to high temperature of PM that its temperature is higher than adiabatic flame temperature of methane-air, the production of NO_x is rather higher while as its soot decreases. Macek and Polasek simulated and studied a PM engine with methane and hydrogen respectively and its potential for practical application was shown. Weclas and Faltermeier investigated penetration of liquid-fuel injection into a PM (as arrangement of cylinders which were mounted on a flat plate with different diameters). The arrangement was changed to obtain optimum geometry which produces the best mixture formation.

Porous regenerator as shown in Fig. 18 has the potential to improve fuel–air mixing and combustion. The porous insert is attached to a rod and moves in the cylinder, synchronized, but out of phase with the piston. During the regenerative heating stroke, the regenerator remains just beneath the cylinder head for most of the period and moves down to the piston (as it approaches the TDC position). During the regenerative cooling stroke, the regenerator moves up and remains in the original position until the next regenerative heating stroke. Following the combustion and expansion, the products of combustion (exhaust gases) retain an appreciable sensible heat. During the regenerative cooling stroke, the hot exhaust gas flows through the insert and stores part of this sensible heat by surface-convection heat transfer in the porous insert (with large surface area). For the proposed engine, a thermal efficiency of 53% was claimed, compared to 43% of the conventional Diesel engines. Macek and Polasek presented a finite volume based simulation of porous medium combustion for reducing emissions from reciprocating internal combustion engines.

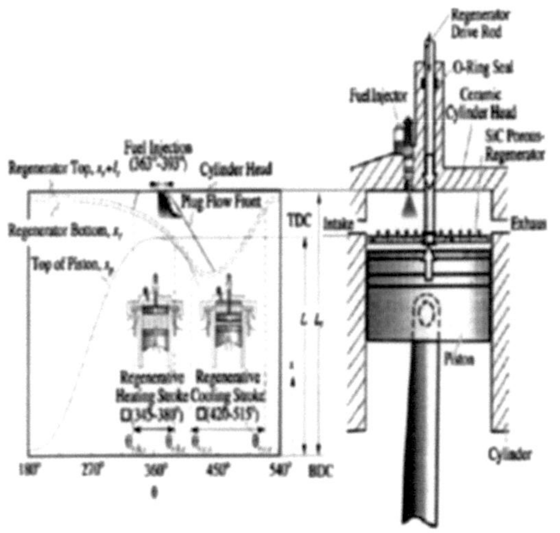

Figure 18. Sequence of motion of the regenerator and physical of fuel injection and air blowing during the regenerative heating stroke (Park and Kaviany, 2002)

The application of a highly porous open cell structures to internal combustion engines for supporting mixture formation and combustion processes was introduced by Weclas. Novel concepts for internal combustion engines based on the application of PMC technology were presented and discussed. His study proved that gas flow, fuel injection and its spatial distribution, vaporization, mixture homogenization; ignition and combustion could be controlled or positively influenced with the use of porous media reactors. The key features of the highly porous medium for supporting the mixture formation, ignition and combustion in IC engines are illustrated in Fig. 19. A study on the use of PMC in direct injection (diesel or gasoline) IC engines was performed by Durst and Weclas. Polasek and Macek presented the simulation of properties of IC engine equipped with a PM to homogenize and stabilize the combustion of CI engines. The purpose of the PIM matrix use was to ensure reliable ignition of lean mixture and to limit maximum in-cylinder temperature during combustion.

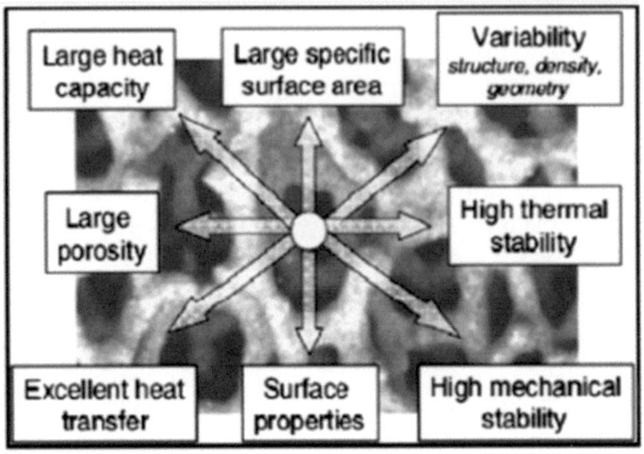

Figure 19. Main feature of porous structure to be utilized to support engine process (Durst and Weclas, 2001)

10.2. Gas turbines and propulsion

A porous burner with matrix stabilized combustion for gas turbine applications. A numerical model for analyzing the evaporation processes in PM for gas turbine applications had been developed. Evaporation of a point wise-injected kerosene spray in a carbon-carbon porous medium was considered. The effects of porous medium temperature, fuel flow rate, air inlet temperature and porous medium geometry on the evaporation of spray can be analyzed. Evaporation characteristics were not found to vary much with porous medium geometry, as the porous medium was modeled as a momentum sink. But thermal effects of PM were found to be more dominant. The characteristics of combustion within porous media which are attractive in a propulsion context are the ability to burn leaner and hotter than a free flame with low emissions, there no cooling requirement for the combustor itself and the potential to operate free from combustion-induced noise. The performance of a PM combustor is applicable for gas turbines, at elevated pressures and inlet temperatures. The combustor was formed of reticulated porous ceramics, untreated to augment or sustain chemical reaction. The results showed that the combustor could operate in a "super-adiabatic" mode, with low emissions.

Author details

Masoud Ziabasharhagh and Arash Mohammadi
K. N. Toosi University of Technology, Iran

11. References

Stanglmaier, R. H., Roberts, C. E., (1999). Homogeneous charge compression ignition: benefits, compromises and future engine applications, *SAE Paper*, 1999-01-3682.

Weclas, M., (2001). Potential of porous medium combustion technology as applied to internal combustion engine, *MECA/AECC*, Nurnberg, Germany.

Trim, D., Durst, F., (1996). Combustion in porous medium – advances and application, *Combustion Sci. and Tech.*, Vol 121, pp. 153-168.

Howell, J. R., Hall, M. J., Ellzey, J. L., (1996). Combustion of hydrocarbon fuels within porous inert media, *Progress in Energy and Combustion Science,* Vol. 22, Issue. 2, pp. 121–145.

Kamal, M. M., Mohamad, A. A., (2006). Combustion in porous media, a review, *Journal of Power and Energy,* Vol. 5,pp. 487–508.

Innocentini, M. D. M., Tanabe, E. H., Aguiar, M. L., Courty, J. R., (2012). Filteration of gases in high pressure : Permeation behavior of fiber-based media used for natural gas cleaning, *J. Chemical Engineering Science,* Vol. 74, pp. 38-48.

Monmont, F. B. J., Van-Odyck, D. E. A., Nikiforakis, N. (2012). Experimental and theoretical of the combustion of n-tridecane in porous media, *J. Fuel*, Vol. 93, pp. 28-36.

Loukou, A., Frenzel, I., Klein, J., Trimis, D., (2012). Experimental study of hydrogen production and soot particulate matter emissions from methane rich-combustion in inert porous media, *Int. J. Hydrogen Energy*, Article in press.

Wood, S., Harris, A. T., (2008). Porous burners for lean-burn applications. *Progress in Energy and Combustion Science,* Vol. 34, pp. 667–684.

Mujeebu, A. A., Abdullah, M. Z., Mohammad, A. A., Bakar, M. Z. A., (2010). Trend in Modeling of Porous Media Combustion, *J. Progress in Energy and Combustion Science,* Vol. 2, pp. 1-24.

Kamal, M. M., Mohamad, A. A., (2006). Development of a cylindrical porous-medium burner. *Journal of Porous Media,* Vol. 9, Issue. 5, pp. 469–481.

Kamal, M. M., Mohamad, A. A., (2007). Investigation of liquid fuel combustion in a cross flow burner. Proceedings of the Institution of Mechanical Engineers: Part A – *Journal of Power and Energy,* 221, pp. 371–385.

Rortveit, G. J., Stromman, A. H., Ditaranto, M., Hustad, J. E., (2005). Emissions from combustion of H2 and CH4 mixtures in catalytic burners for small-scale heat and power applications, *Clean Air: International Journal on Energy for a Clean Environment,* Vol. 6, Issue. 2, pp. 187–194.

Contarin, F., Saveliev, A.V., Fridman, A. A., Kennedy, L. A., (2002). A reciprocal flow filtration combustor with embedded heat exchangers: numerical study, *International Journal of Heat and Mass Transfer,* Vol. 46, pp. 949–961.

Bingue, J. P., Saveliev, A.V., Fridman, A. A., Kennedy, L. A., (2002). Hydrogen production in ultra-rich filtration combustion of methane and hydrogen sulfide. *International Journal of Hydrogen Energy,* Vol. 27, Issue. 6, pp. 643–649.

Bingue, J. P., Saveliev, A.V., Kennedy, L. A., (2004). Optimization of hydrogen production by filtration combustion of methane by oxygen enrichment and depletion. *International Journal of Hydrogen Energy,* Vol. 29, pp. 1365–1370.

Slimane, R. B., Lau, F. S., Khinkis, M., Bingue, J. P., Saveliev, A. V., Kennedy, L. A., (2004). Conversion of hydrogen sulfide to hydrogen by super adiabatic partial oxidation:

thermodynamic consideration, *International Journal of Hydrogen Energy,* Vol. 29, pp. 1471–1477.

Raviraj, S. D., Ellzey, J. L., (2006). Numerical and experimental study of the conversion of methane to hydrogen in a porous media reactor. *Combustion and Flame,* 144, pp. 698–709.

Hendricks, T. J., Howell, J. R., (1994). Absorption/scattering coefficients and scattering phase functions in reticulated porous ceramics. Radiative Heat Transfer: Current Research ASME HTD-276, pp. 105–113.

Barra, A. J., Diepvens, G., Ellzey, J. L., Henneke, M. R., (2003). Numerical study of the effects of material properties on flame stabilization in a porous burner. *Combustion and Flame,* 134, pp. 369–379.

M. Weclas, *porous media in internal combustion engine,* M. Scheffle, P. Colombo, editors, Cellular ceramics-structure , manufacturing, properties and application, Wiley, 2005.

Durst, F., Weclas, M., (2001). A new type of internal combustion engine based on the porous medium technology, *Proc Inst Mech Eng,* Vol. 215, pp. 63-81.

Park, C. W., Kaviany, M., (2002). Evaporating combustion affected by in cylinder reciprocating porous regenerator, *ASME J. Heat Transfer,* Vol. 124, pp. 184-194.

Polasek, M., Macek, J., (2003). Homogenization of combustion in cylinder of CI engine using porous medium, *SAE* Paper, 2003-01-1085.

Mohammadi, A., (2010). *Numerical Simulation of Spark Ignition Engines, Numerical Simulations – Examples and Applications in Computational Fluid Dynamics,* Lutz Angermann (Ed.), ISBN: 978-953-307-153-4, InTech, Austria.

Amsden., A. A., O'Rourke, P. J., and Butler, T. D., (1989). KIVA-II: A Computer Program for Chemically Reactive Flows with Sprays, Los Alamos National Laboratory Report LA-11560-MS, Los Alamos.

Amsden., A. A., (1997). KIVA-3V: A Block-Structured KIVA Program for Engines with Vertical or Canted Valves, Los Alamos National Laboratory Report LA-13313-MS, Los Alamos.

Wakao, N. and Kaguei, S., (1982). *Heat and Mass Transfer in Packed Beds,* Gordon and Breach Science Publications, New Yourk, USA.

S. R. Turn, (1996). *An introduction to combustion,* McGra-Hill, New York, pp. 399-400.

Modest, M., F., (2003). *Radiative Heat Transfer,* Academic Press, California, USA.

Zhdanok, S., (1995). Super Adiabatic Combustion of methane air mixture under filtration in a Packed Bed, *Combustion and Flame,* Vol. 100, pp. 221-231.

Henneke, M. R., Jellzey, J. L., Modeling of Filtration Combustion in a Packed Bed, *Combustion and Flame,* Vol. 117, pp. 832-840.

Mujeebu, M. A., Abdullah, M. Z., Abu Bakar, M. Z., Mohamad, A. A., Muhad, R. M. N., Abdullah, M. K., (2009). Combustion in porous media and its applications – A comprehensive survey, *Journal of Environmental Management,* Vol. 90, pp. 2287–2312.

Patankar. S. V. (1980). *Numerical Heat Transfer and Fluid flow,* McGraw-Hill, ISNB 0-07-048740-5, USA.

Chapter 23

Numerical Simulation of Slab Broadening in Continuous Casting of Steel

Jian-Xun Fu and Weng-Sing Hwang

Additional information is available at the end of the chapter

http://dx.doi.org/10.5772/47768

1. Introduction

Broadening is the deformation of materials in the vertical direction of force in the steel rolling process. Slab broadening in continuous casting increases the slab width in the secondary cooling zone. Continuous casting is a process in which the temperature drops sharply. The drop in temperature leads to slab shrinkage; the linear shrinkage of carbon steel is about 2.5% in the width direction. The decrease in slab width from the initial shell to the cooling slab is considered to be almost negligible and the width may even increase under some conditions.

Although the slab shrinks in the secondary cooling zone, the width of the slab is sometimes greater than that of the entrance of the corresponding mold. The change in slab width is due to broadening being greater than shrinkage. It is rarely well-know that this phenomenon often occurs for slab in continuous casting. Slab broadening makes it difficult to accurately control the size of the slab and has adverse effects on the subsequent rolling processes. Slab broadening becomes increasingly obvious with increasing casting speed. If no vertical miller is used in the rolling process, the broad part of the slab is cut off, wasting material. With a vertical miller, the broad part of the slab is rolled in the width direction, which leads to fluctuation in the slab thickness. The study of slab broadening in the continuous casting process is thus necessary. The present work (FU JianXun et al. 2010(a-c),2011(a-b)) investigates slab broadening in continuous casting using mathematical simulation, industrial measurements, and experiments. Assessments of slab width in several continuous casting factories indicate that slab broadening is common in the continuous casting process. Slab broadening occurs in the secondary cooling zone, as confirmed by experiments. The effects of the productive factors on the slab broadening were also derived. The mechanism of slab broadening is investigated and discussed.

2. Research method

2.1. Index definition

In order to measure slab broadening, the ratio of apparent shrinkage (RAS) and the ratio of ultimate broadening (RUB) were defined respectively as:

$$RAS = \left(U/W - 1\right) \times 100\%, \tag{1}$$

$$RUB = \left(S/T - 1\right) \times 100\%, \tag{2}$$

where:
U is size of mold on the top entrance (mm);
W is the measured width of the slab (mm);
T is the ultimate width of the slab (in mm);
S is the width of the slab (in mm).

The value of the RAS, which denotes the degree of mold shrinkage, is positive when the top width exceeds the slab width. This index can be used to set the mold size. The value of the RUB, which denotes the degree of broadening, is positive when the slab width exceeds the ultimate width.

2.2. Online measurements

An online measurement system was designed to measure slab broadening at the exit of the caster.(FU JianXun et al. 2011(b)) The system comprises an optical lens, a digital camera, a data cable (IEEE 1394), and a computer. The system is controlled using the computer. The digital camera is used to take infrared images of the hot slab. Data is read from the camera at a preset frequency.

Figure 1. Online width measurement system for hot slabs.(FU JianXun et al. 2011(b))

Then, the graphics module creates images of the hot slab according to color aberration, and saves the images as files. The accuracy of the online system is 1 mm. A photograph of the system is shown in Figure 1.

2.3. RAS and RUB investigation

Table 1 lists the RAS and RUB values obtained for five companies. The data in the right column is from a handbook (XIONG Yi-gang, 1994). The RAS values range from 0.47% to 2.16%, with most being higher than the handbook data. The linear shrinkage of carbon steel from the initial shell to the cooled slab is 2.5%. The RUB values range from 0.34% to 2.03%, which is the result that the linear shrinkage subtracting the RAS. In general, the width of a slab is smaller than the top width of a mold. Broadening may overcome shrinkage under certain operating conditions for some particular grades of steel.

The width of a cooled slab is larger than the ultimate width when broadening exists. To obtain a slab with the desired dimensions, the top and bottom widths of the mold must be reset. Therefore, the measured width (W) could replace the ultimate width (T). The RAS of a slab can thus be set by changing the values of the top and bottom widths of the mold. Then compare these values with the linear shrinkage of each steel grade, and it could consequently be found out whether the slab broadening exists and the approximate range of it could also be derived.

	CompanyA	Company B	Company C	Company D	Company E	Handbook
RAS (%)	0.47~0.54	1.81	1.93~2.16	1.70~1.90	1.10 ~2.11	2.1
RUB (%)	1.96~2.03	0.69	0.34~0.57	0.60~0.80	0.39~1.40	0.4

Table 1. RAS and RUB values at various manufactures (FU JianXun et al. 2010(a))

The data show that slab broadening is common in continuous casting. The slab width is the result of shrinkage and broadening. The linear shrinkage of a carbon steel is about 2.5%, which is slightly larger than the slab broadening.

2.4. Mechanics calculations (FU JianXun et al.2011(a))

In the secondary cooling zone, the slab has to release sensible heat and latent heat to avoid complete solidification and to maintain the surface temperature according to the technical requirements of the metallurgy process. In this zone, the stress and strain of the slab are the result of mechanical action and thermal effects (S. Kobayashi et al,1988). Some parts of the slab may have a low temperature, which causes thermal stress in the secondary cooling zone. The thermal stress of the slab in the secondary cooling zone is small enough to be ignored compared to the stress caused by the bulging and the roller disalignment. Thus, mechanical stresses, includes the bending stress, straightening stress, roller-misalignment stress, the stress of rollers acting on the slab, and the static pressure of molten steel, determine the degree of slab broadening.

The bulging stress of a slab is defined as (Sheng Y et al ,1993) :

$$\delta = \frac{pl^4}{32E_xS^3} + \frac{pl^4}{32E_xS^3}(1\mathrm{sqrt}(t)), \tag{3}$$

where Ex is the equivalent elastic modular ratio, expressed as:(Sheng Y et al ,1993)

$$E_x = \frac{T_{So} - T_m}{T_{so} - 100} \times 10^6, \tag{4}$$

The stress of bending and straightening is expressed as:(Lei H et al ,2007)

$$\varepsilon_i = \left(\frac{D_s}{2} - S_i\right)\left(\frac{1}{Ri - \frac{D_s}{2}} - \frac{1}{R_{i+1} - \frac{D_s}{2}}\right) \times 100\%, \tag{5}$$

The stress of disalignment is expressed as: (Chen J,1990)

$$\varepsilon_q = \frac{300 s_i \delta}{l^2} \times 100\%, \tag{6}$$

The values of these stresses calculated for the Q235 slab are listed in Tables 2 and 3. The calculations were based on the parameters of the continuous casters of Maanshan Iron and Steel Co. Ltd. A casting speed of 0.0167 m·s-1 was used. The bending zone of the continuous caster is at the 10th~15th rollers of the 2nd segments, and the straightening zone is at the 60th~65th rollers of the 9th segments. A negative stress indicates that a pushing stress acts on the contact surface between the slab and rollers whereas a positive stress indicates a tensile stress acting on the contact surface.

Roller ID	Slab shell thickness (10^{-2} m)	Casting speed ($m \cdot s^{-1}$)	Bulging (10^{-2} m)	Bulging strain(%)	Disalignment strain(%)	Bending strain(%)
10	4.10	0.0167	0.101	0.115	0.0128	-0.0011
11	4.28	0.0167	0.097	0.115	0.0134	-0.0011
12	4.45	0.0167	0.093	0.115	0.0139	-0.0012
13	4.62	0.0167	0.090	0.115	0.0144	-0.0013
14	4.78	0.0167	0.087	0.115	0.0149	-0.0011
15	4.93	0.0167	0.084	0.115	0.0154	-0.0010

Table 2. Comparison of slab stresses in the bending zone(FU JianXun et al.2011(a))

Roller ID	Slab shell thickness (10^{-2} m)	Casting speed ($m \cdot s^{-1}$)	Bulging (10^{-2} m)	Bulging strain(%)	Disalignment strain(%)	Bending strain (%)
60	10.4	0.0167	0.14	0.196	0.0160	0.0160
61	10.5	0.0167	0.09	0.152	0.0197	0.0197
62	10.6	0.0167	0.08	0.149	0.0198	0.0198
63	10.7	0.0167	0.08	0.147	0.0200	0.0200

Roller ID	Slab shell thickness (10^{-2} m)	Casting speed ($m \cdot s^{-1}$)	Bulging (10^{-2} m)	Bulging strain(%)	Disalignment strain(%)	Bending strain (%)
64	10.8	0.0167	0.08	0.145	0.0202	0.0202
65	10.9	0.0167	0.08	0.142	0.0203	0.0203

Table 3. Comparison of slab stresses in the straightening zone(FU JianXun et al.2011(a))

Tables 2 and 3 reveal that the bending, straightening, and disalignment stresses are far lower than the stress of bulging. Therefore, the stresses of bending, straightening, and disalignment do not cause the broadening of a slab.

3. Model and parameters

3.1. Finite element model

Building a satisfactory three-dimensional (3D) finite element model for the numerical simulation of continuous casting in the secondary cooling zone is quite complex. Thus, to simplify the problem, the following assumptions are made, as in our previous work((FU JianXun et al. 2010(b-c); 2011(b)):

1. The bending and straightening effects of the slab are ignored, and the slab is considered to be a linear object.
2. In the simulations, time, space, the characteristics of steel, and the temperature field in the slab are continuous, and the effects of the initial mechanical conditions of the slab on the deformation are ignored. The continuous caster in the secondary cooling zone is divided into several stages.
3. Because of symmetry, 1/4 of the slab and rollers on one side is used for the calculation.
4. The slab is deformable, the rollers are stiff, and the gap between rollers is variable. The calculation boundaries are placed at the rollers.

Based on these assumptions, the thermal-mechanical coupled model of the whole secondary cooling zone is divided into 6 independent sub-models for calculation. The 15 segments of the secondary cooling zone are divided into 6 groups. The first 5 groups each contain 2 segments; the remaining 5 segments make up the last group as a completely solidified slab. A 2-m slab is used for the simulation. The slab goes through the roll arrangement at a given speed. The simulation is performed continuously from the first group to the last group, and the results of a group of rollers are taken as the initial inputs for the subsequent group.

Eight-node isoparametric elements are used for the geometric discretization of the computational domain in the model. The slab comprises 4500 elements and 5250 nodes. Figure 2 shows the finite element models of the rollers and the slab in the caster. Figure 3(a) shows the rollers and the slab in the 3rd independent sub-model. Figure 3(b) shows the 6th independent sub-model.

Due to the symmetry of the slab in the width direction, one half of the slab was simulated. The grid units at the start plane of the slab move forward at a given speed. The static pressure of molten steel is taken as a mechanical boundary condition. The boundary is applied to the solidifying front of the slab, which is defined as the position with zero-strength temperature (ZST). Considering the effects of solidification-induced segregation and solid fraction (*fs*), the temperature of the units is the ZST where *fs* is equal to 0.8, and the units are considered a solidified shell where $fs \geq 0.8$. T_{80} denotes the temperature at the boundary between the solid phase and the liquid phase (T_{80}=ZST). Static pressure acts on the units where the temperature is higher than T_{80}. The boundary conditions of heat transfer and contact are also applied to the model.

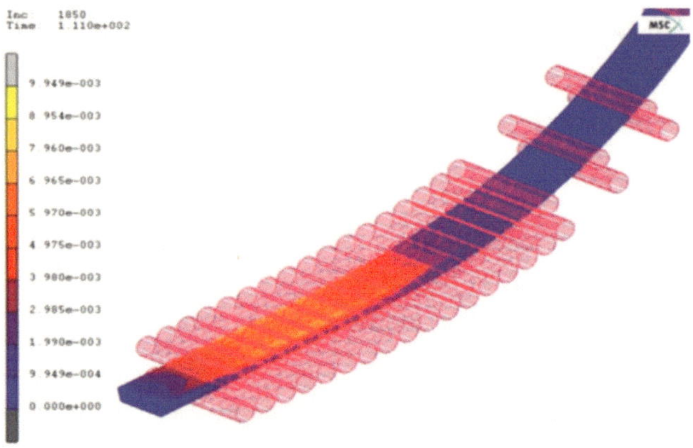

Figure 2. Finite element model of all the rollers and the slab (FU JianXun et al. 2011(b))

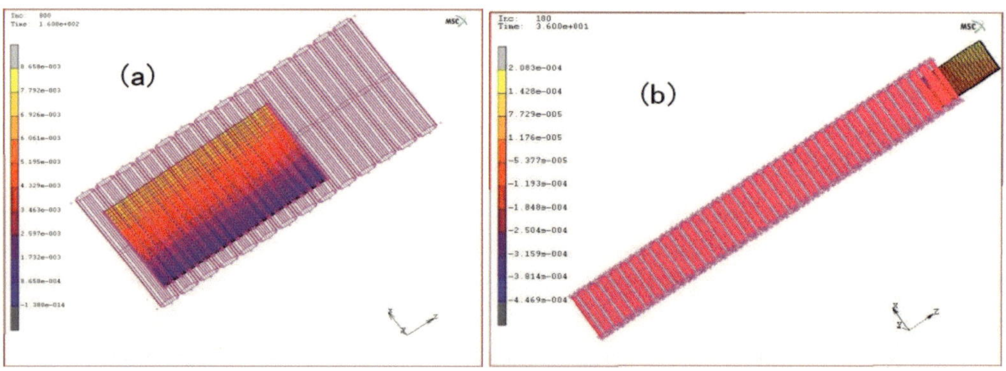

Figure 3. Finite element models of (a) the third group of rollers and the slab (b)the sixth group of rollers(FU JianXun et al. 2010(c))

3.2. Constitutive equations

The key factors that determine the accuracy of a model for analyzing the stress in a slab are included in the constitutive equation of the slab. These factors are heat transfer, mechanical load, stress relaxation, and plastic strain, all of which are time-dependent. The constitutive equation of steel at high temperature, which determines the accuracy of numeric simulations, is expressed as:

$$\varepsilon_{ij} = \varepsilon_{ij}^{e} + \varepsilon_{ij}^{ie} + \varepsilon_{ij}^{T}. \tag{7}$$

where:

ε_{ij} is the total strain;
ε_{ij}^{e} is the elastic strain;
ε_{ij}^{ie} is the non-elastic strain;
ε_{ij}^{T} is the thermal strain, and ij is the strain tensor.

The non-elastic strain ε_{ij}^{ie} is composed of time-independent inelastic strain and time-dependent creep deformation. A viscoelastic-plastic model is used to describe the solidifying behavior of the slab under the conditions of continuous casting, which is expressed as: (Chen J,1990)

$$\dot{\varepsilon}_{ij}^{ie} = f(\sigma_{ij}, T, \varepsilon_{ij}^{ie}). \tag{8}$$

where: $\dot{\varepsilon}_{ij}^{ie}$ is the non-elastic strain ratio; σ_{ij} is the stress; and T is the temperature.

This equation indicates that the non-elastic strain ratio is a function of the stress, temperature, and non-elastic strain.

The constitutive equation of time-dependent plastic deformation is used to describe the stress of carbon steel under various temperatures and strain ratios; it is expressed as: (S. Kobayashi et al.,1988)

$$\begin{cases} \dot{\bar{\varepsilon}}_P = A\exp(-Q/RT)[\sinh(\beta K)]^{1/m}, \\ \bar{\sigma} = K \cdot (\bar{\varepsilon}_P)^n, \end{cases} . \tag{9}$$

where:

$\dot{\bar{\varepsilon}}_P$ is the equivalent plastic strain ratio;
R is the gas constant;
Q is the activation energy of deformation;
σ is the equivalent stress;
$\bar{\varepsilon}_P$ is the equivalent plastic strain;
K is the strength factor;
n is the factor of hardening; and A, β, m are constants.

When carbon steel becomes plastic, strain hardening is observed. The coefficient of strain hardening can be obtained from the following equation:

$$H = K \cdot n \cdot (\bar{\varepsilon}_P)^{n-1}. \tag{10}$$

In this work, the user program includes the strain hardening coefficient in the elastic-plastic model of the MSC. Marc solver to describe the viscoelastic-plastic behavior of the cast slab under high temperature. The work hardening of carbon steel is described by the equations given by Sorimachi and Brimacombe (K. Sorimachi et al.,1977);

$$K_1 / E = 0.13\exp(-0.023\theta), \tag{11}$$

$$K_2 / E = \begin{cases} 0.045 - 3.87 \times 10^{-5}\theta \ , \ \theta < 1050^{\circ}C \\ 0.385 \cdot \exp(-0.00422\theta) \ , \ \theta \geq 1050^{\circ}C \end{cases}, \tag{12}$$

$$K_3 / E = \begin{cases} 0.0197 - 1.68 \times 10^{-5}\theta \ , \ \theta < 1050^{\circ}C \\ 0.0226\exp(-0.00223\theta) \ , \ \theta \geq 1050^{\circ}C \end{cases}, \tag{13}$$

where: E is the elastic modulus; K_1~K_3 are factors of hardening; Θ is the temperature (°C).

Equations (11)~(13) are applied when the strain is smaller than 0.01~0.02, and greater than 0.02, respectively. The factors of hardening are incorporated into the elastic-plastic model in the software package Marc by the user programs.

3.3. Parameters

All simulation parameters are taken from the technological parameters of the #2 continuous caster (SMS-Demag) of Maanshan Iron and Steel Co. Ltd. The parameters of the continuous caster are listed in Table 4.

Segment No.	Shrinkage between rollers (mm)	Slab thickness (m)	Roller diameter(m)	Slit width between rollers (m)	Distance from meniscus (m)
1-2	0.20/0.46	0.2375	0.200	0.240	0-4.374
3-4	0.46/0.46	0.2370	0.245	0.284	4.374-8.388
5-6	0.46/0.44	0.2362	0.255	0.297	8.388-12.592
7-8	0.44/0.44	0.2354	0.265	0.310	12.592-16.992
9-10	0/0.30	0.2346	0.283	0.322	16.992-21.254
11-15	0.30/0.30	0.2343	0.300	0.335	21.254-33.249

Table 4. Parameters of the slab and caster at various segments

Casting temperature: T=1533 °C;
Liquidus temperature T_l=1513 °C;
Solidus temperature T_s =1446.0 °C;
T_{80} = 1459.6 °C;
Environmental temperature: 25 °C;
Roller temperature: 100 °C;
Coefficient of contact heat transfer: 25.0 W/(m·K) (Y. S. Xi and H. H. Chen,2001) ;
Coefficient of fraction: 0.3; Distance tolerance: 0.01 (Y. S. Xi and H. H. Chen,2001).

When the casting speed is in the range of 1.0~1.2 m/min, the SMS-Demag casting machine uses a fixed cooling water intensity in the secondary cooling zone. The parameters of the SPHC steel and Q235 steel are listed in Table 5.

Steel	C (%)	S i(%)	Mn(%)	P(%)	S(%)	Al(%)	Tl(°C)	Ts(°C)
SPHC	0.05	0.05	0.20	≦0.02	≦0.012	0.03	1528.9	1493.0
Q235	0.18	0.20	0.40	≦0.025	≦0.022		1517.0	1446.0

Table 5. Compositions of SPHC steel and Q235 steel

The coefficient of thermal expansion, Young's modulus of elasticity, and Poisson's ratio of the steel as functions of temperature are required for simulation. The elastic modulus of carbon steel for various temperatures during continuous casting is given in equations (14) and (15).(Ueshima Y et al; 1986, I.Ohnaka,1986)

$$\begin{cases} E=(347.6525\text{-}0.350305{*}T)*10^9 & ,\ T<900\ , \\ E=(968-2.33*T+(1.9*10^{-3}){*}T^2-(5.18*10^{-7})*T^3)*10^9 & ,\ Ts>T\geq 900, \end{cases} \quad (14)$$

$$E=\frac{(f_S-f_{ZST})\cdot E_S+(1-f_S)\cdot E_{ZST}}{1-f_{ZST}},\quad T_{80}>T>T_S(f_{ZST}\leq f_S\leq 1), \quad (15)$$

When E=E(Ts) and $Ezst$=E(Tzst), Ezst takes a small non-zero value in order to restrain the deviatoric stress in the liquid phase region to maintain hydrostatic pressure. When the temperature is lower than *Ts*, the elastic modulus is expressed by (14); when it is higher than T_s, it is expressed by (15).

When the temperature is lower than *Ts*, Poisson's ratio can be defined as equation (14); when the temperature is higher than T_s, with decreasing f_s, Poisson's ratio gradually increases from the value at Ts to a certain value which is close to 0.5; it remains at this value above ZST, as expressed by equations (16) and (17). (Uehara M et al.,1986)

$$\nu=\frac{(f_s-f_{ZST})\cdot\nu_s+(1-f_s)\cdot\nu_{ZST}}{1-f_{ZST}},\quad \mathrm{T}>\mathrm{T_L}\left(f_{ZST}\leq f_S\leq 1\right), \quad (16)$$

$$\nu=\nu_{ZST},\quad T\geq T_{80}\quad ,\quad (f_S\geq f_{ZST}). \quad (17)$$

Where f_{ZST} is the solid phase ratio at ZST, often taken as 0.80. ν_{ZST} is the Poisson's ratio at ZST; it is very close to 0.5. The Poisson's ratio of the steel for various temperatures is shown in Figure 4(a). The coefficient of thermal expansion values of Q235 and SPHC are taken from the local measurement results shown in Figure 4(b).

4. Effects of casting speed on slab broadening (Jian-Xun Fu et al , 2011b)

4.1. Numerical simulation

By tracing one node of the slab at the side-face and recording its width, the width of the slab at various positions in the secondary cooling zone can be obtained. The RUB can then be derived from the simulated width of the slab. The simulated RUB values of Q235 and SPHC steels at three casting speeds are shown in Figure 5(a) and (b), respectively.

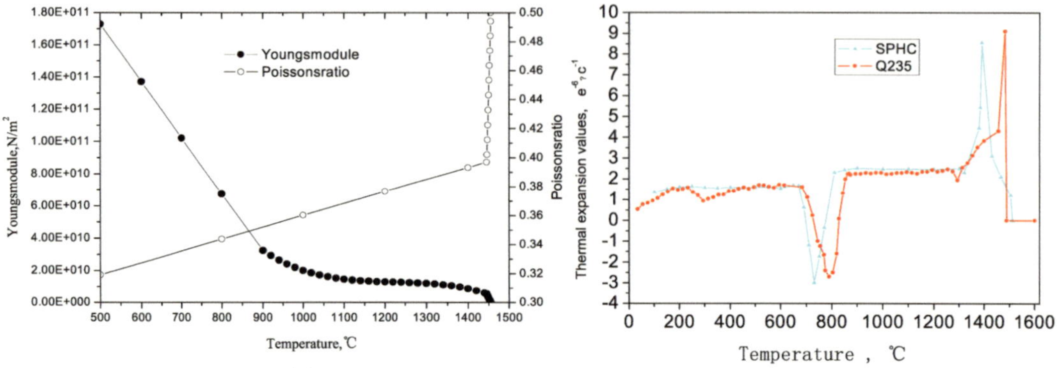

(a) (b)

Figure 4. (a) Young's modulus of elasticity and Poisson's ratio of Q235 steel for various temperatures; (b)Coefficient of thermal expansion of Q235 and SPHC. (Jian-Xun Fu et al , 2011b)

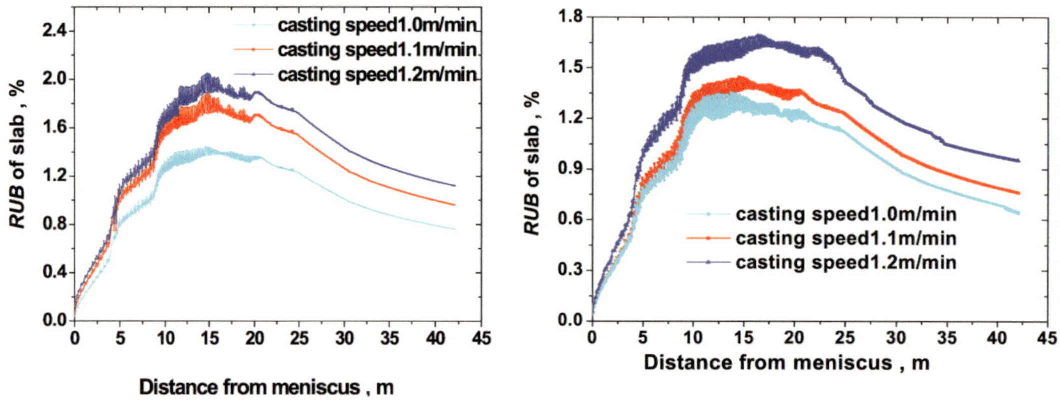

(a) (b)

Figure 5. (a) RUB values versus distance from meniscus of a Q235 steel;.(b) RUB values versus distance from meniscus of a SPHC steel at three casting speeds. (FU JianXun et al. 2011(b))

Slab broadening for Q235 and SPHC steels at three casting speeds shows similar characteristics. The values of the RUB at the three casting speeds are all positive in the whole secondary cooling zone, which means that slab broadening existed for Q235 and SPHC steels at these speeds. The RUB changed from one segment to another for the first five segments. The RUB increased and then gradually decreased after reaching its maximum at the fifth and sixth segments. Near the tenth segment, the RUB decreased smoothly; the slab became completely solidified at this location.

The simulations of Q235 and SPHC steels produced similar results. The RUB increased with increasing casting speed. For Q235 steel, when the casting speeds were 1.0, 1.1, and 1.2 m/min, the maximum RUB values were 1.44%, 1.88%, and 2.04 %, respectively, and the RUB values at the exit of the caster were 0.76%, 0.96%, and 1.14%, respectively. For SPHC steel, when the casting speeds were 1.0, 1.1, and 1.2 m/min, the maximum RUB values were 1.34%, 1.44%, and 1.69%, respectively, and the RUB values at the exit of the caster were 0.64%, 0.76%, and 0.95%, respectively.

Slab broadening is closely correlated with casting speed, which may be due to the slab's temperature changing with casting speed. When the casting speed increased, the liquid core length and temperature of the slab both increased. With increasing temperature of the slab, the high-temperature mechanical properties of the slab changed; ductility increased and the strength and resistance to external pressure decreased, increasing the RUB.

With increasing casting speed, a given cross section of the slab takes up the same amount of space. At 25 m away from the meniscus, the surface temperature in the wide face at a casting speed of 1.2m/min is 11.6 °C and 21.7 °C higher on average than those at casting speeds of 1.1 and 1.0 m/min, respectively (see Figure 6). Under a given set of conditions, increasing the casting speed increases production. However, high casting speed can lead to slab broadening.

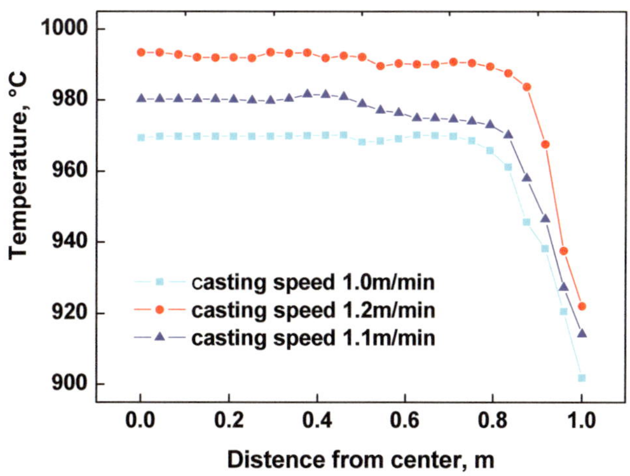

Figure 6. Surface temperature on the slab at various positions.(FU JianXun et al. 2011(b))

4.2. Verification of simulation results

For continuous caster #2 at Maanshan Iron and Steel Co. Ltd., the slab widths of two steel grades were tracked online at the exit of the caster (the end of the 15th segment); the slab width was measured once per minute. For each grade of steel, measurements were taken for more than 70 minutes. The data are shown in Figures 7(a), and (b), respectively.

Figure 7(a) shows the slab width and the RUB of SPHC steel at various moments. Slab broadening can be clearly seen. The RUB of SPHC steel ranges from 1.4% to 2.4%, with an average of 1.96%. The average RUB is greater than the ratio of linear shrinkage, indicating that the width of the slab after cooling was greater than the top width of the mold. This result shows that slab broadening occurred in the secondary cooling zone.

The slab width changed smoothly except from 45 to 55 min, during which time a sharp trough appears on the RUB curve. In the initial 6 minutes of this period, the RUB decreased to 1.4% from 2.25%, and in the following 4 minutes, the RUB increased to 2.1% from 1.4%. This trough was caused by the changing of the tundish, during which the casting speed decreased sharply, and then quickly recovered to normal; i.e., the change in casting speed caused the change in slab broadening.

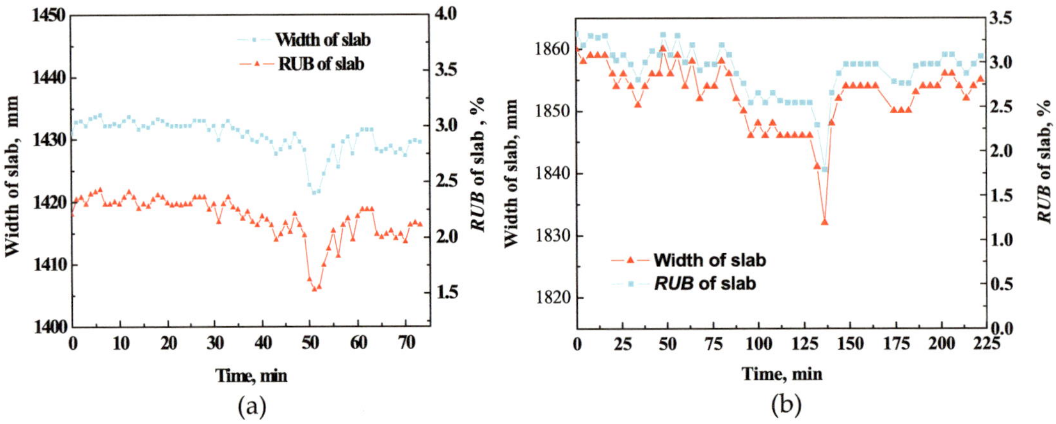

Figure 7. (a) Width of slab and RUB for SPHC steel at various moments; (b) Width and RUB for Q235 steel at various moments. (FU JianXun et al. 2011(b))

Figure 7(b) shows the slab width and the RUB for Q235 steel at various times. The RUB for Q235 steel ranges from 0.77% to 2.91%, with an average of 2.04%. There are five sharp corners on the RUB curve for Q235 steel. By comparing the curve with the production process of Q235, it was found that each sharp corner corresponds to an unsteady production stage. The biggest one corresponds to the changing of the tundish, the last one corresponds to the end of casting, and the remaining three correspond to the changing of ladles.

Figure 8 shows the relationship between the RUB and the casting speed for Q235 steel. The shapes of the RUB curve and the casting speed curve are very similar. When the tundish was changed, the casting speed decreased to 0.5 m/min over a 10-minute period and then recovered to normal in 5 minutes; this change formed a sharp trough in the casting speed curve. At nearly the same time, the RUB decreased to 1.91% from 0.77% in 10 minutes and then increased to 2.1% in 5 minutes, producing a sharp trough in the curve. When the ladle was changed, a similar change happened. When the casting speed was maintained at 1.0 m/min, the RUB remained stable at about 2.0%. The RUB is thus closely correlated with casting speed.

There is a small lag between the RUB curve and the casting speed curve in Figure 12. The change in casting speed curve occurred earlier than that in the RUB curve. For example, the casting speed curve exhibits a sharp trough at about 100 minutes; a sharp trough appears in the RUB curve at about 110 minutes. Comparing Figure 7 and Figure 8, it can be seen that the simulation results generally agree with the industrial measurement results.

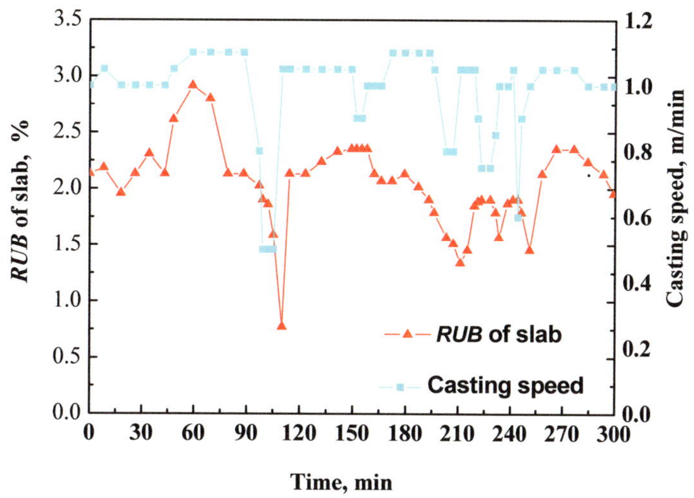

Figure 8. Relationship between the RUB and casting speed. (FU JianXun et al. 2011(b))

5. Effects of width and thickness on slab broadening (FU JianXun et al. 2010(b))

5.1. Numerical simulation

One node of the slab was traced and the width was recorded at various positions of the secondary cooling zone. The RUB was derived from the calculated width of the slab.

The calculated RUB of Q235 steel slab with a cross section 2000 mm × 230 mm at speed of 1.0m/min is shown in Figure 9(a). The RUB changes from one segment to another; its value is over 0 throughout the secondary cooling zone, indicating slab broadening. The RUB increases in the first five segments, and then drops down gradually after reaching its maximum in the sixth segment. In the sixth segment, the width of the slab reaches its maximum with a large fluctuation due to the bulging of the slab in the direction of thickness. Figure 9(b) shows the simulated deformation of the slab in this direction. The shell of the slab has low yield strength and high plasticity; thus, the slab at the points contacting the rollers is depressed and bulges at the slit between the two rollers. Similar to the periodicity of bulging, the width of the slab fluctuates periodically.

The simulated broadening and bulging of the slab in the sixth segment are shown in Figure 10. There is an obvious correlation between broadening in the width direction and bulging in the thickness direction. The position in the slab where the smallest bulging is observed has the greatest broadening. This is due to the depression of slab in the thickness direction contributing to slab broadening in the width direction.

5.2. Effects of slab width on broadening (FU JianXun et al. 2010(b))

230-mm-thick slabs of Q235 with various widths were simulated at a casting speed of 1.0 m/min. The RUB values for various segments are shown in Figure 11. It shows that the simulated RUB of slab slightly increases with the increase of width. The maximum values are 1.27 %, 1.36 %, and 1.44 %, respectively. The RUBs at the exit of caster are 0.63 %, 0.70 %, and 0.76 %, respectively. There is no obvious increase of RUB for slabs with increasing the width, but the increase of broadened size is noticeable. In conclusion, slabs with great width have great broadening.

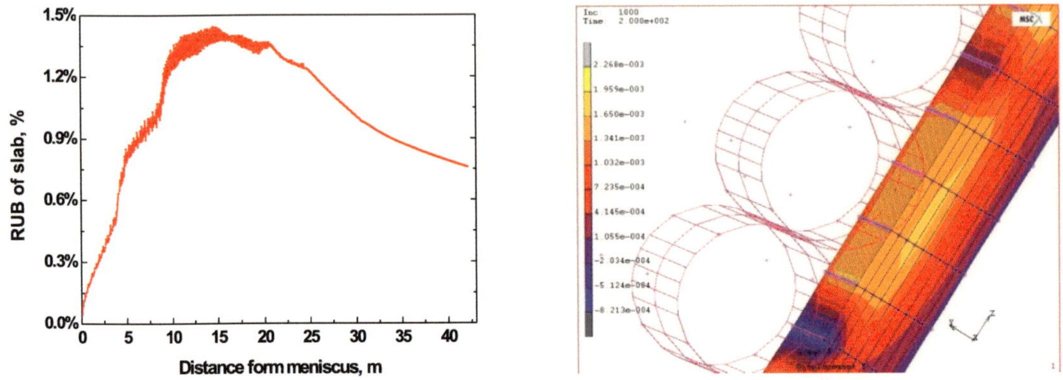

(a) (b)

Figure 9. (a) Calculated RUB of Q235 steel in the secondary cooling zone; (b)Calculated deformation of slab between rollers. (FU JianXun et al. 2010(b))

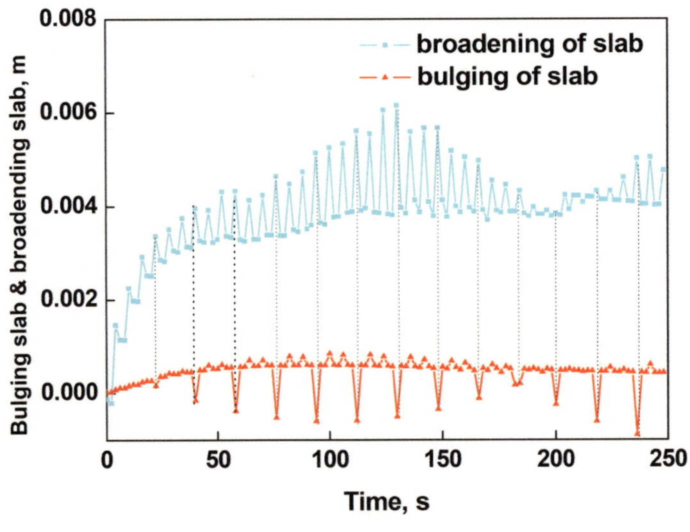

Figure 10. Broadening and bulging of slab in the sixth segment. (FU JianXun et al. 2010(b))

Under the same conditions, the wide slab has greater broadening than narrow slab because of compound effects of temperature and stress. Compared with wide slab, narrow slab has a larger range for heat flow distribution and hence the greater equivalent von Mises stress. But the wider slab has more enthalpy to be removed. So in the same position of caster, the narrow slab has higher yield strength and lower plasticity, and the solidified shell is able to resist great stress.

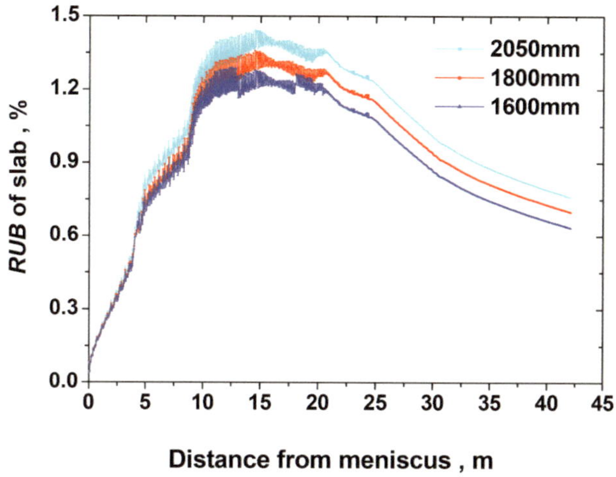

Figure 11. Calculated RUB values for slabs of various widths . (FU JianXun et al. 2010(b))

5.3. Effects of slab thickness on broadening

To study the effect of slab thickness on broadening, 2050-mm-thick Q235 slabs with thicknesses of 230 and 250 mm, respectively, were simulated at a casting speed of 1.0 m/min; the results are shown in Figure 12.

The calculated broadening values for the two slabs are slightly different. The maximum RUB values are 1.4% and 1.38% for 250- and 230-mm-thick slabs, respectively. The RUB values are 0.74% and 0.71% at the exit of the continuous caster, respectively. The difference of broadening is just 0.6 mm between the two slabs. This is because the bulging changes little with increasing thickness.

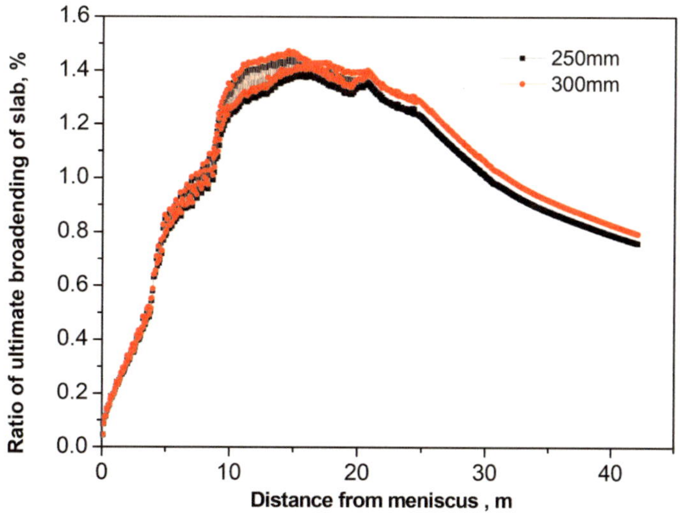

Figure 12. Calculated RUB with different thicknesses. (FU JianXun et al. 2010(b))

5.4. Verification of simulation results

To verify the obtained simulation results, the slab broadening cast on the #2 caster in Maanshan Iron and Steel Co. Ltd was measured. The online measuring system was designed to measure the width of the slab. The digital camera was fixed above the exit of the caster. Q235 steel was used for the experiments. The parameters of the continuous caster and measured results are listed in Table 6.

The online measured RUB values are greater than the simulation results for all the experimental slabs. This is because the preset width of a cold slab in the experiments was the upper width of the mold. The upper width is always greater than the defined width. For the slab with a preset width of 2050 mm, the upper width of the mold is 2081.3 mm (a broadening of 1.56%). With this difference taken into account, the experimental results well agree with those of the simulation.

Defined width (mm)	Upper width (mm)	Lower width of mold (mm)	Measured width (mm)	Measured RUB (%)	Measured broadening (mm)	Calculated broadening (mm)	Deviation rate (%)
1600	1623.8	1610.4	1630.4	1.90	6.6	7.04	6.7
1850	1877.7	1867.3	1885.9	1.94	8.2	9.25	12.8
2050	2081.3	2067.5	2091.4	2.02	10.3	11.69	13.5

Note: the measured broadening of the slab is the difference between the measured width of the slab and the upper width of the mold, and the calculated broadening of the slab is that between the calculated width and the defined width.

Table 6. Measured and calculated widths of slabs

6. Analysis of slab broadening (FU JianXun et al.2011(a))

6.1. Change of mold size

The slabs broaden in width, which varies with the operating parameters of steel produced. The statistical data of 76 taper samples of the mold revealed that the change is very small for the taper of the mold. The average change of a one-sided taper was 0.37 mm, and only a few samples had changes of 1~2 mm. The slight change of the taper is due to metering errors, wear, and deformation. Slab broadening is thus independent of the mold size.

6.2. Exception of equipment or operating parameters

The secondary cooling process is the most important procedure in continuous casting. The temperature field of the slab was checked with the data provided by the producer of the caster. A good agreement was found, indicating that the caster worked well in the secondary cooling process. The monitoring records obtained in a controlled room also reveal that the caster worked well. However, the width of the produced slabs exhibited obvious broadening during the process. It is thus concluded that slab broadening is independent of exceptions of equipment or operating parameters.

6.3. Soft reduction

Soft reduction may strengthen slab broadening and even cause side bulging. For SPHC and Q235 steels, the slabs were broadened in the process of continuous casting with soft reduction set to 0.5~2.5 mm. The broadening width ranges are 2~19 mm and 2~8 mm for SPHC and Q235 steels, respectively. The ratios of broadening are 0.1%~1.46% and 0.15%~0.62% for SPHC and Q235 steels, respectively. Therefore, soft reduction contributes to slab broadening, but is not the main cause.

6.4. Contraction of roll gap

For the continuous caster #2 in Maanshan Iron and Steel Co. Ltd, the ultimate thickness of a produced slab is 230 mm, and the bottom thickness of the mold is 237.5 mm. With a casting speed of 1.1 m/min, the molten steel completely solidifies at the start of the 11th sector where the thickness of the slab is 234.3 mm and the roll gap contraction is 3.2 mm. In this zone, the linear shrinkage ratio is 0.5%~0.7% (1.2~1.7 mm) due to the drop of temperature. Without the contribution of the temperature drop, the roll gap contraction is 1.5~2.0 mm. This amount of shrinkage equals soft reduction of medium or light scale. The roll gap contraction is uniformly distributed. The roll gap contraction acts on the slab and affects the fluctuation of the liquid level of molten steel. However, the slab broadening is far less than that induced by soft reduction. So roll gap contraction is not the main cause of broadening.

6.5. Summary

The static pressure of the molten steel core and the force of the driving rollers may be the main cause of slab broadening.

When there is no support on the narrow face of a slab, the slab deforms in the width direction under the static pressure of molten steel. The high-temperature mechanical properties of the slab are worse than those under normal temperature(Lei H et al,2007; Chen J,1990; S. Kobayashi et al,1988). The slab has good ductility under high temperature and is unable to resist the static pressure of molten steel in the width direction. Therefore, the slab greatly deforms at the edges, and thus the width is broadened. Previous studies found that the hardness of the solidified shell and the ability to resist the static pressure of molten steel are determined by the thickness of the shell and the formation of ferrite-austenite with a dual phase.(Mizukami H et al,1977; Uehara M et al, 1986; Ramacciotti A,1988)

The shell of the slab is clamped under the pressure of the driving roll cylinders so that it moves forward with the rotation of the driving rollers. The solidifying and soft slab is extended and broadens under the pressure of the driving rollers when passing through the cast-rolling segment. The degree of extension and broadening increases with casting speed.

6.6. Creep deformation

The forces acting on the slab shell in the secondary cooling zone can be modeled as the bending of a rectangular thin plate under loading (i.e., static pressure of molten steel). One segment of the slab along the strand direction is taken to build the model. In the model, the slab is a rectangular thin plate fixedly supported along two sides and simply supported along the other two sides. In addition, the thin plate is subjected to lateral loads, and the temperature field linearly changes in the thickness direction of the slab. Because the width of the slab is much greater than the gap between the rollers, the effects of the slab boundary on the internal side of the slab can be ignored according to the Saint-Venant principle. According to plate theory, the slab shell is viscoelastic at high temperature, and the stress and deformation satisfy the Maxwell creep law. As shown in Figure 13.

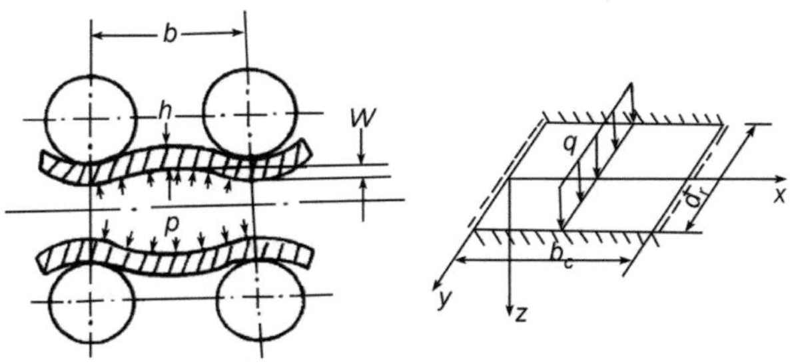

Figure 13. Model of slab shell and the force model of slab creep. (Sun J et al,1996)

In the secondary cooling zone, the total stress equals the sum of elastic strain and creep strain, when the slab shell creepily bends under the static pressure of molten steel. The elastic strain changes little with time. The elastic deflection is expressed as: (Sun J et al,1996):

$$
\begin{aligned}
W_e(x,y) = W_{qe} + W_{Te} &= \frac{4q\alpha^4}{\pi^5 D}\sum_{i=1,3\ldots}^{\infty}\frac{1}{m^5}\times \\
&\left(1-\frac{\alpha_m ch\alpha_m + sh\alpha_m}{\alpha_m + sh\alpha_m ch\alpha_m} ch\frac{2\alpha_m}{b}y + \frac{\sigma_m sh\alpha_m}{\alpha_m + sh\alpha_m ch\alpha_m}\cdot\frac{2y}{b} sh\frac{2\alpha}{b}y\right) \qquad (18) \\
&\times \sin\frac{m\pi}{\alpha}x + \frac{48\alpha a T_0}{\pi^3 h^3(1-2\gamma)(1-\gamma)}\times\sum_{i=1,3\ldots}^{\infty}\left(1-\frac{ch\frac{2\alpha_m}{b}y}{ch\alpha_m}\right)\sin\frac{m\pi}{a}x.
\end{aligned}
$$

where: $T_0 = \int_{-h/2}^{h/2} T(z)\cdot z\cdot \mathrm{d}z$.

The expression of elastic deflection has the series of hyperbolic function, and converges rapidly, thus setting m=1 is sufficiently accurate for calculation. Using equation (18) and the Cauchy equation, the creep deformation of slab shell on the narrow side can be derived as:

$$\begin{cases} \varepsilon_{xe} = -\dfrac{\partial^2 W_e}{\partial x^2} z, \\ \varepsilon_{ye} = -\dfrac{\partial^2 W_e}{\partial y^2} z, \\ \gamma_{xye} = -\dfrac{\partial^2 W_e}{\partial x \partial y} z. \end{cases} \tag{19}$$

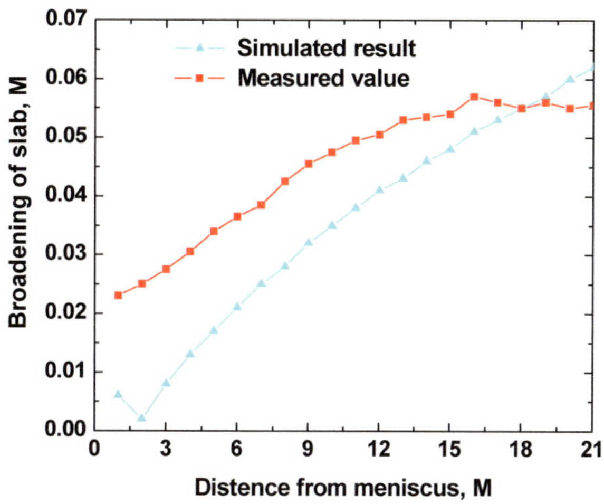

Figure 14. Comparion of calculated and measured side creep results. (FU JianXun et al.2011(a))

The amount of creep deformation for the narrow side of the slab was calculated using Matlab software; the results are shown in Figure 14. The figure also shows the measured results from the experiments of a stagnant slab. The agreement between the calculated results from the Maxwell model and the measured results illustrates that the Maxwell model is able to reveal deformation behavior at high temperature.

6.7. Industrial experiments of stagnant slab (FU JianXun et al.2011(a))

If the static pressure of molten steel is the main reason for the broadening of a slab, the broadening must happen at the forepart of the continuous caster where the slab has a high temperature and a thin shell. If the stress of the rollers is the main reason for broadening, the broadening must happen at the middle part of the continuous caster, specifically the position near the completely solidified zone. Because the molten steel is fluidic before this part(Lin Q Y et al ,2004), decreasing the roller gap does not broaden the slab.

Since the continuous caster is a vertical bow type, it is very dangerous to keep close to it, and thus it is impossible to measure the width of the slab directly. Therefore, when the caster stopped to for the tundish replacement, the width of the stagnant slab was measured to determine where slab broadening happens. When the tundish is to be replaced, the casting speed gradually slows down to zero. This process takes about 4-5 min to form a stagnant slab, which is cooled down continuously by secondary cooling water. The slab in the continuous caster is composed of three parts:

1. For the fully solidified part during casting, the slab broadening is the sum of broadening of the molten steel core.
2. For the part solidified during the stopping period, because it reveals the slab broadening at specific position, and corresponds to the real broadening amount of slab, this part is focused on in our experiments.
3. For the unsolidified part until restarting the casting, the slab broadening continues during subsequent casting, as the molten steel core still exists in the slab shell. However, because the slab shell is very thick, little broadening happens.

Using the square-root law of solidification, the fully solidified normal position and stagnant position can be derived, and thus the above three parts of the slab could be determined.

The slab was Q235 steel, the casting speed was 0.0167 $m \cdot s^{-1}$, the cross section of the slab was 2.050 m × 0.230 m, the upper width of the mold was 2.0813 m, the lower width of the mold was 2.0675 m, the casting temperature was 1533°C, T_l was 1513°C, and T_s was 1546°C.

The width of the front slab was also traced. It remained at 2.040 m, indicating that nearly no broadening of the slab happened at this position. It may be because it was cooled so rapidly that there was no time for broadening. Therefore, the width of the front slab was used as the standard width for assessing slab broadening.

The absolute broadening of the slab was derived from the slab width, which was measured while the slab was pushed through the exit of the continuous caster, subtracting the width of the front slab. The broadening values of the slab are shown in Figure 15(a) and (b).

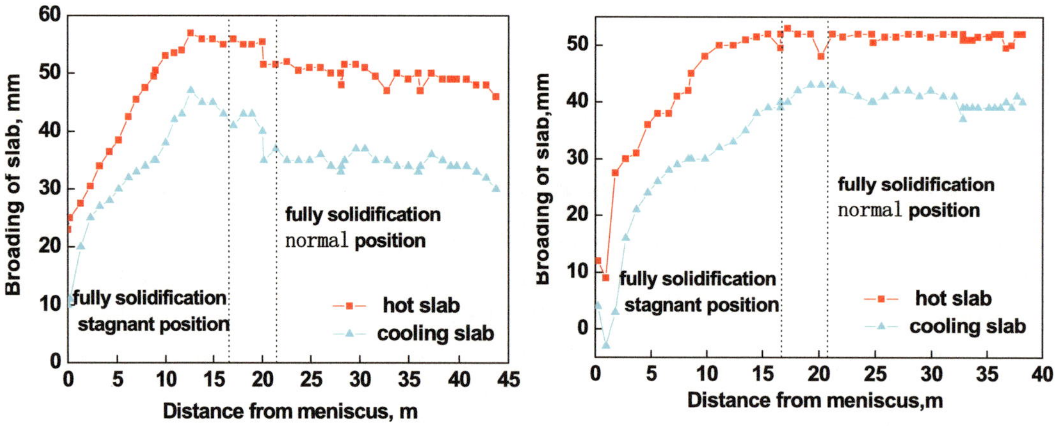

(a) (b)

Figure 15. (a) Absolute broadening of slab in the first strand of stagnant slab; (b) Absolute broadening of slab in the second strand of stagnant slab.(FU JianXun et al.2011(a))

Slab broadening mainly happened in the front 6 segments (before 12.6 m). In these sectors, the broadening increases linearly with the distance from the meniscus. At the position of

12.6 m, the slab broadening was at its maximum, and then decreased slowly with distance from the meniscus. These results confirm that the stress of the roller is not the main reason for broadening. Otherwise, the slab broadening will happen before the slab is fully solidified near the 9th and 10th segments. The trend of slab broadening is consistent with that of the static pressure of molten steel, which confirms that the slab broadening is dependent on the static pressure of molten steel.

7. Mechanism of slab broadening

The static pressure of molten steel deforms the slab shell. The coupled thermo-mechanical viscoelastic-plastic 3D finite element model was built with the secondary development of the commercial software MSC.Marc. The calculated and measured results of slab width are shown in Figure 16.

The figure reveals that the calculated deformation agrees very well with the measured deformation. Slab broadening is the result of slab deformation under the pressure of static melting at high temperature. The deformation of the slab in the direction of thickness is shown in Figure 17(a). The temperature field of the slab is shown in Figure 17(b).

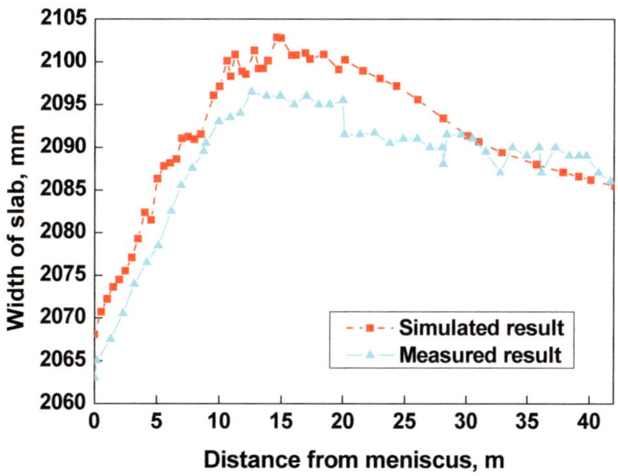

Figure 16. Simulated and measured widths of slab;(FU JianXun et al.2011(a))

The on-site investigation, force analysis, calculation from Maxwell creep model, and numerical simulation from the coupled thermo-mechanical viscoelastic-plastic 3D finite element model reveal that the slab broadening is due to slab deformation under the static pressure of molten steel. The slab shell deforms without constraints on the narrow side.

Creep deformation appears when the material plastic gradually deforms with time under certain conditions. Plastic deformation only happens when the stress exceeds the elastic limit. However, creep deformation happens when the acting time of stress is sufficiently long, even if the stress is very small. The creep deformation of metal is obvious only if the temperature is over the creep temperature (about 0.3 T_m). The slab deforms for a long time under the pressure of static molten steel at high temperature. The creep rate depends on the composition of the compound metal, and the processes of refining and thermal treatment. Creep deformation causes slab broadening because it makes the material keep stress relaxed, reduces hardness, and enhances plasticity.

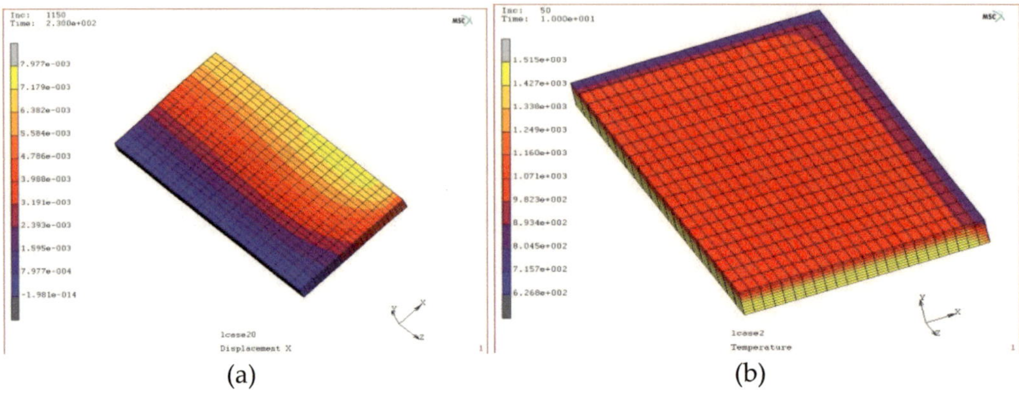

Figure 17. (a) Deformation of slab in the direction of thickness at 230 mm; (b) Temperature field of slab at 1150 s. (FU JianXun et al. 2010(c))

The amount of broadening depends on the forces acting on the slab and the properties of the slab material, especially those at high temperature. Specifically, it depends on the static pressure of molten steel, the high-temperature mechanical properties of steel, the composition of the slab material, the thickness of the slab shell, secondary cooling intensity, casting speed, and the constitution of the caster.

The static pressure of molten steel is the driving force for the deformation of the slab shell. It is related to the type and constitution of caster. At present, vertical-bending casters are most common. For these casters, the static pressure is related to the density of molten steel and the height of the caster.

Under the conditions of high casting speed and constant cooling water, the fully solidified zone extend, the length of molten core increases, and the shell becomes thinner. Because of the higher temperature, the slab shell also has lower yield strength and better malleability. Consequently, the slab broadening increases. However, if the cooling water supply is changed when the casting speed is increased, the problem will become sophisticated.

The effects of steel grade on the broadening result from differences in material properties at high temperature, and hence differences in resistance to plastic deformation and creep deformation. With an increase in the carbon percentage, the ratio of ferrolite and austenite in the two phase regions changes. The increase in austenite is helpful to the reduction of slab broadening.

Intracell dislocation climb and intercell slide are two forms of creep deformation. Solution strengthening, precipitation strengthening, and dispersion strengthening insert a lot of defects into the crystal structure of steel, which hinder dislocation movement and thus reinforce steel. Thus, micro-alloying of steel could enhance the hardness of the slab and reduce slab broadening.

In summary, higher casting speed, lower intensity of secondary cooling, thinner slab shell, larger static pressure of molten steel, and lower hardness of steel at high temperature increase slab broadening.

8. Conclusion

1. The mechanism of slab broadening is that the slab with high temperature exposes to no constraint at the direction of narrow face, and because of the static pressure of molten steel, the slab deforms in this direction.
2. Slab broadening is a common problem in continuous casting. The average RUB for the three grades of steel studied was in the range of 1.27%~3.00%, with a maximum of 4.4%.
3. Stagnant slab measurement experiments reveal that slab broadening happens in the 6 front segments, and that roller compaction is not responsible for slab broadening.
4. The agreement between the calculated results from the Maxwell model and the measured results illustrates that the Maxwell model is able to reveal the deformation behavior of a slab at high temperature.
5. Higher casting speed, lower intensity of secondary cooling, thinner slab shell, larger static pressure of molten steel, and lower hardness of steel at high temperature increase slab broadening. The micro-alloying of steel improves the hardness of the slab and reduces slab broadening.

Author details

Jian-Xun Fu and Weng-Sing Hwang
Research Center for Energy Technology and Strategy & Department of Materials Science and Engineering, National Cheng Kung University, Tainan 701, Taiwan

Acknowledgement

The authors gratefully acknowledge the guidance of Prof. Jingshe Li, Prof. Hui Zhang, Prof. Xingzhong Zhang, et al. The authors would like to thank the National Science Council of Taiwan (NSC100-2221-E-006-091-MY3) for funding this work.

9. References

Chen J. Hand Book of Continuous Casting (in Chinese). Beijing: Metallurgical Industry Press, 1990,

Fu JianXun, Li Jingshe, Zhang Hui, Zhang Xing-zhong. Industrial Research on broadening of slab in continuous casting. JOURNAL OF RON AND STEEL RESEARC INTERNATIONAL. 2010. 17(8):20-24,

Fu JianXun, Li Jingshe, Zhang Hui, Zhang Xingzhng, Mechanism of broadening of slab in the secondary cooling zone of continuous casting. SCIENCE CHINA- Technological Sciences. 54 (2011), No.5: 1228–1233,

Fu JianXun, LI Jingshe, ZHANG Hui,. Effects of Width and Thickness of Sab on Broadening in Continuous Casting. International Journal of Minerals, Metallurgy and Materials. 17 (2010), No. 6, 723,

Fu JianXun, Li Jingshe, Zhang Hui, Viscoelastic–Plastic Analysis of Broadening of Slab in the Secondary Cooling Zone of Continuous Casting. Acta Metallurgica Sinica, 46 (2010), No. 1, 91-96 (in chinese),

Jian-Xun Fu, Weng-Sing Hwang, Jing-she Li, and Zhang Hui. Effect of Casting Speed on Slab Broadening in Continuous Casting. steel research int. 2011 (82) No. 11. 1266- 1272,

I.Ohnaka. Mathematical Analysis of solute redistribution during solidification with diffusion in solid phase. Transactions of ISIJ, 1986, 26: 1045-1051,

K. Sorimachi, J. K. Brimacombe: Ironmak Steelmak, 1977; 4: 240,

Lei H, Yang L D, Zeng J, et al. Discussion of computational methods for the forces incurred in the bending phase in slab casting (in Chinese).Heavy Mach, 2007, (3): 41–45,

Lin Q Y, Jiang H J, Zhu M Y. Analysis of reduction parameters of dynamic soft reduction in continuous casting. J Mater Metall, 2004, 3(4): 261–265,

Miyazawa K, Schwerdtfeger K. Computation of Bulging of Continuously Cast Slab With Simple Bending Theory. Ironmaking and Steelmaking, 1979(2) : 68,

Mizukami H , Murakami K, Miyashita Y. Mechanical Proper ties of Continuously Cast Steel at High Temperatures [J]. Tetsu-to-Hagane. 1977. 63: 146 (in Japanese),

Ramacciotti A. Thermo-Mechanical Behavior of the Solidified Shell in a Funnel-Shaped Mold for Continuous Casting of Thin Slabs rJ1. Steel Research, 1988. 5gr 438,

Sheng Y, Sun J, Zhang M. Calculation for bulging deformation of continuously casting slab (in Chinese). Iron Steel, 1993, 28(3): 20–25,

S. Kobayashi, T. Nagamichi and K. Gunji: Transactions of ISIJ, 28(1988), 543,

Sun J, Sheng Y, Zhang X. Analysis of bulging deformation and stress in continuous cast slabs (in chinese). J Iron Steel Res, 1996, 8 (1): 11–15,

Uehara M. Samarasekera I V, Brimacornbe J K. Mathematical Modeling of Unbending of Continuously Cast Steel Slabs. Ironmaking and Steelmaking, 1986(12) : 138,

Ueshima Y, Mizoguchi S, Matsumiya T, et al. Analysis of solute distribution in dendrites of carbon steel with δ/γ transformation during solidification. Metallurgical and Materials Transactions B, 1986, 17B(4): 845-859,

Xiong Yi-gang. Continuous Casting of Slab [M]. Beijing: Metallurgical Industry Press, 1994 (in Chinese),

Y. S. Xi and H. H. Chen: MSC.Marc Manual for Analysis Using Temperature Field and the Coupled Field, MSC. Software user manual, 2001 (Iin Chinese),

Chapter 24

3D Finite Element Simulation of T-Joint Fillet Weld: Effect of Various Welding Sequences on the Residual Stresses and Distortions

Nur Syahroni and Mas Irfan Purbawanto Hidayat

Additional information is available at the end of the chapter

http://dx. doi. org/10. 5772/50192

1. Introduction

Due to the nature of welding process involving localized heat generation from moving heat source (s), rapid heating in the welded structures, and subsequent rapid cooling, problems such as residual stresses and distortions of welded structures remain great challenges to welding practitioners, designers and modeler. From modeling point of view, it will be very useful if the parameters of interest which contribute to the residual stresses and distortions in various types of welded joint and structure application can be simulated numerically so that welding performance with respect to the various aspects could be assessed and evaluated in an efficient manner (Goldak & Akhlagi, 2005; Lindgren, 2006; and Zacharia et al., 1995). Thorough consideration and assessment of the welding quality could then also be performed in earlier stage in a virtual environment. Moreover, dimensional inaccuracies due to the welding deformation giving rise problems in subsequent assembly and fabrication processes could also be predicted along with the necessary justification needed.

In recent years, various aspects and interests in the numerical modeling of welding residual stresses and distortions, mostly using finite element method, have been elaborated by researchers. Teng & Lin (1998) predicted the residual stresses during one-pass arc welding in steel plate using ANSYS software and discussed the effects of travel speed, specimen size, external mechanical constraints and preheating on the residual stresses. Tsai et al. (1999) studied the distortion mechanisms and the effect of welding sequence on panel distortion and utilized 2D finite element model. Residual stresses and distortions in T-joint fillet welds with the effects of flange thickness, welding penetration depth and restraint condition of welding was simulated by Teng et al. (2001) using thermal elasto-plastic finite element techniques. Further, effect of welding sequences on residual stresses of multi-pass butt-welds and circular patch welds was also investigated by Teng et al. (2003). Moreover, Chang & Lee (2009) performed the finite element analysis of the residual stresses in T-joint fillet welds made of similar and dissimilar steels.

The present study extends the previous work of Teng et al. (2001) and focuses on numerical simulation of welding sequence effect on temperature distribution, residual stresses and distortions of T-joint fillet welds. Several welding sequences were considered and the resulted distribution of welding temperature, longitudinal and transverse residual stresses and angular distortions were simulated utilizing three dimensional finite element models. Four welding sequences considered were one direction welding, contrary direction welding, welding from centre of one side and welding from centres of two sides. Further, a welding sequence producing the smallest residual stress, distortion as well as distortion difference between both flanges was then investigated. The numerical simulation was done in ANSYS environment.

2. Theoretical background

Basic mechanisms of welding residual stress and distortion together with the finite element formulations used in the 3D numerical simulation are described in the following sub-sections.

2.1. Basic mechanism of welding residual stresses

Complex heating and cooling cycles encountered in weldments lead to transient thermal stresses and incompatible strains produced in region near the weld. After heat cycles of welding diminished, the incompatible strains remain and provoking locked stresses or frequently termed as welding residual stresses. In general, term of residual stress deal with those remaining stress in a structure even though no external load applied (Masubuchi, 1980). Several terms having similar meaning with residual stress were found in some literatures, namely: internal stress, initial stress, inherent stress, reaction stress, lock-in stress, etc. In term of welding process, residual stress are the remaining internal stresses after welding and cooling down to room temperature.

There are two basic mechanisms to explain how residual stress produced by welding process, namely: the structural mismatch and the uneven distribution of non-elastic strain composed by plastic and thermal strains.

2.1.1. Residual stress due to mismatch

The residual stress mechanism due to mismatch may be simply illustrated in Fig. 1. Consider three carbon-steel bars of equal length and cross section connected together with two rigid blocks at the ends. The middle bar is heated up to 600°C and then cooled to room temperature while no applied heating on the other two bars. Since the expansion of the

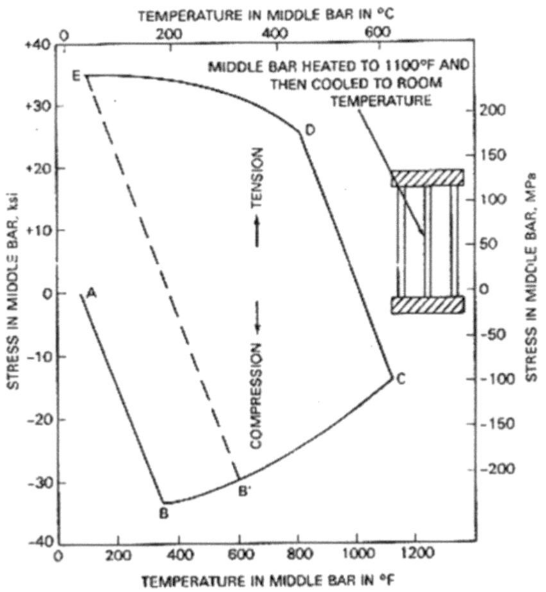

Figure 1. Illustration of residual stress mechanism in welding (source: Masubuchi, 1980)

middle bar is restricted by other bars, compressive stress is encountered at the middle bar and the two side bars are subjected to opposite tensile stress. The compressive stress on middle bar, increases in linear elastic manner when it is heated (AB curve) until the yield stress of material in particular temperature reached, then plastic deformation is encountered which affects in decreasing compressive stress (BC curve). During cooling stage, the stress sign in middle bar is dramatically changed from compressive to tension stress and increases in linear elastic way (CD curve) up to the yield stress at point D. Then, non-linear plastic behaviour takes place (DE curve) in room temperature resulting in a tensile residual stress in the middle bar and contrary a compressive residual stress in both side bars which are equal to one-half of tensile stress in the middle bar.

2.1.2. Residual stress due to uneven distribution of non-elastic strains

When a metal bar is subjected to a uniform heat, it produces a uniform expansion lead to no thermal stresses. However, when it is subjected to non-uniform heat as the case of welding, thermal stresses and strains will be formed. Residual stress field in plane stress condition ($\sigma_z = 0$) can be expressed by the following formulas:

- Elastic and plastic strains:

$$\begin{aligned} \varepsilon_x &= \varepsilon_x' + \varepsilon_x'', \\ \varepsilon_y &= \varepsilon_y' + \varepsilon_y'', \\ \gamma_{xy} &= \gamma_{xy}' + \gamma_{xy}''. \end{aligned} \qquad (1)$$

where:

$\varepsilon_x, \varepsilon_y, \gamma_{xy}$ is components of the total strain,

$\varepsilon'_x, \varepsilon'_y, \gamma'_{xy}$ is components of the elastic strains,

$\varepsilon''_x, \varepsilon''_y, \gamma''_{xy}$ is components of the plastic strains.

- Relationships of stress vs. elastic strain by Hooke's law:

$$\begin{aligned} \varepsilon_x' &= \frac{1}{E}\left(\sigma_x - \nu\sigma_y\right), \\ \varepsilon_y' &= \frac{1}{E}\left(\sigma_y - \nu\sigma_x\right), \\ \gamma_{xy}' &= \frac{1}{G}\tau_{xy}. \end{aligned} \tag{2}$$

- The stress must satisfy the equilibrium conditions:

$$\begin{aligned} \frac{\partial \sigma_x}{\partial x} + \frac{\partial \tau_{xy}}{\partial y} &= 0, \\ \frac{\partial \tau_{xy}}{\partial x} + \frac{\partial \sigma_y}{\partial y} &= 0. \end{aligned} \tag{3}$$

- The total strain must satisfy the conditions of compatibility:

$$\left[\frac{\partial^2 \varepsilon'_x}{\partial y^2} + \frac{\partial^2 \varepsilon'_y}{\partial x^2} - \frac{\partial^2 \gamma'_{xy}}{\partial x \partial y}\right] + \left[\frac{\partial^2 \varepsilon''_x}{\partial y^2} + \frac{\partial^2 \varepsilon''_y}{\partial x^2} - \frac{\partial^2 \gamma''_{xy}}{\partial x \partial y}\right] = 0. \tag{4}$$

The second term of Eq. (4), which is called the incompatibility term, *R,* is determined by plastic strain. When the value of R is not zero, thus residual stresses will exist in the weld joint.

$$R = -\left[\frac{\partial^2 \varepsilon''_x}{\partial y^2} + \frac{\partial^2 \varepsilon''_y}{\partial x^2} - \frac{\partial^2 \gamma''_{xy}}{\partial x \partial y}\right]. \tag{5}$$

More realistic illustration of the residual stress mechanisms during welding in typical plate joints is shown in Fig. 2. Welding bead is made along *x*-axis on the plate. Welding is carried out by moving the welding arc at speed *v,* and presently it is located at the origin O, as illustrated in Fig. 2a. Temperature distributions along particular points at weldline are shown in Fig. 2b, while stress resulted in the respect points are shown in Fig. 2c.

Along point A-A which is located ahead of the welding arc is not affected by heat yet. Section B-B experiences highest heat distribution (Fig. 2b. 2) which results in compressive stresses at just besides of weldline and surrounded by opposite tensile stresses in the side far

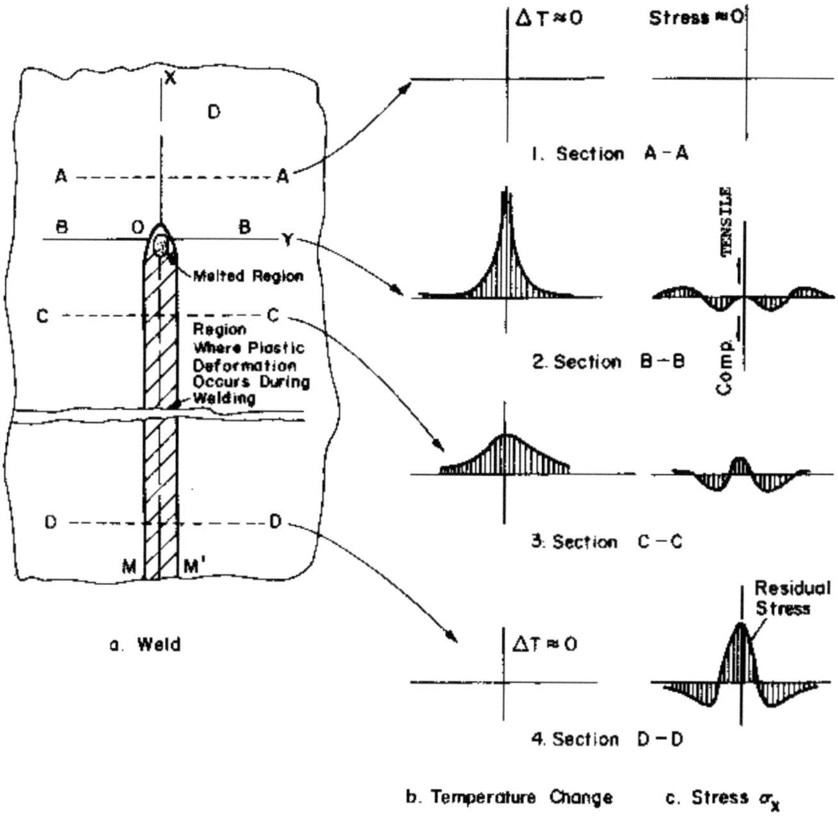

Figure 2. Schematic illustrations of heat cycles in welding and residual stress results (source: Masubuchi, 1980)

away from weld line, whilst at weldment has zero stress due to metal melted (Fig. 2c. 2). Section C-C which is located at some distance behind welding arc is subjected to moderate heat (Fig. 2b. 3) due to cooling stage started in this section in which the condition at this section is similar to those CD curve in Fig. 1. Some distance far away from heat source, cooling down into room temperature is achieved which results in residual stresses in similar way to those in the end of DE curve in Fig. 1.

Furthermore, typical distributions of butt joints in plate are presented in Fig. 3. Components of residual stress are categorized into transverse and longitudinal, designated as σ_x and $\sigma_y$respectively (Fig. 3a). Across the weldline, tensile residual stress in longitudinal direction parallel to the weldline is found in the weldment region and compressive residual stresses occur in the others region away from weldline (Fig. 3b). Transverse residual stresses distributions along weldline are typically compressive part in the ends of plate, otherwise are tensile part with magnitude of stresses is lower than longitudinal residual stress (Fig. 3c). Masubuchi & Martin (Masubuchi, 1980) have developed the distribution of longitudinal residual stress σ_x which can be estimated as follows:

$$\sigma_x = \sigma_m \left\{ 1 - \left(\frac{y}{b} \right)^2 \right\} e^{-\frac{1}{2}(y/b)^2} . \tag{6}$$

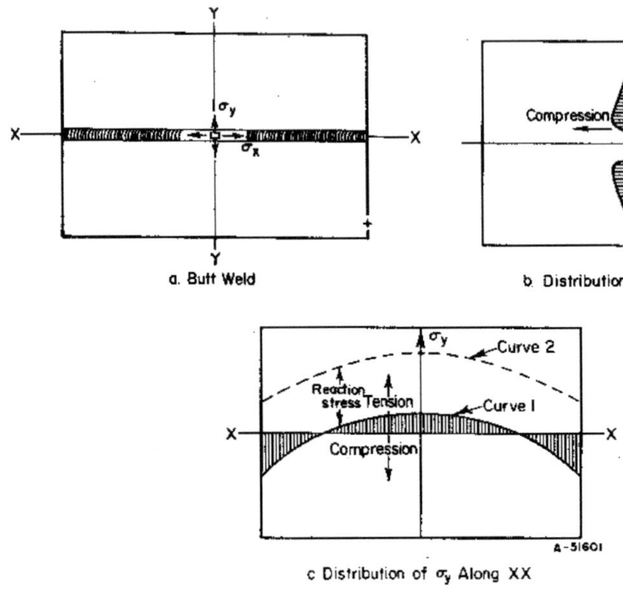

Figure 3. Typical distributions of residual stress in plate butt joints (source: Masubuchi, 1980)

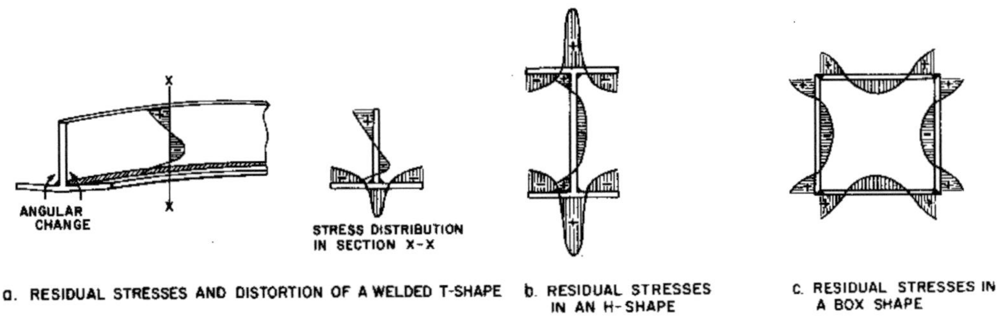

Figure 4. Typical residual stresses in welded structural profiles (source: Masubuchi, 1980)

Fig. 4a shows residual stresses produced in welded T-shape and the residual stresses distributions. As can be further seen, high tensile residual stresses parallel to the axis are produced in areas near the weld in section away from the end of the column. In addition, stresses in the flange are tensile near the weld and compressive away from the weld. The tensile stresses near the upper edge of web are due to longitudinal bending distortion caused by longitudinal shrinkage. Furthermore, Figs. 4b and 4c show the typical distribution of residual stress in an H-shape and a box shape, respectively, particularly the distributions of residual stresses parallel to the weld line, in which the residual stresses are tensile in areas near the welds and compressive in area away from the welds.

2.2. Welding distortions

Distortion is closely related to the amount of residual stress and the degree of joint restraint during welding process. The correlation between distortion and residual stress is illustrated in Fig. 5. As rule of thumb, the welded joint with lower degree of restraint has an advantage due to less residual stress but it tends to get higher distortion. Conversely, the welded joint with higher degree of restraint has less distortion but it will further result in higher residual stress.

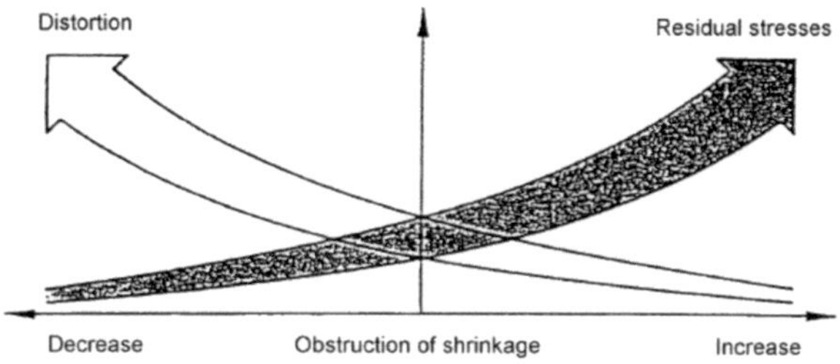

Figure 5. Welding residual stress and distortion correlation (source: Bette, 1999)

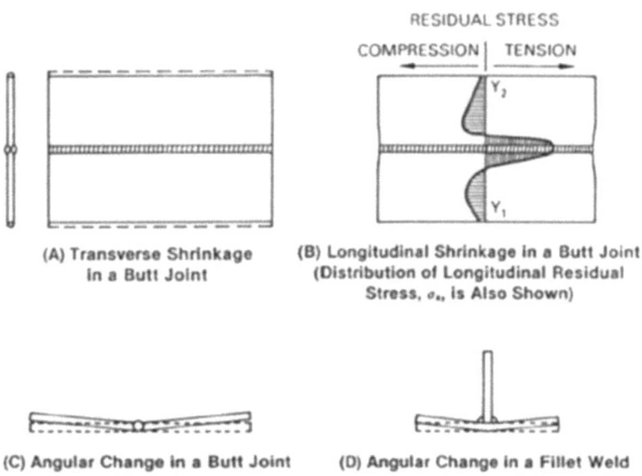

Figure 6. Three basic dimensional changes during welding (source: AWS Welding Handbook, 1987)

There are three basic dimensional changes during welding process with which we can easily understand the mechanism of distortion, namely:

- Transverse shrinkage, Fig. 6A, is a distortion perpendicular to the weld line
- Longitudinal shrinkage, Fig. 6B, is a distortion parallel to the weld line
- Angular change, in butt joint and T joint fillet weld, as shown in Figs. 6C and 6D, respectively, deformation in rotation form around the weld. It happens when the transverse shrinkage is not uniform in the thickness direction

In actual structures, the welding distortions are frequently more complex than these basic distortions or taking place with some conditions. For examples, pure transverse or longitudinal shrinkage will only take place when the following conditions apply, i. e.

thickness of member is large enough and centre of gravity of the welds is in line with the neutral axis of the components. When it is not the case, the rotational deformations such as the angular, bending and buckling distortion may be happened.

The empirical formula to estimate the quantity of transverse shrinkage of carbon and low alloy steel butt welds can be found in American Welding Society (AWS) Welding Handbook (1987) as follows:

$$S = 0.2\frac{A_w}{t} 0.05d. \tag{7}$$

where:

S is transverse shrinkage, in,
A_w is cross sectional area of weld, in^2,
t is thickness of plate, in,
d is root opening, in.

In fillet weld, the amount of transverse shrinkage is less than that happened in butt weld. The transverse shrinkage in fillet weld may be expressed by the following formulas found in AWS Welding Handbook (1987):

- For T-joint with two continuous fillet welds:

$$S = C_1\left(\frac{D_f}{t_b}\right). \tag{8}$$

where:

S is transverse shrinkage, in. or mm,
D_f is fillet leg length, in. or mm,
t is bottom plate thickness, in. or mm,
C_1 is 0. 04 or 1. 02 when using unit in. or mm, respectively.

- For lap joint with two fillet welds (the thickness of two plates are equal):

$$S = C_2\left(\frac{D_f}{t}\right). \tag{9}$$

where:

S is transverse shrinkage, in. or mm,
D_f is fillet leg length, in. or mm,
t is plate thickness, in. or mm,
C_2 is 0. 06 or 1. 52 when using unit in. or mm, respectively.

Compared to transverse shrinkage, the quantity of longitudinal shrinkage for butt joint is much less, approximately 1/1000 of the weld length. King, 1944 (as cited in AWS Welding

Handbook, 1987) proposed a formula to estimate the longitudinal shrinkage of butt joint as follows:

$$\Delta L = \frac{C_3 I L}{t} 10^{-7}. \tag{10}$$

where:

ΔL is longitudinal shrinkage, in. or mm,
I is welding current, A,
L isweld length, in. or mm,
t is plate thickness, in. or mm,
C_1 is 12 or 305 when using unit in. or mm, respectively.

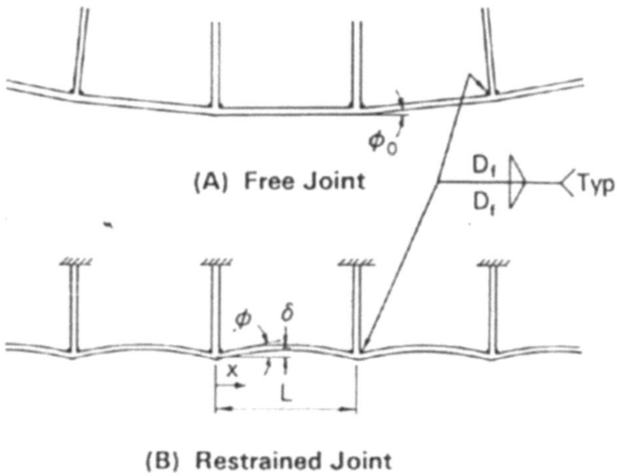

Figure 7. Angular change in T-joint fillet weld, (A) free restrained stiffeners, (B) restrained stiffeners

The primary source of angular change is due to non-uniform of transverse shrinkage in thickness direction. Fig. 7a shows angular change of the free restraint T-joint fillet weld. When the stiffeners are prevented from moving, a wavy distortion occurs as can be seen in Fig. 7b. Masubuchi et al., 1956 (as cited in AWS Welding Handbook, 1987) established a relationship between angular change and distortion at fillet weld using a rigid frame analysis in the following expression:

$$\frac{\delta}{L} = 0.25\phi - \left[\left(\frac{x}{L}\right) - 0.5\right]^2 \phi. \tag{11}$$

where:

δ is distortion,
L is length of stiffener spacing,
ϕ is angular change,
x is distance from centreline of frame to the point at which δ is measured, Fig. 7b.

To summary this section, many factors affect the welding process, thus the produced residual stresses and distortions, such as types of material, types of welded joints, structure thickness, joint restraint, heat input as well as welding sequence, which is the subject of the present study.

2.3. Thermal and Mechanical Finite Element Equations

The corresponding finite element equations of thermal and mechanical are obtained by choosing a form of interpolation function representing the variation of the field variables, namely temperature, *T* and displacement, *U*, within the corresponding finite elements of the structural model and by applying further the weighted-residual or variational argument to the mathematical models. Furthermore, with imposing the boundary and initial conditions, the discritized equations obtained are solved by finite element techniques through which the approximated solution over the finite element model considered could then be obtained.

The thermal finite element equation including boundary condition may be written as follows:

$$[C]\{\dot{T}\}+[K]\{T\}=\{F_T\}, \tag{12}$$

in which:

$$[C]=\int_V \varrho c[N]^T[N]dV, \tag{13}$$

$$[K]=\int_V k[B]^T[B]dV + \int_S h_f[N]^T[N]dS, \tag{14}$$

$$\{F_T\}=\int_V Q[N]^T dV + \int_S h_f T_{ref}[N]^T dS. \tag{15}$$

where:

ρ is the density (kg/m^3),
c is the specific heat (J/kg. K),
k isthe conductivity (W/m. K),
h_f is the convective heat transfer coefficient (W/m^2. K),
Q isthe rate of internal heat generation per unit volume (W/m^3),
[N] is the matrix of element shape functions,
[B] is the matrix of shape functions derivative, and
$\{T\}$ is the vector of nodal temperature.

The results of temperature distribution and history obtained from Eq. (12) are then inserted into the mechanical model in the form of thermal load. Incorporating the elasto-plasticity analysis, the mechanical finite element equation may be written in the form of incremental as:

$$^{i+1}\left[K_1\right]\left\{\Delta U\right\} - {}^{i+1}\left[K_2\right]\left\{\Delta T\right\} = {}^{i+1}\left\{R\right\} - {}^{i}\left\{R\right\}, \tag{16}$$

in which:

$$\left[K_1\right] = \int_V \left[B\right]^T \left[D^{ep}\right]\left[B\right] dV, \tag{17}$$

$$\left[K_2\right] = \int_V \left[B\right]^T \left[C^{th}\right]\left[M\right] dV, \tag{18}$$

$$\left\{R\right\} = \int_S \left[N\right]^T \left\{p\right\} dS + \int_V \left[N\right]^T \left\{f\right\} dV, \tag{19}$$

$$\left[D^{ep}\right] = \left[D^e\right] + \left[D^p\right]. \tag{20}$$

where:

$\{\Delta U\}$ is the incremental of nodal displacement,
$\{\Delta T\}$ is the incremental of nodal temperature,
[B] is the matrix of strain-displacement,
$[D^e]$ is the matrix of elastic stiffness,
$[D^p]$ is the matrix of plastic stiffness,
$[C^{th}]$ is the matrix of thermal stiffness,
[M] is the temperature shape function,
$\{p\}$ is the vector of traction or surface force,
$\{f\}$ is the vector of body force, and
i is the current step of analysis.

The vector of nodal displacement at the next step of analysis, $^{i+1}\{U\}$ could be obtained from:

$$^{i+1}\left\{U\right\} = {}^{i}\left\{U\right\} + \left\{\Delta U\right\}. \tag{21}$$

Furthermore, the updated condition of stress in the structure could be obtained from the following stress-strain relation:

$$^{i+1}\left\{\sigma\right\} = {}^{i}\left\{\sigma\right\} + \left\{\Delta\sigma\right\}, \tag{22}$$

$$\left\{\Delta\sigma\right\} = \left[D^{ep}\right]\left[B\right]\left\{\Delta U\right\} + \left[C^{th}\right]\left[M\right]\left\{\Delta T\right\}. \tag{23}$$

Commonly, the iterative method of Newton-Raphson is employed in the finite element solver to solve the nonlinear equations. For further treatment, see (Bathe, 1996). Note also that from the thermal analysis results, the updated stress and displacement conditions are now obtained.

3. Material and methods

In this study, material used for the welding simulation was SAE 1020 with the material properties vary according to the temperature history (Teng et al, 2001 and ASM, 1990). In addition, the welding parameters used in this analysis were as follows: single pass GTAW welding method, welding current, $I = 260$ A, welding voltage, $V = 20$ V, and welding speed, $v = 5$ mm/s.

3.1. The variations of welding sequence

Several welding sequences (WS) were considered in this study and the numerical investigation of the resulted temperature distribution, longitudinal and transverse residual stresses and angular distortions due to the welding sequences was then carried out. Four welding sequences considered were the one direction welding (WS-1), the contrary direction welding (WS-2), the welding from centre of one side (WS-3), and the welding from centres of two sides (WS-4), which are illustrated in Fig. 8.

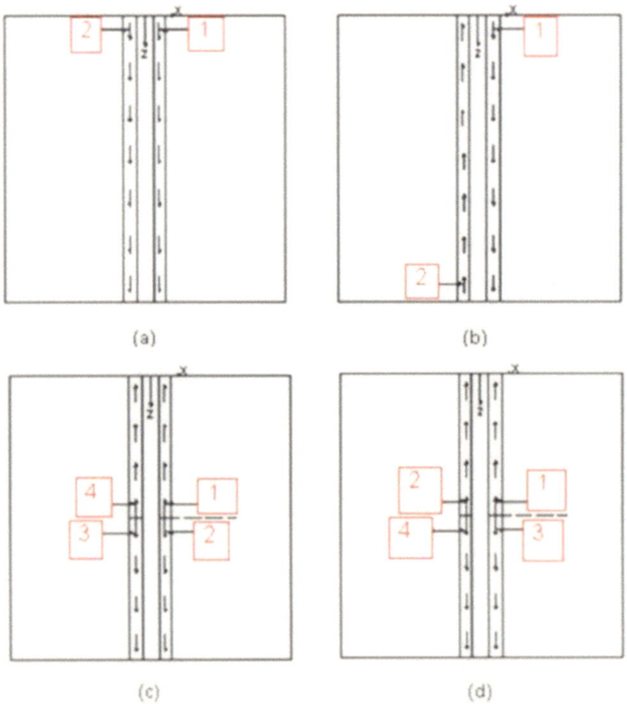

Figure 8. Variation of welding sequence employed in this study: (a) the one direction welding (WS-1), (b) the contrary direction welding (WS-2), (c) the welding from centre of one side (WS-3), and (d) the welding from centres of two sides (WS-4).

3. 2. Finite element simulation of welding

In the present study, a thermal elasto-plastic finite element procedure was employed to simulate the thermo-mechanical response of welding problem. In the procedure, two sequenced thermal and mechanical analyses were carried out independently (uncoupled) to obtain the total or desired response of the welding structure modelled.

A transient thermal analysis of heat conduction was carried out in the first step to obtain temperature distribution histories over the structural model. In the thermal analysis, the welding heat input, Q_a was calculated according to Masubuchi (1980) and the arc efficiency, η_a for GTAW was assumed to be 0. 60 (Grong, 1994). Also, the values of convective heat transfer coefficient, h_f and reference temperature were taken, respectively, to be 15 W/m^2. K and 25°C (298. 15 K).

In the next step, a structural analysis was carried out to now obtain the mechanical response of the structural model, where the temperature history obtained from the first step was employed as a thermal load in the analysis. The material model of elasto-plastic based on the von Mises yield criterion and isotropic strain hardening rule was chosen, in which its response over the history was determined by the temperature-dependent material properties inputted. The boundary condition or constraint on the structural model needs also to be assigned accordingly.

Fig. 9 represents the mesh of T-joint fillet weld employed in this study along with the position of constraint assigned on the finite element model. The total number of nodes and elements utilized for the 3D model were 3654 and 2961, respectively. The analyses were implemented in ANSYS environment utilizing the element type of SOLID70 for the thermal analysis and that of SOLID45 for the structural analysis.

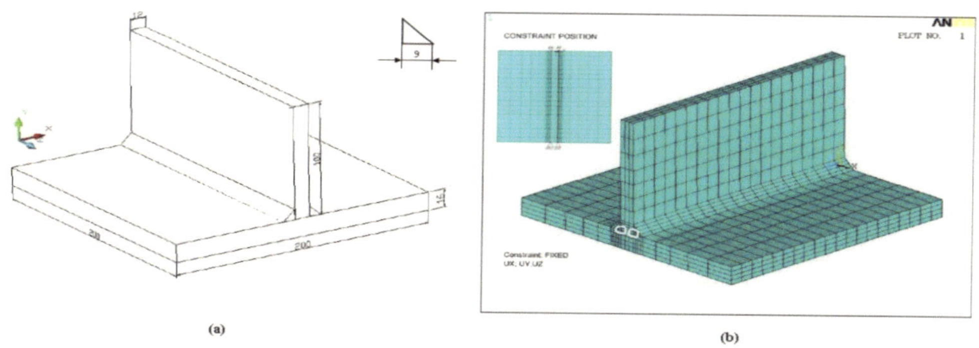

Figure 9. (a) Geometry of T-joint fillet welds, (b) Mesh of T-joint fillet weld along with its constraint position.

4. Results and discussion

With the finite element procedures described in the previous section, results on the problem considered are presented in this section. The finite element simulation for all the variation of welding was completed in 45 load-steps (LS). During the number of load-steps, the welding process took for 40 load-steps, while the cooling one took for the rest of the LS. For the presentation of welding simulation, the results of the LS which respectively represent the conditions of the peak temperature and the beginning of cooling processes were taken and plotted. Note that the temperature went down towards the reference (room) temperature after the LS of 41. Accordingly, the longitudinal and transverse residual stresses and the distortions occurred due to the welding sequences were presented and discussed.

4.1. Welding simulations and temperature distributions

First, thermal profile produced during welding as the heat source travels is presented as shown in Fig. 10. Fig. 10 represents the thermal profiles on several selected nodes along one fillet weld taken from WS-1 simulation results. It was shown that heat was moving as the welding heat source travelled. This can also be seen from the high temperature of the next adjacent node when the previous node has achieved its peak temperature. In addition, the next adjacent node's peak temperature was higher than that of the previous one, which also indicated that heat was accumulated. Subsequently, it has been distributed through the welding structure and the heat release to the surroundings was due to convective heat transfer.

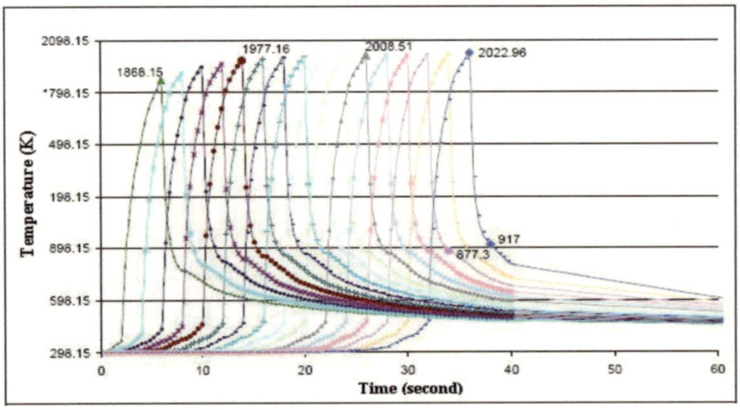

Figure 10. Thermal profiles on several selected nodes along the fillet weld.

Figs. 11 - 14 illustrate the welding simulation showing the peak temperature for each welding sequence and the temperature distribution after welding towards the room temperature. From the temperature distributions, it is clear that the peak temperature achieved in the welding was greatly affected by the welding sequence. The welding sequences produced different interaction between the current step and the accumulation of heat carried out from the previous steps due to the sequential path followed.

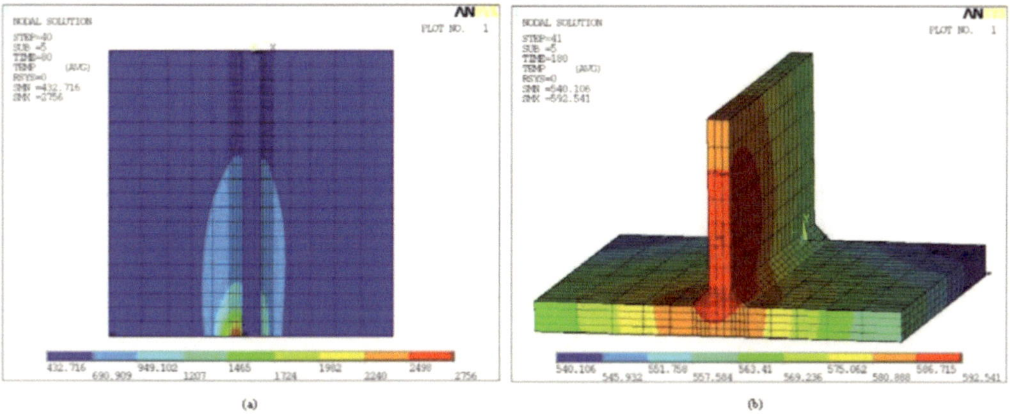

Figure 11. The welding simulation for WS-1: (a) the peak temperature achieved at the LS of 40, and (b) the temperature distribution after the welding process at the LS of 41.

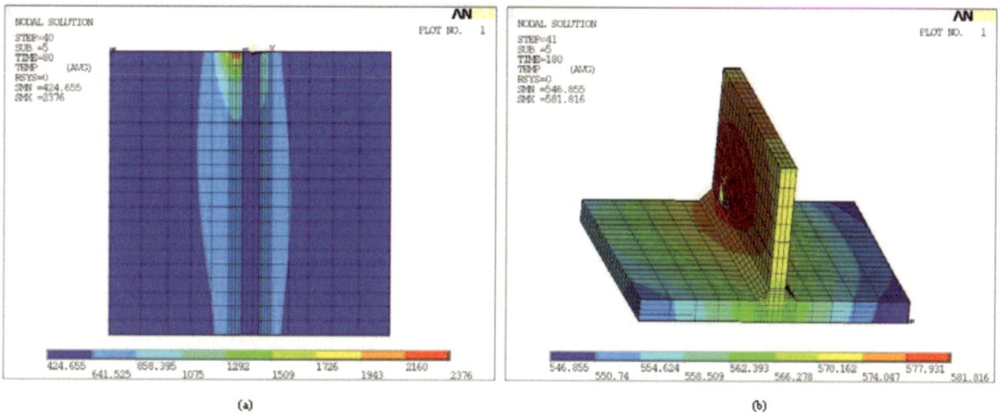

Figure 12. The welding simulation for WS-2: (a) the peak temperature achieved at the LS of 40, and (b) the temperature distribution after the welding process at the LS of 41.

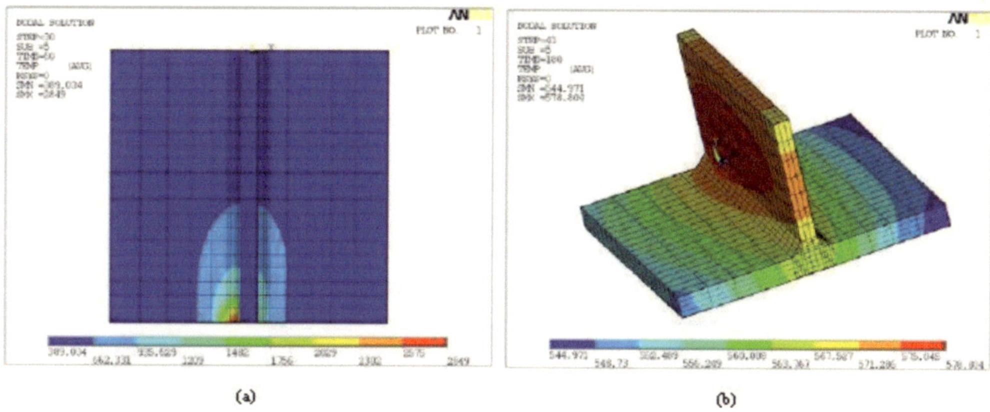

Figure 13. The welding simulation for WS-3: (a) the peak temperature achieved at the LS of 30, and (b) the temperature distribution after the welding process at the LS of 41.

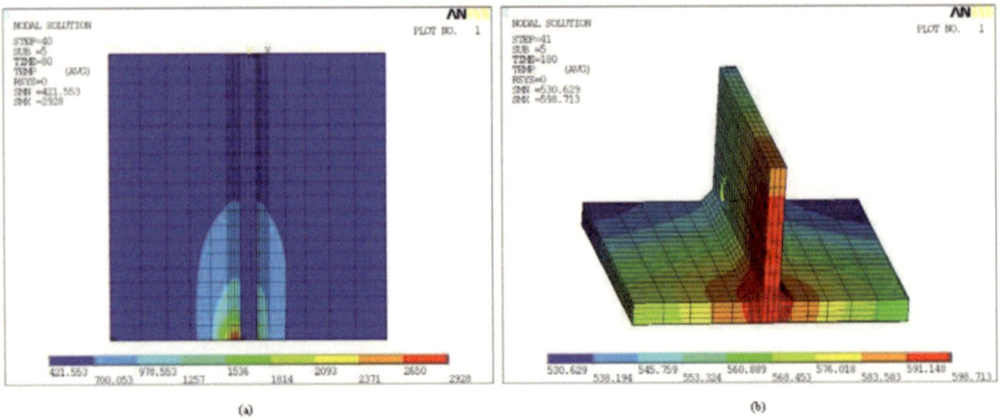

Figure 14. The welding simulation for WS-4: (a) the peak temperature achieved at the LS of 40, and (b) the temperature distribution after the welding process at the LS of 41.

The peak temperature achieved for each welding sequence as well as the peak temperature difference between WS were summarized in Table 1, in which the highest peak temperature of 2928 K belongs to WS-4 having the highest heat accumulation at the end of the welding process. The shapes of the temperature profile at the fillet welds during welding were depicted in Fig. 15.

From Fig. 15, it can be seen the differences of the temperature profile at the fillet welds during different WS. It is interesting to note that in general the temperature profiles of WS-1 and WS-2 tend to be similar. In a less extent, it also happened for those of WS-3 and WS-4, as the peak temperature of WS-3 was achieved at the LS of 30. Nevertheless, the peak temperature achieved was very different, even for the WS having similar temperature profiles such as WS-1 and WS-2. This verified again that the peak temperature achieved in the welding was greatly affected by the welding sequence.

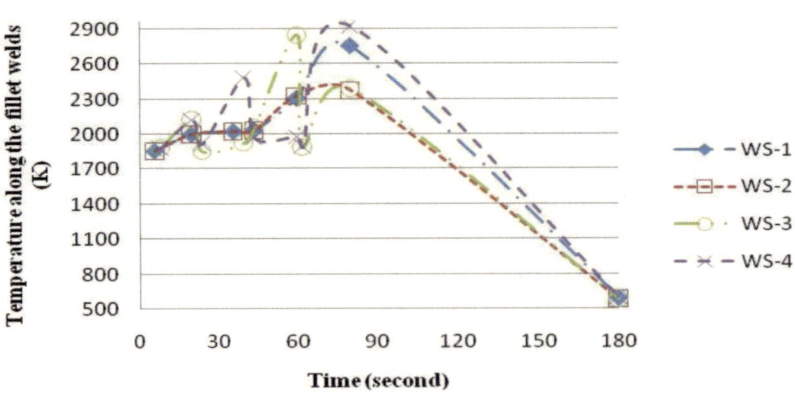

Figure 15. Peak temperature for each welding sequence.

Table 1 describes further the peak temperature achieved in a WS and the peak temperature difference between WS, in which the smallest and largest peak temperature differences between WS were 79 and 552 K, respectively.

Moreover, it may be also interesting to note how the peak temperature achieved in a WS may be related to the corresponding residual stresses and angular distortions produced.

Welding sequence (WS)	Load-step (LS)	The peak temperature achieved [K]	The peak temperature difference between WS [K]
4	40	2928	-
3	30	2849	79
1	40	2756	93
2	40	2376	380

Table 1. The peak temperature achieved for each welding sequence.

4. 2. Residual stress distributions

Fig. 16 and 17 shows respectively the simulated distributions of longitudinal and transverse residual stresses for each welding sequence investigated in this study. It is seen from Fig. 16 and 17, the maximum values of the longitudinal and transverse residual stresses occurred in the weld bead region for all the welding sequences. Note also that the distribution of the residual stresses produced from each of the welding sequences.

It can be seen that the smallest longitudinal and transverse residual stresses occurred in WS-2. It is interesting to note that the welding sequence also had the lowest peak temperature as indicated in Table 1. Also, for longitudinal residual stresses, their distributions due to the welding sequences tend to be similar. For transverse ones, the distributions were different. It seems that for the later, it could be related to the way of the welding had been performed.

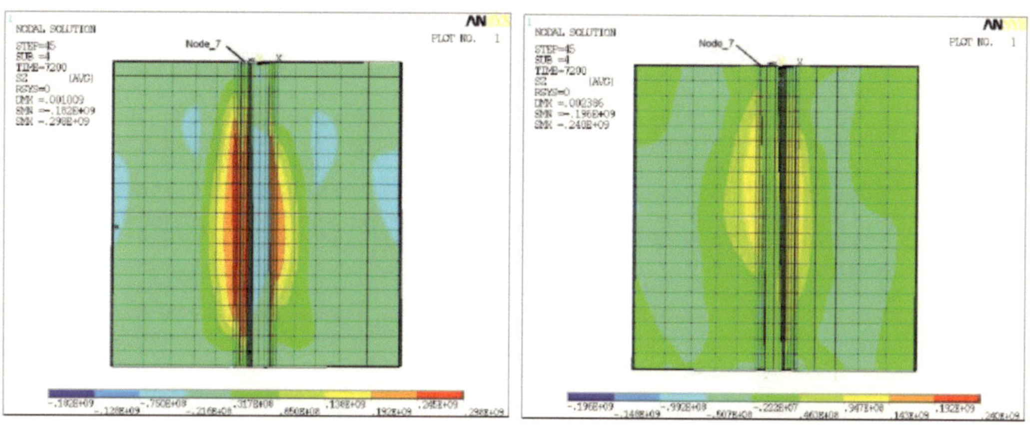

(a) (b)

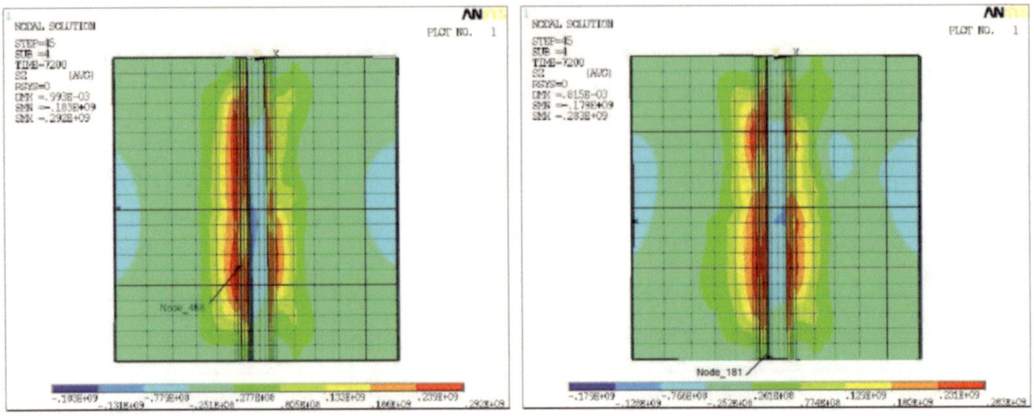

(c) (d)

Figure 16. Simulated distributions of longitudinal residual stresses for: (a) WS-1, (b) WS-2, (c) WS-3, and (d) WS-4.

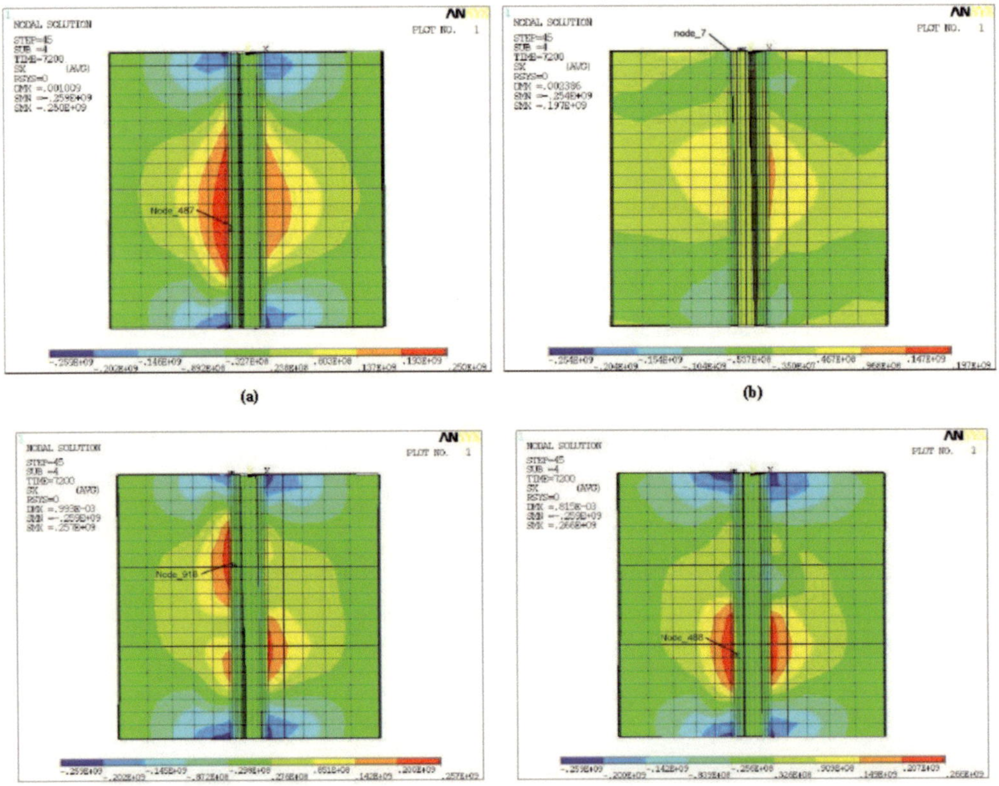

(a) (b) (c) (d)

Figure 17. Simulated distributions of transverse residual stresses for: (a) WS-1, (b) WS-2, (c) WS-3, and (d) WS-4.

Fig. 18 describes the transverse residual stress distribution along the fillet weld for each WS. The maximum values of longitudinal and transverse stresses as well as von Mises stress for each welding sequence were summarized in Table 2. The ratio between the longitudinal and the transverse residual stress values for the problem considered varies from 1. 06 to 1. 22.

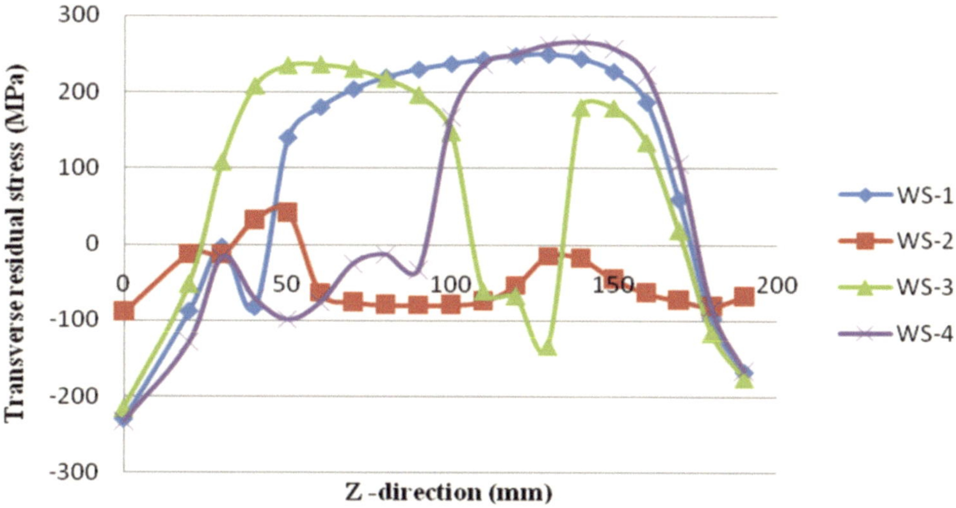

Figure 18. Distribution of transverse residual stress along the fillet weld for each welding sequence.

Observing further Fig. 18, it is also interesting to note the consistency of trends of the transverse residual stresses distributions produced by the WS simulated in the present study. It can be clearly observed that the distributions of transverse residual stresses produced by WS-3 and WS-4 and WS-1 and WS-2, respectively, are in consistent nature with respect to the welding sequences.

Welding sequence (WS)	The maximum longitudinal stress value [MPa]	The maximum transverse stress value [MPa]	The maximum von Mises stress value [MPa]
2	240	197	117
4	283	266	251
3	292	257	249
1	298	250	250

Table 2. The maximum longitudinal and transverse stress values for each welding sequence.

4.3. Distortions

Fig. 19 illustrates the distortions of the welding structure due to the welding sequences. The initial undeformed configurations were also shown. From Fig. 19, it can be seen the angular distortions occurred in both flanges. It can be further revealed that there was the difference of distortion between the flanges showing that the distortion was unsymmetrical. The maximum value of angular distortion took place on the right flange for all the welding sequences, unless that of WS-2 which took place on the left one. The simulation results obtained also clearly indicate the influence of the welding sequences examined in the present study to the angular distortions of the T-joint fillet weld considering the same boundary conditions appliedin the corresponding FEM models of the T-joint fillet weld.

Furthermore, Table 3 summarizes the vertical displacements and the angular distortions of both flanges due to the welding sequences. The angular distortion differences were also shown in Table 3.

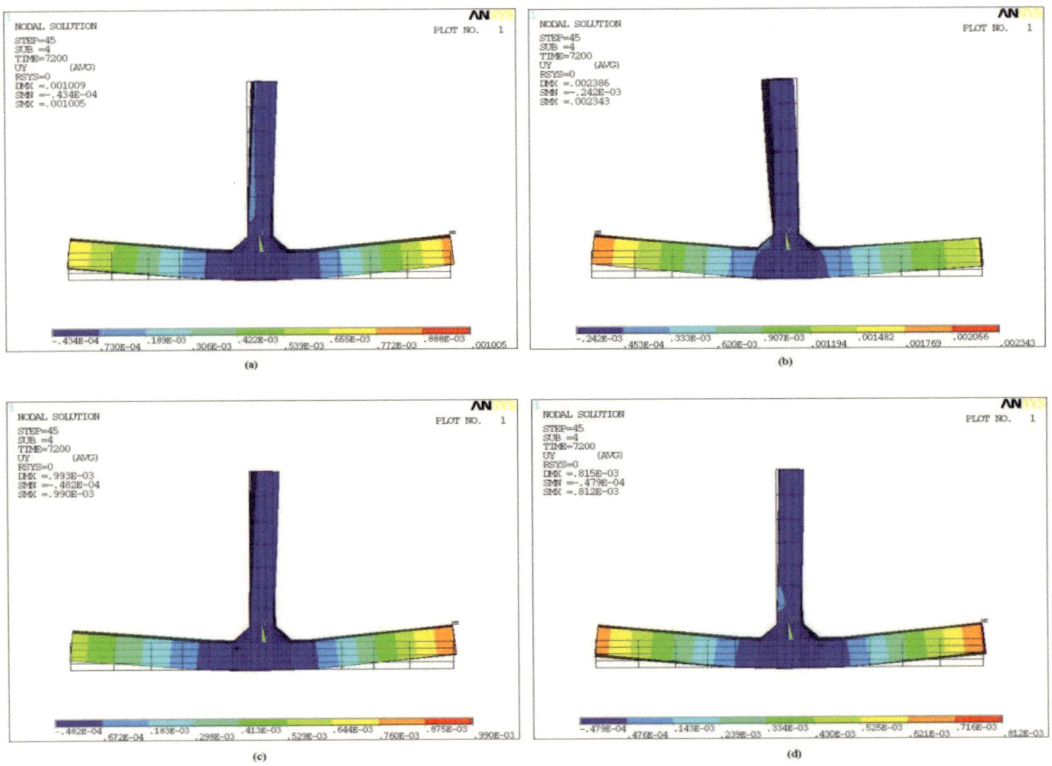

Figure 19. Distortions of the welding structure due to the welding sequences: (a) WS-1, (b) WS-2, (c) WS-3, and (d) WS-4.

Welding sequence (WS)	The left flange (X = -100 mm)		The right flange (X = 100 mm)		Angular distortion difference [rad]
	Uy [mm]	Angular distortion [rad]	*Uy* [mm]	Angular distortion [rad]	
1	0. 897	0. 0090	1. 005	0. 0101	0. 0011
3	0. 755	0. 0076	0. 990	0. 0099	0. 0023
2	2. 344	0. 0240	0. 897	0. 0090	0. 0150
4	0. 783	0. 0078	0. 812	0. 0081	0. 0003

Table 3. The vertical displacements and the angular distortions of both flanges due to the WS.

4.4. Discussions and recommendation for further research

From the results, it seems that, for the problem considered in this numerical study, two welding sequences, namely WS-2 and WS-4, have taken the attention. The WS-2, which is called as simple alternating welding, has produced the lowest peak temperature and the smallest longitudinal and transverse residual stresses as well. Meanwhile the WS-4, which is called as multiple crossing welding, has produced the smallest angular distortion and angular distortion difference, although it produced the highest peak temperature.

The information appears to be consistent with respect to the welding sequences performed. The corresponding value of the von Mises stress and the distortion difference produced as shown respectively in Table 2 and 3 indicated this as well. In particular, the results were also in contrast to those of WS-1 and WS-3. Not only did the welding sequences produce high angular distortions, but also they resulted in relatively high values of the von Mises stresses. Furthermore, the distortion results obtained appears to be match with the ones usually found in the welding practice incorporating alternating welding.

Also, considering limited literatures concerning welding simulation of T-joint fillet welds in 3D (Chang & Lee, 2009 and Deng et al., 2007), the results obtained would be very valuable and useful to welding designers and practitioners, because the results have been describing the predicted or anticipated residual stresses and distortions with respect to the welding sequences, varied from simple to multiple crossing welding. In addition, the assessment of welding performance which can be taken in an efficient and fast manner allows the designers to integrate it in their subsequent design plans.

Furthermore, the 3D simulation results of T-joint fillet weld may be further used as validation model for 3D welding simulations as well as for other numerical technique implementations such as mesh-less techniques, where no predefined mesh is required to build interpolation of the potential field variables investigated thus reducing cumbersome mesh preparation and increasing the related simulation time.

Moreover, the relationship between the input and output variables of the welding process may be further investigated and optimized using techniques from artificial intelligence (AI) family, such as neural networks and genetic algorithm. For examples, in the single pass GTAW welding method presented in this study, the variables of welding current, voltage, welding speed and welding sequences have been examined, in which more output variables may be also examined, such as the nature and dimensions of weld bead. Thus, much more information and insights can be revealed in such a welding process, which is in turn very useful to optimize the welding process.

It is noted here that the aspects of shrinkage were not discussed in the present paper. The aspects could be also related to the variation of welding speed. Also, it may be interesting if some welding paths in one WS are performed and simulated simultaneously thus allowing the exploitation of symmetry and anti-symmetry boundary conditions in the finite element model. The aforementioned aspects would be the subjects of further investigations.

5. Conclusions

Welding sequences effect on temperature distribution, residual stresses and distortions of T-joint fillet welds has been studied numerically in this paper. The simulation results revealed that peak temperature achieved in the welding was greatly affected by the WS and residual stress and angular distortion produced cannot both hold in minimum for a WS. The smallest longitudinal and transverse residual stresses occurred in WS-2, while the smallest angular distortion and difference in WS-4. The distributions of temperature, longitudinal and transverse residual stresses as well as angular distortions were also presented.

Investigating the aspects of shrinkage and simultaneous welding as well as the implementations of other related numerical techniques for further and better understanding of the welding process and its optimization would be the subjects of further publication in the future time.

Author details

Nur Syahroni
Department of Ocean Engineering, Institut Teknologi Sepuluh Nopember (ITS), Surabaya, Indonesia

Mas Irfan Purbawanto Hidayat
Department of Materials and Metallurgical Engineering, Institut Teknologi Sepuluh Nopember (ITS), Surabaya, Indonesia

Acknowledgement

Funding provided by Institut Teknologi Sepuluh Nopember (ITS) Surabaya is gratefully acknowledged.

6. References

ASM (1990). Metals Handbook Vol. 1, 10th ed. , Properties and Selection: Irons, Steels, and High-Performance Alloys, ASM International USA.

Bathe, K. J. (1996). Finite Element Procedures, Prentice Hall, Inc. , New Jersey.

Bette (1999). Fabrication, Applications Engineering, in: The Welding Engineer's Current Knowledge ed. 2000, EWE-3/4. 12 pp. 8-11, SLV Duisburg Gmbh, Germany.

Chang, K. H. & Lee, C. H. (2009). Finite Element Analysis of the Residual Stresses in T-joint Fillet Welds Made of Similar and Dissimilar Steels, Int. J. Adv. Manuf. Technol. , Vol. 41, 250-258.

Deng, D. , Murakawa, H. & Liang, Wei (2007). Numerical Simulation of Welding Distortion in Large Structures, Comput. Methods Appl. Mech. Eng. , Vol. 196, 4613-4627.

Goldak, J. A. & Akhlaghi, M. (2005). Computational Welding Mechanics, Springer, Inc. , New York.

Grong, O. (1994). Metallurgical Modelling of Welding, The Institute of Materials, Cambridge.

Lindgren, L. E. (2006). Numerical Modelling of Welding, Comput. Methods Appl. Mech. Eng. , Vol. 195, 6710-6736.

Masubuchi, K. (1980). Analysis of Welded Structures: Residual Stress, Distortion, and their Concequences, Pergamon Press Ltd, London.

Teng, T. L. & Lin, C. C. (1998). Effect of Welding Conditions on Residual Stresses due to Butt Welds, International Journal of Pressure Vessels and Piping, Vol. 75, 857-864.

Teng, T. L. , Fung, C. P. , Chang, P. H. & Yang, W. C. (2001). Analysis of Residual Stresses and Distortions in T-joint Fillet Welds, International Journal of Pressure Vessels and Piping, Vol. 78, 523-538.

Teng, T. L. , Chang, P. H. & Tseng, W. C. (2003). Effect of Welding Sequences on Residual Stresses, Computers and Structures, Vol. 81, 273-286.

Tsai, C. L. , Park, S. C. & Cheng, W. T. (1999). Welding Distortion of a Thin-Plate Panel Structure, Welding Research Supplement, 156-165.

Zacharia, T. , Vitek, J. M. , Goldak, J. A. , DebRoy, T. A. , Rappaz, M. & Bhadeshia, H. K. D. H. (1995). Modeling of Fundamental Phenomena in Welds, Modelling Simul. Mater. Sci. Eng. , Vol. 3, 265-288.

Chapter 25

Numerical Simulation of Fully Grouted Rock Bolts

Hossein Jalalifar and Naj Aziz

Additional information is available at the end of the chapter

http://dx.doi.org/10.5772/48287

1. Introduction

This chapter describes the application of numerical modelling to civil and mining projects, particularly rock bolting, developing a Final Element (FE) model for the bolt, grout, rock, and two interfaces under axial and lateral loading, verifying the model, analysing the stress and strains developed in the bolt and surrounding materials.

Numerical methods are the most versatile computational methods for various engineering disciplines because a structure is discritised into small elements and the constitutive equations that describe the individual elements and their interactions are constructed. Finally, these numerous equations are solved together simultaneously using computers. The results from this procedure include the stress distribution and displacement pattern within a structure. Numerical modelling includes analytical techniques such as finite elements, boundary elements, distinct elements, and other numerical approaches that depend upon the material. The finite element method "FEM" is considered to evaluate the behaviour of materials and their interactions in a fully grouted bolt which is installed in a jointed rock mass. The simulations were carried out by ANSYS code.

2. FE in ANSYS

ANSYS is a powerful non-linear simulation tool, *Bhashyam.G.R* (2002).The ANSYS software is a commercial FE analysis programme, which has been in use for more than thirty years, *Pool et al.* (2003). The software can analyse the stress and strain built up in a variety of problems, especially designing roof bolts and long wall support systems.

The original code developed around a direct frontal solver has been expanded over the years to include full featured pre and post processing capabilities which support a comprehensive list of analytical capabilities including linear static analysis, multiple non-linear analyses, modal analysis, contact interface analyses and many other types.

In this chapter only structural analysis is considered. Structural analyses are available in the ANSYS Multiphysics, ANSYS Mechanical, ANSYS Structural, and ANSYS Professional programmes only. Statistical analysis is used to determine displacement and stress and strain under static loading conditions (both linear and non-linear statistical analyses). Non-linearity can include plasticity, stress stiffening, large deflection, large strain, hyper-elasticity, contact surfaces, and creep behaviour.

3. A review of numerical modelling in rock bolts

A number of computer programmes have been developed for modelling civil and geo-technical problems. Some of them can be partially used to design and analyse roof bolting systems. It is noted that 3D software is necessary to simulate the whole characters of a model, such as modelling the joints, bedding planes, contact interface and failure criterion. Several numerical methods are used in rock mechanics to model the response of rock masses to loading and unloading. These methods include the method (FEM), the boundary element method (BEM), finite difference method (FDM) and the discrete element method (DEM).

A number of studies were carried out on bolt behaviour in the FE field, including those by *Coats and Yu* (1970), *Hollingshead* (1971), *Aydan* (1989), *Saeb and Amadei* (1990), *Aydan and Kawamoto* (1992), *Swoboda and Marence* (1992), *Moussa and Swoboda* (1995), *Marence and Swoboda* (1995), *Chen et al.* (1994, 1999, 2004), and *Surajit* (1999).

One of the earliest attempts to use standard FEs to model the bolt and grout was done by *Coats and Yu* (1970). The study was carried out on the stress distribution around a cylindrical hole with the FEmodel either in tension or compression. It was found that the stress distribution was a function of the bolt and rock moduli of elasticity. The presence of grout between the bolt and the rock was not considered and there was no allowance for yielding. The analysis was only carried out in linear elastic behaviour with two-phase materials, which limited the model. *Hollingshead* (1971) solved the same problem using a three phase material (bolt-grout and rock) and allowed a yield zone to penetrate into the grout using an elastic, perfectly plastic criterion, according to the Tresca yield criterion, for the three materials (Figure 1). How the interface behaved was not considered in the model.

John and Dillen (1983) developed a new one-dimensional element passing through a cylindrical surface to which elements representing the surrounding material are attached (Figure 2). They considered three important modes of failure for fully grouted bolts, a bi-linear elasto-plastic model for axial behaviour, elastic- perfectly plastic, and residual plastic model for bonding material, was assumed. Although this model eliminated many previous limitations and agreed with the experimental results, it neglected rock stiffness and in-situ stress around the borehole. They claimed that critical shear stress occurred at the grout - rock interface, which is not always the case in the field or laboratory. Aydan (1989) presented a FE model of the bolt. He assumed that a cylindrical bolt and grout annulus is connected to the rock with a three-dimensional 8-nodal points.

Two nodes are connected to the bolt and six to the rock mass. The use of boundary element and FE techniques to analyse the stress and deformation along the bolt was conducted by Peng and Guo (1992) (Figure 3). The effect of the face plate was replaced by a boundary element. The effect of reinforcement because of the assumption of perfect bonding was overestimated.

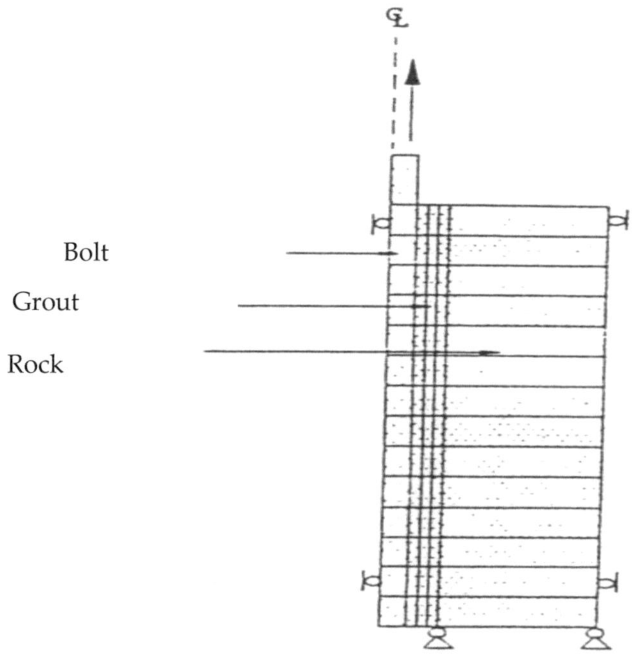

Figure 1. FE Simulation of bolted rock mass (after Hollingshead, 1971)

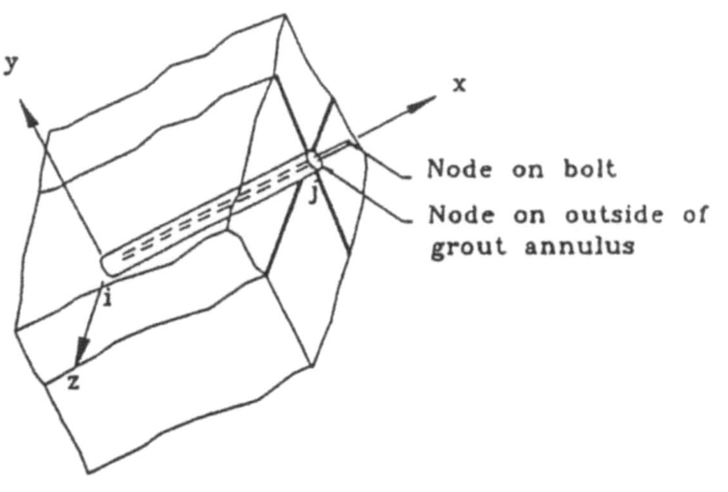

Figure 2. Three-Dimensional rock bolt element (after John and Dillen, 1983)

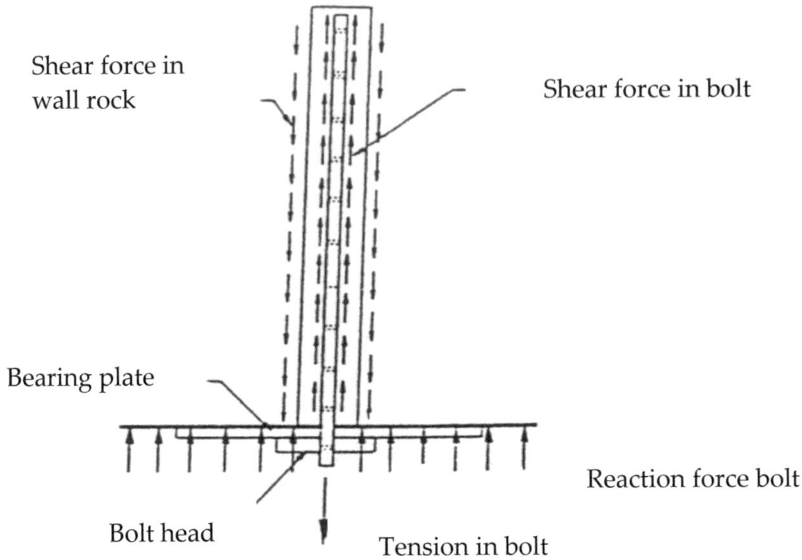

Figure 3. Bolt-Rock interaction model (after Peng and Guo, 1992)

Stankus and Guo (1996) investigated that in bedded and laminated strata, point anchor and fully grouted bolts are very effective, especially if quickly installed at high tension after excavation. They used three lengths 3300, 2400, and 1500 mm and three tensions, 66, 89, and 110 kN and found that:

- Bolts with higher pre-tension induce a smaller deflection
- The longer the bolt, the larger the load,
- In bolts with the same length and high tension, there is small deflection,
- Large beam deflection was observed in long bolts and small deflection in short bolts.

They developed a method for achieving the optimum beaming effect (OBE). However there were some assumptions in their methodology such as, the problem with the gap element, which is not flexible for any kind of mesh, especially with thin grout. Many relevant parameters about the contact interface cannot be defined in gap element. All materials were modelled in the elastic region.

Marence and Swoboda (1995) developed the Bolt Crossing Joint (BCJ) element that connects the elements on both sides of the shear joint. It has two nodes, one each side of the discontinuity. The model cannot predict the de-bonding length along the bolt, grout interface and hinge point position.

It was realised that to further facilitate data analysis and the stress and strain build up along a bolt surrounded by composite material and their interaction, a powerful computer simulation was needed. FE modelling is considered to be the only tool able to accomplish this goal. There is still a lack of an adequate global models of grouted bolts to analyse bolt behaviour properly, particularly at the contact interfaces.

In this chapter, three-dimensional formulations and non-linear deformation of rock, grout, bolt, and two interfaces are taken into account in the reinforced system. A description of the numerical model developed is presented below.

4. Materials design model

The FE method is the most suitable computational method to evaluate the real behaviour of the bolt, grout, and surrounding rock when there are composite materials with different interfaces. A three dimensional FE model of a reinforced structure subjected to shear loading was used to examine the behaviour of bolted rock joints. Three governing materials (steel, grout, and concrete) with two interfaces (bolt-grout and grout-concrete) were considered. To create the best possible mesh, symmetry rules should be applied. To reduce computing demand and time (when a fine mesh is used) the density of the mesh has been optimised during meshing. The division of zones into elements was such that the smallest elements were used where details of stress and displacement were required. The process of FE analysis is shown in Figure 4.

4.1. Modelling concrete and grout

Care was taken to develop the best model for concrete and grout that could offer appropriate behaviour. 3D solid elements, Solid 65 that has 8 nodes was used with each node having three translation degrees of freedom that tolerates irregular shapes without a significant loss in accuracy. Solid 65 is used for the 3-D modeling of solids with or without reinforcing bars (rebar). The geometry and node locations for this type of element are shown in Figure 5 a. The solid element is capable of plastic deformation, cracking in tension, crushing in compression, creep non-linearity, and large deflection geometrical non-linearity, and also includes the failure criteria of concrete Fanning (2001), Feng et al. (2002) and Ansys (2012). Concrete can fail by cracking when the tensile stress exceeds the tensile strength, or by crushing when the compressive stress exceeds the compressive strength. A FE mesh for concrete is shown in Figure 5 b. Figure 6 shows the FE mesh for grout. Due to symmetry only a quarter of the model needed to be treated.

4.2. Modelling the bolt

The steel bar, which resists axial and shear loads during loading, due to rock movement, is the main element within the rock bolt system,. The steel bar was modelled appropriately, particularly with regard to the type of element designed and bolt behaviour, in the linear and non-linear region. 3D solid elements, solid 95 with 20 nodes, was used to model the steel bar, with each node having three translation degree of freedom. The approach adopted is to reveal that the experimentally verified shear resistance of fully grouted bolt can be investigated by numerical design. Elastic behaviour of the elements was defined by Young's Modulus and Poisson's ratio of various materials. The stress, strain relationship of steel is assumed as the bi-linear kinematic hardening model and the modulus of elasticity of strain hardening after yielding, is accounted as a hundredth of the original one, *Cha et al.* (2003),

Hong et al. (2003) and *Abedi et al.* (2003). Figure 7 displays the solid 95 elements and FE mesh for bolt.

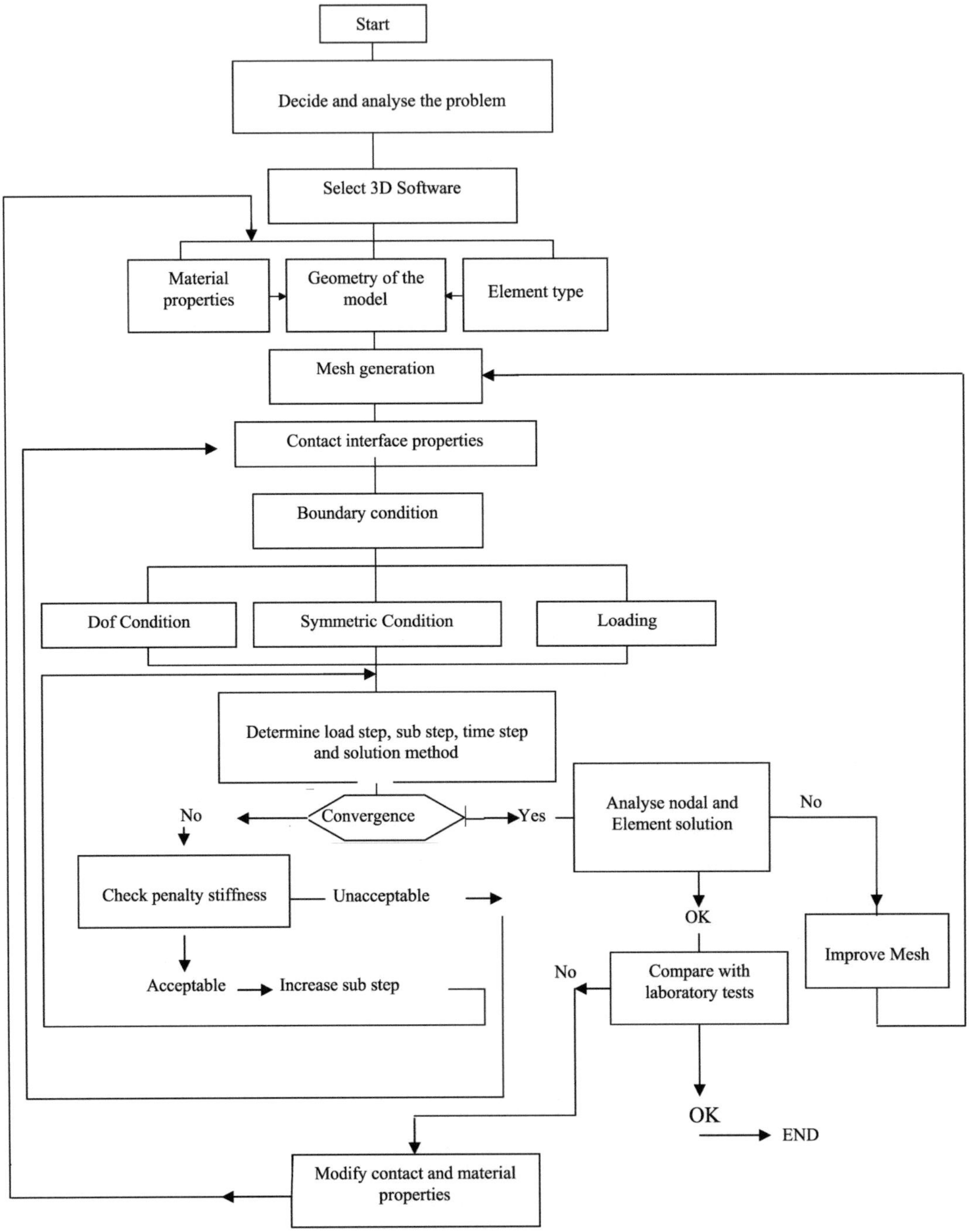

Figure 4. The process of FE simulation (Dof = degrees of freedom)

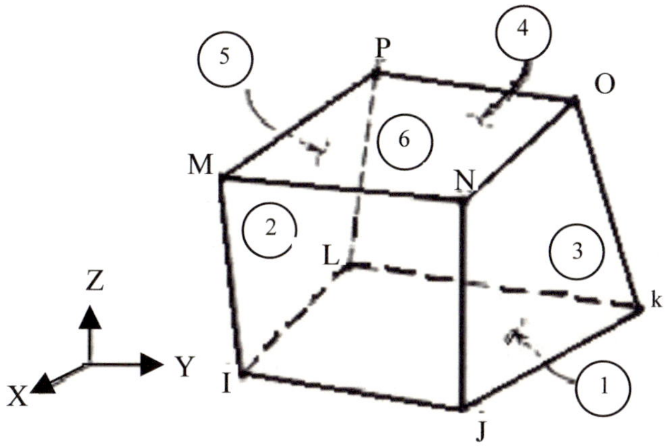

(a)

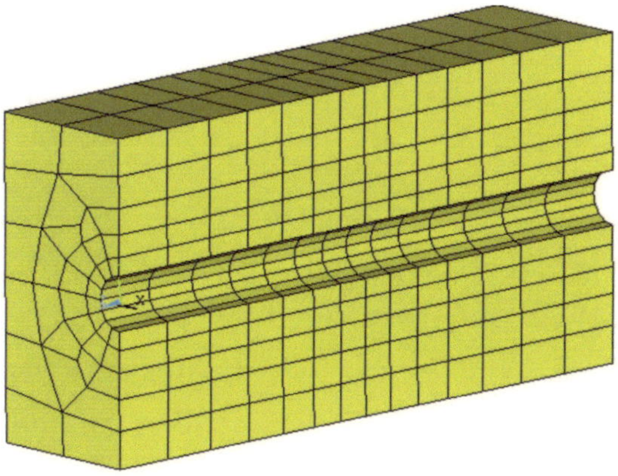

(b)

Figure 5. (a) 3D Solid 65 elements; (b) Concrete mesh

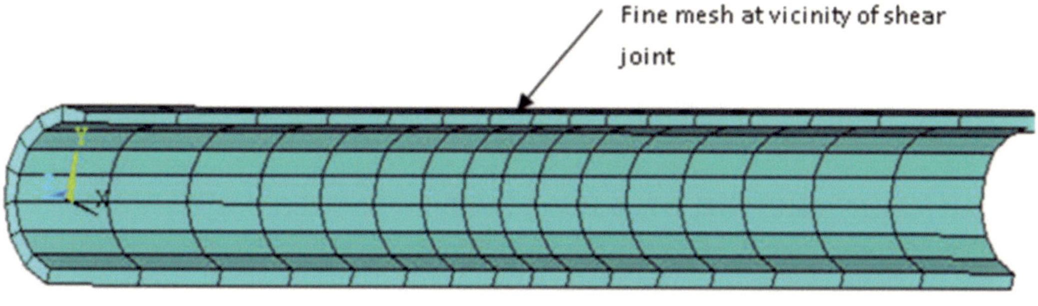

Figure 6. FE mesh for grout

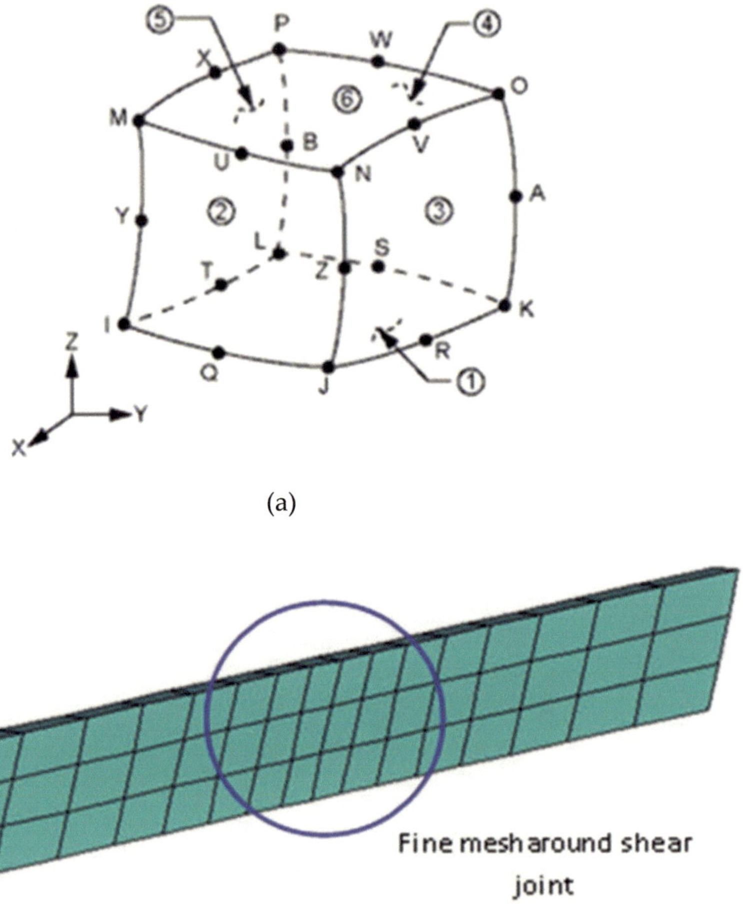

(a)

(b)

Figure 7. (a) 3D Solid 95 elements (b) FE mesh for bolt

4.3. Contact interface model

The main difficulties with numerically simulating a reinforced shear joint are the bolt- grout and grout-rock interfaces. An important parameter controlling the load transfer from the bolt to the rock through resin is bond behaviour between the interfaces. If they are not designed properly it is difficult to understand their behaviour, when and where de-bonding occurs, how a gap is created between the interfaces, and how the load is transferred. Thus the contact interfaces were designed to act realistically. To study the stress, strain generation through numerical modelling, it is very important to model the interfaces accurately, *Pal et al.* (1999). *Ostreberge* (1973) also emphasised the bond strength between two adjacent mediums for an accurate load transfer. *Nietzsche and Hass* (1976) proposed a model for bolt, grout-rock that assumed a linear elastic behaviour for all materials, and perfect bonding for all contact interfaces (bolt- grout and grout- rock). It has to be noted that perfect bonding, particularly between the bolt-grout interface could not be considered to be the right behaviour, because there is no cohesion strong enough between them. In addition, there are large stresses and strains concentrated near the shear joints, which restrict perfect bonding. The interface between the grout and concrete was considered as standard behaviour where normal pressure changes to zero when separation occurs. As found from laboratory results, a low cohesion (150 kPa) was adopted for the contact interface, which was determined from the test results under constant normal conditions.

3D surface-to-surface contact element (contact 174) was used to represent contact between the target surfaces (steel-grout and rock - grout). This element is applicable to 3D structural contact analysis and is located on the surfaces of 3D solid elements with mid-side nodes. This contact element is used to represent contact and sliding between 3-D "target" surfaces (Target 170) and a deformable surface, is defined by this element. The element is applicable to three-dimensional structural and coupled thermal structural contact analysis. This element is also located on the surfaces of 3-D solid or shell elements with mid-side nodes. It has the same geometric characteristics as the solid or shell element face to which it is connected. Contact occurs when the element surface penetrates one of the target segment elements on a specified target surface. The contact elements themselves overlay the solid elements describing the boundary of a deformable body and are potentially in contact with the target surface. This target surface is discritised by a set of target segment elements (Target 170) and is paired with its associated contact surface via a shared real constant set. Figure 8 displays the target 170 geometry.

4.4. 3D geometrical model

An actual 3D geometrical model was created to simulate the rock-bolt- grout behaviour and their interactions. The model bolt core diameter (D_b) of 22 mm and the grouted cylinder (D_h) of 27 mm diameter had the same dimensions as those used in the laboratory test. Due to the symmetry of the problem, only one fourth of the system was considered. Figure 9 shows the geometry of the FE model with mesh generation.

5. Verification of the model

A numerical representation model for a fully grouted reinforcement bolt was developed and its validity assessed with laboratory data conducted in a variety of rock strengths and pre-tension loadings. A comparison of experimental results with numerical simulations showed that the model can predict the interaction between bolt, grout, and concrete, and how the interfaces behave. The consistency of the experimental observations with a numerically design model is presented by typical shear load, shear displacement curves shown in Figure 10. It is clear that when the strength of the concrete was doubled there was a twofold reduction in shear displacement.

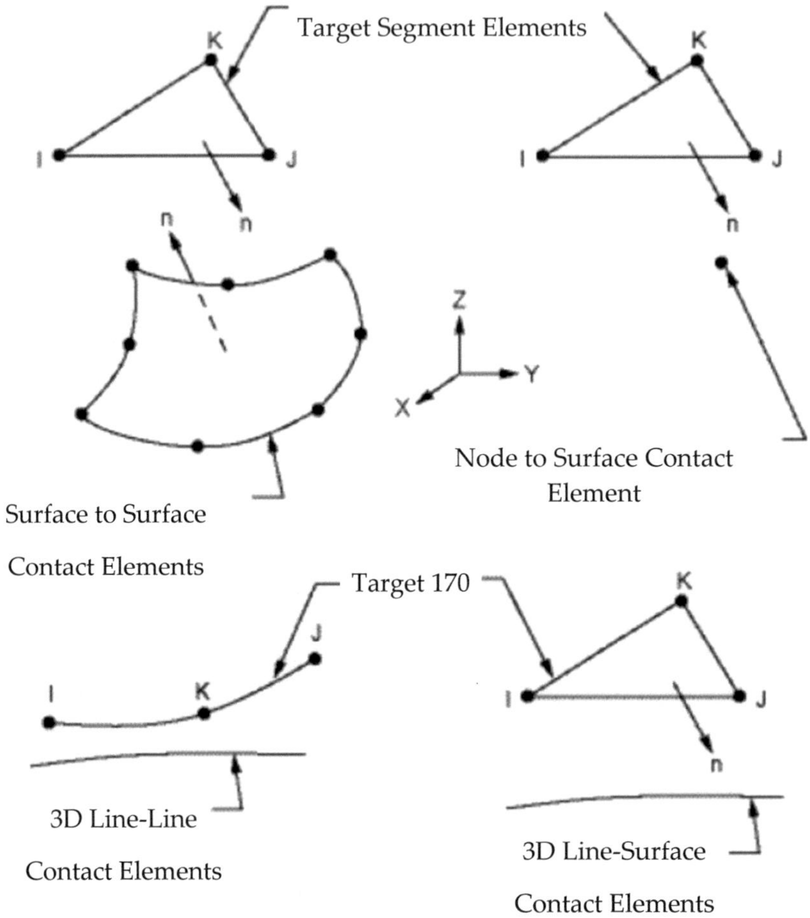

Figure 8. Target 170 geometry (Ansys 2012)

6. Modelling bolts under lateral loading

An extensive series of laboratory tests to analyse the bending behaviour of fully grouted bolts in different strength rock, bolt pre-tension and thickness of resin were carried out. Three governing materials (steel, grout, and rock) with two interfaces (bolt-grout and grout-rock) were considered for 3D numerical simulation.

By this three dimensional FEM, the characteristics of elasto - plastic materials and contact interfaces are simulated. Numerical modelling in different strength rock (20, 40, 50 and 80 MPa) and different pre-tension loads (0, 20, 50, and 80 kN) were carried out and the results were analysed. As the output results were large, only the main results of 0 and 80 kN pre-tension are presented here.

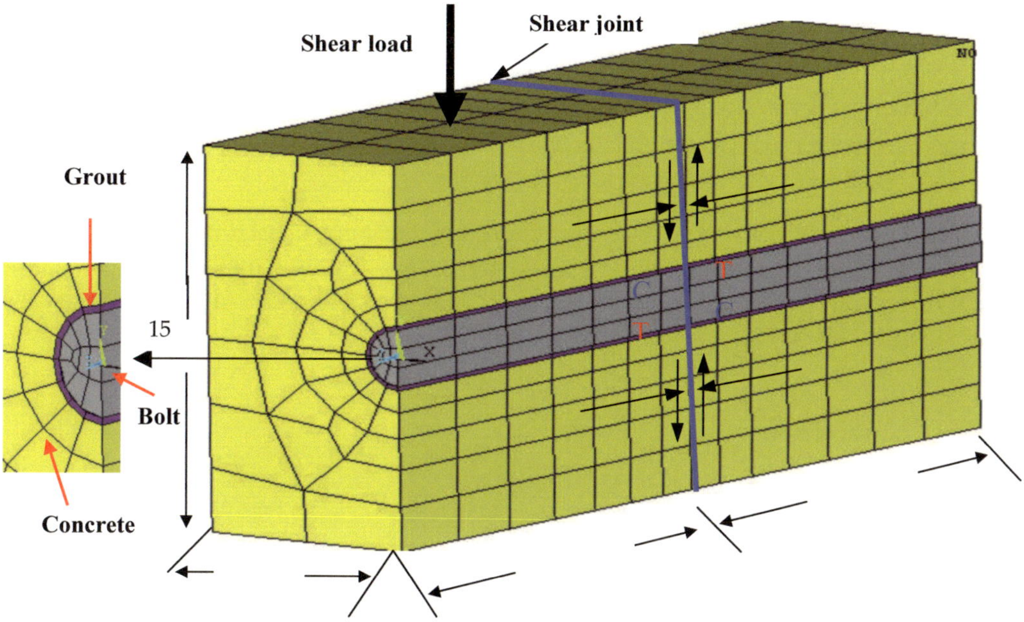

Figure 9. Geometry of the model and mesh generation

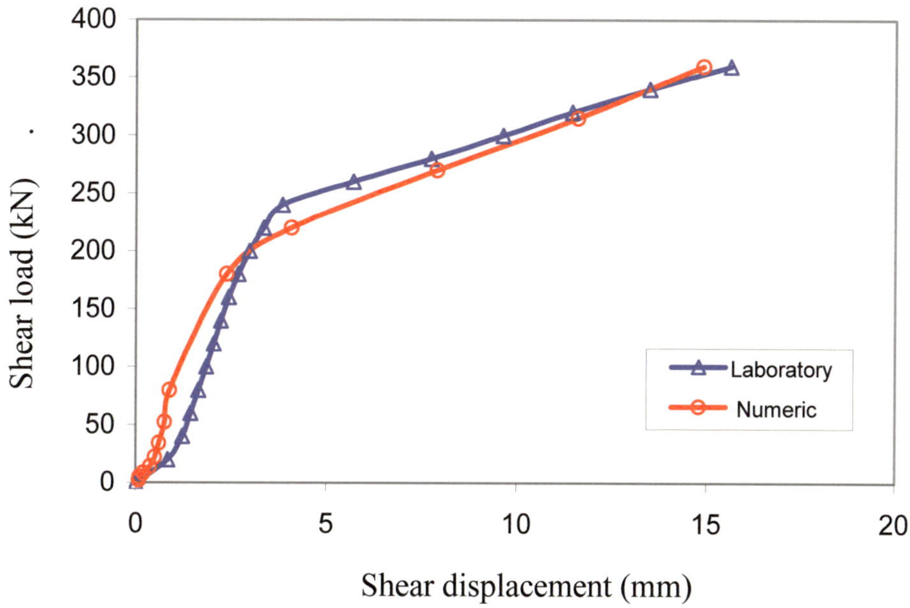

Figure 10. Load-deflection in 80 kN pretension bolt load and 40 MPa concrete

6.1. Bolt behaviour

6.1.1. Stresses developed along the bolt

When a beam with a straight longitudinal axis is loaded laterally, its longitudinal axis is deformed into a curve, and the resulting stresses and strains are directly related to the deflection curve, which is affected by the surrounding materials. Figure 11 shows a quarter of the model with induced loads along the shear joint.

When the beam was bent there was deflection and rotation at each point. The angle of rotation α is the angle between the bolt axis and the tangent to the deflection curve, shown as point o. α was measured for the bolts tested. The deflection trend in 20 MPa concrete is shown in Figure 12.

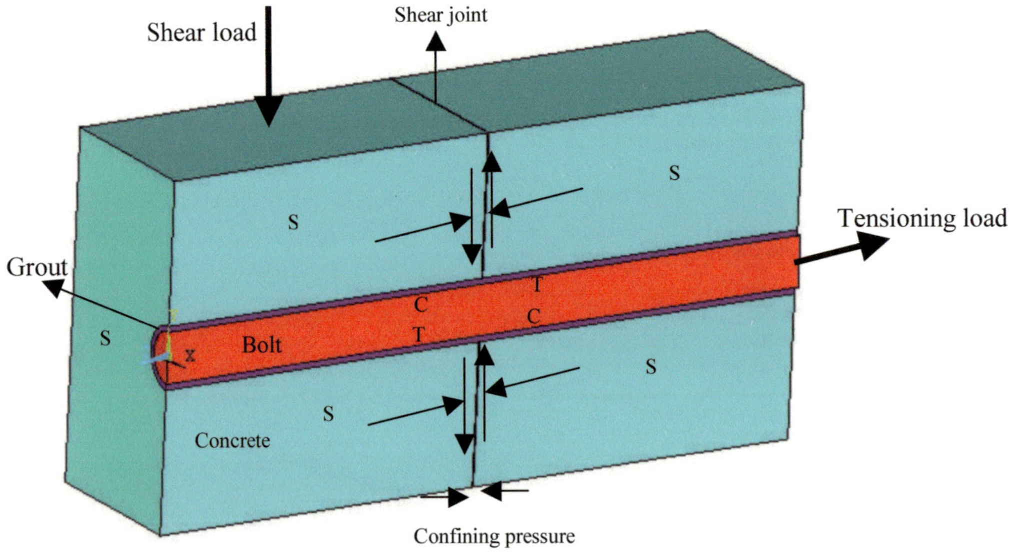

Figure 11. Numerical model (s = symmetric planes, c = compression zone, T = tension zone

Also to find the relationship between deflection and each point along the axis of the bolt, raw output data from the numerical simulation were classified and entered as input data to Maple software. Equation 3 and Figure 13 were established.

$$\tan\alpha = \frac{dv}{dx}, \tag{1}$$

$$\alpha = \arctan\frac{dv}{dx} \tag{2}$$

$$U_y = -40.76 + 26 Arc\tan(e^{(0.05x-7.2)}) \tag{3}$$

where;

- U_y = Shear displacement (mm)
- x = Distance from the bolt centre to the end (mm), from A to B.

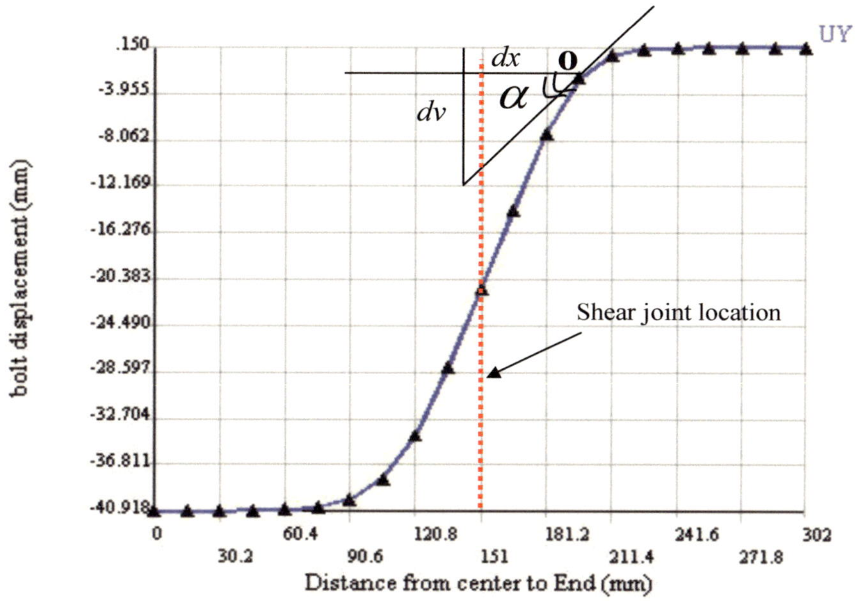

Figure 12. Bolt displacement in 20 MPa, without Pre-tension

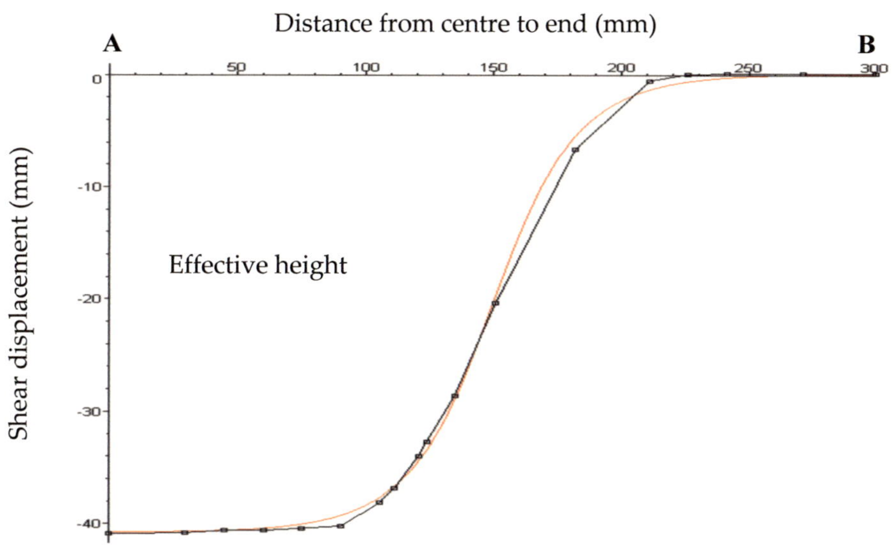

Figure 13. Shear displacement as a function of bolt length sections in 20 MPa concrete

The relationship between vertical displacement at the bolt-joint intersection and hinge point is:

$$Uy\ (hinge) = (0.15\text{-}0.2)\ Uy\ (joint)$$

Which is consistent with the laboratory results. Figure 14 shows the bolt deflection in 40 MPa concrete.

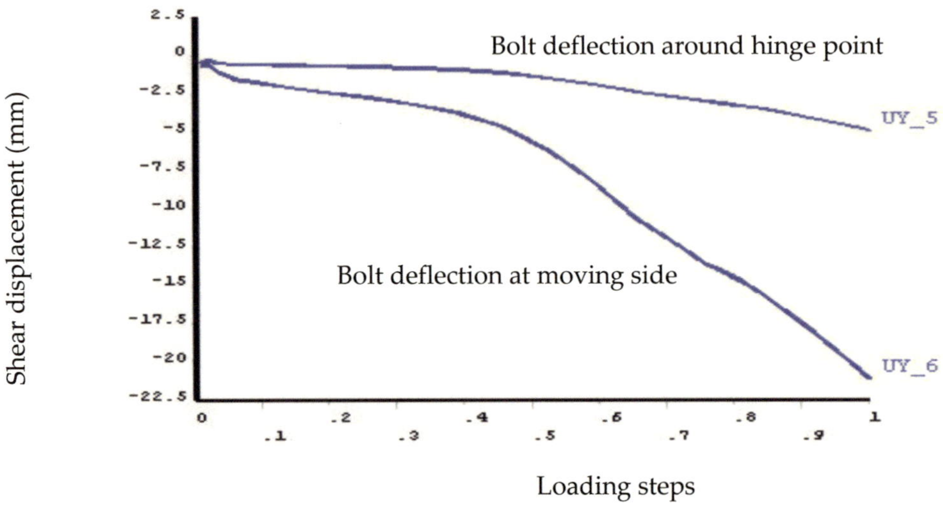

Figure 14. Bolt deflection at the moving side and hinge point versus loading process, in 40 MPa concrete without pre-tension load

Figure 15 shows the contours of stress developed along the bolt in 20 MPa concrete, where the stress in the top part of the bolt and towards the perimeter are tensile and compressive at the centre. However, the stress conditions at the lower half section of the bolt are reversed. In addition, the shape of the bolt between the hinges can be considered as linear. The rate of stress changes in the post failure region is plotted in Figure 16.

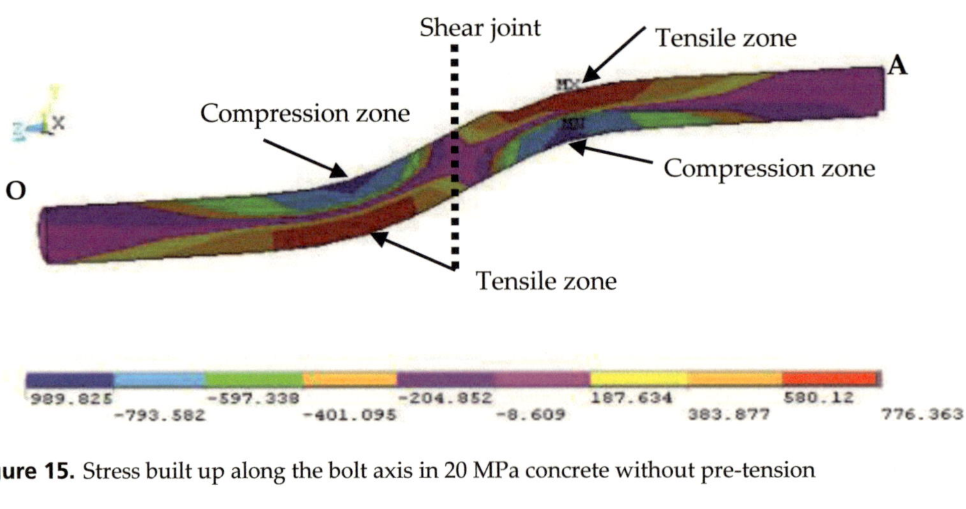

Figure 15. Stress built up along the bolt axis in 20 MPa concrete without pre-tension

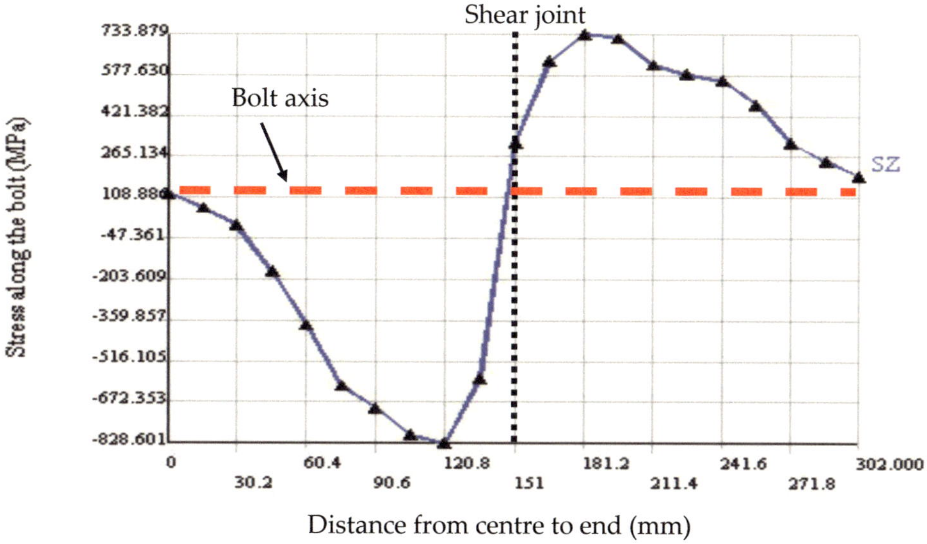

Figure 16. Trend of stress built up along the bolt axis 20 MPa concrete with 80 kN pre-tension

It can be seen that induced stresses at these tensile and compression zones are high and the bolt appears to be in a state of yield. At the two hinges the yield limit of the bolt is reached quickly. However, a further increase in the shear load has no apparent influence on the stress built up at the hinge point. From this stage afterwards, only tensile stresses are developed and expanded between the hinge points, and may lead the bolt to fail at some distance between the hinge points located near the shear joint, as the maximum stress and strain occurs between them.

From analysing the results in different pre-tension loads it was found there are no significant changes in induced stresses along the bolt with an increase in pre-tension load in the tension zone. However there is a slight reduction in compressive stress with an increasing pre-tension load. Induced stresses are higher than the yield point and less than the maximum tensile strength of the steel bolt in both situations (with and without pre-tension in all strength concrete). Moreover, in different strength concrete it was observed that the strength of the concrete affects shear displacement and bolt contribution. However there were no meaningful changes in induced stress beyond the yield point along the bolt axis with increasing rock strength but stress was reduced slightly with high pre-tension loading and strength of concrete. The Von Mises stress trend along the bolt axis perpendicular to the shear joint in 20 MPa concrete is plotted in Figure 17. Comparing the results in 20 MPa concrete with and without pre-tension, Von Mises stress decreased slightly, with an increase in bolt pre-tension. However, this difference is insignificant.

Figure 18 shows the concentration of shear stress along the bolt and the rate of change along the axis is shown in Figure 19. Figure 20 shows the trend of shear stress along the length of the bolt in one side of the joint surrounded with soft concrete.

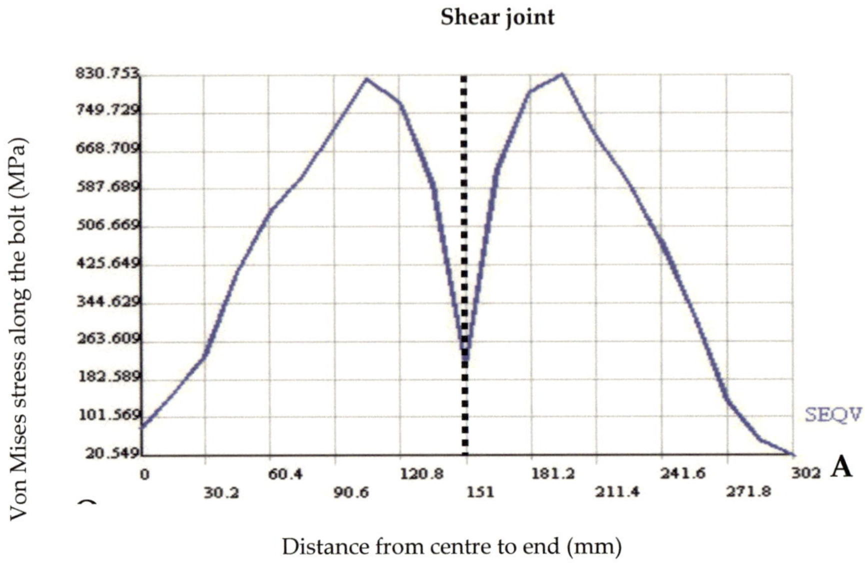

Figure 17. Von Mises stress trend in 20 MPa concrete without pre-tension

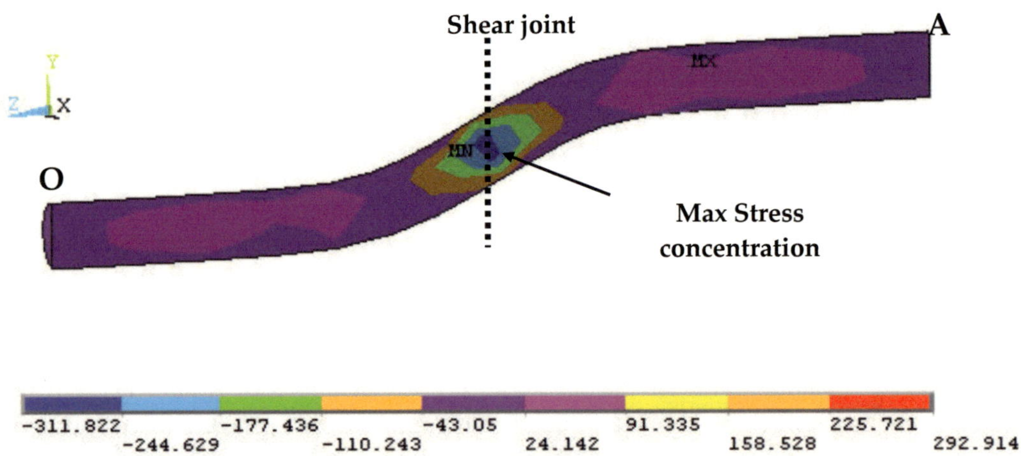

Figure 18. Shear stress contour in the concrete 20 MPa without pre-tension

As it shows the maximum shear stress is concentrated in the vicinity of the joint plane, and according to structural analysis, the bending moment at this point is zero. These stress slowly increase, beginning with plastic deformation, and end with a stable situation. The shear stress reduces dramatically from the shear joint towards the bolt end. This trend reaches zero at the hinge point. In the two hinges, the yield limit of the steel is reached quickly, at about 0.3 P and 0.4 P in concrete 20 and 40 MPa respectively, (P is the maximum given applied load). Further increase in the shear force has no apparent influence on stress in the hinges. The distance between the hinge points is reduced as the strength of the concrete is increased.

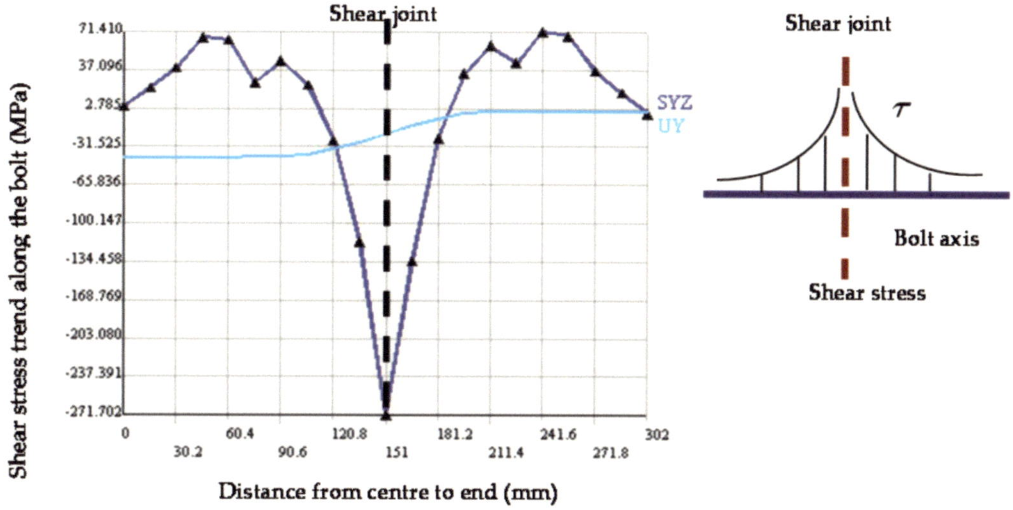

Figure 19. The rate of shear stress change along the bolt axis in concrete 20 MPa without pre-tension

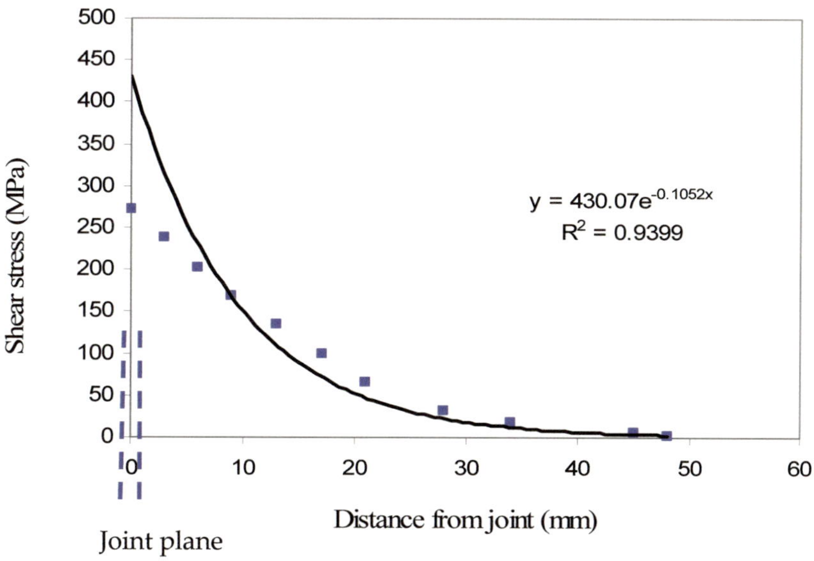

Figure 20. The rate of shear stress along the bolt axis in concrete 20 MPa without pre-tension in one side of the joint plane

Figure 21 shows the trend of changes in shear stress profile with the shear stress tapering off to a stable state past the yield point. It shows the shear stress trend is not exceeded during further loading after the yield point.

Eventually, a combination of this stress with induced tensile stress at the bolt - joint intersection leads the bolt to fail. By increasing the initial tensile load on the bolt, the shear stress was decreased, which was seen in different strength concrete but there was no significant changes with increasing shear load after the yield point. Any reduction in shear stress causes an increase in the resistance of the bolt to shear. It can be noted that the shear stress increased slightly with an increasing strength of concrete.

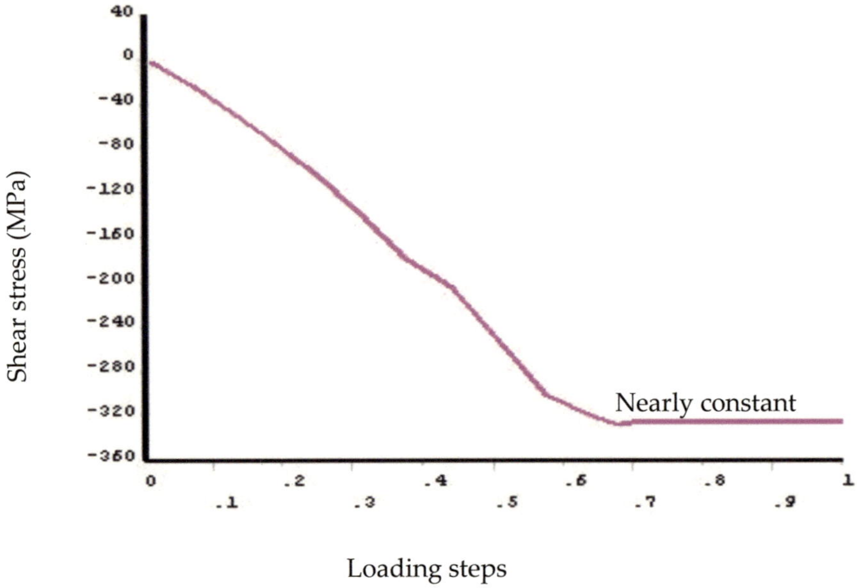

Figure 21. Shear stress trend in bolt –joint intersection in concrete 20 MPa at post failure region without pre-tension load

6.1.2. Strain developed along the bolt

Strain was generated along all the surrounding materials as the shear load increased, particularly along the axis of the bolt. As deflection increased, plastic strain is induced in the critical locations in all three materials (bolt - resin and concrete). Figure 22 shows the location of maximum plastic deformation along the bolt while bending. It shows there are two hinge points around the shear plane approximately 50 mm from the shear joint in 20 MPa concrete.

However an increasing pre-tension load has not affected hinge point distances, which are around 2.3 D_b (D_b is bolt diameter). This value in the laboratory test is around 44 mm that is 2 D_b. The strain and the rate of strain changes along the bolt in 20 MPa concrete are shown in Figures 23 and 24.

As Figure 23 shows that the outer layer of the bolt yielded, whereas the middle section remained in an elastic state.

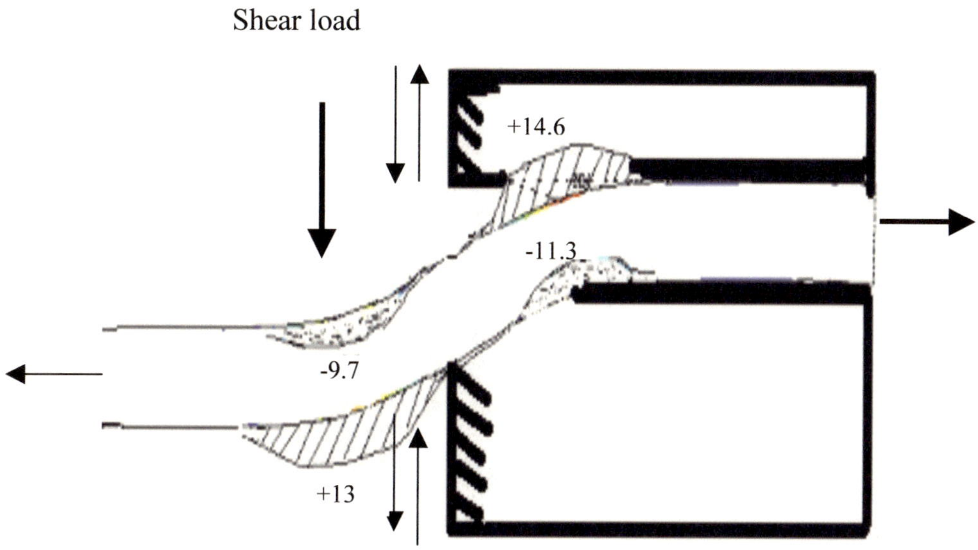

Figure 22. Deformed bolt shape in post failure region in 20 MPa concrete

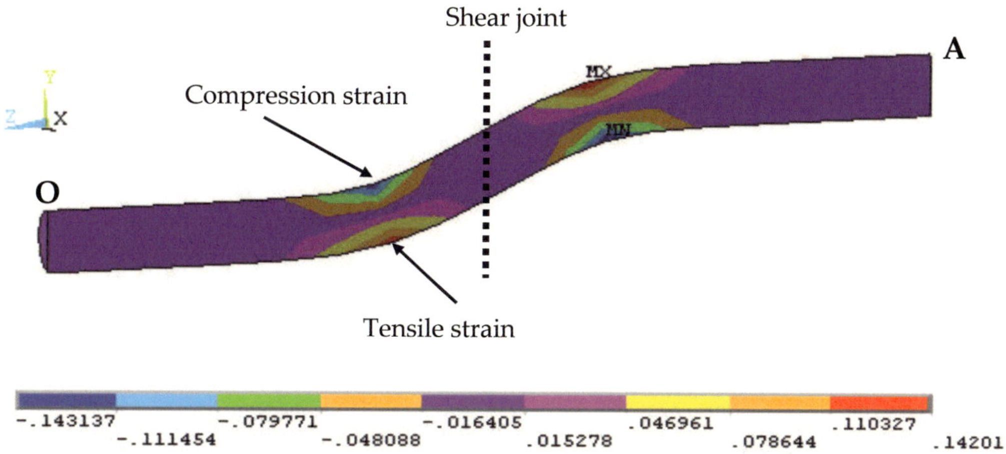

Figure 23. Plastic strain contour along the bolt axis in concrete 20 MPa without pre-tension

Figure 25 shows the beginning of plastic strain during shearing and a trend of strain developing as a function of load stepping. It notes that both the tensile and compression strain around the bolt started approximately 27-30 % after loading began and increased with an increasing shearing load. However, the rate of increase in the tensile zone is higher than the compression zone. It also showed these strains appeared in the early stage of loading with a small displacement (around 3 mm), which increased with increase in shear deflection.

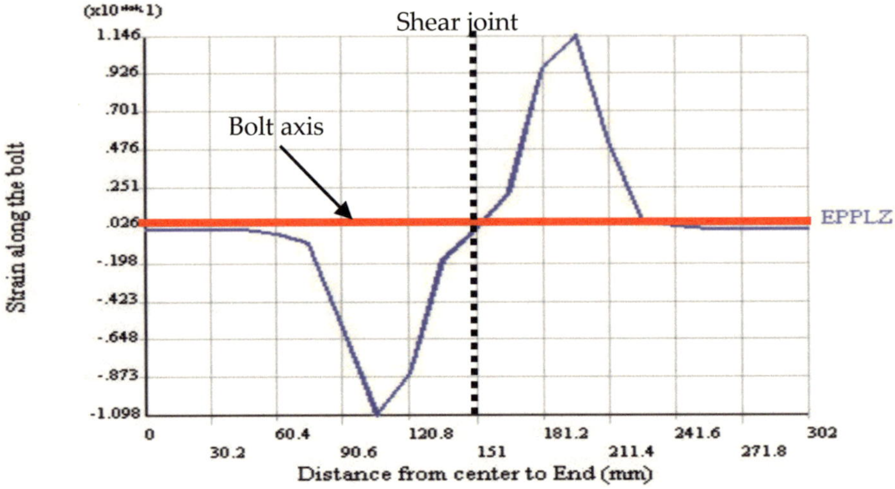

Figure 24. Strain trend along the bolt axis in concrete 20 MPa without pre-tension in upper fibre of the bolt

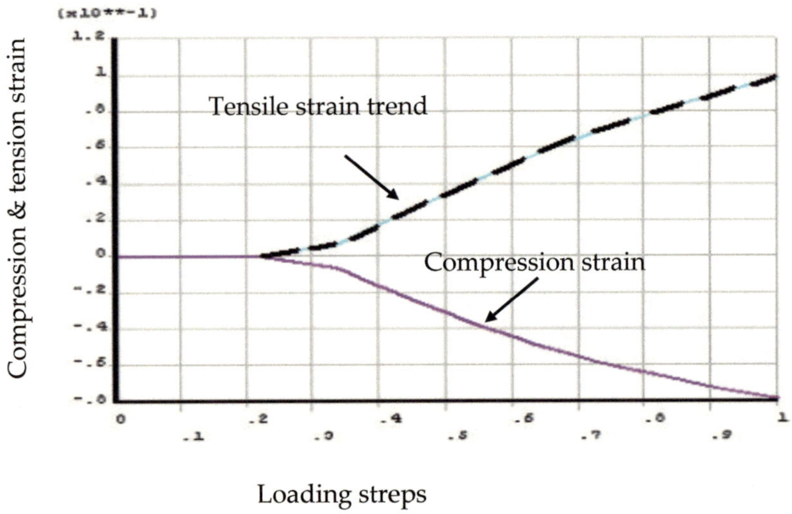

Figure 25. Yield strain trend as a function of time stepping concrete 20 MPa in 20 kN pre-tension load

With an increase in loading, shear displacement was increased. There was a significant increase in shear displacement after 35% of loading time. Bending of the bolt is predominant at a low loading time. plastic strain begins at the hinge point around 35 % of loading. A comparison of the data (with and without pre-tension) shows that the intensity of the strain along the axis of the bolt is slightly reduced with an increase in pre-tension load. However the affected area in the tensile zone expands towards the shear joint. The strains in the compression and tension zones were reduced in higher strength concrete.

6.2. Concrete behaviour

6.2.1. Stress developed in concrete

The behaviour of the centre concrete under shear load in double shearing assembly was analysed in different strength concrete and different pre-tension loads. During shearing the middle part of the assembled system was displaced downwards with increasing shear load. Figure 26 shows the deflection rate after failure. Reaction forces are developed during the middle concrete block displacement, which increased in critical locations (at the vicinity of the shear joint), affected by the bolt. The reaction forces induce and propagate stress and strain in sheared zones. Figure 27 shows the high-induced stress near the shear joint as the maximum reaction forces are expected there. When induced stress is larger than the ultimate stress the concrete will be crushed. Figure 28 displays the rate of induced stress at the interface near the shear joint. It shows that induced stresses are much higher than the compressive strength, and the concrete at this location would be severely crushed. From the figure it can be seen that the high stress is approximately 60 mm from the shear plane. At an early stage of loading, the concrete was crushed and stresses propagated throughout, with bolt yield to start at around 2 mm from the edge of the intersection. Beyond this point stresses increased quickly near the joint intersection and reaction zones. Induced stresses near the shear joints were reduced slightly with increase in the pre-tension load on the bolt. In addition the trend of induced stresses and strains built up along the concrete interface in 40 MPa concrete was the same as with 20 MPa concrete. However, the value of stresses and strains were slightly reduced in higher strength concrete.

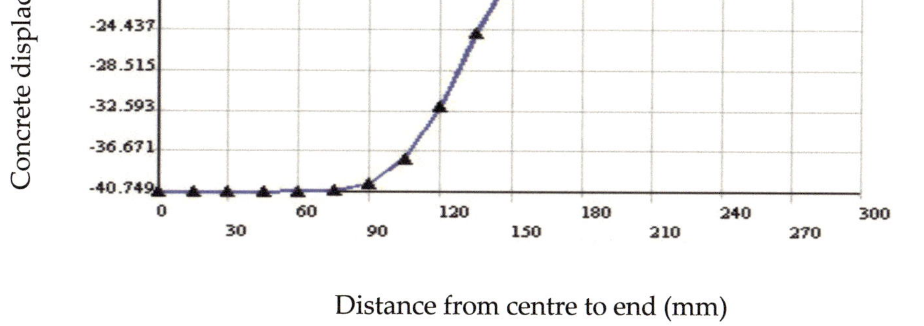

Figure 26. Concrete displacement in non-pretension condition in 20 MPa concrete

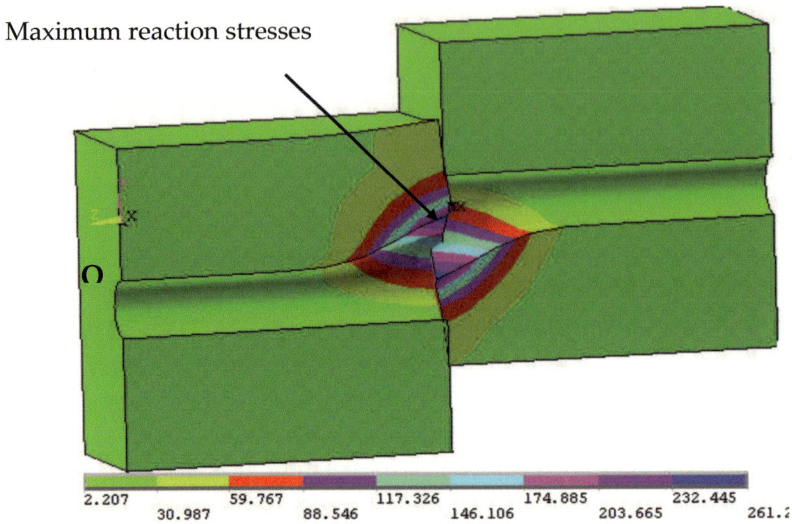

Figure 27. Yield stress induced in 20 MPa concrete without pre-tension condition

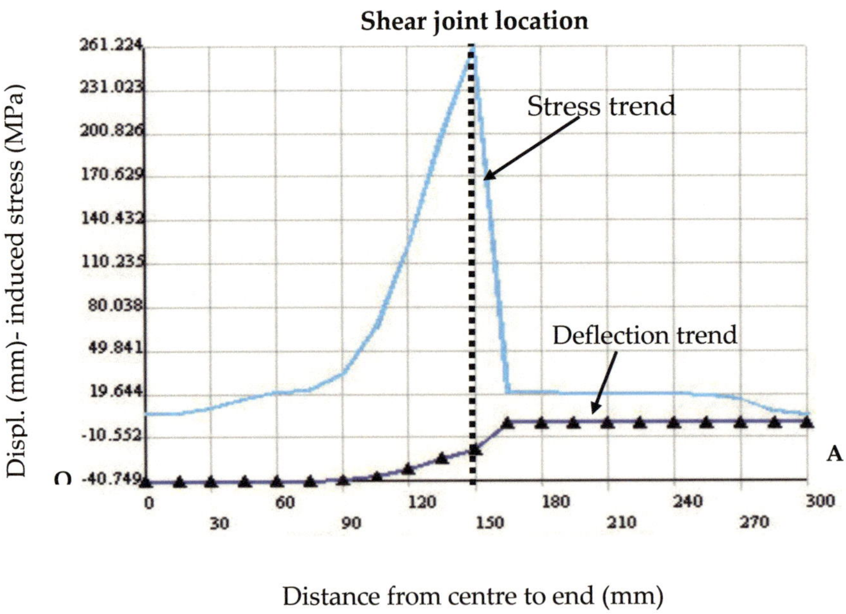

Figure 28. Induced stress and displacement trend in 20 MPa concrete without pre-tension

6.2.2. Strain developed in concrete

The highest level of induced stress was near the shear joint, so it is expected that strain would be highest around this zone. Figure 29 shows the induced strain contours at the high pressure zone. Figure 30 shows induced strain in terms of loading time in grout and concrete. It shows that the strain generation begins in the concrete before it is seen in the resin grout because lower strength concrete is one third the strength of grout. There is an approximate exponential relationship in the strain trend as loading increases. After 20% of loading steps, plastic strain is induced along the contact interface near the shear joint. This value in soft concrete (20 MPa) is at an earlier stage, which is around 15% of loading step. This shows the strain built up along the axis of the bolt is lower than in the shear direction.

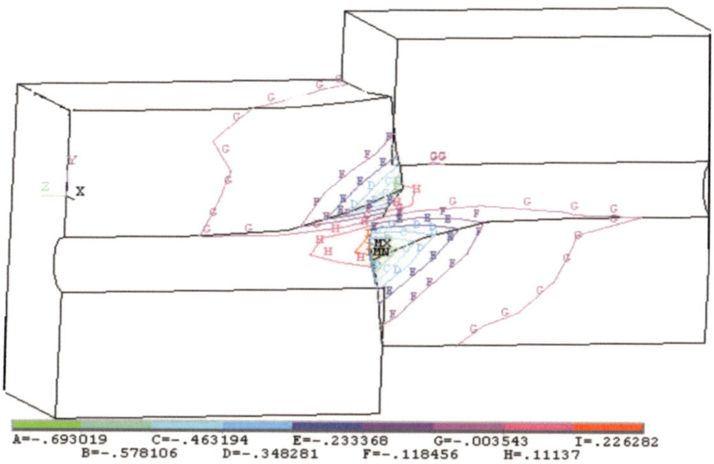

Figure 29. Strain contours in 20 MPa concrete without pre-tension

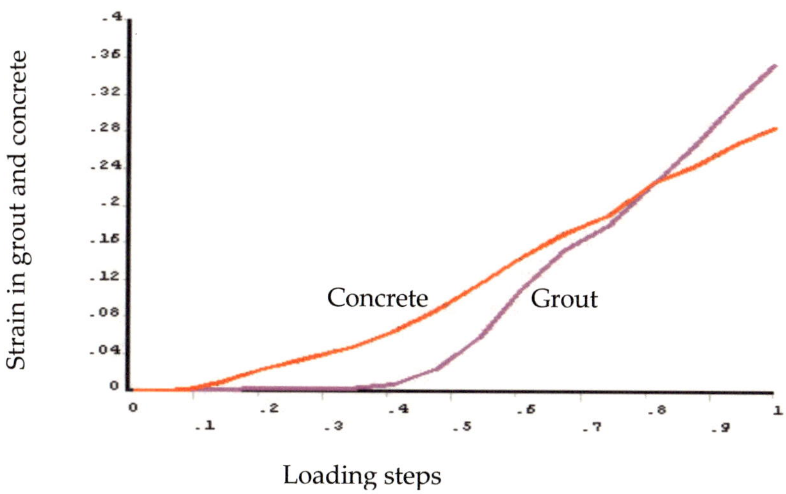

Figure 30. Induced strain in concrete 20 MPa in grout and concrete versus loading without a pre-tension and 27 mm diameter hole

A comparison of induced strain along the joint interface with and without pre-tension found that the strain in the shear direction is reduced (around 15%) with increasing pre-tension. In the axial and shear direction strain was concentrated near the shear joint.

Figure 31 shows the deformation behaviour of both concrete medium and bolt. Plastic deformation of concrete occurs nearly 15 % of the maximum shear load while the deformation of the bolt occurs at 33% of the loading steps. From the graphs it can be inferred that in very low values of bolt deflection and time steps, fractures happen in the concrete, which is in the elastic range of the bolt. Any further increase in shearing does not influence the stress at the hinge points, however induced stress in the concrete blocks causes extensively fractures and eventually leads to failure.

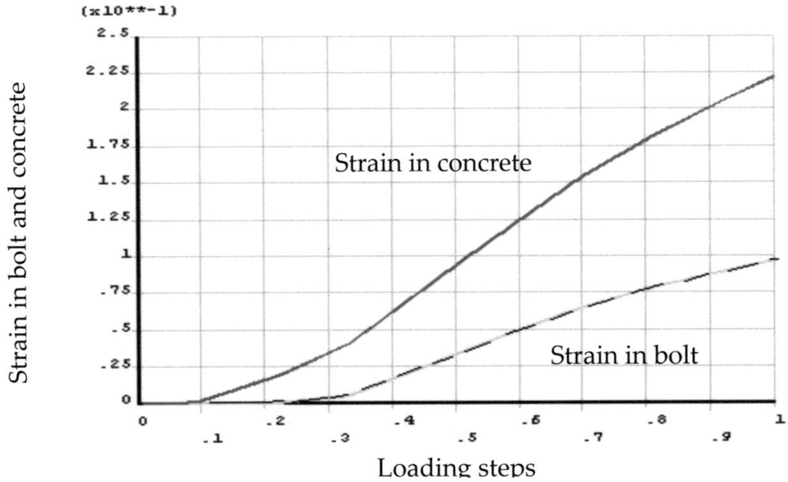

Figure 31. Induced strain in concrete and bolt as a function of loading steps in 20 MPa concrete with 80 kN pre-tension

6.3. Grout behaviour

6.3.1. Stress in grout

It is known that grout bonds the shanks to the ground making the bolt an integral part of the rock mass itself. Its efficiency depends on the shear strength of the bolt - grout, and grout - rock interface. Figure 32 shows the contours of induced stress through the resin layer surrounded by 20 MPa concrete, without pre-tension. It was revealed that the induced stress exceeded the uniaxial compressive strength of the grout near the bolt - joint intersection which crushed the grout in this zone. It shows that the value of induced stress in the grout near the shear joint is much higher than the uniaxial strength, and grout in this location can be crushed. The broken sample showed that the grout was crushed around this zone. The damaged area on the upper side of the grout was approximately 60 mm from the shear joint. Figures 33 and 34 show the gap formation after bending in the numerical and laboratory methods respectively. It is noted that the induced stresses were slightly reduced as the pre-tension increased (nearly 10 %). However, it shows they are slightly expanded.

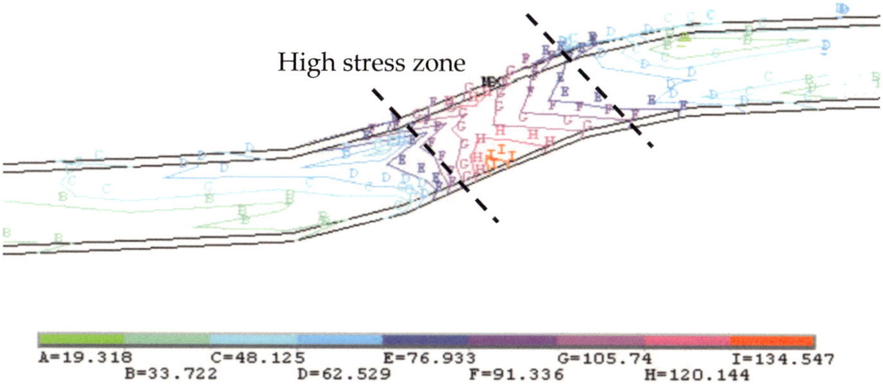

Figure 32. Maximum induced stress contours in grout layer without pre-tension and 20 MPa

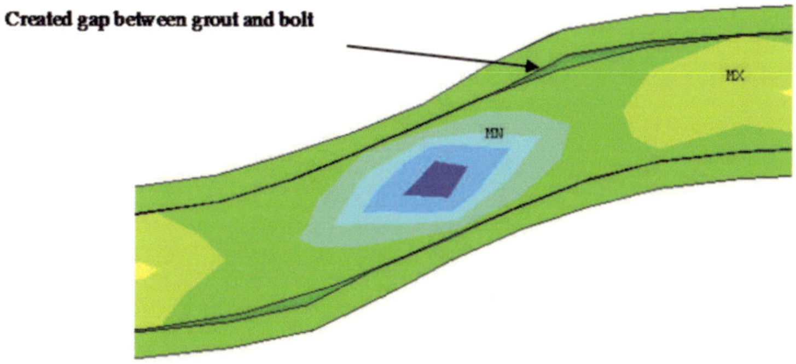

Figure 33. Gap formation in post failure region in 20 MPa concrete in the Numerical simulation

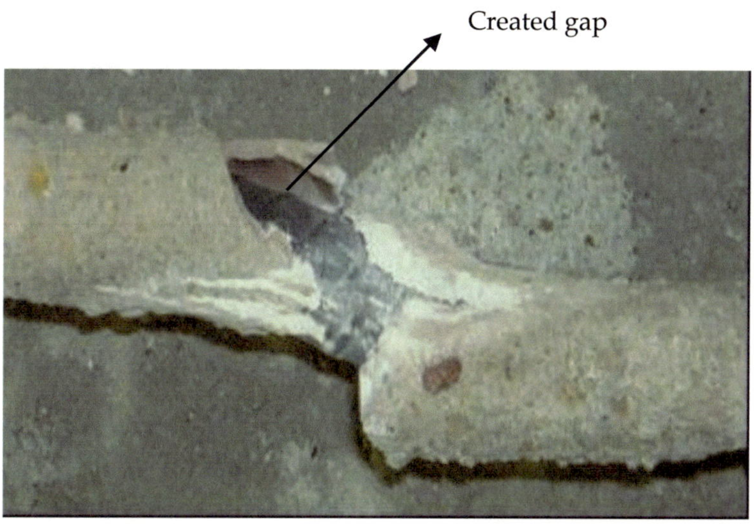

Figure 34. Gap formation in post failure region in 20 MPa concrete in the laboratory test

6.3.2. Strain in grout

While shearing takes place, strains are induced through the grout near the shear joint and reaction zones. The strain in the grout was around ten times greater than the linear region at critical zones. This means that the grout in those areas had broken off the sides that were in tension. The rate of induced strain along the grout in an axial direction is shown in Figure 35.

A comparison of the strain along the joint interface in the grout showed that it decreased between 3% and 5% in the compression and tension zones with increasing pre-tension to 80 kN, which is due to higher shear resistance and lower lateral displacement. It was also found that the grout layer at the bolt - joint intersection will start to crush after slight movement along the joint, which causes plastic strain in the grout layer.

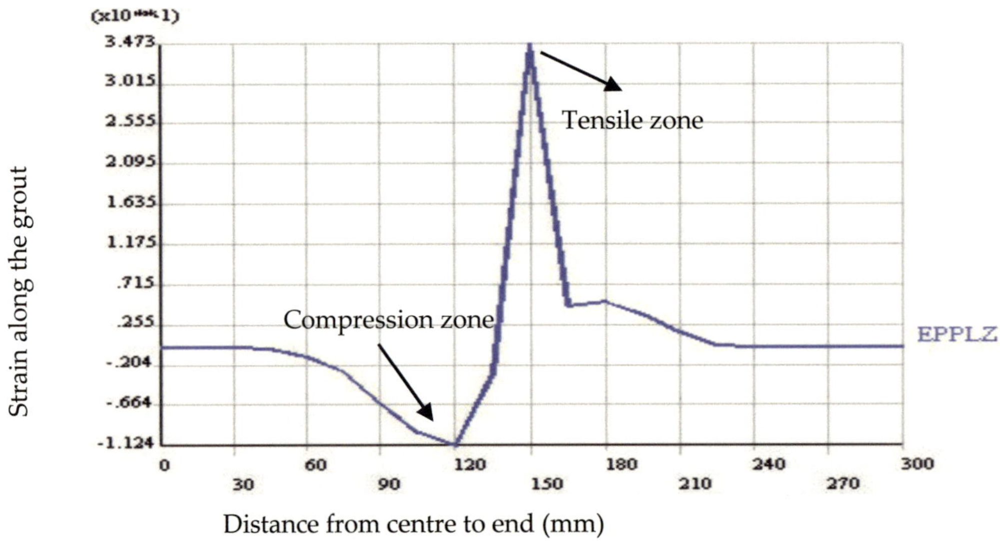

Figure 35. The rate of induced strain along the grout layer without pre-tension in an axial direction

In high strength concrete induced stress was reduced slightly and pre-tension reduces induced stresses along the bolt - grout interface.

From the results at contact pressure in the bolt-grout-concrete it was found that there is an exponential relationship between contact pressure and loading process at the bolt - grout interface, which started after around 15% of the loading process. However, the contact pressure trend in the concrete - grout interface was formed by 2 parts. From the beginning to around 15% of the loading, there is an approximate linear relation followed by an exponential relationship till the end of the load stepping process.

7. Bolt modelling under axial loading

A numerical model was developed to investigate the contact interface behaviour during shearing under pull and push tests. The same 3D solid elements and surface-to-surface contact elements were used to simulate grout and steel. The numerical simulation of the cross section of the bolt and its ribs was complicated, and is almost impossible with the range of software available in the market today. However an attempt was made to model the bolt profile configurations by taking into account the realistic behaviour of the rock - grout and grout - bolt interfaces based on laboratory observations. To achieve this end, the coordinates of all nodes for all materials were defined then all these co-ordinates were inter-connected to form elements, which were extruded in several directions to obtain the real shape of the bolt.

Figure 36 shows the FE mesh. Figure 37 shows the bolt under pull test. Two main fractures were produced as a result of shearing the bolt from the resin. The first one begins at the top of the rib at an angle of about 53^0 running almost parallel to the rib, and the second one has an angle of less than 40^0 from the axis of the bolt. When these fractures intersect they cause the resin to chip away from the main body because it is overwhelmed by the surface roughness of the rib while shearing. Internal pressure produced by the profile irregularities of the bolt induces tangential stress in the grout. The grout fractures and shears when the induced stress exceeds the shearing strength, allowing the bolt to slide easily along the sheared and slikenside fractures in the grout interface.

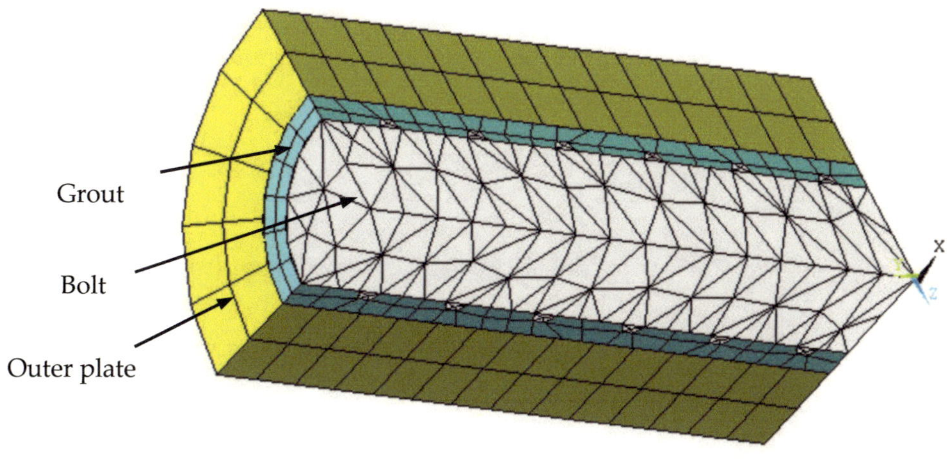

Figure 36. FE mesh: a quarter of the model

7.1. Bolt behaviour

From the simulations it was found that there will be an increase in grout - bolt surface de-bonding, and this decrease in diameter due to Poisson's effect in the steel, contributes to an axial elongation of about 0.084 mm at the top collar where the load is applied. This value in push test is around 0.05 mm as shown in Figure 37.

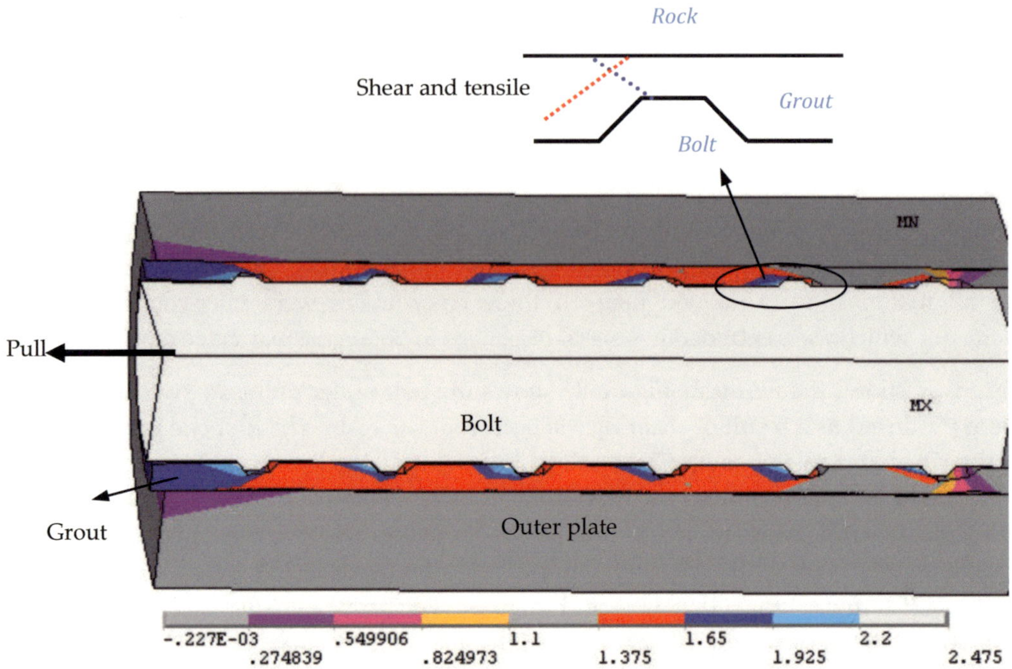

Figure 37. The bolt movement in pulling test

Figure 38 show the maximum induced strain near the applied load position in both the pull and push results. The strain is around the elastic strain and therefore the bolt is unlikely to yield.

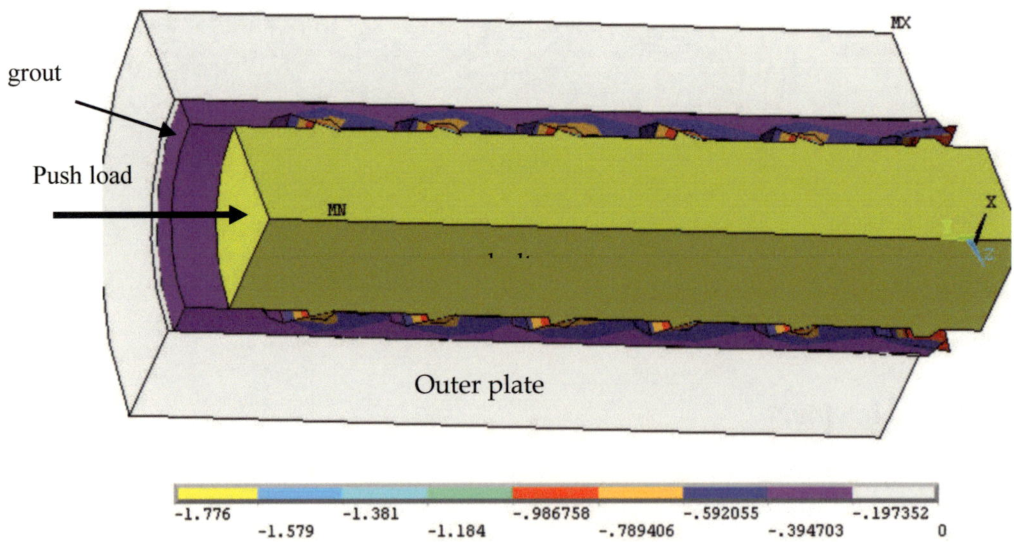

Figure 38. Bolt displacement contour in Bolt Type T1 in case of push test

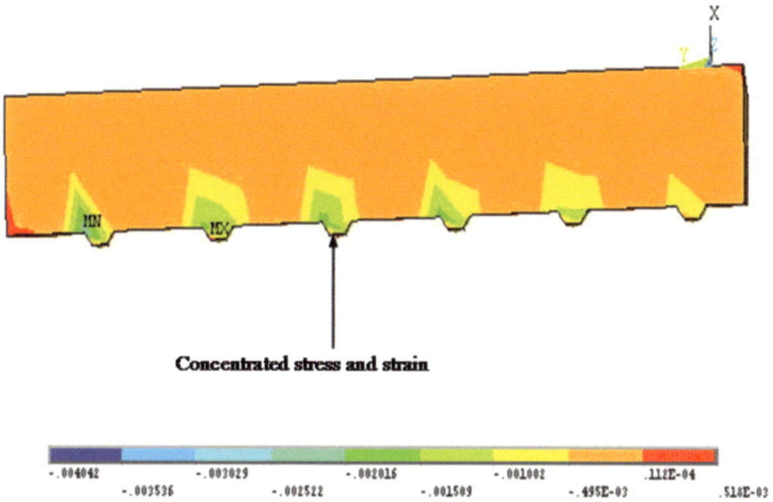

Figure 39. Shear strain in bolt ribs in push test

Maximum tensile stress along the bolt is 330 MPa. This is one half of the strength of the elastic yield point of 600 MPa. This means the bolt behaves elastically and is unlikely to reach a yield situation. Axial stress developed along the bolt is given by:

$$\sigma_t = \frac{4T}{\pi D_b^2} \tag{4}$$

and

$$T = \frac{\pi D_b^2 * \sigma_t}{4} \tag{5}$$

Where, σ_t is the tensile stress, T is the axial load, D_b is the bolt diameter and σ_y is the yield strength of the bolt. The bolt behaves elastically as long as the following expression is satisfied:

$$\sigma_t < \sigma_y \tag{6}$$

So in this situation with failure along the bolt-grout interface will not yield.

7.2. Grout behaviour

The behaviour of interface grout annulus is assumed to be elastic, softening, residual, plastic flow type. This behaviour was developed by Aydan (1989), and is given as:

$$\tau = G\gamma \quad \tau < \tau_{\max} \tag{7}$$

$$\tau = \tau_{max} - \frac{\gamma - \gamma_{max}}{\gamma_r - \gamma_{max}}(\tau_{max} - \tau_r) \tag{8}$$

$$\tau = \tau_r \tag{9}$$

where;

- G = Shear modulus of grout interface
- γ = Shear strain at any point in the interface
- γ_r = Shear strain at residual shear strength
- γ_{max} = Shear strain at peak shear strength
- τ_r = Residual shear strength of the interface
- τ_{max} = Peak shear strength of interface
- τ = Shear stress at any point in interface

The grout material is in elastic conditions if the following expression is satisfied;

$$T_t < T_y \tag{10}$$

where;

- T_t = Actual bond stress in the grout
- T_y = Yield stress of the grout in shear

From the strain generated along the grout interface it was found that the surface of the grout was disturbed by shear stress induced at the interface and this strain is higher than the elastic strain that damaged the grout at the contact surface. Figure 39 shows the shear stress contour at the grout interface. The whole contact area of the grout was affected by the shear stress and consequently the induced shear strain dominated. The maximum bonding stress was approximately 38% of the uniaxial compressive strength of the resin grout. The stress produced along the grout contact interface was greater than the yield strength of the grout of 16 MPa, and beyond the yield point only a slight increase in load is enough to damage the whole contact surface. Shear displacement increased as a result bonding failure. The shear stress at the bolt - grout interface can be calculated by Equation (11), which agrees with the results from the numerical simulation.

Thus,

$$\tau = \frac{f}{A} = \frac{\sigma \pi D^2}{8 \pi r l} = 23.2 MPa \tag{11}$$

where;

- τ = Shear stress in the grout - bolt interface (MPa)
- f = Axial force in the bolt (kN)

- A = Contact interface area (mm^2)
- D = Bolt diameter (mm)

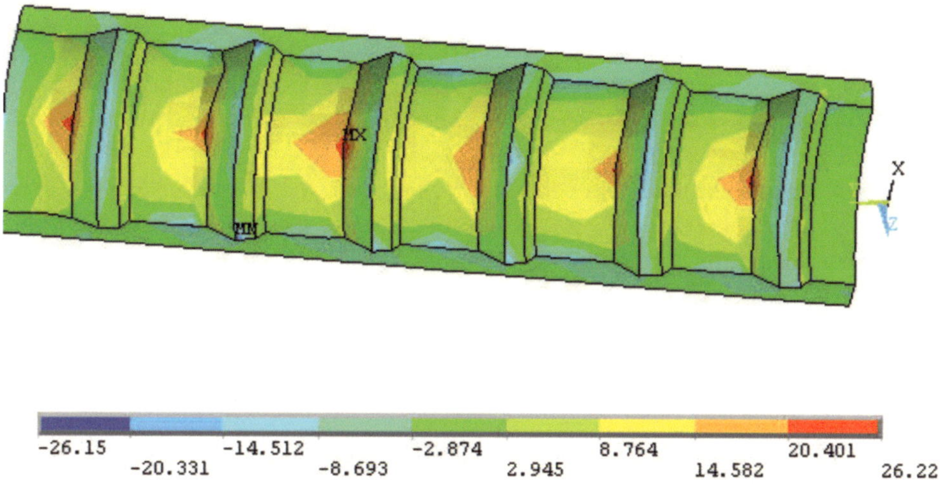

Figure 40. Shear stress contours along the grout interface

Using the *Farmer* (1975) equation the shear strength was equal to 27 MPa.

$$\frac{\tau}{\sigma} = 0.1e^{-(\frac{0.2x}{a})} \tag{12}$$

where;

- τ = Shear stress along the bolt grout interface
- σ = Axial stress
- a = Bolt radius

During shearing the outer plate of the bolt was influenced by the stresses and strains of the resin. From the analyses it was found that induced stress along the surface of the outer plate was insignificant at about 30 % of the yield stress, which is not sufficient to cause the outer plate to yield. In addition, grout de-bonding occurred around 50 to 60 kN at different levels of applied load.

8. Summary

Numerical analysis of the grout – concrete - bolt interaction has demonstrated that:

- There were no significant changes in induced stresses along the bolt with increasing pre-tension load, particularly in the tension zone. However, there was a small reduction in compression stress.
- The yield limit of the bolt at the hinge point depends on the strength of the concrete. In 20 MPa concrete the yield limit was 0.3P and in 40 MPa concrete it increased to 0.4P. A

further increase in the shear force has no apparent influence on stress at the hinges. The distance between the hinge points reduced with increasing strength of concrete.

- The strength of the concrete greatly affects shear displacement and bolt contribution. However, no significant change was observed in the induced stresses beyond the yield point along the axis of the bolt with increasing concrete strength.
- The maximum shear stress was concentrated near the bolt - joint intersection.
- There was an exponential relationship between the shear stress and distance from the shear joint.
- The shear stress was not exceeded during further loading after the yield point. Eventually, a combination of this stress with induced tensile stress at the bolt - joint intersection caused the bolt to fail.
- Shear stress at the bolt - joint intersection increased slightly with an increasing strength of concrete.
- There was no significant change in the hinge point distances with an increase in bolt pre-tension.
- There was a significant increase in shear displacement beyond 35% of the loading step, which is the likely yield point.
- The strain in the shear direction along the concrete was reduced (around 15%) with increasing the pre-tension loading. In both axial and shear directions the strain concentrated near the shear joint.
- The induced stresses exceeded the uniaxial compressive strength of the grout near the bolt - joint intersection, crushing the grout.
- The damaged area in the upper side of the grout was approximately 60 mm from the shear joint.
- Induced stress along the grout was reduced by increasing the pre-tension load nearly 10%. However they have expanded slightly.
- The strain was decreased by around 3% and 5% in the compression and tension zones where the bolt pre-tension load increased to 80 kN.
- Failure of the bolt - resin interface occurred by the grout shearing at the profile tip in contact with the resin.
- Numerical simulation provided an opportunity to better understand the stress and strains generated as a result of the bolt - resin interface shearing. Such an understanding is supported both analytically and by simulation.
- Findings from the experimental test agreed with the numerical simulations and analytical results.

Author details

Hossein Jalalifar
Shaihid Bahonar University of Kerman-Iran

Naj Aziz
Wollongong University- Australia

9. References

[1] Pool.G, Cheng.Y and Mandel.J (2003). Advancing analysis capabilities in Ansys through solver technology. Electronic transactions on numerical analysis 15: 106-121.

[2] Bhashyam.G.R (2002). Ansys Mechanical-A powerful nonlinear simulation tool, 2004. Ansys,Inc. 275 Technology Drive Canonsburge,PA 15317.

[3] Coates.D.F and Yu.Y.S (1970). Three dimensional stress distribution around a cylindrical hole and anchor. Proceeding of 2nd Int. Cong. Rock Mechanics.175-182.

[4] Hollingshead.G.W (1971). Stress distribution in rock anchors. Canadian Geotechnical Journal 8: 588-592.

[5] Aydan.O (1989). The stabilisation of rock engineering structures by rock bolts. Geotechnical Engineering.Thesis. Nagoya, Nagoya: 202.

[6] Saeb.S and Amadei.B (1990). Finite element implementation of a new model for rock joints. Int. Symp. of Rock Joints.707-712.

[7] Aydan, O. and T. Kawamoto (1992). Shear reinforcement effect of rockbolts in discontinious rock masses. Int.Sym. of Rock support in mining and underground construction, Canada.483-489.

[8] Swoboda.G and Marence.M (1992). Numerical modelling of rock bolts in interaction with fault system. Int.Sym. of Numerical modelling in Geomechanics.729-737.

[9] Moussa.A and Swoboda.G (1995). Interaction of rock bolts and shotcrete tunnel lining. Int.Sym. of Numerical models in Geomechanics.443-449.

[10] Marence.M and Swobodea. M (1995). Numerical model for rock bolt with consideration of rock joint movements. Rock Mechanics & Rock Enginnering 28.(3): 145-165.

[11] Chen, S. H. and G. N. Pande (1994). Rheological model and finite element analysis of jointed rock masses reinforced by passive, fully-grouted bolts. International Journal of Rock Mechanics and Mining Science & Geomechanics Abstracts 31.(3): 273-277.

[12] Chen, S. H. and P. Egger (1999). Three dimensional elasto-viscoplastic finite element and its application. Int. J. for Numerical and analytical methods in geomechanics 23: 61-78.

[13] Chen, S. H., S. Qiang and S. F. Chen (2004). Composite element model of the fully grouted rock bolt. Rock mechanics and rock engineering 37.(3): 193-212.

[14] Surajit, P. and G. Wije Wathugala (1999). disturbed state model for sand-geosynthetic interfaces and application to pull-out tests. Int. J. for Numerical and analytical methods in geomechanics 23: 1873-1892.

[15] John.C.M and Van Dillen.D.E (1983). Rock bolts: A new numerical representation and its application in tunnel design. Proc.24th U.S. Symp. Rock Mech., Texas A&M University.13-25(Cited in Moosavi 1994).

[16] Peng, S. and S. Guo (1992). An improved numerical model of grouted bolt-roof rock interaction in underground openings. Rock support in mining and underground construction, Canada.67-74.

[17] Stankus.J.C and Guo.S (1996). Computer automated finite element analysis-A powerful tool for fast mine design and ground control problem diagnosis and solving. 5th Conference on the use of computer in the coal industry, West Virginia-USA.108-115.

[18] Fanning, P. (2001). Nonlinear models of reinforced and post tensioned concrete beams. Structural engineering: 111-119.

[19] Feng.P, Lu.X.Z and Ye.L.P (2002). Experimental research and finite element analysis of square concrete column confined by FRP under uniaxial compression. 17th Australian Conference on the Mechanics of Structures and Materials, Gold Coast, Australia.60-65.

[20] Ansys. 2012. Manual.

[21] Cha.E.J, Choi.S.M and Kim.Y (2003). A moment-rotation curve for CFT square column and steel beams according to reliability analysis. Int. Conference on Advances in Structures, Sydney-Australia.943-950.

[22] Hong.S.D, Choi.S.M and Kim.Y (2003). A moment-rotation curve for CFT square columns and steel beams. Int. Conference on Advances in Structures, Sydney-Australia.951-956.

[23] Abedi, K., H. Afshin and A. Ferdousi (2003). Investigation into the behaviour of a novel steel section for concrete filled tubular columns under axial and cyclic loadings. Advances in structures, Australia. 891-897.

[24] Pal.S and Wathugala.G.W (1999). Distribution state model for sand-geosynthetic interfaces and application to pull out tests. Int.J. for Numerical and Analytical Methods in Geomechanics 23: 1873-1892.

[25] Ostreberge. J.O and Gill. S.A (1973). load transfer mechanism for piers. Proceedings of the 9th Canadian rock mechanics symposium, Montreal , Canada, Mines Brance, Departement of Energey, Mines and Resources.235-262.

[26] Nitzsche. R. N and Haas. C. J (1976). Installation induced stresses for grouted roof bolts. International Journal of Rock Mechanics and Mining Science & Geomechanics Abstracts 13.(1): 17-24.

[27] Farmer, I. W. (1975). Stress distribution along a resin grouted rock anchor. Rock mechanics and mining science 12: 347-351.